W9-BOB-834

# THE HARPER ATLAS OF WORLD HISTORY

# THE HARPER ATLAS OF

# WORLD HISTORY

1817

HARPER & ROW, PUBLISHERS, New York
Grand Rapids, Philadelphia, St. Louis, San Francisco
London, Singapore, Sydney, Tokyo, Toronto

This work was first published in France under the title *Le Grand Livre de l'histoire du monde*, © Hachette, Paris, 1986



Printed and bound in France.

SECOND EDITION

---

**Library of Congress Cataloging-in-Publication Data**

The Harper atlas of world history.

Translation of: Le grand livre de l'histoire du monde.
1. Atlases. I. Vidal-Naquet, Pierre, 1930–
II. Title. III. Title: Atlas of world history.
G1021.H5893 1987 912 87-675015
ISBN 0-06-181884-4

---

90 91 92 93 94 10 9 8 7 6 5 4 3 2 1

# ACKNOWLEDGEMENTS

Editor: Pierre Vidal-Naquet
Cartographer: Jacques Bertin

Text by:

Guillemette Andreu, Françoise Aubin, Michel Barbaza, Elie Barnavi, Irène Beldiceanu, Louis Bergeron, Jean-Noël Biraben, Robert Bonnaud, Jean Bottéro, Habid Boussouf, Olivier Buchsenschutz, François Caron, Roger Chartier, Jean-Pierre Darmon, Christian Décobert, Marie-Danielle Demélas, Elisabeth Deniaux, Jacques Dupâquier, Christian Duverger, Marc Ferro, André Fontaine, Raoul Girardet, Pierre Gouthier, Chantal Grell, Jean Guilaine, Ran Halévi, Mohammed Harbi, Daniel Gémery, Clarisse Herrenschmidt, Christian Jacob, Pierre Jeannin, Gerard Jorland, Alain Joxe, Ahmed Koulakssis, Jean Lacoste, Jean Levi, Claude Lévy, Claude Liauzu, Claude Lutaud, Charles Malamoud, Elise Marienstras, Emilia Masson, Gilbert Meynier, Pierre Milza, Henri Moniot, Christos Mortzos, Jacques Népote, Claude Orrieux, Alain Piessis, Madeleine Rebérioux, Fabienne Reboul, Pierre Riché, Jean-Pierre Rioux, Agnes Rouveret, Yves Saint-Geours, Jean-Claude Schmitt, Pauline Schmitt, Irene Sorlin, Pierre Souyri, Jovier Teixidor, Wladimir Vodoff, Claudie Weill

**Translated from the French by Chris Turner (Material Word Ltd), Leslie Hill, Jean McNeil, Stuart Hammond, Ruth Harvey, Barbara Lewis, Celia O'Donovan and Stuart McKinnon-Evans. Translation co-ordinated and edited by Chris Turner.**

# Introduction

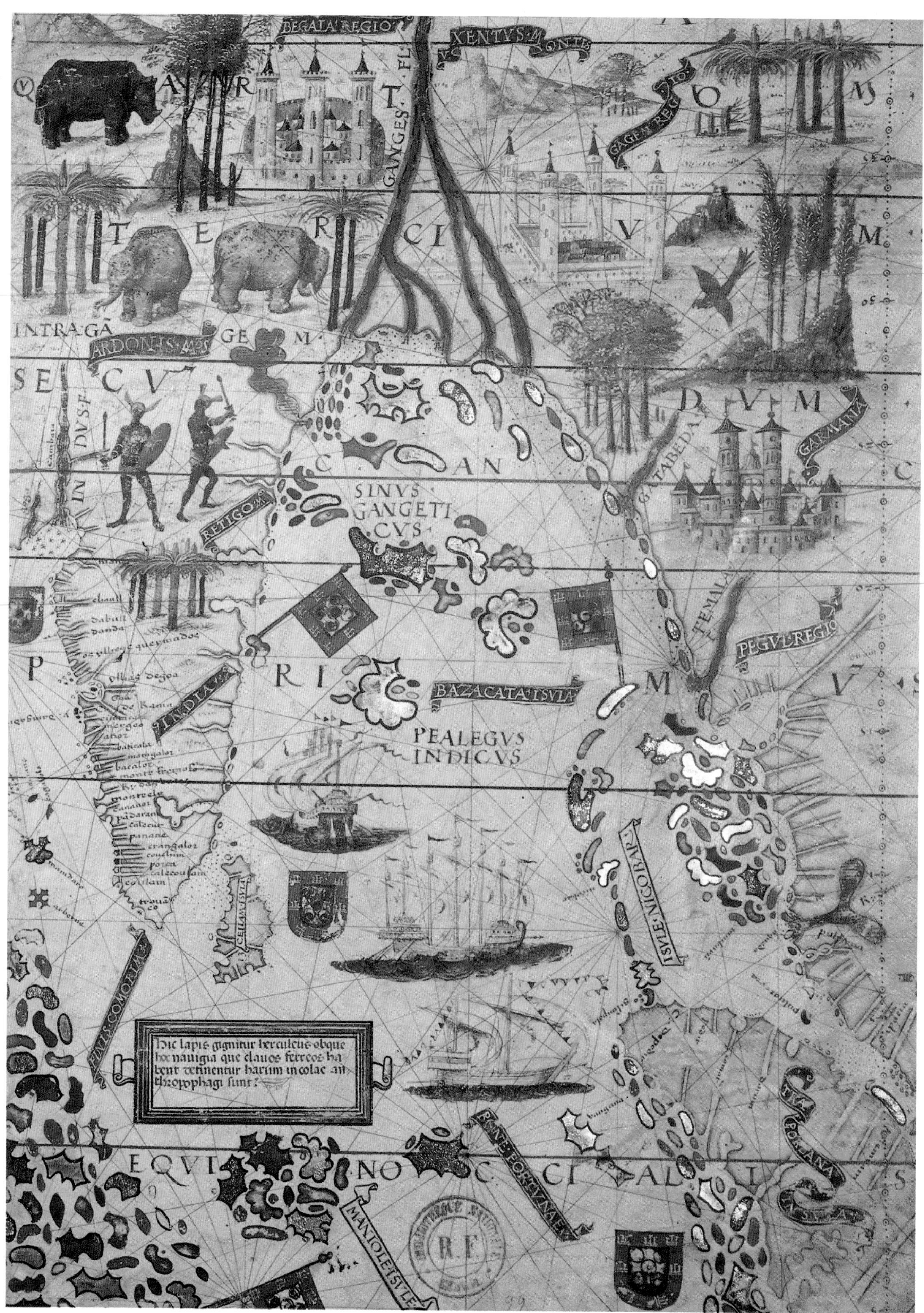


1. *A detail from Lopo Homen's* Nautical Atlas, *(Portugal, c. 1519), showing the coasts of India and the 'islands of the East'.*

# A History of Cartography

The history of the science of map-making is a story of continual development in succeeding cultures through the ages. To summarize the history of maps is also to enquire into their very identity: it is to examine how they are produced and to enquire into the nature of the traces that go to make them up, traces in which writing, painting and geometry are combined. It is also to examine their effectiveness – whether practical and political or imaginary and intellectual – for maps embody a society's knowledge. An historical atlas is, by its very nature, representative of this last function.

*There are maps and maps.* How maps are drawn depends to a large extent on their physical substratum. Some maps are portable while others are not; some stand alone while others form part of a book; some are hand-drawn while others are printed. These are all factors which make for different kinds of map, for projection on to a flat surface is only one solution among many. The Eskimos sculpt bone and wood to represent the outline of a coast; the inhabitants of the Marshall Islands assemble wooden sticks to produce a picture of the movements of wind and tide. The Touaregs make 'concrete maps' on the ground out of sand and gravel. A Babylonian clay tablet (from the end of the sixth century BC) has upon it a map drawn with compasses: the land is surrounded by the 'cruel' ocean and the stars. The first Greek maps were drawn on tablets of wood or metal. These bulky materials were doubtless very quickly supplanted by papyrus. It was on this fragile medium that the ancient Egyptians drew their maps (e.g. the chart of gold mines on the Turin papyrus, c. 1320 BC). In the first centuries of our era, parchment became the principal material. The use of this more solid and manageable medium made it easier for maps to be preserved. This was undoubtedly the case from Ptolemy's *Guide to Geography* (second century AD) onwards. The Portolan charts of thirteenth to fifteenth century Europe were drawn on sheepskin or calfhide. Not until the second century did the Chinese begin making paper. This new material, which did not reach the West until later, was to revolutionize writing and drawing.

There have also been maps of many different sizes. The *mappemondes* or planispheres of the Middle Ages had diameters ranging between 3 centimetres and 3 metres. The Ebstorf monastery map, which covers thirty sheets of parchment, has a surface area of 3.58 metres by 3.56 metres (c. 1284). Its monumental size reflects its decorative, religious function – which was to bear witness to God's majesty – as well as providing space for a great number of names and abundant ornamentation. A hand-drawn map like this is unique; any copy of it is a distortion.

Printing, which was first applied in the map-making field by the Chinese in 1155, was introduced into Europe around 1450. The first schematic printed world map is to be found in a book published by Isidore (Augsburg 1472). However, the main effect of the new technique was to make it possible for a great number of editions of Ptolemy (with maps from 1477 onwards) to be produced. This was how many Germans and Italians discovered map-making. Printing meant that a map could be republished, revised and corrected and, consequently, Ptolemy's map could now be modernized with the engraver replacing the scribe and the illuminator. In the days of wood engraving, only limited print runs and rough lines were possible; however, copperplate engraving, which was introduced in 1477, made more delicate work possible. In the nineteenth century, lithography, which was even more economical, enabled printers to introduce colour. With this step we reach the beginning of modern cartography. Maps were now produced either to stand alone or to be part of a larger work, as illustrations to a text or as a colour plate in an atlas. Alone, they were autonomous objects, serving either a utilitarian or a decorative purpose; in a book, they interacted with the text. In Greece, maps figured in scientific treatises as early as Anaximander (sixth century BC); they were particularly prominent in the work of Eratosthenes (third century BC), who explained how his map had been drawn, what sources he had used and provided a commentary on it; and lastly, they figured in the work of Ptolemy (second century AD) who accompanied his maps with lists of place-names and positions. The rediscovery of Ptolemy in the fifteenth century played a major role in the upsurge in the production of *Cosmographiae* in the sixteenth century (Münster, Thévet, Belleforest).

An atlas was initially a collection of maps assembled to order for a client. Each volume was unique, both in the selection and lay-out of its documents. But an atlas could also have a precise plan. Thus the hand-drawn *Atlas of Islam* (tenth century) included a map of the world, three charts of the principal seas and seventeen maps of individual countries. Printed atlases spread throughout Europe in the sixteenth and seventeenth centuries (the term itself being introduced in 1585 by Mercator), though the first modern atlas, Abraham Ortelius's *Theatrum Orbis Terrarum* had been published in 1570. An atlas gave its reader a symbolic mastery of the world (cf. Coronelli's *Atlante Veneto*, 300 maps, 1690–96).

*Who were the map-makers?* What was their place in society? When did maps begin to be drawn by professionals? The first Greek cartographers (Miletus, sixth century BC), who were geometers and astronomers, speculated on abstract forms. Eratosthenes was a mathematician and geometer, as well as being a philologist and a grammarian. The profile of the medieval cartographer cannot be so clearly drawn. The men who made the hand-produced world maps were scholars: in their maps the earth was divided into three continents (the so-called T and O maps: 'the T in the O') or the globe was divided into climatic zones. These clerics and monastery scribes remained faithful to theological dogma and their maps were more symbolic than geographical. The development of Mediterranean trade in the sixteenth century gave rise to a new utilitarian cartography, providing up-to-date information. The 'Portolan charts' were drawn by specialists, the most celebrated of whom worked in Italy, Catalonia, Majorca or the Balearics. Map-making became a subject to be taught, as it was for example in Majorca (fourteenth century) and Dieppe (sixteenth century). German cartography developed in the universities in the sixteenth century, where it benefited from advances in mathematics and geometry (trigonometry). The methods of the cartographers, long kept secret, became public knowledge. They were now craftsmen working not in isolation, but as members of institutions – often religious institutions, for monks and missionaries played a major role in early map-making. The work of the Jesuits in China for example is well known. At the very beginning of the seventeenth century, Father Matteo Ricci imported a copy of Ortelius. This prototype was distributed and reproduced under the aegis of the Emperor. Subsequently, throughout the seventeenth century and in the eighteenth, the Jesuits re-worked 231 maps of Chinese origin and gathered them into an Atlas (1717–18). But theological dogma also played an inhibiting role. In Medieval times, the T & O map was more often reproduced than the map of terrestrial zones, all of which left unresolved the question of whether the antipodes were populated. Meanwhile, in the Islamic world, cartographers were faithful to another sacred text, the Quran.

2. A Babylonian clay tablet, Mesopotamia, sixth century BC.

It was not only religious power that influenced cartographers. They were also subject to political pressure, since it was sovereigns who provided most of the commissions for maps. Al-Idrisi, geographer to Roger II of Sicily (after

1140) dedicated his first map of the world to his king; the second was made for Roger's son and successor, William the Bad. From the sixth century BC onwards, the Chinese cartographer was a civil servant, charged with drawing up maps and keeping them up to date (Pei Hsiu, minister and map-maker, third century BC). In 1644, the first Manchu emperor instituted a reform of map-making, as if to demonstrate that political renewal required a re-affirmation of the symbolic mastery of space. Between the fourteenth and sixteenth centuries, the kings of Portugal and Castile employed official cartographers. These were men who moved easily from one court to another and some sovereigns paid fortunes to obtain recent maps of overseas discoveries. The great cartographic undertakings were financed by state power. The King of England gave Greenland Collins the task of mapping the country's coasts (1681): the result was a set of 120 charts. In 1666, Louis XIV founded the body of *Ingénieurs du Roi*, whose labours resulted in the *Neptune Français* of 1693 and the *Neptune Oriental* of 1745. Political centralization tended to stimulate greater production of maps. In 1747, the government financed a project to produce a topographical map of France, that had been proposed to them by F. Cassini de Thury. The undertaking continued until the revolution, though by then it was privately financed. The state intervened to complete the project in 1818. Similarly George Washington gathered senior military men together to draw up a map of the United States (1809: first general map of the USA). And we may add that in France, the *Atlas Universel de Géographie* of Vivien de Saint-Martin and Franz Schrader appeared in 1919–22 thanks to assistance from the War Ministry.

The cartographer has also been an actor in, and on occasion a hostage to, commercial strategies. Discoveries reveal untold sources of wealth. Can the map-maker be permitted to reveal this information to the world? Must he not rather conceal it from potential competitors? On Fra Mauro's map of 1459, there is no trace of the recent Portuguese discoveries along the coast of Africa. May we not perhaps attribute the rarity of sixteenth century Portuguese maps to a deliberate policy of concealing information? In the seventeenth century, the Dutch East India Company did not publish documents which could give its competitors information. W. Blaeu, the company's hydrographer had access to the most up-to-date charts, but he did not use these sources for his own publications. It was only in 1675 that the West India Company published its maps of North America. Similarly, the Napoleonic Wars were responsible for a curb on the circulation of sea charts, though in the nineteenth century, these ceased to be regarded as military secrets and the survey departments of the various navies exchanged charts with one another.

However, trading companies did also play a positive role: the Casa da India in Lisbon and its counterpart in Seville were centres of map production in the sixteenth century, as was the Hydrographic Bureau of Seville which, from 1508 onwards, supervised the drawing of charts, checked that they conformed to a fixed prototype and officially authenticated them. The cartographers had at their disposal pilots' logs and the notes made by navigators on old maps. The British companies played a similar role (Hudson Bay Company etc.). Three functions – those of draughtsman, engraver and writer – are involved in map production: historically these have either been assumed by a single individual or by persons joined together in a contractual relationship. From Mercator (1570) onwards, Holland was the main European centre of cartography; this was due particularly to the publishing houses (Blaeu, Hondius) that produced maps there and saw them through from conception to sale.

It was in the trading nations that maps were drawn. When, at the end of the sixteenth century, maritime supremacy passed from the Mediterranean nations to the Low Countries, map-makers followed, obeying the fluctuations of economic history. In the eighteenth and nineteenth centuries, Britain occupied the dominant position. Maps were also produced in the centralized, monarchic states, where a large territory had to be administered (e.g. France in the seventeenth century). We may be sure that where there were important printing centres map-makers were to be found nearby: from the fifteenth century onwards, these centres were in Germany and Italy. Later, supremacy

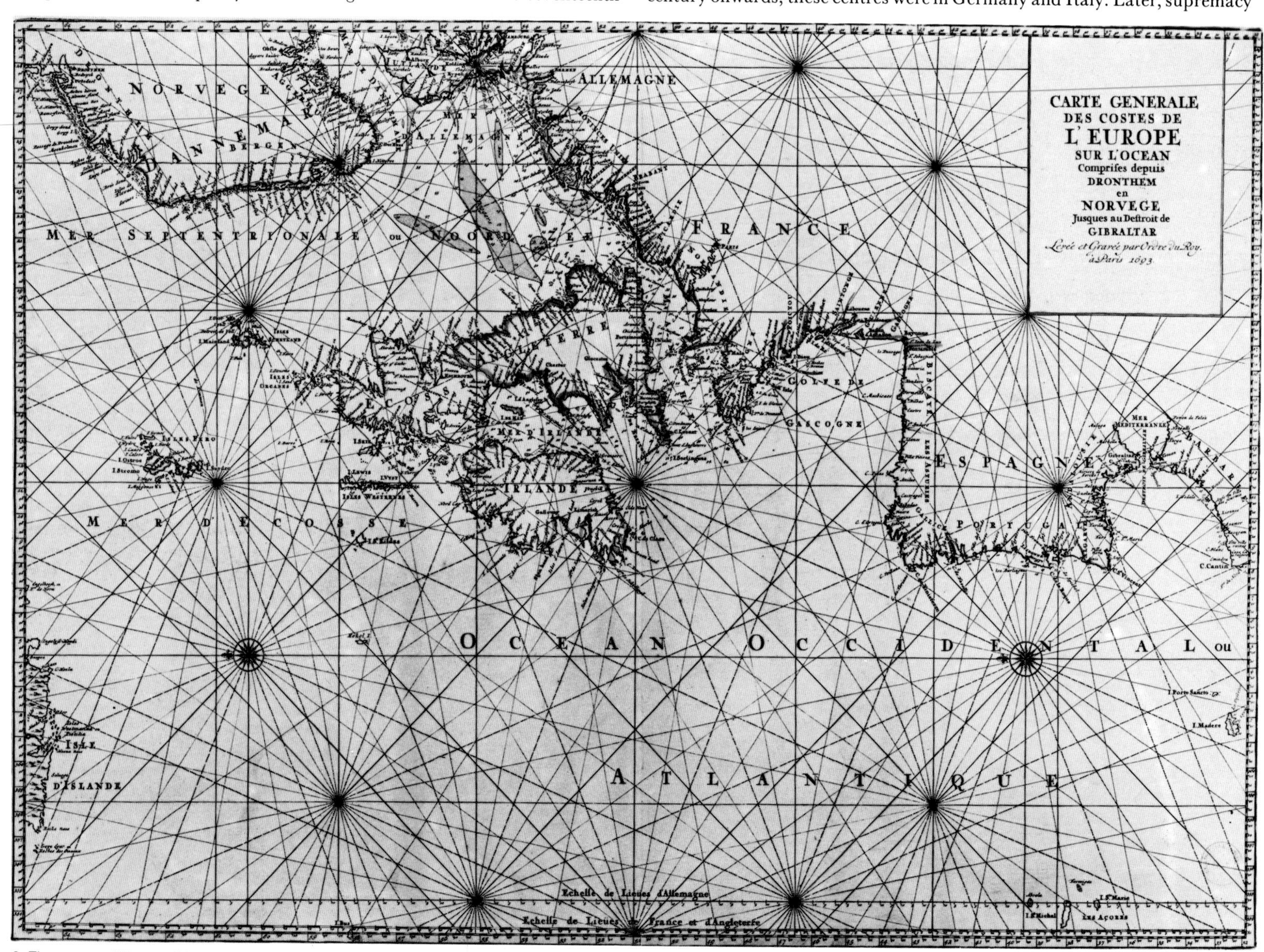


3. *The coasts of Europe. Map taken from the* Neptune Français *engraved by H. van Loon in*

passed to the Netherlands, which became famous for its atlases. In the eighteenth century, France dominated the market: it was there that the first scientific maps were produced.

Map-making developed over time into an institution. It was the aim of the French Academy of Sciences (seventeenth century), the *Ingénieurs du Roi* and the Royal Society of London (1660) to offer the scholar both a place of residence and a centre of learning, as the Museum of Alexandria (third century BC) and the Bayt al-Hikmah (House of Wisdom) in Baghdad (ninth century) had done before them. In the nineteenth century, geographical societies in France and Great Britain made an important contribution to the mapping of the colonial empires. The *Ordnance Survey* was founded in 1791 to draw up a map of England on the basis of a set of triangulations. The French Army Geographical Service, whose role its was to produce maps for the General Staff, was replaced in 1940 by the Institut Géographique National. Inevitably, the day had to come when international bodies would be set up to plan, co-ordinate and standardize maps. As early as 1891, a project was launched to produce an international map of the world, but it was hampered by a lack of co-ordination between the participants and by nationalist rivalries. The project was taken up again in its entirety after the Second World War by the Cartographic Department of the United Nations. Between 1919 and 1921, an attempt was made to standardize the symbols used on maps and they were re-drawn according to simpler, less expensive conventions. One of the routes through the history of map-making runs, then, right from the Portolan workshops to the UN.

*Map-making techniques.* How a map is made determines not only its appearance, but also its function. Purely geometrical maps were not intended to represent geographical reality, which knows no such straight lines and order. Anaximander's map (sixth century BC), which plays on the graphic possibilities of the circle, is of this type. The medieval map also stylized geographical reality to arrive at an essential structure, with the T & O map, which was divided into three by the Nile, the Don and the Mediterranean, and the map with climatic zones laid out in tiers on either side of the Equator. Perpendicular lines on maps brought them new depth. It now became possible to make calculations, as well as to check and correct a map. Eratosthenes (third century BC) could thus project positions and distances from one region of a map to another by employing the analogical operations that were available to him from Euclidian geometry. On Chinese maps of the Han dynasty (third century BC to third century AD), we also find a rectangular canvas with lines marking out regular squares. Ptolemy's grid (second century) allows us to find locations on the basis of their latitude and longitude: the network of parallels and meridians thus introduces a new rigour into position-finding. Between Anaximander and Ptolemy, maps change their meaning: we pass from the map as model to the map as inventory.

In the eighteenth century, the Portolan charts also had a linear framework. Their 'rhumb lines' were straight lines radiating out from the centres of adjacent circles in the direction of the compass-points and were usually thirty-two in number. If these circles were drawn, the points of intersection with the rhumb lines could be joined up to form a quadrangular figure. Rhumb lines were guides for the navigator, who followed a course parallel to them. They did not serve to locate positions on the map. The Portolan charts had, moreover, no 'projection': they neither took into account the spherical shape of the earth nor the convergence of meridians.

The rediscovery of Ptolemy in the fifteenth century made it possible to formulate the rules of map-making in a new way. He in fact advocated two systems of projection. In the first – conical projection – the meridians were straight lines running outwards from the North Pole (which was the centre to the arcs formed by the parallels); in the second, the meridians were curves which became increasingly accentuated as one moved outwards from a straight meridian in the centre. The parallels were drawn in conformity with the proportions of latitude.

In the fifteenth century, Ptolemy's maps were re-drawn. Nicholas Germanus (1466) became an authority in this sphere, both for his trapezoidal projection and the quality of his representation of relief. The editions of 1477 to 1482 were drawn using a rectangular projection. From 1482 onwards (the Ulm edition), the conical projection was used once again. Ptolemy thus introduced a new rigour into European cartography and on H. Martellus Germanus's map of the world (1488–90) we find meridians drawn and graduated. Ptolemy's grid was adopted in the Portolan charts, where it was added in over the rhumb lines. In this way, the representation of the east–west axis of the Mediterranean was rectified (1529, Ribero). Between 1500 and 1520, degrees of longitude and latitude began to appear on maps and from this point on, Portolan charts took account of the earth's spherical shape.

In 1569, Mercator invented a new projection: the meridians were drawn as parallel lines, and as latitude increased, so did the distance between the parallels, which distorted the shapes of the countries. In using this map, a sailor knew that a line drawn with compasses which intersected all the meridians at the same angle represented a straight line and he was therefore able to determine his course from one port to the next. The map was also embellished with topographical information, the quality of which depended on the instruments used. From the Han period onwards in China (third century BC to third century AD), surveying and geodesic instruments such as the chain measure and the plumb line were employed which the West did not discover until much later. It thus became possible to calculate distances and altitudes; in short, by using trigonometry, one could orientate oneself. The mariner's compass (which appeared in Europe in the tenth and eleventh centuries) gave a stimulus to the production of Portolan charts. In the fifteenth century, use of the astrolabe enabled sailors to determine their latitude. In the seventeenth century, the Germans worked out the principles of spherical trigonometry, published astronomical tables and systematized the calculation of latitude and longitude. In the eighteenth century, the telescope, the pendulum clock and logarithmic tables were all developed.

At the end of the nineteenth century, the use of radio signals introduced the greatest possible precision into the calculation of positions. Technical advances enabled countries to undertake cartographic projects on a national scale. A prime example of this is Cassini's map of France. In 1669–70, the Abbé Picard measured an arc of the Paris meridian using a chain of triangles. By 1718, the chain stretched from Dunkirk to the Pyrenees, enabling cartographers to make a great number of calculations of latitude and longitude. Using this triangulation of the national territory, the Cassini family was able to produce its 182-sheet *Carte Géométrique de la France* (1789). Even in the nineteenth century, national surveys were still carried out in much the same way. In the case of far-off lands, the explorer collected data, charted road networks, and measured noteworthy distances and relief features. From 1858 onwards, the technique of aerial observation was developed, using dirigible balloons. The two world wars gave a fresh stimulus to the development of aerial photography. This method, which made it possible to map coasts and inaccessible regions with great precision, created a need for the rigorous interpretation of photographs (nature of the soil, rock formations and vegetation).

*The Map and the Text.* In a geographical treatise, the text provides a gloss on the contents of the map. It renders it intelligible and the map, for its part, allows us to form a visual image of the over-abstract features of the description. This is the case in the treatises produced by Eratosthenes and Ptolemy or in Al-Khuwarizmi's *Curat al-Ard* (c. 820). Tenth century Islamic geography followed two paths. The Balkhi School, with its *Atlas of Islam* gave more prominence to the text than to the maps; the other school subordinated the geographical commentary to the construction of globe and maps. For them, the text had an informative function, whilst the map played a 'theoretical' role, visually condensing geographical science. Maps must provide the information that we need to understand them: the ascription of place names is the point at which the map as simple drawing meets the encyclopaedia. A proliferation of place-names does not necessarily represent topographical richness in a map, but it is evidence of a different project from that of the T & O schema. Naming places is a way of exorcizing the troubling power of blank spaces, as we can see from those Portuguese Portolan charts which are festooned with anachronistic or imagined place names (sixteenth century). The age of discovery was also an age of inventing place names. Everyone wished to impose their particular set of names, which on many occasions only lasted for the lifetime of a map. The New World had Catholic symbolism and hagiography, the names of sovereigns or even the names of European countries foisted upon it. Sometimes it was an intrinsic quality of the land being named that was emphasized, as in 'Tierra del Fuego', or in some cases a native name was borrowed, as with 'Canada'. We owe the name 'America' more to a decision of the map-makers (Waldseemüller's *World Map* of 1507, Mercator's *Map of the World* of 1538, which distinguished North from South America) than to any desire on the part of the man it was named after (Amerigo Vespucci). Meanwhile, Ptolemaic, Christian and Portuguese names co-existed merrily in the maps of the Old World. Place names were an integral part of maps, but names often proliferated at the expense of the map's readability or its decorative elements. A map's aesthetic value derived from the choice of typography or calligraphy (sixteenth century Italy and Holland). On the Portolan charts (thirteenth to fourteenth centuries), the names, which were written in black with the initial letter in red, served to pick out the coast lines more boldly. Written perpendicularly and to the left of the littoral, they formed a verbal fringe which marked the map's edge. The user of the Portolan chart could not simply view it at a single glance; he had to turn it round to read the legend.

Maps contain a great many other texts: the author's signature, the name and address of the printer and the engraver, the dedication and royal licence, the title written in its ornamental cartouche, the scale and sometimes even an explanation of the system of projection, along with fragments of description and references to sources. On his map of the world, Fra Mauro (fifteenth century) apologizes for not having enough space to report all the information brought back by explorers and declares his scepticism with regard to Ptolemy's maps. In some sixteenth century maps, authors provided

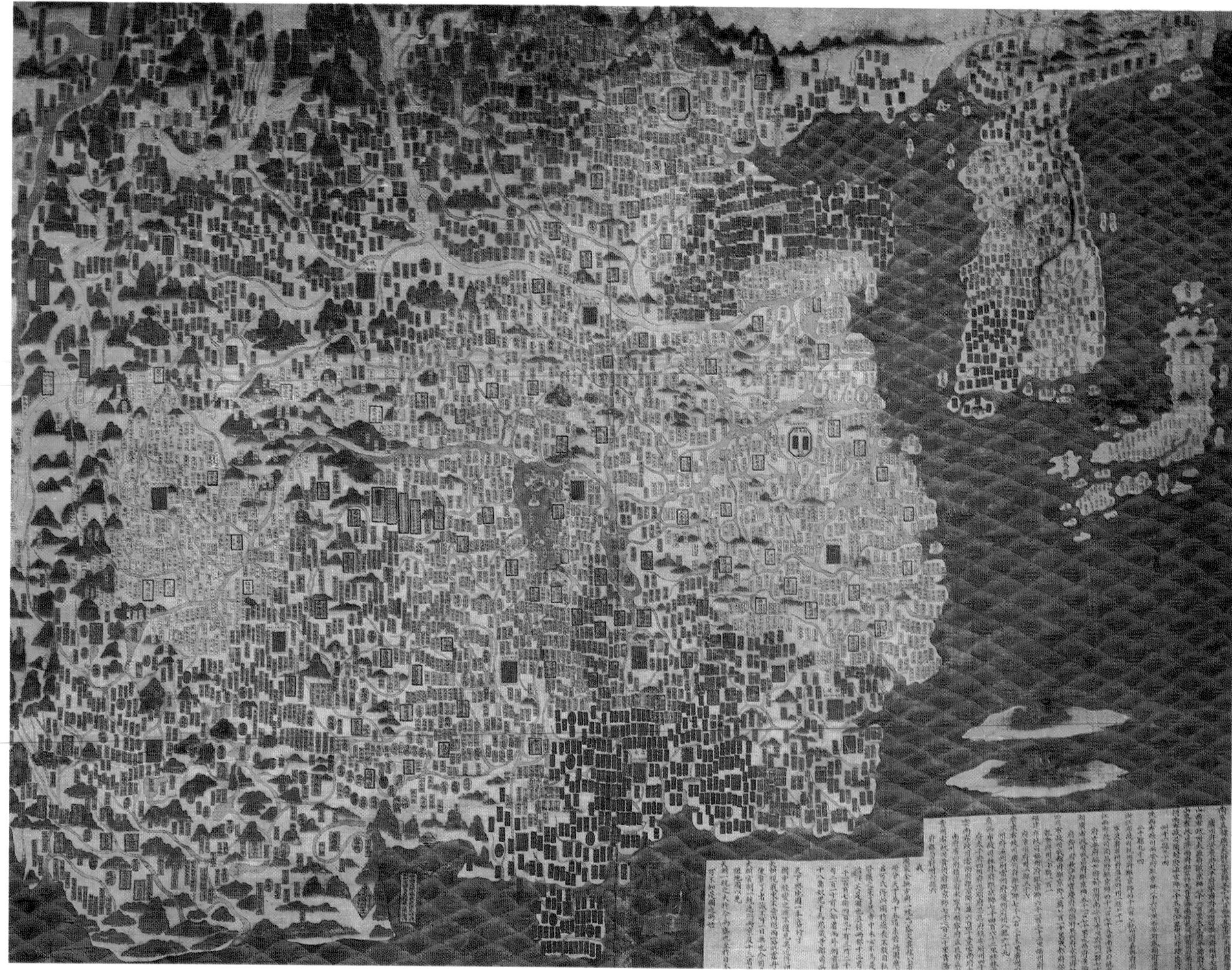

4. Map of the Chinese Empire by Wang P'an, 1594.

explanations and self-justifications. Certain of these notices are often as important as the map itself (Waldseemüller, Mercator).

In some cases, such commentaries were situated on the map itself. On N. Di Caveri's *Mappemonde* (sixteenth century) we read around *Chingirina* (Japan?): 'This island is very rich and there are Christians upon it; this is where Malacca porcelain comes from; benzoin, aloe and musk are also to be found there.' Thus the map-makers assessed potential wealth, determined levels of civilization and, on occasion, noted the names of contemporary rulers or sovereigns from the past of myth and legend; all these practices tended to transform maps into encyclopaedias.

*Geometry and painting*. As visual objects, maps lend themselves to aesthetic appreciation. A 'readable' map is, above all, one you can look at easily, one in which sea and land are distributed in harmonious proportion and where space is filled with clear graphic signs. The geometrical abstraction of Anaximander's maps or of the T & O renderings is not really compatible with a work of descriptive geography. A map must accommodate itself to the accidental contours of real forms even if it subsequently sublimates them in an image which is itself figurative. For example, there is a Chinese map of the world which uses the human profile, the head representing the central continent (China), the front part of the hair Korea and the back part the Western countries, while the chin and neck form India and Indo-china. Sometimes some small act of graphic violence is done to geographic forms to impose a familiar image on the eye. Maps doubtless suggested such parallels, which became proverbial in Greek texts: thus the Pelopponese were seen as the leaf of a plane tree, the Iberian peninsula a stretched-out ox-skin etc. The *Atlas of Islam* (tenth century) adopts this same procedure. To be legible, a map must include a figurative dimension which introduces an empirical motivation into its arbitrary lines.

Advances were also made in the recording of topographical data. The representation of towns, mountains and rivers developed from the figurative mode towards the symbolic. Until the end of the seventeenth century, a mountain was indicated by a picture which sought to represent it 'realistically'; it was an isolated shape, which, in late fifteenth century editions of Ptolemy, looked like the tooth of a saw or a mole-hill. It was not therefore possible to differentiate between a hill and a mountain, nor *a fortiori* to discover the structure of a mountain range or determine a particular altitude. But there was an increasing move towards abstraction. Efforts were made to project altitude onto the horizontal plane and to suggest valleys, peaks and mountain ridges by a graphic code. The nineteenth century saw two major innovations in this regard. In 1802, a decision was taken to take sea-level as the basis of all such calculations, enabling the surveyors who produced the so-called 'General Staff' maps in France (published, 1881) to put altitudes on them. In 1830 or thereabouts, the introduction of lithography made it possible to use colour to represent relief: this marked the passage from the 'landscape' to the 'abstract' map; later, the user would be able to determine altitudes with the aid of contour lines. The representation of towns underwent a similar development. The Portolan charts indicated them with flags or little castles: this generic symbol was often accompanied by veritable descriptive vignettes in the case of the most important towns. Cassini's map in fact contains plans of the main cities.

Another important element in the external appearance of maps is colour. Colour certainly plays a decorative role (sixteenth century maps painted *al fresco*); it also has a symbolic function. In the tenth-century *Atlas of Islam*, it is used to distinguish rivers from mountains. The medieval Portolan charts also used a precise and consistent colour coding.

For many years, printed maps were coloured by hand. In the seventeenth century, when an ordinary buyer acquired a Jaillot atlas, he bought one in which only the contours of the maps were highlighted with colour. More well-to-do clients, however, could purchase lavishly decorated atlases. On modern maps colour has an exact meaning and a contemporary map of the world requires the use of a wide range of colours sufficient to indicate the different bands of altitude, from the depths of the oceans to the peaks of the Himalayas.

The first maps were abstract and geometric in appearance. Figurative representation only appeared at a later stage. Medieval maps contain a plethora of miniatures (animals, plants and monsters) and with these the global overview provided by the world map becomes fragmented into a number of partial scenes. On one contract for a Portolan chart (c. 1400), both the quantity and the type of illustrations are specified: 165 persons and animals, 25 ships, 100 fish, 140 trees, 340 banners. Maps served as a microcosm and an inventory. The seas were studded with ships, which were both a means of discovery and functioned as guarantees that the New World could indeed be reached. This pictorial pedagogy acquainted the reader with exotic animals, Indians and cannibals, though the monsters of the sea could neither be conquered nor assimilated into the fund of human knowledge. The human monsters that inhabited the bowels of the earth were drawn from ancient encyclopaedias and represented a dream-horizon where the fantasy images of the Christian West could be exorcised. The Ebstorf *Mappemonde* (c. 1284) had as its background a picture of Christ crucified with his head at the top (the east) and his arms outstretched to north and south, holding up the world. It was an inventory of Creation in all its profusion and diversity. The Hereford map (c. 1300) is an encyclopaedia: its surface is a classification table for images that are organized into veritable taxonomies of history, ethnography and the natural sciences. These documents bear little resemblance to such 'scientific' works as the Ptolemaic maps.

As the Middle Ages drew to a close, map-makers were faced with a choice. They could either follow the tradition of decorative world maps and increase the figurative component at the expense of the map's geographical content and readability, or they could separate the figurative dimension from the cartographic project altogether. The printed Ptolemy maps mark a break with medieval map-making. The Catalan cartographers had already begun to limit the space given over to miniatures and, from the sixteenth century onwards, under the influence of Mercator and Ortelius, the pictures of natives, fruits, flora and fauna and towns had been moved from the centre of maps to the edges. With his *Atlas de la Chine*, D'Anville introduced a new type of decoration; the titles of the maps were surrounded by large illustrations depicting the customs or resources of a particular area: from this point on, pictures left the map's interior to become part of its periphery.

*Maps as images of the world.* Maps provide the eye and the memory with a single complete picture. It is an essential feature that they should close off space. It matters little that until the fifteenth century, an entire continent remained unknown, and that in some maps there were many blank areas representing uncharted territories. Maps are organized around a centre and move outwards from the known and familiar towards the unknown and exotic. This was the case with the first Greek maps, which were circular and centred on Delphi. It was also true of medieval maps centred on Jerusalem, or of oriental planispheres centred on India or the Pamir plateau. A map's horizon corresponds to the needs and knowledge of a society. The first maps produced by the Japanese contained only those countries known to them by trading links (China and Korea). The map of the Islamic empire (tenth century) runs from Spain in the West to the Indus and Central Asia. The Italian Portolan charts cover only Western Europe and the Mediterranean, while the Catalan charts range as far as Scandinavia and even China. These maps are evidence of two different types of curiosity and two different commercial strategies.

The history of maps merges at points with the history of discovery. The fifteenth and sixteenth centuries represent a turning-point in this regard. While the knowledge of the Old World increased (1427: Nicolas Clavus's map of northern Europe), the Portuguese, by their explorations along the Atlantic coast, modified European perceptions of Africa. In 1448, Andrea Bianco mapped the coastline of Senegal and Cape Verde and in 1459 Fra Mauro completed this work, drawing perhaps on Arabic sources. The coasts of the Congo and the Cape of Good Hope, which were discovered by the Portuguese, are shown on Martellus's map of 1490. On a map printed in 1508, all of Africa south of the equator appears for the first time as a vast peninsula. Advances in the discovery of Asia occurred less rapidly. Martellus drew the islands of the Orient and Cipangu (Japan). Texeira's map of Japan was regarded as authoritative throughout the seventeenth century. Thanks to the British, the map of India became clearer during the eighteenth century.

In the midst of all these advances came a crucial event – the discovery of America. J. De la Cosa's world map of 1500 included information from Columbus's first three voyages and from John Cabot's discoveries in North America. In 1502, Cantino produced a map which drew together all the material from the new discoveries in America and Africa. There were, however, many problems to resolve. To begin with, was the newly discovered land an archipelago or a continent? Was it in Asia and, if so, was it far from Cipangu and Cathay? Contarini was the author of the first map to show the New World. In the north, he recorded the findings of Cabot and Corte-Real, attaching these lands to the province of Tangut (Asia). He placed the West Indies in the centre and the south was occupied by a vast land mass. The cartographic birth of America in fact occurred in 1507, when Waldseemüller drew the intuitive conclusion that all these individual discoveries were connected. He separated America from Asia and, in the process, invented the Pacific Ocean eight years before it was actually discovered! Ribero produced a more precise map of the eastern coastline of America, including the Magellan Strait and Labrador. Cabot traced the outline of the Gulf of the St Lawrence, California and the complete course of the Amazon. From this point on, America was shown with a continuous coastline extending as far as Tierra del Fuego. Cook's voyages between 1773 and 1784 (which led to the production of seven volumes and an atlas) brought enormous progress in the mapping of the Pacific and Australia and New Zealand.

We can see, then, three key stages in the history of the representation of the earth. These were the discovery of America, the re-discovery of Ptolemy (and his model of projection) and the development, in the eighteenth century of surveying techniques that made it possible to fill in what had previously been blank areas on the map.

*Maps, their uses and users.* The primary function of a map is, of course, to allow users to determine their position and find their way. The Marshall Islanders' stick constructions, Portolan charts and road maps all have this same function. From the Islamic world to China and from ancient cadastral surveys to the modern land register, maps have provided a way of resolving problems of boundary lines.

But maps cannot be reduced to one single function. They may at one and the same time serve utilitarian, decorative, political and scientific purposes. They provide information in a condensed form and yet they may also at times be akin to works of art, especially when hand-drawn and illuminated, or printed from a fine engraving and hand-painted. In cathedrals, monasteries and palaces or in the houses of the well-to-do, maps have had a decorative role alongside their educative function. They have also been political gifts exchanged between kings; as such, they may be regarded as signs of 'social distinction'. In the seventeenth century, they were purchased by teachers, lawyers, clergymen, the older nobility and the bourgeoisie.

To read an atlas is to experience the joys of a journey in one's mind's eye. But maps can also be sources of religious edification. In both Christianity and in Islam, the map's order is seen as reflecting God's order. It allows the reader to decipher Creation. The 'T and O' maps were theological symbols: the tripartite division of the continents echoed the Trinity and the three sons of Noah. But maps are also bound up with temporal power. They are instruments of government; they have a preparatory role in military action and in decision-making 'in the field', whether it be the field of battle or that of broader geopolitical strategy. They offer the state symbolic control of its territory. Surveying the extent of that territory means stabilizing its frontier, making it available for organization into administrative units. The imperial geography of Islam was oriented towards the assessment of taxes, defence and the provision of messenger services. Chinese tax-collectors used atlases of the various provinces with statistical charts and maps of grain stocks.

Maps can provide a means for affirming national unity, or even nationalist sentiment. They are also a source of knowledge, and one that is indispensable to the decision-maker. Early in their development, it was seen as part of their encyclopaedic vocation that they should provide an inventory of a country's resources, modes of life and cultural heritage. However, as the decorative illustrations were squeezed out towards the edges, maps increasingly lent themselves to new uses. They became vehicles for transmitting any data that lent itself to treatment in terms of spatial distribution. They became heuristic objects, revealing to the eye what could only be imperfectly conveyed by a written text. The first geological maps appeared at the beginning of the nineteenth century. The thematic map was born in 1875 with Crome's comparative map of European populations, but it owes its development largely to German geographers. A. von Humboldt and K. Ritter used maps to reveal the spatial distribution and interaction of the natural phenomena studied by meteorology, climatology, hydrology and hydrography, geology, zoology, agronomy and ethnography, together with such variables as vegetation and terrestrial magnetism. These thematic maps later benefited from progress made in the field of statistics. The new tool was also used by history: in 1894, in his *Atlas Général*, Vidal de la Blache gave a visual representation of the relations between historical development and the environment.

Today, we are able to convey information through a map which is of equal status with that conveyed by a written text or a picture. A new discipline – 'graphic semiology' – has evolved to examine just what it is that determines the didactic or heuristic effectiveness of maps. Its theoretical principles have only recently been formulated by this volume's principal cartographer Jacques Bertin and *The Collins Atlas of World History* is just one of its most recent practical applications.

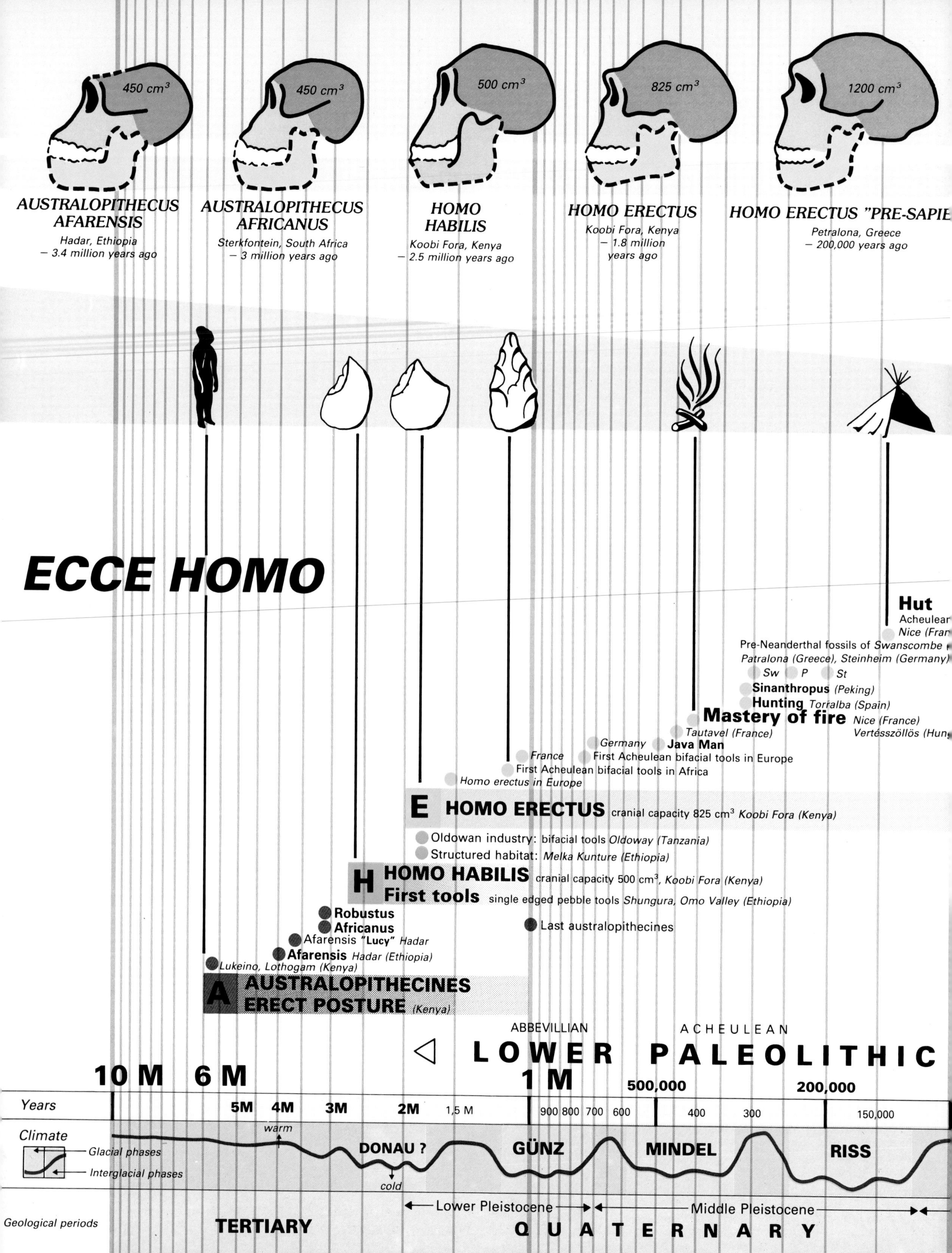

450 cm³
450 cm³
500 cm³
825 cm³
1200 cm³
AUSTRALOPITHECUS AFARENSIS
Hadar, Ethiopia – 3.4 million years ago
AUSTRALOPITHECUS AFRICANUS
Sterkfontein, South Africa – 3 million years ago
HOMO HABILIS
Koobi Fora, Kenya – 2.5 million years ago
HOMO ERECTUS
Koobi Fora, Kenya – 1.8 million years ago
HOMO ERECTUS "PRE-SAPIE
Petralona, Greece – 200,000 years ago
ECCE HOMO
Hut
Acheulear
Nice (Fran
Pre-Neanderthal fossils of Swanscombe
Patralona (Greece), Steinheim (Germany)
Sw
P
St
Sinanthropus (Peking)
Hunting Torralba (Spain)
Mastery of fire Nice (France)
Vertésszöllös (Hun
Tautavel (France)
Germany
Java Man
France
First Acheulean bifacial tools in Europe
First Acheulean bifacial tools in Africa
Homo erectus in Europe
E HOMO ERECTUS cranial capacity 825 cm³ Koobi Fora (Kenya)
Oldowan industry: bifacial tools Oldoway (Tanzania)
Structured habitat: Melka Kunture (Ethiopia)
H HOMO HABILIS cranial capacity 500 cm³, Koobi Fora (Kenya)
First tools single edged pebble tools Shungura, Omo Valley (Ethiopia)
Robustus
Africanus
Last australopithecines
Afarensis "Lucy" Hadar
Afarensis Hadar (Ethiopia)
Lukeino, Lothogam (Kenya)
A AUSTRALOPITHECINES
ERECT POSTURE (Kenya)
ABBEVILLIAN
ACHEULEAN
LOWER PALEOLITHIC
10 M
6 M
1 M
500,000
200,000
Years
5M
4M
3M
2M
1,5 M
900
800
700
600
400
300
150,000
Climate
warm
Glacial phases
Interglacial phases
DONAU ?
cold
GÜNZ
MINDEL
RISS
Lower Pleistocene
Middle Pleistocene
Geological periods
TERTIARY
QUATERNARY

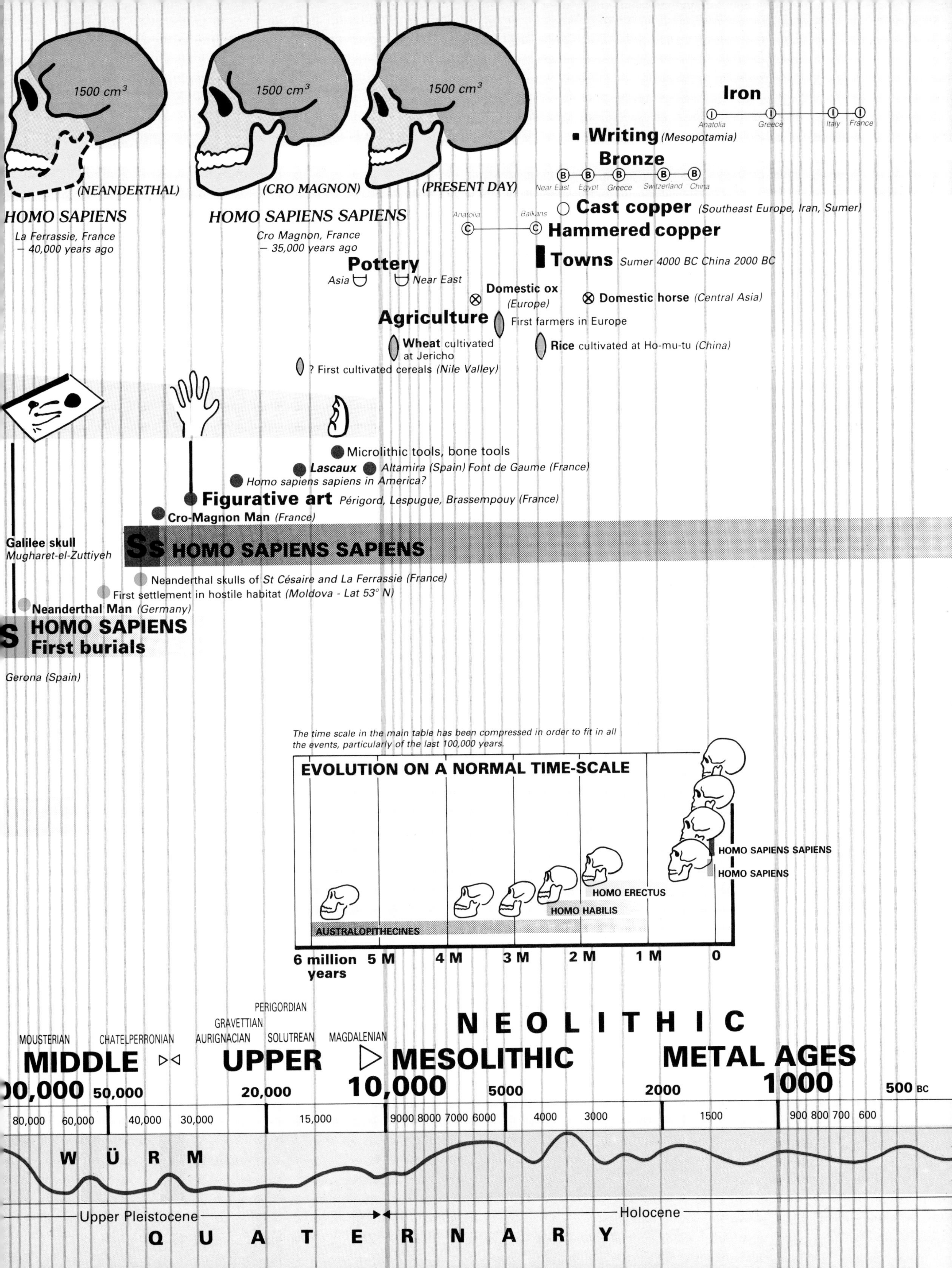
1500 cm³
(NEANDERTHAL)
HOMO SAPIENS
La Ferrassie, France
– 40,000 years ago
1500 cm³
(CRO MAGNON)
HOMO SAPIENS SAPIENS
Cro Magnon, France
– 35,000 years ago
1500 cm³
(PRESENT DAY)
Iron
Anatolia
Greece
Italy
France
Writing (Mesopotamia)
Bronze
Near East
Egypt
Greece
Switzerland
China
Cast copper (Southeast Europe, Iran, Sumer)
Anatolia
Balkans
Hammered copper
Towns Sumer 4000 BC China 2000 BC
Pottery
Asia
Near East
Domestic ox (Europe)
Domestic horse (Central Asia)
Agriculture
First farmers in Europe
Wheat cultivated at Jericho
Rice cultivated at Ho-mu-tu (China)
? First cultivated cereals (Nile Valley)
Microlithic tools, bone tools
Lascaux
Altamira (Spain) Font de Gaume (France)
Homo sapiens sapiens in America?
Figurative art Périgord, Lespugue, Brassempouy (France)
Cro-Magnon Man (France)
Galilee skull
Mugharet-el-Zuttiyeh
Ss HOMO SAPIENS SAPIENS
Neanderthal skulls of St Césaire and La Ferrassie (France)
First settlement in hostile habitat (Moldova - Lat 53° N)
Neanderthal Man (Germany)
S HOMO SAPIENS
First burials
Gerona (Spain)
The time scale in the main table has been compressed in order to fit in all the events, particularly of the last 100,000 years.
EVOLUTION ON A NORMAL TIME-SCALE
HOMO SAPIENS SAPIENS
HOMO SAPIENS
HOMO ERECTUS
HOMO HABILIS
AUSTRALOPITHECINES
6 million years
5 M
4 M
3 M
2 M
1 M
0
PERIGORDIAN
GRAVETTIAN
MOUSTERIAN
CHATELPERRONIAN
AURIGNACIAN
SOLUTREAN
MAGDALENIAN
NEOLITHIC
MIDDLE
UPPER
MESOLITHIC
METAL AGES
00,000
50,000
20,000
10,000
5000
2000
1000
500 BC
80,000
60,000
40,000
30,000
15,000
9000 8000 7000 6000
4000
3000
1500
900 800 700 600
W Ü R M
Upper Pleistocene
Holocene
Q U A T E R N A R Y

# The First Tools, Fire, Ritual

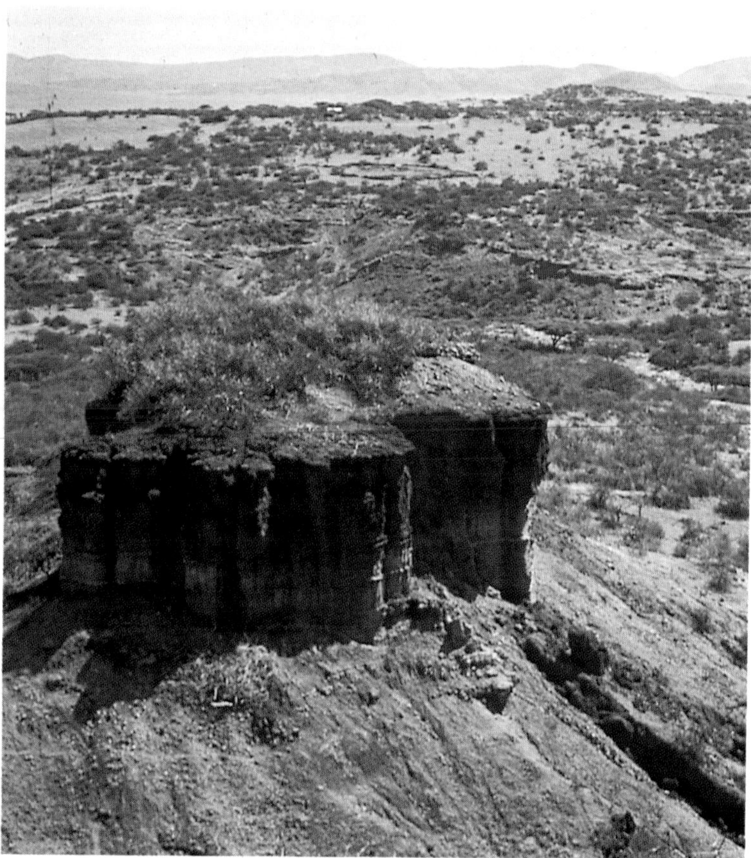

*1. Olduvai gorges in Tanzania, site of Zinjanthropus skeleton, type of* Australopithecus robustus *contemporary of* Homo habilis *(1.7 million years ago).*

THE RIFT VALLEY, a vast tear in the surface of the planet, where the secrets of the earth's history can be glimpsed, is where human life is thought to have begun. Geologists, paleontologists and prehistorians have focused their research here, on the horizon of the *Australopithecines*, a multiform, adaptable genus that gave birth, as far as we know today, to representatives of the genus *Homo*. The species *Homo habilis* began to differentiate themselves about 2.5 million years ago from *Australopithecus africanus*, a gracile, though not particularly specialized form with great evolutionary potential. Thanks to the genetic vigour of some of its members, the evolutionary process was able to continue and give rise, about 1.8 million years ago, to *Homo erectus*.

*Homo habilis* lived in small groups in the varied habitat of the savanna, frequenting in particular, in an amphibian manner, the banks of lakes and rivers. For millions of years their lifestyle evolved little; they were eclectic in their eating habits, feeding as a rule on small animals that were easy to catch, gathering plants and even scavenging the odd carcass or carrion. What was new about these humans was that the dialogue between hand and brain had given birth to tools that developed their capacity for action and made it more effective, and these tools could be used in turn to make other instruments. The methodical chipping away at stones to produce a cutting edge is valuable evidence of coherent thinking and planning. Another particularly human feature of *Homo habilis* is their variety of habitats, from small temporary shelters to large encampments with specialized living areas. At Melka Kunture, an Ethiopian site 1.7 million years old, rest areas marked out with blocks of stone and pebbles but devoid of remains alternate with zones where carcasses were cut up, which are full of tools and fragments of bone.

The human group *Homo erectus* grew rapidly. They occupied the whole territory of Africa and their representatives spread over the totality of the warm and temperate zones of the Old World. Several branches have been found in numerous sites: *Atlanthropus* in Ternifine in Algeria, *Pithecanthropus erectus* in Java, *Sinanthropus pekinensis* at Chou-k'ou-tien in China, pre-Neanderthal humans in Europe etc. The tradition of chipped stone instruments persisted for a long time, then evolved around 1.5 million years BC in Africa (not until 700,000 BC in Europe) into an industry of bifacial tools which clearly show a sense of symmetry and a feeling for the beauty of an instrument. Patterns of life did not evolve at the same pace, haphazard gathering continuing for a long time to form the basis of the economic system. Gradually, perhaps under pressure from less favourable environments, this way of life changed and humans evolved genuine strategies for the hunting of larger mammals around 400,000 BC. At about the same time the use of fire began to be widespread and dwellings no longer consisted of natural shelters roughly adapted for use, but of caves or more elaborate enclosed structures in the open air. With archaic man a totally new dimension was introduced: cultural evolution, an intensification of the natural tendency towards creating ever greater complexity.

**70 million years ago:** End of Secondary Era, beginning of Tertiary. Appearance of first primates.
**15 million years ago:** Possible emergence of first Hominids. Erect posture.
**6–3.7 million years ago:** Earliest remains of *Australopithecus* genus in Kenya: Lukeino tooth, Lothogam jawbone, Kanapoi humerus.
**3.7 million years ago:** Various remains and footprints of *Australopithecus* at Laetoli, Tanzania, provide evidence of perfect erect posture. Oldest fossils of *Australopithecus afarensis* found in Hadar (Ethiopia).
**3.4 million years ago:** Probable date of fossilized skeleton of *Australopithecus afarensis* AL 288 of Hadar, known as 'Lucy'.
**3 million years ago:** Appearance of *Australopithecus africanus* and *Australopithecus robustus*.
**2.5 million years ago:** Probable appearance of *Homo habilis* and first tools.
**2.3 million years ago:** Chopper and adapted stone slab from Shungara in the Omo Valley (Ethiopia).
**1.8 million years ago:** Skull KNM-ER 3733 (cranial capacity 835 c.c.) from Koobi Fora, east of Lake Turkana (Kenya). Attributed to *Homo erectus*.
**1.7 million years ago:** Structured habitat with specialized zones at Gombore, Melka Kunture (Ethiopia) built by *Homo habilis*. Industry found at Oldoway in Tanzania.
**1.5 million years ago:** Spread of *Homo erectus*, evidence of presence in Europe. Site of Chilhac in Auvergne occupied – the oldest tools in Europe.
**1.2 million years ago:** Upper portion of skull of Venta Micena (Granada, Spain).
**1.1 million years ago:** First *Acheulean* bifacial tools manufactured in Africa.
**1 million years ago:** Last *Australopithecines*.
**900,000 BC:** Cave of Vallonnet (Roquebrune-Cap-Martin, France) occupied.
**700,000 BC:** First early *Acheulean* bifacial tools made in Europe.
**630,000 BC:** Probable date of jawbone found at Mauer, Baden-Württemberg, Germany.
**450,000 BC:** Remains of pre-Neanderthal Man of Tautavel, Caune de l'Arago, France. *Homo erectus*.
**400,000 BC:** Hearths of Terra Amata, Nice and Vertésszöllös in Hungary. *Homo erectus* masters fire.
**300,000 BC:** Sites of Torralba del Moral and Ambona (Spain). *Homo erectus* develops strategies for hunting very large mammals.
**250,000 BC:** Appearance of the Levalloisian method of cutting stone, enabling flakes of predetermined form to be produced.
**130,000 BC:** Building of *Acheulean* hut, Lazaret cave, Nice.
**90,000 BC:** Probable age of jawbone found at Bañolas (near Gerona, Spain), attributed to *Homo erectus*.

*4. Bifacial tool found in the region of Liège, Belgium (Acheulean).*

# 70,000,000–90,000 BC

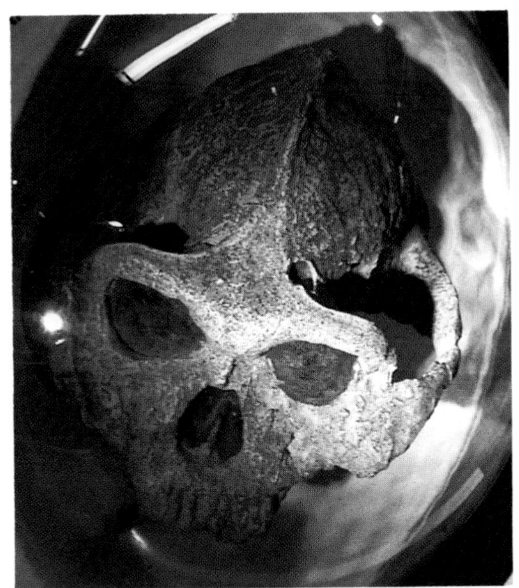
2. *Skull of* Australopithecus robustus *found in Kenya.*

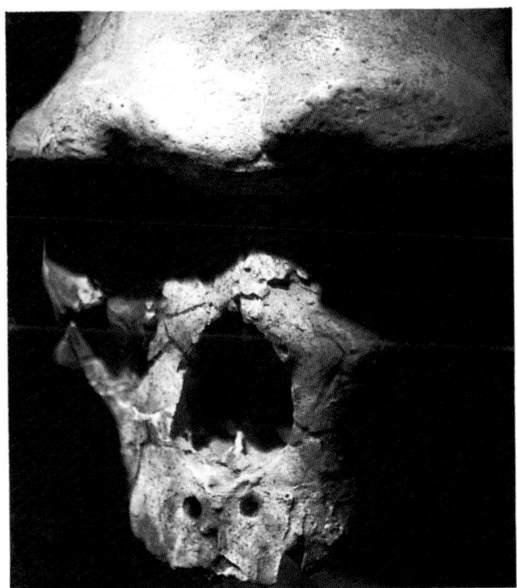
3. *Skull of* Homo erectus*: Tautavel Man.*

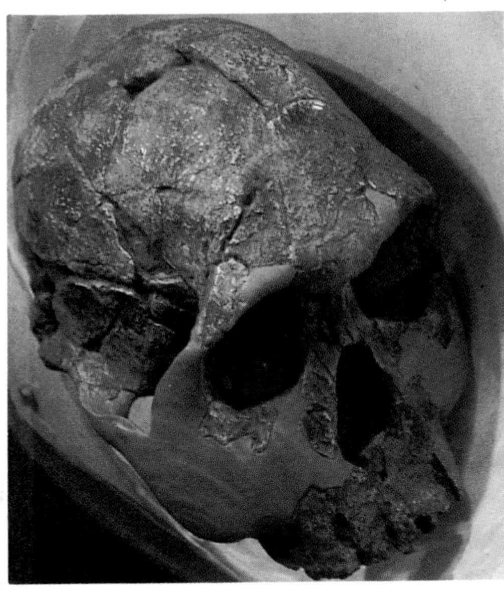
5. *Skull of* Homo habilis *found in Kenya.*

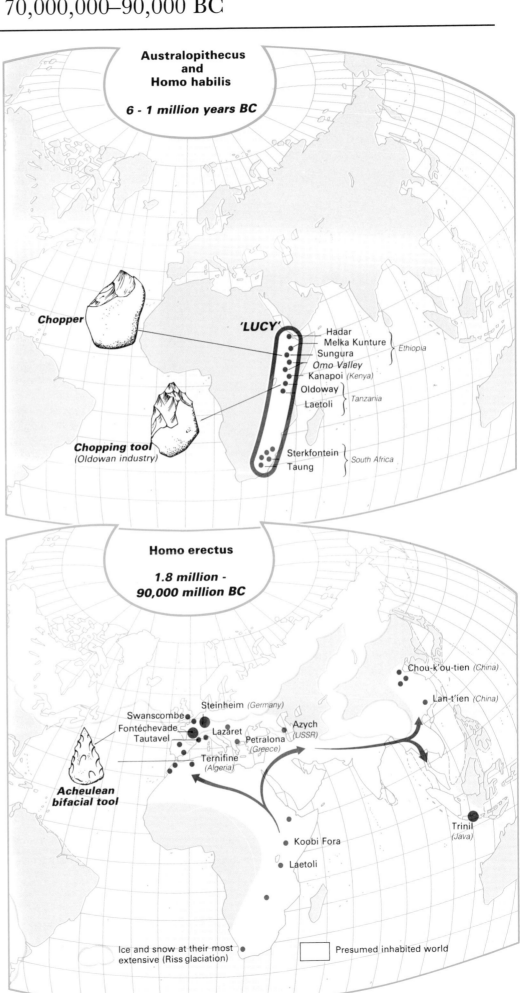

**Australopithecus and Homo habilis**

***6 - 1 million years BC***

**Chopper**

***Chopping tool***
*(Oldowan industry)*

***'LUCY'***

Hadar
Melka Kunture
Sungura
Omo Valley
*Ethiopia*
Kanapoi *(Kenya)*
Oldoway
Laetoli
*Tanzania*
Sterkfontein
Taung
*South Africa*

**Homo erectus**

***1.8 million - 90,000 million BC***

***Acheulean bifacial tool***

Swanscombe
Fontéchevade
Tautavel
Steinheim *(Germany)*
Lazaret
Petralona *(Greece)*
Azych *(USSR)*
Ternifine *(Algeria)*
Koobi Fora
Laetoli
Chou-k'ou-tien *(China)*
Lan-t'ien *(China)*
Trinil *(Java)*

Ice and snow at their most extensive (Riss glaciation)

Presumed inhabited world

# Hunting and the Development of Man 200,000–20,000 BC

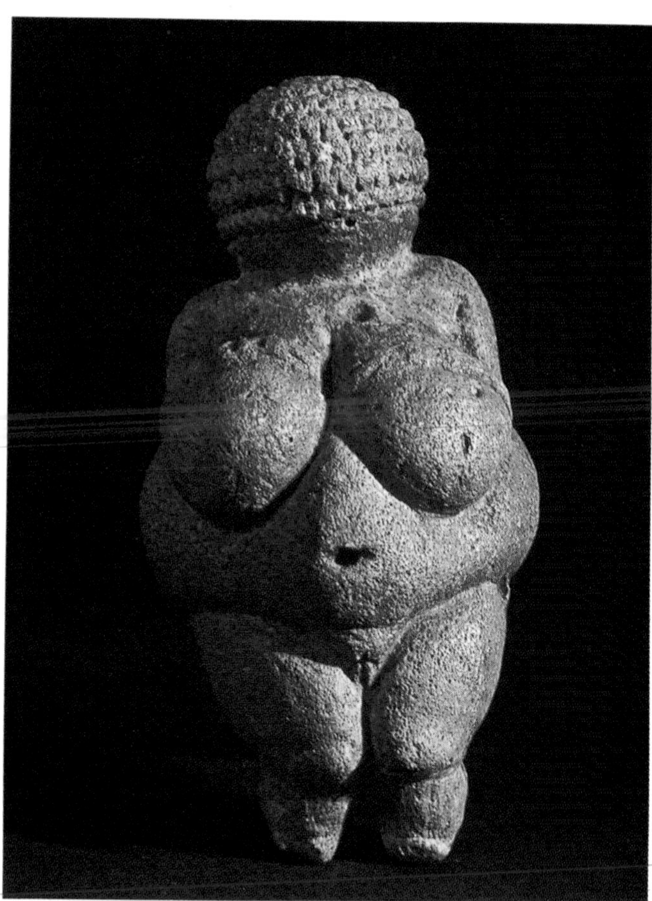

*1. Venus of Willendorf, Austria. Limestone Gravettian statuette.*

After a maturation period lasting thousands of millennia during which major leaps in development occurred, in the last 100,000 years the daring experiment of intelligence at last began to pay off. Progress was irregular and took many false trails, but eventually *Homo erectus* gave way to a new form of humanity, *Homo sapiens*. The first group of these humans was located in Europe and western Asia and was possibly retreating before advancing glaciation: *Homo sapiens neanderthalensis* or Neanderthal Man. They date from between 80,000 and 35,000 BC and their anatomical features were still archaic. From the end of the Lower Paleolithic era, as shown by the fossilized remains of Mugharet el-Zuttiyeh in Israel, a second human grouping began to form alongside the Neanderthalers and the last representatives of *Homo erectus*. The characteristics of modern humans were crystallized in *Homo sapiens sapiens*, who was to go from strength to strength.

Cultural evolution is not apparently sensitive to a profusion of minor variations; it tends to respond only to major ones. Implements that had already been tried out during the Lower Paleolithic evolution, standardized tools made from flakes of brittle stone, were produced in great quantities by all human groups of the Middle Paleolithic. These industries, known as Mousterian after the cave of Le Moustier in the Dordogne, usually comprise a great number of scrapers, points and serrated tools. Surprisingly, bifacial tools from the Acheulean tradition (early Paleolithic) have been found to exist side by side with lighter, smaller tools cut from slivers of stone (scrapers, burins, backed knives). In Europe and southwest Asia, after fifty millennia of Mousterian stability, material culture evolved rapidly in the Upper Paleolithic era, and the latter type of tool, more functional and varied, became increasingly important.

The Neanderthalers were not only concerned with the practicalities of life; as clearly shown by their burial customs, they had a very definite attitude to death, and must therefore have had a particular conception of life.

*Homo sapiens* now looked on the world with a new consciousness of their place in it. From then on, all cosmogonies and spiritual practices, in particular those shown in Paleolithic art after 30,000 BC, arise from the special place humans felt themselves to occupy among living things.

From the end of the Lower to the beginning of the Upper Paleolithic period, lifestyles changed little. This was the era of the great hunters; they did not specialise in a particular species, they knew how to exploit the resources of different environments to the full and were capable of tackling any game. They developed sophisticated, well-adapted dwellings: seasonal encampments of light tents along with much more solid constructions enabling them to withstand the rigours of the Würm Glaciation. Around 40,000 BC *Homo sapiens sapiens* reached Australia, and in 23,000 BC, if not earlier, penetrated America through the Siberian route.

The multiplicity of cultural responses made to daily problems by human societies was rapidly rendering synonymous the habitable and the inhabited regions of the world.

**200,000 BC:** Minimum age of pre-Neanderthal fossilized remains of Steinheim an der Murr (Germany).
**130,000 BC:** Beginning of Riss-Würm interglacial period.
**100,000 BC:** Probable date of remains found at Mugharet el-Zuttiyeh: possible ancestor of proto-Cro-Magnons of Near East. Rise of stone flake industries.
**80,000 BC:** Beginning of Würm glaciation. Appearance of stable characteristics of classical Neanderthalers (*Homo sapiens*) in Europe and Western Asia. Birth of Middle Paleolithic culture; Mousterian industries, first burials, beginnings of religious thought.
**70,000 BC:** Ritual cannibalism detected from remains of about twenty Neanderthalers found at Krapina (Yugoslavia).
**50,000 BC:** Site at Moldova on the Dniester (53°N), first permanent settlement in hostile habitat.
**40,000 BC:** Probable average date of Neanderthalers of La Chapelle-aux-Saints, La Ferrassie, La Quina (France) and of Cro-Magnon-type humans at Skhül and Kafzeh (Israel). Probable arrival of humans in Australia.
**35,000 BC:** End of Mousterian stage, beginning of Upper Paleolithic. Rise of stone implements cut from flakes and slivers of stone and of bone and horn industries. Probable average date of Cro-Magnon-type humans found at Combe-Capelle and Brno (*Homo sapiens sapiens*) and Neanderthaler found at Saint-Césaire (France).
**30,000 BC:** Average date of first obvious appearance of figurative art (Cellier shelter at Tursac, Blanchard shelter at Sergeac and Reindeer shelter at Belcayre, all in the Dordogne region of France).
**27,000–19,000 BC:** Gravettian culture (Paleolithic site of La Gravette, Dordogne). Period of female statuettes, in particular those of Lespugue and Brassempouy (France), Savignano (Italy) and Avdeeno (USSR) etc.
**23,000 BC:** Probable arrival of humans in America.

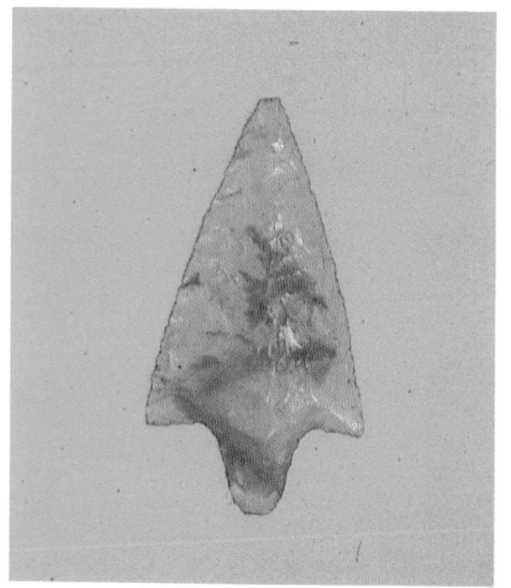

*2. Arrowhead found in Mauritania, Mousterian period.*

*3. Grave at the 'Grotte des Enfants', Grimaldi, Monaco. Aurignacian period, Grimaldi race.*

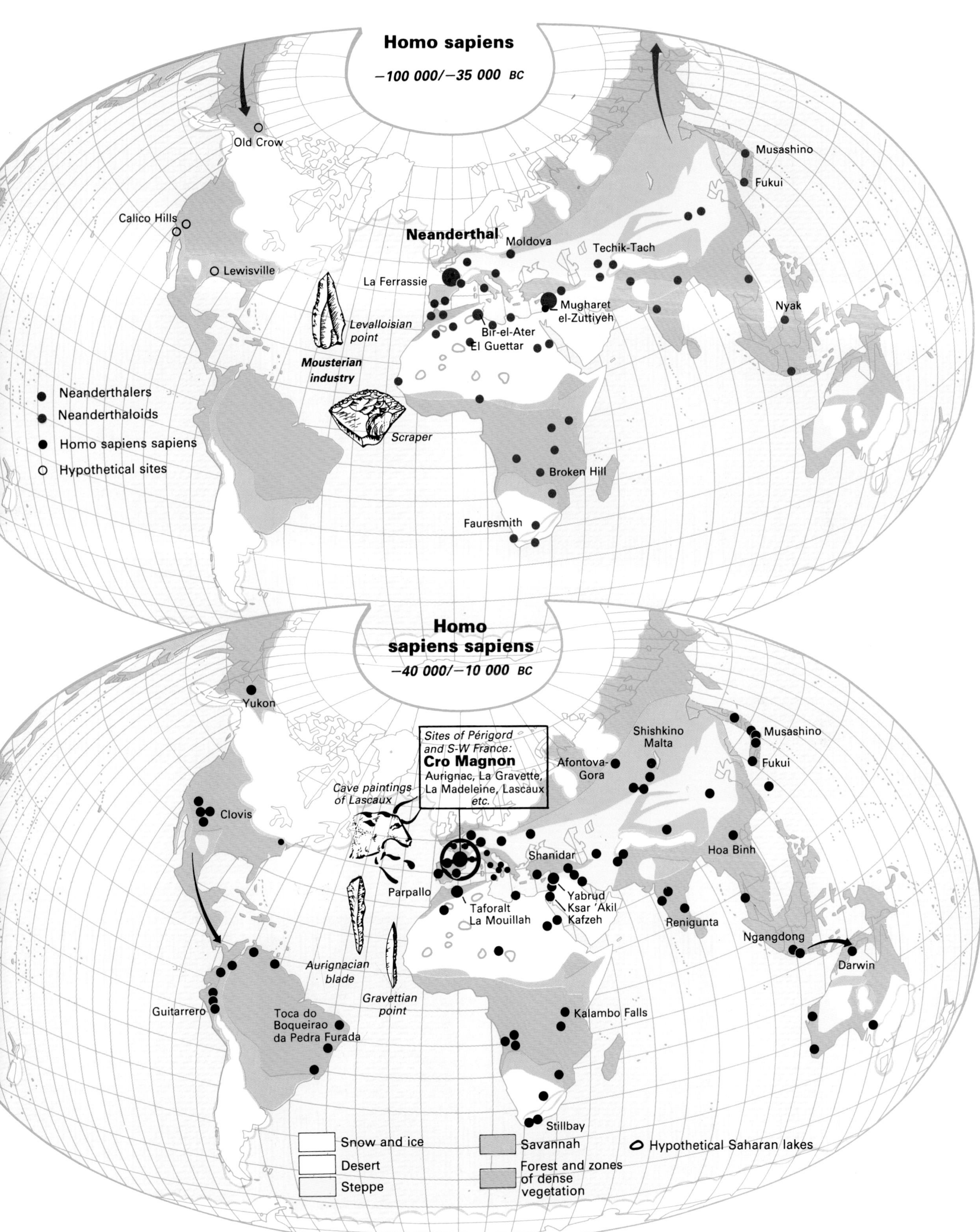

Homo sapiens
−100 000/−35 000 BC
Old Crow
Calico Hills
Lewisville
Neanderthal
Moldova
Techik-Tach
Musashino
Fukui
La Ferrassie
Mugharet el-Zuttiyeh
Levalloisian point
Mousterian industry
Bir-el-Ater
El Guettar
Nyak
Scraper
Broken Hill
Fauresmith
Neanderthalers
Neanderthaloids
Homo sapiens sapiens
Hypothetical sites
Homo sapiens sapiens
−40 000/−10 000 BC
Yukon
Sites of Périgord and S-W France:
Cro Magnon
Aurignac, La Gravette, La Madeleine, Lascaux etc.
Cave paintings of Lascaux
Shishkino Malta
Afontova-Gora
Musashino
Fukui
Clovis
Shanidar
Hoa Binh
Parpallo
Yabrud
Ksar 'Akil
Kafzeh
Taforalt
La Mouillah
Renigunta
Ngangdong
Darwin
Aurignacian blade
Gravettian point
Guitarrero
Toca do Boqueirao da Pedra Furada
Kalambo Falls
Stillbay
Snow and ice
Desert
Steppe
Savannah
Forest and zones of dense vegetation
Hypothetical Saharan lakes

# The Upper Paleolithic Explosion

1. Valley of the Vézère, Dordogne, France. An important centre of hunting and settlement from Paleolithic times.

THE RIGOROUS CLIMATE of the Würm Glaciation produced a mosaic of contrasting landscapes which were often surprisingly conducive to life. Between northern or mountainous areas covered with forbidding masses of ice and arid zones enlarged by a marked increase in rainfall lay an area where conditions were much more hospitable, offering sheltered valleys and sites exposed to favourable, temperate influences. Alternating with hilly, windswept regions and sparse plateaus of steppe and tundra lay zones of open parkland that became refuges for many vegetable and animal species and, of course, for humans.

By setting up permanent, sizeable shelters at the meeting point of several natural zones Paleolithic hunters benefited from complementary eco-systems. During the fine season in particular the clan could

2. Magdalenian burial reconstructed by Abbé Henri Breuil (1887–1961), world authority on prehistory.

**20,000–18,000 BC:** Coldest point of Würm Glaciation.
**20,000 BC:** Last phases of various cultural horizons of European Upper Perigordian.
**18,500 BC:** Beginning of Solutrean civilization (European Upper Paleolithic) in France.
**18,000 BC:** Beginning of Ibero-Marusian civilization (cultural horizon of Late Paleolithic of North African Maghreb), development of arrowhead industry (lighter stone implements evolved), probably influenced by cultures further to the east. Mediterranean Epigravettian civilizations (named after materials found at Gravette site).
**16,000 BC:** Coldest point of glaciation. Mean date of monumental stone bas-relief sculptures. Solutrean sites of Roc de Sers (Charente) and Fourneau du Diable (Dordogne) in France. Probable signs of short-lived cereal cultivation in Nile Valley.
**15,500–10,000 BC:** Development of Magdalenian (evolution of bone industry, improvement in quality of portable and mural art) and Gravettian: climax of Paleolithic art.

4. Magdalenian bone sculpture of bison with turned head found in the cave of La Magdeleine, Dordogne.

**15,000 BC:** Probable date of paintings and engravings on cave walls at Lascaux (Dordogne), France.
**14,000–11,000 BC:** Development of El-Kebareh civilization in southwest Asia (Israel). First free-standing round cabins.
**12,500–9500 BC:** Flowering of Magdalenian civilization. Rise of bone and antler industries (assegais, harpoons, fishing spears) of Upper Magdalenian.
**11,000 BC:** Probable median date of Altamira paintings (Santander, Spain) and Niaux drawings (Ariège, France). Optimum climate of Natufian in Near East. Increase in rainfall changes arid land into grasslands with deciduous trees. Birth of Natufian civilization (from Wadi-al-Nattuf site near Jerusalem), formation of first permanent settlements. Hunting and systematic gathering, storing of wild cereals.
**9800 BC:** Beginning of climatic improvement of Allerod (Denmark). Last manifestations of Magdalenian culture in Europe. Rise of late Gravettian and Alizian cultures in

split up and station itself either next to a ford, on a migratory route or by a beaten track to exploit abundant if ephemeral resources. The obvious risks of an economy based on predation hardly affected its success, as shown by the diversity of material cultures, the strength of religious traditions underlying a cycle of artistic creation that lasted over twenty millennia and above all the multiplicity of sites. The systematic extension of hunting to smaller species such as birds and fish, aided by marked technological improvements such as the bow may have been due to the pressure of population growth.

We do not know what this tension might have produced had the environment remained unchanged; however, the improvement in climate around 12,000 years ago might well be seen in the context of Western Europe as a negative factor. It produced a profound renewal of eco-systems in an increasingly wooded, overgrown environment and for a while put an end to large groupings of people in favour of the most adaptive segment of society, the nuclear family. Hunting became less productive and was supplemented by intensive gathering of smaller animals such as rabbits and snails and new vegetable species such as pulses.

These groups of hunters now benefited from more diverse resources brought about by an increase in the biomass (total mass of living organisms) in a now temperate environment; they adapted their social structures and were able to respond to the post-glacial challenge, making a smooth transition to the Mesolithic period. According to data relating to southwest Asia, particularly the mountainous zones of Palestine, Commagene and Zagros in Asia Minor, the marked rise in rainfall around 13,000 years ago was a particularly dynamic factor.

The optimum climate of the Natufian (Mesolithic cultural horizon of Palestine) produced a sort of savanna with trees eminently favourable to human settlement. The natural presence of animal and vegetable resources, particularly wild cereals which were easy to store, favoured a sedentary existence and the formation of the first real villages about 12,000 years ago.

These successful adaptations began a process in which demographic forces played an essential role and which led – depending on the advantages and constraints of each zone – to an ever greater mastery of the natural environment.

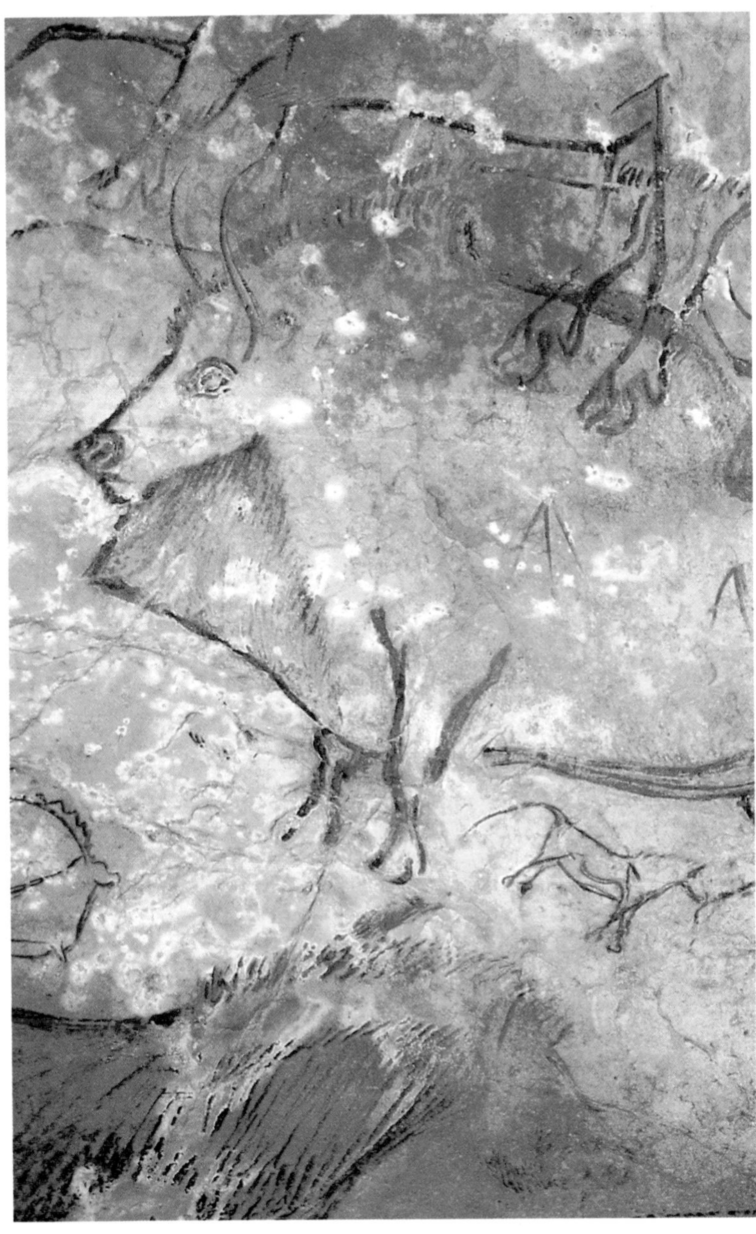

*3. Bisons of the Salon Noir, Niaux, Ariège, France. Magdalenian cave paintings.*

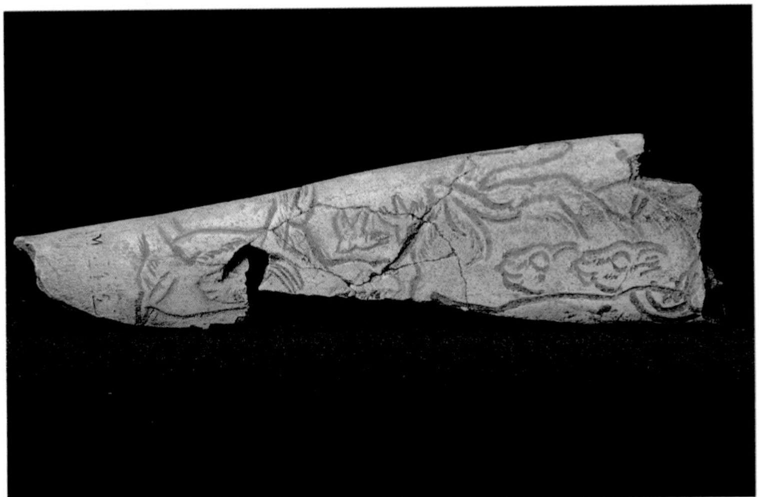

*5. The game found in the Vézère Valley. Magdalenian carved bone.*

Mediterranean Europe. Alizian pebbles painted and engraved with abstract designs (from Mas-d'Azil, Ariège, France).
**8200 BC:** End of third and last glaciation.
**8000 BC:** Systematic harvesting of pulses at La Balma de l'Abeurador (Hérault, France). First one-off attempt at pottery at Mureybet (Syria).
**7600 BC:** First agriculture in southwest Asia.
**7500–5000BC:** Western European Mesolithic. Sauveterrian and Tardenoisian designs of triangles and trapeziums.
**5500 BC:** Appearance of early forms of cattle farming in Mediterranean regions of Western Europe.

*6. Pebble decorated with geometric design found at Mas-d'Azil, Ariège. Azilian period.*

# The Domestication of Plants and Animals

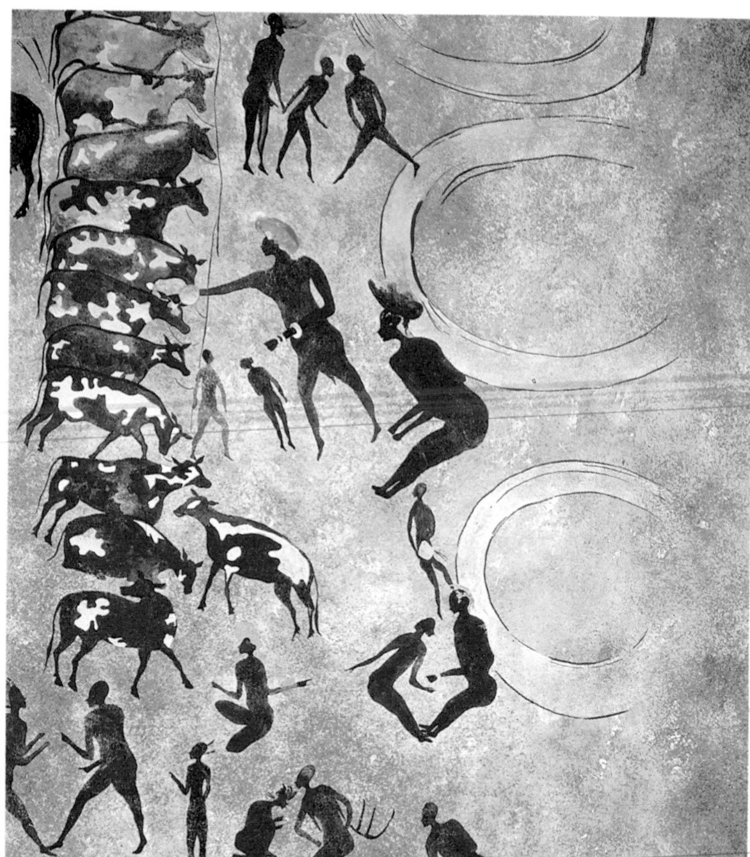

*1. African herdsmen gathering their cattle. Cave painting of Tassili-n-Ajjer, Algerian Sahara, 4th millennium BC.*

A MUTATION of tremendous importance in human history began to occur about 10,000 years ago with the appearance of animal breeding, agriculture and pottery and the first farming communities. These practices spread more or less rapidly to the main populated areas of the world apart from a few resistant pockets of isolated people still living from hunting and gathering. This new epoch – the Neolithic – when settlement in villages became widespread, was the beginning of a crucial stage in human evolution; it laid the foundations for past and present rural societies. This was no instant, decisive revolution; today's prehistorians see it rather as the outcome of a long conditioning of the natural habitat by humans, the establishment of new relations with the environment as societies became more developed.

Several regions of the world shared this development, each in its own way and quite independently. Southwest Asia or the Near East offer examples of advanced settlements with underground homes built of wood, clay and partly of stone, although the economy was still based on hunting (Mallaha-Eynan in Palestine, tenth millennium BC). This budding architecture was to make further progress as the climate became drier towards the end of the ninth millennium (Jericho). A millennium and a half later, around 6500 BC, Catalhuyuk in Turkey presents a typical example of a prosperous Neolithic settlement. Towards the middle of the eighth millennium, from Anatolia to Palestine, barley and certain types of wheat were grown for the first time. In the same geographical area sheep, goats, pigs and oxen were more or less rapidly brought into domestication; stone was still the preferred material for receptacles, with terra cotta coming into general use around 6500 BC.

The Near-Eastern Neolithic cultures were a powerful influence that encouraged the setting up of the first farming communities in Egypt and Europe; these also spread to the Caucasus and Iran and to Afghan, Indian, Yemeni and Cushitic lands. In Africa pottery was introduced very early, appearing in the Sahara before animal farming and agriculture, in the eighth and seventh millennia. On the African continent numerous indigenous plants were progressively brought into cultivation: sorghum, millet, African rice, yam. In China the first permanent villages took root along the Huang Ho River on land rich with deposits of silt (loesslands) (Yang-shao civilization of the fifth and fourth millennia). Rice-growing, either indigenous or imported from more southerly regions, appeared early on in the lower Yanze Valley at Ho-mu-tu.

Horticulture was established very early in Southeast Asia and Oceania. On the American continent permanent settlements predated the advent of agriculture (Anáhuac, Mexico); here marrows, beans and perhaps already maize were grown progressively from the sixth millennium. Around the same period the Andes (Guitarrero caves) then the Pacific coast of Ecuador and Chile were prime centres of agricultural development.

At different points of the globe production economies appeared and gradually took over until the process became irreversible.

**11,000 BC:** Japanese pottery with relief and intaglio decoration (Fukui cave, Kyushu) followed by Jomon cord-marked pottery (Jomon means cord-print). Early centre for pottery-making develops in East Asia.
**From 10,000 BC:** Near-Eastern Natufian 'villages' with round houses (Syria, Palestine), first permanent settlements. Stone polishing techniques applied to objects of adornment. Southeast Asia: horticulture in New Guinea (find of polished axes or adzes dating from c. 9000 BC at Kafiavana). Near East, northwest Europe and North America (Jaguar cave): dogs are domesticated.
**c. 8500–8000 BC:** First cereals – wheat and barley – grown at Jericho in Jordan, at Tell Aswad and Mureybet in Syria. Fleeting appearance of terracotta at Mureybet. Tower and wall of Jericho, pre-ceramic Neolithic.
**c. 8000 BC:** Pottery appears in the Sahara. Domestication of pigs in progress in Crimea.
**c. 7500–7000 BC:** Definitive domestication of goats and sheep in the Near East (Iran, Jordan). Oxen are domesticated a little later, in the Eastern Mediterranean (7th millennium). First work of hammered copper at Cayonutepes, Turkey.

*2. Mother-Goddess of Catalhuyuk, Turkey, 7th millennium BC.*

**c. 6500–5700 BC:** Catalhuyuk, important Neolithic village of Anatolia: houses and sanctuary made of unfired bricks and frescoes of goddesses and bulls.
**c. 6000 BC:** First farming communities of southeast Europe.
**c. 5500 BC:** Progressive cultivation of capsicums and beans in the Andes. Agriculture develops a little later on the Peruvian coast.
**c. 5000 BC:** First settlements in Anáhuac, Mexico (Zohapilco). First Western European farmer.
**From c. 5000 BC:** Beginning of domestication of camelids (lama, alpaca) in Andes (Lauricocha, Junin). Spread of marrow, bean and maize cultivation in Mexico (Tehuacán).
**c. 4500 BC:** First flowering of Megalithic phenomenon: dolmens, menhirs in Western Atlantic regions (Brittany, Portugal).
**c. 4000 BC:** Evidence of rice cultivation in Ho-mu-tu in China (Ch'ing-lien-kang

*3. Ceramic pot, Longshan culture, China, end of 3rd millennium BC.*

# 11,000–2000 BC

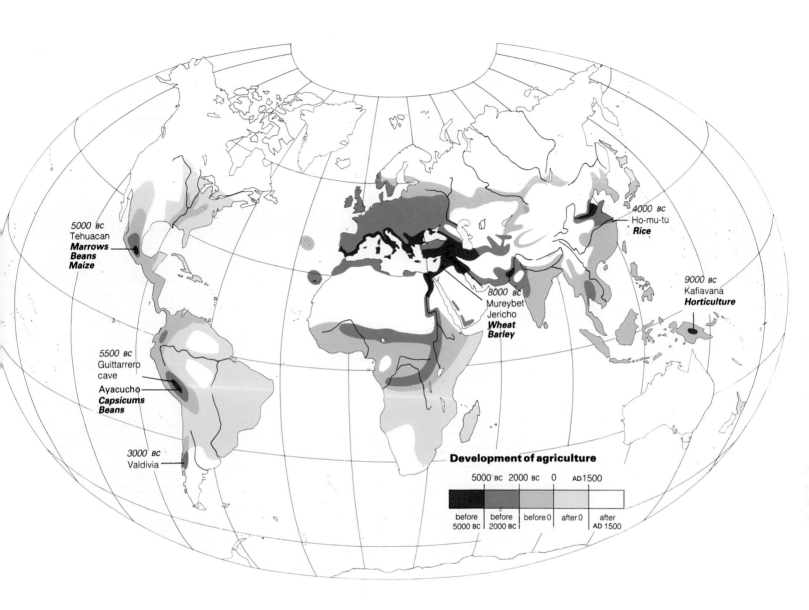

5000 BC
Tehuacan
***Marrows***
***Beans***
***Maize***

5500 BC
Guittarrero cave

Ayacucho
***Capsicums***
***Beans***

3000 BC
Valdivia

8000 BC
Mureybet
Jericho
***Wheat***
***Barley***

4000 BC
Ho-mu-tu
***Rice***

9000 BC
Kafiavana
***Horticulture***

**Development of agriculture**

5000 BC | 2000 BC | 0 | AD 1500

before 5000 BC | before 2000 BC | before 0 | after 0 | after AD 1500

*4. Bone comb from the Island of Gotland, Sweden, 1st millennium BC.*

civilization). Large Chinese Neolithic villages (Yang-shao culture) with pottery, hoes, polished axes, weights for digging sticks and millet cultivation. Development of metalwork in Central Europe.

**c. 3000–2500 BC:** Progressive transition to Bronze Age in Central-western Asia, Europe, Egypt, China.

**Climatic variations from the Neolithic age to the present day**

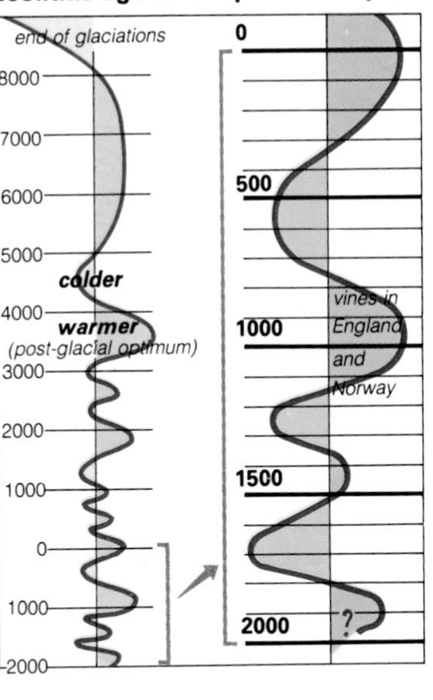

# The Birth of Art

Abstract and figurative art already exist side by side in the prehistoric world. There is no general chronological law governing the unfurling of prehistoric art: its canons and its evolution vary according to time and place. In Europe the Upper Paleolithic (between 30,000 and 9000 BC) produced exceptionally fine works, including engravings, sculptures and mural paintings in caves, rock shelters and in the open, and also objects of bone, ivory or stone. Portable artefacts are the most widely distributed, from the Atlantic to Siberia, from Belgium to the south of Italy, but mural art is only found in particular areas such as Périgord, the Pyrenees and Asturias, with a few exceptions such as the cave of Kapora in the Urals. Its main theme was the large fauna of the Quaternary period, which is depicted realistically; human forms are much rarer and are represented in a schematic or distorted manner; abstract or more or less unintelligible signs complete the motifs. The same differentiation is found in portable artefacts: in Périgordian art (25,000–20,000 BC) figures of women predominate (statuettes with rounded forms). The meaning of European Paleolithic art has been hotly debated: at first it was considered purely aesthetic, then the images were thought to be magical, serving to cast hunting spells. Today's researchers think it could be the expression of a complex cosmogony, a mythology based on sexual symbolism or perhaps the representation of systems of alliance between social groups.

In post-Glacial times (8000–5000 BC) Mediterranean Spain evolved an original art form known as Iberian Levant. It is characterized by fast-moving narratives full of vitality, such as boar and deer hunts and battle scenes.

The Sahara and regions bordering on it had their own particular cave art, the oldest of which dates from just before the sixth millennium BC. The earliest works are essentially naturalistic, with human figures and an abundant fauna; the paintings of Tassili-n-Ajjer are original in their portrayal of round-headed people. Oxen then became the favourite theme of the cattle herders of the Middle Neolithic period, and these in turn gave way, in the second millennium, to stiffer representations of equine animals and carts. The cave art of Southern Africa, most of which is attributed to the Bushmen or their predecessors, shows mainly predatory scenes. In northeast Brazil traces of paintings dating back at least 15,000 years BC are evidence of a very varied figurative cave art.

In general terms we can say that cave art in the last stages of prehistory and the first historical times was more or less universal, from the stone engravings of the Neolithic forest period in the USSR to the schematic Metal Age schools of the Val des Merveilles, the Iberian peninsula or Scandinavia.

Neolithic art in southern Asia, the Mediterranean and Europe often takes the form of a multiplicity of idols of stone or bone. The first statues in Europe – menhir statues – draw their motifs from deities or heroes of the period; the finest examples of these are in Anatolia and Malta.

Because it is found in so many different locations and spans such a long period, prehistoric art is a very complex phenomenon; the themes, styles and meanings of the recognized schools defy reduction to a single explanation.

1. *Hunters and animals. Cave engraving from Tanum, Sweden, 2nd millennium BC.*

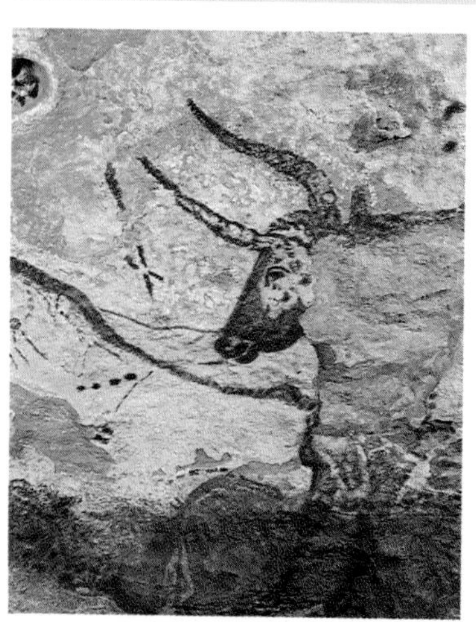

3. *Cave of Lascaux, Dordogne, wild oxen of the rotunda. Early Magdalenian cave paintings.*

**c. 35,000 BC:** Beginnings of European Paleolithic art. Pre-figurative period: Mousterian or Chatelperronian incisions in bone or stone slabs.
**30,000–23,000 BC:** Aurignacian art. Scribblings, vulvar forms, heads or forequarters of animals (stone slabs of La Ferrassie, rock shelters at Castenet and Cellier).
**23,000–19,000 BC:** Early Gravettian and Solutrean art. Depiction of animals with sinuous spines and ill-defined extremities. Bas-reliefs of Laussel (Dordogne). Carvings of Pair-non-Pair (Gironde). Sculpted 'Venus' figurines of Brassempouy, Lespugue, Willendorf (Austria).
**19,000–13,000 BC:** Early Solutrean and Magdalenian art. Sculpted blocks of stone of Roc de Sers, Cap Blanc and Bourdeilles. Cave drawings of Lascaux and Pech-Merle.
**From 15,000 BC:** Beginnings of cave art in South America (Brazil). Shelter of Toca do Boqueirao de Pedra Furada.
**13,000–9000 BC:** Middle and Upper Magdalenian art. Paintings of Font-de-Gaume, Niaux, Rouffignac, Altamira, engravings of Teyjat and Limeuil in the Dordogne. Bisons and modelled figures of bears (Tuc d'Andoubert, Bedeilhac, Montespan).
**8000–7000 BC:** Art of the Arctic zone, including Scandinavia, northern Russia and Siberia. Dotted figures of large mammals, birds, fishes, reptiles and also boats and people wearing skis. (The Neolithic art of Carelia (around 3000 BC) belongs to the same cultural area.) Beginnings of Iberian Levant art.
**From 6000 BC:** Art of Sahara and Maghreb, early phase (giant buffaloes). Around 4000 BC, art of cattle herders of Hoggar, Tibesti, Fezzan, Libya, Nubia, Harran. First South African art (engravings of Orange and Vaal Valleys, paintings of Drakensberg); beginning

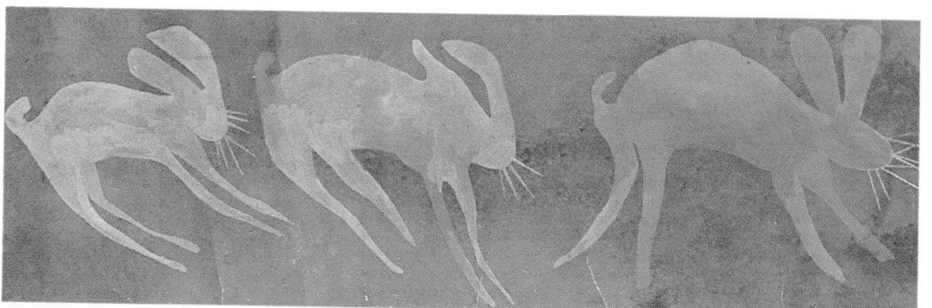

4. *Hares of Tassili-n-Ajjer, Algerian Sahara. Neolithic cave painting, c. 4500 BC.*

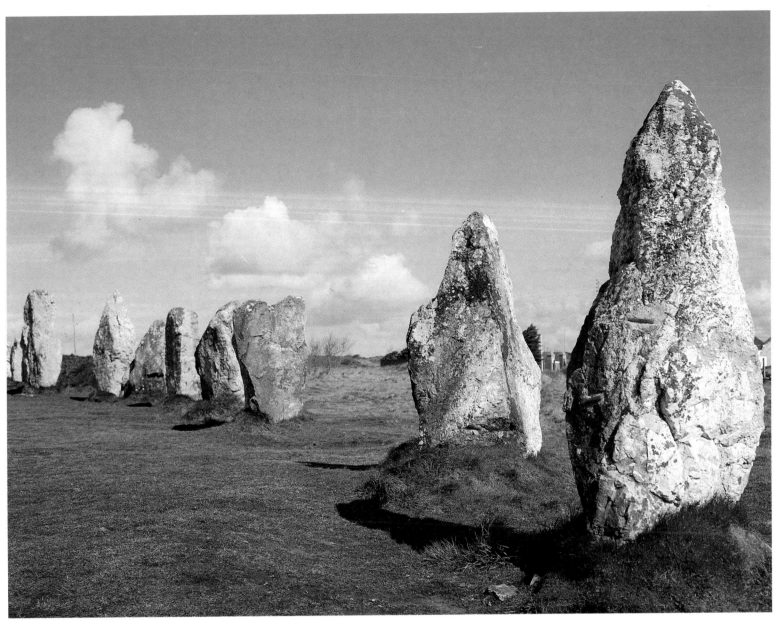

2. *Alignment of stones at Lagat-Jar, Brittany, Neolithic period.*

5. *Carnac cave in the Lot, a reindeer. Early Magdalenian cave painting.*

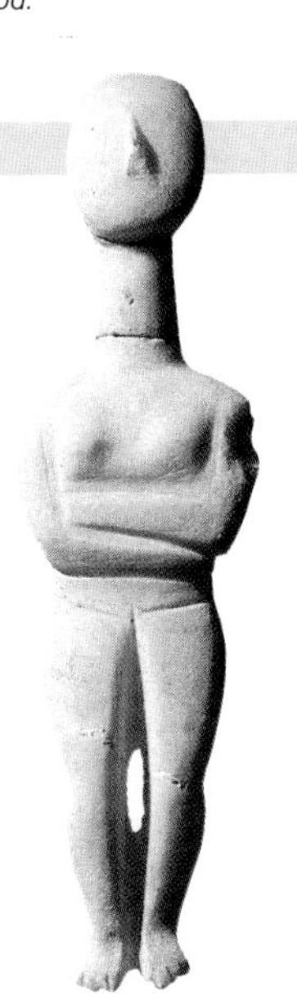

6. *Marble Cycladic idol from Amorgos, Greece, c. 2500 BC.*

of a long line of development.
**c. 6000 BC:** Wall paintings of Catalhuyuk in Turkey.
**From 5500 BC:** Neolithic statuettes of South-Eastern Europe.
**c. 5000 BC:** Fish idols of Lepenski-Vir (Yugoslavia).
**From 4000 BC:** Megalithic art of Western Europe.
**c. 2500 BC:** Cycladic figurines. Menhir statues of Sardinia and southern France.
**c. 2500–500 BC:** Art of Val Camonica in Northern Italy.
**c. 2000–1500 BC:** Cave engravings of Mont Bego (Alpes Maritimes, France).
**c. 1500 BC:** Scandinavian bronze engravings. Horses and carts of Sahara.
**c. AD 1800–1900:** 'X-ray' art of Australian Aboriginals

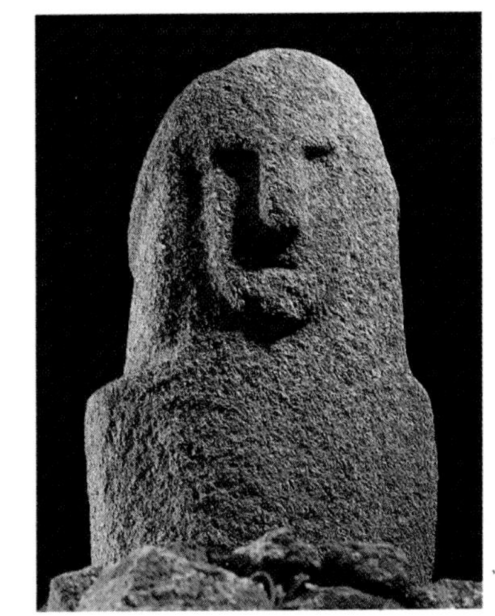

7. *Menhir statue from Filitosa, Corsica, c. 1500 BC.*

# Sumer and Akkad: Cities and Writing

1. A powerful and remarkably well-organized army.

2. A hierarchical society, a diversified economy and a rich, unifying culture.

MESOPOTAMIAN CIVILIZATION was born in the fourth millennium in Lower Mesopotamia. In this gradually emerging alluvial territory, there came together diverse populations who had come down from the mountain country to the north and east, as the ground drained. Vestiges of their cultures remain, but we have no means of identifying them. Only two groups, who came later on the scene and were more significant, have emerged into the light of history. These are the Sumerians, who came from the south-east, having severed all ties with the rest of their people (if indeed they left any of them behind) and who are totally isolated linguistically, and a Semitic population, who are connected to a known cultural and linguistic branch of humanity, which still flourishes today. The first people to arrive, as early as the fourth millennium, had originally belonged to the group of semi-nomadic sheep and goat rearers in the north of the Syrio-Arabian desert. From there, throughout the whole of history, they repeatedly came, singly or in waves, to settle among the Mesopotamians. First these Semitic peoples, who were more numerous in the north of the country, and the Sumerians in the south had to assimilate the old 'underlying' populations, and they grew progressively closer together in their cultural life, giving birth by this pooling of their cultural capital to the local civilization. The land was particularly well suited to livestock-rearing and to large-scale cereal cultivation, so long as the meagre levels of precipitation were supplemented by artificial irrigation. It was the undertaking of vast canal-building works which furthered both the prosperity of the region and the uniting of these populations under a single leader, who was capable of planning, commanding and governing, and ensuring the circulation of goods, even over long distances, as means of obtaining, by commerce or war, the materials lacking in this land of clay, reeds and asphalt, namely wood, stone and metal. These groupings of people gave rise to the formation of city-states, types of principalities which divided the territory into areas of land around the administrative and religious centre constituted by a city. At that point, along with a complex political organization of a monarchic type, monumental arts, metalworking, both in copper and later in bronze, underwent considerable development, together with a number of other techniques against the background of an ever-expanding economy. Around 3000 BC, to smooth the running of that economy, Sumerians developed the first forms of writing. At first picto- or ideographic, the phonetic value of signs was soon discovered and from being a mere aid to memory, this writing became a prodigious instrument for acquiring and propagating knowledge. The division into city-states was solely political: these all shared the same culture, as is very clearly shown by the establishment of a single pantheon and a single religious metropolis for the whole country. Quite early on, the Sumerians merged into the Semite population, the ranks of which were continually being swelled by new arrivals. It is, however, a sign of their acknowledged cultural supremacy that the Sumerian language continued to be used for cultural and liturgical purposes. Around 2300 BC the first unification of the country and the surrounding lands into an empire stretching from the Mediterranean to southwest Iran with Agade as its centre was achieved by Semites, who came subsequently to be known as 'Akkadians', under the leadership of the king known as 'Sargon the Great'. This enormous edifice lasted little more than a hundred years before it collapsed, but its political model was to mark the country for ever, as well as enshrining Semite hegemony. The kingdom of Ur (Ur III), which closes the millennium, would not weaken that hegemony, even though the official language was still Sumerian and the century turned out to be the golden age of Sumerian literature.

**First Uruk archives.**

**3000 BC**

**4th millennium:** Sumero-Semitic symbiosis: first towns (city-states) and emergence of local civilization.
**c. 3000 BC:** First Uruk archives. Writing invented: initially the tablets are used only for administrative operations and systematic lists of characters; they are pictographic and ideographic.
**c. 2900 BC:** First traces of the discovery of the phonetic value of written signs (in the Uruk archives).
**2750–2650 BC:** First Kish dynasty with the oldest known 'historic' king, Enmebaragesi (c. 2700 BC). First Uruk dynasty with its legendary kings: Gilgamesh. Fortifications are built around the towns. First dynasty of Ur: ancient archives and the 'royal cemetery' (the king's household is killed at his death to accompany him into the afterlife).
**c. 2600 BC:** At Fa'rah (Shuruppak) and Tell Abu-Salabikh, the first properly literary texts are produced (hymns, 'incantations' and myths).
**2500–2350 BC:** First Lagash dynasty (c. 2490 BC: Ur-Nanshe; c. 2400 BC: Eannatum:

**Gilgamesh king of Uruk.**

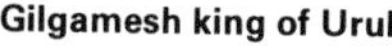

**2700 BC**

3. Man and woman at prayer. 3rd millennium BC.

c. 2350 BC: Uru'inimgina (Urukagina)) and royal archives. Ebla archives. First Mari kings.
**2334–2279 BC:** Sargon, a former officer of Ur-Zababa, King of Kish, kills Lugalzaggesi, takes over his kingdom, which he unifies around his capital Agade and expands it in the course of a series of military campaigns to the east and the west. He becomes master of a vast area of Near-Eastern territory, from the Mediterranean to the south-west marches of Iran. He thus founds and organizes the first Mesopotamian empire and inaugurates an important cultural fermentation of which few vestiges remain today. His descendants and successors – right down to Naram-Sin (2254–2218 BC) – will endeavour to maintain this edifice against both the internal revolts and external attacks which will ultimately destroy it in the reign of the Shar-kali-sharri, last king of the dynasty (2217–2193 BC). A period of anarchy ensues.
**c. 2200 BC:** The Gutians, mountain dwellers from the Zagros Mountains, invade and probably destroy a large part of the country, especially in the north.

# 3500–2000 BC

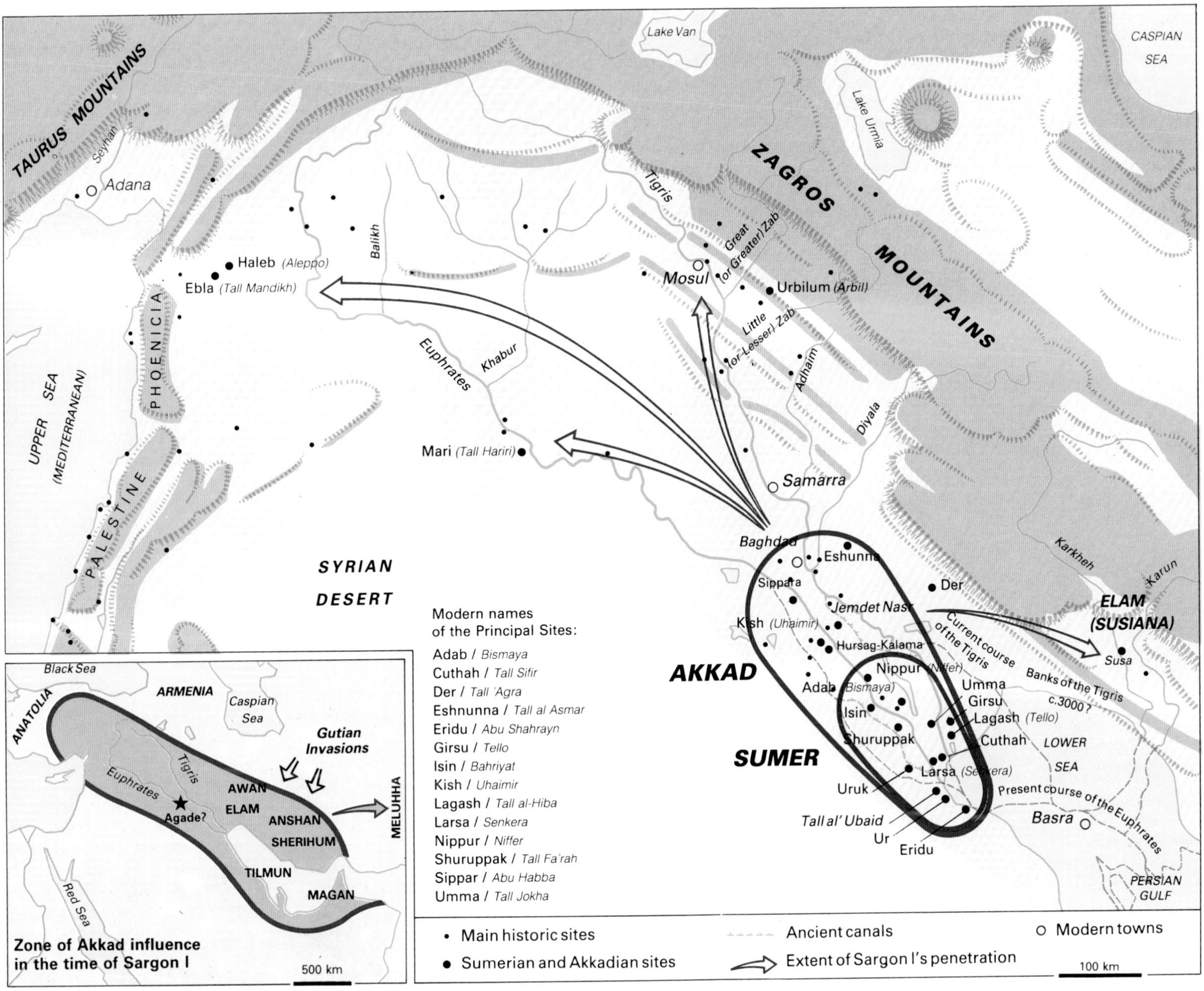

Lake Van
CASPIAN SEA
Lake Urmia
TAURUS MOUNTAINS
Seyhan
Adana
ZAGROS MOUNTAINS
Tigris
Great (or Greater) Zab
Little (or Lesser) Zab
Haleb (Aleppo)
Ebla (Tall Mandikh)
Balikh
Mosul
Urbilum (Arbil)
PHOENICIA
UPPER SEA (MEDITERRANEAN)
Euphrates
Khabur
Adhaim
Diyala
Mari (Tall Hariri)
Samarra
PALESTINE
SYRIAN DESERT
Baghdad
Eshnunna
Sippara
Der
Karkheh
Karun
Jemdet Nasr
ELAM (SUSIANA)
Kish (Uhaimir)
Hursag-Kalama
Current course of the Tigris
Susa
AKKAD
Nippur (Niffer)
Banks of the Tigris c.3000 ?
Adab (Bismaya)
Umma
Girsu
Isin
Lagash (Tello)
Shuruppak
Cuthah
LOWER SEA
SUMER
Larsa (Senkera)
Uruk
Present course of the Euphrates
Tall al' Ubaid
Basra
Ur
Eridu
PERSIAN GULF
Modern names of the Principal Sites:
Adab / Bismaya
Cuthah / Tall Sifir
Der / Tall 'Agra
Eshnunna / Tall al Asmar
Eridu / Abu Shahrayn
Girsu / Tello
Isin / Bahriyat
Kish / Uhaimir
Lagash / Tall al-Hiba
Larsa / Senkera
Nippur / Niffer
Shuruppak / Tall Fa'rah
Sippar / Abu Habba
Umma / Tall Jokha
Black Sea
ARMENIA
Caspian Sea
ANATOLIA
Gutian Invasions
Tigris
Euphrates
AWAN
ELAM
Agade?
ANSHAN
SHERIHUM
MELUHHA
TILMUN
MAGAN
Red Sea
Zone of Akkad influence in the time of Sargon I
500 km
Main historic sites
Sumerian and Akkadian sites
Ancient canals
Extent of Sargon I's penetration
Modern towns
100 km

**Sargon king of Akkad.** — **2334 BC**

**Gutian invasion.** — **2200 BC**

**Gudea king of Lagash.** — **2141 BC**

**Ur-Nammu king of Ur.** — **2112 BC**

**Between 2155 and 2111 BC:** An independent dynasty exists in Lagash which seems to have brought prosperity to this city-state. Its most famous sovereign is Gudea (2141–2122 BC).

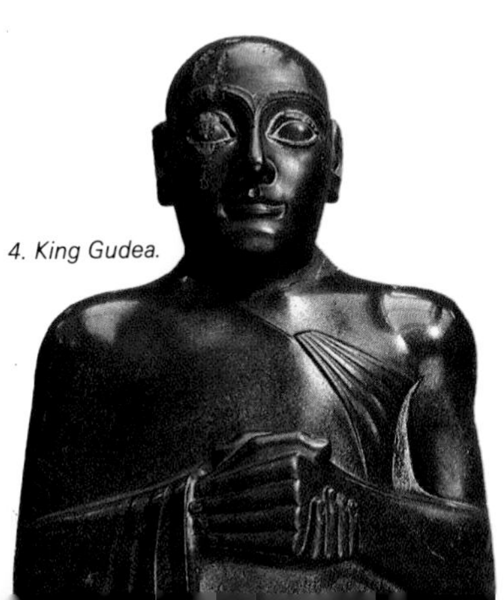

4. King Gudea.

**2123 and 2113 BC:** Ut-khegal of Uruk expels the Gutians and recaptures a large part of the country.

**2112–2095 BC:** Ur-Nammu, one of his officers, supplants him and founds the third Ur dynasty (Ur III), thus opening up a brilliant and productive century in which Sumerian art flourishes. This is also, however, a period of many battles, both offensive and defensive (largely against the Elamites of southwest Iran, fought both by Ur-Nammu and his successors, Shulgi (2094–2047), Amar-Sin (2046–2038), Shu-Sin (2037–2029) and Ibbi Su'en (2028–2004 BC). The last-mentioned succumbs to the Elamites in 2004 BC and the dominance of Ur dies with him. It is during the Ur III period that the first Amorite Semites began to infiltrate into the kingdom after several threats against and attacks upon its northwestern flank.

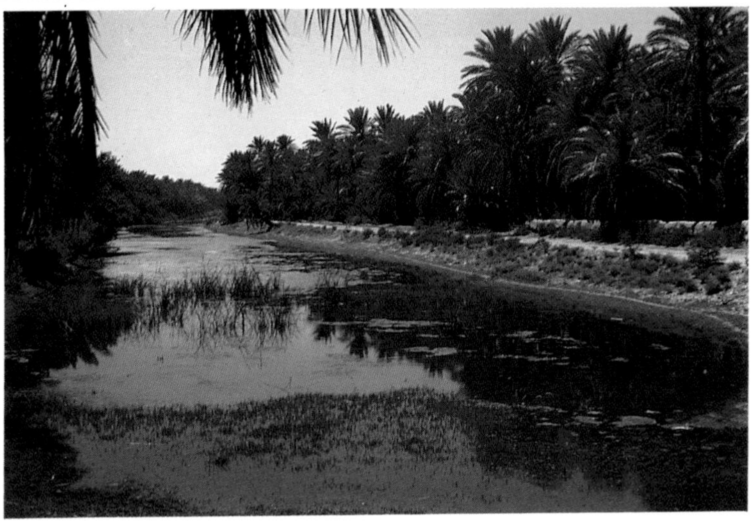

*5. Land of clay, reeds and asphalt.*

# The Nile and the First Pharaohs

The Nile Valley is bathed daily in the sun's rays and inundated each year by a flood that fertilizes the land around it at the height of summer. From 3000 BC onwards it was the cradle of an original civilization ruled over by a human god, the pharaoh. Menes, who, according to Herodotus, was the first Egyptian pharaoh, united Upper and Lower Egypt and imposed his authority upon a hard-working, disciplined peasant population. They were to show little inclination to challenge the foundations of a system that lasted for almost three thousand years. Exercising a power inherited from his divine forefathers, the pharaoh was master of the water and the land. A god among men, he was considered the guarantor of cosmic equilibrium and of the sound running of the country. As early as the first dynasty, the system of hieroglyphic writing was becoming highly developed; it would prove to be a vehicle for the expression of all the subtleties of human thought.

Menes, who had been born in the southern town of This, took up residence on the site of what was to become Memphis, on the borders of the Delta and Upper Egypt. The Old Kingdom (third to sixth dynasties) was the age of the great pyramid-builders. It was Imhotep, the architect of King Djoser (or Zoser) of the third dynasty, who had the revolutionary idea of abandoning sun-dried brick and using stone to build the step pyramid of Saqqarah. Djoser's successors would be buried beneath the famous Giza pyramids, then beneath those at Abu Sir (fifth dynasty) and along the whole of the Memphis plateau. The pyramids, which represented petrified sun rays, made it possible for the king to be united in the afterlife with the Sun God Ré, as did the magic formulas which covered their walls. These 'pyramid writings' are evidence of the dominant influence upon official theology of the priesthood of Heliopolis, who were sun-worshippers. By contrast, the popular pantheon was still very much influenced by archaic forms of worship, and major deities were beginning to be created by the amalgamation of the multitude of local animal gods. From Memphis, the administration organized the country's economy: at the head of this leading élite we find a class of privileged functionaries who had themselves buried in great 'mastabas' (low oblong tombs) built around the royal pyramids.

Being under no external threat, the pharaohs of the Old Kingdom launched no colonial wars; the major external activities of which there is evidence were commercial and mining expeditions (the former in Phoenicia and Nubia, the latter in Sinai). Following the long reign of Pepi II (2330–2240 BC), a grave social crisis shook the country: the provinces threw off the authority of the central monarchy and set themselves up as little kingdoms; Bedouins invaded the Delta and there was widespread famine and violence (seventh to eleventh dynasties).

1. Djoser's pyramid at Saqqarah.

2. Scene from a wall of a princess's 'mastaba'.

The family of the pharaohs of the twelfth dynasty, which originated in Thebes in Upper Egypt, extended its rule over the whole of the country and transferred the capital to Lisht in Middle Egypt. Schools of scribes produced propagandist literature with the aim of restoring monarchist ideology. The great economic achievement of the Middle Empire was the development of the Faiyum region. Abroad, Nubia was colonised, Palestine fell under Egyptian tutelage and expeditions into Libya became more frequent. At the end of the Middle Kingdom the invasion of the Hyksos, who were Canaanite in origin, led to the break-up of the kingdom. A new capital, Avaris, became the residence of these foreigners who ruled over most of Lower Egypt.

**First Pharaoh.** | **First pyramid (Djoser).** | **Giza.** | **Jubilee shrine at Karn**

**3000BC** |  **2660 BC** | **2600 BC** | **1972 BC**

**3000–2660 BC: THINITE PERIOD (1st and 2nd dynasties).** Menes and his successors organized the kingdom by developing irrigation. The establishment of the Sothiac (Sirius-based) calendar with a 365-day year. Building was carried out in sun-dried brick (Abydos, Saqqarah), and the making of statues developed.

**2660–2180 BC: OLD KINGDOM (3rd–6th dynasties).**
**2660–2600 BC:** 3rd Dynasty. Djoser, Sekhemkhet and Huni are the major figures of this dynasty, together with Imhotep, Djoser's vizier and architect. First stone pyramids; beginning of 'mastabas' for individuals.

**2600–2480 BC:** 4th dynasty. Snefru, Khufu (Cheops), Retdjedef (Djedfre), Khafre (Chephren) and Menkaure (Mycerinus), builders of the great pyramids (Maydum, Giza, Abou Roash). The statue of the Great Sphinx stands in front of Khafre's at Giza. Statuary, both royal and private, reached a peak of perfection which was to constitute a benchmark for artists of later periods.

5. The seated scribe, 4th dynasty, Saqqarah.

**2480–2330 BC:** 5th dynasty. Userkaf, Sahure, Neferirkare, Shepseskare, Neuserre, Menkauhor, Izezi and Onas succeeded one another on the throne. Their pyramids were smaller and are today less well preserved than those of their predecessors (Saqqarah, Abu Sir). It is in Unas's pyramid that 'pyramid writings' first make their appearance. The great court figures had scenes from daily life depicted on the walls of their 'mastabas' (Giza, Saqqarah).

**2330–2180 BC:** 6th dynasty. Teti, Userkare, Pepi I and Merenre precede the long reign of Pepi II. Marked increase in the power of provincial governors, who began to gain some independence from central government. The provincial necropolises become more ornate. at Meir, Dayr el Gabrawi, Aswan, Edfu and Dendera the tombs are decorated with great refinement.

**2180–1990 BC: FIRST INTERMEDIATE PERIOD (7th–11th dynasties).**
Anarchy and the dismantling of pharaonic organization. War between various kinglets, particularly between the Heracleapolitans (Middle Egypt) and the Thebans (Upper Egypt). With a few rare exceptions, art was very undeveloped, but under the 11th dynasty there was an appreciable renewal in this field with the accession of Intef and Montuhotep, who re-established unity.

**1990–1780 BC: MIDDLE EMPIRE (12th dynasty).**
Amenhemhat I, Sesostris I, Amenhemhat II, Sesostris II, Sesostris III, Amenhemhat III, Amenhemhat IV and Queen Sebeknefru made up this glorious dynasty. The royal pyramids built in the Faiyum were of modest dimensions. From this point on, the funereal inscriptions were 'democratized' and the 'sarcophagus writings' helped each individual to accede to the realm of Osiris. Numerous sanctuaries were built in various parts of the valley. The royal sculpture workshops were reopened.

# 3000–1560 BC

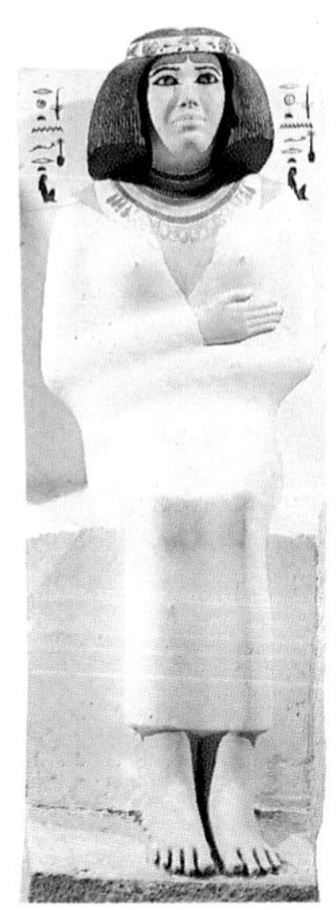

3. Nefertiti, wife of the high priest of Heliopolis, 4th dynasty, Maydum.

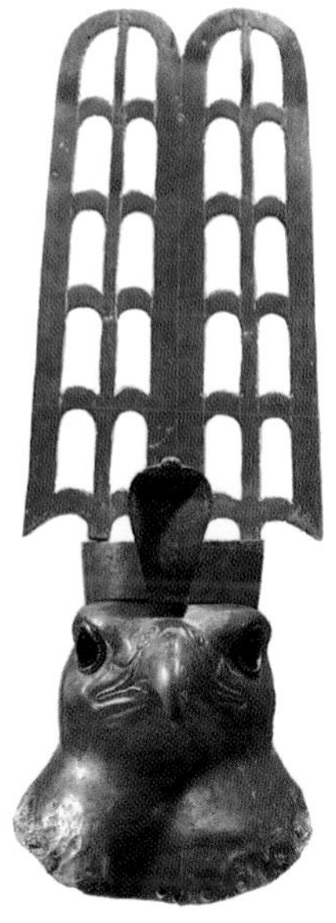

4. The royal symbol of the falcon, 6th dynasty, Hierakonopolis.

**Classical Egyptian language established.**

**1878 BC**

**1780–1560 BC: SECOND INTERMEDIATE PERIOD (13th–17th dynasties).**
Hyksos invasion of the Delta. Social and political disturbances.

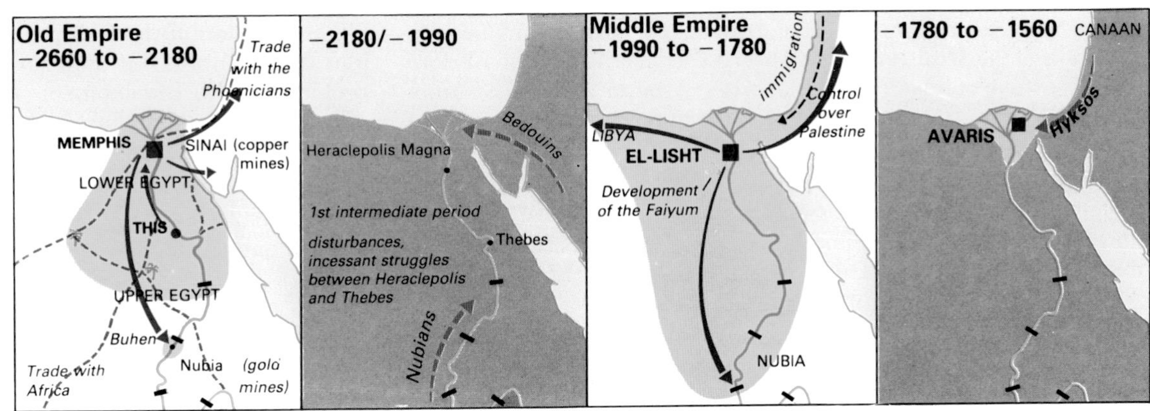

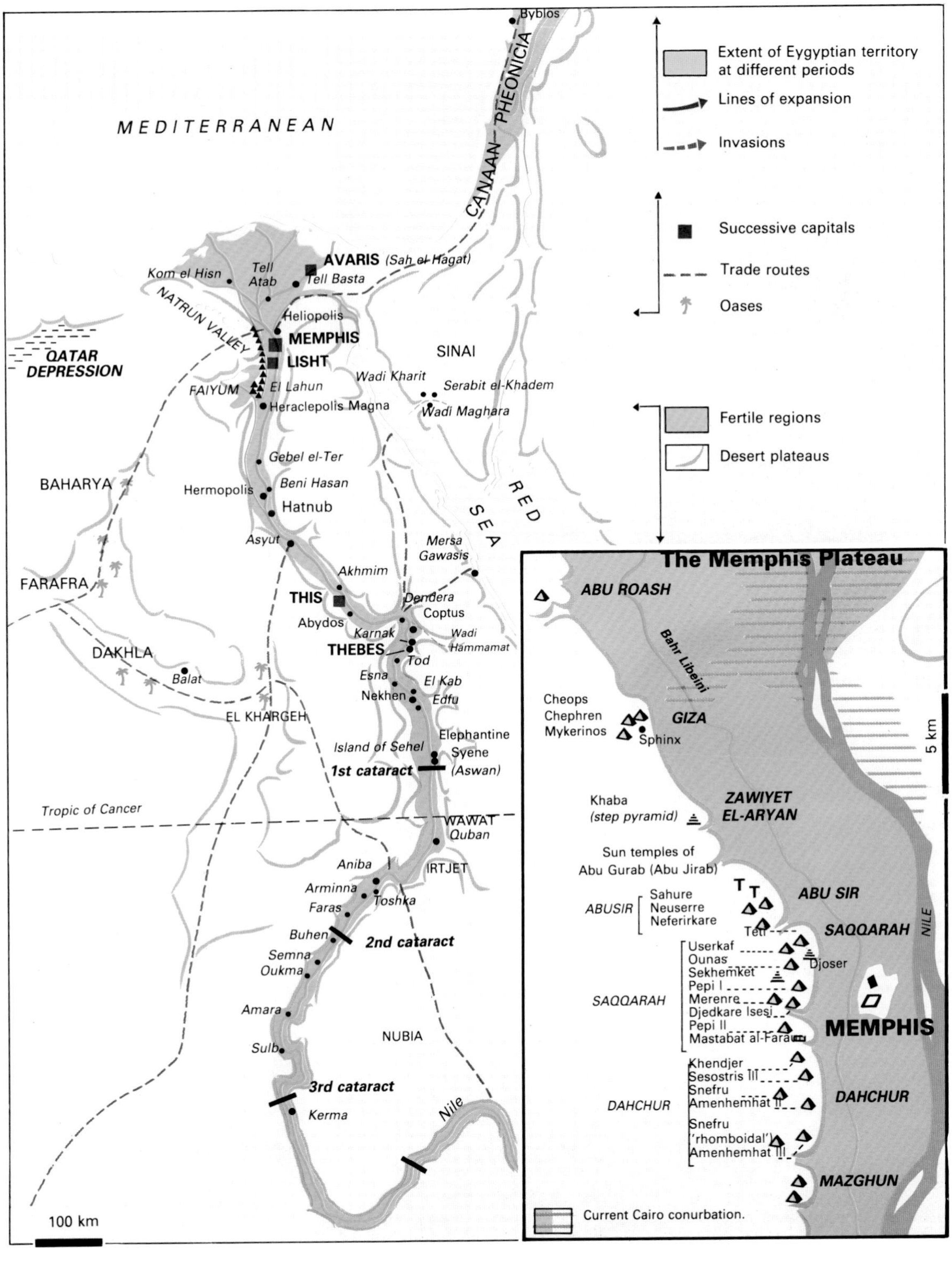

Old Empire
–2660 to –2180
Trade with the Phoenicians
MEMPHIS
SINAI (copper mines)
LOWER EGYPT
THIS
UPPER EGYPT
Buhen
Trade with Africa
Nubia
(gold mines)
–2180/–1990
Heraclepolis Magna
Bedouins
1st intermediate period
disturbances, incessant struggles between Heraclepolis and Thebes
Thebes
Nubians
Middle Empire
–1990 to –1780
immigration
Control over Palestine
LIBYA
EL-LISHT
Development of the Faiyum
NUBIA
–1780 to –1560
CANAAN
AVARIS
Hyksos


Byblos
CANAAN–PHEONICIA
MEDITERRANEAN
Extent of Eygyptian territory at different periods
Lines of expansion
Invasions
Successive capitals
Trade routes
Oases
Fertile regions
Desert plateaus
Kom el Hisn
Tell Atab
AVARIS (Sah el-Hagat)
Tell Basta
NATRUN VALLEY
Heliopolis
MEMPHIS
LISHT
QATAR DEPRESSION
FAIYUM
El Lahun
Heraclepolis Magna
Wadi Kharit
SINAI
Serabit el-Khadem
Wadi Maghara
Gebel el-Ter
BAHARYA
Hermopolis
Beni Hasan
Hatnub
RED SEA
Asyut
Mersa Gawasis
FARAFRA
Akhmim
THIS
Dendera
Coptus
Abydos
Karnak
Wadi Hammamat
THEBES
Tod
DAKHLA
Balat
Esna
El Kab
Nekhen
Edfu
EL KHARGEH
Elephantine
Island of Sehel
Syene
1st cataract
(Aswan)
Tropic of Cancer
WAWAT
Quban
Aniba
IRTJET
Arminna
Faras
Toshka
Buhen
2nd cataract
Semna
Oukma
Amara
NUBIA
Sulb
3rd cataract
Kerma
Nile
100 km
The Memphis Plateau
ABU ROASH
Bahr Libeini
Cheops
Chephren
Mykerinos
GIZA
Sphinx
5 km
Khaba (step pyramid)
ZAWIYET EL-ARYAN
Sun temples of Abu Gurab (Abu Jirab)
ABUSIR
Sahure
Neuserre
Neferirkare
ABU SIR
Teti
SAQQARAH
NILE
SAQQARAH
Userkaf
Ounas
Sekhemket
Djoser
Pepi I
Merenre
Djedkare Isesi
Pepi II
Mastabat al-Faraun
MEMPHIS
DAHCHUR
Khendjer
Sesostris III
Snefru
Amenhemhat II
DAHCHUR
Snefru ('rhomboidal')
Amenhemhat III
MAZGHUN
Current Cairo conurbation.

# The Destiny of Babylon

At the beginning of the second millennium BC, Mesopotamia was in the hands of the Semites, who had been joined nearly a century before by a new wave of invaders, the Amorites. Around 1750 BC the Amorites, headed by Hammurabi, put an end to the regime of city states which had been more or less revived after the third dynasty of Ur, and gave the country its definitive structure as a kingdom with Babylon as its capital. This political triumph marked the climax of the powerful cultural movement started by Sargon of Akkad. Institutions developed, techniques were perfected, thinkers ventured further into old and new realms, such as legal theory, lexicography and grammar, mathematics, divination, medicine, mythology (the 'philosophy' of the time). A great original literature was born.

1. *Clay walls of the town of Nimrud, capital of Assyrian Empire, 9th century BC.*

The invasion of the Kassites around 1600 BC plunged Babylonia into three centuries of political stagnation, but this was a climate propitious to the development of culture and literature in particular. Meanwhile, the Near East had changed its face: Egypt was increasingly involved in the international arena, and new and powerful kingdoms began to make their influence felt, the Hittites in Anatolia, the Mitanni in Syria and in northern Mesopotamia, and the Assyrians, who had regained independence around their original capital of Ashur. In addition, a new Semitic wave was unfurling, the Aramaeans, who were to prove resistant to assimilation. When Babylon, now reduced to its sole southern territory, finally awoke around 1100 BC it was not at first an impressive force. Between 1000 and 700 BC it was obscured by the military might of Assyria, which went from conquest to conquest, particularly on the western front, reaching its peak of glory after 700 BC with the Sargonid dynasty. But culturally it remained dependent on Babylon, the unrivalled intellectual and spiritual capital, which was alone capable of original thought and literature. When Nabopolassar, allied to the increasingly powerful Medes, destroyed Nineveh and forever wiped Assyria off the map, the glorious and awe-inspiring New Babylonian Empire had only a century to live. In 539 BC the founder of the Achaeminid Empire, Cyrus the Great, took Babylon without a struggle and reduced it to the provincial capital of one of his satrapies.

Babylon remained an intellectual centre, but the Aramaean language with its alphabet gradually replaced Akkadian in everyday usage. As Sumerian had done before, Akkadian became a high-brow language protected by its cuneiform script; it was confined, along with the culture it transmitted, to erudite circles whose task was not to create but to defend and promote the intellectual heritage. It was even transcribed in Greek for the Hellenistic world after Alexander's conquest of Mesopotamia in 331 BC, at the beginning of the Seleucid era. From now on, up to its final annihilation by the Parthians in 144 BC, Mesopotamia could only fade away. It had already dispensed the best of its creations over three millennia to lands as far distant as Israel and Greece, who, after adapting and assimilating this precious heritage, handed it down to us in turn.

Babylon sank into obscurity for two millennia. Then it took over fifty years, between 1800 and 1870, to unlock the secret of its extraordinary writing and its languages, to gradually unearth its clay archives spanning 3,000 years. Today we have managed to recover some 500,000 pieces, our oldest 'family archives'.

**Hammurabi accedes to throne.**

**1792 BC**

**Kassite domination.**

**c.1570 BC**

**The *Creation Epic*.**

**c. 1120 BC**

**Library of Ashurbanipal.**

**c. 650 BC**

**2000–1800 BC:** The main political configurations – Isin (Ishbi-Erra, 2017–1985 BC), Larsa (thirteen sovereigns, 2035–1763 BC), Babylon from Sumuabum (1894–1881 BC) onwards, and outlying kingdoms of Assyria and Mari – all appear to be manipulated by the powerful Amorites.
**1792–1750 BC:** Hammurabi, sixth king of the first dynasty of Babylon, unites the whole country around Babylon in a centralized monarchic system never to be challenged. His illustrious reign marks the climax of the period known as Old Babylonian. All fields of thought and literature flourish; not only are old masterpieces in Sumerian copied out with zeal, but a new literature in Akkadian is born.
**1750–1595 BC:** Hammurabi's successors, from Samsuiluna (1749–1712 BC) to Ammisaduqa (1646–1626 BC) did their best to preserve his heritage until it was destroyed during the reign of Samsuditana, when the Hittites destroyed Babylon in 1595 BC.
**c. 1570 BC:** The Kassites from the northeastern mountains establish political domination over the country: this lasts three centuries.

**1365–1330 BC:** The reign of Ashur-uballith I marks the awakening of Assyria: it shines for a century or two under a few great sovereigns (Shalmanesar I, 1274–1245 BC, Tukulti-Ninurta I, 1244–1208 BC) and then falls into obscurity.
**1124–1103 BC:** Nebuchadnezzar I restores Babylon's greatness, freeing the city from the Kassites in 1157 BC. The *Creation Epic*, published at this time, confirms Marduk's promotion to head of the universe and makes Babylon into the spiritual capital of the country. But Babylon is repeatedly invaded by nomads; it never recovers its political ascendency.
**911–891 BC:** From the reign of Adad-Nirari, Assyria reappears on the scene and begins to build a formidable empire which reaches the height of its military, political, economic and intellectual glory under Sargon II (731–705 BC) and his successors, Sennacherib (704–681 BC); Esarhaddon (680–669 BC) and, above all, Ashurbanipal (669–627 BC). Under attack from Babylon and the Medes in 612 BC, Nineveh falls and Assyria disappears.

**From 604–562 BC** (Nebuchadnezzar II) **to 555–539 BC** (Nabu-Na'id), Babylon is left alone to bear the standard for Mesopotamia. It recovers its former supremacy for a while. Aramaean influence grows.

4. *Cuneiform characters.*

**539 BC:** Cyrus conquers Babylon, relegating it to a mere local capital of a satrapy of the Achaemenid Empire. Mesopotamia survives, but its culture languishes under a total lack of political autonomy.
**331 BC:** Alexander conquers it along with the whole of the Orient. He dies in 323 BC and the Seleucid period begins in 311 BC.
**144 BC:** Arrival of Parthians in Babylon sounds the death-knell for Mesopotamia; it is taken over by new political and cultural systems, stripped of its original features, its fabulous innovations plundered by other cultures.

# 2000–144 BC

2. Crowned woman. Ivory statuette, Nimrud, c. 800 BC.

3. Fragment of Enuma elish or Creation Epic. Cuneiform tablet, c. 600 BC.

**Fall of Babylon.** **539 BC**

**Death of Alexander at Babylon** **323 BC**

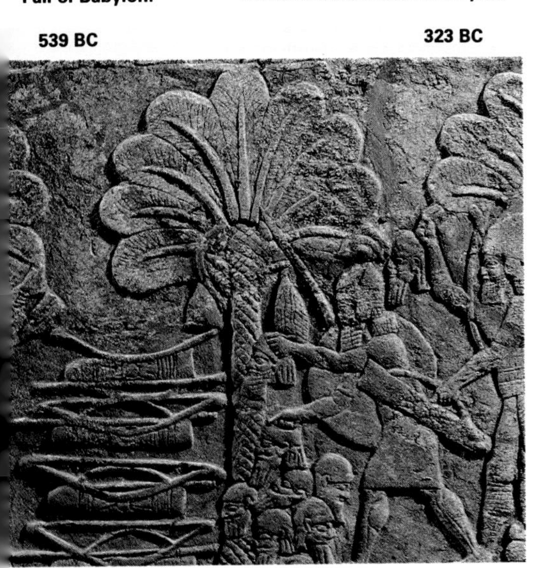

5. Head count: two scribes record bows, quivers and heads of the vanquished. Nineveh, 7th century BC.

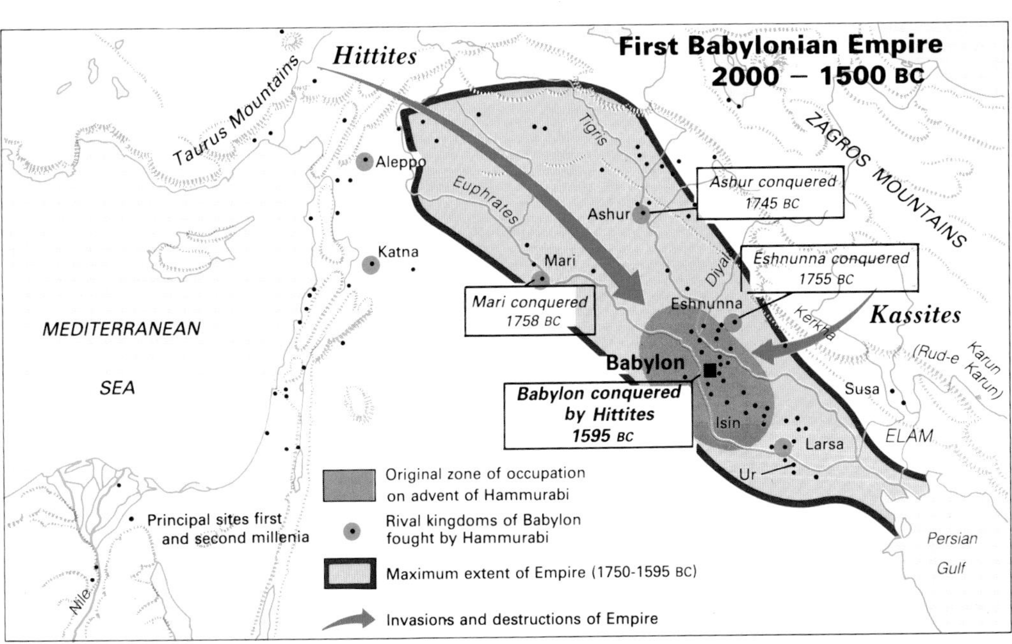


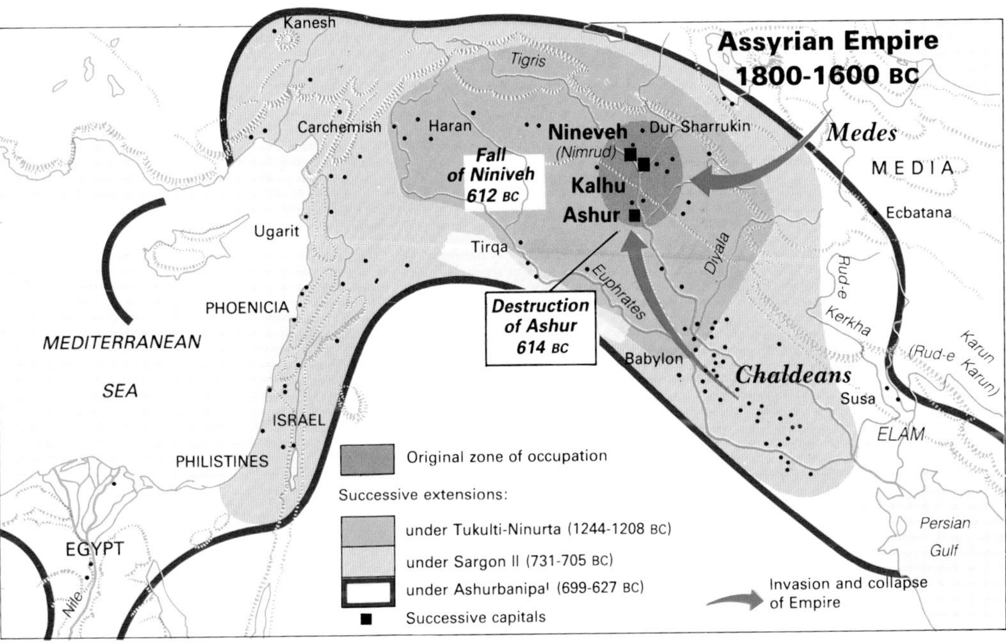


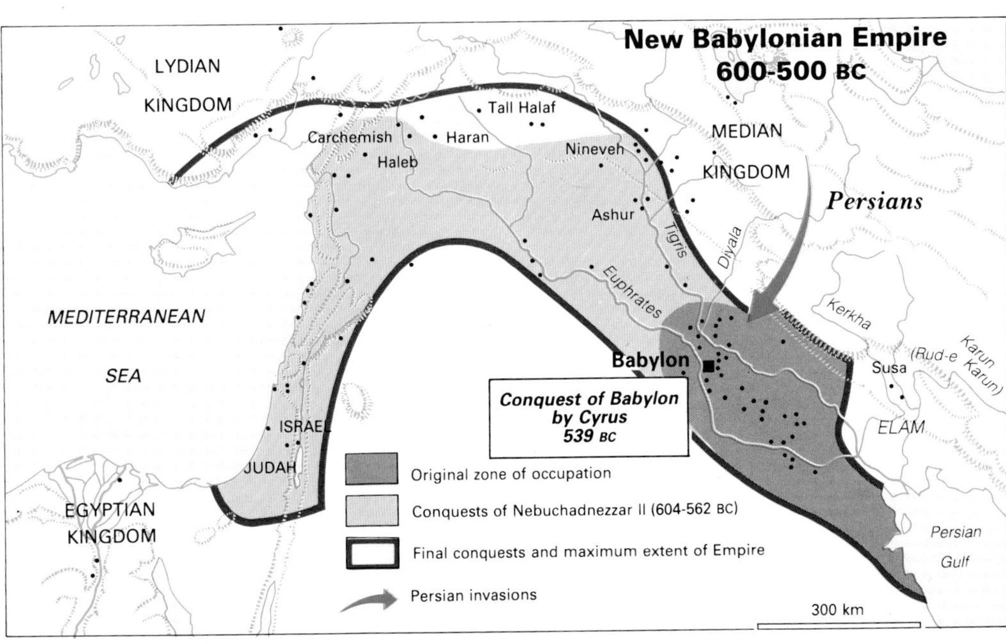

# The Hittite Empire and its Legacy

Hittite civilization was born on the high Anatolian plain in the heart of Turkey. It is both a rather arid region, and inaccessible, being surrounded by mountains which offer excellent natural protection. The population which modern scholars have named the 'Hittites' after the term 'Hatti' (which designated the ethnic group that were the original natives of the region and who were, in the course of time, assimilated into the new population) began to penetrate into Anatolia around 2000 BC, settling initially in its southeastern corner. The Hittites spoke an idiom belonging to the vast group of languages known as Indo-European; indeed, their language is now its oldest known dialect. The creation of the Hittite State, which was to have Hattusa (the present village of Bogazkoy, 150 kilometres east of Ankara) as its capital, took place around 1650 BC. From that point onwards its power was continually extended and increased, until the little kingdom became a great power. It was to occupy a major place on the early political landscape of the Near East, alongside Egypt and Assyria.

The Hittites are one of the rare peoples to have used two parallel systems of writing. They used, first of all, a cuneiform script borrowed from Mesopotamia, in which their long texts were written on clay tablets. These documents were found in their thousands in the various archives of Hattusa. Along with Hittite, these archives reveal the use of a number of other languages on this site, including Palaite, Luwian (Indo-European dialects), Hatti, Sumerian, Akkadian and Hurrite. The same types of texts – political, religious and literary – were found there as had already been found in the neighbouring civilizations. The second system of writing, which was of the pictographic type (known, for that reason, as 'Hurrite hieroglyphics') was created in Anatolia itself around the year 1500 BC. It was used for ceremonial inscriptions which were most often carved on rocks. In the course of the centuries, the Hittites were to create a unique civilization in which Oriental influences and the underlying Hatti component would ultimately remain the essential ingredients.

The Hittite Empire collapsed around 1200 BC, radically modifying the ethnic and political geography of Anatolia and Syria. It was a violent end to a powerful state created by a warrior people, a state summed up in the following prayer: 'Strength and vigour to the King, the Queen, the Princes and their troops, and may their land be bounded on the left by the sea and by the sea on the right.'

2. *The Lion Gate of Hattusa, 17th century BC.*

After an obscure period lasting some two centuries and involving many transformations, a new situation emerged. Cohesiveness was followed by fragmentation. Though the high plateau was deserted, little kingdoms or Hittite city-states formed in the south-east of Anatolia and in northern Syria, where old traditions survived: chief among these were Tabal, made up of a federation of principalities located to the west of the Taurus Mountains, and Melitene, Gurgum, Commagene, Carchemish and Sam'al beyond that mountain chain. Whilst cuneiform writing disappeared, hieroglyphs remained in use and were indeed improved; they now came to be used in the writing of long texts. These so-called neo-Hittite states gave a three century reprieve (1000–700 BC) to the illustrious Anatolian civilization.

1. *The armed gods of Yazilikaya. Rock carving, c. 1250 BC.*

**Assyrian merchants in Anatolia.**

**1900 BC**

**Hattusa capital.**

**1650 BC**

**The Hittites take Babylon.**

**1595 BC**

**1900–1800 BC:** Assyrian trading posts established in Anatolia between Kanesh (the present Kültepe) in the south and, following the Halys Valley (today, Kizil Irmak), the Black Sea in the north (Sinope). Assyrian tablets relating to commercial transactions represent the oldest vestiges of writing in Anatolia. The proper names of Indo-European origin which are found on these documents constitute the first evidence of the arrival in these regions of the Hittites, Luwians and Palaites.
**c. 1650 BC:** Accession of Hattusili I, who creates the Hittite state and sets up its capital at Hattusa.
**1650–1600 BC:** Period of the great military exploits of Hattusili I; they foreshadow the emergence of a powerful kingdom and mark the first territorial gains, notably Zalpa, Alalakh, Arzawa etc. The oldest texts in the Hittite language date from this same period. They are written in cuneiform characters and the most remarkable specimens are the historical annals, the laws and, above all, the political testament of Hattusili I, a unique document in ancient Near Eastern literature.

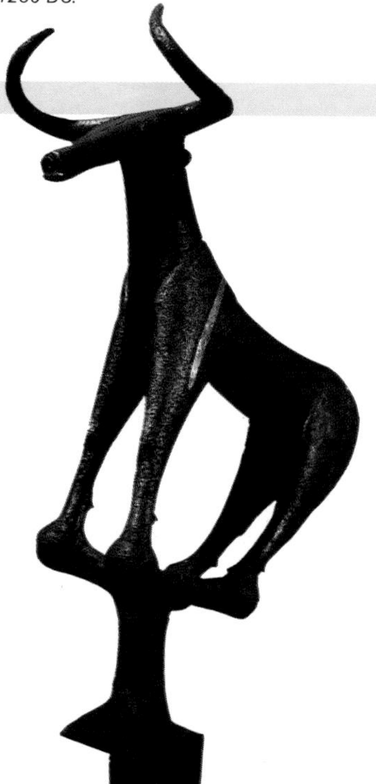

**1595 BC:** Mursili I sacks Babylon.
**c. 1500 BC:** The first documents in hieroglyphic characters appear in the south-east of Anatolia. This script, which was a transcription of a Luwian dialect, spreads progressively over a large part of the territory.
**c. 1300 BC:** The Hittite Empire is at its height. Its frontiers are pushed forward in the east, south and west and it exerts substantial power and influence. Such a situation is not without its effects upon Hittite cultural and religious life, where syncretism becomes more and more evident. The majority of written documents date from this period.
**1285 BC:** Egyptians and Hittites fight at Kadesh for the domination of Syria. After the battle, its territory is divided up between them.
**1250–1225 BC:** Reign of Tuḏhaliya IV. The King completes the building of the Yazilikaya rock shrine (2 km from Hattusa), an extraordinary monument formed out of two

3. *Early Bronze Age standard from the royal tombs of Alaca Hüyük. Beginning of 2nd millennium BC.*

4. *Cuneiform tablet in Babylonian syllabic script bearing the seal of King Mursili II (1344–1315 BC).*

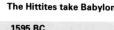

# 1900–700 BC

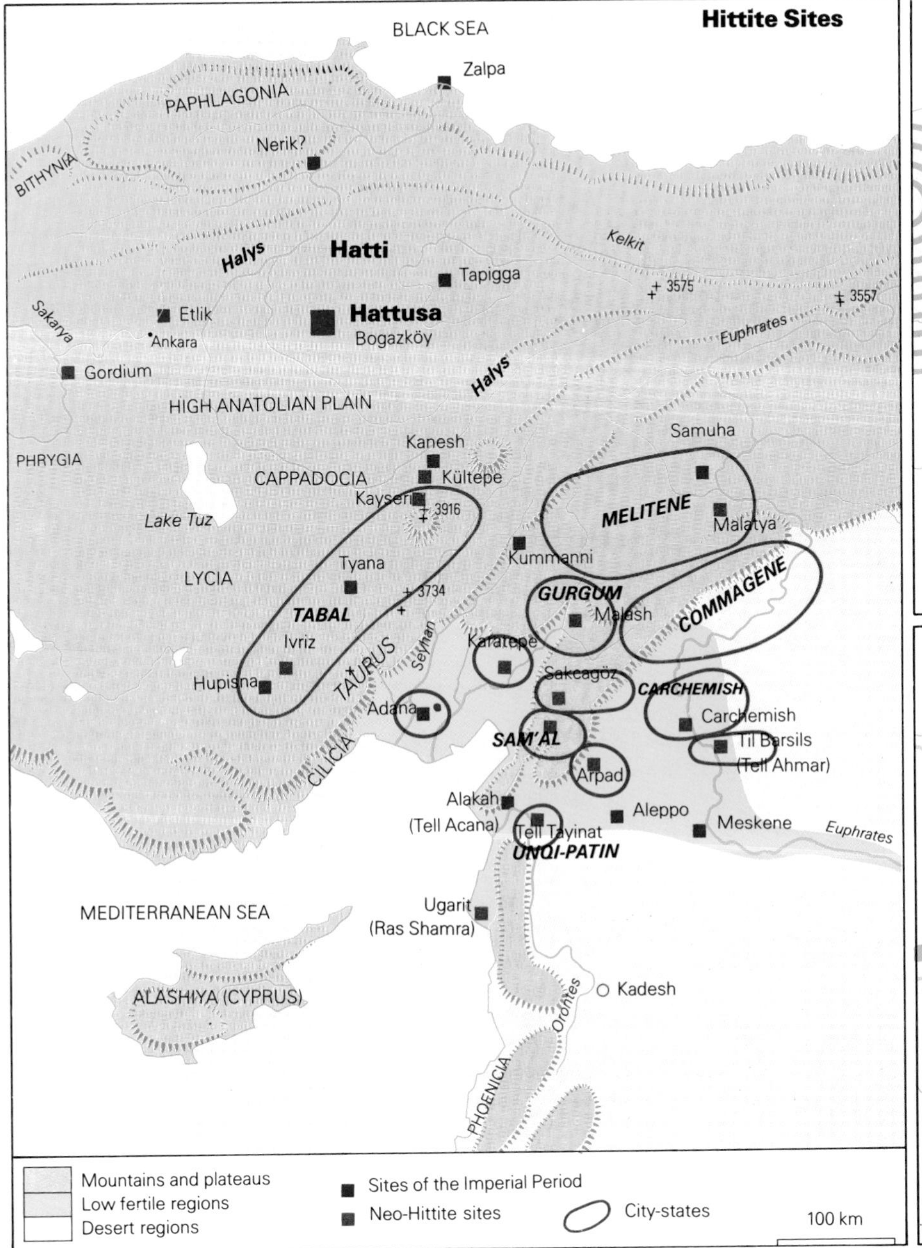


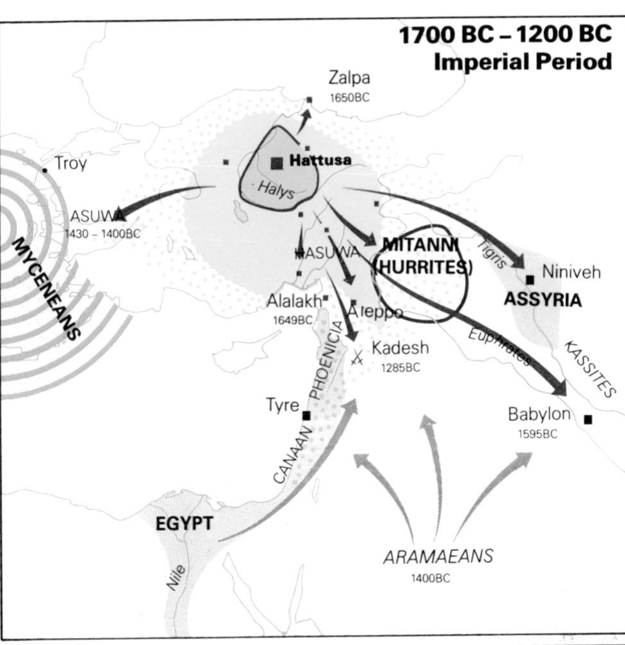


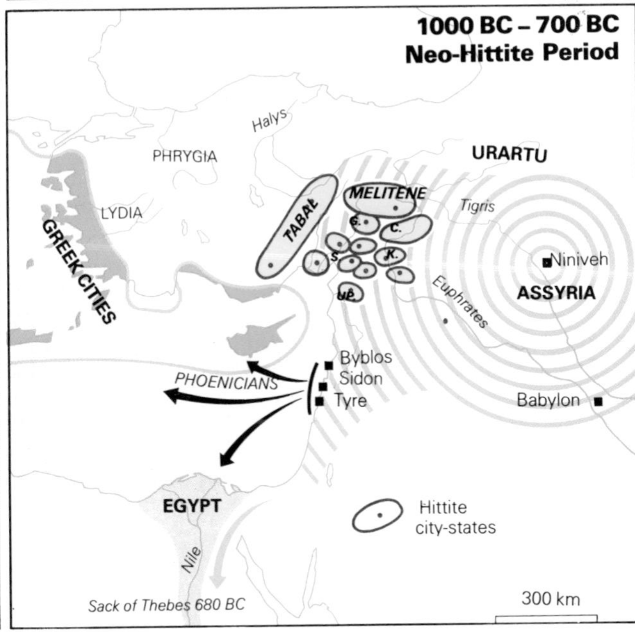


| Battle of Kadesh. | Yazilikaya sanctuary is finished. | Fall of the Empire. |
|---|---|---|
| 1285 BC | c. 1230 BC | c. 1200 BC |

5. *The town of Alaca Hüyük, c. 1300 BC.*

natural galleries, whose walls are covered with reliefs representing 71 divinities from the official pantheon. This king was also responsible for laying out the royal fortress of Büyükkale (in the centre of Hattusa).

**c. 1200 BC:** Fall of the Hittite Empire during the great disturbances which shook the Near East at this time and which are known as the Invasion of the Sea Peoples. Hattusa is destroyed.

**c. 1000 BC:** Formation of neo-Hittite principalities where multiple cross-fertilizations give rise to an art known as 'Syro-Hittite' as well as to the writing of bilingual or trilingual texts (Luwian, Phoenician, Aramaic) until 700 BC.

6. *Inscription in Hittite hieroglyphics from the neo-Hittite period, c. 800 BC, Carchemish.*

# The Aegean World

1. The first circle of royal tombs at Mycenae. 16th century BC.

During the first centuries of the Bronze Age, civilizations of farmers, herdsmen and trading seamen, all virtually undifferentiated from a technological, economical or social point of view, succeeded each other in the Aegean, continental Greece and the Peloponnese. These civilizations, which might be termed regional, are nonetheless distinguished by certain individual traits: marble working in the Cyclades (statuettes, vases), funerary architecture of a monumental type in Crete (communal tombs in the Mesara Plain), production of gold artefacts at Troy and Poliochni (Lemnos).

In this same period, there are striking affinities in material culture between Troy and Lemnos, the Cyclades, Crete and mainland Greece, and the presence of imported objects reveals that there was a continuous movement of people and objects and doubtless also of ideas. Everywhere, except in Crete, sites were fortified, which testifies to the importance of war in these cultures. In Crete specifically, between 2000 and 1600 BC, we can see a civilization developing that was centred on the palace and the town. This was an isolated development in the Aegean world, but one linked to a process that went back thousands of years in the Near East. The archaeological findings tell a story of the progressive formation of a stratified society and the increasing concentration of power in a few great cities, characterized by the presence of a central group of buildings – the palace – which was the focal point of economic, political and religious life. The development of writing using clay tablets (Linear A) helped to facilitate administration. In all the palace/urban centres, evidence of destruction is found, which is most often attributed to earthquakes. It is one such catastrophe which marks the end of the period of the 'first palaces'. The gradual reconstruction of Cretan towns and palaces around 1600 BC leads to the apogee of Minoan civilization and its period of greatest influence in the Aegean world.

In mainland Greece and in the Peloponnese, the transformations leading to a complex and stratified society appear some four centuries later than in Crete. Between 2000 and 1600 BC (Middle Helladic), there developed an homogeneous civilization at the same technological, economic and social level as the societies of the ancient Bronze Age period. It is generally thought that the bearers of this civilization, who came from the north, spoke an Indo-European dialect that was a forerunner of Greek. It is around 1600 BC that the Mycenaean civilization developed on this substratum (period of the deep shaft graves at Mycenae). The Mycenaean kingdoms of mainland Greece and the Peloponnese consolidated their position and prospered thanks to the systematic exploitation of agricultural resources (for example, by the draining of Lake Copais) and a highly centralized, bureaucratic administrative system: the centres of power were impressively fortified and detailed inventories of goods were kept on clay tablets (in Linear B and Greek). The progressive expansion of the Mycenaeans challenged the maritime supremacy of Crete and the Cyclades. The general destruction of Minoan sites around 1450 BC, which is attested by excavations, marks the end of Cretan domination and the beginning of Mycenaean power in the Aegean world. Between 1400 and 1200 BC, Mycenaean trade developed in the central and eastern Mediterranean, clearly promoting the establishment of permanent settlements in some part of the region. Mycenaean material culture, heavily influenced in its beginnings by Minoan artistic tradition and by that of the civilizations of the Near East, is remarkably homogeneous. The brusque and violent destruction of the towns and palaces and the progressive disintegration of the elements characteristic of Mycenaean culture were for many years attributed to the invasion of new Greek populations, the Dorians. But other factors may have played a part, such as climatic changes affecting agricultural production and, most importantly, social upheavals which might have weakened or even overturned the power of the ruling castes.

**Arrival of the Greeks.**

**2000 BC**

**Destruction of the 'first palaces' on Crete.**

**1700 BC**

**3200–2000 BC: Early Bronze Age**
**Pre-hellenic regional civilizations:**
*Helladic* (mainland Greece, Peloponnese and neighbouring islands. Main sites: Eutresis, Orchomenos, Hagios Kosmas, Lerna, Aegina).
*Cycladic* (Cyclades. Main sites: Myrtos, Vassiliki, Lebena, Mochlos, Knossos, Hagia Triada).
*Civilizations of the north-east Aegean region* (Main sites: Troy, Poliochni, Thermi, Emporion).

**2000–1600 BC: Middle Bronze Age**
*Mainland Greece:* Arrival of the first Greek-speaking Indo-European populations.
*Crete:* First rise of a complex urban civilization; 'first palace' period (main sites: Phaistos, Knossos, Mallia).
**c. 1700 BC:** Destruction layers in all the Minoan centres. End of the 'first palace' period.

2. Pitcher in the Kamares style. Minoan art, beginning of 2nd millennium.

**1600–1100 BC: Late Bronze Age**
**1600–1500 BC:** *Crete and Cyclades:* 'Second palace' period. Apogee of the palace/urban civilization (main sites: Kato Zacro, Palaikastro, Gournia, Mallia, Phaistos, Hagia Triada, Knossos, Khania-Kastelli). Expansion of Minoan culture in the Aegean (main sites: Phylakopi, Hagia Irini, Akrotiri).
*Mainland Greece and Peloponnese:* First rise of Mycenaean civilization; shaft graves of Mycenae.
**c. 1500 BC:** Volcanic destruction of Thera (Santorini). The town of Akrotiri buried under volcanic ash.
**c. 1450 BC:** Vast destruction in Cretan sites. Knossos occupied – possibly by Mycenaeans.
**c. 1400 BC:** Final destruction of Knossos.
**1400–1200 BC:** Great rise of Mycenaean civilization. Mycenaean kingdoms in mainland Greece and in the Peloponnese (main sites: Iolkos, Thebes, Orchomenos, Gla, Athens, Mycenae, Tiryns, Pylos, Peristeria). Mycenaean influence in the Aegean islands and Crete. Progressive expansion of the Mycenaean states in the

3. 'The lyre-player', Paros marble, found on the island of Amorgos. Cycladic art, c. 2300 BC.

# 3200–1100 BC

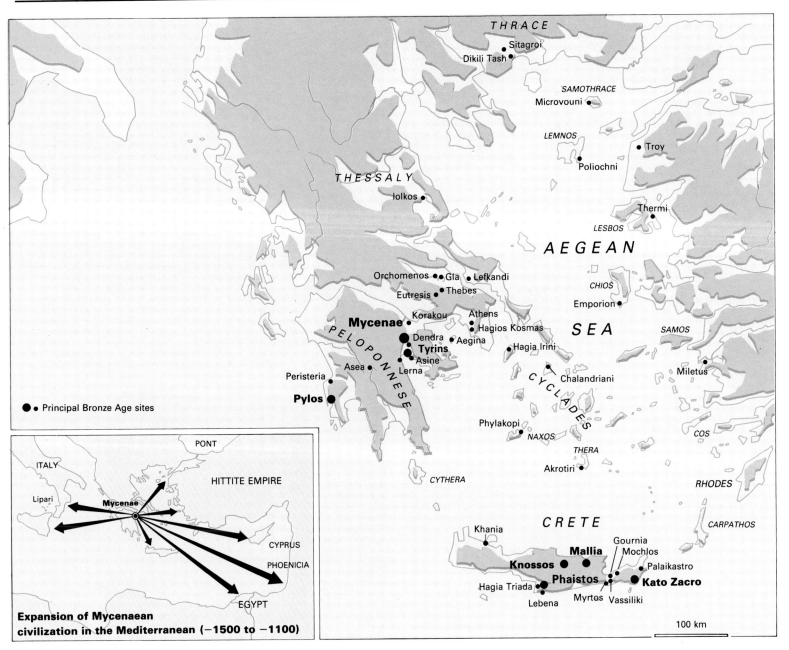

● • Principal Bronze Age sites

100 km

**Expansion of Mycenaean civilization in the Mediterranean (−1500 to −1100)**

| 1500 BC | 1450 BC | 1400 BC | 1200 BC |
|---|---|---|---|
| **Volcanic eruption at Thera (Santorini).** | **Destruction of the 'second palaces' on Crete.** | **Destruction of Knossos.** | **Invasion of the Sea Peoples.** |

central and eastern Mediterranean (southern Italy, Sicily, Sardinia, Malta, Asia Minor, Cyprus, Syria, Palestine, Egypt).
**1200–1100 BC:** Population movements. Disturbances in all the regions of the eastern Mediterranean. Invasions of the Sea Peoples in Egypt. Successive invasions of Dorian tribes in Greece. Destruction of Mycenaean centres of power. Disintegration of Mycenaean culture.

*4. The two antelopes of Santorini, Minoan art, c. 1500 BC.*

*5. Woman bearing offerings, Santorini, c. 1500 BC.*

*6. Painted limestone head, Mycenae, 13th century BC.*

# The Indus Civilization

In 1921 and 1922 archaeologists unearthed the remains of two cities in the Indus valley: Mohenjo-daro, 320 kilometres north of Karachi, and Harappa, 650 kilometres further north. The visible ruins of Harappa had already been described in 1834 by an English traveller who recorded local legends about its destruction. Excavations of the deepest strata of the cities established the existence of an Indian civilization contemporary with that of Egypt and Mesopotamia and covering a much wider area. Remains of the same type were found on the coast 500 kilometres east of Karachi, near Simla, near Delhi, and in the Gulf of Cambay. In all, there were about a hundred widely dispersed sites of this type. Older farming and cattle-breeding villages had paved the way for these two major towns; they were not, as had been thought, Mesopotamian colonies.

What is not known is whether they were capitals of two distinct states or alternate capitals of the same empire. Both have a perimeter of six kilometres and are built on a grid system, with rectangular blocks of dwellings; eight-metre-wide major streets are criss-crossed by smaller lanes. On the western flank stands a mound surrounded by fortifications of mud bricks: the 'citadel'. On the Mohenjo-daro citadel there is an enormous granary on a brick base, equipped with an air-drying system, and at Harappa twelve small silos with the same total capacity as the single one at Mohenjo-daro. The Mohenjo-daro citadel also includes a 'Great Bath', possibly for ritual bathing, with a flight of steps for access and a drainage system; it is surrounded by cells. The lower town was protected from flooding by a brick wall and houses and streets were equipped with a sophisticated system of drains also built of brick. At Harappa workers' barracks stood between the ramparts and the river.

The people of the Indus valley used not only stone tools but also copper and bronze implements. They domesticated horned animals, poultry and probably elephants. They grew wheat and barley, and the oldest traces of cotton have been found in the two cities. Their script is remarkable: they have left us thousands of square, round or cylindrical seals engraved with figures of animals or humans which also bear short inscriptions; these are based on 270 different signs undeciphered to this day. The seals are thought to have been used by traders to seal bundles of merchandise, as examples were found in Mesopotamia dating from 2300 BC; this is confirmed by Mesopotamian records of active trading with ports near the Indus. It is strange that this script should not have been used in longer texts or on material other than the steatite of the seals. Equally mysterious, it would seem, is the absence of temples or palaces in such a highly developed urban environment. We are left wondering also about the terracotta figurines and stone and bronze sculptures of human or divine beings: what religion do they point to? Are they forerunners of post- or para-Vedic Indian deities, proto-Śivas, Great Mothers? We know nothing of their language except that it may be related to the Dravidian group. The social structure and political history are equally mysterious, although these would appear to be centralized bureaucracies, judging by the standardized system of weights and measures (stone weights, for example), the regularly levied taxes on surrounding rich farmland and the fact that the two cities subsisted for six centuries without the slightest sign of change.

The final mystery is: how did this civilization disappear? All we can be sure of is that the skeletons found in the most recent stratum at Mohenjo-daro show signs of violent death. Could there have been a massacre by invaders and could these invaders be forerunners of the Aryans?

1. Site of Mohenjo-daro citadel with Great Bath in centre.

**Neolithic settlements in Baluchistan. Beginnings of cattle breeding and agriculture.**

**Settlements in the Indus Valley.**

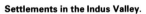

**c. 6000 BC**

**c. 3000 BC**

3. Bust of a man known as the 'High Priest', found at Mohenjo-daro.

4. Detail of Great Bath surrounded by cells at Mohenjo-daro.

5. Bronze dancer, Mohenjo-daro.

# 6000–1700 BC

*2. Steatite seals with animal designs and inscriptions.*

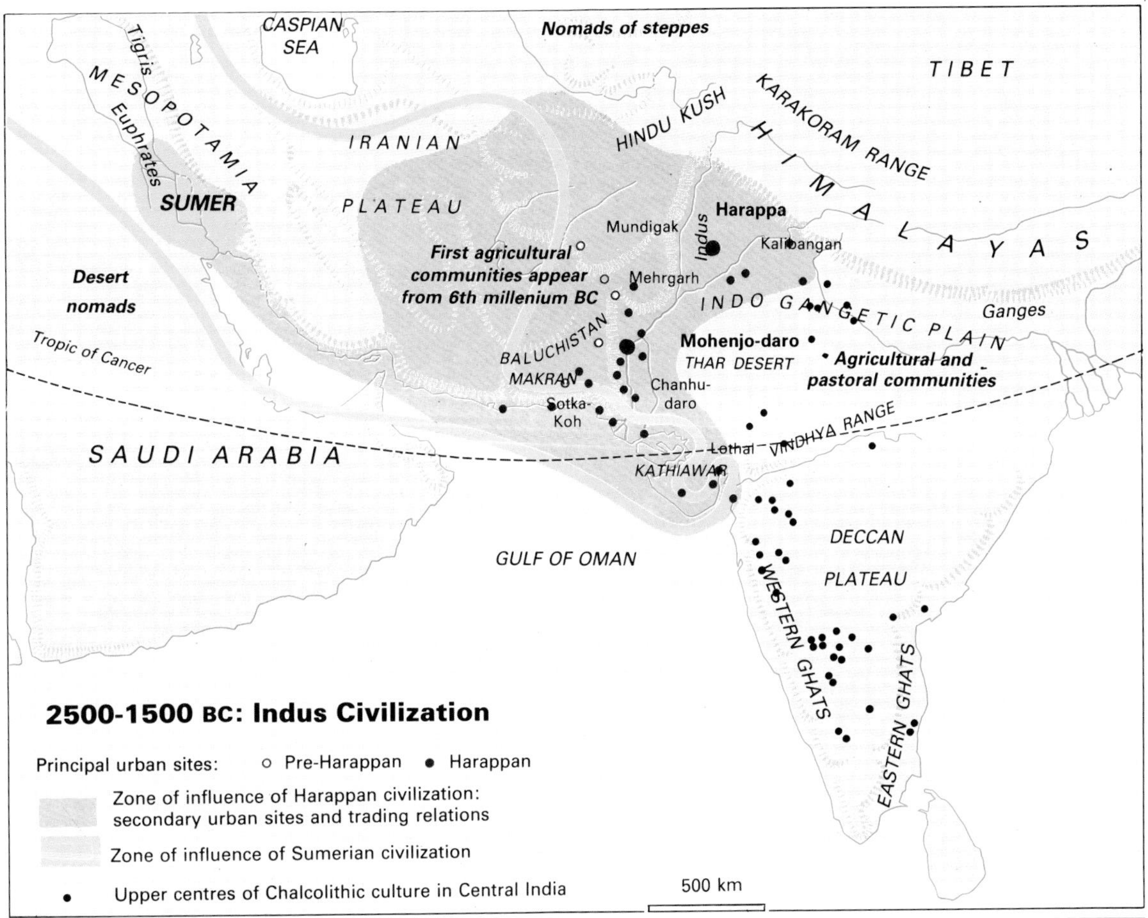

CASPIAN SEA
Nomads of steppes
TIBET
Tigris
MESOPOTAMIA
Euphrates
SUMER
IRANIAN PLATEAU
HINDU KUSH
KARAKORAM RANGE
HIMALAYAS
Harappa
Mundigak
Indus
Kalibangan
First agricultural communities appear from 6th millenium BC
Mehrgarh
Desert nomads
INDO GANGETIC PLAIN
Ganges
Tropic of Cancer
BALUCHISTAN
Mohenjo-daro
THAR DESERT
Agricultural and pastoral communities
MAKRAN
Chanhu-daro
Sotka-Koh
SAUDI ARABIA
Lothal
VINDHYA RANGE
KATHIAWAR
DECCAN PLATEAU
GULF OF OMAN
WESTERN GHATS
EASTERN GHATS

## 2500-1500 BC: Indus Civilization

Principal urban sites: ○ Pre-Harappan ● Harappan

Zone of influence of Harappan civilization: secondary urban sites and trading relations

Zone of influence of Sumerian civilization

● Upper centres of Chalcolithic culture in Central India

500 km

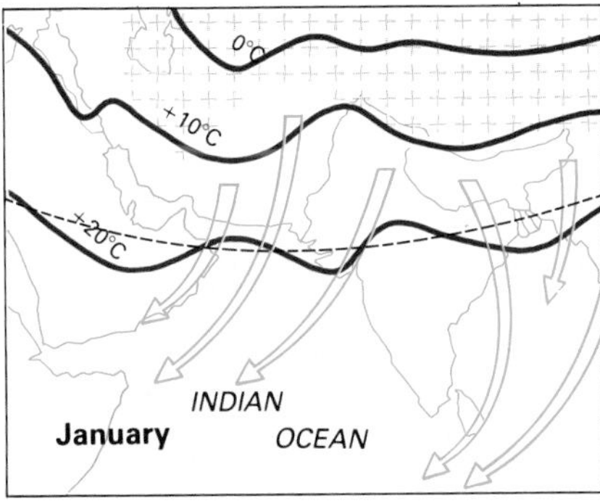


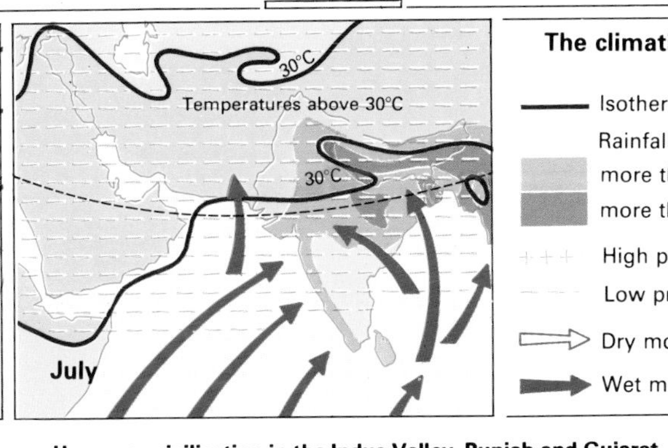


**Pre-Harappan villages.**

**2800–2600 BC**

**Harappan civilization in the Indus Valley, Punjab and Gujarat.**

**2300–1700 BC**

*6. Mohenjo-daro: remains of brick houses and streets.*

*7. Ritual bronze statuette of buffalo, Mohenjo-daro.*

*8. The docks of Lothal in the Gujarat, dating from c. 2500 BC.*

# The Phoenician Middle East

In classical antiquity, the term 'Phoenicians' designated the Semitic peoples who inhabited the Syrian coast between Mount Casius in the north and Mount Carmel in the south, whose best-known towns were Aradus, Simirra, Byblos, Berytos, Sidon, Tyre and Akko (Acre). The origin of the word *Phoenicia* is unknown, since the words derived from the root *ponike* that are to be found in the Linear B texts of Knossos and Pylos (*c.* fourteenth century BC) and which signify not only 'purple' but also a type of spice and the fruit of the palm tree, do not seem to have had any precise ethnic connotation. The *Iliad* considers Phoenicians and Sidonians to be the same people, describing them first as artisans and then as navigators. On the other hand, the traditional accounts collected by Herodotus and Androsthenes, Alexander's explorer, present the Phoenicians as originating in the Gulf region, but these do not take account of the cultural elements which establish long-standing connections between the Phoenicians and the old so-called Canaanite culture of the Syro-Palestinian coast for which the texts of Ugarit are the best source. Some of the Phoenician ports must have been in contact with Egypt since very early times, as fragments of alabaster vases found in Byblos bear the names of pharaohs of the first dynasty who reigned at the beginning of the third millennium. Throughout the second millennium, the commercial relations of the coastal towns with Cyprus, Crete and Egypt became regular. The Akkadian texts from the age of Akhnaton (1364–1347 BC) found at Tell el Amarna reveal the existence along the coast of principalities like those of Byblos and Tyre whose fate was bound up with Egyptian policy in relation to other powers, such as the Hittite Empire. After the social upheaval that was produced in the whole of the Near East around 1200 BC by the invasion of the sea peoples, the Phoenicians acquired the historical identity which the classical authors attribute to them and they began to use alphabetic writing. The shape of the letters was inspired by hieroglyphic script and differs from the texts of Ugarit, which are in a cuneiform alphabet. In Mesopotamia, the Syro-Palestinian hinterland and the western Mediterranean at the beginning of the first millennium, the Phoenicians appear as architects, artisans and merchants. At that point, Tyre and Sidon became the most important cities, a fact recognized by the Assyrian kings, who only maintained diplomatic relations with those cities. Certain elements in Greek mythology and Phoenician religion suggest that the Phoenicians' genuine contacts with the outside world – and, in particular, with the Greeks – date from the beginning of the first millennium. The most recent researches within the domain of West-Semitic paleography show, moreover, that the Phoenician alphabet was taken over by the Greeks in this period and it is in the context of such exchanges that the similarities between the Greek and Phoenician gods must have developed.

Phoenician overseas expansion was the joint achievement of Tyre and Sidon, which were united in a single kingdom around the middle of the ninth century BC, but it was Tyre that played the leading role in that development. In general, the Phoenician cities did not form confederations as the Greek city states did, and their kings generally pursued individualistic policies towards neighbouring powers. But for a brief period after the conquest of Tyre by Nebuchadnezzar in

1. *The ornamental pool of the Ugarit Palace, 14th–13th centuries BC.*

573 BC, the cities were governed by a king. Under Persian domination (539–333 BC), Phoenicia formed part of a satrapate which also included Syria and Cyprus, and the navy of Sidon was placed at the service of the military interests of the Achaemenean kings. After the capture of Tyre by Alexander (332 BC), the Phoenician monarchies were abolished; in the Hellenistic period the cities were governed by Archons and by an assembly whose importance for the Phoenicians resident in overseas trading posts is attested in their inscriptions right up to the Roman epoch.

**Akhnaton corresponds with the Phoenician kings.**
**c. 1350 BC**

**The victorious Rameses III withdraws into Egypt.**

**c. 1177 BC**

**Solomon and Hi**
**c. 960 BC**

**c. 2620 BC:** Snefru, 4th dynasty Egyptian pharaoh, has cedar wood brought from Mount Lebanon.
**c. 2320 BC:** Pepi I (6th dynasty) directs military expeditions against the Syro-Palestinian coast.
**c. 1468–1436 BC:** Tuthmosis III (18th dynasty) maintains garrisons at Tyre, Aradus and Simirra.
**c. 1200 BC:** Invasion of the Sea Peoples. Destruction of Ugarit, Tyre and Sidon.
**1177 BC:** Rameses III's last military campaign (20th dynasty) in Syria and in Palestine. After his victory over the Sea Peopleş, the Pharaoh, much occupied with internal strife, withdrew into Egypt.
**1114–1076 BC:** Tiglath-Pileser I, the King of Assyria, reaches Mount Lebanon, takes cedar wood and receives tribute from Byblos, Sidon and Aradus, 'the island in the deep sea'; with the ships of this latter, he reaches the coast again at Simirra.
**c. 1095 BC:** Zakarbaal, King of Byblos, asserts his independence vis-à-vis Wen-Amun, the envoy of Hrihor, high priest of Amun at Thebes. The Egyptian account of this voyage shows that his father and grandfather had sent cedar wood to the temple of Amun.
**c. 1000 BC:** Ithobaal, King of Byblos, has a sarcophagus made for his father Ahiram bearing an inscription which, for the first time, uses the whole Phoenician alphabet but for two letters.
**c. 995 BC:** Hiram, King of Tyre, a contemporary of Solomon, develops a policy of trade with neighbouring kingdoms.
**c. 887–856 BC:** Ithobaal, high priest of Astarte and King of Tyre and Sidon, gives his daughter in marriage to Ahab, King of Israel.
**883–859 BC:** Ashurnasirpal II, King of Assyria, conducts a campaign against Phoenicia and exacts tribute from the Kings of Byblos, Tyre and Aradus.
**c. 814 BC:** Traditional date of foundation of Carthage by the Tyrians.
**End of 8th century BC:** Luli, King of Tyre and Sidon, crosses the sea and subjugates Kition (Cyprus) which has risen in revolt. Shortly afterwards he is deposed by Sennacherib, King of Assyria, and Luli seeks refuge in Cyprus.

4. *The Phoenician goddess, Anath.*

5. *Helleno-Phoenician sarcophagus from Tyre, beginning of Hellenistic period.*

# 2620–332 BC

2. Phoenician sphinx, an ivory from Nimrud (Assyria), 9th–8th centuries BC.

3. Byblos, landscape with Phoenician mortars.

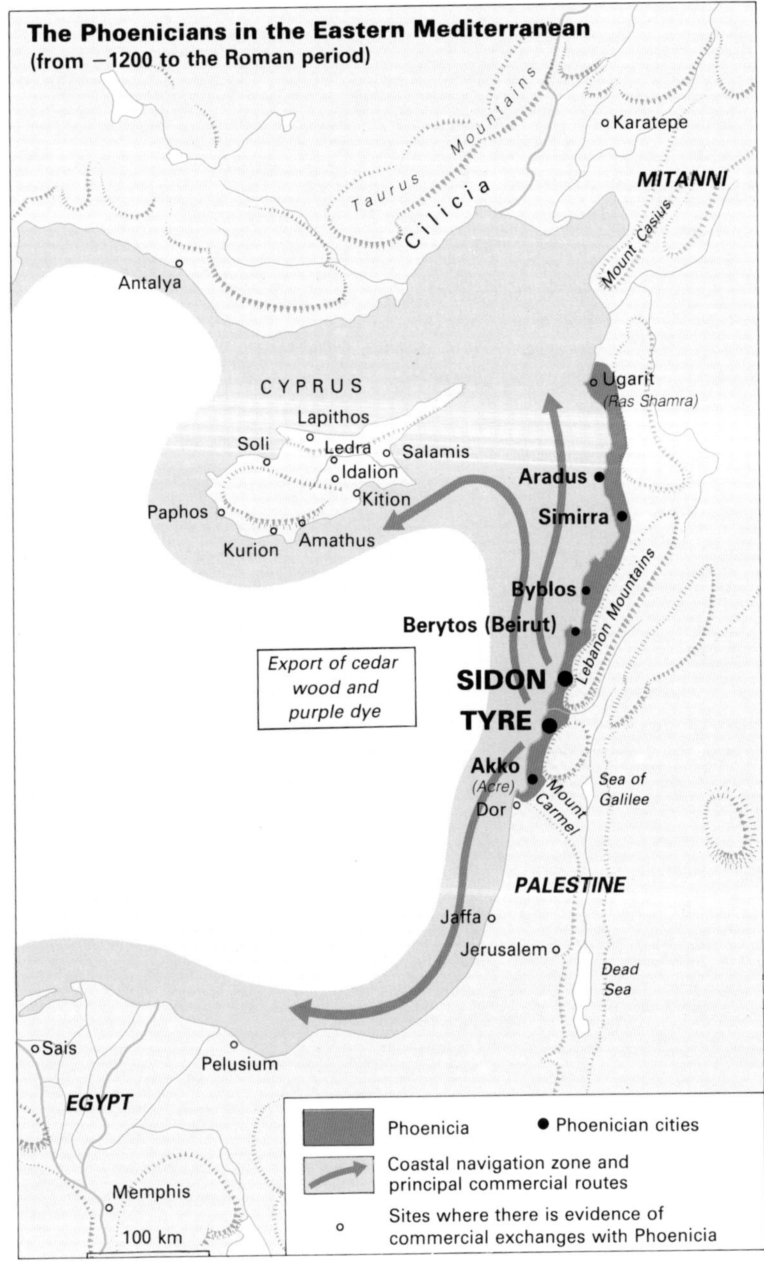


**Capture of Tyre by Nebuchadnezzar II.**

**c. 573 BC**

**667 BC:** Esarhaddon, King of Assyria and Babylon, imposes a humiliating treaty on Baalu, King of Tyre. The Akkadian inscriptions also mention a certain Abdimilkuti, King of Sidon, who was captured and decapitated by Esarhaddon.
**573 BC:** Nebuchadnezzar II, King of Babylon, captures Tyre after a thirteen-year siege.
**539 BC:** Cyrus captures Babylon. Beginning of Persian domination in the East.
**First part of 4th century:** The kings of the Eshmunazar dynasty at Sidon distinguish themselves by the military aid they bring to the Achaemenid kings. As a reward, they receive Dor, Jaffa and the Plain of Sharon in Palestine.
**Middle of 4th century BC:** Athens accords Strato I, King of Sidon, the title of *Proxenos*.
**333 BC:** Alexander arrives in Phoenicia after the battle of Issus. The Kings of Aradus and Byblos fall in with Alexander. Strato II of Sidon is deposed. After a long siege, Tyre is captured in 332 BC.

6. Phoenician ship on coin from Sidon, 375 BC.

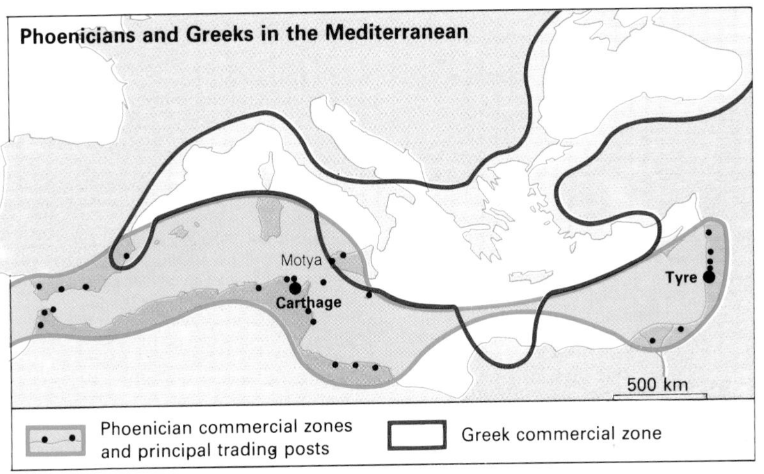

# From the Hebrews to the Jews

THE ANCIENT HISTORY of Israel is mainly known to us through the documents and writings of various periods which, after undergoing revisions and adaptations, went to make up the Bible. The choice of these documents and the modifications made to them were determined by essentially religious criteria: not only must a great deal of critical work be done before they can be used as history, but we also have to expect to find in those documents that the past narrated there – the past of a people which has always claimed its radical religiosity – will be centred on its religion. The long wanderings of its ancestors in the 'Fertile Crescent' between Mesopotamia and Palestine very probably took place, but our information on them, which is provided largely by legends, does not allow us to say any more. After a more or less nomadic sojourn in the south of Palestine, part of this group settled in Lower Egypt, where life was ultimately made very difficult for them. Moses, the man who led them out of Egypt at the beginning of the thirteenth century BC, planned to reunite and consolidate his people by a covenant with the protecting deity, Yahweh, and perhaps also intended to launch them on the conquest of an area of Palestinian territory. This explains the detour via 'the Mountain' (probably beyond the Gulf of Aqaba) on which Yahweh manifested himself by means of seismic phenomena. The Covenant was formed there, marking out Israel as the special people of Yahweh, attached to him alone and ready to serve him by the observance of a sort of moral code of nomadic, tribal life. When they had returned to Palestine, the wanderers reunited with their brothers who had stayed at home and began their campaign of conquest. It took more than two centuries of peaceful penetration and wars to reshape the lives of these wandering shepherds, after they had settled down as peasants or town-dwellers. When finally they became the masters of the country, they gave themselves a king and made Jerusalem their capital. The prosperity and glory they enjoyed under their second monarch, David (*c.* 1010 BC) rapidly disappeared when a part of the population split off to found the northern kingdom of Israel, in opposition to the southern kingdom of Judah. Being richer and more closely involved in international politics, Israel found itself more exposed to the Assyrian conquerors who finally destroyed it in 722 BC. A group of more fervent religious teachers – the prophets – explained this tribulation and others as a punishment sent by Yahweh for their many failures to observe the Covenant after they had become settled, and warned that if things did not change radically the worst was to be feared. A reform organized on these lines, codified in *Deuteronomy* and sanctioned by King Josiah (*c.* 610 BC) failed to remedy matters. A new prophet, Jeremiah, then called for a more inward religious sense and prophesied that Judah would surely be ruined by Babylon. Events also proved him to be right. In 587 BC Jerusalem fell to the forces of Nebuchadnezzar and its elite was exiled to Mesopotamia. This collapse and the isolated exile which followed both confirmed the prophets' doctrines and turned minds towards fundamental reform. A great mind, of whom little is known but whom we call the Second Isaiah, called for Israel to devote its efforts henceforth to making known throughout the whole universe the teachings of its God, whose absolutely unique and universal character had now been discovered. Another doctrine, spread by Ezekiel in particular but probably responding more closely to the popular inclination, advocated that an Israel turned in upon itself should devote its energies exclusively to following the will of its God – now codified as the 'Law' – to the letter. When Cyrus the Great, the conqueror of Babylon (539 BC), opened the gates of their gaol to the exiles, it was this path they would choose and on this foundation that they would build Judaism.

*1. The foothills of Mount Sinai, where Moses received the Tablets of the Law.*

**The Exodus.** 1260 BC — **King David.** 1010 BC — **The separation of Israel and Judah.** 931 BC — **The prophet Amos.** c. 750 BC — **Death of prophet Is** 687 B

**Before the 13th century BC:** The forerunners of the Israelites, a people of Aramean extraction, were nomads who wandered over an indeterminable period westwards along the 'Fertile Crescent' till they finally reached the central and southern regions of Palestine. A group of them – most likely a very small one – then travelled down the Nile delta and were detained there against their will.
**c. 1280–1250 BC:** Moses guided them from Egypt towards what was probably Midian, to make a covenant with Yahweh, whom he identified with their principal traditional god. In exchange for special ties ensuring them of divine protection, they undertook to serve only that god.
**1250–1030 BC:** The members of the various tribes of Israel mingled in with the local Canaanite population in some places, and in others made war on them. They gradually eliminated them, though they adopted both their sedentary way of life – becoming town-dwellers and peasants – and their customs, rendering all the more difficult the observance of those clauses of the Covenant based on a collective and frugal nomadic existence.
**1030–1010 BC:** After the election of a first king, namely Saul, his successor David (1010–970 BC) took Jerusalem as his first capital and brought the greatest success, prosperity and glory to his country.
**931 BC:** Under Jeroboam, the more numerous northern tribes broke away from the rest of the country, taking with them the name of Israel. They founded a kingdom based first on Tirzah and later on Samaria, which was ranged against that of Judah, which continued to have Jerusalem as its centre. The breaches of the Covenant increased and Israel, which had dealings with the neighbouring kingdoms, was attracted to their gods.
**9th century BC:** First religious literature and first zealots of Yahweh (prophets). The most vigorous of them, Elijah of the family of Tishbi, issued dire warnings against the choice of any other official god but Yahweh.
**Middle of 8th century BC:** The Assyrian conquest threatened all the western kingdoms. Second generation of prophets (Amos and Hosea, c. 760–750 BC, then Isaiah, 740–687 BC), who added written propaganda to preaching and threatened their compatriots who were unfaithful to the Covenant with the direst collective punishments.
**722 BC:** The capture of Samaria by Sargon II and the ruin of Israel confirm their prophecies, but the fall of Assyria (612 BC) and the unexpected death of the devout king Josiah, which seemed 'scandalous' to the pious, caused the failure of a first reform that had been prepared in accordance with the prevalent interpretation of the teachings of the prophets. A new prophet, Jeremiah (c. 630–580 BC), arose, calling for a personalized and more inward conception of the Covenant, but his efforts came to nothing.
**587 BC:** Nebuchadnezzar captured Jerusalem and sacked the city. All its leading personalities were exiled in Mesopotamia and, in its turn, Judah ceased to exist as a political entity. Both an important literary complement to what was to become our Bible and a permanent reorganization of religious life were born out of the remorse that was felt and the ideas that were developed during that time of exile (which officially came to an end with the fall of Babylon in 539 BC).

*4. Deportation of the Hebrews after the capture of Lachish by Sennacherib in 701 BC.*

# 16th–6th centuries BC

2. The captivity of the women of Israel at Nineveh. Relief at Sennacherib's palace, beginning of 7th century BC.

3. Pool of Siloam, engineered by Hezekiah in 700 BC.

| Exile at Babylon. | Second Isaiah. |
|---|---|
| 587 BC | c. 550 BC |

5. The Assyrians torture the Hebrews after the capture of Lachish.

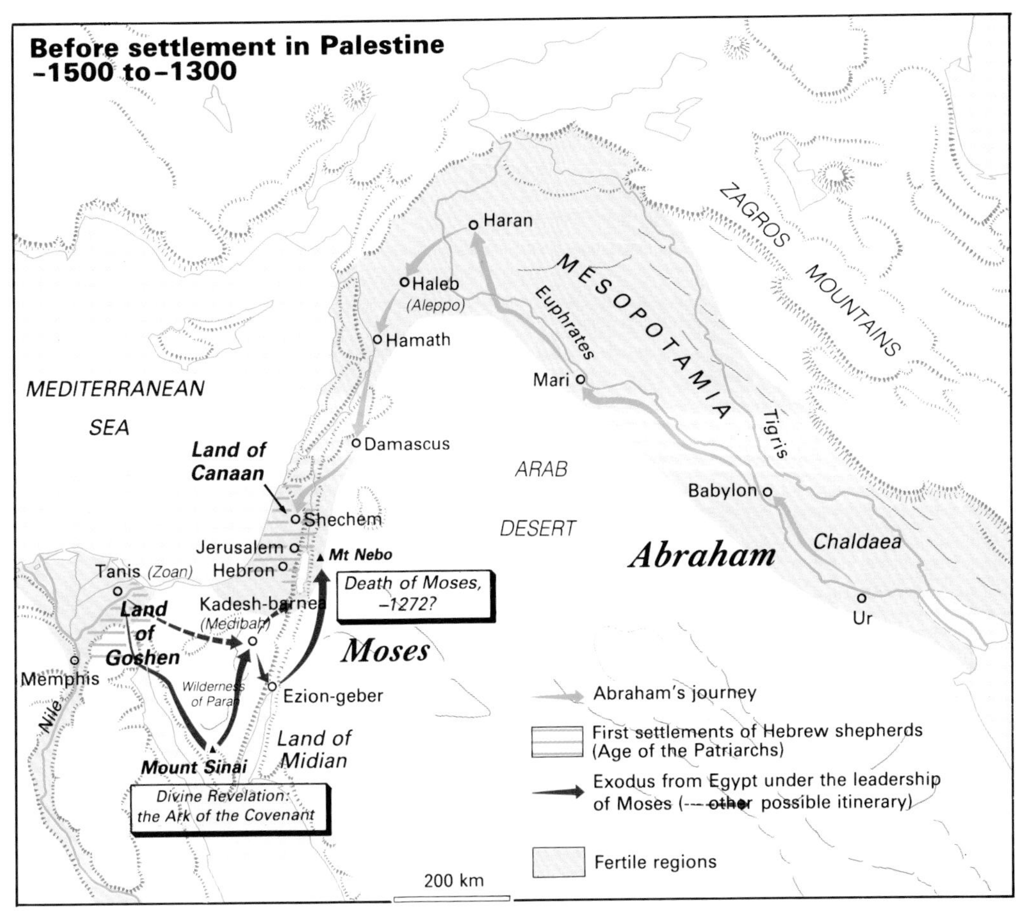



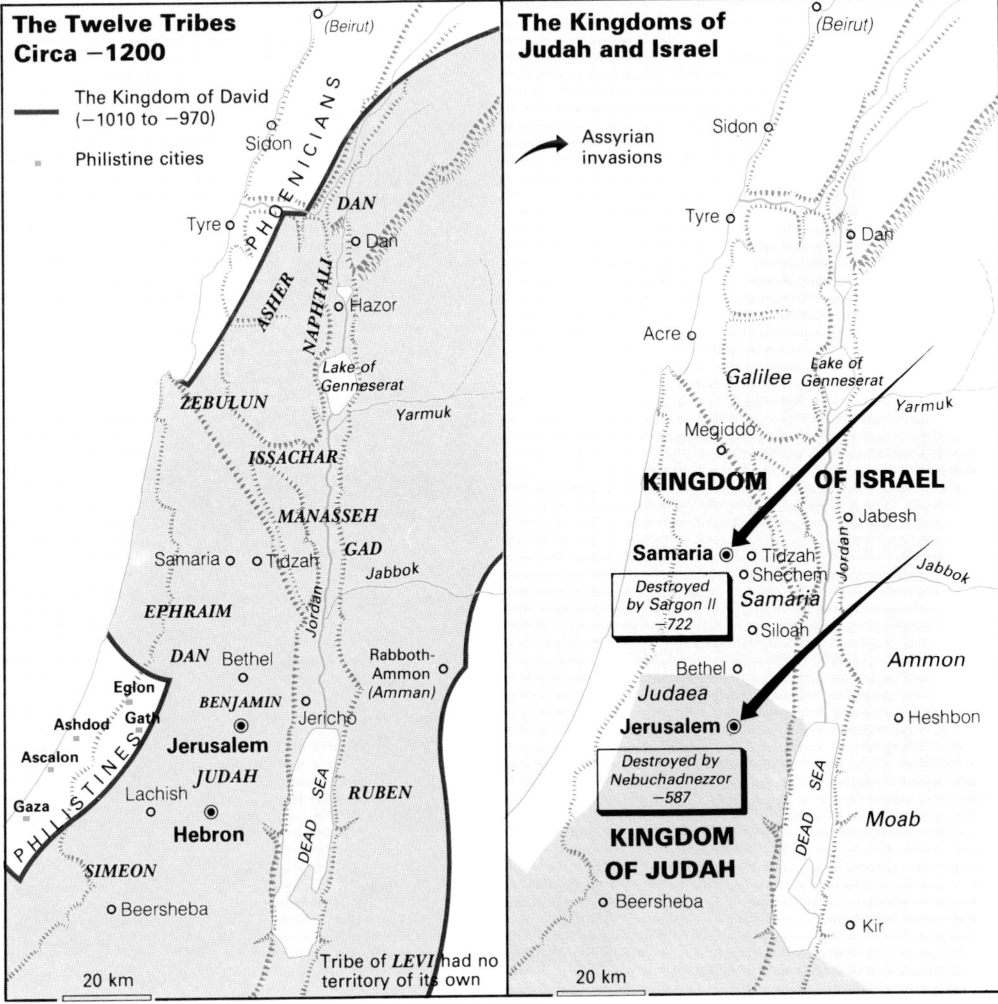

# Imperial Egypt

FOLLOWING A PERIOD of invasions and disorder, the New Empire represents an era of renaissance, conquest and glory in the history of pharaonic Egypt, which can still be seen today in the enormous splendour of its architectural and artistic heritage. Freeing Egypt from domination by the Hyksos, Ahmose, the founder of the eighteenth dynasty, set the country on its feet again by restoring its unity and agricultural prosperity. His capital was at Thebes (Luxor), and it was to that city that wealth would flow, both to the pharaohs' courts and to the temples. In spite of a serious dynastic crisis, in which the personality of Queen Hatshepsut was the main factor (she reigned alone for twenty-two years, arrogating all power to herself and keeping from the throne the future Thutmose III), the Egyptian monarchy had its greatest years under the pharaohs of the eighteenth dynasty. The colonial empire was vast: Thutmose III imposed a protectorate upon Palestine, Phoenicia and Syria; Thutmose IV allied with the Mitannian kingdom of inner Asia by marrying a princess from that country. To the south, Theban domination extended as far as the fourth cataract of the Nile. Everywhere in these new provinces, royal agents levied labour and substantial tribute in raw materials and rare commodities. The privileged class of society was the army, and its power was enhanced by the appearance on the scene of horses and chariots. From the reign of Ahmose onwards the god Amun became the protector of the ruling dynasty. His sanctuaries provided it with wealth and its priests exercised a growing influence on the country's affairs. Gradually the temple of Amun at Karnak became a state within the state.

1. The banks of the Nile, cradle of civilization....

It was at that point that Amenhotep IV-Akhenaton had a revolutionary effect by radically opposing the policies of his forefathers and destroying the religious and social equilibrium which prevailed at the time of his accession to the throne. Akhenaton abolished Amun's privileges and confiscated his goods, founded a new capital at Tell el Amarna (Middle Egypt) and turned Aton from a celestial pharaoh into a universal god. Aton was the sun's disc that gave life and spread goodness: the new religion of Akhenaton and his wife Nefertiti was founded on a doctrine of love, goodness, justice and humanity. At the death of the heretical pharaoh, there was an almost immediate return to traditional orthodoxy and the former order was re-established. Under Tutenkhamun, whose original name was Tutankhaton, Thebes once again became capital and the Valley of the Kings on the western bank once again became the pharaohs' burial ground. It was there that Tutankhamun, who died in adolescence, was buried. The discovery of his intact tomb has enabled us to appreciate the refinement of eighteenth-dynasty art. At the end of that dynasty General Horemheb came to prominence. When he took power he completed the job of eliminating the last vestiges of the Atonian heresy.

2. Agricultural work. Fresco from Menna's tomb at Thebes.

The nineteenth and twentieth dynasties were the work of the pharaohs named Ramses, the most famous of whom was Ramses II. He covered the country with gigantic buildings (cities and temples) and fought unrelentingly in numerous battles in defence of the kingdom (the Battle of Kadesh, campaigns in Syria and Palestine). His reign was very long (sixty-six years). In spite of his efforts, the Egypt he bequeathed to his successors was very much weakened. Invasions, social upheavals, palace plots and scandals eroded the state's authority and the country's prosperity. At the end of the second millennium, poverty and decadence had overtaken the country, which once again forfeited its unity. In the first millennium Persian domination, followed by conquest by the Greeks and Romans, put an end to the local dynasties and reduced Egypt to being one of the larger provinces of these new empires.

**First tomb in the Valley of Kings.** — **1506 BC**

**Terraced temple of Dayr al-Bahri.** — **1490 BC**

**Temples of Karnak and Tell el Amarna.** — **1364 BC**

**1552–1306 BC: 18TH DYNASTY**
**1552–1527 BC:** Ahmose. End of Hyksos domination of Egypt.
**1527–06 BC:** Amenhotep I. Seeks political restoration of the country. Military campaign as far as the Euphrates.
**1506–1494 BC:** Thutmose I. Conquest of Nubia up to the third cataract and victory over the Mitannians. Beginning of the great works on Amon's temple at Karnak.
**1493–1440 BC:** Thutmose II, brother and first husband of Queen Hatshepsut. After his death, crisis over the succession.
**1490–1468 BC:** Hatshepsut rules as regent and arrogates to herself the powers and attributes of royalty. She has herself represented as a man and declares herself to be of the stock of the god Amon. The architect Senmut, the Queen's favourite, takes charge of the building of the funerary temple of Dayr al-Bahri.
**1468–1436 BC:** Thutmose III. One of the most brilliant reigns in ancient Egyptian history. 17 military campaigns in Asia (Megiddo, Kadesh). Numerous additions to the temple at Karnak.

4. Akhenaton, Karnak.

**1438–1412 BC:** Amenhotep II, the son of the previous king, maintained the expansionist policy and repressed two revolts in Asia.
**1412–1402 BC:** Thutmose IV. Pursued a policy of colonization towards the south and the east.
**1402–1364 BC:** Amenhotep III. Egypt is at the height of its glory and splendour. Building of the temple of Luxor.
**1364–1347 BC:** Amenhotep IV (changes his name to Akhenaton). The Asiatic kingdom is threatened by Hittite attacks. Diplomatic correspondence conducted in Akkadian (cuneiform tablets found at Tell el Amarna).
**1347 BC:** Smenkhkare. Brief reign of one of Akhenaton's sons-in-law.
**1347-1338 BC:** Tutenkhamun. End of the schism caused by Akhenaton: return to traditional ways.
**1337–1333 BC:** Ay, a commoner, legitimates his accession to the throne by marrying Tutenkhamun's widow.
**1336–1306 BC:** Horemheb, a soldier backed by the priesthood of the god Amun, marries a royal princess and reorganizes the country.

5. Nefertiti, wife of Akhenaton, Tell el Amarna.

# 1552–1070 BC

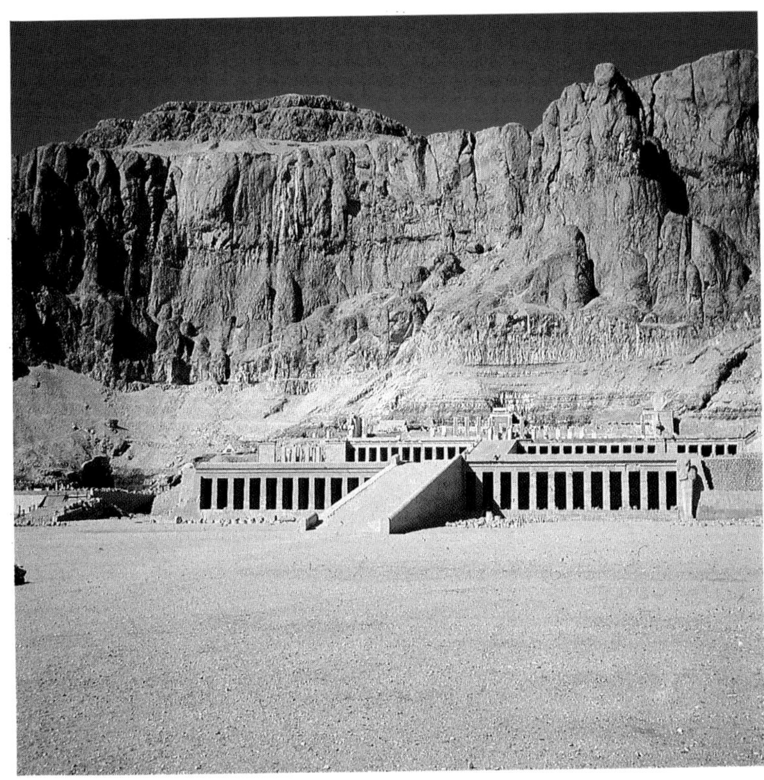

3. Hatshepsut's temple at Dayr al-Bahri, 18th dynasty, Thebes.

Valley of the Kings
Hatshepsut's temple
Mentuhotep's temple
Dayr al-Bahri
Temple of SETHOS I, KURNA
Dayr al-Medina
Temple of RAMSES II (Ramesseum)
Enclosure of temple of MONT
Valley of the Queens
Colossi of MEMNON
Enclosure of temple of AMON
Great Temple
Karnak
Temple of RAMSES III at Madinat Habu
Ruins of AMENOPHIS III'S Palace at MALKATA
Enclosure of temple of MUT
Temple of LUXOR
THEBES (Luxor)
THEBES
1 km

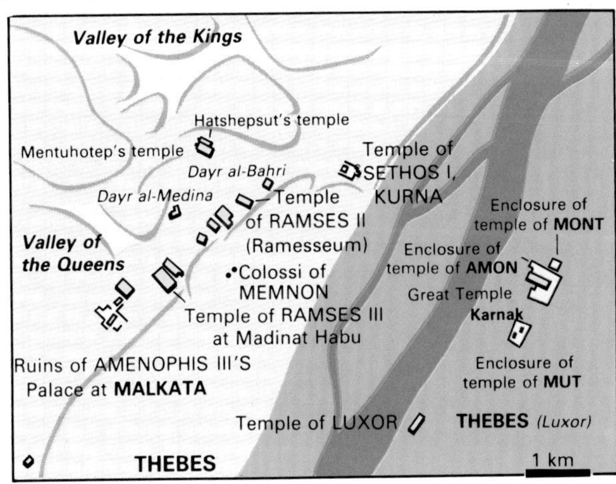

**bu Simbel.** **Madinat Habu.**

**1290 BC** **1184 BC**

**1306–1186 BC: 19TH DYNASTY**
**1306–1304 BC:** Ramses I.
**1304–1290 BC:** Seti I. Consolidates the position of the new dynasty. Victory over the Hittites at Kadesh.
**1290–1224 BC:** Ramses II. Last great figure of the New Empire. Completion of the Great Hypostyle Hall of Karnak and the temple of Luxor. Building of the Ramesseum at Thebes.
**1224–1186 BC:** Merneptah (13th son of Ramses II), Seti II, Siptah and Tausert succeed one another on the throne. At the end of this period, under a Palestinian usurper, there is anarchy.
**1186–1070 BC: 20TH DYNASTY**
**1186–1184 BC:** The Egyptian Setnakht founds the 20th dynasty.
**1184–1153 BC:** Ramses III. Intense struggles against the Sea Peoples and the Libyans. Building of the temple of Madinat Habu at Thebes.
**1153–1070 BC:** Ramses IV to Ramses IX. Decline of the Egyptian Empire.

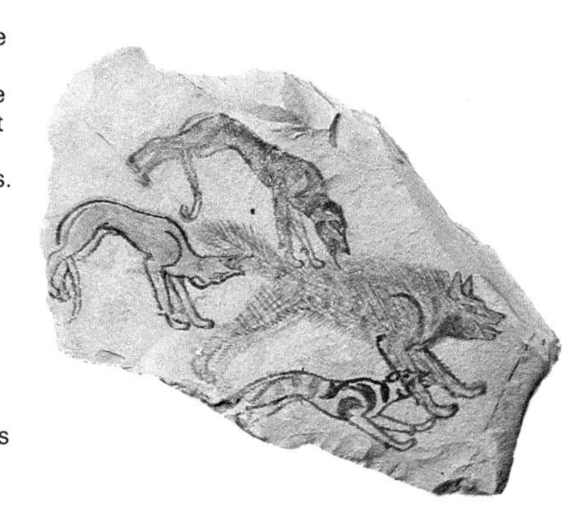

6. Dogs and a hyena; a sketch from the Ramses period.

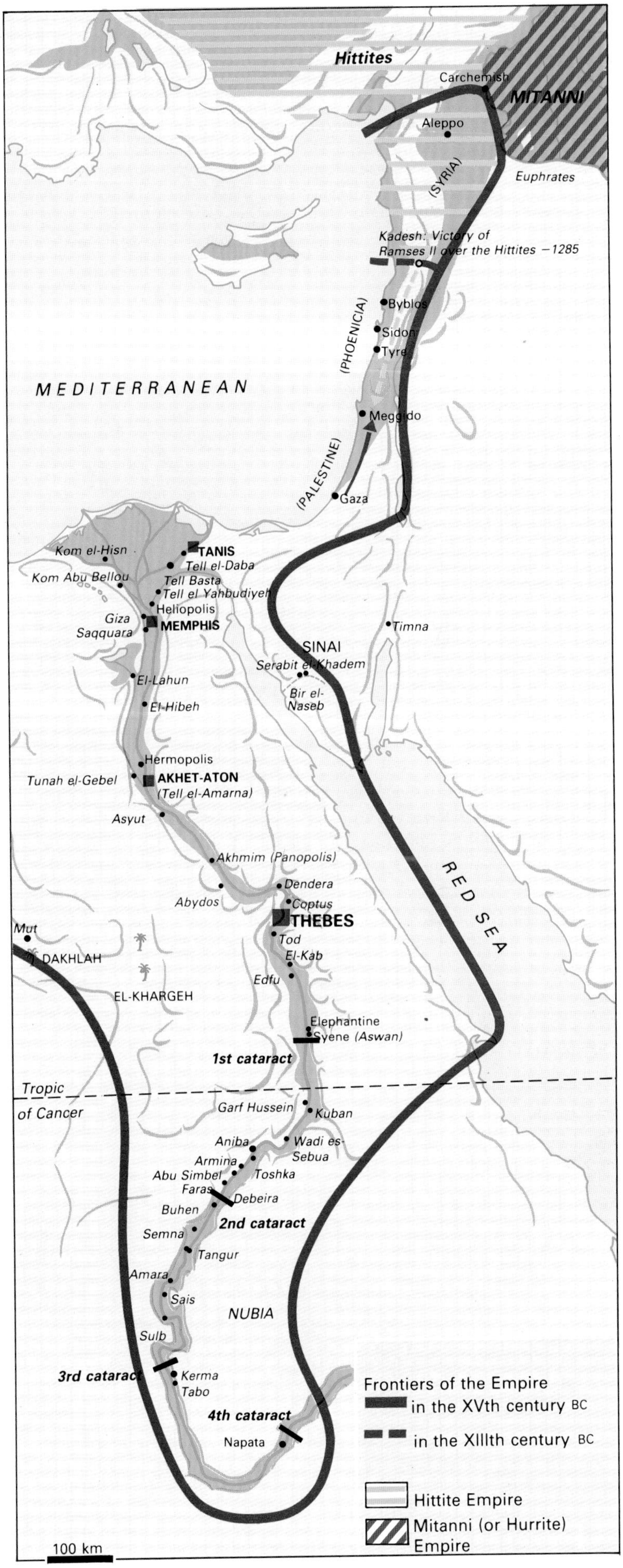

Hittites
Carchemish
MITANNI
Aleppo
(SYRIA)
Euphrates
Kadesh: Victory of Ramses II over the Hittites –1285
Byblos
Sidon
Tyre
(PHOENICIA)
MEDITERRANEAN
Megiddo
(PALESTINE)
Gaza
TANIS
Kom el-Hisn
Tell el-Daba
Kom Abu Bellou
Tell Basta
Tell el Yahbudiyeh
Heliopolis
Giza
Saqquara
MEMPHIS
Timna
SINAI
Serabit el-Khadem
El-Lahun
Bir el-Naseb
El-Hibeh
Hermopolis
Tunah el-Gebel
AKHET-ATON (Tell el-Amarna)
Asyut
Akhmim (Panopolis)
RED SEA
Dendera
Abydos
Coptus
THEBES
Mut
Tod
DAKHLAH
El-Kab
Edfu
EL-KHARGEH
Elephantine
Syene (Aswan)
1st cataract
Tropic of Cancer
Garf Hussein
Kuban
Aniba
Wadi es-Sebua
Armina
Abu Simbel
Toshka
Faras
Debeira
Buhen
2nd cataract
Semna
Tangur
Amara
Sais
NUBIA
Sulb
3rd cataract
Kerma
Tabo
4th cataract
Napata
Frontiers of the Empire
in the XVth century BC
in the XIIIth century BC
Hittite Empire
Mitanni (or Hurrite) Empire
100 km

# The Origins of the Chinese Empire

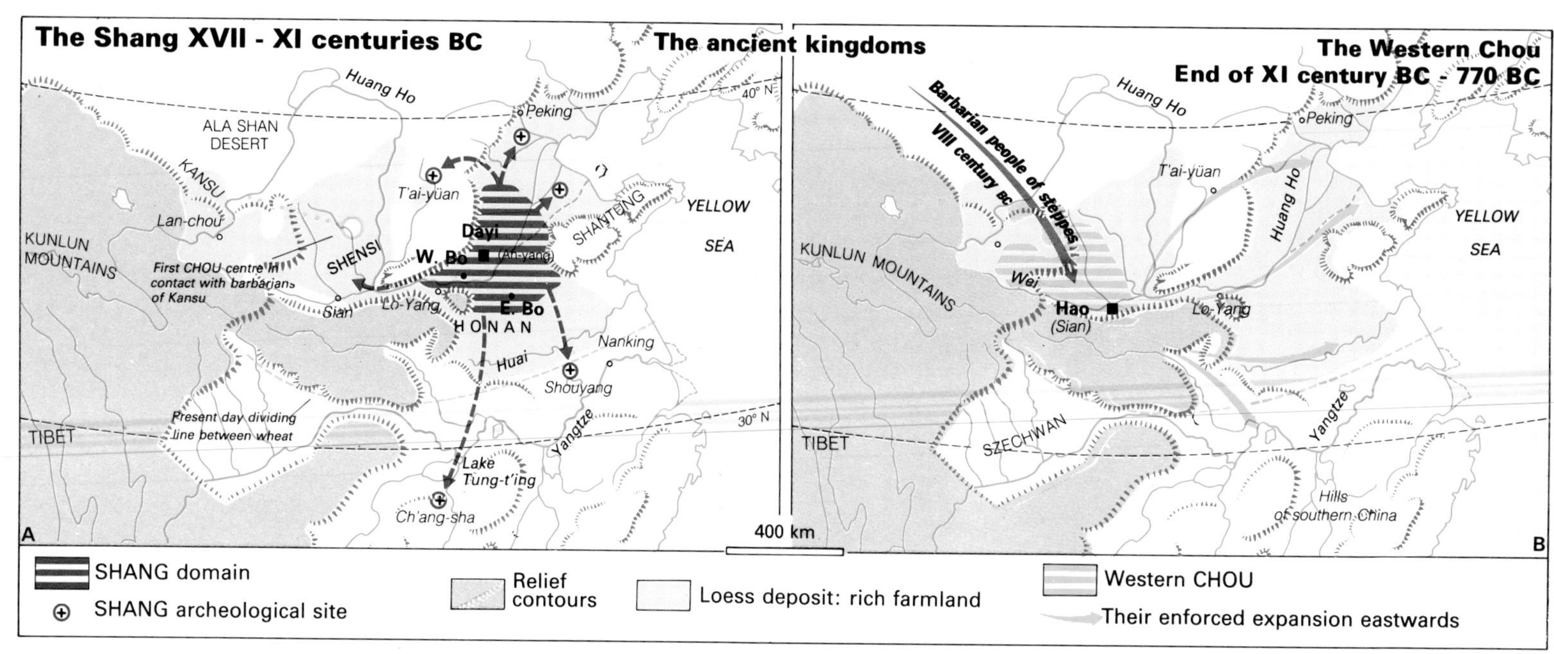


The Shang or Yin dynasty made its appearance in the seventeenth century BC at the juncture of two Neolithic cultures, Yang-shao and Lung-shan, in the fertile, silt-enriched lands (loesslands) of the middle Yellow River basin. With it appeared features typical of ancient Chinese civilization, such as the harnessed cart, writing, bronze, divination by bones and tortoise shells and a political structure that revolved around the royal city. The society was governed by a unitary principle: ancestor worship provided a framework into which each individual was integrated. This enabled the Shang to expand over a vast territory (as far south as Lake Tung-t'ing) with a very elementary political organization mirroring patterns of kinship. Their relations with their neighbours were sometimes based on alliances or vasselage but more usually they were conflictual. They practised the immolation of prisoners to feed the souls of the ancestors, who were the true rulers of society. The expansion of Shang culture provoked tensions in a rigid society and brought about its eventual downfall.

The ancient monarchy was given a new lease of life by the Chou dynasty, founded by a people from the western borders. Family-based ancestor worship was transformed, leading to a more flexible, segmented society. Domains gave way to fiefdoms granted by the king to overlords who presided over the ancestor worship. Although progressively weakened by pressure from the 'barbarians', the monarchy was able to maintain religious and moral ascendancy over the powerful overlords up to the eighth century BC. Hierarchization of forms of worship reached its highest degree of sophistication. Confucius undertook to adapt and reinterpret behavioural roles in a humanist direction; this led to ritual becoming a universal norm of conduct and to the elaboration of classical Chinese codes of behaviour. The nobility was threatened by the formation of large, autonomous political units. While the central principalities remained fragmented into tiny feudal states jealously guarding their privileges, more peripheral states were wresting new territories from the barbarians; their conquered lands became provinces directly under central government. The Chin, the Ch'i, the Ch'u and the Ch'in began to play a dominant role (hegemon states) because of their military and economic power. The army was formed by conscripting independent farmers, which led to the downfall of the heroic code of the warlord; infantrymen were given precedence over charioteers. The previous balance was

**Appearance of bronze.**

**First inscriptions on ritual vases.**

**17th century BC**

**12th century BC**

*2. Bronze wine vessel of Kuang type. Shang period, 17th–11th century BC.*

**17th century BC:** Founding of Shang-Ying dynasty on site of present-day Erh-li-t'ou.
**1384 BC:** Capital moves to Ta-Yeh (now An-Yang).
**1273 BC:** Emperor Tsu Chia reforms religious practice by instituting regular sacrifices to ancestors linked to yearly cycle.

**12th century BC:** First ritual inscriptions on bronze vases.
**11th century BC:** Shang dynasty overthrown by Chou. King Wu Wang founds new dynasty, divides territory between members of his family and allies.

**771 BC:** Raid by Rong barbarians in league with royal family forces King P'ing to move his capital further east, to Lo-Yang. Chou becomes dependent on rulers of Cheng, Wei, Chin and Song.
**772 BC:** Beginning of period known as 'Spring and Autumn' recorded in annals of Lu principality.
**667 BC:** Economic and fiscal reforms made by his prime minister, Kuan Chong, lead to Duke Huan Kung of Ch'i becoming head of Chinese confederation.
**632 BC:** Chin hegemony.
**597 BC:** Hegemony of Duke Chuang Ch'u following victory over Chin.
**590 BC:** Lu introduces first conscription system, which is soon copied by other states.
**536 BC:** First legal code inscribed on bronze braziers and put on public view.
**c. 510 BC:** Spread of iron smelting.
**506–473 BC:** Wars between Wu and Yüeh, two states of southeast China, started by a quarrel between two little girls gathering mulberry leaves and resulting in total destruction of Wu after a series of defeats suffered by Yüeh.

*3. Chariot ornament, bronze encrusted with gold and silver. Ch'u dynasty.*

**481 BC:** End of period recorded in Lu annals rewritten by Confucius.
**479 BC:** Death of Confucius.
**453 BC:** China is split among three high-ranking officers, thus creating three kingdoms of Chao, Han and Wei. This event marks the beginning of the 'Warring States' period.

# 1600–250 BC

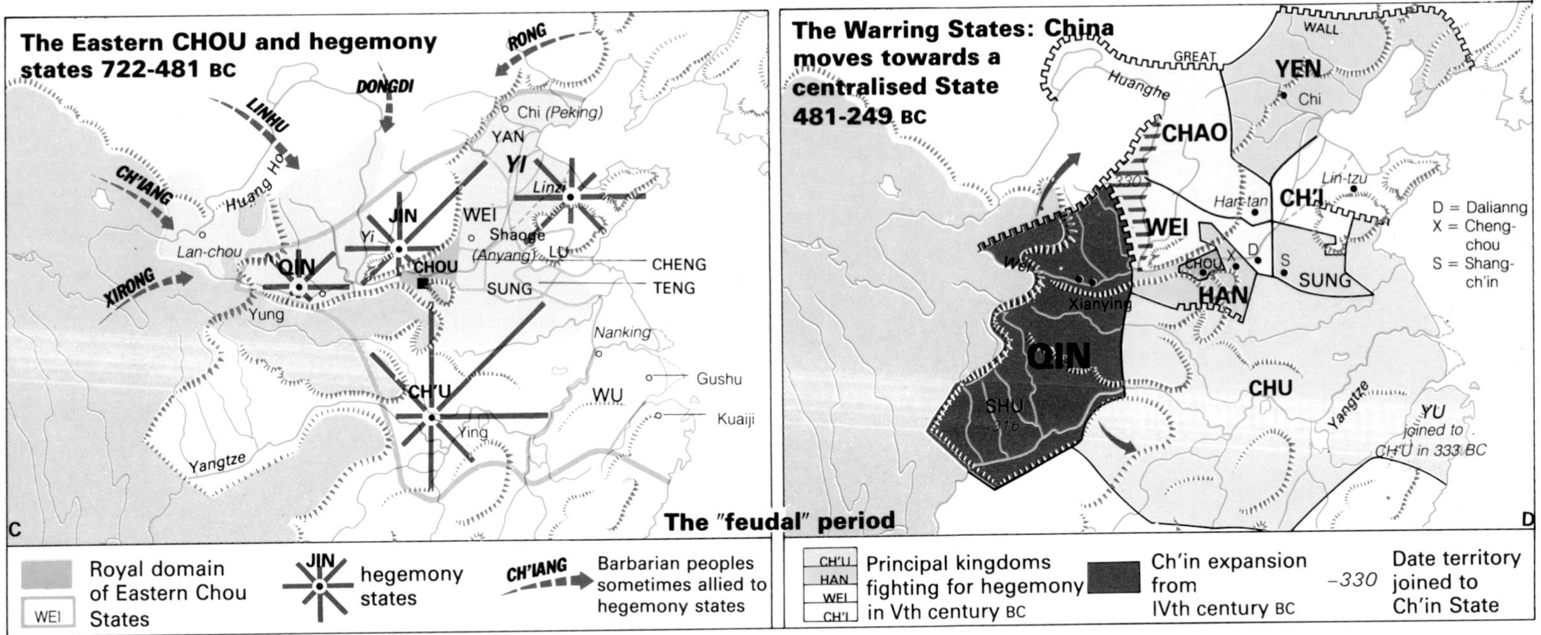

1. *Terracotta mould for casting bronze mask. Warring States period, 481–249 BC.*

disturbed as ritual prestige gave way to naked power; the harsher side of society was reinforced. The sovereign – seen as an incarnation of social and cosmic laws – imposed a feudal system of duties on his subjects. At the same time the growth of iron smelting in the sixth century BC resulted in the peasants being subjected to central government or to large entrepreneurs linked to the state. Social upheaval led to intellectual ferment; a multitude of schools blossomed: Sophistry, Taoism, Legalism, Moism.

As the small principalities disappeared, power tended to be concentrated in the heads of the fiefs, who became veritable monarchs; they were now aided by competent administrators recruited according to ability, not birth. The state of Ch'in undertook a series of reforms that gave it ascendancy over its rivals. Neither reversals of alliances nor the banding together of the large states succeeded in containing the eastward march of the Ch'in. Their annexation of Chou territory merely sanctioned what had already been a fact for two centuries.

**Iron smelting becomes widespread.**

**6th century BC**

**Writings of Lao-Tzu.**

**4th century BC**

**Suicide of poet Ch'ü Yüan for political reasons.**

**277 BC**

**386 BC:** T'ien family usurp power in Ch'i.
**c. 350 BC:** Reforms made by lawyer-administrator Shang Yang give King Hsiao-Wen of Ch'in military superiority over other states.

**311 BC:** Ch'u is defeated in war against Ch'in.
**c. 300 BC:** Death of Taoist philosopher Chuang-tzu. Building of walls by states of Yen, Chao and Ch'in against incursions by barbarians of the steppes.

**284 BC:** Yen, aided by Ch'in, Ch'u and the three kingdoms born of Chin secession, inflicts a bitter defeat on Ch'i. The capital is sacked and the sovereign forced to flee.
**269 BC:** Chao and Wei defeat Ch'in armies.
**260 BC:** During the battle of Changping the commanding general of Ch'in puts to death 200,000 Chao soldiers who had surrendered.
**259–257 BC:** Siege of Handan (capital of Chao) by Ch'in ends in defeat.
**256 BC:** King of western Chou surrenders his throne to Ch'in.
**250 BC:** Destruction of eastern Chou by Ch'in marks the end of the dynasty.

4. *Bronze cooking receptacle, Ting type. Shang period, 17th–11th century BC.*

5. *Knocker in shape of fabulous beast. Warring States period.*

# Celtic Europe

1. Frieze of Gundestrup cauldron representing the god Teutates receiving human sacrifices. Repoussé gilded silver, 1st century AD.

THE NAME 'CELTS' does not appear in texts until the fifth century BC, that of 'Germans' still later, but all the archaeological data seem to indicate that the population of temperate Europe was permanently settled, with a definable culture evolving steadily from the end of the Bronze Age up to the Roman conquest. Farmsteads occupied the richest plains as far north as Scotland, southern Scandinavia and west of the Vistula; hunter gatherers had virtually disappeared from these areas. The farmers divided the land into a complex system of plots ('Celtic fields'); they developed the swing plough, farmed heavy soils and corrected and fertilized poor soils. Intensive mixed farming enabled them to export their surplus: cereals and salt provisions were sent to southern Europe. Trade with the Greek colonies and Italy in other raw materials, such as tin, amber and copper reached a peak in the sixth century BC. Economic dependency of a colonial type developed: the social group who benefited were those who controlled foreign trade and the distribution of imports, now seen as marks of social status. Their rise is linked to the end of the Bronze Age, when increased metal production led to hoarding and inequality of wealth, and also to the appearance of heavily armed professional soldiers in the style of the Greek hoplites.

Although horse-riding was introduced by oriental peoples, the cart was still typical of these cultures, for transport, war and funerary rites. Iron technology spread slowly at the beginning of this period, but in the fifth century BC it was put to good purpose for improving agricultural production, clearing new land and arming the surplus population that were making inroads into Italy and would soon be unfurling over the entire northern Mediterranean. Celtic mercenaries, in their contacts with local populations, introduced new

**Peak of bronze production.**

**1250–800 BC**

**1250 BC:** Rise of Urnfield burial cultures in Lusatia, Central Europe, Switzerland-Rhine. Toughened bronze alloy produced in Atlantic regions. Explosion of bronze production; draught horses; climate becomes wetter. Development of rye, oats, millet and flax. First traces of stables.

**1100–1000 BC:** First burial chariots with furniture imported from the south.

**750 BC:** First Iron Age. Climate changes to very wet and cold sub-Atlantic, crops recede on impermeable soil and at higher altitudes. Iron produced locally. First horsemen. Burial mounds, ritual of burial.

**600 BC:** Massalia (Marseilles) founded by Phoceans.

**600–450 BC:** Chieftains' graves (Vix and Hochdorf), Hallstatt culture (Heuneburg). Imports and colonial-type contacts with Mediterranean. Poland: group of fortified dwellings at Biskupin.

**Chieftains, horsemen, tradesmen.**

**750–450 BC**

**500 BC:** Development of Second Iron Age, known as La Tène culture, in agriculture-oriented environment. Cemeteries of burial mounds or flat tombs, linked to hamlets and organized in family groups. Appearance of 'Celtic Art' style.

**Spread of Celtic farmers.**

**500–250 BC**

**400 BC:** First Celtic raids in Italy. Celts settle in Italy, expeditions to Greece. Spread of La Tène culture to western France and colonization of heavy soils of Eastern Europe. Storage of agricultural produce developed in selected hill forts in Brittany.

3. Mask and hands of hammered bronze from a tomb in Styria, Austria, 7th century BC.

**Specialized craftsmen appear.**

**250–100 BC**

4. 'Severed heads' from the hill fort of Entremont, France, 2nd century BC.

# 13th–1st centuries BC

techniques both in art and in production: compasses, the potter's wheel and the rotary millstone were the most spectacular innovations. In the second century BC artisans with specialized tools began to mass-produce objects which sometimes survived in the same form up to the eighteenth century AD. Iron was made in such quantities that it was employed for the first time in building.

The Roman conquest chased the Celts out of Italy, then southern Gaul. Massive commercial penetration by the Romans, as shown by the wine amphoras found on every site, preceded their occupation of Gaul and gave birth to a civilization based on *oppida*, or hill forts, stretching from Brittany to Hungary. Artisans, tradesmen and part of the landed aristocracy came together to found these important settlements, which were sometimes as big as 100 hectares. The use of bronze coinage and the very first Celtic texts mark the end of protohistorical times. The scene was now stolen by the Roman conquest and by invasions of northeastern European peoples. Today the Celts are still better known to us through what Caesar had to say about them than through the plentiful evidence they have left in the ground or in mediaeval manuscripts.

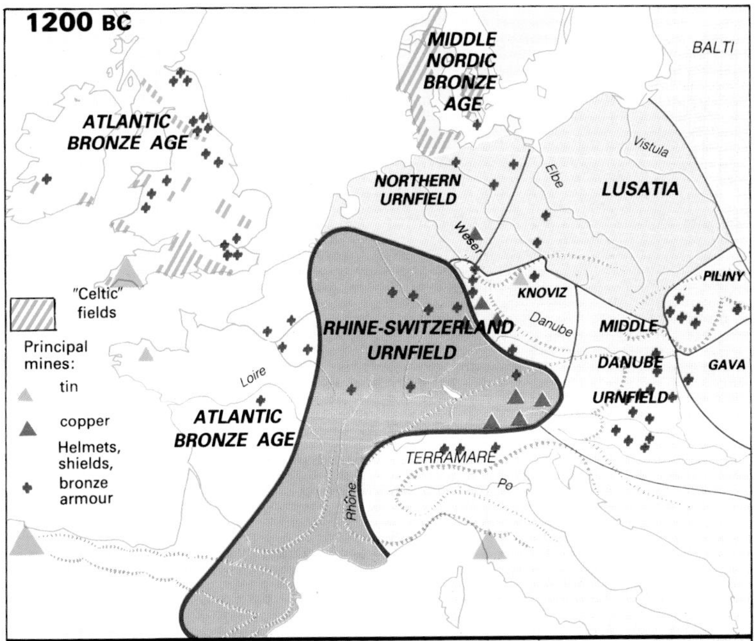

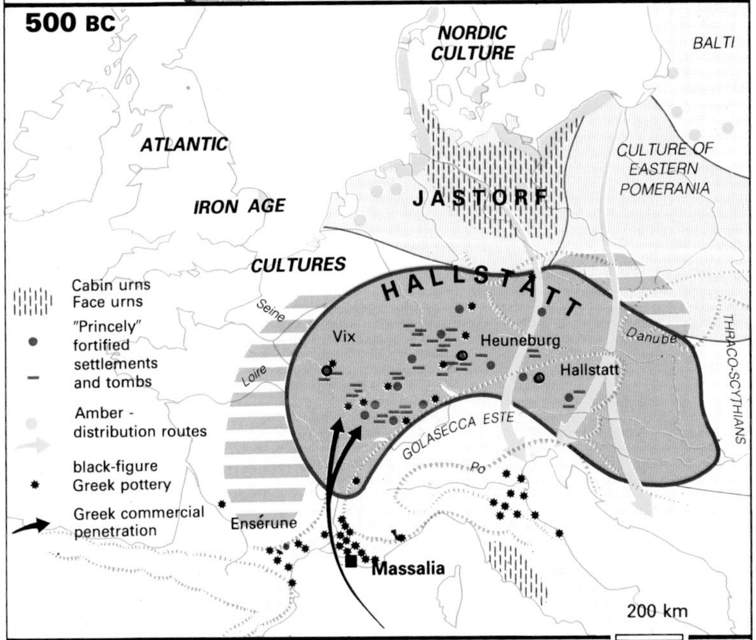

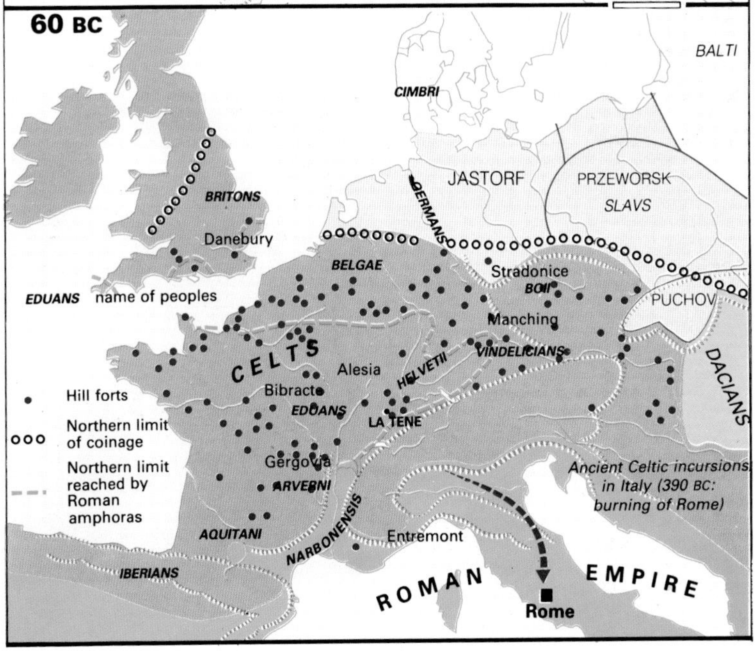

2. Entrance to hill fort of Finsterlohr, Baden-Württemberg, 1st century BC.

**fort civilization.** **Celts retreat before Romans, Germans and Marcomanni.**

**00 BC** **58 BC–AD 1**

**225 BC:** Defeat of Gauls at Talamone.

**189 BC:** Bononia (Bologna) founded. Italian Celts reduced to subjection. Development of craftsmen.

**124 BC:** Defeat of Celts and Salians at Entremont. Founding of Aquae Sextiae (Aix-en-Provence) in Roman Province of Narbonensis (created in 118 BC).

**109–102 BC:** Invasions of Cimbri and Teutoni. Rise of hill fort civilization. Circulation of first low-denomination coins.

**58–52 BC:** Caesar intervenes in Gaul, Brittany, western Germany. Conquest of Gaul.

**c. 50 BC:** Dacians defeat Boii in Pannonia.

**25 BC:** Romans pacify tribes of the Alps.

**25–1 BC:** Romans control south bank of Danube. Marcomanni invade Bohemia.

**15–1 BC:** Hill forts abandoned, founding of present-day provincial capitals.

**AD 43:** Romans occupy south of British Isles.

5. Breton helmet, 1st century BC.

# The Grandeur of Carthage

PHOENICIAN EXPANSION in the western Mediterranean is amply illustrated by recent archaeological discoveries. Tyrians and Sidonians were guided towards Sicily, Malta, Sardinia, the North African coasts and southern Spain by a desire to extend their commercial activities, and perhaps also to alleviate the weight of Assyrian domination over the Near East which had reached its climax in the eighth century BC. However, the stages in this expansion are not well known, and attempts to establish a chronology are necessarily somewhat speculative. An inscription found at the archaeological site of Nora (Sardinia) does, however, provide evidence of a Phoenician presence at that location in the ninth century BC; pottery discovered in Malta and at Motya (Sicily) dates from the eighth century BC and the Phoenician settlements at Toscanos (Andalusia) are from the same period. This archaeological evidence cannot be taken to indicate the initial date of Phoenician presence in these areas; rather it suggests that there had been such a presence there for several generations. The same must also be true of Carthage. If the traditional date of its foundation by Tyre is 814 BC, it may be assumed that regular exchanges between the metropolis and the African coast must have taken place several decades before Kart Hadasht (the 'new city') was founded. With the founding of Ibiza by Carthage in 654–653 BC, the Phoenician presence in the Mediterranean took on a new dimension.

Carthage, governed by two sufets or annually elected chief magistrates, a council of elders and an assembly of the people, was itself capable of founding new colonies or developing existing ones. In this manner, an empire was created in the western Mediterranean basin in the centre of which Sardinia and Sicily were to become the principal stakes in the international political struggle. It was in Sicily indeed that the Greeks and the Carthaginians clashed on several occasions. In 264 BC the intervention of Rome in the affairs of Messina caused the First Punic War, which ended in Rome's naval victory at the battle of the Aegates islands. After its seizure of Sicily, Rome forced Carthage in 237 BC to renounce its claim to Sardinia by a treaty which Carthage always considered an act of brigandage. The period preceding the Second Punic War (218–202 BC) saw the apogee of the Barca family, whose founder Hamilcar Barca undertook the conquest of Spain in the name of the government of Carthage. He was succeeded by his son-in-law, Hasdrubal, the founder of Carthago Nova (*c.* 227 BC), then by his son Hannibal: all three ruthlessly exploited Spain's mineral wealth.

*1. Lid of Greco-Punic sarcophagus, Carthage, c. 300 BC.*

The capture of Saguntum, an ally of Rome, by Hannibal in 219 BC was considered a *casus belli* by the Roman Senate and provoked a declaration of war. Hannibal then decided to cross Gaul and enter Italy by way of the Alps. His army remained there for fifteen years. After his victory at Cannae (216 BC) Hannibal gave a new turn to his Italian policy by signing a treaty with Philip V of Macedonia; however, isolated in Italy shortly afterwards and then recalled to Africa, he was defeated at Zama. From 150 BC onwards Rome decided to put an end to the Carthaginian threat and declared a preventive war against her. The city was disarmed by treason and besieged; after three years' resistance and a final battle fought out in the streets, Carthage was conquered and razed to the ground by Scipio Aemilianus in April 146 BC. At the moment of its fall, Carthage was said to be the richest city in the world (Polybius), and its political institutions had won the admiration of Aristotle, who considered the constitution of Carthage the equal of the best Greek regimes. The organization of its ports, the competence of its generals, its fleet and its cavalry, the possession of the Spanish mines and of a close-knit network of trading posts and colonies had made a clash between Carthage and Rome inevitable.

| c. 520 BC | 508 BC | 480 BC | 264 BC | 217 BC |
|---|---|---|---|---|
| **Himilco's expeditions to northwest Europe. Hanno's voyages on the coast of Africa.** | **First treaty between Rome and Carthage.** | **Himera and Salamis.** | **Beginning of the Punic Wars.** | **Hannibal's victory at Lake Trasimenus.** |

**814 BC:** Traditional date for the foundation of Carthage by the Tyrians.
**8th century BC:** Phoenician presence near Seville is attested by a statuette of the Phoenician goddess Astarte.
**c. 600 BC:** Naval victory of the Phocaeans, founders of Massalia, over the Carthaginians (according to Thucydides).
**535 BC:** Carthaginian and Etruscan victory over the Greeks at Alalia, Corsica (modern Aleria).
**c. 508 BC:** First treaty between Carthage and Rome (according to Polybius): mutual recognition of the right to trade.
**c. 500 BC:** Velianas, King of Caere (Cerveteri), dedicates a shrine in the port of Pyrgi (San Severa) to the goddess Astarte: the text is written in Etruscan and Phoenician.
**480 BC:** Hamilcar, son of Mago, is defeated by Gelon of Syracuse at Himera.
**405 BC:** Dionysius the Elder, 'tyrant' of Syracuse, signs a treaty with Carthage and recognizes the Punic possessions on the island.

*2. Stelae of the Tophet of Tanit and Baal, 5th–4th centuries BC.*

**4th century BC:** Power passes to the family of Hanno the Great, rival of the Barcidae during the Punic Wars.
**348 BC:** Second treaty of Carthage with Rome (according to Polybius).
**264–241 BC:** First Punic War. By the peace treaty of 241 BC, Rome forces Carthage to evacuate Sicily and to pay a war indemnity of 2,200 talents.
**228 BC:** Hamilcar Barca begins the conquest of Spain.
**221 BC:** Assassination of Hasdrubal. Hannibal, the son of Hamilcar Barca, is immediately chosen as leader by the army and is subsequently invested ruler by the Senate and people of Carthage.
**218–202 BC:** Second Punic War.
**216 BC:** Victory of Hannibal at Cannae. Treaties with Capua and other important Italian cities. Rome refuses to sign a treaty with Carthage.
**207 BC:** The army of Hasdrubal the Younger, Hannibal's brother, leaves Spain and manages to reach Italy to reinforce the Carthaginian troops, but it is wiped out at the battle of the Metaurus, where Hasdrubal is killed.
**203 BC:** Hannibal is recalled to Carthage.
**202 BC:** Victory of Scipio Africanus at Zama followed by a peace treaty.

*3. Molten glass mask, 4th–3rd century BC.*

# 814–146 BC

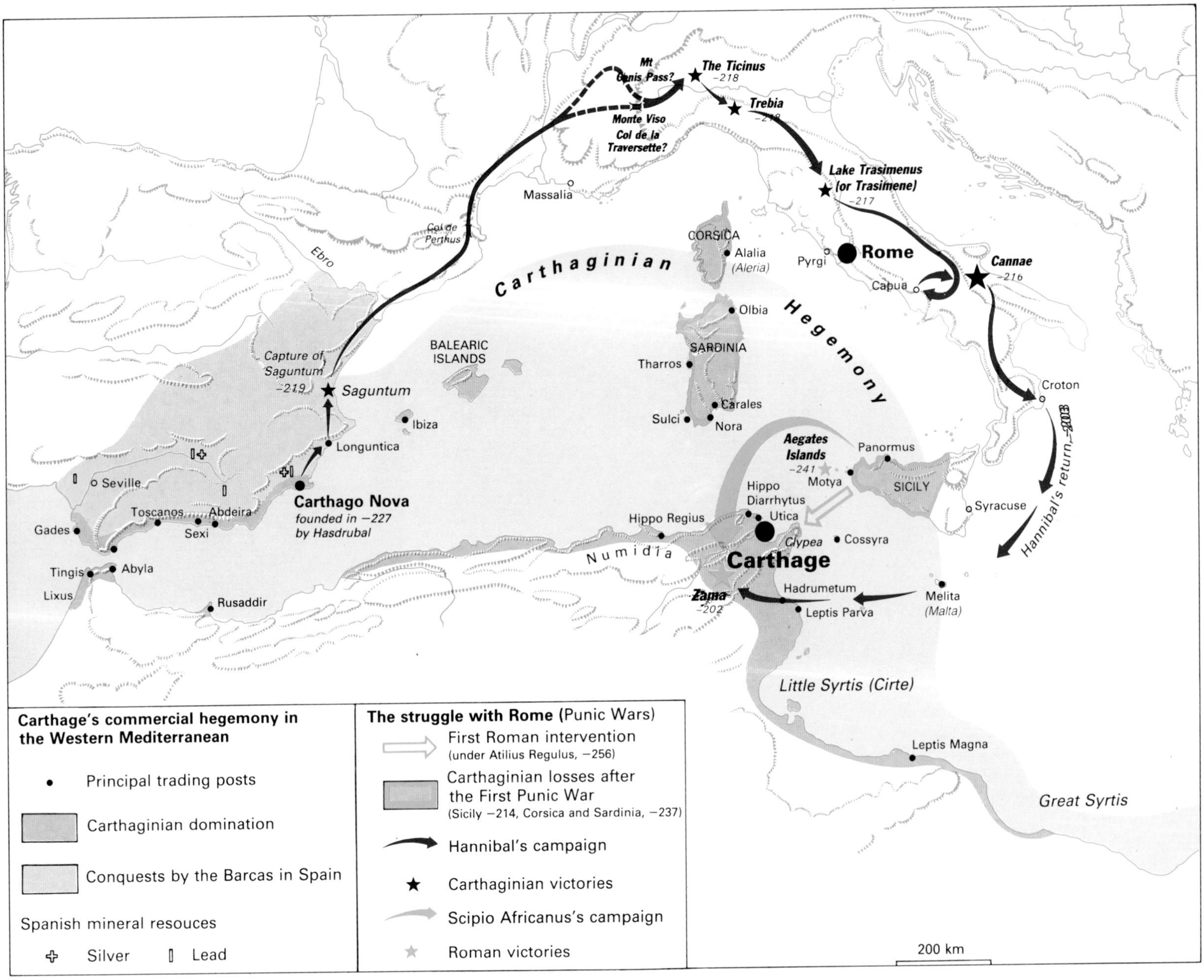

**Carthage's commercial hegemony in the Western Mediterranean**

- • Principal trading posts
- Carthaginian domination
- Conquests by the Barcas in Spain

Spanish mineral resouces

- ✥ Silver
- ▯ Lead

**The struggle with Rome** (Punic Wars)

- First Roman intervention (under Atilius Regulus, −256)
- Carthaginian losses after the First Punic War (Sicily −214, Corsica and Sardinia, −237)
- Hannibal's campaign
- ★ Carthaginian victories
- Scipio Africanus's campaign
- ★ Roman victories

200 km

**Hannibal poisons himself at Libyssa (Bithynia).**

**183 BC**

4. *Punic armour.*

**196 BC:** Hannibal is elected sufet and undertakes administrative reforms. He is denounced by his enemies at Rome.
**195 BC:** Hannibal seeks refuge with Antiochus III, King of Syria.
**Beginning of 2nd century BC:** Masinissa, chieftain of the Numidians, attacks and finally annexes a part of Carthaginian territory.
**189–188 BC:** By the Treaty of Apamea between Rome and Antiochus III, the latter is to deliver Hannibal to Rome. Hannibal is forced to take refuge with Prusias, King of Bythinia.
**c. 167 BC:** Rome grants Masinissa authority to take over the emporia of Cirta (coasts of Cyrenaica and Tripolitania).
**c. 153 BC:** Cato the Elder visits Carthage; he is struck by its prosperity and the extent of its rearmament: *Delenda est Carthago*.
**149 BC:** The Carthaginians reject the order to abandon the city and prepare to resist. They inflict severe losses on the army of the consul Manilius.
**146 BC:** Destruction of Carthage.

**Rome destroys Carthage and Corinth.**

**146 BC**

5. *Barcide coinage in Spain in the Second Punic War period.*

6. *The mole of the war port of Carthage.*

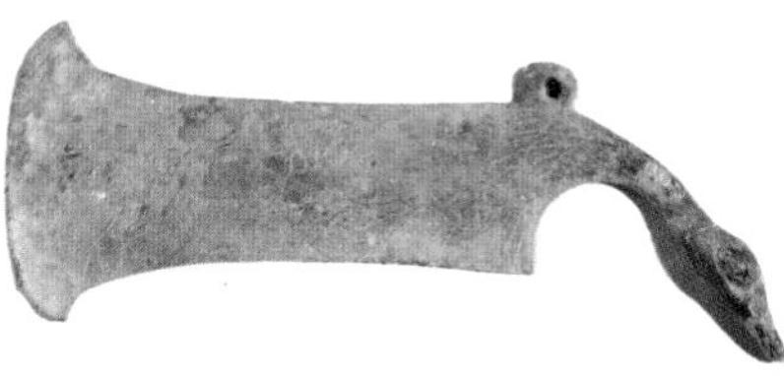

7. *Punic razor in bronze with goose head.*

# Bronze and Iron, Commerce and Money

*1. Hauling up of the great winged bull of Nimrud at the entrance to the palace of Ashurnasirpal II, 9th century BC. Reconstruction by A. H. Layard.*

REVOLUTIONARY INNOVATIONS in technology happened in the Mesolithic and Neolithic periods, before the turning point of 3300 to 2800 BC, but the revolution that took place around 3000 BC was a socio-political one. The birth of the first nations marked the beginning of history seen in terms of growth. These nations could almost be compared to the 'mega-machine' of the modern state in their total regulation of the freedom and leisure of the individual: human labour was exploited, work systematically organized. What better evidence than the ancient myths and formidable constructions of the time: the pyramids of Egypt, the towers of Mesopotamia, the megaliths of Europe and the Mediterranean dating from the second and third millennia BC, monuments to the fabulous human effort that went into their making?

The use of metals, at least of copper which was hardened by hammering, dates from Neolithic times. But bronze, a copper and tin alloy, began in the third and particularly the second millennium to play a major role, linked to changes in society. The use of iron was introduced in Asia Minor from 1500 or 1400 BC and continued to develop well into the first millennium. The iron revolution – with the discovery of abundant ore that could easily be put to use – had tremendous consequences, transforming everyday implements and agricultural activity.

**Beginning of 3rd millennium BC:** Copper is common in Egypt, bronze is known in Mesopotamia. Grandiose constructions.

**c. 2500–2400 BC:** Businessmen in Mesopotamia.

**c. 2200 BC:** Horses are harnessed.

**2100–1900 BC:** Metalwork highly developed among Celts (the 'torque wearers', Anatolia, Europe).

**From c. 2050 BC:** Bronze becomes common in Mesopotamia.

**c. 2000 BC:** Bronze is made in Egypt.

**c. 1600 BC:** The Hittite cart. Cretan domination over the seas.

**c.1500 BC:** Egyptian trade developed with Black Africa. Trade between India and Near East. 'King Solomon's Mines' near the Red Sea, profusion of mines and metal works.

**c. 1500–1400 BC:** Marked development of iron working in the Hittite Empire.

*4. Gold dagger and sheath from Ur, second half of 3rd millennium BC.*

**c. 1400 BC:** Shang bronzes, the finest in the world, Shang-Yin and Chou in China. Period of commercial expansion. Cowrie shell money.

**14th century BC:** Rise of Achaean seafaring, progress of naval technology.

**c. 1200 BC:** Rise of Indian trade. Beginning of Iron Age in Greece. Breton metalwork (bronze axes). First known naval battle, the Egyptians against the Sea People. Specialized war ships developed. Appearance of Olmec civilization in Central America. Importance of trade.

**End of 2nd millennium BC:** Rise of camel-rearing in the Near East, herding and caravans.

**c. 950 BC:** Phoenician sea-going ships are perfected; use of bitumen and the ribbed hull. Kingdom of Solomon plays a role of intermediary in trading.

**c. 900(?) BC:** Chinese coins in form of knives.

**c. 800 BC:** Beginning of Hallstatt civilization (iron).

# 3000–200 BC

Around 200 BC the water wheel took hold in the countries of the Mediterranean and China; hydraulic power began to replace muscle power. This is probably the most important technical innovation of the period.

Meanwhile, in the field of transport important progress was being made. The horse was domesticated in two stages which affected both war and material life: from around 2000 BC carts and harnessed horses appeared, and from around 1300 BC mounted horses and cavalry. Ships, with both sails and oars, were perfected.

From the third millennium onwards Mesopotamia developed powerful corporations of businessmen. They stocked goods, speculated, used various types of goods as currency, and used ingots, especially of silver, carved into particular weights and sizes and sometimes bearing authentication marks. The period beginning around 1400 BC, although marked by catastrophic crises, was one of considerable commercial development in the Mediterranean, India and China. The usual means of exchange – heads of cattle (*pecus*, cattle, gave the Latin *pecunia*), iron brooches (the Greek *obolus*; a *drachma* is a 'handful' of brooches), ingots, shells, coins in the forms of spades and knives – no longer sufficed, being too imprecise and arbitrary. Coins as we know them appeared in the seventh century BC, as the small states of the Mediterranean and the Chinese principalities began to assert their independence and their prerogatives (the levying of taxes, recruitment of mercenaries or civil servants etc.). Coins were in abundant use from around 500 BC. In the Mediterranean the centuries that followed were so marked by the development of trade, money, banks, transport, that several historians have compared them to the capitalist era, an understandable if exaggerated opinion in view of the very real originality in this and other fields of the classical Greek and Hellenistic world.

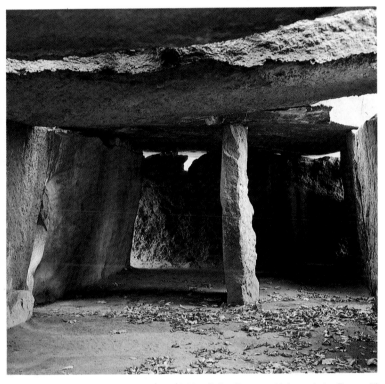

*2. Burial chamber of megalithic monument with galleries, Bagneux, Maine-et-Loire, France, 4th century BC.*

*3. Detail of facing of Pyramid of Mykerinos, Egypt, built around 2600 BC.*

**7th century BC:** Etruscans dominate the seas. Rise of the Phoenicians. Banks in Mesopotamia. Indian navigation. Building of Assyrian fleet. First naval battles in Greece (?). First triremes (ships with three rows of oars). First anchors (?). Greek and Chinese traditions date the appearance of proper coinage from these times; in China, the state of C'hi in Shantung may have played a role in their introduction.

**c. 650–600 BC:** Lydian and Ionian coinage (excavations of Ephesus).

**Late 6th and early 5th centuries BC:** Rise of the mercantile economies of Greece and the Mediterranean. Sea merchants play a role in primitive Buddhism. Proper coins appear in India.

**From c. 500 BC:** Abundant coinage in China, both copper and bronze. Rise of mercantile and urban economy in China. Celtic civilization of La Tène in continental Europe: iron, trade. Bronze Age civilizations in Southeast Asia. Iron working in Nigeria (?). Iron smelting in China.

**4th century BC:** Written texts on work. Major constructions. Progress of metalwork, particularly in China. Working of iron in Meroe in present-day Sudan (?).

**From c. 200 BC:** The water wheel.

*5. Coin made of electrum minted in Asia Minor, early 6th century BC.*

*6. Greek trireme, 5th century BC, marble (Acropolis, Athens).*

# The Population of the Planet

Like all animal populations, prehistoric human populations were subject to the laws of biological equilibrium, with alternate periods of growth and regression according to the way the climate treated them.

However, by the adaptation of its techniques, humanity gradually liberated itself from environmental constraints. Certain technical advances were responsible for a substantial population growth. This was the case with fire and clothing, which allowed the human race at a very early – and very distant – stage to extend its habitat to almost all the climatic regions of the earth. A second demographic revolution occurred when there was a decisive improvement in hunting techniques in the Upper Paleolithic age. A third was produced by the Neolithic revolution. Although climatic variations were still an important factor, capable of producing prolonged declines in population, the cultural milieu began at that point slowly to take over from the natural one in importance and most of the advances made were lasting ones.

The graph shows these advances and declines from 40,000 BC onwards for the whole population of the globe. The substantial leaps in population growth at the beginning of the Upper Paleolithic and Neolithic ages (similar to those which occurred during our own industrial revolution) can be clearly seen.

The elements making up the Neolithic period, which were developed over several millennia in a variety of different (relatively independent) centres and in quite diverse ways, formed, in certain places, particularly expansionist complexes. In a single millennium, the population of the globe was multiplied by a factor of 8 or 10.

More precocious, complete and dynamic than the others, the Near East centre was growing and spreading outwards as early as the seventh millennium. First of all, it expanded towards the Nile Valley in 6300 BC, then to the valleys of the Tigris and Euphrates from 5300 BC onwards. In 6000 BC population began to spread towards the north-west (Balkans, Ukraine, Central Europe) and the shores of the Mediterranean (Italy, southern France, eastern Spain, Andalusia, North Africa and as far as Portugal and Morocco). It expanded also towards the Caucasus in the north, towards Iran in the east, on to the southern shores of the Caspian Sea towards Turkestan in the north-east and Yemen in the south. Finally, far to the east, villages began to develop on the margins of the plateaus of Baluchistan which overlook the lower Indus Valley.

It is at this date that the map '4000 BC' gives a picture of the population of the world. At this period an important climatic change exacerbated the drought in the Sahara and the Near East, producing lower crop yields and casing occasional decreases in population. By contrast, in the Balkans, Ukraine and Central Europe, a peasant agriculture was developing in favourable conditions and was beginning to humanize the landscape. In northern China the same was true of peasant millet-growing, which spread into fertile valleys – particularly those in the east. In the south, however, rice-growing remained very basic and the yields remained at a derisory level, as did the yields of horticulture in Papua New Guinea. The same was true in Mexico and Peru, where the maize, bean and potato harvests were still at very low levels of productivity. Everywhere else, hunting, fishing and gathering were only able to support very sparse populations.

At the beginning of our era, the world population had again multiplied by a factor of 8 or 10 relative to 4000 BC. Every point on the lower map opposite is the equivalent of five points on the preceding map. Proportionally, the Near East, where the land was becoming exhausted or gorged with salt as a result of irrigation, lost some of its importance to India and, to a lesser degree, to China, where the population was expanding.

*1. Transcription at Lyon of Claudius's speech calling for Gauls to be admitted to the Roman Senate, AD 48.*

**10,000 BC:** Beginning of settlement in the Near East.
**8000–6500 BC:** Pre-ceramic Neolithic period in the Near East: the appearance of a first centre of high population density (from Iran to Greece, stretching through Anatolia, Syria and Palestine). This also extends, at a very early date, to Egypt.
**6000–4000BC:** First beginnings of population centres on the Mediterranean coasts, in the Balkans, Ukraine and Central Europe.
**5000–4000 BC:** First beginnings of centres of population in Mexico and, later, on the Peruvian coast. Colonization of the Tigris and Euphrates valleys in the Near East and the spread of population to Turkestan.
**4500 BC:** First Chinese population centre emerging in the Wei Ho basin. Beginning of population of Yemen.
**4000 BC:** First Indian population centre emerging in Indus valley. The populated Wei Ho area extends into the lower valley of the Huang Ho. In southwest China the beginnings of itinerant rice cultivation in areas of burnt forest produced no fixed population centres. In black Africa, the beginnings of agriculture and settlement in the Sudan ran up against the hostility of the climate (desiccation of the Sahel, lateritization of the soil, tropical forest).
**4000–3000 BC:** Rapid extension of agriculture and population in Western Europe (France, north Germany, north Poland, southern Scandinavia, Netherlands, British Isles and Spain), in India (Indus valley), in China (Yellow Sea and China Sea coasts, first inhabitants of Yangtze or Chang Jiang valley). Population growth in the Near East was reduced by drought, as was that of North Africa. The discovery of writing in Sumeria furthered the accumulation of knowledge.
**3000–2000 BC:** Population growth in southern Japan and on the western coasts of Korea. In Ukraine, Western Europe and the Balkans, invasions by peoples from the steppes brought about a serious decline in both agriculture and population growth. In the Near East, too, wars produced devastation. In India, population extended into the Ganges valley, and in the south it spread along the western coast of the sub-continent.
**2000–1500 BC:** In the Near East and Europe wars became more and more lethal and there was a substantial decline in population. In India, the Indus civilization collapsed suddenly and population levels with it. In China, population spread slowly towards the south, whereas in Japan it spread northwards. In America, the spread of population both in Mexico and in Peru was much slower.
**1500–500 BC:** After some large population movements in Europe and the Near East, societies became more stable and population began to increase again.
**500 BC–AD 0:** Founding of a number of great empires: Persian, Macedonian, Chinese, Indian (Maurya) and Roman – which took in almost all the world's organized states – promoted long-distance trade and stimulated the economy. Everywhere, population was in rapid progress.

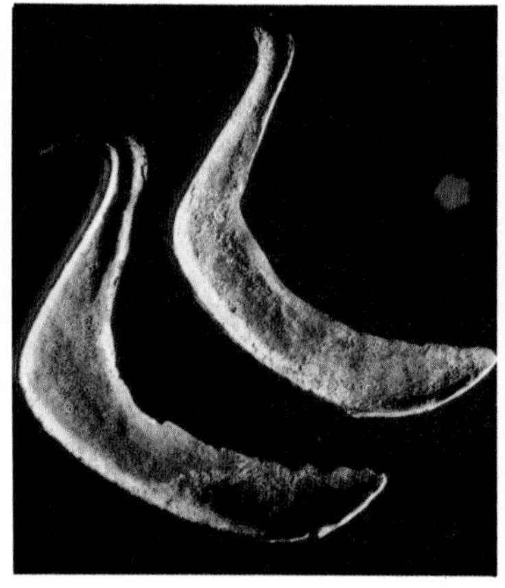

*2. Bronze sickles, c. 1000 BC.*

# From the Neolithic Revolution to Jesus Christ

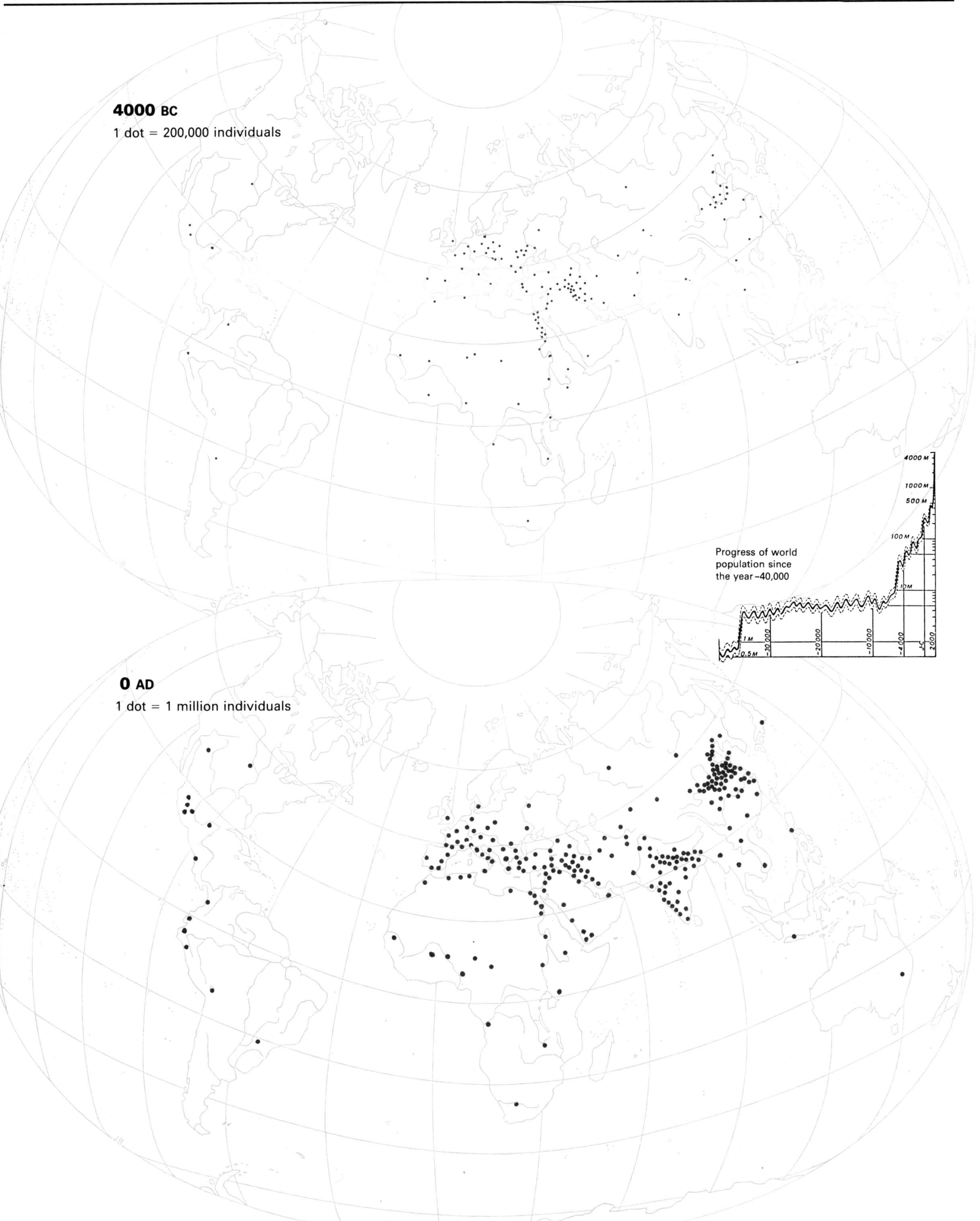


Progress of world population since the year -40,000

# The Greek World between Myth and History

Between the world of the Mycenaean palaces and that of the Greek city-states, between, that is, the years 1200 and 800 BC, four centuries passed which are an enigma to historians. They are known as 'the dark centuries' or the 'Greek Middle Ages', formulae which reveal the irritation which this little-known period provokes among historians (though it has, for precisely the same reason, often stimulated the literary imagination). The absence of any written text (Mycenaean linear script had fallen out of use) confers a primordial importance upon the archaeological record, and it is the recent works of synthesis in this field that allow us to put together an, as yet fragmentary, picture of the Greek world.

*1. The Lelantine Plain in Euboea. In the top left of the picture is the hill on which Lefkandi, the site of the first Eretria, stands.*

The wave of destruction that occurred at the end of the thirteenth century BC was accompanied by the abandonment of the majority of the Mycenaean sites and by population movements towards safe areas where new habitats were created. The break-up of the Mycenaean world doubtless did not occur in an even manner; archaeologists have found that zones of continuity existed at such sites as Athens, Lefkandi in Euboea and in Cyprus. Certainly the collapse was not followed by any permanent settlement of populations that had arrived from elsewhere (the 'Dorian invasions' seem to have been a mirage). At most, what occurred was not a real conquest, but a rapid passing through of migrants. After more than a century of disturbances, from the eleventh century BC onwards, innovations were introduced in a number of fields. The ceramic art that is known as protogeometric made its appearance, iron replaced bronze in the manufacture of tools and there were changes in burial practices. At the end of the century there began the long process of the migration and settlement of Greek communities from continental Greece along the coasts of Asia Minor and in the islands, whilst Cyprus played a major role as go-between with the Middle Eastern civilizations (there existed a Cypriot syllabic script). Little by little, the Aegean became a Greek sea.

Archaeology allows us to eliminate certain false theories which have attempted to project models derived from elsewhere on to these centuries. As a science, it lays stress on geographical diversity and encourages the historian to be prudent and develop a subtle view. Burial customs offer a good example of this. The map of necropolises reveals the variety of funeral rituals and casts doubt on the idea that there was a uniform transition from inhumation to incineration. It brings out the really new developments in this field: the spread of individual graves and the adoption of the cist tomb. The cemeteries also provide a glimpse of how the world of the living was organized. It is possible to perceive distinctive marks between ages, sexes and social groups in them, even if the step from tomb archaeology to social analysis is a difficult and necessarily speculative one. The documents which really bring this world to life are the *Iliad* and the *Odyssey*. These two epic poems attributed to Homer tell the story of the Trojan War and Ulysses's return to Ithaca. These were stories that had possibly been passed on in the oral tradition from as early as the Mycenaean period, but which were not written down until the eighth century BC. These stories essentially provide a picture of the world of the period between Mycenae and the Greek cities, the world of Greece's 'dark age'. They show Greece coming to life. It covered itself with a sprinkling of kingdoms, organized relations with the gods and between men, made the *oikos* (household, domain) the centre of economic and social power and the place in which kinship was expressed. It also peopled itself with 'heroes' – those who announced themselves 'the best' both as soldiers and as givers of banquets.

Our current knowledge of this period does not make it possible to draw up any detailed chronology. The major reference points are provided by the history of pottery. Other innovations cannot be dated in such a precise manner. They all relate to relatively long periods, whether we are considering population movements in Greece itself and in particular in the Peloponnese (1200–1000 BC), migrations in Asia Minor and in the Cyclades (*c.* 1100–800 BC), the spread of the use of iron (1100 BC onwards) or a particular burial site. The dark centuries are periods of long-term processes; within them, however, what one might call 'material culture' provides some markers to guide us.

**Destruction of Mycenaean palace civilization.**

**12th century BC**

**Beginning of Iron Age. Protogeometric cerami**

**1100–900 BC**

*2. Cart drawn by three bulls, Crete, 11th century BC.*

**End of 13th century BC:** Destruction of Pylos.
**12th century BC:** Destruction of Mycenae. Mycenaean palace civilization and Mycenaean script gradually disappear.
**1150–1000 BC:** Sub-Mycenaean ceramics. The motifs of Mycenaean ceramics are simplified.
**1025–900 BC:** Protogeometric ceramics. Vases are decorated with circles drawn with a compass and concentric semi-circles painted with a 'multiple brush'. The only other objects known are bronze buckles and clay statuettes. Nothing is known of domestic o temple architecture.
**900–725 BC:** Geometric ceramics. Decoration takes the form of continuous bands of triangles, wavy lines or zigzags separated by lines. The entire vase is decorated. Excavations have made it possible to reconstruct the structure of the living environment at the very beginning of the ninth century BC (modest cabins as at Smyrna) and of the structure of its defences. The sites whose chronology is best known

*3. Small model granaries, Athens, c. 850 BC.*

# 12th–8th centuries BC

Cist tombs
Other forms of inhumation
Cremation

**Funerary rites: inhumation and cremation**

From A. Snodgrass. *The Dark Age of Greece*. Edinburgh, 1971

**...ration of Greeks into Asia Minor.**

**c. 1100–800 BC**

**Geometric ceramics.**

**900–725 BC**

*4. The Mistress of Beasts (Artemis). Attic vase of the geometric period, 8th century BC.*

are the necropolises. The first cities appeared in the course of the **9th century BC**.

It may be thought that there is one date missing from this brief chronology, that of the 'third Greek invasions: the Dorians'. This omission is deliberate. Did the 'Dorian invasion' really take place? The question has long been a controversial one, but the latest archaeological syntheses find no trace of such a phenomenon. The 'Dorian myth' and the central structuring opposition in Greek discourse between 'Dorians' and 'Ionians' are of the greatest historical interest. They are not, however, by any means proof of the arrival of vast numbers of invaders between the 13th and 12th centuries BC.

At the beginning of the **8th century BC**, figurative decoration appears. This same century sees the diversification of objects and techniques: the sanctuary sites and the rich tombs are filled with magnificent bronze tripod-cauldrons, weapons, bronze figurines, clasps, jewels and statuettes.

*5. Stone tripod, Plataea, 7th century BC.*

# The 'Archaic' Greek World

During these three centuries the geographical limits, mental universe and political structures of what the Greeks called *oukouméné* (the inhabited world) were set in place. The term 'archaic' is only accurate if one takes a view which assumes classical Athens as a model. It would seem more reasonable to view this period as a time in which an enormous number of innovations were tested out, ranging from the appearance of cities to the emergence of rational thought.

We have no means of knowing at what precise date the Greek cities originated; we see them only when they are already functioning, when they have emerged into history (from end of ninth/beginning of eighth centuries BC) and not all the regions of Greece developed at the same pace. A city (*polis*) was a group of people freely governing themselves: the Greeks always referred to the cities by the collective name of their citizens, e.g. the Athenians or the Megarans. Each city was independent, possessed its own institutions and often came into conflict with others. It was made up of a rural territory with a number of villages and a more or less urbanized centre which was the seat of common institutions. Greece was fragmented into several hundred cities, many of which are only names for us today. Lastly, there were a number of Greek regions where organization into cities was not known. The political unit in these regions was the 'people' (*ethnos*) (e.g. the Thessalians or the Locrians). Little was known of their history during these three centuries.

The various cities had very different histories. The close study of a specific community would reveal many features that diverge considerably from the broad outline we are able to present here. There are also gaps in the story owing to the lack of historical evidence. There are few written texts from the period and the archaeological record is often difficult to interpret.

A city was made up of different social groups. Some of these were free; others were slaves. Among the free men there was a fundamental distinction between citizens and non-citizens. As the cities developed, the boundaries between the various categories became more sharply drawn, and access to citizenship – which meant gaining the right to participate in assemblies, tribunals and the magistracy, to fight in wars and possess land – was either expanded or restricted depending upon the particular circumstances.

The lack of cultivable land and its inevitable consequences – debt, slavery and famine – were one of the causes of the great migratory movement which lasted for two centuries. This period of 'colonization' involved the creation of new cities all round the perimeter of the Mediterranean, land being claimed at the expense of the indigenous populations. It did not, however, resolve the internal problems of the cities of continental Greece, but it did ease them in certain cases and produced channels of cultural exchange which had a unifying effect on a considerable area of the Mediterranean world, from Spain to the Crimea. The existence of these new cities and of what had now become metropolises gave legislators the task of framing new laws. These generally introduced more equity into social relations, though only in exceptional cases (as for example at Sparta) did they take account of the clamour for land reform. In some cases, a small number of great families shared power (aristocratic government); in others, one of these families held power illegally for several generations (tyrannic government). This was the only alternative that existed until Athens made equality before the law a principle of government.

*1. The Temple of Apollo at Corinth, 6th century BC. In the background the Citadel of Acrocrinthus.*

**First cities.** **First games at Olympia.** **Beginning of Greek 'colonization'.**

**800 BC** **776 BC** **770 BC**

**End of 9th century BC:** Appearance of first cities.
**Beginning of 8th century BC:** Adoption of a new alphabet with letters adapted from the Phoenician alphabet. The earliest extant inscriptions date from the end of the 8th/beginning of 7th century BC (scratched on pottery) and include the verse inscription on the Bowl of Nestor at Pithecusa (Ischia).
**776 BC:** Traditional date of the first Olympic Games. They were held during a festival in Zeus's honour at Olympia and comprised athletic, musical and poetry competitions. Of these, the athletic events were the most famous. They included running, throwing the discus and javelin, boxing, wrestling and chariot racing.
**770–706 BC:** Greek 'colonization' begins (in the west). Greek settlement at Pithecusai (island off the coast of Naples). Foundation of Naxos and Cumae by Chalcis, Syracuse by Corinth and Tarentum by Sparta.
**Middle–end of 8th century BC:** Iliad and Odyssey, epic poems attributed to Homer, written down. Writings of Hesiod.

*2. Dorian-style Attic Kore, late 6th century BC.*

**747–657 BC:** The family of the Bacchiadae holds power in Corinth: an example of aristocratic government.
**736–720 and 650–620 BC:** Sparta stakes out its territory in the Messenian wars.
**700–675 BC and after:** Greek 'colonization' in the east. Megara founds Chalcedon (c. 687 BC); Paros founds Thasos (c. 682 BC); Megara founds Byzantium. Other cities were also founded along the coast of the Black Sea (Pontus Euxinus), such as Istros and Olbia (by Miletus) around 650 BC. New settlements were created in southern Italy and Sicily and in the far western Mediterranean. This expansion continued until the end of the century.
**680–670 BC:** First appearance of coinage in Lydia and in Ionia. The minting of coins did not develop in the Greek cities for another century. The pottery of this period is known as 'Orientalizing'. First stone temples built.

**7th century BC:** Saw the rise of 'tyrannies' (illegal government by one man) in the Greek cities. Examples are Kypselos and Periandres in Corinth (657–585 BC) or Orthagoras to Cleisthenes at Sikyon. Codes of law were also elaborated under the auspices of such 'legislators' as Zaleucus of Locri (660 BC?), Charondas of Catana and Draco (620 BC) and Solon at Athens.
**600 BC:** Massalia (Marseille) founded as a colony of Phocaea.

*3. Gold buckle in the shape of a falcon. From the Temple of Artemis at Ephesus, c. 550 BC.*

# 8th–6th centuries BC

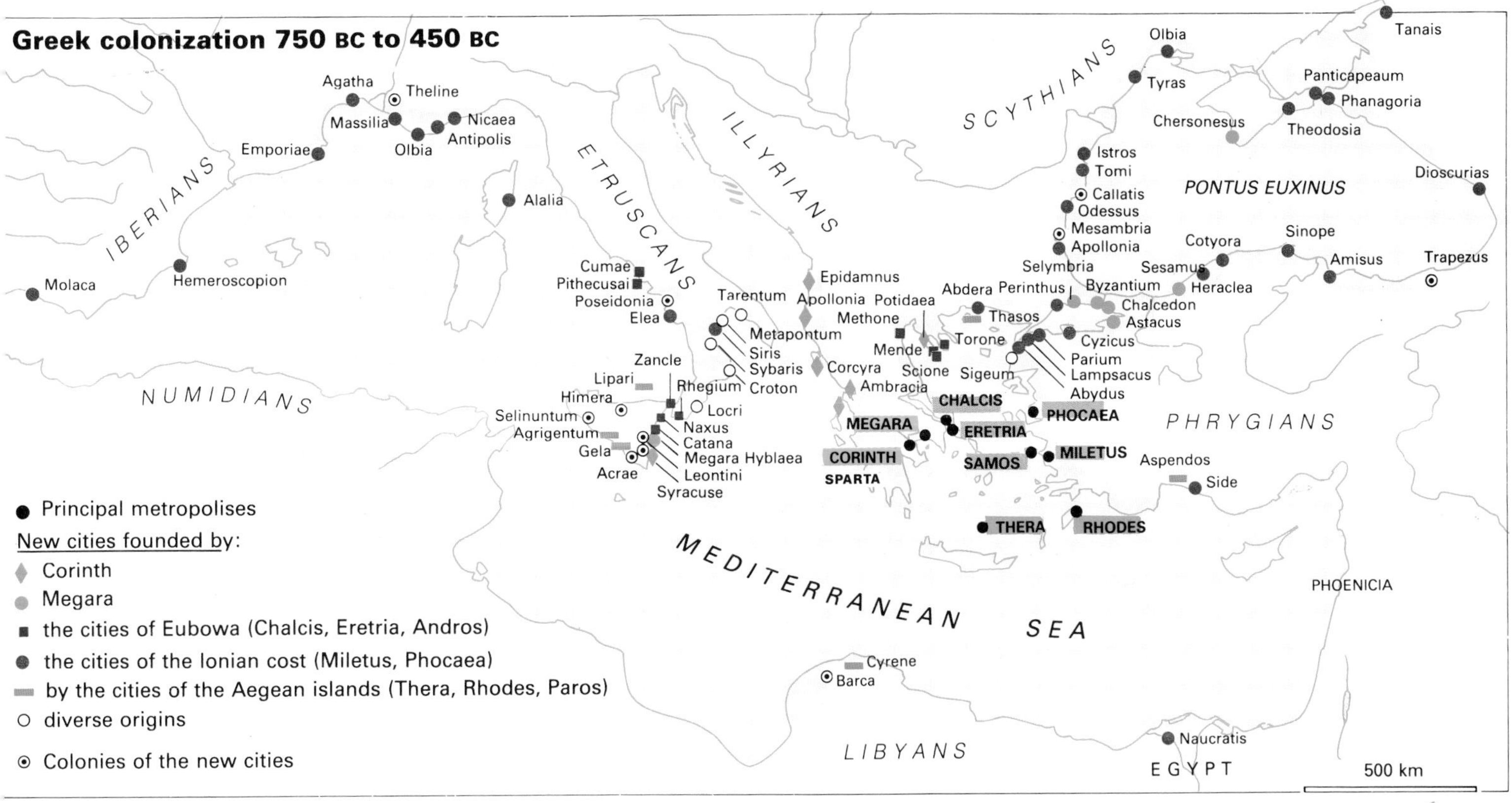

## Greek colonization 750 BC to 450 BC

- ● Principal metropolises

New cities founded by:

- ♦ Corinth
- ● Megara
- ■ the cities of Eubowa (Chalcis, Eretria, Andros)
- ● the cities of the Ionian cost (Miletus, Phocaea)
- ▬ by the cities of the Aegean islands (Thera, Rhodes, Paros)
- ○ diverse origins
- ⊙ Colonies of the new cities

500 km

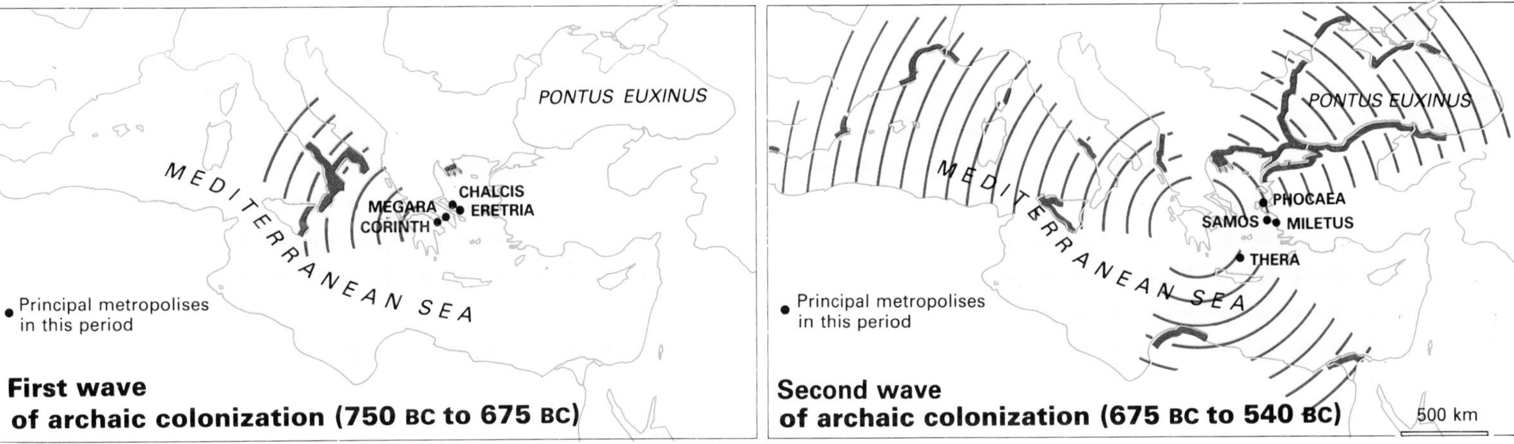


| c. 620 BC | 594 BC | 507 BC |
|---|---|---|
| First coins. | Solon archon at Athens. | Cleisthenes's reforms at Athens. |

*A hoplite. Detail from the 'Krater of Vix', Corinthian art (?), 6th century BC.*

**7th and 6th centuries BC:** Centuries of innovation in all fields: the 'origins of Greek thought' are indissociable from the history of the cities.
**594BC:** Solon, archon at Athens, abolishes enslavement by debt, removes the 'mortgages' that are oppressing the small landowners and introduces a new system of weights and measures. Certain of the constitutional reforms attributed to him (Areopagus council, etc.) were perhaps inventions of the 4th century BC (and Aristotle in particular).
**561–528/7 BC:** Peisistratos rules intermittently as tyrant at Athens.
**528/7–510 BC:** The tyrant Hipparchos (assassinated in 514 BC) is succeeded by the tyrant Hippias.
**508–507 BC:** Cleisthenes's reforms at Athens. The structures which will allow for the introduction of democratic rule are put in place.

*5. The cyclops intoxicated and blinded by Ulysses and his companions. Laconian bowl, 6th century BC.*

# A Universal Empire: Persia

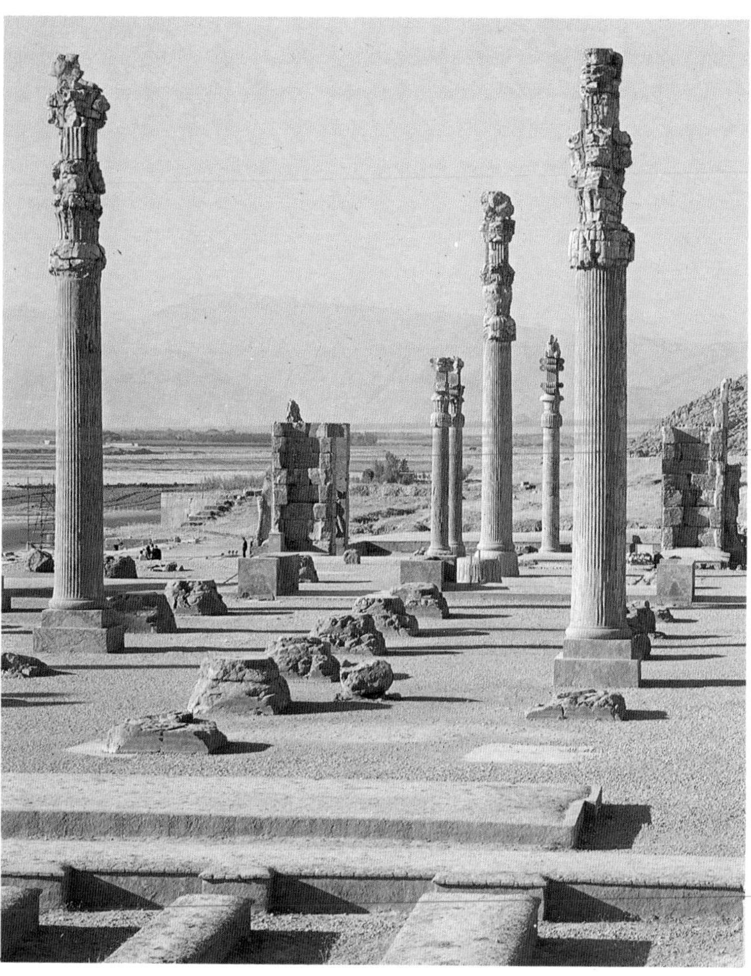

1. The Apadana (Hall of a Hundred Columns) of the palace of Persepolis, 6th–5th century BC.

THE PERSIANS AND THE MEDES were the foremost peoples among the 'barbarians' (the non-Greek-speakers). In forty years, they rose from being mere Oriental provincials to become masters of the world. The conquests of Cyrus, Cambyses and Darius I brought together the Indus region, the Scythians beyond Sogdiana, Egypt and Ionia into a vast single body whose heart beat in Persia. Though there were revolts within the Empire and though it suffered some defeats, particularly at the hands of the Greeks, a state of peace was established (albeit one defended by a vast deployment of arms).

Darius I played an organizing role in the Empire. Firstly, he placed garrisons in all the regions, especially those that were vital on account of their wealth (Egypt, Babylonia) or their location (Ionia, Bactria). The conquered populations were made to pay tribute by providing ships, soldiers or provisions. Secondly, he appointed satraps, governors and Persian officers who, being bound to the Great King by blood or honour, were entirely under his command. The king was the focus of the whole system: he was the theoretical owner of all land, commander-in-chief and supreme judge. He was also the representative of Ahura-Mazda among men, the junction between the divine and the human, the hub of the entire cosmic order. And within an immense network of land, river and sea communications (the royal road from Ephesus to Bactria; the Nile–Red Sea canal dredged in the reign of Darius I), each region continued to live under its own legal system. Greek money reached as far as Bactria, Iranian customs took root in Asia Minor and Egyptian, Greek and Ionian scholars and artists came together in Susa and Persepolis.

Evoking former nomadic times, the court had three residences. In winter it was based at Persepolis or Susa and in summer at Ecbatana(Hamadan). Persepolis was the domain of the Achaemenid clan and by that token, the capital. Built in the days of Darius I and enhanced by constant improvements, it was the centre of the royal economy, the theatre of the New Year festivals and the jewel of Achaemenid art. That art, which welcomed a variety of influences – it looked to Greece in matters of stone working, to Mesopotamia for iconography and to Iran for the representation of animals – was a royal art, in which the delegations lined up to offer their gifts to the king represented the vastness of the whole world showing allegiance to a single sovereign.

The Persians worshipped Ahura-Mazda; he was their great god, together with Mithra and the goddess Anahita; but the king acknowledged Amun-Ré in Egypt and Apollo at Delphi, whilst the Persian administration respected the cult of the Elamite gods at Persepolis.

A great number of centrifugal tendencies, constant dynastic difficulties, and the superior quality of the Greek hoplites, not to mention Alexander's good fortune, put an end to the Persian Empire. A whole chapter in the development of ancient oriental civilization was thus concluded, but Alexander's conquests brought the peoples of Central Asia and Iran on to the historical stage for the first time and opened up distant lands first to the Greco-Macedonians and later to the Romans. It is from these years of integration, in particular from the view that the contemporary Greeks had of the Persians, that we have derived the picture of the Orient that still haunts the Western imagination today, a picture made up of despotism and intrigue, lust and luxury. There is little difference between the writings of classical authors like Ctesias and Plutarch and those of seventeenth-century European travellers in Persia. Both share the same fascination made up of conflicting emotions of surprise, desire and repulsion.

**Union of Medan princes at Ecbatana.**

**700 BC**

**Cyrus builds Pasargades.**

**c. 540 BC**

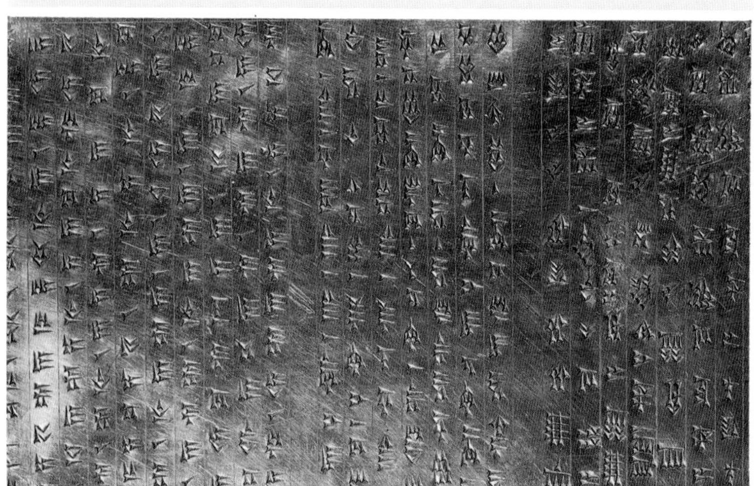

2. King Darius says: 'This is the kingdom I possess. ... Here is what Ahura-Mazda has granted me.' Trilingual golden plaque, Darius I, c. 500 BC.

**612 BC:** A coalition of Median princes destroys Nineveh and the Neo-Assyrian Empire; the Persians become vassals of the Medes.
**550 BC:** Cyrus II the Great defeats the last Median king and conquers Asia Minor, including Croesus's Lydian kingdom and the whole of Iran.
**539 BC:** Cyrus conquers Babylon and allows the Jews, who were captive there, to return to Palestine and rebuild the Temple at Jerusalem.
**525 BC:** Cambyses II conquers Egypt.
**521 BC:** Dynastic problems enable Darius I to usurp the throne by eliminating Cambyses II's brother. With a section of the Persian nobility he represses uprisings throughout the Empire. The inscription at Bagistana in Media recounts his version of events in four languages (Old Persian, Akkadian, Elamite and Aramaic). He then conquers the Indus valley, Thrace and Macedonia.
**510 BC:** Building work at its height at Persepolis. The Elamite tablets – records of the wages paid to workers, peasants and artisans employed there – reveal a centralized, hierarchical economy.

3. Gold rhyton (animal-shaped vessel), Achaemenid art, c. 500 BC.

# 550–331 BC

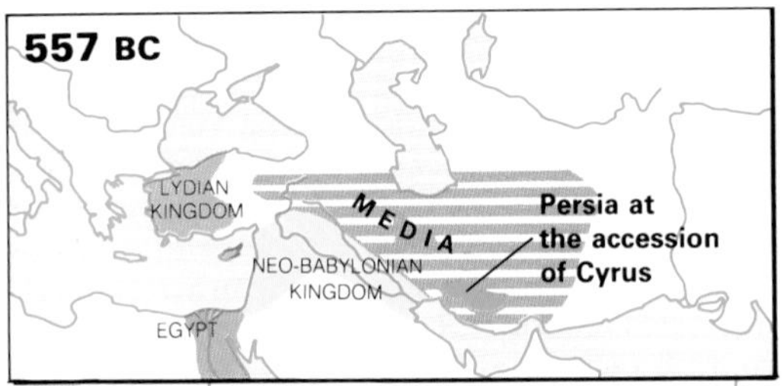

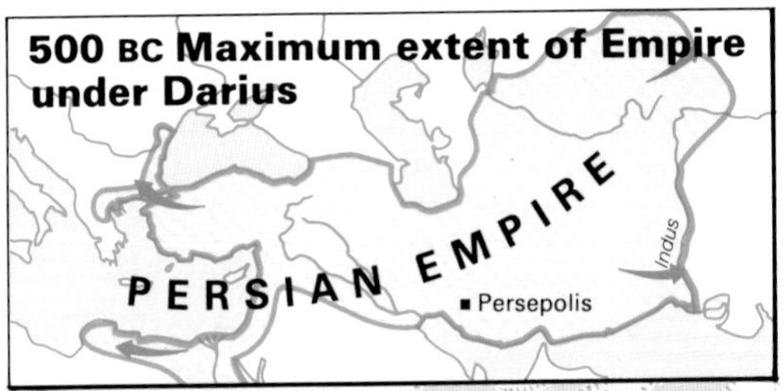

**557 BC**

LYDIAN KINGDOM
MEDIA
Persia at the accession of Cyrus
NEO-BABYLONIAN KINGDOM
EGYPT

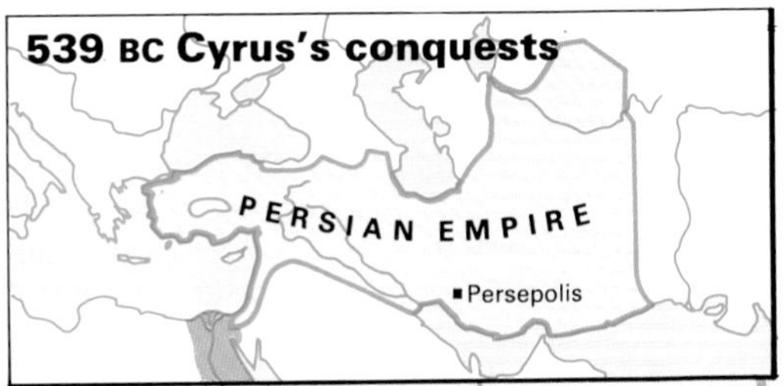

**539 BC Cyrus's conquests**

PERSIAN EMPIRE
Persepolis

**500 BC Maximum extent of Empire under Darius**

PERSIAN EMPIRE
Persepolis
Indus

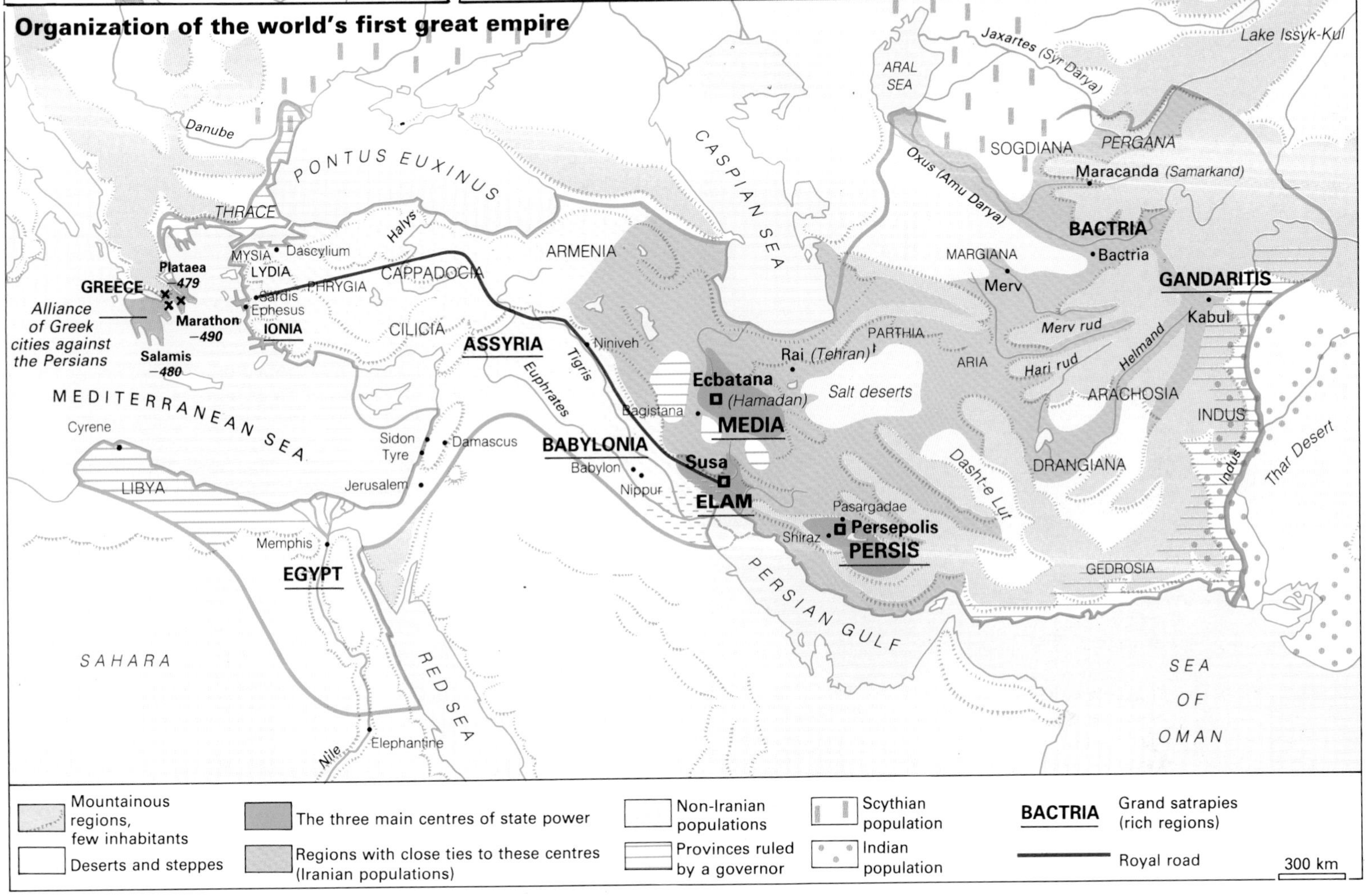

## Organization of the world's first great empire

Mountainous regions, few inhabitants
Deserts and steppes
The three main centres of state power
Regions with close ties to these centres (Iranian populations)
Non-Iranian populations
Provinces ruled by a governor
Scythian population
Indian population
BACTRIA Grand satrapies (rich regions)
Royal road
300 km

| Darius I. | Elamite tablets of Persepolis. | Artaxerxes II. |
|---|---|---|
| 521 BC | 519–465 BC | 404 BC |

**498 BC:** The revolt of Ionia sparks off the Persian Wars. Darius is defeated at Marathon in 490 BC and dies in 486 BC. He is buried at Naqsh-i-Roustem.
**482 BC:** Revolt in Babylonia and Xerxes is defeated by the Greeks at Salamis (480 BC), Plataea and at the Mycale (479 BC).
**c. 450–430 BC:** Herodotus of Helicarnassus, a subject of Artaxerxes I, describes the Persian Empire in his *History*.
**449 BC:** Peace of Callias. This treaty, negotiated at Susa by Callias the Athenian, establishes a demilitarized zone along the coast of Asia Minor and puts an end to the Persian Wars.
**404 BC:** Artaxerxes II, son of Darius II, is challenged by his ambitious brother, Cyrus the Younger, who engages 10,000 Greek mercenaries in order to win the throne, but loses the battle of Cunaxa (401 BC) and dies. Xenophon describes the Retreat of the Ten Thousand in his *Anabasis*; on his return to Greece he writes the *Cyropaedia*, an idealized portrait of Cyrus the Great.
**c. 403 BC:** Revolt and secession of Egypt. Under Nectanebes I and his 30th dynasty, Egypt will enjoy independence and relative prosperity.

4. *The tomb of Darius I at Naqsh-i-Roustem.*

**End of 5th/beginning of 4th centuries BC:** The Greek doctor Ctesias, author of a *History of Persia*, lives at Susa and Persepolis.
**386 BC:** The Peace of Antalcidas dictated by Artaxerxes II, permits the Great King to act as a 'broker' among the Greeks. The Persian king makes good use of his gold both for war and for diplomacy.
**362 BC:** Revolt of the satraps of Asia Minor, amongst whom was a certain Mausolus whose tomb gave us the word mausoleum.
**358 BC:** Artaxerxes III endeavours to restore royal power within the Empire. He eliminates the opposition, reconquers Egypt (343–341 BC). He runs up against the ambitions of Philip II of Macedonia and dies at the hands of an assassin in 338 BC.
**334 BC:** Alexander III, the Great, lands in Asia Minor.
**333 BC:** The Persians lose the Battle of Issus in Cilicia; two years later they lose the Battle of Gaugamela.
**331 BC:** Persepolis is sacked and burnt. In Bactria and Sogdiana, Alexander becomes orientalized as Iran is hellenized.

5. *Lapis Lazuli head of an Achaemenid prince, Persepolis, end of 5th century BC.*

# Hellenism Triumphant

THERE HAS BEEN no shortage of positive expressions – the classical era, the Golden Age of city-states, the high point of Hellenism – deployed to describe this period, and yet it was also an era of incessant battles, plagues, famines, intolerance, civil war and confrontations between rich and poor. To see this, one has only to turn one's gaze away from the shining new statues of the Acropolis to the Ceramicus cemetery where the dead were buried, or from the processions of pilgrims who climbed the sacred path to the sanctuary of Apollo at Delphi to the inscriptions on the temple walls which, in their thousands, bear witness to the existence of slavery.

*1. Athens: the Acropolis and the Parthenon. In the background, Mt Lycabettus (also known as the Hill of St George).*

The fifth century BC was dominated by two conflicts. The one set the Greeks against the Persians, the other saw almost all the Greek cities, with Athens at their head, ranged against Sparta. What was at stake in the struggle against the Persian Great King was the freedom of the Greek world. The opposition between Athens and Sparta was, however, more complex and cannot be reduced to a confrontation between two models of government, one oligarchic, the other democratic. There was indeed a great divide – and one which constantly increased throughout the fifth century – between the rigidity of the Spartan social and political system, which had been frozen in its forms since the Archaic period, and the evolution towards greater power being given to the people (*demos*) which characterizes the internal history of Athens from Cleisthenes to Pericles. But war was in any event one of the primordial aspects of Greek life, an eternal competition which was carried on in every field by individuals and communities for whom rivalry was the only worthy mode of being.

The cult of war was bound inextricably together with the general life of the community through the medium of the gods. Not only fields of battle, from the farmland plains which offered opportunities for the skilful manoeuvring of infantry (hoplites) to the sheltered coves where the battleships (triremes) rammed each other, but also the more peaceful sites where only opinions clashed (assemblies, tribunals), and even the most humble domestic space, all were places where the gods were potentially present, invoked by a sacrifice, a libation, or a simple prayer. Greece certainly had its sanctuaries where marble statues were to be seen looming out of the smoke from roasting meat (who has not heard of Delphi, Olympia, Delos or the Acropolis at Athens?), but it should be stressed that every act of public and private life had a sacred dimension. This dimension was part and parcel of the daily round, which took the Greek from the gymnasium to the agora (public square), from the sanctuary to the banqueting hall, and from the field to the theatre where Aeschylus, Aristophanes, Sophocles and Euripides were performed.

A great deal of experimentation and innovation that had its beginnings in earlier periods was brought to completion in the fifth century. For the Greek city-states as a whole, there were more continuities than radical breaks. The most crucial new development was the immense breakthrough made by written documents, from stone-carved inscriptions to literary texts. Such documents both allow us to discover even the least significant little decree from some obscure city in the Pelopponese and at the same time they privilege a particular vision of the world of the city-states, namely that of Athens, whence most of the texts derive. The modern historian of the 'classical world' has a better understanding of the ethnocentrism of his 'sources', but it is very difficult for that historian to speak with anything but the voice of Athens, a city which saw itself as the model of the Greek world.

**Marathon.** **490 BC**

**Salamis.** **480 BC**

**Delian League.** **477 BC**

**Birth of Socrates.** **470 BC**

**525–456 BC:** Aeschylus.
**508–507 BC:** Cleisthenes' reforms at Athens.
**499–493 BC:** Ionian revolt. The Greek cities rise against the tyrants set in power by the Persians. In 498 BC the Persian town of Sardis is captured and burnt. In 494 BC Miletus is razed to the ground. Peace treaties between Darius and the cities.
**497–406 BC:** Sophocles.
**492–479 BC:** Persian Wars. The Persians under the direction of Darius and, later, Xerxes, invade Greece. They are defeated at Marathon (490 BC), Salamis (480 BC), Plataea and Mycale (479 BC) by a coalition of cities. Athens comes to the fore both by virtue of its place in the front line of the fighting (the Acropolis was burnt by the Persians) and of the part played by Themistocles, the strategic head of the Greek army. See Herodotus's *History*.
**c. 485 BC:** Birth of Herodotus.
**485–406 BC:** Euripides.
**477 BC:** Delian League founded. This was an alliance of Greek cities around Athens to prosecute war against the Persians; Athenian hegemony became more and more marked and the allies were unable to leave the alliance (470 BC, the revolt of Naxos) even after a peace treaty, the Peace of Callias (449–448 BC) had been signed with the Great King.

*2. Athenian decadrachma bearing motif of owl with outstretched wings. Persian Wars period.*

*3. Artemis and Acteon. Bell-shaped krater by the painter of Pan, c. 470 BC.*

**472 BC:** Themistocles ostracized. Ostracism was a vote of the citizen body of Athens condemning to exile a political personality whose presence was thought to endanger the stability of the *polis*. Many Athenian politicians fell victim to it (Cimon in 461 BC; Thucydides in 443 BC).
**472–387 BC:** The tragedies of Aeschylus, Sophocles and Euripides and the comedies of Aristophanes made the theatre of Dionysos at Athens a significant site of civic discourse.
**464 BC:** Earthquake at Sparta. Revolt of the helots, a peasant population of serfs. These revolts, frequent in the 5th century BC, weakened Sparta, which was forced to struggle on several fronts at once. Athens, which employed vast numbers of bought slaves of non-Athenian origin, did not face such internal disturbances.
**462 BC:** Ephialtes' reforms at Athens. The aristocratic Areopagus Council lost part of its prerogatives to the People's Assembly, the Council of the Five Hundred (*Boulê*) and the Heliaea tribunal. An important step towards democracy.

# 5th century BC

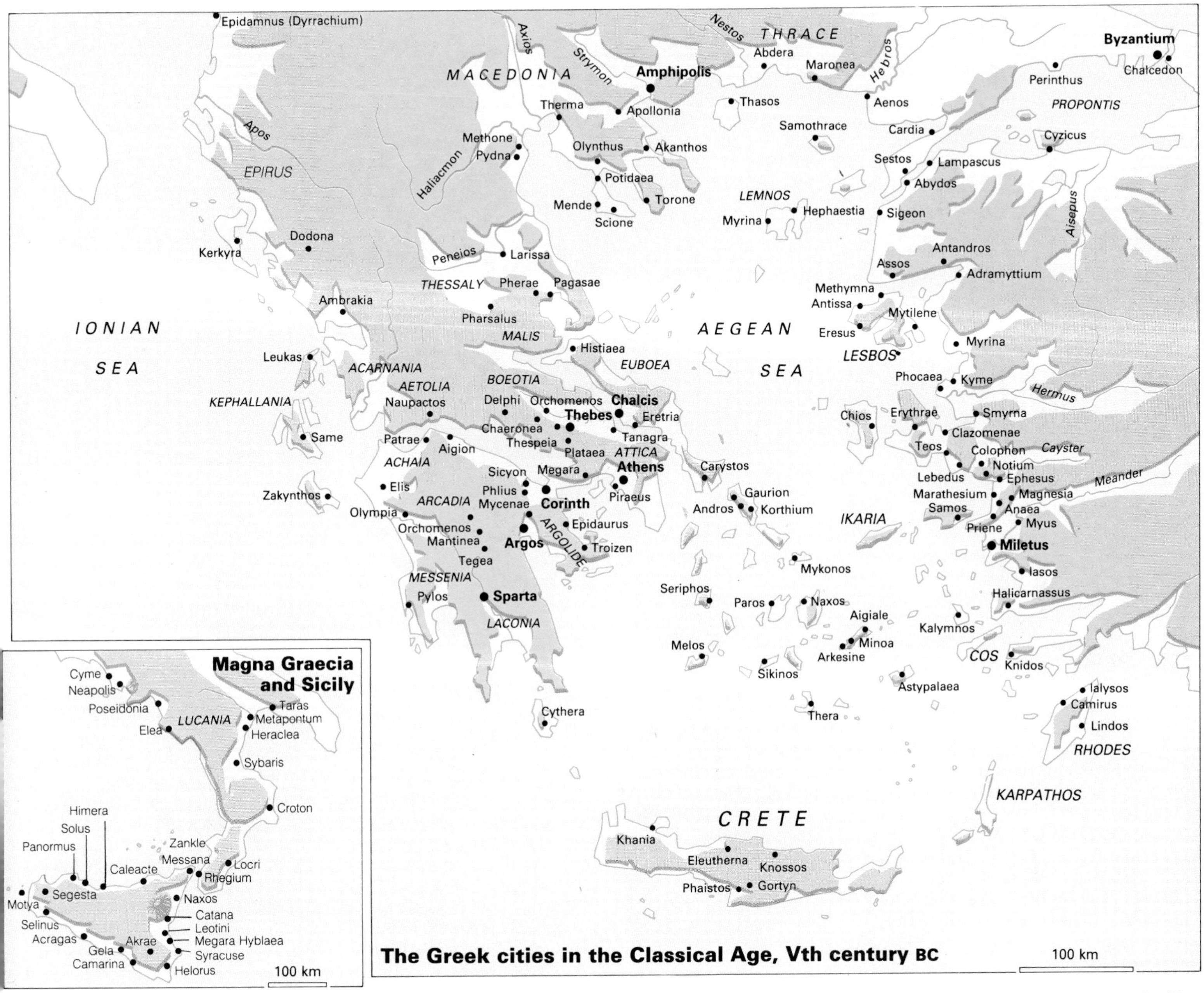

Epidamnus (Dyrrachium) · MACEDONIA · THRACE · Axios · Strymon · Nestos · Hebros · Abdera · Maronea · Amphipolis · Byzantium · Chalcedon · Perinthus · PROPONTIS · Therma · Apollonia · Thasos · Aenos · Samothrace · Cardia · Cyzicus · Apos · EPIRUS · Methone · Pydna · Haliacmon · Olynthus · Akanthos · Potidaea · Sestos · Lampascus · Abydos · Mende · Scione · Torone · LEMNOS · Myrina · Hephaestia · Sigeon · Aisepus · Dodona · Kerkyra · Peneios · Larissa · Antandros · Assos · Adramyttium · THESSALY · Pherae · Pagasae · Methymna · Antissa · Ambrakia · Pharsalus · Mytilene · IONIAN SEA · MALIS · Histiaea · AEGEAN SEA · Eresus · Myrina · Leukas · ACARNANIA · EUBOEA · LESBOS · AETOLIA · BOEOTIA · Phocaea · Kyme · KEPHALLANIA · Naupactos · Delphi · Orchomenos · Chalcis · Hermus · Thebes · Eretria · Chios · Erythrae · Smyrna · Chaeronea · Tanagra · Clazomenae · Same · Patrae · Aigion · Thespeia · Plataea · ATTICA · Teos · Colophon · Cayster · ACHAIA · Sicyon · Megara · Athens · Carystos · Notium · Lebedus · Ephesus · Meander · Elis · Phlius · Piraeus · Gaurion · Marathesium · Magnesia · Zakynthos · ARCADIA · Mycenae · Corinth · Andros · Korthium · Samos · Anaea · Olympia · Epidaurus · IKARIA · Priene · Myus · Orchomenos · ARGOLIDE · Mantinea · Argos · Troizen · Miletus · Tegea · Mykonos · Iasos · MESSENIA · Seriphos · Halicarnassus · Pylos · Sparta · Paros · Naxos · Aigiale · LACONIA · Kalymnos · Minoa · Melos · Arkesine · COS · Knidos · Sikinos · Astypalaea · Ialysos · Camirus · Cythera · Thera · Lindos · RHODES · KARPATHOS · CRETE · Khania · Eleutherna · Knossos · Phaistos · Gortyn

**Magna Graecia and Sicily**

Cyme · Neapolis · Poseidonia · Taras · LUCANIA · Metapontum · Elea · Heraclea · Sybaris · Croton · Himera · Solus · Panormus · Zankle · Messana · Locri · Caleacte · Rhegium · Segesta · Naxos · Motya · Catana · Selinus · Leotini · Acragas · Akrae · Megara Hyblaea · Gela · Syracuse · Camarina · Helorus · 100 km

**The Greek cities in the Classical Age, Vth century BC**

100 km

**Death of Pericles.** **429 BC**

**Death of Sophocles.** **406 BC**

**End of the Peloponnesian War.** **404 BC**

**458 BC:** Aeschyslus's *Orestes, Agamemnon, The Libation Bearers* and *Eumenides*.
**447–438 BC:** Rebuilding of the Parthenon temple on the Acropolis.
**443–429 BC:** Pericles repeatedly re-elected General at Athens.
**431–404 BC:** Peloponnesian War opposed Sparta and its allies to Athens and its allies (Delian League). Thucydides is its historian.
**428 BC:** Birth of Plato.
**421 BC:** Peace of Nicias.
**415–413 BC:** Athenian expedition to Sicily. Alcibiades takes on a political role.
**411–404/3 BC:** Attempts to install oligarchic governments at Athens with the support of Sparta. Double failure.
**404 BC:** Collapse of Athens. Sparta imposes its peace. The Athenian 'Empire' disappears.

*4. Zeus or Poseidon? c. 460 BC. Bronze found in the sea off Cape Artemisium.*

*5. The tomb of the diver of Posidonia (Paestum). Greek painting, 5th century BC.*

*6. Poseidon, Apollo. Eastern frieze of the Parthenon, c. 440 BC.*

# Philosophers and Sages

*1. Buddhas seated on lotus thrones. Dunhuang, 8th century.*

THE IDEA that the years between 600 and 300 BC constitute an 'axial period' in human history is an old one given new life in the twentieth century in the works of Lewis Mumford and Karl Jaspers. On the one hand, we find radical innovation in the socio-political field, where some uniquely productive advances were made; on the other, significant advances in the dimension of intellectual creativity, of philosophical, scientific and artistic invention. From this second point of view, the period 600–200 BC is particularly exceptional and may be compared with the seventeenth and eighteenth centuries in the West or the years 1890–1920 in Europe. One is struck by the sudden burgeoning of genius in every corner of the inhabited world, by the emergence of philosophers, sages and scholars whose teachings and reputations will endure among later generations. What we know of the Olmec civilization, the mother of the Meso-American cultures, even allows us to add America to this panoramic picture. Another impressive feature is the sudden emergence of competing schools, which seem astonishingly modern to us even today (the 'hundred schools' of China, the 'sixty schools' of India). But are there, beyond this mere quantitative simultaneity, this planetary explosion of thought, qualitative similarities, analogies or homologies of content between these separate cultural achievements?

The sixth century BC was a century of intense moral disquiet, of religious agitation and reform; it was a century of mystics and ascetics. But something else was in gestation and even before the end of the century the precursors of world enlightenment were at work in the form of Ionian cosmologists, the Indian materialists, and the Chinese ancestors of legalist rationality and cynicism. Pythagoras, who was a priest and a thaumaturge, was also the forerunner of the mathematically-based science of the fourth century BC (and that of the eighteenth century AD). The monotheism of the Second Isaiah (the first true monotheism in history) is related to 'nationalist' fanaticism (the one God is the God of the Jews), but this purging of the sacred contributed to the 'disenchantment' of the world.

From the last decades of the sixth century BC onwards, this movement gained momentum. Gotama the Buddha with his godless wisdom undermined the hegemony of the priests. Confucius flaunted his agnosticism, desacralizing both writing and ritual. Theagenes rationalized Homer and Hecataeus mocked the Greek myths. The fifth century saw the flowering of a critical, utilitarian cast of mind, particularly after 450 BC (Sophists in Greece, Mozu (Mo-tsu) and his disciples in China, the Twelve Tables and their laicised law in Rome). The fourth century, with its immoralist tendencies, was the great

**Jeremiah.** **627–585 BC**

**Zarathustra.** **627–585 BC**

**The Twelve Tables.** **450 BC**

**1400 or 1300 BC to 300 or 200 BC:** The formative millennium in Central America (the Olmecs), in Oceania (Fiji, Tonga, Samoa, the cradle of Polynesian civilization), in India (the *Vedas*) and in the Mediterranean and China.

*4. Sun Stone, known as Aztec calendar.*

**600–200 BC:** The 'axial' period.

**c. 600 BC(?):** Zoroaster and the dualism of Good and Evil.

**6th century BC:** Anaximander and Anaximenes: cosmologies.

**2nd half of 6th century BC:** Xenophanes criticizes Greek polytheism. Pythagoras. Second Isaiah.

**c. 530 BC:** Gotama the Buddha begins preaching. Rise of materialist schools in India. Confucius (Kong fu-tsu, or Kung-tzu) begins teaching. From about 495 BC onwards, he was a sort of itinerant political adviser: rites, history.

**c. 525 BC:** Theagenes.

**522 BC (?):** Massacre of the Magi (Zoroastrian priests) in Persia.

**508–507 BC:** Cleisthenes's reforms at Athens: rationalization.

**c. 500 BC:** Hecataeus, critical historian and geographer. Calendar and mathematics among the Olmecs.

*5. Epicurus. Roman copy of a Greek original.*

**End of 6th/beginning of 5th centuries BC:** The first great Greek philosophers. Heraclitus: universal flux and rhythm. Parmenides: the oneness of Being. Empedocles: the unity of opposites.

**End of 6th to beginning of 3rd centuries BC:** World Enlightenment.

**Middle of 5th century BC:** Sophist revolution in Greece (critical spirit, progressive anthropology). Anaxagoras at Athens: rationalist humanism, friendship with Pericles. Herodotus: rationalist history.
**c. 450 BC:** The Twelve Tables at Rome, laicization of law.
**444 BC:** Calculation of the solar year in China (365¼ days).
**c. 440 BC:** Mozi reacts against Confucian traditionalism; strong utilitarian tendencies.

**5th–6th centuries BC:** Democritus: atoms and progress. Decline of prophetic activity among the Jews. The 'Chinese sophists': paradoxes and dialectics. Panini, Indian grammarian and linguist.
**c. 400 BC:** Thucydides: historical necessity.

# 600–200 BC

epoch of Greek, Chinese, Indian and Amerindian rationalism. Astronomy was the first of the sciences to be born. Naturalists produced classifications and general rules. History would never be the same again after Thucydides and the Bamboo Annals, nor politics the same after Aristotle and the Artha-sastra, Plato and Zou Yan (Tsou Yen). Logicians and theorists of all kinds flourished. Fourth-century rationalism leaned towards a mathematical, even mystical idealism (Plato, Mengzi, Zhuangzi). At its highest point, the invention of rationalism was internally contradictory and laid the ground for the movements that were to follow.

In the third century, observation reclaimed its due. Scholars designed machines, and moral and practical preoccupations won out once again over ontology and theory. In the religious sphere, the great transformations which were to characterize the following period, either side of the birth of Jesus, were beginning to take shape. For the rationalism of the 500–300 BC period, this was the beginning of the end.

This rationalism, though quite different from ours, is nonetheless of the same lineage. This is particularly true of Greek rationalism, which has had inheritors in the West since the fifteenth century who have brought that inheritance to fruition, disciples who have followed and surpassed the masters. The Chinese or Indian rationalists of the 'axial' period have had only mediocre followers in modern times. Their own grandeur is not, however, thereby diminished.

*2. Plato teaching geometry. Roman mosaic, 1st century BC.*

*3. Confucius. Chinese painting of 18th century.*

**Plato's Academy.**

**387 BC**

**Xun zi.**

**3rd century BC**

*6. Isaiah by Claus Sluter, Dijon, c. AD 1400.*

**399 BC:** Trial of Socrates: conflict of free thinking with the state.

**4th century BC:** Rome provides itself with a history. In China, the *Bamboo Annals*; the *Zhouli*: highly systematic and utopian treatise of administration. Zou Yan: the cycles of the five elements, political cycles. Yang Zhu (Yang Chu) opposes all values. The Greek cynics oppose taboos.
**387 BC?:** Plato founds the Academy: idealism, mathematicism, political theories and utopias.
**335 BC?:** Aristotle founds the Lyceum. Deductive logic and encyclopaedism. High point of Greek rationalism.

**End of 4th century BC:** The Indian(?) *Artha-sastra*: politically rationalist, imbued with spirit of system, immoralistic. Mengzi (Mencius in Latin): idealist rationalism. Zhuangzi: mystical idealism. Shang Yang: Legalism. Euclid's(?) *Elements*.
**306 BC?:** Epicurus founds his school (atomism and happiness).
**Since c. 300 BC:** The Stoics.

*7. Socrates. Roman copy of a Greek original.*

**3rd century BC:** Greek scholars Aristarchus of Samos, Archimedes, Eratosthenes. Xun zi, Chinese empiricist philosopher.
**Since 3rd century BC:** Hellenistic technology. Signs of religious revival throughout the world.

*8. Astronomical papyrus of 2nd century referring to the doctrines of Eudoxus of Cyzicus, 4th century BC.*

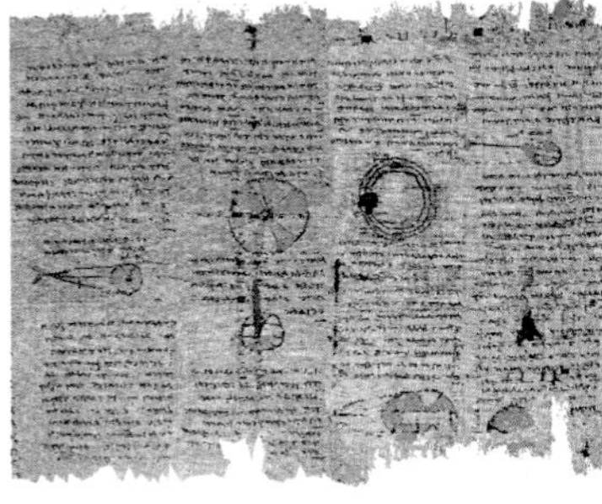

# The Division of the Hellenistic World

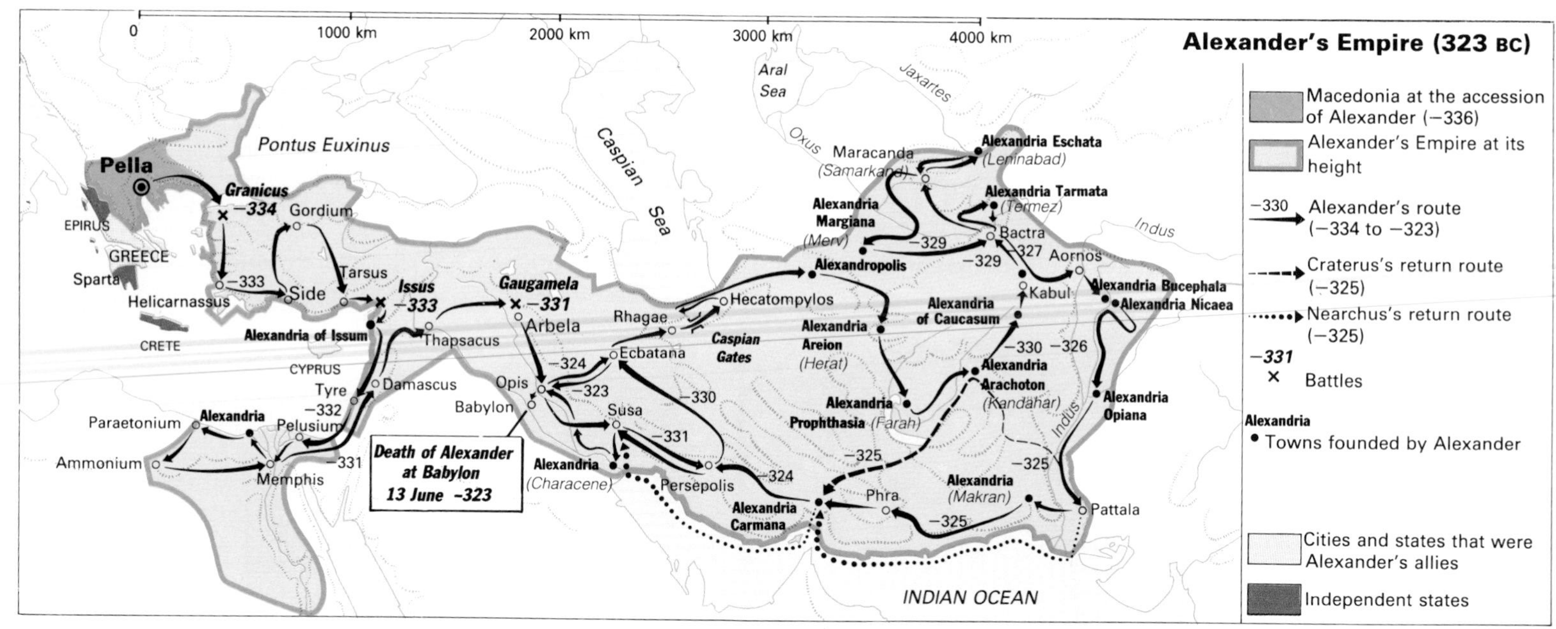


In the middle of the fourth century BC, the idea of an inhabited world (*oikoumene*) with the Aegean Sea at its centre and the city as its model was to produce, among the Greeks, the fantastic ambition of establishing hegemony over the West and conquering the East. However, the high point reached in 325 BC and the decline which set in thereafter reveal the vulnerability of this goal to advances in military tactics: the Macedonian phalanx was all-conquering after Cheronaea, but the Roman legion became dominant after Cynoscephalae. Instead of remaining the centre of the world, as it had hoped, Greece reverted to being part of the periphery.

The years 403–338 BC appear to be a mere prolongation of the preceding century. The need to unite against the 'barbarian' (the argument Demosthenes applied against Philip of Macedon) still met resistance in the shape of the particularism of the individual city-states. We can also see here the renewed rise of the Persians – established in the position of power-brokers ('king's peace') – and of monarchy, in the person of Philip.

The sequence of events between 338 and 168 BC demonstrates the inability of the Greek states to administer a world empire. Setting out symbolically from Troy, within two years Alexander had conquered the Mediterranean façade of the Persian Empire. He needed only one more year to make the legacy of the assassinated Darius III his own. After difficult campaigns in the oriental satrapies, he crossed the Indus in 326 BC, but his troops forced him to stop on the Hyphases. After his death, the wars between the separatist kings (Diadochi) produced an unwieldy arrangement unsuited to the functioning of a great empire in which the principal seats of power were at capitals such as Pella, Alexandria and Antioch, none of which occupied a central position, either in relation to the hinterland or to the Mediterranean area as a whole.

Torn between Europe and Asia, the Antigonids inherited the divisions of the Hellenic world. From this point of view, 281 BC is a key date. The Battle of Corupedium put an end to the Asian ambitions of continental Greece and left the Ptolemies and the Seleucids face to

**Restoration of democracy in Athens.** **403 BC**

**Persian 'King's Peace'.** **386 BC**

**Macedonian 'King's Peace'.** **337 BC**

**Foundation of Alexandria.** **331 BC**

2. *Crown of gold oak leaves.*

**403 BC:** After the bloody tyranny of the 'Thirty Tyrants', a moderate democracy restored the power of Athens.
**401 BC:** The revolt of Cyrus the Younger, supported by Sparta, against his brother Artaxerxes fails at Kunaxa.
**386 BC:** The Persians impose the 'King's Peace', which safeguards the autonomy of the cities.
**377 BC:** Athens reconstitutes its maritime league.
**371 BC:** Defeated at Leuctra, Sparta yields supremacy to Thebes.
**355 BC:** Philip, King of Macedon, extends his power over Thessaly and Thrace at the expense of Athens, which was defeated in the 'War for Amphipolis'.
**338 BC:** Philip wins the Battle of Cheronaea and gains hegemony over the new League of Corinth against the Persians.
**336 BC:** After Philip's murder, his son Alexander represses revolts in Greece (sack of Thebes) and conquers the Persian possessions as far as the Indus (334–324 BC).

**331 BC:** Alexandria founded.
**323 BC:** Death of Alexander at Babylon. War of the 'Diadochi' (successors) (→ 281 BC).
**322 BC:** Failure of revolt at Athens. Demosthenes commits suicide.

*3. Portrait presumed to be that of Alexander the Great. Ivory from a royal tomb, Verghina, c. 330 BC.*

# 4th–1st centuries BC

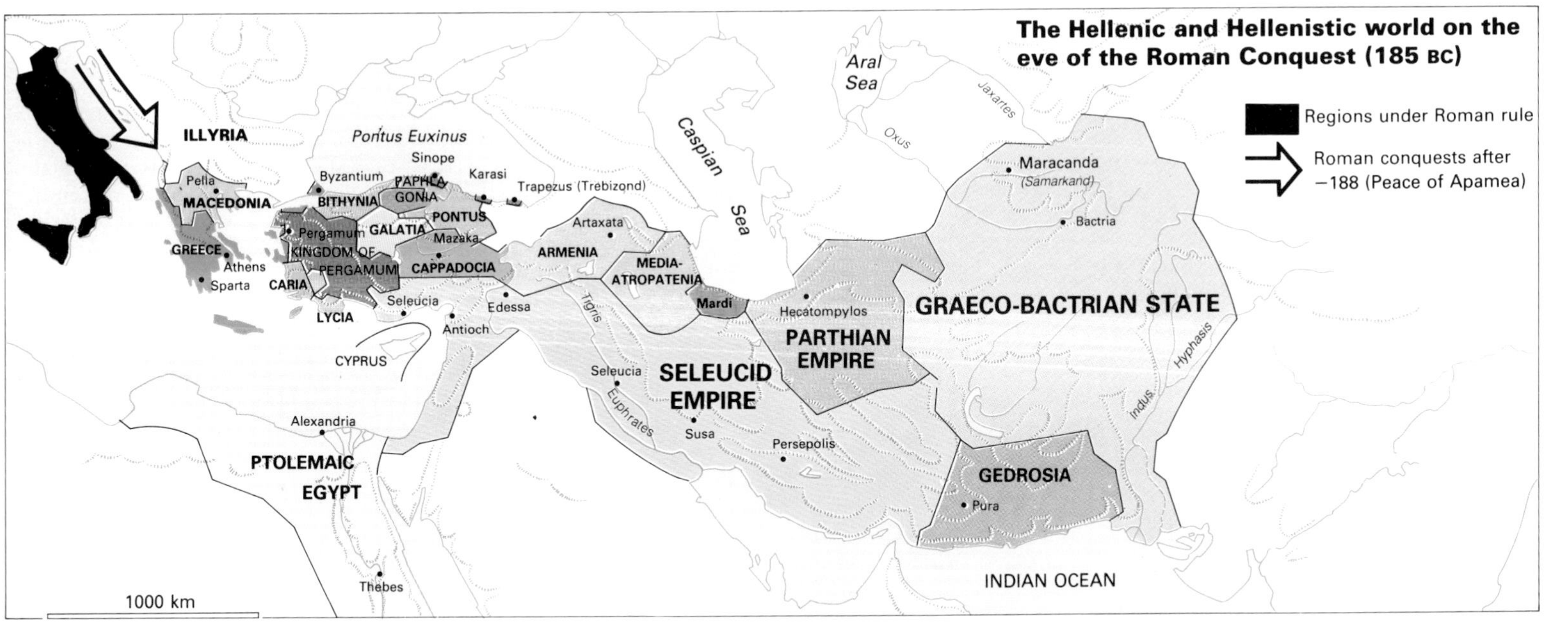


face. These two powers were to be exhausted by the 'Syrian Wars' of which there were six (culminating in the famous circle of Popilius Laenias). Tarentum's appeal to Pyrrhus, the king of Epirus, against Rome, then that of the Syracusans against Carthage, set in train a series of chain reactions in which the Greeks were soon to be reduced to playing only a marginal role. The Battle of Pydna concluded this process, finally eliminating Macedon from the political scene, at the very moment at which the two basins of the Mediterranean entered a common historical process, of which Rome was to be the arbiter.

The Ptolemies enjoyed the most homogeneous territorial base, in the form of Egypt. By methodically exploiting their dynastic possessions in the service of maritime supremacy, Ptolemy II (283–246 BC) and Ptolemy III (246–222 BC) were the only men to create a truly imperial economy.

The Seleucids possessed the most extensive continental land mass (4,000 km from the Aegean to Afghanistan). In spite of the energy of Antiochus I (281–261 BC), Antiochus III (223–187 BC) and Antiochus IV (175–164 BC), their history is one of a progressive erosion. As early as 240 BC, a large strip of land had been lost in the north (Bithynia, Galatia, Cappadocia, Atropatenia), in the east (Parthia, Bactria) and in the west (Pergamum, Ptolemaic possessions). In the south, Coele-Syria, finally conquered in 200 BC, would in 143 BC, during the reign of the Hasmonean dynasty, have an independent Jewish state carved out of it.

*1. Demetrius, King of Bactria, with an elephant-skin headdress. Silver tetradrachma, early 2nd century BC.*

**dom of Bactria founded.** **240 BC**

**Testament of Attalus III.** **133 BC**

**The Greeks encounter the Chinese.** **100 BC**

**306–304 BC:** The Diadochi take the title of king. Macedonia remains in the hands of the Antigonid dynasty (→ 168 BC), Asia under the Seleucid control (63 BC) and Egypt under the Ptolemies (→ 30 BC).
**303 BC:** Alliance between Seleucus I Nicator and Chandragupta, founder of the Maurya Empire, opens India up to exchanges with the West.
**300BC:** Antioch founded.
**281 BC:** Battle of Corupedium. Tarentum appeals successfully to Pyrrhos, King of Epirus, against Rome.
**247 BC:** East of the Caspian Sea, Arsaces founds the Parthian kingdom.
**241 BC:** Attalus proclaims himself king of Pergamum.
**240 BC:** Diodotus creates a kingdom of Bactria (→ 100 BC).
**200 BC:** Battle of Panium gives Coele-Syria to the Seleucids.
**197 BC:** Philip V of Macedon defeated at Cynoscephalae.
**189 BC:** After his defeat at Magnesia, Antiochus III abandons the Seleucid possessions beyond the Taurus by the Treaty of Apamea.
**168 BC:** The Battle of Pydna puts an end to the Kingdom of Macedon. Halted outside Alexandria by the circle of Popilius Laenias, Antiochus IV attempts to end the disturbances in Judaea by outlawing the Jewish religion. Despite the restoration of worship at the Jerusalem Temple in 165 BC the insurrection continues.
**155 BC:** In the Indus Valley, Menander founds an Indo-Greek kingdom (→ 50 BC).
**143 BC:** Jerusalem becomes the capital of a Jewish state (→ 63 BC).
**133 BC:** Attalus III of Pergamum bequeaths his kingdom to the Romans.
**100 BC:** Conquest of Bactria by the Yueh'chih. China's first contacts with the West through Pamir.
**95 BC:** The Parthians sign a treaty of friendship with Sylla, fixing their frontier on the Euphrates.
**66 BC:** Pompey's Eastern Campaigns.
**63 BC:** End of the Seleucid monarchy and the Jewish state. Pompey organizes the eastern territories of the Roman Empire as far as the Euphrates.

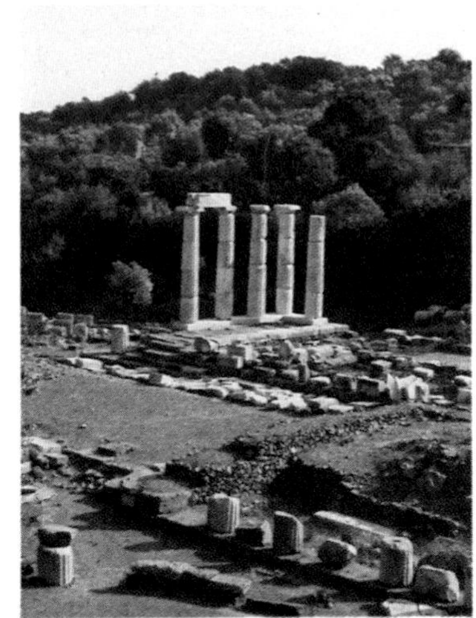

*4. View of the sanctuary of the great gods at Samothrace, Ptolemaic period.*

*5. The Delphi column of the dancers. Attic art, c. 330 BC.*

# Italy, the Etruscans and the Birth of Rome

THE IDEAS OF ANCIENT HISTORIANS on the appearance of cities and peoples were shaped by the model of colonial settlement. They attributed the birth of cities to founder-heroes like Romulus, combining local origins and migratory movements to explain the distribution of peoples or to justify their genealogical ties: the arrival of the Trojans and Aeneas in Latium; the departure of a group of Lydians for Italy under the leadership of Tyrsenos (the eponymous ancestor of the Tyrrhenians, which , as Herodotus tells us, was the Greek name for the Etruscans). Conditioned by these ancient sources, modern historians have until recently tended all too often to pose the problem of the formation of the cultures of Italy in terms of ethnic origins and population movements. Moreover, the heterogeneity of the Etruscan language in relation to the other Italic tongues, all of which are related to the Indo-European family of languages – a diversity emphasized in ancient ethnography, which regards language as a primordial criterion in the differentiation of peoples – has contributed in no small measure to the invention of the 'Etruscan mystery'. This takes on all the more importance in the light of the fact that the Etruscans occupied an essential place in the very birth of Rome, the period of the Etruscan monarchy being a decisive one. Moreover, 'before the Roman Empire, the Etruscans had extended their power far abroad on land and sea' (Livy, Book V), acting as precursors of Rome's own foreign policy. Current analyses are based on the findings of archaeological research and propose a history of the populations of Italy which lays stress on two types of process. On the one hand, there is the internal structuring of economies and societies. We are thus looking here, between the end of the Bronze Age and the beginnings of the Iron Age, at sets of cultural features which can be more or less exactly related to the different peoples settled in Italy in this historical period. Secondly, there are external factors (Mycenaean sea voyages, contacts with the Phoenicians, Greek colonization) which produced real transformations in the parts of Italy where local cultures were sufficiently structured to react positively to outside influence. The single most important phenomenon in determining such transformations was the Greek colonization of southern Italy, which began with the settlement of the Euboeans at Pithecusa (Ischia). It was these settlers who purchased the ores which Etruria possessed in such quantities, and they also carried on trade between the eastern Mediterranean (Al Mina) and the West. This development gave rise to the formation of Etruscan, Latin and Campanian aristocracies, all characterized by the same luxurious, Hellenized style of life (consumption of wine and perfumed oil, the introduction of writing). Etruscan civilization is therefore a particular case of a more general evolution, not the result of a migration (the hypothesis of the transfer of a small nucleus of settlers from the East during the Bronze Age being of no relevance to the socio-economic transformation of the Villanovan milieu). The bipartite onomastic formula (forename plus family name), which distinguishes the peoples of Italy throughout the whole of antiquity and is the basis of our present system, also first appeared in this same period. At the end of this developmental phase, the coming of towns produced a decisive qualitative leap within these societies. The best-known case is that of Rome, where at the end of the seventh century BC a public and religious space appeared alongside the huts. Thus, at the end of the sixth century, a very sharp dividing line separated the regions which had an urban organization of one specific form or another (Roman and Etruscan cities being different in nature) and the rest of Italy, which had not yet reached this stage of development. The subsequent history of these populations is one of changes born out of their reactions to contact with the Greek city-states on the one hand and to interaction with the cities that had grown out of the Italian Iron Age cultures on the other.

*1. An Etruscan couple represented on an urn in the Cerveteri necropolis, 6th century BC.*

**The Euboeans at Ischia.** 775 BC

**Rome founded.** 753 BC

**Syracuse founded.** 734 BC

**Middle of 2nd millennium:** Middle Bronze Age (Apennine culture).
**14th–13th centuries BC:** Mycenaean interest in central Italy (they had been in southern Italy and Sicily since the 16th–15th centuries).
**13th–12th centuries:** Mention in Egyptian chronicles of the Sea Peoples: amongst them the Trs.w (supposed by some to be the Tyrsenoi).
**11th–10th centuries BC:** Late Bronze Age (Proto-Villanovan).
**9th century BC:** First Iron Age: development of Villanovan and Latin cultures (Latium), and the culture of deep-shaft graves.
**814 BC:** Traditional date for the founding of Carthage.
**800 BC:** Traditional date for the founding of Capua.
**c. 775 BC:** First Greek (Euboean) settlements at Pithecusa (Ischia).
**21 April 753 BC:** Traditional date for the founding of Rome by Romulus.
**750 BC:** Cumae, then Zancle and Rhegium (shortly after the middle of the century) founded by the Chalcidians.
**734 BC:** Founding of Syracuse, a colony of Corinth.
**c. 730 BC:** Beginning of the Orientalizing period: development of local aristocracies in Etruria, Latium and Campania; rise of Etruscan civilization.
**728 BC:** Date traditionally given for the founding of Megara Hyblaea, a colony of Megara.
**720 BC:** Achaean cities of Sybaris and Croton founded. They in turn produce further urban settlements, the former at Posidonia (Paestum) and Metapontum, the latter at Caulonia.
**706 BC:** Founding of Tarentum, a Spartan colony.
**688 BC:** Gela, a Rhodo-Cretan colony, founded.
**640/630–580 BC:** Transformation of the major population centres of southern Etruria and Rome into cities. Increased Etruscan presence in Campania. The texts mention the existence of a confederation of 12 cities, modelled on the organization of central Etruria.

*2. Detail from a fresco in the Tomb of the Jugglers at Tarquinia, representing an Etruscan ritual dance, 6th century BC.*

**628 BC:** Selinuntum founded by settlers from Megara Hyblaea. The Ionians journey to the extreme west.
**616–579 BC:** Beginning of the Etruscan monarchy at Rome. The reign of Lucius Tarquinius, the son of the Corinthian Demaratus, exiled at Tarquinia.
**580 BC:** Agrigentum founded by settlers from Gela.
**579–534 BC:** Reign of Servus Tullius, known in the Etruscan texts (according to the Emperor Claudius) as Mastarna. Roman tradition attributes to him the census system and the division of the citizens into tribes.
**c. 550 BC:** Etruscan 'colonization' of the plain of the River Padus, where Villanovan culture had developed since the 9th century BC. Tradition relates that there was a confederation of 12 cities there.
**546–525 BC:** Persians conquer Ionia and Egypt.
**c. 535 BC:** Victory of the Carthaginians and the Etruscans over the Phocaeans at Alalia (Aleria) which comes under Etruscan domination. The Phocaeans found Elea.

# 1500–470 BC

## –530 to –520: The High Point of Etruscan Civilization

Regions structured around:

- Etruscan and Latin cities (▫ Etruscanized centres)
- Greek colonial centres
- Carthaginian colonies

Etruscan mineral resources

▲ Iron ● Copper ✚ Silver

Etruscan maritime trade

100 km

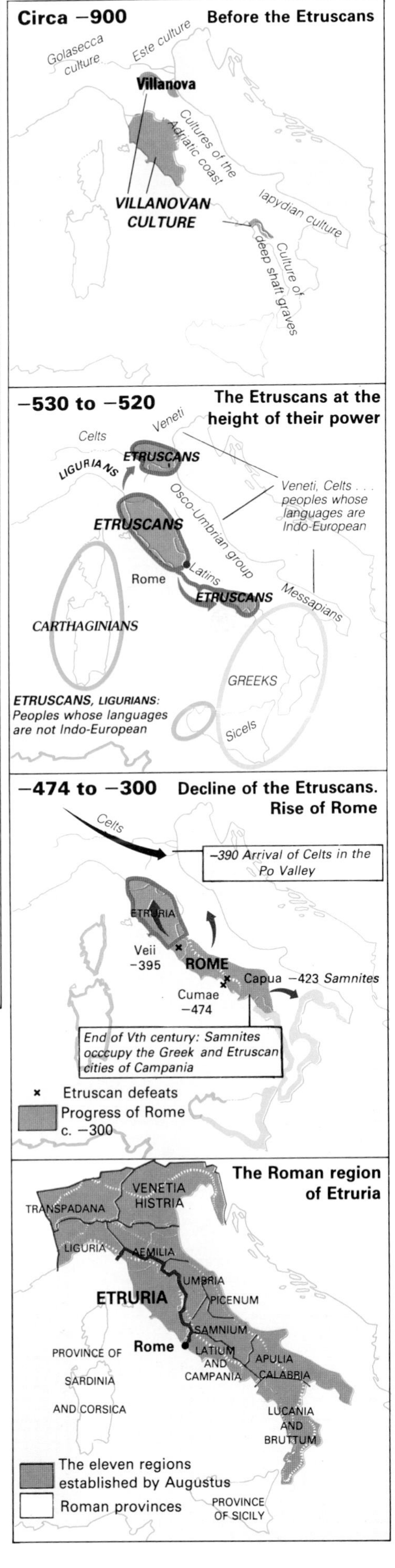


**e Cnidians at Lipari.**

**580 BC**

3. *Votive offering glorifying maternity. Capua, 4th century BC.*

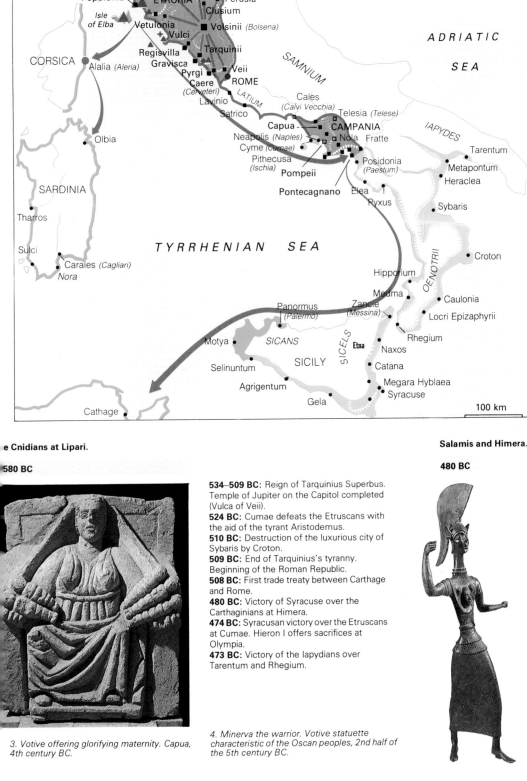

**534–509 BC:** Reign of Tarquinius Superbus. Temple of Jupiter on the Capitol completed (Vulca of Veii).
**524 BC:** Cumae defeats the Etruscans with the aid of the tyrant Aristodemus.
**510 BC:** Destruction of the luxurious city of Sybaris by Croton.
**509 BC:** End of Tarquinius's tyranny. Beginning of the Roman Republic.
**508 BC:** First trade treaty between Carthage and Rome.
**480 BC:** Victory of Syracuse over the Carthaginians at Himera.
**474 BC:** Syracusan victory over the Etruscans at Cumae. Hieron I offers sacrifices at Olympia.
**473 BC:** Victory of the Iapydians over Tarentum and Rhegium.

4. *Minerva the warrior. Votive statuette characteristic of the Oscan peoples, 2nd half of the 5th century BC.*

**Salamis and Himera.**

**480 BC**

# China under the Ch'in and Han Dynasties

1. *Dignitary and servant: Funeral statuettes made of bronze, from the era of the Eastern Han, 2nd century.*

After the collapse of the eastern Chou, the expansion of the kingdom of Ch'in proceeded more quickly. It led to the unification of the whole of China by 221 BC. This expansion was accompanied by the imposition of much greater uniformity across the country resulting from the application on quite a major scale of a system of administrative repression. The imposition of common standards on to society, the criss-crossing of the country by newly established administrative districts which took the place of the former fiefs and kingdoms, went hand in hand with a massive programme for the resettlement of the population. Over the same period, the first emperor undertook a policy of major public works, which resulted in the construction of a network of roads radiating out from the capital, Ch'ang-an, to the remotest towns in the country, in irrigation canals and defensive walls, as well as gigantic palaces and tombs. The reaction of the nobles and the peasants in the principalities of the east, and of the Ch'u under the second emperor, led to the fall of the dynasty and, after a period of confusion, to the arrival on the throne of the house of Han. They reapplied the administrative principles of their predecessors, but made more concessions to the nobles. Once the disturbances marking the change of dynasty had quietened down, the policy of imposing uniformity tried out earlier under the Ch'in emperor Shih Huang Ti was taken up again with greater determination. The threat from the Hsiung-nu, which already existed under the fighting kingdoms, became more substantial when the different tribes undertook to form a federation under the command of a single chief. A policy of reconciliation through marriage having failed, the Chinese government, under the Han emperor Wu, decided to extend its domination towards the west in order to take control of the trade and communication routes leading to and from Eurasia. As a result, Asia became almost totally Sinicized in progressive stages: the setting up of embassies and trading links and colonies was followed by total cultural integration. While the south remained resistant, the borderlands of the north-west were soon being defended by a number of half-

2. *During the Han era, cavalry made a major contribution to reinforcing the power of the Empire.*

Sinicized tribes who formed a buffer against the enemy and provided China with its troops. This cultural and military expansion soon began, however, to threaten the very state organization which had made it possible in the first place. The development of trade stimulated industry and business, and these were soon beyond the control of the central authorities. Social inequalities increased, bringing about the ruin of the peasant-soldier, who was the backbone of the Han system, provoking a number of serious difficulties in the state treasury. An agrarian crisis broke out at the end of the first century and after the aborted usurpation attempt of Wang Mang, which led to more unrest, the Han re-established order by moving their capital further east. This restoration of the eastern Han was the opportunity, in fact, for the arrival on the scene of a new social class of merchants and landowners with large estates. These estates in turn were the cause of the second agrarian and economic crisis, which dragged the dynasty into a series of messianic popular revolts. In parallel to the breaking down of the economic system, the political system itself became threatened by the ever-growing importance of the eunuchs, who had sole access to the emperor's private apartments, and who were a token of the isolation of the monarch.

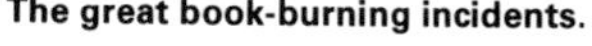

**The great book-burning incidents.**

**213 BC**

**Discussions held on state monopolies.**

**81 BC**

**247 BC:** The Ch'in seize western Shansi. The coup attempt by Lao Ai, the lover of the mother of the Ch'in king and future first emperor, Shih Huang Ti, fails.
**237 BC:** Li Su, a legal expert, succeeds Lu Pu-Wei, who was a rich merchant become statesman, and had been implicated in the Lao Ai affair, as adviser to the Ch'in.
**221 BC:** Ch'in dynasty founded by King Shih Huang Ti, after the annexation of the principalities of Han, Chao, Wei, Ch'u, Yen and Ch'i. Chinese writing, weights and measures, and the axles on carts are all normalized as a result, and the Ch'in system is extended to the whole of China.

**215 BC:** Various expeditions to the south are undertaken.
**213 BC:** The burning of books, the banning of the classics, and the resettlement of many people nearer the Great Wall and further to the south are characteristic of the new regime.
**211 BC:** Intellectuals are persecuted (460 were buried alive), and there are massive deportations towards the Great Wall.
**210 BC:** First emperor dies.

3. *Tomb of the Han emperors in Shansi province.*

**206 BC:** Fall of the dynasty.
**202 BC:** Han dynasty proclaimed after the elimination of Hsiang Yu by Liu Pang. Fiefs are granted to his more humble comrades in arms.
**200 to about 195 BC:** First restrictions imposed on the nobility.
**188/187 BC:** Regency of Empress Lü, who introduces less harsh penal laws.
**180 BC:** After her death the clan of Empress Lü is exterminated.
**158–144 BC:** The pressure from the Hsiung-nu becomes more threatening.
**141 BC:** Emperor Wu Ti of the Han dynasty comes to the throne.
**124–121 BC:** Major Chinese offensives carried out against the Hsiung-nu.
**119 BC:** A monopoly on salt and iron production is imposed and a tax on boats and carts levied to replenish the coffers of the state.
**110 BC:** The kingdoms of Yüeh (Fukien) and of Nanyueh (Canton and northern Vietnam) are annexed.
**108 BC:** Annexation of Korea.
**101 BC:** The victory of Fergana follows the

# 250 BC–AD 220

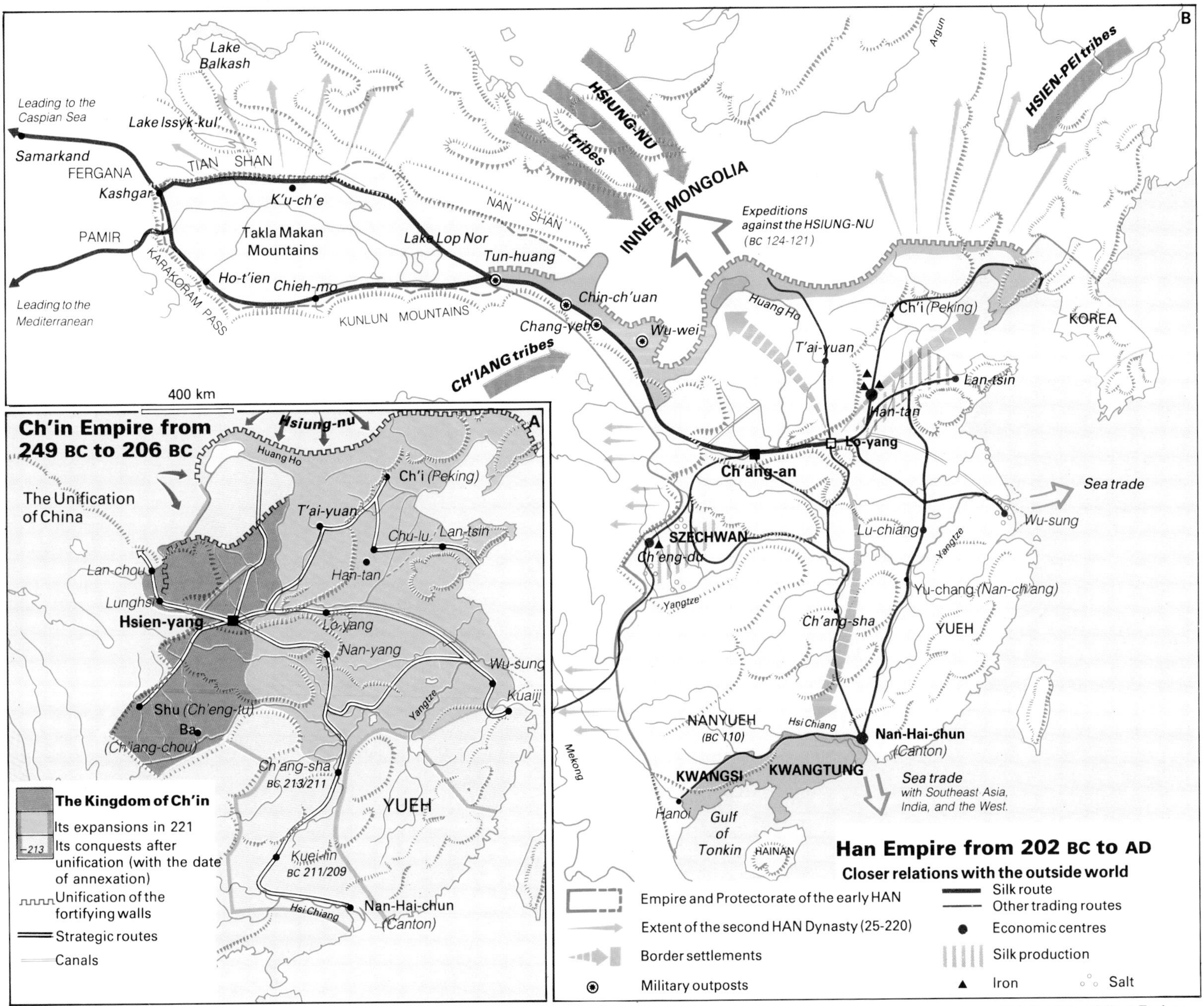

## Han Empire from 202 BC to AD
### Closer relations with the outside world

Lake Balkash
Leading to the Caspian Sea
Lake Issyk-kul'
Samarkand
FERGANA
Kashgar
TIAN SHAN
K'u-ch'e
Takla Makan Mountains
PAMIR
KARAKORAM PASS
Ho-t'ien
Chieh-mo
Leading to the Mediterranean
KUNLUN MOUNTAINS
Lake Lop Nor
NAN SHAN
Tun-huang
Chin-ch'uan
Chang-yeh
Wu-wei
CH'IANG tribes
HSIUNG-NU tribes
INNER MONGOLIA
Expeditions against the HSIUNG-NU (BC 124-121)
Argun
HSIEN-PEI tribes
Huang Ho
T'ai-yuan
Ch'i (Peking)
KOREA
Lan-tsin
Han-tan
Lo-yang
Ch'ang-an
Sea trade
Wu-sung
SZECHWAN
Ch'eng-du
Yangtze
Lu-chiang
Yu-chang (Nan-ch'ang)
Ch'ang-sha
YUEH
NANYUEH (BC 110)
Hsi Chiang
Nan-Hai-chun (Canton)
Mekong
KWANGSI
KWANGTUNG
Sea trade with Southeast Asia, India, and the West.
Hanoi
Gulf of Tonkin
HAINAN
400 km

- Empire and Protectorate of the early HAN
- Extent of the second HAN Dynasty (25-220)
- Border settlements
- Military outposts
- Silk route
- Other trading routes
- Economic centres
- Silk production
- Iron
- Salt

## Ch'in Empire from 249 BC to 206 BC
### The Unification of China

Hsiung-nu
Huang Ho
Ch'i (Peking)
T'ai-yuan
Chu-lu
Lan-tsin
Han-tan
Lan-chou
Lunghsi
Hsien-yang
Lo-yang
Nan-yang
Wu-sung
Kuaiji
Yangtze
Shu (Ch'eng-tu)
Ba (Ch'iang-chou)
Ch'ang-sha BC 213/211
YUEH
Kuei-lin BC 211/209
Hsi Chiang
Nan-Hai-chun (Canton)

- The Kingdom of Ch'in
- Its expansions in 221
- -213 Its conquests after unification (with the date of annexation)
- Unification of the fortifying walls
- Strategic routes
- Canals

**First Buddhist community established.** — AD 65

**Paper invented.** — 105

**Revolt of the Yellow Turbans.** — 184

conquest of the whole of Central Asia.
**87 BC:** Death of Emperor Wu Ti, whose place is taken by the regent Huo Kuang, an ally of the family of the Empress.
**81 BC:** Major discussions take place concerning how opportune it is to continue with the state monopolies.

*4. Guardian of the tomb of Emperor Shih Huang Ti.*

*5. Model of a tower in varnished terracotta. From the era of the eastern Han, 2nd century.*

**76 BC:** Liao-tung colonized by the barbarians.
**AD 9:** Throne usurped by Wang Mang, who introduces a number of reforms which lead to rebellion.
**25:** Han dynasty is restored by a descendant of the Liu house, Kuang Wu Ti.
**42–3:** General Ma Yuan puts down the rebellion of the Trung sisters.
**91:** The Han invade Mongolia.
**c. 94:** Campaign of repression in Central Asia under the leadership of General Pan Ch'ao.
**125–150:** Chinese control is re-established over Central Asia.
**141:** The power of the Ch'iang (who were proto-Tibetans) becomes threatening for the Han.
**175:** The eunuchs hold the real power.
**184:** The great popular uprising of the Yellow Turbans takes place. So called because of the colour of their turbans, which acted as a sign of allegiance, these were rebels who numbered 300,000 through Shansi, Shensi and Hupeh provinces.

**192:** The Revolt of the Yellow Turbans put down by Ts'ao Ts'ao, who became the new strong man of the regime after the assassination of Tung Cho, who had threatened to take over the throne for himself. The Celestial Masters, a Taoist sect, set up a community organization in Szechwan.
**220:** Fall of the Han dynasty and partition of the Empire into three parts.

*6. Tiger and serpent attacking a wild boar: a bronze ornamental plaque from the era of the western Han.*

# The Indian Empire: From the Maurya to the Gupta

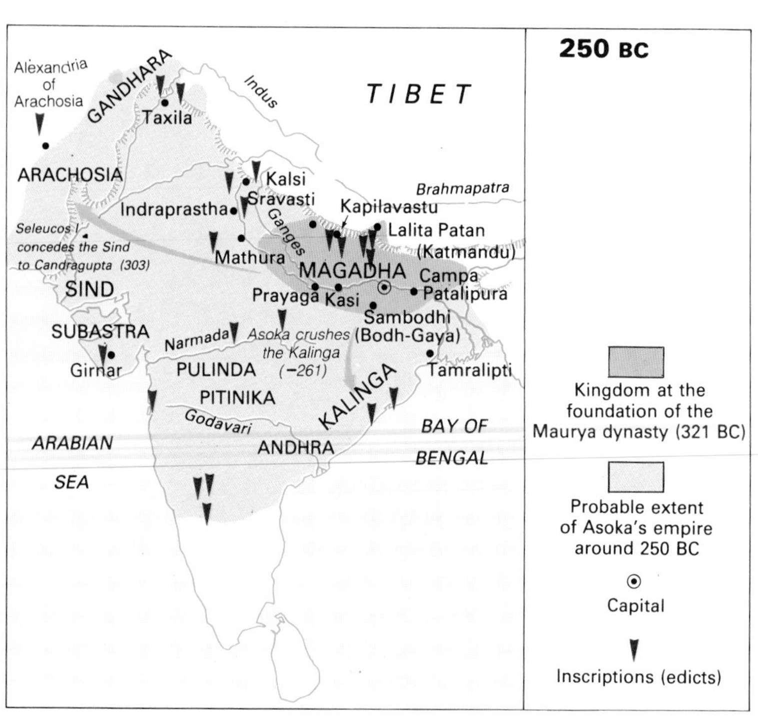


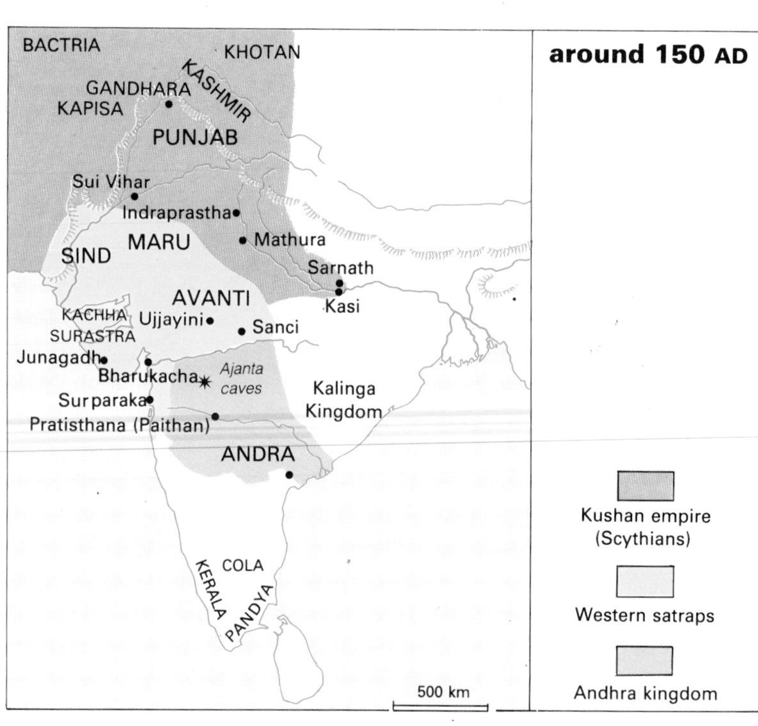


Indian antiquity can be divided into two periods: before and after the expeditions of Alexander – the first really datable event in the history of India. For the period preceding that, the historian has to content himself with hypotheses and conjecture based on the interpretation of myths and legends. After this, there is much documentary evidence in the form of inscriptions, monuments, foreign reports (by Greeks and Chinese): India truly becomes part of history and fits into general chronology. Some uncertainty persists, however, in some cases over several centuries, as to the most notable figures in Indian civilization. There was Panini, the founder of grammar, Patanjali, creator of the theory of yoga, Kautilya, author of a treatise on the art of government, and even the emperor Kaniska (it is uncertain whether his reign began in 58 BC or in AD 78 or even AD 144), without mentioning texts like the two epics, Mahabharata and Ramayana or the Laws of Manu. The outlines of Indian historical development during these two millennia can, however, be described.

The Arya clans were dominant for about ten centuries over the country between the Persian Gulf and the Bay of Bengal, the Himalayas and the Vindhya mountains (the Aryavarta), and the Deccan north of the Godavari: the peoples of these regions adopting their language, religion and social system. Their language was Sanskrit, of Indo-European origin. The Indian-style languages developed from Sanskrit in the various regions of the Arya territory. The first inscriptions were written in these Indian-style idioms. Then Sanskrit, which had been kept as a religious language, became secularized and used as the vehicle for profane works of literature. The dividing line between the north and the south is in the language. In the north, only Sanskrit or languages drawn from it were used. The south, although it had adopted Sanskrit at the beginning of our period as a literary and religious language, kept alive the Dravidian languages, notably Tamil, which was used in the first centuries AD in some outstanding poetry.

In religion, beliefs and rites set out in the Veda (a form of polytheism which gave increasing precedence to sacrificial ceremonies) were the order of the day. But as it came into contact with native

**Beginnings of the Iron Age. Irrigated rice farming in the Kaveri delta.**

**c. 1000 BC**

**Appearance of money in the Magadha.**

**c. 500 BC**

*1. Eastern portico of the Great Stupa, a Buddhist monument, at Sanci in Madhya Pradesh. 2nd century AD.*

**c. 1400 BC:** The Arya moved into the Punjab. During the following centuries they would advance towards the east and the south; by 600 BC they would have conquered the entire Ganges Valley.
**c. 650 BC:** 'Second urbanization'; towns in the Magadha.
**518 BC:** Gandhara and Sind were satraps of the Persian Empire.
**483 BC:** Date normally given for the death of the Buddha.
**467 BC:** Presumed date of the death of the Jina.
**327–325 BC:** Alexander's expedition to India. Having seized Taxila, which was at that time a major centre of Brahman culture, Alexander vanquished the Indian armies of King Puru (Poros in Greek), but because his troops refused to go further he retreated towards the mouth of the Indus.
**322 BC:** In the Magadha, Candragupta the Maurya founded a state whose control extended in the end throughout northern India.
**272–232 BC:** Ashoka. Completely under the spell of Buddhism, this grandson of Candragupta built up an empire which covered the whole of the sub-continent apart from the south of the peninsula. Throughout the whole of the Empire, inscriptions/engravings on pillars and rocks proclaim (in various Indian idioms) the political and religious principles of Ashoka. After his death, the Empire broke up.
**160–140 BC:** The Indo-Greek king Milinda (Menander) ruled over the Punjab.
**1st century BC:** Scythians and Parthians destroyed the Indo-Greek kingdoms, and replaced them in the northwest of India with dynasties which quickly became Indianized.
**1st century AD:** The Kushans swept in. They came from Central Asia and seized Gandhara and the Punjab and conquered the Ganges Valley as far as Patalipurra. In the northern Deccan, around Pratisthana (Paithan), the Andhra (Satavahana dynasty) had supremacy. In the extreme south a powerful Cola kingdom was established. Indian kingdoms were created in Indochina and Malaysia.

# 15th century BC–7th century AD

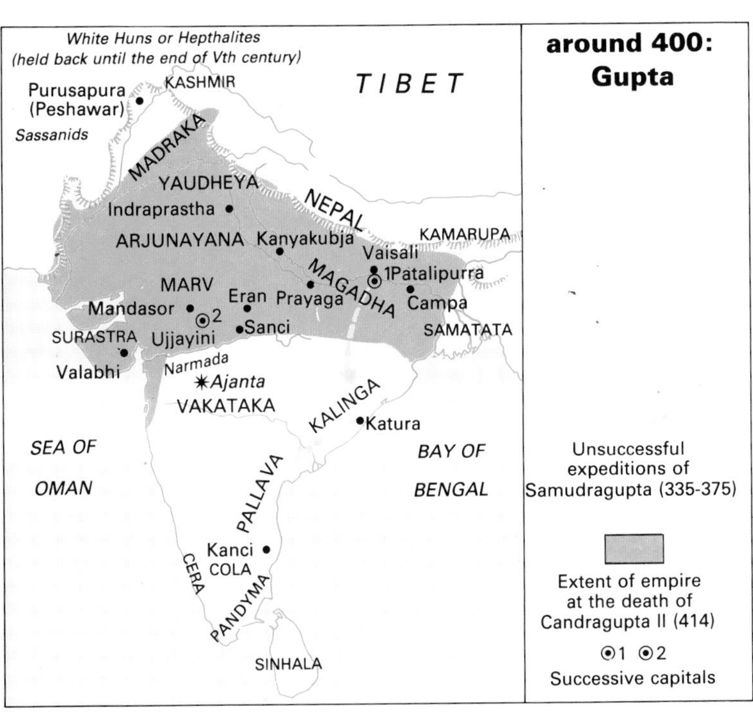


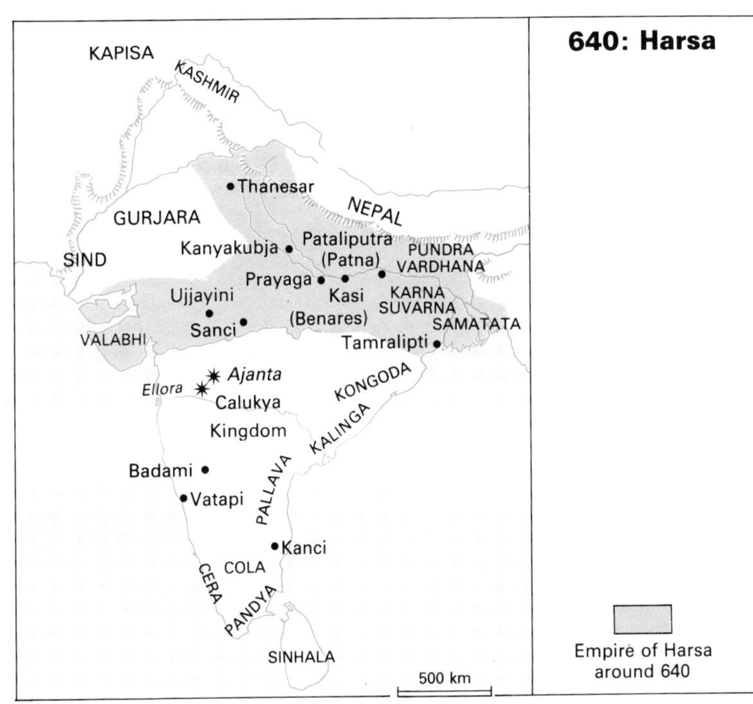


peoples, Vedism took up the cult of images, incorporated other gods, and balanced the ritual with a warm personal relationship between the devout and the divinity. This is Hinduism as we know it today. In the sixth century BC, two new religions came into being in the middle Ganges kingdoms, which advocated non-violence, detachment, and the formation of monastic communities: Jainism, founded by the Jina Mahavira, would remain exclusively Indian, and for the minority (but still alive today); Buddhism, however, would spread throughout the whole of Asia.

As regards society, because of what the Veda taught, the Arya were split into four 'classes' (*varna*): the Brahmans, religious specialists; the Ksatriya, warriors and political leaders; the Vaisya, wealth producers (farmers, craftsmen, merchants); and the Sudra, who served the first three *varna*. Outside the country, the tribal people were considered to be barbarians. These theoretical groups formed the framework within which were arranged hierarchically the real groups making up the whole of society: the castes (*jati*).

When they went into India, the Arya, who were shepherds and farmers, destroyed the towns. But in the sixth century BC a new urban civilization grew up in the Magadha. Later on, new towns appeared which were centres of an economic and intellectual lifestyle much admired by the Chinese pilgrims. They were linked by caravan trails: one linked Tamralipti to Taxila, another went from Prayaga to Ujjayini and Pratisthana (Paithan) and towards the ports of Surastra.

After the death of Candragupta the Maurya, the country was alternately divided into huge imperial blocks with changing frontiers, and small kingdoms. The most famous of the emperors, the most perfect ruler in the whole of India's history, was Ashoka, who, having taken over political power, declared his avowed hatred of war and his desire to bring about the Buddhist ideal of universal goodwill. Empires consisting of the whole continent were the work of the northern sovereigns, Indians or Central Asian invaders. The southern dynasties looked more towards foreign lands and trading links with Eastern Asia and the Roman world: from antiquity, the export of spices, precious stones and cloth brought gold from Europe to India.

**Embassy of a Pandya king to the Emperor of Rome.**

**Aryabhata's mathematical treatise: decimal numbering, zero, value of pi.**

**AD 20** — **c. 500**

**c. 50:** The Parthian king Gondophares of Taxila welcomed and then martyred Thomas the Apostle.
**78?/144?:** Presumed and contested dates given for the beginning of the reign of Kaniska, the most prestigious Kushan sovereign.
**270–500:** The Gupta Empire. From their initial territory, the Magadha, the Gupta princes extended their direct sovereignty or their protectorate over India to the north of Narmada and over part of the Deccan.
**375–414:** Reign of Candragupta II, who made Ujjayini his capital. Golden age of Indian civilization: the work of the poet Kalidasa symbolized this.
**400–500:** First Sanskrit inscriptions from Cambodia, Java, Borneo.
**c. 450:** The Hepthalite Huns (Hunas) moved into Bactria, then settled in the Indus basin. Skandagupta held them back. But the Gupta Empire fell apart.
**c. 550:** The Calukya of Badami became the major power in the northwest of the Deccan.

*2. Ajanta Caves, Rupestrian (?) shrine in the Deccan. 3rd–6th centuries AD.*

**End of the 6th century:** Supremacy of the Pallava of Kanci over the south-east of the peninsula, which would last until the 9th century. They attempted to conquer Ceylon and helped Indian kingdoms in Southeast Asia to develop.
**606–47:** Reign of Harsa. The capital of his empire was Kanyakubja (Kanauj): last truly outstanding period of the Hindu-Sanskrit culture in northern India.
**630–44:** Voyage of the Chinese pilgrim Hsuang-tang.

*3. One of the 21 celestial, heavenly nymphs of the site of Sigirya. AD 485, Sri Lanka.*

# Rome: City of Conquest

ROME WAS INITIALLY similar in nature to the other Mediterranean cities. It formed itself into a state by assimilating Italy and conquered an empire by striving to extend its boundaries to the limits of the known world. The political centre of that empire grew into what, for the ancients, was the greatest city ever known. Greek observers like Polybius praised the excellence of its constitution and the cohesiveness of its social body: all its citizens served in the legions, paid taxes, elected the magistrates, and decided the laws, as well as questions of peace and war. Politics was everyone's affair; it was the *res publica*. In reality, it is possible to discern a political class of privileged individuals set apart from the mass of the citizenry, a citizenry from which women, foreigners and slaves were, in any case, excluded. The censors kept watch over the fortune and honour of each citizen and regulated his role in political life – along with his military and fiscal contribution. The richest citizens and those who were fortunate enough to be high born formed an oligarchy which shared out among itself the offices of magistrate, military commander and priest. The struggles between patricians and plebeians in the early years of the republic had led to an expansion of this 'nobility'. Later, however, it was only very rarely that this class opened itself up to 'new men' who had revealed outstanding political – or particularly military – talents.

*1. The Appian Way linking Rome and Brundisium.*

The Roman city-state was first and foremost a community of warriors. The existence of military service, which meant that citizens could be mobilized between the ages of seventeen and sixty, distinguished it from Carthage and from the Hellenistic kingdoms which only possessed mercenaries. The defeated powers also had to provide soldiers for Rome's further conquests.

Control over the city-state's expansionist inclinations, which were bound up initially with its desire to ensure its own security, was in the hands of the Senate – a kind of permanent council consisting of former magistrates – which received ambassadors and ruled on the allocation of the budget.

Rome's early conquests were confined to Italy. Through the elaboration of a variety of diplomatic contacts with the peninsula's ethnically and culturally heterogeneous communities, and in organizing the Italian geographical area by building roads and founding colonies, Rome laid the basis of a unification which Hannibal's political strategy did little to damage. Presenting himself as the liberator of Italy, Hannibal was only able to win support among a section of the Campanians. The accession of more than a million Italians to Roman citizenship after the Social War was to revolutionize the structures of the city once and for all.

When Rome attacked Carthage, which controlled the western Mediterranean, it was entering upon a conflict with incalculable consequences. It was its first military intervention as a sea-power and its first outside Italy. The Second Punic War extended the field of hostilities to Spain, Italy, Sicily and Africa, as well as to the Greek world. The Third Punic War showed that Rome was henceforth capable of totally destroying those who resisted her. Rome conquered Carthage and also established her power over all the Hellenistic kingdoms. The profits from these conquests were so substantial that, after 167 BC, Romans no longer paid any direct taxes. But social tensions were growing. Rome had to modify its conditions for recruiting soldiers under Marius, and the way in which great commands were allocated in the first century BC. In spite of attempts at reform, such as those of the Gracchi, the economic and social system began to come under strain and the cohesiveness of the political system diminished. The clash of ambitions between the military leaders who had, in their turn, dominated parts of the East (Sulla, Pompey) or the West (Caesar) led to the Empire.

**390 BC** — **Brennus at Rome: *'Vae victis!'* (Woe to the vanquished!)**
**272 BC** — **Rome mistress of southern Italy.**
**247 BC** — **Birth of Hannibal.**
**c. 200 BC** — **Birth of Polybius.**
**149** — **Death of Cato the Eld**

**406 BC:** Siege of Veii.
**390 BC:** Capture of Rome by the Gauls. A wall is built around Rome (the 'Wall of Servius Tullius').
**367 BC:** Consulship opened up to plebeians.
**343–341 BC:** First Samnite War.
**338 BC:** Rome dissolves the Latin League. Founding of the first Roman colony.
**334–326 BC:** Rome controls Campania.
**326–304 BC:** Second Samnite War.
**312–308 BC:** Appius Claudius becomes censor. Building of the Via Appia and the first aqueduct.
**300 BC:** The pontificate (civic priesthood) is opened to plebeians.
**295 BC:** Gauls, Etruscans and Samnites defeated at Sentinum.
**287 BC:** The votes of the plebeian assemblies given force of law.
**279–275 BC:** Expeditionary corps of Pyrrhus, King of Epirus, in Italy 'to defend the independence of the Greek cities'.
**272 BC:** Capture of Tarentum.
**268 BC:** Colonies of Ariminum (Rimini) and Beneventum.
**265 BC:** Fall of Volsinii and the subjugation of the Etruscans.
**264 BC:** First Punic War. First funerary games in Rome with gladiator fights.
**260 BC:** Naval victory at Mylae.
**256–255 BC:** Failure of Roman campaign in Africa.
**254 BC:** Birth of the comic author Plautus.
**242 BC:** Creation of the Peregrine Praetor to judge legal disputes between Romans and foreigners.
**241 BC:** Rome is victorious over Carthage and occupies Sicily.
**240–237 BC:** The Romans in Corsica and Sardinia; revolt of mercenaries at Carthage.
**239 BC:** Birth of the poet Ennius.
**222 BC:** Occupation of Cisalpine Gaul.
**220 BC:** Flaminius is censor; the Via Flaminia and Circus Maximus are built at Rome.
**219 BC:** Capture of Saguntum. Beginning of the Second Punic War.
**218 BC:** Hannibal crosses the Alps.
**216 BC:** Hannibal victorious at Cannae. Defection of Capua.
**215 BC:** Creation of the companies of publicans to provide supplies for armies.
**212 BC:** Archimedes dies at Syracuse.
**211 BC:** Hannibal at the gates of Rome.
**210 BC:** Scipio in Spain.
**204 BC:** Scipio in Africa.
**203 BC:** Hannibal returns to Africa.
**202 BC:** End of the Second Punic War.
**200–197 BC:** Macedonian War against Philip V, who had supported Carthage.
**197–181 BC:** Cisalpine Gaul is annexed and colonized.
**196 BC:** The 'freedom of the Greeks' is proclaimed by Flaminius at Corinth.
**192–188 BC:** War against Antiochus III, King of Syria.
**184 BC:** Cato is censor. Construction of the first basilica at Rome.
**168 BC:** Polybius held hostage in Rome.
**167 BC:** Delos becomes a free port.
**154–133 BC:** Spanish Wars (Scipio Emilio at Numantia).
**149 BC:** First permanent tribunal to rule on the exactions of provincial governors.
**149–146 BC:** Third Punic War.
**148 BC:** Macedonia becomes a Roman province.
**146 BC:** Rome destroys Carthage and Corinth.
**136–132 BC:** First revolt of slaves in Sicily.
**133 BC:** Titus Gracchus becomes people's tribune.
**129 BC:** Creation of the province of Asia.
**125 BC:** Romans enter Transalpine Gaul.
**118 BC:** Colony of Narbo founded.
**112–105 BC:** War against Jugurtha.
**107 BC:** Marius's military reforms.
**104–101 BC:** Marius fights against the Cimbri and the Teutoni in Gaul.
**91–88 BC:** Social War: the defeated Italians receive Roman citizenship.
**88 BC:** Mithridates, King of Pont, invades the province of Asia and massacres the Italians at Delos. Sulla is given charge of the Roman troops.
**87–83 BC:** Marius and his associates in power.
**83–72 BC:** Rising in Spain. Sertorius defeated.
**82 BC:** Sulla occupies Rome. 'Proscriptions'.
**74 BC:** Licinius Lucullus at war with Mithridates.
**73–71 BC:** Revolt of slaves in Italy (led by Spartacus).
**70 BC:** Prosecution of Verres, Governor of Sicily.

# 4th–1st centuries BC

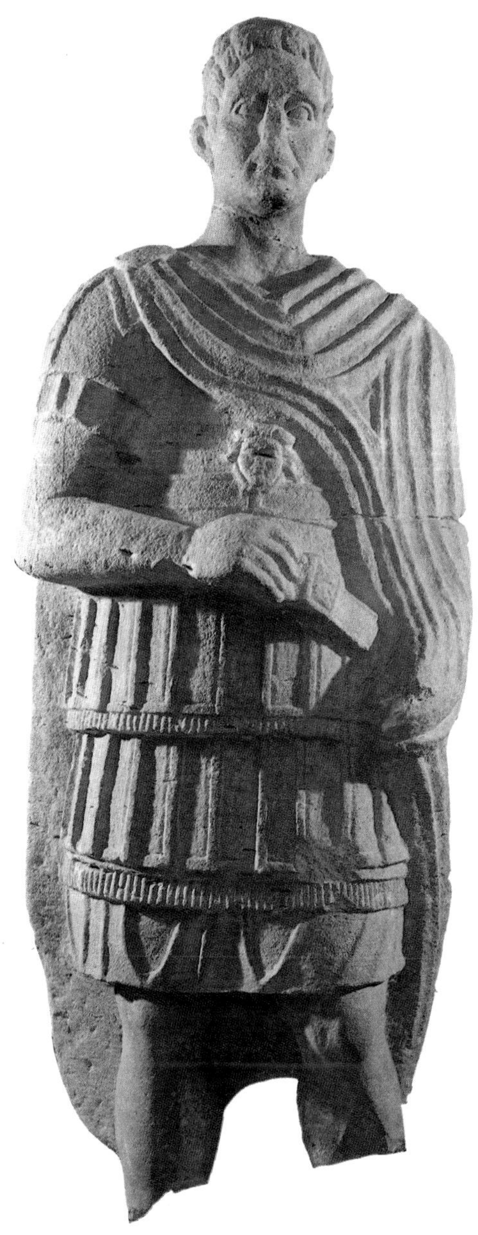

*2. Samnite warrior, 3rd century BC.*

Rome in Italy 406 BC to 88 BC
Aquileia
Ticinus
(–218)
Placentia
Cremona
Trebia
(–218)
Genoa
Bononia
Ariminum
Pisa
Faesulae
Sentinum
Ancona
Arretium
Lake Trasimenus
(–217)
Saturnia
Volsinii
Castrum Novum
CORSICA
Veii
Corfinium
Rome
Cannae
(–216)
Ausculum
Bari
Capua
Beneventum
Brundisium
Caudine Forks
Tarentum
(–272)
SARDINIA
Lake Trasimene
Herclea
Mylae
Panormus
Drepanum
Rhegium
Messina
SICILY
Utica
Carthage
Agrigentum
Ecnomus
Syracuse
The advance of Rome's frontiers
– 300 – 264 – 241 – 90
Roman roads
Aquileia: Latin or Roman colonies
Carthaginian possessions
Under Carthaginian influence until –241
Territories allied to Hannibal
Cannae: Battles against (–216) Hannibal
Battles against
Etruscans – 406/– 265
Samnites – 343/– 295
Pyrrhus – 280/– 275
Carthage – 264/– 241
Territories of the insurgents in the Social War
– 91/– 88

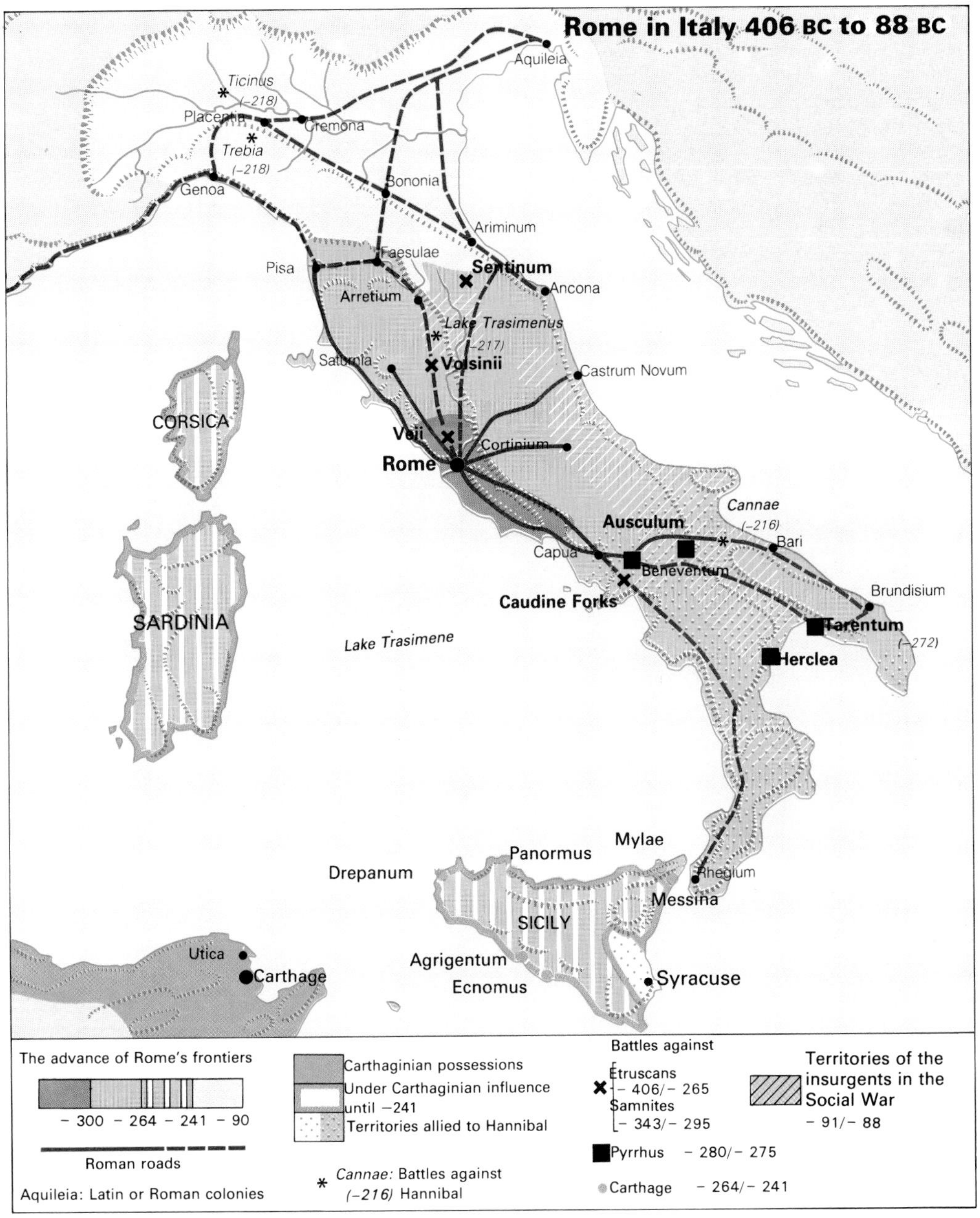

**Death of Spartacus.** **71 BC**

**Caesar crosses the Rubicon.** **49 BC**

**66 BC:** Pompey's army fights Mithridates.
**63 BC:** Cicero consul. Catiline conspiracy.
**59 BC:** Caesar is consul.
**58–52 BC:** Caesar conquers Gaul.
**53 BC:** Licinius Crassus defeated by the Parthians.
**52 BC:** Pompey is made sole consul.
**49 BC:** Caesar marches on Rome.
**48 BC:** Pompey defeated at Pharsalus. Caesar in Egypt.
**46–45 BC:** The Pompeian forces defeated in Africa (Thapsus) and Spain (Munda).
**46–44 BC:** Caesar's dictatorship.
**44 BC:** Caesar assassinated on 15 March.
**43 BC:** The Triumvirate: Mark Antony, Lepidus, Octavian. Proscriptions.
**42 BC:** Victory over Brutus and Cassius at Philippi.
**36 BC:** Lepidus eliminated from Triumvirate.
**31 BC:** Antony defeated at Actium. Conquest of Egypt.

Rome in the world 241 BC to 27 BC
GALLIA
Alesia
COMATA
– 51
TRANSALPINE
GAUL
– 125
CISALPINE
GAUL
– 222
ILLYRICUM
– 167
Narbo
Numantia
NEARER
SPAIN
– 197
Saguntum
FURTHER
SPAIN
– 197
Carthago Nova
ROME
– 241
MACEDONIA
– 148
Pydna
Cynocephales
Actium
ACHAEA
– 146
Corinth
Sparta
Pergamum
ASIA
– 129
Magnesia
BITHYNIA – 74
and PONT – 65
PHRYGIA
– 103
CILICIA
– 101
Carrhae
Antiochia
SYRIA
– 64
Carthage
AFRICA
– 146
AFRICA
NOVA
– 46
Jerusalem
– 63
Alexandria
CYRENE
– 74
EGYPT
– 31
Roman Possessions
– 241 – 197 – 133 – 101 – 27
Battles

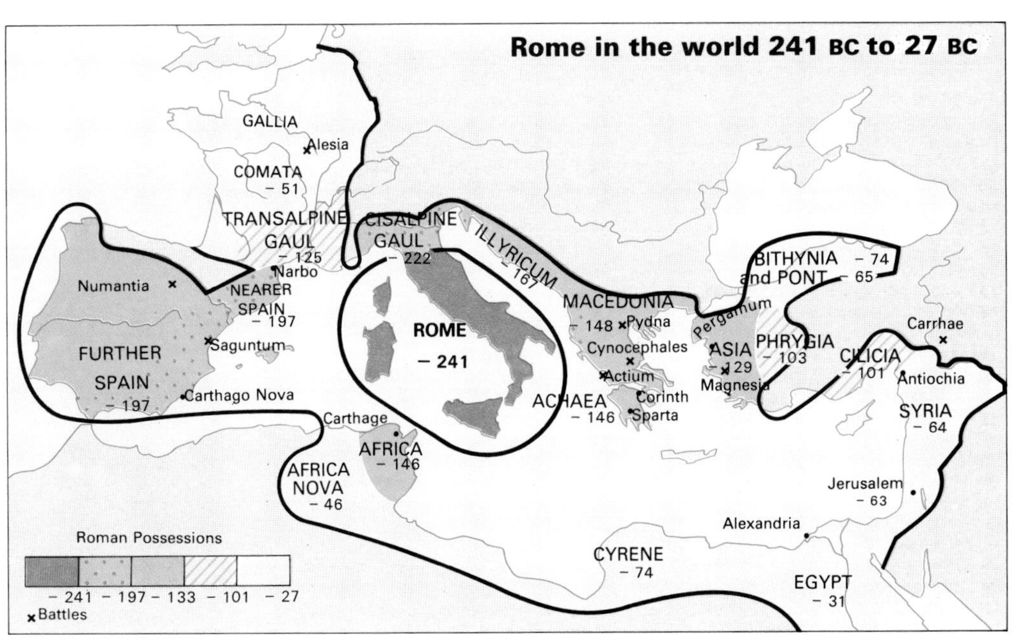

# Towards an Integrated Roman World

Augustus, *Imperator Caesar Augustus*, was, first and foremost, 'the conqueror'. A commander-in-chief was hailed with the title *Imperator* after a victory. It was during Augustus's reign that the ideology of a victorious emperor unifying the world according to an order ordained by the gods was first elaborated. The military victories of Augustus and his successors – Trajan in particular – were always widely celebrated with triumphal arches and commemorative monuments and paved the way for certain military leaders to become emperors (Vespasian, Septimius Severus).

Augustus was also the founder of a political regime to which the name of empire was given. He transformed the republic into a monarchy. Caesar had attempted to achieve this by way of dictatorship. Paradoxically, his adopted son Octavian, presented as the providential saviour of republican institutions, was the man who established an hereditary monarchy in Rome. This was sustained by the Italian municipal oligarchies, who hoped to share the prerogatives of the traditional Roman nobility. He could not have acted without the existence of a very broad consensus. The Senate, which saw its role diminished, the population of Rome that was protected from crises by imperial benevolence and the provincial populations who organized to celebrate his cult, all wished for peace after the civil wars. Sure in the knowledge of this support, Octavian even assented to abandoning his exceptional powers; as a mark of gratitude the Senate accorded him the title of Augustus, which was subsequently borne by all his successors.

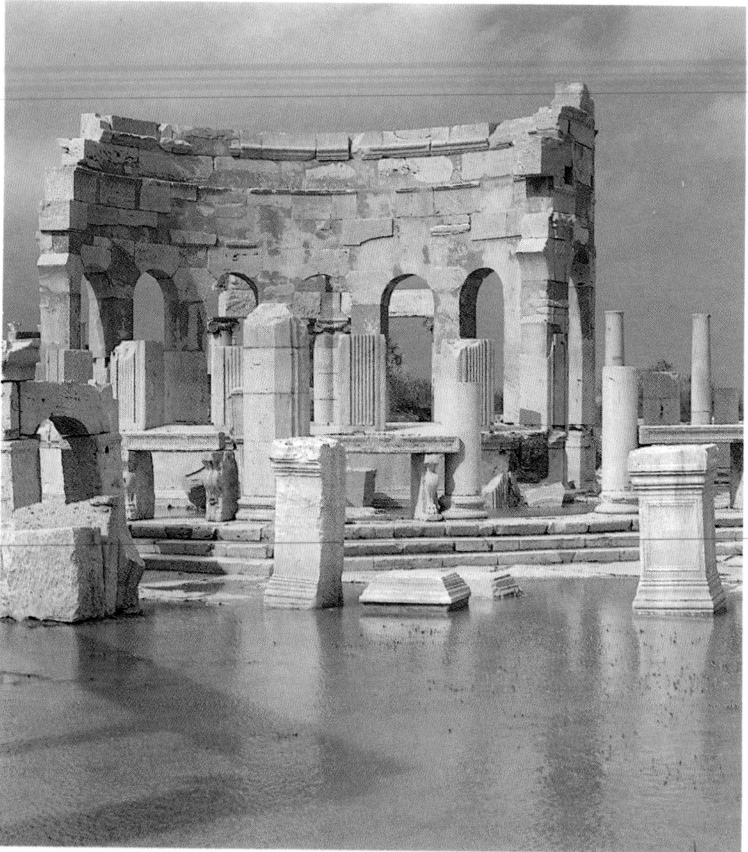

1. Forum of Leptis Magna, 3rd century.

Augustus became the sole ruler of an immense empire in which the world of cities encountered that of tribes. That empire was run by an administrative service which would later assume specialized functions and be protected by a standing army. Within it, a regular fiscal system and a universally recognized legal system were established. It is this image of empire which is still ours today.

The peace Rome enjoyed under Augustus, which guaranteed it that prosperity celebrated by poets and artists, was an armed one. Maintaining peace required a solid military infrastructure of some 300,000 men, a road network that permitted them to intervene rapidly, and a frontier (*limes*) that was reinforced to a great depth by an agricultural colonization that had necessitated the organizing of large-scale population movements (into Germany and the Agri Decumates). The destabilization of this latter area only began in the reign of Marcus Aurelius. The *pax romana* was also largely guaranteed by a willingness to allow the former conquered peoples to share in the profits of empire. From as early as Augustus's time, a subtle diffusion of citizenship made certain privileged individuals the equals of Romans. Under Claudius, Gauls participated in the Roman Senate. Under the Antonine emperors, the senators of Rome were drawn from Spain, Gaul, Greece and the East, as well as from Italy. The knights (*equites*) who provided the Empire's civil service were most commonly recruited among notables from the various provinces. The most humble of them could also become Roman citizens by joining the army. Finally, in 212, Caracalla accorded citizenship to all the free inhabitants of the Empire. Caracalla himself provides a perfect illustration of this policy of integration, being the son of the first emperor of non-Roman origin, Septimius Severus.

This was the final stage in an earlier policy of assimilation: in the West, the progression of the Latin language, adaptation to the spatial and institutional framework of the city and to Roman models of behaviour, made for the development of a Romanization process, the traces of which can still be seen today.

**29 BC** — **Virgil begins the *Aeneid*.**

**AD 30** — **Death of Jesus.**

**48** — **Gauls in the Senate.**

**79** — **Destruction of Pompeii and Herculaneum.**

**27 BC:** Octavian receives the title of Augustus. Supervision of provinces shared between the Senate and the emperors. Dedication of the Odeon of Agrippa.
**26–25 BC:** Pacification in Spain and Gaul. Beginning of the imperial cult in Spain.
**19 BC:** Death of Virgil.
**18 BC:** Augustus receives the tribunician power.
**13 BC:** Altar of Augustan Peace built.
**12 BC:** Augustus becomes *pontifex maximus*. Beginning of the imperial cult in Gaul. Campaigns of Tiberius and Drusus (who goes as far as the Elbe) in Germania.
**9 BC:** The disaster which befalls the legions of Varius puts an end to the brief campaigns of conquest in Germania.
**8 BC:** Deaths of Horace and Maecenas.
**AD 13:** Testament of Augustus.
**14:** Death of Augustus. Germanicus's campaign on the Rhine.
**14–24:** African insurrections.
**15–31:** Sejanus becomes prefect of the Praetorian Guard.
**17:** Death of the historian Livy.
**42:** Construction of the port of Ostia.
**43:** Beginning of the conquest of Britain.
**48:** Claudius's speech in favour of the admission of Gauls into the Senate.
**50:** Adoption of Nero by Claudius.
**55–65:** Seneca, philosophical works.
**58–63:** Armenian campaigns.
**64:** Rome burns. Persecution of Christians. Nero's Golden House.
**66–70:** Revolt in Gaul (Vindex) and in Judaea. Nero's suicide. End of the Julio-Claudian dynasty. Civil wars: Galba, Otho, Vitellius.
**69–96:** Flavian dynasty.
**70:** Vespasian, proclaimed emperor in 69, becomes ruler of the Empire. Capture of Jerusalem by his son Titus.
**71:** Vespasian's Forum and Temple of Peace.
**74:** Spain receives Latin rights.
**77–84:** Agricola pacifies Britain.
**79:** Death of Pliny the Elder.
**80:** Dedication of the Coliseum. Arch of Titus built.
**85–6:** Wars against the Dacians.
**96:** Assassination of Domitian. Nerva adopts Trajan.
**97–8:** Forum of Nerva. Tacitus writes the *Life of Agricola* and the *Germania*.

2. Two legionnaires of the Roman army in Germany.

**98:** Trajan reinforces the *limes* of the Rhine.
**101:** First war against the Dacians.
**105:** Arabia becomes a Roman province.
**108:** Creation of the *alimentia*, an institution giving aid to young Italians.
**111–13:** Correspondence between Pliny, the governor of Bithynia, and Trajan.
**111–14:** Trajan's forum, the work of Apollodorus of Damascus.
**114:** War against the Parthians: annexation of Armenia.
**116:** Trajan conquers Assyria and Mesopotamia and reaches the Persian Gulf.
**c. 116:** Tacitus writes *The Annals*.
**117:** Hadrian withdraws from the eastern lands conquered by Trajan.
**120:** Suetonius writes the *Lives of the Caesars*. Death of Plutarch, author of the *Parallel Lives*.
**122–7:** Building of Hadrian's Wall in Britain.
**125–35:** The Villa Hadriana at Tivoli.
**132–5:** Second Jewish War.
**135:** Hadrian in Judaea. Capture of Jerusalem.
**142:** Antonine Wall in Scotland.

# 1st century BC–3rd century AD

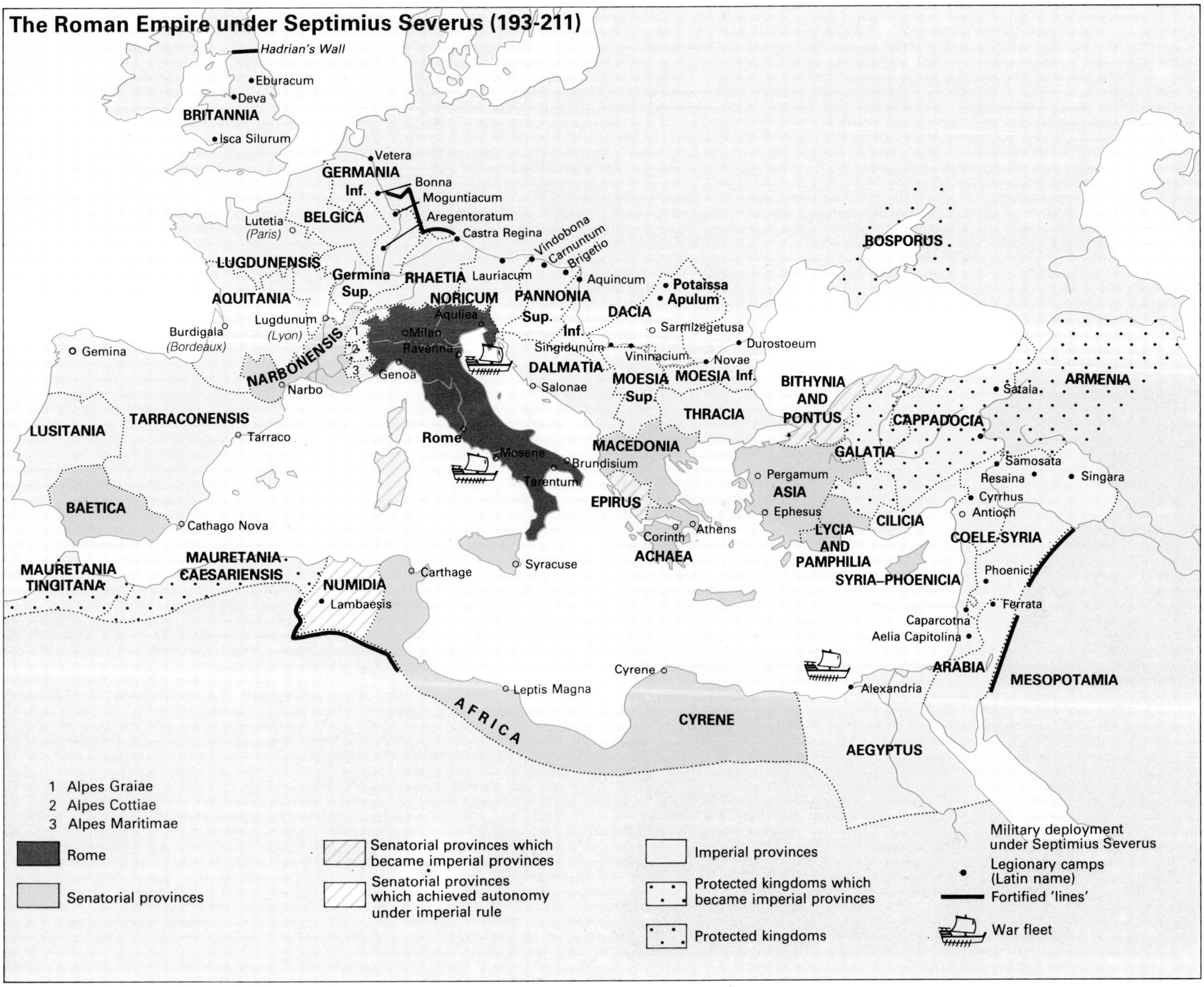

## The Roman Empire under Septimius Severus (193-211)

1 Alpes Graiae
2 Alpes Cottiae
3 Alpes Maritimae

Rome

Senatorial provinces

Senatorial provinces which became imperial provinces

Senatorial provinces which achieved autonomy under imperial rule

Imperial provinces

Protected kingdoms which became imperial provinces

Protected kingdoms

Military deployment under Septimius Severus

Legionary camps (Latin name)

Fortified 'lines'

War fleet

**Death of Tacitus.**

**c. 120**

**All communities of the Empire enfranchised.**

**212**

**143:** Aelius Aristides writes his panegyric of Rome.
**161–6:** War against the Parthians.
**167:** Great plague in Rome.
**169:** Death of Lucius Verus, who had been made co-emperor by Marcus Aurelius.
**172–5:** Marcus Aurelius writes his *Meditations*.
**172–80:** Campaigns on the Rhine and the Danube.
**184–5:** Troubles in Britain. The Antonine Wall abandoned.
**192:** Assassination of Commodus. Political crisis. End of the Antonine dynasty.
**193:** Septimius Severus proclaimed emperor.
**211:** Death of Septimius Severus in Britain. He is succeeded by his sons, Caracalla and Geta.
**212:** Assassination of Geta. Edict of Caracalla granting citizenship to all the inhabitants of the Empire.
**216:** Baths of Caracalla built.
**218–22:** Development of sun worship (of Eastern origin) in Rome under Elagabalus.
**226:** The Sassanian dynasty in Persia.

*3. Slaves serving at a banquet, Carthage, 3rd century.*

**234:** The Alamanni invade Germania.
**235:** Assassination of Severus Alexander. End of the dynasty of the Severi.

*4. The Emperor Caracalla.*

# Roman Gaul

The Gauls burst on to the scene of Roman history in the fourth century BC: they swept through Italy and settled in the plain of the River Po, the future province of Gallia Cisalpina. Rome first took an interest in the Hellenized Gallia Transalpina in the third century BC, in response to an appeal from Marseille, which was concerned at the Carthaginian advance in Spain. Hannibal's campaign across the Alps had no lasting effects, and the *Provincia* of Transalpina was founded as early as the second century. The invasion of the Germanic tribes, the Cimbri and the Teutoni, and their repulsion by Gaius Marius, soon placed Rome in the role of protector of the Gauls, and the halt that Julius Caesar put to the migration of the Helvetii stabilized the frontiers of the cities. But Caesar needed a victory. His attempt to conquer the Gauls and Britons sparked off a general revolt. The leader of that revolt, Vercingetorix (who struck his own coinage like a Hellenistic king), won great victories. However, Caesar, though he came near to disaster, emerged victorious at Alesia; the cities submitted to his rule and Marseille was taken after a long siege. On the death of Caesar in 44 BC, Rome controlled the whole territory of Gaul.

Augustus reorganized the conquered areas. Old *Provincia*, now known as *Provincia Narbonensis*, remained a senatorial province and received Latin rights: all the other Gallic cities were grouped into the three imperial provinces of Aquitania, Lugdunensis and Belgica. Colonies were founded, native population centres displaced and towns built on the Roman model, local aristocracies liberally receiving the benefit of Roman law. The death of Augustus reawakened desires for independence under his successor Tiberius, but Claudius, who knew Gaul well, opened the Roman Senate up to its élites and associated these provincials very closely with the destinies of the Empire. This decision set a precedent that was followed in the case of other provinces.

*1. Roman Games in Gaul. Mosaic of chariot racing, Lyon.*

From this point on Gaul became an essential part of the Roman world. It provided soldiers, administrators and governors and each year, on the Altar of the Three Gauls at Lyon, it renewed its allegiance to the Empire. The wide reputation enjoyed by its centres of ceramic production (La Graufesenque and then Lezoux) attests to its prosperity, as do the thousands of inscriptions, mosaics, sculptures, bronzes, terracotta pieces and the rich hoards of coins and gold artifacts that have been discovered, not to mention its great architectural achievements, such as the Maison Carrée, the amphitheatre at Nîmes, the theatre at Orange, the Pont du Gard, the temples of Glanum, Vienne and Autun, and the Cluny thermal baths in Paris. Arles was a great port and received produce from the East. Jews were among those who landed there, and it became a centre of Christianity. These provinces retained their specific local features, as can be seen in such material symbols as the use of the *tonneau* and the wearing of breeches. Their gods and the forms of worship accorded to them retained local characteristics. During political crises, the Gauls willingly organized themselves as an autonomous empire, as can be seen in the troubled years of the third century AD when the Gallic emperors took charge of the Roman Empire's western defences.

Reorganized into two dioceses, they contributed to the fourth century Renaissance: Trêves (Trier) became the imperial capital and its Porta Nigra and Basilica are magnificent relics of that period. The villas of Aquitania and Mid-Gaul are proof of the continued prosperity of the country areas, in spite of the endemic agitation of the Bagaudae (bands of Gallic peasants in rebellion against Roman rule); the towns, which were fortified, in some cases retained their splendour. The aristocracy, converted to Christianity, provided the Empire with some personalities of the first rank. When the military defences fell, the Germanic peoples who had settled in Gaul were not long in becoming Romanized in their turn.

**Sack of Rome by the Gauls.**

**390 BC**

**4th century BC:** Gauls in northern Italy.
**4th–3rd century BC:** La Tène civilization in Gaul.
**231 BC:** Marseille seeks Roman diplomatic intervention in Spain.
**218 BC:** Hannibal passes through southern Gaul and crosses the Alps to attack the Romans in Italy.
**122–121 BC:** Domitius Ahenobarbus in Gallia Transalpina; foundation of Aix; defeat of the Allobroges, then of Bituitus, king of the Arverni; Rhône valley brought under Roman rule as Provincia.
**118 BC:** Foundation of the Roman colony of Narbo Martius (Narbonne).
**109–103 BC:** Invasion of the Cimbri and the Teutoni.
**102–101:** Marius defeats the Teutoni at Aix, then the Cimbri at Vercelli.
**1st century BC:** La Tène III civilization.
**87?–52? BC:** Catullus, a Cisalpine poet of Verona.
**70–19 BC:** Virgil, a Cisalpine from Mantua.
**?–26 BC:** Cornelius Gallus, Gallic elegiac poet from Fréjus.

**Caesar in Gaul.**

**59–49 BC**

**61 BC:** The Aedui appeal to Rome against the Germanii.
**59–17 BC:** Livy, a Cisalpine from Padua.
**59–58 BC:** Migration of the Helvetii, halted by Caesar at Bibracte.
**57–56 BC:** Caesar in Belgium; Crassus in western Gaul; Caesar among the Veneti.
**55–54:** Caesar in Brittany.
**53 BC:** Vercingetorix leads revolt of the towns of Gallia Comata; Gallia Transalpina supports Caesar.
**52 BC:** Roman defeat at Gergovia; siege and capture of Alésia. Vercingetorix taken prisoner.
**51–50 BC:** Towns of Gaul surrender.
**49 BC:** Marseille, the last independent Greek city in the Mediterranean, is besieged and captured by Caesar.
**46–44 BC:** Colony of Arles created.
**43 BC:** Colonies of Lyon and Augst in Switzerland founded.
**27 BC:** Augustus at Narbo; Transalpine Gaul divided into four provinces.
**6 BC:** Definitive subjugation of the Alpine peoples; monumental trophy of La Turbie built.

**Claudius's speech on the extension of the *jus honorum* to the Gauls.**

**AD 48**

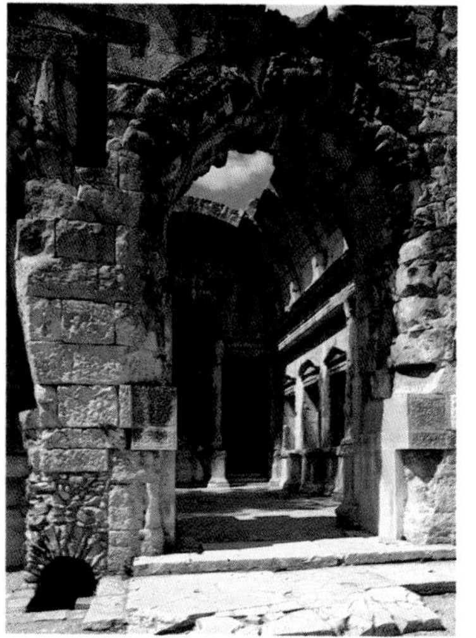

*2. The Temple of Diana at Nîmes, 1st century.*

**1st century AD:** Trogus Pompeius, Gallic historian.
**2–4:** Dedication of the Maison Carrée.
**14:** At the death of Augustus, Béziers, Fréjus, Orange, Valence, Vienne and Nyons also become *coloniae* under Roman law; Apt, Nîmes and Carcassonne become *coloniae* under Latin law.
**21:** Revolt of Florus and Sacrovir.
**26–7:** Dedication of the Arch of Orange.
**41:** Claudius, who spent his youth in Gaul, becomes emperor.
**48:** Aedui admitted to the Senate.
**c. 50:** Trêves becomes *colonia*; building of theatre at Orange.
**68–70:** Vindex, Civilis and the ephemeral first Gallic Empire.
**69–79:** Vespasian; Avenches becomes *colonia*; marble land survey map of Orange.
**?–113:** Pliny the Younger, a Cisalpine from Coma.
**121–2:** Hadrian visits the northwest provinces.
**135–61:** Reign of Antoninus Pius, who is partially of Gallic descent.
**177:** Christians persecuted at Lyon.

# 4th century BC–5th century AD

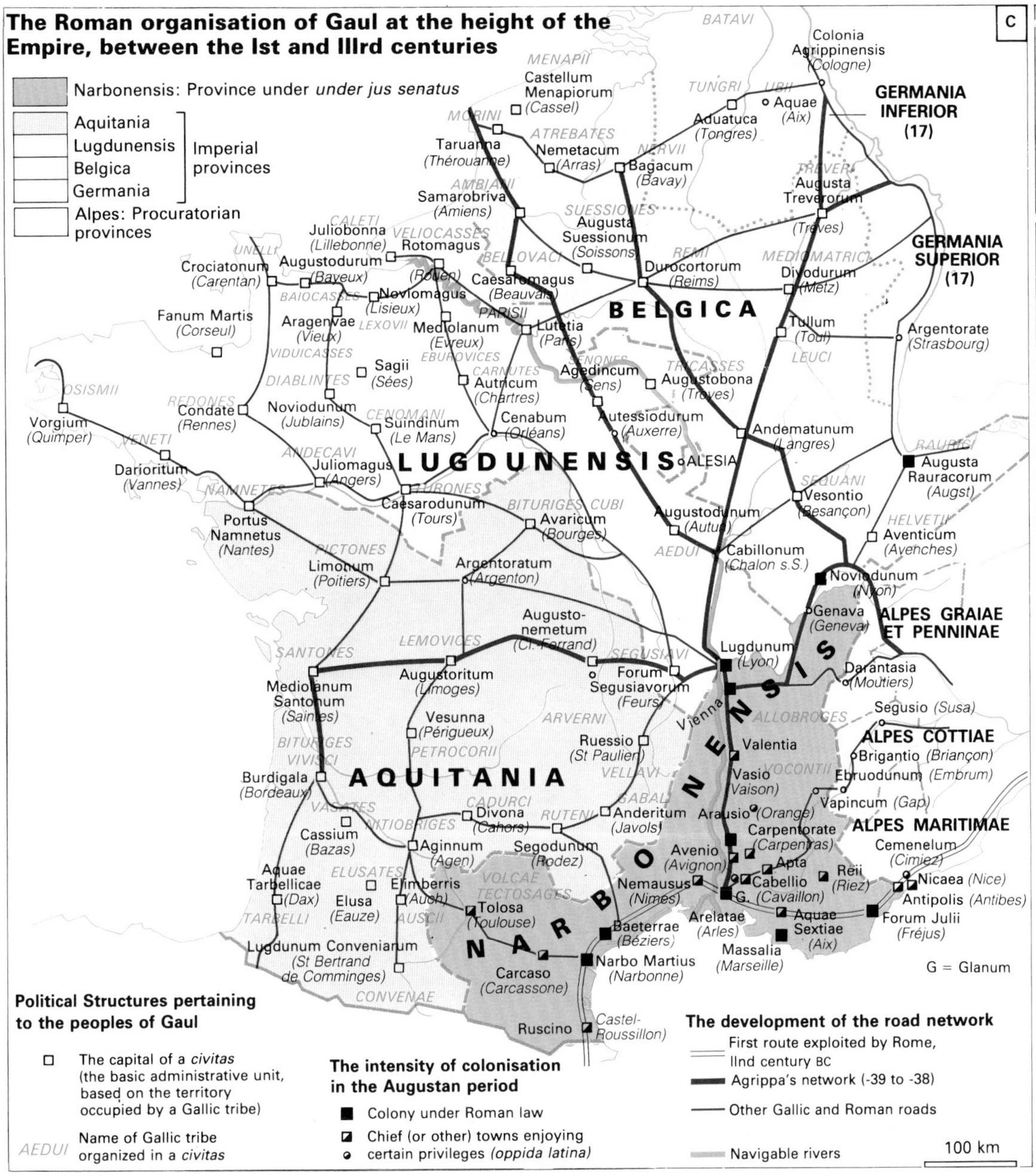

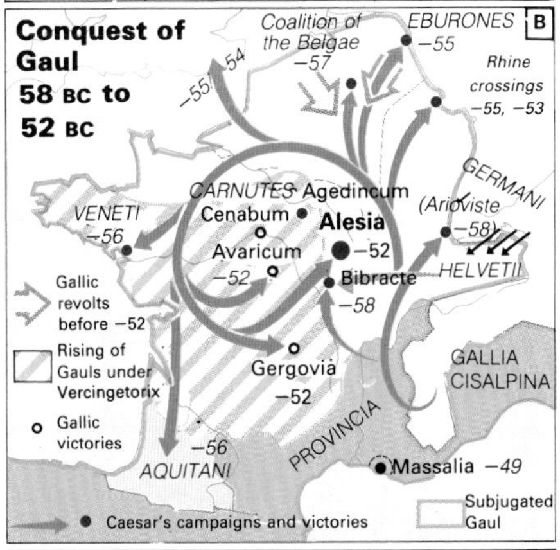

### The Roman organisation of Gaul at the height of the Empire, between the Ist and IIIrd centuries

C

Narbonensis: Province under *under jus senatus*

Aquitania, Lugdunensis, Belgica, Germania: Imperial provinces

Alpes: Procuratorian provinces

GERMANIA INFERIOR (17)

GERMANIA SUPERIOR (17)

BELGICA

LUGDUNENSIS

AQUITANIA

NARBONENSIS

ALPES GRAIAE ET PENNINAE

ALPES COTTIAE

ALPES MARITIMAE

G = Glanum

**Political Structures pertaining to the peoples of Gaul**

- The capital of a *civitas* (the basic administrative unit, based on the territory occupied by a Gallic tribe)
- *AEDUI* Name of Gallic tribe organized in a *civitas*

**The intensity of colonisation in the Augustan period**

- Colony under Roman law
- Chief (or other) towns enjoying certain privileges *(oppida latina)*

**The development of the road network**

- First route exploited by Rome, IInd century BC
- Agrippa's network (-39 to -38)
- Other Gallic and Roman roads
- Navigable rivers

100 km

### Before the conquest

A

Via Domitia: military highway to Spain

Roman Province

The Romans 'aiding' the Gauls against the Teutoni (–102)

Massalia and its territory, allies of Rome since the IIIrd century BC

### Conquest of Gaul 58 BC to 52 BC

B

Gallic revolts before –52

Rising of Gauls under Vercingetorix

Gallic victories

Caesar's campaigns and victories

Subjugated Gaul

### The Late Empire, late IIIrd to beginning of Vth century

D

Diocese of the Gauls

Diocese of Vienna

D = Darantasia

| Second Gallic Empire. | Trêves (Trier) capital of the empire in the West. | Eumenius's speech on the restoration of the schools of rhetoric at Augustodunum (Autun). | The Vandals in Gaul. |
|---|---|---|---|
| 8–273 | 285 | 298 | 406–7 |

**196:** Albinus's rebellion in Gaul against Septimius Severus.
**197:** Battle of Lyon; death of Albinus.
**212:** Edict of Caracalla (*Constitutio Antoniana*) confers Roman citizenship on all the free men of the Empire.
**258–68:** Postumus, Emperor of the Gauls, defends against invasions by Germanic tribes.
**268–73:** Tetricus, Emperor of the Gauls, is ultimately forced to surrender to Aurelian.
**269:** First mention of the troubles caused by the Bagaudae.
**275–7:** Barbarian invasions.
**276–82:** Probus drives the invaders out of Gaul.
**286:** Maximian suppresses the Bagaudae.
**303–4:** Diocletian's persecution of Christians.
**306–11:** Constantine in Gaul.
**309–90:** Ausonius, Bordeaux poet and tutor of Gratian.
**314:** Council of Arles.
**355:** Invasions. Julian the Apostate Caesar.
**356–7:** Julian wins victories.
**360?–425?:** Sulpicius Severus Aquitanian historian.
**361:** Julian proclaimed Augustus at Paris.
**363–4:** Invasion. Jovian wins victories.
**386:** Council of Trêves.
**430–80:** Sidonius Apollinaris, letter-writer, Bishop of Clermont and poet.
**435–7:** Bagaudae.
**455:** Capture of Trêves by the Franks.

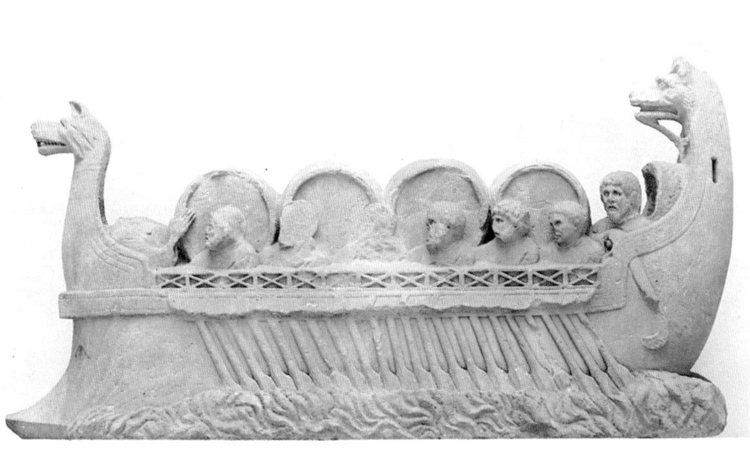

3. *The* tonneau, *a Gallic invention. 2nd-century relief, Rhineland.*

4. *The Apollo of the Maison Carrée, Nîmes.*

# Christianity Persecuted and Triumphant

Pluralism was at the heart of ancient religion: each group of humanity expressed its cohesion by honouring its own gods, who were adapted to the local setting and social needs. In Rome, as in Athens, the reception of new divinities obeyed the same rules as applied to the welcome of foreigners: that is to say their followers were required – upon pain of death – not to disturb the social order (Socrates' trial in 399 BC; Bacchanalian scandals of 186 BC). The Roman Empire even tolerated the exclusivism of the god of Israel, granting the Jews the right not to worship Rome and Augustus.

So long as the 'supporters of Christus' were identified with the Jews, they enjoyed the same privileges, which in part explains why Christianity was able to spread so rapidly (it was established in Damascus and Antioch before AD 38, in Asia Minor as early as AD 45, in Rome before AD 49, and at Corinth in AD 50). But the proselytism of the missionaries, which was often foolhardy, caused disruption almost immediately among the lower classes. The journeys of the apostle Paul are studded with civil disturbances which did not simply come from within the Jewish communities, who were indeed accustomed to showing discretion. The ease with which the unjust condemnation of the Christians as fire-raisers in AD 64 was accepted reveals a deep hostility towards them in public opinion. The persecutions unleashed by local magistrates when Christians were denounced were for a long time seen as simple public order measures. It was Trajan who brought these under control.

Everything changed at the beginning of the third century, when the barbarian threat became serious. Christianity, then quite widespread among the upper classes and even stretching beyond the frontiers of Rome as far indeed as Rome's enemies, the Sassanians, seemed to the soldier-emperors to smack of treason at a time when all energies had to be mobilized to save the Empire. This was a grave political error, for the Christians were generally loyalists where the state was concerned. Decreed from on high, the great persecutions were not reflections of popular pressure. Not only were they ineffective, they created new ferments of disintegration.

The 'conversion of Constantine' reflected the same concern as had inspired the Edicts of Diocletian: at all costs the unity of the Roman world had to be maintained. And one soon saw emperors – whether usurpers or not – imposing the same repressive measures on the traditional cults that had been decreed by their predecessors against Christianity. Thus the former sufferers became in their turn persecutors, even on occasion persecutors of their own co-religionists, accused of schism or heresy.

The church, though called upon by its founder to observe and promote unity, was in fact very soon prey to internal splits, in which local differences were revived, which neither the great schools of theology (Alexandria, Antioch, Caesarea) nor the development of monarchism would be able to contain. The mother community in Jerusalem, which inherited the divisions within the Jews, was split between 'Hellenists' and 'Hebrews' on the question of observance of the Mosaic customs. The Jewish–Christian schism (Ebionism) was the first of a long series, chief among which were Montanism in Phrygia and Donatism in Africa. The difficulty of reconciling the divinity of Jesus with monotheism was the cause of the first heresies (Gnosticism in Syria, Marcionism in Pontus, Sabellianism in Cyrenaica, Arianism in Egypt). To repress these disturbances of public order, the emperors in their turn became theologians and presided over synods. Thus was Roman continuity maintained.

*1. The Good Shepherd. Catacombs of St Priscilla, c. 260.*

**Birth of Jesus Christ.** 4 BC

**Peter and Paul killed at Rome.** AD 64

**First heresies.** c. 100

**30:** Jesus of Nazareth condemned to death by Pontius Pilate, Governor of Judaea, for having proclaimed himself King of the Jews.
**37:** Stoning of Stephen. The dispersion of the 'Hellenists', who proclaimed the Gospel to the Gentiles. Conversion of Paul.
**45–9:** Paul in Asia Minor. The Council of Jerusalem declares Gentiles free of obligations under the Mosaic law.
**50:** Claudius expels from Rome the 'Jews who are agitating at the instigation of Christus' (Suetonius).
**50–2:** Paul in Greece. Epistles to the Thessalonians.
**53–8:** Paul in Asia Minor. Epistles to the Corinthians and the Romans. Arrested in Jerusalem for disturbances in the Temple, he is judged at Rome before Caesar and discharged (63).
**64:** Burning of Rome and persecution of Christians accused of being fire-raisers.
**66:** Revolt of Judea. The Christians take refuge at Pella.
**After 70:** The synoptic Gospels. The Ebionites accept Jesus as Messiah but deny his divinity.

**95:** Under Domitian, new persecutions. Writings of St John.
**c. 100:** The Gnostics argue that Jesus's humanity is mere appearance.
**111:** Trajan's reply to Pliny the Younger fixes the procedure to be followed in the trials of those denounced for the crime of Christianity.

*2. Judea vanquished. Coin struck by Vespasian in 71.*

**c. 150:** The Marcionists reject the Old Testament.
**c. 170:** The Montanists form a charismatic church.
**177:** Martyrdom of the Christians of Lyon.
**202:** Edict of Septimius Severus forbidding proselytism.
**217:** Sabellius denies the personal distinction between Father and Son.
**250:** Edict of Decius ordering participation in a general sacrifice. Repression of those who refused. Many renunciations of Christianity ensue.
**260:** Gallienus's Edict of Toleration.
**297:** Diocletian's Edict against the Manichaeans.
**303–5:** Edicts of Diocletian forbidding Christian worship, ordering the torture of priests who refuse to renounce that religion and condemning to death or hard labour those refusing to take part in a general sacrifice to the tutelary gods of Rome.
**311:** Galerius's Edict of Toleration. Anthony the Hermit.
**312:** The Donatists reject the validity of the sacraments conferred by priests who had

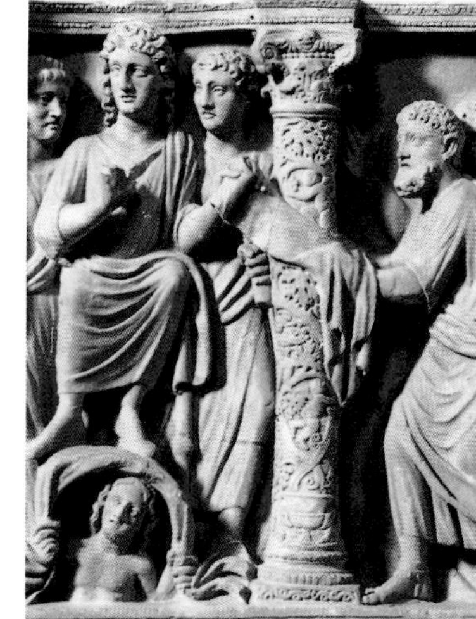

*3. Jesus giving the law to Peter. 4th century sarcophagus.*

# AD 30–392

## The Spread of Christianity

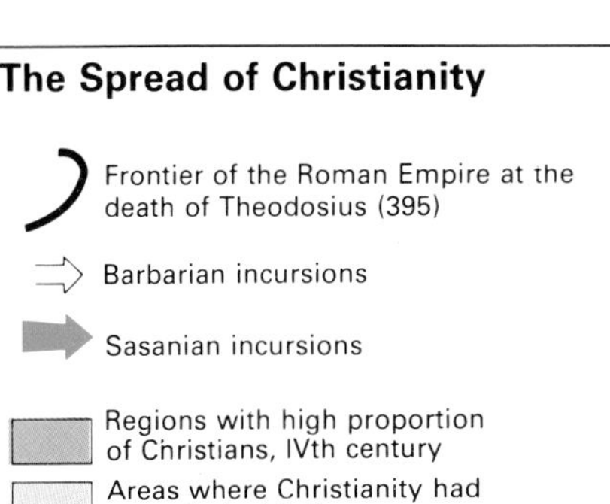


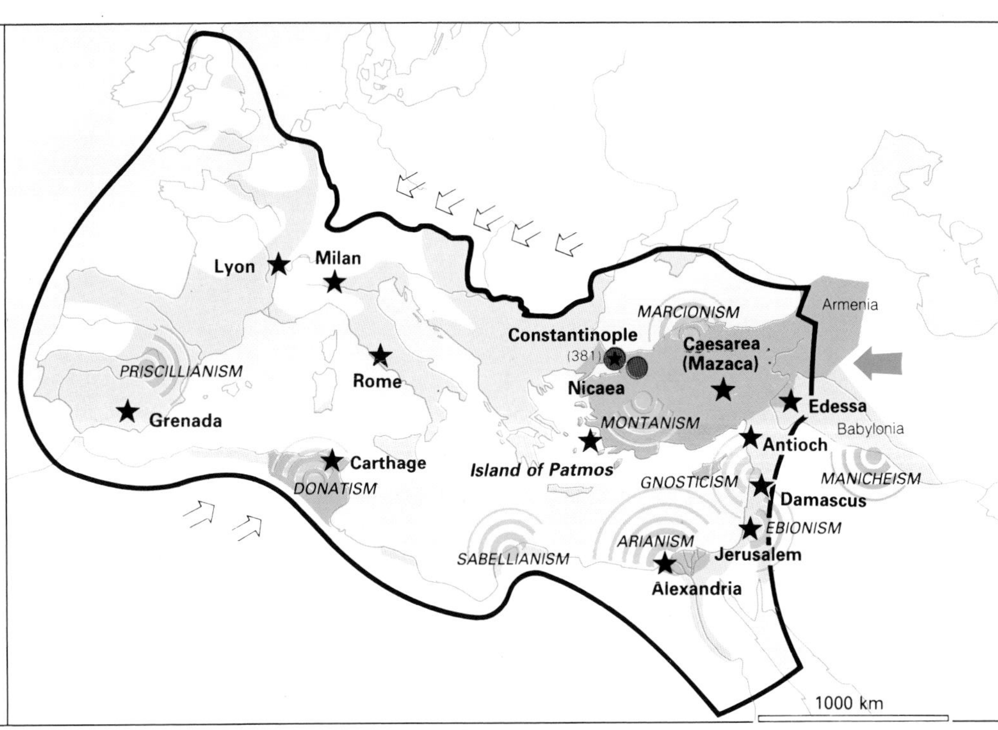


## The Journeys of Paul and the Churches of the *Apocalypse*

Paul's journeys

From Antioch

First journey (45-49)

Second journey (50-52)

Third journey (53-58)

From Caesarea

Journey in captivity to Rome (60-62)

The Seven Churches of John's *Apocalypse*

1 - Ephesus
2 - Laodicea
3 - Pergamos
4 - Philadelphia
5 - Sardis
6 - Smyrna
7 - Thyatira

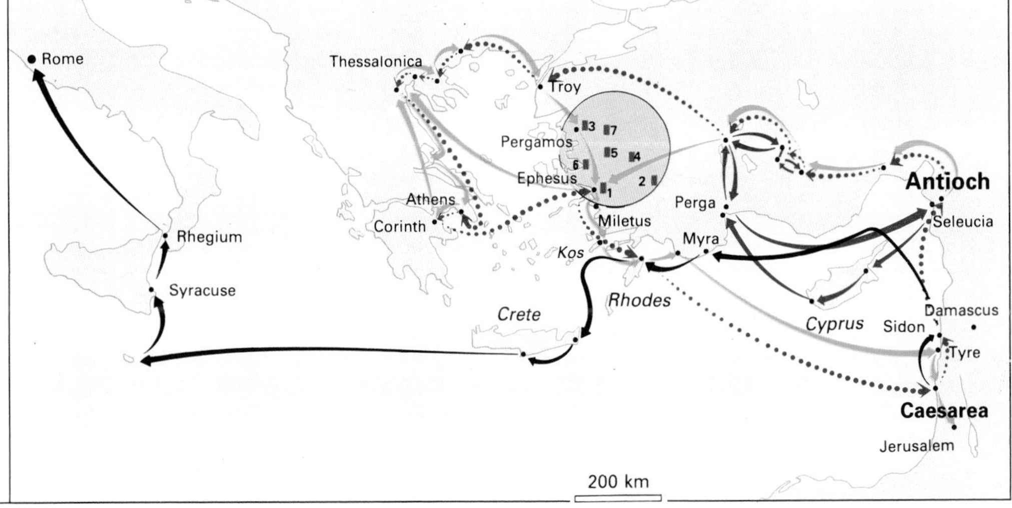


**250** Decian persecution.

**311** Serdica Edict of Toleration.

**363** Death of Julian the Apostate.

*4. Sarcophagus of Eutropos, a Christian sculptor, c. 350.*

forsworn their religion during the period of persecution.
**313:** Constantine and Licinius accord freedom of worship to all the inhabitants of the Empire.
**c. 320:** In Egypt, Arius professes that the Father and the Son are not of the same nature. Pachomius founds the first monastery.
**325:** The ecumenical council of Nicaea condemns Arianism.
**c. 340:** Wulfila spreads Arianism among the Goths.
**347:** Constant I orders the prosecution of the Donatists.
**361:** Julian gives aid to promote anti-Christian resistance.
**381:** The ecumenical council of Constantinople defines the consubstantiality of Father and Son.
**385:** Priscillian is executed at Trier as a heretic.
**391–2:** Theodosius outlaws all pagan cults.

*5. Folio of the Gospel according to St John, Codex Sinaiticus, 4th century.*

# Expansionist Tendencies

The historical turning-point which marks the beginning of a clear trend towards homogenization, which the Greek historian Polybius situated around 220 BC – the point at which Rome began to exert its power over the other Mediterranean countries – can also be seen in Chinese history, where it is, if anything, even more marked. It was in 221 BC that China was first unified. These two parallel developmental processes make the third century AD one of the crucial moments in human history. Might it be said that the year 221 BC marked the end of an era for China and the beginning of a new one for Rome? In fact, the process of Roman conquest outside the peninsula began around 269 BC (according to Polybius himself). It quickened first around 260 BC, then in 229 BC and, once again, around 220 BC. It began again, after a pause, in 154 BC. The beginnings of the Chinese Empire obeyed a somewhat similar chronology.

Several factors do, however, to some degree temper the importance of the events of the late third century. The preceding period was an exceptionally fruitful one, since it saw the birth of such remarkable new phenomena as Greek democracy, Roman law, Jewish nationalism and the legalist Chinese state. It also saw the Persian Empire and Alexander's. Though these were not very long-lived and may even seem positively ephemeral alongside the Roman and Chinese Empires, they were more cosmopolitan, 'imperial' and adventurous. The fact was, however, that after the turn of the third century BC history passed into a phase of banalization and growing uniformity. And the socio-political units that emerged at that time were generally of a defensive, rather timid and prudent nature. The Chinese grouped together against the nomads from the Steppes. The Romans organized a common front of the Hellenized peoples against the Western Semites and the 'barbarians' of Germany. Central Asia, Iran and Mesopotamia rejected Hellenism. India, after Ashoka, reacted against Buddhist internationalism and reverted to Brahminism. Elsewhere, as ever, progress took an internally contradictory course: 'horizontal' integration occurred at the expense of 'vertical' segregation; the rich supported centralizing states, while the poor suffered.

There was, however, a great deal of progress, much of it occurring – most strikingly as it now seems – at around the same time. This can be seen in the many new peoples who 'entered history' (Vietnamese, Japanese, Ethiopians, the Slavs and the Numidians), in the numerous new contacts between peoples and in the evidence of the restless human spirit shown by the Jews in the West; the Teutons in Germany; the Polynesians in their travels to the Marquesas and Society Islands more than 3,000 kilometres from Samoa; the Bantus of the Cameroon and Congo forests advancing into the savannahs of the south and east of Africa, taking with them agricultural skills and iron; migrants from the Indian archipelago journeying to Madagascar and the east coast of Africa; the South American Arawaks sailing to the West Indies; Roman coins finding their way to Indochina etc. The face of progress could also be seen in those states which arose after the end of the third century BC in North Africa or in Celtic, Dacian and Hun territory, which opened the way to the development of empires. And it is also seen in the missionary religions, the sudden explosion of religious univeralism in Judaism, Mahayana Buddhism, the conversion of Southeast Asia to Brahminism (the Indian form of expansion – at once religious, political and commercial) and the conversion of the Mediterranean and Western Europe to Christianity. Then, finally, there was also the establishment of Teotihuacan on the Mexican plateaus which, by its immense political and religious influence, would leave its definitive stamp on the whole of Central American history.

*1. Augustus imperator, marble, Rome, 1st century.*

**272–232 BC:** Ashoka – Indian unity and Buddhist missions. There followed a Brahman reaction and the Indianization of Southeast Asia.
**c. 270–265 BC:** The Ch'in state (which was to give its name to China, at least in European languages) adopted the markedly legalist orientation, which was to be the foundation-stone of its greatness. Rome became interested in Sicily, where she was subsequently to encounter Carthage.
**c. 270–250 BC:** Bible translated into Greek.
**c. 260–241 BC:** Roman victory over Carthage. The Ch'in state became the dominant power in China.
**Second half of 3rd century BC:** The Arsacid Parthians freed themselves from Greek domination. Central Asia detached itself from the Seleucid Empire. The Teutons left their peninsulas and marched towards the south. The Celts fell back and sought to unite. The Slavic people was taking form. A Japanese people and culture made its appearance. A Hun kingdom (Hsiung nu) and Numidian and Moorish kingdoms emerged. The King of Meroe conquered Ethiopia.

*3. The soldiers of the dead ruler's army. Tomb of the first Chinese emperor, Shih Huang Ti, in Shensi province.*

**229–222 BC:** The Romans crossed the Adriatic and occupied Cisalpine Gaul. The Ch'in state reduced its rivals to the status of provinces.
**221 BC:** The Ch'in Empire. Hannibal's Empire. The decisive conflict with Rome imminent.
**219–202 BC:** Second Punic War. In 202 BC the Han Empire replaced the rapidly dismembered Ch'in Empire: this had a 'federal' or 'feudal' structure, with great autonomy granted to the provinces.
**2nd century BC:** The Mongol Huns formed a bastion against the Indo-European Yueh-chih, who surged back into Central Asia, destroying Hellenism there. In their westward march the Jews reached Greece and Rome. Attempts at unification among the Dacians. First buildings at Teotihuacan. First Mayan layer.
**154 BC:** Rome, which had subjugated Spain, North Africa and Greece, was coming out of a relatively quiet period. New imperial impetus in China. End of provincial autonomy.
**c. 130 BC:** The Roman legions in Asia. Chinese offensives against the barbarian

# 3rd century BC–1st century AD

2. The Great Wall of China, built in the reign of Shih Huang Ti (221–206 BC).

4. Capital of the pillar erected by Ashoka at Sarnath, India, 3rd century BC.

north and south-west.
**1st century BC:** Aksum – the formation of historic Ethiopia. Hellenism again in retreat in the Near East. Expansion of Indian trade with the Mediterranean and the Far East.
**Middle of 1st century BC:** High point of Roman conquest. Stabilization and consolidation of the Empire. Rise of Italians and western provincials. Further successful Chinese expansion followed by a tendency for such expansion to decelerate. Promotion of provincial élites.
**AD 50:** Beginning of Christian expansion.
**End of 1st millennium BC/beginning of 1st millennium AD:** Bantu migration in Africa. Polynesian migration in Oceania. Indian migration into Southeast Asia and Indonesia. The Arawaks in the West Indies.

5. Mythic account of the migration of the Aztecs. Detail from the Boturini codex.

# Fall of the Roman Empire in the West

AT THE END of the crisis of the third century, the 'Late' Empire – as it is known – underwent a profound transformation, becoming an absolute monarchy with capitals at Ravenna, Milan, Trier, Constantinople and Sirmium. Rome was now merely a cultural and religious centre. At the Empire's frontiers, the emperors had installed barbarian peoples as *foederati* and reinforced the *limes* – fortified lines between the Rhine and the Danube – to contain the Germanic tribes. Diocletian divided the Empire into fifteen large dioceses, each one being itself divided into provinces (of which there were seventeen in Gaul) and each province into cities. When, by the Edict of Milan, Constantine decided to grant freedom to Christians, the ecclesiastical hierarchy was laid down: the 'metropolitan', later to be called an archbishop, was placed at the head of a province, whilst the role of a bishop was to direct the church in a city. Once converted to Christianity, Constantine considered himself head of the church. He called the first Ecumenical Council at Nicaea to fight against the Arian heresy. It was in the reign of Theodosios I that Catholicism became a true state religion. Contrary to common belief, the Late Empire was not a 'decadent' period; in the field of philosophy and the arts one might more accurately speak of a 'Constantino-Theodosian Renaissance'. On the death of Theodosios, the Empire was split into two. Ravenna became the capital in the west and Constantinople capital of the East. At the end of the fourth century, under pressure from the Huns – a Turco-Mongol people – the barbarians moved west in successive waves. Iranian nomads, Sarmatae and Alans were among the first, followed by the Goths. The Visigoth people requested asylum from the Emperor Valens in 376 and crossed the Danube. Two years later the Gothic cavalry defeated the Roman army at Adrianople and Valens was killed. The Visigoths dispersed about the Empire and captured Rome in 410. The fall of the Eternal City sent a shock wave through the Christian world, though Augustine did seek to reassure the faithful with his *City of God* (413–26). The Visigoths finally settled, with imperial authorization, in southern Gaul and Spain. Alans, Suebi and Vandals, who had crossed the Rhine in 406, passed through Gaul and Spain. Under the leadership of Genseric, the Vandals continued their advance into Africa. When he had conquered Carthage, the great grain exporting port, King Genseric persecuted the Catholics. Attila's Huns, who had settled in the Danube Basin, invaded the West in 451. They were unable to take either Paris, which was defended by Genevieve, or Orleans, and were finally defeated by Aetius and his barbarian soldiers at the Campus Mauriacus (near Troyes). Attila attempted to invade Italy in 452, but, yielding to the entreaties of Pope Leo the Great, he declined to advance south of Mantua.

In the second half of the century, the barbarian peoples formed themselves into political units. The Burgundi settled between Langres and Avignon in Sapaudia (origin of the modern 'Savoy'). The Angles, Jutes and Saxons invaded Britain and forced the Celts back to the west. The Visigoths extended the area of their domination from the Loire to southern Spain. Veritable playthings of the barbarian princes, the emperors succeeded one another rapidly at Ravenna until Odoacer decided to put an end to the fiction by taking the place of the last emperor, Romulus Augustulus, and by sending the imperial insignia back to Constantinople, a symbolic gesture which spectacularly sealed the refound unity of the Empire.

*1. Diptych of the consul Boethius. Ivory carving, 5th century.*

**Diocletian's monetary reforms.** — **294**

**Council of Nicaea.** — **325**

**St Martin becomes bishop of Tours.** — **371**

**Death of Augustine at Hippo.** — **430**

**284–305:** Reign of Diocletian. Maximian is nominated to serve alongside him in 287 (dyarchy). Constantius Chlorus and Galerius proclaimed Caesars in 193 (tetrarchy). He reorganized the tax system (297: first revision of the fiscal assessment or *indictio*) and controlled prices (*Maximum* edict, 301). In 303 he resolved to persecute the Christians and ultimately abdicated with Maximian in 305. Diocletian retired to his palace at Salonae (Split).
**306–37:** Reign of Constantine, son of Constantius Chlorus. He triumphed over his rivals and in 312 won the Battle of Pons Mulvius (Ponte Molle).
**313:** Edict of tolerance towards the Christians. 314: Council of Arles; 46 Western bishops meet – including two from London and York. In 325 Constantine calls the Council of Nicaea. In 330 he founds the new city of Constantinople. Pope Sylvester I, who has been given the Lateran Palace, dies in 335.
**337–64:** Constantine's successors come up against the Arian problem. Wulfila is made a bishop in 341 and converts the Goths to Arianism. 355: The Alamanni and the Franks invade Gaul. 357–359; Three councils meet at Sirmium. In 360, St Martin founds Licugé, the first Western monastery. Julian the Apostate reigns between 361 and 363 and attempts to restore paganism.
**364–78:** Valentinian I and Valens divide up the Empire. In 370 the Huns arrive on the Don. The Visigoths cross the Danube in 376 and win a victory at Adrianople in 378. In 382 they will be considered as foederati in Lower Moesia.
**379–95:** Reign of Theodosios I in the East. Later, ruler of the whole Empire. The Second Ecumenical Council meets at Constantinople in 381. The pagan temples are closed down in 391.
**395–450:** Reign of Arcadius and his son Theodosios II in the East. Invasions of the Germanic tribes in the West. The barbarians cross the Rhine in 406 and the Visigoth, Alaric, takes Rome. Gallia Placidia, sister of Honorius, the second son of Theodosios, having been taken hostage, marries Ataulf in 413; the Visigoths are legally settled as foederati in the south-west of Gaul. Genseric's Vandals take Hippo, St Augustine's city, in 431, then Carthage in 439. They sack Rome in 455. Aëtius governs the Western Roman Empire from 434 to 454 in the name of Valentian III. He allows the Burgundi to settle in Sapaudia, the Alans on the Loire. He fights back the Franks. Attila is beaten in 451 by Aëtius and his barbarian auxiliaries. 452: Attila fails in northern Italy. He dies in 453 and his 'empire' falls apart. Aëtius is assassinated in 454 and Valentinian III in 455.
**455–76:** The Visigoth Theodoric II as Avitus proclaimed emperor. Marjorian is the last great emperor (457–61). Ricimer, from the Suebi, has real power over the emperors until 472. The Frank Childeric governs the north of Gaul at the request of the Roman general Aegidius. Euric, the Visigoth, becomes chief at Narbonne (470), then in the Auvergne. The Christians are persecuted. 472: The Burgundian Gundobad in power at Lyons. He imposes Glycerius as emperor in 473. Orestes, Attila's former adviser, installs his son Romulus Augustulus as emperor. Odoacer re-establishes the unity of the Empire in 476.

*3. Bronze colossus at Barletta in Apulia.*

# 3rd–5th centuries

2. Chariot race in the Constantinople hippodrome. Ivory panel, c. 450.

| odosian Code. | Sidonius Apollinaris becomes bishop of Clermont. |
|---|---|
| 50 | 470 |

ecorated bronze belt buckles from a prince's tomb, 5th tury.

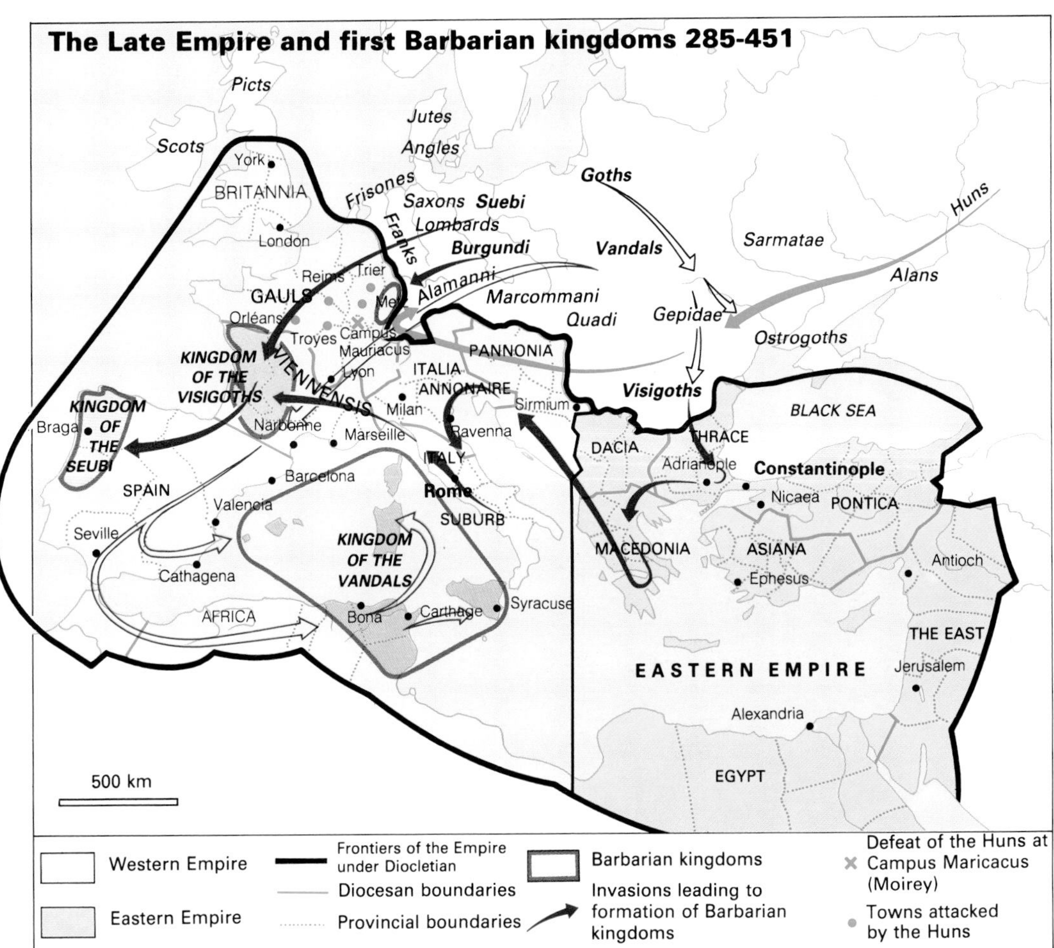


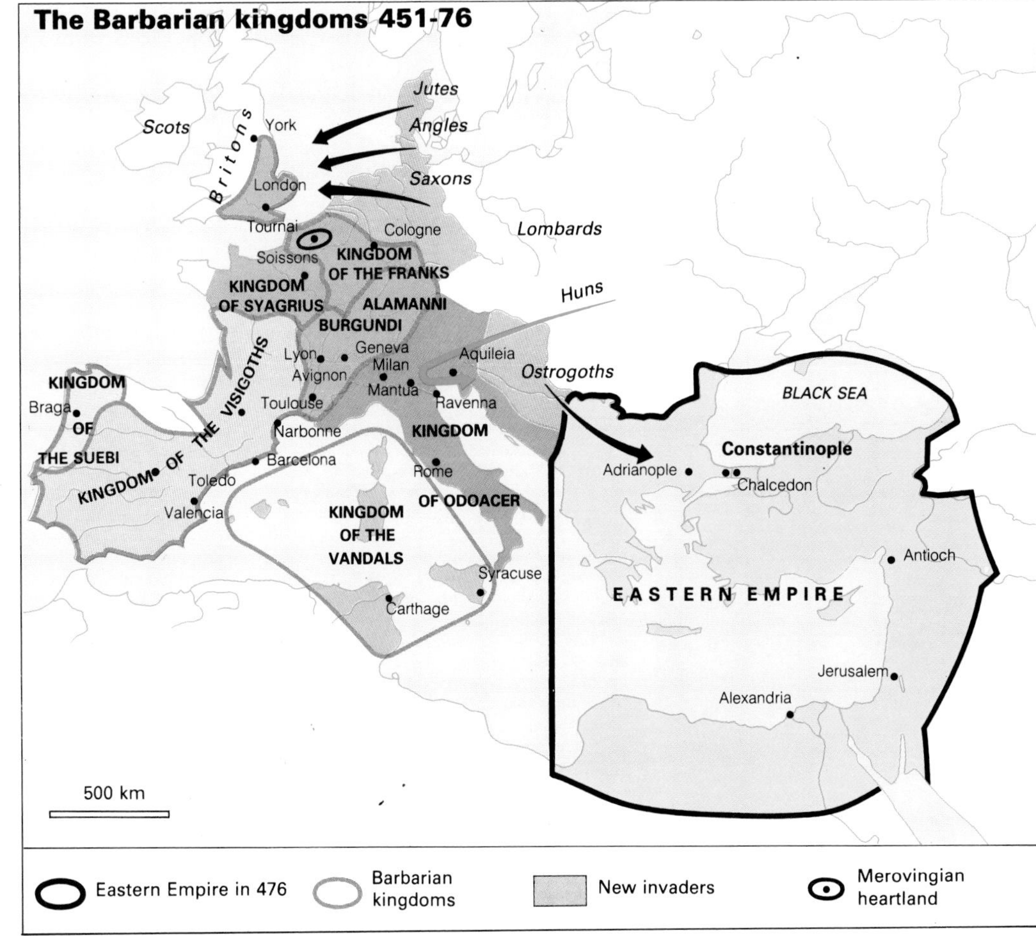

# Iran and Central Asia: Between Two Worlds

*1. Royal hunt. Silver dish of the Sassanian period. c. 500.*

AT THE END of the third century BC western Iran was under the control of the Arsacid Parthians, while the east was ruled by the Graeco-Bactrian sovereigns. Later the Kushan Empire appeared, from its centre in Kabul, linking Central Asia to India. If it is particularly remembered for its coinage, this is because its trade in precious goods flourished, especially with the Romans. Two centuries of peace under the Kushans enabled Afghanistan to become urbanized and also allowed the expansion of Buddhism and a flourishing of Graeco-Buddhist art, known as Gandhara, which combined local themes with Greek techniques and which became predominant in India and Asia as far as China.

It fell to the Sassanian Ardashir to re-found an Iranian empire based on Ctesiphon, which brought together Iran, Afghanistan and Mesopotamia. The latter was almost constantly at war with the Roman and Byzantine Empires; similarly the Iranians and the Romans (the Persian word for Roman – *roumi* – is the origin of the Arabic word for 'European') fought over northern Mesopotamia and Armenia. In the east, Iran was invaded first by the Hepthalite Huns and then the Oghuz Turks and lost the former Kushan region in the fifth century. In the end, neither the maintenance of the Arab vassal kingdom of Hira nor the Iranian presence on both shores of the Persian Gulf could prevent the Arabo-Muslim campaign of conquest in the seventh century.

Centralized state control, an objective of the first Sassanian kings, was only achieved under Khosrow I. By supporting the lesser gentry against the upper aristocracy, and by setting fixed rates of taxation and establishing a coherent legal system, he brought the Empire to the height of its power and laid the political and economic foundations for the Umayyad and Abbasid Empires. Art flourished in this period, with the accent on character and essential forms rather than on elements situated in a specific time or place; this was a period of Iranian artistic rebirth in which symbolic values and the search for new decorative forms combined in the celebration of an eternal glory.

Zoroastrianism became the state religion and its clergy, the magi, wielded enormous power. Whilst in Iran, the Avesta was being written down in a language which by that time was already dead, but certain parts of which had been preserved in the oral tradition for more than a thousand years, in Babylon the Jews, who formed an ancient and stable community, were writing the Talmud, which extolled the virtues of rabbinical discipline and study. However, the stringencies of the Zoroastrian ritual and a sense of social injustice led the Iranian Mazdak to found a new religion in which the victory of good over evil would be achieved by the redistribution of wealth. Though popular, the movement was brutally suppressed.

The Sogdians, who were still independent from the Iranian kingdom, continued to conduct trade between China and the West through the towns of Samarkand, Bukhara and Pendzhikent, providing a means of circumventing the taxes the Sassanians imposed in the sixth century on caravans passing through their territory. Though they founded no state, they were the ambassadors of the Turks to the Byzantine Empire, importers of wine into China, and they also supplied believers to all the religions of the age, especially to their own form of Zoroastrianism that was less strict and less priest-dominated than that of Iran. Their art bears the stamp of Iranian, Chinese and Indian influences.

The culture of Iran, Afghanistan and of the Russian Tadzhiks has its roots in these centuries. It is a many-faceted culture with its own distinctive place in the Islamic world.

| 130 BC | AD 78? | 14th April 216 | 224 | 488 |
|---|---|---|---|---|
| Yüeh-chih invasions. | Kaniska. | Birth of Mani. | Ardashir I, founder of the Sassanian dynasty. | Kavadh I. |

*2. Shapur I defeats the Emperor Valerian. Carving at Naqsh-i Roustem, c. 265.*

**130 BC:** Saka (Scythians) and Yüeh-chih lay waste the Hellenized regions of Bactria and India and settle there.
**AD 20–200?:** Kushan Empire; reaches its peak in the reign of Kaniska (78?–120?). He initiates the *saka* system of dating still in use in India today and builds Purusapura (Peshawar).
**224–40:** Ardashir I defeats the last Parthian king: it is probably during his reign that eastern Iran (the former Kushan kingdom) is conquered.
**240–72:** Empire grows and is strengthened under Shapur I. Valerian, the Roman Emperor, is taken prisoner in 259 and works at Shushtar on the Karun dam, which is still known today as 'Caesar's dam'.
**270:** The Mani religion takes root in Iran.
**273–6:** Under Bahram I and Karter, the most influential magus, a Zoroastrian reaction sets in. The prophet is executed and his followers isolated.
**309–79:** Shapur II. During his reign the Roman Empire and Armenia are converted to Christianity. The borders with the Byzantines are bitterly disputed. The Iranian Christians are seen as internal enemies until 484, when the Iranian Nestorian Church is founded (it is independent of Byzantium).
**313:** Tün Huang's letters show that the Sogdians were in western China.
**5th century:** Royal power weakened in Iran: nobility and clergy elect the kings. Situation stable in the west. In the east, the Hepthalite Huns appear and the Iranians are forced to pay tribute to them around the middle of the century.
**488–531:** Kavadh I ascends the throne, thanks to the Huns, uses the Mazdakites against the nobles and re-establishes the power of the monarchy.
**531–79:** Khosrow I Anushirvan ('of the immortal soul'). He defeats the Huns and welcomes the Neo-Platonists to Ctesiphon when Justinian closes the Academy in Athens in 529. The Persians claim (wrongly) that he invented the game of chess, though 'check mate' is indeed the English version of a Persian expression meaning 'the king is dead'. Regarded as both good and wise, he was the model pre-Islamic ruler.
**565:** Oghuz Turkish Empire founded in the

*3. Horse's head in gilded silver, 4th-century Sassanian art.*

# 130 BC–AD 751

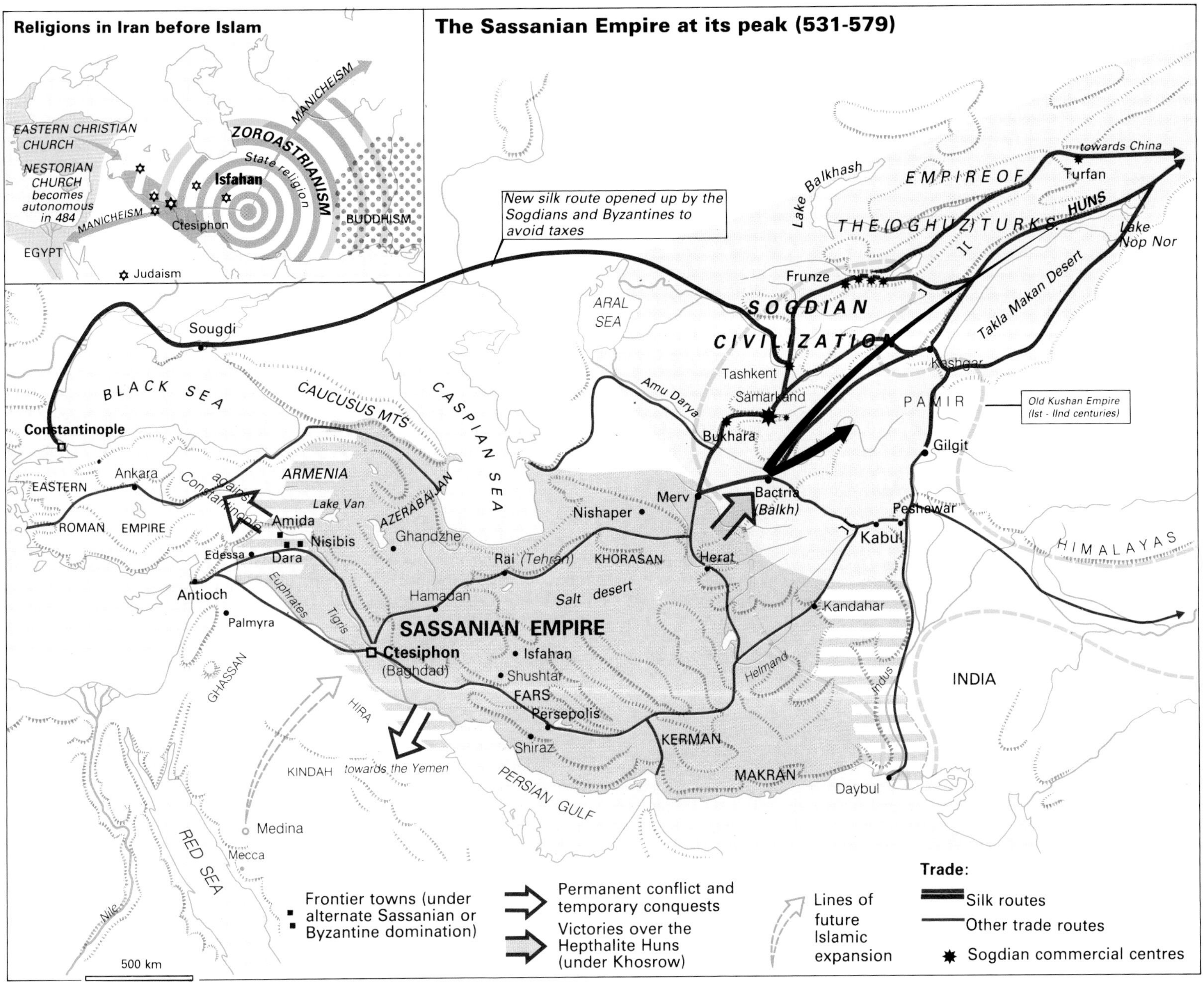

**Religions in Iran before Islam**

EASTERN CHRISTIAN CHURCH
NESTORIAN CHURCH becomes autonomous in 484
MANICHEISM
ZOROASTRIANISM State religion
Isfahan
Ctesiphon
BUDDHISM
EGYPT
✡ Judaism

**The Sassanian Empire at its peak (531-579)**

New silk route opened up by the Sogdians and Byzantines to avoid taxes

Sougdi, BLACK SEA, Constantinople, Ankara, EASTERN ROMAN EMPIRE, CAUCUSUS MTS, ARMENIA, Lake Van, AZERABAIJAN, against Constantinople, Amida, Nisibis, Edessa, Dara, Antioch, Palmyra, Euphrates, Tigris, GHASSAN, HIRA, KINDAH, towards the Yemen, Medina, Mecca, RED SEA, Nile, CASPIAN SEA, ARAL SEA, Ghandzhe, Rai (Tehran), Hamadan, SASSANIAN EMPIRE, Ctesiphon (Baghdad), Isfahan, Shushtar, FARS, Persepolis, Shiraz, PERSIAN GULF, KERMAN, MAKRAN, Salt desert, KHORASAN, Nishaper, Merv, Herat, Helmand, Kandahar, Amu Darya, Bukhara, Samarkand, Tashkent, SOGDIAN CIVILIZATION, Frunze, Lake Balkhash, EMPIRE OF THE (OGHUZ) TURKS, HUNS, Turfan, towards China, Lake Nop Nor, Takla Makan Desert, Kashgar, PAMIR, Old Kushan Empire (Ist - IInd centuries), Gilgit, Bactria (Balkh), Kabul, Peshawar, HIMALAYAS, Indus, INDIA, Daybul

▪ Frontier towns (under alternate Sassanian or Byzantine domination)

Permanent conflict and temporary conquests

Victories over the Hepthalite Huns (under Khosrow)

Lines of future Islamic expansion

**Trade:**

Silk routes

Other trade routes

✸ Sogdian commercial centres

500 km

**Khosrow I.** **Fall of Samarkand.**

4. *Boddhisattva.*

steppes of Asia and Sogdiana: the Sogdian merchant Maniakh is sent as Turkish ambassador to Byzantium. A new silk route is opened and a Sogdian trading post is opened on the Black Sea at Sougdi, which, in years to come, will be one of Marco Polo's ports of call.

**591–628:** Khosrow II Parviz ('the victorious') leads lightning campaigns in Asia Minor, Syria and Egypt. While he is away, the Byzantine Emperor Heraclius sacks Ctesiphon (627).

**628–36:** Five sovereigns, including Queen Boran, succeed one another. The last of them, Yazdegerd III, loses the Battle of al-Qadisiyah against the Arabs and is assassinated in 651 during his flight to the east.

**650:** Sogdiana under the nominal protectorate of Tang China and the mercantile oligarchies of Pendzhikent prosper. However, the country is ravaged by the Arabs in 712–22. The Sogdians appeal in vain for China to come to their aid. Victory of the Arabs over the Chinese in 751 at the Battle of the Talas. The Abbasid caliphate effectively takes control of Sogdiana.

5. *The preaching of the Buddha. Fresco at Qizil, Hsin-hsiang, influenced by Sogdian art, c. 600.*

6. *Episode in the life of the Buddha. Graeco-Buddhist art, Paitava.*

# The Barbarian Kingdoms of Europe

THE BARBARIAN KINGDOMS took shape during the sixth century, but were very different from north to south. In Britain, pagan Anglo-Saxon states were established. In Gaul, the Franks under Clovis, the son of Childeric, advanced from Tournai to Soissons, where Syagrius, 'the last of the Roman rulers', was defeated, then to Paris and the Rhine. Clovis, the first barbarian king to be baptized according to Catholic ritual, defeated the Arian Visigoths at Vouillé before being recognized as king by the Eastern Emperor. His sons completed the conquest of Gaul with the occupation of the Kingdom of Burgundy and of Provence. But the Germanic influence was still dominant, and resulted in the Kingdom of the Franks being partitioned into Neustria, Austrasia, Burgundy, and Aquitaine, the last of these being the most Romanized area. In the barbarian kingdoms on the Mediterranean, Roman influence was maintained. Theodoric the Ostrogoth won Italy from Odoacer and surrounded himself with Roman senators, like Cassiodorus and Boethius. But the barbarian kings were Arians, the result of which was that the Eastern Emperor Justinian decided to reconquer the western kingdoms. He retook Carthage, and took control of Italy after twenty years of war and settled his representative in Ravenna. Italy, which was ruined, fell to the Lombards in 568. The Visigoths resisted and made Toledo their capital. Justinian was able to repossess only the south of Spain. The Arian Leovigild, king of the Visigoths, dreamed of bringing about religious and political unity in the Iberian peninsula. He subjugated the Basques and founded Vitoria. But when his son Recared abandoned Arianism and became a convert to Catholicism in 587, a new era in the history of Spain began. In Italy, the Middle Ages began with the Lombard invasion. These Arian barbarians settled in northern Italy, in Spoleto and Benevento, while the Roman Empire retained only the Tiber valley, Ravenna, the coast and islands. Pope Gregory the Great, the first monk to be pope, was caught between the Byzantines and the Lombards whom he hoped to convert to Catholicism. He decided to convert the pagan Anglo-Saxons, and the conditions of religious and cultural life in the West were to be profoundly altered as a consequence. During the same period, Celtic monks settled in Gaul. In Spain, the Catholic kings drove out the Byzantines and took control of a prosperous kingdom. St Isidore, the Bishop of Seville, gave his name to a kind of 'Renaissance'. In Gaul, Chlotar II and Dagobert I re-established the unity of the kingdom. The Irish monks restored religious life. But after 639 the kingdom was partitioned once again, and the aristocracy, controlled by the mayors of the palace, held power. Over this period the Byzantine Empire was being attacked on all sides: in Italy by the Lombards, in the Balkans by the Slavs, and in particular by the Arabs, who left them holding only Asia Minor. In addition, religious issues set the emperors at odds with the papacy. At the beginning of the eighth century Arabs and Berbers from North Africa invaded Spain, drove the Goths back as far as the Asturias and tried to enter Gaul. But the Austrasian mayors of the palace re-established their authority in the Kingdom of the Franks. Charles Martel triumphed over the aristocrats and the neighbouring barbarian peoples. His sons Pepin III and Carloman reigned in the name of the Merovingian kings and, with St Boniface, reformed the Frankish Church. The popes, who were increasingly threatened by the Lombards and were opposed to the religious policy of the emperors, turned to the West and to the Franks.

*1. Visigoth manuscript illustrating an episode from the life of Moses. 7th century.*

| **Baptism of Clovis.** | **Rule of St Benedict.** | **Luxeuil founded by Columban.** | **The Venerable Bede retires to the Monastery of St Paul in Jar** |
|---|---|---|---|
| 498 | 534 | 590 | 685 |

**481–511:** Reign of Clovis, the son of Childeric I. 486: Victory at Soissons. 494: Clovis comes to the assistance of the Rhenish Franks attacked by the Alamanni at Zülpich (Tolbiac). Under the influence of the Burgundian Princess Clotilda, Clovis becomes a convert to Catholicism, and is baptized in Reims by Bishop Remigius. He defeats the Arian Visigoths (under Alaric II) at Vouillé in 507 and calls a Church Council at Orleans in 511 to reorganize the Church of the Gauls.

*4. Merovingian eagles in cloisonné enamel. End of the 5th century.*

**493–526:** Reign of Theodoric, the Ostrogoth king, who restores Italy, builds churches and allies himself with the Vandal, Burgundian and Visigoth princes. In 508–9 he prevents Clovis from reaching the Mediterranean coast. In 523 he breaks with the Emperor. Boethius is condemned and executed in 524. **527–65:** Reign of Justinian I. 533: Vandal North Africa is reconquered in an effort to come to the aid of the persecuted Catholic community. 536: Belisarius recaptures Naples, then Rome. 538: The Ostrogoth Witiges lays a year-long siege to Rome. 540: Ravenna is captured. 543–6: The Ostrogoth King Totila retakes Naples, then Rome. 552: Totila is defeated and killed. Italy is rebuilt as a result of the promulgation by Justinian of the *Pragmatic Sanction* (13 August 554). 555: The Ostrogoths capitulate. The Byzantines take southern Spain. Toledo becomes the Visigoth capital.
**568:** The Lombards, pressed by the Avars from Pannonia, invade Italy. Pavia is captured in 569–72. The Byzantines set up the Exarchate of Ravenna in 584. Benedictine monks from Monte Cassino arrive in Rome.

**590–604:** Gregory I, 'the servant of the servants of God', is pope. Rome is besieged by the Lombards. 600: The Slavs attack Salona. 601: Recared, the first Catholic Visigoth king, dies. 605: Augustine of Canterbury, who had been given the task of evangelizing the Anglo-Saxons by Gregory the Great, dies.
**610–41:** Reign of the Eastern Emperor Heraclius. 613: King Chlotar II has sole power in the Frankish kingdom. 614: The Irish monk Columban founds the monastery at Bobbio with the help of Agilulf. 626: The Avars lay siege to Constantinople. 629: The Byzantines are driven out of Spain. 633: Bishop Isidore of Seville presides over the Fourth Council of Toledo, and dies in 636.
**629–39:** Reign of Dagobert I. He embarks on campaigns against the Basques, the Bretons and the Slavs. 632: Death of the prophet Mahomet. 634: Start of the Arab conquests. 636: Heraclius is defeated at the Battle of the Yarmuk River.
**641–68:** Constant II becomes Eastern Emperor. 643 sees the Edict of the Lombard king Rothari, which codifies Lombard customs. 650: Founding of Saint-Wandrille and Nivelles. 653: The Lombards convert to Catholicism. Pope Martin I is deported to Constantinople. 654: Foundation of Jumièges. 663–79: Struggles break out between Léger, the aristocratic Bishop of Autun, and the mayor of the palace, Ebroin.
**687–751:** The Merovingian mayors of the palace govern Gaul. 711: The Arabs defeat the Visigoths at the Rio Guadalete. 714: Pepin II of Herstal dies. 718: Pelayo defeats the Arabs at Covadonga. 732: Battle of Poitiers.
**715–44:** Conflicts break out between the popes Gregory II, then Gregory III, the Lombard king Liudprand and the Byzantine Emperor, Leo III. The Lombards make further inroads. The Iconoclastic Controversy begins.
**735–51:** Anglo-Saxon monks are sent as missionaries to Frisia and Germania. 735: The Venerable Bede dies. Councils of reform are held. 744: Founding of the monastery at Fulda. 751: Ravenna captured by Aistulf the Lombard. Pepin III, the Short, becomes king.

# 5th–8th centuries

2. Apsidal chapel in Venasque (Vaucluse). An example of Christian art in the 7th century.

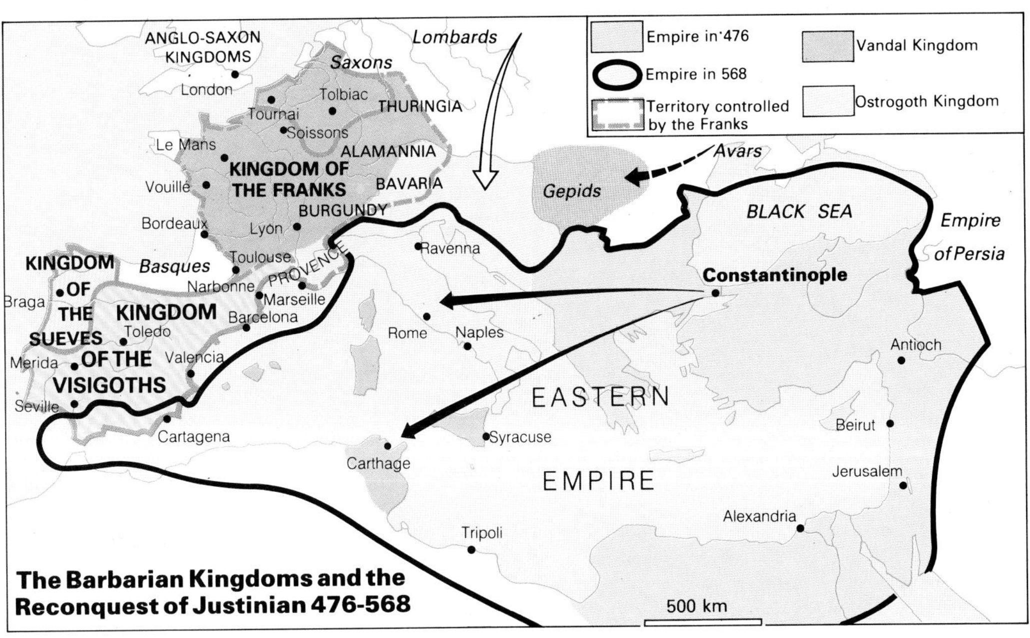

3. Inlay of a Lombard shield in the form of a horseman. Gilt moulded bronze, 7th century.

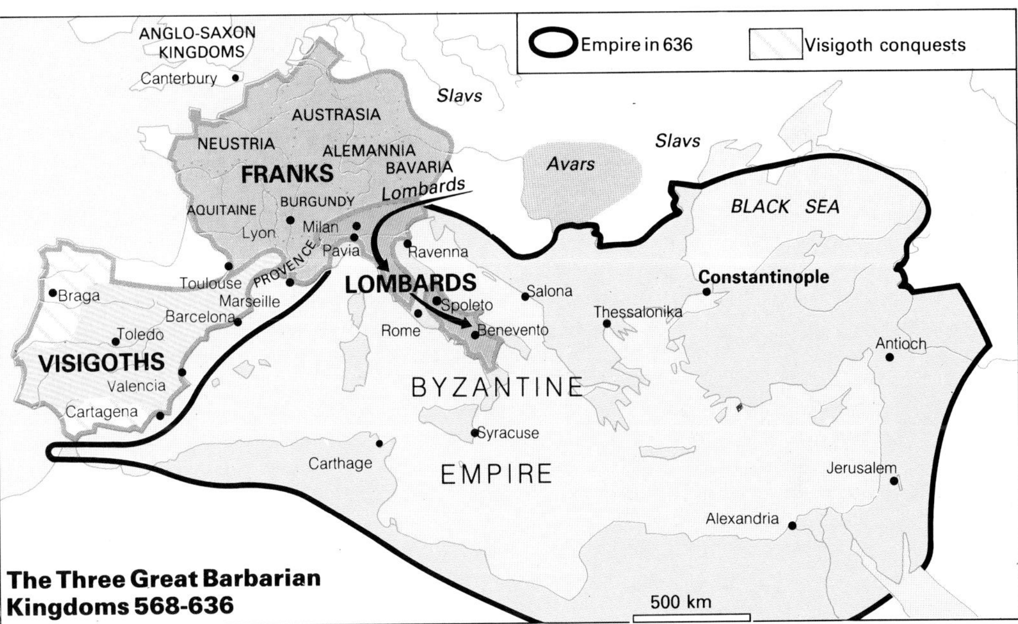


**Ravenna captured by the Lombards.**

**751**

5. Ornamentation from the helmet belonging to Agilulf, the 7th-century Lombard king.

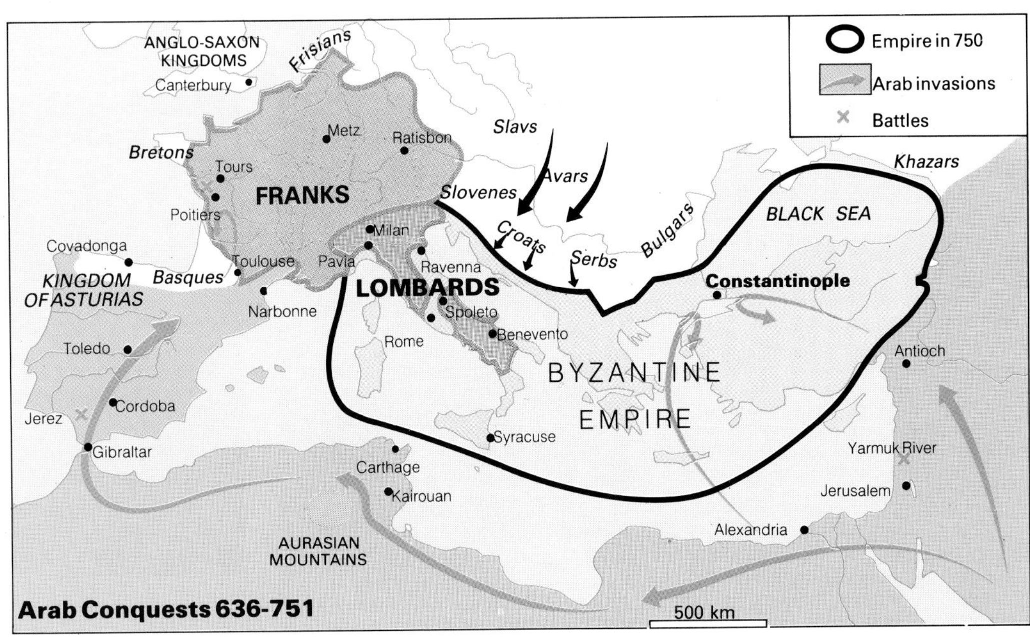

# Constantinople and the Byzantine Empire

1. A naval battle illustrates a Greek manuscript of the 11th century.

THE TRANSFER of the Roman capital to Constantinople in 330 was a sign of the Emperor Constantine's desire to reunite the western and eastern parts of the Empire, which had been effectively divided by Diocletian in 286. In spite of such attempts at unification, the distance between east and west continued to grow.

Constantinople was 'the new Rome'. As the phrase suggests, the Byzantine Empire was thus founded under a dual impetus, on the one hand towards continuity and on the other, change. Though Byzantium inherited a territory whose boundaries were continually changing as a result of invasion, the same theoretical frontiers were always claimed by the emperors. It thought of itself as the inheritor of the Roman Empire (its emperor would always bear the title 'Emperor of the Romans'), which indeed it was in terms of its institutions, even though these underwent some transformation over the centuries. The Byzantine state was based upon a strictly hierarchical central administration, which lasted in an effective form into the thirteenth century. Social exchanges were regulated by Roman law, which was recognized and taught throughout the Empire. A healthy level of monetary circulation made for an active economy. Byzantium derived profit both from its gold reserves and its role as intermediary in the East-West trade in luxury goods. From the reign of Constantinople onwards, it imposed upon its subjects the use of its gold currency, which remained stable right up to the eleventh century and became the standard currency of Mediterranean commerce.

Here the Roman legacy ends, for it was its Hellenistic culture, rather than its institutions, which gave Byzantium its unity. In the seventh century the Empire consisted of all the Greek-speaking territories under the emperor's rule. Greek, which was the language of culture for the Oriental elites, and which after Justinian became the language of administration, was also, most importantly, the language of the Eastern Christians. The Hellenistic tradition (Byzantium was never to reject the heritage of secular Greek culture) and the language of the Gospels and the liturgy gave the diverse peoples who made up the Empire an identity which at a very early stage was formed by setting itself against the Western and barbarian worlds. This opposition is emphasized in the organization of the church. The church was modelled on the administrative structures of the Empire, which led to ecclesiastical jurisdiction being split between east and west. Byzantium's loss of its western territories after the Teutonic invasions led the bishops of Rome, as early as the fourth century, to claim independence from the temporal power. In the east, by contrast, the imperial power over the church became more precise. Theodosios I made Christianity the state religion. From that point onwards, the internal history of Byzantium merges with that of Christianity. The Eastern Orthodox Church, which was more conservative that its Roman counterpart, would seek to preserve the tradition of the original Christian church, a tradition expressed in its forms of worship and liturgy. It therefore resisted the theological innovations introduced in Rome. Right up to the twelfth century there would be many political and theological disputes between the two churches, without the unity of the Christian faith being compromised. It was a political crisis – the diversion of the Crusades on to Constantinople and the conquest of that city by the Westerners – that was to make the division irreversible.

**Definitive division of Eastern and Western Empires.** **395**

**Collapse of the Persian Empire.** **628**

**Arab attack on Constantinople.** **674–8**

**330:** Constantine inaugurates the new capital, giving it his own name. Constantinople develops on the site of the old Hellenistic town of Byzantium. The fortifications built by the emperors will make Constantinople impregnable for many years. Situated at the junction of many East-West trade routes, Constantinople enjoys enormous economic prosperity; it will be the greatest town in the medieval world (almost 500,000 inhabitants in the 6th century).
**337–518:** The Empire is threatened by the Huns and the Teutons, whom the emperors divert, by conceding territories and tribute, towards the West. Between 410 and 493, Italy, Gaul, Spain and North Africa are lost. But the oriental territories remain intact.
**518–610:** The Emperor Justinian (527–65) reconquers North Africa, Sicily, southern Spain and the great Italian cities. But he ruins the Empire and leaves its eastern front exposed. His successors, attacked in the east by the Persians and by the Slavs and the Avars (a Turko-Mongol people) on the Danube, abandon Italy. Byzantine civilization is at its height at this point. Roman law and jurisprudence are enshrined in the *Justinian Code*.
**537:** Building of Hagia Sophia completed: this domed edifice is a fine example of Byzantine architecture. The mosaics at Ravenna mark the birth of a new figurative style.
**610–717:** Heraclius (610–41) and his successors have difficulty defending the Empire. The Persians are contained, but the Slavs cross the Danube. The Bulgars set up a powerful kingdom in Thrace. The Arabs conquer Syria, Egypt, Palestine and North Africa. Though halted before Constantinople in 677, they remain a threat.
**717–867:** The Empire is reduced to Greece and Asia Minor. It is shaken by a deep religious crisis. Outbreak of iconoclasm (or the destruction of images). This is in keeping with oriental sensibility which sees representations of the divinity as a form of idolatry. The emperors, who are natives of Asia Minor, support the movement from inner conviction and also to detach the eastern provinces from Arab influence. They are supported by the higher clergy (the

*2. The central nave of Hagia Sophia, Constantinople, 6th century. Lamps and coat of arms from the Ottoman period.*

*3. Capital and mosaic from St Vitale, Ravenna, 6th century.*

# 330–1057

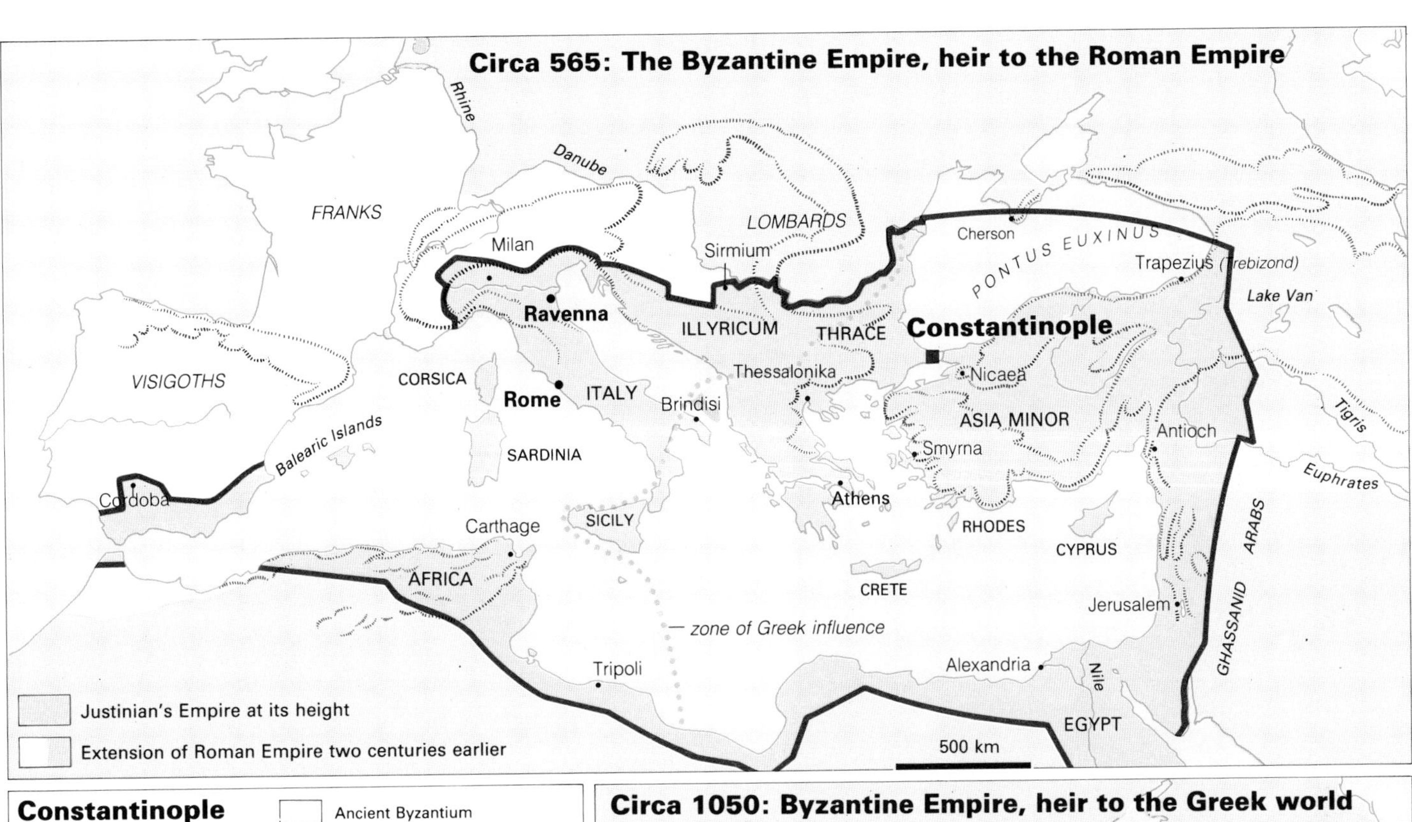


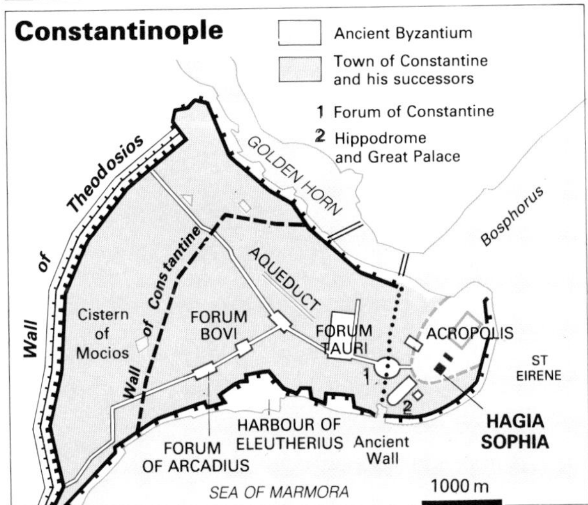

**Beginning of the Iconoclastic Controversy.**

**726**

**Eastern Church's first break with Rome.**

**867**

**Constantinople's second break with Rome.**

**1054**

councils of 730 and 754 forbid the worship of images) but opposed by the monks whose possessions they seek to confiscate. The worship of images is restored in 843.
**867–1057:** With the descendants of Basil I (867–86) in power, the idea of the family as a source of political legitimacy develops. The 'Macedonian' emperors conquer Syria, Crete and Cyprus. Armenia is subjugated. In the West, Byzantium establishes a foothold in southern Italy. In 1014, Bulgaria has to bow to Byzantine rule. The new economic prosperity is paralleled by a remarkable burgeoning of cultural activity (legislative writings of the emperors, flowering of humanist culture, etc.).

*4. Imperial Quadriga, silk and gold, Constantinople, 8th century.*

*5. Scenes of pastoral and farm life. Illustration from an 11th-century manuscript, Constantinople.*

*6. The baptism of Christ. Mosaic at St Luke's Monastery, Phocis, c. 1050.*

# From Arab Conquest to Islamic Empire

THE ARAB CONQUESTS were the direct product of the preaching of Muhammad (Mohammed). In his teachings, monotheistic revelation is accompanied by exaltation of a way of life based on warrior virtues. The Quran (Koran), God's word, says precisely this: the sincere believer is the warrior, the one who accepts exile, and the spoils of war shall be his viaticum. These conquests, which Islam needed if it was to survive beyond its early years, proceeded swiftly. When Muhammad died in 632, western Arabia was under his control. The caliphs who followed him as leaders of the true believers roved far and wide in their campaigns of conquest, sweeping aside the Sassanian kingdom and amputating the Syrian and Egyptian provinces from the Byzantine Empire. The Arab advance, which slowed under 'Ali, quickened again under the Umayyads: in 711 the Berber Tariq ibn Ziyad entered Spain and the following year Hajjaj's troops advanced up the Indus as far as Multan.

This sweep of conquest was blocked by some effective resistance put up by opposing armies and populations, especially by the Berbers and the Byzantines, who sealed off the north of Syria against them. It was also disrupted by internal conflicts: a model of a closed community of equal warriors was set against one based on a spiritual hierarchy. The origin of the various Muslim sects (Kharijites, Shi'ites etc.), these two models constituted, broadly, the two poles between which the Islam of the first centuries oscillated, without really settling on any one solution and without confronting the problems of caliphal power and the status of converts.

The pattern of Arabs stationed in garrisons levying tribute was fast disappearing. At the end of the seventh century some converts joined the army, others entered the administrative service of their conquerors. In the following century conversions were carried out on a much greater scale and increasingly in country areas. The regions under Islamic rule were not so much occupied as administered, and were so in a way that took account of the local cultures, whether Persian, Syrian or Coptic. A nascent system of law aimed at unifying all the conquered lands, whilst the science of geography developed to provide a conceptual grasp of the different regions.

Under the Umayyads (660–750) an empire was built, though it was one in which control of territory by the arts of war was replaced by submission to the divine order. Among its first acts were the choice of ancient Damascus as capital (far from the sanctuary of Mecca) and Arabic as the official language. They also began minting their own coinage and introduced a new division of the provinces along military lines. The garrisons were moved into the towns, where they grew rapidly (at Kufa, Basra, Fustat, Kairouan etc.). What is known as the Abbasid 'Golden Age' (middle of eighth to middle of ninth centuries) was characterized, in spite of the disturbances which occurred at the time, by a gigantic siphoning off of levied goods towards a few metropolises, where mosques, palaces and canals were constructed. In these centres the Greeks were translated. The authority of the caliph was both divine and human in its essence; this meant that he embodied the cohesiveness of the community and guaranteed the application of the law. However, the forces which provided the Islamic state's strength in the provinces were also its undoing: in the ninth century the governors became autonomous and founded local dynasties, first on the margins of the Empire, then later at its centre. The demands of the leaders of the Turkish warriors became more pressing, as did those of the jurists and doctors of the law (*'ulama*), who sought a share in the heritage of the prophetic mission. From the tenth century on, other caliphates, including the Fatimids in the Eastern Maghreb (909) and the Umayyad caliphate of Cordoba (929) competed with that of the Abbasids.

*1. The Great Mosque of Cordoba with its nineteen naves, each with a double layer of vaults. 8th–10th centuries.*

| Hijra. | Capture of Syria. | 'Ali becomes caliph. | Arabs land in Spain. | Defeat at Poitiers. |
|---|---|---|---|---|
| 622 | 633 | 656 | 711 | 732 |

**622:** Flight (Hijra or Hegira) of the prophet Muhammad and his followers from Mecca to Yathrib (Medina): beginning of the Hegiran era.
**624:** Victory of Muhammad's troops over the Meccans at Badr.
**632:** Death of Muhammad: Abu Bakr becomes caliph (successor).
**634:** Beginning of the caliphate of 'Umar.
**636:** Victory in the Battle of the Yarmuk over the Byzantines; Arab settlement in Syria.
**637:** Capture of al-Qadasiyah on the Euphrates and sack of the Sassanian capital Ctesiphon.
**640:** 'Amr ibn al-'As enters Egypt. Fustat founded.
**642:** Capture and sack of Alexandria; victory at Nehavand which opens up the Iranian plateau.
**644–56:** Caliphate of 'Uthman: conquest of Khorasan, Kirman and, in the west, of Cyrenaica.
**656:** Controversial choice of 'Ali, son-in-law of the Prophet, as caliph: civil war.
**660:** Mu'awiyah, the Umayyad governor of Syria, proclaims himself caliph and takes up residence at Damascus.
**661:** Assassination of 'Ali.
**670:** Conquest of Ifriqiya (Eastern Maghreb). Kairouan founded.
**680:** Death of Mu'awiyah: his son Yazid succeeds him; al-Husayn, second son of 'Ali and Fatima is killed at Karbala.
**685–705:** Caliphate of Abd al-Malik: supported by the remarkable governor of Iraq, Hajjaj, he creates an Arabized administration and divides the provinces into military districts under Syrian control.
**711–14:** In the west, Tariq ibn Ziyad enters Spain: conquest of Cordoba and of the Visigothic kingdom of Toledo; in the east, the Indus is reached.
**732:** The Arabs are defeated by Charles Martel at Poitiers.
**744–50:** Revolt of Arab settlers and converts in the Khorasan: this will bring the Abbasids (another branch of the Prophet's family) to the office of caliph.
**750:** Caliph Marwan II is killed. Abu al-Abbas as-Saffah takes over power.
**756:** Umayyad amirate of Cordoba.
**762:** Abbasid capital of Baghdad founded.

*2. From Byzantium to Islam: façade of the Umayyad mosque, Damascus, 8th century.*

**777:** Beginning of the first regional Islamic dynasty, the Rustamids of central Maghreb.
**786–809:** Caliphate of the colourful Harun ar-Rashid.
**821:** Beginning of the Tahirid dynasty in the Khorasan.
**833:** The caliph al-Ma'mun dies shortly after ordering that those writers who claim the Quran to be 'not of God' be subjected to inquisition; the dispute masks a struggle for the legacy of the Prophet's teaching and for religious power.
**836:** Foundation of the short-lived capital at Samarra; al-Mu'tasim settles there and surrounds himself with an army of Turkish slaves.

*3. 9th-century ceramic dish.*

# 7th–10th centuries

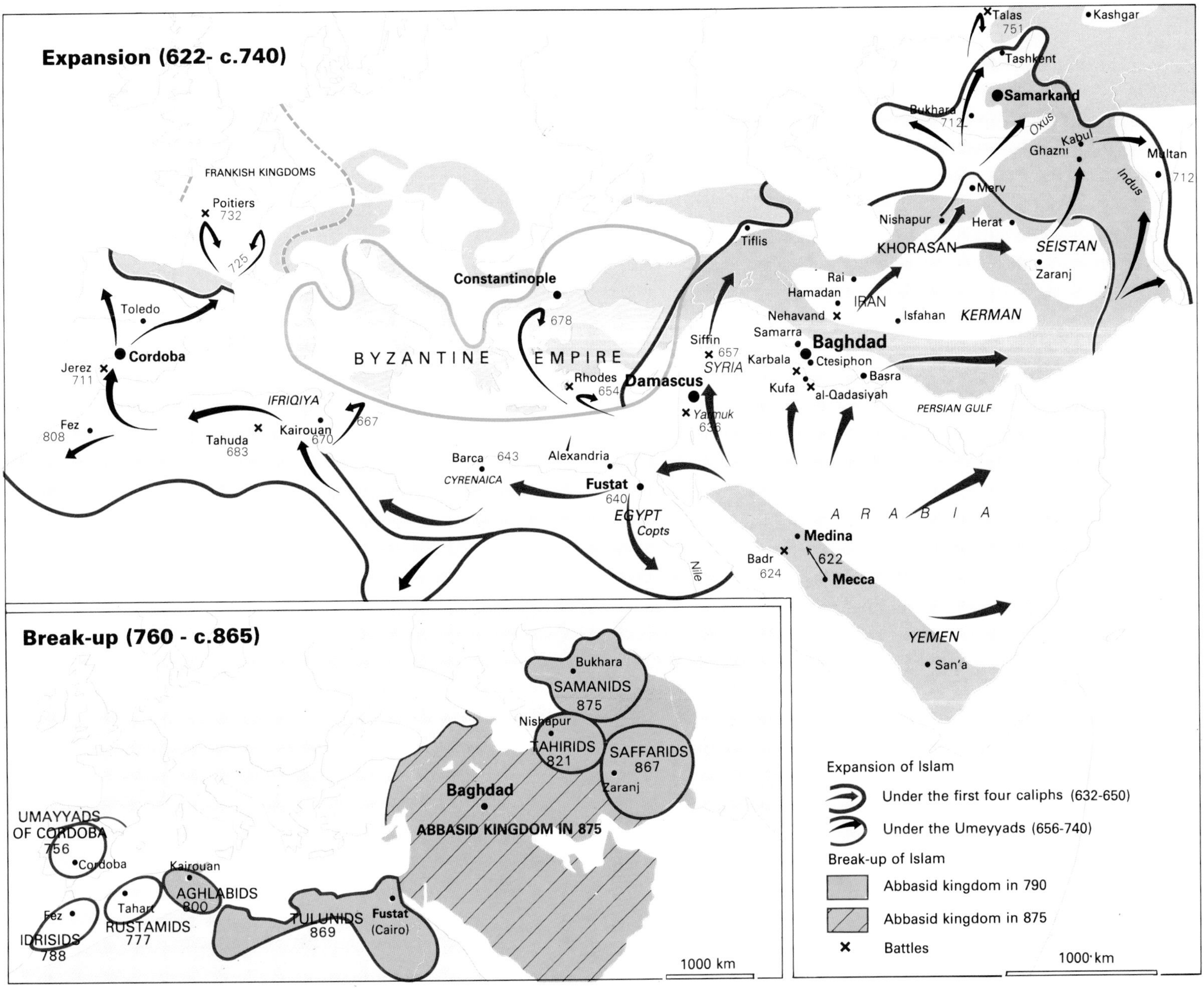

## Expansion (622- c.740)

FRANKISH KINGDOMS
Poitiers 732
725
Toledo
Cordoba
Jerez 711
Fez 808
IFRIQIYA
Tahuda 683
Kairouan 670
667
Constantinople 678
BYZANTINE EMPIRE
Rhodes 654
Damascus
Siffin 657
SYRIA
Yarmuk 636
Barca 643
CYRENAICA
Alexandria
Fustat 640
EGYPT
Copts
Nile
Tiflis
Rai
Hamadan
IRAN
Nehavand
Samarra
Baghdad
Ctesiphon
Karbala
Kufa
al-Qadasiyah
Basra
Isfahan
KERMAN
PERSIAN GULF
ARABIA
Medina
Badr 624
622
Mecca
YEMEN
San'a
Talas 751
Kashgar
Tashkent
Bukhara 712
Samarkand
Oxus
Kabul
Ghazni
Multan 712
Indus
Merv
Nishapur
Herat
KHORASAN
SEISTAN
Zaranj

## Break-up (760 - c.865)

UMAYYADS OF CORDOBA 756
Cordoba
Fez
IDRISIDS 788
Tahart
RUSTAMIDS 777
Kairouan
AGHLABIDS 800
TULUNIDS 869
Fustat (Cairo)
Baghdad
ABBASID KINGDOM IN 875
Bukhara
SAMANIDS 875
Nishapur
TAHIRIDS 821
SAFFARIDS 867
Zaranj
1000 km

Expansion of Islam
Under the first four caliphs (632-650)
Under the Umeyyads (656-740)
Break-up of Islam
Abbasid kingdom in 790
Abbasid kingdom in 875
× Battles
1000 km

**Foundation of Cairo.**

**969**

4. *Minaret of the Great Mosque of Samarra, Iraq, 850.*

**867:** The Saffarid amirs take over power in the province of Seistan.
**868:** The governor of Egypt, Ahmad ibn Tulun, secedes.
**909:** Conquest of Ifriqiya by the Fatimids (Ismailian Shi'ites).
**928:** The Qarmatians (a populist Ismailist movement) occupy Mecca.
**929:** The Umayyad amir of Cordoba, Abd ar-Rahman III proclaims himself caliph.
**945:** The Buyid amirs (Shi'ites from the Daylam region) occupy Baghdad; end of the imperial age of Islam.
**969:** The Fatimids conquer Egypt and found Cairo.
**972:** Inauguration of the al-Azhar Mosque at Cairo.
**996:** al-Hakim becomes caliph of Cairo at the age of 11; his (25-year) reign is marked by bizarre deeds and even more by rigorous anti-Coptic policies.

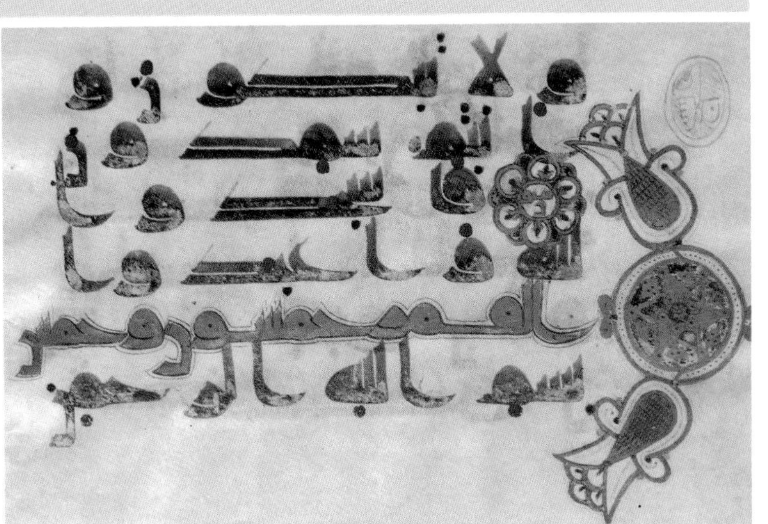

5. *Page of a Quran, Tunis, 9th century.*

# The New Western Empire: Charlemagne

BETWEEN THE MIDDLE of the eighth century and the middle of the ninth, the Carolingians proceeded to combine a large part of the West into a single unit once again. Having first struck an alliance with the papacy, Pepin the Short was elected and crowned king of France. He defeated the Lombards and created a separate political state for the Pope: from this point until 1870 the popes were to be both temporal and spiritual potentates. He also expelled the Arabs from Spain in preparation for the reign of his son. Charlemagne made Austrasia, which was richly endowed with abbeys and palaces, the centre of his kingdom. After thirty years of warfare, he brutally subjugated Saxony. He also annexed the kingdom of Lombardy and Bavaria and thwarted the powerful Avars on the Danube. When he had finished building his empire, Charlemagne set about protecting its frontiers by creating 'marches': those of the Slavs in the east beyond the Elbe, those of Slovenia and Friuli in the south-east, in the south that of Spain (after the defeat at Roncesvalles) and in the west that of Brittany. Ruler of a kingdom extending over a million square kilometres, he was crowned emperor by the Pope. The Byzantine Emperor, who found Charlemagne's elevation difficult to accept, held on to Venice, southern Italy and Sicily.

After the fashion of the Byzantine Emperor, Charlemagne considered himself master of the church. He intervened in theological questions and had an impressive palace built for himself at Aix-la-Chapelle (Aachen). In order to govern his empire more effectively, he divided off the kingdoms of Aquitaine and Italy, which he bestowed on his sons. Bavaria became a prefecture, responsibility for which he delegated to his brother-in-law. Lastly, the Austrasian aristocrats who allied with the imperial family were designated counts, bishops and *missi* (agents of the king who travelled about the Empire in his name and submitted their findings to him). In his way of life, Charlemagne remained a Frank. He loved hunting and swimming and had numerous concubines.

His son Louis the Pious was very different in character. During his reign the bishops played a genuine political role: as guarantors of the unity of the Empire, they stood out against the Emperor's sons, who favoured the division of the territory along the lines laid down by Germanic tradition. This tension was to give rise to the wars between Louis and his sons and, after his death (840), to the famous Treaty of Verdun, by which the Empire was divided into three parts in 843 and then into five in 855. Popes Nicholas I and John VIII took advantage of this situation to recapture the authority they had lost. They intervened in the churches of the various kingdoms – and even in the lives of the princes – and sought to recover some influence over the Eastern Church.

Charlemagne and his successors stimulated a religious, intellectual and artistic renaissance. Dozens of monasteries, cathedrals and palaces were built in this period, particularly north of the Loire in France, in Germany and in Italy. Schools and scriptoria were established in the monasteries. Some 8,000 manuscripts from this period are still extant: thanks to them, numerous classical authors have been saved from oblivion.

We should note that the Carolingians did not conquer the whole of Europe. The Celtic and Anglo-Saxon kingdoms remained independent, but maintained good relations with the emperors. The kingdom of Asturias was governed from its capital at Oviedo by the Visigothic kings, who dreamed of recapturing Spain from the Arabs. The Basques of Navarre also retained their independence.

In sum, the Carolingian Empire achieved a successful balancing of the perennially opposed tendencies towards unification and fragmentation.

*1. The Eagle of St John. Carolingian ivory, northern Italy, 9th century.*

**Pope Stephen II at Ponthion.** **754**

**Alcuin abbot of Saint-Martin-de-Tours.** **796**

*2. Illuminated manuscript of St Augustine's* Quaestiones, *copied in the 8th century, northern France.*

**751–68:** Reign of Pepin the Short. 754: Stephen II comes to Ponthion to meet Pepin, whilst Emperor Constantine V assembles the iconoclastic Council of Hiereia. Boniface dies a martyr's death at Dokkum in Frisia. In 755, and again in 756, Pepin intervenes against the Lombards and gives the territories won in the battle to the Pope. But the new Lombard king Desiderius refuses to submit.
**752–68:** Septimania won back from the Arabs and first stages of the subjugation of Aquitaine. Tassilo III, Duke of Bavaria, asserts his independence. The Irish monk Virgil is appointed Bishop of Salzburg. 765: Exchange of ambassadors with Baghdad. 767: Synod of Gentilly with the Byzantine envoys.
**768–72:** Early years of Charlemagne's reign. 771: Death of his brother Carloman; break with Desiderius. 772: Accession of Pope Adrian I. Beginning of war with the Saxons.
**772–8:** Policy of expansion. 774: Kingdom of Lombardy annexed. First journey to Rome. 776: Saxons subjugated. 777: Paderborn Assembly, which lays the basis for ecclesiastical organization of the defeated countries. 778: Expedition to Spain.

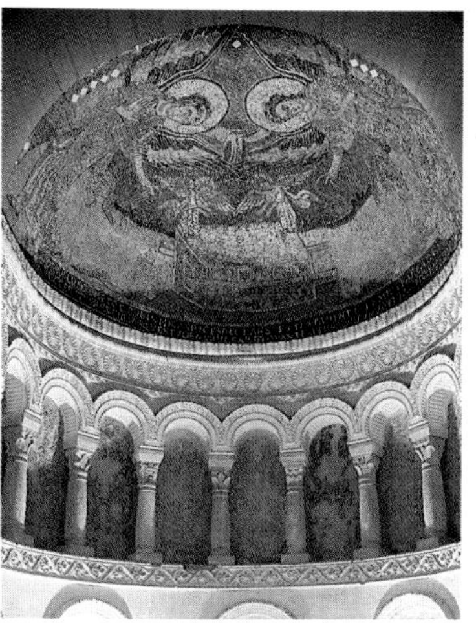

*3. The Ark of the Covenant. Mosaic in the Chapel of St Theodulf's Palace at Germigny-des-Prés (Loiret), early 9th century.*

Roncesvalles disaster. Revolt of the Saxon Widukind and Arichis of Benevento.
**778–92:** The decisive years. 780: Second stay at Rome. 781: Pepin King of Italy. Louis King of Aquitaine. 783–5: War in Saxony. 785: Third stay in Rome. Benevento subjugated. 788: Bavaria annexed. 789: *Admonitio generalis* capitulary. Frisia subjugated. Conquest of Gerona.
**792–3:** Crises – revolts of Benevento and Saxony, Muslim attacks, famines.
**793–814:** End of period of conquest.
**794:** Council of Frankfurt in response to 2nd Council of Nicaea of 787. Conflict with Byzantium over icons. Charlemagne moves to palace at Aix-la-Chapelle. 796: The Avars defeated. 797: Rising in Saxony quelled. 797–801: Spanish march constituted. Capture of Barcelona. 799: Pope Leo III takes refuge at Paderborn. Empress Irene reigns alone in Byzantium. 800: Imperial coronation. The *De villis* capitulary lays down how the royal domains are to be organized. 811: Campaign in Bohemia. 812: Peace between Charles and the Byzantine Emperor. 813: Louis made co-emperor.

# 8th–9th centuries

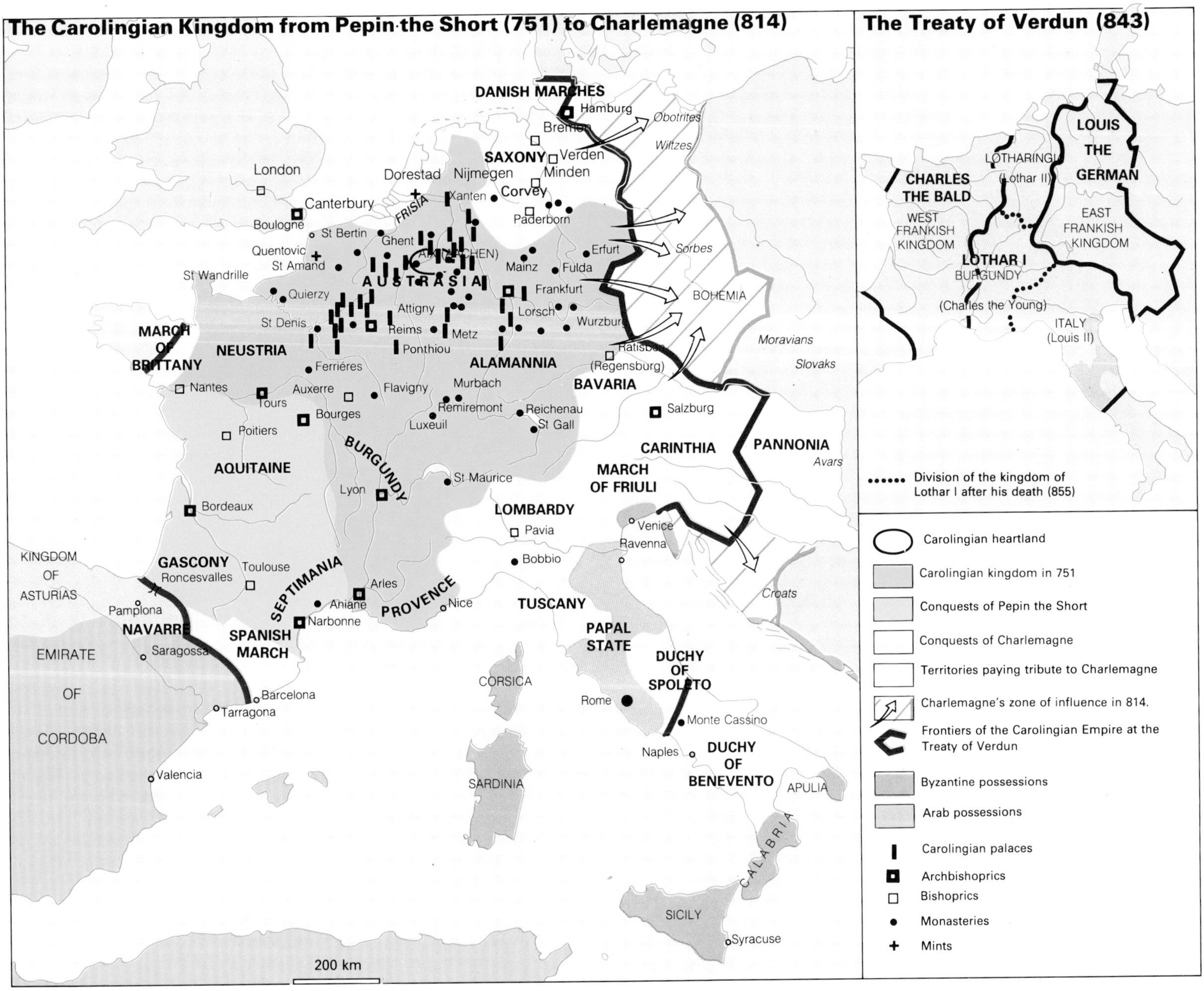

## The Carolingian Kingdom from Pepin the Short (751) to Charlemagne (814)

DANISH MARCHES
Hamburg
Bremen
Obotrites
Wiltzes
SAXONY
Verden
Minden
London
Dorestad
Nijmegen
Canterbury
FRISIA
Xanten
Corvey
Paderborn
Boulogne
St Bertin
Ghent
AIX (AACHEN)
Quentovic
St Amand
Erfurt
Sorbes
Mainz
Fulda
St Wandrille
AUSTRASIA
Frankfurt
BOHEMIA
Quierzy
Attigny
Lorsch
Wurzburg
St Denis
Reims
Metz
MARCH OF BRITTANY
NEUSTRIA
Ponthiou
Moravians
Ratisbon (Regensburg)
Slovaks
Ferrières
ALAMANNIA
Nantes
Auxerre
Flavigny
Murbach
BAVARIA
Tours
Remiremont
Reichenau
Salzburg
Bourges
Luxeuil
St Gall
Poitiers
CARINTHIA
PANNONIA
BURGUNDY
Avars
AQUITAINE
St Maurice
MARCH OF FRIULI
Lyon
Bordeaux
LOMBARDY
Pavia
Venice
Ravenna
KINGDOM OF ASTURIAS
GASCONY
Roncesvalles
Toulouse
SEPTIMANIA
Bobbio
Arles
Aniane
Pamplona
PROVENCE
Nice
TUSCANY
Croats
Narbonne
NAVARRE
SPANISH MARCH
PAPAL STATE
EMIRATE OF CORDOBA
Saragossa
DUCHY OF SPOLETO
CORSICA
Barcelona
Tarragona
Rome
Monte Cassino
Naples
DUCHY OF BENEVENTO
Valencia
SARDINIA
APULIA
CALABRIA
SICILY
Syracuse
200 km

## The Treaty of Verdun (843)

LOUIS THE GERMAN
LOTHARINGIA (Lothar II)
CHARLES THE BALD
WEST FRANKISH KINGDOM
EAST FRANKISH KINGDOM
LOTHAR I
BURGUNDY (Charles the Young)
ITALY (Louis II)

•••••• Division of the kingdom of Lothar I after his death (855)

- Carolingian heartland
- Carolingian kingdom in 751
- Conquests of Pepin the Short
- Conquests of Charlemagne
- Territories paying tribute to Charlemagne
- Charlemagne's zone of influence in 814.
- Frontiers of the Carolingian Empire at the Treaty of Verdun
- Byzantine possessions
- Arab possessions
- Carolingian palaces
- Archbishoprics
- Bishoprics
- Monasteries
- Mints

| **Building of Saint-Riquier.** | **Discovery of relics of St James of Compostela.** | **Oath of Strasbourg.** | **Treaty of Verdun.** |
|---|---|---|---|
| **800** | **839** | **842** | **843** |

**814:** Death of Charles I.
**814–29:** Imperial unity maintained by Louis the Pious and his eldest son Lothar. 816–7: St. Benedict of Aniane presides over the Councils of Aachen (Aix-la-Chapelle).

4. *The crystal of Lothar II. Gold and quartz, depicting the biblical episode of Susannah and the Elders, 9th century.*

5. *Copy of the* Breviary of Alaric, *made in the 9th century, representing the organization of power in the Carolingian Empire: the king, the bishop, the duke and the count.*

*Ordinato imperii*: Lothar becomes co-emperor. 818: Louis the Pious marries Judith of Bavaria. 821: Birth of Charles the Bald. Louis's brother Drogo Bishop of Metz. 824: Embassy of Emperor Michael II to Louis's court. 826: Harald I of Denmark baptized at Ingelheim. Ansgar leaves with him.
**829–40:** Revolt of the sons against the father. 829: Plan for Empire to be divided in Charles's favour. Revolt of Lothar. 831: New plan for a division. Revolt of Pepin and Louis. 833: Louis the Pious deposed at Soissons. 835: Restoration of Louis. 838: Death of Pepin in Aquitaine. Lothar in Italy. Norman incursions.
**840–3:** Fighting between the three brothers. 843: The Treaty of Verdun.

6. *Charlemagne depicted in a 10th-century manuscript.*

# The Nordic Peoples

*1. Prow of the Oseberg ship, southern Norway, 9th century.*

By the start of the fifth century the Roman legions had left Britain, giving the Celts the opportunity to organize themselves. The Britons now fought against the Picts and the Scots. The Welshman Patrick converted Ireland to Christianity around 430. The Briton chief, Vortigern, called on the Saxons to fight the Picts. The Jutes invaded Kent, the Angles the eastern coasts. Small kingdoms were set up named after those who invaded them. The Christian Celts gathered in Wales, Cornwall and Cumberland, taking no notice of their pagan neighbours. Britons moved into Armorica. At the end of the sixth century Gregory the Great sent the Roman monk, Augustine, to convert the pagans in Kent. Canterbury became the episcopal centre of the new church. The other kingdoms were converted gradually. The Irish founded monasteries in Northumbria (Lindisfarne, Whitby) and ended up by taking over Roman liturgical customs. Between Christian Britain and the Continent there were important links. The Channel and the North Sea became a sort of 'Nordic Mediterranean'. The ports of Quentovic, Dorestad, London and Hedeby were used by the Frisians. It was through the tradings of these pirates and merchants that coins (sceattas) spread through Northern Europe. The Carolingian *denier* was based on them. The Frisians held out for a long time against conversion. The Anglo-Saxon Willibrord's follower, Boniface, died a martyr at Dokkum.

In the eighth century the Scandinavians began their attacks. The Vikings ('bay men') steered their fast-moving and steady boats, with rectangular sails and ornamental monsters on the prows, towards the river mouths. For a century Danes and Norwegians pillaged the West. Eastern Ireland was occupied, as was the north of England and the islands off Scotland. King Alfred the Great, one of the most remarkable princes of the time, succeeded in stopping the Danes after the Treaty of Wedmore. His successors gradually took over the Danelaw lands. In France, Charles the Simple set up the Normans of Rollon on the Lower Seine (Treaty of Saint-Clair-sur-Epte). The Norwegians colonized Iceland and Greenland, and arrived around the year 1000 in Canada in a land they called 'Vinland'. The Swedes, known by the name 'Varangians', traded with the Baltic countries, Courland and Novgorod, and contributed to the formation of the first state of Kiev. They formed the 'Varangian guard' in Byzantium.

Christianity spread into the Scandinavian countries through Hamburg, and three bishoprics were created in Jutland. Harald Bluetooth was converted around 960, and had the Jelling Stone erected to commemorate the event. The first Christian Norwegian king, Olaf Tryggvason, brought in priests and bishops from Britain. These first steps towards the conversion to Christianity did not prevent the Scandinavians from preserving many aspects of their pagan past.

At the end of the tenth century the Danes, the toughest soldiers in this region, went to conquer England. King Ethelred fled to Rouen and left his kingdom to Svend I (Swein) Forkbeard. Many generations would come and go before his ancestors' plan would finally work out, and all his descendants would play their part. When Svend disappeared, his son Cnut the Great extended his power over southern Sweden and Olaf's Norway. The empire was divided between his sons in the following generation. Edward the Confessor, son of Ethelred II, finally returned to England, and it was William of Normandy who eventually had the honour of conquering England.

| **Victory of Britons over Picts and Saxons at Verulamium.** | **Death of St Patrick.** | **Plague.** | **Dublin founded.** | **Sack of Dorestad.** | **Dunstan Archbishop of Canterb** |
|---|---|---|---|---|---|
| **429** | **460** | **668** | **839** | **863** | **95** |

**408–600:** Period of invasions. 408: The Romans leave Britain. 432: Patrick begins the conversion of Ireland. Great Welsh monasteries set up. 444: Mission of Germain, the Bishop of Auxerre, against the Pelagian heretics. Vortigern in conflict with Ambrosius Aurelianus, the Briton equivalent of King Arthur. Middle of the 5th century: The Anglo-Saxon invasions. Briton victory at Mount Badon. 500: Resumption of invasions. 563: The Irish on the island of Iona. 590: Columban in Gaul. 597: Augustine of Canterbury converts Kent.
**600–99:** Beginnings of Christianity in England. Ethelbert of Kent dies in 616. Paulinus, the Archbishop of York, baptizes Edwin, King of Northumbria, in 627. c. 630: The tomb at Sutton Hoo. 633–55: Disputes between Mercia and Northumbria. 664: Synod of Whitby. 668: Arrival of Theodore and Hadrian in Canterbury to reorganize the Church after the plague epidemic. 681: Foundation of Jarrow. Coinage struck at Dorestad.
**680–754:** Conversion of Frisia. 680: Radbod's attacks against the Franks. 690: Willibrord in Frisia. Victory of Pepin II over Herstal. 717: Boniface in Frisia. 733: Charles Martel conquers Frisia. Wera Bishop of Utrecht. 754: Boniface martyred.
**757–96:** Reign of Offa of Mercia who constructed Offa's Dyke separating England from Wales. 766: Alcuin in control in York. 787: First Viking raids on England. Pillage of Lindisfarne. 795: The Norwegians in Ireland.
**802–39:** Reign of Egbert of Wessex. Beginning of this kingdom's supremacy. 820: Ansgar at Hedeby. 830: First church at Birka. 839: Foundation of Dublin. c. 850: End of Frisian trade with Jutland.
**850–910:** Great Scandinavian invasions. 851: They set up winter quarters on the Thames and the Seine. 863: Destruction of Dorestad. 867: Capture of York. 870: *Annus terribilis*. King Edmund martyred by the Danes. 875: Foundation of Reykjavik in Iceland. Victories of Alfred the Great over the Scandinavians. 879: Peace of Wedmore. Military reforms, revival of scholarship. 900: Death of King Alfred.
**910–91:** Height of the Anglo-Saxon kingdom. 911: Treaty of Saint-Clair-sur-Epte. 921: Edward the Elder joins with Constantine III, King of the Scots. 924–39: Aethelstan reconquers York. 957–9: Reign of Edgar the Peaceful, King of all England. 966: Baptism of Harald Bluetooth. 980: Colonization of Greenland.
**991–1035:** More Danish attacks on England. 991: Ethelred the Unready beaten at Maldon. Olaf I Tryggvason beaten by Svend (Swein). 1014: Svend (Swein) King of England. Death of Ethelred in Normandy. 1016–35: Reign of Cnut the Great. 1018: Alliance between England and Denmark. 1028–30: Conquest of Norway. Death of Saint Olaf. Cnut's pilgrimage to Rome. 1042–66: Reign of Edward the Confessor, the last Anglo-Saxon king.

*3. Helmet from the royal tombs of Sutton Hoo, Great Britain, gold and silver, 7th century.*

# 5th–11th centuries

2. *Irish Celtic cross, St Columcille's Monastery, Drumcliff (Sligo), 10th century.*

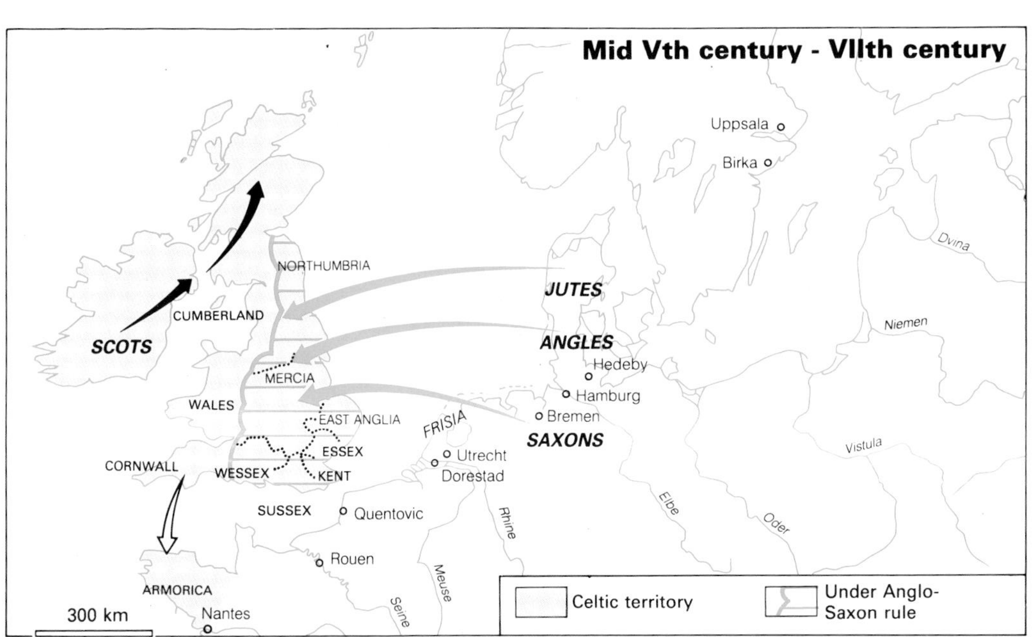


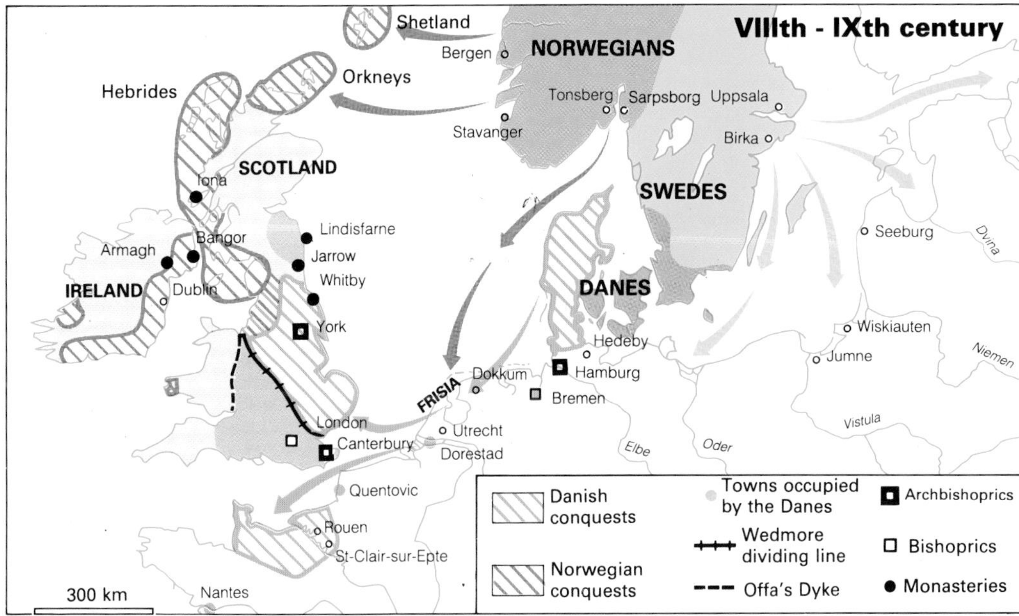


**William the Bastard Duke of Normandy.**

**1035**

4. *Ornament from the Oseberg ship, which served as a tomb for a Viking princess.*

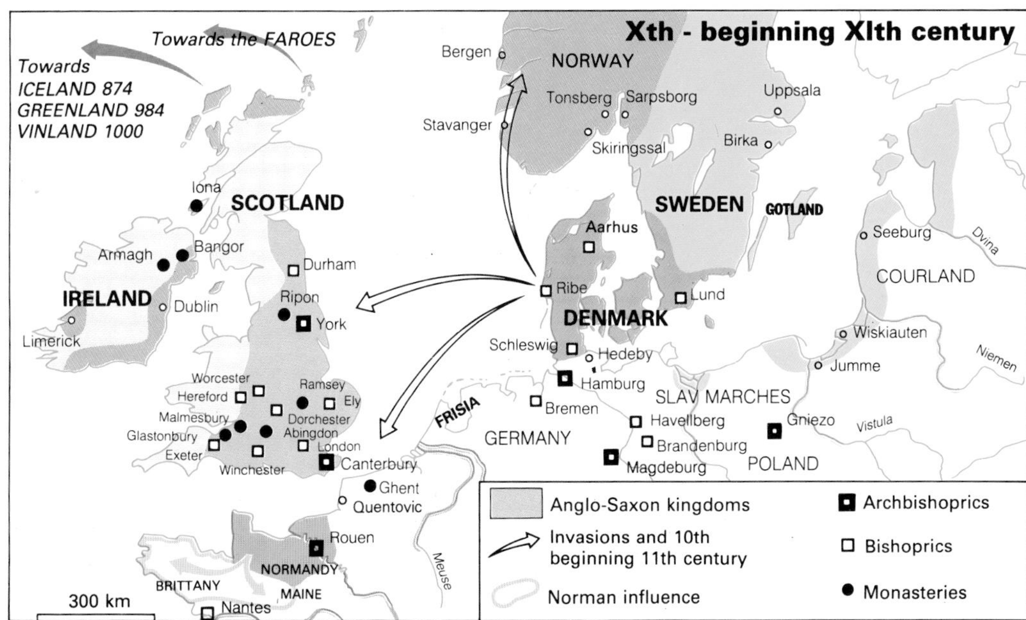

# China from the Six Dynasties to the Sung

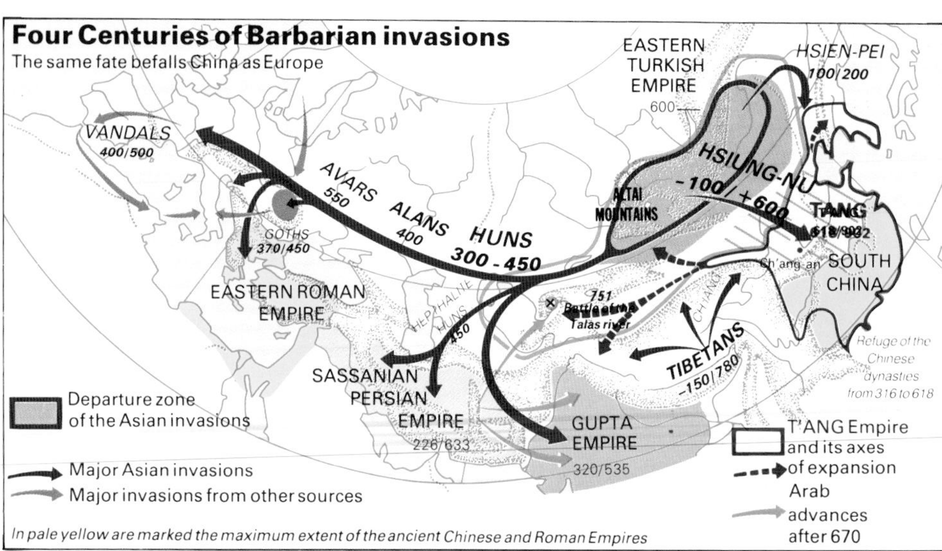

1. Ladies-in-waiting belonging to the Princess Yung T'ai, from the T'ang tombs at Ch'ien Hsion.

Broken up into three separate kingdoms, China was unable to resist the pressure of the barbarians (the Hsiung-nu, the Hsien-pei, and the Toba, who were Turks, Mongols or Tibetans) and the north was invaded. It was during this period of unrest that the economic importance of the Blue River basin became manifest with the influx of refugees from the north. Now subject to foreign pressures, China also became more open to foreign influence, essentially to Buddhism. Partition marked an unprecedented upturn in religious fervour.

Reunited by the usurper Yang Chien, who was of barbarian descent and who founded the Sui dynasty, China entered a long period of unity and prosperity with the T'ang and Sung Empires, the history of which is marked by a threefold movement – political, economic and ethnic. A multiracial and aristocratic state, most of whose trade was done with its own interior, was about to transform itself into a trading state, governed by a class of civil functionaries whose view of the world was entirely xenophobic. The dynasty of the T'ang, more in its administrative organization than in the make-up of its ruling class, was the direct heir to the barbarian states. Having at its disposal a strong military tradition as well as vast troops of horses (which were the main tool it used in service of its policy of conquest), the dynasty established control over Eastern and Central Asia from the seventh century. The practice of setting up military colonies had eased the process of conquest, but the victory of the Arabs in the battle of the Talas River put a final stop to expansion. Having gained control of the mainland communication routes, China became very open to foreign penetration. This was the golden age of Buddhist pilgrimages to India. Persian and Arab influence was evident in every field, particularly in religious matters. In addition to the might of their armies, the success of the T'ang rested on the remarkable organization of their system of government. It owed its integrity to the recruitment by special competition of state officials whose influence counterbalanced the

**China partitioned.**

**Great Canal built.**

**220**

**605**

**220:** Han Empire divided up into the kingdoms of Wei, Wu and Shu-Han.
**280–316:** Reunification of China (under the Chin dynasty).

3. A celadon jar, from the Chin era, at the end of the 3rd century.

**316:** Barbarian invasions force the Chin to retreat to the Yangtze.
**386:** Kingdom of the Toba, or northern Wei, founded.
**557:** Northern Chou founded.
**577:** North China unified by the Chou.
**581:** Sui dynasty founded.
**589:** China reunited by the Sui dynasty.
**618:** Generalized uprisings bring the T'ang dynasty to power.
**666–8:** After Central Asia, it is the turn of Korea and Manchuria to come under Chinese control.
**690:** Reign of Empress Wu Han, who founded the Chou dynasty.
**700:** Death of Judge Ti.
**751:** Imperial armies defeated by the Arabs at the battle of the Talas River.
**756–63:** Rebellion of An Lush-an. The Emperor flees to Szechwan.
**762:** The capital, Ch'ang-an, looted by the Uighurs.
**763:** The Tibetans, after breaking their alliance with the Chinese, sack Ch'ang-an.

4. Pagoda of the Great Wild Goose at Hsian, which was erected in 652.

**780:** A harvest tax is substituted for the family tax levied in copper coin. The salt tax is instituted.
**790:** The T'ang lose control of all the territories to the west of western Kansu.
**845:** Buddhism and foreign religions are proscribed.
**860–70:** The southern kingdom of Nanchao extends to Vietnam and Szechwan.
**879–84:** As a result of economic difficulties,

5. A vase from the T'ang era.

# 3rd–13th centuries

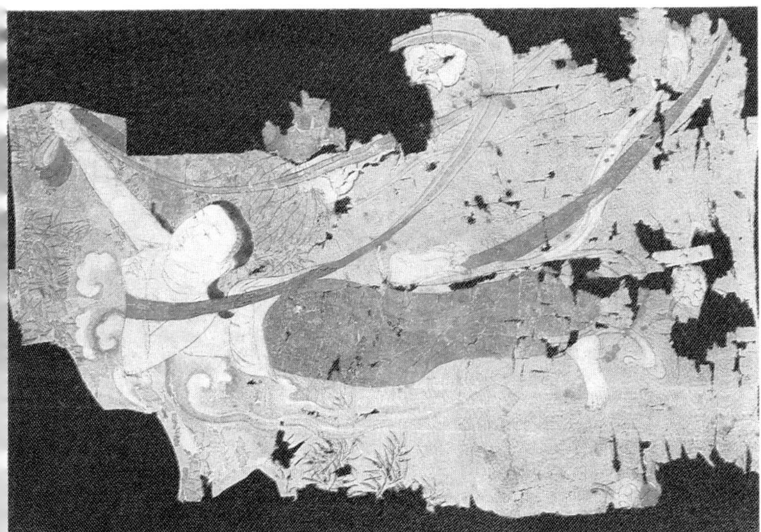
2. Apsaros, the Buddhist spirit, from a silk painting from Tun-Huang in the 9th century.

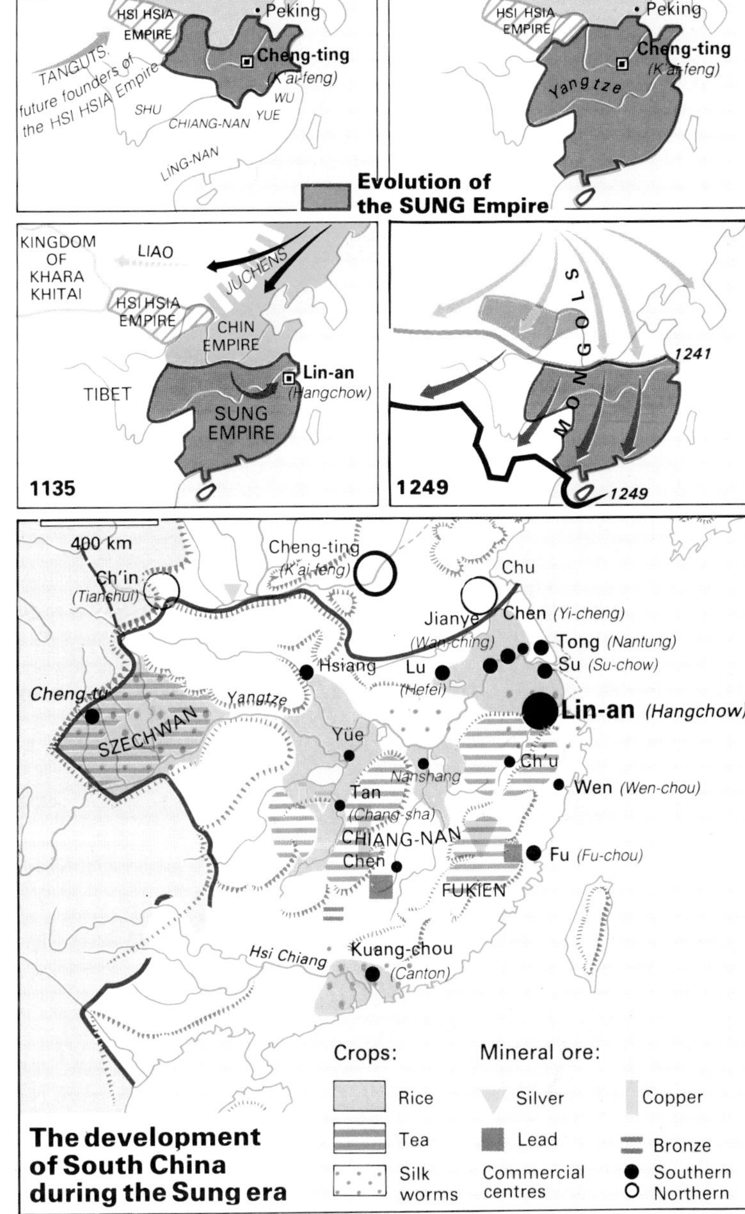


power of the nobles. The conflict, which was initially latent between the two classes, came to the surface in the great military rebellion of the non-Chinese generals led by An Lu-shan in the middle of the eighth century. The date marked a turning-point in Chinese history Foreign traditions became highly suspect (Buddhists were persecuted and Muslims massacred), and attempts were made to find the authentic source of tradition in Confucianism. The loss of its stud farms made China very vulnerable to invasion from the nomads, from the Tibetans in the west and before long from the Khitans in the north-east, who took possession of Manchuria and north China and founded, on the Chinese model, the dynasty of the Liao, before falling victim in their turn to another nomadic people, the Jürcheds. These, after driving out the Khitans, their former masters, towards the west, pushed the Sung back to the Yangtze. This retreat accelerated the process of economic redeployment begun two centuries earlier. The building of the Grand Canal by the Sui had turned east-central China into the crossroads for all trade between the north and the south, by linking together the Yangtze basin with that of the Yellow River. The Yangtze, because of its high output, fed the northern region, which was no longer self-sufficient in food. The economic and then political centre of gravity shifted from the north to the south: a technical (printing, compasses, gunpowder), commercial and cultural blossoming ensued.

**The monk Hsüan-tsang returns from pilgrimage to India.** — **645**

**Introduction of reforms by Wang An-shih.** — **1067**

**Death of the neo-Confucian philosopher Chu Hsi.** — **1200**

rebellion breaks out under the leadership of Hung Ch'ao. Lo-yang is destroyed, Ch'ang-an is occupied and the head of the rebels is proclaimed emperor.
**902–60:** The Empire is broken up into ten kingdoms, founded by the commanders of the military regions.
**947:** Liao Empire founded by the Khitans.
**960:** The Sung dynasty is founded by Chao K'uang-yin, who adopts K'ai-feng as his capital.
**977:** Official recruitment competitions are reintroduced.
**991–7:** Khitan influence is extended.
**1004:** A peace treaty is signed between the Sung and the Liao according to the terms of which the Sung are to pay a tribute of silks and silver.
**1038:** The kingdom of Hsi Hsia is founded by the Tanguts.
**1044:** The Sung conclude a peace treaty with the Hsi Hsia in return for a tribute of silks, silver and tea.
**1067–1100:** Struggle for influence between conservative forces (led by Sima Kuang) and reformers (led by Wang An-shih).

6. Boddhisattva, found in Kuan-yin, from the 11th century.

**1126:** The Jurcheds, having taken the title of Chin, destroy the kingdom of the Liao and take possession of K'ai-feng, thus reigning over the whole of north China and the Yellow River.
**1135:** After retreating to the Yangtze, the Sung use Lin-an (the present-day Hangchow) as their capital.
**1142:** The Sung sign a peace treaty with the Chin after the death of Yo Fei, who advocated the reconquest of the lost territory.
**1162:** The Sung win a great victory over the Chin at Kai-shi after the Chin had invaded the north of the territory.
**1225:** The Mongols seize the northern Chin capital (Peking).
**1234:** The alliance between the Chinese and the Mongols leads to the destruction of the Chin Empire.
**1279:** The Mongols take over the whole of China. The last Sung emperor commits suicide.

7. Portrait of the poet Li T'ai-po, by Liang Kai, from around 1200.

# Ancient Japan

JAPAN WAS MENTIONED for the first time by Chinese chronicles in the first century of our era. It was a country then divided into a large number of communities already familiar with techniques of metallurgy and paddyfield rice-growing brought in from the continent. In 239, Himiko, a queen of the Yamatai kingdom, sent an embassy to China. But the first real evidence of a political centre in the Kinai plain dates only from the fourth century. Japanese society was then controlled by an aristocracy known to historians by the ornamental tombs or *kofun* which they had built. During the fifth and sixth centuries, Yamato dominance continued, both over Japan and beyond its frontiers. They had acquired a base of operations in the territory of Mimana, and this was maintained until 562, when it was finally destroyed by the Korean kingdom of Silla. During the whole period, Korean cultural influences were of great importance and were instrumental in bringing about the rapid transformation of Japanese society.

Between the end of the sixth century and the beginning of the eighth, Japan passed from protohistory to a high degree of civilization. The Yamato became the centre of a state which followed the Chinese model. Buddhism was introduced around 538 and adopted by the court, although Shinto animism was not rejected. The regent Shotoku Taishi (593–622) decreed a constitution styled on the Confucianist ethic. After the great reform of Taika in 646, the principles of an imperial government were set out. Land reform was instituted which would transform the aristocracy into a bureaucracy paid by the state. Cultivated land was declared state property and there was a census of peasant families, who would now have to undergo periodic redistribution of their land. Finally, at the beginning of the eighth century, the imperial court promulgated administrative and penal codes and had great historical chronicles compiled.

The bureaucratic monarchy of the Codes operated only for a short time, because the families of the court tried to monopolize the remunerated posts. After the capital of Nara had been transferred to Heian (Kyoto) in 794, the Fujiwara clan took more than a century to take full control. By installing their grandsons as emperors, the Fujiwara ministers were able to acquire the role of regent. The system reached its peak around the year 1000 under Michinaga. For several centuries the Heian aristocracy had a cultivated life style, with a host of ceremonies and poetry competitions. The break in official relations with China in 894 is a sign of the extent to which Japanese culture and aesthetics had reached maturity.

From the eighth century onwards the law had made provision that land reclaimers were allowed to maintain possession of their fields. Local officials and monasteries gradually formed estates, the *shoen*, with various tax exemptions and immunities. These were outside the control of central government. To ensure that they kept possession of their property, the land-clearing barons kept in favour with those in power at court. They became the local managers of the *shoen* of the Heian aristocracy. At the end of the ninth century the emperor succeeded in breaking away from the supervision of the Fujiwara and established *Inseid* (rule by the retired emperor). In the east of the country in particular, where the minor officials were taking up arms, groups of vassal warriors of independent spirit were formed and these bands began to threaten order in the provinces.

*1. The monk Ganjin in meditation, Nara period.*

**PROTOHISTORY.** **ANTIQUITY.**

100 200 300 400 500 600 700

**STATE OF THE YAMATO.** **STATE OF THE CODE**

645 71

**57:** A king of the country of Wa (Japan) sends an embassy to the Han.
**107:** Further embassy.
**235–9:** Himiko (a Shaman priestess?) reigns over the country of Yamatai (?).
**391:** The Yamato advance into Korea and take over there, at the expense of the Koguryo and Silla kingdoms. Japan seems to have been unified by the Yamato dynasty, ancestors of the imperial clan.
**538:** Introduction of Buddhism.
**587:** Fall of the Mononobe clan and rise of the Soga clan, who seek Chinese-style reform.
**604:** Proclamation by the regent Shotoku Taishi of the '17-article Constitution'.
**607:** First official Japanese embassy to the Sui emperors. Construction of the Horyuji near Nara.
**630:** First embassy to the Tangs.
**645–6:** Coup d'état against the Soga clan and beginning of the great Taika reform.
**701:** Promulgation of the Daiho code.
**712:** Compilation of the *Kojiki – Chronicle of Ancient Things*.
**718:** Yoro code.
**720:** Compilation of the *Nikon Shoki – Chronicle of Japanese History*.

*2. Funerary ornament from the period of the Kofun tombs.*

*3. Pagoda at the Temple of Horyuji, Japan's oldest sanctuary, beginning of the 7th century.*

**743:** Land reclaimers granted possession rights. First step towards the appearance of private estates.
**770:** The fall of the monk Dokyo brings about a decline in the influence of the monks of Nara on the court. Around this time the *Man'yoshu*, a great anthology of poetry, is written.
**801:** Tamuramaro is appointed shogun to fight against the barbarian peoples of the north, who are still undefeated.
**805:** The monk Saicho, on his return from China, founds the Tendai sect at Mount Hiei.
**806:** The monk Kukai founds the Shingon sect at Mount Koya.
**858:** Fujiwara no Yoshifusa is imperial regent.
**901:** Dismissal of Sugawara no Michizane the scholar, who opposes the policies of the Fujiwara.
**Early 10th century:** Publication of a large number of literary works – *The Tale of the Bamboo Cutter, The Tale of Ise, Anthology of Things of Yesterday and Today*.

# 1st–12th centuries

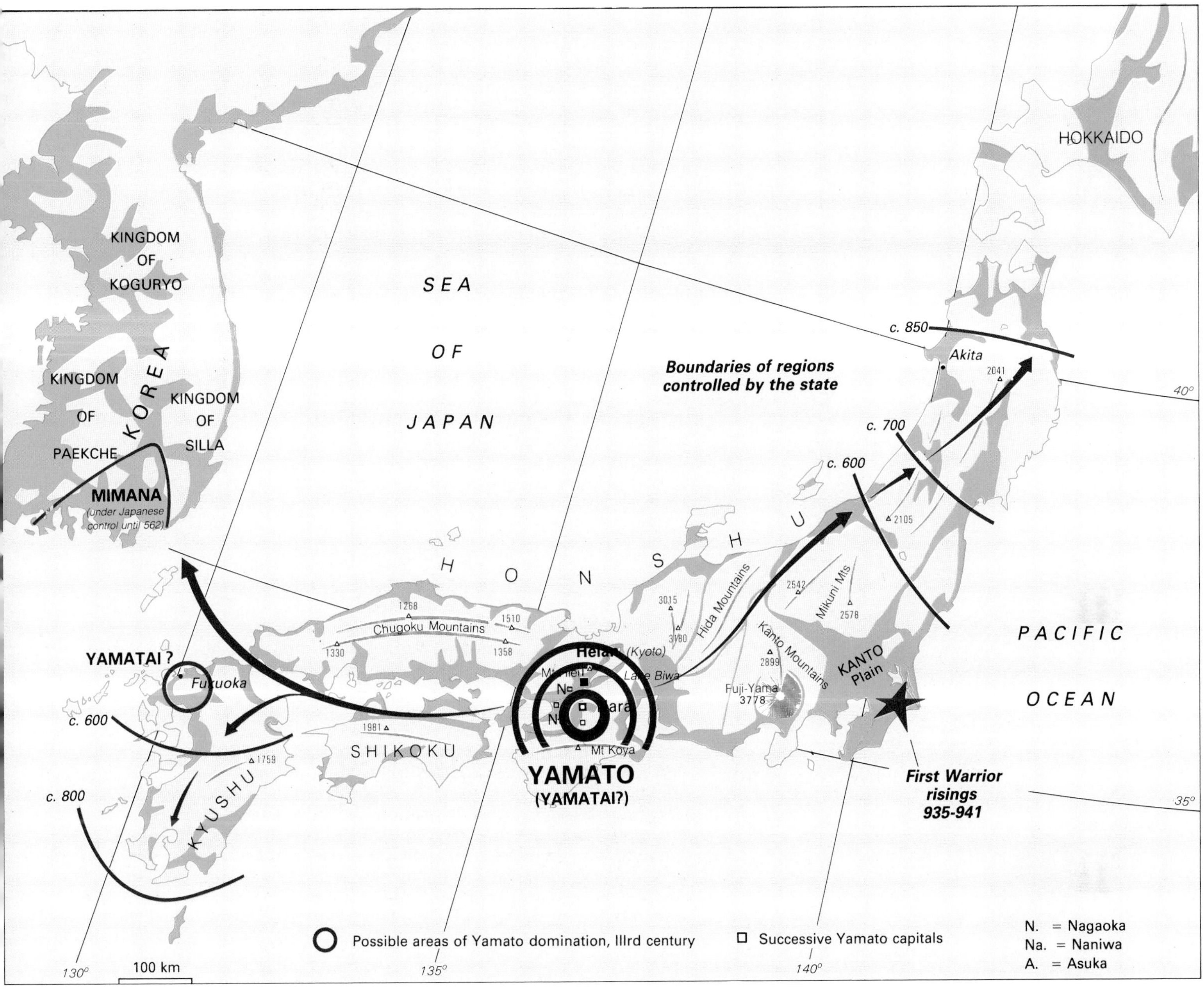

HOKKAIDO
KINGDOM OF KOGURYO
SEA OF JAPAN
KOREA
KINGDOM OF PAEKCHE
KINGDOM OF SILLA
MIMANA
(under Japanese control until 562)
Boundaries of regions controlled by the state
c. 850
Akita
2041
40°
c. 700
c. 600
2105
H O N S H U
Hida Mountains
Mikuni Mts
2542
2578
3015
3180
1268
1510
Chugoku Mountains
1330
1358
Heian (Kyoto)
Lake Biwa
Kanto Mountains
2899
KANTO Plain
PACIFIC OCEAN
YAMATAI ?
Fukuoka
c. 600
Fuji-Yama 3778
Mt Hiei
Nara
Mt Koya
1981
SHIKOKU
1759
KYUSHU
c. 800
YAMATO
(YAMATAI?)
First Warrior risings 935-941
35°
Possible areas of Yamato domination, IIIrd century
Successive Yamato capitals
N. = Nagaoka
Na. = Naniwa
A. = Asuka
130°
100 km
135°
140°


MIDDLE AGES.

| 800 | 900 | 1000 | 1100 | 1200 |
|---|---|---|---|---|
| | PERIOD OF FUJIWARA DOMINANCE. | | RULE BY THE RETIRED EMPERORS. | SHOGUNATE OF KAMAKURA. |
| ara Period. 784 | | Heian Period. | | 1185 |

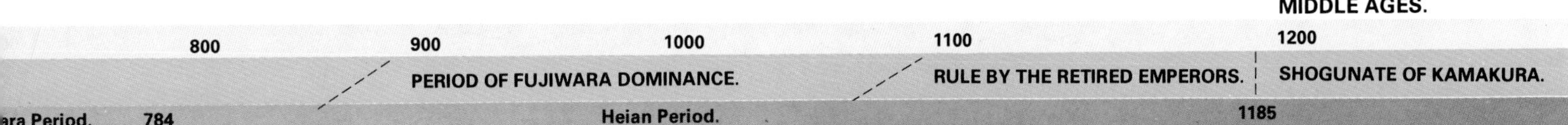

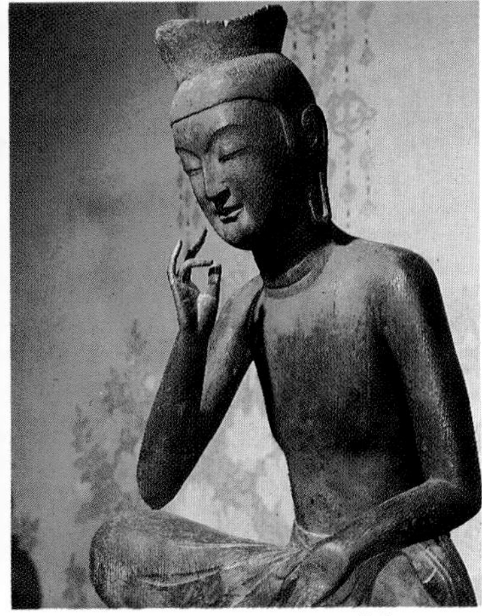

4. *The Buddha of the future, sitting prophesying. Wood from the Asuka period, 7th century.*

**935–41:** Revolts of Taira no Masakado in the Kanto and of Fujiwara no Sumitomo in the Inland Sea.
**995–1016:** Fujiwara no Michinaga all-powerful at the court.
**c. 1000:** *Pillow Book* by Sei Shonagon and *Tale of Genji* by Murasaki Shikibu; women's writing at its height.
**1051–87:** Violent wars in the northern provinces for control of these regions by the warrior clans. Beginning of the rise of the Minamoto in eastern Japan.
**1053:** Fujiwara no Yorimichi has the Byodoin built.
**1086:** The emperor Shirakawa abdicates and continues to hold real power at court from his 'retirement' residence.
**c. 1120:** Stories of *What Is Now Past*.

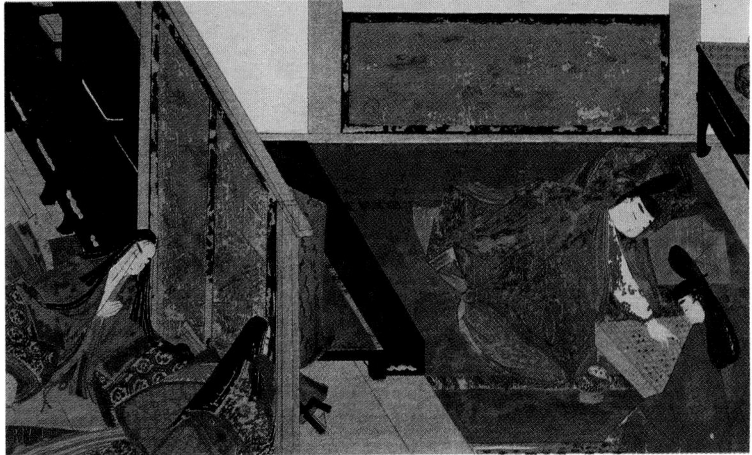

5. *'The prince playing backgammon', scroll from the* Tale of Genji.

# Southeast Asia

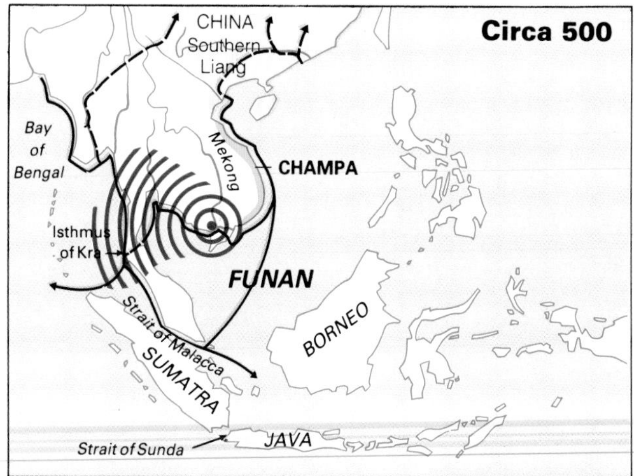


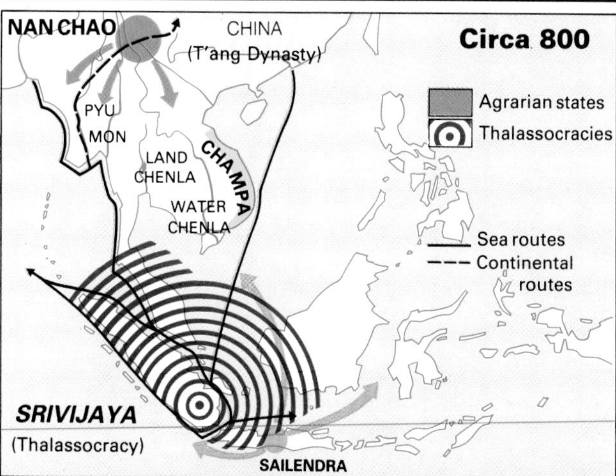


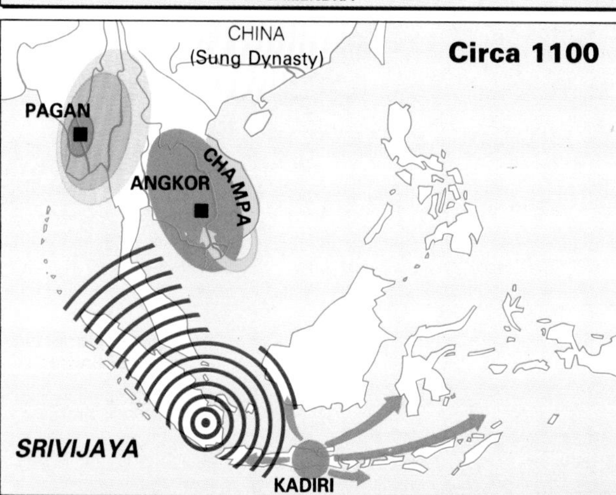


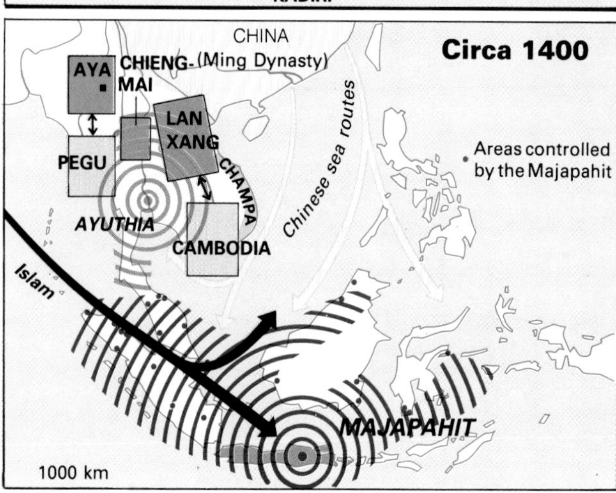


THE PROTOHISTORIC SOCIETIES of Southeast Asia, endowed as they were with precious goods, such as spices, gold or camphor, developed in their own indigenous manner, as was the case, for instance, in Burma in the second century BC, where there were already signs of the beginnings of urbanization. In the following centuries, these societies were progressively influenced by the Chinese and, later, Indian civilizations. Chinese influence, which was based on the country's importance as a commercial and technological centre, went hand in hand with a policy of annexation, the effects of which, however, did not extend beyond the Tonkin delta (the present-day North Vietnam). Beyond this line, China contented itself with the increasingly symbolic policy of placing the local leaders in the position of tributaries. On the other hand, Indian influence, outside of any political link, endowed these selfsame local communities with more sophisticated cultural offerings (from religion, writing and art to political expertise) which reinforced their identity. The combination of these two influences created fertile ground for the transformation of the indigenous principalities into kingdoms which, in the main, appeared 'Indianized'. Given this dual heritage, the geopolitical logic of the region was for it to maintain the movement of trade between India and China by the establishment of maritime kingdoms centred on the trading network. The first of these thalassocracies was Funan, which for almost three centuries dominated the shipping lanes from the Malay peninsula to the mouth of the Mekong. By the sixth century, its inability to control Champa, and the region around the Malay straits and the strait of the Sunda, brought about its collapse. In the course of the seventh century, the shift in the central focus of trade to the straits region provided the basis for a more ambitious thalassocracy in the shape of Srivijaya. On its periphery, some communities which were already established in the agricultural basins found that it was possible to follow a different continental and territorial course, as a result of a new idea of royalty and the perfecting of irrigation techniques. This gave rise to a fresh disposition of agrarian land, as is demonstrated by the great religious monuments of the region. The finest example is that of the 'hydraulic city' of Angkor. From the second half of the eighth century, the new policy was already burgeoning on Java, as is shown by the building of Borobudur, although the states centred there still clearly entertained maritime ambitions. At the end of the ninth century, the new approach was developed most of all in Angkor by the Khmers, then in the eleventh century in Pagan by the Burmese ethnic group. The Mongolian surge of the thirteenth century split this regional balance into two competing halves, each of which attempted to accomplish the synthesis between maritime state and agrarian state. On the Indonesian archipelago, the Majapahit Empire was partly successful in this and managed to recentre the maritime trade network on Java. In Indochina, on the other hand, the efforts of the Thais, who were newcomers to the area, were more or less in vain: although they dominated the region territorially, they remained nevertheless largely dependent on Chinese traders for the management of their trading networks. These two attempts at synthesis remained all the more partial because the new peninsular order rested on 'Small Vehicle' (Hinayana) Buddhism, which maintained the divisions between the different kingdoms and bore the seeds of future clashes between the Thais and the Burmese. As for Majapahit, it did not control the markets at the end of the Chinese sea networks and Islam was soon to take over.

| First inscriptions in the Khmer language. | Campaigns by Śrivijaya. | Nan chao founded. |
|---|---|---|
| 611 | 683–6 | 728 |

*3. Site of the former capital of the kingdom of Pagan, in present-day Burma (9th–13th centuries).*

**2nd century BC:** Earliest archaeological evidence of urbanization can be dated to this century (on the site of Bekthano, in Burma).
**1st century BC:** Trade grows in the China Sea.
**1st century AD:** Appearance of the first 'kingdoms' for which there is historical proof.
**2nd century:** There are beginnings of some political harmonization along the trade routes between the Malay archipelago and the Mekong delta.
**Mid-3rd century:** The thalassocracy of Funan has links with India and China.
**4th–5th centuries:** There is significant archaeological and epigraphic evidence of Indianization.
**Late 5th century:** Funan makes unsuccessful attempts to take control of the kingdom of Champa with Chinese support.
**Early 6th century:** Funan is at its height.
**Second half of 6th century:** Funan is dismembered and its regional economic role is taken over by Champa.
**Late 6th century:** The earliest architectural monuments to be preserved date from this period. The major states are organized, and

# 2nd century BC–16th century AD

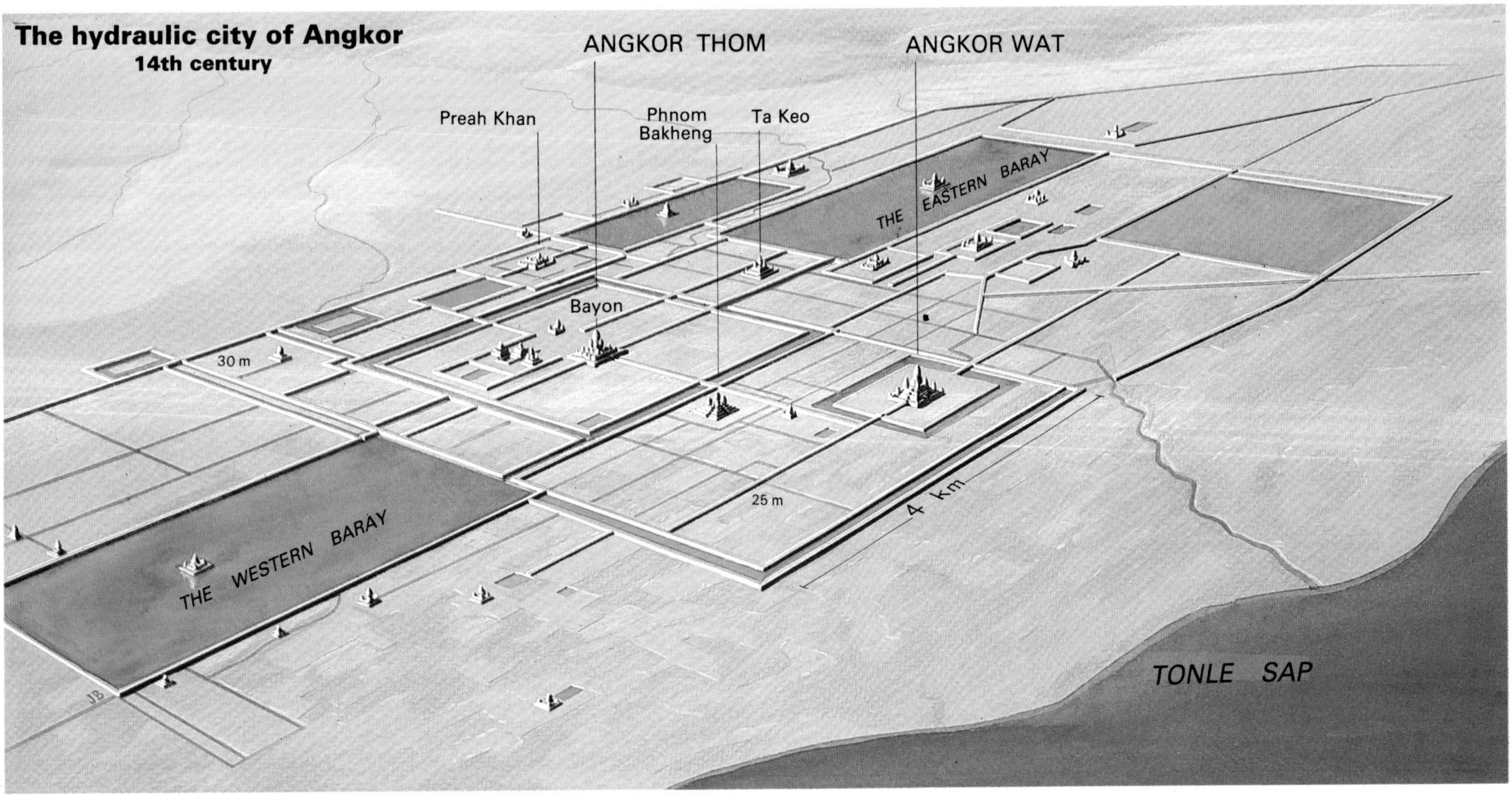

## The hydraulic city of Angkor
### 14th century

ANGKOR THOM
ANGKOR WAT
Preah Khan
Phnom Bakheng
Ta Keo
THE EASTERN BARAY
Bayon
30 m
25 m
4 km
THE WESTERN BARAY
TONLE SAP

*Great reservoirs (called* baray*), held in by high dams, are fed by rivers and rainwater. They provide water for irrigation during the dry season.*

*1. Frontal of Khmer dancing women in the Bayon of Angkor Thom (late 12th century).*

*2. The Khmer temple of Angkor Wat (12th century).*

| c. 800 | 889 | 1058 | 1253 | 1350 | 1431 |
|---|---|---|---|---|---|
| **Building of Borobudur.** | **Angkor founded.** | **First inscriptions in the Burmese language.** | **Nan chao occupied by the Mongols.** | **Ayuthia founded.** | **Khmer court is transferred from Angkor to Phnom Penh.** |

there is the development of a local style of art in sculpture and building.
**7th century:** The Khmers are unsuccessful in their attempt, from a continental base, to take over the pre-eminent role previously filled by Funan.
**Late 7th century:** The new thalassocracy of Śrivijaya is formed.
**Second half of 8th century:** The Śailendra rulers establish in Java a dominant agrarian state, but one which still harbours maritime ambitions.
**822:** Nan chao invades the territory of the Pyu, followed by the ethnic Burmese, who take control of the country.
**877:** Unification of the two Chenla (Land Chenla and Water Chenla) by Indravarman I (the nephew of the first Angkor king), and the building of the first Khmer 'hydraulic city'.
**Early 10th century:** The Javanese centre of government shifts to the east of the island, which begins to spread its trade network towards eastern Indonesia.

*4. Terraces of rice fields on Bali.*

**Mid-10th century:** Vietnam becomes independent and the Cham withdraw.
**Mid-11th century:** The Burmese conquer the territory belonging to the Mon and set the seal on the unity of Burma.
**Late 12th century:** The last 'hydraulic city' is built.
**Mid-13th century:** The Thais rise up against the authority of the Khmer.
**Late 13th century:** Independence is restored to the Mon and Pagan is overrun by the Mongol armies (in 1287).
**Early 14th century:** The rise of the kingdom of Majapahit (on Java) puts an end to Śrivijaya.
**Mid-14th century:** Re-establishment of a Khmer state beyond the influence of the Thais in the lower Mekong valley.
**1446:** Islam triumphs in Malacca.
**1471:** Champa is reduced to three principalities.
**Early 16th century:** Majapahit is no longer a powerful state.

*5. The Buddhist stupa of Borobudur, in the centre of Java, built around 800.*

# The Last Barbarian Invasions

1. Panel of an altar frontal made of gold, belonging to Otto II, depicting Christ as judge.

AFTER THE PARTITIONS of 843 and then 855, the former Carolingian Empire was broken up into various separate kingdoms and principalities. Despite the resistance of the church, the Germanic practice of partition at each succession prevailed over the principle of unity. Nonetheless the imperial dignity was safeguarded, at least until the beginning of the tenth century. Pope John VIII crowned Charles the Bald emperor in 875, then, after his death, Charles the Fat, who was forced by ill-health to abdicate in 887. The various royal titles fell to representatives of the great aristocratic families, such as Arnulf in Germania, Guy of Spoleto then Berenger in Italy, Rudolph I in Burgundy, Boso in Provence, and Eudes (the ancestor of the Capetians) in France. The last Carolingians competed for power with the Capetians until 987. Within these kingdoms themselves, dukes sought to set up independent principalities, as in Germania (Saxony, Swabia, Bavaria, Lorraine and Franconia) or Italy (Friuli, Ivrea and Tuscany) or in France (Aquitaine, Gascony, Burgundy, Normandy, Flanders etc.). Both dukes and counts endeavoured to appropriate for themselves the various regal privileges, like levying indirect taxes, minting coins, building castles, or administering justice.

Fortifications had become all the more essential, since, from the middle of the ninth century, the Vikings had been invading the Western countries, looting rich monasteries and laying siege to cities, notably Paris, first in 845, then again in 885. Princes had to pay a tribute (or *danegeld*), and monks fled, taking their holy relics with them, like those from Noirmoutier who ended up in Tournus. Charles the Simple installed the Normans along the lower Seine and made Rollo count of Rouen, though this did not stop the Normans pushing into Brittany and the Maine area. From Africa and from Spain came waves of Muslim pirates. They looted Rome in 846 and forced Leo IV to surround the Vatican with a defensive wall, which can still be seen today. They destroyed Monte Cassino, captured Bari and settled in Sicily, where they remained for 200 years. The Italian princes and the Pope stopped them in 911 along the Garigliano. In Provence, the Muslims used Fraxinetum (La Garde-Freinet) as a base for their raids. Last, arriving from Asia as the Huns and Avars had done, were the Magyars, who settled in the Danube basin and launched attacks into Lorraine, Burgundy and Italy. Indeed, more than thirty Magyar incursions took place within the first fifty years of the tenth century. Without being as aggressive, the Slavs sought to set up their own states like the Slavic kingdom of Moravia, which was Christianized by the Byzantine monks Cyril and Methodius and then was broken up by the Magyars.

It was not until the middle of the tenth century that the kings counter-attacked. Henry I of Germania, then his son Otto the Great, won convincing victories over the Magyars. In defence against the Slavs, Otto organized buffer territories between the Elbe and the Oder and along the Danube. He brought Christianity to these areas and created bishoprics dependent on the archbishopric of Magdeburg. Bohemia was converted, as well as Poland and Hungary. In the year 1000, Otto III and Pope Sylvester II bestowed a national hierarchy on the two states. The frontiers of Roman Christianity henceforth reached as far as the Vistula and the Danube.

| 858 | 885 | 948 | 992 |
|---|---|---|---|
| **Nicholas I becomes pope.** | **The Normans lay siege to Paris.** | **Synod of Ingelheim.** | **Building of Langeais Castle.** |

**840–55:** The Empire is partitioned and invaded. 841: Lothair is defeated at Fontenoy-en-Puisaye by Charles the Bald. 842: Meeting between Charles the Bald and Louis the German to swear the Oath of Strasbourg. 843: Treaty of Verdun sees the Empire partitioned between the three brothers. The Normans reach the Loire Valley. 845: First siege of Paris. 846: The Muslims attack Rome. 850: The Normans overrun Frisia. 855: Lothair I dies, and his kingdom is divided up between Lothair II, who claims the north (Lotharingia), Charles (Burgundy and Provence) and Louis II, who receives Italy and is given the title of Emperor.
**855–88:** The Carolingians resist invaders. 860: The Muslims reach Campania. The Magyars reach the Dnepr. 866: Robert the Strong, the ancestor of the Capetians, is killed at Brissarthe. In Bulgaria, Boris asks Pope Nicholas I to send him missionaries. 869: Death of Lothair II and of Cyril. who had introduced the Slavonic liturgy. 871: Emperor Louis II and the Byzantines recapture Bari. 875: Pope John VIII bestows the title of emperor on Charles the Bald and calls for his assistance against the Muslims. The monks of Noirmoutier arrive in Tournus. 879: Boso becomes king of Provence. 881: Charles III, the Fat, becomes emperor, and restores the unity of the Empire in 884. The Normans are defeated at Saucourt-en-Vimeu. 885: Paris is under siege. 887: Emperor Charles III, the Fat, is deposed.
**888–936:** Invasions continue, and many principalities are created. 888: Eudes wins a victory over the Normans at Montfaucon. The Muslims establish their base in La Garde-Freinet. 898: Magyar invasions into Italy and Bavaria. The Slavic kingdom of Moravia is destroyed. 911: Treaty of Saint-Clair-sur-Epte. Lorraine is annexed by Charles the Simple. 918: Count William I of Aquitaine, founder of the Abbey at Cluny, dies. 919: Henry I the Fowler, Duke of Saxony, becomes king of Germania. 926: Hugh of Arles becomes king of Italy. 927–35: Herbert of Vermandois pursues his campaign against King Rudolph of Burgundy. Henry I the Fowler recaptures Lorraine and defeats the Magyars. 932: Alberic II takes control of Rome and the papacy.
**936–1000:** The kingdoms reassert themselves. Otto I becomes king of Germania. In France the Carolingian Restoration takes place. The kingdom of Burgundy is annexed. 942–8: Struggles break out between Duke Hugh the Great and Louis IV d'Outremer ('from overseas'). Otto intervenes on Louis's side. The Synod of Ingelheim is held. 951: Otto I becomes king of Italy. 955: Otto defeats the Magyars and the Slavs at Lechfeld and Recknitz. Pope John XII, the son of Alberic II, crowns Otto emperor. Otto is deposed in 963. The Polish Duke Mieszko is Otto's first vassal, and is baptized in 966. The dioceses suffragan to the archbishopric of Magdeburg are established. 972: Otto II marries the Byzantine princess Theophano and succeeds his father in 973. The Bishopric of Prague is founded. 982: Gerbert of Aurillac is abbot at Bobbio. Otto II is defeated by the Arabs in southern Italy (in 982) and dies a year later. The Slavs revolt. 985: Stephen I of Hungary is baptized and is king from 1000 to 1038. 987: Death of Louis V, the last Carolingian monarch. Hugh Capet accedes to the throne. 996: Otto III, the Emperor, takes up residence in Rome. 999: His master Gerbert is appointed Pope and takes the name of Sylvester II. Otto II undertakes a pilgrimage to Gniezno and Aix-la-Chapelle (Aachen).

3. La Garde-Freinet (Fraxinetum), the site of a Moorish fortress.

# 9th–10th centuries

2. St. Paul. Ivory of the Ottonian era.

**eace Assemblies take place.**

**994**

4. The Judgement of Solomon. A Catalonian manuscript of the Bible from Saint-Pierre de Rodas, c. 1000.

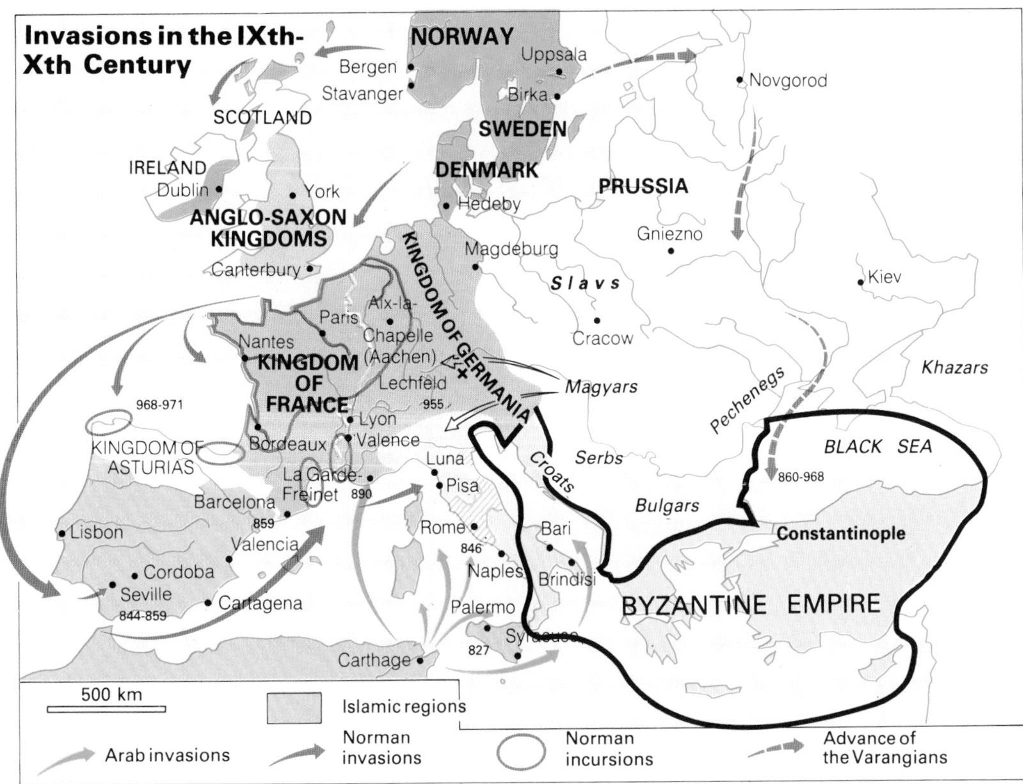

Invasions in the IXth-Xth Century
NORWAY
Bergen
Stavanger
Uppsala
Birka
SWEDEN
Novgorod
SCOTLAND
IRELAND
Dublin
York
DENMARK
Hedeby
PRUSSIA
ANGLO-SAXON KINGDOMS
Canterbury
KINGDOM OF GERMANIA
Magdeburg
Gniezno
Slavs
Kiev
Paris
Aix-la-Chapelle (Aachen)
Cracow
Nantes
KINGDOM OF FRANCE
Lechfeld
955
Magyars
Khazars
Pechenegs
968-971
Lyon
Valence
KINGDOM OF ASTURIAS
Bordeaux
Luna
Pisa
Serbs
Croats
BLACK SEA
La Garde-Freinet
890
860-968
Barcelona
859
Bulgars
Lisbon
Valencia
Rome
846
Bari
Constantinople
Cordoba
Seville
844-859
Cartagena
Naples
Brindisi
BYZANTINE EMPIRE
Palermo
Syracuse
827
Carthage
500 km
Islamic regions
Arab invasions
Norman invasions
Norman incursions
Advance of the Varangians

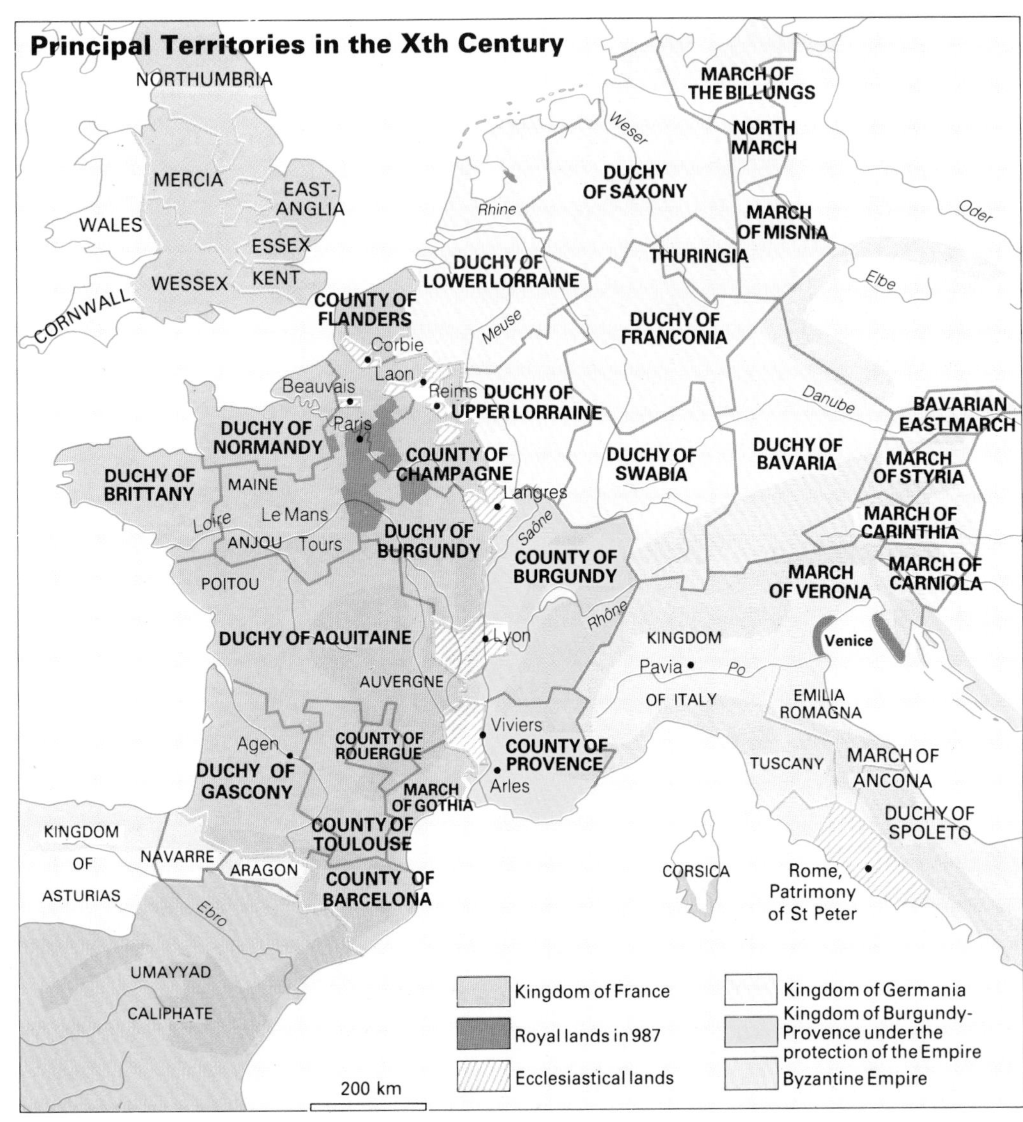

Principal Territories in the Xth Century
NORTHUMBRIA
MARCH OF THE BILLUNGS
Weser
NORTH MARCH
MERCIA
EAST-ANGLIA
DUCHY OF SAXONY
Rhine
Oder
WALES
ESSEX
MARCH OF MISNIA
THURINGIA
DUCHY OF LOWER LORRAINE
WESSEX
KENT
Elbe
CORNWALL
COUNTY OF FLANDERS
DUCHY OF FRANCONIA
Corbie
Meuse
Laon
Beauvais
Reims
DUCHY OF UPPER LORRAINE
Danube
BAVARIAN EAST MARCH
Paris
DUCHY OF NORMANDY
COUNTY OF CHAMPAGNE
DUCHY OF SWABIA
DUCHY OF BAVARIA
MARCH OF STYRIA
DUCHY OF BRITTANY
MAINE
Langres
Loire
Le Mans
MARCH OF CARINTHIA
Saône
ANJOU
Tours
DUCHY OF BURGUNDY
COUNTY OF BURGUNDY
MARCH OF CARNIOLA
POITOU
MARCH OF VERONA
Rhône
DUCHY OF AQUITAINE
Lyon
KINGDOM
Venice
Pavia
Po
AUVERGNE
OF ITALY
EMILIA ROMAGNA
Viviers
Agen
COUNTY OF ROUERGUE
COUNTY OF PROVENCE
TUSCANY
MARCH OF ANCONA
DUCHY OF GASCONY
Arles
MARCH OF GOTHIA
DUCHY OF SPOLETO
KINGDOM OF ASTURIAS
COUNTY OF TOULOUSE
NAVARRE
ARAGON
COUNTY OF BARCELONA
CORSICA
Rome, Patrimony of St Peter
Ebro
UMAYYAD CALIPHATE
Kingdom of France
Royal lands in 987
Ecclesiastical lands
Kingdom of Germania
Kingdom of Burgundy-Provence under the protection of the Empire
Byzantine Empire
200 km

# The Innovations of the Dark Ages

1. Chinese pilgrim monk, carrying scrolls of manuscripts. Painting of the Tun-huang school, 9th century.

THE PERIOD FROM the fourth to the tenth centuries remains mysterious and uncertain, yet numerous technical innovations were introduced. In China, for instance, it was the age of the first major upsurge in irrigated rice cultivation, of the crucial introduction of the technique of planting out, and of the emergence of tea and sugar cane (as a result of these changes the economic centre of gravity moved south, towards the Yangtze River). Cambodia had considerable success in the use of hydraulics. India adopted the elevating wheel for irrigation, and Ethiopia started growing coffee. In the Islamic world, which shared with China the passion for horses, whole agricultural estates were established, as notably at Tahert (in North Africa). In the West, the forests were slowly being turned into grazing land: the use of ploughs with wheels, and ploughshares with mouldboards and coulters, became systematic. The recourse to scythes, to marling, to the three-field system of crop rotation (itself the most important agricultural innovation of the European Middle Ages), became generalized. The energy of animals was mastered with the domestication of the horse: the use of stirrups, shoeing, 'modern' harnesses with shoulder collars (representing a true technical revolution) spread throughout the ancient world. In addition to the utilization of animal energy, other new energy sources such as water and wind-power began to be harnessed to human activities. The water-mill, which first appeared in the second century BC, became quite common and its many technical applications grew in number. The windmill, which was used in Iran and Afghanistan in the sixth or seventh century, was used in China in the ninth century, during which period gunpowder was also discovered. From the seventh century onwards, Byzantium possessed 'Greek fire' (a mixture of saltpetre and bitumen). The Buyyids of Iraq-Iran, in the tenth century, used burning missiles, while China and Europe at the same period were armed with crossbows with metal springs. By the tenth century Western Europe had perfected the chimney and stained glass. The spread of new materials was spectacular: by the tenth century silk came to be used by the Byzantines and the Arabs, and no longer just by the Chinese and Indians. Paper had been used in China since the sixth century and had reached the Islamic and Byzantine world by the eighth centuries. China had been making proper porcelain since the seventh or eighth century. In the tenth century Western architects began using stone again, while the Pueblo Indians (from what is now the south-west of the United States) did the same. The progress made in the use of metals, iron and steel, was enormous.

The efforts to explore and master space, in these centuries of the nomad, were sometimes sufficient to overcome the long periods of stagnation in trade (conditions improved somewhat between 750 and 900). Particularly worthy of mention are the explorers and travellers of the sixth and seventh centuries (like St Brendan of Ireland, Cosmas from Byzantium, and the Buddhist pilgrims), the Vikings and

**6th century:** The breeding of silkworms begins in the Byzantine world. John Philiponus, in Alexandria, merges pagan science and Christianity, while Dionysius Exiguus invents the Christian calendar.
**c. 540:** Chinese book written on methods of cultivation.
**After c. 550:** Growth of steel-making in China.
**From the 6th or 7th centuries:** Introduction of the technique of planting out, of new tools, and cranking gear for the raising of water in China.
**6th–7th centuries:** Writing of *Geoponica*, a Byzantine treatise on working the land. 'Indian' and 'Frankish' swords are used. Chain-mail is introduced. Growth in the use of gold for fine metalwork. This, in turn, spreads across Turkey, Central Africa and America. Almost everywhere the trend is towards 'industrialization', with the standardization and mass production of tools, jewellery and weapons. In India, the decimal system (nine digits and zero) is devised, as is algebra. The golden age of the Mayas is reflected in their dizzying preoccupation with complex calculations. The *Codex Justinianus* is written and Western custom law is codified. The influence of these was to be long-lasting.
**Late 6th–7th centuries:** Collapse of Mediterranean trade. Contacts between India and the Mediterranean become looser. The circulation of money in the majority of the developed areas slows down considerably.
**After c. 600:** In India, the number of trading groups declines, and the number of artisan castes increases. 'Greek fire', a mixture of sulphur and saltpetre, is invented.
**Early 8th century:** Japanese legal code written down. It was to remain in force till 1868. The T'ang code in China, similarly, remained in force till the 20th century. Sugar cane and tea are grown in China. Paper is made in the Muslim and Byzantine countries. China has its first escapement clock.
**c. 710:** Liu Chi-shi, the first Chinese theorist of history.
**After c. mid-8th century:** There are signs of economic recovery in Europe and the Mediterranean, in North Africa and the Sahara region, in India and China.
**8th–9th centuries:** Invention of the shoulder collar and of horseshoes.
**After 800:** Chinese xylography (the engraving in relief on wooden slabs) is used for calendars and books as well as pictures. Szechwan seems to have played a central role in this.
**c. 800:** Harun ar-Rashid offers Charlemagne a water clock. New writing systems are introduced, including Carolingian minuscule, Greek minuscule and the Japanese syllabary. The Carolingian, Byzantine and Chinese 'Renaissances' take place, leading to the rediscovery of ancient writers.

4. Horse and harness: a three-coloured pottery figure of the T'ang era, 7th–8th century.

5. Remains of the palace built by the Umayyad sultan Hisham (724–43) at Rusafa, near Jericho

# 6th–10th centuries

Varangians (especially in the ninth century), the wonderful map-makers (from the ninth century onwards), the sea compasses invented by the Chinese (in the eighth or ninth century) and, in the same spirit, the introduction of 'flying money' (or paper currency) by the ninth-century T'ang dynasty, or the use of gold in the Sudan. ...

The struggle to conquer time was equally active during this period. It gave rise to inventions such as Harun ar-Rashid's water clock and the Chinese forebear of the mechanical escapement clock. It also produced the transformation represented by Chinese xylography, and other new, and quicker, modes of writing. It slowly became possible to reach back into time, through memory, history and writing. The result was the various rediscoveries of ancient writers, notably the renaissance of Greek science and philosophy in the Islamic world, saved by translators to be enriched and passed on later to the Western world.

The pragmatism of the sixth to tenth centuries, the technical approach it promoted, was of a piece with its abstract rationalism, and fostered the establishment of major legal monuments and the development of the law as a practical discipline, though one dedicated to generalization and uniformity. Abstract rationalism was also behind the mathematical computations of the Mayas and the Indians, whose major achievements were quickly taken up in China and by the Islamic world. The same combination of pragmatism and abstraction also lay behind philosophy, behind the desire to master the world by philosophical concepts. ...

2. Traditional architecture of the Pueblo Indians (New Mexico).

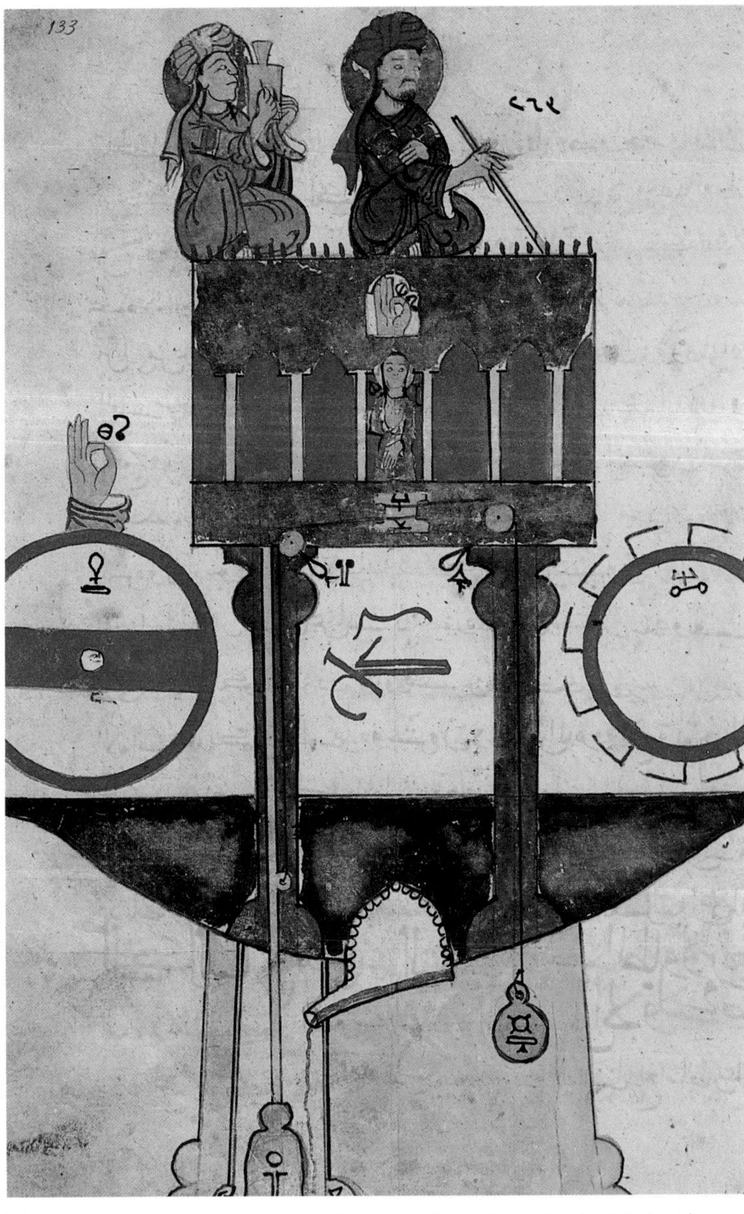

3. Water clock with automatic movement, from a painting in the Book of Knowledge of Mechanical Processes, by Al-Djazani, from the Seljuq copy of 1206.

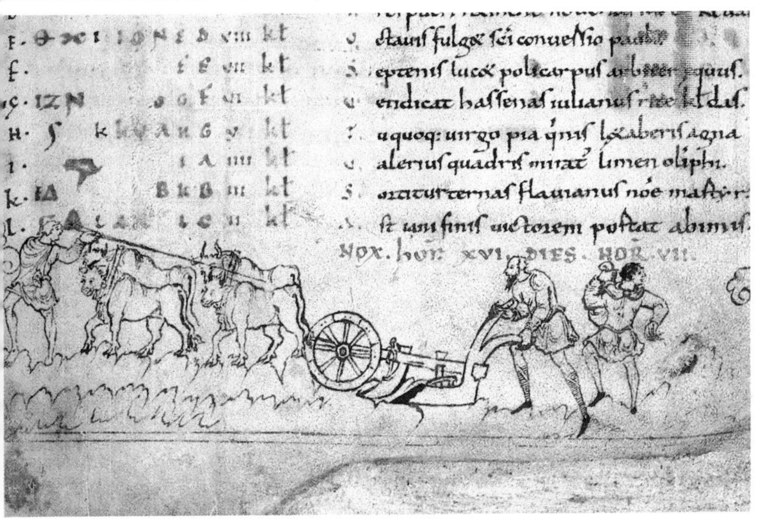

6. A Saxon ploughman directing a team of oxen. Pen drawing from England, 8th century.

**800–50:** The Indian Philosopher Sankara (780–820) elaborates his monistic idealist system. The Irishman Johannes Scotus Erigena combines rationalism and Platonism, while the Arab philosopher al-Kindi mingles Aristotelianism with Platonism.
**832:** al-Mamun founds the House of Wisdom in Baghdad. Translations are made from the Greeks. A world atlas is made. There is much traditionalist resistance to the rationalist offensive.
**After c. 850:** Muslim map-makers are active.
**9th century:** Invention of gunpowder in China.
**10th century:** Growth of cotton as a crop and of new farming methods in Mexico. The West goes back to stone building. Chimneys and stained-glass are perfected. The Pueblo Indians construct their buildings (in the south-west of the United States). The Japanese have sabres. The Toltecs show their prowess as workers in fine metal. The metal-spring crossbow is introduced.
**c. 960:** Chinese treatise on the history of technology is written.

7. 'Greek fire' used to set a tower alight. From a Byzantine manuscript, 10th century.

# Europe in the Year 1000

On the eve of the millennium, Europe was experiencing radical changes in all fields. Unprecedented demographic and agricultural growth meant that Europe had developed considerably more than neighbouring regions and, in the course of the resulting drive to expand, it acquired firm territorial outlines which, broadly speaking, remain the same today. The old Holy Roman Empire still constituted Europe's central axis. In theory this comprised Italy and Germany, to which in the eleventh century were added Provence and Burgundy.

1. *The Four Horsemen of the Apocalypse. Illumination from an 11th-century manuscript from St Sever in southwest France.*

In the year 1000 the emperor Otto III and Pope Sylvester II (Gerbert of Aurillac, one of the most learned men of his day) dreamed of 'restoring the Roman Empire', but new geopolitical powers were forming in the West: from 987 Capetian France and, from 1066, the Anglo-Norman kingdom would play an increasingly important part in events. The changes taking place on the fringes of Europe were no less significant: the Carolingians had already subdued and converted the Saxons to the east. The archbishopric of Magdeburg on the Elbe became a base for expeditions against the Slavs. The conversion of these peoples, however, was achieved less by means of armed force than by missionary activity and as a result of the matrimonial alliances of princes whose subjects followed their example in observing the new faith. Christianity had already been adopted throughout most of Bohemia in the tenth century. In 973 Duke Boleslas I, who had recognized the imperial suzerainty, established the see of Prague, whose second incumbent, St Adalbert, died a martyr's death in Prussia. Duke Mieszko I of Poland was baptized in 966, and the whole of his kingdom constituted the diocese of Gniezno, which was directly subject to Rome. The Hungarians had settled the land following their decisive defeat by Otto I at Lechfeld in 955: they were converted to Christianity during the reign of Vaik (997–1038), who was baptized as Stephen and later canonized. The incorporation of all these kingdoms into Latin Christendom halted the further advance of the Eastern Church, which by this time had established itself in the Russian principality of Kiev, and then in Bulgaria and Serbia. The schism between the two churches had in actual fact been brewing for a long time, fostered as much by mutual linguistic and cultural incomprehension as by divergence of dogma: when it finally came in 1054 the frontiers of the two observances were fixed once and for all. The Christianization of Central Europe also prevented the 'Drang nach Osten' of the German peoples, a barrier breached only by the violent conquest of pagan Prussia by the Teutonic Knights in the thirteenth century. Around the year 1000 the Scandinavians had also become Christian: Denmark under Harald Bluetooth (950–986); Norway under Olaf Tryggvason (995–1000) and lastly Sweden. Between 1000 and 1035 Cnut, King of Denmark, created an empire comprising his own country, southern Sweden and Norway and extending as far as England. Expansion was equally vigorous in the Mediterranean: the Norman Robert Guiscard conquered Campania, and his brother Roger, Sicily. Roger II united the whole kingdom of 'greater' Sicily under his control. In Spain the *Reconquista* first opened up the pilgrim route to Santiago de Compostela and in 1085 Toledo was taken. The decisive battle was fought at Las Navas de Tolosa in 1212 and by the mid-thirteenth century only the kingdom of Granada was left in Arab hands: this finally fell to the Christians in 1492.

**Vikings settle in Normandy.** 911

**Baptism of Mieszko I.** 966

**Accession of Holy Roman Emperor Otto** 996

**911:** The Vikings settle in Normandy under the terms of the Treaty of St-Clair-sur-Epte between Rollo and Charles the Simple. This region forms their base for expeditions against England (1066) and southern Italy.
**955:** Hungarians defeated by Otto I at Lechfeld (Bavaria). This marks the end of their raids across Europe: they settle the land and adopt Christianity.
**966:** Baptism of Mieszko I of Poland, who founds a centralized state ruled by 'ducal law'. Creation of the archbishopric of Gniezno.
**973:** Creation of the see of Prague, but Duke Boleslas I accepts the suzerainty of Emperor Otto I.
**985:** Baptism of Vaik (St Stephen), founder of the Christian kingdom of Hungary, who is crowned in 1001 in the new metropolitan see of Esztergom. The pagan uprising which follows his death is put down by King Béla I.
**996–1002:** Reign of Otto III, son of Otto II, and the Byzantine princess Theophano. The Emperor installs his old tutor, Gerbert of Aurillac, in the Holy See as Pope Sylvester II. Both dream of restoring the Roman Empire, the Senate and the Code of Justinian. The Emperor orders the tomb of Charlemagne at Aix-la-Chapelle to be opened and venerates his relics. He is deeply influenced by the apocalyptic ideas which become widespread as the millennium approaches.
**1000:** The terrors foretold for this time fail to materialize, but ecclesiastics find in the Book of Revelations the prediction that the Devil, bound in chains since the coming of Christ, would be set free and would reign on earth. Wonders, the appearance of comets or the birth of monsters are interpreted as signs of the impending end of the world.

2. *Reliquary of St Foy de Conques, 9th–10th century.*

3. *Monogram of Hugh Capet, King of France 987–96.*

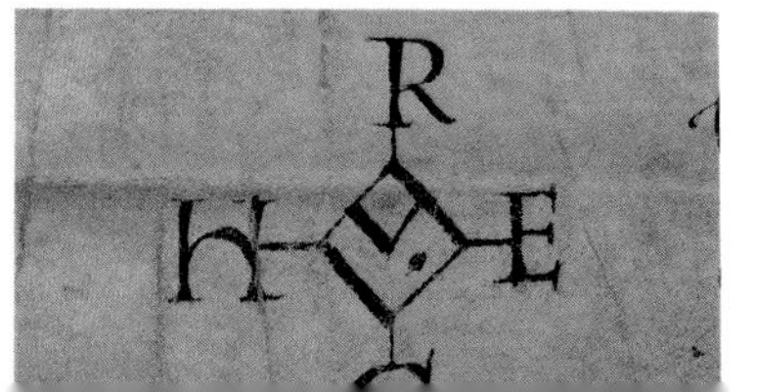

4. *Ivory box inscribed with the name Al Mughira, Cordoba, 10th century.*

# Tenth and eleventh centuries

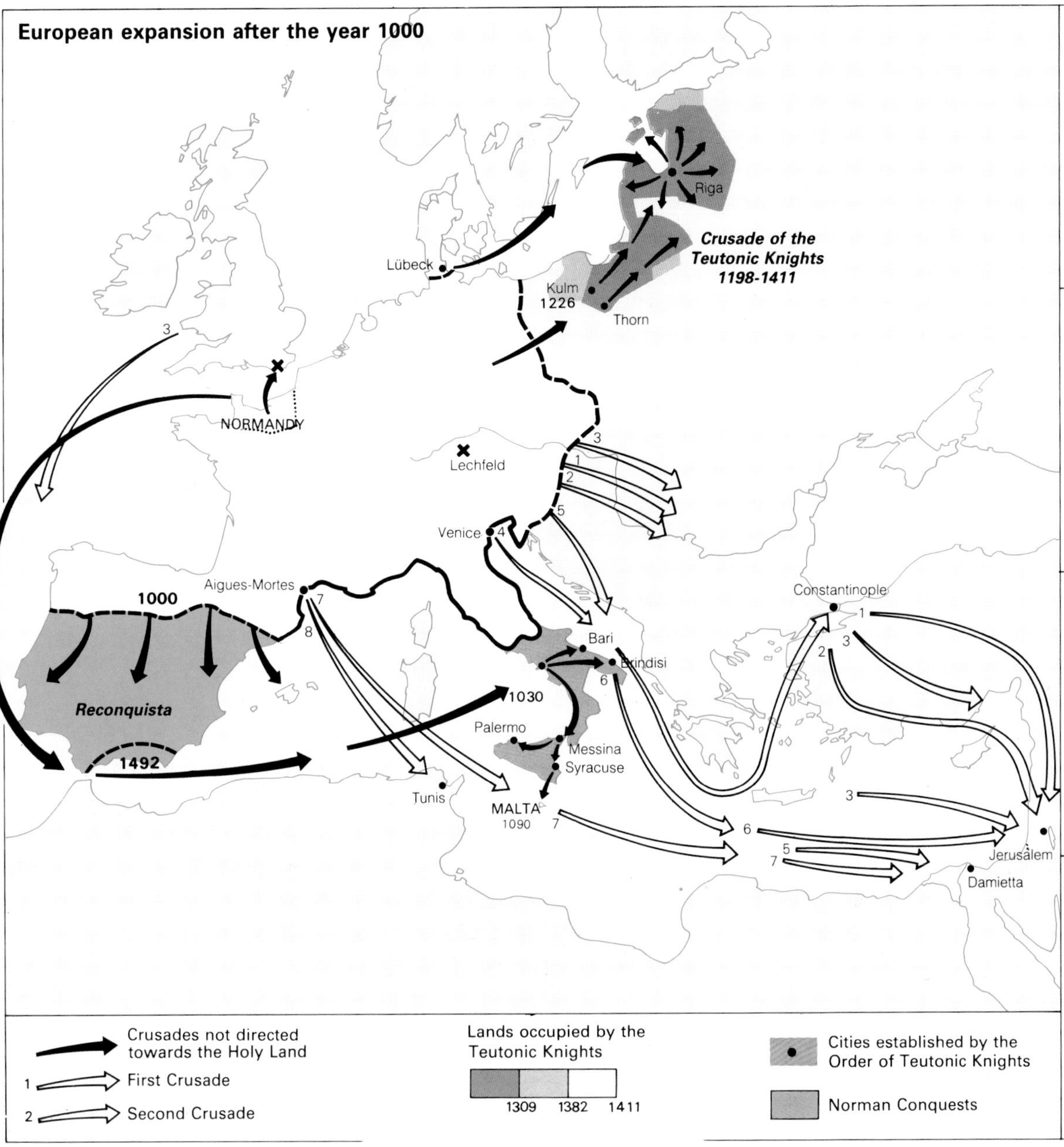

## European expansion after the year 1000

Lübeck
Kulm 1226
Thorn
Riga
*Crusade of the Teutonic Knights 1198-1411*
NORMANDY
Lechfeld
Venice
Aigues-Mortes
1000
*Reconquista*
1492
Bari
Brindisi
1030
Palermo
Messina
Syracuse
Tunis
MALTA 1090
Constantinople
Jerusalem
Damietta

Crusades not directed towards the Holy Land
1 First Crusade
2 Second Crusade
Lands occupied by the Teutonic Knights: 1309, 1382, 1411
Cities established by the Order of Teutonic Knights
Norman Conquests

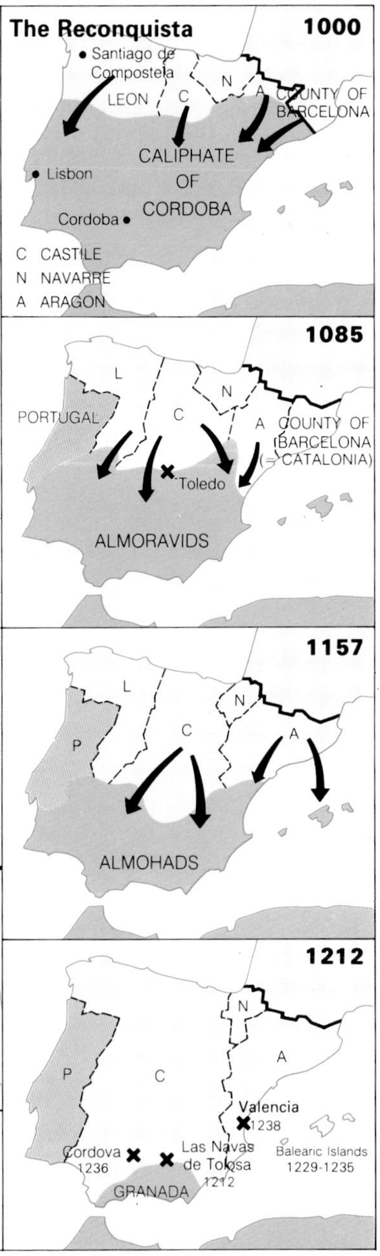

## The Reconquista

**1000**
Santiago de Compostela
LEON
C
N
A
COUNTY OF BARCELONA
CALIPHATE OF CORDOBA
Lisbon
Cordoba
C CASTILE
N NAVARRE
A ARAGON

**1085**
L
N
C
A
PORTUGAL
COUNTY OF BARCELONA (= CATALONIA)
Toledo
ALMORAVIDS

**1157**
L
N
C
A
P
ALMOHADS

**1212**
N
A
P
C
Valencia 1238
Balearic Islands 1229-1235
Cordova 1236
Las Navas de Tolosa 1212
GRANADA

**Death of Cnut the Great.**
**1035**

5. *St Stephen, King of Hungary. Fragment of coronation robe, 1031.*

**1018–35:** Reign of Cnut the Great, King of Denmark, which was converted to Christianity in the 10th century. The bishopric of Lund rapidly becomes independent of the see of Hamburg.
**1060–91:** Norman conquest of Sicily. By 1131 Roger II controls the whole kingdom of Sicily, including Calabria and Apulia. In 1194 the kingdom passes to the Hohenstaufens of Swabia as a result of a marriage alliance.
**1066:** Norman conquest of England. Duke William the Bastard had been designated heir by the last Anglo-Saxon king, Edward the Confessor. Harold opposes William but is defeated at Hastings. These events are illustrated in the Bayeux Tapestry.
**1075–1122:** Construction of the cathedral of Santiago de Compostela. The *Reconquista* makes progress. Toledo is captured from the Moors in 1085.

6. *Stave church of Hopperstad, Norway, c. 1150.*

# The Crusades in the East

WESTERN EXPANSION was not slow to upset the balance of power in the Mediterranean world. In the west there was Latin Christendom; to the north-east the Byzantine Empire; and in the south Islam, stretching from Almohad Spain to the Middle East, which was gradually conquered by the Seljuk Turks, who cut off Christian pilgrims' access to the holy places. Already in the eleventh century the Spanish *Reconquista* had familiarized the French and Burgundian knights who took part in it with the notion of 'Holy War', while at the same time the impulse for religious reform had glorified Christian values: promotion of the 'Peace of God', which sought to limit the violent depredations of the warrior classes within Western society, made it possible for this energy to be turned against the infidel to liberate the Holy Sepulchre. For a society deeply imbued with millenarian ideas, 'taking the cross' meant identifying oneself with the Redeemer and, in the certainty of salvation, going to relive the sufferings of His Passion at their actual scene. The First Crusade was preached by Urban II at Clermont in 1095. Flemish and northern French knights such as Godfrey of Bouillon set out in response to this appeal, preceded by crowds of humbler folk, many of whom perished on the way, victims of the hardships of the journey and the attacks of the Turks. A third contingent under the leadership of Raymond, Count of Toulouse, set out from southern France; they, too, followed the overland route. Jerusalem fell to the crusaders on 15 July 1099, but the crusade also led to the creation of four Latin states in the East: the County of Edessa, the Kingdom of Jerusalem, the Principality of Antioch and the County of Tripoli. Thenceforth the defence of these lands became the prime consideration in the launching of crusades: St Bernard preached the Second Crusade (1147–9) at Vézelay following news of the fall of Edessa, and again in 1189–92 a third expedition set off in response to the loss of Jerusalem. Apart from their disappointing results, these new enterprises were notable for the participation of Western monarchs (Louis VII and Philip Augustus of France, Richard the Lionheart of England, and the German emperors Conrad III, Frederick Barbarossa and finally, in the thirteenth century, Frederick II). In all cases the faster sea-route was used, though this meant that political and commercial agreements had to be reached with the Italian cities, who alone possessed the necessary fleets, with the result that rivalry of interests among the crusaders themselves, considerable as these already were, became ever more pronounced. If the Muslims benefited from this trend, the Byzantines were its first victims: in 1191 Richard the Lionheart took from them Cyprus, which became a Frankish kingdom under the Lusignan family, and, after the capture of Zara in Dalmatia (which the Venetians demanded as compensation), the Fourth Crusade culminated in the crusaders' sack of Constantinople (1204) and the partition of the Byzantine Empire among the Frankish lords, who established the Principality of Morea (Achaea), the Lordship of Athens and the Kingdom of Thessalonika. The attention of the West was thus diverted from the Holy Land: Jerusalem was recovered only temporarily between 1229 and 1244, and it was in the face of public opinion that Louis IX went on crusade to Egypt and the Holy Land (1248–1254). He died on crusade outside Tunis in 1270, fulfilling an anachronistic dream.

*1. Crusaders' assault on Antioch. Manuscript of Chronicles of William of Tyre, 12th century.*

**Urban II preaches the First Crusade.** — 1095

**Crusaders take Jerusalem.** — 1099

**St Bernard preaches the Second Crusade at Vézelay.** — 1146

*2. Ramparts of Caesarea in Palestine, 13th century.*

**1062–4:** Pope Alexander II grants a plenary indulgence – the forgiveness of all sins – to those who fight the Muslims. This encourages the participation of many northern French and Burgundian knights in the *Reconquista*. Toledo is taken in 1085.
**1095:** Pope Urban II preaches the First Crusade at Clermont.
**1096–9:** First Crusade – involving knights and separate contingents of simple people led by itinerant preachers such as Peter the Hermit. Many pogroms against the Jews take place in the course of this movement. Jerusalem is taken on 15 July 1099 and the Kingdom of Jerusalem, governed by Godfrey of Bouillon, is created, along with the Principality of Antioch and the Counties of Edessa and Tripoli.
**1147–9:** Second Crusade, prompted by the loss of Edessa to the Muslims and preached by St Bernard at Vézelay in 1146. Louis VII of France and the emperor Conrad III take part.

*3. Cross of a knight who participated in the First Crusade, end of 11th century.*

# 11th–13th centuries

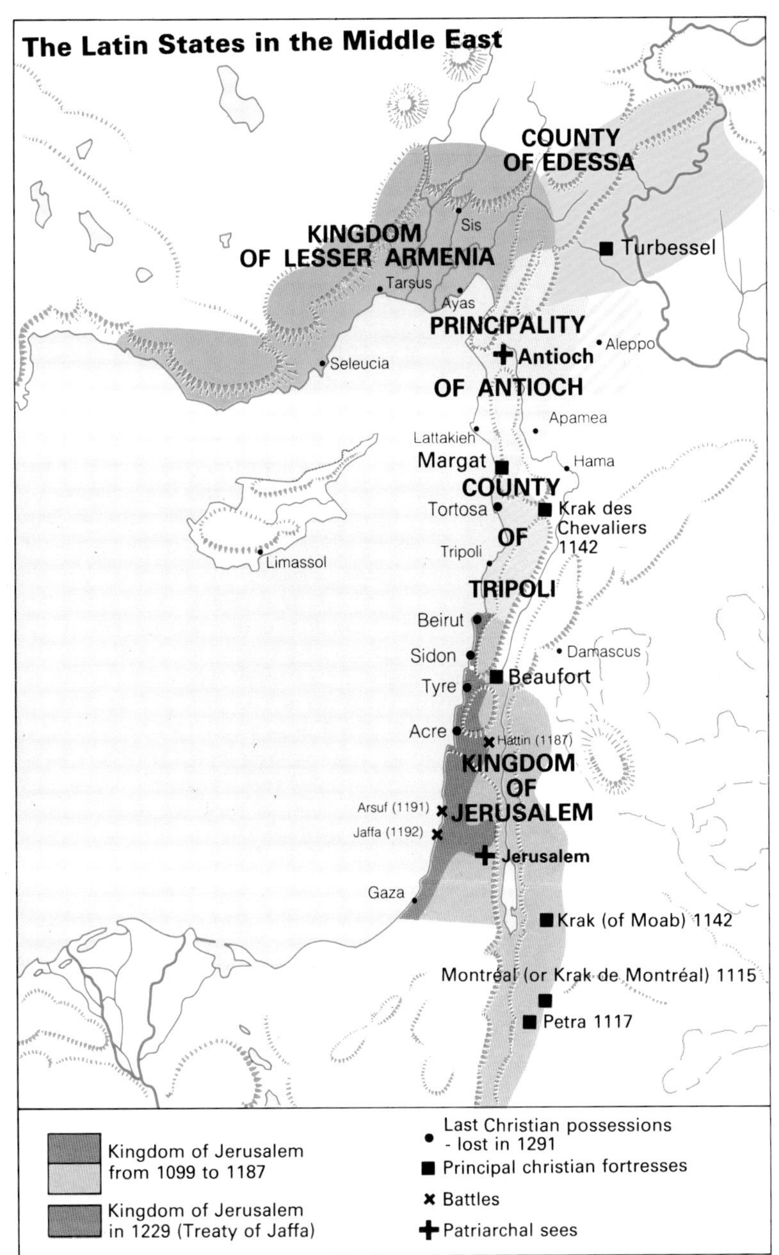


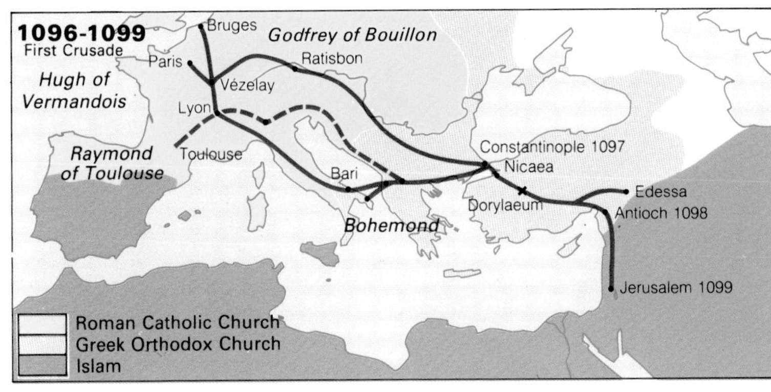


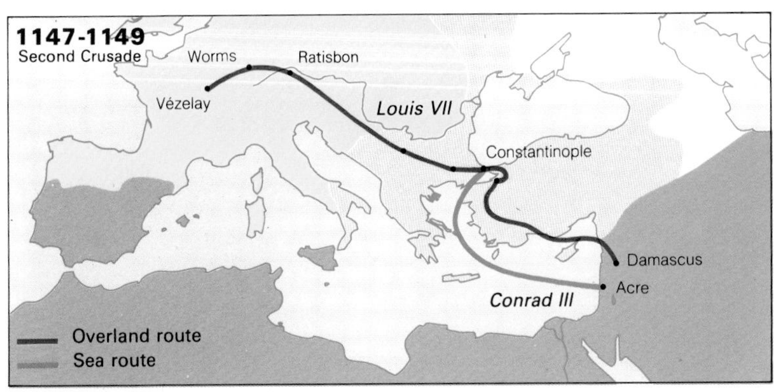


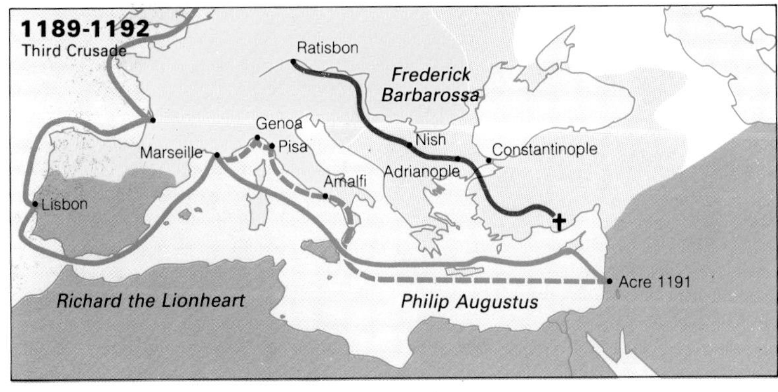


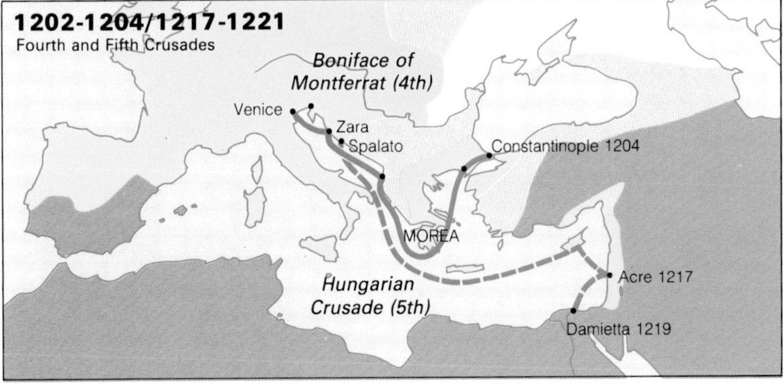


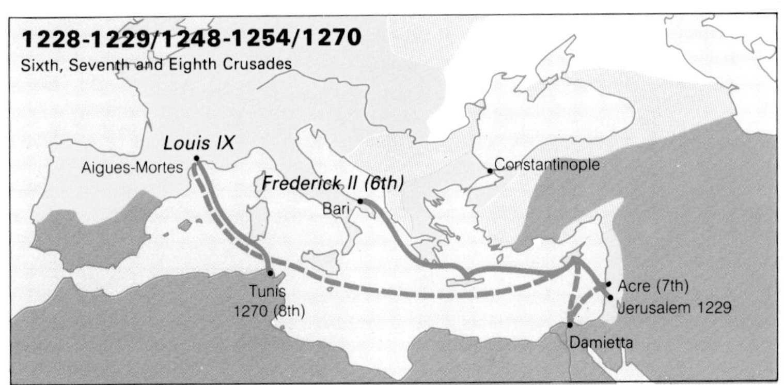


**adin recaptures Jerusalem.** | **Death of Louis IX outside Tunis.**

**187** | **1270**

**1189–92:** Third Crusade, following the recapture of Jerusalem by Salah ed-Din Yusuf (Saladin) in 1187. Emperor Frederick Barbarossa takes the cross but is drowned in Anatolia. Richard the Lionheart and Philip Augustus, King of France, take part.
**1202–4:** Fourth Crusade, instigated by Pope Innocent III. The demands of the Venetians – who provide the crusaders with sea transport – lead to the capture of the Byzantine town of Zara, then of Constantinople itself (1204). A Latin empire replaces the Byzantine and its capital is established at Nicaea. Frankish nobles carve out fiefs for themselves in Greece.
**1208–13:** Albigensian Crusade against the Cathar heretics of southern France.
**1217–21:** Fifth Crusade, originated by Innocent III. The crusaders take Cyprus, Acre and Egypt. Damietta is taken but then lost. This expedition is preceded by the Children's Crusade – in reality composed of young people, the majority of whom die on the journey.
**1228–9:** Sixth Crusade, organized by Frederick II although he has been excommunicated. The Emperor negotiates with the Sultan for the right to reoccupy Jerusalem, which is finally lost in 1244.
**1248–54:** Seventh Crusade, to Egypt. Led by Louis IX: he takes Damietta but is defeated and captured at Mansourah. After he is freed on payment of a ransom, he spends four years in the Holy Land.
**1270:** Eighth Crusade, to Tunisia, under the leadership of Louis IX, who dies outside Tunis.
**1291:** Fall of Acre, last bastion of resistance among the Latin kingdoms in the East.

# Kiev and the Birth of the Russian State

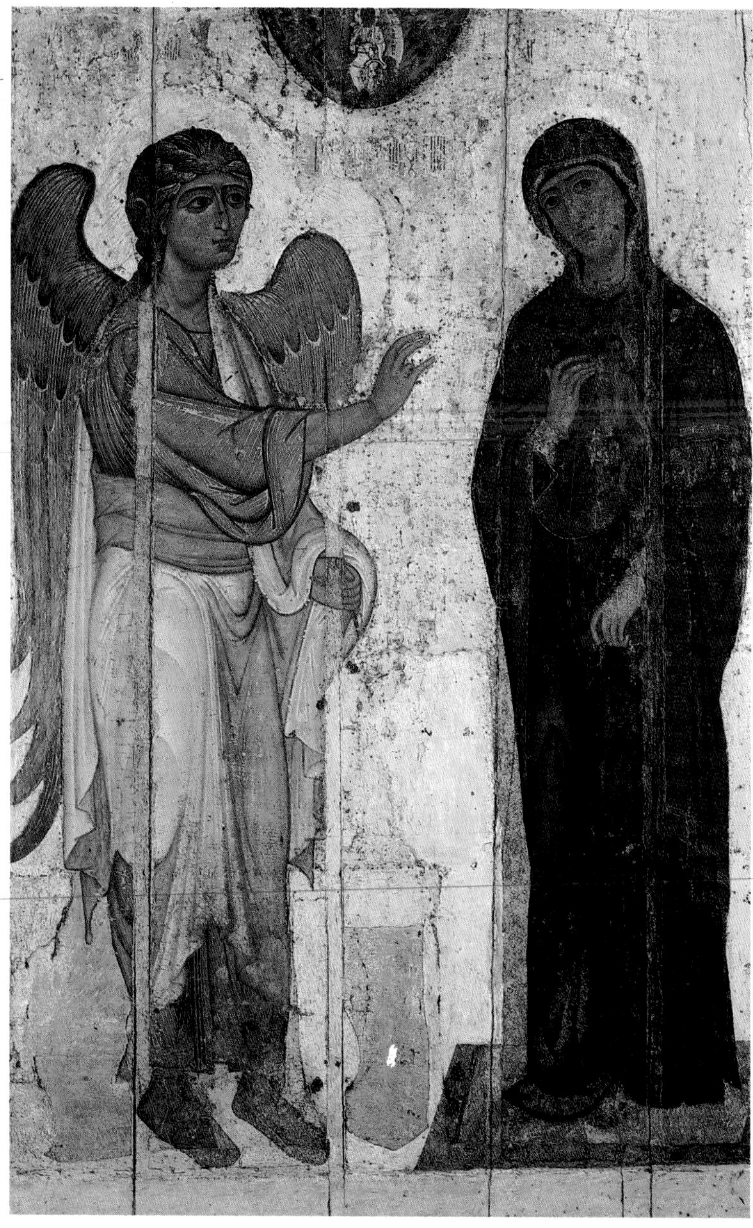

*1. The Annunciation by Ustiug. Novgorod school, 12th century.*

At the end of the ninth century Russia emerged as a geographical and political unit. But the word Russian, which is often used to refer to its population, is somewhat misleading and the reality is more complex. Slav peoples had occupied the vast area of land spreading from the Baltic to the Black Sea and from the Bug to the Oka. There is clear evidence of settlements along the coastal regions of the Black Sea going back to the fourth century. The Slavs mixed with older populations of Iranian origin (the Scythians and Sarmatians), who, living from agriculture and from animal husbandry, had taken up a sedentary existence and reached a high level of civilization. In the north, settlements followed later. Slav tribes settled in the region around Novgorod and along the upper reaches of the Dniepr River around the seventh century. These were nomadic peoples and made their living as hunters and gatherers. Their mode of life was similar to that of the Finno-Ugric peoples who were their near neighbours to the north-east of the Volga. But these small autonomous groups with their own local leaders remained separate from the Finns and the Balts essentially because of their language, which also laid the foundation for their own unity. Between the eighth and ninth centuries urban centres sprang up along the rivers (which were the only means of communication), the first of these being Novgorod. Very early on, the area around Novgorod was occupied by Scandinavian peoples, no doubt coming from Norway. In the ninth century the arrival of the Vikings added to these peaceful settlements. The rivers criss-crossing Russia gave the Scandinavians more direct access than was possible by sea both to the Arab countries, along the River Volga and the Don, and to Byzantium. Coming down the Lovat from the Dniepr, the Scandinavian warrior traders (Varangians) reached the Black Sea, then Constantinople, where their goods and services were paid for in gold: they brought with them slaves as well as furs, wax and honey levied from the Slavs on their route.The first Russian leaders were drawn from these bands of adventurers. By forming alliances or by force of arms, they subjugated the Slav tribes who lived along the commercial routes, founded cities, and carved out vast properties for themselves. In the tenth century Kiev, which was an ancient city occupying a key position on the 'road from the Varangians to the Greeks', fell into the hands of the Rurikid princes, the first royal line for whom there exists documentary evidence. These princes subjugated Novgorod and put their families in control of neighbouring towns. Very quickly they became integrated into the Slav population. To reach the markets in Constantinople, which they at first attempted to win over by force, the Russian princes concluded treaties of alliance and trade with Byzantium. In order to negotiate successfully with the emperors they had to demonstrate their own unity and organize themselves according to some definite hierarchical order. This is emphasized, after the conversion of the Russians to Christianity, by their ecclesiastical structure. Directly subordinate to the patriarch of

**The Russians lay siege to Constantinople.** **Oleg becomes prince of Kiev.** **Baptism of Prince Vladimir and the Christianization of Russia.** **Reign of Jaroslav the Wise.**

**860** **c. 900** **988–9** **1019–54**

**860:** The first date in Russian history according to Byzantine sources. The Russians lay siege to Constantinople. The Patriarch Photius attempts to convert them to Christianity (864–7).
**911–71:** At the beginning of the 10th century a prince from the line of Rurik, Oleg, settles in Kiev and subjugates Novgorod. In 911 he signs a peace and trade treaty with Byzantium. The alliance is renewed in 955 by his successor, Igor, after a short campaign against Constantinople in 943. These two documents, preserved in the first Kievan Chronicle, almost certainly had Greek originals. Together with a document from the middle of the 10th century, from the hand of Emperor Constantine VII Porphyrogenetus, they are extremely informative about social and political conditions in Russia. After Igor (who died in 945), his son Svyatoslav seeks to consolidate his control over the commercial routes. In the east, he attacks the Khazar kingdom, and threatens the Byzantine lands in Cherson (965–6). In 968 he undertakes an expedition against Bulgaria and attempts to occupy the lower regions of the Danube. Byzantium counter-attacks. Defeated at Dorostolon, Svyatoslav signs a new peace treaty in 971. In 972 he is killed by the Pechenegs (a nomadic Turkic people established since the beginning of the 10th century on the northern shores of the Black Sea), almost certainly at the instigation of the Byzantines.
**972–1015:** Vladimir, Svyatoslav's younger son, captures Novgorod in 978, and then Kiev, with the help of Scandinavian mercenaries. Emperor Basil II asks for his assistance to quell a military rebellion; in exchange he receives the hand in marriage of the Emperor's sister Anne. The alliance is preceded by the Prince's conversion to Christianity (989). Though Christianity had begun to penetrate into Russia before this official ceremony, the attempts at the forced conversion of the Russian people, particularly in rural areas, were to meet with strong resistance.
**1019–54:** Jaroslav takes power in 1019. Under his reign, Kievan Rus enjoys its most successful period. The Prince concludes alliances with several European courts. The Patriarch of Constantinople bestows the status of metropolis on Kiev. Cathedrals are built, including the cathedrals of St Sophia in Kiev and Novgorod, which are amongst the finest examples of stone architecture. There is intense literary activity. The first Russian chronicles are written.
**1054–1110:** After Jaroslav, the influence of Kiev collapses. The Kievan princes are no longer able to restrain the internal feuding between the principalities or prevent their break-up. External threats become more serious, both in the west, in Poland, and in the east, where the Cumans had settled permanently in the plains of southern Russia, making trade with Byzantium more difficult. From this period of upheaval date many important literary landmarks: the first versions of Russian law (*Russkaja Pravda*), which ordered social relations according to princely law, and the *'Russian Primary Chronicle'* or *'Tales of Bygone Years'*, the first Russian historical work, which was written around 1110.

*3. The Vladimir Madonna, an icon of the early 12th century from Constantinople.*

# 9th–12th centuries

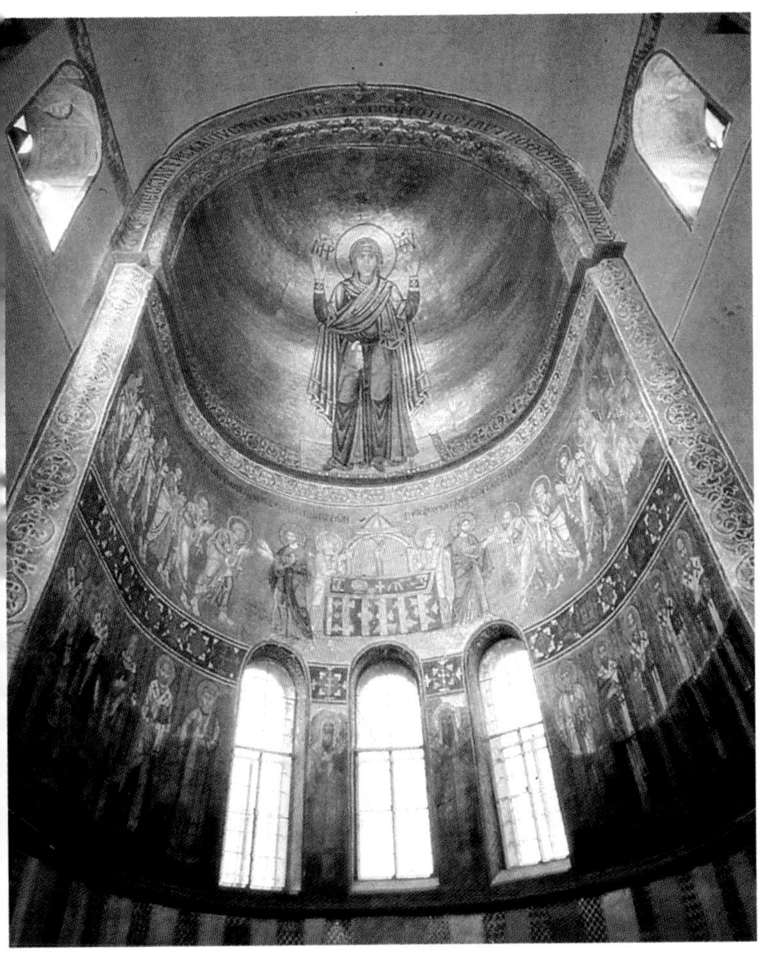

2. *Apse of Cathedral of St Sophia in Kiev, 12th century.*

Prior to 900
Slav settlements
Nomadic
Sedentary
Centres of unification of Russia
Forests
Rich lands
Steppes
'Road from the Varangians to the Greeks' and Eastern trade route
CARELIA
Lake Onega
Lake Ladoga
SCANDINAVIANS
FINNO-UGRICS
Ladoga
Novgorod
Gotland
BALTIC SEA
FINNO-UGRICS
Lovat
Volga
West Dvina
Nema
Oka
BALTS
SLAVS
Vistula
Pripet
Marshes
Kiev
Ros
Bug
Dnestr
CARPATHIANS
Don
Donetz
Volga
Olbia
Dniepr
Sarkel
Itil
KHAZARS
Tmutarakan
CASPIAN SEA
Danube
Cherson
BLACK SEA
CAUCASUS
Constantinople
Sinope
BYZANTINE EMPIRE
A
900-1100
Kievan Rus
in 912
in 972
in 1054
BALTIC SEA
Ladoga
Novgorod
Pskov
West Dvina
Lovat
Tver
Rostov
Murom
Volga
Nema
Polotsk
Oka
POLAND
Smolensk
Vistula
Ryazan
Ecclesiastic structure
Patriarchy
Metropolis
Bishoprics
Turov
Chernigov
Vladimir
Kiev
Galich
Belgorod
Pereyeslavl
Dniepr
Don
Dnestr
Bug
HUNGARY
PECHENEGS
Sarkel
Volga
Olbia
Itil
KINGDOM OF THE KHAZARS
Danube
Cherson
Tmutarakan
Dorostolon
BULGARIA
BLACK SEA
Constantinople
BYZANTINE EMPIRE
2000 km
B

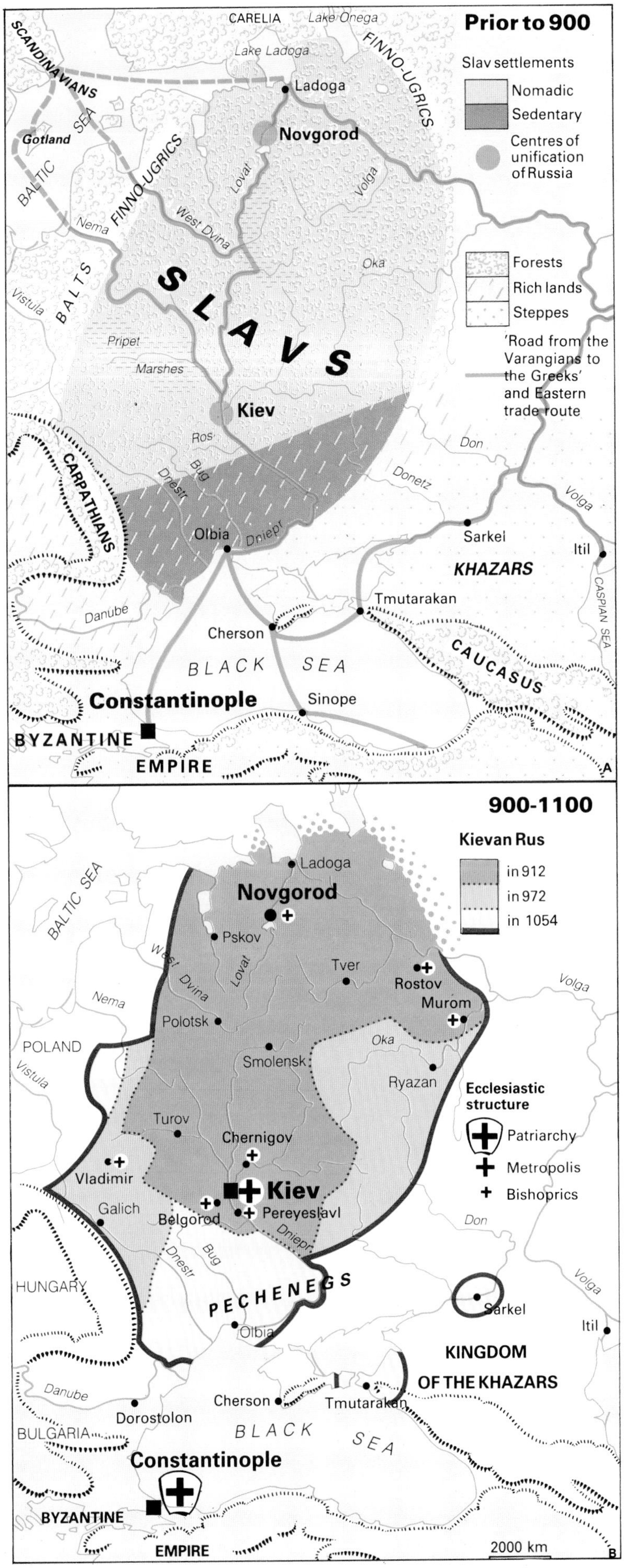

Constantinople, Kiev became the metropolitan centre of 'all of Russia'. The political image of Russian unity was sustained by a religious ideal, which was much called upon in times of crisis. The culture of Kievan Rus, which was at its height in the eleventh and twelfth centuries, owed its first literary works and first monuments to the clerics and artists of Byzantium. After the destruction of Kiev by the Mongols in 1240, the Russian principalities of the north were to invoke this cultural and spiritual heritage as a way of consolidating their own hegemonic position.

**nastery of the Caves founded in Kiev.** **Reign of Vladimir II the Monomakh.**

**1** **1113–25**

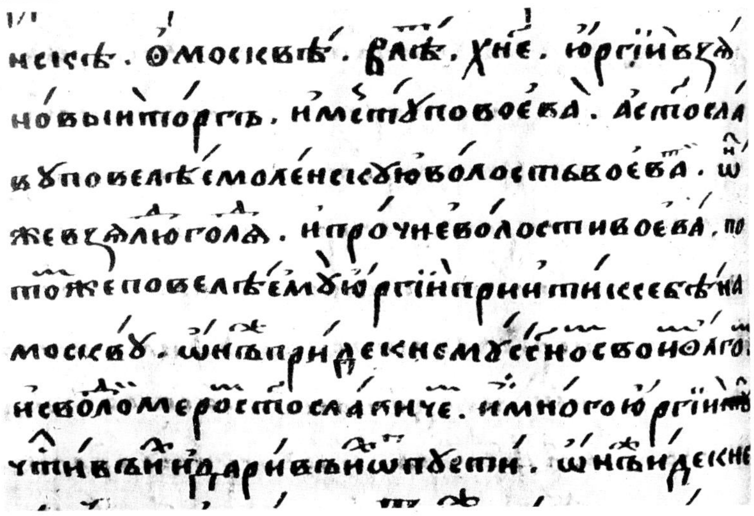

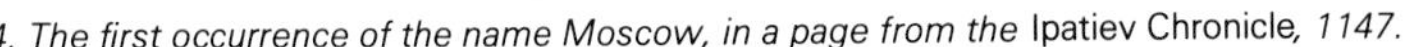

4. *The first occurrence of the name Moscow, in a page from the* Ipatiev Chronicle*, 1147.*

# Popes and Emperors

1. Christ blessing the Emperor Otto II. Byzantine ivory, 10th century.

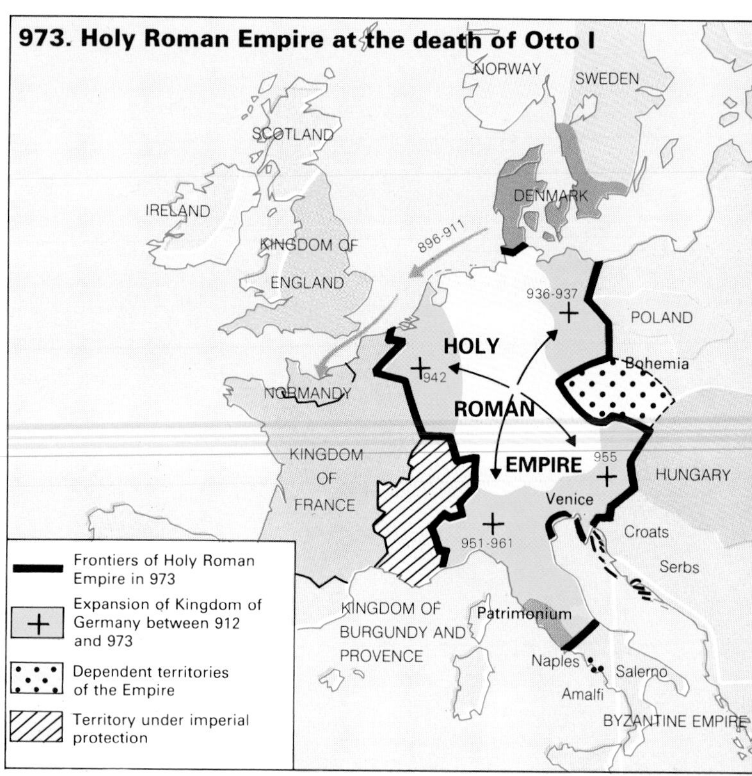


Between the Rhine and the Elbe, which is to say between the Latin world and the Slavic, the process of disintegration of the Carolingian Empire gave birth to four duchies: Saxony, Franconia, Swabia and Bavaria. This group of territories was soon augmented by the addition of Upper and Lower Lorraine, then in 1033 of Burgundy, giving a western border that ran along the Seine and the Rhône, as established by the Treaty of Verdun of 843. In the east, between the Elbe and the Oder, Bohemia, Austria, Carinthia, Styria, the Marches of Brandenburg, and Upper and Lower Lusatia were progressively conquered and converted to Christianity. Around 1190, the old Empire was then divided up into some seventeen duchies. In the south the Kingdom of Italy and the Mark of Verona also theoretically belonged among this number, though the emperors had repeatedly to return to assert their rights against the claims of local dynasties or towns or the Holy See. The reunification of the Empire, with the German regions as its new focus, was the work of the Saxon dynasty: Otto I, conqueror of the Hungarians at the Lech (955) received the imperial crown from the hands of the Pope at Rome, in exchange for the re-affirmation of papal

**Gregory VII's *Dictatus Papae*.** 1075

**Henry humiliated at Canossa.** 1077

**Frederick Barbarossa crowned emperor.** 1155

**962:** Otto I crowned emperor at Rome.
**962–1002:** Ottonian dynasty of Saxon origin.
**996–1002:** Otto III emperor. With Gerbart of Aurillac, who becomes Pope Sylvester II, he dreams of re-establishing the Roman Empire.
**1024–1138:** Salian dynasty of Franconian origin.
**1075–1122:** 'Quarrel over investiture of bishops' between the Pope and the Emperor. In 1075 *Dictatus Papae* (the Pope's instructions) is promulgated by Gregory VII (1073–85), the former Cardinal Hildebrand – central figure in the 'Gregorian Reforms' – whose object is to prevent church appointments being controlled by the laity and who declares the pope's right to depose the emperor. In 1077 the emperor Henry IV is forced to make submission to the Pope at Canossa. In 1122 the two parties come to an agreement in the Concordat of Worms: the Pope reserves the right to the spiritual induction of prelates, the Emperor receives rights of temporal investiture. This accord is ratified by the First Lateran Council in 1123.
**1122–1250:** 'Struggle between the priesthood and the Empire': revival of the

2. Emperor Otto the Great among the monks. 13th-century illuminated manuscript.

quarrel between the Emperor and the Pope on the more general question of universal sovereignty.
**1138–1250:** Hohenstaufen dynasty, of Swabian origin.
**1155–90:** As a descendant of the two rival families, the Guelphs and the Ghibellines, Frederick Barbarossa is chosen as emperor. He proves to be a bitter adversary of Pope Alexander III. Dies during the Third Crusade, drowned in a Cilician river, thus gathering around his name the legend of 'the Emperor of the Last Days', according to which he is waiting on the Kyffhäuser mountains to return to lead the German people.
**1177:** Peace of Venice between Frederick Barbarossa and the Pope. It allows the Emperor, though weakened, to recover his power very quickly in Italy.
**1179:** Third Lateran Council, which decides that the Pope will henceforth be elected by a two-thirds majority of the cardinals and takes various measures aimed at bringing about church reform.
**1202:** Innocent III's *Venerabilem* decretal affirms Pontifical Theocracy, the doctrine of

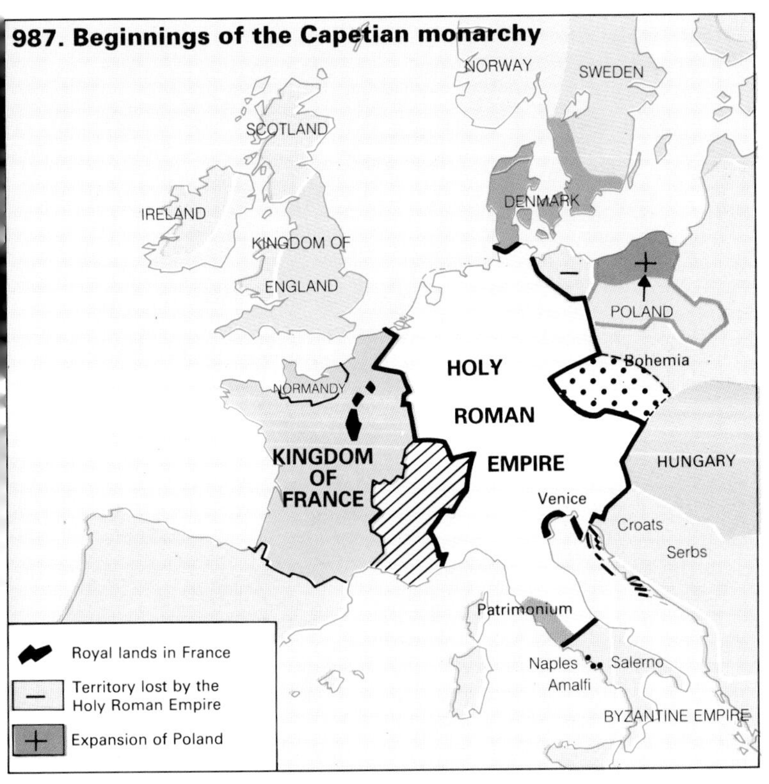


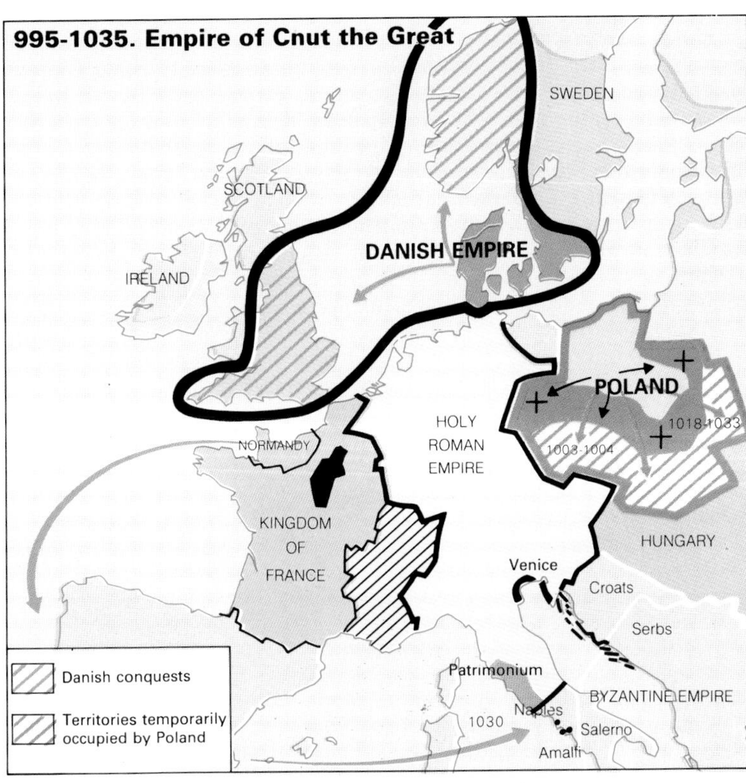


rights over the Patrimony and over southern Italy, which was held by the Byzantines. The emperor did, however, obtain a right of supervision over the election of the pope and gained control of the German church; for their part, the German prelates took a considerable share in the exercise of and benefits accruing from imperial power. However, the emperor, unlike the French king, for example, possessed no lands of his own; and, most importantly, the elective principle put in question the extent of his power at each succession. The princes, who were mainly ecclesiastics, chose the new emperor from one of the ducal families. The emperors certainly attempted to designate successors during their own lifetimes, thus ensuring a certain dynastic continuity to the Ottonians of Saxony, the Salians of Franconia (1027–1152) and the Swabian Hohenstaufens (1138–1250). But, by contrast with the kingdom of France, for example, the Empire was not in the hands of a single dynasty that might have strengthened it vis-à-vis the papacy. The Pope, undertaking a general reform of the church and Christianity, denied the Emperor his right of intervention in the papal election (*Dictatus papae* of 1075) and his right of ecclesiastical investiture. With the emperor Henry IV and Pope Gregory VII the conflict came to a head. In 1122, the Concordat of Worms recognized that the pope alone had control over the spiritual consecration of bishops ('by the ring and staff'), the emperor merely retaining the power of temporal investiture ('by the sceptre'), but the political and ideological question as to which of these powers took precedence over the other was not resolved. In the Peace of Venice (1177), Frederick Barbarossa had to acknowledge that the cardinals were free to elect the pope. Worse still from the emperors' point of view, Innocent III was able, at the beginning of the thirteenth century, to affirm his right to arbitrate between two candidates for the imperial crown (in the decretal *Venerabilem* of 1202) and he also elaborated the theory of the universal power of the pope in juridical terms (pontifical theocracy). Frederick II did not succeed in restoring dignity, or its former power, to the imperial throne, which, shortly after his death in 1250, was to remain vacant for many years (interregnum of 1256–73). The Empire would never recover from this two-century-long confrontation with the papal monarchy.

**e Innocent III's decretal, *Venerabilem*.** **Death of Frederick II.**

**1202** **1250**

the universal sovereignty of the Holy See.
**1220–50:** Frederick II becomes emperor. He is son of Emperor Henry IV and Constance, daughter of Roger II of Sicily, which enables him to become king of Sicily in 1198. He resumes the struggle against the papacy, now represented by Innocent III and Honorius III. In 1229, though excommunicated, he leads the Crusade and negotiates the return of Jerusalem. At Palermo, with his harem and menagerie, he leads the life of an oriental prince. He is a fascinating character who, like Barbarossa before him, is thought of as incarnating the legendary idea of the 'Emperor of the Last Days'.
**1250–73:** Interregnum. The imperial throne remains vacant, the princes being unable to agree on a candidate. The Empire comes out of the struggles with the papacy very weakened. This is also the end of the Hohenstaufen dynasty.

*3. The imperial globe. 12th-century Germanic.*

*4. Castel del Monte, the castle of Frederick II of Hohenstaufen in Apulia.*

# Feudal France

As EARLY AS 888–898 the crown of the kingdom of 'Western Francia' passed out of the hands of the Carolingian dynasty to King Eudes. Hugh Capet, one of his descendants, was elected king by the magnates of the realm in 987, and thereafter the crown remained with the Capetians. Thanks in part to their practice of having their eldest sons crowned during the king's own lifetime – a practice observed even by Louis VII – the Capetian succession was remarkably untroubled. Moreover, they excelled in exploiting the concept of sacral kingship, which was glorified by symbolism, ritual and myth such as the legends of the holy oil of consecration borne by the Holy Spirit to Clovis's baptism and the king's purported ability to cure scrofula. The king also made the most of his demesne, which was extremely well placed in the heart of the rich wheat-fields of the Ile-de-France. Powerful barons such as the Dukes of Normandy and Aquitaine, held lands much more extensive than the king's but his symbolic authority offset his comparative lack of effective political power. The Capetians also benefited from their alliance with the church and, in contrast to the German emperors, generally supported the reform movement. Even in the south of France 'royal bishoprics' served as the advance guard of Capetian influence in the kingdom. In the twelfth and thirteenth centuries the increase in royal authority was evident everywhere. In the east Louis VI forced the Emperor to withdraw from Champagne in 1124. In the west the accession to the English throne of the seigneurial family of the Counts of Anjou, the Plantagenets, had catastrophic consequences for the French king when Henry II married the Duchess Eleanor of Aquitaine and thereby acquired sole control over England, Normandy and all western France with the exception of Brittany. The first hundred years of conflict between these two powers, which were marked by Philip Augustus's noteworthy victory at Bouvines (1214), culminated in the Treaty of Paris in 1259, according to which Louis IX accepted Henry III as his vassal for Guyenne and the county of Ponthieu. In the south the crusade against the Albigensian heretics (1208–1213) enabled the French crown to drive back the Aragonese in Catalonia and to annex the seneschalcies of Nîmes-Beaucaire and Béziers-Carcassonne (Treaty of Paris, 1229), while the county of Toulouse, which had formed the apanage of Alphonse of Poitiers, reverted to the crown at Alphonse's death in 1271. By the mid-thirteenth century the king

1. *Philip the Fair receiving a sealed document from a monk. Illumination from the* Livre de Dina et Kalila *(collection of fables), 1313.*

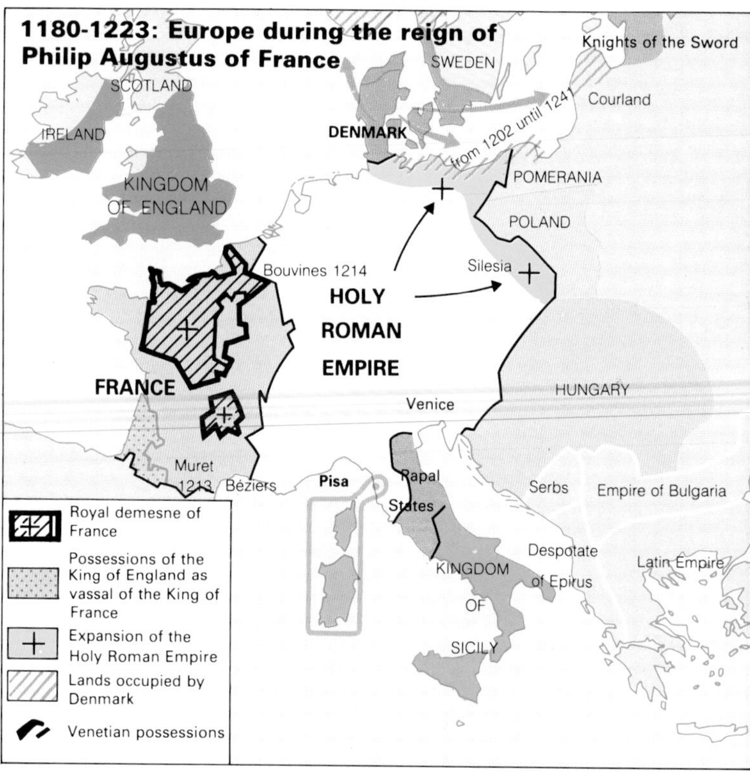


**Accession of Hugh Capet.**

**987**

**Louis VII repudiates Eleanor of Aquitaine.**

**1152**

**987–96:** Reign of Hugh Capet. Hugh, a descendant of King Eudes, is elected king over Charles of Lorraine, the Carolingian candidate. Archbishop Adalbero of Reims, and Gerbert, master of the schools and future Pope Sylvester II, play a decisive part in this change of dynasty.
**996–1031:** Reign of Robert the Pious, consecrated during his father's lifetime. His sanctity is praised by Archbishop Adalbero in his *Life of Robert the Pious*, although he is excommunicated by the Pope for marrying his cousin, Bertha of Burgundy, and has to repudiate her.
**1031–60:** Reign of Henry I, during which the first conflicts arise with the increasingly powerful Duke of Normandy.
**1060–1108:** Reign of Philip I, who adds the Gâtinais, the French Vexin and Berry to the royal demesne. Once Philip's conflict with the papacy is resolved, the Capetians, in contrast to the German emperors, maintain good relations with the Holy See.
**1108–37:** Reign of Louis VI, who pacifies the Ile-de-France, subduing in particular the Sire de Coucy. In 1124 he repels an invasion of Champagne by the emperor Henry V, ally of the King of England.
**1137:** The union of the kingdom of Aragon and the county of Barcelona creates a threat to the south of France which is removed only in 1213.
**1137–80:** Reign of Louis VII. He marries Eleanor, daughter of the Duke of Aquitaine, only to repudiate her in 1152 after the Second Crusade. She marries Henry Plantagenet, who becomes king of England.
**1151:** Death of Suger, Abbot of St Denis and Louis VI's chief advisor.
**1180–1223:** Reign of Philip Augustus, who crushes the King of England and his allies at Roche-au-Moine and Bouvines (1214).
**1208–13:** Albigensian Crusade, led by Simon de Montfort. He defeats and kills Peter II of Aragon at the Battle of Muret in 1213. After Louis VIII's intervention the Treaty of Paris in 1229 leads to the royal annexation of the seneschalcies of Nîmes and Beaucaire. The war against the Cathar heretics continues until the fall of Montségur in 1244.
**1223–6:** Reign of Louis VIII, who annexes the Poitou region.

3. *Nave of the Abbey of St Denis, 13th century.*

4. *Knight on a prancing horse. 13th-century French manuscript.*

# 10th–14th centuries

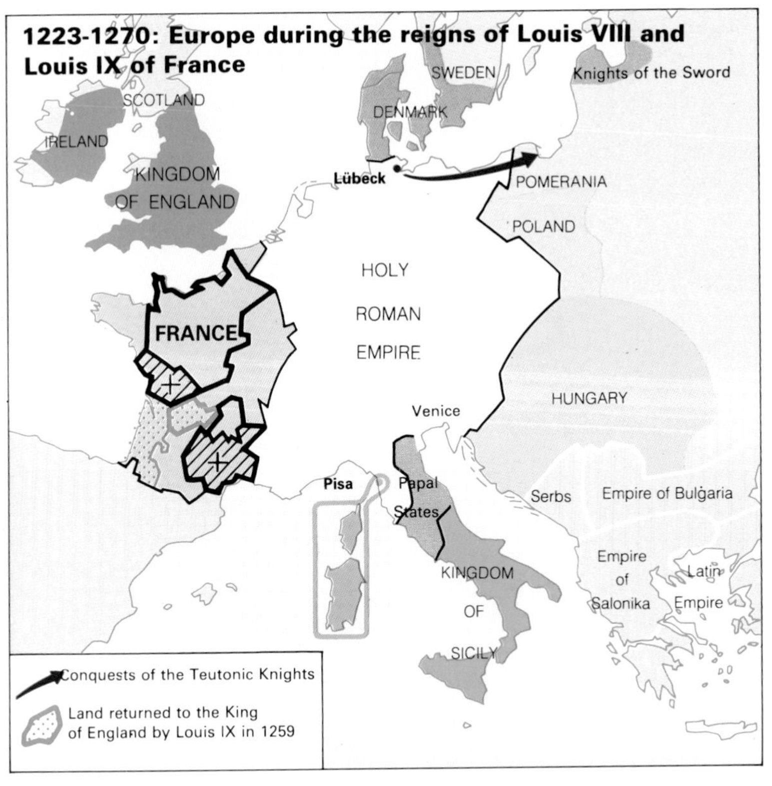


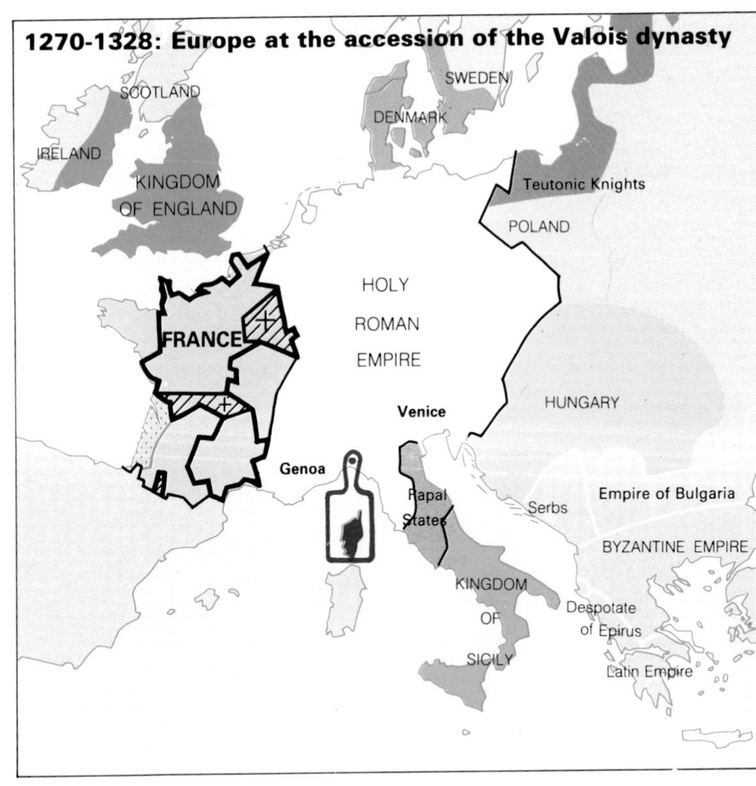


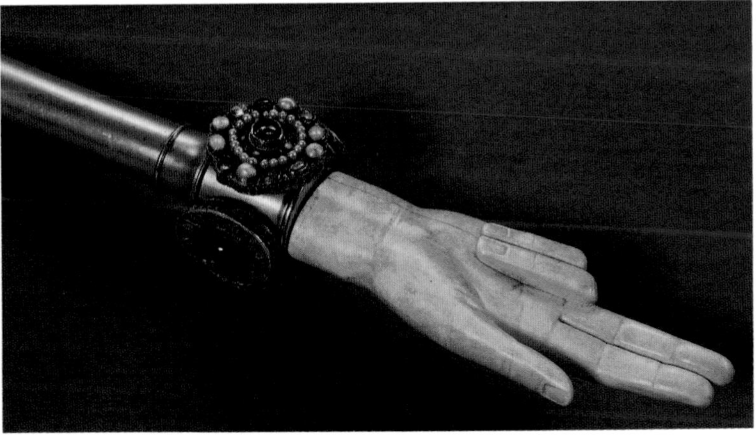

2. *Hand of Justice of the kings of France, 12th century.*

controlled almost all of a kingdom of some 14 million inhabitants, by far the most populous in the West. Paris was already generally thought of as the political capital and centre of learning. Under Philip Augustus and Louis IX there emerged stable organs of monarchical government and administration which were already highly centralized: the *Parlement* developed from having been an offshoot of the feudal *curia* into the supreme judicial body; bailiffs and seneschals were the king's representatives throughout the country and they submitted annual accounts to the *Chambre des Comptes* (Accounting Chamber). The Grand Ordinance of 1254 set out in detail the administrative organization of the kingdom. Under Philip the Fair the French monarchy emerged strengthened from its conflict with the papacy: the humiliation which Gregory VII had inflicted on the Emperor in 1077 was reversed when in 1303 the King's envoys seized the Pope; the King's lawyers pointed to Roman law to justify royal sovereignty, but the destruction of the Templars (1307–1314) also demonstrated the awesome degree of efficiency which state policing had by then attained.

**Battle of Bouvines.** 1214

**Treaty of Paris between France and England.** 1259

**Canonization of St Louis.** 1297

5. *Statue of St Louis, painted wood, c. 1300.*

**1226–70:** Reign of Louis IX (his mother, Blanche of Castile, is regent until 1242). The King of England is defeated at Taillebourg and Saintes, but in 1259 (Treaty of Paris) Louis IX restores to him Quercy, Perigord and the Limousin. After Louis's unhappy experiences on the Seventh Crusade, he dies outside Tunis during the Eighth Crusade. His piety, concern for justice and death on crusade lead to his canonization in 1297.
**1270–85:** Reign of Philip III. At the death of his uncle, Alphonse of Poitiers, in 1271 he incorporates Languedoc into the kingdom of France.
**1285–1314:** Reign of Philip the Fair. He endows France with an efficient and modern government but clashes with Pope Boniface VIII (1294–1303), who is humiliated by the King's officers in 1303, and destroys the Templars (1307–1314).

6. *Illumination from* The Coronation Ordines of the kings of France, *c. 1250.*

# Feudal England

THE ENGLISH MONARCHY in the eleventh and twelfth centuries was essentially the product of conquest. King of England by his victory at Hastings in 1066, William the Conqueror, Duke of Normandy, replaced the Anglo-Saxon monarchy with a political system modelled for the most part on the centralized administration of Normandy. The continental influence dominated every aspect of English society, institutionally as well as linguistically, and French remained the language of the aristocracy until at least the beginning of the thirteenth century. With the lands confiscated from the Anglo-Saxon nobility the King created a substantial personal demesne (amounting to one-seventh of the country) and endowed his companions-in-arms, who became his tenants-in-chief owing him personal allegiance. In 1085 he ordered the compilation of the Domesday Book, an inventory drawn up under oath of his kingdom's estates and wealth. The crown

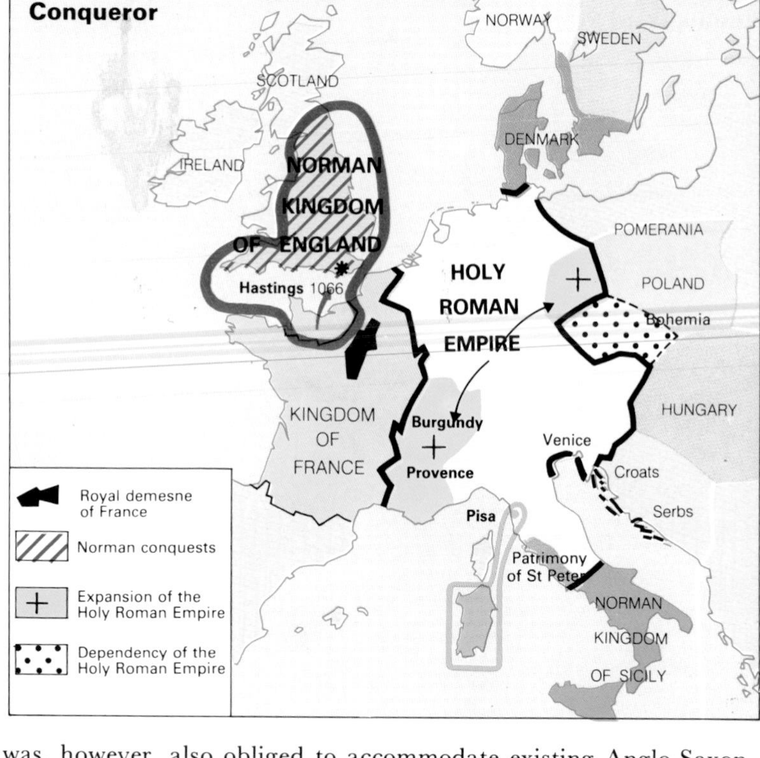

1. Chapter house of Wells Cathedral, 13th century.

was, however, also obliged to accommodate existing Anglo-Saxon traditions, in particular the right of all free men to sit in session at the local courts of shires and hundreds. The local office of sheriff was preserved, with its judicial and fiscal responsibilities, but these people became the king's personal representatives in the counties and were inspected regularly by itinerant justices. At the level of central government the king legislated for all the realm through the holding of general assizes: at the Assize of Clarendon in 1166 steps were taken to deal with lawlessness in the country, the Grand Assize of 1179 reorganized the administration of justice, and both the Assize of Arms (1181) and the Assize of the Forest (1184) introduced important new measures. From an early date a highly organized system of taxation provided the crown with large revenues, which account for England's military strength relative to the more populous France. In the same period England also acquired permanent and centralized institutions of government: King's Bench became a court of appeal from local tribunals, and the Exchequer audited the sheriffs' accounts. In the thirteenth century the King's Council replaced the feudal *curia*. Eng-

**Battle of Hastings.**

**1066**

**Marriage of Henry II to Eleanor of Aquitaine.**

**1152**

**1066:** Conquest of England by William, Duke of Normandy and designated heir of the last Anglo-Saxon king, Edward the Confessor. William crushes his rival, Harold, at Hastings. The Bayeux Tapestry, which depicts these events, is completed shortly afterwards. William reigns from 1066 to 1087. **1085:** Commissioning of the *Domesday Book*, an exhaustive inventory of land-ownership in England after the Conquest. **1087–1100:** Reign of William Rufus

3. Harold meeting William. Bayeux Tapestry, 11th century.

4. West front of Salisbury Cathedral, 13th century.

# 11th–14th centuries

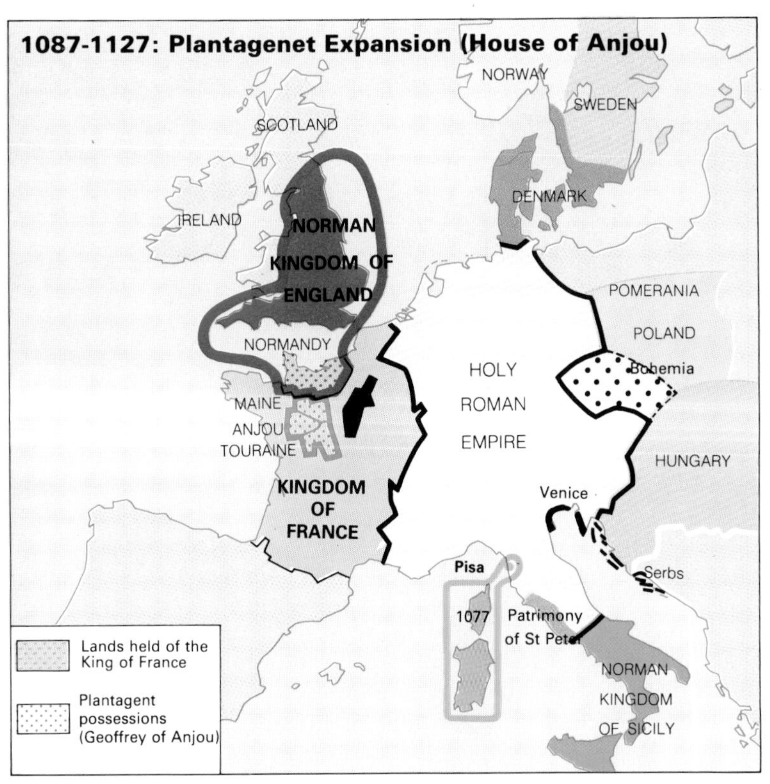


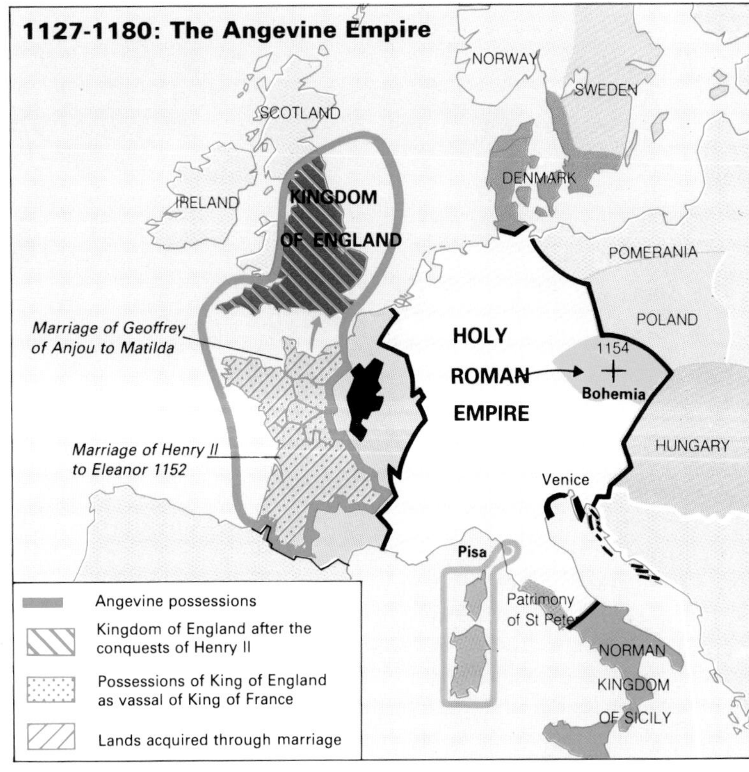


land distinguished herself from France by the early introduction of central governmental institutions. Paradoxically, however, while France later came to be governed by a powerful centralized authority, England's institutional history was one of development towards a limited monarchy. During Henry II's reign the English crown seemed to reach the height of its power: following Henry's marriage to Eleanor of Aquitaine in 1152 the king ruled over all western France with the exception of Brittany. But conflicts with baronial factions (who rebelled in 1173–4), with the Church (culminating in the murder of Thomas Becket, Archbishop of Canterbury, in 1170 – a grave political miscalculation from which the monarchy never quite recovered), the war against Capetian France and the defeats of 1214 finally forced the crown to accept the conditions of Magna Carta in 1215 and the Provisions of Oxford in 1258. Thereafter power would be shared with Parliament, which represented the various communities of the kingdom and whose consent was needed for the raising of any taxation. On this basis the English monarchy recovered a measure of stability during the reign of Edward I (1272–1307), while the conquest of Ireland, the subordination of Wales to the crown and the pressure exerted on Scotland set the seal on its increasingly insular destiny. The outbreak of the Hundred Years' War in 1337 was to upset this balance again.

*2. Richard the Lionheart fighting Saladin during the Third Crusade. Luttrell Psalter.*

**Magna Carta.** **1215**

**Organization of Parliament.** **1294**

*5. The Sower. Window of Canterbury Cathedral, 13th century.*

(William II), son of the Conqueror.
**1100–35:** Reign of Henry I, brother of William Rufus. 1106: Defeat of Robert Curthose at Tinchebrai. Henry I becomes Duke of Normandy as well as King of England.
**1135–54:** Reign of Stephen of Blois.
**1138:** Outbreak of civil war between the supporters of Matilda – whom her father, Henry I, designated as his successor – and Stephen of Blois, grandson of William the Conqueror through his mother.
**1154–89:** Reign of Henry II, grandson of Henry I through his mother Matilda, and Count of Anjou through his father Geoffrey Plantagenet. By marrying Eleanor, the recently repudiated wife of the King of France, he also rules over all Aquitaine. Conflict between Henry and the French king is henceforth inevitable. But the murder of Thomas Becket, Archbishop of Canterbury, in 1170 turns the church against Henry II. In 1173–4 the barons rebel. Between 1166 and 1184 the King reforms the administration of the kingdom through several important assizes.
**1189–99:** Reign of Richard the Lionheart, son of Henry II. Between 1189 and 1192 he participates in the Third Crusade, but on the return journey he is captured by Duke

*6. 14th-century enamelled casket depicting the murder of Thomas Becket in 1170.*

Leopold of Austria and handed over to the German Emperor Henry VI, ally of the King of France. During this period his brother, John Lackland, usurps power in England. Once he is freed, Richard reassembles his troops and makes war on Philip Augustus of France.
**1199–1216:** Reign of John Lackland. In 1214 he is defeated by the Capetian Philip Augustus at Roche-au-Moine, and his allies (Otto IV of Brunswick and the Counts of Flanders and Boulogne) are crushed at the Battle of Bouvines. His barons take advantage of this to force him to accept the conditions of Magna Carta.
**1216–72:** Reign of Henry III. He is forced to agree to the Provisions of Oxford (1258) and also to conclude the Treaty of Paris (1259), by whose terms Henry retains Quercy, Perigord and the Limousin as a vassal of Louis IX.
**1272–1307:** Reign of Edward I. In 1265 he puts down Simon de Montfort, leader of the rebellious barons, and as king conquers Wales (Treaty of Aberconway, 1277), but Scotland holds out against him. The basis of Parliament's organization is settled in 1294.

# Monasticism in the West

1. *Episodes from the life of St Dominic by Fra Angelico.*

MONASTICISM, a way of life quite distinct from that of laymen and clerics living in the community, is a characteristic feature of Christianity from the first centuries onwards. Between the eleventh and thirteenth centuries it underwent many changes as it adapted to new conditions in the surrounding economy and society. New religious orders appeared which claimed to reform the Benedictinism that had been prevalent since the sixth century. The diversity of orders is particularly characteristic of the central period of the Middle Ages, reflecting a society marked by an increased division of roles and occupations. By setting up networks of congregations independent of political and linguistic frontiers, the new orders gave the Christian world a systematic structure. The Benedictine order underwent two very important reforms – those of Cluny and Citeaux in 910 and 1098 respectively. Directly dependent on the Holy See, Cluny flourished under its first six abbots, who had total control over more than 1,100 affiliated priories and abbeys, mainly situated in France, Spain and Italy. Other less important congregations appeared at the same time: Hirsau in southern Germany, Gorze in Lorraine. The 'White Monks' of Citeaux, who were also from Burgundy, rapidly spread outwards from that abbey and its four 'daughter-houses' (La Ferté-sur-Grosne, Pontigny, Clairvaux – founded by St Bernard – and Morimond). In 1153 the order had some 350 houses; by 1200 it had 530. The emphasis was on asceticism and humility rather than (as at Cluny) on the liturgy. Alongside traditional monasticism there was a new interest in the reclusive life, and a number of new orders were created: the Camaldolesi (1002), Vallombrosa (1039) in central Italy and the Carthusians founded by St Bruno in 1084. Combining hermit-like solitude with community life, this latter order had 39 monasteries by 1200 and almost 200 by the end of the Middle Ages. The 'Rule of St Augustine', which married communal life to secular action, inspired the foundation of new congregations of regular canons: in 1120 Norbert of Xanten founded the Premonstratensians, an order which after his death in 1134 had 614 monasteries, particularly in Flanders, northern France and Germany. The same rule was followed by the nursing and military orders such as the Templars (1118–1314), the order of St John's Hospital of Jerusalem (1113) (the origin of the Order of Malta), the Teutonic Knights and the Order of the Brothers of the Sword (these last were the principal agents of German penetration into Prussia). However, the need to work among the laity, particularly in the towns, the urgent need for a more effective fight against the rebirth of heresy, and the promotion of the spiritual value of poverty as a reaction to the growth in the wealth of the monasteries and of the church, led to the creation of mendicant orders at the beginning of the thirteenth century. The Order of Preachers – founded by St Dominic to combat the Cathar heresy – followed the rule of the canons of St Augustine; the Friars Minor, founded by St Francis, set even more store by poverty, which was to be the source of internal rifts within the order throughout the thirteenth century. The less important orders, the Carmelites and the Hermits of St Augustine, completed the 'family' of mendicant orders during this century.

**Cluny founded.**

**910**

2. *'St Matthew'. Masterpiece of Irish illumination, taken from the* Great Gospel of St Colomba, *Kells, early 9th century.*

**910:** Foundation of Cluny on land given by the Count of Aquitaine, William the Pious: the Abbot Odon restores the Rule of St Benedict. The order is directly dependent on the Holy See. The abbots Maieul, Odilon and Hugh ensure its prosperity, which lasts until the abbacy of Peter the Venerable (middle of 12th century). But the economy of Cluny – too closely linked to the manorial system – adapts badly to the growth of trade links from which the Cistercians profited.

**1002–39:** Foundation of two congregations of ascetic monks in Tuscany: the Camaldolese Benedictines set up by Romuald and the congregation of Vallombrosa by John Gualberto.

**1059:** Foundation of the reformed Benedictine congregation of Hirsau, which rapidly spreads throughout Germany.

**1084:** Foundation of the Grande-Chartreuse near Grenoble. Each monk has a small cottage and hermit's garden in which to do both mental and manual work; communal services.

**Foundation of Cite**

3. *Consecration of the high altar of the Abbey of Cluny by Pope Urban II in 1095. Painting taken from the manuscript of the* Chronicle of Cluny.

**1098:** Foundation of Citeaux by Robert de Molesmes in a deserted region south of Dijon. The legate Hugues de Die approves the austere and contemplative life of the Cistercian monks. The lay brothers, who perform the material tasks, are not subject to that rule. In 1112 Bernard de Fontaines joins the community with a group of young knights. The first 'daughters' of Citeaux are founded in the following three years: La Ferté, Pontigny, Clairvaux run by St Bernard and Morimond. With the general economic boom, the order grows to 530 monasteries at the end of the 12th century.

**1110:** Foundation of St Victor de Paris (Regular Canons of St Augustine) by William of Champeaux.

**1113, 1118:** Foundation of the military orders of the Knights Templar and St John of Jerusalem, who were to defend the Latin states in the East.

**1117:** Death of Robert d'Arbrissel, founder of the double monastery of Fontevrault, where the abbess also has authority over the monks.

# 10th–13th centuries

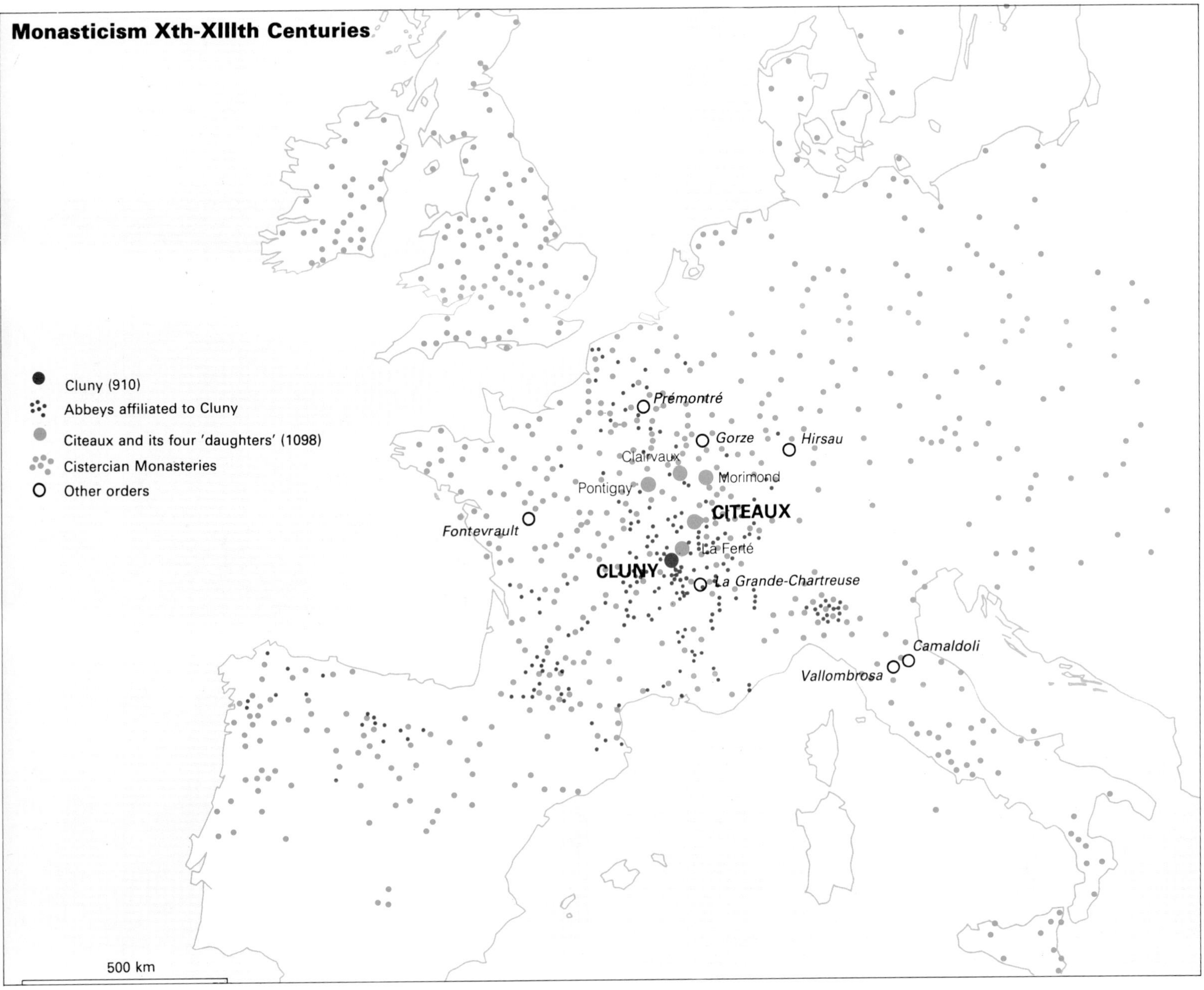

## Monasticism Xth-XIIIth Centuries

- Cluny (910)
- Abbeys affiliated to Cluny
- Citeaux and its four 'daughters' (1098)
- Cistercian Monasteries
- Other orders

Prémontré, Gorze, Hirsau, Clairvaux, Morimond, Pontigny, CITEAUX, Fontevrault, La Ferté, CLUNY, La Grande-Chartreuse, Camaldoli, Vallombrosa

500 km

**Death of St Bernard.**

**1153**

**Foundation of Dominican and Franciscan Orders.**

**1207–9**

**1120:** Foundation of the Abbey of Prémontré by Norbert of Xanten: these regular Canons who follow the rule of St Augustine, of whom there are a large number in Germany, turn to preaching.
**1153:** Death of St Bernard.

*4. Seal of the Templars.*

*5. St Benedict receives the* Commentary on the Rule of the Order *from the hands of the Abbot John. 11th-century manuscript, Monte Cassino.*

**1198, 1202:** Foundation of the German military orders – the Teutonic Knights and the Brothers of the Sword – who subdue Prussia.

**1207–12:** Foundation of the Order of the Friars Preachers by St Dominic, in Languedoc (1221), to convert the heretics and preach to the laity. He adopts the Rule of St Augustine. In the 13th century he plays an important intellectual role, alongside Albert the Great and Thomas Aquinas.

**1209:** Foundation of the Minor Friars by St Francis of Assisi. He receives the stigmata of the wounds of Christ in 1224 and dies in 1226. He imposes strict poverty on his friars. But only the Spiritual Franciscans follow this rule to the letter. The Conventuals take over in the order, with St Bonaventura among them, after a very violent struggle.

**1243–7:** Foundation of the Hermits of St Augustine and resettlement of the Holy Land by the Carmelites: these two orders are linked to the mendicant orders.

*6. Teaching monk. Illumination from a Latin vocabulary, Austria, c. 1350.*

# Religious Dissidence: Jews and Heretics

THE UNITY OF FAITH and of practices of worship is a fundamental principle of medieval Christianity and one that was forcefully reaffirmed from the eleventh century onwards when the rapidly expanding West came up against Islam (first in Spain, then in the Holy Land), Slav and Magyar paganism, and the Greek schism (from 1054 onwards). Within the Christian world attitudes also changed towards the Jews and the church had to confront a new upsurge of heresy. The period – especially from the thirteenth century onwards – is characterized by a hardening of attitudes and the establishment of a system of social exclusion which was also directed against the poor, lepers, prostitutes and homosexuals. The First Crusade was accompanied by numerous pogroms which are attributable to Christian anti-Judaism; there was as yet, however, no anti-Semitism as we know it. The Fourth Lateran Council gave a juridical basis to the exclusion of Jews and imposed on them the wearing of a distinctive mark (a piece of yellow or crimson cloth). At the dawn of the fourteenth century Jews were banished from the kingdom of France.

The birth of popular heresies at the beginning of the eleventh century was in part a product of the church's success, the result of the spread of its teachings and a manifestation of the moral exigencies consequent upon the reform of manners and society which it had itself proposed. The resonances of such movements among the laity were all the greater for the fact that social tensions, caused by the rise in Europe's material prosperity, had produced aspirations towards greater social justice, and the church was by far the richest and most powerful institution in Christendom.

Medieval heresies were various in nature, but they all had in common a desire to return to the letter of the Gospels, to the precept of poverty and the apostolic spirit; they criticized the church's worldly dealings, the clerical monopolization of holiness and particularly of preaching; they wished to strip the Christian religion of the rites and beliefs that had been added to it in the course of history, such as the cults of the Virgin and saints, belief in Purgatory etc. The first seedbeds of heresy appeared in France and northern Italy around the year 1000. At the end of the century the movement first accompanied, then violently overspilled from, the campaign for ecclesiastical reform (Milanese *Paterines*). In the twelfth century heresiarchs sprang up everywhere (Peter of Bruys, Tanchelm). The most important group, the Waldensians, was formed in Lyon in the 1170s; in spite of persecution, it spread rapidly in Italy and even as far as Central Europe. Catharism was not so much a genuine heresy as a wholly different religion, inspired by the Balkan Bogomils and founded on a doctrinal dualism between good and evil, discounting the Fall. It was an awareness of the danger represented by the Cathars that was at the origin of the creation of the Dominican order, the crusade against the Albigensians and the formation of the Inquisition (which was entrusted to the mendicant orders in 1232). Heresies, however, merely grew in number and intensity at the end of the Middle Ages, even undermining the Franciscan order itself (the *fraticelli*, inspired by the eschatology of Joachim of Flora) and becoming more and more bound up with social demands – or even revolts. Thus the preaching of John Wyclif in England inspired the English Lollards and, more importantly, Jan Hus's teachings lay behind the Hussite rising against the church and the Empire in Bohemia.

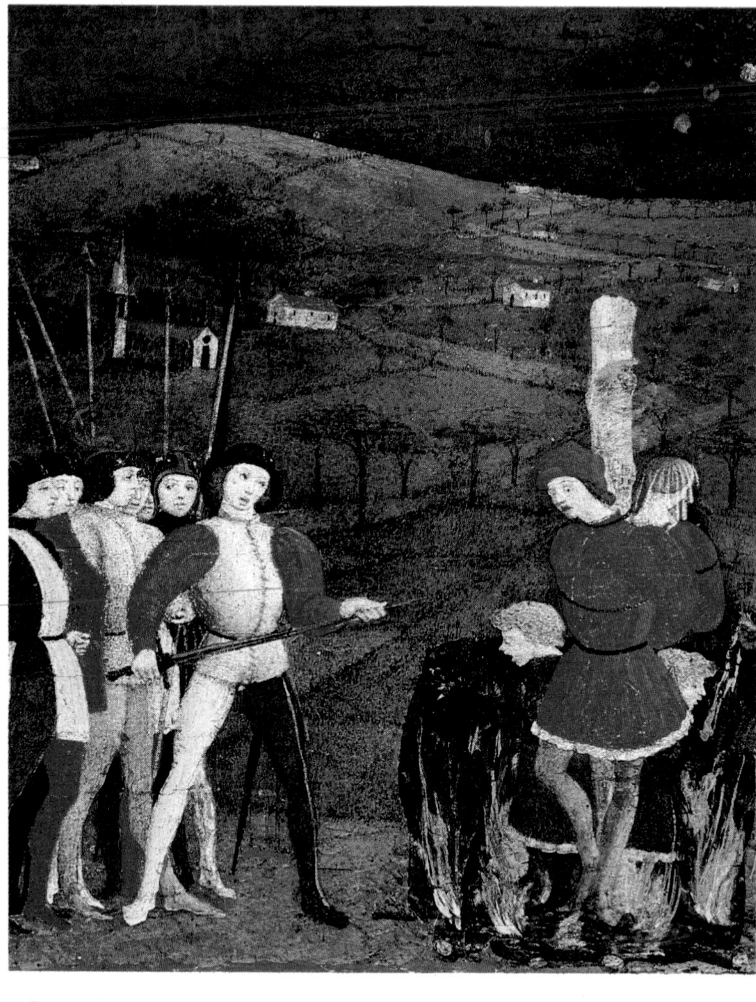

*1. Episode from the* Legend of the Profanation of the Host *by Paolo Uccello, 1469.*

**Leutard, the heretic, in Champagne.** 1000

**Organization of the Cathar Church in Languedoc.** 1167

**Waldo at Lyon.** 1170

**Albigensian Crusade.** 1208

**1000:** Leutard, the heretic at Vertus (Champagne): first manifestation of popular heresy. In the same period, other seedbeds of heresy at Orleans, Chalons, in Aquitane, Arras and around Milan.

*2. Sarcophagus of a follower of the Bogomil heresy, prevalent in Serbia in the 11th century.*

The Paterines are poor people vigorously critical of the unreformed clergy. A long period of mutual incomprehension and doctrinal divergences ends in schism from the Byzantine Church.

**1096–7:** Departure of the First Crusade. Anti-Jewish pogroms.

**c. 1140:** Death of the heretic Peter of Bruys. His disciple, Henry of Lausanne, is denounced by St Bernard.

**1146–55:** The heretic Arnold of Brescia, a disciple of Abelard, in power at Rome.

**1167:** Cathar Council of Saint-Felix-de-Camaran; this organizes the Cathar Church of the Languedoc with its bishops and clergy made up of the 'perfected', who are distinct from simple 'believers'. The third Lateran Council pronounces the first condemnation of the Cathars.

**1170:** Waldo preaches at Lyon: he advocates voluntary poverty and presses the right of lay people to preach. Waldensians condemned in 1184.

**1184:** Creation of Episcopal Inquisition. In 1232 it is entrusted to friars of the Dominican order. The Inquisition uses the procedure of

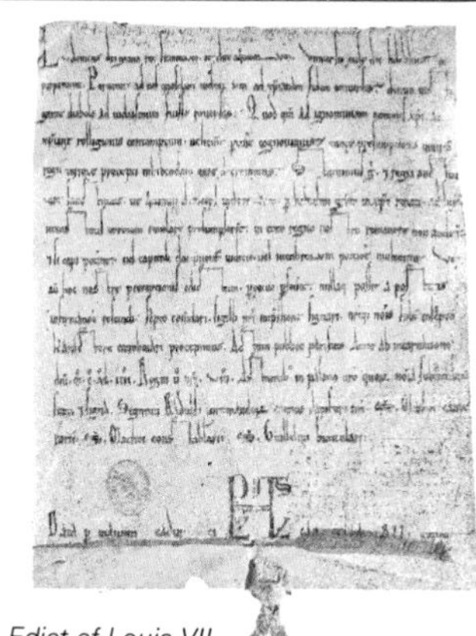

*3. Edict of Louis VII banishing relapsed Jews from the kingdom of France, 1145.*

interrogation and also torture to obtain confessions from suspects charged with heresy. The guilty, once reconciled with the church, are condemned to the 'broad' or 'narrow' 'wall' (*murus largus* or *murus strictus*), i.e. life imprisonment. Relapsed heretics are handed over to the secular arm – the temporal powers – and burned at the stake.

**1202:** Death of the Calabrian Cistercian, Joachim of Flora. His conception of universal history being divided into three ages – those of the Father (Old Testament), the Son (incarnation in the present age) and the Holy Spirit (yet to come) – led him to predict the imminent disappearance of the church and the coming of a reign of saints and monks; this millenarianism inspired the Spiritual Franciscans (fraticelli) who will later be accused of heresy.

**1207:** Preaching of St Dominic in Languedoc. At Fanjeaux he founds a community of converted female heretics.

**1208–13:** Crusade against the Albigensians, led by Simon de Montfort. This prepares the ground for the King of France to intervene in

# 11th–15th centuries

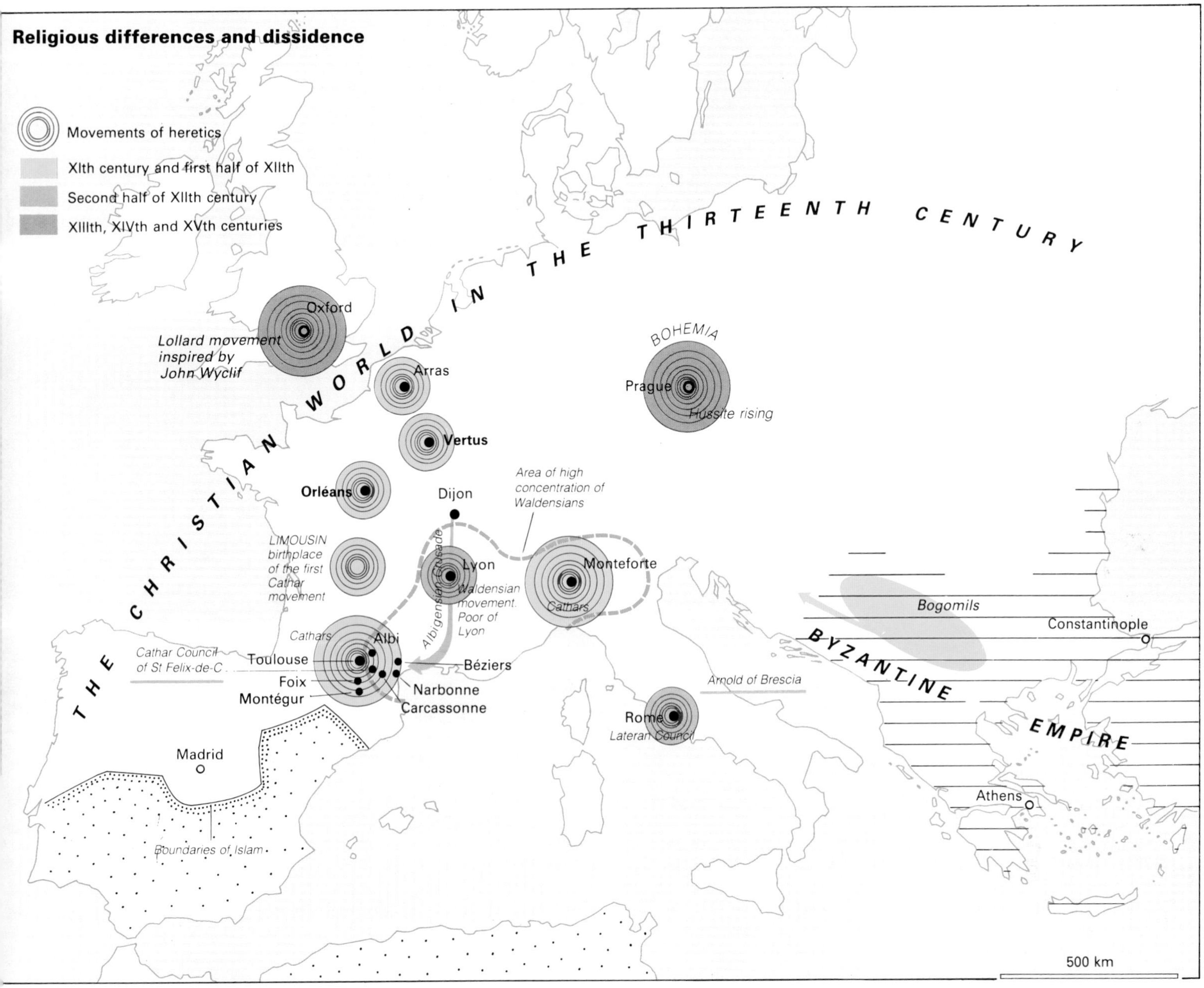

## Religious differences and dissidence

Movements of heretics
- Xlth century and first half of Xllth
- Second half of Xllth century
- Xlllth, XlVth and XVth centuries

THE CHRISTIAN WORLD IN THE THIRTEENTH CENTURY

Oxford
Lollard movement inspired by John Wyclif
Arras
Vertus
Orléans
Dijon
LIMOUSIN birthplace of the first Cathar movement
Lyon
Waldensian movement. Poor of Lyon
Albigensian Crusade
Area of high concentration of Waldensians
Monteforte
Cathars
BOHEMIA
Prague
Hussite rising
Cathars
Albi
Cathar Council of St Felix-de-C.
Toulouse
Foix
Montégur
Béziers
Narbonne
Carcassonne
Madrid
Boundaries of Islam
Arnold of Brescia
Rome
Lateran Council
Bogomils
BYZANTINE EMPIRE
Constantinople
Athens
500 km

**Jan Hus executed at Constance.**

**1415**

4. *Chateau de Peyrepertuse in the Aude (France), a Cathar bastion besieged during the Albigensian Crusade.*

5. *Inquisition scene: the exhibition of condemned heretics. Detail from a painting by Pedro Berruguete.*

the south. The last outpost of Cathar resistance, the Château of Montségur, falls in 1244.

**1215:** Fourth Lateran Council. Canon 21, *Omnis utrusque sexus*, obliges all Christians to make confession once a year – a measure which some see as directed at identifying heretics – and forces Jews to wear a piece of yellow or crimson cloth as a distinguishing mark.

**1240:** Dispute over the Talmud between clergy and rabbis at the court of the King of France. The copies of the Talmud are burnt.

**1306:** Jews expelled from the kingdom of France.

**1377–82:** Lollard movement in England.

**1415:** Council of Constance posthumously condemns John Wyclif for heresy. Execution of Jan Hus, a Bohemian reformer who was in fact less radical than Wyclif. In Bohemia, after the moderate Hussites or Calixtines – who demanded the communion in both kinds – returned to the fold, the radical Hussites or 'Taborites' are crushed at the Battle of Lipary (1434).

6. *Death of Jan Hus at the stake in 1415. From Diebold Schilling's* Spiezer bilder-chronik, *1485.*

# Decline and Fall of Byzantium

*1. Mistra (Peloponnese), showing the Church of the Hodegetria, 14th century.*

THE BYZANTINE EMPIRE reached its zenith between the ninth and eleventh centuries. By that point it had consolidated its territorial possessions and enjoyed great economic prosperity. The renewed circulation of gold in the Mediterranean in the period following the Arab conquest made the Empire for a while the great beneficiary of East-West trade. However, this wealth, which took on mythic proportions in Western accounts, provoked on the one hand the greed of the Normans and on the other the rivalry of the Italian republics, who as a result sought direct trading access to the Levant. The Western drive to go in search of the wealth of the Orient is at the origin of the crusades; it was the principal cause of the ruin of the Empire and its incapacity to defend itself against the Turks. Internal factors also contributed to this decline. The end of the Macedonian dynasty (1057) opened up a power vacuum which was only filled by the coming to power of provincial military families, whose fortune was based on the ownership of great estates. In the course of the eleventh and twelfth centuries the emperors distributed territories, privileges and tax exemptions to their own families and to those military families to which they were allied. The division of the land into small estates on which the fiscal assessment was based began to disappear and large sectors of land fell outside of the control of the central administration. Independent governments were formed even before the Empire was divided up by the Latins. The state's monopoly on the sale and production of luxury goods and the aristocratic tendencies of Byzantine society did not help to promote the development of a class of merchants capable of competing with the Italian republics. Byzantine trade was a passive trade. The customs concessions granted to Venice, then later to Pisa and Genoa, in exchange for aid against the

*2. 'The Sufferings of Job'. Byzantine manuscript, 1362.*

Normans and Turks, and the monopoly granted to Venice in the eastern Mediterranean after the Fourth Crusade, deprived the Empire of all its revenue. The sack of Constantinople by the crusaders in 1204 took from it its last remaining wealth and precipitated its dislocation. A Latin emperor was crowned at Constantinople, whilst the Frankish lords divided up the western regions of the Empire between them, founding principalities of a feudal type. In the second half of the thirteenth century the Greek emperors succeeded in reconquering the capital, but the emperors of the Paleologus dynasty

**The Normans take Bari; Seljuq Turks win a victory at Manzikert. Capture of Constantinople by the crusaders. Michael VIII Paleologus signs the Treaty of Nymphaeum with Geno**

**1071** **1204** **13 March 1261**

**1057–81:** The Empire is attacked on all sides. In the west the Normans settle in Byzantine Italy. In the Balkans the Petchenegs (Turkish tribes) take control of Macedonia and Thrace. In the east the Seljuq Turks (so named after their first chief, Seljuq) penetrate into Asia Minor, inflicting defeat on Byzantium at the Battle of Manzikert (1071). They establish the Sultanate of Iconium.
**1081–1185:** The Comneni dynasty provides a period of internal stability, but external attacks continue. In the Balkans the Petchenegs are repulsed in 1091, but the Hungarians and Serbs pose a new threat. In Asia Minor the Seljuq Turks consolidate their position and win the decisive victory of Myriokephalon in 1176. In the west the Normans occupy Dyrrachium (Durazzo) and threaten Constantinople (1081). To combat them, Alexis Comnenus calls on aid from Venice and accords that republic a monopoly on trade throughout the Empire (1082). The mistrust between Greeks and Latins (Westerners of Roman Catholic obedience) leads to the massacre of the Latin population of Constantinople (1182).

*4. Carpenter at work. Mosaic of St Mary of Otranto, 12th century, southern Italy.*

**1185–1204:** The failure of the first crusades has in the West been unjustly attributed to the treachery of the Greeks. The Fourth Crusade is openly directed against Byzantium by Venice. In 1204 Constantinople, overrun by the crusaders, is looted and pillaged. Baldwin, Count of Flanders, is crowned at Hagia Sophia. He appoints a Venetian patriarch. Venice takes over Byzantium's ports and most of its islands.
**1204–1261:** The Greek emperor Theodore Laskaris founds the Empire of Nicaea in the west of Asia Minor. His successors recapture territory in Thrace, Macedonia and Epirus. In 1261 the Latin Empire of Constantinople collapses.
**1261–82:** The Empire is reduced to the territory of the Empire of Nicaea, Thrace and a part of Macedonia. Serbs, Bulgars and Turks threaten its frontiers. Michael VII Paleologus turns to the West and achieves some diplomatic successes. To thwart Charles of Anjou, who has designs on the Empire, he accepts papal supremacy over the Eastern Church at the Second Council of Lyon in 1274. This decision is met with strong

*5. The wedding at Canaa. Mosaic in the Monastery Church of Chora, 13th century.*

# 1057–1453

3. *The Virgin and the Apostles. Dome of the Monastery Church of Chora, which is now the Kariye Mosque, Constantinople, early 14th century.*

(1261–1453) were unable to prevent the disintegration of the Empire, nor to restore the economic situation. Under threat from their Slav neighbours and, more importantly, from the advancing Turks, they appealed in vain to the West. Their attempts at *rapprochement* with Rome, which were viewed very unfavourably by a population hostile to the Latins, only exacerbated tensions within the Empire, and the aid they requested did not materialize. The political decline of Byzantium was accompanied, paradoxically, by a remarkable flowering of culture. Great artistic centres emerged in the provinces at Mistra (in the Peloponnese) and at Mount Athos. Byzantine painting exercised a profound influence upon the Greek Orthodox Slav countries. There was also a brilliant renaissance of philosophical and theological speculation, and we are indebted to the Byzantine humanists who took refuge in the West after the Turkish conquest for our knowledge of many of the great authors of classical antiquity.

**uncil of Lyons.** **Reunion of Eastern and Western Churches at Council of Florence.**

**274** **1438–9**

religious opposition in Byzantium, which leads eventually to schism.

**1282–1453:** The greatest danger now comes from a new Turkish tribe, the Osmanlis or Ottomans (so called after their chief, Uthman), who carved out for themselves a state in Asia Minor (at the expense of the Seljuqs), then continue their advance into Byzantine territories. By 1341 they have become masters of Asia Minor and enter Europe. Between 1363 and 1389 they conquer Thrace, Macedonia, Serbia and Bulgaria. In 1444 they defeat the Hungarians at Varna and become masters of the Balkans. Constantinople, defended only by its own troops, is taken on 29 May 1453. Sultan Mehmed II goes on to take Morea and Trebizond (1460, 1461), after which nothing remains of the old Empire.

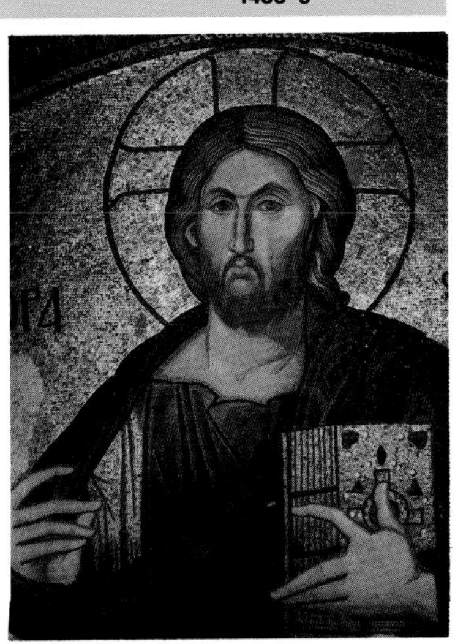

6. *Christ Pantocrator. Mosaic in the Monastery Church of Chora, early 14th century.*

**1080-1204**

Venice, Genoa, PETCHENGS, Danube, PONTUS EUXINUS, Adrianople, Constantinople, Trebizond, Dyrrachium, Thessalonika, NORMANS, Manzikert, SELJUQ TURKS, Myriokephalon, Athens, Antioch, MEDITERRANEAN SEA, Euphrates

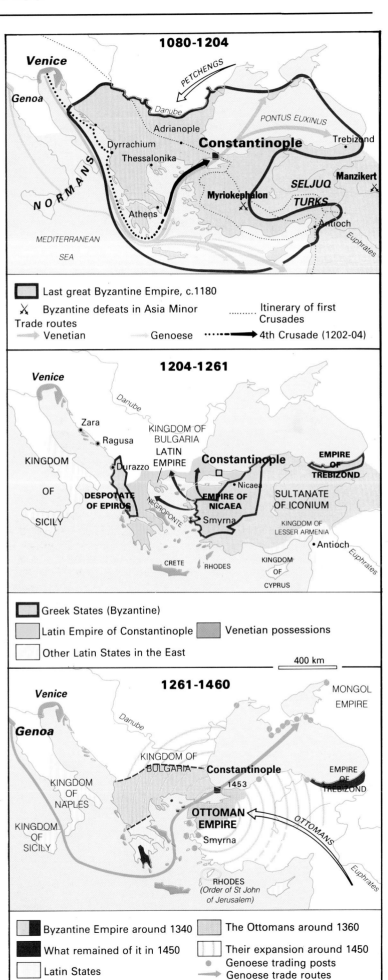

Last great Byzantine Empire, c.1180
Byzantine defeats in Asia Minor
Itinerary of first Crusades
Trade routes
Venetian
Genoese
4th Crusade (1202-04)

**1204-1261**

Venice, Danube, Zara, Ragusa, KINGDOM OF BULGARIA, LATIN EMPIRE, KINGDOM OF SICILY, Durazzo, Constantinople, EMPIRE OF TREBIZOND, Nicaea, DESPOTATE OF EPIRUS, NEGROPONTE, EMPIRE OF NICAEA, SULTANATE OF ICONIUM, Smyrna, KINGDOM OF LESSER ARMENIA, Antioch, Euphrates, CRETE, RHODES, KINGDOM OF CYPRUS

Greek States (Byzantine)
Latin Empire of Constantinople
Venetian possessions
Other Latin States in the East
400 km

**1261-1460**

Venice, Genoa, Danube, MONGOL EMPIRE, KINGDOM OF BULGARIA, Constantinople, 1453, EMPIRE OF TREBIZOND, KINGDOM OF NAPLES, OTTOMAN EMPIRE, OTTOMANS, KINGDOM OF SICILY, Smyrna, Euphrates, RHODES (Order of St John of Jerusalem)

Byzantine Empire around 1340
The Ottomans around 1360
What remained of it in 1450
Their expansion around 1450
Genoese trading posts
Latin States
Genoese trade routes

# Islam's New Edifice Breached

At the end of the tenth century the Islamic world had lost its imperialist designs. They had been laid to rest by forces to which it had itself given rise. Local administrations became more powerful, wealth was distributed on a more regional basis and institutional life and legal matters were structured by the diffuse group of *'ulama* (doctors of the law). The Empire, which had been founded on war, could not survive Islamization and the adherence of the majority to Islamic law. In the period of change which followed, religious values (based in theory either on a community of equal believers or a spiritual hierarchy) became mere rationalizations of other interests: the Almoravids (Sanhaja Berbers, 1056) from the outer Maghreb saw themselves as a community of warriors for the faith and stood out against the Fatimids – with their 'inspired' caliph – who were installed in Cairo. Whilst the latter imposed their foreign rule over a non-Shi'ite population, the Almoravids were striving to extirpate Kharijitism from the Maghreb. In the east, the Seljuq Turks moved over a few years from Transoxiana to Iraq, passing through Aleppo (Haleb) as they went and forcing the Byzantines back to a narrow coastal strip of land. With the support of an Islamic Iranian aristocracy, they established solid administration everywhere and defended strict observance of tradition (*sunna*), though they in fact used their power to subordinate the caliph to their own authority. Also in the eleventh century, the Islamic world discovered the Christian West. Trading links began cautiously, with southern Italy and the Normans in Sicily. But the arrival of the crusaders (First Crusade, 1095) came as a shock. The Latin states created by the knights were isolated entities with few settlers. They paid little heed to the Eastern Christians who spoke Arabic and who saw themselves as belonging to the Muslim world come what may. They were also unable to turn to advantage the commercial routes which were developing between the Italian towns on the one hand (Pisa, Venice and later Genoa) and Egypt and Syria on the other. In response to the interest shown in Islamic philosophy and science in cultured Western circles, Muslim scholars travelled to Sicily and Spain.

1. The citadel of Haleb (Aleppo).

One man, Salah ad-Din Yusuf ibn-Ayyub (Saladin), destroyed the Fatimid caliphate (1171) and through a holy war against the infidel brought about unity in the Near East and dealt a lethal blow to hopes of a Latin Orient (Battle of Hittan, 1187). His real achievement was to turn Islam into a system in which the power exercised by the strong man – the amir or sultan (usually not an Arab) – was recognized and ratified by a caliph whose only power was that accorded him by the political authority. The sack of Baghdad by the pagan Mongols of Hülegü (1258) and the seizure of power by the Cairo Mamluks (emancipated slaves) in Egypt (1250) came as a confirmation of that development.

2. Aristotle and his followers. 13th-century Seljuq manuscript by the Arab author Al-Mubassir.

Eastern Islam now became centred on Egypt, where the Mamluks (1250–1517), though welcoming a powerless caliph to Cairo, imposed a strictly military regime, which in the time of the Circassians was not dynastic. It was an efficient system which provided protection against the Mongols: however, a long series of epidemics (from 1348 onwards) and the decline of certain internal commercial routes weakened a country whose economic exchanges with the northern coast of the Mediterranean were becoming increasingly unequal.

**Conquest of the Punjab.** — 1001
**The Seljuq Turks at Baghdad.** — 1055
**El Cid captures Valencia.** — 1094
**Saladin takes power in Egypt.** — 1171
**Capture of Jerusalem.** — 1187

**1001:** Muslim troops penetrate into the Punjab.
**1009:** Destruction of the Holy Sepulchre by order of al-Hakim; this will later be taken as a pretext for the Crusades.
**1031:** Quarrels over succession lead to the demise of the Spanish caliphate.
**1036:** The Almoravids leave the western Sudan and march on the Maghreb.
**1038:** The Seljuq amirs take Nishapur (in Khorasan).
**1052:** The Banu Hilal tribe are sent by the Fatimids to ravage Ifriqiya.
**1055:** The Seljuqs at Baghdad; the caliph al-Qa'im confers the title of sultan on Toghril Beg. Despite their dislike of the settled life and the fact that there are younger independent dynasties, the Seljuqs are to dominate the Middle East for more than two centuries (1038–1194), during which they will impose an occasionally hectoring guardianship on the caliph.
**1085:** Alfonso VI of Castile recaptures Toledo.
**1091:** Normans take Sicily.
**1094:** El Cid (El Campeador) takes Valencia.
**1095–9:** First Crusade and capture of Jerusalem. Four states created: Kingdom of Jerusalem, County of Edessa, Principality of Antioch, County of Tripoli.
**1130:** The Almohads take the eastern Maghreb, then Spain and the rest of the Maghreb: Abd al-Mu'min, a disciple of the founder Ibn Tumart, becomes caliph.
**1147–9:** Second Crusade.
**1169:** Shirkuh, a Kurd, the new vizier of the Fatimid caliphate, dies and is succeeded by his nephew Saladin.
**1171:** Saladin overthrows the Shi'ite caliph and returns Egypt to Sunni orthodoxy and the rule of the caliph.
**1187:** Saladin defeats the Crusaders at Hattin and retakes Jerusalem.
**1191:** Capture of Acre by the Third Crusade: Richard I ('the Lionheart') occupies the Byzantine island of Cyprus.
**1228:** Hafsids in Ifriqiya (until 1574); this puts a definitive end to the unity of the Maghreb.
**1235:** Abd al-Wadid dynasty in Tlemcen (until 1557).
**1236:** The Castilians recapture Cordoba.
**1248:** Recapture of Seville.
**1250:** The Cairo Mamluks take over Egypt: Louis IX taken prisoner at El-Mansura (Egyptian delta), then freed after the surrender of Damietta and payment of a ransom.

4. Arab astrolabe.

**1256–60:** Mongols in Iran, Iraq and Syria.
**1269:** End of the reign of the Almohads in the Maghreb.
**1269–1465:** Marinid dynasty in the western Maghreb (Morocco).
**1279–1290:** Sultanate of the great Qala'un in a prosperous Egypt.
**1291:** Mamluks destroy the last Latin bastion at Acre.
**1382:** The Circassian Mamluks take power.
**1387:** Taking of Isfahan by Tamerlane: at least 70,000 beheaded.
**1492:** The Catholic kings complete the 'Reconquista' by taking the small Nasrid amirate of Granada.
**1517:** Selim I's Ottoman Turks invade Egypt.

# 11th–15th centuries

3. Manteq ot-teyr (The Conference of the Birds). *15th-century manuscript.*

| **Tamerlane.** | **Fall of Granada.** |
|---|---|
| **1336–1405** | **1492** |

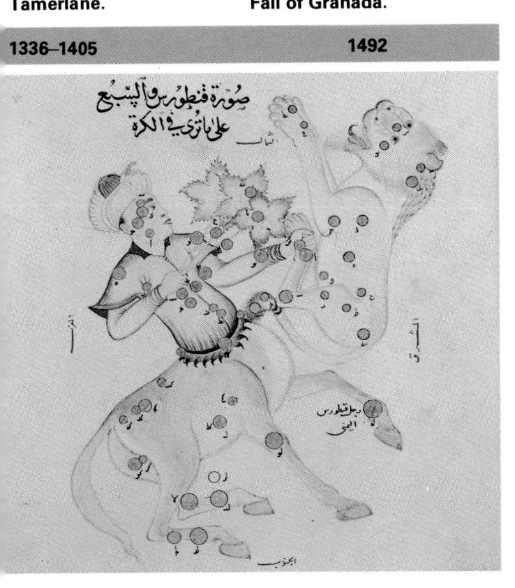

5. *Detail from a manuscript copy of the* Suwer al-Kawakib al-thebitah (Book of the Fixed Stars) *by Abd ar-Rahman ibn 'Umar as-Sufi.*

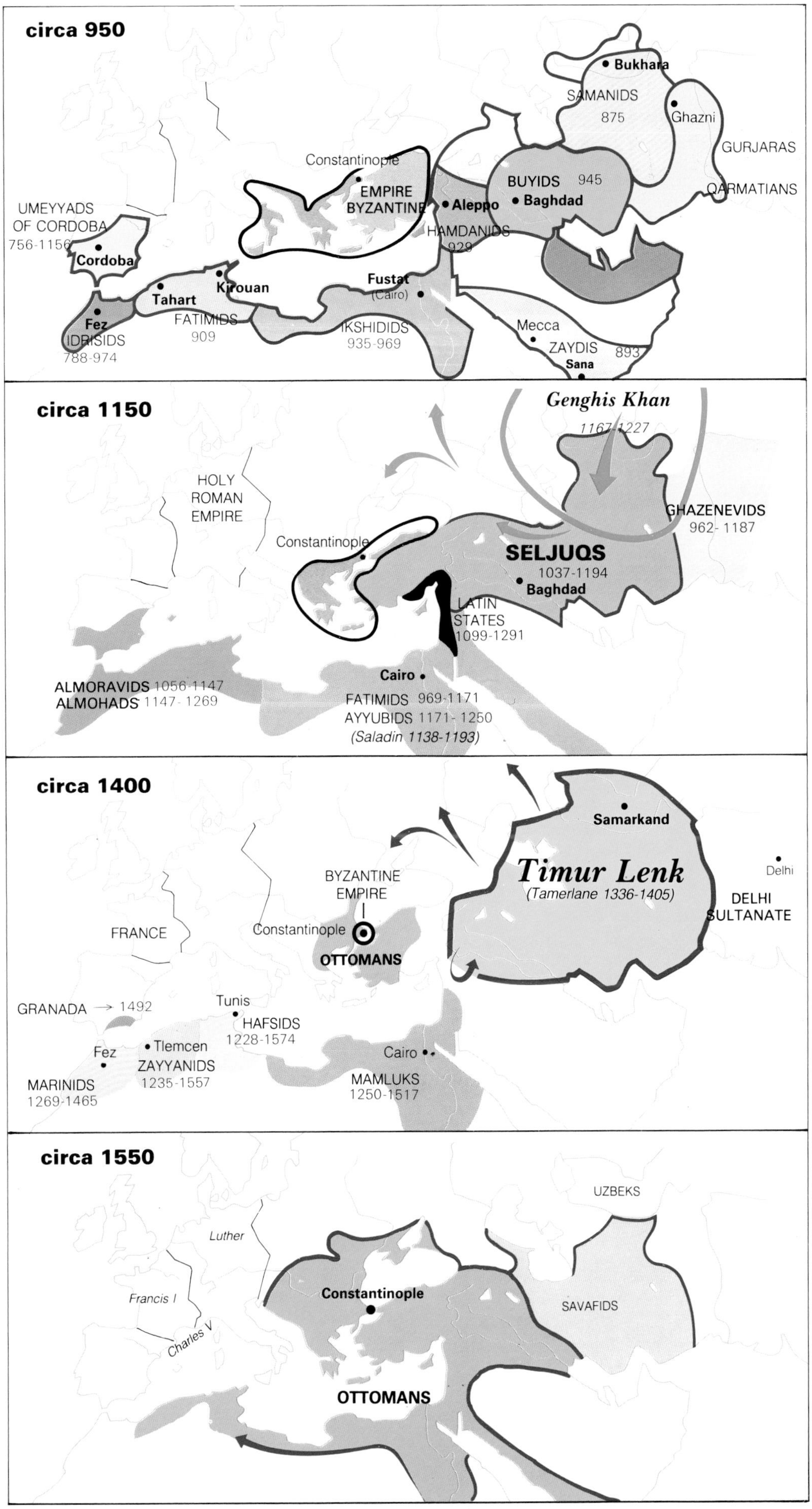

**circa 950**

Bukhara
SAMANIDS 875
Ghazni
GURJARAS
QARMATIANS
Constantinople
EMPIRE BYZANTINE
BUYIDS 945
Aleppo
Baghdad
UMEYYADS OF CORDOBA 756-1156
Cordoba
HAMDANIDS 929
Kirouan
Tahart
Fustat (Cairo)
Fez
IDRISIDS 788-974
FATIMIDS 909
IKSHIDIDS 935-969
Mecca
ZAYDIS 893
Sana

**circa 1150**

*Genghis Khan*
*1167-1227*
HOLY ROMAN EMPIRE
GHAZENEVIDS 962-1187
Constantinople
**SELJUQS** 1037-1194
Baghdad
LATIN STATES 1099-1291
ALMORAVIDS 1056-1147
ALMOHADS 1147-1269
Cairo
FATIMIDS 969-1171
AYYUBIDS 1171-1250
*(Saladin 1138-1193)*

**circa 1400**

Samarkand
***Timur Lenk***
*(Tamerlane 1336-1405)*
Delhi
DELHI SULTANATE
BYZANTINE EMPIRE
FRANCE
Constantinople
OTTOMANS
GRANADA → 1492
Tunis
HAFSIDS 1228-1574
Fez
Tlemcen
ZAYYANIDS 1235-1557
Cairo
MARINIDS 1269-1465
MAMLUKS 1250-1517

**circa 1550**

UZBEKS
*Luther*
*Francis I*
*Charles V*
Constantinople
SAVAFIDS
OTTOMANS

# The Nomadic Empire of the Mongols

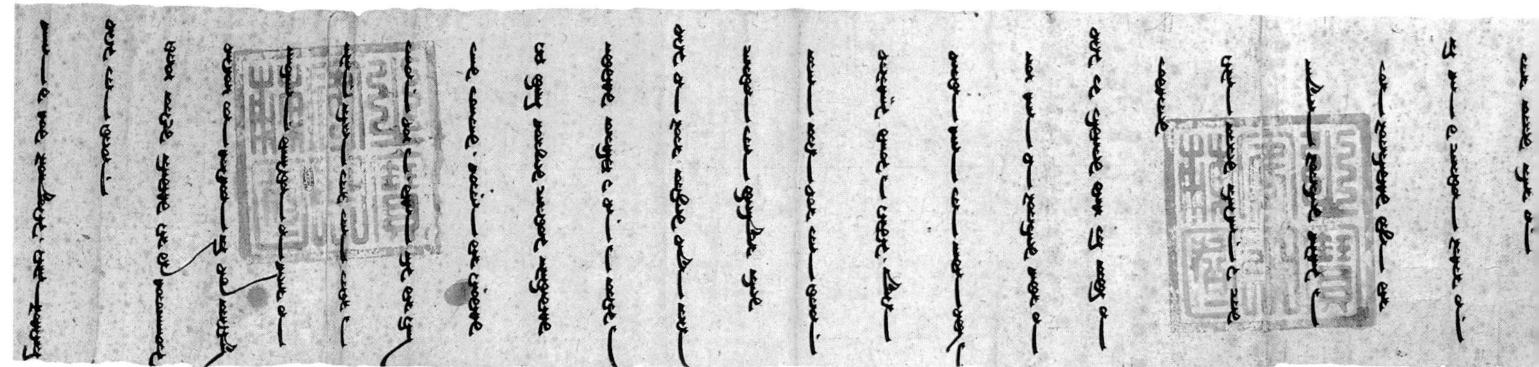

*1. Letter written by Arghun, Mongol ruler of Persia, to Philippe le Bel (Philip the Good), announcing the Mongol victory over the Arabs in Egypt.*

Genghis Khan, the thirteenth-century 'Conqueror of the World', did not appear from nowhere. For fifteen centuries before his day the 'Empires of the Steppes' – unstable confederacies controlled by the ancestors of the Turks, the Mongols or the Manchus – succeeded one another in Central Eurasia and even, from time to time, took power in the north of China. These were original civilizations of great richness, as the archaeological record reveals, and their whole economy was based on nomadic pastoralism.

The Mongols burst on to the world scene with a cleverly organized campaign of terror. Their history is composed entirely of conquests, sieges and massacres. When Genghis Khan died in 1227 the Mongol Empire stretched from the Pacific to the Black Sea, from northern China to the Siberian taiga, the Volga Plain and Persia. Fourteen years later the horsemen of the Steppes went even further, reaching right to the gates of Vienna. The Western world trembled, convinced that the Anti-Christ had come to sweep away Christianity, when suddenly the terrible invaders turned back, recalled by domestic intrigues of imperial succession. They were never to return. China was less fortunate. For the first time in its long history, it fell totally under the domination of a dynasty of barbarian origin. The Mongols' conquests stretched as far as Cambodia, Burma and Annam.

European travellers – missionaries and traders – started to journey through Eurasia. Luxury goods from the Far East now became an essential feature of life in the upper echelons of Italian and French society. The rulers of Christendom nurtured dreams of allying with the Mongols to destroy the forces of Islam. But the decline of the Mongol Empire was as sudden as its growth had been quick. From the 1250s onwards the khanates, founded by sons or grandsons of Genghis Khan, began to assert their independence. Those in the west became Turkish and Islamic in character. The Great Khan now only ruled over China. The epic period of Genghis Khan's rule was, however, more than just a series of wars of conquest and domestic strife; it was also more than might be gleaned from the tales of Marco Polo. It marks the period in which the Mongol peoples finally settled in the territories that were to become their own. The unity of the population assisted in the creation of a cultural identity – both material and spiritual – which can be seen to have been remarkably continuous from the thirteenth century up until our own times. We possess written records of this process in both Eastern and Western languages – Chinese, Persian, Syriac, Armenian, Russian, Greek, Latin, Italian etc. The abundance of such material contrasts markedly with the poverty of sources from earlier periods of civilization in the Steppes.

To understand thirteenth-century Mongol civilization from the inside, the key document is the *Secret History of the Mongols*, a splendid chronicle in narrative form, written to glorify Genghis Khan and the line descended from his youngest son (that of Möngke and Kubilai, who were in conflict with the descendants of Ogedei). Its pages reveal the operation of a morality based on loyalty and respect for age which is still very much alive in the Steppes. In the name of the 'Eternal Blue Sky', Genghis Khan and his successors also imposed a code of law whose influence is visible in the Mongol legal codes of later centuries. So much so, indeed, that up until recent times Genghis Khan was seen as the great protector of his people; in all Mongol regions his name was venerated and his glorious return awaited. In 1980 the People's Republic of China reconstructed his pseudo-mausoleum in the Ordos Desert (Inner Mongolia), in order themselves to share in some of the glory still attaching to his memory.

| Genghis Khan. | Ogedei. | Guyuk. | Möngke. |
|---|---|---|---|
| c. 1155–1227 | 1229–41 | 1246–8 | 1251–9 |

**2nd century BC:** Confederation of the Hsiung-nu: rich Bronze Age civilization, powerful cavalry.
**6th–8th centuries AD:** Confederation of the T'u-chueh (Chinese transcription of 'Turk'); first Turkish Empire.
**8th–10th centuries:** Confederation of the Uighur Turks, a great civilization which was to influence the Mongols.
**907–1118:** Khitans control northern China (Liao dynasty).
**1115–1234:** The Jurchen tribes control northern China (Chin dynasty).
**1206:** Temujin takes name Genghis Khan and founds the Mongol state.
**1215:** Capture of Peking, capital of the Chin, and northern China is gradually conquered.
**1219–23:** First invasion of the Muslim world and the Russian Steppes.
**1227:** Death of Genghis Khan.
**1229–41:** Reign of Ogedei, third son of Genghis Khan; capital at Karakorum.
**1231–44:** Conquest of Asia Minor resumed.
**1234:** Whole of northern China occupied (end of the Chin).
**1236–40:** Conquest of Russia.
**1241:** Invasion of Europe is halted after reaching its most westerly point.
**1245–7:** John Plano Carpini is sent by Pope Innocent IV to the court of the Great Khan.
**1245–48:** Reign of Guyuk, son of Ogedei.
**1251–9:** Reign of Möngke, son of Genghis Khan's fourth son.
**1253–5:** William Rubrouck, a Flemish Franciscan, journeys to the court of the Great Khan on behalf of Louis IX.
**1260–94:** Reign of Kubilai Khan, younger brother of Möngke and founder of the Chinese dynasty of the Yuan.
**1271–95:** Journey of the young Venetian Marco Polo through Europe and Central Asia to China.
**1276–7:** Conquest of China completed.
**1294–1328:** John of Montecorvino is sent to Khanbaliq (Peking) as apostolic legate by Pope Clement V. He becomes bishop there and later Oriental Patriarch.
**Late 13th century:** Mongol Empire breaks up into rival states. In the Russian steppes, the Golden Horde, led by the descendants of Jochi, eldest son of Genghis Khan, is won over to Islam. The khanates of Crimea, Astrakhan, Bukhara, Kasimov, Khiva and Khokand were to result from this process. Until 1335: Iran is governed by the Likhans, descendants of Möngke and Kubilai Khan converted to Islam. Chagatei khanate in Turkestan, founded by the second son of Genghis Khan, was Turkish and Islamic. Dominated by Timur Lenk (Tamerlane) in 1370; khanates of Transoxiana, Mogholistan and Kashgar result. In the east, the Yuan dynasty, Sinified and Buddhist.
**1345–6:** Journey of the Arab writer Tanger Ibn Battuta to southern China and Khanbaliq (Peking).
**1368:** Yuan overthrown by the Ming. Mongols return to the steppes.

*3. The Mongol ruler of Persia, Mahmud Ghazan, and his wife surrounded by their court. Mongol manuscript, late 13th century.*

# 12th–14th centuries

2. Hunting scenes. Details of a painting on silk by Zho Mongfu, a Chinese painter in the service of the Mongols.

**Kubilai Khan.**

**1260–94**

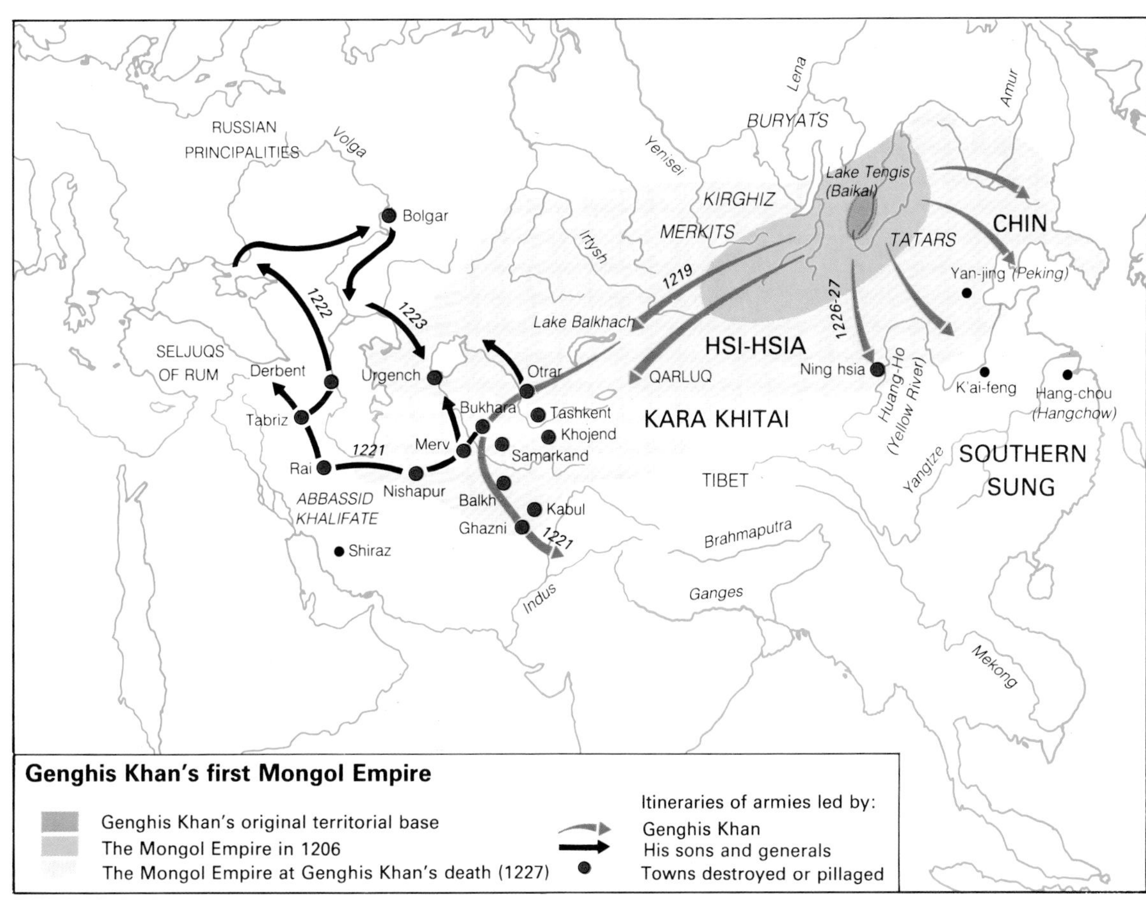


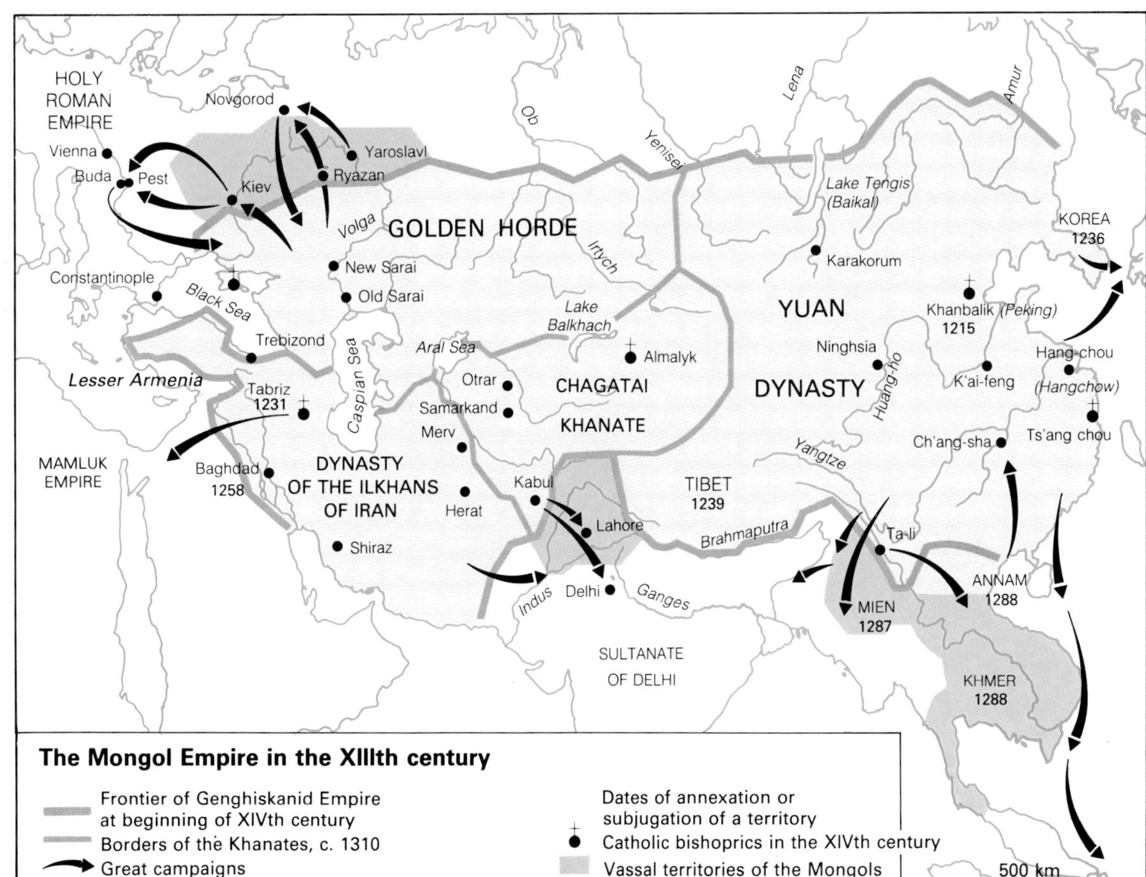

4. 13th-century tortoise at the entrance to the site of Karakorum, former capital of the Genghiskhanids in Mongolia.

# Medieval Japan

In the Kanto at the end of the twelfth century the warriors were becoming increasingly active. In 1156, and again in 1159, the aristocracy called upon the great warrior clans to settle their internal disputes. For some twenty years the Taira clan eclipsed the Fujiwara at court, but they were themselves displaced by the head of the Minamoto clan, who set up his government at Kamakura and took the title of *shogun* in 1192. The old imperial regime, which had been based on an aristocracy dedicated to state service, lost power to the warriors, who took over the administration of the landed estates to carve out fiefs for themselves. As in the West, the Japanese chivalric system was based on vassalage. The suzerain of the warriors (the shogun), or his regent from the Hojo clan, took over political power, while the former Kyoto aristocracy which remained the titular owner of the *shoen* existed alongside. The liegemen of the shogunate were given key positions in the provinces and in the estates. It could be said that the power held by the warriors in a way complemented that of the civil and religious aristocracy.

The thirteenth century was a relatively stable period, which saw slow but even commercial expansion. The attempted invasions by the Mongols forced the warriors to bear the costs of war, with Kamakura in no position to pay its vassals. Outbreaks of fighting, banditry and private wars started up again. In 1333 the Emperor succeeded in restoring the old regime, but was unable to control the warriors' lust for land. Ashikaga Takauji founded a new shogunate at Kyoto, but the civil war continued with only occasional interruption by truces.

The thirteenth and fourteenth centuries were periods of great religious activity. New sects advocating salvation through a simple faith in the Buddha Amida (Amidaist sects) took root among the lower levels of society. The Zen sects, with their rigid moral standards, meditation techniques and mastery over the body, exerted a strong influence on the thinking and way of life of the warriors. The shogunate encouraged the Zen monasteries, which were arranged in a hierarchical system known as that of the Five Mountains. 'Intimist' and poetic literature gave way to great war epics. In the fifteenth century increased homogeneity between local economies, technological advances in farming and the exploits of pirate-traders at sea brought Japanese civilization to one of its highest points. The former aristocracy, the shogunal court and the growing bourgeoisie invented new artistic forms: Zen gardens and the tea ceremony, architectural masterpieces and the Noh theatre. But this growth brought social upheavals in its train. Some warrior clans collapsed; others extended the area of their control. Revolts in the countryside, sometimes organized by the Ikkoshu (Single-Minded sect), made the control of central Japan impossible for the shogun, who was now a mere puppet of his vassals. Merchant oligarchies at the head of 'free towns' liberated themselves from seigniorial tutelage. It was a prosperous but divided land that the Portuguese found when they landed in 1543, bringing with them Christianity and firearms.

*1. Portrait of Yorimoto, ruler of Japan from 1192.*

**ANTIQUITY** | **MIDDLE AGES**

**1100** | **1150** | **1200** | **1250** | **1300**

**RÉGIME OF RETIRED EMPERORS** | **TAIRA RÉGIME** | **SHOGUNATE OF KAMAKURA**

**Heian period.** | **1159** | **1185** | **Kamakura period.** | **1333** | **1338**

**1156:** The aristocracy in the capital calls upon the Taira and Minamoto warriors to control its internal conflicts.
**1159:** New coup d'état. The Taira take over from their rivals, the Minamoto.
**1167:** The head of the Taira family, Kiyomori, is 'prime minister' at court.
**1175:** Honen founds the Pure Land sect (or Jodo).
**1180:** Revolt of Minamoto-no-Yoritomo in the Kanto.
**1185:** The Minamoto are victors over the Taira in the west. Yoritomo makes his followers military governors (*shugo*) and land stewards in the estates (*jito*).
**1191:** Eisai founds the Rinzai sect.
**1192:** Yoritomo appointed *sei-i-tai shogun*.
**1203:** Hojo Tokimasa becomes regent of the shogunate. Beginning of the dominance of the Hojo family.
**1221:** The retired emperor Go-Toba tries to suppress the shogunate. Unsuccessful, he is exiled. The Hojo confiscate many estates and consolidate their power. Shinran founds the True Sect of the Pure Land.
**1227:** Dogen teaches the Zen doctrines of the Soto sect.
**1232:** The regent Hojo Yasutoki establishes a legal code, the *Joei Shikimoku*.
**c. 1240:** Composition of the greatest warrior epic, the story of the Taira family, *The Tale of the Heike (Heike Monogatari)*.
**1253:** Nichiren founds an original sect committed to the teachings of the Lotus sutra; they wished to make Japan the birthplace of a doctrine that would be spread throughout the world.
**1274:** Failure of the first Mongol invasion on the coasts of Kyushu.
**1281:** Further failure for the Mongols.
**c. 1320:** *Tsurezure gusa (Idle Jottings)*.
**1333:** General revolt against the Hojo of Kamakura. Kemmu restoration.
**1338:** Ashikaga Takauji founds his shogunate. The imperial dynasty is divided into the northern court, supported by the

*2. 13th century silk scroll depicting an episode in the war against the Mongols.*

# 12th–16th centuries

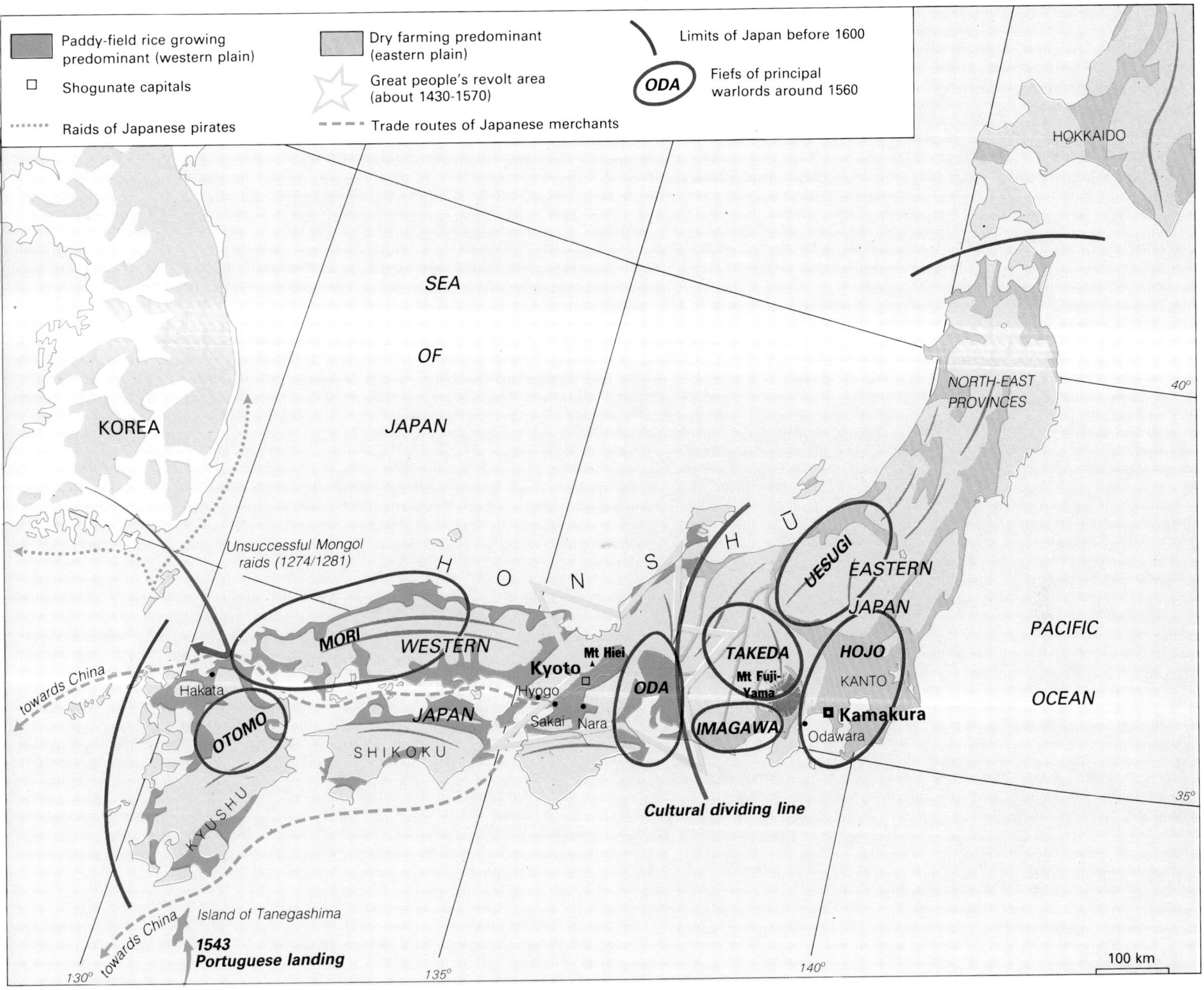

**MODERN TIMES**

1350 | 1400 | 1450 | 1500 | 1550 | 1600

**ASHIKAGA SHOGUNATE**

**…rs between the southern and northern courts. 1392 Muromachi period. 1477 Warlord/Shokuho period. 1573**

3. *The moss garden at Kyoto, created in the 15th century.*

Ashikaga, and the southern, which refuses to recognize the shogun.
**1378:** The third shogun, Ashikaga Yoshimitsu, has the 'Villa of Flowers' built at Muromachi.
**1392:** Reunification of the two imperial courts.
**1395:** Yoshimitsu has the 'Golden Pavilion' built.
**c. 1400–20:** Zeami fixes the rules of the Noh Theatre.
**1401:** Yoshimitsu re-establishes official links with Ming China. He takes the title in Chinese of 'King of Japan'.
**1428:** First great peasant revolt.
**1441:** The shogun Yoshinori is assassinated. The peasants around Kyoto rise up and demand the abolition of debts.
**1467–77:** Civil wars in Onin.
**1485:** Start of the great revolt of the province of Yamashiro. The shogun Yoshimasa has the 'Silver Pavilion' built.
**c. 1530:** The peasant and religious leagues, the *ikki*, at their peak. The warlords consolidate their fiefs.
**1543:** The Portuguese land in the south of Japan.
**1546:** The first firearms are made by the Japanese.
**1573:** Oda Nobunaga drives the last Ashikaga shogun out of Kyoto.

4. *Old Age, 15th century.*

# Muslim India

THE CONQUEST of the Sind by the troops of Muhammad ibn al-Qasim was one aspect of the spectacular Arab expansion in the first decades of Islam, yet it happened at a time when everywhere else the momentum was declining: the new Arab province could not act as a base for the conquest of the rest of India. The Arabs showed tolerance and subtlety in the way they treated their Hindu subjects: they gave them the status of *dhimmi* or 'protected ones' (which is normally only applied to the 'People of the Book'), leaving them free to practise their religion and to live by their own customs as long as they paid the special tax known as the *jaziyah*. They also took an interest in the culture and in particular in the accumulated knowledge of the Indians. In the next three centuries, then, Islam was to remain on the margins of India.

*1. The great monolithic Buddha of Pollonnoruva, Sri Lanka (Ceylon), 11th century.*

The situation became quite different when the Turk, Mahmud of Ghazna, began a series of raids and massacres in the Indian towns and Hindu temples. Some two centuries later the process was repeated, this time under Muhammad of Ghur, who carried out campaigns of extermination and created the sultanate. The rise of Islam resumed, this time in the hands of warriors from Central Asia whose power base was located in a number of Afghan principalities. The end result was the creation of a Muslim state which was to dominate India, though which was only to become Indian slowly and partially, bringing about profound transformations in Indian society in the process. Three stages can be distinguished. First there was the Slave (or Mamluk) dynasty. Iltutmish introduced a bureaucratic administration that consolidated the sultanate's power over the whole of northern India. Then came the Khaljis. The sultanate – under Ala ud-Din – was now at the height of its political, territorial and cultural power. Last of all came the Tugluqs, under whose rule regional Muslim states were founded: Indian Islam would now no longer be a mere emanation of the sultanate, the break-up of which was soon to be hastened by Tamerlane's incursions.

At the end of the thirteenth century Muslims apparently made up a quarter of the population. There were several different groups, including people who were of Muslim origin, Turkish and Afghan courtiers who were paid hereditary tenures (*jagir*) by the sultan, and warriors from Central Asia, who along with their families and sometimes their entire clans came to replenish and reinforce the ranks of the conqueror's armies. Their common language was Persian and this became the language of government and prestige (even for Hindus). Persian culture was their ideal. The largest part of the Muslim population was, however, made up of converts, of whom there were a great number throughout the north and particularly in the Punjab and Sind regions and also in Bengal, where Islam had supplanted the previously dominant Buddhist faith. Hinduism proved more durable because it was solidly built into the social structure. A large number of converts were, however, made from Hinduism. It is not the case, as has been argued in the past, that most of them came from the lower castes, seeking to escape the oppression of the system, for in Muslim society, though technically egalitarian, the caste system was to some degree re-established: this was how Islam became integrated into Indian culture. The Hindu Indians – especially upper-class ones – adopted Muslim customs, such as *purdah*. There also developed an Indo-Muslim style in the arts and the Urdu language, a mixture of Persian and Hindi, appeared at this point. In spite of the savagery of its wars, India prospered. The account of the Hindu town of Vijayanagar given by the Muslim Abd al-Razzaq is an eloquent testimony to the splendours of India in the later part of this period.

**Kashmir: independent Hindu kingdom and centre of Sanskrit culture.** **725–1339**

**Sultanate of Delhi: dynasty of the 'Slaves'.** **1206–90**

**Khilji dynasty.** **1290–1320**

**712:** The Arab Muhammad ibn al-Qasim conquers Sind for the Umayyad caliphate.
**c. 760:** The Great Temple of the Kailasa is hewn out of rock at Ellora.
**780–820:** The Hindu philosopher Sankara lives in Kerala. He professes 'Nondualism'.
**783:** Gurjara-Pratihara dynasty founded. It dominates northern India until 885, constituting an obstacle to Arab expansion.
**c. 850:** The Cola become the ruling power in southern India. Cola 'thalassocracy' lasts for two centuries.
**950–1050:** The Chandelas of Prayag build the temples of Khajuraho.
**933:** Founding of Delhi.
**1000–27:** Mahmud of Ghazna launches looting raids against towns and temples in India, including Mathura, Thanesar and Kanauj. During his reign, al-Biruni, the historian, geographer and astronomer, compiles an important anthology of observations and reflections on India.
**1173:** The Afghan princes of Ghur seize Ghazni.
**1192:** Battle of Thanesar. Muhammad of Ghur conquers and kills the Rajput king, Prthviraja. His troops enter the Ganges valley, destroy Benares and the Buddhist and Hindu centres of Bihar and Bengal.
**1206:** Qutb-ub-Din Aybak founds the Sultanate of Delhi.
**1211–36:** Iltutmish becomes Sultan of Delhi. He fights off Genghis Khan's Mongols and builds the Qutb Minar.
**c. 1250:** Construction of the Temple of the Sun at Konarak in Orissa.
**1288 and 1293:** Marco Polo visits southern India.
**1303:** Ala ud-Din Khalji seizes Chitor in Rajasthan. Queen Padmavati burns herself alive along with thousands of women to avoid being captured by the conquerors (*jauhar* rite).
**1310:** Malik Kafur, Ala ud-Din Khalji's general, brings almost all of the Deccan under Delhi's rule: the extreme south and pockets of resistance in Rajasthan and on the Malabar coast are the only parts to escape his control.
**1325–51:** Muhammad Tugluq, Sultan of Delhi. He has part of the population of Delhi transported to his new capital at Daulatabad. Bold but unsuccessful attempts at monetary

*3. Illustration from a Kalpasutra, a Jain text portraying the life of the Jina Mahavira.*

# 8th–16th centuries

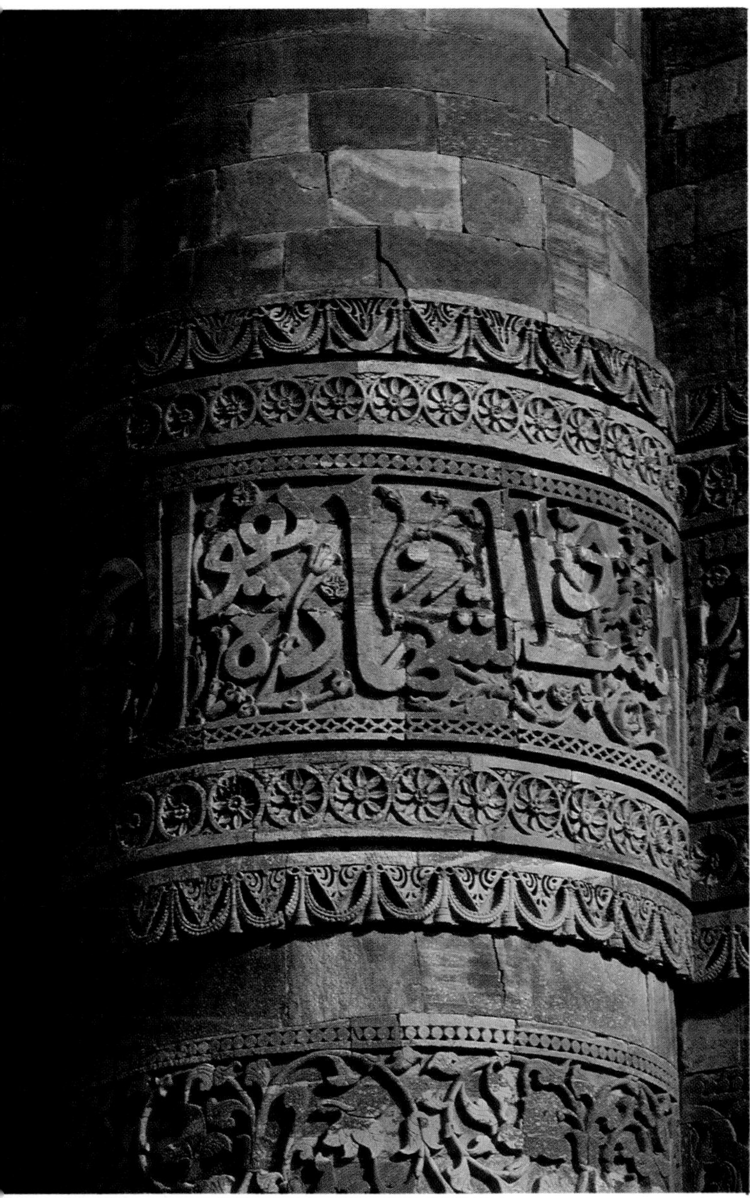

2. Verses from the Quran on a column of the Mosque of Quwat ul-Islam, near the Qutb Minar tower (Delhi), 13th century.

**Tugluq dynasty.**

**1320–88**

reform and fiscal centralization.
**1336:** Foundation in Mysore of the Hindu kingdom of Vijayanagar, which was to control southern India until 1565. A centre of Sanskrit culture.
**1347:** Bahman Shah establishes an independent sultanate based on Bijapur, Bidar and Gulbarga, which will develop fruitful relations with the whole of the Muslim world. Constantly in conflict with Vijayanagar over two centuries.
**1387:** Death of Sayana, author of a commentary on the Veda.
**1398:** Tamerlane raids Delhi.
**1420:** The Italian voyager, Niccolo dei Conti, visits Vijayanagar.
**1470:** The Russian merchant Nikitin visits Bidar.
**1440–1518:** Life of Kabir, a mystic poet, who dreams of uniting the Hindu and Islamic cultures.
**1469–1539:** Life of Nanak, founder of the Sikh community.
**1498:** Vasco da Gama lands at Calicut: first time a European journeys to India entirely by sea.

**Lodi dynasty.**

**1450–1526**

**1510:** Portuguese admiral Albuquerque seizes Goa and massacres the Muslim population.
**1534:** Bishopric of Goa founded.

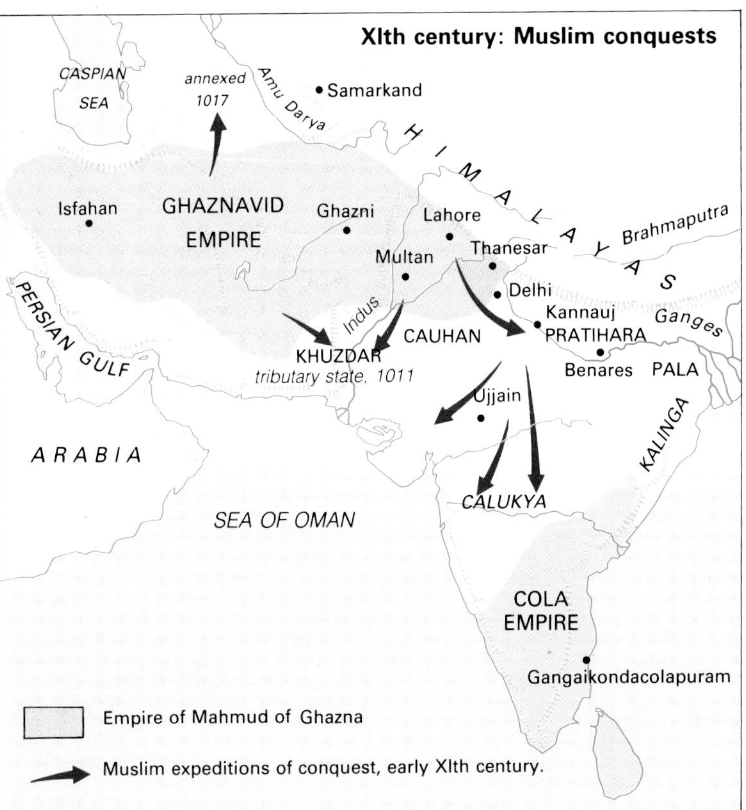


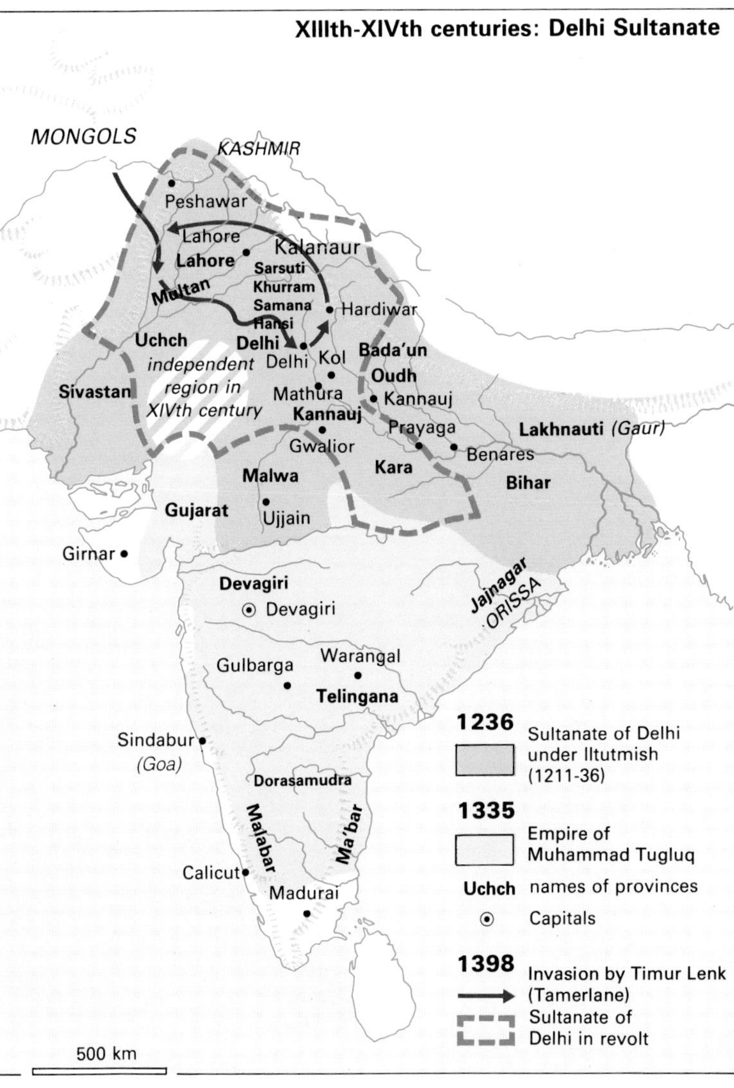

# The Rise of the Towns in the West

BETWEEN THE TENTH and the thirteenth centuries Western Europe underwent a series of profound material and social changes on a scale not seen again until the Industrial Revolution. Since medieval society was organized around cultivation of the land, it is in the great expansion of agricultural production that we must seek the origins of these transformations. New social bonds were created which reflected the organization of manorial demesnes and an increase in the feudal dues which the aristocracy exacted in kind, in labour (the *corvée*) and, more and more frequently, in money. Greater productivity was therefore required of the only class able to furnish it – the peasantry. A number of other factors contributed to this agricultural boom. Europe was entering a period of drier, colder climatic conditions which favoured the growth of cereals, the Hungarian and Scandinavian invasions came to an end and workers were now better protected, thanks to the 'Peace of God'. More efficient tools and machinery (such as the wheeled plough with mouldboard, the collar-harness, the harrow, the water-mill and later the wind-mill) came into widespread use,

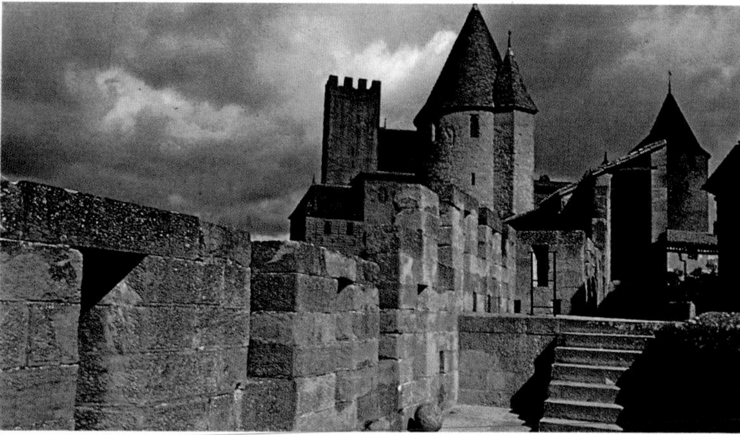

*1. Town walls and towers of Carcassonne. 13th century.*

together with improved agricultural techniques. Three-year crop rotation became the practice in the most fertile areas in the thirteenth century. In these conditions cereal harvests increased to give a yield of 5 or 6 to 1. The dramatic rise in production was, however, due less to intensified cultivation than to the increase in the area of arable land through scrub clearance, marsh drainage and reclamation of land in coastal regions (*polder*), and the expansion was sustained by that universal driving force of land acquisition – demographic growth. Over three centuries the population of Europe more or less doubled, to reach a figure of around 60 million inhabitants. They settled either in the villages which sprang up in this period or in the towns, whose growth picked up again for the first time since late antiquity. In addition to the long-established episcopal cities, there grew up *portus* (urban centres of trade and craft industries), and 'new towns' (or the French *sauvetés*) were built from scratch. Town life gave rise to new forms of organization of trades (guilds), new political structures (the communes) and new religious associations (the confraternities). All these were concessions which the townspeople extracted from the lay and ecclesiastical overlords. The urban economy increasingly dictated that of the surrounding countryside (the Italian *contado*), but it was above all tied up with long-distance trade. Commerce benefited greatly from increased monetary circulation, which boosted the minting of silver *deniers* (necessary for large transactions) and later, in the thirteenth century, the issue of gold coins. The entire European economy was stimulated by trade between the two great economic zones – on the one hand the Italian ports of Pisa, Genoa and Venice with their maritime trading links with the Levant, and on the other the northern European cloth towns of Ghent, Ypres and Bruges. The merchants of these two complementary regions met annually at the fairs in Champagne, which reached their peak during the twelfth century at Troyes, Provins, Bar-sur-Aube and Lagny. Merchants there employed new financial and commercial practices such as using bills of exchange which enabled them to circumvent the church's prohibition of usury. Towards the end of the fourteenth century, however, there were increasing signs that Western Europe's economic and demographic boom was running out of steam.

*2. The Lendit Fair at St Denis. Manuscript of the* Grandes Chroniques*, 14th century.*

**First 'Peace of God'.** **989**

**Creation of the Commune of Laon.** **1112**

**941–2:** Famine in western France.
**c. 950:** Earliest evidence of land clearance and of use of water-mills for grinding grain and also in dyeing, forging and pressing: this is a crucial factor in the economic expansion of Europe.
**989:** Synod of Charroux – beginning of the 'Peace of God' imposed by the church on the knightly classes. Most of the time, however, the church has to settle for imposing the 'Truce of God' on certain days of the week or dates of the year. This nevertheless affords some degree of protection to church property as well as to the defenceless peasantry and to the material basis of the economy. In this respect the 'Peace of God' movement contributes significantly to the economic revival.
**992:** First commercial treaty between Venice and Byzantium. This marks the beginning of Venetian maritime power in the Mediterranean.
**1005–6:** Famine in Western Europe.
**1032–3:** Chroniclers, alert to signs announcing the coming of the Antichrist, record a famine in France.

*3. The windmill. Illumination from a 14th-century French manuscript of the* Roman d'Alexandre.

**c. 1097:** Completion of the Bayeux Tapestry, which carries in its lower border the earliest picture of a harrow.
**c. 1100:** Increasing importance of the fairs in Champagne – halfway between the towns of Flanders and those of northern Italy. The counts of Champagne have an interest in protecting and promoting these fairs. The scratch plough tends to be replaced by the wheeled plough, whose mouldboard and heavier ploughshare enable farmers to increase their yields.
**1112:** Creation of the Commune of Laon. The townspeople assassinate the bishop who is also their secular lord. King Louis VI intervenes to put down the uprising.
**1120–50:** First statutes of the trade guilds, which are drawn up under the aegis of the princes or town governments. They are intended to preserve equality between master craftsmen or merchants and to protect them from competition, either internal or external. In 1121 Louis VI grants privileges to the Parisian corporation of water-carriers, whose provost becomes in effect mayor of the capital city.

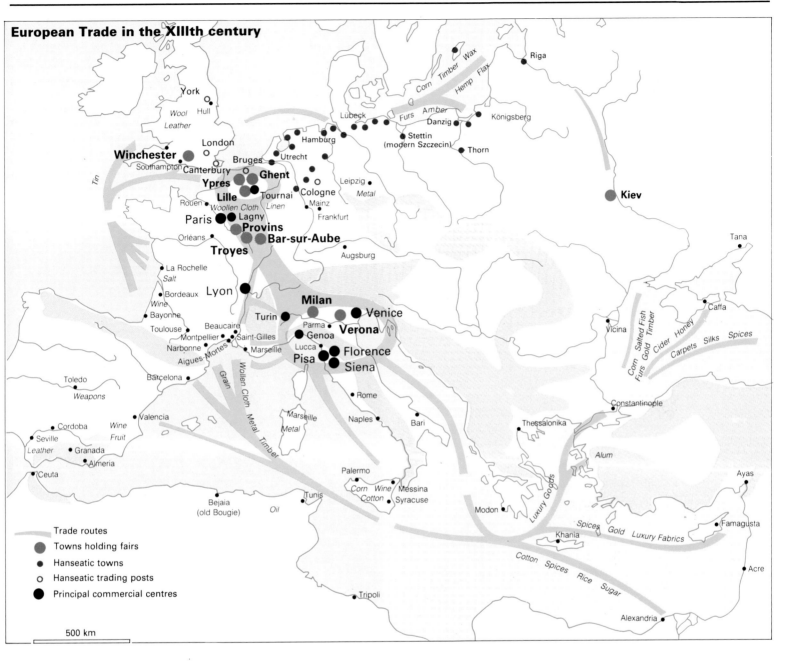

## European Trade in the XIIIth century

Riga
Corn Timber Wax
Hemp Flax
York
Wool Hull
Leather
Lübeck
Furs Amber
Danzig
Königsberg
London
Hamburg
Stettin
(modern Szczecin)
Thorn
Winchester
Southampton
Canterbury
Bruges
Utrecht
Ghent
Ypres
Lille
Tournai
Cologne
Leipzig
Metal
Tin
Kiev
Rouen
Woollen Cloth
Linen
Mainz
Paris
Lagny
Frankfurt
Provins
Orléans
Bar-sur-Aube
Troyes
Augsburg
Tana
La Rochelle
Salt
Bordeaux
Lyon
Wine
Milan
Bayonne
Turin
Venice
Caffa
Toulouse
Beaucaire
Parma
Verona
Montpellier
Saint-Gilles
Genoa
Narbonne
Marseille
Lucca
Florence
Vicina
Aigues-Mortes
Pisa
Siena
Corn Salted Fish
Furs Gold Timber
Cider Honey
Carpets Silks Spices
Toledo
Barcelona
Grain
Wollen Cloth Metal Timber
Weapons
Rome
Constantinople
Valencia
Marseille
Metal
Naples
Bari
Thessalonika
Cordoba
Wine
Fruit
Seville
Leather
Granada
Almeria
Alum
Ceuta
Palermo
Ayas
Luxury Goods
Corn Wine
Cotton
Messina
Syracuse
Tunis
Bejaia
(old Bougie)
Oil
Modon
Spices Gold Luxury Fabrics
Famagusta
Khania
Cotton Spices Rice Sugar
Acre
Tripoli
Alexandria

Trade routes
Towns holding fairs
Hanseatic towns
Hanseatic trading posts
Principal commercial centres

500 km

**Sack of Constantinople by the crusaders.**

**1204**

**Minting of gold coins resumed.**

**1252**

*4. The punishment of adulterers: the guilty couple are paraded through the town. 13th-century Cistercian manuscript.*

**1124–6:** Severe famine in the countryside of Flanders.
**c. 1180:** Appearance of windmills in the West. A mill represents a considerable capital investment: ownership is consequently restricted to lords, who reserve the exclusive right to operate them as a public right or 'ban': the fees charged for use of the mill make up an increasingly important part of the lord's income.
**1204:** Capture and sack of Constantinople during the Fourth Crusade, enabling the Genoese to set up trading posts on the shores of the Black Sea.
**c. 1237:** The St Gothard Pass is opened up: this assists the economic growth of southern Germany.
**1250:** Great increase in the numbers of charters of liberties granted to rural communities. Large numbers of serfs are freed. The peasants' tithes and labour services are commuted to monetary dues.
**1252–82:** Resumption of minting of gold coins and of the bimetallic currency system (gold and silver) which had disappeared in late Antiquity. In 1231 Emperor Frederick II issues the *augustale*, Genoa mints the *genovino*, Florence the florin and, from 1284, Venice issues ducats. The King of France issues the *ecu* (1263).

*5. Seal of town of Saint-Omer depicting the échevins (aldermen). 13th century.*

# Romanesque Art

Around the year 1000, in the monk Rodulfus Glaber's words, Christendom became covered with a 'white mantle of churches'. The flowering of art and architecture during this period is best understood in the context of a whole range of mutations, economic, demographic, technical and religious. It is directly linked with the dynamism of religious orders such as Cluny and later Citeaux, the rapid growth in the number of monasteries, the birth of villages and towns which needed places of worship and the abundance of gifts received by the church, enabling them to finance expensive buildings. Important, too, was the development of hoisting, stone-cutting and vaulting techniques and, finally, the increasing popularity of relics and pilgrimages: Santiago de Compostela, Vézelay and Conques have magnificent churches.

Romanesque is characterized above all by its new architecture. Between 1000 and the twelfth century techniques of construction which were already known but had not found the right context for their development were brought together in an original synthesis. The basilical plan with nave and two aisles and the column with a capital came from Antiquity. The use of the dome and the taste for polychromy may have had oriental and Arab origins. The Romanesque style derived directly from the Carolingian (Germigny-des-Prés, Aachen) but the synthesis was new, whether the plans adopted the transept with dome over the crossing or the circular or octagonal form. The forms of worship were important in structuring space: chapels radiating from the apse were built to accommodate separate altars (Oliba Monastery at Ripoll in the Spanish Pyrenees has seven), ambulatories for processions, crypts for the relics of the saints. However, it was the revolution in building techniques which allowed the realization of daring projects: exclusive use was made of hewn stone, which called for vaulting on a grand scale. Within this framework various formulae were used: the barrel vault (Saint-Savin-sur-Gartempe) or the vault formed by intersecting arches. Where two barrel vaults met, groin vaults had to be erected.

Around 1125–1130 in the Ile de France (Morienval and ambulatory of Saint-Denis) rib vaulting was used for the first time; it soon became characteristic of Gothic architecture. But a major technical problem was caused by the considerable pressure on the outer walls; the answer was increasingly thick, windowless walls and powerful buttresses. In some regions such as Aquitaine (Saintes, Périgueux, Angoulême, Cahors) the solution was a series of domes rather than barrel vaults. The variety of styles – according to 'school', region (Catalonia, Burgundy, Auvergne, Germany, Lombardy etc.) or monastic order financing the church (Cluniac, Cistercian styles) – is as important as the unifying influence of Romanesque.

Other forms of art were closely linked to architecture: the sculptures of tympana and capitals (great Romanesque tympana of the first half of the twelfth century, Moissac, Vézelay, Conques, Autun etc.) were the church's way of explaining Christian eschatology. Mural paintings (San Clemente de Tahull in Catalonia) had an edifying function, but the harmony of their colours was also designed to accompany the liturgical chants. Gold and silverwork and illuminations represent the most precious expression of the spirituality of the times.

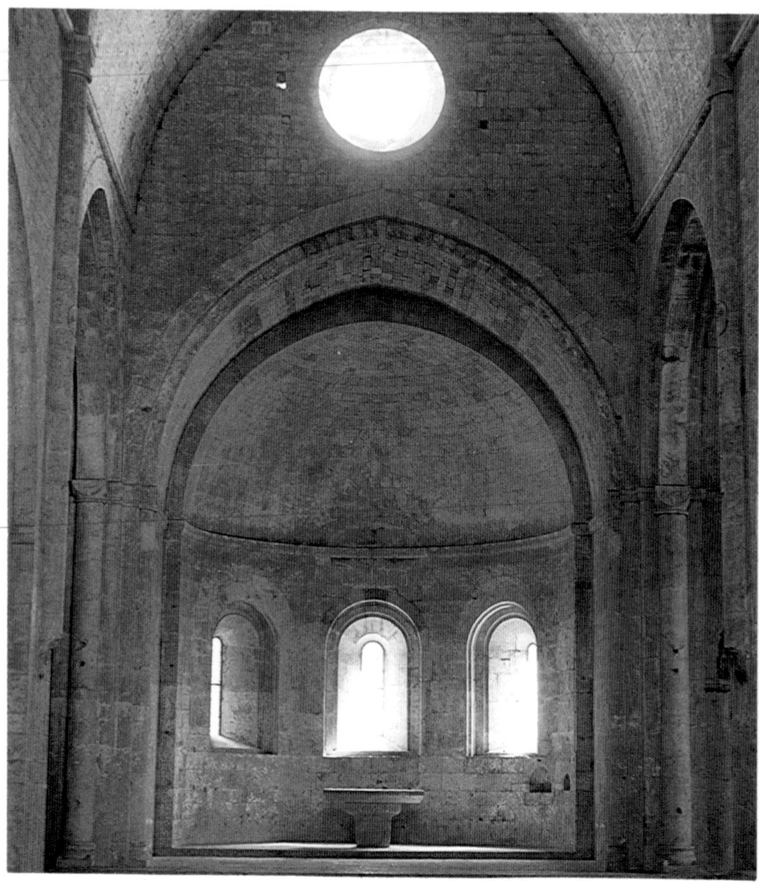

*1. Apse of Cistercian Abbey of Le Thoronet, Provence, c. 1160–80.*

***Book of Miracles of Saint Foy of Conques.*** **1030**

**Fleury Abbey completed.** **1068**

**Work begins on Santiago de Compostela.** **1075**

*2. Elephants and flowers. Capital of Perrecy-les-Forges, Saône-et-Loire, 12th century.*

**997–1004:** Building of Saint-Martin at Tours, one of the first important Romanesque churches, now almost entirely destroyed. The choir was surrounded by an ambulatory with five radiating chapels.

**1000–30:** Statue of Saint Foy at saint's shrine, Conques: wooden figure covered in gold leaf and precious stones; the head probably dates from 5th century. It was worshipped as an idol and was the object of an important 11th-century pilgrimage.

**1006–13:** Building of the abbey church of Saint-Philibert at Tournus, remarkable for the Saint-Michel Chapel above the entrance porch and for transverse barrel-vaulted aisles.

**1007:** Rotunda of Saint-Bénigne at Dijon based on basilical plan.

**c. 1015–24:** Basle altar-front in repoussé gold, one of the masterpieces of Romanesque work in precious metals, now in the Musée de Cluny, Paris.

*3. Head of Christ at Lavandieu, Loire, 12th century.*

**c. 1025:** Frescoes of Saint-Savin-sur-Gartempe painted on the barrel vaulting of one aisle. Old Testament scenes: the Flood and Noah's Ark, the Tower of Babel, etc.

**1045:** Building of octagonal church of Ottmarsheim (Upper Rhine), inspired by the Palatine Carolingian chapel of Aachen.

**1067–8:** Construction of Fleury Abbey (Saint-Benoît-sur-Loire) with vast narthex (vaulted porch beneath belfry).

**1075–1122:** Cathedral of Santiago de Compostela built to accommodate crowds of pilgrims coming to St James the Great's tomb. A Moslem raid in 997 had destroyed the primitive church. The porch (Pórtico de la Gloria) is related to those of Moissac and Saint-Sernin at Toulouse.

**1088–1130:** Building of Cluny III to replace two other abbey churches: Cluny I which dates from the early 10th century and Cluny II dating from 955–91. The new church is

# 10th–12th centuries

Hildesheim
Paderborn
Ely
St Albans
Winchester
NORMANDY
Jumièges
Morienval
Trier
Lorsch
Speyer
St-Georges-de-Boscherville
Caen
RHINELAND
Orléans
St-Benoît-sur-Loire
Tours
Vézelay
Reichenau
Dijon
Cîteaux
Autun
Tournus
Cluny
St-Savin-sur-Gartempe
Aulnay-de-Saintonge
Saintes
Angoulême
Périgueux
BURGUNDY
Milan
Pavia
Torcello
Le Puy
SOUTHWEST FRANCE
Conques
Moissac
Santiago de Compostela
Pamplona
Arles
St-Michel-de-Cuxa
Tahull
St-Martin-du-Canigou
CATALONIA
Ripoll
Rome
Monreale
Cefalu
500 km

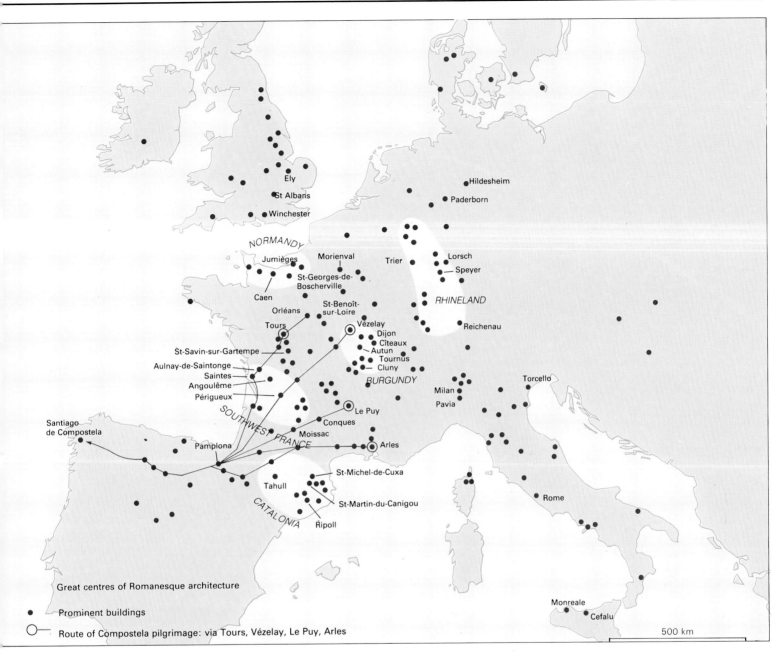

Great centres of Romanesque architecture

Prominent buildings

Route of Compostela pilgrimage: via Tours, Vézelay, Le Puy, Arles

**Moissac tympanum.**

**1115**

**Cluny Abbey completed.**

**1130**

181 metres long, has four aisles and a double transept; its scale reflects the power of the Cluny order. It was unfortunately almost entirely destroyed during the French Revolution.

**1096–1132:** Construction of Vézelay Abbey, famous for the sculptures of the main tympanum and those of the capitals in the nave.

**1115:** Moissac tympanum heralds the series of great Romanesque tympana of the first half of the 12th century: Saintes, Aulnay in Saintonge, Conques in Rouergue, Vézelay, Autun in Burgundy. All show themes of the Apocalypse and are organized around the figure of Christ presiding over the Last Judgement and the Resurrection of the Dead.

**1130–47:** Construction of the Cistercian Abbey of Fontenay, still remarkable for the close relation between its religious and its utilitarian buildings, such as the forge.

**1132:** Ambulatory of Morienval: its groin vaults emphasized by thick cylindrical mouldings mark the transition from Romanesque to Gothic.

*4. The Animals of Creation. Catalan tapestry, 12th century.*

*5. The porch at Aulnay-de-Saintonge, 12th century.*

# Gothic Art and the Twelfth-Century Renaissance

1. Porch of Cologne Cathedral, 13th century.

2. Nave and north transept of Amiens Cathedral, 13th century.

In the mid-twelfth century towns became the main centres of material and intellectual life, the source of all innovation. The founding of universities and the building of cathedrals are vivid evidence of this urban renaissance. The transfer of learning from the monasteries to the city schools went along with a complete transformation of the content, form and object of intellectual activity. To begin with, schools remained dependent on the bishop and chapter, as in Laon, Chartres and Orleans. They were also identified with new religious communities, such as the Abbey of Saint-Victor in Paris. The rediscovery of ancient philosophy and science (Plato, Aristotle, Hippocrates) through Arab authors (Avicenna, Averroës) stimulated the most advanced thinking. The seven liberal arts – 'literary' trivium, 'scientific' quadrivium – formed the basis of study. In the thirteenth century universities emerged, at Paris, Bologna and Oxford, at first in the form of corporations of masters and students. Paris included an Arts faculty and three specialized faculties: Medicine, Canon Law and Theology. The masters were either clerics paid by the students or, increasingly, members of mendicant orders. Teaching and examinations were based on the *disputatio*, the confrontation and synthesis of opposite arguments. The effort to reconcile Christian culture and pagan philosophy caused serious tension, with the church authorities stepping in to maintain orthodoxy. In 1270 and 1277 the Bishop of Paris, Etienne Tempier, proscribed the doctrine of the 'double truth' taught by the followers of Averroës. In 1337 William of Ockham's Nominalism was denounced as a source of scepticism in matters of faith. The great theological *summa* of the scholastic age have been compared to the cathedrals of the same period, in that they present the same logic of articulation and subdivision, the same breadth. They also both originated in the prosperous heart of the Ile-de-France, where Abbot Suger of Saint-Denis erected around 1140 the first example of the new art. New architectural techniques took Romanesque a step further: the crossing of pointed arches meeting in a crown enabled the force of gravity to be spread equally among four pillars. Walls were freed of their load-bearing function; large windows could now be cut in them, and stained glass could express Gothic aesthetics and spirituality in glowing colours. The edifice could reach undreamt-of heights; storeys of arcades, tribunes, triforia and clerestory windows graced the interior, while the structure was visible outside in the design of the façade framed by towers and spires. There was, however, great variety among Gothic churches, depending on the finance available, the size of the population and the period, from the first buildings of the twelfth century (Noyon, Senlis, Laon, Notre-Dame, Paris) to the 'classical' period of Reims, Amiens, Bourges and the Sainte-Chapelle at Paris and finally the 'flamboyant' Gothic of the late Middle Ages. Regional variations play a part, too (the brick cathedral of Albi, the Mudejar style of Spain, the rectangular forms of English cathedrals with flat chevet, as in York, Lincoln, Durham), as do various specific requirements, as can be seen in the spacious churches of the mendicant orders which were adapted to preaching and are similar all over Europe.

**Suger abbot of Saint-Denis.**

**The *Sentences* of Peter Lombard.**

1122

1152

**1132–44:** Suger builds abbey church of Saint-Denis. The ambulatory is the first example of Gothic art.
**1140:** Council of Sens. Abelard condemned at the instigation of St Bernard. Two conceptions of theology are revealed, rational for the master of dialectics, mystical for the monk.
**c. 1140:** *Decretum Gratiani*, critical synthesis of church legal texts or canon law.
**1145–55:** Royal portal of Chartres. On the tympanum, Christ in His Majesty and symbols of the evangelists above figures of the apostles. On either side of the porch the *pieds-droits* (column-statues) represent the prophets and kings of Israel.
**1152:** The Parisian master Peter Lombard writes the *Four Books of Sentences* or *Sentences*, which becomes the basic text of biblical interpretation at the university.
**1152–1211:** Construction begins on principal Gothic cathedrals of northern France: Le Mans, Laon, Notre-Dame, Paris, Chartres, Bourges, Reims.
**1168–83:** French romances in verse by Chrétien de Troyes: *Lancelot* or *le Chevalier à la Charette*, *Yvain* or *Le Chevalier au Lion*, *Perceval* or *Le Conte du Graal*.

3. Stained-glass window of Saint-Denis basilica, 12th century.

**1215:** Statutes of the University of Paris deriving from the schools of the 12th century. The 'University of Masters and Students', governed by the Pope, soon becomes independent of royal and episcopal power. Fourth Lateran Council takes a stand on all major questions of the period.
**1220–70:** Stained-glass windows of Chartres.
**c. 1234:** First part of *The Romance of the Rose* by Guillaume de Lorris, French didactical and allegorical poem in octosyllables. Completed by Jean de Meung (1275–80), who gave it an encyclopaedic form.
**1240:** Translation of Aristotle's *Ethics* by William of Moerbeke. Now better known, Aristotle's works revolutionize orthodox theological, political and scientific ideas.
**1243–8:** Louis IX has the Sainte-Chapelle built to accommodate Christ's Crown of Thorns.
**1245–59:** Dominicans Albertus Magnus and Thomas Aquinas teach at Paris University.

4. Psalter of Queen Ingeborg of Denmark, wife of Philip II Augustus, 1210.

# 12th–14th centuries

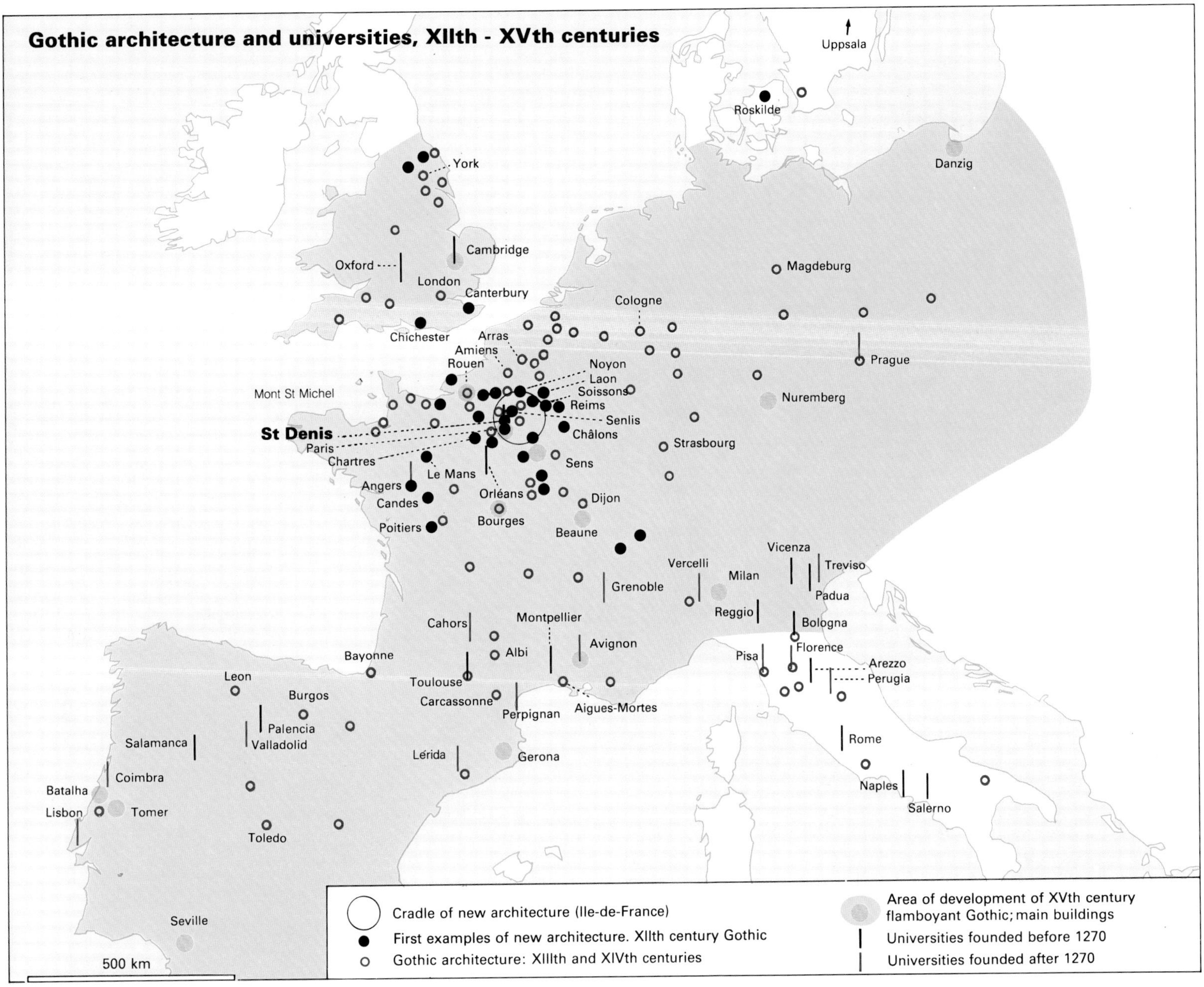

## Gothic architecture and universities, XIIth - XVth centuries

Cradle of new architecture (Ile-de-France)
First examples of new architecture. XIIth century Gothic
Gothic architecture: XIIIth and XIVth centuries
Area of development of XVth century flamboyant Gothic; main buildings
Universities founded before 1270
Universities founded after 1270

500 km

**Fourth Lateran Council.**

**1215**

**Averroism condemned.**

**1277**

From 1266 to 1273 the latter publishes his *Summa Theologiae*.
**1265–1321:** Dante Alighieri, author of *The Divine Comedy*.
**1270–7:** Averroism condemned by Bishop of Paris, Etienne Tempier. The Arab philosopher Averroës (died 1198) originated a doctrine unacceptable to the church, of a 'double truth', that of reason and of faith.
**1310–15:** William of Ockham teaches Nominalism at Oxford. This doctrine, originated by Abelard in the 12th century, stipulates that general ideas (or universals) do not have any reality in themselves but are only names, thus demolishing the traditional realism of medieval theology.

*5. Virgin and Child, painted stone statue from the Ile-de-France, early 14th century.*

*6. The Virgin of Calvary, 14th-century English embroidery work.*

*7. Statute book of Hubant College, French manuscript of 1387.*

# Italy: The Era of Merchants and Artists

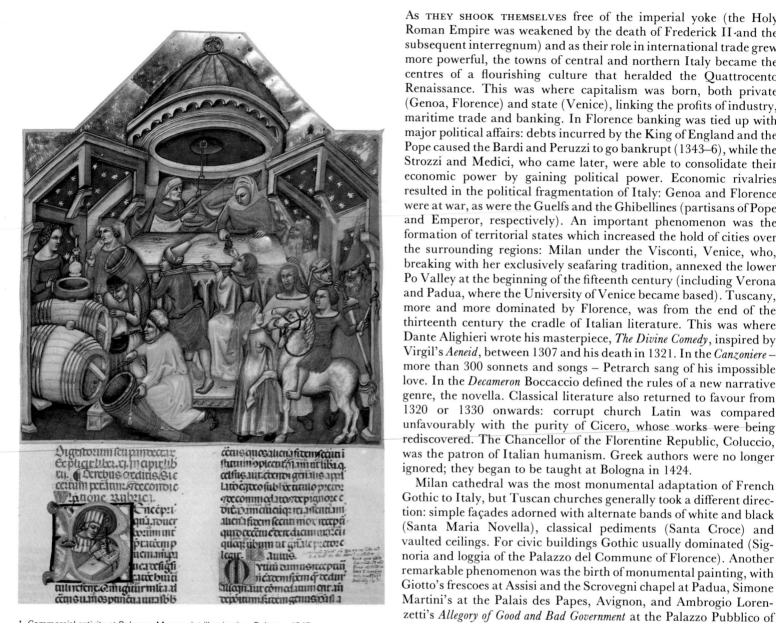

1. Commercial activity at Bologna. Manuscript illumination, Bologna, 1345.

As THEY SHOOK THEMSELVES free of the imperial yoke (the Holy Roman Empire was weakened by the death of Frederick II and the subsequent interregnum) and as their role in international trade grew more powerful, the towns of central and northern Italy became the centres of a flourishing culture that heralded the Quattrocento Renaissance. This was where capitalism was born, both private (Genoa, Florence) and state (Venice), linking the profits of industry, maritime trade and banking. In Florence banking was tied up with major political affairs: debts incurred by the King of England and the Pope caused the Bardi and Peruzzi to go bankrupt (1343–6), while the Strozzi and Medici, who came later, were able to consolidate their economic power by gaining political power. Economic rivalries resulted in the political fragmentation of Italy: Genoa and Florence were at war, as were the Guelfs and the Ghibellines (partisans of Pope and Emperor, respectively). An important phenomenon was the formation of territorial states which increased the hold of cities over the surrounding regions: Milan under the Visconti, Venice, who, breaking with her exclusively seafaring tradition, annexed the lower Po Valley at the beginning of the fifteenth century (including Verona and Padua, where the University of Venice became based). Tuscany, more and more dominated by Florence, was from the end of the thirteenth century the cradle of Italian literature. This was where Dante Alighieri wrote his masterpiece, *The Divine Comedy*, inspired by Virgil's *Aeneid*, between 1307 and his death in 1321. In the *Canzoniere* – more than 300 sonnets and songs – Petrarch sang of his impossible love. In the *Decameron* Boccaccio defined the rules of a new narrative genre, the novella. Classical literature also returned to favour from 1320 or 1330 onwards: corrupt church Latin was compared unfavourably with the purity of Cicero, whose works were being rediscovered. The Chancellor of the Florentine Republic, Coluccio, was the patron of Italian humanism. Greek authors were no longer ignored; they began to be taught at Bologna in 1424.

Milan cathedral was the most monumental adaptation of French Gothic to Italy, but Tuscan churches generally took a different direction: simple façades adorned with alternate bands of white and black (Santa Maria Novella), classical pediments (Santa Croce) and vaulted ceilings. For civic buildings Gothic usually dominated (Signoria and loggia of the Palazzo del Commune of Florence). Another remarkable phenomenon was the birth of monumental painting, with Giotto's frescoes at Assisi and the Scrovegni chapel at Padua, Simone Martini's at the Palais des Papes, Avignon, and Ambrogio Lorenzetti's *Allegory of Good and Bad Government* at the Palazzo Pubblico of Siena (1338). Religious painting on wood, influenced by Byzantine

***Maestà* of Siena Cathedral by Duccio.** 1311

**Death of Dante Alighieri.** 1321

**Death of Giotto.** 1337

**1228:** Construction begins on basilica at Assisi, two years after death of St Francis.

**1240–1302:** Cimabue, Tuscan painter influenced by Byzantine art. Painter of crucifixes of Arezzo and Santa Croce at Florence (the latter damaged in 1966 flood).

**1245–1302:** Arnolfo di Cambio. Begins work on Duomo at Florence in 1300. Santa Croce and Palazzo Vecchio attributed to him.

**1250:** Death of Emperor Frederick II. As King of Sicily he was mainly concerned with Italian affairs. At his court at Palermo he was host to Greek, Arab, Jewish and Italian scholars. A man of wide culture, he wrote a treatise on hunting, had Aristotle and Averroës translated, founded Naples University in 1224.

**1255–1319:** Duccio di Buoninsegna. Painter of the *Maestà* of the Virgin in Siena Cathedral, 1311.

**1265–1321:** Dante Alighieri. From a Florentine Guelf family, he played a diplomatic role before being exiled. In *De monarchia* he advocates the independence of temporal power from spiritual power. *Il convivio* (The Banquet) is a philosophical treatise in the classical tradition. *De vulgari eloquentia* is written in Latin but advocates the use of Italian as a literary tongue. His lyrical works include the *Canzoniere*, in which he celebrates his love for Beatrice, *Vita nuova* and, above all, *The Divine Comedy* (1307–21), inspired by Virgil, a vast portrait of the human condition.

3. The Virgin with Angels *by the Sienese painter Cimabue, Pisa, 13th century.*

**1266–1337:** Giotto di Bondone. Painter of frescoes in upper church at Assisi (1296–9) and Scrovegni chapel at Padua (1303–5).

**1284–1344:** Simone Martini. Painter of the *Maestà* at the Palazzo Pubblico of Siena and frescoes at Notre-Dame-des-Doms and the Palais des Papes, both at Avignon.

**1303–74:** Petrarch. Lived mainly in Avignon; his *Canzoniere*, which include *I trionfi* and *Le rime*, inspired by Ovid, Seneca, Cicero and

*4. Portrait of Dante illustrating a manuscript of* The Divine Comedy, *Sienese studio, 1403.*

# 13th–15th centuries

art and Franciscan spirituality, is represented by Cimabue (1240–1302) in Florence and Duccio di Buoninsegna, who painted the *Maestà* of the Virgin in 1311 for Siena cathedral. Nicola Pisano was the first in a brilliant line of sculptors, notably, Giovanni Pisano, Arnolfo do Cambio (who began the Duomo at Florence around 1300) and Andrea Pisano, who sculpted one of the bronze doors of the Baptistery at Florence, completed by Ghiberti in the next century.

*2. The prosperity of the city, a result of 'Good Government'. Fresco by Ambrogio Lorenzetti, Siena, 1338.*

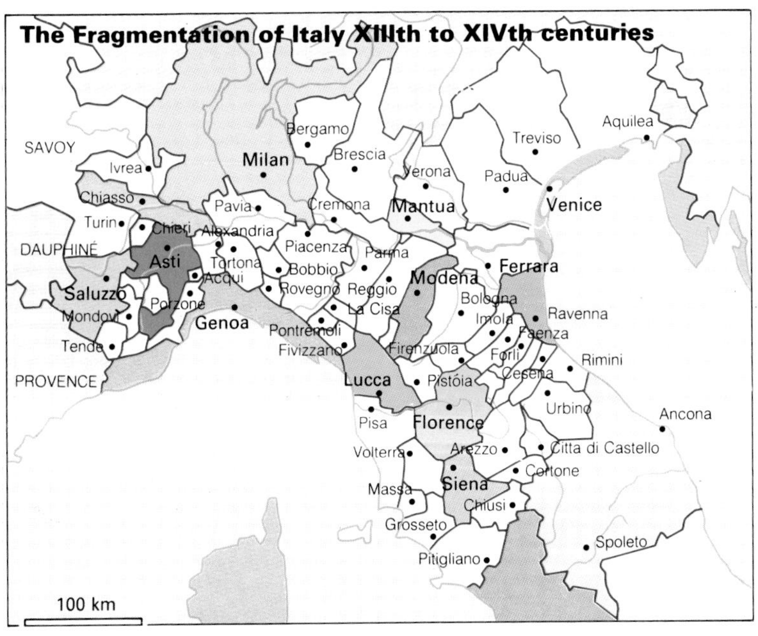


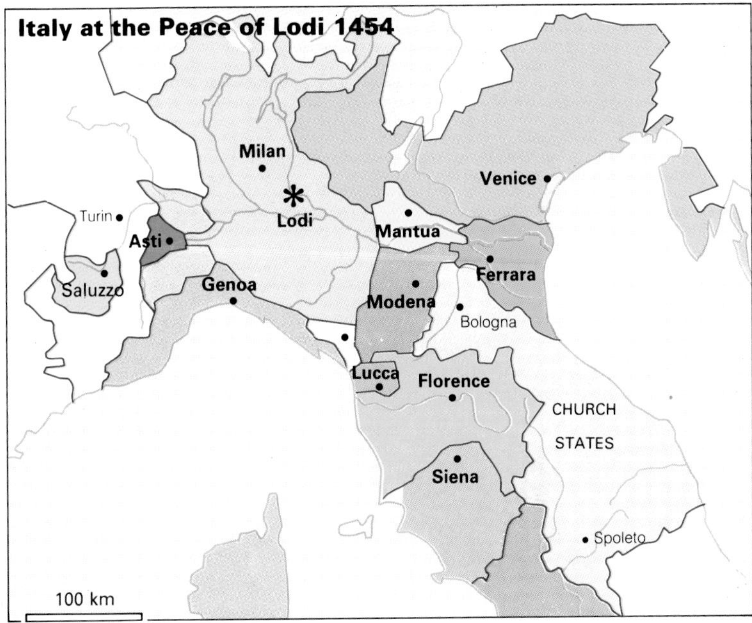


**Death of Boccaccio.**

**1375**

Virgil, tell of his lost love for Laura.

**1313–75:** Giovanni Boccaccio. Born of a Tuscan father and a French mother, lived in Florence and at the court of Charles I at Naples. Between 1348 and 1353 he wrote the *Decameron*, founding the literary genre of the Italian novella. In 1360 he wrote *De claris mulieribus*, a collection of biographies of illustrious women.

**1337–9:** Ambrogio Lorenzetti paints *Allegories of Good and Bad Government* at the Palazzo Pubblico of Siena.

**1424:** Teaching of Greek introduced at Bologna.

**1429:** Venice conquers Po valley up to the Adda. Padua becomes university of Venice and a flourishing centre of humanism.

**1434:** Cosimo de' Medici takes de facto power in Florence.

*5. The Palazzo d'Este, Ferrara, 14th century.*

*6. Lady with the arms of the Visconti. Miniature illustrating Cicero's* De natura deorum, *early 15th century.*

# The Hundred Years' War and the Great Schism

THE MODERN STATE was born in the later Middle Ages. The economic crisis which occurred at that point both adversely affected the resources of the various states and contributed indirectly to their formation. The survival of governments, confronted with the expenses incurred by permanent warfare, depended on their capacity to raise taxes, if necessary by submitting to the prior consent of assemblies such as the Parliament in England or the Estates – both national and provincial – in France, which met at the moments when the monarchy was at its weakest (in 1356–8, during Étienne Marcel's revolutionary uprising and the 'Jacquerie' which followed, in 1380–2 on the accession of Charles VI and in 1415–20 when Paris was occupied by the Anglo-Burgundians). The growing role of representative assemblies and the attempts to have the élites participate in decision-making were characteristic features of the political and institutional evolution of the period. This tendency could also be seen in the church with the Conciliary movement, which, given further impulsion by the Great Schism, considerably weakened the papal monarchy (Councils of Constance, Ferrara, Basle). Another striking feature was an increasing national particularism, which crystallized in wars but which also expressed itself in a rise in nationalist sentiment. The clearest examples of this are to be seen in anti-English feeling in Scotland, Bohemian disaffection with the Empire and Rome, and Polish opposition to the Teutonic Knights. For its part, the church, in its divided condition, was unable to avoid espousing these nascent nationalisms: national forms of Christianity found expression in Gallicanism, Anglicanism and Bohemian Utraquism. At the time of the Great Schism, the two (and subsequently three) rival allegiances flowed quite naturally into the pre-existing mould of the political alliances between the various states. The 'Clementine' party – partisans of the Avignon Pope – consisted of France, Scotland, the Iberian Peninsula and the Kingdom of Naples. Ranged behind the 'supporters of Urban', who favoured the Pope of Rome, were England, and with her Burgundy, the Empire, Flanders and Northern Italy. The internationalization of conflicts was therefore a further dominant characteristic of fourteenth and fifteenth-century Europe. It explains their generality and their inevitable repercussions, both on the level of rivalry between nations (France, England, Burgundy etc.) and that of the schism within the church and the struggle between rival ecclesiastical allegiances. For the first time, the whole of Europe seemed to suffer and fear at the same rhythm. Thus around 1380 the social upheavals which struck England, Italy and France coincided with the beginning of the Great Schism. In 1417 the Schism was healed, but France was torn by the bloody struggle between the Armagnacs and the Burgundians; the Lollards rose in England, the Taborites in Bohemia and the Conciliary movement seemed to be winning out within the church. After 1453 England and France were no longer in conflict, but the former was entering upon the Wars of the Roses, which set the houses of York and Lancaster against each other, and over the latter there hung the increasingly dangerous threat of encirclement by the states of the Duke of Burgundy, Charles the Bold. Only the defeat and death of Charles in 1477 would see an end to that threat.

*1. Charles the Bold presiding over a chapter of the Order of the Golden Fleece. From the book of the same name by Guillaume Filastre, late 15th century.*

**Great Schism begins.** 1378

**Battle of Agincourt.** 1415

**Council of Constance: end of Schism.** 1417

**1309–77:** Papacy installed at Avignon, where seven popes succeed one another.
**1311–12:** Council of Vienna, which orders the suppression of the Templars.
**1337–1453:** Hundred Years War. The King of France, Philip IV, is initially defeated by Edward III of England, who takes Calais. In 1356 John the Good is defeated and taken prisoner at Poitiers. By the Treaty of Brétigny (1360), France loses Calais, le Ponthieu and Aquitaine.
**1348–51:** Black Death.
**1364–80:** Charles V king of France. With his constable, Du Guesclin, he reconquers the territories occupied by the English.
**1378–1417:** The Great Schism divides the church into two allegiances – 'Clementine' in Avignon, 'Urbanist' in Rome. In 1409 the Council of Pisa causes the birth of a third allegiance. The election of Martin V puts an end to the Schism in 1417.
**1380–1422:** Charles VI king of France. His madness promotes rivalry between the Armagnac party (that of Duke Louis of Orleans, assassinated in 1407) and the Burgundian party. The latter allies with the English king Henry V, who has triumphed at Agincourt (1415). After the assassination of the Duke of Burgundy, John the Fearless, at Montereau in 1419, his party choose Henry V, the king of England, as king of France (Treaty of Troyes, 1420).
**1386:** The Swiss Confederation defeats Leopold III of Austria at Sempach.
**1411–33:** King Sigismund II calls the Council of Constance.
**1414–18:** Council of Constance. Execution of Jan Hus (1415).
**1422–61:** Charles VII denounces the Treaty of Troyes and reconquers his kingdom (in 1429 Joan of Arc liberates Orleans). The King is crowned at Reims, but Joan is executed in 1431. The alliance with Philip III the Good, Duke of Burgundy, allows the King to recapture Paris in 1436, then to reconquer Normandy (1449–50) and Guyenne (1450–53).
**1431–9:** Council of Basle, where the conciliary theory limiting the Pope's authority triumphs and where an agreement is struck with the Hussites (*Compactata* of 1436).
**1438:** Pragmatic Sanction at Bourges

*2. Court life. Scene from a falcon hunt. Fresco by Matteo di Giovanetti da Viterbo, 14th century, Palais des Papes, Avignon.*

*3. The future emperor, Sigismund, receives homage from his Hungarian subjects at the Council of Constance in 1414. Engraving, 1483.*

# 14th–15th centuries

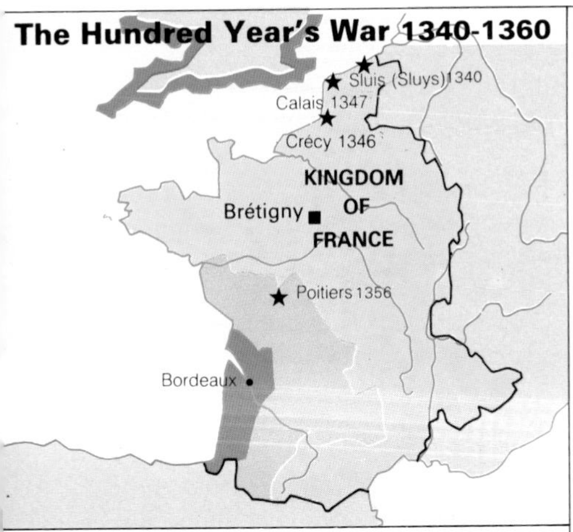

## The Hundred Year's War 1340-1360

Sluis (Sluys) 1340
Calais 1347
Crécy 1346
KINGDOM OF FRANCE
Brétigny
Poitiers 1356
Bordeaux

English possessions
Lands acquired by the Treaty of Brétigny, 1360
★ English victories

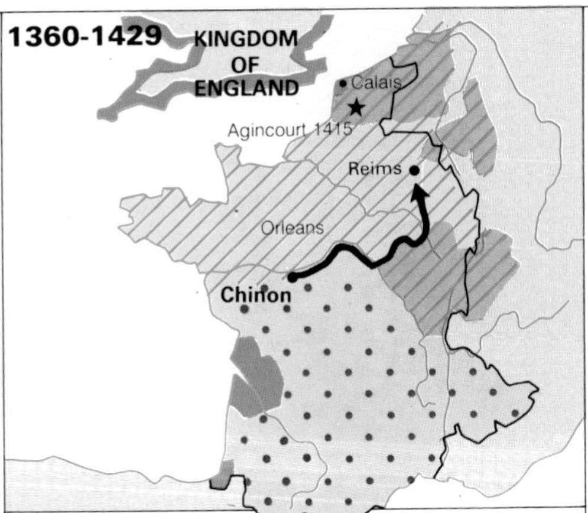

## 1360-1429

KINGDOM OF ENGLAND
Calais
Agincourt 1415
Reims
Orleans
Chinon

Territory owing allegiance to the King of England
Territory loyal to the King of France
Possessions of the Duke of Burgundy
Territory under the Duke of Burgundy's control
Path followed by Joan of Arc

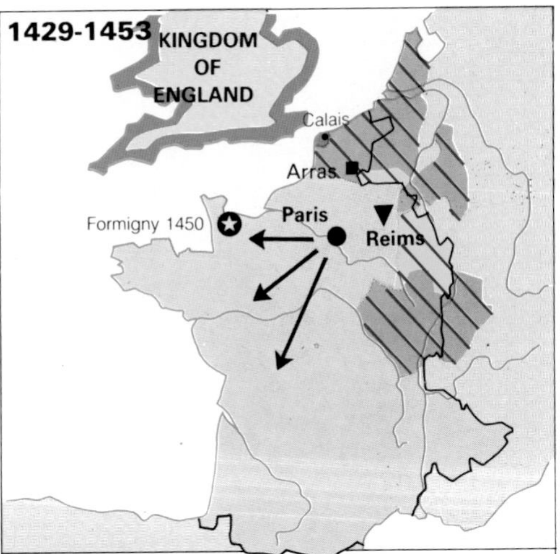

## 1429-1453

KINGDOM OF ENGLAND
Calais
Arras
Formigny 1450
Paris
Reims

Burgundy allied to the King of France by the Peace of Arras (1435)
French victories
Coronation of the King of France in 1429
Lands recaptured by Charles VII

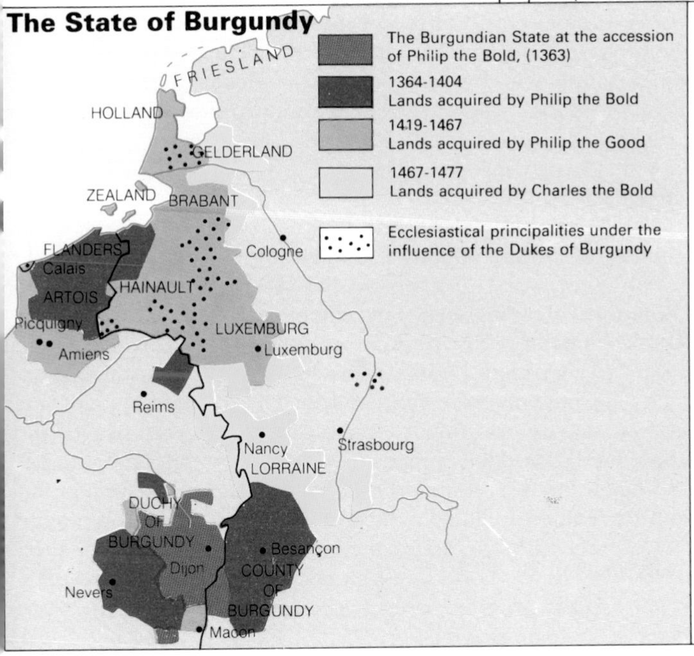

## The State of Burgundy

The Burgundian State at the accession of Philip the Bold, (1363)
1364-1404 Lands acquired by Philip the Bold
1419-1467 Lands acquired by Philip the Good
1467-1477 Lands acquired by Charles the Bold
Ecclesiastical principalities under the influence of the Dukes of Burgundy

FRIESLAND
HOLLAND
GELDERLAND
ZEALAND
BRABANT
FLANDERS
Calais
ARTOIS
HAINAULT
Cologne
Picquigny
Amiens
LUXEMBURG
Luxemburg
Reims
Nancy
LORRAINE
Strasbourg
DUCHY OF BURGUNDY
Dijon
Nevers
Besançon
COUNTY OF BURGUNDY
Macon

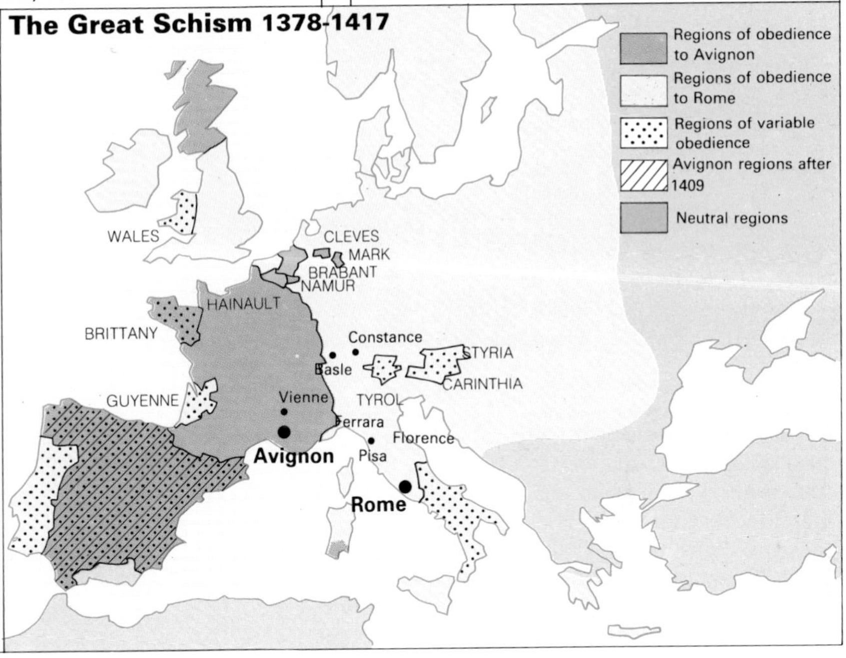

## The Great Schism 1378-1417

Regions of obedience to Avignon
Regions of obedience to Rome
Regions of variable obedience
Avignon regions after 1409
Neutral regions

WALES
CLEVES
MARK
BRABANT
NAMUR
HAINAULT
BRITTANY
Constance
Basle
STYRIA
CARINTHIA
GUYENNE
Vienne
TYROL
Ferrara
Florence
Avignon
Pisa
Rome

**Execution of Joan of Arc.** **1431**

**Defeat and death of Charles the Bold.** **1477**

between the Pope and Charles VII. The election of French prelates henceforth requires the king's consent.

**1438–9:** Councils of Ferrara and of Florence, which oppose the Pope. The union of the Greek and Latin churches is proclaimed, but the capture of Constantinople by the Turks (1453) will render it obsolete.

**1450–85:** Wars of the Roses in England between the houses of York (White Rose) and Lancaster (Red Rose). A scion of the latter house will found a new dynasty in 1485.

**1461–83:** Louis XI king of France. He opposes François II of Brittany and Charles the Bold, Duke of Burgundy. In 1468 at Péronne, where Charles is holding Louis prisoner, Charles forces him to cede Champagne. But the King makes an agreement with Edward IV of England against Charles (Treaty of Picquigny, 1475). Charles is finally defeated and killed at Nancy in 1477. His states fall to the Emperor Maximilian, husband of Mary of Burgundy. By the Treaty of Arras (1482), Burgundy and Picardy are ceded to Louis XI.

*4. Ferdinand I re-entering Naples after his victory over the Angevins at Ischia in 1462. Anonymous Neapolitan artist.*

# Crisis and Change in the West

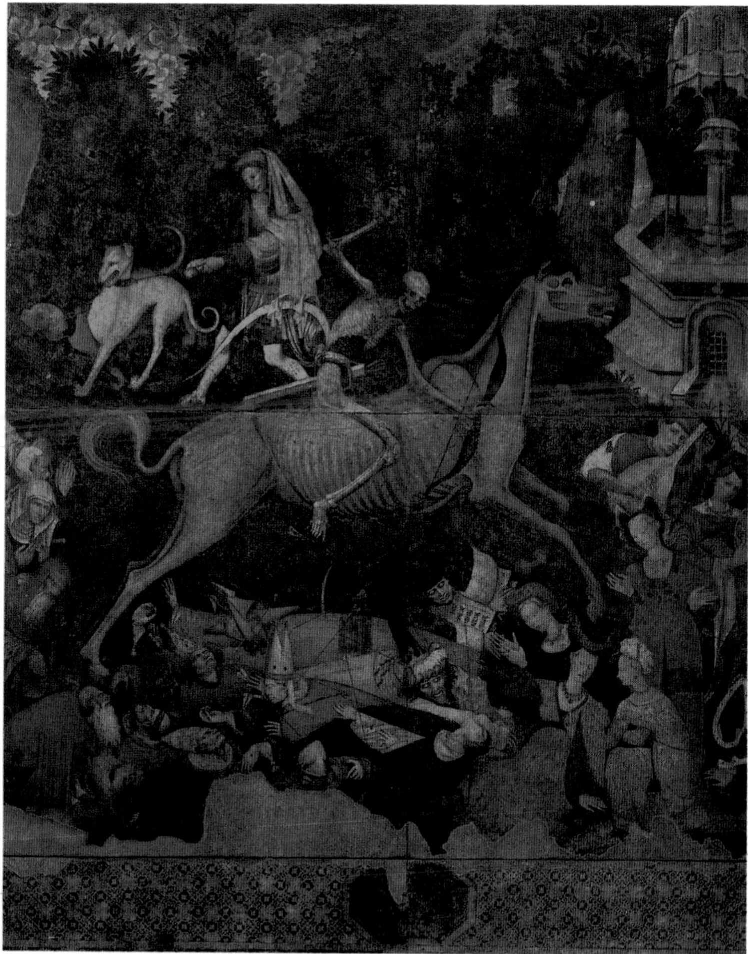

1. The Triumph of Death. 15th-century Sicilian fresco.

FROM THE END OF THE THIRTEENTH CENTURY Western economic and demographic expansion began to show definite signs of stagnation. The general depression which then set in was to last until the mid-fifteenth century, making deep inroads into medieval life, yet also creating the conditions for a new social and economic order.

The crisis first appeared in the rural economy. The consistent fall in agricultural prices, the tendency of a reduced pool of labour to increase wages, and an even more marked rise in the cost of manufactured products combined to cause growing instability. Grain crop failures, as in 1315 and 1316, brought famine and unrest for short periods to town and country. The years of dearth rendered the population particularly vulnerable, and in 1348–50 it suffered the full impact of the Plague. Not since the sixth century had the West experienced a scourge of such magnitude: in the space of three years the Black Death claimed a quarter to a third of Europe's population. Demographic and economic factors thus combined to alter the face of society drastically. Whole villages were deserted; agricultural activity converted away from staple food products to more profitable specialized crops and stock-rearing; rural populations moved into the towns, causing mass impoverishment.

It is against this background – further aggravated by constant war and political tension – that the numerous uprisings characteristic of the period must be set. On occasion, as in Flanders after 1323 or in the Ile-de-France in 1357, peasant insurgents sought to join forces with groups in the towns, where the issues of pay and working hours, the exclusion of journeymen from the mastery, and the effect of monetary changes on purchasing power were the source of extremely violent conflicts.

The depression, however, gradually brought about a modification of social and economic structures, the most obvious being the growing influence of state intervention, which henceforth determined fiscal and monetary policy and even attempted by decree to limit salaries and control the labour market. The economic attitude of the state was principally one of protectionism, defending home markets and granting monopolies to privileged merchants, e.g. Jacques Coeur in France under Charles VII, and the Medicis in the Papal States with their monopoly on Tolfa alum. New forms of capital organization emerged: the Medicis introduced affiliated companies, while large international monopolies were built up by the Hanseatic League in the Baltic. Equally evident is the shift in centres and axes of the European economy, the opening of the Saint Gotthard Pass in 1237 providing new impetus to central and northern Switzerland and southern Germany. The decline of trade fairs in the Champagne region was accompanied, on the one hand, by the rise in importance of the Rhône-Saône axis, the development of Marseille as a port, and fairs in Lyon and Chalon; and, on the other hand, by increasing activity on the Atlantic seaboard (La Rochelle, Brouage) and the growing importance of maritime countries such as Spain and Portugal – soon to discover the New World – England with its nascent woollen industry, and Holland, developing at the expense of Flanders, especially Bruges.

**Bardi and Peruzzi bankruptcies in Florence** — **1343–6**

**Black Death.** — **1348**

**'Ciompi' revolt in Florence.** — **1378**

**1315–16:** Grain crisis.
**1323–7:** Revolt in coastal Flanders.
**1337–45:** Strike by weavers in Ghent. Notable among their demands: a cut in working hours.
**1343–6:** Failures of the Florentine bankers Bardi and Peruzzi, following non-repayment of debts on the part of the Pope and the King of England.
**1348–50:** Black Death. Introduced via the Mediterranean, the Plague spread within three years to almost every country, killing up to a third of the European population.
**1356–8:** Political and fiscal disruption in Paris. Taking advantage of the imprisonment of French king, John II, the Good, merchants' provost Étienne Marcel imposed on Dauphin Charles the 'Grande Ordonnance' of 1357 which rendered the levying of taxes subject to the approval of the Etats Généraux. The Dauphin's escape and the subsequent murder of E. Marcel enabled the rebellion to be quelled.
**1358:** Peasant uprisings ('Jacquerie') in the Ile-de-France, Champagne and Picardy, suppressed by Charles II of Navarre at the cost of 20,000 dead.
**1377–83:** Revolts throughout Europe. In Florence textile workers (the *'Ciompi'*) forced the inclusion of commoners (*'il populo minuto'*) in the Republic's political bodies.

*4. Leper-house in France, 14th century. Miniature from Vincent de Beauvais's* Miroir Historial.

Peasant revolts in England, also affecting London. Their leader, a priest named John Ball, preached equality for all. Rebellion in Rouen against new tax levies. 'Maillotin' uprising in Paris (so called after the insurgents' leaden hammers) in protest against a new tax. 'Tuchin' revolts in rural areas. Revolt, turning to insurrection, of the Lollards, a popular heretical movement in England inspired by the doctrines of John Wyclif.
**1397–1456:** Jacques Coeur, French merchant, native of Bourges, where he erected a magnificent palace. Established trading posts in all commercial centres in Europe and the Middle East. Banker to Charles VII, who entrusted important public functions to him. Financed the reconquest of Normandy before being arrested for embezzlement.
**1411, 1434, 1438, 1441:** Popular revolts in Scandinavia.
**1413–14:** Revolution in Paris led by butcher Simon Caboche in alliance with the Burgundians against Dauphin Charles VI. Imposition of the 'Ordonnance Cabochienne'. The revolution was later quelled by the Armagnacs.
**1414–20:** Hussite uprising in Bohemia, rapidly weakened by its division into the moderates of Prague, who negotiated with the Council of Basle, and the 'Taborites', a popular radical movement based at Tábor. The latter, who preached social revolution, were finally defeated at Lipany in 1434.
**1420:** Royal charters granted by French king to Lyon fairs.
**1450–70:** Beginning of European economic revival.
**1476:** Niklashausen revolt in Thuringia, prelude to the Peasants' War of 1525.
**1494–8:** Florence: the waning power of the Medicis succeeded by the theocratic régime of Savonarola. Savonarola excommunicated by the Pope and later assassinated.

# 14th–15th centuries

357: Massacre at Meaux after revolt of the 'Jacques'. From anuscript of the Grandes Chroniques de France, 15th tury.

panish fortress, c. 1450. Artist unknown.

**Execution of Savonarola.**

**1498**

Fruit and grain merchants, 15th century. Italian manuscript.

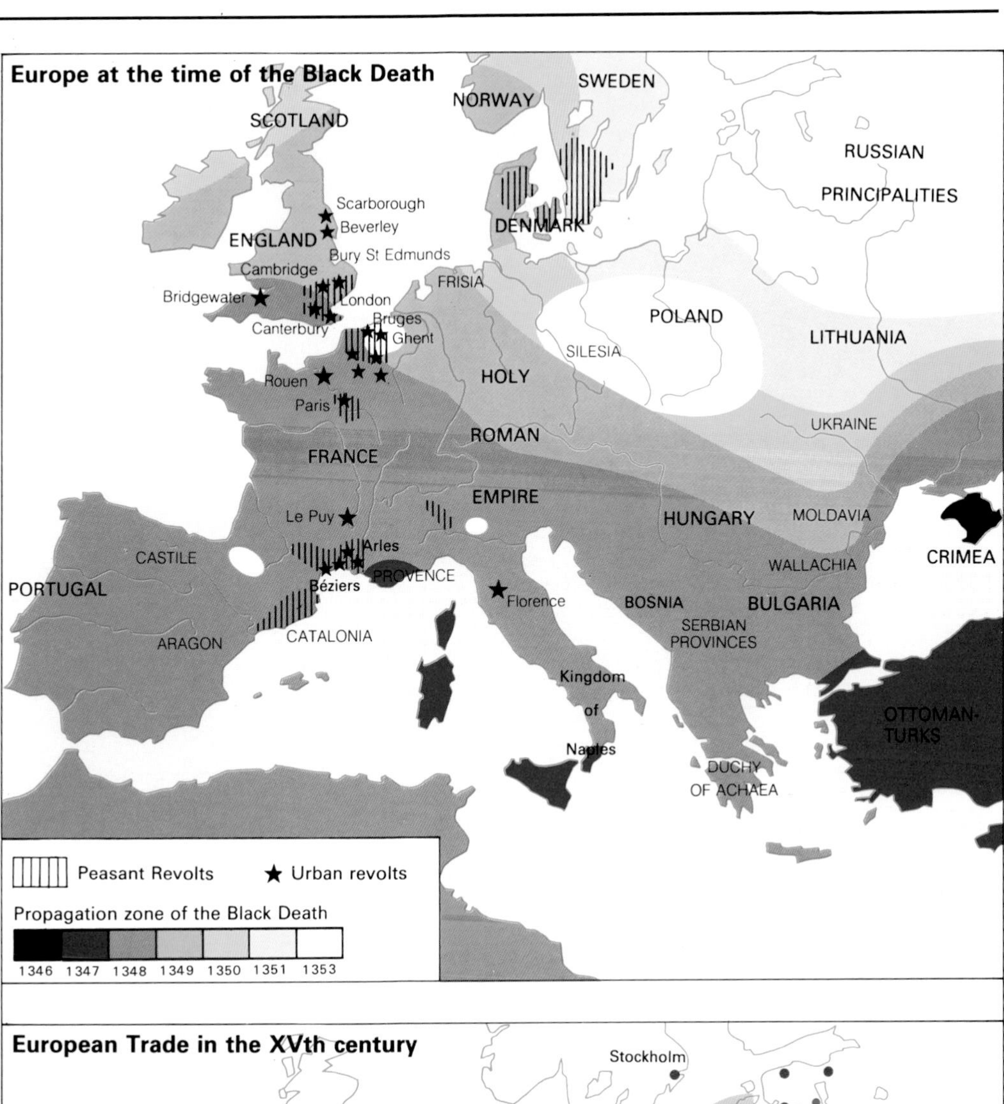


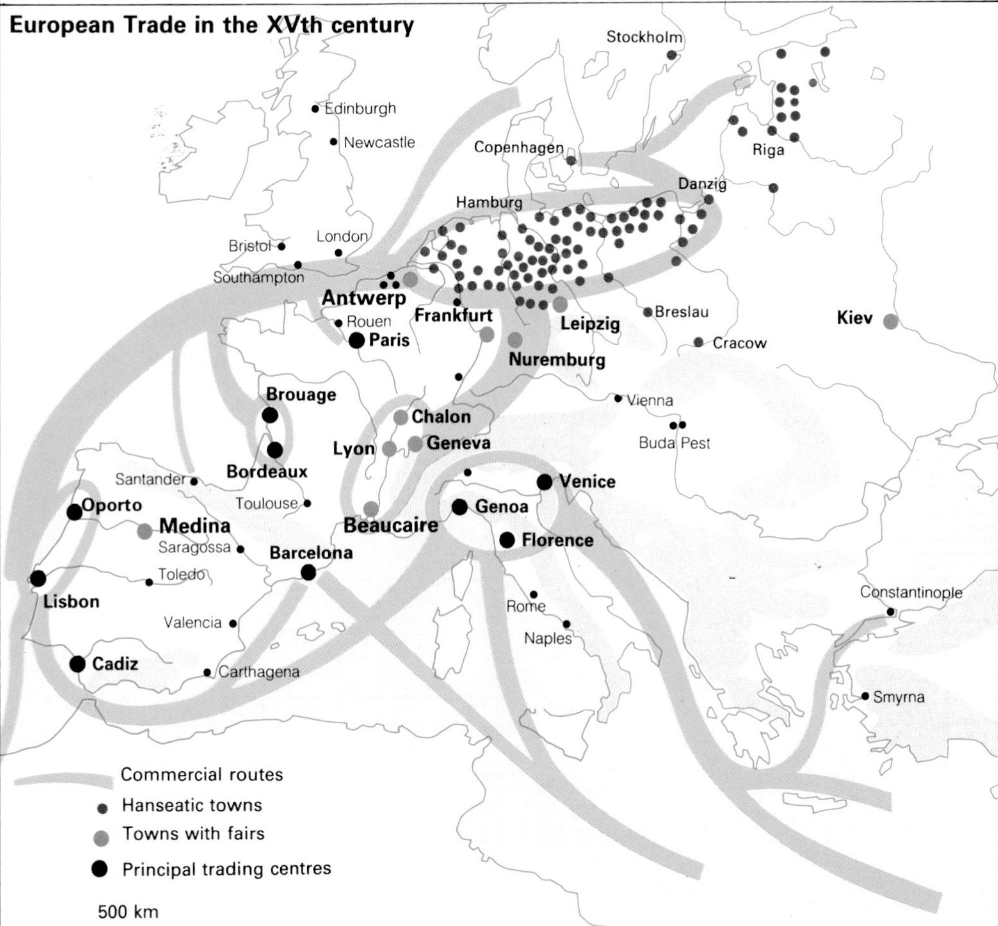

# Medieval Africa

Muslim and, later, European sources reveal to us that external forces exerted some influence within Africa during the 'medieval' period. The taming of the camel and Islamic dynamism opened up the Sahara, through which there had previously only been a trickle of travellers, and linked the Sudan, both intellectually and economically, to the outside world. The traditional openness of the eastern coast to the countries of the Indian Ocean took on a new dimension in this period, particularly on account of Islam. The Atlantic, however, was still one of the ends of the earth: this would not really change until the fifteenth century, when it first became a historic frontier.

These external forces have, however, often blurred the issue. Progress in archaeology and the development of more cogently argued historical theories have combined to cast some doubt on the aptness of applying the term 'medieval' to Africa. Settlements, developments in agriculture and animal husbandry and advances in metal-working are thought to have predated, in some instances, the medieval period, and indeed to have done so quite considerably. The political entities referred to in 'medieval' written (or sometimes oral) sources clearly stood on ground prepared by long processes of technological development of indigenous origin, however much these societies may subsequently have benefited from external contributions.

The foundations of the fifteenth-century Luban political society, for example, were laid by the earlier Kisalian culture. Another case is that of the peoples found on either side of the mid-Limpopo and from there to the Zambezi. The industrious society of that plateau – which was rapidly strewn with enclosures (Zimbabwe) – derived an important source of wealth from cattle-rearing. Evidence of the blossoming of that civilization can be seen at Mapungubwe, Mapela and, most importantly, at Great Zimbabwe, a major political and monumental centre. The flame of that culture is taken up in the fifteenth century by the Matapa and Butua states. On the eastern coast, from the ninth century onwards, an influx of Arabian, Persian and even more distant immigrants and cultural influences contributed to the formation of trading centres. To the south of Kismayu these factors also combined, over a number of years, to produce the Swahili language and civilization, which are African in origin but which contain some imported elements.

Though the kingdom of Aksum withered away in the tenth century, Christian Ethiopia continued to survive. After 1270 it enjoyed a two-century-long revitalisation which saw it assert its power over its – Muslim and non-Muslim – neighbours and consolidate the unity of Church and State. By contrast, though Christian Nubia flourished for several centuries, the influence of Islam eroded its power in the twelfth and thirteenth centuries and the Christian kingdoms finally disappeared between 1365 and 1500.

In the west, Jenne, Niani, Igbo-Ukwu and the Sao sites of the lower Chari are evidence of settled societies and the development of ancient techniques. From the eleventh century onwards Ife became the political and religious centre of the Yoruba country, and Benin was later to take certain technical and ideological elements from that source. The new trans-Saharan links stimulated the growth of empires. A western centre of power was provided successively by Ghana, Mali and the Songhai empire, whilst in the east Kanem-Bornu held sway. Alongside these empires, the Hausa and Senegambian states, amongst others, contributed to the rich political and human tapestry of that region.

*1. Rock church in Lalibela, Ethiopia, 13th century.*

**Cathedral of Faras, Nubia.**

**7th century**

**400–900:** Development of the Jenne settlement.
**7th–8th centuries:** Faras (or Pachoras) Cathedral (architecture, painting). Empire of Ghana, traces of which date back to the 8th century.
**8th–9th centuries and after:** Kukiya kingdom, then that of Gao, another partner in trans-Saharan relations.
**9th century:** Igbo-Ukwu remains (Bronzes, burial chamber of a high-ranking figure, long-distance trade links).
**9th–10th centuries:** Emergence of Kanem. New dynasty in second half of 12th century and sovereign converted to Islam.
**10th century:** Major disturbances in Christian Ethiopia.
**10th–11th centuries:** High point for the trading city of Awdaghost.
**10th–14th centuries:** Kisalian culture in the Upemba valley and around Lake Kisale (fishing, agriculture, long-range trade links, crafts).
**11th century:** Islam in Takrur (mid-Senegal).
**Second half of 11th century:** Almoravid militancy, originating among the Sanhajah

*3. Part of the ruins of Great Zimbabwe, discovered by Europeans in 1868.*

**Empire of Ghana.**

**8th–13th centuries**

Berbers of Mauritania. In the Sudan its effect is to reinforce the presence of Islam and increase relations with the Maghreb.
**11th–15th century:** The Ife assert political, technical, artistic and religious dominance in Yorubaland.
**Beginning of 12th century:** King of Ghana converted to Islam.
**12th–13th century:** Boom years for Mogadishu on the east coast.
**c. 1200–c. 1450:** Intensive occupation of the (long inhabited) Great Zimbabwe site; clear signs of its political dominance and its distant economic relations.
**13th century:** Kanem becomes very powerful and subjugates the Fezzan for a time at the end of the century.
**First quarter of the 13th century:** Reign of Lalibela in Ethiopia; rupestrian churches in his capital (which takes his name).
**Mid-13th century:** Mali becomes prominent under Sundiata (d. 1255); the Empire remains at its peak until the mid-14th century (reign of Mansa Musa, 1312–37).
**1270:** New dynasty in Ethiopia which proclaims legitimate descent from Solomon.

# 7th–15th centuries

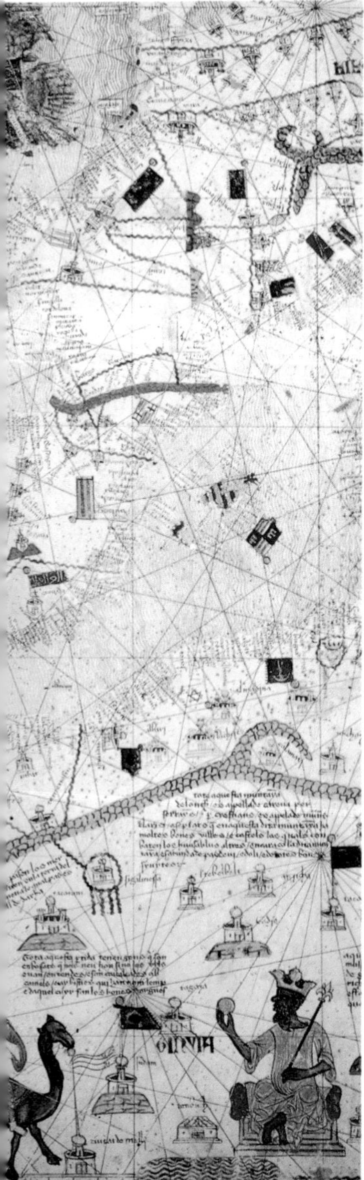
*. The king and the camel-driver, a detail from he Great Catalan Atlas,* 1373.

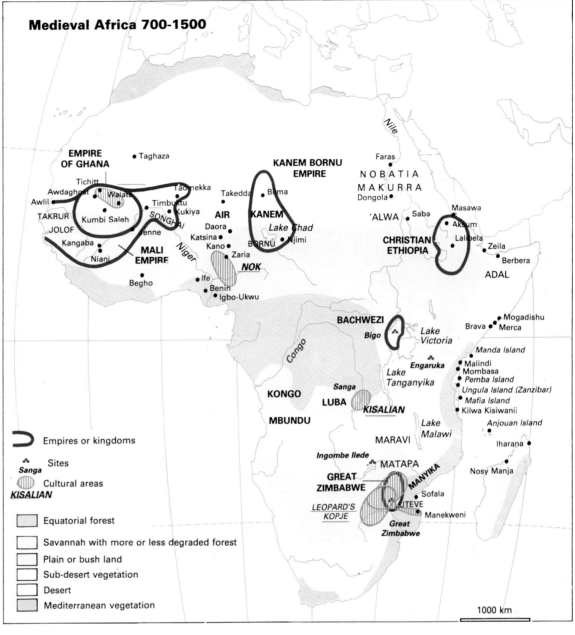

## Medieval Africa 700-1500

Empires or kingdoms
Sites
Cultural areas
Equatorial forest
Savannah with more or less degraded forest
Plain or bush land
Sub-desert vegetation
Desert
Mediterranean vegetation

1000 km

**Great Zimbabwe.** c. 1200

**Reign of Mansa Musa in Mali.** 1312–37

**Mwene Matapa kingdom.** c. 1450–1500

**14th century?:** Rise of Benin. Empire of Jolof.
**1314–44:** Reign of Amda Tseyon; militant religious policies based on a combination of Ethiopian nationalism, Christian tradition and the conversion of conquered peoples.
**End of 14th century:** Decline of Mali. Around 1400, its capital is pillaged by the Songhai Empire, which is in the ascendant during the first half of the 15th century. The Empire of Kanem is reduced to the Bornu territory.
**c. 1400?:** Kongo kingdom.
**14th–15th centuries:** In the interlake zone, the Bachwezi political culture (nothing is known of the people involved). Kilwa on the east coast is powerful and prosperous.
**1434–68:** Reign of Zara Yacob in Ethiopia; warrior leader and spirited reformer, who combated heresy both practically and intellectually.
**Mid-15th century:** Rapid decline of Great Zimbabwe; Matapa in the north and Butua in the south-west rise in its place.

*4. Bronze bust, made by lost wax technique, representing a king of Ife, Nigeria, c. 12th to 15th centuries.*

*5. Traditional Dogon urban habitat, Mali.*

*6. Ivory breastplate. 15th century Benin art.*

# The Aztec Empire and its Antecedents

1. Teotihuacan, metropolis of the central plateau: the Pyramid of the Sun.

When the Spaniards invaded Mexico at the beginning of the sixteenth century, the Aztecs ruled over a powerful empire which opened on to two oceans, controlling the trade routes through Central America. That rapidly expanding empire was, however, quite a new creation. The ruling dynasty had only been in power for 150 years, whilst the history of the indigenous civilizations of Meso-America went back several millennia.

Around the year 1500 BC there existed in various parts of Mexico villages of sedentary farmers who had learnt how to cultivate maize and make pottery and who modelled feminine figurines which, it is assumed, represent the first images of the native gods. The population was already large, heterogeneous and differentiated. It is from this context that the Olmecs emerged. Originating in the low tropical lands along the coast of the Gulf of Mexico, they were to extend their influence over the central high plateau and the Pacific coast as far as Costa Rica. They were the bearers, in particular, of a religion based on the worship of the jaguar. It is the Olmecs who are responsible for the first ceremonal centres in Central America, the first monumental sculpture, the first carved jade objects and the first traces of writing. Around the year 300 BC the Olmecs disappeared as suddenly as they had appeared. Regional cultures then developed, amongst which we can distinguish those of the west (Colima, Jalisco, Nayarit) and those of the Basin of Mexico (site of Cuicuilco).

It was to be some six centuries before two new cradles of civilization – Teotihuacan and the Mayas – emerged. If there was no 'Teotihuacan Empire' in the strict sense of the term, the great metropolis of the central plateau nonetheless exerted an influence across a wide zone, stretching from Nayarit to Guatemala, by way of Monte Alban. Teotihuacan thus disseminated certain cultural features – like the step pyramid or the cult of the rain god – all of which contributed to establishing a homogeneous culture in Central America.

In the same period the other contending centre of power was located in the lands of the Maya, a constellation of city-states which, contrary to a widespread fallacy, fought a great deal among themselves. This highly cultivated society, which produced an exuberant art, declined during the course of the ninth century. It seems that, having turned in upon itself, it collapsed from within.

It is at this point that northern Mexico saw great migrations. Tribes of nomadic hunters who came from the north and spoke Nahuatl invaded the central plateau and rapidly won control of that region. Among the first to rise to prominence were the Toltecs. By contrast, the first Aztecs would be the last Nahuas to arrive in the valley of Mexico, at the end of a long migration. The Aztecs settled in Mexico-Tenochtitlan on an island in the middle of a vast lake. After modest beginnings, the town soon took on the appearance of a capital. Sustained by an élite army, the Aztec regime asserted its crushing superiority. It organized the state not only in its administrative functioning but also, and most importantly, in its ideological underpinnings. Emperor Motecuhzoma I and his brother Tlacaelel invented a new religion, a synthesis of northern tribal traditions and the preceding indigenous cultures. Holy war and its correlate, human sacrifice, which skilfully united the priesthood and the army, served as the cornerstones of a systematic expansion policy pursued from 1428 onwards. This policy would find only one obstacle in its path: the Tarascan empire of Michoacan which was definitively to block the Aztecs' westward thrust. In 1519 Motecuhzoma II reigned over 20 million subjects and the valley of Mexico, which probably alone had five million inhabitants, was at that time the greatest urban concentration in the world.

It was this empire which Cortes would conquer with the aid of 600 soldiers, sixteen horses, ten cannons and thirteen arquebuses.

**Start of the Nahua invasions**

**850**

**Aztecs settle at Tenocht**

**1325**

**850:** Beginning of the great Nahua invasions from the north of Mexico. Founding of Tula by the Toltecs.
**900:** Collapse of the Maya civilization (Yucatan and Guatemala).
**970–985:** Reign of Topiltzin Quetzlcoatl at Tula. The death of the sovereign marks the beginning of the dispersion of the Toltecs throughout the whole of Mexico.
**1100:** The Nahuas dominate the central plateau. Mexican dynasties also rule over most Mayan cities. The Aztecs are still merely a nomadic tribe wandering through northern Mexico.
**1325:** Aztecs settle at Mexico-Tenochtitlan.
**1376:** Accession of Acamapichtli, founder of the Mexica (Aztec) dynasty.
**1428:** Victory of Tenochtitlan over the rival city of Azcapotzalco; the Aztecs rule over the Basin of Mexico. Enthronement of Itzcoatl.
**1429:** Triple Alliance constituted (Mexico, Tetzcoco, Tlacopan).
**1440:** Motecuhzoma I crowned. The Aztecs reign over Cuernavaca and the hot lands of Morelos.
**1450–4:** Natural calamities produce a long and deadly famine.
**1468:** Axayacatl succeeds Motecuhzoma I and pursues expansionist policies.
**1469:** Occupation of the Totonac region on the coast of the Gulf of Mexico.
**1478:** Failure of Michoacan's campaign. The Tarascans will remain outside the Empire.
**1486:** Emperor Ahuitzotl, seventh Aztec sovereign. Newly elected, he extends the Templo Mayor in Mexico City and inaugurates it by sacrificing 20,000 prisoners of war.
**1487–8:** Beginning of the campaigns of conquest over the Huaxteca, Guerrero and Oaxaca.
**1492:** Christopher Columbus discovers the Bahamas.
**1496:** Conquest of Tehuantepec by the Aztecs.
**1500:** Conquest of Soconusco at the frontier of Mayan territory.
**1502:** Motecuhzoma II succeeds Ahuitzotl: the expansion of the Aztec Empire marks time; Mexico's rivalry with Tlaxcallan becomes exacerbated.

4. Codex tro-cortesianus *or* Madrid Codex. *Mayan divinatory manuscript.*

**1517:** First reconnaissance of the coasts of Mexico by Hernandez de Cordoba.
**1518:** Juan de Grijalva's expedition reaches the Veracruz region. The Spaniards are forced back.
**1519:** Having set out from Cuba, Hernan Cortes lands near the site of modern Veracruz (22 April), marches on Mexico (August), enters Tlaxacallan (23 Sept.), destroys Cholula (18 Oct.), and enters Mexico (8. Nov.), where he takes power.
**30 June 1520:** The *Noche triste*; rout of the Spaniards and their flight from Mexico.
**1521:** Cortes besieges Mexico, which falls on 13 August. The Aztec Empire becomes New Spain under the authority of Cortes, who is named Captain General.

# 850–1521

...la: columns of the front hall of the Toltec Temple of the ...ning Star.

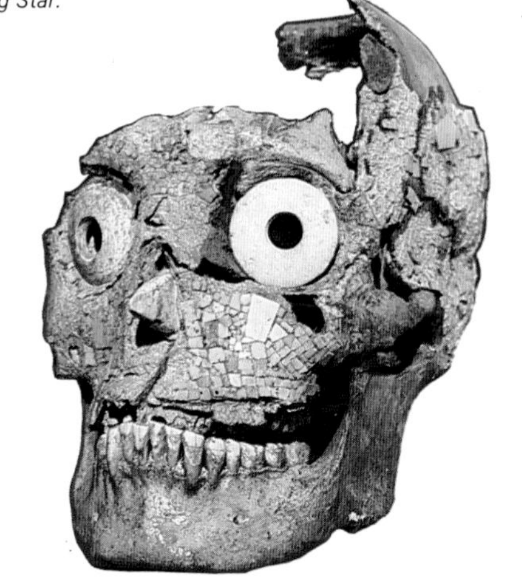

...kull decorated with mosaic of turquoises and ivory, Oaxaca ...ey.

| Inaugural sacrifices at the Templo Mayor | Fall of the Aztec Empire |
|---|---|
| 1486 | 1521 |

...tatue from Las Limas (Vera Cruz), Olmec civilization.

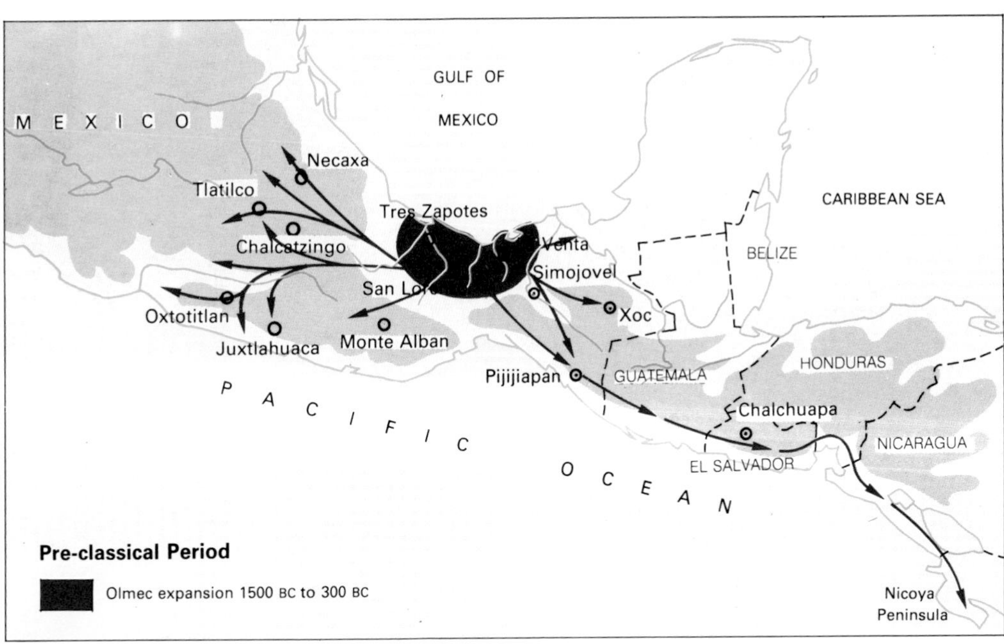


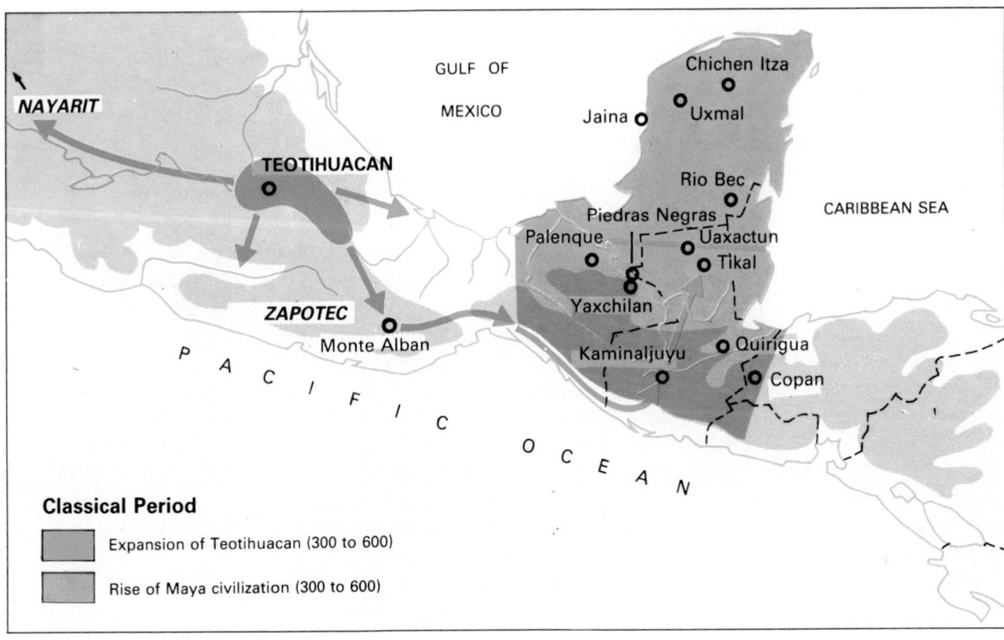


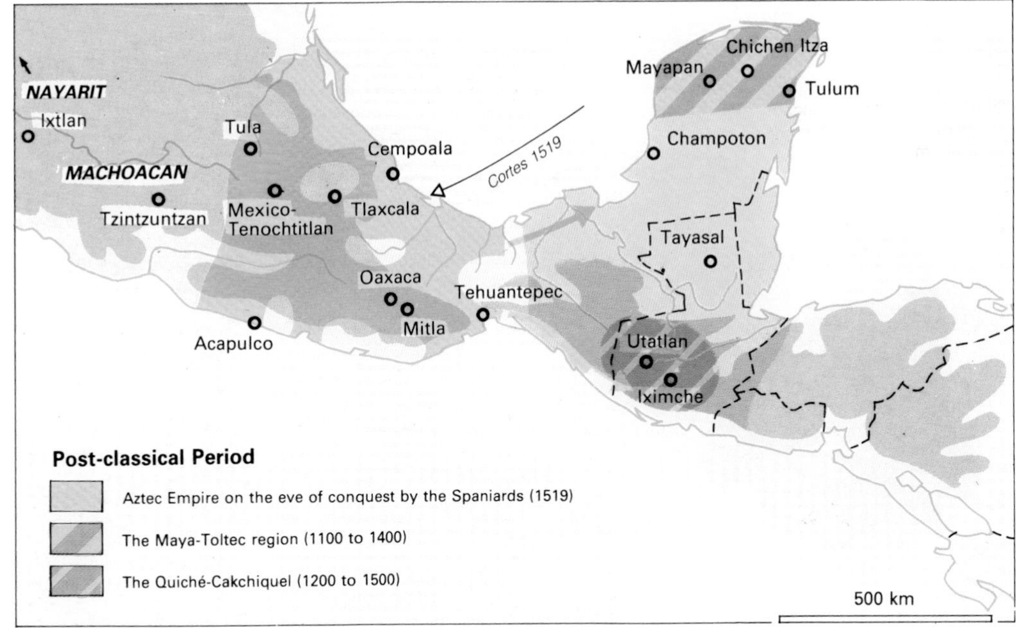

# The Inca Empire and its Antecedents

As though there existed some kind of historical symmetry between North and South America, the chronology of pre-hispanic Peru is not appreciably different from that of pre-Columbian Mexico. It is around the year 1500 BC that the first farming settlements appear, together with the first monumental constructions, which had a religious function. Then the dawn of the first millennium BC sees the emergence of the parent civilization of the Andean world: Chavin culture, characterized by the worship of a feline god, was to see its influence spread not only in the north of Peru but also on the southern coast. The theme of the semi-human, semi-divine jaguar, for example, recurs on the pottery and multi-coloured cotton funeral garments of the inhabitants of Paracas. This Chavin influence, which in certain respects is reminiscent of that of the Olmecs in Mexico, seems to have produced the beginnings of a uniform culture in Peru.

Towards 300 BC, however, the influence of Chavin declined and regional variations began to assert themselves. Peru became fragmented. Each coastal valley, each Andean basin developed its own original culture. On the coast, metalwork, weaving and ceramics attained an artistic quality which remained unsurpassed. In the north, the most dynamic civilization was that of the Mochica; in the south, the Nazca, the brilliant inheritors of Paracas traditions, were dominant. By comparison, the highlands of the interior did not experience the same magnificent development. It was not until the ninth century that Peru's cultural centre of gravity shifted. The motive force for this shift came from Tiahuanaco, which was situated 4,000 metres above sea level near Lake Titicaca. A much more militarist culture soon emerged and the government of Tiahuanaco, after having built a second capital at Huari (Ayacucho), succeeded in unifying the previously very fragmented Andean world. This supremacy of the high plateaus over the coast lasted for approximately two centuries.

Around 1200 AD the country again became split. In the south the Inca state was founded, whilst in the north the Chimu established themselves in the ancient territory of the Mochica. They founded a capital at Chanchan and ruled for more than two centuries over a sort of coastal empire, controlling some 1,200 kilometres of littoral. Their advance was not to be halted until the rise of the Incas in the middle of the fifteenth century.

The Inca state was born at Cuzco, in the heart of the Andes. Its origins are obscure. In the thirteenth and fourteenth centuries the Incas were not really distinguishable from the other tribes who lived a half-peasant, half-warrior life on the Andean plateau. But after the enthronement of Pachacuti, which followed victory over the Chanca (1440), the Inca triumph was stunning. Pachacuti behaved like a

*1. The Inca city of Machu Picchu, looking towards Huyana Picchu.*

**Cuzco capital of the Incas.**

**The Incas reach Qu**

**1250**

**147**

**1250:** Incas settle at Cuzco.
**1400:** Reign of Viracocha, eighth sovereign of the Inca dynasty: his authority only extended over a 40 km radius around Cuzco.

*3. Mochica pottery.*

**1440:** Battle of Cuzco: the Incas defeat the Chanca. In triumph, Viracocha's son deposes his father and reigns under the name Pachacuti.
**1441–4:** Campaigns of conquest – Vilcas in the west, Lake Titicaca in the east, Arequipa in the south.
**1463–70:** Expeditions of Capac Yupanqui, brother of Pachacuti Inca – conquest of the north, subjugation of the Chimu; the Incas reach Quito (Ecuador).
**1471–4:** Inca domination extends as far as the southern coast of Peru.
**1473:** Death of Pachacuti; accession of Topa Yupanqui, his son.
**1473–5:** The Amazonian dream. Topa, at the head of the Inca army, descends the Amarumayu (Rio Madre de Dios) and reaches the tropics. Expedition ends in disappointment. A rebellion on the Shores of Lake Titicaca brings him back to Cuzco.
**1480:** The 'pacification' of Bolivia.
**1484:** Conquest of northern and central Chile. Garrison set up at Coquimbo, at the southernmost tip of the Inca Empire.
**1485–9:** Topa's Great Progress. The Inca took four years to travel around and inspect the whole of his empire.
**1492:** Christopher Columbus lands on the coast of the West Indies.
**1493:** Death of Topa at Chinchero, near Cuzco. Palace intrigues. Accession of Huayna Capac, aged five, who governs with his elder brothers.
**1500:** Portuguese explorer Cabral discovers the Brazilian coast.
**1511:** Huayna Capac leads a military campaign into the far north against the Carangui of Ecuador.
**1511–26:** The Inca king dedicates himself to the 'pacification' of the north. A regent is installed in Cuzco.
**1513:** Having crossed the Panama isthmus, the Spanish conquistador Balboa discovers the Pacific.
**1514:** Smallpox, brought by the Spaniards, begins to decimate the Indian populations.
**1523:** Induced to do so by the Portuguese, who have gone into Brazil, the Chiriguano launch a raid on the Inca Empire's Bolivian frontier.
**1524:** First expedition of Francisco Pizarro, from Panama to the Columbian coast.
**1526:** Huayna Capac dies of smallpox at Quito. Pizarro's second voyage, which touches land on the coast of Ecuador.
**1527:** Pizarro reaches Peru, then returns to Panama. Huascar proclaims himself king at Cuzco, whilst his brother Atahuallpa has himself acclaimed sovereign of Quito. Partitioning of the Empire.
**1530:** War between the feuding brothers; defeat of Huascar.
**1531:** Pizarro's third voyage. The conquistador lands with less than 200 soldiers.
**16 November 1532:** Battle of Cajamarca. The Spaniards impose their superiority. Atahuallpa is taken prisoner.
**29 August 1533:** Atahuallpa is hanged by Pizarro at Cajamarca.
**15 November 1533:** The Spaniards enter Cuzco.

conqueror, but also like a wise organizer. In order to integrate the conquered populations, he imposed *Quechua* as the common language of the entire empire, set in train a policy of forced resettlement and made sun worship obligatory. Tribute and corvées made possible the opening up of roads, the building of terraces to grow maize and the construction of forts built in cyclopean blocks. When Topa Inca progressed around his empire at the end of the fifteenth century it extended over more than 900,000 square kilometres, and covered 4,000 kilometres of coastline. The very size of the Inca Empire was the cause of its fragility. Before the Spanish conquistadors landed the state had split in two and various hotbeds of agitation were appearing. It was easy for Pizarro to exploit these internal rivalries and conquer the country.

2. Pre-Inca ceremonial knife (Chimu culture).

**ɔpa Inca journeys**
**t around his empire.**
**85–9**

**Fall of the Inca Empire.**
**1533**

4. The Inca fortress of Sacsahuaman, near Cuzco.

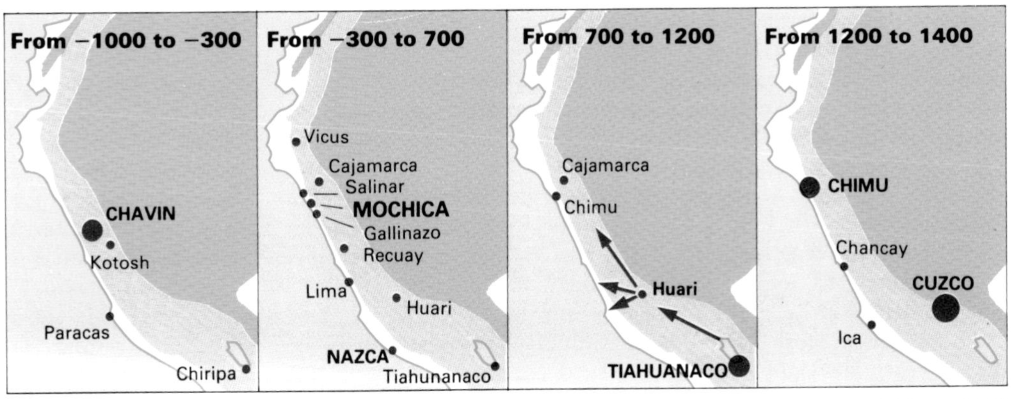

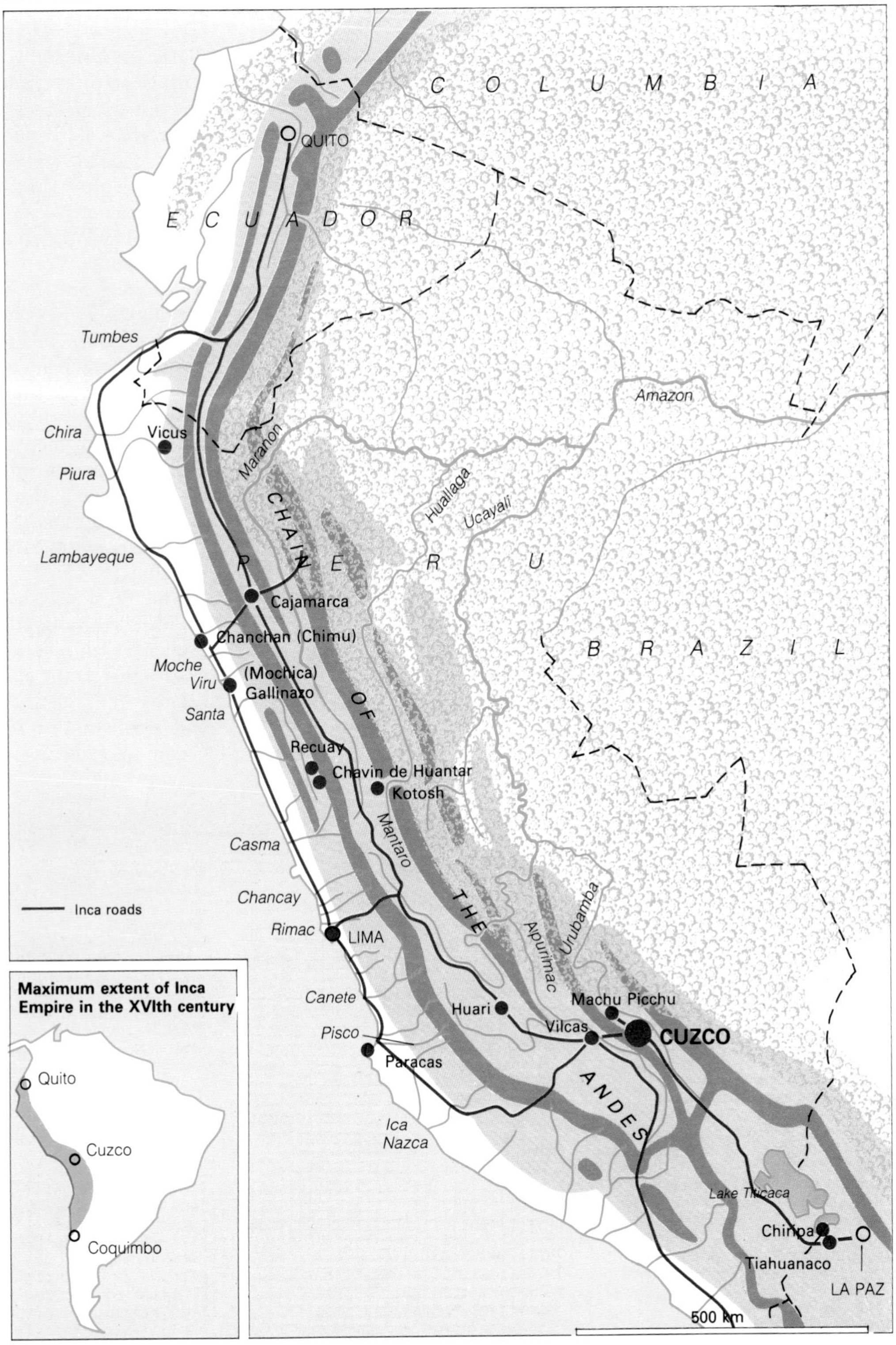

# China, Europe and World Exploration

THE FIFTEENTH CENTURY is one of those turning-points in history, like the centuries around 3000 BC and the first three decades of the twentieth: it laid the foundations of capitalism and the world market. But it also had its own distinct sub-periods and turning-points, the most important of which was the period 1465–70. This was when the Equator was crossed, the terrors of the unknown overcome; the circumnavigation of Africa was within sight and Africa's gold fell into European hands. In fact, the West had begun to take off. The last third of the fifteenth century is the period that recurs whenever historians try to locate the beginnings of 'modern' economic development in the regions of Western Europe.

The medieval world (like that of Antiquity) was less unbalanced than our own; development was more even, countries did not progress at such widely different rates. In spite of this, Europe before the fifteenth century lagged behind the Orient – particularly China – in almost every field. Admiral Cheng Ho, who headed Chinese maritime exploration from 1405 to 1433, had enormous resources at his disposal. The cockleshells and paltry fleet of Dias and Columbus were no match for the enormous junks and tens of thousands of men under Cheng Ho's command. The Chinese made seven expeditions to the South Seas; they visited Southeast Asia, Indonesia, India, Persia, Arabia, Somalia and Kenya. They exchanged sumptuous and exotic presents, received promises of friendship and vows of submission. Then, strange as it may seem, they ceased their wanderings. They were not there when the Portuguese reached the Cape; they did not overtake them at La Miña, nor did they encounter them at Cape St Vincent or Lisbon. Why was it the Westerners who, almost without realizing it, ended the isolation of separate civilizations? Why were they the ones who, to their own glory and great profit, put the peoples of the world in touch with each other? Answers suggest themselves when we compare the two blocs. The West was poor, it coveted gold and spices. China, on the other hand, had banknotes, the silver of Japan, the tropics on its doorstep; it had no need to seek the solution of forging new geographical links. The West was under threat: the Turks occupied the Near East and were moving westwards; trade with Eastern countries meant parting with precious metals and was not advantageous to the middle man. Alternative solutions were imperative. The 'middle part' of China was peaceful and stable; if it were to push southwards too forcibly it would leave the northern frontier vulnerable and risk unleashing the only real peril – the perennial peril of the Steppes. The West was divided into many weak states, even if the rivalries between them could be positive (Venetians and Genoese, Portuguese and Spaniards). Whereas imperial China was strong and it was not easy to evade its grasp or disobey its commands. The West needed to come out of itself, but how? Its physical space was beset on all sides by the sea, so it was naturally drawn to navigation. Portugal, because of the Trade Winds, was drawn to the southern seas. The West had for centuries been fed on Greek cosmography, Latin cartography, Italian and Norman naval daring, not to mention the Crusades. For a long time technology in the West had been far ahead of political and social organization, which had remained rudimentary, feudal. And for some time now, Western high culture, particularly painting, had been obsessed by space, by the rendering of perspective, the pushing back of horizons....

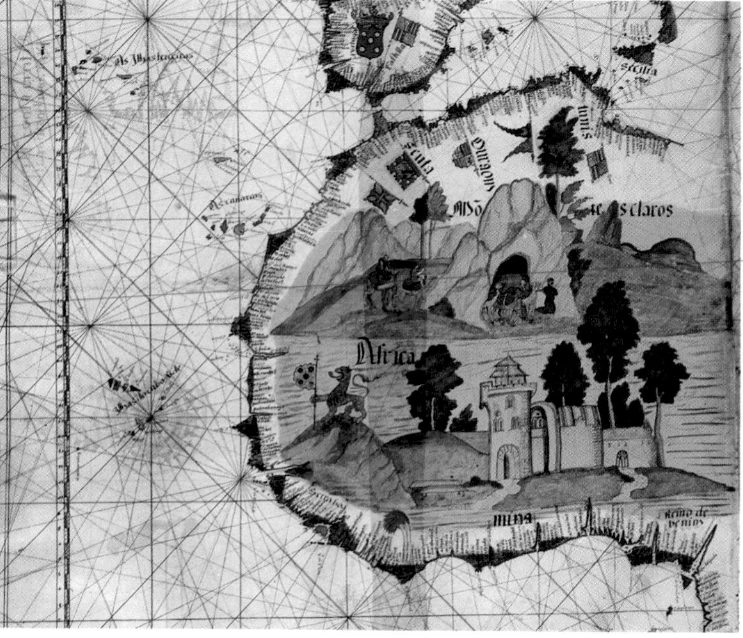

1. Western Africa according to a Portuguese atlas of 1563.

The West was not alone in this adventure. Discovery was not simply the monopoly of the Portuguese and Spanish, aided by numerous Italians, a few French at the beginning of the century and a few English at the end. On the contrary, many and diverse lands were caught up in the fascination for distant parts, but the West preceded and outdistanced them all. For four centuries the world was to become Western.

**From c. 1400:** Major improvements made in Western sailing ships.
**1402:** Korean map shows tip of Africa.
**1402–6:** French explore the Canary Islands.
**1405:** First major Chinese sea expeditions.
**1406:** Ptolemy rediscovered in the West.
**From 1407:** Chinese missions to Central Asia.
**1409–11 and 1411–15:** Second and third Chinese sea expeditions to Indonesia, India etc.
**1413:** Pierre d'Ailly's work *Imago mundi* inspires Christopher Columbus.
**1415:** Ceuta in Morocco captured. Portuguese maritime expansion begins. Kenyan giraffes shown at court of Nanking.
**1417–19:** Chinese ships reach east coast of Africa.
**c. 1418:** Gypsies reach Western Europe. In 1418 Henry the Navigator, Prince of Portugal, organizes Cape St Vincent as a base for Portuguese expeditions.
**From 1419:** Portuguese on Madeira. Voyages of Venetian Niccolo Dei Conti to Vijayanagar in India (1420) and Southeast Asia.
**1419–22:** Persian traveller in China.
**c. 1420:** First caravels (?). Indian or Arab ship rounds Cape of Good Hope and sails into the Atlantic.
**1425:** Celebrated Korean geographical work.
**1431–3:** Seventh and last Chinese expedition in Indian Ocean. Chinese ships again reach Africa (Somalia, Kenya and possibly Tanzania and Mozambique).
**c. 1436:** Cape Bojador is rounded (coast of western Sahara); Portuguese reach Rio de Oro.
**1437:** Tangier expedition proves disastrous for Portuguese.
**c. 1442:** Development of caravel. Pope recognizes African 'Crusade'. First African base on Arguin Island. First black slaves to Portugal. Discoveries multiply. Cape Blanc reached in 1441, Cape Verde in 1444.
**1455:** First African spices reach Portugal.
**1461:** Major geographical directory printed in China.
**From 1462:** Nautical treatise of Ahmad ibn Madjid, possible future pilot of Vasco da Gama on Indian Ocean expedition.
**From 1465:** Russian expeditions to Siberia. Abortive Chinese plans for sea expeditions.
**From 1465–70:** Marked progress of stellar navigation in West. Portuguese explore Gulf of Guinea and cross Equator. Gold from La Miña (now Ghana) reaches Europe. Slave trade develops. Idea of sailing round Africa spreads. Portuguese crown now allied to private capital.
**1466–72:** Russian Nikitin travels to India.
**c. 1470:** An Italian visits Timbuktu. English reach Newfoundland (?).
**From 1470:** First pivoted front axles developed on four-wheeled vehicles.
**1476:** Christopher Columbus in Portugal.
**Last decades of 15th century:** Migrations of Nilotic peoples to East Africa. Arrival of Somalian-Ethiopian peoples in Madagascar. Migration of Brazilian Indians. Inca expansion. Aztec expansion.
**c. 1484–5:** New developments in navigational techniques.
**1485–6:** Columbus leaves Portugal for Spain, where he is welcomed by Queen Isabella.
**1485–8:** Diego Cão and Bartholomeu Dias reach the tip of Africa.
**1487:** Chinese memorandum advocating maritime trade.
**1492:** The 'Columbus of mountaineering' climbs the Mont Aiguille in the French Alps. Martin Behaim produces a globe in Germany. Columbus discovers the Caribbean Islands.
**1493:** Pope dictates limits of Spanish and Portuguese expansion ('Inter caetera' Bull).
**1496–7:** John Cabot, an Italian in the service of the King of England, explores North Atlantic and discovers Labrador.
**1497–8:** Vasco da Gama reaches India via the Cape.
**1498:** On his third journey Columbus discovers American continent.

# 1400–1500

. Giraffe brought back from Africa by Chinese dmiral Zheng He in 1414, by the artist Shen Tu.

. Portuguese warrior portrayed by Benin artist. 6th-century brass plaque.

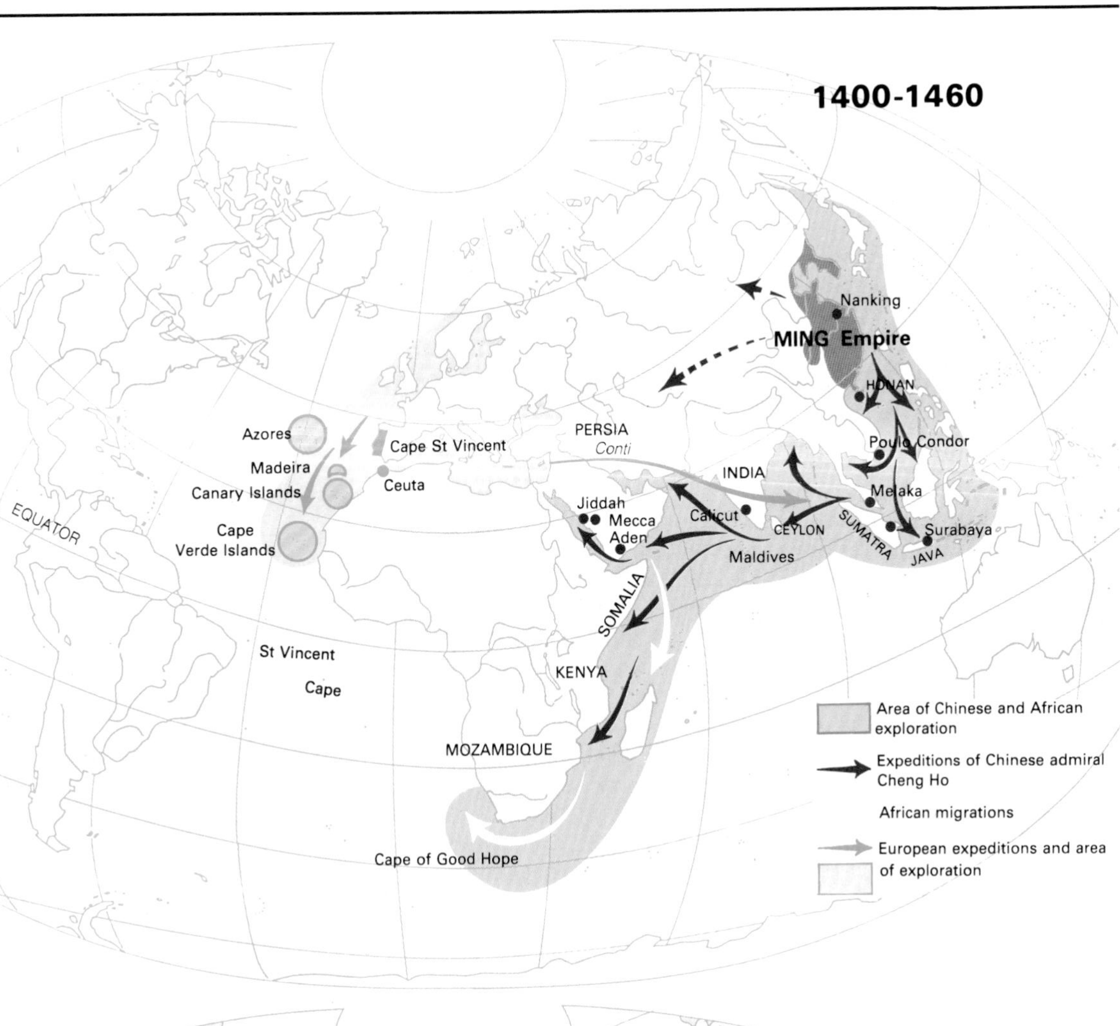


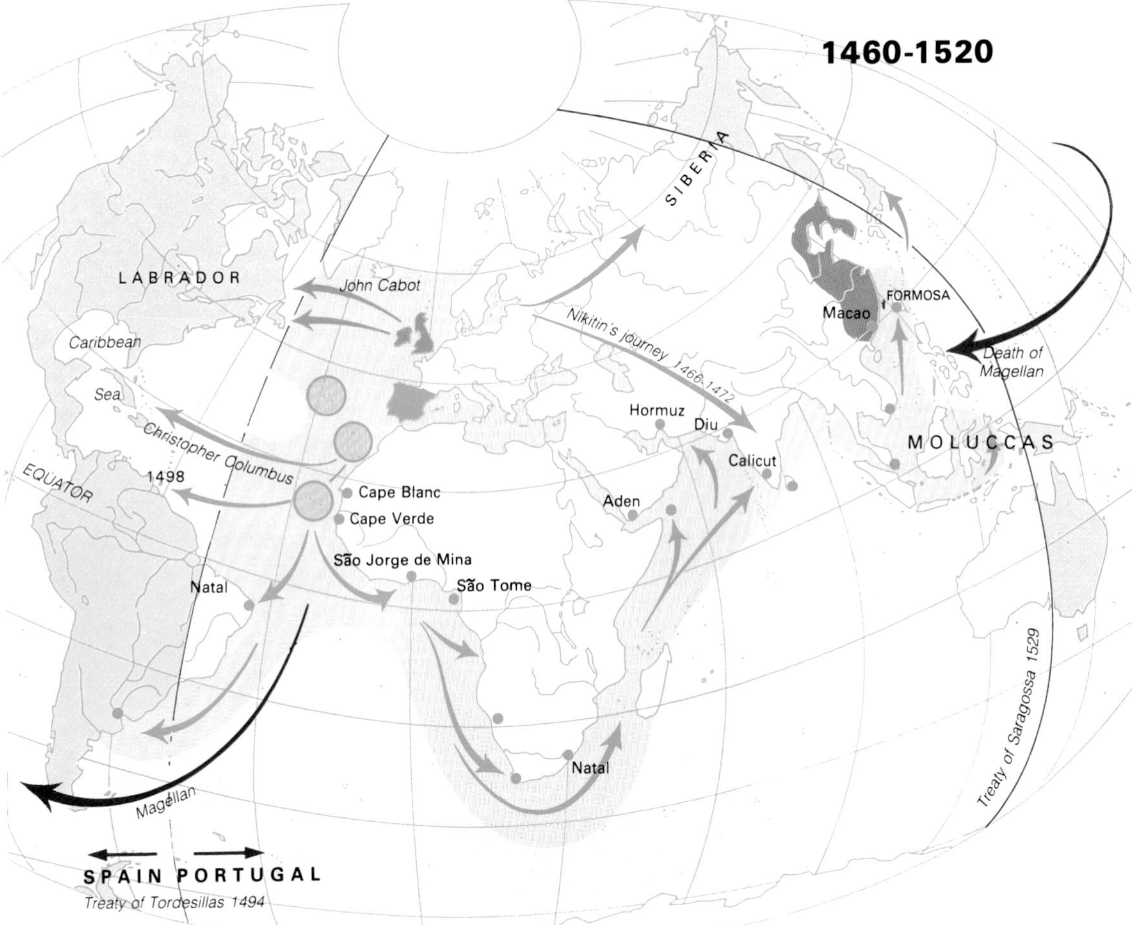

# The First Division of the World

AFTER THE ERA of the discoverers came the age of the 'conquistadors'. Strengthened by the blessing of the Pope ('Inter caetera' Bull, 1493) and the agreement of the Chancelleries (Treaty of Tordesillas, 1494), urged on by the taste for riches and adventure, and by missionary zeal as well, intrepid men left to conquer new worlds. In 1519, with 600 men and sixteen horses, Hernán Cortez seized Mexico, the great Aztec Empire. Ten years later, with fewer than 200 men and twenty-seven horses, Francisco Pizarro decided the fate of the Inca Empire of Peru. In one generation, Central and South America became 'Latin', that is to say Spanish or, in the case of Brazil, Portuguese. Between 1540 and 1550 the discovery of the silver mines in Mexico and Peru – especially Potosí in upper Peru – was to help the Spanish maintain a fifty-year political and military hegemony over Europe.

The Portuguese pushed down towards the south, along the west coast of Africa and then up the east coast, moving out into the Indian Ocean. They settled on the west coast of the sub-continent, took Ormuz, then Malacca, seized the principal spice market, the Moluccas (or Spice Islands) in 1512, and finally gained a foothold in Japan (1543) and China (1557). At the same time they colonized Brazil, which had quickly become the world's main sugar producer. But Spanish and Portuguese hegemony could not last. The future of imperialism belonged to the northern nations, who were richer in human and material resources and more modern in terms of state and social structures. Late entrants in the race and confined to 'lands of no worth' in North America and seeking the famous 'passage' to India, the French and Dutch settled where they could, the former in the St Lawrence valley and around the Great Lakes and the latter in the Hudson valley. Although they arrived last, the British moved in in more tightly closed groups and enjoyed the support of the mother country. They were eventually to acquire control of the continent.

The latecomers did not resign themselves, however, to a Spanish and Portuguese monopoly over the 'prime' sites, from which flowed gold, silver, spices, sugar and slaves. Practising first piracy (French and Dutch Calvinists, and English corsairs such as Drake and Hawkins), then open war, they eventually seized entire colonies, the British through the East India Company, founded in 1600.

In 1602 the Dutch created their own company, which was by far the most powerful, and systematically chased the Portuguese from their bases along the length of the spice route to the Moluccas, then – from their stronghold at Batavia (Djakarta) – from Malacca and Ceylon. All the while, the coasts of India, the Caribbean and Africa became the private property of the British and the French. In the seventeenth century the Spanish and Portuguese imperial monopoly was finally broken in favour of the northern powers – a situation which was repeated in Europe itself (see below).

Within three generations the face of the whole globe had changed.

*1. Beginnings of Spanish America: Francisco Pizarro, conqueror of Peru.*

The sword of the conquistadors, the 'microbic unification of the world' and the brutality of the colonists had depopulated the American continent. The slave trade had bled Africa and given a tremendous lift to the European economy, now effectively a 'world economy', and the white man had imposed his total rule and his civilization everywhere. From this time on, even those adversaries who attacked him were to do so with his weapons and his concepts.

**Voyage of Christopher Columbus.** **1492**

**Cabral discovers Brazil.** **1500**

**Cortez among the Aztecs.** **1519**

**Pizarro among the Incas.** **1531**

**1479:** Treaty of Alcacovas between Spain and Portugal concerning the Atlantic islands.
**1493:** 'Inter caetera' Bull recognizing Castillian sovereignty over lands already discovered and as yet undiscovered beyond an imaginary line passing 100 leagues west and south of the Azores and Cape Verde.
**1494:** Tordesillas Treaty: Portugal and Spain divide the New World between them.
**1501:** Beginning of the African slave traffic to the Americas.
**1505–15:** The viceroys Almeida and Albuquerque build the Portuguese trade empire – Ormuz, Goa, Ceylon, Malacca, East Indies.
**1508–11:** Conquest of Puerto Rico. Colonization of Jamaica.
**1511–15:** Conquest of Cuba by Diego Velasquez.
**1519–21:** Hernán Cortez conquers the Aztec Empire and refounds Mexico.
**1521–30:** Portuguese colonization of Brazil.
**1523–35:** Conquest of Guatemala, El Salvador, Honduras, Yucatan.
**1524:** Seville receives the monopoly of Spanish colonial trade.

*2. Francisco de Almeida.*

*3. Alfonso de Albuquerque.*

**1529:** Treaty of Saragossa between Spain and Portugal fixes the demarcation line in the Far East.
**1531–4:** Francisco Pizarro conquers the Inca Empire.
**1535–8:** Conquest of Columbia by Gonzalo Jimenez de Quesada.
**1546:** Foundation of Potosí, silver mining centre of Peru.
**1557:** The Portuguese gain foothold in Macao.
**1562:** John Hawkins is the first Englishman to trade in slaves between West Africa and the New World.
**1565–71:** Legazpi subjugates the Philippines and founds Manila (1571).
**1565:** The Portuguese found Rio de Janeiro.
**1574:** Beginnings of Portuguese colonization in Angola.
**1577–80:** Voyages of Francis Drake along the Pacific coasts.
**1584:** Sir Walter Raleigh founds Virginia.
**1600:** Founding of the British East India Company.
**1602:** Dutch East India Company.
**1608:** Samuel de Champlain founds Quebec.

# 15th–17th centuries

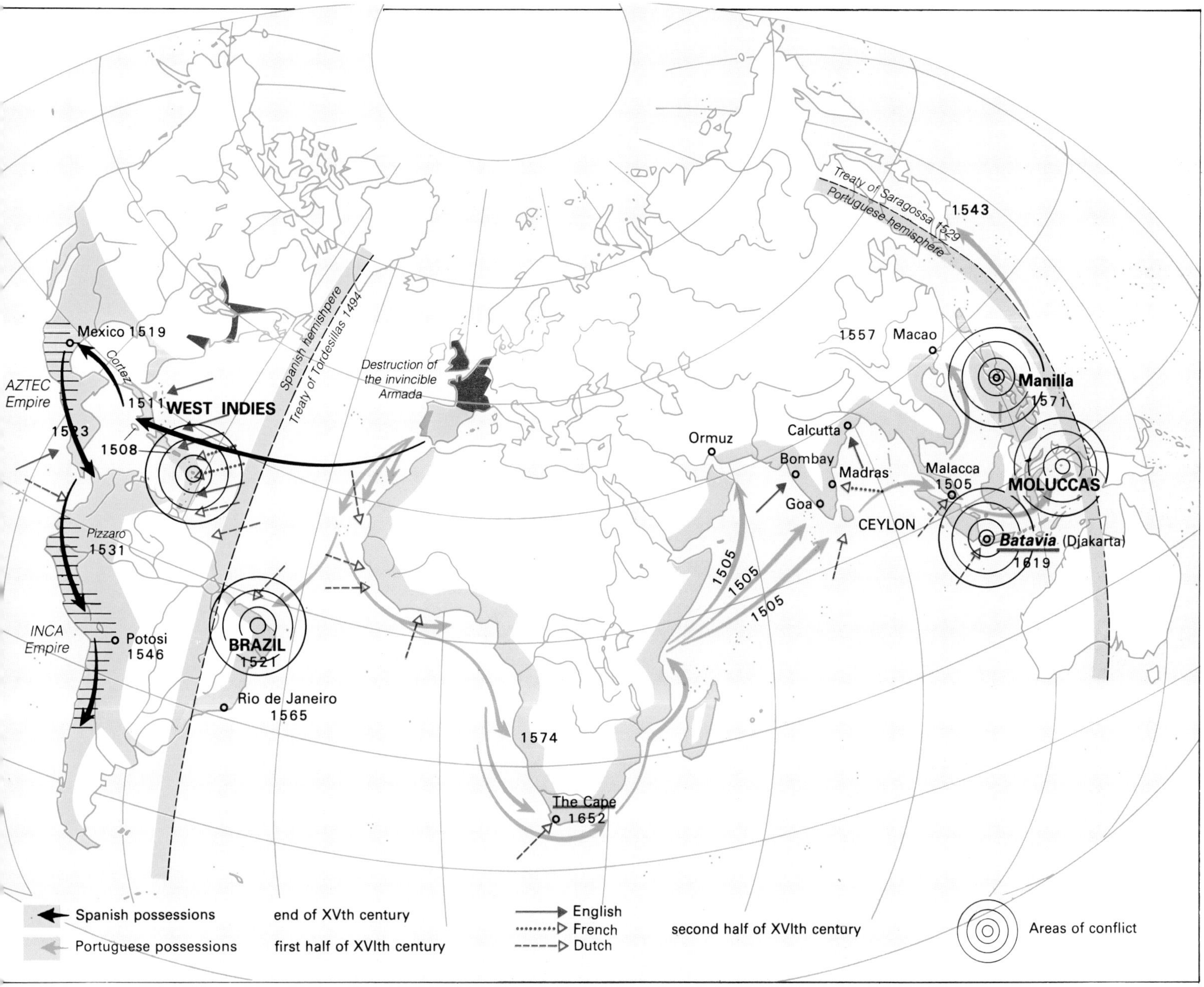

Treaty of Saragossa 1529
Portuguese hemisphere
1543
1557 Macao
Manilla 1571
MOLUCCAS
Malacca 1505
Batavia (Djakarta) 1619
CEYLON
Calcutta
Bombay
Madras
Goa
Ormuz
1505
1505
1505
1574
The Cape 1652
Destruction of the invincible Armada
Spanish hemisphere
Treaty of Tordesillas 1494
Mexico 1519
Cortez
AZTEC Empire
1511 WEST INDIES
1523
1508
Pizzaro 1531
INCA Empire
Potosi 1546
BRAZIL 1521
Rio de Janeiro 1565

Spanish possessions — end of XVth century
Portuguese possessions — first half of XVIth century
English
French
Dutch
second half of XVIth century
Areas of conflict

**Sir Walter Raleigh founds Virginia.**

**1584**

**The French in Senegal.**

**1637**

**1609:** The Portuguese lose Ceylon to Holland.
**1619:** The Dutch found Batavia.
**1620:** Voyage of the Mayflower, the vessel of the Pilgrim Fathers.
**1621:** Dutch West India Company.
**1624:** The Dutch gain a foothold in Taiwan.
**1624–54:** Dutch-Portuguese wars over Brazil.
**1625–64:** The French settle in the West Indies.

4. *A caravelle.*

**1637:** French settlements throughout the length of Senegal.
**1641:** The Dutch take Malacca from the Portuguese.
**1642:** Founding of Montreal (Ville-Marie).
**1652:** The Dutch found the Cape.
**1664:** Colbert founds the French East India Company; New Amsterdam, founded in 1626, becomes New York.
**1682:** Cavelier de la Salle takes possession of Louisiana.
**1686:** Louis XIV annexes Madagascar.
**1697:** Treaty of Ryswick; France receives Haiti.
**1699–1702:** Start of French colonization in Louisiana.

5. *The massacre of Aztec chiefs at Tenochtitlan in 1521, codex of Diego Duran, 1579.*

# The Expansion of Financial and Commercial Capitalism

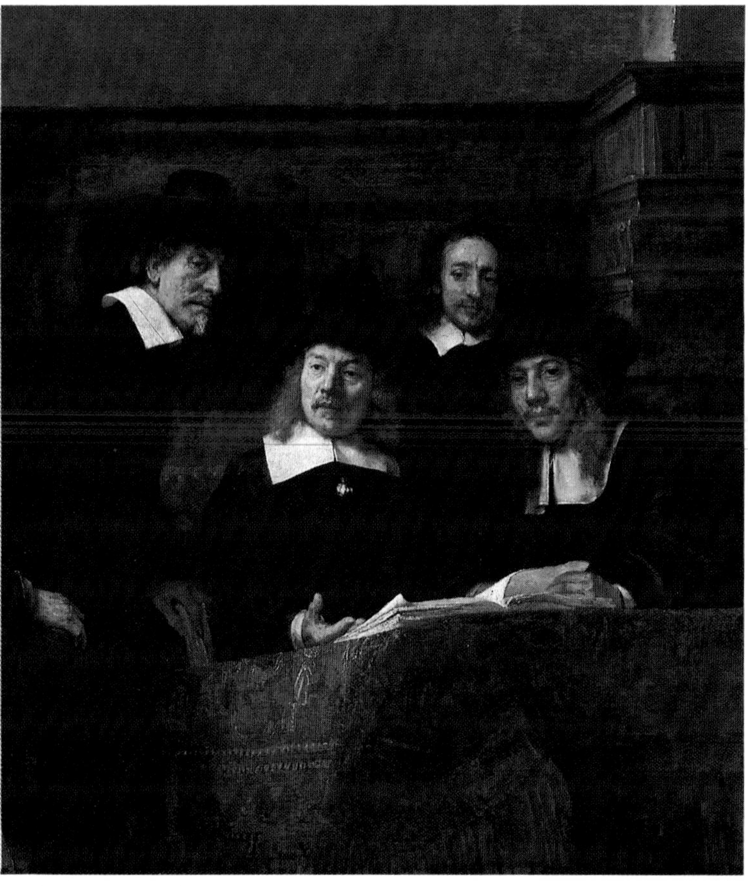

*1. Urban oligarchic forces: the cloth-making syndics of Amsterdam, as seen by Rembrandt.*

From the second half of the fifteenth century the crisis during the latter part of the Middle Ages was brought to a halt, the population curve stabilized and the Western world entered a long period of economic progress. Although the structures remained essentially medieval, beyond any doubt the advent of colonialism, the emergence of 'new monarchies', the enormous concentration of capital in the hands of great 'merchants' (whose role was that of banker, manufacturer and trader) and the appearance of state and private monopolies of international size and scale all created the conditions for the first capitalist age. The powerful bourgeois – individualistic, hard-working, something of an adventurer, concerning himself with the business of princes (in order to improve his own) and dealing ever more effectively with them – became a perfectly defined social type, the complete opposite of the medieval *miles christianus*. In Europe itself, the main axes of trade did not undergo significant changes. In the fifteenth century Venice had a virtual monopoly in spices from the East, which were distributed by Venetian and German merchants along a southwest–northeast trade route (from France and Spain to Germany, the Baltic and Scandinavian states) with an extension towards the north-west (Netherlands and England). From the Scandinavian countries came wheat, wood and skins to be exchanged for salt, wine and manufactured goods from the more developed European countries. Arab merchants brought to Mediterranean ports exotic products from those parts of the world with which Europe had not yet forged direct links: slaves and African gold, Chinese silks, Indian spices. ...

The great fortunes of the late Middle Ages and the beginnings of the modern era had their origins in the south and were centred on the Mediterranean. There were first of all the Florentines, then the Genoese and the south Germans. The organization of trade may well have been archaic still, but commercial techniques had made notable progress and the first commodity markets allowed speculative business to be carried out on a large scale. Later, the appearance of public banks was to bring new facilities to international trade. In the wake of further discoveries, direct contacts were established and the Venetian monopoly declined. Europe, Africa and America formed an enormous three-way trading bloc: ships loaded with alcohol, arms and glass beads traded their cargoes all along the African coast against slaves destined for the sugar plantations of America; there, in the holds of the same boats, sugar cane, and later tobacco and cotton were loaded, destined for the European ports, replacing human flesh. The American money that passed through Seville paid for the products needed by the colonists and flooded the money markets in Genoa, Piacenza, Lyons, London and Antwerp. At the same time, the Portuguese maintained trade with India and the fabulous Spice Islands of eastern Asia. Spices were used to pay for German copper, iron and silver, among other things. But the Portuguese and the Spanish were soon to be shouldered aside by the French, the British and the Dutch.

In the sixteenth century Antwerp was the centre of European and Atlantic trade. The bankruptcies suffered by nations in the fifties and sixties, war and the religious troubles all hastened its decline, and in the seventeenth century Amsterdam took over the torch before itself being supplanted by London a century later. The significance of this enormous shift to the west and north is clear: the Spanish and Portuguese had revolutionized the world economy and the Protestant powers and France were to benefit from it.

**1503** **Casa de Contratación.** — **1517** **Le Havre.** — **1554** **Muscovy Company.**

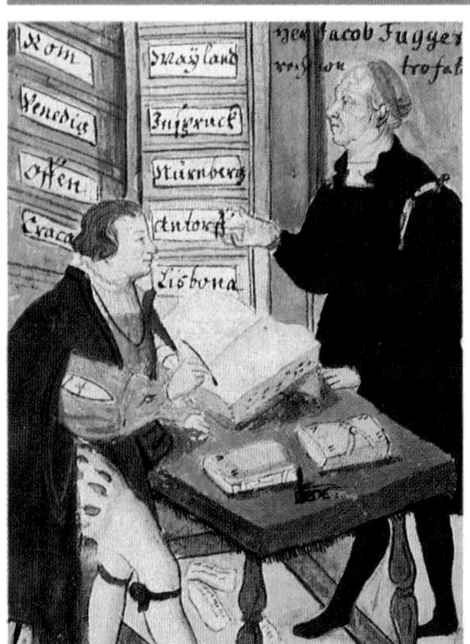


*2. A builder of empire: Jakob II Fugger 'The Rich' and his accountant.*

**1462:** Protectionist edict of Louis XI ensuring the prosperity of the Lyon fairs.
**1487:** The Fuggers secure control over the silver mines in the Tirol, then Thuringen and Hungary, and become the sponsors of the imperial crown.
**1488:** Bruges loses its commercial advantages to Antwerp.
**1503:** Founding of the Casa de Contratación in Seville.
**1506:** The King of Portugal reserves the monopoly in spices for himself.
**1513:** The Fuggers become agents for the distribution of indulgences in Germany.
**1517:** François I founds Le Havre de Grâce.
**1519:** The Fuggers ensure the election of Charles V to the Empire.
**1522:** François I inaugurates the system of irredeemable securities on the Hôtel de Ville in Paris.
**1525:** Death of Jakob Fugger, whose capital, destined to double in twenty years, is valued at two million florins.
**1526:** Rise of the Genoese Bank.
**1531:** Opening of the new Antwerp Stock Exchange.

*3. The centre of the Western economy: the Antwerp Stock Exchange at the height of its power.*

# 15th–17th centuries

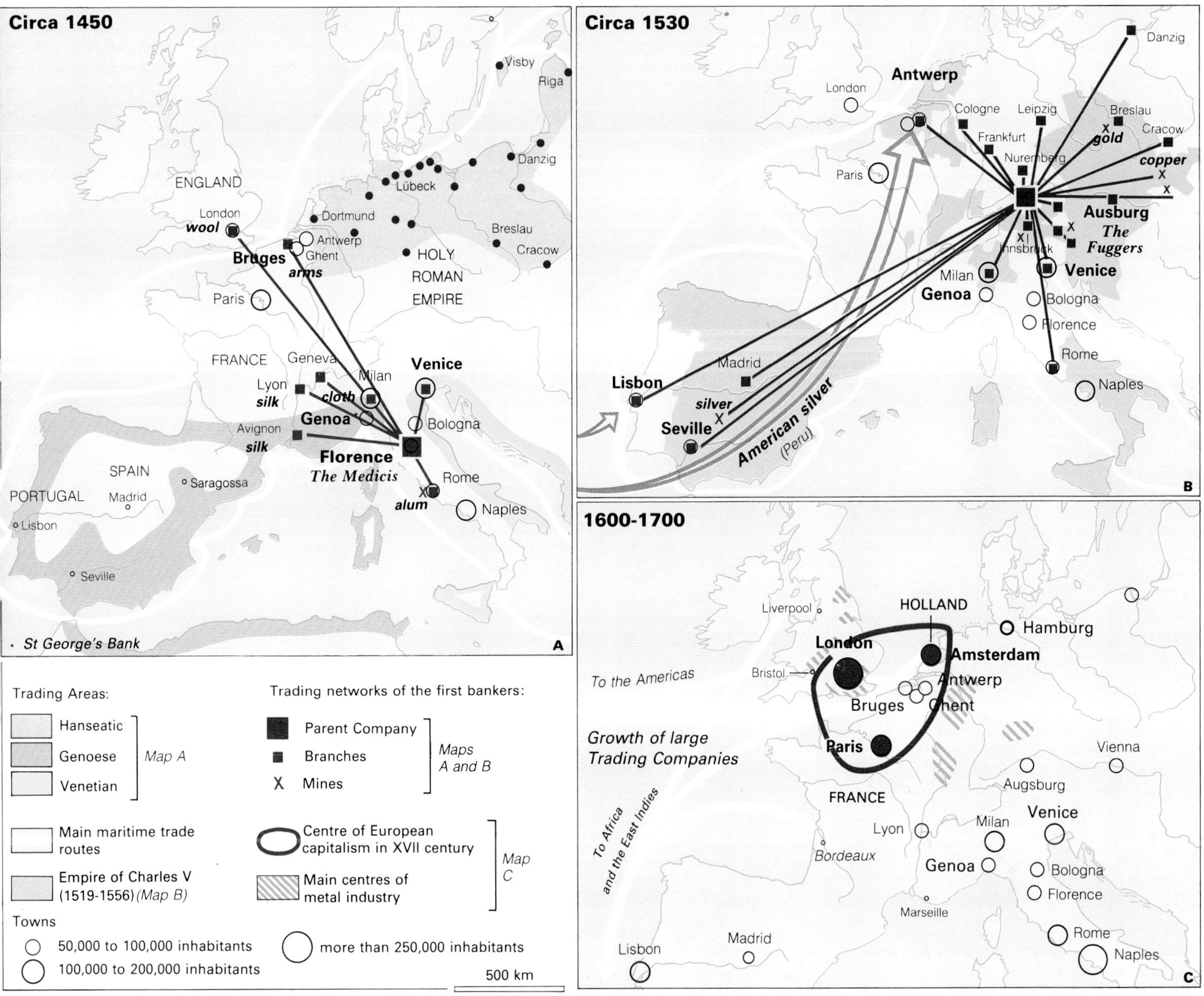

**Circa 1450**

ENGLAND
London
*wool*
Visby
Riga
Danzig
Lübeck
Dortmund
Antwerp
Ghent
Bruges
*arms*
Breslau
Cracow
HOLY ROMAN EMPIRE
Paris
FRANCE
Geneva
Milan
Lyon
*silk*
*cloth*
Genoa
Venice
Bologna
Avignon
*silk*
Florence
*The Medicis*
SPAIN
Saragossa
PORTUGAL
Madrid
Lisbon
Rome
*alum*
Naples
Seville
· *St George's Bank*
A

**Circa 1530**

London
Antwerp
Cologne
Leipzig
Breslau
Cracow
Danzig
Frankfurt
Nuremberg
*gold*
*copper*
Paris
Ausburg
*The Fuggers*
Innsbruck
Milan
Venice
Genoa
Bologna
Florence
Rome
Naples
Madrid
Lisbon
*silver*
Seville
*American silver (Peru)*
B

**1600-1700**

Liverpool
HOLLAND
Hamburg
London
Amsterdam
Bristol
Antwerp
Bruges
Ghent
*To the Americas*
*Growth of large Trading Companies*
Paris
FRANCE
Vienna
Augsburg
Venice
Milan
Lyon
*To Africa and the East Indies*
Bordeaux
Genoa
Bologna
Florence
Marseille
Madrid
Lisbon
Rome
Naples
C

Trading Areas:
- Hanseatic, Genoese, Venetian — *Map A*
- Main maritime trade routes
- Empire of Charles V (1519-1556) *(Map B)*

Trading networks of the first bankers:
- Parent Company, Branches, X Mines — *Maps A and B*
- Centre of European capitalism in XVII century; Main centres of metal industry — *Map C*

Towns
- 50,000 to 100,000 inhabitants
- 100,000 to 200,000 inhabitants
- more than 250,000 inhabitants

500 km

**British East India Company.** **1600**

**French East India Company.** **1664**

**1540:** Decree of Charles V in connection with the Netherlands, legalising bank interest.
**1540:** Start of massive influx of American money.
**1545:** Calvin refutes scholastic arguments against loans with interest.
**1554:** Creation of Muscovy Company.
**1556:** The 'Grand Parti' of Lyon.
**1557:** Bankruptcy of the King of Spain.
**1559:** Bankruptcy of the King of France.
**1560:** Death of Anton Fugger: beginning of the decline of the house.
**1566:** M de Malestroit. *Remonstrances . . . on wealth . . .*
**1568:** In his *Reply to the paradoxes of M de Malestroit . . .* Jean Bodin examines the mechanism of inflation and shows the main cause to be the influx of precious metals from America.
**1581:** Creation of the British Company of the Levant.
**1600:** British East India Company.
**1602:** Dutch East India Company.
**1609:** Creation of the Bank of Amsterdam.
**1614:** Dutch North Company: Levant Company.
**1615:** Antoine de Montchrestien, *Treaty on Economic Policy*.
**1619:** Creation of the Bank of Hamburg.
**1621:** Dutch West Indies Company.
**1627:** Richelieu creates the Company of One Hundred Associates.
**1660–80:** General fall in prices due to the economic crisis.

*4. Trade in Venice in 1616.*

**1664–7:** Colbert's protective tariffs.
**1664:** Colbert creates the French East India Company and the French West India Company.
**1669:** French North Company. Jacques Savary *The Perfect Merchant*.
**1670:** Colbert creates the Levant Company.
**1685:** Creation of the Guinea Slave Trade Company and the Privileged Royal Company of Senegal.
**1694:** Creation of the Bank of England.
**1698:** Creation of the China Company by Jourdan: creation of the Saint-Dominique Slave Trade Company.

*5. Louis XIV visiting the Gobelins factory.*

# The First Industrial Age

CAN WE CALL THIS a period of industrial capitalism in the same sense as we have spoken (above) of commercial and financial capitalism? Only to a certain extent, for traditional craft production remained the most widespread form of manufacture. This was organized in small workshops where the independent producer worked with one or two assistants, produced for a local market and was a member of a guild with its strict regulations, quality control and fixed prices. In short, this was an economy much closer to that of the twelfth than the nineteenth century. However, in certain branches of industrial production a class of entrepreneurs possessing capital and the means of production could be seen clearly emerging, whilst opposite them there arose a class of workers selling their labour power. The classic example of a purely capitalist – in fact state-capitalist – enterprise was the Venice arsenal, where thousands of workers built, repaired and armed the republic's fleet. The mining and iron industries, which required large quantities of investment, were organized along similar lines, as increasingly was the textile industry. If there was nothing spectacular about the technological innovations that took place between the Middle Ages and the Industrial Revolution (rather than producing new developments, the spread of printing in fact enabled the sixteenth century to make available to a wider audience what had been invented in the Middle Ages), the organization of work developed rapidly: 'rural' industry allowed the 'merchant' to escape the tentacular grasp of municipal regulations. In the large production units, more rational methods of exploiting labour power, growing demand from both courts and armies and a great number of technological innovations, especially in mining, metallurgy (notably with the introduction of the high furnace, forerunner of the present blast furnace) and the textile industry all indubitably created the conditions of a modest but genuine 'industrial age'. At the beginning of our period, this was particularly true for the area stretching from Flanders to Tuscany, including southwest Germany and northern Italy. This was an area on which the rest of Europe was largely dependent. In the course of the sixteenth and seventeenth centuries, other centres of production emerged – especially France, Holland, Sweden and England (we may again observe here a displacement of the centre of gravity of the European economy towards the north-west, cf. p. 140). Textiles remained the dominant industry with Florentine, Flemish (Hondschoote, Lille) and, increasingly, Dutch (Leyden, Haarlem) and English woollen cloth. Linen came from Saxony and Picardy, and silk, initially the Italian product par excellence (Lucca), was later produced by the Spanish (from Seville and Toledo) and, finally, by the French with the development of the Lyon silk industry. The mining industry – without doubt the most 'modern' – was undergoing rapid expansion: silver came from the Tyrol, Carinthia and Upper Silesia, areas that were soon to lose their dominant position with the arrival of American imports; iron and copper from Sweden, coal from the Liège region and the north of England, which towards the end of the sixteenth century had become the principal source of energy for iron-smelting. As the sixteenth and seventeenth centuries were indisputably an age of war, they saw a real boom in the armaments industry. We must also mention printing, an industry in the forefront of technology (see below), naval shipbuilding (England, France – especially in the second half of the seventeenth century – and the Netherlands) and the glass industry (Venice, France and England).

Spain lost ground considerably in these years; the old centres of production – Italy, Flanders and south Germany – also showed a relative decline; meanwhile England, France, the Netherlands and Sweden emerged as economic powers. Industrial Europe was some way off, but it was already possible to discern its future contours.

*1. Work in the Kutna Hora mine.*

**Arms manufacture at St Étienne.** **1516**

***De re metallica.*** **1556**

**1460:** Discovery of the Tolfa alum mines.
**1460:** Introduction of the blast furnace.
**1464:** Edward IV prohibits the importation of foreign cloth.
**1470:** Manufacture of precision astronomical instruments at Nuremberg (Regiomontanus).
**1500:** Rise of the Venetian, English and Dutch woollen industries and decline of the Flemish and Florentine. Appearance of the musket (Germany).
**1516:** First firearms manufactured at St Étienne (France).
**1529:** Strike of the Lyon printing workers (Grande Rebeyne).

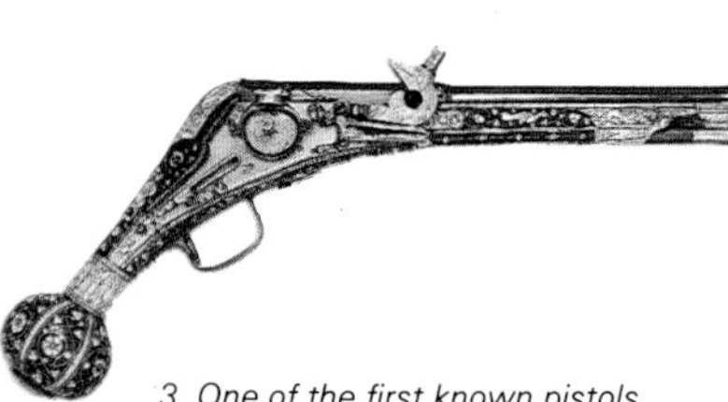

*3. One of the first known pistols.*

**1531:** Beginnings of Lyon silk industry.
**1540:** V. Biringuccio, *De la pirotechnia.*
**1540:** Use of railways in mines; casting of iron cannons in England.
**1543:** 400 ironworks in France.
**1552:** Prohibition of the export of Spanish cloth to the Americas.
**1556:** Georg Agricola, *De re metallica*. The *patio* amalgam process for the extraction of silver is introduced into the mines of Peru and Mexico.
**1563:** Elizabeth I's *Statute of Artificers.*
**1569:** The textile industry is prohibited in the Spanish colonies.
**1570:** Increased iron and copper production in Sweden. Mining begins at the Huancavelica mercury mine.
**1572:** First use of gunpowder in mining (Sicily).
**1578:** Jacques Besson, *Théâtre des instruments.*
**1580:** The windmill-driven saw; the Dutch freighter (fluyt); Delftware; coal is increasingly used in England.
**1588:** Agostina Ramelli, *Le Diverse Artificiose Machine.*

*4. Rapidly expanding industries: a cannon foundry in the 16th century.*

# 15th–17th centuries

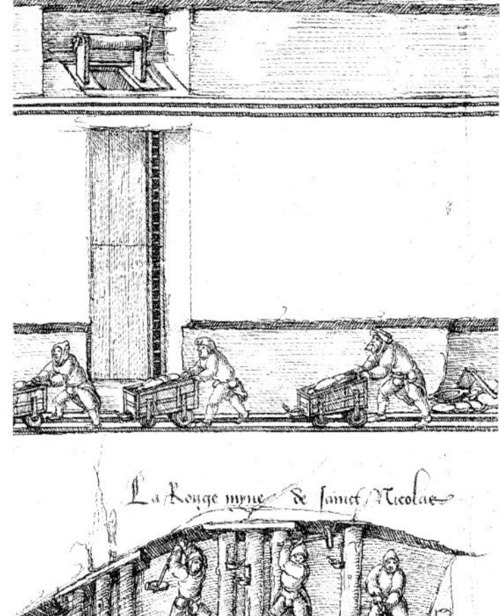

*2. Stages in the search for and processing of ore in a German silver mine, drawn by Heinrich Gross (16th century).*

| ***Alchemia.*** | **The royal Gobelins manufactory.** | **The steam engine.** |
|---|---|---|
| **1597** | **1667** | **1687** |

**1589:** William Lee's knitting machine.
**1590:** Introduction of railways into English coal mines.
**1597:** Andreas Leibau, *Alchemia*, the first manual of chemistry.
**1600:** Claude Dangon's loom (Lyon). 800 ironworks in England.
**1611:** Royal foundries at Seville for the Indies fleet.
**1615:** Use of coal in the manufacture of glass in England.
**1650:** Leyden becomes the major centre of the woollen industry.
**1667:** The Gobelins company becomes a royal manufactory.
**1670:** Cannon-making works set up in the Angoumois, Périgord, Nivernais, Lyonnais, Dauphiné and Burgundy by Colbert; creation of the great royal factories of France: cloth at Abbeville (Van Robais), tapestries at Beauvais (Hinard), glass (Du Noyer).
**1687:** Denis Papin's steam engine.
**1692:** Creation of the Saint-Gobain company.
**1695:** H. Gautier, *Traité de la construction des chemins.*

*5. Few inventions, many innovations: a crane, as seen by Agostino Ramelli.*

*6. First products of applied science: Pascal's calculator.*

# The Development of Printing

THE MODERN WESTERN BOOK is a product of two revolutions. The first of these in the first centuries AD introduced a new form of book, the stitched book (or codex), which gradually supplanted the scroll (volumen). The second in the mid-fifteenth century revolutionized the conditions of reproduction of texts: we refer, of course, to the invention of printing.

It was from 1452–3 onwards that Gutenberg, in Mainz, produced the first European printed texts using movable metal type: the type was pressed onto paper with the aid of a hand press. The technique, which greatly reduced the cost of book manufacture and allowed the reproduction of several hundred copies of an identical text (an average print run in the fifteenth century was of the order of 500 copies), had evolved in response to unprecedentedly high levels of demand that had been poorly met by the manual copying of books, where manufacture was on an individual basis and remained slow and expensive. Increased demand arose in part because the lay community was becoming more literate and educated; there was, in this period, an unprecedented thirsting after a new spirituality to be achieved through the reading of works of piety. In part also it was due to the new demands of emerging state structures. Two sets of technological developments had made Gutenberg's invention possible in the fifteenth century. On the one hand, there was the newly-acquired expertise in metalworking, in particular by German goldsmiths (Gutenberg was the son of a goldsmith and was himself a member of the goldsmiths' guild of Strasbourg before his return to Mainz); on the other, there was a great increase in the number of paper mills, which had spread across the whole of Europe from Italy, where they had first appeared at the end of the thirteenth century.

The printing of texts by means of movable type was not peculiar to Europe. During the Sung dynasty (between the eleventh and thirteenth centuries) printing had reached a peak in China, whilst in Korea movable metal characters had been used for the first time during the thirteenth century. However, in neither of these two countries was printing to find the place it was to have in the West, a fact doubtless to be explained by the large number of characters required (several tens of thousands), which meant that its use was confined to state publications alone. Interestingly, it does not seem that Gutenberg, or, indeed, any of his European contemporaries, knew of these earlier Oriental examples.

In the fifteenth century the new invention quickly spread throughout the whole of Europe, carried initially by the early German printers on their travels. Between 1452 and 1470 the new art conquered nine German towns, four Italian centres, Paris, which had its own printing shop at the Sorbonne in 1470, and Seville. Six years later, William Caxton began printing at Westminster, and by 1480 printing had won a temporary or permanent place in 108 towns, and by the year 1500 it was established in 226. In the age of incunabula (i.e. before 1500) we may suppose that the European printing shops printed between 35,000 and 40,000 publications, of which more than three-quarters were in Latin. At that stage Venice was the printing capital, followed by Rome, Paris and Cologne, and the three great bastions of book production were Italy (42% of incunabula), Germany (30%) and France (15%).

*1. Printing shop in the 15th century.* Manuscrit des chants royaux.

In the sixteenth century the spread of printing continued, but production became concentrated in the university towns and the great trading centres. Venice continued to dominate the book market and Paris maintained its position (production there was doubled between 1500 and 1540), but some new centres appeared – Lyon, Basle, Antwerp and Frankfurt – and a first shift in European printing became evident, the balance moving from Italy towards Northern Europe, where Gutenberg's invention lent its support to the spread of humanism and the Reformation.

**Movable type in use in China.** **First paper in the W**

**1000** **1276**

*2. 'Thousand Buddha' scroll. Chinese xylograph, 7th–9th centuries.*

**Beginning of the 11th century:** Appearance in China of printing with movable type.
**11th century:** First use of paper in Western manuscripts, in Spain. The technique of paper-making had been introduced to the West from China by the Arabs.
**13th century:** Oldest known Korean publication, printed with metal movable characters.
**c. 1276:** Beginning of paper-making at Fabriano in Italy.
**c. 1340:** Paper mills set up at Troyes.
**c. 1452–3:** First pieces printed at Mainz with movable type.
**c. 1455:** Gutenberg's forty-two line Bible (perhaps 150 copies).
**1457:** Mainz Psalter – first book with a title page and publisher's name: Fust and Schöffer of Mainz.
**1461:** Albrecht Pfister prints the first known illustrated printed books at Bamberg.
**1465:** First book printed outside Germany in the printing shop of the Monastery of Subiaco in Italy.
**1470:** Foundation of the printing shop at the Sorbonne and the first book printed in France.

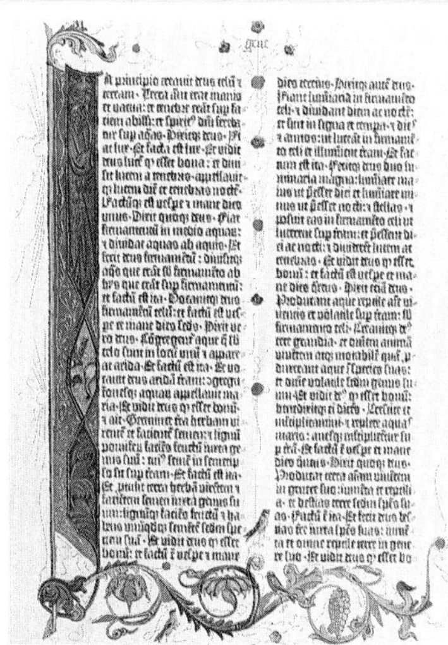

*3. Illuminated folio from Gutenberg's thirty-six-line Bible.*

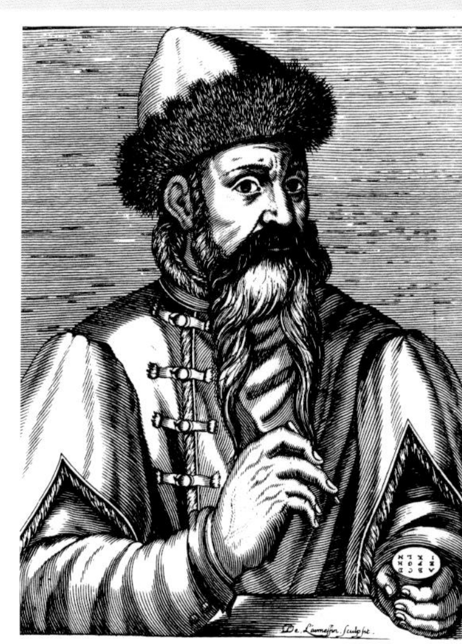

*4. Portrait of Gutenberg engraved by Larmessin, 1682.*

# 11th–16th centuries

## Before 1471

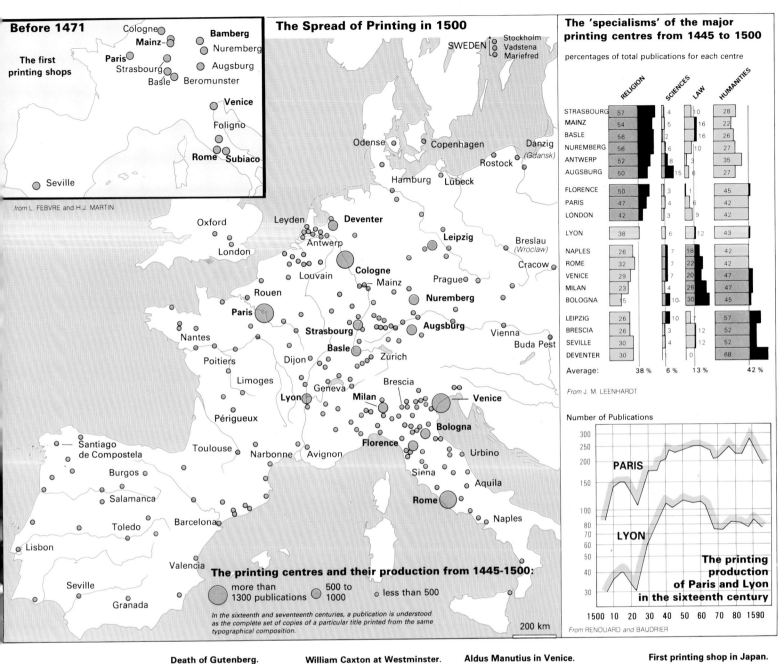

The first printing shops

Cologne, Mainz, Bamberg, Nuremberg, Paris, Strasbourg, Augsburg, Basle, Beromunster, Venice, Foligno, Rome, Subiaco, Seville

*from* L. FEBVRE and H.J. MARTIN

## The Spread of Printing in 1500

SWEDEN: Stockholm, Vadstena, Mariefred

Odense, Copenhagen, Danzig *(Gdansk)*, Rostock, Hamburg, Lübeck, Oxford, Leyden, Deventer, London, Antwerp, Leipzig, Breslau *(Wroclaw)*, Cracow, Louvain, Cologne, Mainz, Prague, Rouen, Nuremberg, Paris, Strasbourg, Augsburg, Vienna, Nantes, Basle, Buda Pest, Poitiers, Dijon, Zurich, Limoges, Geneva, Brescia, Lyon, Milan, Venice, Périgueux, Bologna, Santiago de Compostela, Toulouse, Narbonne, Avignon, Florence, Urbino, Burgos, Siena, Aquila, Salamanca, Rome, Toledo, Barcelona, Naples, Lisbon, Valencia, Seville, Granada

**The printing centres and their production from 1445-1500:**

more than 1300 publications — 500 to 1000 — less than 500

*In the sixteenth and seventeenth centuries, a publication is understood as the complete set of copies of a particular title printed from the same typographical composition.*

200 km

## The 'specialisms' of the major printing centres from 1445 to 1500

percentages of total publications for each centre

| | RELIGION | SCIENCES | LAW | HUMANITIES |
|---|---|---|---|---|
| STRASBOURG | 57 | 4 | 10 | 28 |
| MAINZ | 54 | 5 | 16 | 22 |
| BASLE | 56 | 2 | 16 | 26 |
| NUREMBERG | 56 | 6 | 10 | 27 |
| ANTWERP | 52 | 8 | 3 | 35 |
| AUGSBURG | 50 | 15 | 6 | 27 |
| FLORENCE | 50 | 3 | 1 | 45 |
| PARIS | 47 | 4 | 6 | 42 |
| LONDON | 42 | 3 | 9 | 42 |
| LYON | 38 | 6 | 12 | 43 |
| NAPLES | 26 | 7 | 18 | 42 |
| ROME | 32 | 7 | 22 | 42 |
| VENICE | 29 | 7 | 20 | 47 |
| MILAN | 23 | 4 | 26 | 47 |
| BOLOGNA | 15 | 10 | 30 | 45 |
| LEIPZIG | 26 | 10 | 7 | 57 |
| BRESCIA | 26 | 3 | 12 | 52 |
| SEVILLE | 30 | 4 | 12 | 52 |
| DEVENTER | 30 | 1 | 0 | 68 |
| Average: | 38 % | 6 % | 13 % | 42 % |

*From* J. M. LEENHARDT

Number of Publications

PARIS

LYON

300, 250, 200, 150, 100, 80, 70, 60, 50, 40, 30

1500 10 20 30 40 50 60 70 80 1590

**The printing production of Paris and Lyon in the sixteenth century**

*From* RENOUARD *and* BAUDRIER

**1468** Death of Gutenberg.

**1476** William Caxton at Westminster.

**1494** Aldus Manutius in Venice.

**1590** First printing shop in Japan.

**1476:** William Caxton begins printing from Westminster.
**1494:** First publications of Aldus Manutius in Venice.
**1501:** First book printed in italic by Aldus Manutius.
**1514–17:** Alcala de Henares's polyglot Bible.
**1522:** Publication at Wittenberg by Melchior Lotter of the first vernacular translation of the New Testament by Luther (with an exceptional print-run of 3,000 copies).
**1531:** Publication at Augsburg of Andrea Alciati's *Liber emblematum*, which fixes the iconographic repertoire employed by book illustrators.
**1539:** First printing shop set up in Mexico.
**1545:** First catalogue of condemned books, published at the instigation of the Sorbonne.
**1544–5:** First papal *Index* of books banned by the church. First printing shop in India.
**1559:** Christopher Plantin printer at Antwerp.
**1564:** Publication of the Council of Trent's *Index* by Paul Manuce at Rome.
**1564:** First general catalogue of books sold at the Frankfurt fair.
**1569–73:** Plantin's Polyglot or Royal Bible.

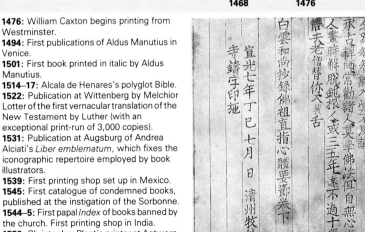

*5. Buddhist treatise printed using movable type, 1377,* Jik ji sim kyong.

**1584:** First printing shop in Peru.
**1588:** Introduction of printing to Macao.
**1590:** First printing shop in Japan.
**1592:** Publication of the papal Vulgate at Rome.

*6. Death and the bookseller. A* Danse macabre, *Lyons, 1499.*

# Renaissance Europe

The Renaissance was born in fourteenth-century Tuscany, came to maturity in the fifteenth century and, in the sixteenth, swept through the whole of Western Europe. Seen by contemporaries as a genuine revolution that would put an end to a thousand years of medieval barbarism and revive the splendours of classical antiquity, it was, first and foremost, a cultural and intellectual phenomenon. The key concept here is humanism. Strictly speaking, this referred only to the *studia humanitatis* (philology, languages, ancient literature), by opposition to medieval scholasticism. In this sense, the humanist was the person who studied the ancients in a new spirit free of dogmatic prejudices; the key features of that spirit were intellectual curiosity, sympathy, the free exercise of critical reason and the appreciation of human values (truth, beauty, glory) for their own sake. In the broad sense, humanism was a system of thought which put the human being in the centre of a universe designed for the greater glory of humanity. The view of the human being as a miserable creature, forever shackled by original sin, gave way to a vision of the free, autonomous, creative being, whose nature was innately good and whose faculties were unlimited. Thus, rather than being a specific philosophy, humanism was a method of working, a doctrine of life and a system of education. In the Graeco-Latin works, the humanist pursued a (moral, aesthetic and social) model of human perfection.

The search for ancient documents put forgotten texts within the reach of scholars. But it was not so much the quantity of ancient treasures that changed as the way they were regarded, the desire to become impregnated with them and identify with them. That divine spark which Pico della Mirandola discerned in every human being had to be brought out. This was the work of the educators of the Renaissance, who developed methods which are even today considered revolutionary, aimed at bringing about the blossoming of the intellectual, moral and physical capacities of the child. Men like Erasmus, Rabelais and Montaigne wrote scornfully of medieval education and sang the praises of the liberal arts of their day, and the humanist schools formed an élite that was small in number, but significant on account of its social position.

We find humanism again in the field which, more than any other, epitomizes the contribution of the Renaissance, the plastic arts. Every theme – even the religious – is treated in a human perspective. The artist imitates nature – for it is beautiful and good – and produces endless representations of the nude male and female forms, seen as the fruit of divine love rather than the miserable product of an original transgression. And in order to paint the human form as it is, or rather as the canon of human beauty requires it, all its aspects – anatomy, perspective, proportions and colour – are studied; where, in Leonardo, for example, does science end and art begin? Delivered from their association with architecture, the plastic arts claimed their autonomy and dignity: accordingly, the painter, who was now fully an artist, would sign his works and deal with princes as an equal.

This handful of heroes invented a social ideal: the *uomo universale*, the most developed representative of which was Leonardo. To those who had not been granted genius, the *Zeitgeist* of the century left a choice between financing the genius (without patrons there would have been no Renaissance) and apeing him, like that 'Courtier' of whom Castiglione demands all the virtues, except that of being a good Christian. But *virtù* is not virtue, and Machiavelli's 'Prince' has nothing of the contemplative about him. We must not forget that the Renaissance was also the crucible in which the modern state was forged (see below) and much blood was shed in the process.

1. *Antonello da Messina,* Annunciation.

**Birth of Petrarch.**

**1304**

**1304–74:** Petrarch, the father of Italian humanism.
**1348–53:** Boccaccio writes the *Decameron.*
**1396–7:** Manuel Chrysoloras, a Byzantine scholar, settles in Florence.
**1425:** Vittorino da Feltre founds his *Casa giocosa*, the celebrated humanist school.
**1440:** Cosimo de Medici founds the Platonic Academy.
**1449:** Lorenzo Valla, *Annotationes in Novum Testamentum.*
**1462–92:** Rule of Lorenzo the Magnificent. Peak of the Florentine Renaissance.
**1469:** Marsilio Ficino begins the translation of the Platonic *Dialogues.*
**1486:** Pico de la Mirandola, *De hominis dignitate.*
**1493:** Dürer, *Self-portrait.*
**1495:** Leonardo da Vinci, *The Last Supper.*
**1500:** The *Adagia* of Erasmus; Botticelli, *Mystic nativity.*
**1501:** Michelangelo, The *Pietà* in St Peter's.
**1504:** Michelangelo, *David.*
**1506:** Jimenez de Cisneros founds the University of Alcala de Henares.
**1507:** Dürer, *Adam and Eve.*
**1508:** Michelangelo begins the ceiling of the Sistine chapel.
**1510:** John Colet founds St Paul's School.
**1511:** Erasmus, *In Praise of Folly.*

2. *Façade of Santa Maria Novella.*

**1512:** Michelangelo, *Moses*. Lefèvre d'Étaples publishes his *Commentaries on the Epistles of St Paul.*
**1514–17:** Publication of the Complutensian Polyglot Bible.
**1515–17:** Ulrich von Hutten, *Letters of Obscure Men.*
**1516:** Machiavelli, *The Prince*; Thomas More, *Utopia*; Ariosto, *Orlando furioso*; Erasmus publishes the New Testament.
**1518:** Titian, *The Assumption.*
**1520:** Lefèvre d'Étaples joins the 'Meaux Circle'.
**1528:** Baldassarre Castiglione, *The Courtier.* Jean Clouet appointed painter to the king.
**1530:** Francis I founds the *Collège des lecteurs royaux.*
**1532–4:** Rabelais, *Pantagruel* and *Gargantua.*
**1541:** Michelangelo, *The Last Judgement*; Marot's *Psalms.*
**1543:** Copernicus, *De revolutionibus orbium coelestium*; Vesalius, *De corporis humani fabrica.*
**1549:** du Bellay, *Defense et illustration de la langue francaise.*
**1550:** Vasari's *Lives*, the first systematic history of art.
**1553–7:** du Bellay, *Antiquités de Rome.*
**1555:** Veronese, *The Coronation of the Virgin.*
**1559:** Amyot translates Plutarch's *Lives.*
**1561:** F. Guicciardini, *History of Italy.*
**1564:** Lescot finishes the façade of the Louvre. Delorme begins his Tuileries façade. Birth of Shakespeare.
**1566:** Bodin, *Methodus ad facilem historiarum cognitionem.*

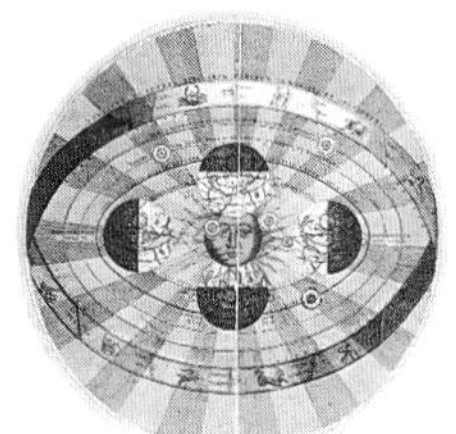

3. The solar system according to Copernicus, *by Andrea Cellarius.*

# 14th–16th centuries

Number of editions

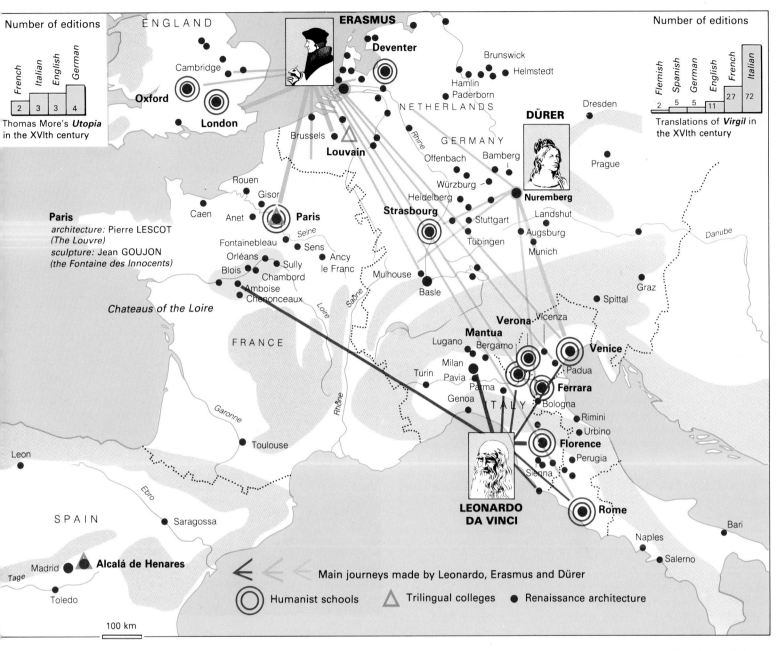

| French | Italian | English | German |
|---|---|---|---|
| 2 | 3 | 3 | 4 |

Thomas More's ***Utopia*** in the XVIth century

Number of editions

| Flemish | Spanish | German | English | French | Italian |
|---|---|---|---|---|---|
| 2 | 5 | 5 | 11 | 27 | 72 |

Translations of ***Virgil*** in the XVIth century

ENGLAND
Cambridge
**Oxford**
**London**
**ERASMUS**
**Deventer**
Brunswick
Helmstedt
Hamlin
Paderborn
NETHERLANDS
Dresden
**DÜRER**
Brussels
**Louvain**
Rhine
GERMANY
Offenbach
Bamberg
Prague
Würzburg
Rouen
Gisor
Heidelberg
**Nuremberg**
Caen
Anet
**Paris**
**Strasbourg**
Landshut
Stuttgart
Augsburg
Tübingen
Munich
Danube

**Paris**
*architecture:* Pierre LESCOT
*(The Louvre)*
*sculpture:* Jean GOUJON
*(the Fontaine des Innocents)*

Fontainebleau
Seine
Sens
Orléans
Ancy le Franc
Sully
Blois
Chambord
Amboise
Chenonceaux
Mulhouse
Basle
Graz
Saône
Loire
Spittal
*Chateaus of the Loire*
Verona
Vicenza
Mantua
FRANCE
Lugano
Bergamo
**Venice**
Milan
Padua
Turin
Pavia
Parma
**Ferrara**
Genoa
ITALY
Bologna
Garonne
Rhône
Rimini
Urbino
**Florence**
Toulouse
Perugia
Leon
Sienna
Ebro
**LEONARDO DA VINCI**
**Rome**
SPAIN
Saragossa
Bari
Naples
Salerno
Madrid
**Alcalá de Henares**
Tage
Toledo

Main journeys made by Leonardo, Erasmus and Dürer
Humanist schools
Trilingual colleges
Renaissance architecture

100 km

| 1452 | 1475 | 1516 | 1564 | 1580 |
|---|---|---|---|---|
| **Birth of Leonardo da Vinci.** | **Birth of Michelangelo.** | **Machiavelli, *The Prince*; Thomas More, *Utopia*.** | **Birth of Galileo.** | **Montaigne and Tasso.** |

4. *Domenico Ghirlandaio,* Four Italian humanists*: Ficino, Landino, Politian and Gentile de'Becchi.*

*5. A manuscript by Francis I and Henry II's Greek copyist, Ange Vergèce, who inspired the French expression 'to write like an angel'.*

**1567:** Bruegel the Elder, *The Land of Cockaigne.*
**1572:** Ronsard, *La Franciade.*
**1576:** Bodin, *Six livres de la République.*
**1580:** Montaigne's *Essays*; Tasso, *Jerusalem Delivered.*

*6.* The anatomist Vesalius *by Pierre Poncet.*

# The Empires: Machiavelli and the Modern State

It was in the later Middle Ages that the modern state was born, out of the ruins of the imperial concept of a universal, double-headed *Respublica christiana* and of feudalism. First France and England – nations which had emerged fully armed from the Hundred Years' War – then Spain – unified morally by the Reconquista and politically by the will of the Catholic monarchs – emerged at the end of the fifteenth century as 'new monarchies'. That is to say, they were solid political entities based upon a broad national consensus with a suitably centralized political system, in which the king's authority over his subjects knew no bounds other than those dictated by custom, morality and religion, and where the only limits to external action were set by the extent of a state's power. Royal absolutism – de jure in Valois France and Hapsburg Spain and de facto in Tudor England – made the prince an 'emperor within his own kingdom' and a 'power' outside it.

Two great political entities did not reach this stage of development. These were the Holy Roman Empire and Italy. The former was a mosaic of principalities, bishoprics and free cities, kept in balance by a constitution which reduced the (elected) emperor to the role of a president-mediator without royal power. For the latter, even this theoretical unifying factor was absent. *Italianità* was powerless to unify a peninsula torn apart by the intense rivalry that existed among the five 'powers' – Venice, Milan, Florence, the Papal States and the Kingdom of Naples – and their satellites. All these states, not to mention the smaller ones, spied on and fought each other, negotiated, made and unmade military coalitions and volatile political alliances. It is easy to understand why Italy was the diplomatic school of the modern age and the laboratory in which *raison d'état*, that cynical ideology, born essentially of impotence, was forged. One can also easily understand why Italy became the major bone of contention between the great national monarchies – and also the battlefield on which they fought out their rivalries. The Angevin heritage of Charles VIII and the Milanese claims of Louis XII dragged France down into the Italian quagmire. Francis I's crushing defeat of the Swiss at Marignano left the French and the Spaniards alone in the field. Four years later Charles V united the Aragon heritage (Naples) with the imperial heritage (Milan). From that point on, the houses of Hapsburg and Valois were engaged in a fight to the death, which finally laid to rest the fiction of Christian unity. Between Charles V's imperial dream and France's desire to break out of Hapsburg encirclement, nothing – not even the Turkish threat – could produce grounds for compromise. Charles V's victories ultimately led nowhere. In the end the Protestant counter-offensive, his inability to bring France to its

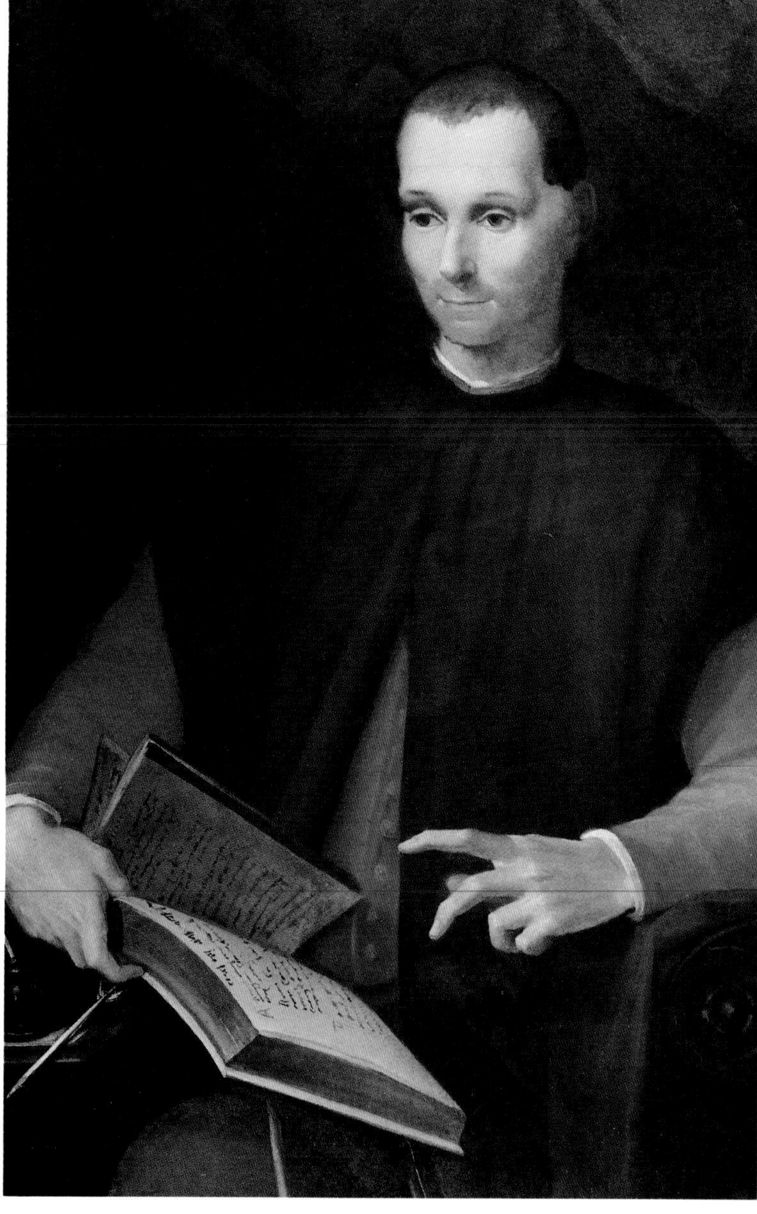

1. Niccolo Machiavelli, *by Rosso Fiorentino.*

**Fall of Constantinople and end of the Hundred Years' War.** **Accession of Francis I.** **Cateau-Cambré**

**1453** **1515** **1559**

**1453:** End of the Hundred Years' War.
**1454:** The Peace of Lodi establishes a balance of power in Italy that lasts until 1494.
**1469:** Marriage of Ferdinand of Aragon to Isabella of Castile.
**1477:** Battle of Nancy. Louis XI defeats Charles the Bold and annexes the Duchy of Burgundy.
**1481:** Annexation of Provence by the French crown.
**1485:** End of the Wars of the Roses: the Tudor, Henry VII, becomes king of England.
**1491:** The marriage of Charles VIII to Anne of Brittany lays the ground for the annexation of the Duchy (1532).
**1494:** Conquest of Naples by Charles VIII of France.
**1499:** Independence of the Swiss cantons.
**1499–1500:** Louis XII takes the Duchy of Milan.
**1504:** Ferdinand of Aragon retakes possession of the Kingdom of Naples.
**1509:** Louis XII wins a victory over the Venetians at Agnadello.
**1511:** The Holy League formed by Pope Julius II, Spain, Venice and the Swiss cantons; later joined by the Emperor and Henry VIII.
**1513:** French defeats at the Battle of the Spurs and Novara; Louis XII withdraws from the Duchy of Milan.
**1515:** Marignano: Switzerland institutes a policy of neutrality.
**1516:** The Bologna Concordat offers the King of France the effective leadership of the Gallican church.
**1519:** Charles V, King of Spain since 1516, is elected emperor.
**1520–2:** Abortive revolt of the *comuneros* in Spain.
**1522:** Imperial victory at Bicocca. France loses Milan.
**1523:** Confiscation of the domains of the Duke of Bourbon, Constable of France.
**1525:** Battle of Pavia. Francis I taken prisoner by Charles V.
**1526:** Treaty of Madrid, which Francis I denounces after his release.
**1526–9:** Holy League of Cognac, which unites Pope Clement VII, Francis I, Milan, Florence and Genoa; second war against France.
**1527:** Sack of Rome by the Lutheran mercenaries of Charles V.
**1529:** Peace of Cambrai (*Paix des Dames*); first Turkish siege of Vienna.
**1535:** Charles V's campaign against Barbarossa; capture of Tunis.
**1536:** Franco-Ottoman alliance and third war.
**1538:** Truce of Nice between Charles V and Francis I.
**1542–4:** Fourth war between Charles V and Francis I.
**1544:** Peace of Crespy: Francis I surrenders his claim to Naples.
**1547:** Death of Francis I. Henry II king of France.
**1552:** Treaty of Chambord. In exchange for the Three Bishoprics (Metz, Toul, Verdun), Henry II of France promises assistance to Maurice of Saxony against Charles V.
**1552–6:** Charles V attempts in vain to recapture the Three Bishoprics.
**1554:** Marriage of Philip II to Mary Tudor; Mary of Guise becomes Scottish regent.
**1556:** Abdication of Charles V. Ferdinand II Emperor. Philip II King of Spain.
**1557:** Spanish victory at St Quentin, where Coligny commanded the French troops.
**1558:** Death of Charles V.
**1559:** Treaty of Cateau-Cambrésis. Death of Henry II. Regency of Catherine de Medici.

3. Elizabeth I of England, *by Zuccaro.*

knees and serious financial problems exhausted the knight-emperor. The rickety Augsburg compromise (see below) set the seal upon his failure. His abdication and the partition of the Empire ensured that Spanish interests would predominate. In 1557 bankruptcy and the acute nature of the religious problem led the weakened belligerents to the negotiating table. At Cateau-Cambrésis, France gave up its

2. Catholic monarchs, Ferdinand of Aragon and Isabella of Castile.

unrealistic Italian ambitions but kept Burgundy. The treaty reflected the drifting of the political centre of gravity towards the West; it opened up a half-century of 'Spanish preponderance', enshrined the lasting decline of Germany and Italy and marked the rise of the great centralized states.

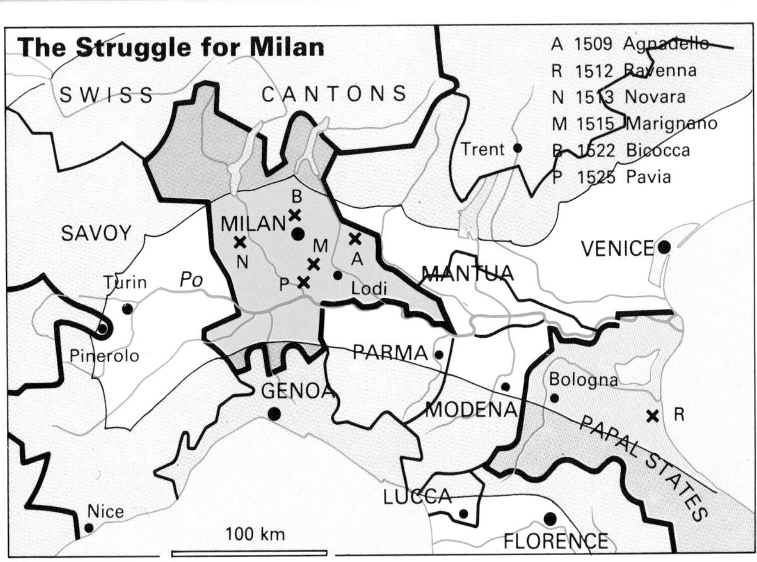


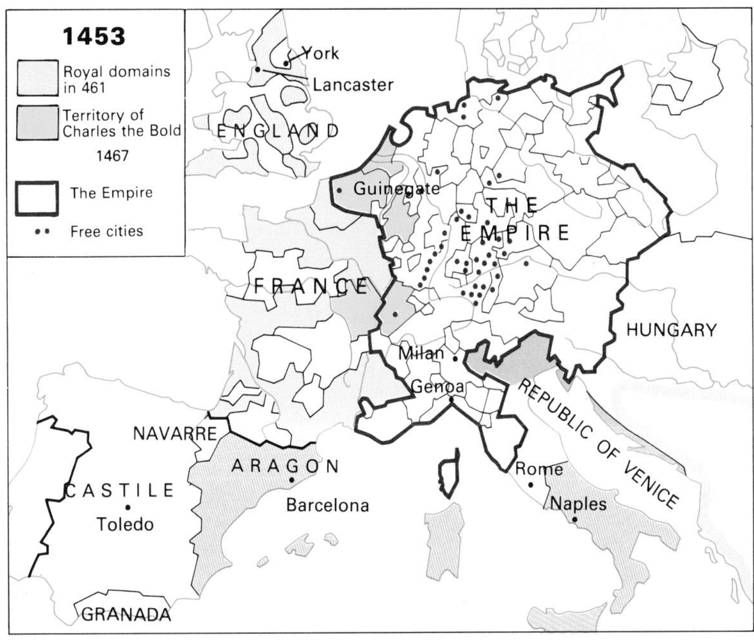


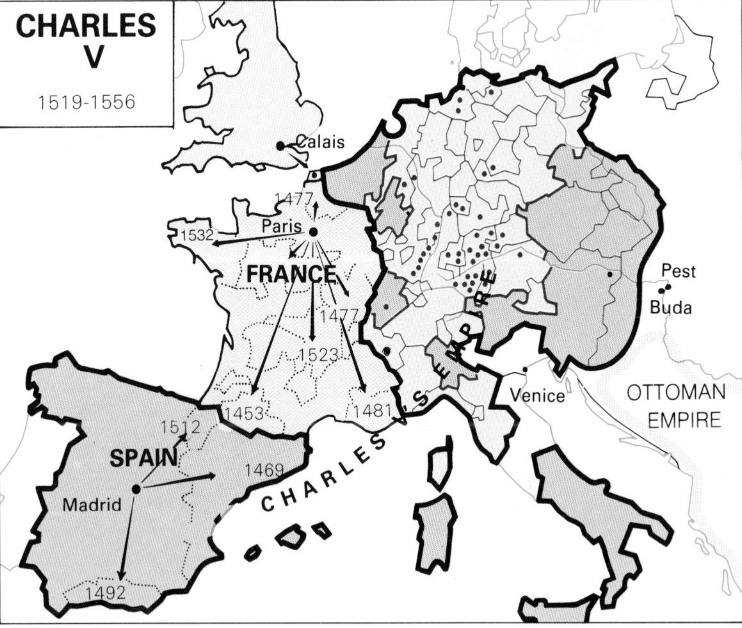

# The Protestant Reformation

AT THE TIME when Luther stood out against Rome, the 'seamless robe' of the Christian West had already been damaged by the long crisis that affected both the church and the faith of the declining Middle Ages, by the 'new monarchs' and by the critique of the humanists, but it was still entire. A generation later it was in shreds. The revolt of this Augustinian monk against the church's abuses (indulgences etc.) and the solution he found to the agonizing problem of his own personal salvation (the omnipotence of Grace, justification by faith alone, the revelation of the Word by Scripture in a church constituted by the community of the faithful, who are all equal in the sight of God) found favourable conditions in a Germany that was disunited, eager for reforms, riven by rivalries between princes and by social tensions and increasingly impatient with Rome's tutelage. A fraction of the lower and middle clergy, humanists, a good proportion of the nobility and the urban bourgeoisie rallied to the movement. Luther offered the towns the means to rid themselves of a rich, idle and detested clergy; to the princes he offered a power that they would at last no longer have to share; to everyone, his was a simple, national, intelligible faith, drawn from Gospel sources. Those whom the revolutionary implications of the Lutheran message might have troubled were reassured by the reformer's reaction to the Peasants' War and subsequently to revolutionary Anabaptism as it manifested itself in Munster in 1534. From the popular movement that it initially seemed to be, the German Reformation became socially and politically conservative, an instrument of state and royal control. On the reformer's death, three-quarters of Germany, fifty-one cities of the Empire out of sixty-five, the Scandinavian countries, Prussia, the Baltic states and Finland were of the Lutheran confession. In a different socio-policital context and under the rule of men of a different sensibility, who in some respects were closer to Erasmus than to Luther – Zwingli in Zurich, Bucer in Strasbourg and, most importantly, Calvin in Geneva – the Reformation established itself in the towns of Upper Germany and Switzerland. From there, it spread to France, the Netherlands, Scotland, England, Bohemia, Poland and Hungary. After some difficult beginnings, the Reformation had become solidly established in Geneva and, from 1541 onwards, Calvin set about turning that city into a theocratic republic. At the same time he directed the French Reformation from afar, imposing doctrinal cohesion and a set method of pastoral training upon it.

It was England which engaged upon the most original Reformation. This was made possible, as on the Continent, by a long hostility to Rome and by the work the lay intellectuals in the great universities had done to undermine the church and its teachings. But it had its immediate origin in a problem that was legal rather than theological, namely the matrimonial difficulties of Henry VIII. The English Reformation stemmed from the King's decision to be divorced, whatever the obstacles. Once he had become 'supreme head of the Church of England', Henry VIII silenced the Catholic opposition and suppressed the monasteries, but the English church was, nonetheless, only 'Anglican' in the way that the French church was 'Gallican'. All that was missing was the pope. After the reign of the Catholic Mary, the pendulum swung back wildly, producing the Elizabethan compromise of an Anglican Church that was Catholic in appearance but Calvinist in inspiration.

The unique character of the English case should not obscure the general truth: the Reformation became established in those places where the secular power wanted it. Luther understood that perfectly, as did the Pope and the Catholic princes, who did all they could to block the Protestant advance. There would indeed be a Catholic Reformation, but there would also be a half-century of religious wars.

1. Martin Luther.

2. Melanchthon, painted by Cranach.

3. Calvin.

4. Zwingli, painted by Hans Asper.

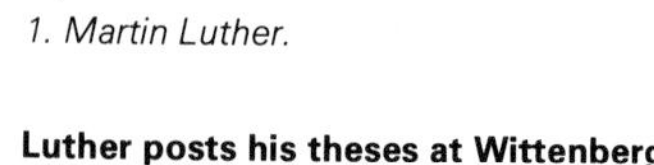

**Luther posts his theses at Wittenberg.** — **1517**

**Luther translates the Bible.** — **1522**

**Peasants' War.** — **1525**

Gottes wort bleibt ewig.

Biblia/das ist/die gantze Heilige Schrifft Deudsch.
Mart. Luth.
Wittemberg.
Begnadet mit Kürfurstlicher zu Sachsen freiheit.
Gedruckt durch Hans Lufft.
M. D. XXXIIII.

5. Martin Luther's rendering of the Bible, 1534 edition.

**1517:** Luther's 95 theses at Wittenberg.
**1519:** The Leipzig disputation with the theologian Johann Eck.
**1520:** Papal bull, *Exsurge domine*. Luther, who is condemned and ordered to retract, burns the bull in public; his three famous treatises: *An den christischen Adel deutscher Nation* (To the Christian nobility of the German nation), *Von der babylonischen Gefangenschaft der Kirche* (On the Babylonian captivity of the Church) and *Von der Freiheit eines Christenmenschen* (On the liberty of the Christian).
**1521:** Diet of Worms. Luther is placed under the imperial ban and is given refuge at Wartburg Castle. Melanchthon, *Loci communes*, the first work of Lutheran theology; an anti-Lutheran pamphlet earned Henry VIII the title 'Defender of the faith'.
**1522:** Luther's German Bible. Rising of the imperial knights led by Hutten and Sickingen: agitation of the (Carlstadt) radicals at Wittenberg, defeated by Luther.
**1523:** Zwingli establishes the Reformation in Zurich: the movement spreads to Basle (Oecolampadius), Berne and then Strasbourg (Bucer).
**1524:** Erasmus, *De libero arbitro*.

6. Leo X flanked by two cardinals, painted by Raphael.

**1525:** Luther, *De servo arbitro*; the Peasants' War; Luther's violent pamphlet, *Wider die mördischen und räubischen Rotten der Bauern* (Against the murderous and thieving peasant bands); defeat of the peasants at Frankenhausen and death of Münzer; bloody repression encouraged by Luther. Grand Master Albert of Prussia secularizes the state of the Teutonic Knights and transforms it into a secular duchy: birth of Prussia.
**1526:** Luther lays down the form of the German communion service; the ecclesiastical organization of the electoral Duchy of Saxony becomes the model for the Lutheran churches.
**1527:** Founding of the first Protestant university at Marburg, followed by Königsberg (1544) and Jena (1588); Riksdag of Vesteras: Gustavus Vasa introduces the Reformation into Sweden.
**1529:** The Marburg Colloquy between Luther and Zwingli runs into difficulties over the problem of the communion: fall of the cardinal-legate Wolsey in England.
**1531:** Death of Zwingli in the Battle of Kappel. Bucer presses for union with the Lutherans. Bullinger opposes this move.

# 1517–1566

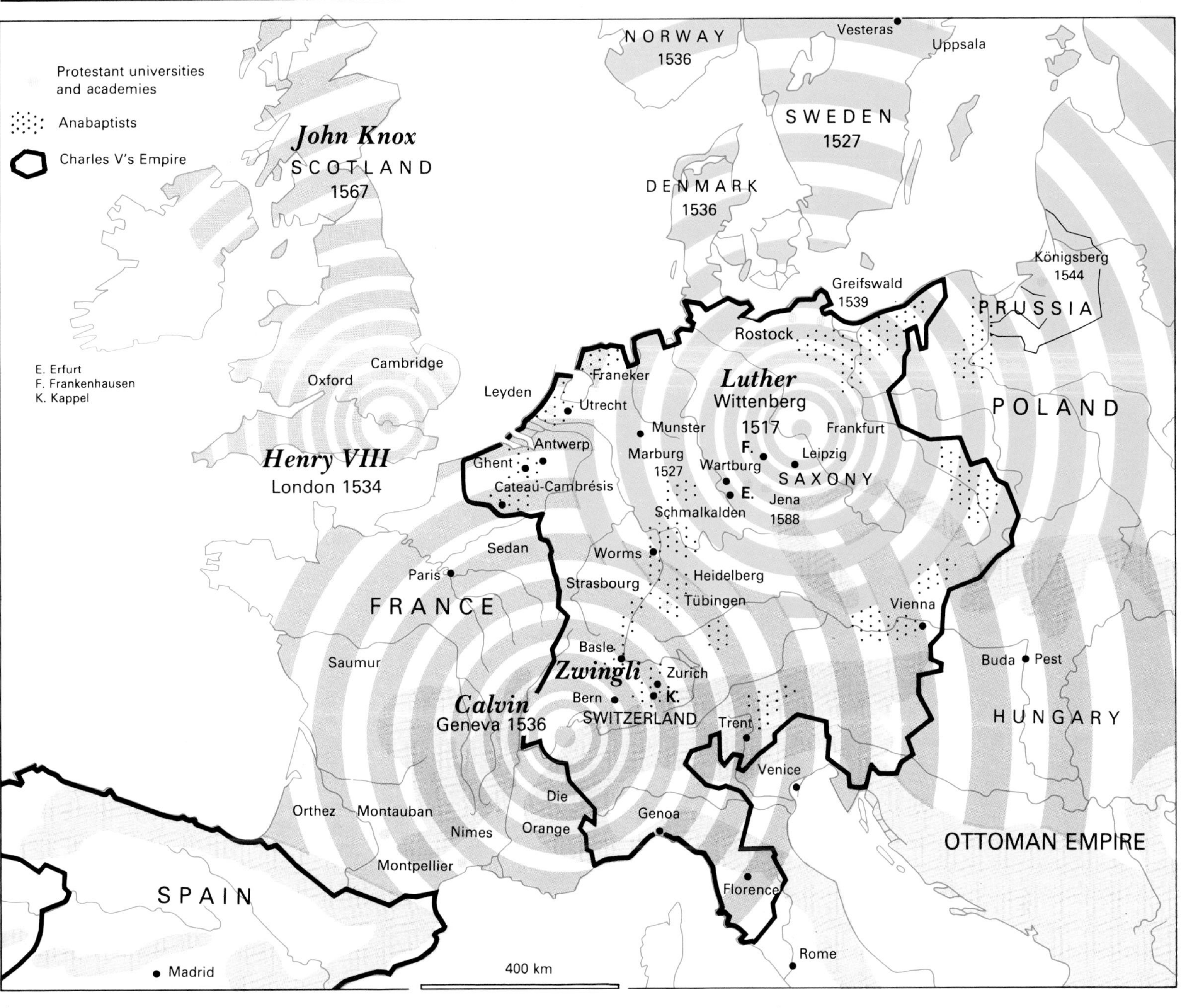


**y VIII founds the Anglican Church.** **1534**

**Calvin at Geneva.** **1541**

**Michael Servetus is burnt at Geneva.** **1553**

*7.* The Peasants' War, *by David Vinckboons.*

*8.* Henry VIII, *by Hans Holbein the Younger.*

**1533:** Divorce of Henry VIII, who marries Anne Boleyn.
**1534:** Henry VIII supreme head of Church of England; the millenarianist kingdom of Johann Matthiesen and John of Leyden at Munster.
**1535:** Execution of Thomas More.
**1536:** Christian III introduces Lutheranism into Denmark and Norway; Calvin publishes *Institutio religionis christianae.*
**1541:** Calvin, French translation of *Institutio.*
**1547:** Death of Henry VIII; in the name of the minor, Edward VI, Cranmer gives the Anglican Church a resolutely Protestant direction.
**1549:** *The Book of Common Prayer.*
**1553:** Execution for heresy of Michael Servetus at Geneva.
**1556:** Execution of Cranmer during the Catholic reaction of Mary Tudor.
**1559:** Academy of Geneva; Elizabeth I's restoration of Anglicanism; first national synod of the reformed churches of France in Paris.
**1560:** Establishment of the Scottish Presbyterian Church, which in 1567 became the established state church.
**1563:** The '39 Articles' of the Church of England.
**1566:** The Synod of Antwerp founds the Calvinist Church of the Netherlands.

# The Counter-Reformation and the Wars of Religion

1. The Holy League in Procession.

THE TERM COUNTER-REFORMATION is an ambiguous one. The nineteenth-century liberal historians who coined it saw the actions of the papacy and Catholic princes as nothing more than an obscurantist reaction to that deeply portentous event, the Protestant Reformation. Incomplete as the view of those historians may have been, it would be wrong to seek to deny this aspect of the phenomenon. There were indeed desperate attempts to arrest the advance of Protestantism and, as far as possible, to win back lost ground. At the local level, this was a matter for the princes, who were the natural defenders of the faith. The first round was fought in Germany, where twenty years of war between Charles V and the Lutheran princes of the Protestant League ended in the compromise of Augsburg: *cuius regio, eius religio* – the ruler alone was to determine the religion of his subjects. This spelled the end of the concept of the universal empire, and it set the seal on the definitive division of the Christian West. The maelstrom then shifted westwards, to France and the Low Countries. The accidental death of that great persecutor of heretics, Henry II, initiated a long power struggle which resurrected the fortunes of the noble families and fostered the development of politico-religious 'parties'. The militarization of the Huguenots after the peace of Cateau-Cambrésis, the crown's devious policies, the rivalry between Catholic Guises and Protestant Bourbons, popular fanaticism and the ambition of faction leaders were all features of the backdrop to the 'Wars of Religion'. In the Low Countries, religious strife also took on a nationalist dimension, since the Calvinist cause became indistinguishable from the struggle for independence. Everywhere extremism and violence were generated by the weakness of central authority and by ancient enmities (dynastic, feudal and social), exacerbated ideologically by religious passions. Increasingly from the end of the 1560s, the battle was fought out on an international stage. Coalitions were formed with French and Dutch Calvinists supported by England on the one side and Catholic French Leaguers and Spain on the other. Philip II's grand design had been to put Mary, Queen of Scots, on the English throne and a Spanish puppet on the throne of France, to reconquer the Low Countries and thus put an end once and for all to heresy. His ambitions foundered with the Spanish Armada. Henry IV finally triumphed over the League and France was to remain Catholic. By the Edict of Nantes, however, for the first time in the Christian West, a religious minority was accorded a place within the national community. This marked a first victory for religious toleration – though admittedly one that was dictated by overwhelming practical considerations. Moreover, even Alexander Farnese, with all his military and diplomatic skills, was unable to restore to the bosom of Spain the seven northern provinces of the Low Countries which had acquired independence under the leadership of Holland.

In the meantime, the church pursued its own reforms. These began in Spain and Italy, scenes of a remarkable Catholic renaissance, and continued under the aegis of the papacy, which armed itself with the instruments of reconquest – the Inquisition, reconstituted on the Spanish model, and, most particularly, those formidable soldiers of the faith, the Jesuits. At the same time, the church was, at the Council of Trent, undertaking the immense task of doctrinal clarification and ecclesiastical reform which left an indelible mark on modern Catholicism. Rome can by no means be said to have succeeded in 'rooting out heresy', but the combined effects of armed action, propaganda, religious art, education and a less corrupt church with a more responsible clergy, made it possible to avoid the worst deviations, and prepared the way for the great Catholic revival of the 'Century of Saints'.

**Birth of Ignatius Loyola.** **Foundation of the Society of Jesus.** **Beginning of the French Wars of Religi**

**1491** **1534** **1562**

2. Ignatius of Loyola, by H. P. Seghers.

**1524–5:** Foundation of the Theatine, Capucin and Ursuline religious orders.
**1526:** *The Spiritual Exercises* of Ignatius Loyola.
**1531:** The Protestants of the Empire form the Schmalkaldic League.
**1534:** Loyola founds the Society of Jesus.
**1540:** Paul III confirms the new order.
**1542:** Roman Inquisition introduced on the Spanish model.
**1545:** First session of the Council of Trent.
**1548:** Charles V imposes the Interim of Augsburg on the Protestants.
**1555:** The Peace of Augsburg.
**1559:** The Peace of Cateau-Cambrésis: death of Henry II; accession of Francis II to the French throne; government by the Guise family.
**1560:** Conspiracy of Amboise; accession of Charles IX to French throne; regency of Catherine de Medici.
**1561:** Colloquy of Poissy; failure of Michel de l'Hospital's policy of conciliation.
**1562:** Massacre of Wassy; beginning of the Wars of Religion.
**1563:** Assassination of Francois, Duc de Guise; Edict of Amboise; dissolution of the Council of Trent.

3. Saint Bartholomew's Day, Nuremberg print.

# 1524–1635

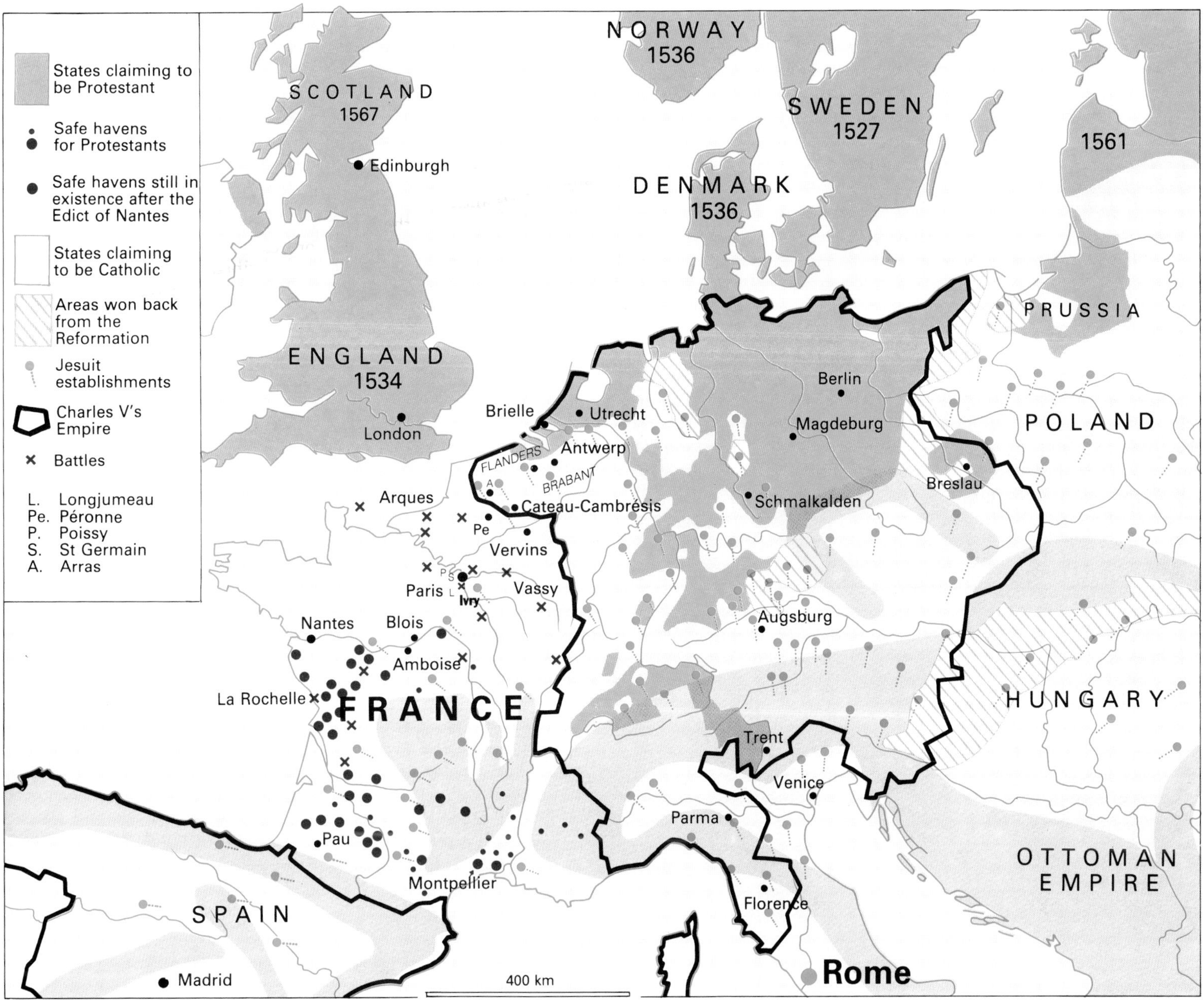

States claiming to be Protestant

Safe havens for Protestants

Safe havens still in existence after the Edict of Nantes

States claiming to be Catholic

Areas won back from the Reformation

Jesuit establishments

Charles V's Empire

× Battles

L. Longjumeau
Pe. Péronne
P. Poissy
S. St Germain
A. Arras

NORWAY 1536 · SCOTLAND 1567 · SWEDEN 1527 · 1561 · DENMARK 1536 · ENGLAND 1534 · PRUSSIA · POLAND · HUNGARY · OTTOMAN EMPIRE · FRANCE · SPAIN · FLANDERS · BRABANT

Edinburgh · London · Brielle · Utrecht · Antwerp · Berlin · Magdeburg · Breslau · Arques · Cateau-Cambrésis · Schmalkalden · Pe · Vervins · Paris · Ivry · Vassy · Augsburg · Nantes · Blois · Amboise · La Rochelle · Trent · Venice · Parma · Pau · Montpellier · Florence · Madrid · Rome

400 km

| …acre of St Bartholomew's Day. | Union of Utrecht. | Edict of Nantes. | Trial of Galileo. |
|---|---|---|---|
| 1572 | 1579 | 1598 | 1633 |

**1564:** Publication of *Index* of works forbidden by the Holy Office.
**1565:** Protestation of the Dutch nobles (dismissed as 'beggars' by Berlaymont).
**1567:** Military dictatorship ('Council of Blood') by Duke of Alva in the Netherlands.
**1568:** Execution of the Counts of Egmont and Hoorn; treaty of Longjumeau; departure of Michel de l'Hospital.
**1570:** Peace of St Germain, favourable to Huguenots.
**1572:** St Bartholomew's Day Massacre; the 'Sea Beggars' take Brill in Zeeland.
**1573;** Publication in Geneva of Francois Hotman's *Franco-Gallia.*
**1574:** Death of Charles IX; accession of Henry III to French throne.
**1576:** The 'Peace of Monsieur'; formation of the first Catholic League at Péronne; the 'pacification' of Ghent; Union of the seventeen provinces against Spain; Philip Neri founds the Congregation of the Oratory in Italy.
**1578:** The Union of Arras returns the southern provinces of the Low Countries to Spain.
**1579:** Union of Utrecht concluded among the northern provinces.
**1581:** Declaration of independence by the Union of Utrecht.
**1582:** Reform of the calendar by Gregory XIII.
**1584:** Assassination of William of Orange; constitution of the United Provinces; Alexander Farnese, Prince of Parma, becomes governor of the Low Countries in the name of Philip II and occupies Flanders and Brabant.
**1585:** Fall of Antwerp to the Spanish; formation of the second Catholic League in Paris.
**1588:** 'Day of Barricades' in Paris; the Estates General meet in Blois; assassination of Duc de Guise and Cardinal de Guise; defeat of the Spanish Armada.
**1589:** Death of Catherine de Medici; assassination of Henry III.
**1590:** Battle of Ivry; Henry IV besieges Paris; new edition of the Vulgate produced in Rome.
**1593:** Meeting of Estates General in Paris dominated by the Catholic Holy League; conversion of Henry IV to Catholicism.
**1594:** Henry IV enters Paris; *Menippean Satire*; execution of the regicide Jean Chatel and expulsion of the Jesuits.
**1598:** Edict of Nantes; Peace of Vervins; death of Philip II.
**1603:** *Introduction to the Devout Life* by St Francis of Sales.
**1609:** Twelve-year truce between Spain and the United Provinces.
**1627:** Company of the Holy Sacrament founded.
**1632:** Galileo's *Dialogue Concerning the Two Chief World Systems, Ptolemaic and Copernican.*

*4. A hanging in Brabant, 1570.*

*5. The golds and blacks of the Gesu church (Giacomo della Porta).*

# Philip II's Spain: The Golden Age

In 1556 the son of Charles V inherited the western half of his father's immense empire. This reserved, hard-working and conscientious man, a home-loving bureaucrat and a fervent Catholic, the master of Spain during the half-century in which Castilian power was at its height, had great ambitions and, it seemed, the means to realize them. Thanks to a tentacular bureaucracy, his empire was as centralized as possible; Spain had been spared religious troubles and, since the failed revolt of the *Comuneros* of Castile, the kingdom had been peaceful. His troops, the redoubtable *tercios*, were reputed to be the best in the world, and the flow of American money was apparently inexhaustible.

During the first half of his reign Philip fought in the Mediterranean against the forces of Islam. Then, when he had removed the Turkish threat at Lepanto, he turned his attentions to the Atlantic, where he opposed the Protestants. The annexing of Portugal and its empire in 1580 marked the high point of his power. This was the period of Philip's 'Grand Design' (see above, p. 152). He dreamt of establishing his domination over a Catholic West from which heresy would be forever banished. So great was the power of Spain and so magnificent its civilization – one thinks of the Christian humanism of a Francisco de Vitoria, the neo-Thomism of Suarez and Molina, the mystical spirituality of Theresa of Avila and of St John of the Cross, but also of *Don Quixote* and *Amadis de Gaul* – that there were very few at the time, apart perhaps from the Venetian ambassador (who portrayed the misery of the Spanish people) or Jean Bodin (1530–1596, French philosopher and economist, who described the dependence of the kingdom on French manufactured goods), who recognized it as a colossus with feet of clay. The fact was that Philip II's Spain was a poor, badly unified country, which produced very little, had to import almost everything, including corn, and whose trade was in the hands of foreign merchants. Its political and military power was artificially preserved by the flow of American ingots. The Reconquista had left the Spaniards with a *hidalgo* mentality (whereby they scorned trade and manual labour), archaic and rigid social structures, and an ardent and exclusive religious faith. The final collapse of Philip's 'Grand Design' was a logical consequence of the country's economy and demography and the outcome of his European war was disastrous: not only did he not succeed in taking France and England, but he also lost the rich 'Low Countries'.

After the peace of Vervins and the death of the King, the decline accelerated. The expulsion of the Moriscoes (Muslims theoretically converted to Catholicism), the great plagues of the beginning and middle of the century and emigration decimated the population and completed the ruin of the economy. The international position of Spain felt the consequences of this. Under mediocre sovereigns and ambitious ministers – Lerma and then Olivares – Spain engaged in ill-fated wars against Holland and France, had to recognize the de jure independence of the former and cede areas of its territory (Roussillon, Artois, Franche-Comté) to the latter. Incapable of internal reform, Spain remained on the margins of Europe's expansion and its imperial power did not usher in capitalism. It would not, for example, occur to the twentieth-century French historian Fernand Braudel, when writing a history of the Mediterranean in the seventeenth century, to include the names of Philip III, Philip IV or, even less, Charles II. All the same, literature and art suffered hardly at all from this decadence; the Spanish 'Golden Age' was still a glowing reality even when the glory of Spanish military deeds had become but a pale memory. The plays of Lope de Vega and Calderon, and the paintings of El Greco, Murillo and Velazquez bear witness to this.

*1. Don John of Austria, champion of Christendom: the Battle of Lepanto definitively ended the Turkish threat to the West.*

**Theresa of Avila, *The Castle of the Soul.*** **1577**

**El Greco, *The Burial of the Count Orgaz.*** **1586**

**Cervantes, *Don Quixote.*** **1605**

**1556:** Philip II becomes king of Spain.
**1556–9:** War against France (see p. 148).
**1557:** Beginning of building of Escorial: bankruptcy.
**1559:** Treaty of Cateau-Cambrésis (see p. 148).
**1568:** St John of the Cross founds the order of the Descalzos or Barefoot Carmelites; mysterious death of Philip's son Don Carlos.
**1568–71:** Revolt of the Moriscoes of Granada.
**1571:** Victory at Lepanto over the Ottoman fleet.
**1575:** Bankruptcy.
**1577:** St Theresa of Avila, *The Castle of the Soul.*
**1579:** El Greco, *Trinity.*
**1580:** Annexation of Portugal. El Greco, *Adoration.*
**1581:** Act of Abjuration: Dutch states reject Philip's claim to sovereignty.
**1584:** Alliance with the Guises and the Leaguers. Alexander Farnese takes Ghent. Completion of the Escorial. Cervantes, *Numancia.*

*3. American treasures flood into Spain but do not remain there: the port of Seville in the 16th century.*

**1586:** El Greco, *The Burial of the Count Orgaz.*
**1587:** Francis Drake raids Cadiz.
**1588:** Wreck of the Invincible Armada. Molina, *Liberi arbitrii cum gratiae donis, divina praescentia, providentia, praedestinatione et reprobatione, concordia.*
**1593:** Molina, *De justitia et jure.*
**1595:** War against France.
**1596:** An English fleet destroys Cadiz. Bankruptcy.
**1597:** Francisco Suarez, *Disputationes metaphysicae.*
**1598:** Peace of Vervins. Death of Philip II. Philip III abandons the management of national affairs to the Count of Lerma. Lope de Vega, *Arcadia, La Dragontea.*
**1605–16:** Cervantes, *Don Quixote.*
**1608:** High point of trade between Seville and America.
**1609–14:** Expulsion of the Moriscoes.
**1612:** Francisco Suarez, *De legibus.*
**1613:** Cervantes, *Novelas exemplares.*
**1618:** Velazquez, *Old Woman (frying eggs).*
**1621:** Philip IV King of Spain. Olivares initiates an ambitious foreign policy.

# 16th–17th centuries

2. *The king of all Spain at the height of his power. Portrait of Philip II by Antonio Moro.*

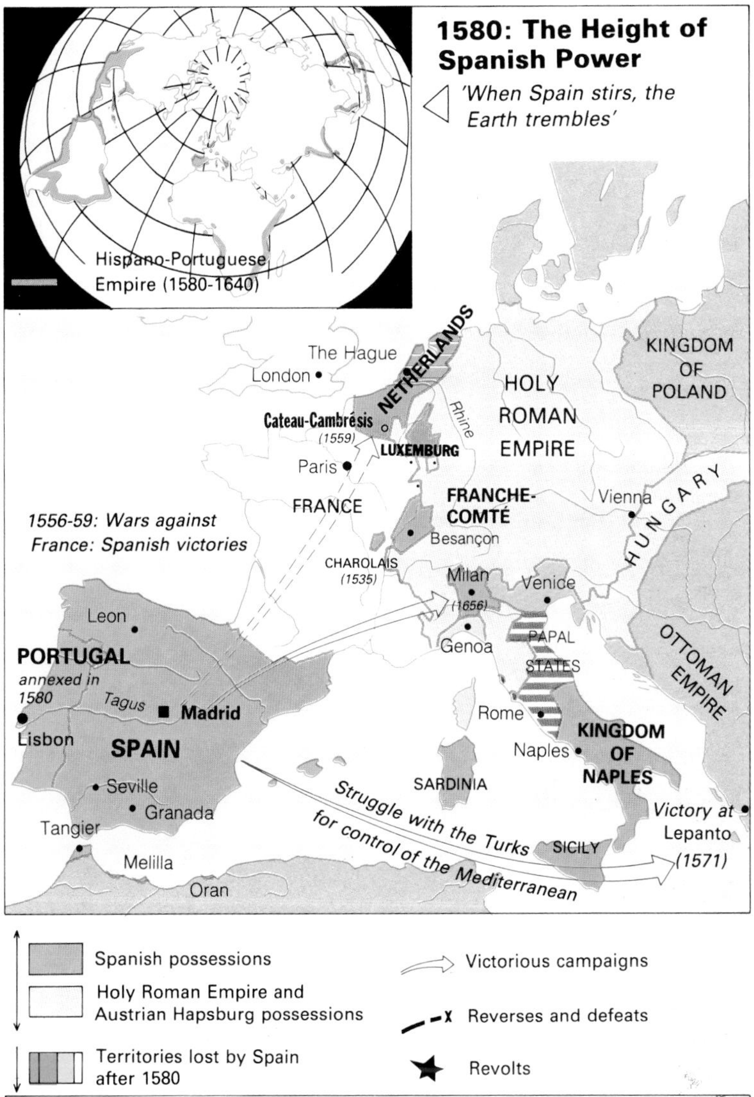

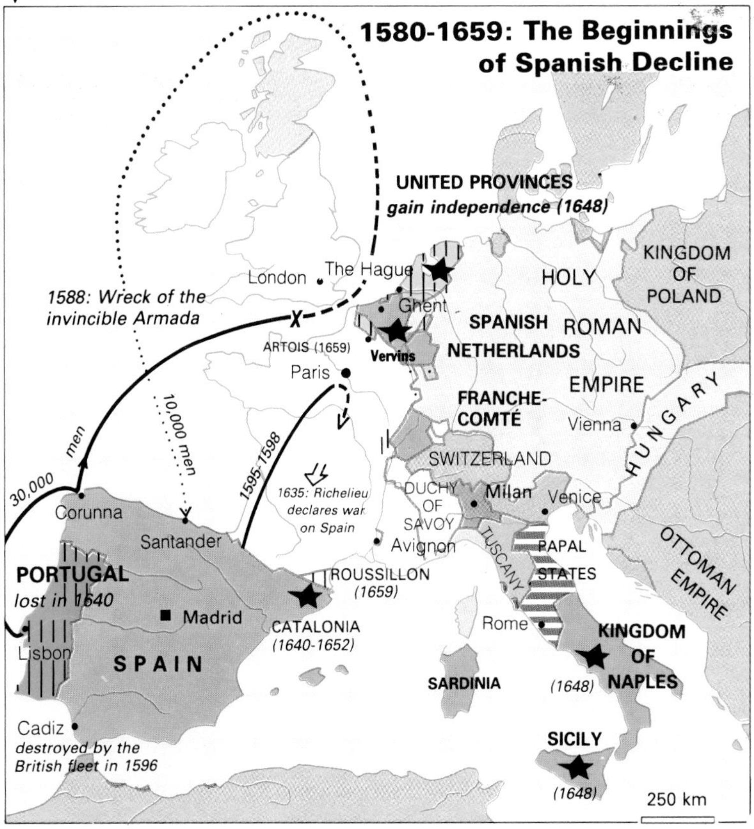

**lderon, *La Vida es Sueño.*** **Velazquez, *Las Meninas.***

**1631** **1656**

EL INGENIOSO
HIDALGO DON QVI-
XOTE DE LA MANCHA,
*Compuesto por Miguel de Ceruantes Saauedra.*
DIRIGIDO AL DVQVE DE BEIAR,
Marques de Gibraleon, Conde de Benalcaçar, y Bañares, Vizconde de la Puebla de Alcozer, Señor de las villas de Capilla, Curiel, y Burguillos.
Año, 1605.
CON PRIVILEGIO,
EN MADRID, Por Iuan de la Cuesta.
Vendese en casa de Francisco de Robles, librero del Rey nuestro señor.

4. *First edition of* Don Quixote.

**1628:** War against the United Provinces recommences. Zurbaran, *Saint Serapian.*
**1631:** Calderon, *La Vida es Sueño.*
**1632:** Lope de Vega, *La Dorotea.*
**1635:** Calderon, *El Médico de sa honra.* Zurbaran, *The Painter before Christ Crucified.* Richelieu declares war on Spain.
**1636:** Taking of Corbie (near Amiens) by Spain.
**1640:** Spain loses Portugal.
**1643:** Lope de Vega, *El castigo sin venganza.*
**1647–52:** Plague kills half a million. Revolt of Naples.
**1647:** Velazquez, *The Surrender of Breda.*
**1648:** End of the Thirty Years War. *De jure* recognition of the independence of the Netherlands.
**1656:** Murillo, *Vision of St Anthony.* Velazquez, *Las Meninas* (The Maids of Honour).
**1657:** Velazquez, *Las Hilanderas* (The Spinners).
**1659:** Peace of the Pyrenees.

## 1580: The Height of Spanish Power

*'When Spain stirs, the Earth trembles'*

Hispano-Portuguese Empire (1580-1640)

The Hague · London · NETHERLANDS · Cateau-Cambrésis (1559) · LUXEMBURG · Rhine · HOLY ROMAN EMPIRE · KINGDOM OF POLAND · Paris · FRANCE · FRANCHE-COMTÉ · Besançon · Vienna · HUNGARY · CHAROLAIS (1535) · Milan (1656) · Venice · Genoa · PAPAL STATES · OTTOMAN EMPIRE · Rome · Naples · KINGDOM OF NAPLES · SARDINIA · SICILY · Leon · PORTUGAL *annexed in 1580* · Tagus · Madrid · Lisbon · SPAIN · Seville · Granada · Tangier · Melilla · Oran

*1556-59: Wars against France: Spanish victories*

*Struggle with the Turks for control of the Mediterranean*

*Victory at Lepanto (1571)*

Spanish possessions
Holy Roman Empire and Austrian Hapsburg possessions
Territories lost by Spain after 1580
Victorious campaigns
Reverses and defeats
Revolts

## 1580-1659: The Beginnings of Spanish Decline

**UNITED PROVINCES** *gain independence (1648)*

London · The Hague · Ghent · ARTOIS (1659) · Vervins · SPANISH NETHERLANDS · HOLY ROMAN EMPIRE · KINGDOM OF POLAND · Paris · FRANCHE-COMTÉ · Vienna · HUNGARY · SWITZERLAND · DUCHY OF SAVOY · Milan · Venice · Avignon · TUSCANY · PAPAL STATES · OTTOMAN EMPIRE · Rome · KINGDOM OF NAPLES (1648) · SARDINIA · SICILY (1648) · Corunna · Santander · ROUSSILLON (1659) · CATALONIA (1640-1652) · PORTUGAL *lost in 1640* · Lisbon · Madrid · SPAIN

*1588: Wreck of the invincible Armada*

30,000 men · 10,000 men · 1595-1598

*1635: Richelieu declares war on Spain*

Cadiz *destroyed by the British fleet in 1596*

250 km

# England: Towards a Bourgeois Monarchy

THE FIRST TUDOR, Henry VII, had put an end to the civil wars. His son Henry VIII succeeded, at the height of the humanist Renaissance and the Lutheran Reformation, in asserting the national, independent character of the English throne. Drawn, whether by concern for a son and heir or by kingly ambition, into a crisis over Rome's refusal of his divorce, he in his turn rejected Rome and proclaimed himself head of the Church of England. There followed a long period of instability. Edward VI, who favoured the Reformation priests, was succeeded by a 'Spanish-style' Catholic reaction under Mary Tudor.

After 1558, Elizabeth I ended the uncertainty. Consolidating the Acts of Supremacy and Uniformity, in the face of the (foreign) 'Papists' and the (rebel) Puritans, she imposed a national religion, later to be called 'Anglican'. This was a compromise between Protestant dogmatism and episcopal discipline and hierarchy, which was based on two documents, the 'Thirty-nine Articles' and the Book of Common Prayer. By manipulating her parliament, the Queen 'allowed' her Franco-Scottish rival Mary Stuart to be executed. She also profited greatly from the catastrophic failure of the Spanish Armada (1588). The forty-five-year-long 'Elizabethan Era' consolidated the English national identity by opening it up to influences from the four corners of the earth. It was also a period of great cultural Renaissance in which Shakespeare stands out as the leading figure.

1. William and Mary crushing tyranny, painted by J. Thornhill.

The year 1603 does not simply mark a change of dynasty. The explicit absolutism of the Stuart, James I, and the financial disorder he created, exasperated both the gentry and the city bourgeois, who were the masters of the Commons, 'God's elect', and therefore men with a vocation to govern. In the great city of London, the word on everyone's lips was 'reform'. Under Charles I, this pressure mounted, and Parliament demanded the power to share in decision-making. Its Petition of Right was punished by eleven years of tyranny in which both crown and bishop joined forces. The failure of the attempt to extend Anglicanism to Calvinist Scotland unleashed revolution in 1640. The key word was now 'revolt'. Under great financial pressure, the King accepted the Remonstrances of the Parliament, which voted to 'extirpate' the bishops and the prerogative courts. Censorship ceased, in practice, to exist. The revolt of the Catholics in Ulster and the violation of the immunity of the Commons provoked civil war. When the 'New Model Army' of the independent parliamentarian Cromwell had crushed the Royalists in 1645, freedom seemed won. Equality, however, was not. 'Leveller' fever ran rife in the towns and among the soldiery. Once Cromwell had purged his ranks of this radicalism, the rest of Parliament judged the King and condemned him to death for having violated the political contract. After the proclamation of the republic, the City found itself in favour (Navigation Act) with the result that from 1653 on it affirmed the personal power of the Lord Protector of the Commonwealth. After his death, there were two years of great upheaval, following which Charles II, the executed king's son, returned from exile.

In a framework of economic vitality, with both dissidents and Papists removed from the scene, the Restoration saw sharply opposed Whig and Tory administrations exchanging power. It also, paradoxically, saw the introduction of the law of *Habeas Corpus*. But the Catholic James II had learnt nothing. He was to be put to flight by a revolution made by the Whigs and spoken of as 'Glorious' (1688). His son-in-law, Stathouder of Holland, and his daughter were crowned monarchs on the basis of a contract by which the king was to be controlled 'in Parliament'.

**Thomas More, *Utopia.***

**1516**

**1485:** End of the Wars of the Roses. Tudor Age begins.
**1517:** Luther's 95 theses produce resonances in Britain.
**1527:** Beginning of the controversy surrounding Henry VIII's divorce from Catherine of Aragon.
**1533:** Excommunication of Henry VIII.
**1534:** Act of Supremacy: King becomes head of the Church of England.
**1535:** Execution of the Catholic humanist Thomas More.
**1536–9:** Dissolution of the monasteries: creation of a nobility based on wealth who were loyal to the state.
**1559:** Act of Uniformity: Elizabeth I head of the episcopal hierarchy of the new Church of England.
**1563:** The Thirty-Nine Articles: faith and order.
**1577:** Francis Drake sets off to circumnavigate the earth.
**1587:** Mary Stuart executed.
**1588:** The 'miraculous failure' of the 'invincible' Spanish Armada.
**c. 1590:** Beginning of Shakespeare's magnificent *oeuvre.*
**1600:** East India Company granted its charter.
**1603:** Beginning of reign of Stuart dynasty (which will end in 1714): uniting of English and Scottish crowns.
**1605:** Failure of the (Catholic) Gunpowder Plot.
**1611:** Authorized version of the Bible.
**1620:** Pilgrim Fathers sail for America.
**1628:** Parliament's Petition of Right.
**1638:** Revolt of Scotland to defend its religious freedom.
**1640:** Long Parliament meets.
**1641:** Execution of the minister Strafford and the Grand Remonstrance.
**1642:** Civil War. Charles I leaves London.
**1644:** Milton's *Areopagitica*: for the freedom of the press.
**1645:** Cromwell's victory over the Royalists at Naseby.
**1647:** Organization of the egalitarian movement, the Levellers.
**1649:** Trial and execution of the King. Republic. Diggers phenomenon (rural socialism). Cromwell crushes Ireland.

**The Thirty-Nine Articles**

**1563**

2. Charles I is beheaded.

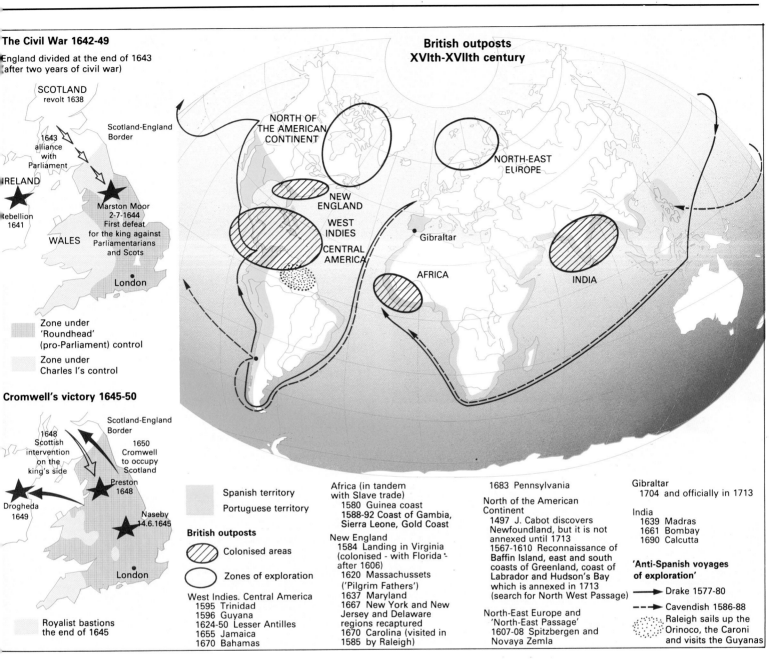

# 1485–1713

## The Civil War 1642-49

England divided at the end of 1643 (after two years of civil war)

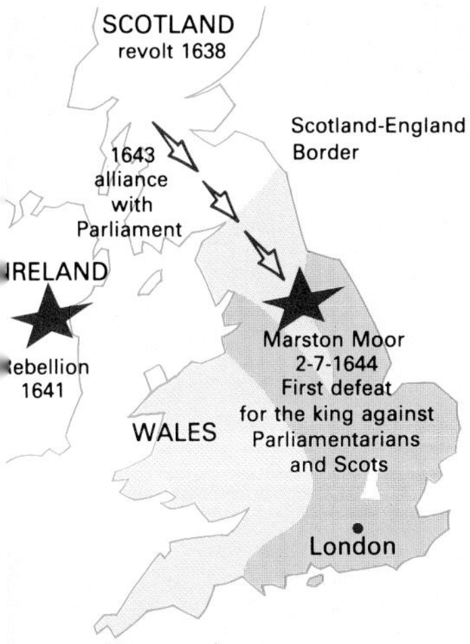

SCOTLAND revolt 1638

1643 alliance with Parliament

Scotland-England Border

IRELAND

Rebellion 1641

Marston Moor 2-7-1644 First defeat for the king against Parliamentarians and Scots

WALES

London

Zone under 'Roundhead' (pro-Parliament) control

Zone under Charles I's control

## Cromwell's victory 1645-50

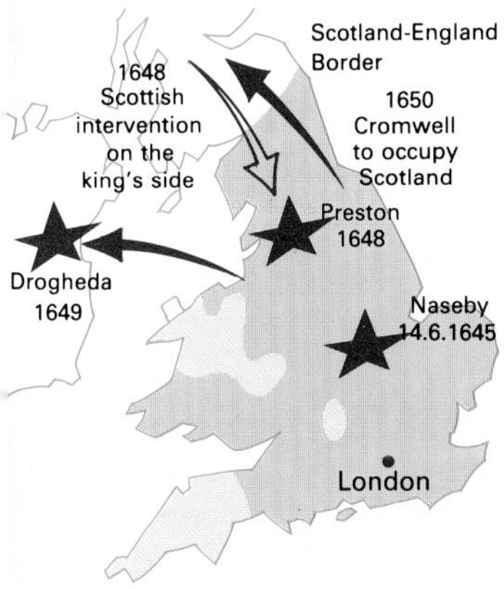

1648 Scottish intervention on the king's side

Scotland-England Border

1650 Cromwell to occupy Scotland

Preston 1648

Drogheda 1649

Naseby 14.6.1645

London

Royalist bastions the end of 1645

## British outposts XVIth-XVIIth century

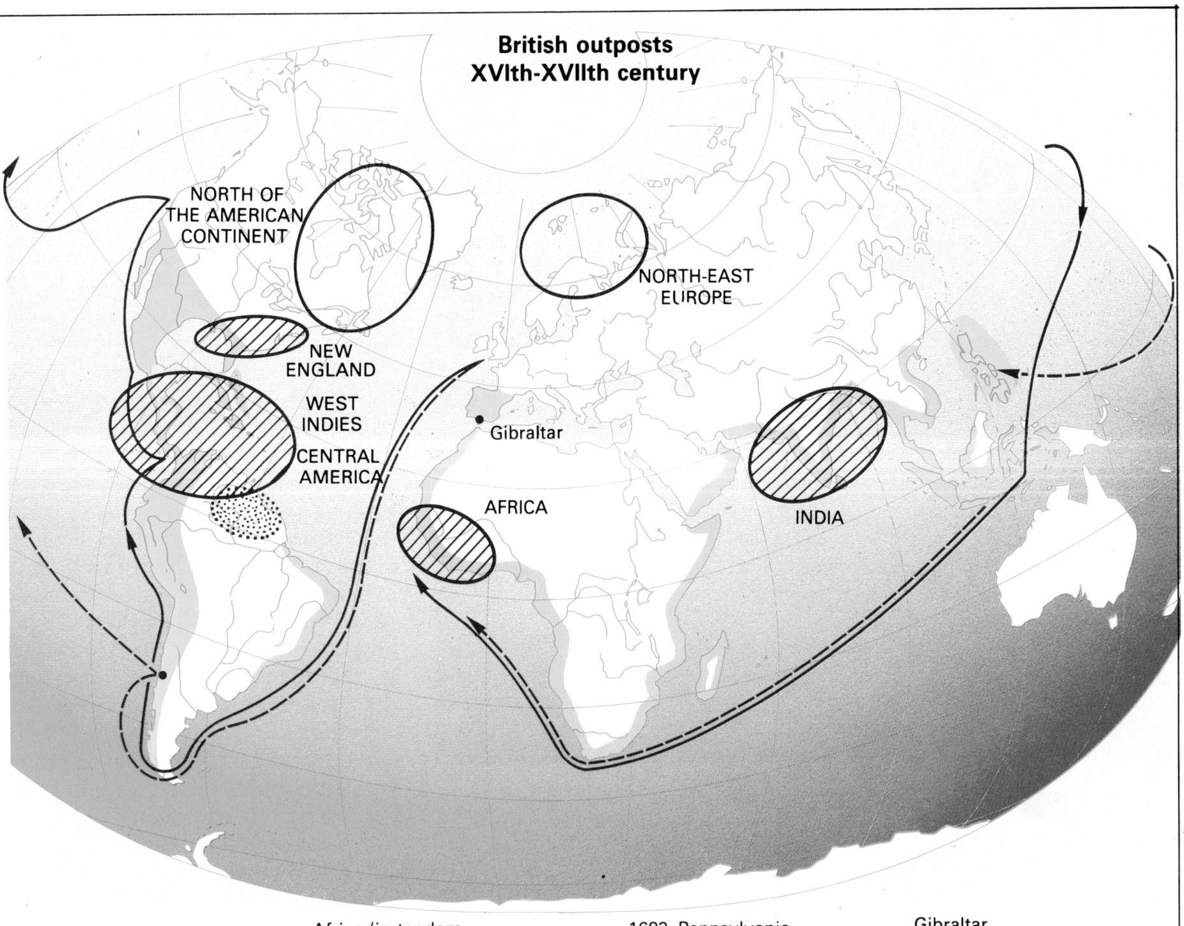

NORTH OF THE AMERICAN CONTINENT

NORTH-EAST EUROPE

NEW ENGLAND

WEST INDIES

CENTRAL AMERICA

Gibraltar

AFRICA

INDIA

Spanish territory

Portuguese territory

**British outposts**

Colonised areas

Zones of exploration

West Indies. Central America
1595 Trinidad
1596 Guyana
1624-50 Lesser Antilles
1655 Jamaica
1670 Bahamas

Africa (in tandem with Slave trade)
1580 Guinea coast
1588-92 Coast of Gambia, Sierra Leone, Gold Coast

New England
1584 Landing in Virginia (colonised - with Florida - after 1606)
1620 Massachussets ('Pilgrim Fathers')
1637 Maryland
1667 New York and New Jersey and Delaware regions recaptured
1670 Carolina (visited in 1585 by Raleigh)

1683 Pennsylvania

North of the American Continent
1497 J. Cabot discovers Newfoundland, but it is not annexed until 1713
1567-1610 Reconnaissance of Baffin Island, east and south coasts of Greenland, coast of Labrador and Hudson's Bay which is annexed in 1713 (search for North West Passage)

North-East Europe and 'North-East Passage'
1607-08 Spitzbergen and Novaya Zemla

Gibraltar
1704 and officially in 1713

India
1639 Madras
1661 Bombay
1690 Calcutta

**'Anti-Spanish voyages of exploration'**

Drake 1577-80

Cavendish 1586-88

Raleigh sails up the Orinoco, the Caroni and visits the Guyanas

**King James Bible.** 1611

**Death of Shakespeare.** 1616

**Charles I executed.** 1649

**Death of Locke.** 1704

**1651:** Navigation Act: Cromwell the 'City's man'. Hobbes: *Leviathan.*
**1653–8:** Cromwell Lord Protector. Personal rule.
**1660:** General Monk restores the monarchy (Charles II).
**1661–5:** Anti-Puritan Restoration (Clarendon Code).
**1665–7:** War with Holland. Acquisition of New York.

3. *Cromwell Lord Protector. Portrait attributed to G. de Crayer.* 4. *The Royal Exchange, London.*

**1666:** Great Fire of London. Reconstruction under the guidance of Christopher Wren.
**1673:** Test Act: confirmed exclusion of Catholics.
**1679:** *Habeas Corpus.*
**1687:** Newton formulates his theory of universal attraction.
**1688:** Birth of a Catholic heir to the throne. Appeal to William of Orange. James II flees to France.
**1689:** Bill of Rights accepted by William and Mary. Act of Religious Toleration (did not include Catholics).
**1690:** Locke, *Treatise on Civil Government*, a justification of 1688.
**1694:** Bank of England. End of censorship.
**1701:** Act of Settlement: Catholics excluded from the throne.
**1707:** Act of Union between England and Scotland.
**1713:** Treaties of Utrecht: Britain henceforth the major maritime and colonial power.

# Contemporary Revolutions

*1. The orator Genuino haranguing the mob during the revolt in Naples, led by Masaniello, 1657.*

WHAT HAD THE various disturbances of the middle years of the seventeenth century in common, if not 'the mood of giddiness which prevailed at the time'? (Voltaire). To this we should add Vauban's equally famous observation, 'There is nothing which stirs and angers the people more than food shortages and the cost of bread.' In Europe, these 'stirrings', both urban and rural, like those in Andalusia in 1652, caused by hunger or, to be more exact, by the fear of hunger, tended to remain circumscribed. But in China, the catastrophic droughts which began in 1627 shook and eventually overturned the power of the Ming dynasty (1644) and paved the way for the Manchurian invasions.

Most uprisings against central government were anti-fiscal in character. Thus, for example, in Russia the common townspeople (*posadskie*), particularly in Moscow, rose in revolt (1648), and this led to the drafting of a new code of law (*Sobornoe Ulozhenie*); the representative assembly, the *Zemski Sobor*, was not summoned after 1653. In England, Charles I's attempts at absolutism encountered the fierce opposition of the Independents, who took full advantage of the general hostility to ship-money (a levy intended to finance the building of warships). The conflict between France and the nebulous Hapsburgs meant an increase in fiscal pressure and imprisonment for debts, and this added to the state of tension in the country. Mazarin was reputed to have put in irons 25,000 prisoners for non-payment of the taille (the major direct tax) and of this large number 6,000 died of starvation in the prisons. In many cases the rebels' justification was the defence of traditional liberties (long-established privileges, representative assemblies). The *Va-nu-pieds* (literally 'those who go barefooted') of Normandy wanted to preserve their right of *quart-bouillon* (a salt tax paid at a lower rate than the standard *gabelle*). The leaders of the 'secret diet of peasants' in Lucerne (Christmas 1652) dressed themselves symbolically in the old costume of the Swiss confederates. Prudently, the revolutionaries claimed to respect legitimate authority; the *croquants* (a group of French peasants) intended to take their taxes directly to the king in the Louvre palace (1637). Cries of 'Long live the King!' punctuated the most unruly outbreaks; Stenka Razin called on the Cossacks to march against the 'enemies of the Tsar'. The antipathy to centralization was fuelled by regionalist and nationalist feeling. The agents of authority were regarded as outsiders. During the Fronde revolt, the fact that the chief minister (Mazarin) was a foreigner was exploited to the full. The rebellion in Naples (1647) was helped by the anti-Spanish sentiments of the nobility, epitomized by Generalissimo Marco Antonio Brancaccio (1570–1650). In 1668 the Sardinian nobility, taking advantage of the War of Devolution, tried to set their island on an anti-fiscal and autonomous adventure. The only successful revolt was that of Portugal, where the long tradition of nationalist feeling kept resistance going until Spain was forced to concede defeat (1 December 1640–January 1668). The Cortes (national assembly) of Catalonia was persuaded to offer sovereignty over the country to Louis XIII (23 January 1641). The Cossack insurrection led by Bogdan Chmielnicki (1648), which began as a defence of ancient privileges, changed into a nationalist movement against the Poles and ended with the Zaporozhians putting themselves under the protection of the Tsar of Moscow.

In the early days of colonialism, anti-colonial uprisings were rare: the people of Ulster, driven from their lands by the Plantations of 1607–11, revolted in October 1641. Cromwell, who in 1637 had been refused permission to emigrate to New England, led the repression. This was a prelude to the confiscation and colonization of land by the British, effectively keeping the Irish confined in Connaught.

**Masaniello's revolt in Naples.** **Barricades in Paris.**

**1647** **1648**

**1637:** Revolt against Shogun by 40,000 Christian peasants in Nagasaki region.
**1 June:** *les croquants* (peasant revolutionaries) crushed at La Sauvetat.
**July–November 1639:** Revolt of the *Va-nu-pieds* (lit. 'those who go barefooted') in Normandy.
**7 June 1640:** Viceroy of Catalonia murdered in Barcelona by insurgents disguised as harvesters (*segadores*).
**22 October 1641:** Irish rebellion in Ulster. Institution by Puritans in January 1642 of public national fast on last Wednesday of each month for duration of revolt.
**1642:** Refusal by parishes of Val d'Aran, led by their priests, to pay taxes to King of France.
**22 August:** Charles I's standard raised at Nottingham.
**1644:** Taking of Peking by Li Zicheng: suicide of last Ming emperor.
**2 July:** Battle of Marston Moor.
**1647:** Disturbances in Seville.
**19 May:** Uprising in Palermo to cries of *'Fuera gabelle. Viva il re e muora il mal governo.'* (Down with the salt tax. Long live the King and death to bad government.)

**7 July:** Insurrection in Naples. Masaniello killed 16 July but struggle continued by partisans until February 1648 against Spanish troops of viceroy Arcos and fleet of Don John of Austria. Republic proclaimed 23 October 1647.
**1648:** Riots in Moscow. Insurrections in Ukraine (1648–54).
**26 August:** Barricades in Paris following arrest of Broussel (a leader of the Parlement).
**9 February 1649:** Execution of Charles I.
**11 September:** Population of Drogheda massacred by Cromwell's army.
**1650:** Riots in Pskov and Novgorod.
**12 January 1651:** Following death (on 6 November 1650) of William II of Nassau, sovereignty of individual Dutch provinces declared at The Hague by general assembly of the seven provinces.
**21 May 1653:** Bern besieged by peasant army of 16,000 men: army defeated on 8 June at Herzogenburg.

*3. A fight between peasants and soldiers, as seen by Gallais.*

# 1630–70

*2. Soldiers pillaging a farm. France, 17th century.*

| 1658 | 1670 | 1671 |
|---|---|---|
| **Death of Cromwell.** | **Spinoza's *Tractus Theologico-politicus.*** | **Execution of Stenka Razin in Moscow.** |

**1658:** Cossack revolt.
**April–August:** Revolt of the *sabotiers* (clog-makers) of the Sologne.
**May–July:** Revolt of the Lustucrus in the Boulogne region put down on 11 July at Hucqueliers.
**28 May 1668:** Assassination of Marquis of Camarassa, viceroy of Sardinia.
**24 June1670:** Capture of Astrakhan by Stenka Razin.
**15 June 1671:** Execution in Cagliari of Marquis of Cea, leader of Sardinian conspiracy.
**20 August 1672:** John and Cornelius de Witt assassinated at The Hague.

*4. 'We are right to rebel' – engraving from the period of the Fronde.*

# Thirty Years of European Wars

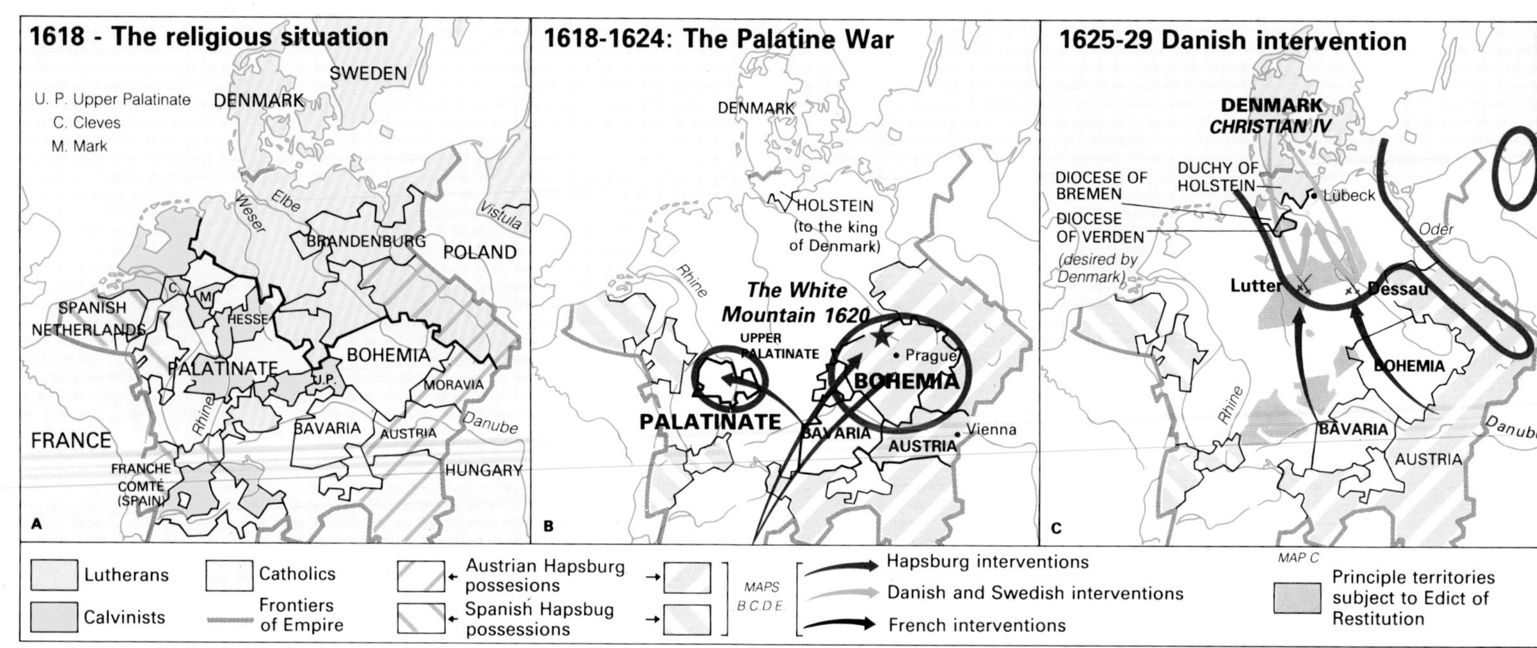


Bohemia, an elective monarchy, was not subject to the principle, *cuius regio, eius religio*. Protected by the Letter of Majesty (1609), which guaranteed freedom of worship, the Utraquists, exploiting an aristocratic reaction against the Hapsburgs on the death of the Emperor Matthias (1619), prompted the inauguration of a *Confederation Bohemica*, and appealed to the leader of the Evangelical Union, Frederick V the Elector Palatine. After the Battle of the White Mountain, the states of Bohemia and Moravia capitulated. The Letter of Majesty was torn to shreds by the public executioner. The Elector Palatine was placed under the imperial ban, his possessions were confiscated and his electoral dignity was transferred to his Bavarian cousin. On the death of the Archduke Albert (1621), the Netherlands became once again a group of Spanish provinces. When the twelve-year truce ended, hostilities recommenced between Spain and the United Provinces: the latter gradually conquered the 'Generality Lands' and won independence.

After the Peace of Augsburg (1555) the Lutherans retained possession of the secularized church property. But the Ecclesiastical Reservation prevented bishops who abandoned Catholicism from conserving their temporal power. In the north of the Empire this clause was often violated, a provisional administrator of the temporal power occupying the vacant episcopal seat until such time as it could be

*1. The Plague at Ashdod, by Nicolas Poussin, 1630.*

**Battle of the White Mountain.** **Wallenstein leader of Empire's armies.** **Nicolas Poussin, *The Plague at Ashd***

**1620** **1625** **1630**

*3. Battle at Prague, 16 September 1620. German engraving.*

**23 May 1618:** Defenestration of Prague.
**4 November 1619:** Frederick V crowned King of Bohemia.
**3 July 1620:** At Ulm, the Protestants undertake not to intervene in the Bohemian war; the Catholics agree to respect the Elector Palatine's states.
**8 November:** Protestants defeated at the Battle of the White Mountain.
**14 May 1621:** Evangelical Union disbands at Heilbronn.
**August:** War between Spain and United Provinces recommences.
**5 March 1626:** Treaty of Monzon: Spanish troops evacuate the Valtelline, whose inhabitants are forced to pay tribute to their old rulers, the Grisons.
**17 January 1628:** Charles I of Gonzaga, Duke of Nevers, takes possession of Mantua, his cousin Vincent II having died on 26 December 1627.
**6 March 1629:** Edict of Restitution.
**22 May:** By the Treaty of Lübeck, Christian IV of Denmark renounces his claims to bishoprics within the Empire.

*4. Count Wallenstein, leader of the imperial mercenaries. A. van Dyck, c. 1630.*

# 1618–48

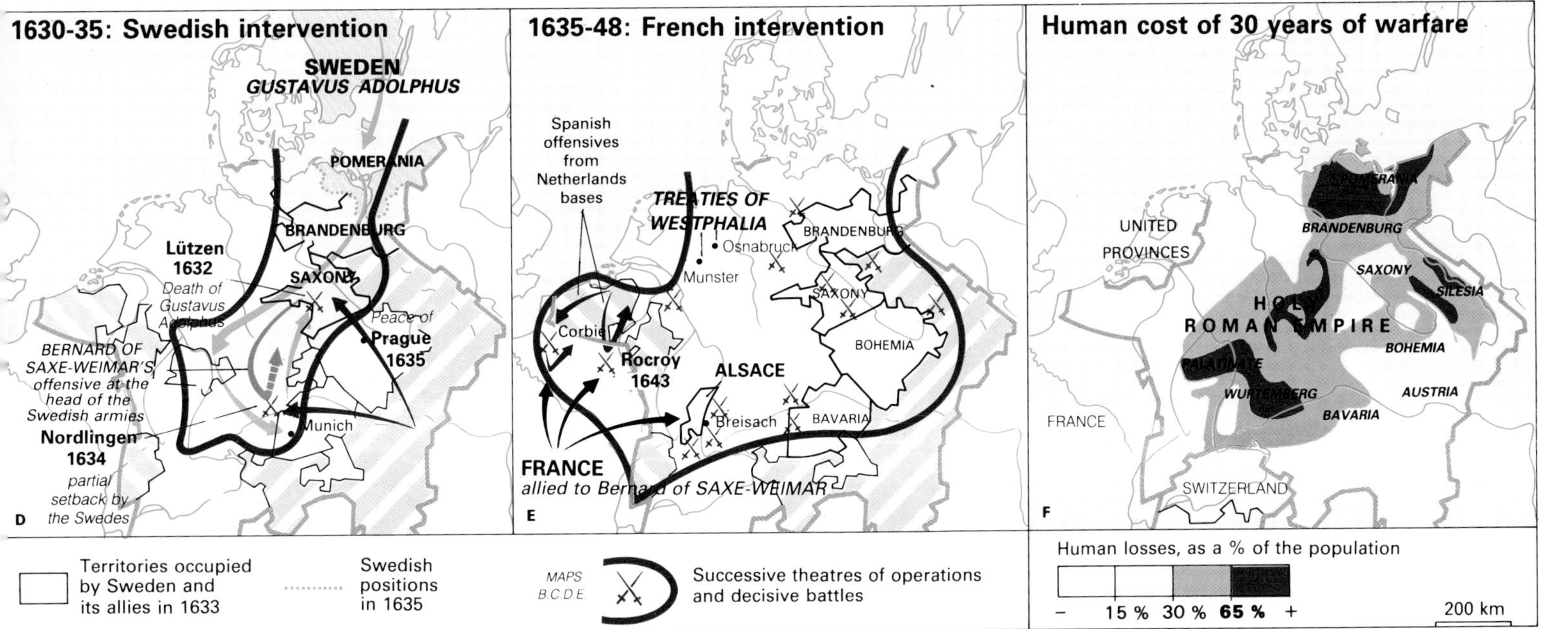


secularized. This explains the clashes over Aachen, Cologne and Strasbourg (1592–1604). Christian IV of Denmark, who had had his youngest son elected administrator of the Bishopric of Verden and arranged matters so that the same son would acquire control of the Archbishopric of Bremen, had a great deal to fear from the success of the Counter-Reformation, and threw himself into war in June 1625. The military genius of Wallenstein forced him to desist (Lübeck, 1629). The Edict of Restitution (6 March 1629) annulled all the secularizations effected since 1555.

Since the Treaty of Vervins (1598), France had sought to weaken Spain's positions. In 1601 she acquired Bresse and Bugey. And in response to the occupation of Jülich-Cleves by imperial forces, she allied with the Evangelical Union and Savoy, though this was interrupted by Henry IV's assassination in 1610. She cut the lines of communication between Spanish and Austrian Hapsburgs in the Valtelline. She intervened against the Spaniards who were laying siege to Casale (Montferrat) in 1629–30. Spain's American money having been cut off (Admiral Piet Heyn had captured it at Matanzas Bay), France remained at Pinerolo, while the Duke of Nevers retained Mantua (1631). With the help of French subsidies he received under the Barwalde Treaty, Gustavus II Adolphus conducted a dazzling campaign throughout the Empire until his death at Lützen. When the Swedes were crushed at Nördlingen, France had itself to enter the war. After some difficult beginnings (Corbie, 1636), her efforts were eventually sufficient to cause the Iberian bastion to totter: Louis XIII was proclaimed Count of Barcelona and concluded an alliance (1641) with the new king of Portugal. If, however, the Emperor was resigned to losing his patrimonial lands in Alsace and what real sovereignty he retained within the Empire, Spain – in spite of Rocroy (1643), Dunkirk (1646) and Lens (1648) – was not so ready to give up the fight. . . .

2. The Miseries of War. *Jacques Callot, 1634.*

**Jacques Callot, *The Miseries of War*** — **1634**

**Peace of Westphalia.** — **1648**

**June 1630:** Gustavus II Adolphus lands in Pomerania.
**July:** Diet of Ratisbon.
**23 January 1631:** By the terms of the Treaty of Barwalde, France promises an annual subsidy of a million pounds to Gustavus Adolphus, who undertakes to respect the neutrality of Bavaria and the Catholic League.
**20 March:** Sack of Magdeburg by Tilly's army rallies the undecided Protestant princes to Gustavus Adolphus's cause.
**16 November 1632:** Victory – and death – of Gustavus Adolphus at Lutzen.
**6 September 1634:** Victory of imperial troops over the Swedes at Nördlingen.
**19 May 1635:** France declares war on Spain.
**30 May:** Treaty of Prague between Emperor Ferdinand II and the Princes of Saxony and Brandenburg.
**11 July:** By the Treaty of Rivoli, Victor Amadeus I of Savoy takes command of the Italian League against Milan.
**7 August 1636:** Spaniards take Corbie.

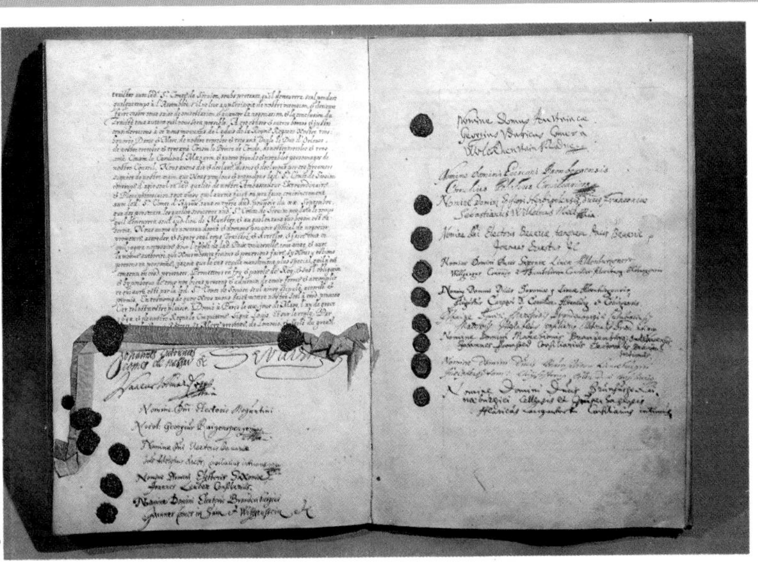

*5. The end of a long war: the French copy of the Treaty of Münster.*

**9 August 1640:** French take Arras.
**25 December 1641:** Preliminary peace treaties between France and the Empire signed: date for negotiations is fixed as 25 March 1642.
**19 May 1643:** Duke of Enghien victorious at Rocroy.
**May 1644:** Münster and Osnabruck conferences open.
**30 January 1648:** At The Hague, Spain recognizes the independence of the United Provinces and cedes the 'Generality Lands' to them (Treaty ratified at Münster, 15 May 1648).
**20 August:** Condé victorious at Lens. Treaties of Westphalia.
**7 November 1659:** Treaty of the Pyrenees between France and Spain.

# The Ottoman Empire: Grandeur and Decline

THE CAPTURE OF CONSTANTINOPLE began the second phase of the Turkish expansion which had come to a halt after the victory of Tamerlane over Bayezid I in 1402. Indeed, less than a century later, the Ottoman state stretched from the Red Sea and the southern coasts of the Mediterranean to the gates of Vienna. There are many reasons for this success. The sultans had at their disposal a powerful army made up of timariots (salaried cavalrymen) and janissaries (infantrymen receiving a fee, recruited from among Christian children instructed in the Muslim faith). This enlistment also allowed capable men of humble origin to rise to high positions, even to the rank of grand vizier. The talent for exploiting internal struggles in neighbouring countries was another strong point. The sultans would be called in to help and would end up taking over power for themselves (cf. the fate of Hungary after the death of Louis II (1526)). The state thus very soon included a large number of ethnic groups, among whom the only common denominator was the duty to serve the ruling dynasty. When a country had been conquered and its military and judicial administration taken over, its ancient customs and laws were left intact. This disparity between the various systems was the source of some of the Empire's earliest problems. Mehmed II, seeking new resources after his costly campaigns, realized that he could not make decrees without knowing what laws governed his empire. It is to him, then, that we owe the first 'book of laws' or legal code. He tried to unify legislation relating to land ownership by reforming the property laws, but created widespread discontent, particularly among the dervishes and the timariots in Anatolia who had hereditary revenues.

In the sixteenth century the conquest of Egypt by Selim I and the surrender of the sherifs of Mecca made possible the appearance of a further unifying factor. Rather than create a single secular constitution, the Holy Law (*Shari'a*) was glorified as the arbiter supreme. This last conferred on those who applied it even greater recognition, since it brought religious prestige to add to military glory. The reign of Süleyman the Magnificent was the high spot of this development, with illustrious jurisconsults such as Kemalpashazade and Abu Su'ud. Constantinople and its court were seen by all as the model to copy. Following the example of the capital, the provincial centres had mosques, schools, libraries, hospitals, soup kitchens, public baths and fountains. Religious foundations also saw it as part of their role to provide for the welfare of the community. In the literary field, writers cultivated a refined style by introducing Persian and Arabic elements into the Turkish texts (the poets Bâkî and Fuzuli).

However, the state had serious economic problems. In the euphoria of conquest, little thought was given to the careful management of the riches so gained. Large sums of money were given to the dignitaries, and the queues of timariots waiting for promotion lengthened. The constant debasement of the coinage diminished purchasing power and had an effect on the equipping of the army. What is more, the young princes, isolated in the harem, no longer learned the art of government in the provincial capitals. The sultans shut themselves away in the seraglio and fell under the influence of the sultan's mother and the favourites. Corruption became rife and even able viziers like the Köprülü in the seventeenth century could only temporarily stall the decline. The overwhelming successes of the Ottomans forced the West to co-ordinate its defence more carefully, with the resulting victory over the Ottoman fleet at Lepanto in 1571, and, on land, with the victory at the Battle of Saint-Gotthard in 1644: this process climaxed with the relief of Vienna in 1683. The wars against Russia, which became frequent from the end of the seventeenth century, would hasten the downward trend.

*1. The siege of Vienna, 27 September 1529, as seen by a Turkish artist (1588).*

| Mehmed II. | Fall of Constantinople. | Bayezid II. | Selim I. | Süleyman the Lawgiver. | Selim II. |
|---|---|---|---|---|---|
| 1451 | 1453 | 1481 | 1512 | 1520 | 1566 |

**1453:** Capture of Constantinople by Mehmed II; death of last Byzantine Emperor.
**1458–9:** Conquest of Serbia.
**1460:** Conquest of Morea.
**1461:** Conquest of Trebizond; end of the great Comneni state.
**1463–4:** Conquest of Bosnia.
**1463–79:** War against Venice.
**1464:** Occupation of Konya, capital of the Karaman emirate; the conquest of the emirate was completed in 1474.
**1468:** Death of Skanderbeg, leader of the Albanian rebels.
**1473:** Mehmed II defeats Uzun Hasan, head of the Ak Koyunlu or White Sheep dynasty, at Otluk-Beli.
**1475:** Capture of Kafa from the Genoese and defeat of the Crimean Khanate.
**1484:** Conquest of ports of Kilia and Akkerman in Moldavia.
**1514:** Defeat of Shah Esma'il I of the Safavid dynasty in Chaldiran.
**1516–17:** Conquest of Syria and Egypt.
**1521:** Capture of Belgrade.
**1522:** Süleyman the Magnificent (also called the Lawgiver) overthrows the dynasty of Zu'l Kadr. Conquest of Rhodes: the Knights now settle on the island of Malta.
**1526:** Victory over Louis II, King of Hungary, at Mohács and capture of Buda.
**1529:** First siege of Vienna.
**1533:** Süleyman appoints Barbarossa (Khayr ad-Din) *kapudan* of Algiers.

*2. Portrait of Süleyman the Magnificent by a Venetian artist, 17th century.*

*3. The fortress of Roumeli Hisari facing Constantinople, 15th century.*

*4. Pottery from Iznik (Nicaea), c. 1580.*

**1534:** Capture of Baghdad.
**1535:** Treaty between Süleyman and Francis I.
**1566:** Conquest of Szigetvár; Süleyman dies during the siege.
**1571:** Capture of Cyprus from the Venetians, but defeat of the Ottoman fleet at Lepanto.
**1577–89:** War against Persia; peace treaty signed in 1590.

# 15th–17th centuries

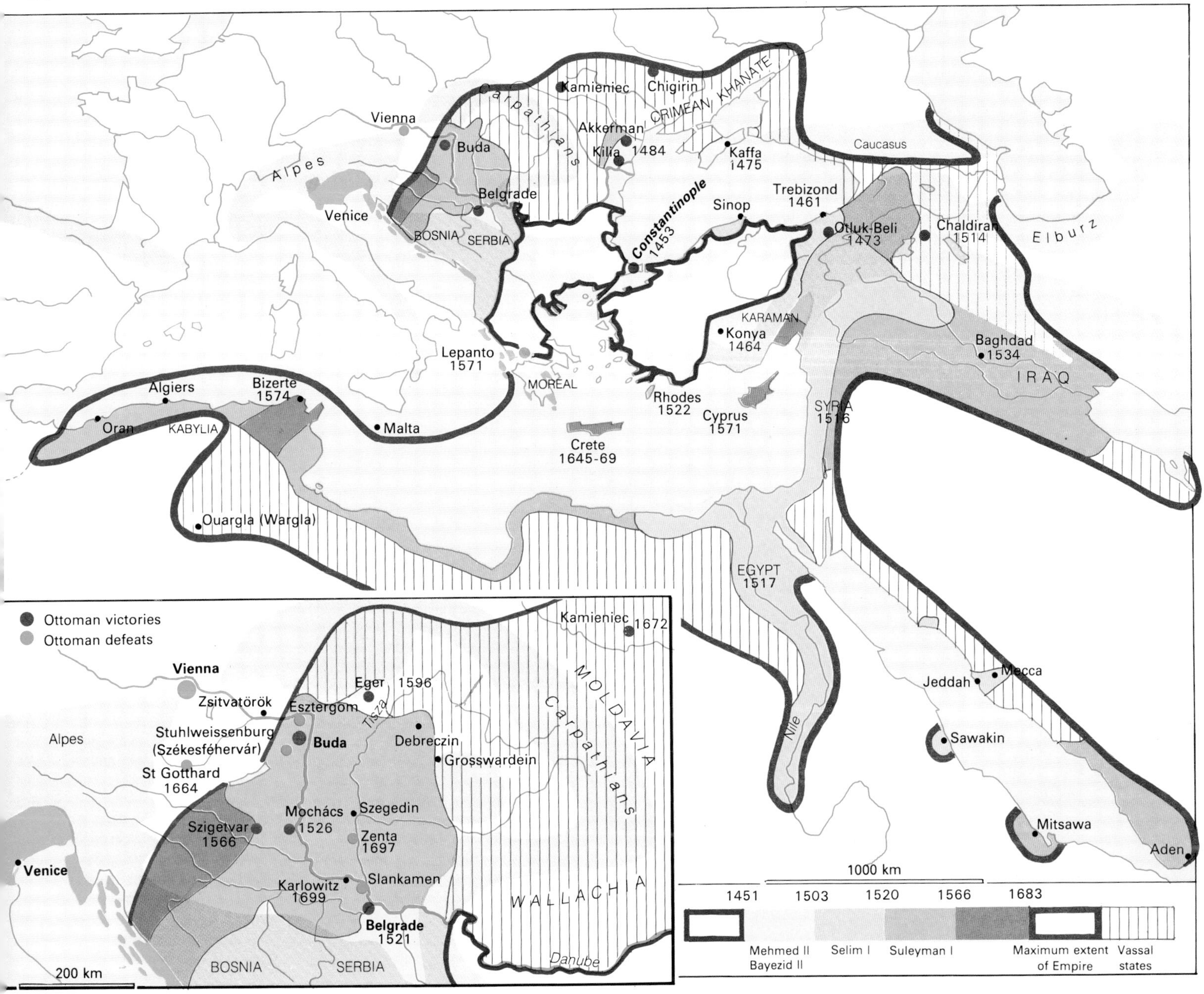

Ottoman victories
Ottoman defeats

1451 | 1503 | 1520 | 1566 | 1683

Mehmed II Bayezid II | Selim I | Suleyman I | Maximum extent of Empire | Vassal states

| ...rad III. | Mehmed III. | Ahmed I. | Mustafa I. | Murad IV. | Ibrahim. | Mehmed IV. | Mustafa II. |
|---|---|---|---|---|---|---|---|
| ...74 | | 1603 | 1617 | 1623 | 1640 | 1648 | 1695 |

5. *The Mosque of Sultan Selim II, designed by Sinan (1569–74).*

**1594:** Capture of Esztergom by the Hapsburgs, who will lose the fortress ten years later.
**1596:** Conquest of Eger by the Ottomans.
**1602:** The Ottomans recapture Szekésfehervar (in present-day Hungary), lost one year previously.
**1606:** Ahmed I signs the Peace of Zsitvatörök, favourable to the Hapsburgs.
**1645–69:** Conquest of Crete.
**1656–61:** Ahmed Köprülü is Grand Vizier.
**1664:** The imperial troops, with French assistance, defeat the Ottomans at St Gotthard.
**1672:** Capture of Kamieniec from the Poles.
**1678:** Capture of Chigirin from the Russians.
**1683:** Defeat of the Grand Vizier Kara Mustafa Pasha at Kahlenberg, near Vienna, due to the arrival of Polish troops under their king, Jan III Sobieski.
**1691:** Defeat of the Ottomans at Slankamen.
**1697:** Victory of Eugene of Savoy over the Ottomans at Zenta.
**1699:** Peace of Carlowitz signed by the Ottoman Empire, the Holy Roman Empire, Poland and Venice (with Russia in 1700).

6. *The Great Hall of the Seraglio, Constantinople.*

# China under the Ming and the Early Manchu

IN THE COURSE of four centuries Chinese society underwent a dual process of change. After an initial agrarian phase there began to appear, towards the end of the sixteenth century, small pockets of an embryonic capitalist economy, which the bureaucratic apparatus sought to restrict. The founder of the Ming dynasty, who was of peasant stock, proceeded to reconquer territory from the Mongols and gave a firm foundation to future prosperity by introducing a policy of major public works (irrigation, reforestation, the building of dams). At the same time, a strict system for control of the population was introduced, accompanied by a massive programme of resettlement. This policy of national reconstruction was a major success. China, rediscovering its former prosperity, saw its influence spread over Mongolia, Manchuria, and over Vietnam, which was momentarily under Chinese rule. Major sea expeditions, the purpose of which was diplomatic as much as commercial, spread the grandeur of Ming culture. Chinese junks sailed the oceans. Nonetheless the maritime expansion was short-lived. Within a short space of time the emperors' lack of interest in the fleet left the way open for the exactions of Japanese pirates, whose incursions into Chinese territory became more and more daring, while the Europeans entered on to the scene, at first discreetly, with the Portuguese, then more assertively with the Dutch. The remarkable prosperity the Empire enjoyed paradoxically undermined its autocratic and agrarian foundations. Industrial development threatened the privileges of the state and its bureaucracy.

While the sixteenth century did mark the development of an urban trading economy, it also confirmed the pre-eminence of the region around the Yangtze within that economy. While cash crops (like cotton or tea) were developed in the area, food crops moved more to the south (to Fukien and Kweichow), which thus became the granary of China. The impoverishment of the peasants as a result of the re-establishment of the great estates and the discontent amongst the city dwellers who felt hemmed in by state regulations led eventually to disturbances which, in conjunction with the external threat from Manchuria, brought the dynasty to an end.

Nevertheless it did prove necessary for the Manchu princes to declare their allegiance to Confucian values and for the mandarin system to be restored before the élite were willing to serve their new masters. The Manchus brought to China immense lands and a remarkable war machine. The Ch'ing ruled the Steppes without challenge. Endowed with vast buffer zones and with well-defended borders, China experienced a period of great prosperity, some measure of which was due to the remarkably efficient use of the land and the introduction of new crops (such as groundnuts, sweet potatoes and maize). A side-effect of this prosperity was a demographic upsurge across the country. Though this was in some respects a positive thing, it turned out to be a major handicap once traditional society had reached the threshold of growth imposed on it by its own pre-industrial mode of production. From the end of the eighteenth century the threat to China became more and more clearly visible, in the shape of Russian and Japanese expansionism in the north and east, and the increasing influence of the Western countries at sea, while internally the regime had to confront a number of social crises of its own.

*1. The entrance to the imperial palace under the Ch'ing dynasty (18th century).*

**Dissertations in eight parts for official examinations.**

**1387**

**Death of Wang Yang-ming, the author of a philosophy of the spirit.**

**1528**

**1368:** The Ming dynasty is proclaimed by Chu Yuan-chang, a former peasant who had become leader of the anti-Mongolian rebellion.
**1370–87:** The whole of China is liberated.
**1380:** Purges culminate in the execution of Chu Yuan-chang's comrade-in-arms, Hu Wei-yang.
**1395:** A policy of major public works is introduced.
**1403:** Chu Di, the younger son of the founder of the dynasty, usurps the throne.
**1405–33:** Great sea expeditions set out for the China Sea, Southeast Asia and to Africa, under the command of the Muslim eunuch, Admiral Cheng Ho.
**1421:** The capital is transferred from Nan-ching to Peking.
**1424:** Successful expeditions are launched against the Oyrats (Kalmycks).
**1449:** The Emperor is imprisoned by the Mongols after a raid.
**1470–80:** A wall is built in northern China to restrict the incursions of the peoples of the steppes.

*2. The Temple of Heaven, built under the Ming dynasty in Peking in 1420.*

**From 1500:** The conflict hardens between eunuchs and Intellectuals.
**1550:** Mongol offensives are launched against the Chinese.
**1555:** Hangchow is sacked by pirates.
**1563:** Japanese pirates run amuck in Fukien.
**1570–80:** The use of money, based on the silver ingot, becomes more widespread.
**1592–4:** First attempted Japanese invasion of Korea is repelled.
**1596–8:** Second invasion attempt of Korea fails.

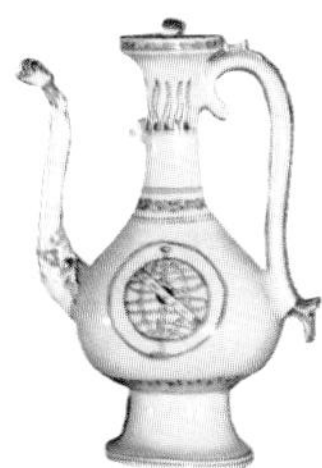

*3. Porcelain ewers from the Ming dynasty with an armillary sphere as a motif (16th century).*

# 1368–1800

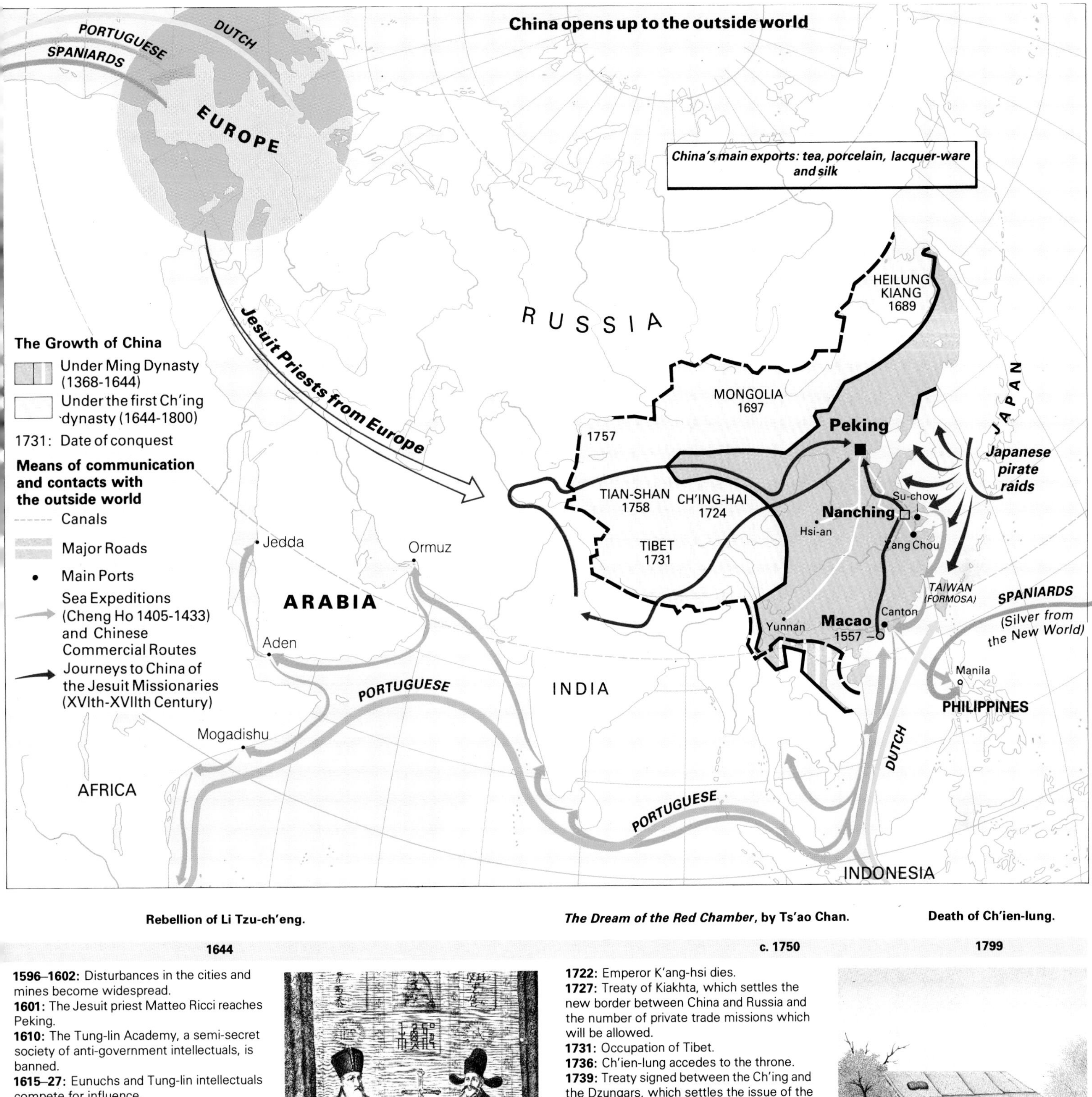

## China opens up to the outside world

PORTUGUESE
DUTCH
SPANIARDS
EUROPE
China's main exports: tea, porcelain, lacquer-ware and silk
HEILUNG KIANG 1689
RUSSIA
Jesuit Priests from Europe
MONGOLIA 1697
JAPAN
Peking
1757
Japanese pirate raids
TIAN-SHAN 1758
CH'ING-HAI 1724
Su-chow
Nanching
Hsi-an
TIBET 1731
Yang Chou
Jedda
Ormuz
ARABIA
TAIWAN (FORMOSA)
SPANIARDS (Silver from the New World)
Canton
Yunnan
Macao 1557
Aden
Manila
PORTUGUESE
INDIA
PHILIPPINES
Mogadishu
DUTCH
AFRICA
PORTUGUESE
INDONESIA

**The Growth of China**
- Under Ming Dynasty (1368-1644)
- Under the first Ch'ing dynasty (1644-1800)
- 1731: Date of conquest

**Means of communication and contacts with the outside world**
- Canals
- Major Roads
- Main Ports
- Sea Expeditions (Cheng Ho 1405-1433) and Chinese Commercial Routes
- Journeys to China of the Jesuit Missionaries (XVIth-XVIIth Century)

**Rebellion of Li Tzu-ch'eng.** 1644

***The Dream of the Red Chamber*, by Ts'ao Chan.** c. 1750

**Death of Ch'ien-lung.** 1799

**1596–1602:** Disturbances in the cities and mines become widespread.
**1601:** The Jesuit priest Matteo Ricci reaches Peking.
**1610:** The Tung-lin Academy, a semi-secret society of anti-government intellectuals, is banned.
**1615–27:** Eunuchs and Tung-lin intellectuals compete for influence.
**1627–30:** Peasant rebellions break out.
**1644:** The rebellion of Li Tzu-ch'eng puts an end to the Ming dynasty. The Ch'ing take control of the north of China and order the wearing of pigtails.
**1657:** After the conquest of the whole of China, official competitions for recruitment begin again in Peking.
**1661:** Koxinga drives the Dutch out of Taiwan, where they had been settled for 30 years. The end comes of the southern Ming and of resistance to the Manchurians.
**1665:** The Ch'ing progress to north of the Amur River.
**1689:** Treaty of Nerchinsk fixes the border between Russia and China in Manchuria.
**1697:** Outer Mongolia is occupied.

*4. The Jesuits in China: on the left, Father Matteo Ricci in mandarin dress, as seen by Father Athanasius Kircher in 1607.*

**1722:** Emperor K'ang-hsi dies.
**1727:** Treaty of Kiakhta, which settles the new border between China and Russia and the number of private trade missions which will be allowed.
**1731:** Occupation of Tibet.
**1736:** Ch'ien-lung accedes to the throne.
**1739:** Treaty signed between the Ch'ing and the Dzungars, which settles the issue of the border in the Altai Mountains region.
**1756–7:** The Dzungars are exterminated and the area around Lli conquered.
**1758–9:** Conquest of the Tarim basin.
**1775:** The population of China reaches 264 million inhabitants.
**1788:** China extends its sovereignty over the upper basin of the Irrawaddy River in Burma.
**1795–1803:** White Lotus Rebellion.
**1799:** Death of Ch'ien-lung.

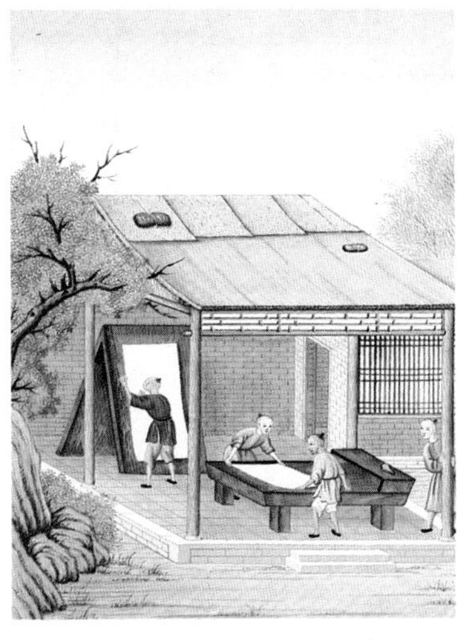
*5. The process of drying in paper-making. From an album on the paper industry (17th century).*

# Japan under the Tokugawa

AROUND 1550, civil war was a constant feature. Whilst the warlords wanted merely to settle in the capital, the Amidaist sects recruited the peasants (farmers) of central Japan, and the city dwellers took over control of the municipal administration. The introduction of firearms and the construction of citadels revolutionized the nature of the war. Oda Nobunaga, and then Toyotomi Hideyoshi, succeeded in breaking up regional resistance and reunified the country under their hegemony. The lords or *daimyo* were overcome or made into vassals (military), the lesser samurai were made to leave the land and to live in towns below castles, and the farmers were disarmed (sword hunt). Thorough land-survey registers were kept enabling taxes relating to real productivity to be levied. When he had wiped out his enemies, Tokugawa Ieyasu took over: in 1603 he took the title of shogun and settled in his new capital, Edo (Tokyo). Christianity was prohibited, and the ports were closed to overseas trade with the exception of Nagasaki, where the Dutch trading post of the East India Company was set up in 1641. Japan closed in on itself.

The seventeenth century was also a century of great economic growth. The population tripled, reaching more than 30 million by about 1700. The daimyo in their fiefs, and the shogun in his estates, increased the range of uses of hydraulic power, allowing land to be reclaimed and the rice fields to be extended. The land-survey registers and the reduction in the number of those having the right to land simplified production procedures. It was in the interests of the farmers to increase and commercialize their production. The samurai, who were forced to live in the towns near to their lord, were cut off from the land and became fief administrators, managing the revenue of the shogun or the daimyo. They had to learn to be efficient and so attended special schools set up for them. The official philosophy of Neo-Confucianism provided an appropriate framework for these warriors-cum-bureaucrats. The shogunal state and the great lords attracted a hard-working population of artisans and merchants to the towns. A bourgeois society grew up in the main towns: by about 1700 Edo had a million inhabitants, Osaka nearly 400,000, and Kyoto almost as many.

A new aesthetic awareness flourished in this urban society. The puppet theatre which came into being at Osaka, and the Kabuki, had rich repertoires, with Chikamatsu Monzaemon the greatest of the playwrights. Basho was one of the great masters of haiku poetry, and in his novels Ihara Saikaku described the 'floating world' of the *ukiya* (pleasure quarters).

In the eighteenth century expansion gave way to stagnation. Social inequalities became more pronounced. Peasant famines and uprisings started up again, and got worse and worse until the final collapse of the regime. Reforms were seen to be inadequate. Literature became more ironic and critical, and new currents of thought, based on the national heritage, untainted by foreign ideas, attacked the official Confucianism, which was now stagnant. Other thinkers were interested in 'Dutch studies' which filtered in through Nagasaki. From the beginning of the nineteenth century uprisings in the country and the towns became more and more common: the southwestern fiefs, which were more prosperous, shook off shogunal control, and pressure from the West to re-open Japan became stronger and stronger. In 1853 the Shogun had to give in to the demands of the American, Perry. The days of the Tokugawa *ancien régime* were numbered.

1. Castle of the White Heron, erected at Himeji, late 16th century.

**MIDDLE AGES** | **MODERN (OR PRE-MODERN) AG**

1500 | 1550 | 1600 | 1650 | 170

**ASHIKAGA SHOGUNATE**

**Warlords Period.** | **1573 Azuchi-Momoyama Period. 1603**

**1549:** Francis Xavier lands in Japan and preaches Christianity. Half a century later there are 600,000 Christians.
**1568–82:** Oda Nobunaga eliminates his rivals, drives out the Ashikaga shogun and destroys the military power of the Buddhist sects.
**1582–98:** Toyotomi Hideyoshi continues the task of unification started by Nobunaga. He conducts a land survey and carries out the 'sword hunt'.
**1600:** Tokugawa Ieyasu wins the Battle of Sekigahara and reaps the political legacy of Hideyoshi.
**1603:** Tokugawa Ieyasu is appointed shogun.
**1615:** With the capture of the citadel at Osaka, the last opposition is defeated.
**1636:** Inauguration of the great temple of Mikko dedicated to the memory of Ieyasu.
**1637:** The great Christian revolt of Shimabara ends in a bloodbath with the aid of the Dutch.
**1641:** Only the Dutch are tolerated in their trading post of Deshima at Nagasaki.

2. Detail from a door at the Toshugu Sanctuary at Nikko, revealing the Chinese influence on Japanese architecture, 17th century.

**c. 1685:** Poetry by Basho and novels by Ihara Saikaku.
**1688–1703:** Genfoku period. The régime of the Tokugawa shoguns at its peak.
**c. 1715:** Chikamatsu Monzaemon writes the major plays in his theatrical repertoire.
**1716–51:** Reign of the shogun Tokugawa Yoshimune. His reformist policies stabilize the shogunal economy, but the social situation deteriorates.
**1772–86:** The minister Tanuma Okitsugu in power. Failure of his reformist and 'liberal' political ideology.
**1782:** Great famine of the Temmei era.
**1787:** More and more revolts, even in the towns. Matsudaira Sadanobu, the Shogun's chief minister, embarks on a new series of reforms aiming to reinforce control of the country by the shoguns, and reverses Tanuma's liberalization programme.
**1792:** Russians in Hokkaido. Sadanobu refuses any opening up of the country.
**1808:** The Japanese explore Sakhalin.

3. Portrait of an actor, by Toshusai Sharaku. Late 18th-century print.

# 1550–1853

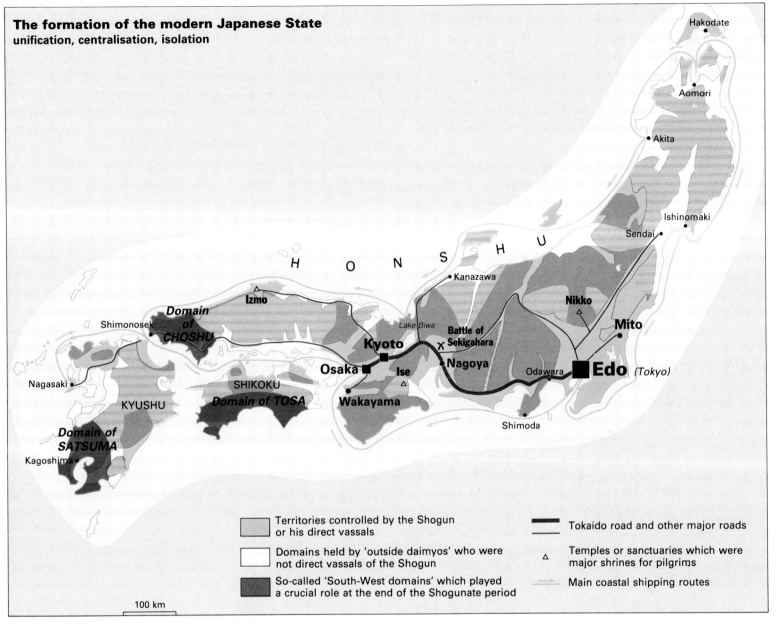

**The formation of the modern Japanese State**
**unification, centralisation, isolation**

Hakodate
Aomori
Akita
Ishinomaki
Sendai
HONSHU
Kanazawa
Izmo
Nikko
Domain of CHOSHU
Shimonoseki
Lake Biwa
Battle of Sekigahara
Mito
Kyoto
Osaka
Nagoya
Odawara
Edo (Tokyo)
Nagasaki
Ise
SHIKOKU
Domain of TOSA
Wakayama
KYUSHU
Shimoda
Domain of SATSUMA
Kagoshima

Territories controlled by the Shogun or his direct vassals
Domains held by 'outside daimyos' who were not direct vassals of the Shogun
So-called 'South-West domains' which played a crucial role at the end of the Shogunate period
Tokaido road and other major roads
Temples or sanctuaries which were major shrines for pilgrims
Main coastal shipping routes
100 km

CONTEMPORARY AGE
1750 1800 1900
OKUGAWA SHOGUNATE | MEIJI ERA
EDO PERIOD 1853 'End of the Shogunate' Period. 1868

**1809:** First engravings in the style known as Ukiyoe.
**1833:** Hiroshige paints his famous '53 views of the Tokaido'.
**1836:** Serious famine of the Tempo era.
**1837:** Great revolt of the people at Osaka.
**1840–5:** The minister Mizuno Tadakuni passes a new series of measures, known as the Tempo era reforms, along the same lines as the previous reforms. These also fail.
**1844:** William II, King of the Netherlands, demands that the Japanese ports should be opened. The shogunate refuses.
**1853:** The American commodore, Perry, moves into the Bay of Edo with his fleet. In the following year, the shogunate agrees to sign a treaty with the United States. End of the political isolation of Japan.

4. Fishing for shellfish. *Hokusai painting on silk.*

*5. The Portuguese arrive in Japan. Detail from a decorated screen, early 17th century.*

# The India of Akbar and the Great Mughals

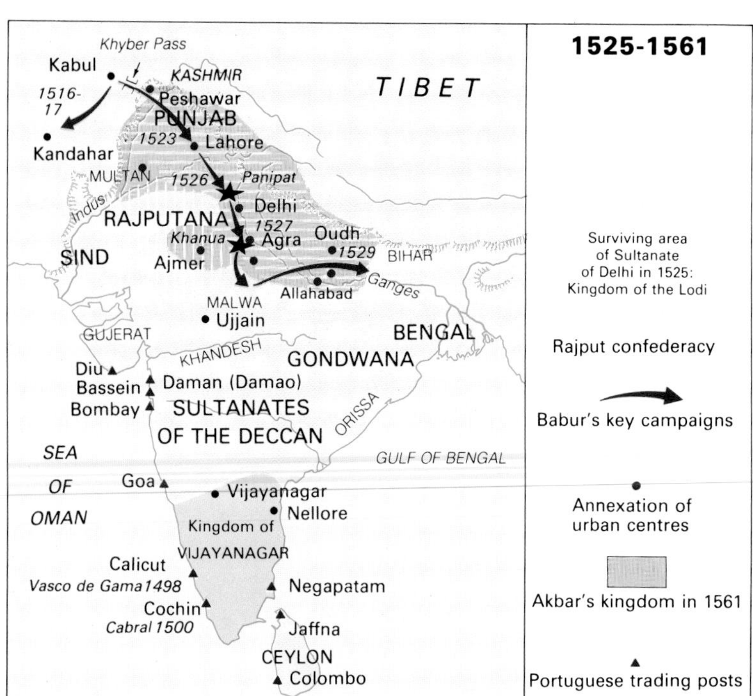


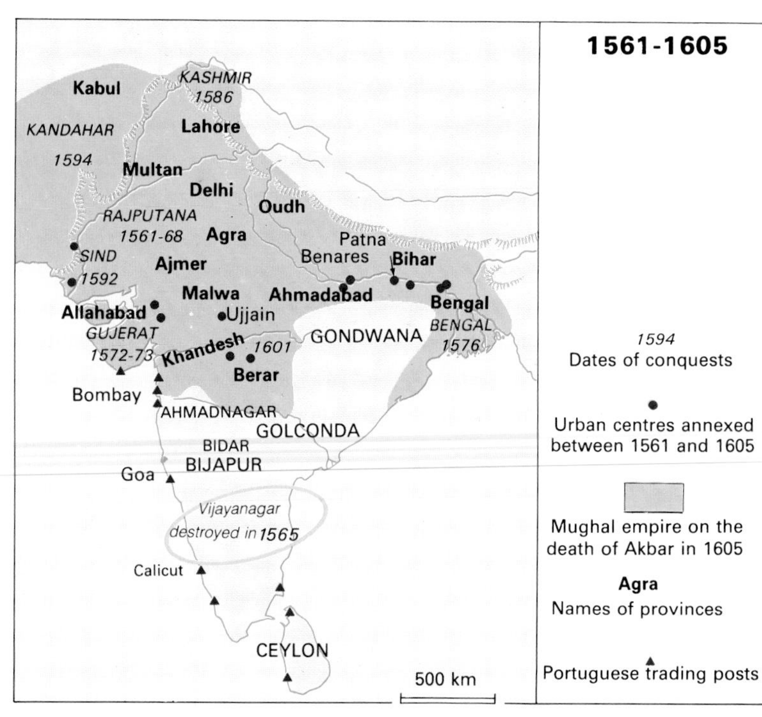


On the death of Akbar, the empire which Babur had founded on the ruins of the old Sultanate of Delhi was at the height of its greatness. It had unified the whole of the country north of the Narbada (and Afghanistan too) and it was on the point of absorbing the sultanates of the Deccan. At that stage a very great number of India's 100 million inhabitants were among its subjects. Sher Shah's land reform had proved effective: the peasants had received rights to land and paid taxes directly to the state (a third of their harvests), assessed on the basis of their plots as they appeared on the land register. The civil servants, now closely supervised, received money wages and were no longer rewarded by large estates, which had a tendency to become hereditary. Artisanal labour remained a great source of wealth (at least for the merchants and the state): European innovations were turned to good account (e.g. book printing inspired colour printing on cotton). There were changes in the relations between Hindus and Muslims: by suppressing the *jiziya* (a poll tax on non-Muslim subjects) and by striving to create a synthesis of Hinduism and Islam, Akbar intended to show that India had ceased to be a conquered country.

But if the splendours of the Mughal courts became even more magnificent under Akbar's successors, many of the reforms he had instigated were reversed. Aurangzeb re-established the jiziya in 1679, which caused a rift with the Rajput warriors with whom Akbar had managed to make an alliance. And the state allowed the tax collectors to develop into a landed aristocracy once again. Moreover, in 1681 Aurangzeb embarked upon a war of conquest in the Deccan which impoverished and weakened the Empire. The decline which set in at the end of the seventeenth century was exploited by the Marathas, who now became the prominent power in the region. Under Sivaji's leadership, the *svarajya* (autonomous kingdom) of the Marathas harassed the armies of Delhi, and extended its power rapidly into the Deccan. It even built a fleet that was capable of defeating the English off Bombay in 1680. Sivaji was regarded as the Hindu national hero and his successors, or rather the chief ministers of their house, the Peshwas of Poona, forced the Mughal emperor to recognize the legitimacy of the power of the Maratha state (now the *samrajya* or imperial confederacy) in the areas where it had supplanted Delhi.

However, India had made its entry on to the stage of world politics,

**Tulsidas: *Ramcaritmanas.***

**Under Akbar, the *Ain-e Akbari*.**

**1504:** Babur (Zahir ud-din Muhammad), a descendant of Tamerlane and Genghis Khan, conquers Afghanistan.
**1526:** Battle of Panipat. Babur, the Great Mughal, takes control of the capital.
**1530:** Death of Babur. He leaves memoirs written in Turki.
**1533–1623:** Tulsidas, author of a vast epic poem in Hindi, the *Ramcaritmanas*.
**1540–5:** Reign of Sher Shah, who had defeated Humayun, Babur's son. A lasting, efficient administration is set in place.
**1542:** Arrival in India of the Spanish Jesuit, Francis Xavier.
**1542–1605:** In Akbar's reign, the *Ain-e Akbari* is composed in Persian by Abu'l-Fazl; it is a systematic description of the resources and the administration of the Empire. A work that is unique of its kind in pre-colonial India.
**1556:** Battle of Panipat. Akbar, son of Humayun, restores the sovereignty of the Great Mughals.
**1569:** Akbar defeats the Rajput Rana Pratap and overcomes the resistance of the Gondwana, who are led by Queen Durgavati.
**1572:** Abolition of taxes on non-Muslims.
**1582:** Akbar creates a new religion, the Din-Illahi or 'Divine Faith', which finds followers only among his immediate entourage.
**1600:** British East India Company founded.
**1602:** Dutch East India Company founded.
**1605:** Death of Akbar. The Spanish Jesuit Roberto de Nobili arrives in India. He settles in Madura.

*2. The Emperor Akbar crosses the Ganges. Detail of a Mughal miniature, late 16th century.*

**1605–27:** Reign of Jehangir. Political and cultural pinnacle of Mughal civilization in India.
**1615:** Delhi grants Thomas Roe the right to open a trading station at Surat.
**1627–58:** Reign of Shahjahan.
**1630–32:** Terrible famine in Gujerat.
**1631:** Death of the Empress Mumtaz. Shahjahan has the Taj Mahal built as a mausoleum for her at Agra.
**1640:** British East India Company establishes a trading post at Madras.
**c. 1640:** Dara Shikoh, son of Shahjahan, has the *Upanishads* translated into Persian.
**1650:** British trading post established at Hooghly, near what will become Calcutta.
**c. 1650:** The great temple to Shiva at Madura (now Madurai) is built.
**1658–1707:** Reign of Aurangzeb. A strict Muslim, he reacts against the tolerant universalism that had been prevalent under Akbar.
**1664:** French East India Company founded.
**1666:** Sivaji, Hindu prince of the rebellious Maratha states, signs a (very temporary) settlement with Aurangzeb.

*3. The temple to Vishnu of Srirangam at Tiruchchirappalli in the state of Tamil-Nadu).*

# 16th–18th centuries

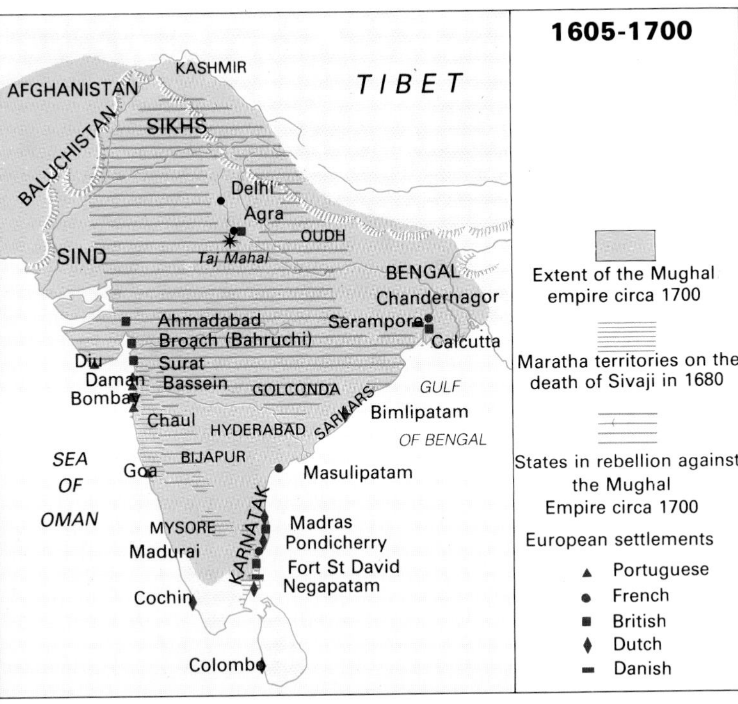


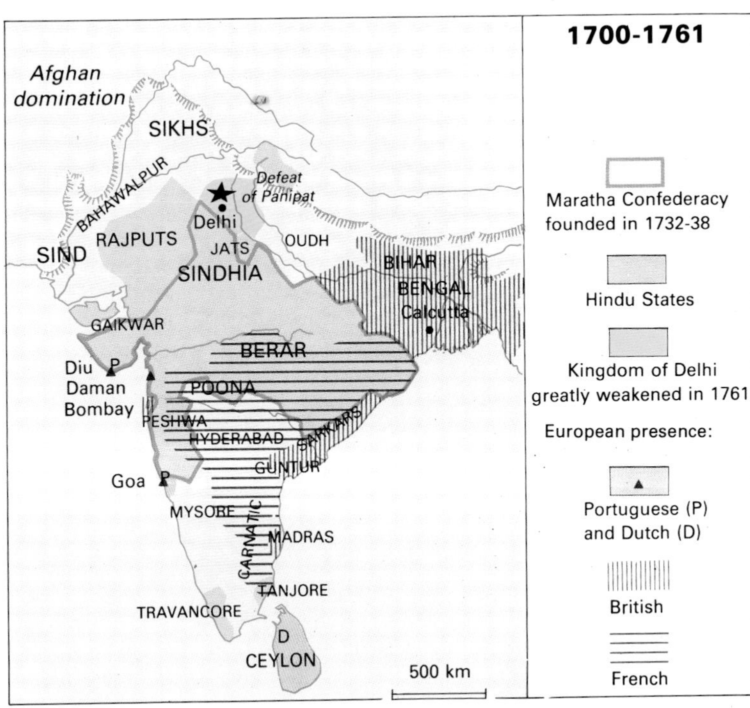


which is to say the stage of European rivalries. What was now beginning was the last phase of a process that had begun at the very moment when the foundations of the Mughal Empire were being laid. As early as 1535, in fact, the Portuguese had obtained the fortress of Diu from the sovereign of Gujerat and established a series of trading posts along the coasts. Their objective was to ensure a monopoly of the seaborne trade between India and Europe and also to obtain a foothold in India from which to spread the Catholic religion. However, they were only able to hold on to the enclave of Goa. Everywhere else they had gradually to give way, first to the Dutch and the Danes, then later to the English and the French. For the Indian sovereigns themselves, these 'trading stations' became an essential element in the export system. A decisive change took place in 1741, when Dupleix, the governor of the French East India Company, received a *jagir* (gift of land) from the Great Mughal. France became a territorial power in India. Britain, which was at war with France, could not allow her a free hand on the sub-continent. Once her army had defeated the French on Indian soil, Britain stood on the verge of what was to be the long adventure of her conquest of India.

*1. Krishna tells how he fell in love. . . . Miniature taken from an 18th-century erotic treatise.*

**Sivaji, the founder of Maratha power.**

1627–80

**Gobind Singh, founder of Sikh power.**

1675–1708

**1669:** Rising of the Jats, Hindu peasants of the Mathura region.
**1674:** On the initiative of François Martin, the French trading post at Pondicherry is opened.
**1700:** The Punjab becomes a Sikh state.
**1714–40:** Maratha territory extended to the gates of Delhi and as far as the southern Deccan.
**1757:** Battle of Plassey. Robert Clive defeats the troops of the Nawab of Bengal.
**1760:** Battle of Wandiwash (near Madras). The British inflict a decisive defeat on the French.
**1761:** Battle of Panipat. The Great Mughal is defeated by an Afghan warlord, in spite of Maratha support. There is no longer an Indian army to stand out against British penetration.

*4. Fort of Golconda, built to resist the Mughal invasion in Andhra Pradesh, 16th–17th century.*

*5. Jaipur, Rajastan. Jantar Mantar astronomical observatory. In the foreground, a solar clock (18th century).*

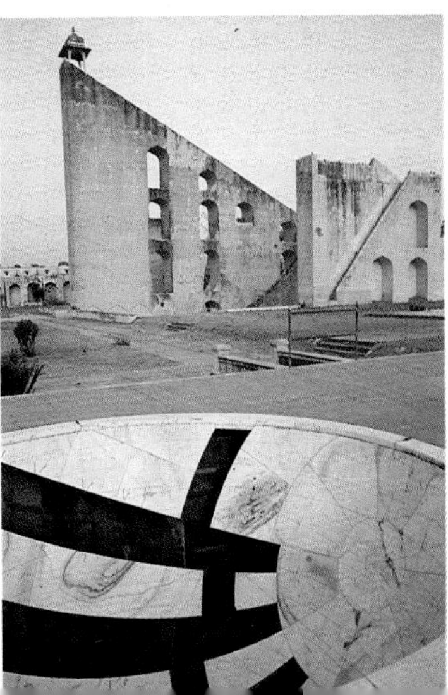

# Africa at the Time of the Slave Trade

BETWEEN 1450 AND 1600, Europeans voyaged to the African coasts, but their presence remained limited and their influence marginal until the nineteenth century; the appearance of this new Atlantic front did not reduce the importance of the Saharan one. The old kingdom of Gao became the great Songhai Empire. It was, however, destroyed in a battle at the end of the sixteenth century. Meanwhile Bornu, which had reconquered Kanem, became a major power. The century is characterized by the rise of a variety of states, including, for example, the kingdoms of the Volta (Mossi, Dagomba) and Sennar. This was also the period in which the Christian and Muslim kingdoms of Ethiopia clashed violently, leaving both sides weak and drained. On the east coast, the Portuguese dismantled the existing trading network between the cities and replaced it with their own. Matapa and Butua prospered and the kingdoms of Luba and Lunda became prominent. The Kongo kingdom took the risk of opening itself up to Christianity and Portuguese technology, though in the long run it lost its vigour.

1. The king of the Kongo receiving Dutch ambassadors. From an engraving of 1700.

**Black Africa from the XVth to the XIXth centuries 1450-1600**

Taghaza
SONGHAI
Timbuktu
Tondibi
Gao
CAYOR
FOUTA TORO
Jenne
Niger
MOSSI
MAMPURSI
DAGOMBA
Oyo
Benin
BENIN
HAUSA STATES
BORNU
Lake Chad
Nile
FUNJ
Sennar
ETHIOPIA
Zeila
ADAL
Harar
Mogadishu
Kismayu
Malindi
Mombasa
Lake Victoria
Congo
LUANGO
KONGO
Lake Tanganyika
LUBA
LUNDA
Luanda
Kilwa
Lake Nyasa
Mozambique
Tete
Sera
MATAPA
BUTUA
Sofala
Orange

SONGHAI EMPIRE
Direct domination at its peak
Partial domination
Portuguese colonisation
Desert
Dense forest
1000 km

Between 1600 and 1800, the Sudan was more fragmented than before, though its territory was still the site of intensive interactions between some old protagonists (Hausa states, Bornu) and some new ones (Segu and Wadai kingdoms). Its coastal traffic mainly centred on the slave trade, which had negative effects in the long term. However, the West African states, particularly the Ashanti and Abomey – two of the new powers – used that trade and adapted it to their own ends, without becoming solely dependent upon it. Oyo was dominant among the Yoruba states. In the southern savannahs, the Luba and the now reduced Lunda kingdoms extended the field of

**Sonni 'Ali Ber Emperor of Songhai.**

**1464–92**

**Afonso I, Christian king of the Kongo.**

**1506–43**

**Reign of Fasilides in Ethiopia.**

**1632–67**

**1464–92:** Reign of Emperor Sonni 'Ali Ber, a great conqueror and administrator, in the Songhai.
**1483:** The Portuguese come into contact with the Kongo kingdom.
**1493–1528:** Reign of Muhammad I Askia, who continues the work of Sonni 'Ali Ber, though in an Islamic framework.

**End of 15th–beginning of 16th centuries:** Restoration of Bornu.
**1504:** Destruction of Soba; emergence of the Funj kingdom.
**1505:** The Portuguese at Sofala.
**1506–43:** Afonso I Christian king of the Kongo.
**1521–42:** Invasion of Ethiopia by Ahmad Gran: intense wars; Ethiopia imperilled but eventually survives.

**Mid-16th century:** Growth of Fouta-Toro.
**c. 1570:** Portuguese settlements around Luanda and in the Zambezi valley.
**1571–1603:** Glorious reign of Idris Alawma in Bornu.
**1591:** Defeat and collapse of the Songhai at Tondibi at the hands of Moroccan soldiers (conflict over the Teghaza salt mines).
**1593:** Portuguese fort built at Mombasa.
**1606–32:** Reign of Suseynos in Ethiopia: forced to abdicate upon conversion to Catholicism.
**1632–67:** Reign of his successor, Fasilides, who drives out the Jesuits and makes his capital at Gonder in 1636.
**1668:** Battle of Ambuila; Portuguese kill the king of the Kongo, which now declines.

**End of 17th–beginning of 18th centuries:** Portuguese driven out of Mombasa. Osei Tutu founds the Ashanti political state (c. 1695).

**Beginning of 18th century:** Creation of the Dyula kingdom of Kong (now Ivory Coast). Reign of Mamari Kulibali (known as the 'Commander'), the Bambara king of Segu (1712–55); successful conqueror and unifier of his people.
**1725:** Muslim state of Fouta Jallon.
**1726:** Muslin state of Fouta Toro.
**1785–1810:** Reign of Andrianampoinimerina in Madagascar.

2. The Ashanti receive the British ambassadors, c. 1815. Anonymous engraving.

# 15th–19th centuries

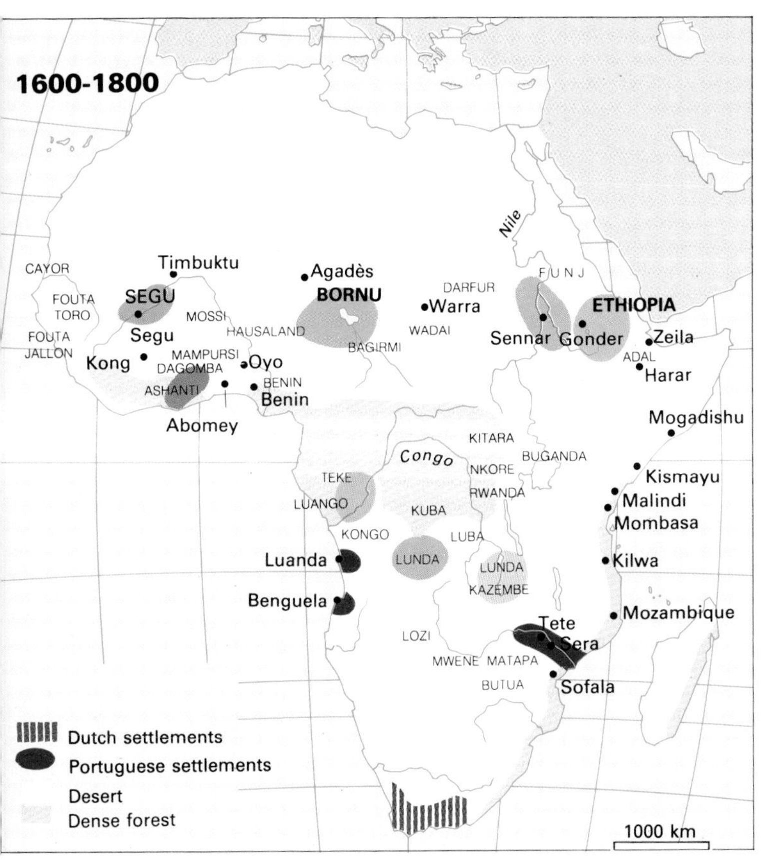



their tributary economy and forged links with coastal traffic through intermediaries (Kasanje etc.). In the east, the coastal cities underwent something of a revival, thanks partly to the presence of Omanis. Ethiopia, which was initially reunited around Gonder, again became fragmented.

Between 1800 and 1875 the slave trade – though now repudiated by Europe – continued, remaining particularly lively in Islamic areas. A dizzy rise in trade links with Europe put the various coastal societies to the test: where states were able to respond to this new situation their power was consolidated; otherwise they were plunged into crisis. There was a generalized penetration of the continent, spurred on by European and Arabo-Swahili trade. However, these developments cannot all be ascribed to a single logic. In the Sudan, as early as the eighteenth century, a series of social and political revolutions gave birth to a number of dynamic, resolutely Muslim states. The process repeated itself throughout the nineteenth century. In Natal, after 1816, Shaka brought the Zulu state to prominence. Dissidents from and imitators of this military society spread its example far and wide in dramatic raids. In Madagascar, around the year 1800, Andrianampoinimerina brought unity, organization and power to the Merina people in the centre of the island. In the middle of the century, Tewodros reconstructed Ethiopia, though not without much bloodshed. Buganda also, which had, by its own efforts, formed itself into a centralized state, opened its frontiers to external trade and foreign ideas.

Should we then regard this as a period in which indigenous African forces dominated? Or did the slave trade economy simply prefigure later relations of dependence? Both perspectives can provide some understanding of nineteenth-century Africa, but only up to 1860. When we reach the 1870s the 'scramble' for the continent begins.

**Reign of Andrianampoinimerina in Madagascar.** 1785–1810

**Muhammad Bello King of Sokoto.** 1817–37

**Reign of Tukulor al-Hajj 'Umar.** 1852–64

**Tewodros II King of kings in Ethiopia.** 1855–1868

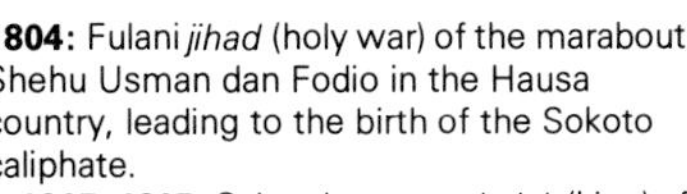

**1804:** Fulani *jihad* (holy war) of the marabout Shehu Usman dan Fodio in the Hausa country, leading to the birth of the Sokoto caliphate.
**c. 1805–1815:** Sabun becomes *kolak* (king) of the Wadai.
**1812:** Muhammad al-Kanami saves the Bornu kingdom from the Sokoto threat and gives it a new lease of life.
**1816–28:** King Shaka creates the Zulu society and state.
**1817–37:** Reign of Muhammad Bello, sovereign and brilliant intellectual, in the Sokoto.
**1818:** Muslim state of Masina.
**1823:** Ndebele kingdom.
**1830:** Disintegration of the Oyo kingdom.
**1833:** Mshweshe unites the Sotho people in a single state.
**1835:** Beginning of the Great Trek of the Boers.
**1852–64:** Tukulor al-Hajj 'Umar conquers Kaarta (1855–6), Segu (9 March 1861) and Masina (16 May 1862).
**1855:** Tewodros II crowned Emperor of Egypt (c. 1868).

*3. Ethiopian popular art: Menelik II depicted as King Solomon, 19th-century manuscript.*

**1862–86:** Lat Dior, leader of the Cayor (Senegal), resists the French.

*4. Three elephants, an Ashanti golden ornament.*

# Art in Europe: A New Vitality

1. Tromp-l'oeil ceiling by Ignazio Birajo di Borgaio in Aglie Castle, Piedmont.

As STAGES ON THE road to modernity, the Renaissance, Mannerism, and the Baroque were each different facets of a multidisciplinary inquiry into the world which drew no distinction between science, art and technology. At the same time as Michelangelo was designing the dome of St Peter's, Cardan, in his *Ars Magna* (1545), was setting out the concepts of positive, negative and imaginary numbers. The catenary curve was used to calculate the arches of Saint-Eustache, even before its function had been defined by Pascal. Stereotomy, the art, according to Charles Perrault, 'of using the weight of stone against itself and supporting it in the air with the same weight as that which makes it fall', through the efforts of Desargue, La Hire, Frézier and Monge, led directly to descriptive geometry.

Challenging Aristotle, a whole sector of European thinking abandoned functionality and privileged appearance. The structure of edifices could no longer be grasped simply and clearly by the eye but was masked by the rigid application of the laws of symmetry. Artists undertook to conquer space, movement, light. The vertical perspective imagined by Mantegna for his *Camera degli Sposi* (wedding chamber) frescoes in Mantua was taken up and extended by Andrea Pozzo, who, in effect, doubled the height of the nave of St Ignazio's in Rome. Michelangelo's *Moses* was ready to leap to his feet, but Giulio Romano's giants in the Sala dei Giganti in the Palazzo del Te on the outskirts of Mantua strained to break down the very walls which contained them. The flame from St Joseph's candle in the *Nativity* attributed to the Master of Flémalle (in the Musée de Dijon) was replaced by the glow of the sun setting over the Roman ruins of a Claude Lorrain. Baroque virility was disciplined into classical virtue, but degenerated into rococo virtuosity.

Classicism was a struggle for order amidst this teeming surge of energy. Order reigned in the rules of perspective, and the gruff accuracy of the engravings of Abraham Bosse was the very reverse of the generous creativity apparent in the etchings of Rembrandt. Order reigned, too, in the use of the palette, and Poussin, emulated by Lebrun, laid the emphasis on clarity of meaning and propriety. The warmth of Rubens was not rediscovered until the time of Watteau. Classicism could soften the impact of the Baroque to the point of freezing it entirely. The façade of the Louvre palace, filled with movement by the skill of a Bernini, lost all its vitality in the hands of a Perrault. In Gabriel's drawings the Place Louis XV was scrupulously arranged and laid out.

The Rococo made its appearance when the dynamic energy of the Baroque had become mere dispersion and movement little more than agitation. Even as Monteverdi's music was being acclaimed in Mantua, the spectacle of the opera in the Tuileries offered only the creaking of machines and monstrous apparitions lit by fireworks. Caravaggio expressed the conversion of Saint Paul with stunning economy, whereas the minor masters found their delight in the illusions of the trompe-l'oeil and the ambiguities created by anamorphosis. The old demons of excess and overstatement re-emerged once order was no longer respected. As a result the achievement of the Escorial remains isolated in the whole of Castile, while elsewhere on the Iberian Peninsula and in Latin America medieval retables were being overlaid with colour. Whilst Saenredam gives an indication of the sobriety of Dutch churches, the gilt decorations of the German churches were periodically brightened up.

**Death of Palladio.** **1588**

**Birth of Boromini and Velázquez.** **1599**

**First performance of Monteverdi's *Orfeo*.** **1607**

3. The statuette of the Immaculate Conception by Alonso Cano (1601–67) in the sacristy of Granada Cathedral.

**1563–4:** Juan de Herrera, El Escorial.
**1568–75:** G. Della Porta, Church of Gesù, Rome.
**1584:** Palladio, Teatro Olimpico, Vicenza.
**1600:** Caravaggio, *The Conversion of St Paul*, Rome. Church of S. Maria del Populo.
**1605:** Building starts on the Place Royale (the present-day Place des Vosges) in Paris.
**1607:** Claudio Monteverdi, first performance of *Orfeo*.
**1617:** Building begins on the Plaza Mayor in Madrid by J. Gómez de Mora.
**1619:** Inigo Jones begins work on the banqueting hall, Whitehall.
**1627:** Simon Vouet returns to Paris.
**1633:** Bernini completes the baldachin over the tomb of St Peter in Rome.
**1638:** Philippe de Champaigne, *Le Voeu de Louis XIII*.
**1642:** Rembrandt, *The Night Watch*. Nicolas Poussin in Paris.
**1656:** Jean de La Vallée builds the Church of St Catherine of Stockholm, with its cupola on a Greek cross.
**1657–63:** Bernini: colonnade over the piazza before St Peter's.
**1665:** Bernini travels to Paris.
**1666:** Great Fire of London. Foundation of the French Academy of Rome.
**1674:** Boileau writes his *Art poétique*.
**1675:** Christopher Wren, St Paul's (work continues till 1710).
**1677:** Roger de Piles, *Conversations sur la connaissance de la peinture*.
**1702:** Building starts on the Abbey of Melk (Austria).
**1703:** Founding of St Petersburg.
**1705:** Sir John Vanbrugh undertakes the

4. The Holy Spirit descending from the cupola, by Francesco Borromini, in the Church of S. Carlo alle Quattro Fontane, in Rome (1641).

# 17th century

2. *The beginnings of the Baroque: the contrast between heaven and earth, as depicted in El Greco's* Burial of Count Orgaz, *1586.*

**1680** **Bernini dies.**

**1720** **Watteau, *L'Enseigne de Gersaint*.**

**1723** **Christopher Wren dies.**

*5. The ecstasy of God's love: St Theresa, as seen by Bernini (1652).*

building of Blenheim Palace for the Duke of Marlborough.
**1707:** Foundation of the Society of Antiquaries in London.
**1717:** Antoine Watteau, *L'Embarquement pour Cythère.*
**1717–31:** Juvarra's basilica on Superga, near Turin.
**1725:** John Wood the Elder begins work in Bath.
**1730:** J. E. Fischer von Erlach, imperial stables in Vienna.
**1735:** Jean-Philippe Rameau, the opera-ballet *Les Indes galantes.*
**1745:** G. W. von Knobelsdorff builds Sans-Souci palace in Potsdam.
**1749–60:** Palace of Amalienborg, Copenhagen.
**1750:** Giambattista Tiepolo begins his cycle of frescoes decorating the rooms of the Residenz in Würzburg.
**1755:** Earthquake in Lisbon.
**1768–75:** Jacques-Ange Gabriel, Place Louis XV in Paris (the present-day Place de la Concorde).

*6. Dam Square in Amsterdam, by J. Van der Ulft, in 1659.*

*7. The sacristy of the convent-palace of El Escorial, as seen by Claudio Coello in 1690.*

# Louis XIV and Absolute Monarchy

The Fronde was many things. It marked a moment of crisis in the authority of an under-age king and was a sign of revolt against an unprecedented fiscal onslaught by central government, as well as a period of self-interested agitation on the part of the privileged classes. It saved Spain from disaster and jeopardized the diplomatic and military achievements of Richelieu and Mazarin.

As a true pupil of Cardinal Richelieu, Louis XIV devoted the bulk of his time to foreign policy. Without having any single fixed idea throughout his personal reign of fifty-four years, he nonetheless pursued an anachronistic battle against Spanish hegemony. It was not a dowry that he married (indeed, the 300,000 gold crowns were never to be paid) but a set of political aspirations: upon the death of Philip IV, he claimed the devolution of Brabant, the freehold of the Hainault and the equal partition of the Franche-Comté. To press home his claims he needed to humiliate the United Provinces, and attract England into the French sphere of influence, as well as to support a good part of Europe financially. However, Louis had not reckoned with the surprising longevity of Charles II of Spain. He had, in the end, no alternative but to accept the terms of his last will and testament (16 November 1700).

For the execution of his policy he had at his disposal a large, well drilled army established by Le Tellier and Louvois and protected by Vauban's fortifications. But its cost was so high that, to improve the yield of indirect taxation, Colbert introduced the system of the five great tax Farms (in 1669). Faced with all the various threats of the last years of the reign, it proved necessary to sell offices, to tax the privileged classes by the introduction of *capitation*, a graduated poll-tax, and to follow Vauban's advice in collecting a tithe (1710). A highly centralized administrative structure held the country in its grip: the office-holders had to give way to *commissaires*, and the 'sovereign' courts became merely 'higher' courts (1665). Restored after the Fronde, the *intendants* administered the provinces, which were progressively unified by the Civil Ordinance of 1667, the Criminal Ordinance of 1699 and the setting up of the post of *lieutenant général de police* in the cities.

Fiscal pressure led inevitably to the development of a mercantile and protectionist economy. Communications were improved, with Riquet, completing, for example, the Canal du Midi. The rise in

2. Versailles viewed from the gardens in 1672.

1. Louis XIV, five years after the start of his personal reign, surrounded by Colbert and various members of the Academy of Sciences, as seen by Henri Testelin, 1666.

manufacturing output, the foundation of the French East India Company, and the 1664 and 1667 changes in the tariff system, brought about the closing of the borders of Holland to French products in 1670 and, subsequently, war with Holland. The competitive Dutch economy was much weakened as a result, and the only beneficiaries were the English. Alarmed by any action which might possibly have some subversive implication or intent, Louis XIV restricted the papal prerogative, dissolved the Company of the Holy Sacrament and revoked the Edict of Nantes. As a result he impoverished the kingdom by forcing the Protestants (Huguenots) to flee, though he did welcome the Irish, who had been declared outlaws by the penal laws of 1702–1705. More a close descendant of Philip II of Spain than Henry IV of France, Louis imposed the rigid etiquette of a cult of monarchy on a domesticated nobility.

**1642** — **Death of Richelieu.**

**1661** — **Death of Mazarin.** **1662** — **Death of Pascal.**

**14 May 1643:** On the death of Louis XIII, Louis XIV comes to the throne.
**19 May:** Victory of the Prince de Condé at Rocroi.
**January 1644:** Imposition of the *toisé*, which ordered the destruction of the dwelling-houses built just outside Paris (where building was prohibited for military reasons), or a fine of 50 sous per *toise* (a unit of measure).
**1647:** Vaugelas, *Remarques sur la langue française*.
**15 June 1648:** Declaration of the Chambre de St Louis imposing a charter on Anne of Austria, the Queen Regent.
**1–2 July 1652:** Battle of the faubourg Saint-Antoine during the Fronde.
**1660:** Company of the Holy Sacrament dissolved.
**9 June:** Marriage of Louis XIV to Marie-Thérèse of Austria, daughter of the King of Spain, in Saint-Jean-de-Luz.
**9 March 1661:** Death of Mazarin.
**1665:** Colbert appointed controller general of finance.
**17 September:** Death of Philip IV of Spain, the father of Marie-Thérèse.
**1667:** Racine writes *Andromaque*.

3. An argument in favour of converting to Catholicism after the Revocation of the Edict of Nantes. A Protestant cartoon from 1688.

**2 May 1668:** The Treaty of Aix-la-Chapelle marks the end of the War of Devolution.
**1670:** The Criminal Ordinance.
**10 May 1678:** 1st Treaty of Nijmegen marks the end of the war with Holland.
**1681:** Annexation of Strasbourg.
**1682:** Declaration of the Four Articles reaffirming the legitimacy of Gallican customs.
**30 July 1683:** Death of Queen Marie-Thérèse.
**15 August 1684:** Truce of Ratisbon between Louis XIV and the Holy Roman Emperor.
**18 October 1685:** Edict of Fontainebleau revokes the Edict of Nantes.
**1688:** Setting up of the militia.
**1694:** First edition of the *Dictionnaire de l'Académie française*.
**1695:** Introduction of *capitation*.
**27 September and 30 October 1697:** The treaties of Rijswijk mark the end of the War of the League of Augsburg.
**1 November 1700:** Death of Charles II of Spain.
**16 November:** Philip V accedes to the Spanish throne.
**1707:** Vauban, *Projet d'une dîme royale*.
**12 June 1709:** Appeal from Louis XIV read out in all the churches in France.

# 1643–1715

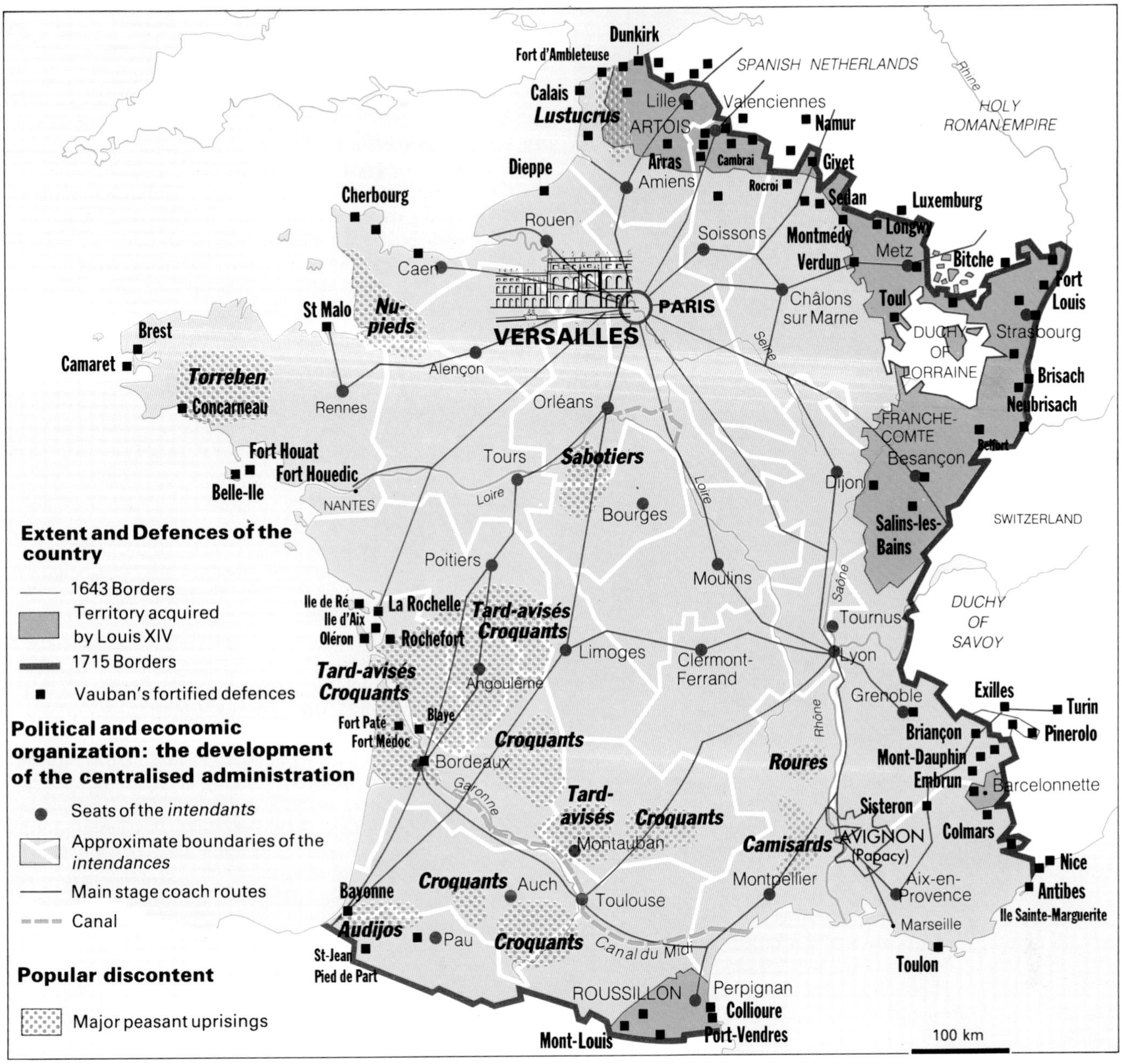

Dunkirk
Fort d'Ambleteuse
Calais
Lustucrus
Lille
ARTOIS
Arras
Amiens
Valenciennes
Cambrai
Rocroi
SPANISH NETHERLANDS
Namur
Givet
Sedan
HOLY ROMAN EMPIRE
Rhine
Dieppe
Cherbourg
Rouen
Caen
Soissons
Montmédy
Verdun
Luxemburg
Longwy
Metz
Bitche
Fort Louis
Toul
Châlons sur Marne
PARIS
VERSAILLES
St Malo
Nu-pieds
Brest
Camaret
Torreben
Concarneau
Rennes
Alençon
Seine
DUCHY OF LORRAINE
Strasbourg
Brisach
Neubrisach
Orléans
FRANCHE-COMTE
Belfort
Besançon
Fort Houat
Fort Houedic
Belle-Ile
NANTES
Tours
Loire
Sabotiers
Bourges
Dijon
Salins-les-Bains
SWITZERLAND
Poitiers
Moulins
Saône
Ile de Ré
Ile d'Aix
Oléron
La Rochelle
Rochefort
Tard-avisés Croquants
Limoges
Clermont-Ferrand
Tournus
Lyon
DUCHY OF SAVOY
Angoulême
Grenoble
Exilles
Turin
Pinerolo
Fort Paté
Fort Médoc
Blaye
Bordeaux
Croquants
Rhône
Roures
Briançon
Mont-Dauphin
Embrun
Barcelonnette
Garonne
Sisteron
Colmars
Tard-avisés
Montauban
Camisards
AVIGNON (Papacy)
Nice
Antibes
Ile Sainte-Marguerite
Bayonne
Auch
Toulouse
Montpellier
Aix-en-Provence
Marseille
Toulon
Audijos
Pau
Canal du Midi
St-Jean Pied de Port
ROUSSILLON
Perpignan
Collioure
Port-Vendres
Mont-Louis
100 km

**Extent and Defences of the country**

- 1643 Borders
- Territory acquired by Louis XIV
- 1715 Borders
- Vauban's fortified defences

**Political and economic organization: the development of the centralised administration**

- Seats of the *intendants*
- Approximate boundaries of the *intendances*
- Main stage coach routes
- Canal

**Popular discontent**

- Major peasant uprisings

| Birth of Voltaire. | Death of Racine. | Death of Louis XIV. |
|---|---|---|
| 1694 | 1699 | 1715 |

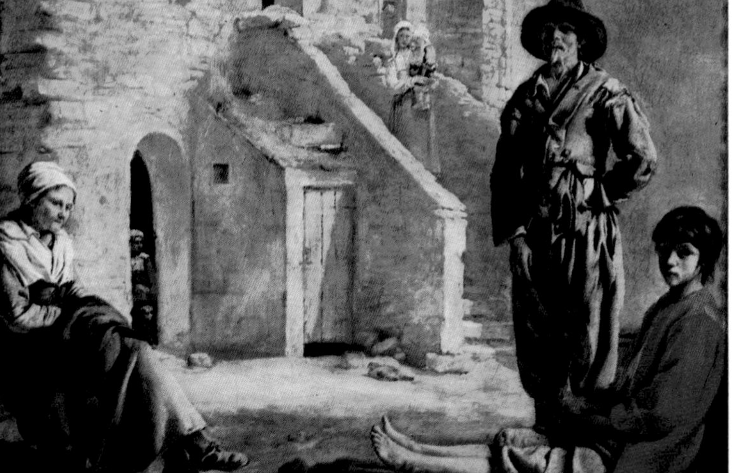

4. *The beginnings of realism: a group of French peasants, by Louis Le Nain.*

**24 July 1712:** Battle of Denain.
**11 April 1713:** Treaty of Utrecht between France on the one hand and England, Portugal, Savoy and the United Provinces on the other, marking the end of the War of Spanish Succession.
**6 March 1714:** Treaty of Rastatt signed with Emperor Charles VI, thus ratifying the Treaty of Utrecht.
**1 September 1715:** Death of Louis XIV.

5. *Louis XIV as the Sun King.*

6. *Louis XIV, at the end of his reign, 21 October 1714, welcomes the Elector of Saxony. Painting by Louis de Silvestre.*

# An Imperial Republic: The United Provinces

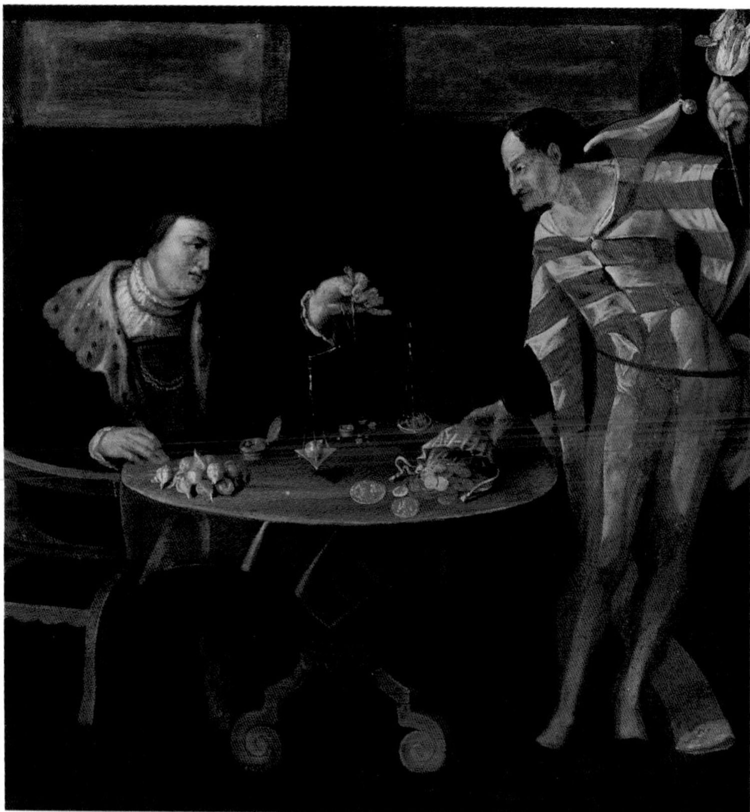

1. Valuing tulip bulbs in gold – picture of the Dutch School, 17th century.

THE NARROW, FLAT LANDS of the United Provinces, bordered by the sea, were claimed first by Spain (1621–48), then by France (1672–8). Each was attracted by the area's prosperity, for if ever there was an agricultural revolution, it sprang from Dutch husbandry.

The Dutch were experienced herring-fishermen in the North Sea and well equipped to inherit the legacy of the Hanseatic League in the Baltic: 'Commanding the trade of the Kingdom of Sweden since they command the trade of copper' (Huet, 1694). With a new type of ship (a bulk carrier – the *fluyt*) and a fleet of ten thousand vessels, they carried Baltic corn as far as the eastern Mediterranean. Van Heemskerck and Barents set out to find a north-eastern passage but became ice-bound in the Arctic Ocean and had to return with only geographical information.

To reach the spices of the Indian Ocean – Lisbon having been closed to the Dutch since 1580 – a first expedition financed by the Far Lands Company and commanded by Cornelius Van Houtman (who had lived in Portugal in his youth) rounded the Cape of Good Hope, made treaties with local rulers and came back with a valuable cargo. In 1602 a number of trading companies were amalgamated to form the East India Company, which was directed by Dutch merchants. In 1605 the company got a foothold in the Moluccas (Spice Islands) and established a garrison at Amboina; in 1616 it obtained the monopoly of trade with Japan, an essential factor in trade with the Far East; in 1619 it occupied Jakarta and established the capital of its colonial empire at Batavia, on the island of Java; in 1624 it founded a settlement on Formosa. The company rid itself of English competition (the massacres of Amboina in 1624), drove the Portuguese from Malacca (1641), Ceylon and the Moluccas and took over the pepper and cinnamon trade. On the spice route, the Dutch stopped periodically at Mauritius and established a station at the Cape of Good Hope (1652), a port of call for its vessels which gradually became a permanent colony. The quest for new routes led Willem Janszoon (1606) and Piet von Nuyts (1628) to Australia, and Tasman to New Zealand and Fiji (1624–44). In 1607 Hudson had tried in vain to find a north-west passage.

The West India Company (1621) set its aims on America. It founded, as stations for the fur trade, both New Amsterdam on the island of Manhattan and, 200 kilometres up-river, Fort Orange (Albany). Disquieted by this, the English invaded New Netherland in 1664 and renamed the colony New York. The company was forced also to relinquish Bahia but nevertheless, between 1621 and 1634, captured 540 Spanish vessels carrying goods worth more than 150 million *livres*. Lured by the sugar of Brazil, the company took Recife from the Portuguese and gradually extended its influence over 2,100 kilometres of coastline. Between 1636 and 1645 it imported 23,000 black slaves. But Portugal's regaining of its independence (1642), the slump in sugar prices in Amsterdam (1644), the uprising – almost nationalist in character – of the *moradores* (Portuguese settlers) in 1644 and the exhausting of sources of black slaves in Angola put an end to the domination of the *Flamengos* (the Dutch). They withdrew to Curacao, a busy centre of smuggling and illegal trade with the Spanish colonies.

In this Protestant society, the profits of trade had to be reinvested: art was the only permitted luxury. But it was a sober luxury, for this art depicted bare churches, quiet interiors and boards of directors and governors. Rembrandt side-stepped such restrictions by making himself the subject of his paintings. ...

**Birth of Rembrandt in Leyden.**

**1606**

**Birth of Spinoza in Amsterdam and Vermeer in Delft.**

**1632**

**1595:** Expedition (4 vessels, 250 men), financed by Far Lands Company, commanded by Cornelius Van Houtmann.
**1602:** Founding of one of first great joint-stock companies – Dutch East India Company (*Vereenigde Oost-Indische Companie*).
**9 April 1609:** Twelve-year truce, signed at Antwerp. In same year, founding of Bank of Amsterdam (*Amsterdamsche Wisselbank*). Publication by Huig Van Groot (better known as Grotius, 1583–1645) of *Mare liberum*.
**1621:** Founding by Usselincx of West India Company (*West Indische Companie*). First long-term Dutch settlement in Guiana.
**10 May 1624:** Bahia captured by expedition (26 ships, 450 cannons, 3,300 men), financed by West India Company, commanded by Jakobs Willekens.
**1626:** Founding of Nieuw-Amsterdam (New York).
**7–8 September 1628:** Seizure by Piet Heyn of 80 tons of silver (15 million florins) from Plate fleet of New Spain.
**1630:** Recife taken by Dutch.
**1639:** Admiral Van Tromp's great victory, off Dover, over Spanish fleet.
**1644:** Revolt of *moradores* in Brazil.
**30 January 1648:** At The Hague, independence of United Provinces recognized by Spain. Agreement by Spain to surrender its right to the 'Pais de la Généralité' and to close Antwerp. (Treaty ratified at Münster on 15 May 1648.)
**5 August 1651:** Navigation Act promulgated by Cromwell.
**28 January 1654:** Loss of Recife to the Portuguese. Treaty of Westminster with England.
**1661:** Dutch driven from Formosa by Chinese (Koxinga).
**4 September 1662:** Treaty with England.
**1665:** Dutch colonial positions attacked by English.
**1667:** Peace of Breda: English possession of New York recognized by Dutch.
**January 1668:** Triple Alliance at The Hague (Sweden, England, Holland) against Louis XIV. In same year, Japanese embargo on export of silver, depriving East India Company of metal money, used to pay in Indies for exports to Europe.

2. The port of Macassar on the Indonesian coast, after its capture by the Dutch in 1660.

# 1595–1689

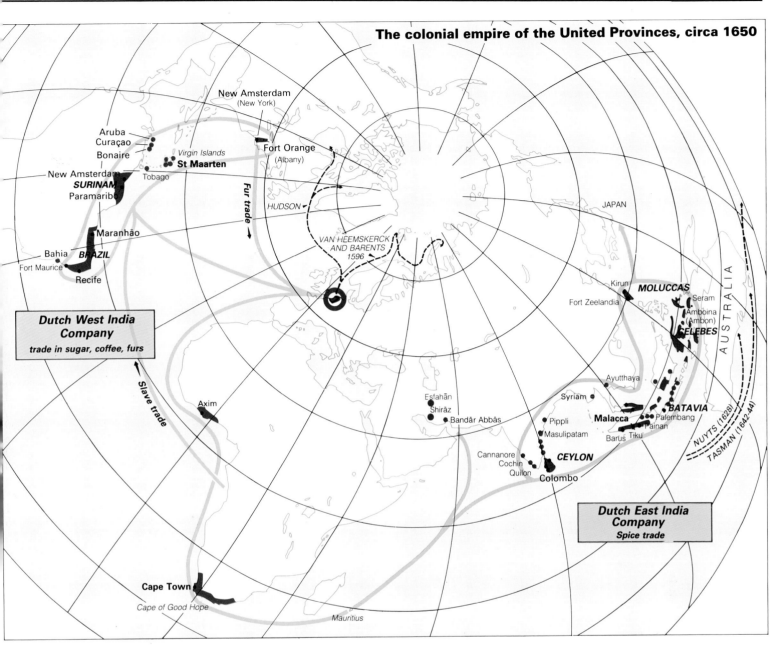

## The colonial empire of the United Provinces, circa 1650

New Amsterdam (New York)
Fort Orange (Albany)
Aruba
Curaçao
Bonaire
Virgin Islands
St Maarten
Tobago
New Amsterdam
SURINAM
Paramaribo
Fur trade
HUDSON
Maranhão
Bahia
BRAZIL
Fort Maurice
Recife
VAN HEEMSKERCK AND BARENTS 1596
JAPAN
Kirun
MOLUCCAS
Fort Zeelandia
Seram
Amboina (Ambon)
CELEBES
AUSTRALIA
Dutch West India Company
trade in sugar, coffee, furs
Slave trade
Axim
Esfahān
Shirāz
Bandār Abbās
Ayutthaya
Syriam
Pippli
Masulipatam
Malacca
BATAVIA
Palembang
Painan
Barus
Tiku
NUYTS (1628)
TASMAN (1642-44)
Cannanore
Cochin
Quilon
CEYLON
Colombo
Dutch East India Company
Spice trade
Cape Town
Cape of Good Hope
Mauritius

| Death of Frans Hals in Haarlem. | Loss of New Amsterdam (New York). | Louis XIV in Holland. |
|---|---|---|
| 1666 | 1667 | 1672 |

3. *The governors of the Handbow Archers' Guild depicted by Van der Helst, 1613–70.*

**1669:** Death of Rembrandt.
**1670:** Publication by Spinoza (1632–77) of *Tractatus Theologico-politicus.*
**12 June 1672:** Crossing of Rhine by Louis XIV.
**1677:** Posthumous publication of Spinoza's *Ethics.*
**10 May 1678:** Peace of Nijmegen.
**1689:** Accession of William III to English throne.

4. *Japanese engraving of a Dutch ship, circa 1700.*

# The Greatness of Russia

AT THE DAWN OF the modern age, the territory of medieval Muscovy expanded considerably, both as a result of military conquest – the product of a strengthening of the state – and also, more importantly, as a result of a vast spontaneous migration of the population. From the fifteenth century the princes were led increasingly to reduce the peasantry to serfdom in order to satisfy the needs of a new class of 'lesser serving landowners' (*dvoriane*), favoured at the expense of the old aristocracy (the *boyars*). This produced a migratory movement, first of all towards the steppes of the Don region – where communities of Russian Cossacks formed parallel to those of the Ukrainian Cossacks on the Polish marches, then towards Siberia. The discontent of the masses also found expression in rural risings in which the serfs were joined by Cossacks, defending their rights against advancing state structures and foreign immigrants. These revolts were often conducted in the name of a legitimate prince, who had disappeared in mysterious circumstances and been usurped by an adventurer. In effect, the image of an authoritarian sovereign, who was the protector of the weak and whose legitimacy derived from hereditary right, was ever present in the popular consciousness. But this utopia could not survive the evidence of the repression practised against both rural and urban uprisings. Even among the more well-to-do sections of society, the possibilities of participation in government that were offered in the seventeenth century by the 'Assemblies of the Land' (*Zemskie Sobory*) – to whom was entrusted among other tasks the resolution of dynastic crises – had come to nothing, because society was not organized into orders and a 'third estate' could not be easily identified. The power of the church was reduced once and for all by Peter the Great. His reign saw the culmination of a process whereby all social groups were subordinated to the needs of the state: the nobles were merged into a single class, whose role was to serve the state, in either a military or a civilian capacity; the peasants were called upon to provide the economy with servile labour on the lands of the nobles or the crown or in the first factories, and to provide the army with recruits. Thanks to the decisive role the nobility played during palace revolutions, its obligations were diminished and its rights reinforced. The nobility, a privileged class, which in fact supplied the state with all its officers, became the solid pillar on which the monarchy rested. The army, a caricatural copy of the Prussian model, contributed to the further petrification of social relations. The European dress which the élite chose to wear simply completed their isolation from the rest of the nation. The cultural unity of Russian society had already been compromised in the seventeenth century by the Old-Believers schism, which put an end to the idea of a Christianity identified with the Russian ethnic group and by the Polish, White Russian and Ukrainian influences on the Muscovite aristocracy. It was shattered when Peter the Great abruptly introduced a policy of Westernizing the beliefs, manners, way of life and even language of the ruling class. The Russian, with its foreign loan-words, which they had spoken was now supplanted by French. Even literary Russian, a combination of the vernacular language and Slavonic, which in Catherine II's reign had boasted Russia's first great modern writers and poets, had distanced itself from the language of the people, who were left only with traditional oral culture and a religion reduced to rituals.

1. The soldiers of Peter the Great, by Kardovski.

2. The Kolichev Estate in the province of Tver, by E. Fedorov, 18th century.

| Ivan IV. | Fyodor I. | Boris Godunov. | Fyodor II, then the first False Dimitri. | Mikhail Romanov. | Alexis. |
|---|---|---|---|---|---|
| 1533 | 1584 | 1598 | 1605 | 1613 | 1645 |

**1547:** Imperial coronation of Ivan IV ('the Terrible'); official adoption of the title of tsar (from the Latin Caesar).
**1549–60:** Government of the so-called 'Chosen Council' (Izbrannaya Rada). Administrative, judicial and military reforms.
**1553:** Arrival in Russia of the English explorer, Richard Chancellor.
**1558–72:** War of Livonia. General exhaustion of the country.
**1564:** First book (Acts and Epistles) printed in Moscow.
**1565–72:** Creation of the *oprichnina*, an instrument of the terror régime, placed under the direct control of the Tsar.
**1571:** Raid of the Crimean Tartars; burning of Moscow.
**1582:** Cossack troops under Ermak penetrate into Siberia.
**1589:** Creation of the Moscow patriarchate.
**1603–19:** Outbreak of social struggles, fanned by famine, dynastic crises and foreign intervention.
**1617–18:** Armistice treaties with Sweden and Poland.
**1630–2:** Creation of army mercenary corps.

3. Muscovite cavalrymen. German engraving, 16th century.

**1648:** Rising of Ukrainian cossacks against Poland. Social disturbances in Moscow and several other cities.
**1649:** Promulgation of a new legal code (the *ulozhenie*), laying down judicial procedures and legalizing serfdom.
**1654:** Proclamation of union of Ukraine with Moscow.
**1654–67:** Liturgical reforms; Old Believers schism.
**1662:** Rioting in Moscow against price rises brought about by the introduction of copper coinage.
**1682:** Abolition of placement in state offices based on internal hierarchy in noble families (*mestnichestvo*).
**1687:** Creation of the Slavo-Graeco-Latin Academy.
**1697–8:** Peter the Great's first journey to Europe.
**1699–1705:** Beginnings of military conscription.
**1700:** Introduction of the Julian calendar.
**1718:** Introduction of a poll-tax.
**1718–21:** Creation of 'colleges', which pre-figured ministries, to replace *prikazy* (executive bureaux of Muscovite administration).
**1721:** Creation of the Holy Synod to replace the patriarchate.
**1722:** Promulgation of the 'Table of Ranks' fixing civil, military and ecclesiastical hierarchies.
**1725:** Academy of Sciences founded.
**1736–9:** War against Turkey (Treaty of Belgrade).
**1753:** Abolition of internal customs duties.
**1754:** Creation of Commercial Bank in St Petersburg.

4. The first False Dimitri, Tsar in 1605.

# 1547–1796

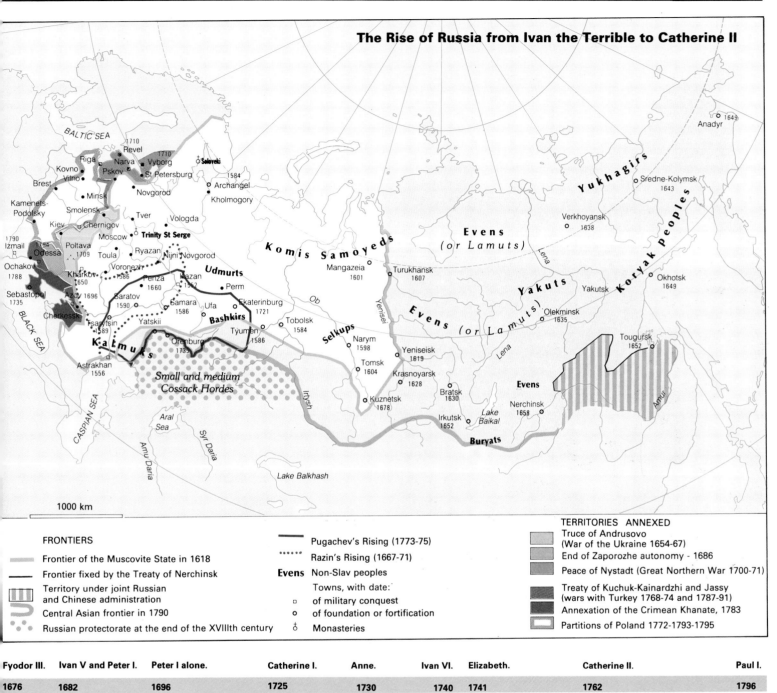

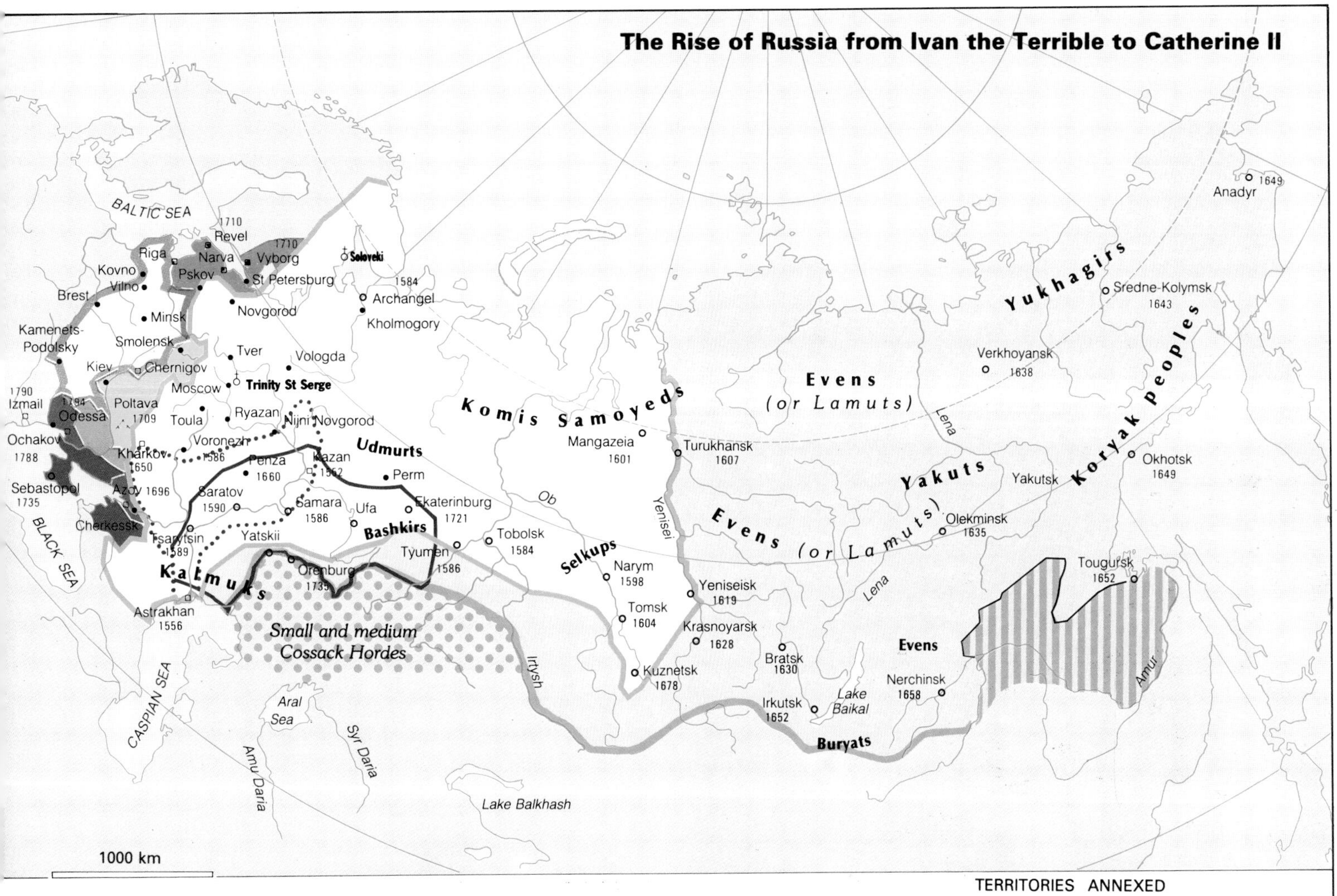

## The Rise of Russia from Ivan the Terrible to Catherine II

1000 km

FRONTIERS

- Frontier of the Muscovite State in 1618
- Frontier fixed by the Treaty of Nerchinsk
- Territory under joint Russian and Chinese administration
- Central Asian frontier in 1790
- Russian protectorate at the end of the XVIIIth century
- Pugachev's Rising (1773-75)
- Razin's Rising (1667-71)
- **Evens** Non-Slav peoples

Towns, with date:
- of military conquest
- of foundation or fortification
- Monasteries

TERRITORIES ANNEXED

- Truce of Andrusovo (War of the Ukraine 1654-67)
- End of Zaporozhe autonomy - 1686
- Peace of Nystadt (Great Northern War 1700-71)
- Treaty of Kuchuk-Kainardzhi and Jassy (wars with Turkey 1768-74 and 1787-91)
- Annexation of the Crimean Khanate, 1783
- Partitions of Poland 1772-1793-1795

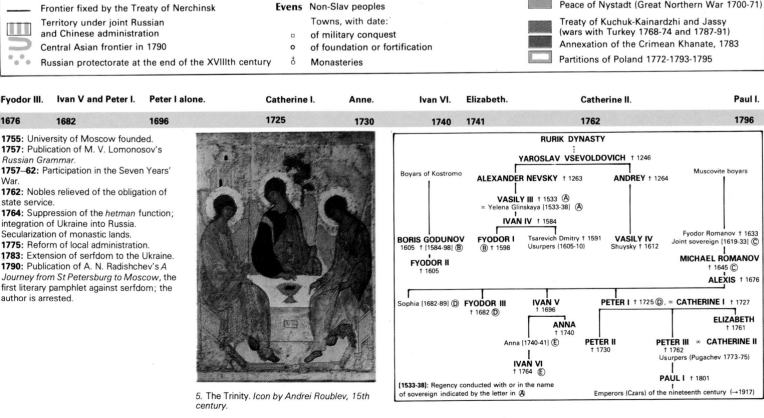

| Fyodor III. | Ivan V and Peter I. | Peter I alone. | Catherine I. | Anne. | Ivan VI. | Elizabeth. | Catherine II. | Paul I. |
|---|---|---|---|---|---|---|---|---|
| 1676 | 1682 | 1696 | 1725 | 1730 | 1740 | 1741 | 1762 | 1796 |

**1755:** University of Moscow founded.
**1757:** Publication of M. V. Lomonosov's *Russian Grammar.*
**1757–62:** Participation in the Seven Years' War.
**1762:** Nobles relieved of the obligation of state service.
**1764:** Suppression of the *hetman* function; integration of Ukraine into Russia. Secularization of monastic lands.
**1775:** Reform of local administration.
**1783:** Extension of serfdom to the Ukraine.
**1790:** Publication of A. N. Radishchev's *A Journey from St Petersburg to Moscow*, the first literary pamphlet against serfdom; the author is arrested.

5. The Trinity. *Icon by Andrei Roublev, 15th century.*

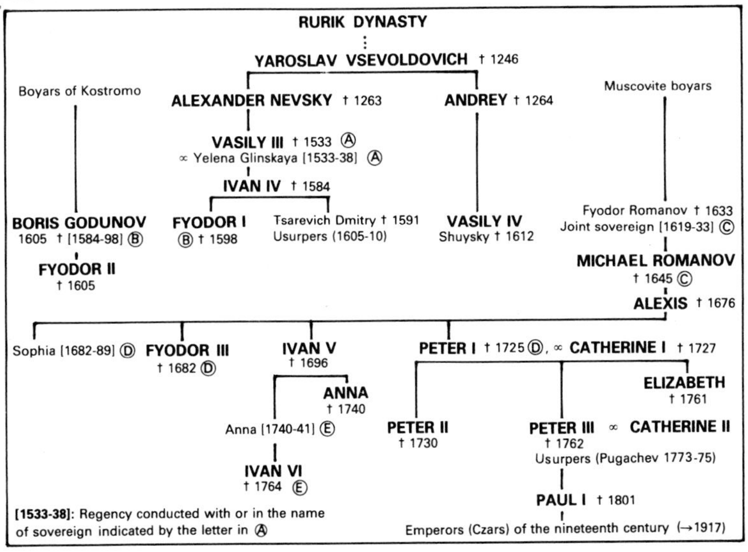

**RURIK DYNASTY**
⋮
**YAROSLAV VSEVOLDOVICH** † 1246

Boyars of Kostromo | **ALEXANDER NEVSKY** † 1263 | **ANDREY** † 1264 | Muscovite boyars

**VASILY III** † 1533 Ⓐ
∞ Yelena Glinskaya [1533-38] Ⓐ
**IVAN IV** † 1584

**BORIS GODUNOV** 1605 † [1584-98] Ⓑ
**FYODOR II** † 1605

**FYODOR I** Ⓑ † 1598
Tsarevich Dmitry † 1591 Usurpers (1605-10)
**VASILY IV** Shuysky † 1612
Fyodor Romanov † 1633 Joint sovereign [1619-33] Ⓒ
**MICHAEL ROMANOV** † 1645 Ⓒ
**ALEXIS** † 1676

Sophia [1682-89] Ⓓ | **FYODOR III** † 1682 Ⓓ | **IVAN V** † 1696 | **PETER I** † 1725 Ⓓ, ∞ **CATHERINE I** † 1727

**ANNA** † 1740
Anna [1740-41] Ⓔ
**IVAN VI** † 1764 Ⓔ

**ELIZABETH** † 1761
**PETER II** † 1730
**PETER III** † 1762 ∞ **CATHERINE II**
Usurpers (Pugachev 1773-75)
**PAUL I** † 1801
Emperors (Czars) of the nineteenth century (→1917)

**[1533-38]:** Regency conducted with or in the name of sovereign indicated by the letter in Ⓐ

# Swedish Expansion and the Rise of Prussia

THE TREATIES OF WESTPHALIA made Sweden a major force in Europe. To go with her Baltic possessions (Ingria, Estonia, Livonia), well secured since 1629, she now received Pomerania, Wismar and the bishoprics of Bremen and Verden, all of which, together with her role in the Empire, exposed her to other nations' jealousies. For his part, the Elector of Brandenburg acquired the bishoprics of Halberstadt (with Magdeburg to follow), Cammin and Minden, the latter a staging-post on the way to the Rhenish territories inherited in 1614. With less than 1.5 million inhabitants (even counting Finland), Sweden was a poor country and its expansion produced internal tensions. The 'alienation' (or acquisition by the nobility) of crown lands (formerly farmed as common land) was endangering the survival of a free peasantry, and the upper aristocracy, who were strong enough to thwart the intentions of the monarchy, met with hostile reaction from the three lower orders of the Parliament (Riksdag), the clergy, bourgeoisie and peasants. King Karl X Gustav, who came to the throne after Queen Kristina's abdication, pushed through a policy of 'reduktion' (reclamation) of a quarter of the 'alienated' lands. He also embarked upon a renewed policy of aggressive expansion. His military campaigns in Poland and Denmark both ended in failure. The maritime powers – the United Provinces and England – could not accept the effective domination of the Baltic by Sweden. The death of Karl X left to a regency the arduous task of maintaining a façade of greatness with insufficient means. The development of export industries (iron, tar) by foreign entrepreneurs augmented resources somewhat and Sweden's external possessions brought in some revenue, but their potential was not integrated into an imperial economy. Faced with the vengeful intentions of the Danish monarch, now no longer hamstrung by his aristocracy, the Swedish polity had need of funds. Alliance with France in 1672 provided them. In 1679 Louis XIV forced the restoration to Sweden of the German provinces she had lost in battle. This put a check on the aspirations of Brandenburg, which Frederick William had built up patiently, establishing his authority at home against the old estates, setting up a permanent administration and army, and winning sovereignty in Prussia by skilfully playing off Poland and Sweden (until 1657 Prussia had been a Polish fief). In 1685 the Great Elector welcomed Huguenot refugees, who provoked new disturbances in Berlin.

Karl XI, who came of age in 1672, fought a fine defence of Skane; his reign was distinguished by the completion of the process of 'reduktion' of former crown lands, which he began in 1680. This was a prelude to the installation of an autocratic, thrifty government which steered clear of alliances. Both the army and the bureaucracy were efficient instruments in Karl XII's hands and, riding on a strong wave of national feeling, he had some initial success in battle against his united neighbours. He became bogged down in Poland, however, and even more irremediably so in Russia, obstinately refusing any compromise settlement. An exhausted Sweden viewed the collapse of these pretensions to grandeur with some relief. In the new northern balance of power, English maritime dominance was placed in the service of Hanover, the elector of which sat on the English throne; the new element in the situation was the considerable presence of Russia installed on the Baltic. Between these two, Prussia made modest progress. Possessing a taste for dynastic pomp, the Great Elector's successor had taken the royal title in Prussia, but his political actions had been unremarkable. Going to war only in 1714, his son Frederick William I gained part of Pomerania including Stettin. Until 1740 he was to use his stern sergeant-king's manner to train up his army, without, however, taking it to war. The real strength of the Hohenzollern state was as yet difficult to discern.

*1. The Great Elector Frederick William and his mother, or 'Solomon and the Queen of Sheba', Mathias Czwieczek, 1648.*

**Descartes dies in Stockholm.** **1650**

**Prussia becomes a sovereign state.** **1657**

**Absolutism in Denmark.** **1665**

**1648:** Treaties of Westphalia. Gains by Sweden and Brandenburg.
**1653:** The agreement of the Brandenburg Estates consolidates the power of the Elector and the subservient status of the peasants.
**1654:** Queen Kristina abdicates. Karl X Gustav becomes king of Sweden (1654–60).
**1655:** Swedish invasion of Poland ('the deluge'). The Swedish Riksdag votes to reclaim a quarter of alienated crown lands.
**1656–7:** Danzig protected by a Dutch fleet. Sovereign independence conferred upon the Duchy of Prussia.
**1657–8:** Unsuccessful Danish attack: by the Peace of Roskilde, Frederik III has to cede six provinces to Sweden.
**1658–9:** Karl X Gustav reopens hostilities, but his siege of Copenhagen ends in failure.
**1660:** The Treaty of Oliva with Poland produces no gains for Sweden. The Peace of Copenhagen gives back Trondheim and the island of Bornholm to Denmark. The Danish monarchy becomes hereditary.
**1661:** The Treaty of Kardis between Sweden and Russia.
**1661–3:** The Diet of Prussia reduced to a subordinate role.
**1662–8:** Construction of the Frederick William Canal (Elbe-Oder).
**1665:** The new constitution of Frederick III codifies absolutism in Denmark.
**1666:** Foundation of Lund University in Swedish Skanie.
**1674–8:** Allied to Louis XIV, Sweden's only successful resistance against the attacks of her united enemies is in Skanie; Prussian victory at Fehrbellin (1675).
**1679:** Louis XIV forces the restitution of all Swedish possessions in the Treaty of Saint-Germain-en-Laye.
**1679–1702:** Publication of *Atland* by Olaus Rudbeck, 'proving' that Sweden was Atlantis.
**1680:** The archbishopric of Magdeburg passes to the Elector of Brandenburg. Karl XI wins assent for his policy of *reduktion* of all alienated crown lands.
**1682:** Swedish monarchy becomes virtually absolute.
**1685:** The Edict of Potsdam grants asylum to Huguenot refugees from France in the states of the Great Elector.

*4. Olaus Rudbeck, as depicted by M. Mijtens in 1696.*

**1688:** Death of the Great Elector, Frederick William, first architect of the might of the Prussian state.
**1694:** Foundation of the University of Halle; spread of Pietism (August Francke).
**1697:** At the age of 15, Karl XII inherits uncontested power in an isolated Sweden.
**1700:** Foundation of the Society of Sciences at Berlin; Frederick IV of Denmark has to withdraw in defeat from the coalition against Sweden. Karl XII defeats the Russians at Narva.
**1701:** The Elector Frederick III has himself crowned king in Prussia (and becomes Frederick I).
**1704:** Karl XII has Stanislaw Leszczynski elected king of Poland.
**1709:** Defeated at Poltava in the Ukraine, Karl XII flees into Turkey.
**1710–14:** All Swedish external possessions are conquered by the allies; desire for peace within Sweden.
**1718:** Death of Karl XII.
**1719–20:** New Swedish constitution reduces the monarch's power almost to nothing. The Treaties of Stockholm cede the provinces of

# 1648–1721

2. Leibniz. Late 17th-century engraving.

NORWAY
Christiania (Oslo)
Trondheim
JAMTLAND
KINGDOM OF SWEDEN
Uppsala
Stockholm
Abo
tar
iron, copper
linen, hemp, copper
Vyborg
Narva
INGRIA
KERALIA
Reval
ESTONIA
Dorpat (Tartu)
LIVONIA
OSEL
Riga
Novgorod
RUSSIA
Dvina
BOHUSLAN
Towards England and the United Provinces
Göteborg
HALLAND
GOTLAND
DENMARK
Sund
BLEKINGS
Halsingborg
Lund
SKANE
Copenhagen
Baltic Sea
cereals
cereals
BORNHOLM
BREMEN AND VERDEN
Lübeck
WISMAR
WESTERN POMERANIA
Bremen
Hamburg
Stettin
HANOVER
Elbe
BRANDENBURG
Danzig
Königsberg
PRUSSIA
Vistula
POLAND
200 km

**Swedish expansion, 1560-1660**

- The Sweden of Gustavus I Vasa (1523-1560)
- Acquisitions between 1561 and 1660
  - Treaty of Altmark (1629) → Baltic possessions
  - Treaty of Brönsebro (1645) → Jamtland
  - Treaty of Westphalia (1648) → Pomerania, Wismar, Bishoprics of Bremen and Verden
  - Treaty of Roskilde (1658) → Southern provinces
- Temporary acquisitions Trondheim and Bornholmk (1558-60)
- ♦ Great Swedish universities

**Decline of Swedish power, 1679-1721**

- to the benefit of Russia
- to the benefit of Brandenburg
- to the benefit of Hanover

**The Baltic Economy**

- ●• Major ports
- Principal sea-trade routes

3. Skokloster Palace in Sweden.

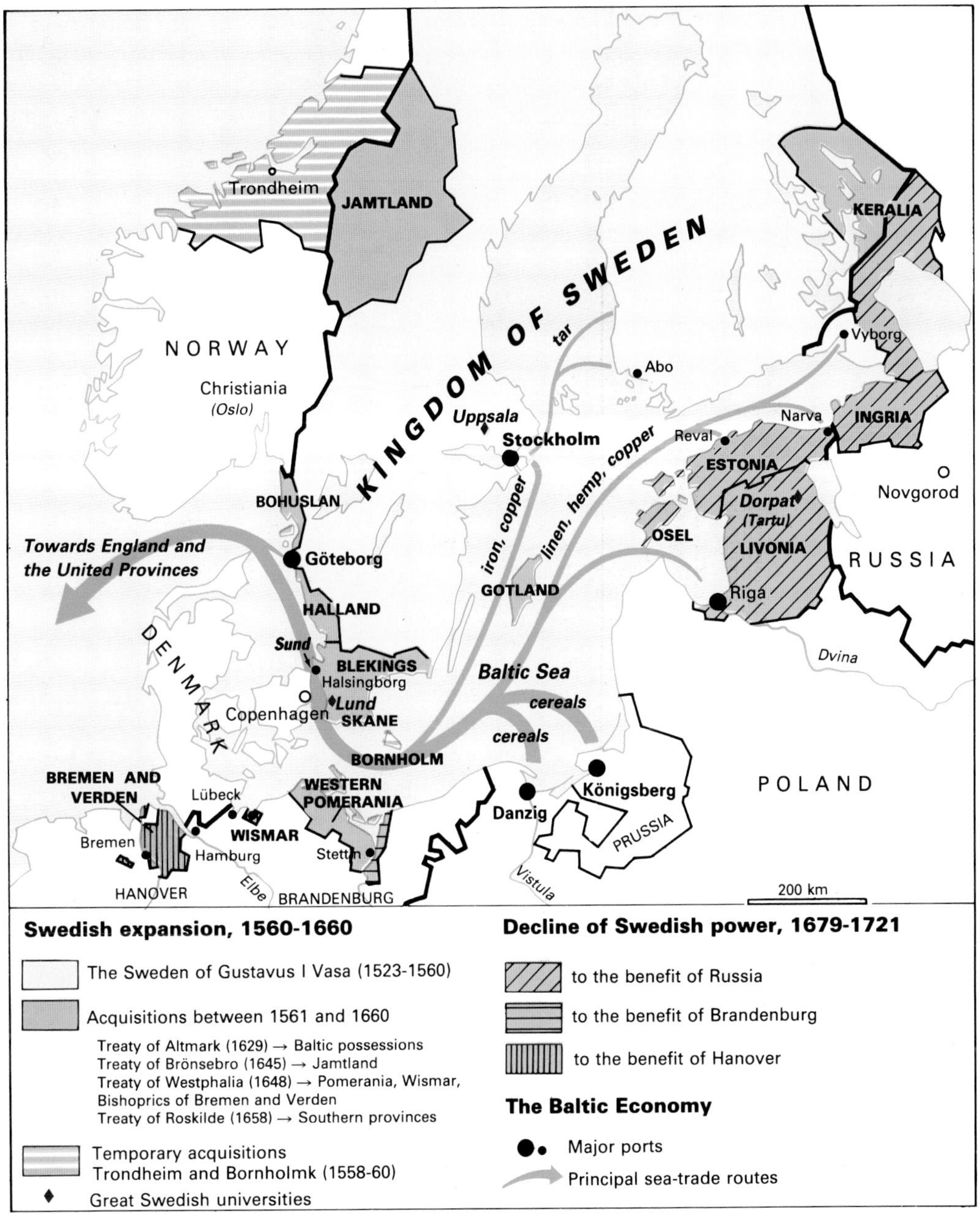

**Huguenots welcomed by Prussia.**

**1685**

**Death of Olaus Rudbeck.**

**1702**

Bremen and Verden to the Elector of Hanover and a part of Swedish Pomerania to Prussia; Denmark makes no territorial gains.
**1721:** The Peace of Nystad cedes the Baltic provinces and a part of Karelia to the Tsar.

5. Charles XII. Engraving after a painting by Craft, 1701.

6. The war between the Russians and the Swedes, from the Zubov Chronicle.

# Colonial Expansion of England and France

THE EIGHTEENTH CENTURY marked a particularly important stage in the history of European expansion in the world. This movement should be considered in terms of its three main features: the development of great voyages of exploration and discovery, the rise of intercontinental trade, and the growth of colonial imperialism.

The great voyages of exploration were made possible by advances in shipbuilding and in navigation techniques. Increasing numbers of expeditions set sail in the second half of the century. The ambitions which inspired these enterprises were born of the spirit of the age: faith in enlightenment and in the advance of knowledge, a passion for science and nature, the desire to make a complete inventory of human activity in the world. The main objective of the expeditions was to explore the uncharted areas of the Pacific Ocean, which some geographers had suggested might hide another continent. By the end of the century, barring a few details, the discovered lands and their coastlines had been mapped definitively. On the other hand, the interiors of both the Asian and African continents – particularly the latter – had been explored very little.

The development of maritime trade was one of the most important factors in the profound economic changes which the countries of Western Europe experienced during this period. Ever-increasing quantities of tropical products – cotton, sugar, coffee, indigo – were sought by Europe and the volume of trade between the continents was growing constantly. The most profitable part of this trade was 'triangular': in exchange for various goods, local rulers on the west coast of Africa handed over slaves; these slaves were sold, on the other side of the ocean, to planters in the West Indies and in both North and South America; the profit from these transactions enabled tropical goods to be purchased and exported at great gain to the markets of Europe. Thus the Atlantic became the centre of international trade, while the ports of Western Europe – Bordeaux, Nantes, Liverpool, London – enjoyed a period of exceptional prosperity.

Bitter commercial rivalry – particularly between France and England – largely explains the lengthy conflicts which ensued over the possession or control of certain colonial territories. When the Treaties of Utrecht were signed, the major colonial powers were still Spain, Portugal and the United Provinces. France and Great Britain began expanding their domains through overseas conquest somewhat later. Each did so during a period of economic expansion, and each was a contender for naval supremacy. So it was, that in the second half of the century, a fierce contest was fought on three fronts: the Caribbean, North America and the East Indies.

The conflict began in 1755 and ended in 1763 with a decisive English victory which was confirmed by the Treaty of Paris. In the West Indies, which were particularly valuable because of their rich plantations, French possessions remained intact. In contrast, however, France lost its vast territories in North America, stretching from the St Lawrence to the Gulf of Mexico. In addition, France renounced its policy of territorial expansion in the East Indies, where it retained only five coastal trading stations. It was the turn of the English to expand their territories in the East Indies, thus marking the beginnings of the British Empire, which would be consolidated in the course of the next century.

*1. Loading cargo bound for the colonies in the port of Rochefort in 1762. Painting by Joseph Vernet.*

**Treaties of Utrecht between England and Holland.**

**French defeat the Allies at Fontenoy.**

**1713** — **1745**

*2. General Louis-Joseph de Saint-Véran, Marquis of Montcalm, dies outside Quebec in 1759. Engraving by Moret, after a drawing by Desfontaines.*

**1715:** Death of Louis XIV. Beginning of policy of *rapprochement* between France and Great Britain, lasting until 1740.
**1740–8:** War of Austrian Succession. France in naval conflict with Great Britain.
**1742–54:** Dupleix, governor of French East India Company's trading stations. Start of policy of territorial expansion.
**26 December 1754:** Godeheu Treaty (from name of Dupleix's successor in the Indies). Agreement by English and French East India Companies to abandon policies of expansion and conquest.
**1755:** Beginnings of Anglo-French hostilities in North America. Seizure by English (under Admiral Boscawen) of more than 300 French ships.
**1759:** Siege and surrender of Quebec.
**8 September 1760:** Capture of Montreal by English.
**1761:** Capture by English of French station at Pondicherry.
**10 February 1763:** Treaty of Paris. Surrender of French territories in North America, with exception of islands of St Pierre and Miquelon and fishing rights off Newfoundland.

**1765:** Robert Clive appointed governor of English East India Company's trading stations. Extension of company's dominion to Bengal and Ganges Valley.
**1766–9:** Bougainville's voyage around world.

*3. Joseph-François Dupleix (1696–1763), French colonial administrator, and Governor General of the French settlements in India.*

**1768–71:** Captain Cook's first voyage. Discovery of New Zealand and east coast of Australia.
**1774:** Extension of Dutch territorial power to Java.
**1774–83:** Revolt of England's 13 American colonies and American War of Independence.
**1779:** Death of Cook in Hawaii.
**1783:** Treaty of Versailles. Granting of independence to British colonies in America.
**1785–8:** La Perouse's voyage of discovery. Expedition wrecked in the New Hebrides.
**1788:** First English settlement in Australia (Botany Bay).

# 18th century

## The world in 1787

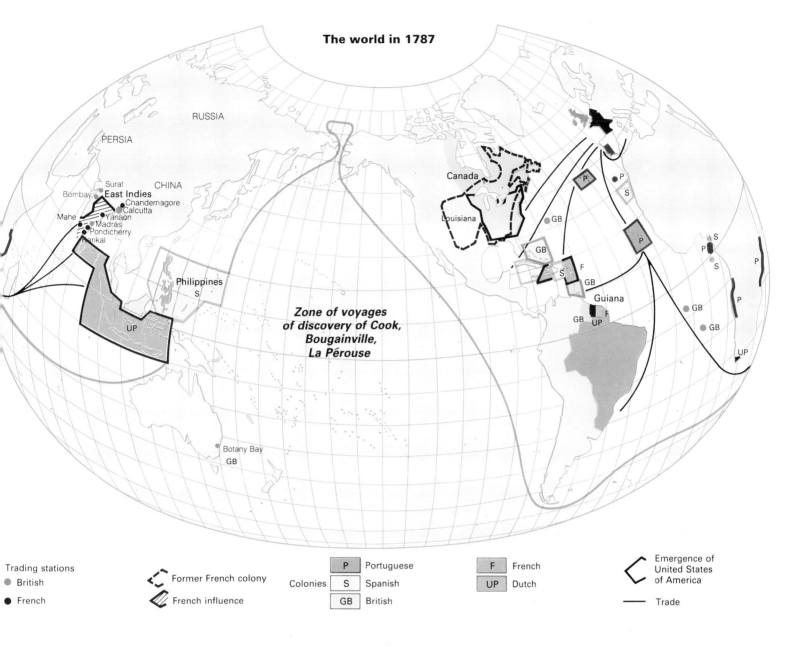

RUSSIA
PERSIA
CHINA
Surat
Bombay
East Indies
Chandernagore
Calcutta
Mahe
Yanaon
Madras
Pondicherry
Karikal
Philippines
S
UP
Zone of voyages of discovery of Cook, Bougainville, La Pérouse
Botany Bay
GB
Canada
Louisiana
GB
GB
P
S
P
S
F
GB
Guiana
GB
UP
F
P
S
P
S
P
P
GB
GB
UP

Trading stations
- British
- French

Former French colony
French influence

Colonies
- P Portuguese
- S Spanish
- GB British
- F French
- UP Dutch

Emergence of United States of America
Trade

| 1763 | 1768–71 | 1785–8 |
|---|---|---|
| **Peace of Paris between France and England.** | **Cook circumnavigates the earth.** | **La Pérouse's voyage.** |

*4. Plan of Madras, trading post of the British East India Company, on the Coromandel coast, captured by La Bourdonnais in 1746 and lost again in 1759.*

*5. The English navigator, James Cook, during his second voyage to Tahiti in 1774, looks on at a human sacrifice.*

# The Enlightened Despots

THE EXPRESSION 'enlightened despotism', widely employed in the nineteenth century, has its origin in the *Literary Correspondence* of Melchior Grimm. It is used to designate both a technique of government enabling backward states to become modernized and a propaganda theme. Among the many countries which attempted this form of government (Pombal's Portugal, Spain, Naples, Parma, Poland and Denmark), there are only three which played a significant 'great power' role: Frederick II's Prussia, the Hapsburg Empire of Maria Theresa and Joseph II and Catherine the Great's Russia. The policies of these sovereigns had certain features in common; in particular, they all regarded Louis XIV as an exemplary figure, and the practices of Frederick II (historically the first 'enlightened' ruler) exerted enormous influence over the others. Their principal concern was for the glorification of the state, of which they themselves were the incarnation. To this end, they began by augmenting their own powers. For Frederick II, who was given, now and then, to theorising, the source of political authority resided in a social contract which gave the sovereign very extensive rights indeed; he therefore suppressed the Diet of Prussia and set out to reduce the powers of the intermediary state bodies. In this he was imitated by Maria Theresa, who drastically reduced the privileges of her dominion states, by Joseph II, who centralized power within his empire, and by the Tsarina, who in her *Nakaz* produced an apology for the despotism of law. Following the example of Frederick II, who had built up his civil service and standardized laws and customs, Catherine II and Joseph II proceeded to initiate thoroughgoing reforms. The latter created a genuine 'civil service' and imposed the use of the German language on his various kingdoms; the education provided by the grammar schools (*Gymnasien*) and the universities was reformed to adapt it to the needs of state service. The army was the principal instrument of these rulers' power: in 1780, with some 200,000 men, Frederick II's army was the most powerful in Europe. Russia and Austria took similar steps to build up their military might. The maintenance of so many troops required new sources of fiscal revenue: these rulers increased their resources by means of customs duties, indirect taxes and monopolies (only Joseph II was so bold as to propose equality of liability to taxation, on the basis of a cadastral survey). Alongside these efforts, they also pursued a goal of enriching their countries; they encouraged agricultural colonization, the building of roads and canals and the creation of industries, all within a strictly regulated framework. Such Colbertist measures enabled these states to meet their own needs and even to export to finance their conquests. Austria, which had lost Silesia, did, however, participate in the dismembering of Poland, completed in 1795. These administrative, military and fiscal reforms did not drastically change society, which remained fixed in its archaic ways: the Prussian and Russian nobilities saw their privileges increase in this period. Joseph II alone dared stand up to the privileged classes, as can be seen in his attempt to abolish serfdom and corvées and his reorganization of the secular clergy along the lines of a civil service. Everywhere, however, the bourgeoisie remained weak and urbanization was still in its initial stages. It is, therefore, more accurate to speak of state despotism than enlightenment in this context. Certain themes borrowed from Enlightenment philosophy (reason, tolerance, happiness) served mainly as an excellent fund of propaganda themes. Voltaire and Diderot hailed Frederick II and Catherine II as 'philosophers'. Frederick II, indeed, kept what was positively a 'philosophical menagerie' at Sans-Souci and at the Berlin Academy. The Austrian monarchs showed some reserve in this matter, though it was in fact Joseph II who attempted the most far-reaching and radical reforms, precipitating his states into a revolt that was quelled only when all his reforming measures were revoked after his death.

*1. The Marquis of Pombal, by J. Guimaraes.*

**Frederick II King of Prussia. Maria Theresa Empress.** — **1740**

**Voltaire in Berlin.** — **1750**

**Catherine II Tsarina.** — **1762**

**1736:** Correspondence between Voltaire and Frederick II begins.
**1739:** Frederick II: *Anti-Machiavel.*
**1740:** Accession of Frederick II (May) and Maria-Theresa (October).
**1740–48:** Christian Wolff, *Jus naturae.*
**1741:** First war in Silesia.
**1742:** Treaty of Breslau. A large part of Silesia becomes Prussian.
**1743:** Frederick II draws up statutes of the East Berlin Academy, whose director is Maupertuis.
**1744:** Frederick II introduces the cotton industry.
**1745:** Construction of the Sans-Souci residence at Potsdam.
**1747:** Johann Sebastian Bach at Potsdam.
**1749:** Frederick II's directory and commission for schools.
**1752:** Maria Theresa creates a system of technical education.
**1753:** Voltaire and Frederick II quarrel. Maria Theresa institutes a judicial commission.
**1756–63:** Seven Years' War.
**1762:** Nationalization of the Bank of Vienna; accession of Catherine II, who corresponds

*2. Frederick II at Sans-Souci.*

with d'Alembert; Maria Theresa, Mining College of Hungary.
**1764:** C. Beccaria-Bonesana, *On Crimes and Punishments.*
**1765:** Death of Emperor Francis; Joseph II Emperor and co-regent. Catherine II buys Diderot's library. Helvetius at Potsdam; creation of the Bank of Berlin.
**1767:** Nakaz ('Instruction') by Catherine II; she translates Marmontel's *Bélisaire*; Mercier de la Rivière at St Petersburg.
**1769:** Catherine II creates the Assignat Banks of Moscow and St Petersburg.
**1770:** Maria Theresa: Royal Academy of Commerce and Penal Code.
**1771:** Voltaire, *Épitre à l'impératrice de Russie*; Maria Theresa's patents on the corvée in Silesia.
**1772:** First partition of Poland.
**1773:** Pugachov's revolt in Russia; Diderot at St Petersburg; Frederick II decrees education compulsory.
**1775:** Catherine II issues decrees on administrative reform, freedom of trade and industry.
**1778:** Equestrian statue of Peter the Great

*3. The Empress Maria Theresa.*

# 18th century

## The Age of Enlightened Despotism

FINLAND
KARELIA
St Petersburg
SWEDEN
ESTONIA 1721
LIVONIA 1721
Pskov
DENMARK
1772
Dwina
Smolensk
EAST FREISLAND 1744
Lübeck
Hamburg
Stettin
POMERANIA
Königsberg
DANZIG
UNITED PROVINCES
Bremen
Lingen
HANOVER
WEST PRUSSIA 1772
DUCHY OF CLEVES 1702
BRANDENBURG
DUCHY OF GELDERLAND 1713
RAVENSBERG
Dortmund
Magdeburg
Berlin
Antwerp
Brussels
COUNTY OF MARK
Potsdam
Elbe
SCHWIEBUS 1742
Vistula
POLAND
Pripet
NETHERLANDS
Aix-la-Chapelle
Cologne
SAXONY
Leipzig
Warsaw
AUSTRIAN
Mainz
Dresden
Breslau
SILESIA 1742
LOWER PALATINATE
Worms
Prague
Rothenburg
Nüremberg
Cracow
FRANCE
Heilbronn
UPPER PALATINATE
BOHEMIA
KINGDOM OF GALICIA AND LODOMERIA 1772
Dniepr
Esslingen
Nördlingen
MORAVIA
Rottweil
Ulm
Augsburg
INNVIERTEL 1779
Vienna
Memmingen
BAVARIA
Danube
BUKOVINA 1775
NEUCHATEL 1707
Kempten
Salzburg
SWITZERLAND
TYROL
SIYRIA
Tisza
Buda
Pest
Trent
CARINTHIA
CRIMEA 1774
1714 MILAN
REPUBLIC OF VENICE
HUNGARY-TRANSYLVANIA
Rhône
PIEDMONT 1738
Milan
CARNIOLA
Trieste
MANTUA 1708
BANATE 1718
PARMA 1735-1748
Florence
TUSCANY 1737
SERBIA-WALLACHIA 1718-1739
Danube
KINGDOM OF NAPLES 1714-1735
OTTOMAN EMPIRE
SARDINIA 1714-1720
300 km

Russia (Romanov)
Prussia (Hohenzollern)
Austria (Hapsburg)
Territories acquired temporarily
SAXONY Electorate
Border of the Holy Roman Empire
1744 Date of annexation
Imperial Free Cities
Towns and cities:
With more than 100,000 inhabitants
With more than 50,000 inhabitants
With more than 25,000 inhabitants
With less than 25,000 inhabitants
---- Polish frontier before 1772

## Partitions of Poland

Riga
Russia
Courland
Danzig
LITHUANIA
Prussia
Torun (Thorn)
Vistula
Poland
Kiev
Cracow
GALICIA
PODOLIA
Austria
1772

Russia
Prussia
Poland
Austria
1793

Russia
Prussia
Austria
1795
300 km

**Joseph II's Edict of Toleration.** **1781**

**Third partition of Poland.** **1795**

(by Falconet) at St Petersburg.
**1778–80:** Lessing, *Gespräche für Freimaurer.*
**1780:** Death of Maria Theresa, who is succeeded by Joseph II.
**1781:** Frederick II, *Essay on Forms of Government*; Kant, *Critique of Pure Reason*; Joseph II, cadastral survey, Edict of Toleration, reform of the regular clergy and abolition of serfdom.
**1782:** Joseph II, reform of the secular clergy; Berlin Academy's competition on the universality of the French language.
**1786:** Joseph II abolishes the guilds. Mirabeau in Prussia. Death of Frederick II (17 August).
**1787:** Triumphal visit of Catherine II to the Crimea; Josephinian Law Code.
**1788:** Risings in Hungary and Belgium.
**1789:** Joseph II, abolition of the corvée; the Austrian Netherlands proclaim their independence.
**1790:** Death of Joseph II (20 February).
**1793:** Second partition of Poland.
**1795:** Third partition of Poland.
**1796:** Death of Catherine II (17 November).

*4. Schönbrunn Palace in Vienna, by Bellotto.*

*5. Catherine II of Russia.*

# Europe of the Enlightenment and the Encyclopaedists

ENLIGHTENMENT EUROPE was characterized by French domination and by the awakening of 'Germany' after 1770. Dutch, English and Italian influence declined: the universities of Leyden, Utrecht and Oxford had lost their vitality, and the Dutch republican model was no longer regarded as particularly inspiring by theorists, who saw it as suitable only for small states. English-style parliamentarism was admired by philosophers but not by sovereigns jealous of their power. Italy, the home of the arts, remained the country most visited by lovers of painting, opera and antiquities (the discovery of Pompeii and Herculaneum). According to Gibbon, 40,000 English people toured Italy in 1785, but there was a considerable decline in the overall number of visitors. After 1750, Italian artists were much less in demand and were replaced more often than not by French ones. In the field of the arts, the classical and neo-classical French influence won out over the baroque. The other states built palaces inspired by Versailles and constructed royal squares. In political matters, Louis XIV served as a model, while, culturally, the *philosophes*, who became the zealots of reason, freedom and tolerance, were a dominant force. Enlightenment culture was an élite culture (nobility and upper bourgeoisie) which was transmitted by way of national and provincial academies, masonic lodges (English and Scottish in origin) and salons (particularly those of Mmes Geoffrin, Deffand and Necker and of Mlle Lespinasse, all in Paris). Paris, the 'model for foreign nations' (Caraccioli) was the capital of taste and fashion, wit and good manners. The diaspora of French Protestants in their Dutch, Swiss and German havens ensured the spread of the language and culture. Holland and Switzerland became the great centres for the printing of banned books and Frankfurt a great market for French works. The principal European courts copied the French model: they wrote and spoke in French (which, since the Treaties of Utrecht, was the language of diplomacy) and they engaged the services of French tutors, scholars, actors, artists and architects. They copied Parisian fashions and they created academies. All this represented a court culture, imposed by the rulers. A reaction did, however, set in very early, especially in 'Germany' with Weimar and Dresden, faithful to their local Germanic culture, giving the lead. In Germany's dynamic universities (Leipzig, Halle, Göttingen, Königsberg) a generation was formed which further developed the specific traits of the German *Aufklärung*. This was rationalist in tendency in the work of Kant, for example, but was also characterized by a nostalgia for origins (Herder) and a certain world-weariness. The new generation was that of the *Sturm und Drang* epitomized by Goethe's *Young Werther*. This triumph of sensibility became a European phenomenon which at times developed into a taste for the morbid: the readers of Rousseau's *La Nouvelle Héloise* also appreciated Young's *The Complaint, or Night Thoughts*, macabre meditations that were translated into all languages. The influence of 'German' culture was strong in the field of music, where Italian supremacy was now fiercely contested. Following on the heels of Handel and Bach, Gluck was a great success in Paris; Mozart, Haydn and, subsequently, Beethoven were also soon to make their reputations. In the later years of the century, the cosmopolitanism of the Enlightenment, illustrated by the diffusion of French culture, was everywhere receding. The first manifestations of nationalism appeared, with the virtues of national languages and heritages being extolled. This was a prelude to a new type of confrontation between states, one unknown in the century of the Enlightenment in which conflicts – localized and few in number (Wars of the Austrian Succession, 1741–8; Seven Years' War, 1756–63) – had remained an affair of princes rather than peoples.

1. From left to right: Condorcet, La Harpe, Voltaire, d'Alembert, Diderot and le père Adam, as seen by J. Huber.

**Birth of Voltaire.** **1694**

**Birth of Rousseau.** **1712**

**1721:** Montesquieu (1689–1755), *Lettres persanes.*
**1723:** J. S. Bach, *The St John Passion.*
**1726:** Voltaire (1694–1778), journey to England.
**1730:** Réaumur's thermometer.
**1731:** Academy of Surgery. Abbé Prévost, *Manon Lescaut.*
**1733:** Boerhaave, *Elements of Chemistry*; Pope, *Essay on Man.*
**1735:** Linnaeus, *Systema Naturae*; Rameau, *Les Indes galantes.*
**1742:** Young, *The Complaint, or Night Thoughts.*
**1744:** Piranesi, *Prisons.*
**1748:** Montesquieu, *L'Esprit des lois*; Hume, *An Enquiry Concerning Human Understanding.*
**1749–51:** Marigny, Cochin and Soufflet journey to Italy.
**1749–67:** Buffon, *Histoire naturelle.*
**1750:** Rousseau (1712–78), *Discours sur les sciences et les arts.*
**1751–72:** The *Encyclopédie* (banned in France in 1759).
**1751:** Voltaire, *Le Siècle de Louis XIV.*
**1753–90:** Grimm, Diderot, Raynal, *Correspondance littéraire.*
**1754:** Rousseau, *Discours sur les origines et les fondements de l'inégalité.*
**1756:** Voltaire, *Essai sur les moeurs.*
**1757:** Academy of Sciences and Fine Arts, Berlin.
**1758:** Russian Academy of Fine Arts.
**1759–81:** Diderot (1713–84), Accounts of the Paris Salons.

2. The owl of Minerva. An illustration to Buffon's work by Martinet.

3. The so-called Temple of Neptune at Paestum, by Piranesi.

# 18th century

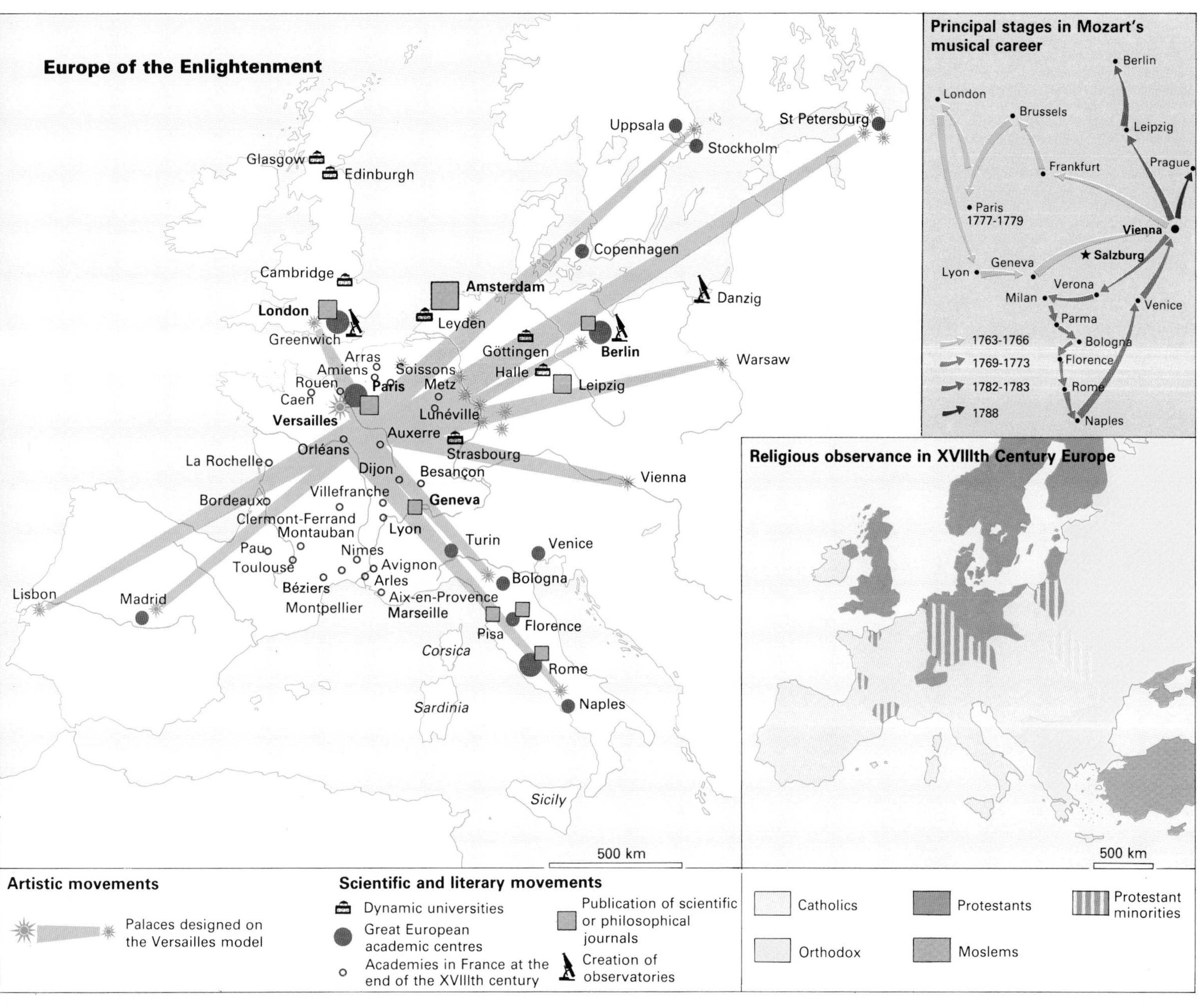


| rit des lois. | The *Encyclopédie*. | Mozart becomes a freemason. | Death of Condorcet. |
|---|---|---|---|
| 1748 | 1751 | 1784 | 1794 |

**1760:** MacPherson, *'Ossian'*.
**1761:** Rousseau, *La Nouvelle Héloise*; Greuze, *L'Accordée du village*.
**1762:** Rousseau, *The Social Contract* and *Émile*; Gluck, *Orfeo*; Gabriel, the Petit Trianon.
**1763–79:** Potsdam, the columns and outbuildings of Sans-Souci.
**1764:** Winckelmann, *History of the Art of Antiquity*; Voltaire, *Philosophical Dictionary*.
**1764–90:** Soufflot, Sainte-Geneviève (Panthéon).
**1765:** Cavendish studies hydrogen.
**1766:** Lessing, *Laokoon*; Bougainville's voyage.
**1768:** Cook's first voyage. Foundation of the Royal Academy (London).
**1768–75:** Gabriel, Place Louis XV (Concorde).
**1774:** Herschel's Great Telescope; Goethe, *The Sorrows of Young Werther*.
**1775–9:** Ledoux builds the salt-works of Chaux at Arc-et-Senans.
**1776:** Adam Smith, *The Wealth of Nations*.
**1777:** *Journal de Paris*, daily newspaper; K. W. Scheele separates hydrogen from nitrogen.

4. Ledoux's stage set for the theatre at Besançon.

**1778:** Mozart (1756-91) and Mesmer in Paris.
**1781:** Herschel discovers Uranus; publication of Rousseau's *Confessions*; Schiller's *Robbers*; Laclos, *Les Liaisons Dangereuses*.
**1783:** Lavoisier's analysis of water. First balloon flight.
**1784:** Beaumarchais, *The Marriage of Figaro*.
**1785:** David, *The Oath of the Horatii*; La Pérouse's voyage.
**1787:** Mozart, *Don Giovanni*; Bernardin de St Pierre, *Paul et Virginie*.
**1788:** Monge, *Traité de statistique*.
**1789:** Kalproth discovers uranium; Abbé Barthélemy, *le Voyage du jeune Anacharsis en Grèce*; William Blake, *Songs of Innocence*.
**1791:** Polish constitution; Mozart, *The Magic Flute*; Haydn, *Orpheus and Euridyce*.
**1793:** Suppression of the Paris Academies.

# World Population

**1500:** Population of the world, before its systematic exploration by the Europeans, approximately 470 million. Main centres of population – India (including present-day Pakistan, Bangladesh, Nepal, Bhutan, Sri Lanka), approximately 95 million; China (including present-day Manchuria, Mongolia, western Turkestan, Tibet and Taiwan), 84 million; Europe, 78 million; central Sudan (including present-day Niger and Nigeria), 25 million; Peru and Mexico, each 12 million; Japan, 10 million.
**1517:** Death of almost one-third of Mexico's population, after spread of smallpox from Haiti. Same fate a little later for other American countries. Smallpox followed by other diseases: measles, typhus, diphtheria in 1531, 1545, 1564, 1576–7 and (the worst epidemic) in 1582. Beginning, nevertheless, of Spanish emigration to New World.

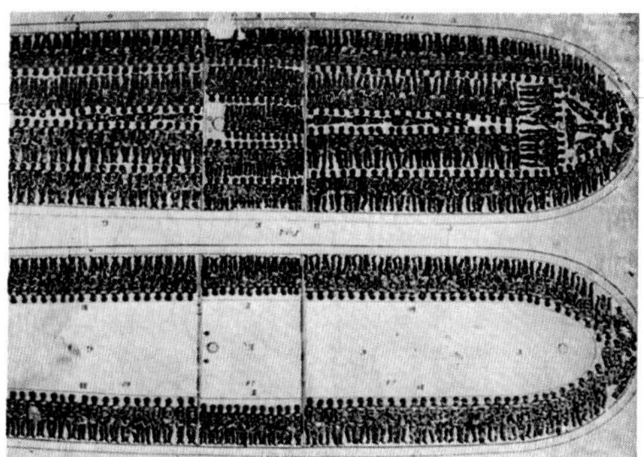

*1. Slave ship at Goree, Senegal, late 18th century.*

**1518:** Slaves from Black Africa taken to America by the Spanish to overcome shortage of manpower; from 1520, slave trade established on coast of Guinea.
**1522–34:** Significant drop in population of Western Europe, caused by famines, wars and epidemics.
**1530:** Beginning of rise of trade with America and India and of prosperity of Atlantic ports. Decline of Mediterranean trade and of economic role of Ottoman Empire. Population of the East at lowest level.
**1542:** Arrival of first shipload of African slaves in Brazil.
**1556:** 800,000 Chinese killed in Shaanxi earthquake.
**1563:** Plague epidemic throughout Europe; continuing increase in population.
**1580–98:** Population of France reduced by four million through epidemics and religious conflicts.
**1582–3:** Famines and serious epidemics in Saharan Sudan.
**1588:** Growth of Chinese population not hindered by great famine and epidemics affecting almost whole of China.

*2. Slave merchants at Goree, Senegal, late 18th century.*

**1500**

1 point: 1 million individuals

**1600**

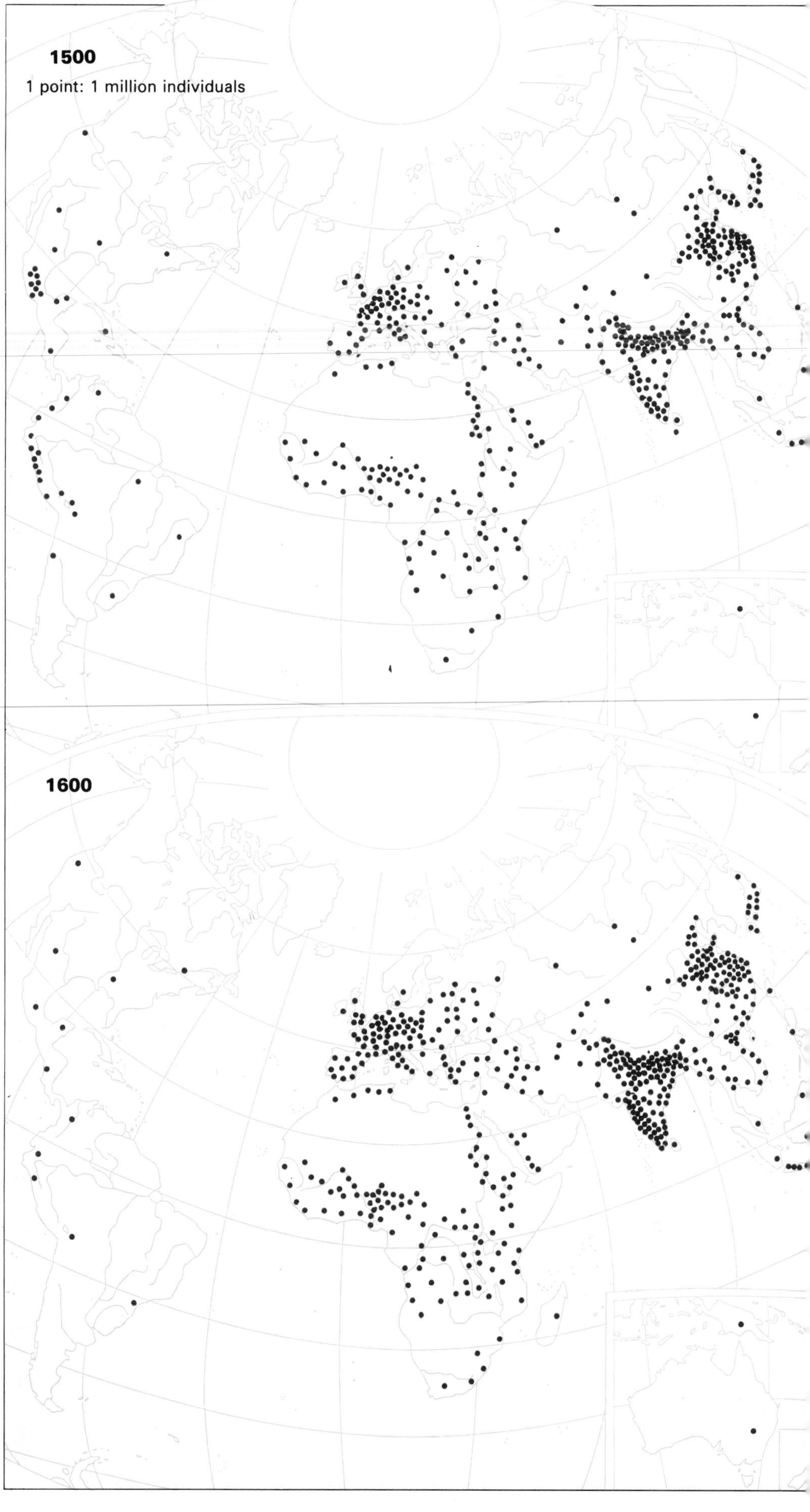

# 16th–18th centuries

THE THREE CENTURIES from 1500 to 1800 form the first phase of an age of transition, the second phase of which we are still living through today: it is the age of the discovery of the world by Europe and of the cultural, technological and biological repercussions of that discovery.

In the sixteenth century the Muslim and Chinese worlds seemed to follow along with the European movements in scientific learning. But from the second half of the seventeenth century the closing of minds – even more than the closing of frontiers – meant that for three centuries (two in the case of Japan) the initiative in both technical progress and cultural development was held by Europe, and Europe alone derived benefit from it. This made for an even greater shock when, from political, commercial, religious or ideological motives, Europe and its influence eventually penetrated into all societies on earth. From the demographic point of view, the exchanges of microbes were particularly deadly to the American peoples: the arrival of smallpox in Mexico in 1517, for example, wiped out more than 30% of the population.

The map for 1500 shows the approximate distribution of the world's population at that date, on the eve of the spate of discoveries and journeys of exploration which would bring all those previously separate worlds into contact with one another. Each had lived until then inside its own system of religion, culture, cosmology and philosophy, which formed a coherent mental whole; its almost complete ignorance of all other societies had preserved this self-sufficiency. The principal centres of population at this time were India, followed by China, Europe, Western Sudan (Niger-Nigeria) and, in the New World, Western Mexico and Peru.

The map for 1600 shows the upheavals which, a century later, followed that initial shock: the terrible reduction – to almost one-fifth – of the American population and the stagnation and, in some cases, decline of the populations of Africa, Asia and the South Sea Islands. Only Europe saw a significant increase in its population.

On the map for 1800, two centuries later, a new demographic order can be seen. The population of Europe was still growing, as was that of China, which had isolated itself from the rest of the world and continued to live at its own rhythm. But the population of India was increasing only slightly, while that of America was stagnating, with the exception of the Atlantic coast of North America, where large numbers of immigrants were beginning to settle. The population of Africa, drained by the slave trade, was decreasing, as was that of the South Sea Islands, decimated by epidemics.

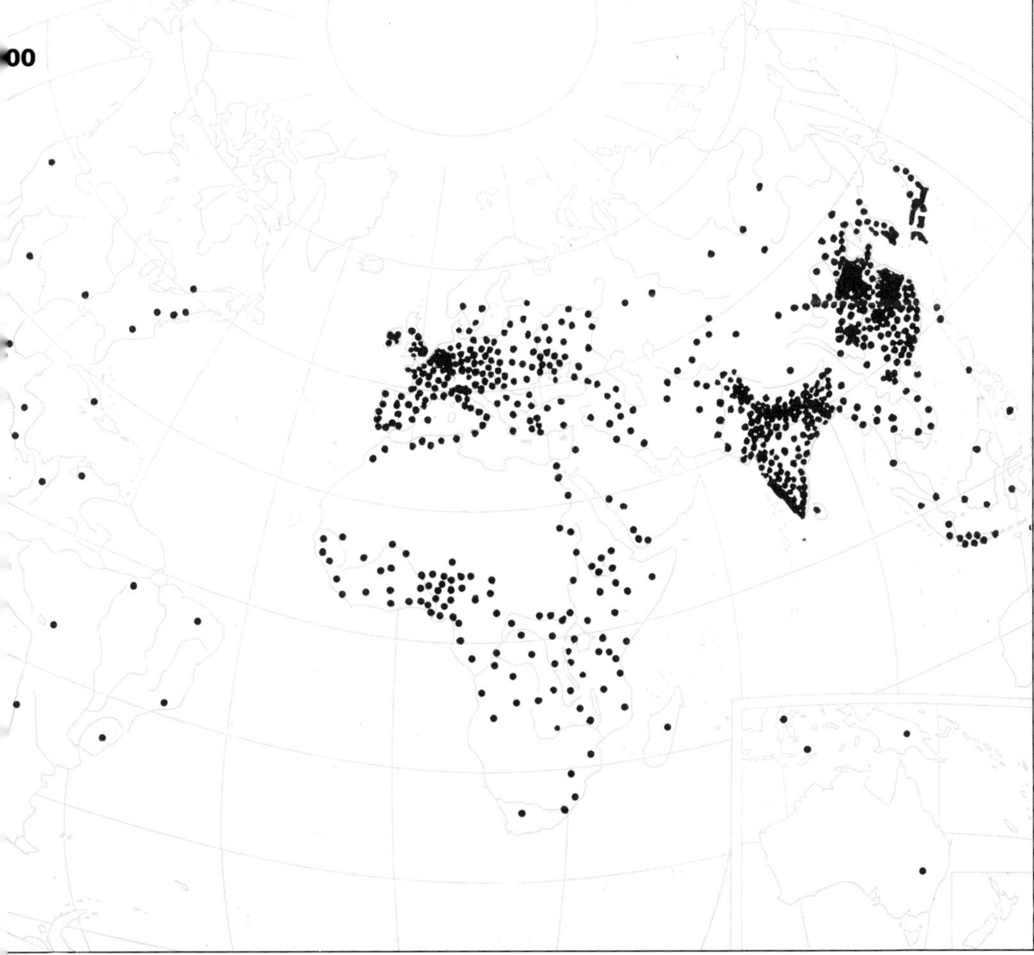


*3. The plague in Marseille, 1720, depicted by Michel Serre.*

**1618–48:** German population reduced through Thirty Years' War and epidemics by almost one-third from 15 million to 10 million.
**1620:** Beginnings of slave trade in English colonies.
**1628–31:** Terrible plague epidemics in Germany, France, northern Italy. Serious uprisings in China.
**1636:** Beginning of slave trade in French colonies.
**1641–4:** Famine, epidemics, uprisings, Manchurian invasions; fall in Chinese population estimated at 13 million.
**1648–51:** One million people killed by plague in Spain; population level not restored until 18th century.
**1650–85:** Population of Great Britain reduced by almost one million by civil war and plague.
**1651–3:** Nearly one million people killed in France by Fronde uprisings and plague.
**1654–7:** One-third of Polish population lost in wars against Russia and Sweden and in epidemics.
**1689:** Beginning of policy of repopulation of the Balkans with German settlers.
**1690–4:** Serious crisis of food shortages and epidemics in almost all Europe. Fall in European population at start of 17th century, from approximately 106 million in 1600 to 103 million in 1650, followed by slight increase to 114 million in 1700. Contrasting rise in Japanese population from 10 million in 1600 to 25 million in 1700.
**1699:** Sultanate of Oman established on east coast of Africa: new impetus to trade – existing since eighth century – of black slaves to Muslim countries.
**1709–10:** Severe winter and food shortages in Europe. Repeopling of northern Poland, east Prussia and Lithuania, following loss of half of population through famine, plague and smallpox.
**1730:** From this date, rapid rise in European population, from 114 million in 1700 to 180 million in 1800. (But in France, beginnings of contraception and fall in birth rate.) Even greater increase in Chinese population, from about 150 million to 330 million in course of century. Population of Japan level at 25 million.
**1740–80:** Slave trading by European merchants at its height – tripled since 17th century. Trade in Muslim countries doubled. In course of 18th century, population of Black Africa reduced by 10 million through slave trade.
**1769–70:** Great famine in Bengal, where the population is reduced from 29 million to 19 million.
**1787:** Beginning of movement in England for abolition of slavery.
**1794:** Abolition of slavery in French colonies decreed by Convention Nationale. Beginning of decline in European slave trade.

# The Beginnings of the Industrial Revolution

The Industrial Revolution – a British phenomenon above all – was at once the product of a specific historical experience limited to a particular geographical area and the result of the very broadest patterns of world historical development. Hence the ambiguous consequences of 'imitating' it and the sometimes tragic setbacks experienced by many of those who have sought to do so. Put simply, it consisted of a wave of particularly significant, sudden innovations, the unexpected, accidental character of which it would be foolish to deny, but which, nonetheless, followed on one from the other in a logical sequence. A series of convergent lines of technical development came together, and, in so doing, formed a new 'system'. Two such 'lines' were of particular importance: developments in textiles (notably the mechanization of the production process and the rise of chemical processes of bleaching and dyeing) and developments in coal fuel technology. Coal now had a double role, both as the principal fuel for treating and refining materials, and as a source of mechanical energy, which it had become thanks to the new 'atmospheric machines'. Each of the significant inventions of the time was in reality only one link in a continuous chain of interactions which continued a developmental process spanning many centuries. The Industrial Revolution was not a 'leap' in technological development; it was the outcome of a long learning process.

1. Open-cast coal mine in Great Britain, c. 1790. Steam pump invented by Thomas Newcomen.

Before 1750 Britain was an advanced pre-industrial country: its agriculture was generally more efficient than Continental farming and its industry, which was expanding within a framework of domestic production, was becoming increasingly diversified. From the seventeenth century onwards Great Britain in fact enjoyed a market whose criteria were distinctly higher than those of Continental markets, and which, moreover, was capable of accepting new partially standardized products. Between 1500 and 1750 the growth in industrial production was of the order of 0.2% per head annually and the overall increase in production 0.45%. New technical avenues were evolved because as different types of production developed they came up against the right bottlenecks: a very early shortage of fuel in the case of the coal sector, a localized but marked shortage of labour in the case of textile mechanization. This pressure became more and more constraining after 1760 and especially after 1780: the increase in industrial production rose from 0.7% a year between 1700 and 1760 to 1.5% between 1760 and 1780, and 2.1% between 1780 and 1800. The role of exports, which was by no means negligible in the eighteenth century, now became crucial. The history of the cotton industry is exemplary in this regard: initially started as part of a substitution process – to displace imported Indian articles – after 1780 it was carried along by the very rapid rise in exports that increasing mechanization made possible.

In order to grasp the opportunities offered, on the one hand by the combination of the science and technology of the period and, on the other, by the pressure of demand, it was necessary for a stratum of industrial entrepreneurs to be formed, possessing a minimum of capital and capable of putting the available labour force to work. Even if the rates of capital accumulation did not achieve the wonderful leap forward that has been suggested, they nonetheless rose progressively throughout the period. On the micro-economic level, a minimal initial input was required, together with the will to reinvest the profits systematically. Here once again historical continuity came into play: the initiative was for the most part taken by traders or merchant producers, the most enterprising of whom transformed themselves into industrialists.

**A. Darby smelts iron with coke.**

**1709**

**J. Kay invents the flying shuttle.**

**1733**

**1698:** Thomas Savery (c. 1650–1715) designs a machine aimed at draining water from mines ('the miner's friend').
**1700:** The rate of capital formation is 4% of gross national product (GNP) and exports represent 8.5% of national revenue.
**1709:** Abraham Darby (1677–1717) first smelts iron with coke at Coalbrookdale in Shropshire.
**1712:** Thomas Newcomen (1663–1729), a Dartmouth locksmith, builds the first piston-driven 'atmospheric machine'.
**1733:** John Kay (1704–64) invents the flying shuttle.
**1740–50:** B. Huntsman (1704–66) perfects the production of steel in a crucible furnace.
**1746:** John Roebuck (1718–94) perfects the iron chamber process for manufacturing sulphuric acid.
**1748:** The Darby process of cast-iron production using coke is improved by selecting ores that contain less phosphor.
**1761:** Adoption of cast-iron rails in the factories of Coalbrookdale.
**1762:** Matthew Boulton (1728–1809) builds his factory at Soho.

2. First entirely automatic loom built by Jacques de Vaucanson in 1745.

**1767:** J. Hargreaves, a Stanhill weaver, perfects the 'Spinning Jenny' for the spinning of cotton.
**1769:** R. Arkwright perfects his 'Waterframe' spinning machine. J. Wedgwood opens his 'Etruria' pottery works. First patents for J. Watt's steam engine.
**1770:** The share of exports in national revenue falls back to 7.6% after having reached 11.6% in 1759.
**1771:** Completion of Richard Arkwright's first factory at Cromford (Derbyshire).
**1776:** Adam Smith, the father of economic liberalism, publishes *An Enquiry into the Nature and Causes of the Wealth of Nations.*
**1777:** Arkwright builds a second factory at Cromford.
**1779:** Samuel Crompton invents the spinning mule. First cast-iron bridge over the Severn (J. Wilkinson).
**1780:** The rate of investment as a proportion of GNP reaches 7%.
**1780–1800:** Average annual growth rate of total production estimated at 1.2%. Growth of industrial production is 2.11%. Production per head is rising by 0.35%.

**1782–5:** Rotative beam steam engine invented by J. Watt. Henry Cort takes out his grooved rail patent.
**1783:** Exports as a proportion of national revenue at 7.8%.

3. Joseph Priestley (1733–1804), British chemist and philosopher, who discovered oxygen in 1774.

# 18th century

## Great Britain's supremacy at the end of the XVIIIth century

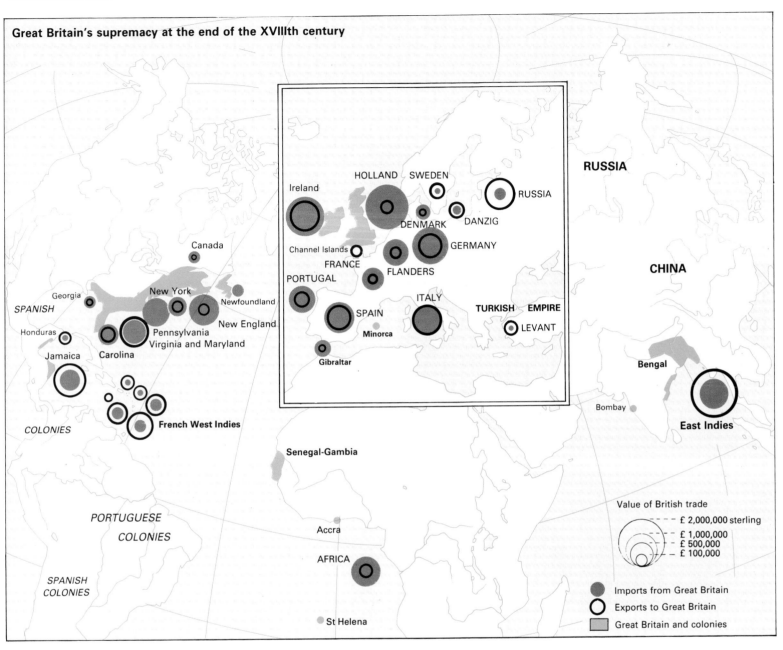

RUSSIA
HOLLAND SWEDEN
Ireland
RUSSIA
DENMARK DANZIG
Canada
Channel Islands
GERMANY
FRANCE
FLANDERS
CHINA
PORTUGAL
Georgia
New York
Newfoundland
SPANISH
ITALY
TURKISH EMPIRE
SPAIN
New England
Honduras
Pennsylvania
Virginia and Maryland
Minorca
LEVANT
Jamaica
Carolina
Gibraltar
Bengal
Bombay
French West Indies
East Indies
COLONIES
Senegal-Gambia
PORTUGUESE COLONIES
Accra
AFRICA
SPANISH COLONIES
St Helena

Value of British trade
£ 2,000,000 sterling
£ 1,000,000
£ 500,000
£ 100,000

Imports from Great Britain
Exports to Great Britain
Great Britain and colonies

**Arkwright's spinning machine.** **N. J. Cugnot invents the steam road-carriage.** **First steam engine on rails by M. Boulton and J. Watt.**

**1769** **1770–1** **1785**

4. *The workshop at Soho near Birmingham, where Boulton and Watt's steam engines were built, c. 1790.*

**1784:** Henry Cort takes out patent for the puddling process.
**1785:** Matthew Boulton and James Watt's first steam engine installed in a Nottingham cotton factory.
**1787:** Cartwright's semi-automatic weaving machine. Adoption of bleaching process using chlorine, invented by C. L. Berthollet in 1785. Foundations laid for Arkwright's New Lanark factory in Scotland.
**1792:** First successful attempt at gas lighting by William Murdoch.
**1797:** Henry Maudsley invents carriage lathe.
**1801:** Exports represent 17.8% of national income. The rate of investment reaches 7.9%.

5. *Galleries in the Bradley coal mine, Staffordshire, c. 1800.*

# Revolutions throughout the World

From around 1760 onwards, the revolutionary upheavals which had characterized the middle of the seventeenth century resurfaced on a wider scale and with even more striking effects. Out of the whole period in which the capitalist world market was being formed and rising to its zenith (from the end of the fifteenth century to the beginning of the twentieth), the years 1760–1800 or, more precisely, 1787–94, were the richest in socio-political innovation. The American Constitution of 1787 is still in force and the French Revolution is still a vital factor today. The reigns of Andrianampoinimerina in Madagascar (1787–1810) and the Tay Son brothers in Vietnam (1786–92) constitute major landmarks in the history of those countries; the movement of Tupac Amaru in Peru has been described as 'the greatest social revolution in Latin American history' (before Mexico in the second decade of this century) and Pugachov's was indisputably the greatest peasant revolt in Russia before 1917.

If the place occupied in this crucial period by Pascal Paoli's Corsica, the Tay Son brothers' Vietnam, Stanislaus II (Poniatowski)'s Poland and Tupac Amaru's Peru forces us to reject the expressions 'Atlantic Revolution' or 'Western Revolution', it is nonetheless true that Western Europe and North America were at the centre of the global historical process. And there is no doubt that the French Revolution was at the heart of the Western part of that process.

*1. Emelyan Ivanovich Pugachov, 'Tsar of the Mujiks and Cossacks', anonymous Russian painting.*

One should not, though, make too rigid a distinction between genuine revolutions and the many and varied vigorous attempts at reform which followed the Seven Years' War. The 'enlightened despots' of these decades and their ministers were great innovators.

Even though Louis XIV, George III of England and Joseph II of Austria were victims of the upheavals of the age, and the 1780s in particular were hardly favourable to the enlightened despots (some curious 'aristocratic reactions' emerged in the period), and though the first large-scale 'republics' known to history were born at that time, princely or royal 'revolutions' and popular revolutions had as much to unite them as to divide them.

If we ask what the common achievement of these revolutions was, the answer must be a rationalization of societies and cultures, a containment of religious influence and a general re-shaping of reality by the new spirit. They also achieved some democratization, the reduction or abolition of privileges, a reduction of differences in status, the passage from caste to class societies, and, therefore, the embourgeoisement of both the old and new élites. Together with this went a liberation of mercantile and productive energies, with, after the 1780s in particular, periods of anti-trade reaction such as are seen in the French Revolution and counter-revolution with their very marked peasant overtones and in Norway, the Ukraine, Rumania, China, Japan, North and South America etc. Finally, in many cases there was a clear restoration or reinforcement of the spirit of patriotism, to the detriment of colonial or cosmopolitan tendencies: there were moves towards integrating the Jews in Western countries, the first concerted abolitionist activities on the part of the North American Blacks, there were Indian and Creole risings throughout the Americas, and anti-Manchu plots and uprisings in China. Other important patriotic movements which surfaced during this period include the first signs of the assertion of Vietnamese identity, the beginnings of armed resistance by the great African peoples against Boer expansion, Greek insurrections against the Turks, the modest beginnings of the Italian *Risorgimento*, and the development of early German nationalism, not to mention the emergence of 'patriots' in France and elsewhere. . . .

**1755–69:** Pascal Paoli is general of the Corsican nation; he is a kind of 'enlightened despot'.
**1756–63:** Seven Years' War: major turning-point in European and world history.
**1759–60 onwards:** Numerous peasant uprisings in Russia, Norway etc.
**1760s:** Democratic stirrings in Geneva, which in 1768 limits the privileges of the oligarchy in favour of the bourgeoisie.
**1760–1820:** George III King of Great Britain and Ireland. Upsurges of nationalist and democratic feeling in the country, which at times seems on the verge of revolution.
**1761–82:** Hyder Ali King of Mysore: reforms; war against the British. His son Tippoo (1782–99) continues his policy.
**1764:** Beginning of the reign of Stanislaus II (Poniatowski) in Poland. End of the nobiliary state. Period of reforms and enlightenment.
**1768:** Peasant rising in the Polish Ukraine; massacres of nobles and Jews.
**1769:** Publication begins of Nikolai Ivanovich Novikov's revue, *The Drone*, in Russia. It deals with peasant problem, problem of relations with Western culture.
**c. 1769:** Beginnings of *Sturm und Drang* literary movement in Germany, with democratic and nationalist tendencies.
**1770:** Anti-Turkish risings in Greece.
**1770–1:** Maupeou's reforms in France: attempt at 'Royal Revolution'.

*2. The eldest of the three Tay Son brothers, the unifier of Vietnam. Stamp issued by the Democratic Republic of Vietnam.*

**1771:** Beginning of the Tay Son insurrection – a national, popular movement – in Vietnam.
**1773–4:** Pugachov's revolt in Russia.
**1774:** Beginnings of anti-Manchu revolts in China – social movements with nationalist tendencies.
**1775–83:** American War of Independence.
**1776:** Revolt of Mapuche Indians in Chile.
**1779–80:** First 'Kaffir War' (Boer expansion comes up against native resistance).
**1780s:** Peasant risings in Norway, Massachusetts, Rumania, Ukraine, Japan etc., generally directed against merchants and speculators.
**1780:** Beginning of the social disturbances in Holland, which rapidly grow into the republican revolution. Grave failure of the King of Poland and his reform attempts.
**1780–2:** Tupac Amaru's rising in Peru.
**1781:** The Californian Indians massacre the Spaniards. Anti-Spanish movements in Colombia and Venezuela.
**1782:** Oligarchic reaction in Geneva.
**1786–92:** Reign of the Tay Son brothers in Vietnam, who carry out an impressive programme of modernization and unification.

*3. Andrianampoinimerina, King of Madagascar. Anonymous painting.*

# 1750–1800

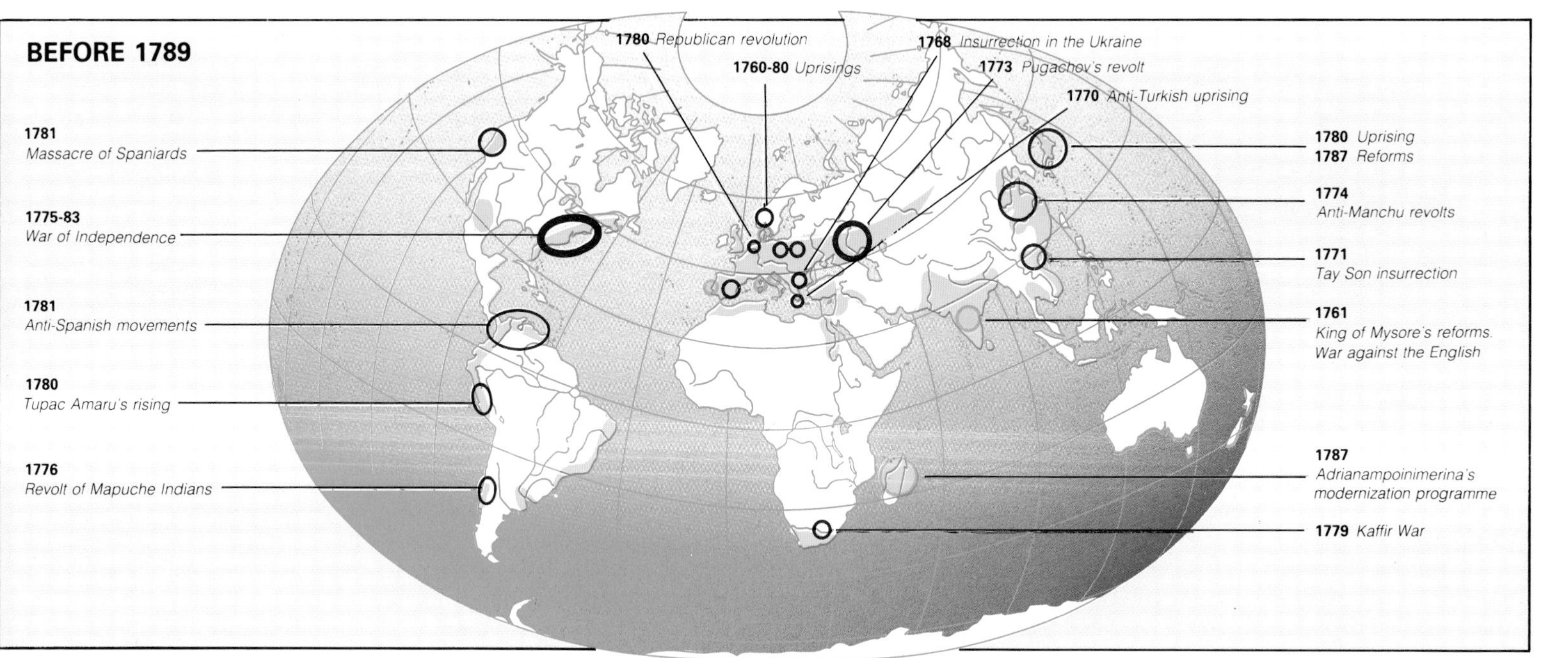


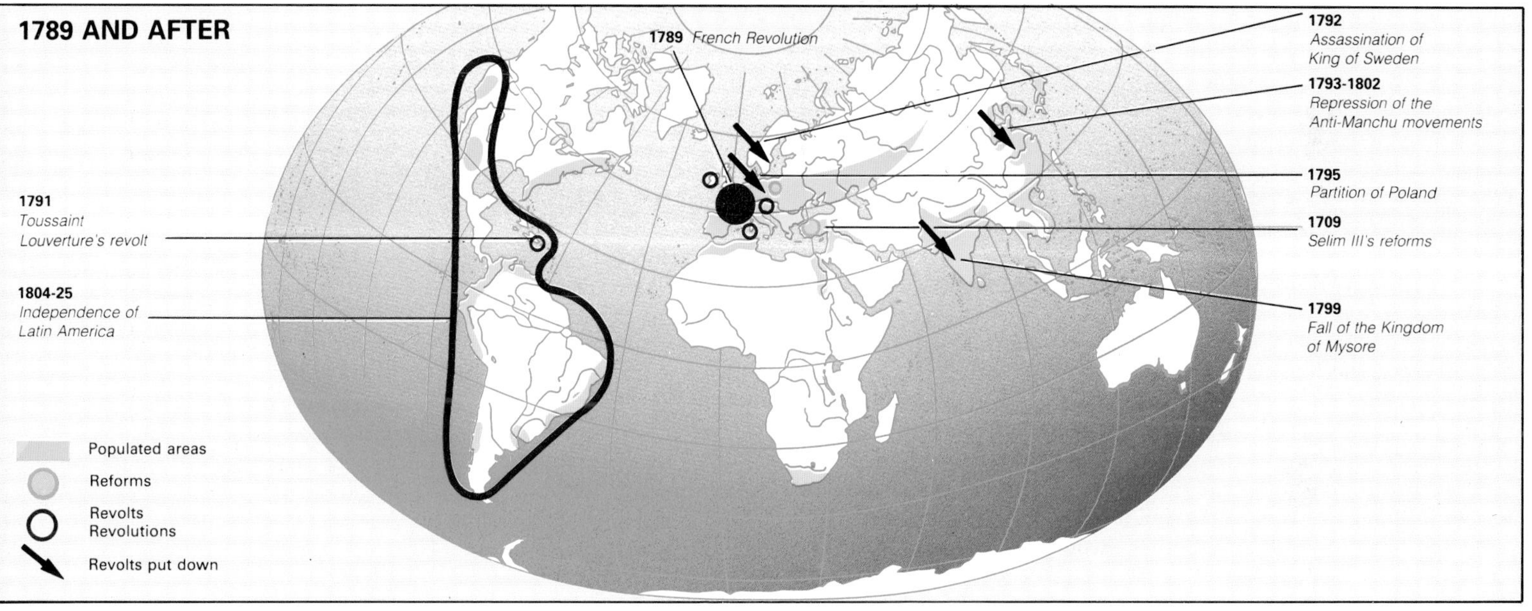

4. *Gustavus III, King of Sweden, 'contemplating revolution beneath the gaze of Minerva and Justice'. Engraving by John F. Martin, 1784.*

**1787:** US Constitution and beginnings of French Revolution. First great democratic reforms in Denmark. Beginnings of the Kansei era reforms in Japan; these had an anti-trade, 'back-to-the-land' aspect.
**1787–1810:** Andrianampoinimerina becomes King of Madagascar. Great programme of modernization and unification carried out.
**1788–92:** Four Years' Diet meets in Poland: great debates, reforms.
**1788–9:** Anti-Portuguese plot in Brazil.
**1789:** Beginning of Turkish sultan Selim III's reforms directed against the traditionalists. Royal anti-aristocratic *coup d'état* in Sweden, but King Gustavus III is assassinated in 1792.
**1793:** Vendéan insurrection in France.
**1793–1802:** Savage repression of anti-Manchu movements in China.
**1795:** Third partition of Poland.
**1799:** Fall of the state of Mysore.

5. *Vendéan leader, Henri de la Rochejaquelin, pictured by Baron Guérin, 1817.*

# The Age of Railways and Steamships

1. The first French railway, from Lyon to Saint-Etienne, in 1832.

In 1840 THERE WERE 8,854 kilometres of railway track throughout the world; in 1860 there were 106,000 kilometres; of these, 50% were in North America and 47% in Europe (excluding Russia). In 1900 the figure was 750,000 kilometres, and in 1920, 1,086,000 kilometres; of these, 24% were in Europe (excluding the USSR) and 43% in America.

The lines which were built in the 1840s, 1850s and 1860s for the most part served areas where there was already considerable economic activity and therefore represented a good investment. Gradually, however, there developed a whole ideology of the railway, according to which railways could populate deserts and bring wealth to undeveloped regions. Building them became a concern of the state and largely exceeded simple criteria of economic rationality. The building of railways was, and remained, till just before the First World War, far and away the single most important reason for the export of capital and the main method of developing new territories. The American transcontinental railways constructed between 1864 and 1890 played a key role in populating and developing huge tracts of land, as did the Trans-Siberian Railway after 1891.

Fairly rapidly, however, it became clear that the building of railways could not of itself bring about the hoped-for prosperity. In this respect the history of railways is to some extent a story of lost illusions. Nevertheless, the returns on investment, even long afterwards, were always considerable. The expansion of the network and the rise in traffic gave the impetus to technical progress and made railways one of the main sources of innovation in the nineteenth century. The decisive turning-point came in the 1870s, which saw the simultaneous adoption of steel rails, electric signals, compressed-air brakes, hydraulic handling apparatus and other inventions. The development of railways thus prompted many of the technical discoveries which were to be fundamental to the civilization of the twentieth century.

The age of sailing ships, which was dominated by American technological expertise, reached its height in the middle of the nineteenth century. It was the era of the clippers which plied from the east coast of America and California, carried on the tea trade with China and shipped convicts to Australia. In the world context the rise of the railway was inseparable from that of the steamship. In 1838 four British steamers crossed the Atlantic. But steam shipping came into its own in a real sense only after 1870, as a result of the completion of the Suez Canal in 1869 and the technical progress which reduced the amount of coal consumed in the steam engine. Sailing ships held their own over very long distances until the 1890s but by 1913 they represented only 8% of world shipping capacity (40% of which was British, whilst the Germans and Americans each controlled 11%).

The economic and geographic consequences of these two innovations complemented one another. Both had the effect of increasing the size of markets as well as the amount of economic activity. The expansion of newly emergent countries like the USA, the Argentine, Siberia and Australia, as well as many others, was closely linked to this. Everywhere new opportunities for trade became available, as was the case, for instance, with wine from the Languedoc or coal from Britain, both of which were exported worldwide. The trade in foodstuffs (which till the 1850s had been an exclusively European concern) now operated within a global market.

But over the same period railways and steamships made competition more acute because of the falls in tariffs. A process of depopulation and deindustrialization had been set irreversibly into motion that was ultimately to cause the Great Depression.

**R. Fulton builds the first submarine.**

**1800**

**George Stephenson builds his first locomotive.**

**1815**

**Building of the Suez Canal.**

**1859–69**

**1814:** George Stephenson builds his first locomotive.
**1825:** First line of railway track using steam traction opened in Great Britain.
**1827:** Marc Séguin invents his multitube boiler.
**1829:** Stephenson's *Rocket*, using the principle of the fire-tube boiler wins Rainhill Concourse.
**1830:** First locomotive built and first line opened in the USA. Stephenson develops in same year a locomotive using cylinders arranged horizontally.
**1832:** First railway line using steam opened in France.
**1836:** First patents granted for properly efficient steam-driven propellers.
**1837:** First railway line opened in Russia. In France, line opened between Paris and St Germain.
**1838:** Isambard Kingdom Brunel's *Great Western* crosses the Atlantic.
**1839:** First application in France of the guaranteed interest system for the financing of the Paris–Orléans line. R. and W. Hawthorn invent their steam superheater.
**1842:** French and Prussian laws defining the modes of concession of railway lines.
**1846:** First three-cylinder locomotive built by Robert Stephenson and William Howe. Concession of the 'ligne du Nord' between Paris and Lille to a consortium headed by Rothschild's Bank. Concession of the Paris–Strasbourg line.
**1848:** Brunel's *Great Britain*, first iron-built propeller-driven steamship.
**1849:** Crampton perfects his express locomotive.
**1850:** First railway line using steam opened in Mexico.

3. St Pancras Station in 1876.

# 19th century

2. A share certificate in a British shipping firm around 1880.

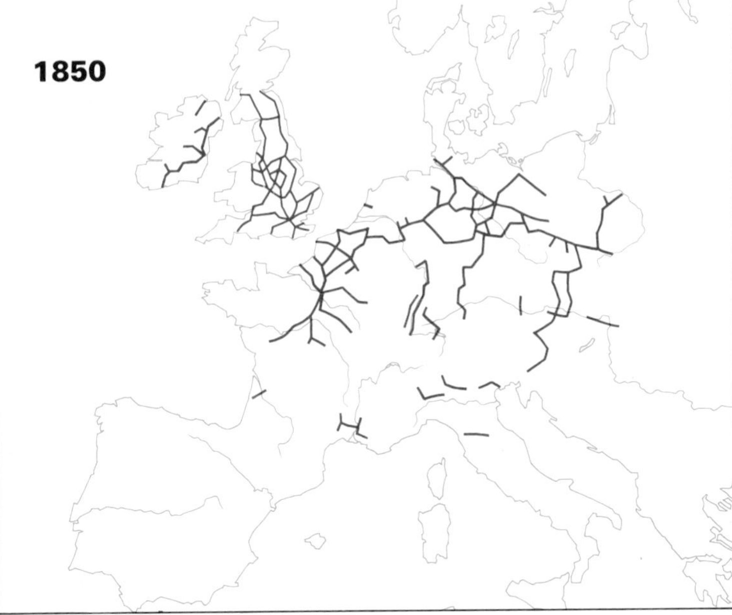


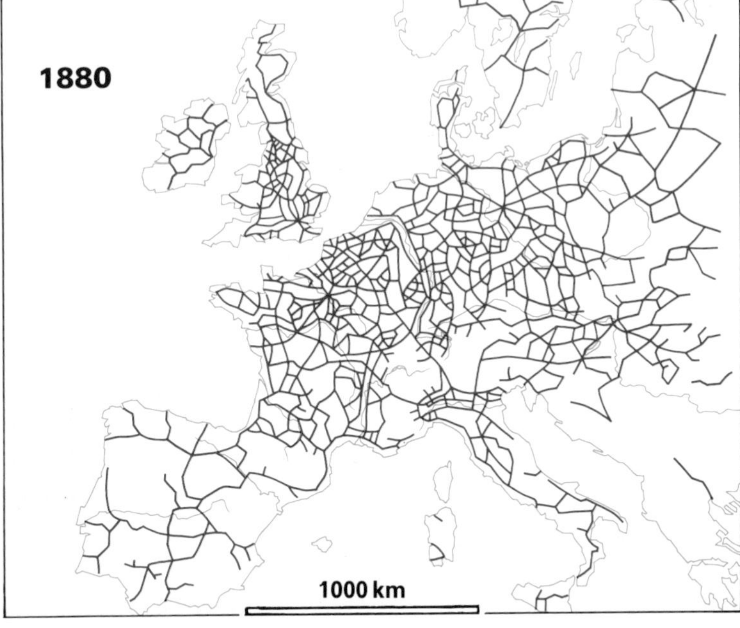


**The Transcaspian Railway.**

**1880–8**

**The Transsiberian Railway.**

**1891–1906 and 1907–17**

**1850–60:** Perfecting of the compound engine, which reduces the consumption of coal by half.
**1853:** First railway line using steam opened in India.
**1854:** First railway lines using steam opened in Brazil, Egypt and Australia.
**1856:** 'La Grande Société des Chemins de fer Russes' formed.
**1859:** Signing of the Franqueville conventions in France between the state and the railway companies. The railways become a national institution.
**1860–70:** First use in Britain, France and the USA of Bessemer steel for the manufacture of rails.
**1862:** The Steamship, *The Banshee*, is the first steel-built ship to cross the Atlantic. First steam railway line opened in Algeria.
**1864–9:** First American transatlantic service.
**1867:** First compound engine locomotive by John Lay.
**1871:** First multiple expansion engines for ships.
**1872:** First railway line using steam opened in Japan. Westinghouse invents his automatic compressed-air brake.
**1876:** A. Mallet invents his twin-cylinder compound engine.
**1883:** First railway line using steam opened in China. Signing of conventions between the state and the French railways which were to be seen as models throughout the world.
**1891:** The Tsar's rescript deciding upon the start of work on the Transsiberian railway.
**1894:** With the invention of radio, ships were no longer cut off from the outside world. Four-cylinder shipboard compound engine.
**1897:** First application of the steam turbine.
**1909:** First fitting of the steam turbine to a cargo ship.

# The Birth of a Nation: USA

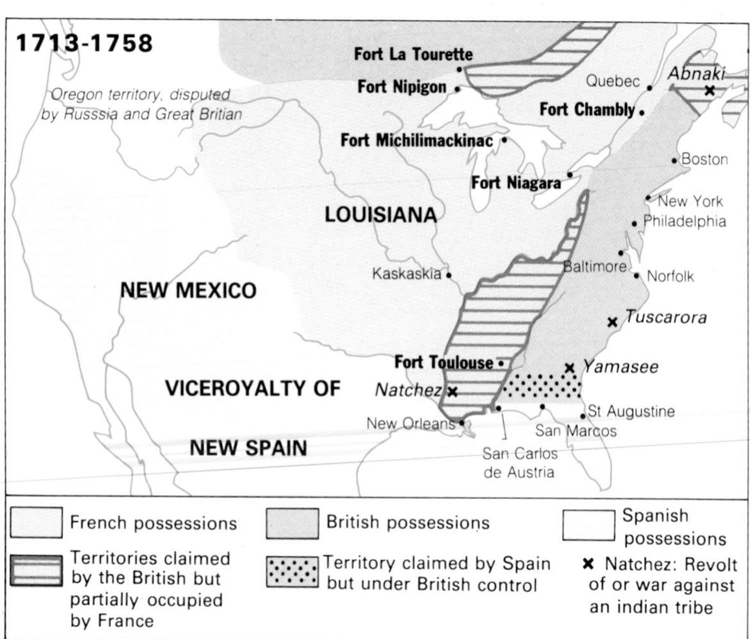


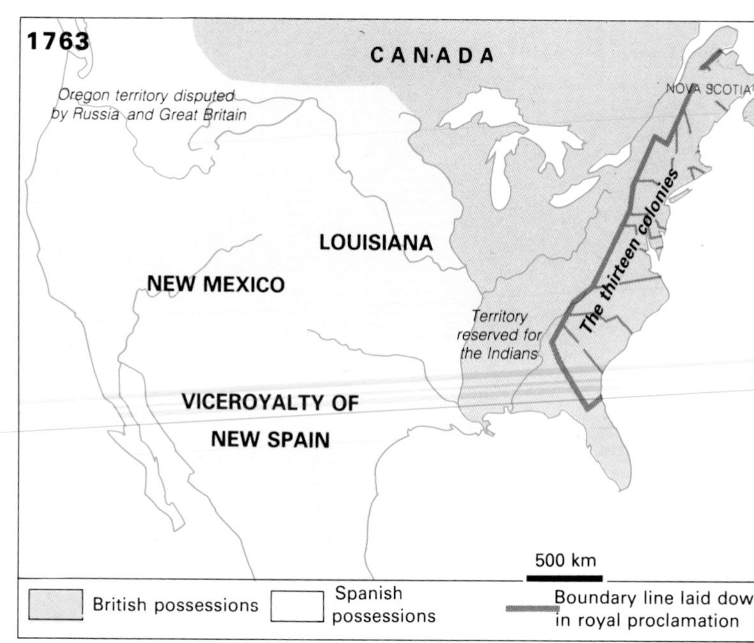

1. The American uprising: the statue of George III knocked off its pedestal, 9 July 1776.

PROSPECTS SEEMED VERY BRIGHT for the British Empire in the second half of the eighteenth century. The thirteen North American colonies had considerably expanded their agriculture, forestry and commerce, as well as their fishing and shipbuilding activities. The Seven Years' War (also known as the French and Indian Wars), which stripped France of its American possessions, rid the settlers of a dangerous rival. Nothing seemed to stand in the way of their territorial and economic expansion. And England, after this 'last war for the Empire', also saw the balance of power in Europe swinging in its favour.

But the war left England heavily in debt, and this new extension of the Empire required administrative and political reorganization. The hesitant, erratic and clumsy political actions of the crown came into conflict with colonial interests. The royal proclamation reserving the land west of the Appalachians for the Indians and the Acts of Parliament extending the English monopoly on maritime trade to new commodities and tightening English control over the colonial settlers were met in the colonies with petitions, pamphlets and a boycott of English goods. Tensions increased until, in April 1775, the first military hostilities broke out. The war, in which the settlers received aid from Louis XVI, was to last eight years. In July 1776 the Second

**France is driven out of America.** 1763

**The 'Boston Tea Party'.** 16 December 1773

**Declaration of Independe**[nce] 1776

**1754–63:** Seven Years' War or French and Indian Wars.
**1763:** Peace of Paris. France loses its possessions on the American continent. War by Pontiac, chief of the Ottawa Indians of the Great Lakes region, against the British. Royal proclamation forbidding the colonists to settle west of the Appalachians.
**1764–5:** Mercantilist laws on sugar, money and stamp duties. Protests in the colonies, including boycott of British products. Intercolonial Stamp Act Congress.
**1766–7:** The above-mentioned Acts are revoked, but the Townshend Act introduces duties on other commodities.
**1773–5:** Boston Tea Party; the Boston 'Sons of Liberty' throw East India Company tea into the sea. Parliament responds with coercive legislation.
**1775:** First clashes at Lexington and Concord between British troops and Massachusetts militia. The Second Continental Congress appoints Washington commander-in-chief of the colonial armies.
**4 July 1776:** Signature of the Declaration of Independence.

3. The 'Boston Tea Party', 16 December 1773.

**1775–83:** War of Independence. The first phase, which produces no definite outcome, ends in 1778 with the coming of the alliance with France (La Fayette and Rochambeau).
**1777–81:** The Articles of Confederation, the first constitution of the USA, are drawn up, then ratified.
**1783:** Peace of Versailles. Recognition of the United States.
**1786:** Revolt of the farmers, led by Shays in Massachusetts.
**1787:** North-West Ordinance, which regulates the admission of new states into the Union and the administration of the West. The Convention of Philadelphia draws up the Constitution.
**1789:** The Constitution is ratified and put into practice. George Washington President. Bill of Rights passed (the first ten amendments).
**1791–2:** Alexander Hamilton's fiscal proposals become law.
**1791–4:** Armed conflicts against the North-West Indian Confederation. Series of American defeats. Battle of Fallen Timbers: the Indians are defeated.

# 1754–1800

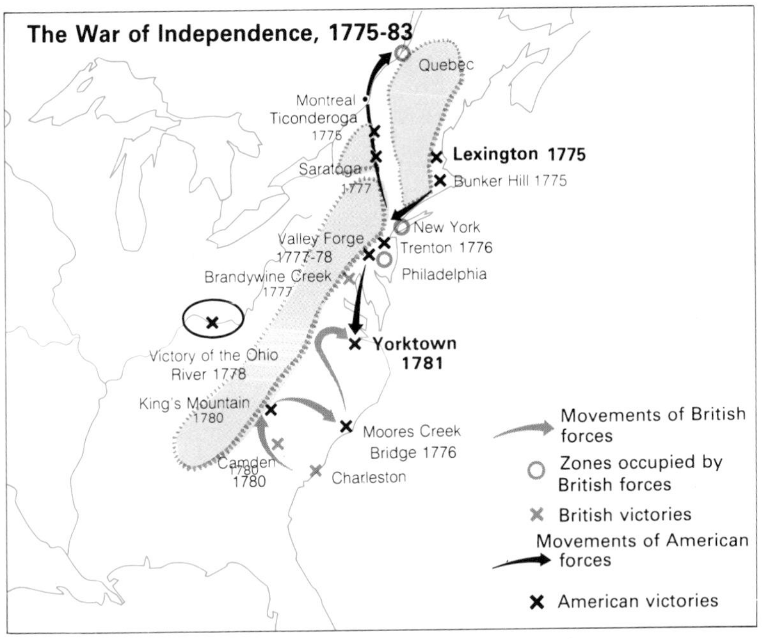


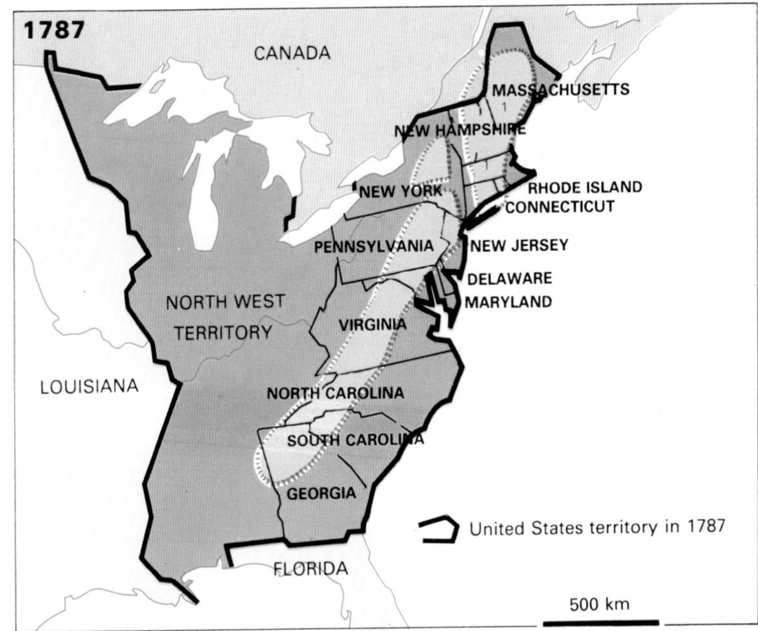


Continental Congress signed the Declaration of Independence of the United States.

But the unity of the new states, initially held together by war against the metropolis, was fragile. Apart from the internecine struggles between Loyalists and Patriots, the former colonies were divided over territorial questions, trade and the relative autonomy that was to be accorded to the individual states of the Union by the central government. The leaders also had to deal with revolts on the part of farmers and artisans against crippling taxes and oligarchic power.

The Articles of Confederation which set out the terms of the Union were thought insufficient by the more conservative of the new leaders. Meeting at Philadelphia in 1787, the delegates of the thirteen states drew up a constitution which established a powerful central government, whilst at the same time ensuring, by the federal system, the relative sovereignty of each member. Individual liberties were guaranteed by the first ten amendments, but Black slavery was maintained and the Indians were excluded from the American nation.

In 1789 George Washington became the first President of the United States; the legislative Congress was made up of two chambers and, with the Supreme Court as third power, a clear separation of powers was maintained, with the various institutions exercising a check on each other. During George Washington's two terms and that of John Adams, the 'federalist' conservatives interpreted the Constitution in such a way as to strengthen the position of the central government. Alexander Hamilton laid the bases for economic nationalism with the quasi-public Bank of the United States, a development plan for manufacturing industry, protectionist customs tariffs and the federal government's acceptance of responsibility for war debts. In foreign policy, the federalists conducted a covert war against revolutionary France. At home, they curbed individual freedom. These policies bred discontent among certain sections of the population and, upon being elected third President of the USA in 1801, Thomas Jefferson, the leader of the Democrats (or Radicals), announced a 'Second Revolution'.

2. The English plenipotentiary as seen by an American caricaturist, 1778.

ace of Versailles. | Constitution. Washington President. | John Adams President. | Thomas Jefferson President.

783 | 1789 | 1797 | 1801

4. White America and a young Black keep vigil at George Washington's tomb, c. 1800.

**1794:** *Whiskey Rebellion* (Pennsylvania farmers' revolt).
**1794–5:** The Jay Treaty with England, Pinkney Treaty with Spain and Greenville Treaty with the Indians ease the course of expansion westwards.
**1797:** The federalist John Adams elected President.
**1798:** Covert war against France. Congress passes laws on aliens and sedition. Opposition leaders Thomas Jefferson and James Madison have resolutions adopted in Virginia and Kentucky declaring any law which infringes individual liberties null and void.
**1800:** Thomas Jefferson is elected President on the thirty-sixth ballot of the Congress. He will revoke the centralizing measures passed by the federalists.

5. William Penn, the father of the constitution of Pennsylvania, a model for American institutions

# The French Revolution

1. The storming of the Bastille, as seen by one of those involved, le sieur Cholat.

THE CRISIS which was to sweep away the *Ancien Régime* was born of a combination of three factors: first, a bad harvest, which produced, as usual, food shortages, unemployment, poverty and unrest; second, the financial deficit suffered by a state that had exhausted both its resources and the range of fiscal measures it could apply; and lastly, the resistance of the *'notables'* (representatives of the privileged orders: great nobles, bishops and *parlementaires*) and the *'parlements'* (sovereign courts of justice which were becoming a forum for political debate) to any reform of the royal finances that was not sanctioned by a meeting of the Estates General, where representation by social 'order' assured them of an automatic majority. When this body did meet, the Third Estate, which popular anger, the appeal to natural rights and the claim for equality before the law had momentarily united, became ever more ferocious in its denunciation of the seigneurs, privileges and despotism. The immediate causes of the revolution here met its deeper origins: the inevitable crisis of absolute power and its manifestations, the divorce between the theory and the actual development of a society of 'orders', the cultural transformations that had been taking place for the past century or more, Enlightenment teachings etc.

In summer 1789 an insurrection in Paris, an agrarian revolt and, most importantly, a political revolution all occurred simultaneously. The political revolution broke with the 'organic' logic of the old social order: sovereignty changed hands, passing from the divine right of the monarch to the nation, the corporate entity was supplanted by the individual and the subject became a citizen. Liberty and equality were established, in theory at least, and privileges abolished. *The Declaration of the Rights of Man and of the Citizen* laid down the principles of a new legal system, that was subsequently enshrined in the constitution of 1791. Meanwhile, the deputies claimed church possessions for the nation and enacted the civil constitution of the clergy.

Successive factions came and went, their various external and internal conflicts all revolving around the same notions of national sovereignty, the popular will and the hydra of counter-revolution. From the monarchists to Robespierre, by way of Feuillants, Girondins, Dantonists and Hébertists, each succeeding group would be either deposed or executed, as Louis XVI was to be in 1793.

This uncontrollable dynamic, periodically re-stimulated by pressure from the street, culminated in the installation of a dictatorship and the Terror, a system of government which created new opponents as fast as it could eliminate old ones (in Paris, Lyon, Nantes, the Vendée etc.) and which finally devoured itself on 9 Thermidor.

These struggles unfolded against a backcloth of foreign war, entered upon, in a wave of enthusiasm, by the Legislative Assembly; the part played in this decision by ideological ambitions was as great as that played by classical reasons of state. Victory at Valmy safeguarded France against invasion; the Battle of Fleurus opened Europe for invasion and led to the subsequent great expeditions of Bonaparte (Italy and Egypt). But between these two dates a long series of reverses (Neerwinden, Valenciennes, Mainz, Toulon) imposed an unprecedented war effort on the young republic. In this regard, Thermidor brought a double respite. However, the advent of the Directory did not restore the republic's institutional stability, nor pacify its citizens. General weariness, an endemic civil war, a crisis of authority and the discredit into which the representative regime had fallen would ultimately sweep it away on 18 Brumaire.

2. Snuff-box of a Parisian sans-culotte, with the inscription, 'Peace to the simple folk, châteaus, death to tyrants', from the Convention period.

**Tennis Court Oath.** **20 June 1789**

**Fall of the Bastille.** **14 July 1789**

**Louis XVI guillotined.** **21 January 1793**

**22 February 1787:** Assembly of Notables meets.
**8 August 1788:** The Estates General are called for 1 May 1789.
**5 May 1789:** Opening session of Estates General at Versailles.
**17 June:** The Third Estate declares itself a National Assembly.
**20 June:** Third Estate takes Tennis Court Oath.
**14 July:** Storming of the Bastille.
**July–August:** 'Great Fear' and peasant uprisings.
**4 August:** 'Feudal régime' abolished.
**26 August:** Declaration of the Rights of Man and the Citizen.
**6 October:** The King is brought back to Paris. The Assembly declares itself inseparable from the King.
**2 November:** The clergy's possessions are put at the disposal of the nation.
**12 July 1790:** Civil constitution of the clergy.
**20 June 1791:** Flight of the King and royal family; they are stopped at Varennes.
**14 September:** Louis XVI gives his sanction to the Constitution.

3. The politicization of women during the Revolution: here, in a picture by Lesueur, a patriotic club discusses the decrees of the Convention.

**1 October:** First session of the Legislative Assembly.
**20 April 1792:** France declares war on Francis II in his capacity as king of Hungary and Bohemia.
**10 August:** The people of Paris invade the Tuileries.
**2–5 September:** Massacres in Paris prisons.
**20 September:** Battle of Valmy.
**21 September:** First session of the Convention. Monarchy abolished.
**21 January 1793:** Louis XVI is guillotined.
**1 February:** The Convention declares war on Holland and England.
**10 March:** Revolutionary tribunal created.
**11 March:** Beginning of the Vendéan War.
**18 March:** Defeat of Neerwinden; French troops retreat from Belgium.
**6 April:** Committee of Public Safety formed.
**31 May:** Day of rioting against the Girondins.
**28 July:** Surrender to the British forces at Valenciennes.
**27 August:** Toulon is occupied by the British.
**5 September.** The Convention puts Terror on the order of the day.
**5 October:** Republican calendar adopted.

4. End of the Capetian monarchy: execution of the former King Louis XVI on the Place de la Révolution (now Place de la Concorde). Popular print, 1793.

# 1787–1799

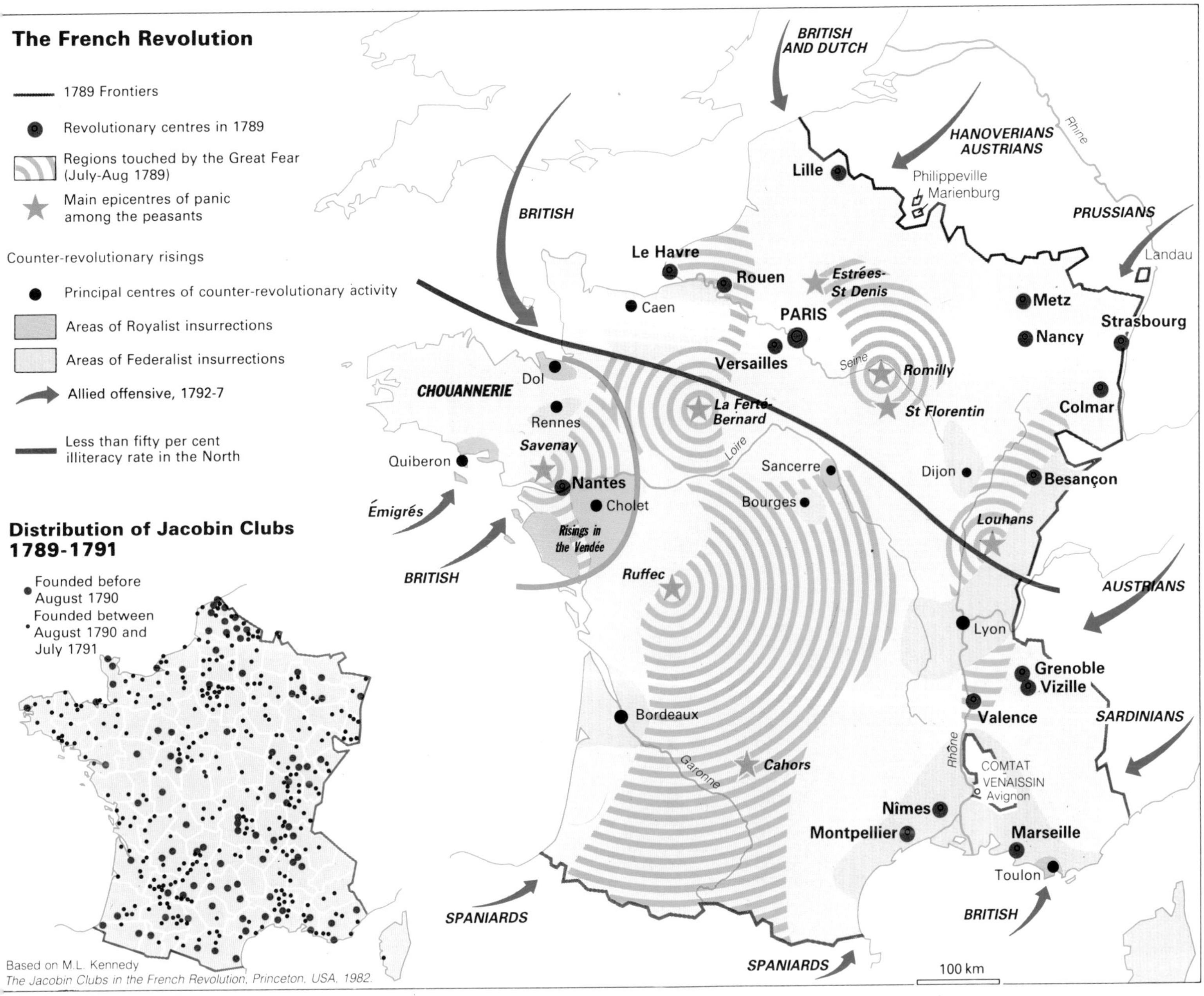

## The French Revolution

1789 Frontiers

Revolutionary centres in 1789

Regions touched by the Great Fear (July-Aug 1789)

Main epicentres of panic among the peasants

Counter-revolutionary risings

Principal centres of counter-revolutionary activity

Areas of Royalist insurrections

Areas of Federalist insurrections

Allied offensive, 1792-7

Less than fifty per cent illiteracy rate in the North

BRITISH AND DUTCH
HANOVERIANS AUSTRIANS
Rhine
Lille
Philippeville
Marienburg
PRUSSIANS
Landau
BRITISH
Le Havre
Rouen
Estrées-St Denis
Caen
PARIS
Metz
Strasbourg
Nancy
Versailles
Seine
Romilly
Dol
CHOUANNERIE
La Ferté-Bernard
St Florentin
Colmar
Rennes
Savenay
Loire
Quiberon
Sancerre
Dijon
Besançon
Nantes
Émigrés
Cholet
Bourges
Louhans
Risings in the Vendée
BRITISH
Ruffec
AUSTRIANS
Lyon
Grenoble
Vizille
Bordeaux
Valence
SARDINIANS
Rhône
Garonne
Cahors
COMTAT VENAISSIN
Avignon
Nîmes
Montpellier
Marseille
Toulon
SPANIARDS
BRITISH
SPANIARDS
100 km

## Distribution of Jacobin Clubs 1789-1791

Founded before August 1790

Founded between August 1790 and July 1791

Based on M.L. Kennedy

*The Jacobin Clubs in the French Revolution, Princeton, USA, 1982.*

| Beginning of the Great Terror. | Victory at Fleurus. | Bonaparte's Coup d'état. |
|---|---|---|
| 10 June 1794 | 26 June 1794 | 18 Brumaire Year VIII |

**19 December:** Recapture of Toulon by French forces.
**8 June 1794** (2 Prairial Year II): Festival of the Supreme Being.
**10 June** (22 Prairial): Beginning of the Great Terror.
**26 June** (8 Messidor): French victory at Fleurus.
**27 July** (9 Thermidor): Warrant issued for Robespierre's arrest. He is guillotined the following day with Saint-Just, Couthon and 19 other Robespierrists.
**21 January 1795** (3 Ventose, Year III): Freedom of worship granted.
**31 May** (12 Prairial): Revolutionary tribunal suspended.
**23 September** (1 Vendemiaire, Year IV): New Constitution proclaimed.
**26 October** (4 Brumaire): The Convention disbands.
**31 October** (9 Brumaire): Executive Directory elected.
**2 March 1796** (12 Ventose): Bonaparte named commander-in-chief of army in Italy.
**4 September 1797** (18 Fructidor, Year V): Coup d'état of the Directory against the councils.
**17 October** (26 Vendemiaire): Peace of Campo Formio between France and Austria.
**11 May 1798** (22 Floreal, Year VI): Coup d'état of the Directory against the left.
**19 May** (30 Floreal): Bonaparte sets out for Egypt.
**25 July 1799** (7 Thermidor, Year VII): Victory at Aboukir.
**9–10 November** (18–19 Brumaire): Resignations of Ducos, Barras and Sieyes. Bonaparte, who had returned from Egypt on 9 October, is appointed commander of the French army in Paris. On 10 November Bonaparte, Sieyes and Ducos are appointed consuls.

*5. The battle of Jemappes: victory of the French general Dumouriez over the Austrians, 6 November 1792. Popular print.*

# Bonaparte and the Lure of Empire

NAPOLEON BONAPARTE'S 18th Brumaire *coup* discomfited only the Parisian 'political class'. Though he was installing a form of political regime in France that had no parallel in contemporary Europe – the enlightened despotism of a general bathed in military glory – he met with the general consent of the majority of the population, which was at once weary of the succeeding manifestations of the republic and yet unwilling to countenance a restoration of the monarchy.

In terms of the perceptions of their own age, the Consulate and the Empire could be thought of as phases of consolidation. The successive constitutions had gradually come to vest all power in a single man. It was self-evident that the period of France's apprenticeship in democracy (or at least in the operation of a representative regime) had been too chaotic. The pursuit of those goals would now be put off to other generations. Admittedly, the proclamation of the first emperor since Charlemagne might seem disconcerting, but was this not merely a means of continuing the consolidation process? The *Code civil*, the guarantee of the inviolability of the *biens nationaux*, the Concordat, the Legion of Honour, the reintroduction of titles of nobility (hereditary if primogeniture was accepted) satisfied the country's deepest needs, which were the confirmation of private ownership of property, the restoration of the values of authority, religion and the family, together with hierarchy and marks of distinction. These were all things for which the bourgeoisie clamoured. The France of 'orders' and privileges gave way to a France of notables, landowners and heads of families.

1. Bonaparte at the Council of Five Hundred, 19 Brumaire, Year VIII.

Being, at least in his early years, a man of 'consensus', Bonaparte found little opposition when he undertook the formidable task of reconstructing the administrative institutions. This reconstruction – completed around 1808 – was a prelude to the effective unification of France as a modern nation-state which, without doubt, was one of the most surprising consequences of the revolution.

Unfortunately, Napoleon Bonaparte had always had two contending sides to his personality: ultimately, his desire to rival Alexander vitiated the actions of the statesman within him. Internal stability was not accompanied by military and diplomatic stability, except during the truce constituted by the Peace of Amiens (1802).

2. Crossing of the Beresina, late November 1812. Gouache by General Fournier-Sarloves.

Europe saw Napoleon as the dangerous knight of the revolution, and he undoubtedly continued to subscribe to its essential political and social principles. He, for his part, saw the continent as the ideal terrain for building a political edifice in which France's frontiers would be extended with vassal states organized in a pyramid around her, allowing the personal ambitions of his own family to be satisfied and the continent to be unified as a trading area that was at once hostile to English commerce and accommodating to France's interests. The overweening nature of his ambitions, as they stand revealed in his attempts to conquer the Iberian Peninsula and the vastness of Russia, led Napoleon, from 1808–09 onwards, first through a series of partial failures and then to total catastrophe. In the process, he threw away not only his own personal success but also many of the achievements of the revolution.

As for Europe, it came out of the adventure profoundly transformed. It was henceforth hostile to France, which was now perceived to be as much a domineering, exploitative state as a land committed to propagating the ideals of the Enlightenment.

**Beethoven: *Pathétique Sonata.*** **Chateaubriand, *La Génie du christianisme.*** **Fichte: *Addresses to the German Nation.*** **Turner, *London seen from Greenwich.***

**1799** **1802** **1807–8** **1809**

**9 November 1799** (18 Brumaire, Year VIII): Transfer of the Assemblies to Saint-Cloud; de facto dissolution of the Directory; Bonaparte made commander of the Paris troops.
**10 November** (19 Brumaire): Bonaparte forces the Assemblies to cede power to three provisional consuls.
**12 December:** Bonaparte imposes the text of the Year VIII Constitution and becomes First Consul.
**7 February 1800:** Results of plebiscite on the Constitution: 3 million vote 'Yes', 1,500 'No'.
**13 February:** Creation of the Bank of France.
**17 February:** Creation of prefects and sub-prefects.
**3 March:** Closure of the lists of émigrés.
**14 June:** Bonaparte crushes Melas at Marengo.
**3 September:** The French surrender at Malta.
**1 October:** San Ildefonso Treaty with Spain: restitution of Louisiana to France.
**24 December:** Rue Saint-Nicaise assassination plot.
**9 February 1801:** Peace of Luneville with Austria: France gains the Left Bank of the Rhine.
**15 July:** Signature of the Concordat.
**25 March 1802:** Peace of Amiens with England.
**8 April:** *Articles Organiques.*
**26 April:** Amnesty granted to all émigrés returning to France before 1 Vendemiaire, Year XI; creation of lycées.
**20 May:** Slavery and slave trade restored in the colonies.
**2 August:** Napoleon Bonaparte appointed First Consul for life.
**23 January 1803:** Bonaparte suppresses the Moral and Political Sciences class at the Institute.
**20 March:** Bonaparte declares the Peace of Amiens breached by the English.
**21 March:** Duc d'Enghien executed. *Code civil* promulgated.
**18 May:** Bonaparte proclaimed Emperor of the French under the title, Napoleon I (Constitution of the Year XII.)
**19 May:** Creation of 18 Imperial Marshalls.
**2 December:** Napoleon I's coronation.
**17 March 1805:** Napoleon made King of Italy.
**21 October:** France and Spain defeated at Trafalgar.
**2 December:** French victory at Austerlitz.
**4 April 1806:** Publication of the *Catéchisme impérial.*
**10 May:** University of France, an 'institution of public education', founded.
**12 July:** Confederation of the Rhine created.
**6 August:** End of Holy Roman Empire; Francis II resigns the Imperial Dignity and becomes Francis I, Emperor of Austria.
**27 October:** Napoleon in Berlin.
**8 February 1807:** Battle ('Butchery') of Eylau.
**25 June:** Meeting between Napoleon and Tsar Alexander I at Tilsit.
**12 October:** French enter Spain (with the aim of attacking Portugal).
**2 May 1808:** The population of Madrid attacks the French soldiers.
**22 July:** French surrender at Baylen.
**13 May 1809:** Napoleon enters Vienna.
**1810:** France annexes Rome (17 February), Holland (9 July), the Hanseatic towns and the Canton of the Valais (10 December).
**2 April:** Napoleon marries the Archduchess Marie-Louise.
**8 February 1811:** The French army sets out discreetly for Russia.
**20 March:** Birth of the 'King of Rome'.
**19 June 1812:** Pius VII interned at Fontainebleau.
**14 September:** Napoleon enters Moscow.
**27–29 November:** Battle of Beresina.
**11 January 1813:** 250,000 Frenchmen technically eligible for military service between 1810 and 1815, called up.
**21 June:** Wellington wins Battle of Vittoria; French forces withdraw from Spain.
**16–19 October:** Napoleon loses Battle of Leipzig.
**31 March 1814:** Allies triumphantly enter Paris.
**6 April:** Napoleon's first abdication.
**3 May:** Louis XVIII enters Paris.
**30 May:** First Treaty of Paris: France loses most of the territory gained since 1792.
**20 March 1815:** Napoleon returns to Paris.
**18 June:** Napoleon defeated at Waterloo.
**22 June:** Napoleon's second abdication.

# 1799–1815

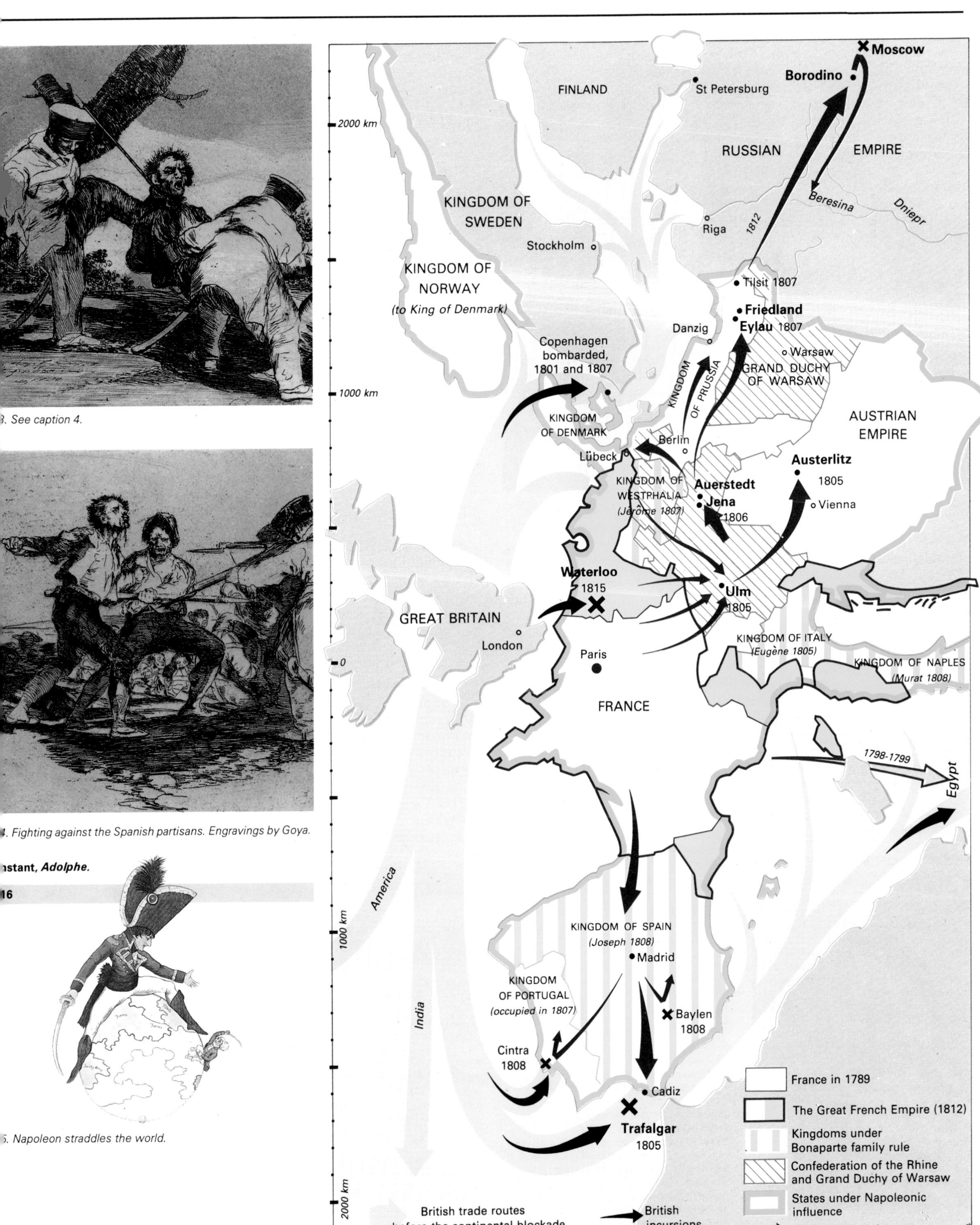


3. See caption 4.

4. Fighting against the Spanish partisans. Engravings by Goya.

**nstant, Adolphe.**

16

5. Napoleon straddles the world.

# Nationalism and Revolution

1. The 'Trois Glorieuses', July 1830. Fighting near the Porte Saint-Denis, as depicted by Delondre.

Political energies during this period were, at first, directed towards the exaltation of nationalist sentiment. Romanticism at its height, with its demands for a return to the simple life, its attachment to folklore and its sympathy for oppressed peoples, paved the way for a considerable intellectual and artistic flowering in the period following the Congress of Vienna. It also laid the ground for an affirmation of cultural identity in Italy and Germany – though each was frustrated in its hopes of achieving unity – and among the peoples of Central Europe, who were subsumed against their will within the Turkish, Russian or Austrian Empires or into the Kingdom of Prussia.

The first insurrections bore the marks of this impulsion, though the wave of uprisings of 1820, which was a product of both nationalist and liberal demands, was quickly crushed. The case of Germany was quite specific and contrasts with the demands for independence and for a constitution that inspired the Spanish liberals, the Italian *carbonari* and later the Russian Decembrists. The problem of German unity had two stages to it. There was an initial need to produce an internal coherence within each of the thirty-nine states, whose frontiers contained within them a number of ancient principalities; then to bring into being a greater German state that would have a more genuine existence than the German Confederation. The cause of unification was championed by groups from the universities, gathered together in an association, the *Burschenschaft*. This was suppressed in 1820 after having had some success in the granting of constitutions. It was Prussia, the principal countervailing power to Austria, which took the initiative in bringing about customs union (*Zollverein*), a sign that those states felt they shared common economic interests.

The support the Western powers gave to the Greek independence movement (after some initial reticence) was, however, as much a response to a public opinion that had been awakened to Romantic accounts of the plight of the Christian populations of the Ottoman Empire as it was the result of diplomatic considerations. The success of the movement showed that nationalist rebellions could only hope to succeed where they could ensure, if not the support, then at least the neutrality of the great powers.

It was the July Revolution in France, which was as much national-

**Rising in Serbia led by M. Obrenovic.**

**1815**

**Chios massacres.**

**April 1822**

3. Anonymous French picture honouring Greek independence fighters, 1821.

**1815–17:** Serbia gains independence.
**1820:** In Naples, Piedmont and Spain, officers lead army rebellions and force their sovereigns to grant constitutions. These risings are crushed by the French and the Austrians.
**1821–32:** First Eastern crisis: Greek independence (7 May 1832).
**December 1825:** Tsar Nicholas I puts down the insurgents in Moscow who were demanding a constitution.
**11 January 1828:** Signature of a treaty of customs union (*Zollverbund*) between Prussia and Hesse-Darmstadt. This is in time extended to the majority of the German states and transformed into the *Zollverein* (from 1 January 1834).
**1830:** Agitation in Germany: the sovereigns of Hanover, Saxony and Brunswick agree to promulgate constitutions. The Diet of the German Confederation presided over by Austria passes six articles limiting the powers of the Constitutional Assemblies and renewing its restrictions on the universities, the press and on the right of assembly.
In Switzerland, the liberal opposition wins electoral successes in various cantons and modifies their constitutions. The seven Catholic cantons will form a separatist *Sonderbund* in 1845.
**27–9 July 1830:** July Revolution in France. After the signature of four reactionary ordinances, three days of rioting and barricades (the 'Trois Glorieuses') leave Charles X no alternative but to abdicate.
**7 August:** The Chamber of Deputies recognizes the King's abdication and calls on Louis-Philippe, king of the French, to reign with a revised charter. Revolutionary fever spreads throughout Europe.
**25 August:** An insurrection of the bourgeoisie and the popular classes in Brussels calls on the Dutch king to respect basic law and the separation of powers. A provisional government proclaims independence in October. France threatens to defend Belgium in case of intervention. In December the London Conference recognizes the independence of Belgium and, on 20 January 1831, its perpetual neutrality. After some minor military excursions the Dutch king accepts the *fait*

4. 'Patriots of all lands, beware!' The execution of two Italian nationalists, 16 June 1831. Lithograph by Daumier.

# 1815–1832

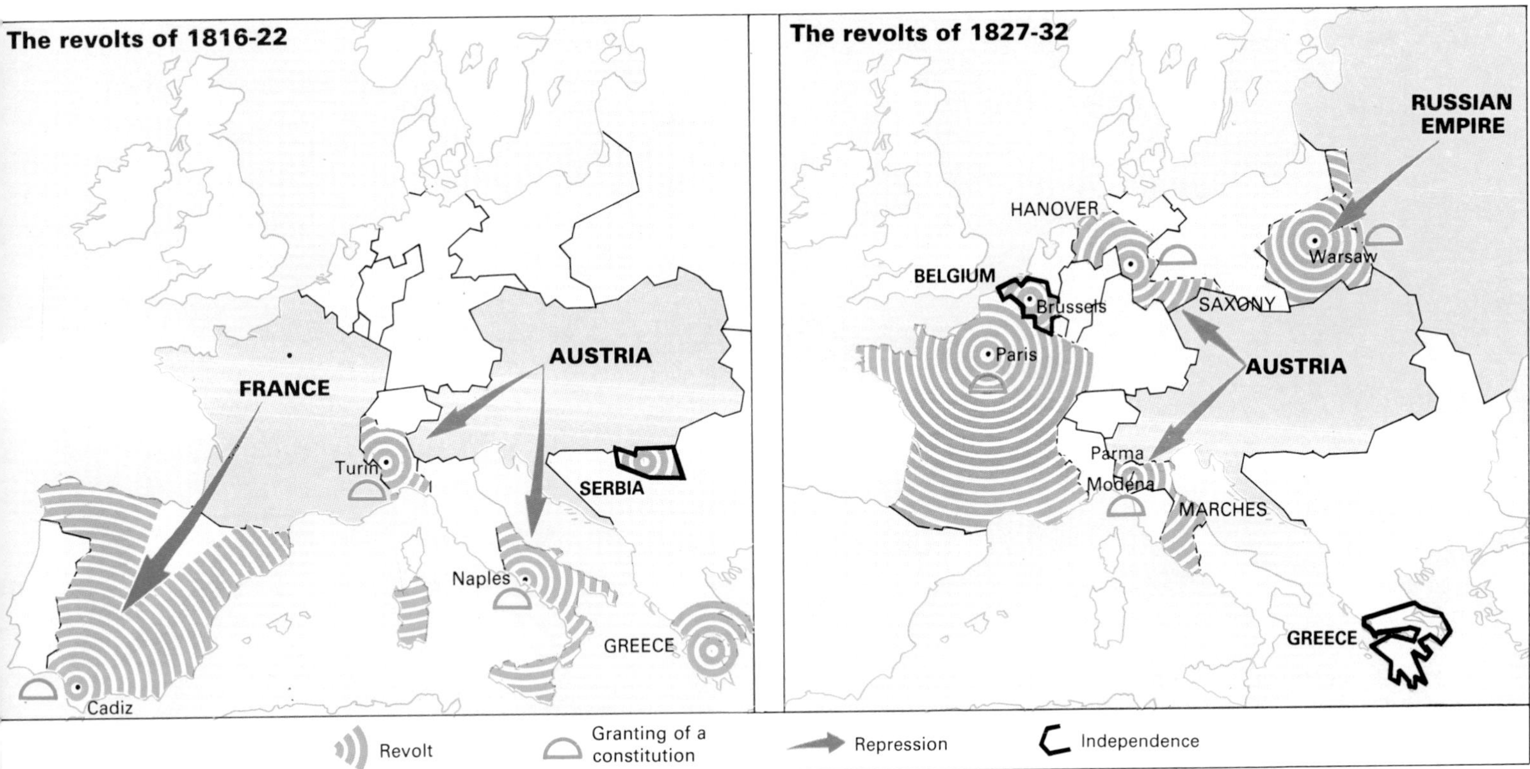

2. The echo of the 'Trois Glorieuses' in Warsaw. Parisian engraving.

ist as liberal in inspiration and which reflected the frustrations produced by both the Treaty of Paris and the Restoration, that gave the signal for a wave of revolutions in Europe. The accession of a bourgeois king, carried to power by street rioting, gave birth to great hopes, as can be seen from the fact that it was immediately followed by the Belgian revolution. One of the members of the Belgian provisional government arrived in Paris to request material aid from Louis-Philippe. Though that aid was refused, the revolutionaries did receive effective diplomatic protection which, when coupled with a military expedition, would prove sufficient to ensure Belgian independence.

There were stirrings of revolt in a great number of countries, including the southern German states, northern and papal Italy and Poland. In spite of sympathy in some quarters for these movements, France refused to intervene and they were rapidly snuffed out.

The July monarchy did not therefore fulfil the hopes it had aroused, either in France or abroad. 1830 remained a passionate but abortive manifestation of the aspirations of the European peoples.

| Battle of Navarino Bay. | Revolution in Paris (the 'Trois Glorieuses'). | Independent Belgian constitution proclaimed. | Greece wins independence. |
|---|---|---|---|
| 20 October 1827 | 27–29 July 1830 | 11 February 1831 | 7 May 1832 |

*accompli.*

**29 November:** Revolt in Warsaw. An insurrectionary government is formed and on 25 January 1831 the Diet of Warsaw announces that Tsar Nicholas has been deposed. Warsaw falls to Russian troops on 8 September and the revolution is crushed.

**1831–2:** Italian revolutionary movements at Modena, Bologna, Parma, Piacenza and in the Marches. The Austrians occupy the Duchy and the north of the Papal States. A French expeditionary force, designed to prevent them from advancing too far in the peninsula, lands at the port of Ancona and remains there till 1838. Sporadic insurrections occur until 1848.

5. Women appear on the barricades, Paris, July 1830. Painting by Manguin.

6. 'Order reigns at Warsaw': a lithograph by Grandville after the crushing of the insurrection.

# From the Holy Alliance to the Eastern Question

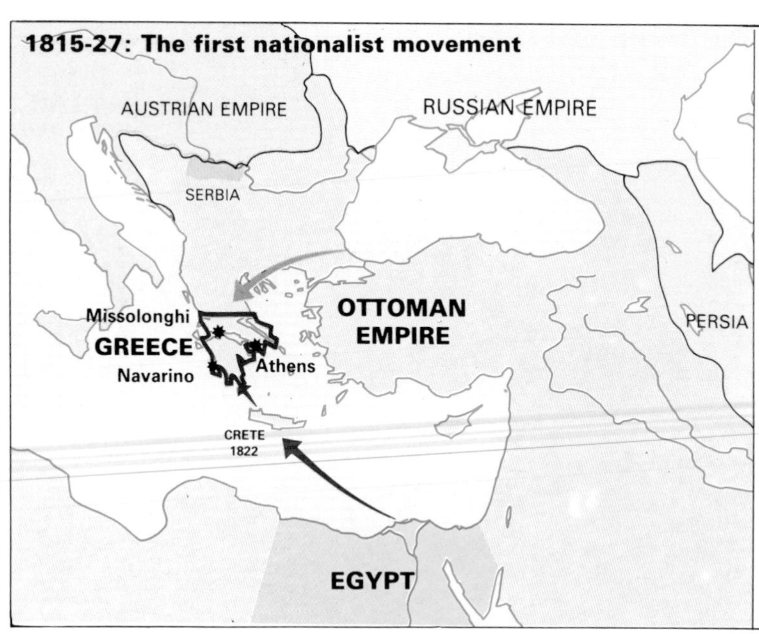

IT WAS AT the Congress of Vienna that the political reorganization of Europe was negotiated between the states allied against Napoleon. Two principles regarded as crucial to the maintenance of order governed those negotiations: dynastic legitimacy and the balance of power. To this purely geographical arrangement, there was added the Holy Alliance, which lacked any real force, and the Quadruple Alliance, which affirmed the solidarity of Prussia, Austria, Russia and England against the revolutionary forces. Provision was made for congresses, which were to provide forums for dialogue and platforms for intervention. It was at such congresses that military expeditions were decided upon, such as the Austrian expedition to Italy and the French one in Spain. Though modern in its preoccupation with collective organization, this diplomatic machinery – largely inspired by the Austrian chancellor Metternich – nonetheless revealed a total inability to understand national and liberal aspirations. The basic underlying idea was one that belonged to the *Ancien Régime*.

The first Eastern crisis (Greece, 1821–32) revealed its weaknesses: the crisis involved an implicit challenge to the dynastic principle, but Western pressures on Sultan Mahmud II were connected rather with the problem of Russian access to the Mediterranean through the Black Sea Straits, which posed a threat to British maritime supremacy. The European revolutions of 1830 modified the Vienna balance: France passed into the camp of liberal nations and supported

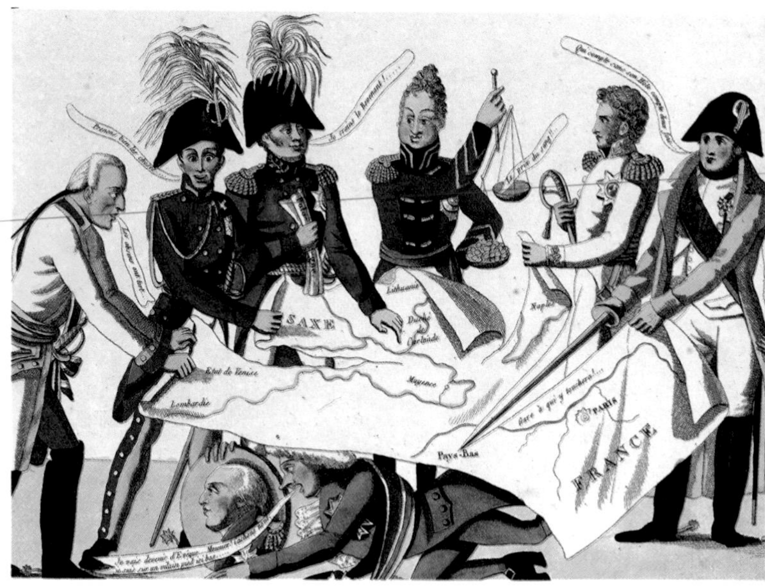


*1. The 'Kings' Cake' or the division of Europe at the Congress of Vienna, as seen by an unknown French caricaturist.*

**Congress of Vienna.** — **September 1814–June 1815**

**Death of Byron at Missolonghi.** — **19 April 1824**

**Navarino.** — **20 October 1827**

*3. Mehemet Ali, Viceroy of Egypt from 1804 to 1849, in the period of his victory over the Mamlukes. Anonymous artist, 1811.*

**23 September 1814–9 June 1815:** Congress of Vienna.
**26 September 1815:** Holy Alliance.
**20 November 1815:** The Second Peace of Paris settles France's new frontiers and the Quadruple Alliance is signed. France is integrated into it at the Congress of Aix-la-Chapelle (30 September–21 November 1818).
**1820–1:** The Austrian Empire is mandated to intervene militarily in Turin and Naples by the Congresses of Troppau (2 October–17 December 1820) and Laibach (26 January–12 May 1821). In 1822, France will be entrusted with the mission of restoring order in Spain.
**March 1821:** The Archbishop of Patras and a member of the Hetaera (a patriotic society) summon the Greeks to insurrection.
**1822:** Turkish sultan Mahmud calls on the help of the Egyptian Pasha Mehemet Ali (Mohammed Ali) in the fight against the Greek insurrection. He wins victories at Navarino, Missolonghi and Athens (1825–7).
**6 July 1827:** A treaty between Britain, France and Russia proposes a settlement whereby the Sultan is to remain suzerain of an autonomous Greece. After Mahmud II's rejection of this proposal, the British destroy the Turco-Egyptian fleet at Navarino (20 October).
**14 September 1829:** By the Treaty of Adrianople, the Turks accept Greek independence under Turkish suzerainty and cede various territories to Russia.
**1830–1:** European revolutions.
**7 May 1832:** The London Convention makes Greece a *de jure* independent kingdom.
**December:** War between Egypt and Turkey. The Egyptian army routs the Turks in Syria and at Konieh. Mahmud II calls on the great powers for aid.
**1833:** At the Conference of Teplitz and Münchengrätz, Russia and Prussia form a conservative alliance. Beginning of the crisis of the Spanish succession.
**February:** The Russian fleet occupies the Bosphorus. France and Britain put pressure on Turkey and Egypt to come to an early settlement.
**May:** The Sultan cedes the whole of Syria to Egypt by the Treaty of Kütahya.
**July:** Treaty of Unkiar-Skelessi (Turkey)

*4. Prince von Metternich-Winneburg (1773–1859), by Sir Thomas Lawrence, 1818.*

# 1814–1846

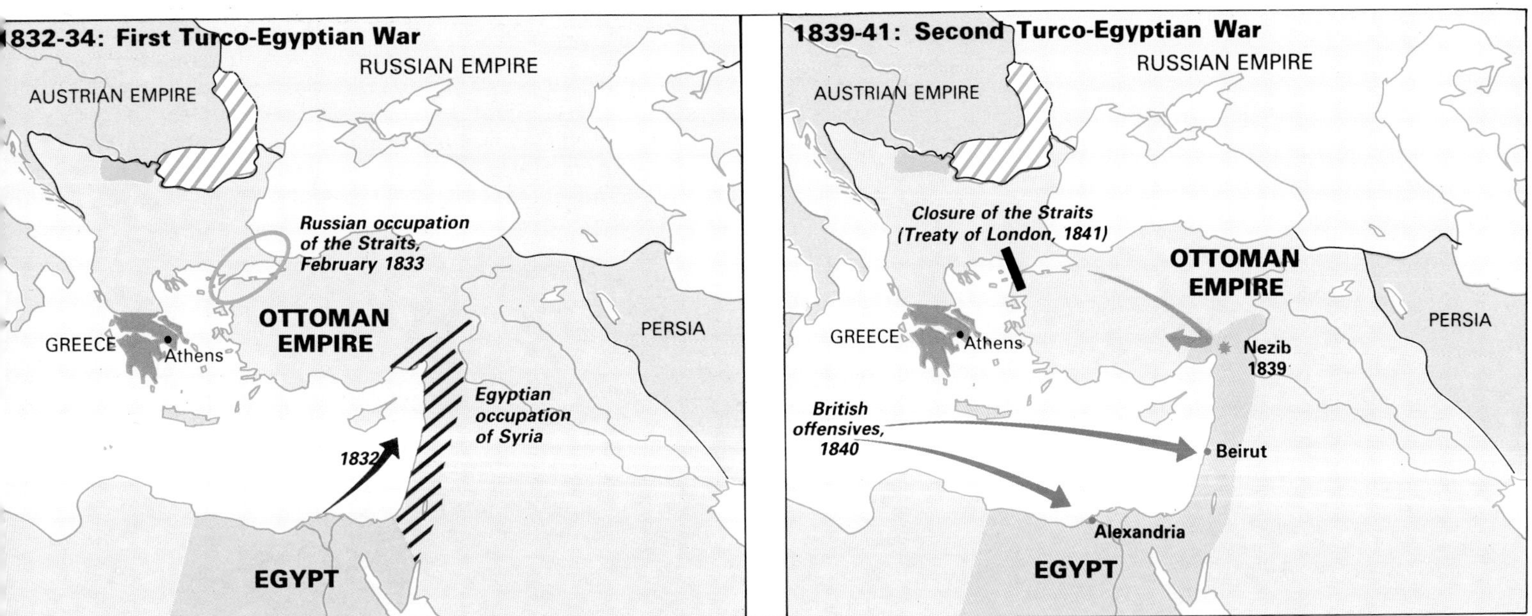


ıe cause of Belgian independence against the Dutch king. The buffer f little states that was intended to isolate Central Europe from ossible French contagion crumbled away. In spite of the formation on the pretext of difficulties in the Iberian Peninsula) of a liberal ront to oppose the conservative alliance, Europe in the period after 830 was dominated by two great antagonisms, the one between Russia and England and the other between Russia and France.

The second Eastern crisis (Egypt 1832–41) saw the liberal states at oggerheads, with France supporting the Egyptian Pasha, Mehemet Ali, who had gone to war against his sovereign. The Treaty of Unkiar-Skelessi, which established a virtual Russian protectorate ver the Ottoman Empire, saved the latter and gave Russia access to he Mediterranean. The defeat of Mahmud II gave England an pportunity to propose the establishment of a collective European protectorate over Turkey at the Conference of Vienna, which effectively snatched away Russia's newly-won advantage. In the final phase of the Egyptian crisis, the Anglo-French antagonism grew, and French blunders allowed the British Prime Minister, Palmerston, to btain the neutralization of the Straits, whilst leaving Mehemet Ali ereditary Pasha of Egypt.

The key feature of the 1840s was European expansionism. The ntente between France and England was re-established, in spite of ome colonial differences. The marriage of Queen Isabella II of Spain to her cousin the Duke of Cadiz in 1846 reawakened a hostility which ruled out the possibility of any middle ground being found; the conservative powers were able to impose their law on the Catholic cantons of Switzerland and on insurgent Polish Prussia.

However, behind the interplay of commercial and territorial rivalries, the rise of nationalist aspirations was laying the ground for the 1848 'Springtime of the Peoples'.

2. Louis-Philippe, king of the French, welcoming Queen Victoria at Le Tréport in September 1843, as portrayed by François-Auguste Biard.

**ireek Independence.** **May 1832**

**The Ottoman Empire defeated at Nezib.** **June 1839**

**Convention of the Straits.** **13 July 1841**

etween the Ottoman Empire and Russia ıakes provision for mutual assistance and ıe closure of the Straits to any foreign fleet or eight years, making the Black Sea a vast Russian roadstead.

**2 April 1834:** Signature of a liberal Quadruple Alliance between France, Britain, Spain and Portugal to prevent the return of bsolutism in Spain (Don Carlos and Dom Miguel).

**une 1839:** Sultan Mahmud II attacks Egypt. He dies after the defeat at Nezib. The powers neet at Vienna to seek a common solution.

**5 July 1840:** After secret attempts at nediation by the French, Britain, Prussia, Russia and Austria sign the Treaty of London, which gives Mehemet Ali hereditary ossession of Egypt and southern Syria for fe. When he refuses the arrangement, Palmerston bombards Beirut and in December, after deploying the British fleet ff Alexandria, wins Egypt's unconditional urrender.

**3 July 1841:** Egyptian crisis ended on terms aid down by Treaty of London. Convention of ıe Straits is signed, closing them to warships of all nations.

**1846:** Austria annexes the Cracow Republic after the uprising in Polish Prussia.

5. Capture of Trocadero, near Cadiz, by the French expeditionary force (31 August 1823). Engraving by Ledoyen.

6. Caricature of Talleyrand, Paris, 15 April 1815.

# South America at the time of the Caudillos

1. *San Martín at the battle of Chacabuco (2 February 1817), by Géricault.*

THE OCCUPATION of Spain and Portugal by Napoleon's armies and threats of a French or English conquest of South America prompted certain South American élites to take over the actual running of their countries and very soon to seek political independence. This movement towards emancipation was general but not unanimous: it took various and sometimes contradictory forms. Spanish America was the scene of fifteen years of civil war that divided every stratum of colonial society; the partisans of independence fought for motives as diverse as religious integration (in Quito) and liberal principles (in Buenos Aires and Venezuela). Others sought to free themselves as much from Southern American powers on whom they were dependent as from the colonial powers; this was the case for Ecuador, Bolivia, Paraguay and Uruguay.

The independence of Spanish America resulted first of all in the fragmentation of the sub-continent into small units, sparsely populated and weakened by war. Much of the countryside was ruined, the population dispersed and decimated, administration reduced to a bare minimum. The new states went through thirty years of instability aggravated by the *caudillos*, local chieftains whose irregular armies fought for domination. Civil wars continued up to the 1860s, with federalists confronting partisans of a centralized state.

Brazil was free of these wars and disturbances. In January 1808 the Portuguese royal family and government officials took refuge in Rio; the administration of the new state was handed over to the Infante Pedro, who was declared Emperor in 1822, and the transition was thus accomplished smoothly. When Brazil became a republic in 1889 this also happened without disruption.

Towards the middle of the century the budding states were able to emerge from their difficulties by exporting their natural resources. Peruvian guano, Ecuadorian cocoa, Brazilian and Venezuelan coffee, Argentine and Uruguayan cattle, Bolivian and Chilean ores, were exported to the United States and Europe, particularly Britain, which controlled a great part of the South American market and invested in the sub-continent.

Argentina, which won its 'frontier' by waging campaigns on the Indians of the interior, and, to a lesser degree, Chile and Brazil were peopled by immigrants from Europe; the gap widened between these states and the others, some of which, such as Peru, Bolivia and Paraguay, suffered from the expansionist designs of their powerful neighbours.

At the end of the century South American governments, converted to liberal economics and influenced by positivist philosophy, attempted to modernize the societies they controlled. They met with resistance from a traditionalist population, provoking revolts among the Indians and messianic movements in the Sertão.

**Death of Aleijadinho in Brazil.**

**1814**

**Death of Bolivar and Sucre.**

**1830**

**End of war that destroyed the Triple Alliance.**

**1870**

**1807–8:** British attempts to conquer the Rio de la Plata meet with resistance from local inhabitants.
**1808:** Spain occupied by Napoleonic armies. Legitimacy of colonial government in question, communications difficult.
**1809–12:** First South American insurrections at Chuquisaca, La Paz, Quito, Santa Fé, Caracas, Buenos Aires.
**1811:** The independent town of Buenos Aires sends expeditionary force to the provinces of the interior to win them over to its cause.
**1814–40:** Dictatorship of de Francia in Paraguay. Communication with other countries outlawed.
**1818:** Chilean independence.
**1819:** Venezuela and Colombia become independent (definitively in 1830).
**1821:** Precarious independence of Peru; San Martin appoints himself protector.
**1822:** Guayaquil conference, following which General San Martin retires from South American scene in favour of Bolívar.
**1824:** Battle of Ayacucho ends war of independence in Peru.
**1825:** Province of Banda Oriental becomes independent and takes name of Uruguay (definitive independence in 1828). Bolivia declares its independence against wishes of Peru and Argentina.
**1825–c. 1855:** Instability becomes general: caudillos engage in civil wars and risk themselves in frontier expeditions.
**1828–38:** Government of Marshal Santa Cruz in Bolivia.
**1830:** Partition of Gran Colombia in three states: Ecuador, Colombia and Venezuela. Assassination of Sucre. Death of Bolívar.
**1831–89:** Reign of Pedro II in Brazil. He abdicates in 1889 and republic is proclaimed.
**c. 1850:** Abolition of slavery in most states except Cuba (1886) and Brazil (1888). New states adopt their own legal systems and abandon Spanish law in force until then.
**1850–60:** Presidency of Marshal Castilla in Peru. The country amasses a shortlived fortune by exporting guano.
**1864–70:** Triple Alliance war. Paraguay is attacked by Brazil, Uruguay and Argentina in coalition and loses nine-tenths of its male population.
**1879–83:** Pacific war between Chile and an alliance of Peru and Bolivia; Bolivia loses its coastline and Peru its saltpetre mines. Chile controls Pacific.
**c. 1880:** End of Indian wars in Argentina and Chile.
**c. 1880–1900:** Conservative but modernizing régimes in most South American states. Programmes of road, rail and telegraph development. Exportation of natural resources.
**1895–1903:** Liberal coups d'état, civil wars between liberals and conservatives in Chile in 1891, Ecuador 1895, Uruguay 1897, Bolivia 1899, Colombia 1899–1902; Thousand-Day War in Venezuela 1899–1903.
**1897–8:** Messianic uprising of the *Canudos* in the hinterland of Bahia, Brazil.

2. *An imperial philosopher: Don Pedro II, in 1855.*

# 1800–1900

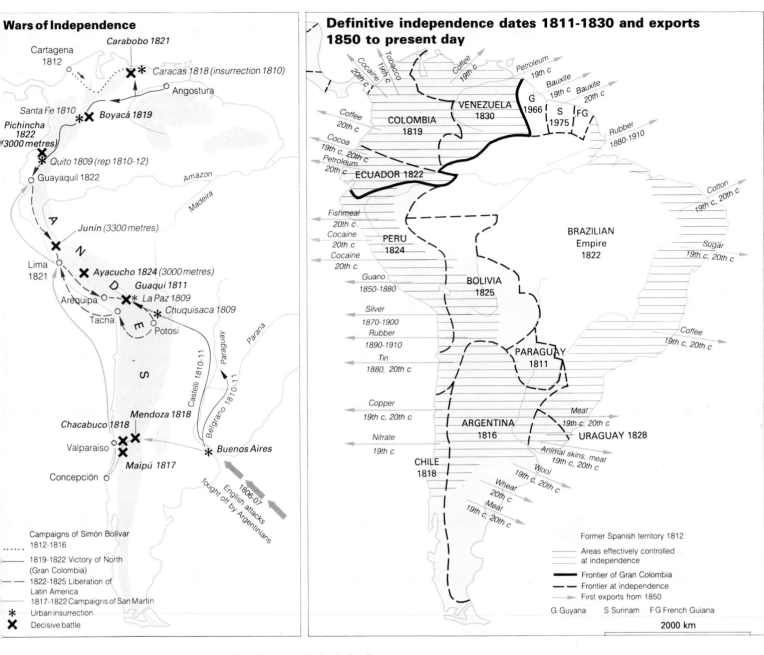

## Wars of Independence

Carabobo 1821
Cartagena 1812
Caracas 1818 (insurrection 1810)
Angostura
Santa Fe 1810
Boyacá 1819
Pichincha 1822 (3000 metres)
Quito 1809 (rep 1810-12)
Guayaquil 1822
Amazon
Madeira
A N D E S
Junín (3300 metres)
Lima 1821
Ayacucho 1824 (3000 metres)
Guaqui 1811
La Paz 1809
Arequipa
Chuquisaca 1809
Tacna
Potosi
Paraguay
Parana
Castelli 1810-11
Belgrano 1810-11
Mendoza 1818
Chacabuco 1818
Valparaiso
Buenos Aires
Maipú 1817
Concepción
1806-07 English attacks fought off by Argentinians

Campaigns of Simón Bolívar
...... 1812-1816
—— 1819-1822 Victory of North (Gran Colombia)
— — 1822-1825 Liberation of Latin America
—— 1817-1822 Campaigns of San Martín
* Urban insurrection
✖ Decisive battle

## Definitive independence dates 1811-1830 and exports 1850 to present day

Cocaine 20th c
Tobacco 19th c
Coffee 19th c
Petroleum 19th c
Bauxite 19th c
Bauxite 20th c
VENEZUELA 1830
G 1966
S 1975
FG
COLOMBIA 1819
Coffee 20th c
Cocoa 19th c, 20th c
Petroleum 20th c
ECUADOR 1822
Rubber 1880-1910
Cotton 19th c, 20th c
Fishmeal 20th c
Cocaine 20th c
Cocaine 20th c
PERU 1824
BRAZILIAN Empire 1822
Sugar 19th c, 20th c
Guano 1850-1880
BOLIVIA 1825
Silver 1870-1900
Rubber 1890-1910
Tin 1880, 20th c
Coffee 19th c, 20th c
PARAGUAY 1811
Copper 19th c, 20th c
Meat 19th c, 20th c
ARGENTINA 1816
URAGUAY 1828
Nitrate 19th c
Animal skins, meat 19th c, 20th c
CHILE 1818
Wool 19th c, 20th c
Wheat 20th c
Meat 19th c, 20th c

Former Spanish territory 1812
Areas effectively controlled at independence
Frontier of Gran Colombia
Frontier at independence
First exports from 1850
G Guyana S Surinam FG French Guiana
2000 km

**José Hernandez: *Martin Fierro***
**1872**

**Republican constitution in Brazil.**
**1891**

*3. Simón Bolívar frees the Colombian slaves, as portrayed by Luis Cancino Fernandez.*

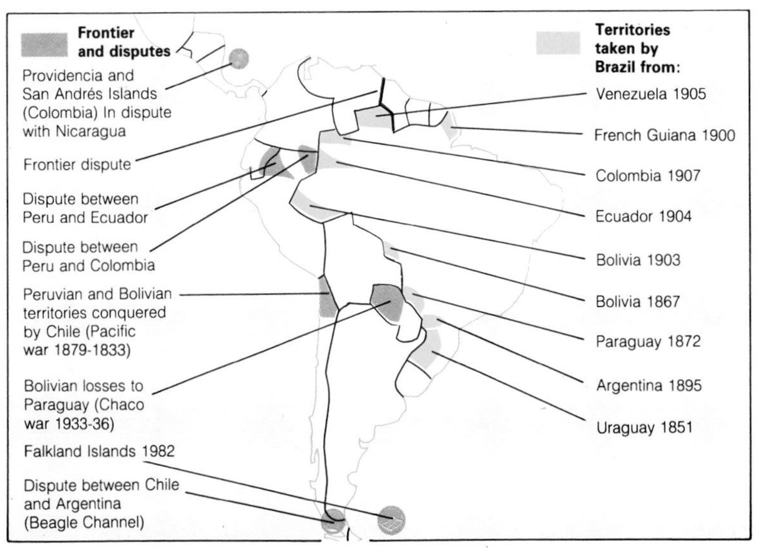

# Central America

Economic expansion based on exports made Latin America in the late nineteenth century a reserve for world capitalism. It generated an embryonic middle class whose vast fortunes were spent in Europe while leaving the greater part of the population in extreme poverty, a situation that led to the eventual downfall of the regimes that had created the new order.

This was to happen in 1910 with the Mexican revolution. The long presidency of Porfirio Díaz (1876–1911), supported by ministers with modernizing, anti-clerical attitudes who were fascinated by the North American example, ended in a civil war bringing into play the reaction of a still largely traditional population and the centrifugal tendencies of a vast and poorly administered country. The confrontation between government forces and opposition armies was followed first by clashes between rival factions, then by the religious war of the *Cristeros* (partisans of Christ the King). The Cárdenas government (1934–40) gave some impetus to agrarian reform and the situation became more stable; the only party (the PRI – Institutional Revolutionary Party) now held power unopposed and a state with unprecedented powers was established.

Central America and the West Indies were then under United States protection. Cuba and Nicaragua were ruled by fierce dictatorships for several decades.

The First World War broke the traditional patterns of trade and immigration; it also brought into question European political and cultural models. In addition, with the opening of the Panama Canal in 1914 and the withdrawal of European powers, the United States acquired a much greater hold on the sub-continent, over and above their historical domination of the Caribbean and Central America by such well-known tactics as the 'big stick' and 'dollar diplomacy'.

The crisis of 1929 dealt Latin America a severe blow: the flow of capital stopped, the price of raw materials collapsed. In the larger countries, however, it was useful in stimulating the creation of industries to replace goods until then imported. But social problems were soon overtaken by political ones.

From 1930 onwards instability became the rule; the military, supported by some politicians, plotted to take over government.

Industrial and office workers and sections of the middle classes withdrew their support from the liberal parties in favour of more immediate solutions confidently offered by popular leaders in direct contact with the masses. This marked the rise of populist movements backed by the trade unions, whose policies were progressive and nationalist but whose practices were often quite moderate. Although some real improvements were made, particularly in conditions of life in the cities, and although the regimes did wish to modernize their countries, no real reforms were made in the countryside, powerful vested interests remained unchallenged and the military stayed close to the seat of power.

In Cuba and then in Nicaragua the 'rebels' went much further in overthrowing the old ruling classes and challenging American domination; however, they paid the price of dependence on the USSR, and the revolutionary societies themselves became militarized. The United States in turn provided massive aid to the enemies of Nicaragua's Sandinista government, the Contras.

Meanwhile, from the 1960s the Caribbean states and Central America were going through a rapid process of decolonization: Jamaica and Trinidad and Tobago became independent in 1962, Barbados in 1966, the Bahamas in 1973, Grenada in 1974, Dominica in 1978, Saint Lucia in 1979, Saint Vincent and the Grenadines in 1979, Antigua, Barbuda and Belize in 1981 and St Kitts and Nevis in 1983.

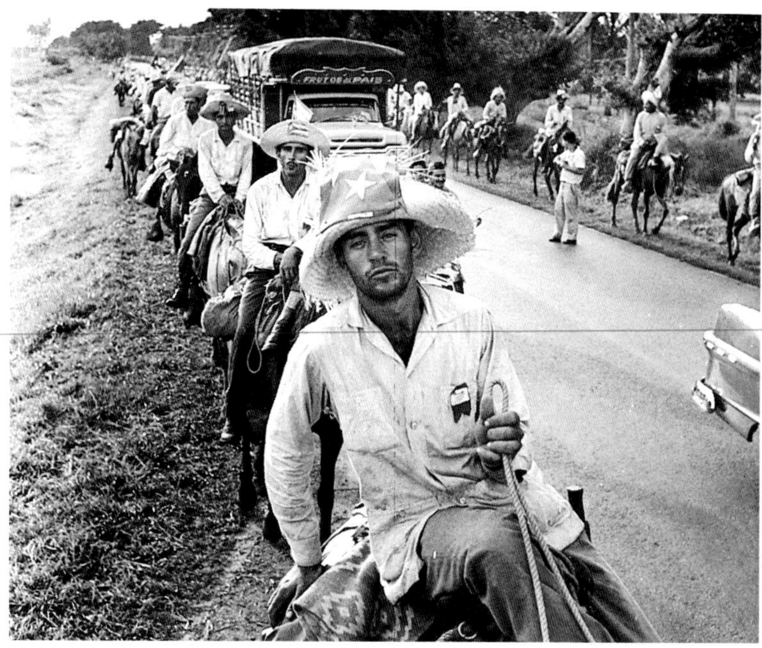

*1. March of Castro's forces on Havana, early January 1959.*

**War between USA and Mexico.** 1846–8
**Emperor Maximilian shot at Queretaro.** 19 June 1867
**Pancho Villa, Mexican revolutionary.** 1878–1923
**D. A. Siqueiros: *The Devil in the Church.*** 1947
**Juan Rulfo: *Pedro Paran*** 1955

*2. The 1810 War of Independence in Mexico, as seen by Diego Rivera, 1929.*

**1810–11:** First popular insurrections in Mexico in favour of independence, led by priests Miguel Hidalgo and José Maria Morelos.
**1824:** Birth of Mexican Republic after an attempt at establishing a Creole empire. In 1833 General Santa Anna sets up a long series of dictatorships punctuated by civil wars (up to 1855).
**1839:** Central America splinters into many states. In spite of all attempts to form a federation during the century (particularly by Rufino Barrios, President of Guatemala), 'Balkanization' is inevitable.
**1861:** Mexican liberals defeat conservatives. Their leader, Juárez, suspends repayment of foreign debt, thus provoking French intervention.
**1862:** French occupation in support of Emperor Maximilian; he is defeated and shot by troops led by Juárez in 1867.
**1867–76:** Period of reform in Mexico, first modernizing and secularizing measures.
**1868–78:** Cuba fights for independence and eventually fails.

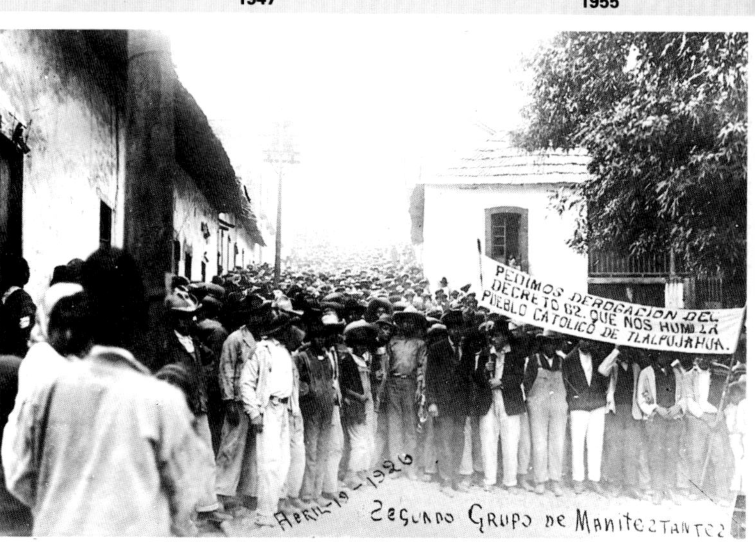


*3. The Cristero rebels, opponents of aggressive anti-church measures, Tlalpujahua, 1926.*

# 19th–20th centuries

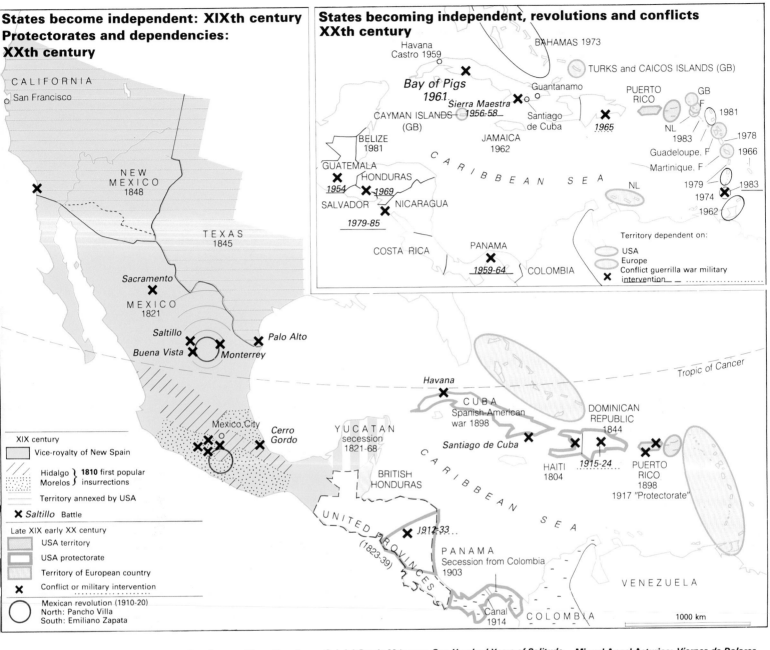

## States become independent: XIXth century Protectorates and dependencies: XXth century

CALIFORNIA
San Francisco
NEW MEXICO 1848
TEXAS 1845
Sacramento
MEXICO 1821
Saltillo
Buena Vista
Monterrey
Palo Alto
Mexico City
Cerro Gordo
YUCATAN secession 1821-68
BRITISH HONDURAS
UNITED PROVINCES (1823-39)
1912-33
PANAMA Secession from Colombia 1903
Canal 1914
COLOMBIA
VENEZUELA
Havana
CUBA Spanish-American war 1898
Santiago de Cuba
DOMINICAN REPUBLIC 1844
HAITI 1804
1915-24
PUERTO RICO 1898 1917 "Protectorate"
CARIBBEAN SEA
Tropic of Cancer
1000 km

XIX century
Vice-royalty of New Spain
Hidalgo } 1810 first popular
Morelos } insurrections
Territory annexed by USA
*Saltillo* Battle

Late XIX early XX century
USA territory
USA protectorate
Territory of European country
Conflict or military intervention
Mexican revolution (1910-20)
North: Pancho Villa
South: Emiliano Zapata

## States becoming independent, revolutions and conflicts XXth century

Havana Castro 1959
BAHAMAS 1973
TURKS and CAICOS ISLANDS (GB)
Bay of Pigs 1961
Guantanamo
Sierra Maestra 1956-58
Santiago de Cuba
CAYMAN ISLANDS (GB)
PUERTO RICO
GB
F
1981
1965
NL
1983
BELIZE 1981
JAMAICA 1962
1978
Guadeloupe, F
1966
Martinique, F
GUATEMALA 1954
HONDURAS
1969
SALVADOR
NICARAGUA
1979-85
CARIBBEAN SEA
NL
1979
1983
1974
1962
COSTA RICA
PANAMA 1959-64
COLOMBIA

Territory dependent on:
USA
Europe
Conflict guerrilla war military intervention

**Alejo Carpentier**: *El Siglo de las Luces.* 1962 | **Jose Lezama Lima**: *Paradiso.* 1966 | **Gabriel Garcia Márquez**: *One Hundred Years of Solitude.* 1967 | **Miguel Angel Asturias**: *Viernes de Dolores.* 1972

**1873–85:** Rufino Barrios dictator in Guatemala.
**1876–1911:** Porfirio Díaz governs Mexico, retaining presidency in six successive elections.
**1898:** Spanish-American War: Cuba gains independence but ends up an American protectorate in all but name.
**1903:** Panama secedes from Colombia, supported by North American intervention.
**1910–20:** Mexican Revolution.
**1912–33:** United States occupies Nicaragua, Haiti (1915–33) and Dominican Republic (1916–24). Founding of APRA (Alianza Popular Revolucionaria Americana) in Mexico City by Peruvian Raúl Haya de la Torre, to regroup revolutionary tendencies in Indian America.
**1925–33:** Dictatorship of General Machado in Cuba.
**1927–9:** War of the Cristeros in Mexico, a popular reaction against anti-religious policies of the revolution.
**1934–40:** Lázaro Cárdenas president of Mexico; reformist policies.
**1936–79:** Dictatorship of Samoza family in Nicaragua; this is overthrown by a massive insurrection led by Sandinista party which takes power.
**1939–59:** Dictatorship of Batista in Cuba; overthrown by guerrilla fighters led by Fidel Castro.
**20 August 1940:** Assassination of Trotsky in Mexico.

*4. Emiliano Zapata.*

**1950–4:** Arbenz Guzman president of Guatemala.
**1957–71:** Francois Duvalier dictator in Haiti.
**21 April 1961:** Attempted landing by anti-Castro forces in Bay of Pigs.
**1962:** International crisis provoked by installation of Soviet missile bases in Cuba. Beginning of Nicaraguan guerrilla war.
**1963–9:** Crisis in Dominican Republic; military intervention by USA.
**1969:** War between El Salvador and Honduras.
**1978:** Dormant civil wars erupt in Central America (Guatemala, El Salvador, Nicaragua).
**1982:** Unprecedented economic crisis in Mexico.
**7 February 1986:** Fall of Haitian dictator Jean-Claude Duvalier.
**1989. 19 March:** In El Salvador, A. Cristiani defeats J. Napoleon Duarte in the presidential elections.
**7 May:** As a result of fixed elections in Panama, General M. Noriega remains in power.
**20 December:** The United States invades Panama to oust Noriega and set up a new government.

*5. Daniel Ortega on the first day of his presidency, Managua, 1985.*

# The Springtime of the Peoples

A TANGLED WEB of anti-feudal, democratic, social and nationalist aspirations existed in Europe in 1848. Widespread revolution was the outcome. The economic crisis in Britain in 1847 and the Chartist movement, the hunger riots caused by the food shortages of previous years, the Polish uprising of 1846 signaling the democratization of the nationalist movement, and the civil war in Switzerland, were all precursory signs of the revolutionary explosion. Italy, as yet still an abstract entity, was ablaze from north to south and Hungary was trying to shake off the Austrian yoke. The monarchy in France had been abolished at the end of February, and the outlines of a modern democratic social system were taking shape with the Luxembourg Commission and the setting up of National Workshops. Starting in southern Germany, the democratic revolutionary movement brought about both a pre-parliamentary body (which was to lead to the Frankfurt elected assembly and to a government devoid of power) and the Vienna and Berlin uprisings. Finally, Prague rose up as the effects of the Czech national movement were felt, and formed a pan-Slavic democratic congress in which the only Russian was Bakunin.

Having returned to Cologne, Marx and Engels took part in the revolution and published the *Neue Rheinische Zeitung*. The counter-revolution celebrated its first victories in Paris during the bloody 'June days' that were triggered off by the announcement that the National Workshops were to be closed, whilst in the elections for the Assembly the rural areas had already enabled the moderate elements to win a triumphant victory. There were victories, too, in Prague, where the uprising was crushed and the pan-Slavic congress dissolved, and in Custozza, where the army of Charles Albert was defeated by the Austrians. In contrast, Vienna continued to resist the inconsistencies of government policy and sided with the Hungary of Kossuth, whose armies in turn supported the Viennese rebellion until it was crushed. In Germany the Frankfurt Parliament's acceptance of the armistice with Denmark marked the final abandonment of the German national cause in Schleswig and Holstein and unleashed the second wave of revolution in Frankfurt and in the south-west. The republican idea gained ground in Italy, where, both in Rome and Florence, the Republic was proclaimed, though not in Manin's Venice (a bastion of resistance to the Austrians). Although international intervention by the revolutionaries – by the French in Germany and Belgium and by the Germans on behalf of the Poles in Posen – had been hesitant and contradictory in nature, reactionary intervention was in a much more offensive style. Under cover of containing the Austrian advance, the French got the better of the Republic of Rome, while Russian troops, called to the rescue by the Emperor of Austria,

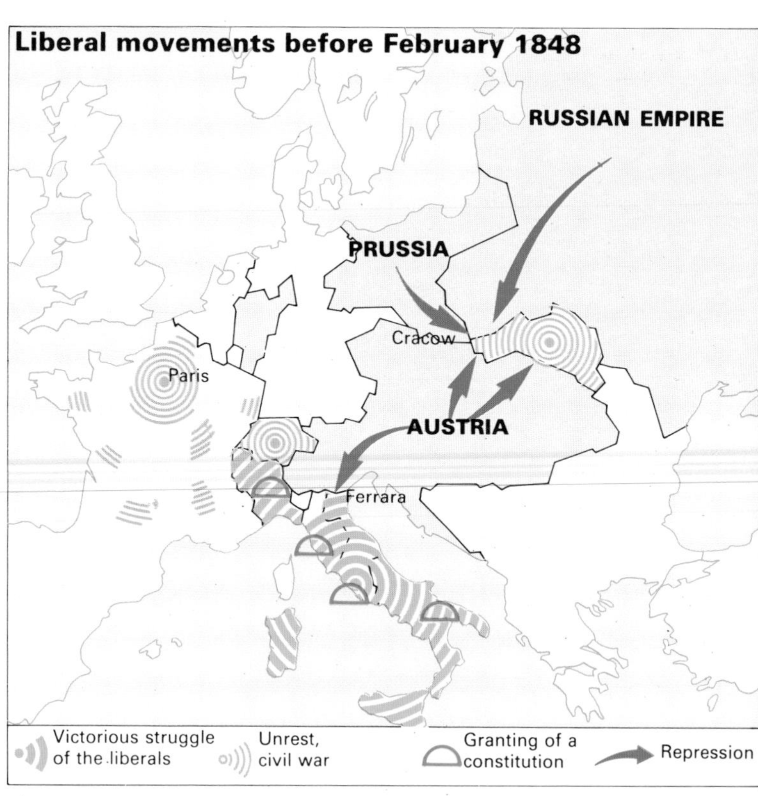

1. *The barricades in the Avenue Brigida in Naples, 15 May 1848. Anonymous painting.*

| Uprising in Paris. | Uprising in Vienna. | Berlin. | Pan-Slavic Democratic Congress of Prague. | Workers' riots in Paris, 'the June Days'. |
|---|---|---|---|---|
| 22–25 February 1848 | 13–15 March 1848 | 18–22 March 1848 | 2–28 June 1848 | 23–6 June 1848 |

**2–4 January 1848:** Cigar workers' riot in Naples.
**12 January:** Palermo uprising.
**10 February:** Constitution granted to Naples and to Florence (17th).
**22–5 February:** Uprising in Paris, proclamation of the Republic, creation of the Luxembourg commission and national workshops.
**March (beginning):** Liberal governments in several German states; peasant uprising in the south-west.
**5 March:** Promulgation of the constitution (Statuto) of Charles Albert, King of Sardinia; German liberals and democrats meeting in Heidelberg decide to assemble a pre-parliamentary body.
**5–6 March:** Troubles in Glasgow.
**13–15 March:** Uprising in Vienna, flight of Metternich.
**14 March:** Rome constitution.
**17–22 March:** Uprising in Venice; Daniele Manin proclaims the Republic.
**18–22 March:** In Berlin, Frederick William IV grants a constitution. Uprising in Milan against the Austrian occupation.

3. *Allegory of the Republic. Anonymous French painting.*

**22 March:** Charles Albert declares war on Austria.
**26 March–7 May:** Riots in Madrid.
**31 March–3 April:** Meeting of the pre-parliamentary body (Vorparlament) in Frankfurt.
**12–20 April:** Uprising in Baden.
**23–4 April:** Extreme left defeated in French elections.
**April–May:** Polish uprising in Posnan.
**15 May:** Demonstrations in Paris and Vienna.
**15–16 May:** Popular uprising crushed in Naples.
**18 May:** First session of the Parliament of Frankfurt.
**22 May:** Start of the Prussian National Assembly.
**2–28 June:** Pan-Slavic Congress of Prague.
**11–17 June:** Prague uprising crushed.
**15 June:** Workers' riot in Berlin.
**23–6 June:** Workers' riot in Paris put down by Cavaignac.
**22 July:** Opening of Austrian Parliament in Vienna.
**22–5 July:** Austria (Radetzky) defeats Charles Albert at Custozza.

**July–August:** Irish rebellion fails.
**23 August:** Uprising in Vienna.
**23 August–3 September:** Congress of Workers' Associations in Berlin.
**7 September:** Abolition of feudal régime in Austria.
**10 September:** Jellačic's Croatian troops attack Hungary.
**16 September:** Parliament of Frankfurt ratifies the Malmo armistice of 26 August, setting off the 18 September uprising in Frankfurt.
**21–4 September:** Failure of the republican endeavour in Baden.
**6–31 October:** Revolution in Vienna.
**15–16 November:** Republican uprising in Rome.
**22 November–7 March 1849:** Austrian Parliament sits at Kremsler.
**2 December:** Franz Josef Emperor of Austria.
**5 December:** Dissolution of the Prussian National Assembly.
**10 December:** Louis Napoleon Bonaparte elected President of the French Republic.
**February 1849:** Republic proclaimed in

# 1848

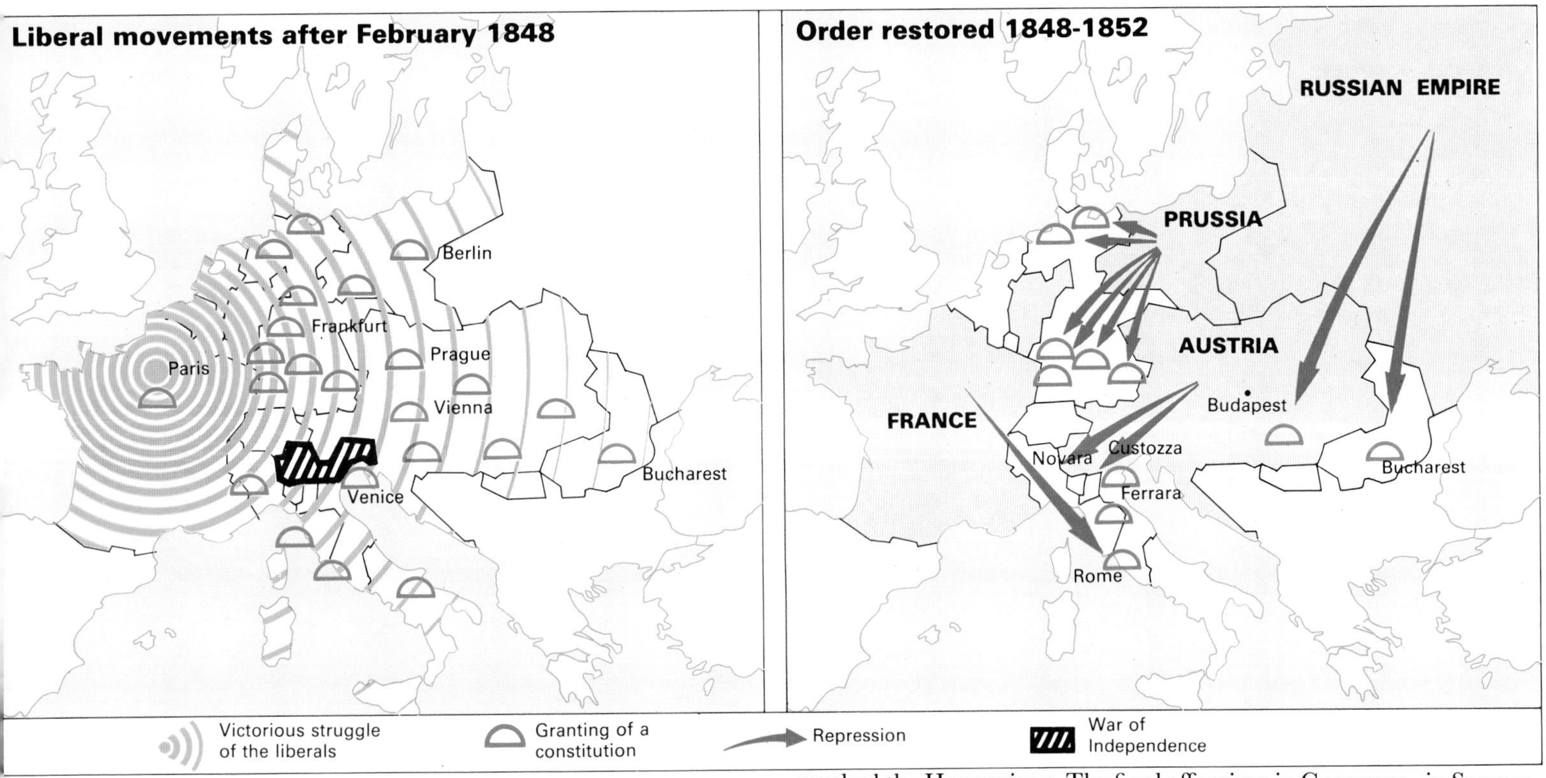

**Liberal movements after February 1848**

Paris
Frankfurt
Berlin
Prague
Vienna
Venice
Bucharest

**Order restored 1848-1852**

RUSSIAN EMPIRE
PRUSSIA
AUSTRIA
FRANCE
Budapest
Novara
Custozza
Ferrara
Rome
Bucharest

Victorious struggle of the liberals — Granting of a constitution — Repression — War of Independence

crushed the Hungarians. The final offensives in Germany – in Saxony with Bakunin, in Baden, in the Palatinate and in the Rhineland with Engels – were launched to support the constitution voted through by the Parliament of Frankfurt, but this was rejected, together with the imperial crown and its 'plebeian' associations, by Frederick William IV. At the same time French intervention in Rome set off the final convulsive movements of the people's revolt in Paris and Lyon.

Despite their general failure, the 1848 revolutions, as well as achieving the abolition of seigneurial privileges, did allow clarification of the division between democrats in general and democratic-socialists, and as the revolutions unfolded the independent organization of the working class began to emerge. But the revolutions also revealed the complexity of radical movements within particular countries; for example, in Hungary, the revolutionaries' refusal to respond to supporters of Slav national liberation – particularly the Croats – made the nationalists allies of the monarchy.

*2. Riot scene in Berlin, June 1848. Engraving by P. C. Geissier, Nuremberg.*

**Revolution in Vienna.** **6–31 October 1848**

**Republic proclaimed in Tuscany and Rome.** **8–9 February 1849**

**Proclamation of Hungarian independence.** **14 April 1849**

*4. The Viennese watch over the German democrat, Robert Blum, after his execution in October 1848. Lithograph by H. Shanes, 1851.*

Tuscany (8th) and in Rome (9th).
**15–30 March:** Ancient powers re-established in Parma, Modena, Florence.
**23 March:** Charles Albert abdicates, defeated at Novara by the Austrians.
**28 March:** The Parliament of Frankfurt adopts the constitution of the Reich and offers the imperial crown to Frederick William, who refuses it (28 April).
**14 April:** Kossuth proclaims Hungarian independence at Debrecen.
**3 May–23 July:** Uprisings in Saxony, Baden, Palatinate, Rhineland.
**11 May:** Restoration of absolute monarchy in the Kingdom of the Two Sicilies.
**23 May–13 August:** Victorious Tsarist intervention against Hungary.
**30 May–18 June:** The Parliament leaves Frankfurt and sits in Würtemberg.
**15 June:** Workers' uprising in Lyon.
**1 July:** Surrender of Rome.
**22 August:** Surrender of the Republic of Venice.

*5. Lajos Kossuth (1802–94), leader of the Hungarian nationalist revolution. Anonymous painting.*

# Europe: From Romanticism to Positivism

IT MAKES GOOD SENSE to speak of a separate historical entity called the nineteenth century, even if this entity does not fit exactly into the chronological frame of a century. Between the Napoleonic era and the First World War we can identify a relatively homogeneous period easily distinguishable both from the period 1640–1800 and from the twentieth century that followed. It is often said that the nineteenth century was a religious century, a century in reaction against the rationalism of the 'Century of Louis XIV', the Enlightenment and the French Revolution. This observation holds true only if one does not attribute the generally high levels of artistic and scientific creativity found during this period to the burgeoning pioneering and avant-garde movements of the time, which were above all rationalist in inspiration: and further if one separates this high level of creativity from the rise of mass production, which can after all be considered to have spread the spirit of the Enlightenment, albeit in a vulgarized form, rather than to have denied it.

Nonetheless, the nineteenth century did challenge excessive faith in reason in the name of morality and the mystical, and what's more, it also put abstraction in the dock in the name of singularity and sensuality. It was 'realistic' after its own fashion, even if subject to some degree of hallucination. It was the century of the concrete, of the novel in literature, of induction and experimentation in science and of the close study of history and geography. There was a general passion for detail and fine distinctions; the age adored local colour, cultivated a feeling for nature and freely indulged in pantheism and pansexualism. Not least, the nineteenth century exalted the individual over the group and tended to contest the disciplines, rules and norms which the classical spirit (and even the revolutionary spirit) considered indispensable.

These characteristics are essentially those of Romanticism. Some further secondary features can be added to this picture. It is clear, for example, that Romanticism developed links at a very early stage with political liberalism and also with nationalism. In Germany, for example, Romanticism cannot be understood unless one takes into account the desire to be free of French influence. In Spain, 'Romantic' meant the opposite of 'servile'.

Yet, if the nineteenth century was the century of Romanticism, it was also the century of Positivism. That is to say, the philosophical and scientific tendency of the age was towards description and induction, as is illustrated by the strong predeliction for the natural sciences and their methods. Ultimately, the nineteenth century can only be seen as homogeneous in relation to what preceded it and what followed it. It can be broken down into three great sub-periods. The second of these (1855–85) saw a reaction against Romanticism properly so-called (1800–55, the first sub-period), appearing less moralistic and religious, and if anything even more obsessed by natural and material realities but also less indifferent to the demands of community, less free in its attitude to conventions. As for the third period (from around 1885: Symbolism, Modernism, Idealism ...), it saw a protest against scientism, a rediscovery of the sacred and a partial rehabilitation of the symbol and the concept. It also saw some staunch battles fought in defence of the individual.

A deeper study would have to go beyond this tripartite chronological schema to produce a more thorough inventory of these longer sub-periods and, in particular, to examine shorter sub-divisions: 1828–44 (Romantic freedoms but also rationalist achievements ...), 1869–79 (religious offensives and resistance, flowering of utopian thinking and poetry ...), 1900–10 (movements towards secularization and social preoccupations ...). We would also have to show the very broadly European and worldwide character of these turning-points in collective sensibility.

*1. Victor Hugo, standard-bearer of Romanticism. Caricature by Montbard in* Gulliver, *c. 1870.*

**1797–1804**: First German Romantic Movement. A.W. and F. von Schlegel (founders of the review Athenäum (1798).
**1798:** Beginnings of English Romanticism: W. Wordsworth, *Lyrical Ballads*; S. T. Coleridge, *Recantation.*
**After 1799:** Strong religious revival.
**1802:** Chateaubriand's *Génie du christianisme.*
**1804:** Birth of Russian prophetic monasticism. Rise of German Romanticism.
**1805:** Chateaubriand's *René.*
**1805–7:** Hegel's thought undergoing development. Primacy of history; hostility to the Enlightenment. The *Phenomenology of Mind* published in 1807.
**1812–22:** Alessandro Manzoni's *Inni Sacri.*
**1816:** The 'Romantic Battle' begins in Italy.
**1816–17:** Leopold von Ranke, the greatest scholarly historian of the century, has elaborated his method.
**1819:** Géricault's *Raft of the Medusa.*
**1828:** Anti-clerical measures in France.
**1830:** Success of Berlioz's *Symphonie fantastique.* The 'battle' over *Hernani* (Hugo's play) in France. Goethe opposes Romanticism. First volume of what will become Balzac's *Comédie humaine* is a satire of romantic dreams, *Scènes de la vie privée* (1830–2).
**1830–42:** Publication of the six volumes of Auguste Comte's *Course of Positive Philosophy.*
**1839–1841:** F. Chopin's 25 *Preludes.*
**1842:** Publication of the first part of N. Gogol's *Dead Souls.*
**1844–5:** Upsurge of Romantic movements in France, Germany and Italy. Realist tendencies developing, especially in painting.
**1846–9:** The 'Forty-Eighters', Romantic revolutions, Christian socialism.
**1853:** Verdi's *La Traviata.*
**1855:** In Piedmont, Cavour launches an attack on monastic property, Gustave Courbet's Exhibition seen as a Realist 'insurrection' (especially *The Burial at Ornans, The Studio*). Offensive of biological evolutionism with Herbert Spencer (*Principles of Psychology*) and A. R. Wallace. L. Büchner's *Kraft und Stoff* (*Energy and Matter*). Materialism has some success. N. G. Chernyshevsky's Anti-Romantic Manifesto. He becomes leader of Nihilist thinkers (*A Vital Question or What is to be done?*, 1863).
**1855–7:** Taine's *Les philosophes français du XIXe siècle.*
**1856:** First publication of Flaubert's *Madame Bovary.*
**1857:** Attacks in Germany on Hegel and metaphysics.
**1859:** Charles Darwin's *The Origin of Species by Natural Selection.*
**1862:** Otto von Bismarck Chancellor. *Realpolitik.*
**1862–3:** E. Renan is appointed to the Collège de France and publishes *The Life of Jesus.*
**1863:** Failure of insurrection in Poland: end of Polish Romanticism.
**1865–9:** Tolstoy's *War and Peace.*
**1866:** Dostoyevsky's *Crime and Punishment.*
**1869:** Meeting between Monet and Renoir. Towards Impressionism.
**1869–70:** Zola and his friends develop Naturalism.
**8 December 1869–18 July 1870:** First Vatican Council. Traditionalism affirmed.
**1872:** Dostoyevsky's *The Possessed.*

*3. Georg Wilhelm Friedrich Hegel, German philosopher (1770–1831). Copy of a portrait by E. Born, 1831.*

# 19th century

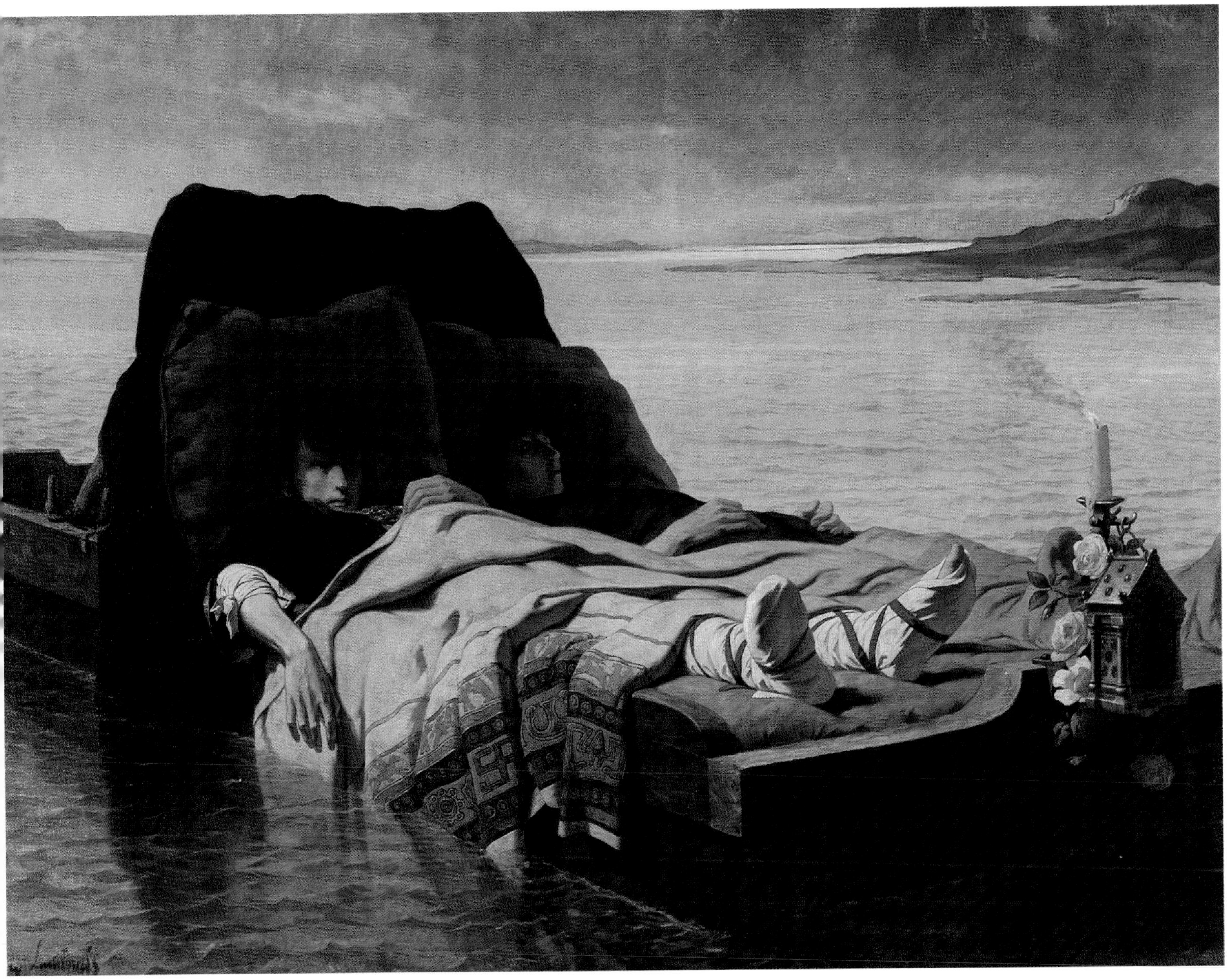

2. Les Énérves de Jumièges, *as imagined by Evariste Vital Luminais (1822–96).*

**1874:** E. Boutroux's philosophical thesis, *De la contingence des lois de la nature.*
**1876:** Inauguration of the theatre at Bayreuth. Wagner's *Ring* cycle performed.
**1878:** Election of Pope Leo XIII, who will attempt to make the church more in touch with the modern world.
**1880:** The *lois laïques* in France.
**1882:** Death of Charles Darwin (national funeral). Triumphal reception of H. Spencer in USA.
**1885:** M. Barrès's *Culte du Moi* (Cult of the Self). Death of Victor Hugo (22 May).
**1886:** Conversion to Catholicism of Paul Claudel, Charles de Foucauld and Theresa of Lisieux. Tolstoy's *Death of Ivan Illich.* E. M. de Vogüé's *Le Roman russe.* Idealist Manifesto. Crisis of Naturalism. 'Symbolist Revolution'. Discovery of Rimbaud. Wagner fashionable in France.
**1886–7:** Policy of appeasement towards Catholics in France. Polish Neo-Romanticism.
**1887–8:** 'Modernism' in Hispanic literature.
**1889:** Henri Bergson's thesis, *Les Données immédiates de la conscience.*
**c. 1890:** Hegemony of Marburg School and Neo-Kantianism in Germany (H. Cohen, P. G. Natorp, E. Cassirer).
**1900–10:** Neo-Classical and anti-individualist trend in literature, rationalist tendencies in philosophy and theology, and laicising ones in politics.
**c. 1910:** New wave of religious converts.
**1911:** Triumph of Bergson at the Bologna Congress.

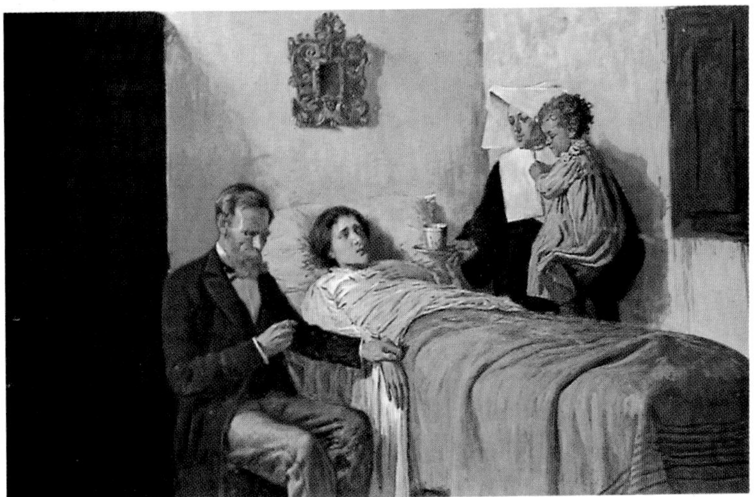

4. Science and Charity, *by Pablo Picasso, 1897.*

# European Migration

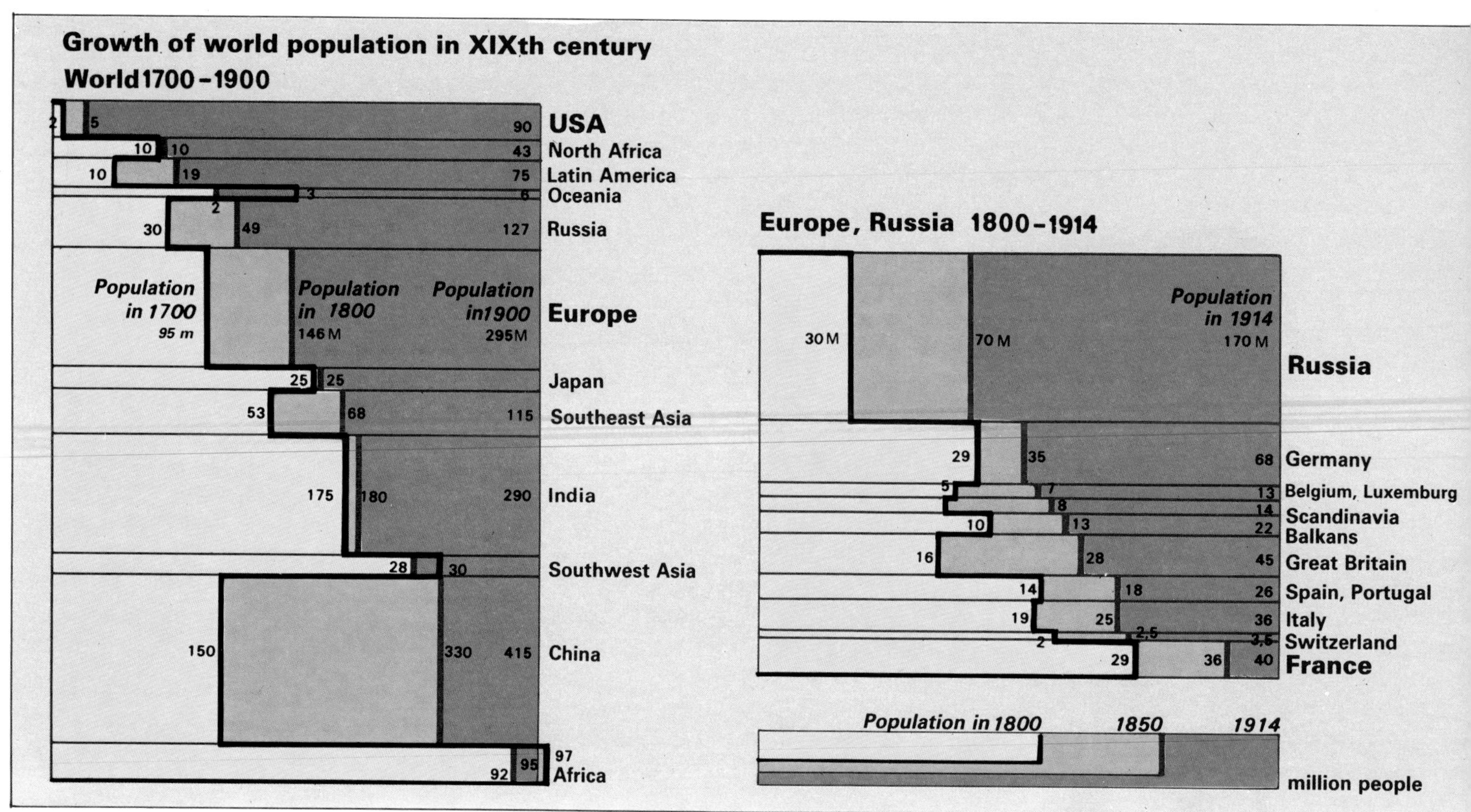


World population growth, estimated at 18% during the seventeenth century and 40% during the eighteenth, speeded up in the nineteenth century: total population went from 680 million in 1700 to 954 million in 1800, 1,241 in 1850 and 1,634 in 1900, a relative rise of 71% in 100 years.

The main causes of this increase are still in doubt; some attribute it to climatic variations (the Little Ice Age may have limited the spread of microbial infections), others to the mix of populations which may have strengthened immune defences. For nineteenth-century Europeans the effects of anti-smallpox vaccination were of major importance, as were improvements in hygiene, particularly the antiseptic techniques popularized by Pasteur from the late 1880s onwards.

Progress in the fight against mortality enabled the European continent to increase its share of world population considerably. In the seventeenth century demographic growth was only 13% compared with 19% for the rest of the world, but in the eighteenth century it reached 56% (rest of the world 37%) and in the nineteenth 106% (rest of the world 63%). In 1770, with approximately 115 million people, Europe made up only one-sixth of the world total; in 1800 it represented 20% (192 million out of 954) and in 1900, 24% (395 million out of 1,634).

During this same century Europe expatriated to other continents about 70 million emigrants (50 million of these permanently), mostly to North America but many to Siberia, Latin America and Australia. These people then reproduced in their new homelands, bringing the total population of European origin to 210 million at the beginning of the nineteenth century and 560 million around 1900 (166% increase), when it represented over a third of the population of the globe!

All the European countries did not share equally in this expansion nor in the creation of new centres of population. In France the early adoption of birth control practices meant that the population was only just reproducing at replacement level; but for an increase in average lifespan it would not have grown, as it did, from 29 million to 40 million. Consequently France contributed little to the great movement of European emigration.

Most other European countries, on the contrary, witnessed both a demographic explosion and a mass exodus of their population.

The British, and especially the Irish, were among the first to leave. Between 1800 and 1850 the population of the British Isles doubled and that of Ireland reached a record level in absolute terms (8 million around 1845).

Even before the Great Famine the Irish had begun to emigrate in large numbers: half a million crossed the Atlantic from 1820 to 1844 and nearly one and a third million in the decade that followed, at which point they represented half the influx to the USA. As for the English and the Scots, 13 million of them emigrated between 1815 and 1914 in four successive waves (around 1850, 1870, 1885 and 1910). 65% settled in the USA, 15% in Canada, 11% in Australia and 5% in South Africa.

About 6 million Germans emigrated, mostly to the USA, with three peaks (around 1850, 1870 and 1885). Two million Scandinavians left, crossing the Atlantic either with the last wave of Germans or with the fourth wave of British.

Italy expatriated 16 million citizens: 4 million to the US, 4 million to Latin America and the rest to Europe. The beginnings of the twentieth century witnessed a veritable tidal wave, with 873,000 departures in the one year 1913.

At the same time there was an exodus from Central and Eastern Europe: 4 million Austro-Hungarians, 2.5 million Russians and the same number of Poles. Over 15 years about 6 million people emigrated to the USA. Many Russians also left for Asia: in 1914, 4 million of them had settled in the Caucasus and 9,600,000 in Siberia.

Between 1800 and 1914 Europeans had progressively peopled the world.

# 19th century

## European emigration

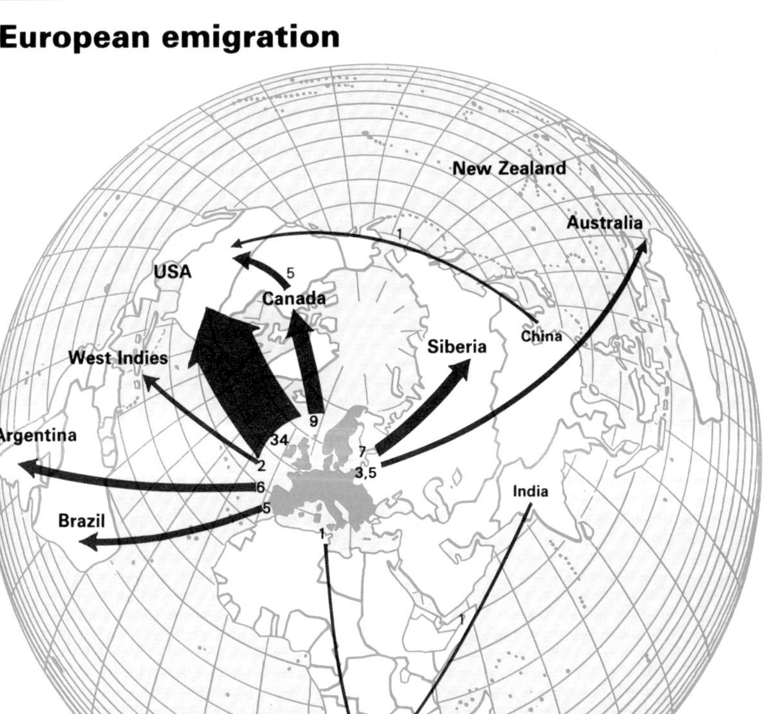

New Zealand
Australia
USA
Canada
West Indies
Siberia
China
Argentina
Brazil
India
South Africa
5
1
9
34
2
6
5
7
3,5
1
1
million people

Immigrants to USA
Population of USA
Immigration
120
100
50 M
10 M
0
1800
1850
1900
1930

Country of origin of immigrants to USA
Ireland
Great Britain
Germany
Scandinavia
Italy
Central and Eastern Europe
Asia
Canada
2 M
1 M
0

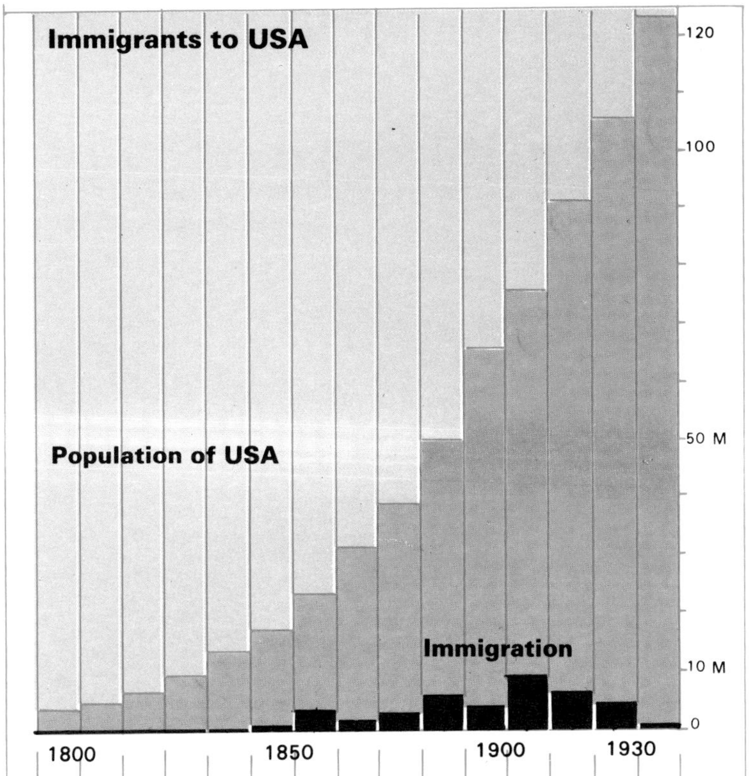

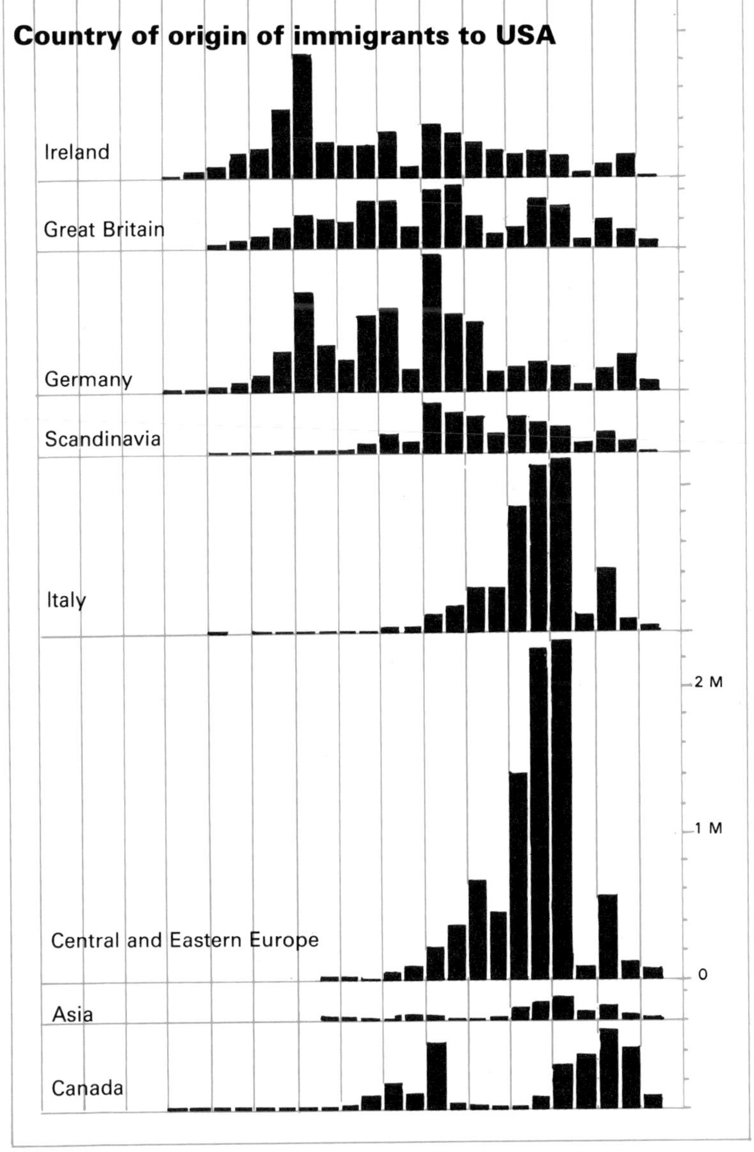

*1. On the Canadian Pacific Railway: immigrants around 1880.*

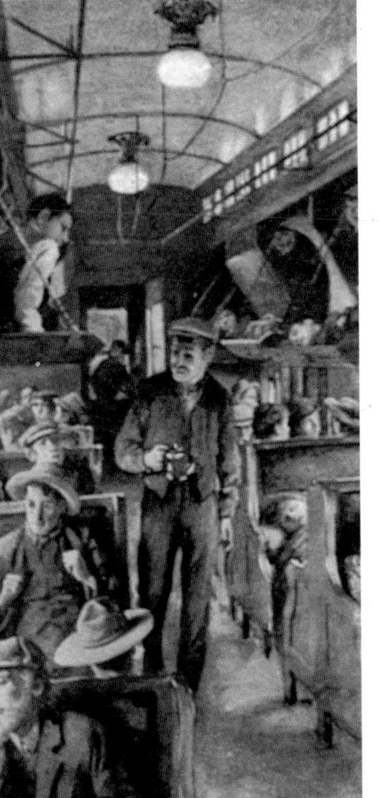

*2. From Genoa to New York: Italian emigrants in 1901.*

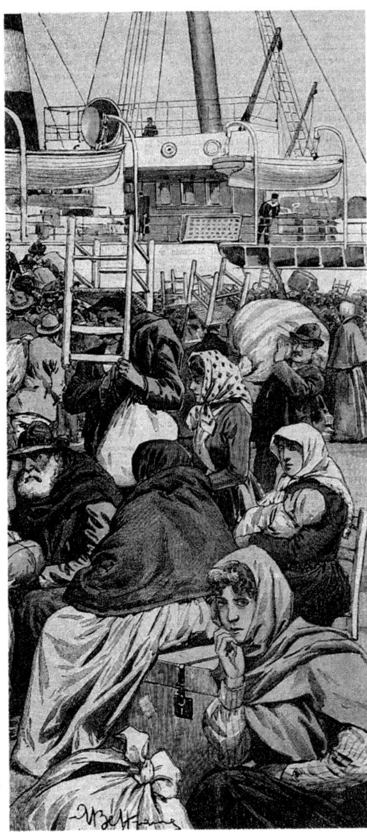

**Population of the United States of America, 1790–1930**

(million people)

| | | | | | | | | | |
|---|---|---|---|---|---|---|---|---|---|
| **1790** | 3.9 | **1820** | 9.6 | **1850** | 23.2 | **1880** | 50.2 | **1910** | 92.0 |
| **1800** | 5.3 | **1830** | 12.9 | **1860** | 31.4 | **1890** | 66.9 | **1920** | 105.7 |
| **1810** | 7.2 | **1840** | 17.1 | **1870** | 38.6 | **1900** | 76.0 | **1930** | 122.8 |

# Capital, Industry and Banking

*1. The new industrial space: a panorama of the Universal Exhibition in Paris in 1867.*

THE GROWTH of industrial civilization in the nineteenth century was marked by a gradual shift from a system of production dominated by 'iron and coal' technology towards a model dominated by the technology of electricity, the internal combustion engine and the chemistry of synthetic materials. The turning point in this process came in the 1890s when technological development in all fields began to accelerate exponentially. The spread of industrialization through the century was confined mainly to a number of European countries together with North America, and can be broken down into three stages. The first began in Great Britain at the end of the eighteenth century, and reached France, Belgium, Switzerland and the United States by the first half of the nineteenth century. All these countries, with the sole exception of the United States, experienced a marked slowing down in growth after the 1860s. While Great Britain was responsible for producing one-third of world industrial output in 1873, its share had fallen to 14% by 1913, while that of the United States went from 23% to 36%. The years from 1840 to 1873, those of the first world boom in railway construction, saw a real industrial revolution spread throughout Europe, particularly to Germany. In Germany's case, this was only the first stage in a much greater economic transformation which, after a severe period of stagnation (from 1873 to 1886), took Germany's share of world economic output from 13% to 16% (the second highest in the world). The last wave of industrialization came at the end of the nineteenth century. By this time Russia, the Scandinavian countries, Italy, various parts of Eastern Europe and Japan were also enjoying a strong surge in economic activity, in a series of great leaps forward. In 1913 Europe was responsible for 44% of world industrial production, as opposed to 62% in 1870. But if one adds North America to this, the figure goes up to 82% in 1913, as compared with 86% in 1870.

The growth and spread of new technology were accompanied by deep-seated changes in how the system of production was organized. Until the 1870s the capitalist system, in its actual workings, simply carried on, without any major disturbance, the commercial capitalism of modern Europe. To this extent its social dynamic was founded essentially on the family, and its modes of internal organization rested on the authority of one man, the all-knowing entrepreneur. Gradually, however, mainly in Germany and in the United States, a new model began to emerge, which reflected the system of continuous production and the organization of business around mass distribution. The shift could be defined as the substitution of the 'visible hand' of the integrated company by the invisible hand of the market. It went hand in hand with the growing concentration of firms, which tended to bring together in one unit the activities of production, marketing and research. These huge corporations, with their multi-functional structure, became organized according to the hierarchical model borrowed from the railways. Some of these companies did retain a family structure, while others evolved irresistibly towards a managerial model, and decision-making passed into the hands of salaried executives. The networks of marketing agreements which became ever closer after the 1880s did no more than set these mergers in motion. Nevertheless, the dynamism of the system was due just as much to the continual emergence of new businesses (which introduced new products like the bicycle, the motor-car, cinemas and aeroplanes), as it was to the successful re-organization and rationalization of these large corporations. It was the existence of these two types of activity side by side which guaranteed the smooth progress of the system.

| 1822 | 1839 | 1856 | 1869 |
|---|---|---|---|
| **Société Générale de Belgique.** | **First steam hammer developed in Great Britain.** | **Bessemer perfects the manufacture of steel.** | **Zénobe Gramme invents the dynamo.** |

**1822:** Société Générale de Belgique founded.
**1825–34:** Development in Great Britain of the wet puddling process. Richard Roberts invents his automatic loom, and the Neilson process for hot-air blasting in smelting furnaces is developed.
**1827:** B. Fourneyron develops the hydraulic turbine by applying Carnot's principles.
**1839:** In Great Britain, Nasmyth builds the first steam hammer. The Daguerrotype is perfected.
**1851:** The Great Exhibition at the Crystal Palace demonstrates simultaneously British pre-eminence and American expertise in certain techniques like the standardization of parts, which was a fundamental aspect of the American system of manufacturing. First Singer sewing machine built.
**1856:** Perkin obtains the patent for manufacturing aniline dye, known as 'aniline purple' or 'mauve'. Bessemer process for the manufacture of steel developed.
**1859:** Laws concerning the setting up of public companies passed in Great Britain.
**1867:** Siemens develops his open-hearth furnace based on the regenerative principle. French legislation is enacted concerning the freedom to create public companies.
**1869:** Zénobe Gramme improves the dynamo. The birth of electromechanics. Synthetic alizarin dye is developed.
**1873:** Hippolyte Fontaine discovers that the dynamo could be operated in reverse as an electric motor at the Exhibition of Vienna.
**1876:** Patent granted for the telephone of Alexander Graham Bell.

*4. The cup-and-ball telephone invented by Alexander Graham Bell in 1876.*

**1878:** Patent granted for an efficient typewriter (Christopher Sholes had sold his patent to Remington and Sons in 1873).
**1880:** Edison develops the light bulb.
**1881:** Patent for the first transformer granted to Lucien Gaulard and John D. Gibbs. First international electricity exhibition held in Paris.
**1882:** First working public power station put in operation in New York. The Standard Oil Trust is set up by John D. Rockefeller and associates.
**1883:** Emil Rathenau founds the DEG, which was to become the AEG combine (Allgemeine Elektrizitäts Gesellschaft).
**1884:** Bayer Research Laboratory founded. Patent for the turbine granted to Charles Algernon Parsons. The CIBA AG founded in Basle. The Comte de Chardonnet granted a patent for artificial silk.
**1888:** Nikola Tesla granted a patent for his induction motor.
**1889:** Eiffel Tower built for the Universal Exhibition. The Michelin Company set up as a limited partnership.
**1891:** First patent granted to the Michelin

NUNC est bibendum!!
c'est-à-dire
À VOTRE SANTÉ
LE PNEU Michelin
BOIT L'OBSTACLE!

*5. The Michelin Man is born, 1898.*

he plans for the Eiffel Tower. A satirical engraving in about 1886.

3. Steel being poured from a Bessemer converter, Germany, c. 1880.

**on produces the first electric light bulb.** **Michelin brothers are granted their first patent.** **Pierre and Marie Curie discover radium.**

**880** **1891** **1898**

factory in the Ruhr, pictured by A. Dressel, 900.

brothers, which was to be the first of many. The Diesel engine developed. Thomson-Houston and Edison General Electric merge to form General Electric.
**1897:** Peugeot Automobile Company founded.
**1898:** Louis Renault begins making motor-cars. Frederick Winslow Taylor develops high-speed steel and Bayer makes aspirin.
**1901:** J. P. Morgan forms the United States Steel Corporation. General Electric sets up its research laboratory.
**1904:** The three major German chemical firms (BASF, Bayer and AGFA) form a cartel, the *Dreibund*, later to become I. G. Farben.
**1911:** The Supreme Court demands the breaking up of Standard Oil under the Anti-Trust Act.
**1913:** BASF develops an economical process for the synthesis of ammonia.

7. The Chicago Stockyards, c. 1910.

# Workers and Socialism in Europe

One of the major consequences of European industrialization was the growth of the working class, the development of its forms of organization and its links with those other social strata that were to some degree unwilling to accept integration into bourgeois society. Three principal periods can be distinguished. The first of these, marked by powerful popular movements and harshly repressed mass strikes, runs from the creation of the International Working Men's Association in 1864 to the founding of the Socialist International, which coincided with the explosion of socialism in Western Europe (1889–93). The second period, which came to an end around1903–5, was characterized by the rise of trade unions and by the entry on to the scene in the newly constituted nation-states of political parties. The dominant feature of the last period, which runs from 1905 to the Great War, was the general expansion of the labour and socialist movement and the appearance of new problems with which it was forced to contend.

The First International, 'a big heart in a little body', as a celebrated expression had it, founded in London in 1864, initially drew its vitality from the British, French, Belgian and Swiss workers' organizations, though subsequently those of Germany, Italy and Spain also became of major importance. It aimed to be a worldwide workers' party, or, at least, a European one. As a breeding-ground of solidarity among workers struggling to improve their conditions, it both radicalized many – if only temporarily – and stimulated them to organize themselves. On the paramount need to organize Marx and Bakunin were in agreement, even if the 'anti-authoritarian' faction came into conflict (especially after 1869) with those followers of Marx who led the International's General Council. After the Paris Commune – which was both the end of an era and a new dawn – it was the very development of the working class which led, in a mere twenty years, to the splintering of the movement into national groups. It gradually became clear that the different forms of action and militancy could not develop according to a single model, even if the German Social Democratic Party had the ambition – legitimated by its seniority, its long resistance to Bismarck's Anti-Socialist Laws, its political power (A. Bebel, W. Liebknecht) and its theoretical capacities (K. Kautsky) – of playing the role of the guiding party. The movement polarized around the two opposing elements, unions and parties. The relative importance of these two bodies varied according to the economic situation, the extent of industrial development and the state of civil liberties. In these conditions, it was only possible for the Second International, which was born in the years 1889–91, to be a loose federation of organizations.

1. Strike of graders at the Courrières mine in 1911, as seen by one of the participants.

2. 'Proletarians of all lands unite!' Swiss trade union banner from the end of the 19th century.

It did, however, contribute to establishing the tenets of the socialist creed, particularly at the London Congress of 1896. To call oneself a socialist, it was necessary to work for the collective ownership of the means of production and recognize the need for political and parliamentary action. In this way the anarchists were swept aside and with them, in many countries, a number of syndicalists, at a time when renewed expansion was producing a general upturn in the

**First International.** **28 September 1864**

**Paris Commune.** **March–May 1871**

**Second Internatio** **188**

**1864:** International Workers' Association founded.
**1869:** Large-scale strikes in France at La Ricamarie and St Aubin.
**18 March–27 May 1871:** Paris Commune.
**1875:** At the Gotha Congress, the two German socialist parties, founded in 1863 and 1869, form the SPD, the German Social Democratic Party.
**1879:** The Federation of the Party of the Socialist Workers of France is born at the Congress of Marseille.
**1883–9:** Bismarck's social insurance laws.
**1884:** In Great Britain, Social Democratic Federation, Fabian Society and Socialist League founded. In Belgium, Belgian Workers' Party.
**1887:** Norwegian Workers' Party.
**1888:** Spanish Socialist Workers' Party. Austrian Social Democratic Party.
**1889:** Second International founded. Social Democratic Party of Sweden. Dockers' strike in London. New unionism.
**1890:** First May Day parades.
**1891:** SPD's Erfurt Programme. Fourmies massacre.

4. The Lyon silk workers live and work in their workshops. Engraving by Moller, 1860.

**1892:** Italian Socialist Party. Polish Socialist Party.
**1893:** Mass strikes in Belgium. Independent Labour Party formed in Britain. Social Democratic Workers' Party founded in Netherlands.
**1895:** CGT formed in France. Death of Engels.
**1896:** In London, the Second International expels the anarchists and a section of the syndicalists.
**1897:** The Bund, the General Jewish Union of Workers of Lithuania, Poland and Russia, is founded.
**1898:** Milan uprising. Social Democratic Workers' Party of Russia founded. Law on industrial accidents passed in France.
**1900:** The International Socialist Bureau meets in Brussels.
**1901:** In Switzerland, the Social Democratic Party is formed; it is an offshoot of the 'Grütli' (the pact founding the Swiss Confederation in 1291). In Russia, the Socialist Revolutionary Party formed.
**1903:** Split between the two wings of the Bulgarian Social Democratic Party and

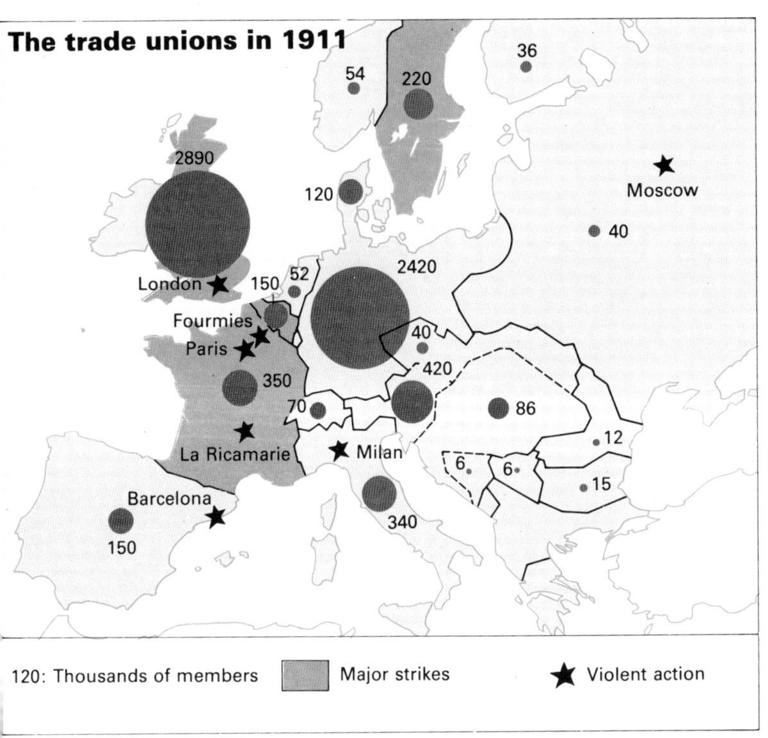


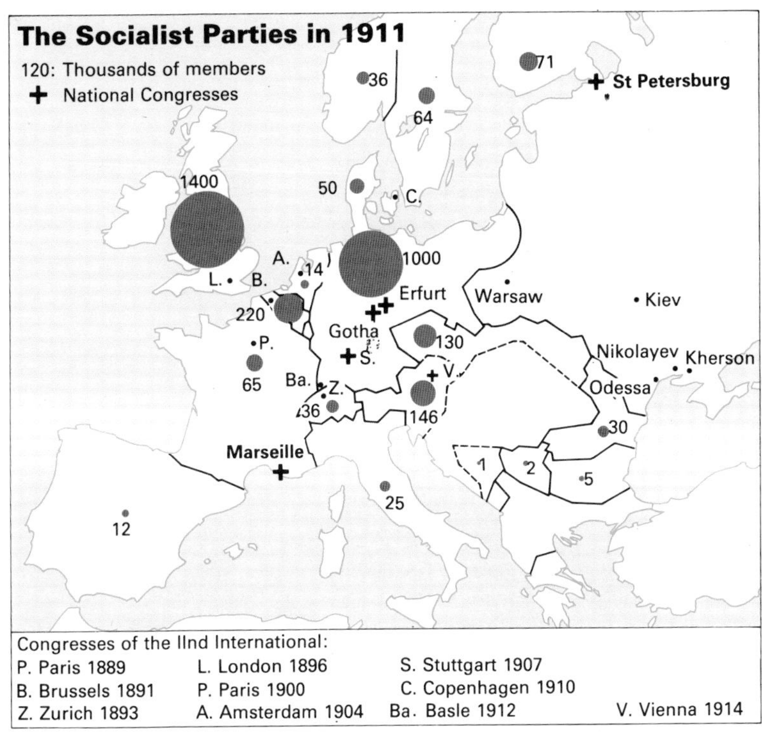


fortunes of trade unions and political parties. These latter began to appear in the Balkans and they even emerged in tsarist Russia – though with enormous difficulties. From this point on, one has to differentiate between those countries where the trade unions (and in some cases co-operatives) and the political parties lived in symbiosis (Great Britain, Belgium, Sweden), where they grew in parallel – though not without difficulties (Germany, Austria, Balkan states) – and those where trade unionism or syndicalism was the vehicle of 'a different type of socialism' (France, Italy, Spain). Strikes were increasingly becoming the union movement's main weapon and the question of the functions of the general strike was placed on the agenda.

At the beginning of the twentieth century the labour movement, proved impotent in the face of the rise of the various nationalisms and imperialism. In spite of Jaurès's efforts in France, at the eleventh hour he gave in to the declaration of war without a fight.

3. *The beginnings of the 'trois-huit'. Advertisement for the Workers' Soap Factory, Paris, 1894.*

**Second International expels the anarchists.** **6**

**First Russian Revolution.** **1905**

**The Stuttgart Congress votes against war.** **1907**

5. *'Forward, the dawn is breaking!' Labour Party poster, 1910, by Gerald Spencer Pryse.*

between the Bolsheviks and the Mensheviks in the Russian SD Party.
**1905:** First Russian Revolution. Socialist unity achieved in France with the creation of the SFIO, the French section of the Workers' International.
**1906:** The Labour Representation Committee takes the name Labour Party.
**1907:** At the Stuttgart Congress, the Second International passes its famous motion against war.
**1909:** General strike in Sweden. 'Tragic week' in Barcelona.
**1910:** Upsurge of labour unrest in Great Britain. French railwaymen's strike.
**1911:** National Confederation of Labour (anarchist) founded in Spain.
**1912–14:** Social legislation in Great Britain after the election of Lib-Labs and the Labour Party.
**31 July 1914:** Assassination of Jaurès.

6. *Jean Jaurès at the Pré Saint-Gervais in May 1913.*

# The United States and the Western Frontier

1. *Evening meal on the trail going west.*

THE TERRITORY coveted by the United States, a domain inhabited by a great number of native communities (there were approximately 10 million American Indians in the fifteenth century), was conquered within a century. In that period the new American nation expanded outwards from the initial narrow Atlantic belt to reach the Pacific coast. This expansion was achieved by negotiation and by purchases from the great powers (Louisiana, Florida, Oregon), by colonization and annexation (Texas), by military conquest (California and New Mexico). In 1867, with the purchase of Alaska from Russia, the United States eliminated her rivals from North American territory. In 1812–14 a war against England led to the acquisition of the Great Lakes region, and fixed the frontier with Canada. In 1823 President Monroe announced the doctrine of European non-interference in the Western Hemisphere, keeping 'America for the Americans'. There remained only the 'savages', who, it was hoped, would disappear with the onward march of civilization.

The winning of the West was, as Benjamin Franklin had predicted, a spur to demographic growth. From 4 million in 1790 the American population rose to 31 million in 1860 and to 75 million inhabitants by the end of the century. The government encouraged migration westward by liberal land laws: in 1862 the Homestead Act allotted 160 acres to every pioneer family free of charge. As the new territories became inhabited, they passed from the status of colonies under the jurisdiction of Congress to that of equal states within the Union. The 'frontier', which mythology has portrayed as a 'wild' area, a domain of individual dynamism and agrarian democracy, was a powerful factor in capitalist development. To join the eastern states to the West, lines of communication were developed, including river routes, canals and, later, transcontinental railroads. These were the source of intense financial speculation, which gave rise to economic crises throughout the entire country. The westward march of farmers from the North-East, planters from the South, immigrants newly arrived from Europe, adventurers and missionaries, produced some rapid successes which led to growth, though there were also some catastrophic collapses. Towards the end of the century, farmers encountered the 'scissors phenomenon' which favoured industrial over agricultural prices; they organized in populist movements, but their movement failed in the face of opposition from the two political parties which held the reins of industry and finance. The frontier was pushed back at a cost to the native populations who, though they put up tenacious resistance, had in 1830 to take the 'Trail of Tears' across the Mississippi. In the second half of the century, in the great central plains, the railway builders and fur traders massacred 15 million bison, the Indians' chief source of subsistence. Defeated by the army, decimated by epidemics and reduced to poverty, the Indians yielded their territories and were left with nothing but small reservations. They lost their independence and were placed under the administrative supervision of the Bureau of Indian Affairs; with the disappearance of collective property and their conversion to Christianity, they forgot their own cultures. In 1890, after the Ghost Dance attempt at cultural revival, the massacre of 300 Sioux at Wounded Knee marked the triumph of the United States' colonization of the West.

**Washington becomes federal capital.** — **1801**

**Spain sells Florida.** — **1819**

**Beginning of the great removal of the Indians.** — **1830**

**Annexation of Texas.** — **1845**

**Unification of the railr**

**1803:** Thomas Jefferson buys Louisiana from Napoleon.
**1803–5:** Lewis and Clarke's expedition to the Pacific.
**1811:** Tecumseh organizes an Indian confederation.
**1812–14:** US war against England.
**1814–18:** Expeditions against the Creek and Seminole Indians.
**1819:** Adams-Onis Treaty: Spain cedes Florida.
**1823:** Monroe Doctrine: Europe is excluded from America.
**1825:** Completion of the Erie Canal.
**1830–8:** The 'Removal Bill': Creeks, Cherokees, Chickasaws, Choctows and Seminoles pushed back towards 'Indian territory'.
**1836:** Texan settlers proclaim an independent republic.
**1841:** By the Law of Pre-emption, squatters are given first rights in the purchase of public lands.
**1842:** The Oregon Trail is opened up: end of the 'definitive frontier' between Whites and Indians.

4. *The California gold rush.*

**1845:** Annexing of Texas to the Union in the name of the doctrine of 'Manifest Destiny'.
**1846–8:** War against Mexico. By the Treaty of Guadalupe-Hidalgo, the US acquires the southwestern regions.
**1847:** Mormons settle in Utah.
**1848:** California Gold Rush.
**1858:** Wells Fargo Company founded.
**1858–64:** Gold rushes and miners' strikes in Colorado, Nevada, Arizona, Idaho and Montana.
**1860:** Invention of the Winchester rifle.
**1861–5:** Cheyenne and Arapaho wars of resistance in the plains. The Cheyenne are massacred at Sand Creek.
**1862:** Homestead Act; 160 acres allotted free to every pioneer householder. Pacific Railway Act: subventions in the form of land to the transcontinental railroad building companies.
**1865:** Beginning of the great migrations of cattle from Texas towards the north and the east.
**1865–8:** Great Sioux Wars against Crazy Horse and his warriors.
**1867:** Organization of Indian reservations in Oklahoma and Dakota. Purchase of Alaska. Agrarian movements.
**1867–85:** Extermination of bisons in the Great Plains.
**1869:** Completion of the first transcontinental railroad.
**1871–86:** Military conflicts with the Apaches.
**1876:** Dakota gold rush. Battle of Little Big Horn against the Sioux: Custer and his regiment are killed.
**1877:** War against the Indians of the North-West.
**1887:** End of the open-range cattle industry boom. Dawes Severality Act: the tribal lands are split up and allotted to families; tribal governments are dissolved.
**1889:** First colonization of Oklahoma.
**1890:** Ghost Dance; and its repression. Massacres of Wounded Knee. The Superintendent of the Census Bureau announces that the frontier is no longer of statistical relevance.

# 1800–1890

2. Wild West heroine Calamity Jane.
3. The Apache chief Geronimo, c. 1895.

**Disappearance of the 'frontier'.**

**1890**

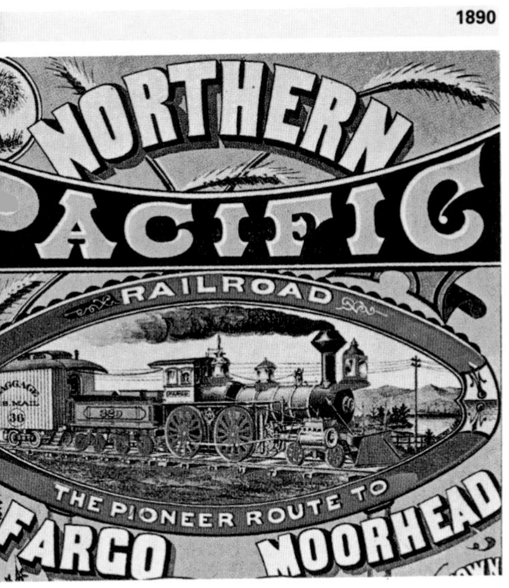
NORTHERN
PACIFIC
RAILROAD
THE PIONEER ROUTE TO
FARGO
MOORHEAD

5. When the pioneers took the railroad.

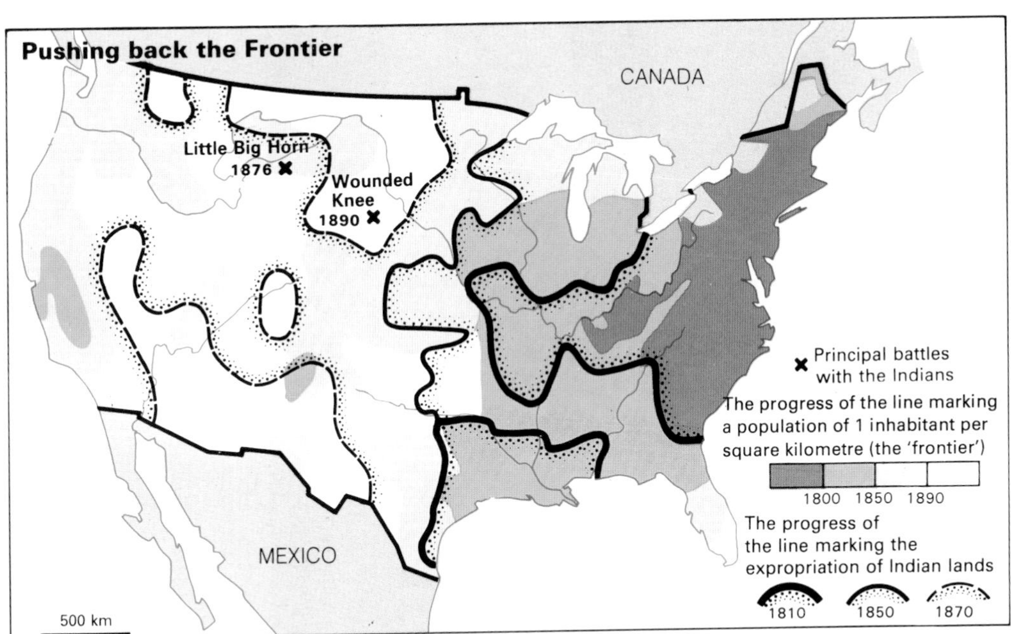
Pushing back the Frontier
CANADA
Little Big Horn 1876
Wounded Knee 1890
MEXICO
500 km
Principal battles with the Indians
The progress of the line marking a population of 1 inhabitant per square kilometre (the 'frontier')
1800 1850 1890
The progress of the line marking the expropriation of Indian lands
1810 1850 1870

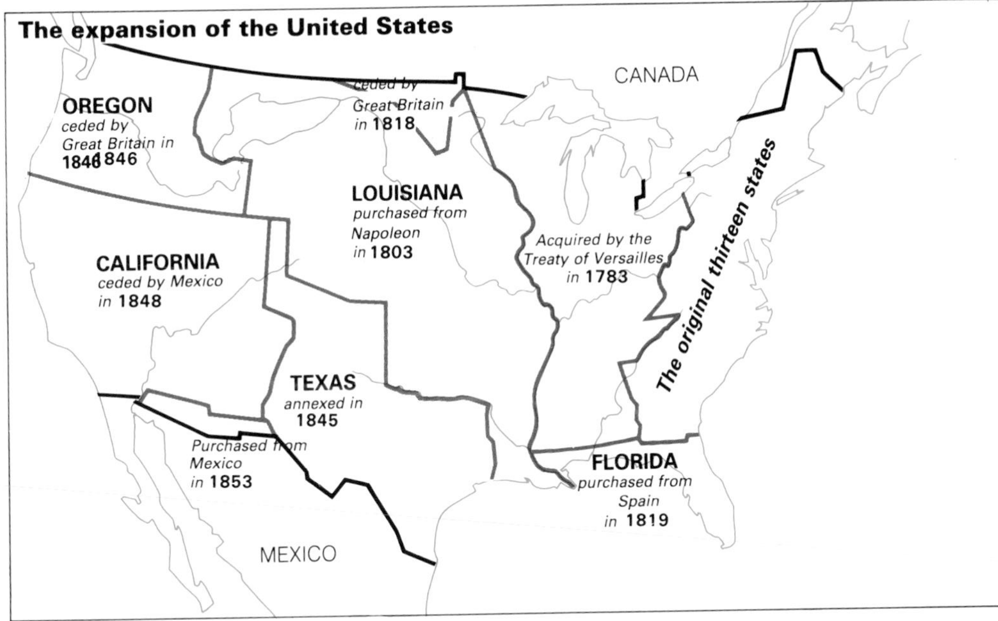
The expansion of the United States
CANADA
OREGON
ceded by Great Britain in 1846
ceded by Great Britain in 1818
LOUISIANA
purchased from Napoleon in 1803
Acquired by the Treaty of Versailles in 1783
The original thirteen states
CALIFORNIA
ceded by Mexico in 1848
TEXAS
annexed in 1845
Purchased from Mexico in 1853
FLORIDA
purchased from Spain in 1819
MEXICO

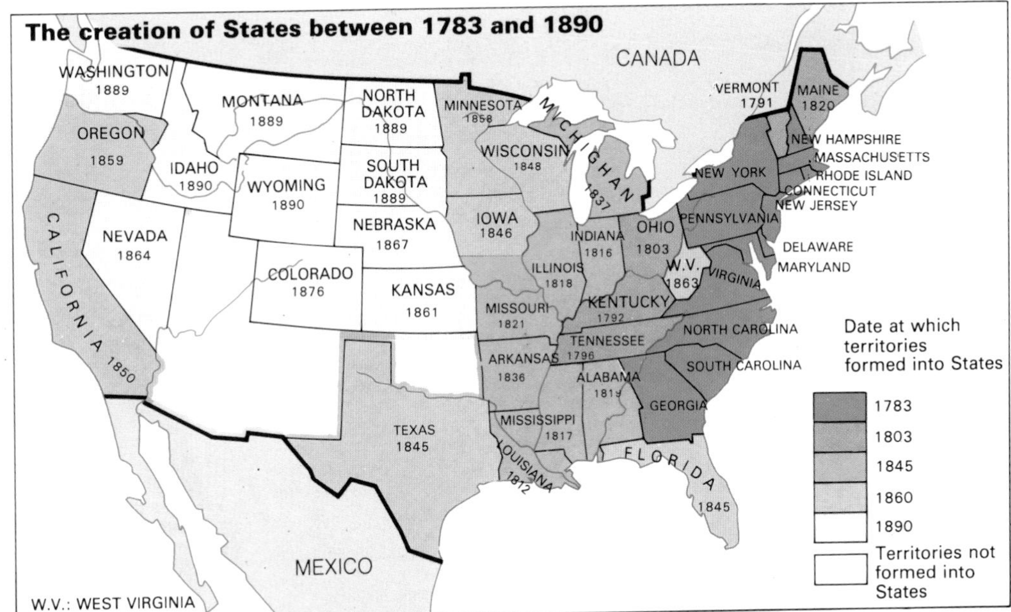
The creation of States between 1783 and 1890
CANADA
WASHINGTON 1889
MONTANA 1889
NORTH DAKOTA 1889
MINNESOTA 1858
MICHIGAN 1837
VERMONT 1791
MAINE 1820
OREGON 1859
IDAHO 1890
WYOMING 1890
SOUTH DAKOTA 1889
WISCONSIN 1848
NEW YORK
NEW HAMPSHIRE
MASSACHUSETTS
RHODE ISLAND
CONNECTICUT
NEW JERSEY
CALIFORNIA 1850
NEVADA 1864
NEBRASKA 1867
IOWA 1846
INDIANA 1816
OHIO 1803
PENNSYLVANIA
DELAWARE
MARYLAND
COLORADO 1876
KANSAS 1861
ILLINOIS 1818
W.V. 1863
VIRGINIA
MISSOURI 1821
KENTUCKY 1792
TENNESSEE 1796
NORTH CAROLINA
SOUTH CAROLINA
ARKANSAS 1836
ALABAMA 1819
GEORGIA
MISSISSIPPI 1817
TEXAS 1845
LOUISIANA 1812
FLORIDA 1845
MEXICO
W.V.: WEST VIRGINIA
Date at which territories formed into States
1783
1803
1845
1860
1890
Territories not formed into States

# The United States: The North–South Conflict

*1. Ruins of Charleston after the Northern victory.*

SLAVERY, which in its ethos ran counter to the ideology of independence, disappeared from the northern states in the early years of the nineteenth century. It was, however, implicitly recognized by the US Constitution, where provision for an end to the slave trade was only made in 1808. The North–South conflict over the slavery issue intensified as economic growth produced greater disparities between the two regions. By 1860, the North had become the home of industry, great ports and banks. The South, where 350,000 families (one-third of the white population) owned some 3 million slaves, the plantation economy, where single crops of tobacco, cotton, rice and sugar were grown, determined a way of life and a set of values quite opposed to those of the industrial capitalism of the North and the family agriculture of the West. Slavery was still at the centre of debate in the first half of the century because it involved a wide range of economic, political and ideological rivalries.

Apart from the campaign of the Abolitionists (Quakers, reformers, industrialists) in the North for the suppression of slavery, the conflict centred on three issues. The first of these was the question of who was to have ascendancy over the Congress and the Presidency; this was important because it would enable the dominant party to obtain legislation favourable to their particular type of economic base. The second was the problem of customs tariffs, which the North wished to keep high to protect its industry, but which threatened the exporting South with economic retaliation on the part of its overseas clients. The third was the issue of control over the West, which became the object of conflict between the Southern planters, who wished to extend their system of life to that area and acquire new land, and the North, which saw the West as the natural outlet for its industry and as a provider of meat and cereals to its urban population.

The problem of the slave or free status of the new states of the West was settled by a series of unsatisfactory compromises in 1787, 1820 and 1850. 1854 saw the founding of the Republican Party, which stood for the abolition of all slavery, the granting of land free of charge to settlers in the West and protectionism. The South campaigned for the maintenance of slavery, an issue championed by the Democratic Party. When the Republican candidate, Abraham Lincoln, was elected President, South Carolina seceded, was followed by ten other states and created a new Confederacy.

A minor military clash in April 1861 led to the outbreak of war. The South, though lacking industry, had the better officers, yet was unable to follow up its early successes. It had to capitulate in April 1865 after a savage conflict. This was, in fact, the first modern war; there were more than a million victims, civilian and military; modern means of transport and warfare were employed; and the Southern countryside was devastated. The war set two conceptions of federal government at odds, that of a contractual union between sovereign states on the one hand and that of an indestructible organic nation on the other. The North, with its nascent industrial capitalism, was to bring about the victory of the latter.

It took ten years to reconstruct the Union. Under the Thirteenth Amendment, Blacks were released from slavery and under the Fourteenth they acquired the right to vote. For a long time the South remained in an inferior economic and political position. Cotton only recovered its previous strong position in 1880. Meanwhile, as the Southern states recovered their freedom of action, they began to apply segregation against the Blacks.

**Arrival of black slaves.** **1619**

**Outlawing of slave trade.** **1808**

**Birth of Buffalo Bi** **184**

**1619:** First twenty Africans sold in Virginia.
**1660–80:** Institutionalization of slavery in English colonies.
**1787:** Slavery is prohibited in the North-West, but the Constitution protects it elsewhere.
**1808:** Congress outlaws slave trade.
**1820:** Missouri Compromise; the 36°30′ parallel separates the slave states from the free states.
**1828:** 'Abominations' tariff; denounced by the South and West.
**1829–37:** Jackson President. Rise of liberal capitalism.
**1848:** Free Soil Party: 'free soil, free speech, free labour and free men'.
**1850:** Clay Compromise: admission of California as a non-slave state. The question of slavery in the new states to be decided by their populations.
**1852:** The Abolitionist Harriet Beecher-Stowe publishes *Uncle Tom's Cabin.*
**1854:** The Free-Soilers are absorbed into the Republican Party. Ostende Manifesto under pressure from the Southern states recommending that Spain purchase Cuba; Kansas-Nebraska Act, which invalidates the Missouri Compromise.
**1856:** Bloody Kansas. Civil war between pro- and anti-slavers.
**1857:** Dred Scott affair. The Supreme Court declares Congress incompetent to decide on the right to slavery.
**1859:** John Brown's raid on the arsenal at Harper's Ferry.
**1860:** Abraham Lincoln elected President. South Carolina secedes in December.
**1861:** February–March: Ten states join South Carolina to form the Confederacy with its capital at Richmond. April: Capture of Fort Sumter by the Confederates. Lincoln declares war on the rebels. Potomac front; Southern victories.
**1862:** March: Missouri front; Lee's Confederates are pushed back towards the South. On the peninsula they fail to break the Northern blockade. September: Proclamation of emancipation of the Blacks by Lincoln. 13 December: Lee is victorious at Fredericksburg.
**1863. January–July:** Victorious march north by Lee. July: Lee is halted by Federal troops at Gettysburg. Grant's campaign in the West. 4 July: Northerners victorious at Vicksburg.
**1864–5:** Northerners, led by Sherman, march towards the South.
**9 April 1865:** Lee abandons Richmond. The Southern capital is captured by the North. Victory of the Union.
**1865:** Thirteenth Amendment: Abolition of slavery in the USA. 14 April: Lincoln is assassinated. Johnson becomes President.
**1867:** Formation of the Ku Klux Klan. Beginning of reconstruction.
**1868:** Fourteenth Amendment: Congress lays down the rules of citizenship.
**1877:** End of reconstruction. The Southern states are re-integrated.

*3. Abraham Lincoln.*

# 1619–1877

. Uncle Tom's Cabin. *An illustration from Harriet Beecher-Stowe's famous work.*

**The white man, John Brown, leads a rising against slavery.** **Ku Klux Klan.**

| 1859 | 1867 |
|---|---|

. *The Mistress's Visit, as seen by Winslow Homer.*

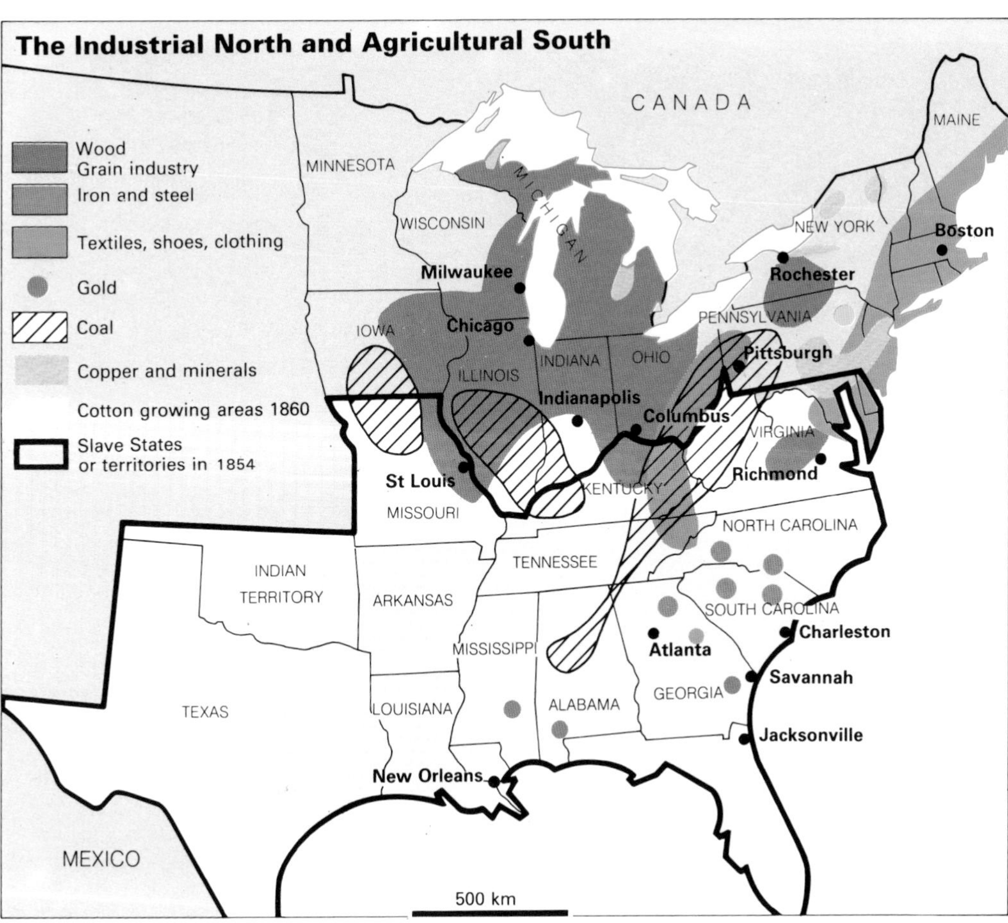


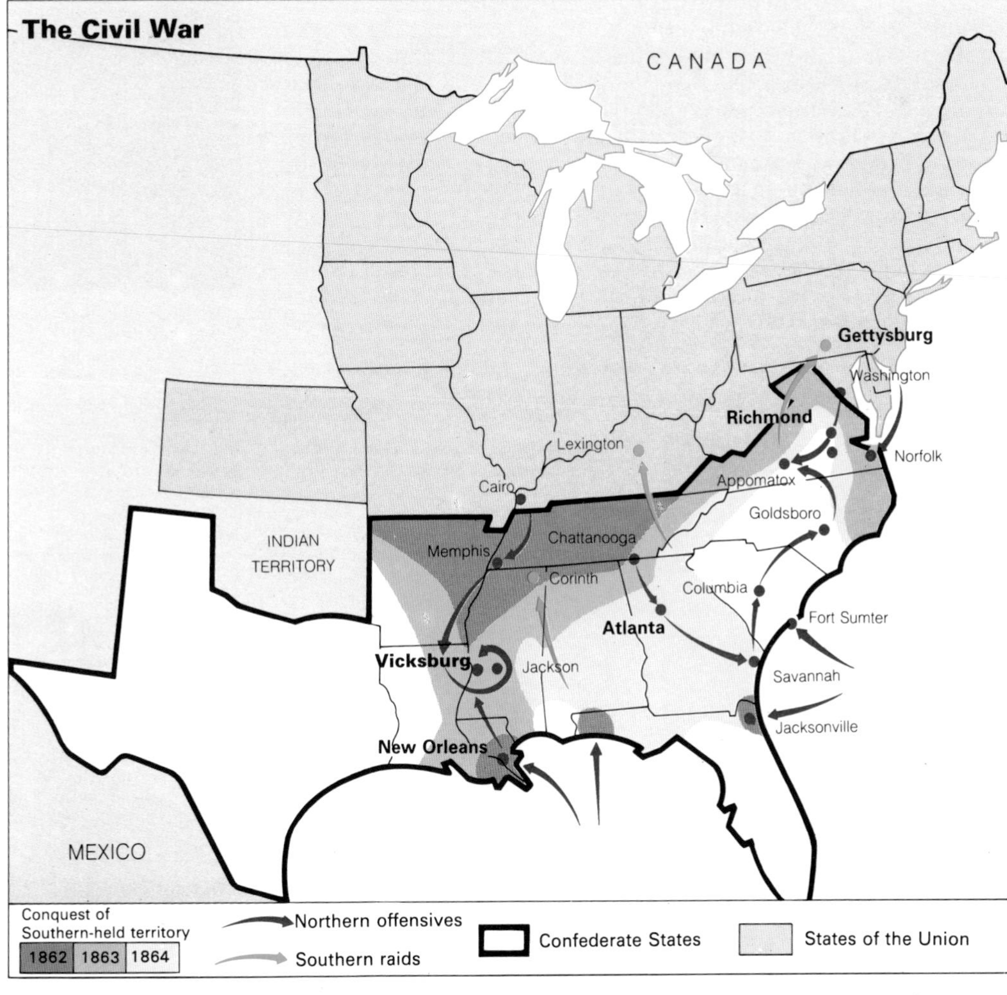

# Italian and German Unification

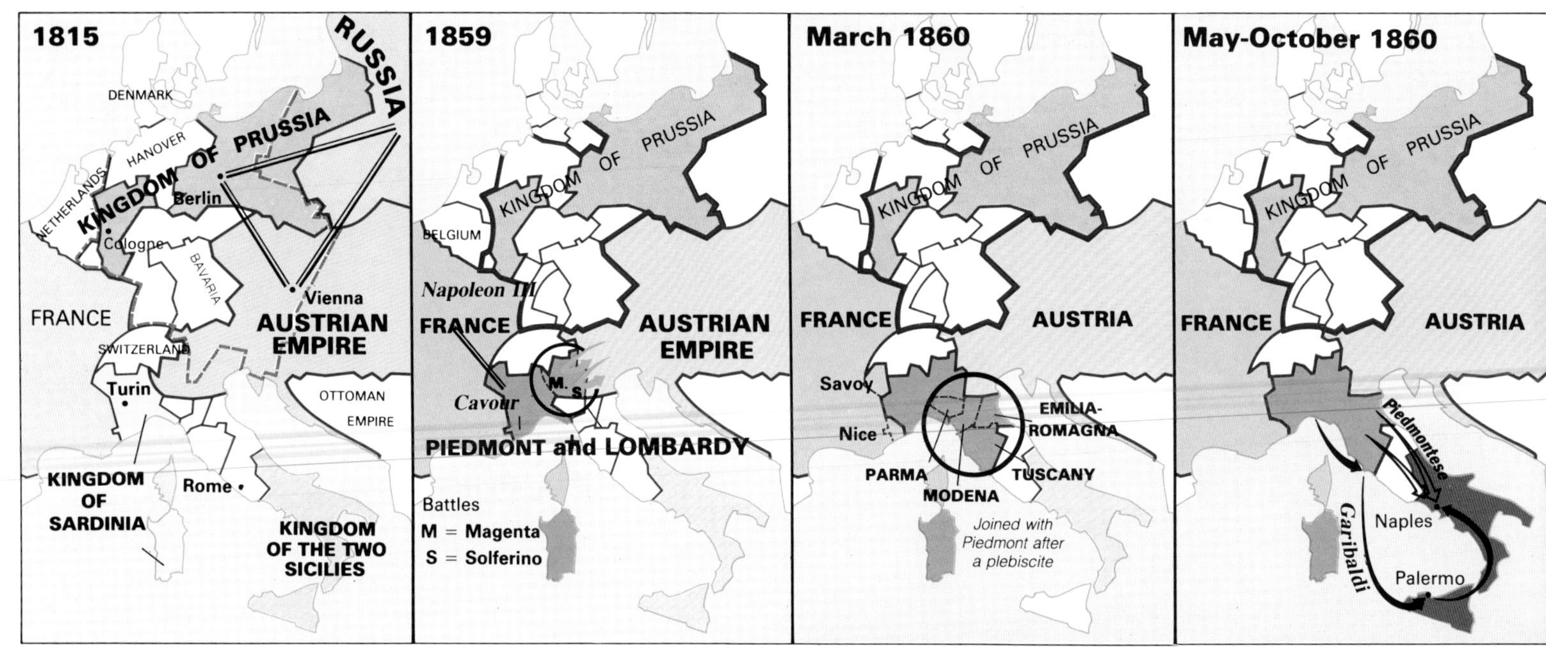


FROM THE BEGINNING of the nineteenth century, nationalist and liberal opinion in Italy had grouped together under the banner of the newspaper *Il Risorgimento*, the organ of the industrial and commercial middle classes of the north, who saw in the achievement of unity and in the setting up of a constitutional monarchy the means of satisfying both their patriotic feelings and their own economic interests. Cavour, the Prime Minister of Piedmont, was to be the principal architect of unity. Fully aware of the need to have recourse to the assistance of a foreign power, Cavour turned to Napoleon III, whose sympathies for the Italian patriots were well known. An alliance was concluded between Piedmont and France, and in April 1859 the two countries went to war together against Austria. In June, the Franco-Piedmontese army won the victories of Magenta and Solferino. But Napoleon III, motivated by the slaughter at Solferino and worried at the reaction of French Catholics to the mobilization of Prussia, signed the armistice of Villafranca and then the Treaty of Zurich with the Austrians, according to the terms of which Piedmont was given Lombardy but Venetia was left in the hands of the Austrians. Despite this setback to unity, Cavour took advantage of the cautious complicity of France to found, in less than two years, the Kingdom of Italy, which was proclaimed in March 1861 after the merging of the three duchies of central Italy (Tuscany, Parma and Modena), Papal

1. The end of the temporal power of the Pope: the Italian Bersagliere at the gates of Rome (20 September 1870).

**First performance of Verdi's *Nabucco* at La Scala, Milan.** **Abdication of Charles Albert in favour of his son Victor Emmanuel II.**

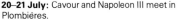

**9 March 1842** **23 March 1849**

2. The making of Italian national banners in Piedmont, in April 1859.

**14 January 1858:** The Italian patriot Orsini makes an attempt on the life of Napoleon III. Orsini's action, which was motivated by a wish to punish the Emperor for abandoning his former comrades-in-arms (in 1831 Louis Napoleon had taken part in an uprising against the Papal States), persuades the Emperor to give military support to the Kingdom of Piedmont.
**20–21 July:** Cavour and Napoleon III meet in Plombières.
**26 January 1859:** Franco-Piedmontese Alliance signed in Turin.
**April:** Austria declares war on Piedmont. France intervenes almost immediately.
**4 June:** Battle of Magenta.
**24 June:** Battle of Solferino.
**12 July:** Unbeknown to Cavour, who resigns the following day, Napoleon III and the Emperor of Austria, Franz-Josef I, sign the Armistice of Villafranca.
**11 November:** Treaty of Zurich. Austria cedes Lombardy to France, who cedes it in turn to Piedmont.
**March 1860:** Annexation of the three duchies of central Italy (Tuscany, Parma and Modena) and of Emilia-Romagna.
**24 March:** Under the Treaty of Turin, France is awarded Nice and Savoy in exchange for its good will.
**May–October:** Expedition of the Thousand. The small army of volunteers recruited by Garibaldi conquers the Kingdom of the Two Sicilies.

3. Count Cavour, the architect of Italian unity, in a painting by Francisco Hayez.

**4 November:** Annexation of Umbria.
**5 November:** Annexation of the Marches.
**14 March 1861:** The Kingdom of Italy is proclaimed, and Victor Emmanuel takes the title of King of Italy.
**6 June:** Death of Cavour.
**29 August 1862:** Garibaldi is defeated and taken prisoner at Aspromonte in Calabria by the Piedmontese, who are forced to intervene under pressure from the French.
**22 September:** Bismarck appointed chancellor of Prussia.
**14 August 1865:** The Convention of Gastein ends the Danish War. Prussia is given the administration of Schleswig, while that of Holstein is handed over to Austria.
**October:** Meeting in Biarritz between Napoleon III and Bismarck. France guarantees Prussia its neutrality in the event of a conflict with Austria.
**April 1866:** Alliance between Prussia and Italy.
**21 June:** Beginning of the Seven Weeks' War between Austria and Prussia.

# 1858–1871

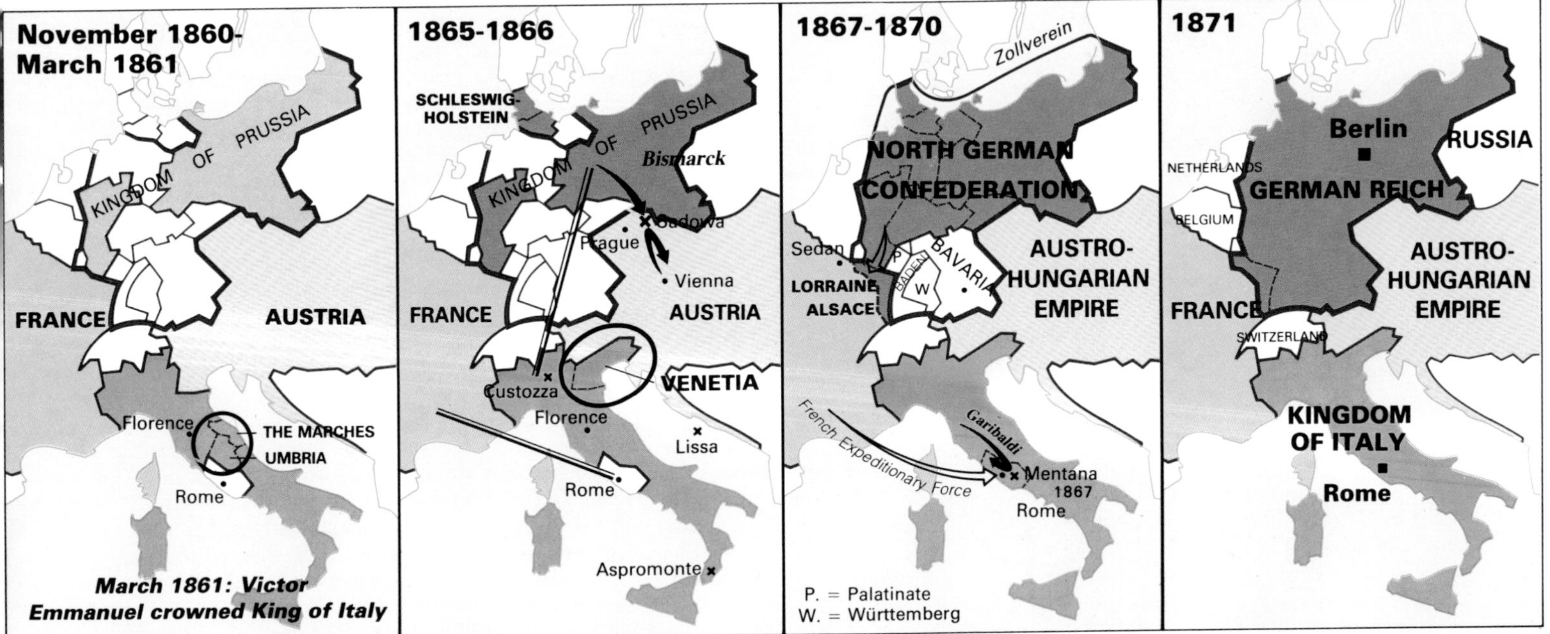


Emilia-Romagna and the Kingdom of the Two Sicilies which had been conquered by Garibaldi and his army of volunteers (the 'Thousand'). France, as a result of her acquiescence, was rewarded in exchange with Nice and Savoy. Under the pretext of arresting Garibaldi, the Piedmontese troops then occupied the Papal States (excepting Rome and the surrounding areas). Venetia was annexed in 1866 as a result of the alliance with Prussia.

The resolution of the Roman question, however, proved more troublesome and was more protracted. On this occasion the French Catholics mobilized and forced the Emperor to intervene, directly as well as indirectly, against the Garibaldians who, in 1862 and 1867, attempted to take the city. It was not until the recall of the French Expeditionary Force in September 1870 that Rome at last became the capital of the Kingdom of Italy, which it did on 1 August 1871.

In Germany, the failure of the bourgeois liberal revolution of 1848 left the initiative for unity to Prussia, which was in the hands of conservative forces. The architect of German unification was Otto von Bismarck, who was made chancellor in 1862. But the unity of Germany under the aegis of Prussia was impossible so long as Austria continued to exert its influence over the German-speaking lands. Bismarck, who had decided to embark on a trial of strength with the Austrian government, grasped the opportunity given him by the issue of Schleswig-Holstein in 1864. The two duchies of Schleswig and Holstein, which were inhabited by a mixture of Germans and Danes, and were under the control of the King of Denmark, declared themselves, on the death of Frederick VII in 1863, in favour of a German prince who had the support of the Prussian chancellor. As a result, Bismarck decided to intervene in a joint action with the Austrians. The two allies, at the end of a rapid campaign, obtained the transfer of the two duchies, which henceforth came under joint Austro-Prussian administration. After having assured himself of French neutrality and concluded an alliance with Italy, Bismarck only had to invoke the pretext of the 'poor administration' of Holstein by the Austrians to invade the territory and declare war on the Hapsburgs. The Austrians won a land battle over Italy at Custozza (24 June 1866) and a sea battle at Lissa (20 July). But in Bohemia, the Prussians won a resounding victory at Sadowa. The peace treaty signed in Prague gave the duchies to Prussia and forced upon Austria the dissolution of the German Confederation.

The following year, after annexing the minor states in the centre of Germany, Bismarck set up the North German Confederation, under the presidency of the King of Prussia. The war with France, by uniting the German princes against a common enemy, put the final seal on unity and overcame the lingering reservations of the southern German states. The German Reich was proclaimed in Versailles on 18 January 1871.

**Victor Emmanuel II crowned King of Italy.** — 14 March 1861
**Death of Cavour.** — 6 June 1861
**Prussian victory over the Austrians at Sadowa.** — 3 July 1866
**Proclamation of the German *Reich* in the Hall of Mirrors at Versailles.** — 18 January 1871

4. *'Be united!' An allegory of Germany according to a patriotic image in 1870.*

**3 July:** The Prussian army routs the Austrians at Sadowa.
**23 August:** Under the Treaty of Prague, Austria cedes Schleswig-Holstein to Prussia.
**19 October:** Under the Treaty of Venice, Austria cedes Venetia to France, who transfers it to Italy.
**1 July 1867:** Establishment of the North German Confederation.
**3 November:** The French Expeditionary Force sent to defend Rome disperses Garibaldi's troops at Mentana.
**19 July 1870:** Napoleon III falls into the trap laid by Bismarck (in the Ems telegram of 13 July) and declares war on Prussia.
**2 September:** France capitulates after the defeat at Sedan.
**20 September:** The Italian Army enters Rome.
**18 January 1871:** Proclamation of the German *Reich*.
**1 August:** Rome becomes the capital of Italy.

5. *Kaiser Wilhelm II proclaims the German Reich in the Gallery of Mirrors at Versailles. From a German engraving dated 1871.*

6. *Giuseppe Garibaldi (1807–82), dressed in his red shirt, which became the uniform of the Garibaldian volunteers.*

# Victoria, Queen and Empress

*1. The Great Exhibition of 1851 at the Crystal Palace, by L. Haghe.*

THE SIX MILLION PEOPLE who in 1851 visited the Crystal Palace, the central attraction of the Great Exhibition, were more or less conscious participants in the burial of the green England of former times, and were joining together in the self-consecration of a triumphant island full of mystical self-confidence in its mission as the workshop of the world. At the heart of this industrial hall of fame was the railway engine: for twenty years 'railway-mania' had mobilized people's savings and transformed the countryside, and the advance of the railways symbolized the technological supremacy of a whole nation. London was the unrivalled financial centre of the world as well as being the capital of the first country to have a majority urban population: in 1851, 50.1% of Britons lived in the city, compared with 16.9% in 1801, and outside of London ten other cities had more than 100,000 inhabitants. This proliferating growth appeared to be limitless; and in 1870 more than a third of world production of manufactured goods came from British factories. In the period leading up to the coronation of Queen Victoria, heated political controversies had heralded the changing balance of forces within what was the first industrial society. The 1832 Reform Act had enfranchized only one in five of the population, and the landowning oligarchy were still in control of Parliament. However, the dynamic of reform had begun, and was to promote slow but steady progress towards democracy. Revolutionary stirrings were to be found, most notably present in the guise of Chartism, which worried the ruling class on three occasions, but the movement turned out in the end to be 'much ado about nothing' and paid the price of its own incoherent demands. It is difficult to see how a programme for the restructuring of the electoral system could successfully be mixed up with a call for the abolition of workhouses (set up under the 1834 Poor Law Act), or be consistent with the backward-looking agrarian ideals of O'Connor, one of the movement's leaders. More effective in their aims were the crusades in favour of free trade, the support for which came from the employers in Manchester. The campaigners grouped themselves together under the name of the Anti-Corn Law League. Its victory was precipitated by the Great Irish Famine of 1846.

It is unsurprising that the values of those who defined themselves as 'the industrious middle classes' characterized Victorianism at its height: the attachment to religion, the family, thrift, the spirit of endeavour, 'respectability', all the virtues embodied by the Queen, herself an emblem of security and unity. But this edifice of certainty slowly developed cracks in the face of the emergence of numerous accounts of an 'other nation' of workers whose living and working conditions were not only difficult to reconcile with Christian values but threatened to cause social unrest. Only in the very last decade of the century was a powerful trade union movement to emerge, when socialists begun to organize and unite, albeit more often inspired by the Bible than by Marx. Twenty-five years earlier a wave of reforms had started up once again, under the dual impetus of Disraeli and Gladstone, preserving social stability by absorbing pressures from 'below'. However, an opportunity to make progress on the eternal Irish question had been lost with the failure of the 1886 Home Rule Bill.

The attack of imperialist fervour which filled most minds at the end of the Queen's reign, was, perhaps, a means of exorcizing anxiety at having to compete with the emergent powers, America and Germany.

**Birth of Chartism.**

**1838**

**Great Famine in Ireland.**
**Corn Laws repealed.**

**1846**

**Gladstone Prime Minist**

**186**

**1837:** Victoria accedes to the throne, at a time when the prestige of the monarchy is low.
**1838:** The first Anti-Corn Law League founded. Dickens publishes *Oliver Twist*, describing the depths of low life in London.
**1839:** Parliament rejects the 1838 People's Charter calling for universal suffrage.
**1842:** England acquires Hong Kong by the Treaty of Nanking.
**1846:** Great Famine in Ireland. Over a five-year period there were 800,000 deaths from hunger, and about the same number emigrated. The protectionist Corn Laws are repealed by Parliament.
**1847:** Ten-hour day introduced for women textile workers.
**1848:** Definitive failure of Chartism.
**1849:** Navigation Acts repealed.
**1851:** First Universal Exhibition in London.
**1855:** Palmerston Prime Minister. The master of Victorian diplomacy from 1830 to 1865 (with a few brief intervals), he remained the symbol, either hated or revered, of British superiority.
**1856:** Development of the Bessemer process, which leads to a boom in steel production.
**1857:** Indian Mutiny put down with great brutality.
**1859:** Darwin's *Origin of the Species* causes great scandal. Samuel Smiles publishes *Self-Help*, which was to symbolize Victorian individualism.
**1865:** William Booth founds the Salvation Army.
**1867:** 1867 Reform Bill gives the vote to 2,250,000 electors, a third of whom are workers.
**1868:** Gladstone forms his first Liberal government. Disraeli made leader of the Conservative Party. The Trades Union Congress is formed, and Sir Charles Dilke publishes *Greater Britain*, the gospel of nascent imperialism.
**1869:** Disestablishment of the Anglican Church in Ireland.
**1870–6:** Numerous reforms are enacted (legal recognition of trade unions, compulsory primary schooling, secret voting etc.).
**1872:** Disraeli delivers his imperialist speech at the Crystal Palace.
**1873:** Onset of economic depression (fall of

*2. Reformers attack the tree of Rotten Boroughs in 1832.*

# 1837–1901

## The British Empire at the death of Queen Victoria in 1901

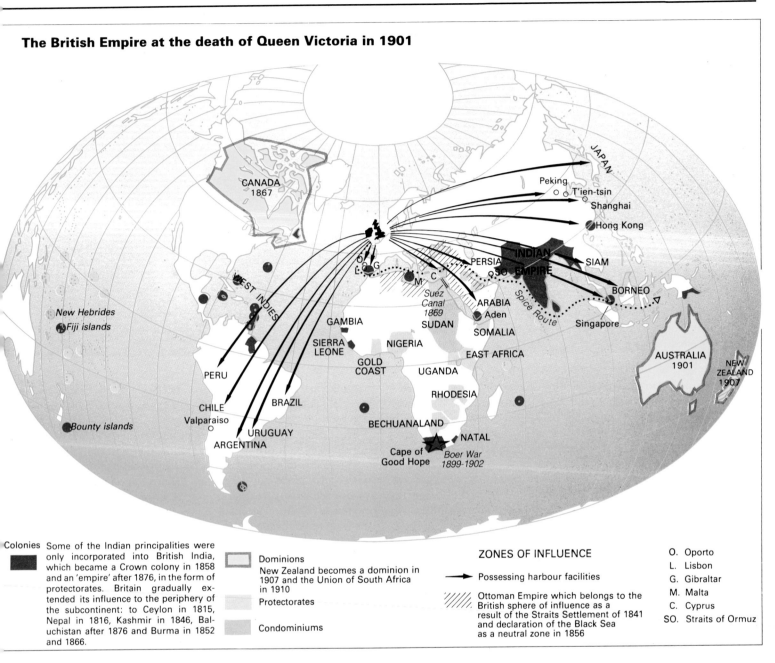

CANADA 1867
JAPAN
Peking
T'ien-tsin
Shanghai
Hong Kong
INDIAN EMPIRE
SIAM
PERSIA
SO
BORNEO
Singapore
Spice Route
O
L
G
M
C
Suez Canal 1869
ARABIA
Aden
WEST INDIES
New Hebrides
Fiji islands
GAMBIA
SUDAN
SOMALIA
SIERRA LEONE
NIGERIA
EAST AFRICA
GOLD COAST
UGANDA
AUSTRALIA 1901
NEW ZEALAND 1907
PERU
RHODESIA
CHILE
BRAZIL
Valparaiso
Bounty islands
BECHUANALAND
URUGUAY
ARGENTINA
NATAL
Cape of Good Hope
Boer War 1899-1902

Colonies: Some of the Indian principalities were only incorporated into British India, which became a Crown colony in 1858 and an 'empire' after 1876, in the form of protectorates. Britain gradually extended its influence to the periphery of the subcontinent: to Ceylon in 1815, Nepal in 1816, Kashmir in 1846, Baluchistan after 1876 and Burma in 1852 and 1866.

Dominions: New Zealand becomes a dominion in 1907 and the Union of South Africa in 1910

Protectorates

Condominiums

ZONES OF INFLUENCE

Possessing harbour facilities

Ottoman Empire which belongs to the British sphere of influence as a result of the Straits Settlement of 1841 and declaration of the Black Sea as a neutral zone in 1856

O. Oporto
L. Lisbon
G. Gibraltar
M. Malta
C. Cyprus
SO. Straits of Ormuz

**kens dies.** **70**

**Fall of Disraeli.** **1880**

**R. L. Stevenson's *Treasure Island*.** **1883**

*3. The Queen Engine and the Fairy Electricity. . . . From Queen Victoria's Jubilee album in 1897.*

world economic indexes and relative slowing down of British economic growth).
**1876:** Queen Victoria proclaimed Empress of India.
**1878:** Near Eastern crisis and British invasion of Afghanistan.
**1879–82:** Irish Land War.
**1882:** Occupation of Egypt.
**1885:** Two out of three Englishmen given the vote.
**1885–7:** Workers' riots as a result of unemployment.
**1886:** The General Election goes against Gladstone and his Home Rule Bill.
**1889:** General strike in London docks.
**1893:** Independent Labour Party founded as a forerunner to the Labour Party (which was itself formed in 1906).
**1896:** The best-seller *Made in Germany* points out the advances made by Germany in various leading technical domains. Birth of *The Daily Mail*, which was to be a focal point of popular imperialism.
**1897:** Queen Victoria's Diamond Jubilee.
**1899:** Beginning of the Boer War.
**1901:** Death of Queen Victoria.

Find Gardeners 'Two' and 'Five'

and 'Gardener Seven.'

*4. '"Off with their heads!" said the Queen', in Lewis Carroll's* Alice in Wonderland.

# From the President-Prince to President Poincaré

*1. Execution of the Communards: the* Mur des Fédérés*, 28 May 1871, by Alfred-Henri Darjou.*

FRANCE'S POPULATION varied as her territorial boundaries shifted – Nice and Savoy were added in 1860, Alsace-Lorraine taken away eleven years later – but on the whole it grew gradually, from 36 million to 39.7 million, mainly due to the early immigration of Italians and Belgians. The mortality rate was relatively high and the birth and fertility rates exceptionally low for the period, leading to a static, aging population.

Economic growth was irregular and unequal. After the crisis of the mid-nineteenth century, the railways stimulated an average growth in revenue of 2% per annum up to 1865 and French industry appeared to be catching up with Britain's; French capital and engineers contributed to the development of many other countries. But a severe depression followed (1873–1896), and a more rapid decline than elsewhere meant that for three decades the growth rate was a meagre 1% per annum. France lagged behind in spite of renewed economic vitality at the beginning of the twentieth century, when the growth rate rose to 3%. However, the *Belle Epoque* witnessed some remarkable achievements in new sectors, such as automobile manufacture, and capital was exported freely. France's new economy was dualistic: ancient forms of production and exchange subsisted side by side with modern ones.

The rural sector was still of major importance, peasants representing about 40% of the active population. The great number of smallholdings slowed down progress and favoured the survival of traditional polyculture: however, some regions were specialized (e.g. Languedoc for wine); in others, such as Beauce, large farms practised modern agricultural methods. Peasants were now less concerned with the state of their crops than with their market value.

Towns varied greatly. Side by side with slow-moving, traditional towns, manufacturing centres sprang up, such as Le Creusot and Roubaix. Paris stood out by its rapid growth and its size (2.9 million inhabitants in 1911). The capital was enlarged and modernized during the Second Empire; bourgeois neighbourhoods in the west abutted poor and working-class suburbs in the north and east. Marked social inequality characterized the whole of French society. Two-thirds of the population left practically nothing at their death.

**Napoleon III Emperor.**

**2 December 1852**

**The Paris Commune.**

**18 March–27 May 1871**

**2 December 1851:** Coup d'état of President-Prince Louis Napoleon Bonaparte.
**1852:** Setting up of Crédit Mobilier and Crédit Foncier (December 10) and large private railway companies.
**1853:** Haussmann prefect of the Seine département.
**1854–6:** Crimean War.
**25 February–30 March 1856:** Congress of Paris convened at end of Crimean War.
**1859:** War between Italy and Austria.
**23 January 1860:** Trade agreement with Britain. Nice and Savoy vote to become part of France.
**1862–7:** Mexican expedition.
**1864:** Law on 'combination'.
**1865:** Bank cheques legally recognized.
**1867:** Law liberalizing the setting up of limited companies.
**1868:** Laws restoring freedom of the press and rights of assembly.
**1869:** Suez Canal opened.
**2 January 1870:** Emile Ollivier government.
**8 May:** Referendum approves the liberal Empire.
**19 July:** War declared on Prussia.
**2–4 September:** Fall of Sedan. Government of national defence set up.
**1871:** Armistice 28 January. Thiers heads government.
**18 March–27 May:** Paris Commune.
**10 May:** Treaty of Frankfurt.
**24 May 1873:** Thiers resigns and is replaced by Mac-Mahon.
**1875:** Wallon amendment (vote on 30 January) and constitutional laws founding Third Republic.
**1877:** Legislative assembly dissolved, Republican victory in legislative elections.
**1878:** Freycinet plan aiding economic expansion (railways, canals etc.).
**1879:** Jules Grévy replaces Mac-Mahon as President.
**1880:** Amnesty of Communards. Official celebration of 14 July as a national holiday.
**1881:** Tunisia becomes protectorate. Law introducing free primary education. Laws on public meetings and the press.
**1882:** Gambetta Prime Minister. Union Générale crashes (economic crisis). Law introducing compulsory lay primary education.

*4.* La Tache noire*: the cultural heritage being transmitted at a lay school, as seen by Albert Bettanier in 1887.*

# 1851–1914

2. *Factories at Le Creusot in 1866. Watercolour by Ignace-François Bonhomme.*

Many working people made a precarious living; over half their revenue was still spent on food, although their diet was now more varied. At the opposite pole, the numerous tiers of the bourgeoisie reached their apogee in the aristocracy of the millionaires, mainly bankers, industrialists and absentee landlords.

The most spectacular changes were in the political field. The Second Empire marked France's first step towards universal suffrage. Then, with hopes of a restoration dashed and those of a revolution fading fast, the French at last enjoyed a stable regime uniting two political principles inherited from 1789 and until now incompatible: democracy and freedom. The Third Republic made France into a great colonial power; she held her rank in Europe thanks to the Triple Entente with Russia and Great Britain. Considerable improvements were made at home, particularly in education. Though there were violent conflicts between radical governments and the Catholics, the Republic did succeed in lessening the age-old differences between the regions and consolidated national unity.

3. *The Separation of Church and State. Postcard, 1907.*

| Emile Zola: *J'accuse.* | Entente Cordiale. | Law on the separation of Church and State. | Jean Jaurès assassinated. |
|---|---|---|---|
| 13 April 1898 | 8 April 1904 | 9 December 1905 | 31 July 1914 |

**1883:** Second Jules Ferry government. Annam becomes protectorate.
**1884:** Trade union and divorce laws.
**1885:** Pasteur administers first anti-rabies vaccination.
**1886–9:** Boulanger crisis.
**1887:** Grévy resigns.
**1888:** First Russian loan.
**1889:** Eiffel Tower built.
**1891:** Fourmies incident.
**1892:** Méline tariff. Panama scandal.
**1893:** Franco-Russian military convention.
**1894:** Anti-anarchist laws.
**23 September 1895:** CGT (Confédération Générale des Travailleurs) formed.
**1898:** Dreyfus Affair. Crisis between France and Britain at Fashoda.
**1899:** Waldeck-Rousseau government.
**1901:** Radical Party founded. Law on associations.
**1902:** Combes government.
**1904:** Entente Cordiale with Britain. Law forbidding religious orders to teach. Break with Vatican.
**23–25 April 1905:** SFIO (Section Française de l'International Ouvrière) founded.

5. Pas-à-Quatre*: pro-Dreyfus caricature on the Affair.*

**1906:** Algeciras conference. 24 hours weekly rest introduced by law. CGT conference at Amiens. Clemenceau Prime Minister.
**1907:** Languedoc vine-growers' revolt.
**1912:** Morocco becomes a protectorate.
**1913:** Poincaré President. Military service increased to three years.
**1914:** Vote to introduce income tax.
**31 July:** Jaurès assassinated.
**3 August:** Germany declares war on France.

# Bismarck and William II

1. Friedrich Krupp's foundry at Essen. Otto Bollhagen, 1873.

THE CREATION of the German Reich, which symbolically took place in the Hall of Mirrors at Versailles, succeeded in producing German unity around Prussia by joining the southern states to the North German Confederation. In spite of the existence of universal suffrage in the elections to the Reichstag, the Reich remained until its demise an authoritarian state, since the government was not responsible before parliament. The parliament itself was, in any case, dissolved on each of the numerous occasions when it displayed opposition to the government. The predominance of Prussia over the other twenty-four states (which included three city-states) forming the federation meant the imposition of a particular civilization and type of government characterized by Junker conservatism and domination of the civil service by a powerful military caste. Bismarck, the Prussian prime minister and chancellor of the Reich, first assured himself of the support of the Liberals and then, in the *Kulturkampf* (campaign for secularization), set about attacking the particularist Catholics of the *Zentrum*. This led to the expulsion of the Jesuits and controls being imposed upon the clergy, which also alarmed Protestants. It was, therefore, a failure. Two attempts on the Kaiser's life then gave Bismarck a pretext for dissolving the Reichstag and promulgating the so-called Anti-Socialist Laws, which were renewed every two years until his fall from power. The great rise in population that the Reich had seen, alongside the disordered growth in investment in the feverish climate of the *Gründerjahre* (foundation years), was temporarily halted by the repercussions of the Viennese Stock Market crash. Expansion continued nonetheless. Heavy industry became more highly concentrated and rapid urbanization was accompanied by a further dramatic population increase, which cannot simply be attributed to decreasing levels of emigration. Agriculture was modernized, in spite of the archaic social relations which still pertained in the east. Germany became the second-strongest world power, practising a unique form of state capitalism. A variety of interest groups stepped into the breach left by the failings of the German parliamentary system: associations of employers and farmers, and colonial and nationalist pressure groups. Falling into line with the aristocracy, the richest industrialists joined in the chorus of hostility to socialists, progressives and trade unionists: hence the repeated attempts to integrate the workers into society by detaching them from the Social Democratic Party (SPD), such as Bismarck's insurance laws and the social legislation passed at the beginning of William II's reign and revamped in the early years of the twentieth century. The Reich was largely dependent for its revenue upon the goodwill of its individual states. It was also faced, on its borders, with a number of national problems, which were aggravated by its policy of Germanization.

In foreign policy, the attempt under Bismarck to consolidate Germany's position in Europe by a series of apparently contradictory treaties was followed, under William II, by the search for 'a place in the sun'. In fact, the colonies were to have more of a strategic than an economic significance, and imperial rivalries posed more of a threat to Germany's ability to carry through a co-ordinated process of modernization and democratization than they did to its overseas empire. The influence of the SPD, the leading force in the Socialist International, increased in this period, and in 1912 it became the largest group in the Reichstag. One of its main objectives, which it backed up by demonstrations and strikes, was to win universal suffrage in the parliaments of those *Länder* where the three-class system was still in force (Prussia, Saxony etc.). This demand figured among its war aims when the SPD accepted Germany's entering the war under a government of national unity on 4 August 1914.

**Creation of the Reich.**
**18 January 1871**

**Triple Alliance.**
**1882**

**Bismarck dismissed.**
**19 March 1890**

2. The founders of the Reich: William I, Crown Prince Frederick William, Prince Frederick-Charles, Bismarck and Moltke. German postcard.

**18 January 1871:** William I, King of Prussia, is proclaimed German Kaiser.
**1871:** Zentrum (German Catholic Centre Party) founded.
**1871–86:** *Kulturkampf* – power struggle against Catholicism.
**May 1873:** Vienna Stock Market crashes.
**May 1875:** The two German socialist parties unite to form the SPD (Social Democratic Party of Germany) and adopt the Gotha Programme.
**1876:** German Conservative Party founded.
**11 May and 2 June:** Assassination attempts on William I.
**June–July 1878:** Berlin Congress.
**October 1878–1890:** Anti-socialist laws.
**October 1879:** Alliance with Austria-Hungary.
**June 1881:** The Three Emperors' League (William I, Alexander II and Franz Josef).
**1882:** Triple Alliance (Germany, Austria-Hungary, Italy).
**1883:** Death of Karl Marx in London (14 March). Law on health insurance.
**1884:** Law on industrial accident insurance.

3. Jules Favre and Adolphe Thiers opposite Bismarck, May 1871. Anonymous lithograph.

# 1871–1914

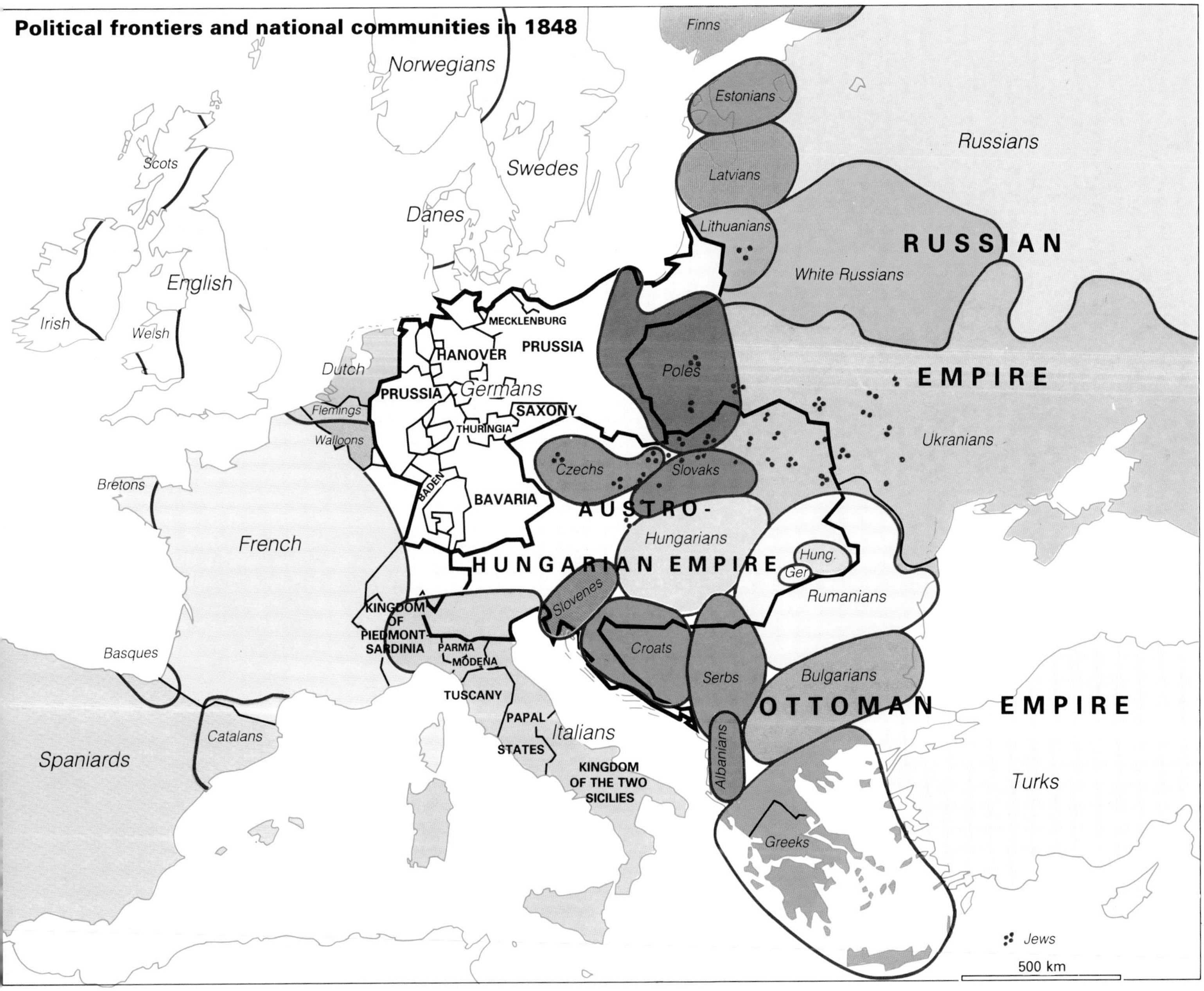

## Political frontiers and national communities in 1848

Norwegians
Finns
Estonians
Scots
Swedes
Russians
Latvians
Danes
Lithuanians
RUSSIAN
English
White Russians
Irish
Welsh
MECKLENBURG
HANOVER
PRUSSIA
Poles
EMPIRE
Dutch
PRUSSIA
Germans
Flemings
SAXONY
THURINGIA
Walloons
Czechs
Slovaks
Ukranians
Bretons
BADEN
BAVARIA
AUSTRO-
Hungarians
French
HUNGARIAN EMPIRE
Hung.
Ger.
Slovenes
Rumanians
KINGDOM OF PIEDMONT-SARDINIA
PARMA
MODENA
Croats
Basques
Serbs
Bulgarians
TUSCANY
OTTOMAN
EMPIRE
PAPAL STATES
Italians
Catalans
Albanians
Spaniards
KINGDOM OF THE TWO SICILIES
Turks
Greeks
Jews
500 km

| Mass movement for universal suffrage in Prussia. | Moroccan crisis. | G. Hauptmann wins Nobel Prize for Literature. | First World War. |
|---|---|---|---|
| 1905 | 1911 | 1912 | August 1914 |

**1884–5:** Beginnings of German colonial empire.
**March 1888:** Death of William I. Frederick III reigns for 99 days.
**1888–1918:** Reign of William II.
**1889:** Law on old age pensions.
**1890–91:** Legislation on working conditions.
**1890–4:** Caprivi Chancellor.
**1891:** SPD adopts the Erfurt Programme.
**1892:** Gerhardt Hauptmann's *Die Weber*.
**1893:** General Commission of German Trade Unions founded.
**1894–1900:** Hohenlohe-Schillingfürst Chancellor.
**1895:** Death of Engels in London.
**1897–9:** Extension of German colonial possessions.
**1898:** Admiral Tirpitz becomes head of Reich Navy Office.
**1899–1907:** Social legislation extended.
**1900–9:** Bülow Chancellor.
**1903:** A German firm begins the construction of the Berlin-Baghdad railway, which is intended to link Constantinople with the Persian Gulf.
**1904:** Textile workers' strike at Crimmitschau.
**1905:** Strike by Ruhr miners, iron and steel and building workers demanding universal suffrage.
**March:** Moroccan crisis provoked by William II's visit to Tangier and followed by the Algeciras Conference (16 January–7 April 1906).
**1906–7:** Reichstag refuses to vote military budget for German colonial policy and is dissolved. The 'Hottentot elections' ensue.
**1908:** Expropriation Law, permitting the confiscation of Polish property.
**October:** William II's controversial *Daily Telegraph* interview, after which his influence on foreign affairs is curtailed.
**1909–17:** Bethmann-Hollweg Chancellor.
**1910:** Progressive Popular Party founded.
**February–May:** SPD demonstrations for universal suffrage.
**May 1911:** New constitution for Alsace-Lorraine.
**July:** Threat of war as a result of German gunboat being sent to Agadir.

*4. The town of Mannheim, c. 1910. German postcard.*

**4 November:** Agreements with France on colonial questions.
**1913:** Saverne affair: conflict between the military and the Alsatian population. Reichstag votes a wealth tax.
**4 August 1914:** Reichstag votes war credits.

# Austria-Hungary and Russia

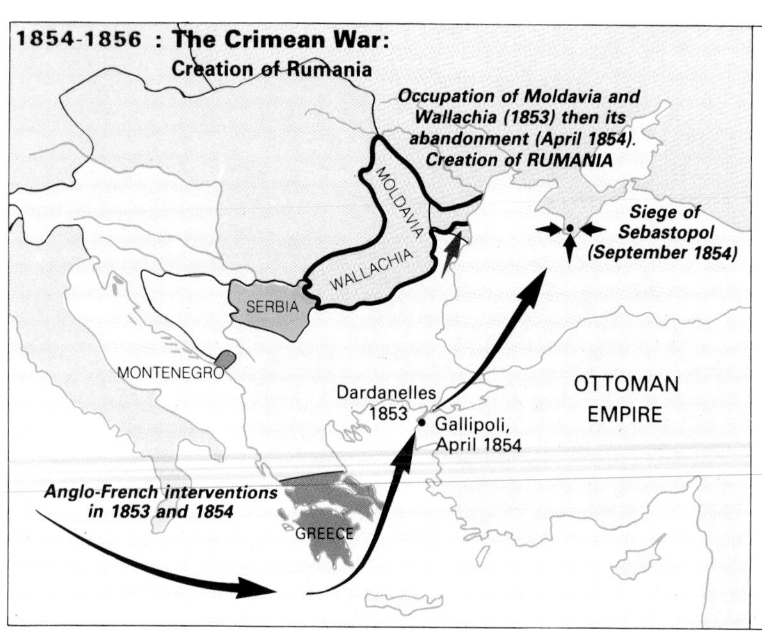

After the revolutions of 1848, the Russian and the Austro-Hungarian Empires emerged as champions of law and order. For both, military defeat proved to be a turning-point, in Russia's case in the Crimean War, in Austria's at Sadowa, ten years later, excluding her from the German Reich. In an age of nation-states, these two multi-national states seemed outmoded even in their style of colonial expansion, Russia finally conquering Caucasia and Central Asia, and Austria-Hungary penetrating deeper into the Balkans. These conquests were accompanied by a policy which encouraged the spread of German, Magyar or Russian national influence, although the controlling nations did not play the same economic role: the Germans were responsible for the development of an essentially finance-based capitalism, whilst in Russia it was the state which encouraged development, with the support of a few large, middle-class, Russian or non-native families. With the accession of Alexander II, the reformist era began; serfdom was abolished and peasants were allowed to buy up land gradually; locally elected councils (*zemstva*) were created; there was legal reform and municipal administrations were established. The assassination of Alexander II can be traced back to the populist movement, *Narodnaya Volya* (the Will of the People), which both originated from and yet constituted an advance over the university youth's campaign of 'going to the people'; but the Polish uprising

1. Naval battle of Petrograd between the Russians and the Germans. Russian illustration 1914.

**Fall of Sebastopol.** **Peasants freed from serfdom.** **Polish uprising.** **Assassination of Alexander II.** **Beginning of the Russian Revolution.**

**8 September 1855:** Fall of Sebastopol during Crimean War.
**1855–81:** Reign of Tsar Alexander II.
**1859:** Surrender of Chamil: completion of the conquest of the Caucasus by Russia.

*3. The diversity of the Hungarian people. German engraving by H. Veber 1854.*

**19 February** [3 March] **1861:** Promulgation of the 'Edict of emancipation of Russian peasants from serfdom'.
**1863:** Polish uprising, suppressed the following year.
**1864–5:** Conquest of Central Asia by Russia.
**13 January 1864:** Administrative reform in Russia; creation of *zemstva* (local assemblies).
**2 December:** Reform of the judiciary in Russia.
**3 July 1866:** Austria is defeated by Prussia at Sadowa.
**18 February 1867:** 'Compromise' between Austria and Hungary: creation of the double monarchy.
**1868:** Croatia becomes the Kingdom of Croatia-Slavonia following a 'compromise' with Hungary.
**1870:** Municipal administrations established in Russia; creation of urban dumas.
**1873:** Alliance between the three Emperors (William I, Alexander II, Franz-Josef).
**May:** Vienna Stock Exchange crash.
**1874:** 'March to the People' in Russia.

*4. The Viennese doctor, Sigmund Freud, founder of psycho-analysis with his wife Martha, circa 1890.*

**19 April 1877–31 January 1878:** Russo-Turkish War.
**5 February 1878:** Vera Zasulič shoots at Trepov, chief of police in St Petersburg.
**13 June–13 July:** Congress of Berlin.
**1879:** Occupation of Bosnia-Herzogovina by Austria-Hungary.
**1 [13] March 1881:** Assassination of Alexander II.
**1881–2:** Wave of pogroms against the Jews in Russia.
**1887:** *Numerus clausus* for the Jews: increase of Russian influence in Poland and the Baltic countries.
**1888:** Founding of the Austrian Social Democratic Party led by V. Adler and O. Bauer.
**1891–3:** Franco-Russian Alliance.
**1 November 1894:** Death of Alexander III: accession of Nicholas II.
**1897:** Creation of the fifth curia (general) for the *Reichsrat* elections. Edicts of K. Badeni (President of the Austrian Council of Ministers) on the equality of languages in Bohemia.
**March 1898:** Founding of the Russian Social

# 1855–1918

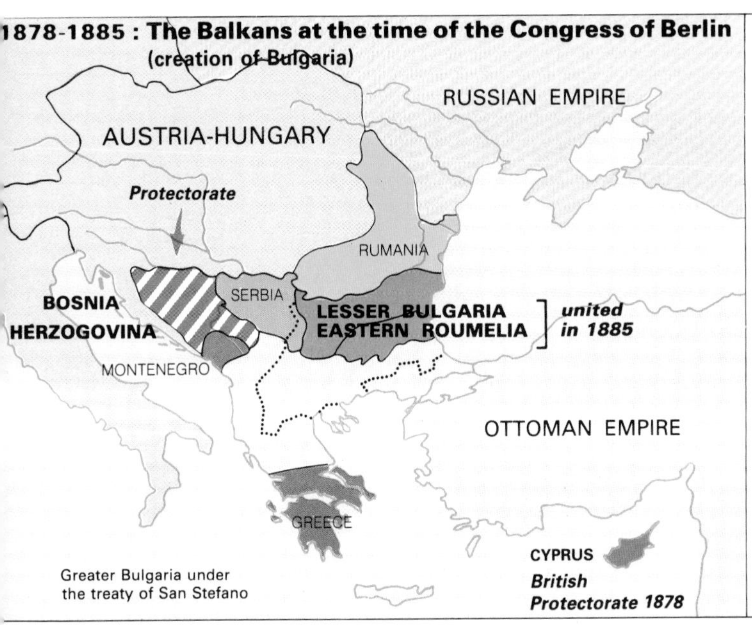

of 1863 had already cooled the movement's reforming zeal, particularly in national affairs.

Within the Hapsburg Empire – founded on clericalism, bureaucracy and the army – recognition of the 'historic Magyar nation' led to the era of 'compromise' (*Ausgleich*). Defence, foreign affairs and their financing were all that Austria and Hungary administered jointly. The Slavs were the overall losers in this arrangement. While the nationalities of Hungary were reduced to silence, the middle classes of the renascent 'nations without a history' were struggling in Austria for a share of power in the state, particularly through obstruction in parliament, which slowed down social progress. Social democracy took its place in the *Reichsrat* (the Austrian parliament) when a fifth curia was created, and in 1907, in the wake of the Russian Revolution of 1905, it won the universal suffrage denied its Hungarian counterpart. A federation of six national parties – German, Czech, Italian, Southern Slav, Polish and Ruthenian (Ukrainian) – set up a model national programme. It was challenged by a strong populist movement which was violently anti-semitic and formed under the wing of the Christian-Social party.

Within the Russian Empire, the socialist parties of the various nationalities also became spokesmen for national demands; the split which occurred between Bolsheviks and Mensheviks in 1903 actually concealed a rift between nations. Preceded by terrorist attacks and anti-Jewish pogroms, the revolution broke out on 'Red Sunday', the catalysing agent being the Russo-Japanese war. The concessions of the Tsar's October Manifesto had been gradually whittled away by the dissolution of the first two Dumas, the first after the St Petersburg Soviet had been crushed, the second after the Moscow uprising.

The First World War was catalysed by rivalry in the Balkans between two powers which were already suffering internal instability because of national dissensions. Even within the Austro-Hungarian army there were deep tensions and last minute concessions could not stop the rot. In Russia, the 'Sacred Union' of nations could only briefly hold the revolutionary movement in check.

2. *Archduke Charles-Louis of Hapsburg, Emperor Franz-Josef, Franz Ferdinand, Hungarian chromolithograph.*

**Universal suffrage in Austria.** **Russian Revolution.**

1907 February [March] 1917

5. *Sailors of the battleship* Potemkin*, June 1905. Anonymous Russian painting.*

Democratic Workers' Party in Russia.
**1901:** Founding of the Russian Revolutionary Socialist Party.
**1902:** Confiscation of Armenian Church property in Russia.
**1903:** Pogroms in Gomel and Kishinev.
**8 February 1904:** Port Arthur attack (start of Russo-Japanese War).
**9 [22] January 1905:** Red Sunday; the police open fire on a large popular peace demonstration in front of the Winter Palace in St Petersburg.
**14–25 June [27 June–8 July]:** Mutiny on the battleship *Potemkin* at Odessa.
**5 September:** Treaty of Portsmouth between Russia and Japan.
**30 October:** October manifesto of Nicholas II, which promises a meeting of the State Duma.
**December:** Uprising in Moscow.
**10 May–21 July 1906:** First Duma.
**1907:** Universal suffrage in the Reichsrat.
**5 March–6 June:** Second Duma in Russia.
**1908:** Annexation of Bosnia-Herzegovina by Austria.
**1912:** Striking miners shot in Lena.

6. Judith, 1909, *by the Viennese Gustav Klimt (1862–1918) co-founder of the Secession* *(see p. 274).*

**December:** Start of the Fourth Duma.
**28 June 1914:** Assassination of Franz-Ferdinand at Sarajevo.
**1 August 1915:** The Duma calls for a government accountable to parliament.
**21 October 1916:** The Social Democrat, Friedrich Adler (son of Victor), assassinates Count Sturgh, Prime Minister of Austria.
**21 November:** Death of Franz-Josef; accession of Charles I.
**February [March] 1917:** Russian Revolution.
**18 October 1918:** Charles I announces the creation of a Federal State of Austria.
**12 November:** Proclamation of the Republic of German Austria.

# The New Division of the World

On the eve of the 1914 war, it seemed that the division of the world among a number of great powers was almost complete. In Africa there were only two independent republics: Ethiopia and the small Republic of Liberia. In Asia the remaining great empires – Turkey, Persia, China – were increasingly being threatened by rival foreign ambitions. In Central and South America, the United States was establishing its economic protection. This general movement of imperialism – which involved not only the old colonial powers such as France and Great Britain, but Germany, Italy, Russia, Japan and the United States as well – took various forms, from territorial conquest and colonial domination to the imposition of such less direct methods of control as the enforcement of political allegiance or the setting up of a state of economic dependency. There were various reasons for this, many of which were closely interrelated, though they were of varying importance depending on the countries involved.

The first causes were economic. After the establishment of free trade in Europe from 1860, there followed a general return to protectionism at the end of the century, except in Great Britain. National markets were shrinking and there developed a determination to appropriate overseas territory possessing natural potential for expansion which would provide markets for industrial production and financial investment. Jules Ferry said that 'Colonial policy is the daughter of industrial policy.' In some instances (Italy, for example) strong demographic pressure was exerted in addition to pressure from all-important business interests.

These economic factors, on the other hand, came to be part of a power struggle inseparable from a nationalism that was asserting itself in increasingly violent terms. The great powers needed to acquire naval bases essential to the protection of the commercial sea routes and to the supply of their fleets of coal-carrying ships. It was also something of a race on a global scale to prevent other states from staking their claims over lands that were considered available. 'No time must be lost,' said King Leopold II of Belgium, 'otherwise we shall see nations more enterprising than ours taking up the best positions, and such positions are few in number already.'

Finally, there were the ideological and moral forces in play. Faith in the values of progress and civilization among Western nations led them to argue that colonization would bring the light of reason, democratic principles and the benefits of science and medicine to those tribes of the interior that were thought of as primitive. Also, there was a desire in religious circles to spread the Christian faith in areas which had not yet been converted. The spread of missionaries had been part of colonial expansion ever since the beginning of the century. For those countries involved, expansionist policies would lead to outbreaks of violent controversy. Pressures from certain groups (businessmen, missionaries, the military, nationalist or progressive idealists, travellers and geographers) often met with lively resistance from many and various quarters (humanitarian arguments or suggestions that caution should be exercised where commitment was considered dangerous and of no value compared with the costs involved). Notions of worldwide policy and global strategy nonetheless did finally become accepted thinking in international relationships. Paul Valéry summed up the situation when he wrote: 'The age of the finite world has begun.'

By overturning people's traditional ways of thinking and the old economic and social structures, colonialism soon aroused hostile reactions in the conquered countries, however. Indian nationalism and the reawakening of the Arab world were direct consequences of this.

*1. The Sudan war: the British Army marching against the Khartoum uprising in 1898.*

**Anglo-French Free Trade Treaty.** — **1860**

**Leopold II, King of the Belgians.** — **1865–1909**

**Colonial Conference in Ber[lin]** — **1884**

**1859–79:** Conquest of the Caucasus and Russian expansion to the south of the Aral Sea in Central Asia.
**1873–4:** French attempt to conquer Tonkin. Hanoi is taken, then evacuated.
**1874–8:** Exploration of the Congo area by Savorgnan de Brazza and Stanley.
**1879–82:** Competition between Brazza and Stanley (acting in the name of the King of the Belgians, Leopold II) for the control of the Congo basin. Question of the Egyptian debt. This brings about increasing political intervention by France and Great Britain in Egyptian internal affairs.
**1881:** French intervention in Tunisia. 12 May: signing of the Bardo treaty by which the *bey* recognizes French protectorate. Touaregs massacre the French reconnaissance mission in the Hoggar.
**1882:** Military intervention and establishment of British control in Egypt. Crisis in Anglo-French relations.
**1883–95:** Conquest of Tonkin and recognition of French protectorate by Annam.
**1883–95:** French rule over the Niger, Guinea, Ivory Coast and Dahomey areas established.

*2. The march of African slaves according to the accounts of Dr Livingstone, c. 1860.*

**1884–5:** Colonial Conference in Berlin. Establishment of a procedure to settle frontier conflicts in Africa and the recognition of the independent state of the Congo under the sovereignty of Leopold II.
**1885:** Franco-Chinese war. China renounces suzerainty over Annam. Anglo-Russian tension over Afghanistan.
**1886:** Burma becomes a province of the Indian Empire.
**1890–1:** Italy conquers Eritrea and Somalia.
**1894–5:** Sino-Japanese war. Victory for Japan, established by the Treaty of Shimonoseki.
**1894–6:** Conquest and annexation of Madagascar by France.
**1895–6:** Attempted Italian take-over of Abyssinia. Disaster at Adowa (1 March). Under the Treaty of Addis Ababa, the Italians recognize Ethiopian sovereignty.
**1898:** Anglo-French crisis over the control of the Upper Valley of the Nile. Marchand mission reaches Fashoda then leaves, 7 November.
**1899:** Establishment of Anglo-Egyptian joint rule over the Sudan. Fouteau-Lamy mission

# 1860–1914

## he division of the world circa 1900

olonies

- British
- French
- German
- Others
- Russian expansion

Colonies

P: Portuguese
S: Spanish
D: Dutch
B: Belgium
Da: Danish
U.S.: United States
I: Italian

d Treaty of Tiantsin between China and France. | Fashoda. 1898 | Algeciras Conference. 1906

rosses the Sahara. Definitive establishment f French rule over the Sahara.
**899–1902:** Boer War originating from pposition between the Boer Republics in )range Free State and Transvaal, and the ritish colonies in Southern Africa. The efeated Boers accept the suzerainty of the ing of England at Vereeniging 31 May 1902.
**900:** Boxers attack the foreign legations in eking, China. An international expedition led y the German general, A. von Waldersee elieves the legations, 14 August.
**904–5:** Russo-Japanese war. Japan is ictorious on land and sea and ensures its wn freedom of action in Manchuria and orea.
**905:** First Moroccan crisis. Germany pposes French ambitions in Morocco. The lgeciras conference (16 January–7 April 906) makes the Moroccan question an nternational issue.
**910:** Annexation of Korea by Japan.
**911–12:** Italian-Turkish war and Italian ccupation of Libya. Second Moroccan crisis. Germany accepts the principle of French rotectorate against certain territorial

*3. One picture of colonialism: a white teacher in Senegal c. 1860.*

concessions in the Congo.
**30 March 1912:** Fez Convention. Establishment of French protectorate over Morocco.

# The Break-Up of the Chinese Empire: Contacts with the West

AT THE END of the reign of Ch'ien-lung two major factors were already in evidence which were to undermine the basis of imperial society at the very moment when, on its borders, the threat from Western imperialism was becoming plain. The first, and most important problem, was the extent to which China's mandarin system and its centralized administration were ill-adapted to pre-industrial society. Secondly, difficulties arose as a result of what has been termed the 'handicap of a prematurely high level of social equilibrium': the agricultural and industrial progress of the eighteenth century brought in its train a demographic explosion which hampered any attempt to industrialize the country, firstly by making mechanization unnecessary, and secondly by causing the pauperization of the whole of society when production stagnated. In this way a chronic economic cycle was set into being, of which China remained the prisoner for more than a hundred years. In the rural areas, for example, poverty gave rise to the endemic problem of peasant revolts, which in their turn made poverty more acute.

In addition to these internal causes were external factors. The

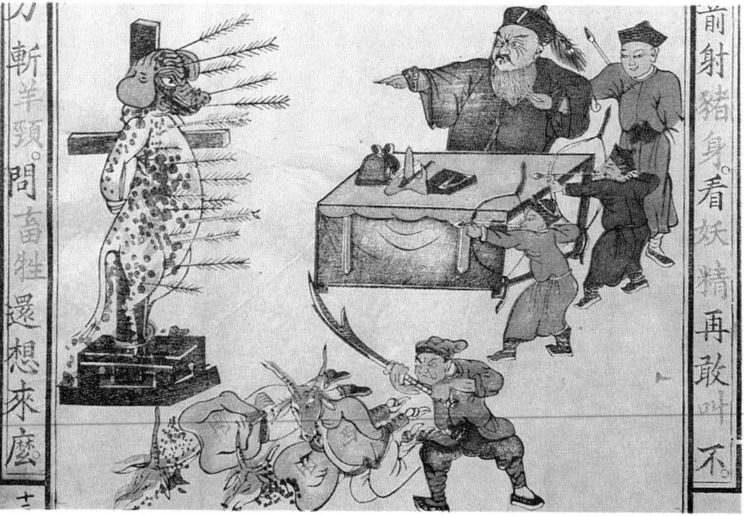


1. 'Shoot the Christian Pig!'. A popular propaganda engraving from around 1810.

opium trade, forced on China by the British, created such a heavy balance of payments deficit that the result was almost catastrophic. This was at the root of the two major events in the history of China in the twentieth century, which were to have a decisive effect on its destiny. The Opium Wars not only left the way open for the foreign penetration of China, they also marked the end of a movement of trade (which till then had always been favourable to the West) and provoked a haemorrhage of capital, which in turn created a financial crisis of the most severe sort.

The collapse of the economy was sparked off by the Taiping Rebellion. This gigantic movement of revolt, under the leadership of Hung Hsiu-ch'uan (who was also a convert to Christianity), had its roots in ancient tradition. It caused irreparable damage in the Yangtze basin, which was the most prosperous area in China. It went hand in hand with other peasant uprisings (of the Nien, for example) with which it at times converged, while it was given further momentum by secessionist moves on the part of the Hui (who were Muslims) in Yunnan and Kansu, then in Sinkiang. In truth, the whole Empire was in turmoil for more than fifty years. These rebellions, which demonstrated the inability of central government to react to the crisis, marked the rise to power of a new generation of provincial administrators who were both reformers and traditionalists, such as Tseng Kuo-fan or Tso Tsung-t'ang. They met, however, with hostility on the part of the imperial court and total lack of sympathy on the part of Empress Tzu-hsi. The inability of Chinese society to effect its own modernization was mirrored in the liquidation of its reforming leaders (the most important of whom, Kan Yu-wei and Liang Ch'i-Ch'ao, were only in government for a hundred days) and in the destruction of the Chinese fleet at the hands of Japan. The Western countries took advantage of China's weakness and divided the country up into zones of influence. The awareness that it had proved impossible to reform traditional society from within led to the emergence of a radical movement which saw the only hope as being total Westernization. The Boxer uprising was only to be the last, archaic convulsion of an empire whose days were numbered. Even though the Republic, proclaimed by Sun Yat-sen, was taken over by General Yüan Shih-k'ai, it did enough to destroy the dynasty for ever.

2. Empress Tzu-hsi in her sedan chair.

***The Mirror of the Hundred Flower Women*** **by Li Ru-chen, the phonetician.**

**Taiping Rebellion.**

**1825** **1850**

**1800:** A decree is passed, banning the importation of opium and the planting of poppy fields.
**1810:** Christian preaching is banned.
**1812:** The population of China reaches 361 million inhabitants.
**1820–5:** A growing balance of payments deficit is caused by the development of the opium market by the East India Company.
**1839:** Energetic measures taken by Lin Tse-hsü to ban the importing of opium cause British retaliation and mark the beginning of the First Opium War.
**1842:** Display of strength by the British leads to the Treaty of Nanking, setting up trading links between China and the West and providing for the transfer of Hong Kong to Britain.
**1843:** China recognises the territorial independence of Hong Kong. Shanghai and Ning-po are declared open ports.
**1850:** The Taiping Rebellion begins. Hung Hsiu-chüan proclaims himself Heavenly King in the Celestial Kingdom of Great Peace.
**1853–4:** After spreading to Hunan and the Yangtze basin, the Taiping establish their capital in Nanking. The Nien uprisings begin. The Taiping movement spreads to the North and threatens Peking.
**1855:** Muslim uprisings in Yunnan.
**1857–60:** Second Opium War, leading to the sack of the Summer Palace by French and British troops and to the ratification of the Peking Treaty.
**1861–2:** Muslim uprisings in Shensi and Sinkiang.
**1863:** The sea-board customs network passes under British control.
**1864:** Nanking is captured and Hung Hsiu-chüan commits suicide.
**1865:** The Nien counter-attack.
**1866:** The Taiping are defeated.
**1867:** Li Hung-chang defeats the Nien as they threaten Peking.
**1876–8:** The Secessionist revolt of Sinkiang is put down.
**1879:** Under the Treaty of Livadia the major part of the area around Ili passes under Russian control.
**1883–5:** War breaks out between China and France as a result of the French intervention in Indochina and ends under a treaty signed after the siege of Ning-po.
**1888:** An armaments factory is set up in Wuhan.
**1894–5:** War between China and Japan, leading to the Treaty of Shimonoseki (under which Taiwan and the Pescadores Islands are given to Japan). China must pay extensive reparations.
**1897:** Chiao-chou Bay in Shantung is annexed by Germany.
**1898:** Wei-hai-wei is annexed by the British, and Dalian by the Russians. The liberal policies followed by K'ang Yu-wei come to an end and reformist circles are repressed.
**1900:** The Boxer uprising breaks out as a result of Western harassment. It leads to the capitulation of the Imperial Court and the paying of reparations.
**1905:** Sun Yat-sen founds the United League (T'ung-meng hui) in Japan.
**1907:** The imperial system of recruitment by written examinations is abolished.

3. The passengers of a British steamship arriving in Canton: mid-nineteenth-century Chinese painting.

# 1800–1916

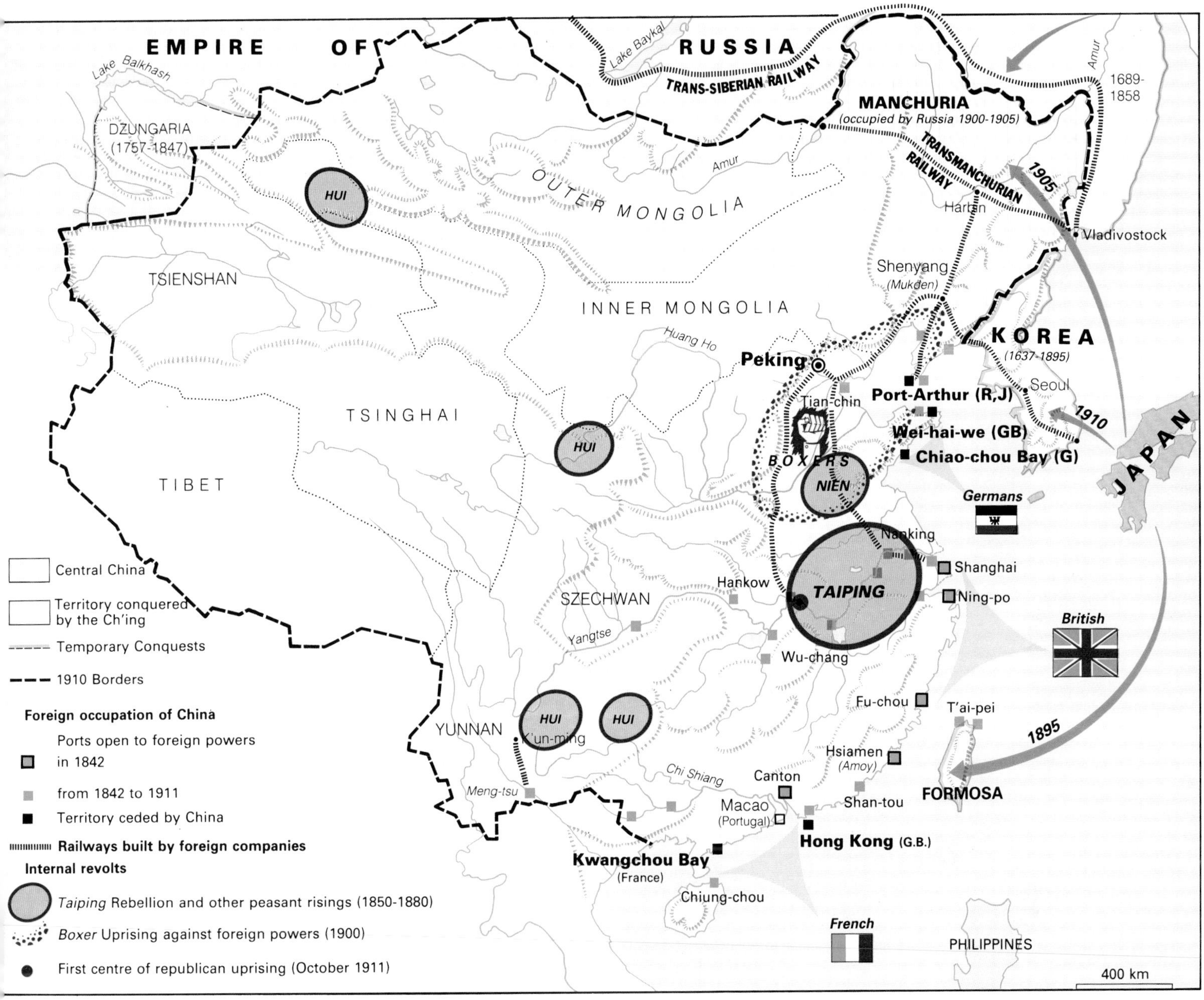

EMPIRE OF RUSSIA

Lake Balkhash
Lake Baykal
TRANS-SIBERIAN RAILWAY
MANCHURIA (occupied by Russia 1900-1905)
TRANSMANCHURIAN RAILWAY
Amur
1689-1858
1905
Harbin
Vladivostock
DZUNGARIA (1757-1847)
HUI
OUTER MONGOLIA
TSIENSHAN
INNER MONGOLIA
Shenyang (Mukden)
KOREA (1637-1895)
Huang Ho
Peking
Seoul
Port-Arthur (R,J)
Tian-chin
1910
TSINGHAI
HUI
Wei-hai-we (GB)
Chiao-chou Bay (G)
JAPAN
BOXERS
NIEN
Germans
TIBET
Nanking
Shanghai
Hankow
TAIPING
Ning-po
SZECHWAN
British
Yangtse
Wu-chang
Fu-chou
T'ai-pei
YUNNAN
HUI
HUI
K'un-ming
1895
Hsiamen (Amoy)
Chi Shiang
Canton
Meng-tsu
Shan-tou
FORMOSA
Macao (Portugal)
Hong Kong (G.B.)
Kwangchou Bay (France)
Chiung-chou
French
PHILIPPINES
400 km

Central China
Territory conquered by the Ch'ing
Temporary Conquests
1910 Borders

**Foreign occupation of China**

Ports open to foreign powers in 1842
from 1842 to 1911
Territory ceded by China
**Railways built by foreign companies**

**Internal revolts**

*Taiping* Rebellion and other peasant risings (1850-1880)
*Boxer* Uprising against foreign powers (1900)
First centre of republican uprising (October 1911)

| 1898 | 1912 | 1915 |
|---|---|---|
| ***The Great Commonwealth*** **by K'ang Yu-wei.** | **Reform of teaching.** | **The magazine** ***New Youth*** **is launched.** |

**1908:** Death of Empress Tzu-hsi.
**1910:** Northeast China is divided up between the Russians and the Japanese.
**1911:** Insurrection in Wu-han leads to the secession of South China.
**1912:** Sun Yat-sen proclaims the Republic in Nanking, and the Emperor Pu-yi abdicates. Sun Yat-sen hands the presidency of the Republic over to General Yüan Shih-k'ai. The education system is reformed.
**1916:** Death of Yüan Shih-k'ai.

*4. Yüan Shih-k'ai before his death in 1916.*

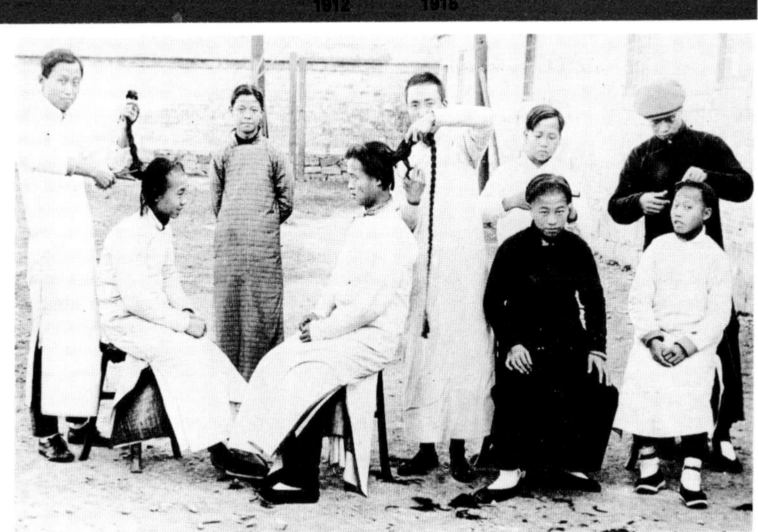

*5. The revolution is also a matter of hair-style.*

# British Colonial Settlement

*1. Queen Victoria visits the Australia exhibit, in May 1886.*

SINCE 1791 CANADA HAD BEEN under the control of a governor appointed by London and an executive council made up of leading citizens and British civil servants. But there were growing demands for a representative system, and Canadians of French descent continued to protest at their exclusion from power. By 1837 the need for change had become clear to all. Lord Durham was commissioned to undertake an inquiry into the roots of the disturbances. His report recommending the granting of responsible self-government was only partly put into effect, though in reality Governor Elgin allowed the assembly elected in 1848 to form the government itself, and this type of self-government quickly created a precedent for other countries. Moreover, the annexationist overtures being expressed by the United States led to the growth of the idea of a federal structure: as a result, in 1867, the Dominion of Canada was created from the joining together of four provinces, including Quebec, with institutions on the British model. The integration of the west and the completion of the Canadian Pacific Railway gave the country a continental dimension.

In the case of Australia, the country had at first been little more than the penal colony of New South Wales. After 1840, the crown made official the settling of vast areas in the country by squatters whose main interest was in wool production, and later in gold mining as the gold rush got under way. The granting of self-government took place smoothly and a second dominion came into being at the start of the twentieth century. Similarly, in New Zealand, where agricultural development took the form of the confiscation of Maori land, the path to self-government was quickly followed and dominion status finally granted in 1907. Durham and those who came after him had understood that as far as the 'White' colonies were concerned the interests of trade and profit were best served by the abandonment of unwieldy and expensive colonial rule.

The strategic importance and mineral wealth of Southern Africa, its ethnic diversity, and the growing number of politicians invoking the supremacy of the Empire, resulted in different conflicts and took the whole region down a different evolutionary path. In the Cape, the attempted process of anglicization and the emancipation of the slaves had, in the years after 1833, sparked off the Great Trek, that is the migration towards the north-east of the country of 10,000 Boers (these were colonial settlers of Dutch descent). After limiting the extent of these movements by the declaration of Natal as British territory, Britain recognized the independence of the Boer states of the Orange Free State and the Transvaal. But the problem became more complicated after the discovery of diamonds along the borders of the Orange Free State in 1867. The British extended the sovereignty of the Cape Colony before granting it self-government. Unrest on the part of the black workers, the mining interests involved and the appeal of the Transvaal for German capital dragged Britain into an abortive project for a South African Federation, and then in 1877 into a disastrous

**The first convicts arrive in Botany Bay, near Sydney.**
**1788**

**Ottawa has its first Parliament.**
**1848**

**Diamonds discovered in the Orange Free Sta**
**1867**

3. The Last of England *by Ford Madox Brown.*

**1788:** The first shipment of convicts arrives in Sydney.
**1791:** Constitutional Act of Canada.
**1815:** Britain has its title to the Cape Colony confirmed.
**1825–1836:** Five new colonial states are founded in Australia.
**1829–1836:** William Lyon Mackenzie launches his campaign for Canadian self-government.
**1834–9:** The Great Trek by the Boers.
**1837:** Rebellion put down in Montreal.
**1839:** The Durham Report is published, opening the way to responsible self-government in Canada.
**1840:** Annexation of New Zealand.
**1841:** Union Act passed, by which the different provinces of Canada are unified.
**1843:** The British occupy Natal. The Orange Free State is founded.
**1848:** Beginnings of parliamentary government in Canada.
**1851:** Gold discovered in Australia.
**1852:** The Transvaal founded. The British recognize its independence (and that of the Orange Free State in 1854).
**1854–9:** Five Australian colonies gain responsible self-government.
**1867:** The Dominion of Canada is established. Diamonds are discovered in the Orange Free State.
**1868:** Basutoland becomes a British protectorate.
**1870–3:** Three new provinces, including British Columbia, join the Dominion of Canada.
**1871:** The diamond mining district of Kimberley is transferred to the Cape Colony.
**1872:** The Cape Colony gains responsible self-government.
**1876:** The British plan for a South African federation fails.
**1877–9:** Disraeli adopts an aggressive policy: the Transvaal is attacked, then the Zulu War breaks out.
**1880:** The Transvaal rises up against the British, and Boer, or 'Afrikaner', nationalism emerges.
**1881:** The British are defeated by Transvaal forces at Majuba Hill.
**1882:** The first cargoes of refrigerated meat leave New Zealand for Britain.
**1885:** Gold is discovered in the Transvaal. Kruger greets the Germans from South West Africa as allies.
**1886:** Completion of the Canadian Pacific Railway.
**1889:** The British South African Company,

*4. President Kruger as seen by Caran d'Ache.*

attempt to annex the Transvaal. The country, vastly enriched by the mining of gold after 1885, rallied around President Kruger to reject any abandonment of sovereignty. The fate of the Uitlanders, who were (often British) workers in the Transvaal mines and enjoyed no political rights, added to the dispute. When in 1899 war broke out, international opinion regarded the Boers as the innocent victims of British imperialism. Two and a half years, 400,000 soldiers and the invention of concentration camps were needed to break their resistance. The annexation of the Boer states was tempered by the assurance that self-government would be granted before long. At last, the Union of South Africa was established. It had the status of a dominion, but one in which the Boers demanded that all civil rights be reserved for the Whites. Racial segregation had found a homeland.

2. The British Lion and the Boer Bull.

**[K]ruger becomes [Pres]ident of the Transvaal.** 1883

**Gold rush in the Transvaal.** 1885

**Australia becomes the second dominion.** 1901

founded by Cecil Rhodes in 1887, is given the territories soon to be named Rhodesia to administer.

**1895:** Failure of the Jameson Raid against the Transvaal.

**1897:** The ultra-imperialist Sir Alfred Milner is appointed High Commissioner in the Cape Colony by the Colonial Secretary Joseph Chamberlain.

**9 October 1899:** The Orange Free State and the Transvaal declare war.

**1900:** In the British General Election the supporters of Empire win a convincing victory.

**1901:** The Commonwealth of Australia is founded. This was the second dominion, after Canada.

**31 May 1902:** The Peace of Vereeniging leads to the annexation of the Boer States.

**1906–7:** The Transvaal and the Orange Free State are given self-government.

**1907:** The Dominion of New Zealand is established.

**31 May 1910:** The Union of South Africa is established, on the basis of racial segregation.

5. Terminus of the Canadian Pacific Railway in Vancouver.

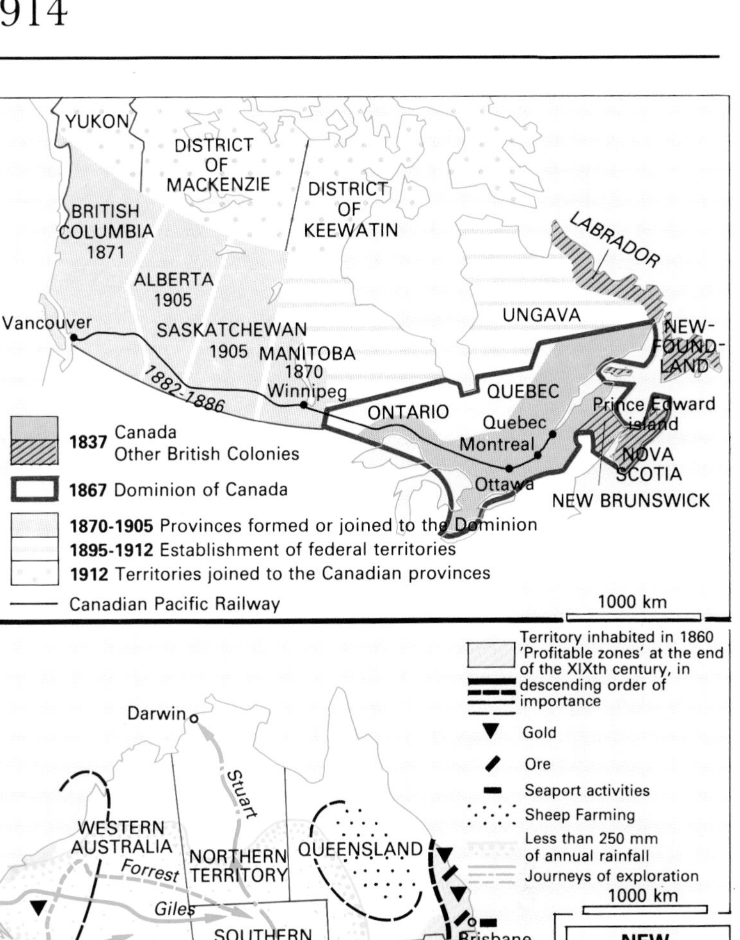


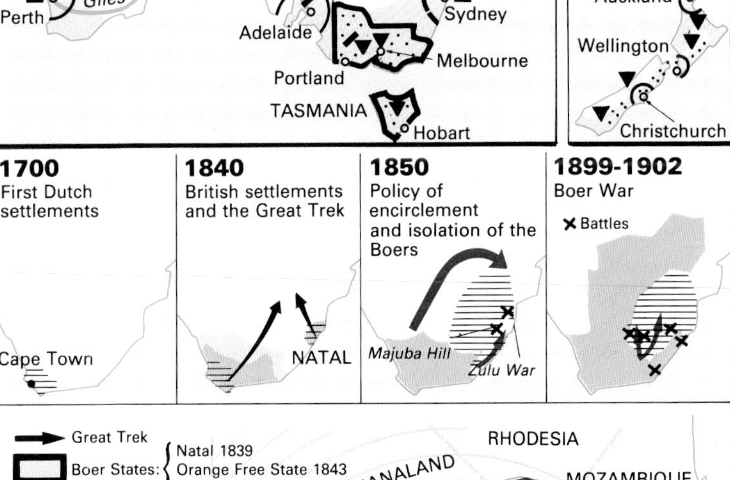


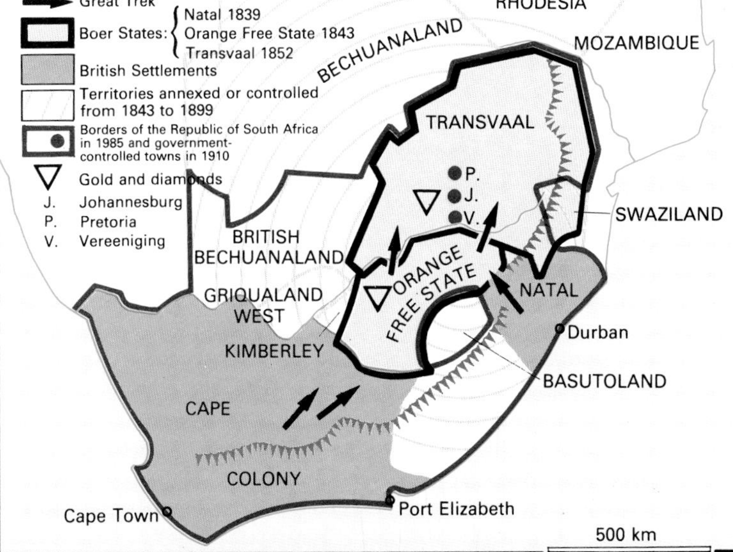

# The United States and Global Expansion

FOLLOWING THE CIVIL WAR, over a period of some twenty years, the United States, which at the time was still mainly an agrarian country, entered the industrial era. The need for war materials, the temporary absence of the Southerners from the political scene and the conquest of the far West stimulated the exploitation and transformation of resources. The rise of the food, textile and iron and steel industries and the growth in coal, mineral and oil production was such that by the end of the century the United States was able to compete with the European powers. Its success was due to the concentration of its industry, both the concentration of its resources – geographic, economic and human – and the financial concentration that came with the formation of trusts and holding companies, which liberal legislation would not succeed in checking. A monopoly capitalism, from which several major figures (Rockefeller, Carnegie, Morgan) had an impact upon political life, became superimposed upon the brute capitalism of the 'robber barons'. Between 1900 and 1920 the movement of reformers fighting against the abuses of capitalism was outflanked by the political strategy of Theodore Roosevelt, who represented a progressive position, and Woodrow Wilson, a Democrat. The First World War, which the US entered in 1917, increased foreign demand for its goods and made the USA the leading world power.

1. Immigrants arriving at Ellis Island c. 1900.

The American industrial revolution would not have been possible without the contribution from immigrant labour. Thanks to that immigration, the American population rose from 31 million in 1860 to 92 million in 1910. At the beginning of the twentieth century, more than a million people a year (in peak years) were entering the USA. Brought there by economic demand, the immigrants – most of whom came from Central and Southern Europe, though there were some from Asia – were badly received by the more established population, who resented them for accepting lower wages and for having different cultures. From 1882 onwards, nativist and trade union movements succeeded in having the Congress pass discriminatory immigrant legislation. The 'melting-pot' was now to admit only those who were by their colour and culture close to the 'White Anglo-Saxon Protestants'. Part of the effect, however, of the newcomers' influence was that the traditionally elitist and reformist American trade unions became radicalized, a process which culminated in the great days of the Haymarket Affair in 1886 and the Pullman strike in 1894 and in the revolutionary movement of the IWW (Industrial Workers of the World) at the beginning of the twentieth century.

Whilst protecting itself from outside influences, in foreign affairs the USA conducted a policy of expansion by investing capital as far afield as Oceania, by implanting colonial settlers in Puerto Rico, the island of Guam and the Philippines, by exerting political, military and financial influence in Cuba, and by its military expedition against Spain in 1898. In the wake of this venture, Hawaii was annexed. Theodore Roosevelt justified this policy in terms of a doctrine of the 'big stick'. Under his leadership, the US participated in the actions of the European powers in China, a decision which was made in the name of the 'open door' theory.

The age of imperialism did not end with the election of the Democrat, Woodrow Wilson, for he intervened in Latin America, combating the Mexican peasant revolution to establish bourgeois democracy. In 1917 the United States entered the First World War on the side of the democracies, but the politics of Wilson's 'Fourteen Points' was to be disavowed by public opinion and Congress, which in 1919 refused to ratify signature of the Treaty of Versailles.

**Blacks granted civil rights.** **Economic crisis and monetary disorder.** **Protectionism.**

**1866** **1873** **1890**

**1866:** Creation of the Freedmen's Bureau; assistance to the emancipated Blacks. The Civil Rights Act guarantees them civil rights.
**1868:** Burlingame Treaty: admission of Chinese workers.
**1869:** C. Vanderbilt organizes the New York Central Railroad Company. Creation of the Knights of Labour, an industrially based union.
**1873:** Crisis caused by railroad speculation.
**1875:** Greenback Party, supporting an inflationary policy.
**1876:** Centenary Exhibition in Philadelphia. Alexander Graham Bell invents the telephone.
**1877:** Major strike by workers in the Baltimore and Ohio Railroad Company.
**1879:** Formation of the Standard Oil Trust.
**1880:** Chicago becomes the capital of meat packing.
**1882:** Formation of the Standard Oil Company. Act prohibiting Chinese immigration (renewed in 1892 and again, definitively, in 1902 when it is extended to all Orientals).
**1886:** Haymarket Riot; explosion of a bomb during a public meeting in Chicago. Four anarchists hanged without evidence. Creation of the American Federation of Labour (A.F. of L.), a federation of craft unions.
**1887:** The Interstate Commerce Act regulates national transport.
**1890:** McKinley protectionist tariff. Anti-Trust Act of Senator Sherman.
**1892:** Homestead strike in the Carnegie works.
**1894:** Strike in the Pullman factories in Chicago.
**1898:** War against Spain in Cuba and the Philippines; annexation of Hawaii.
**1900:** McKinley assassinated. Theodore Roosevelt President.
**1901:** Currency Act: gold made the sole monetary standard.
**1903:** Revolution in Panama: United States accorded contract for management of a trans-isthmian canal.
**1905:** The appearance of revolutionary syndicalism in the shape of the Industrial Workers of the World (IWW).
**1908:** Appearance of *The Octopus* by Frank Norris, *The Jungle* by Upton Sinclair and *The Iron Heel* by Jack London, all critiques of capitalism.
**1912–20:** Woodrow Wilson President.
**1912–25:** Occupation of Nicaragua.
**1913:** Federal Reserve Act: government control over money supply.
**1914:** US intervention in Mexico.
**1915:** Intervention by the marines and occupation of Haiti.
**1917:** Literacy Test Act: immigrants have to be able to read. 6 April, US declares war on Germany.
**1919:** Volstead Act on the prohibition of alcohol.
**November 1919:** The Senate rejects the Treaty of Versailles.
**1920:** 20th Amendment. Women granted the right to vote. Election of the Republican, W. G. Harding.
**1921 and 1924:** Quota Acts fixing the number of immigrants at 3% of nationals of the same country in the USA in 1910, then at 2% of the 1890 figure.

3. In the streets of New York: barrel organ c. 1910.

# 1865–1920

2. *First view of America.*

**Wilson is elected President.** **USA enters First World War.**

**1912** **1917**

## U.S. expansion in the Pacific and the West Indies

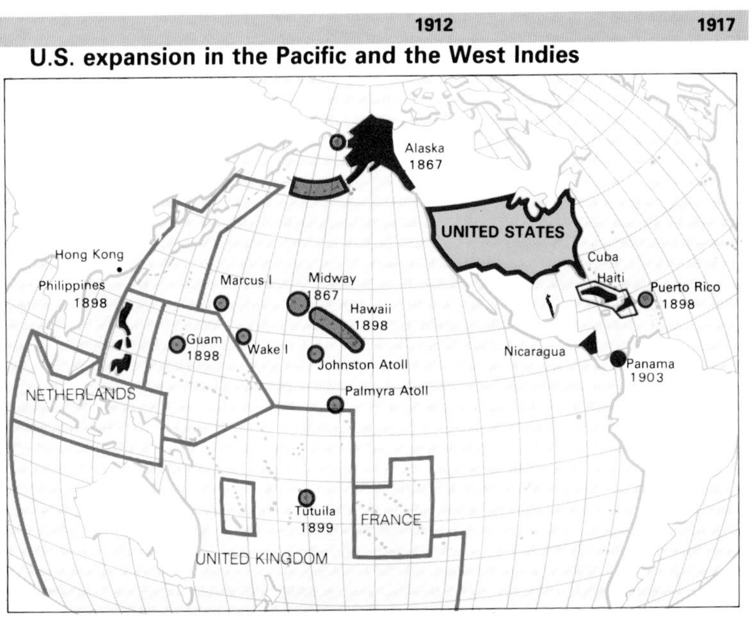

Alaska
1867
UNITED STATES
Hong Kong
Philippines
1898
Marcus I
Midway
1867
Hawaii
1898
Guam
1898
Wake I
Johnston Atoll
Palmyra Atoll
Cuba
Haiti
Puerto Rico
1898
Nicaragua
Panama
1903
NETHERLANDS
Tutuila
1899
FRANCE
UNITED KINGDOM

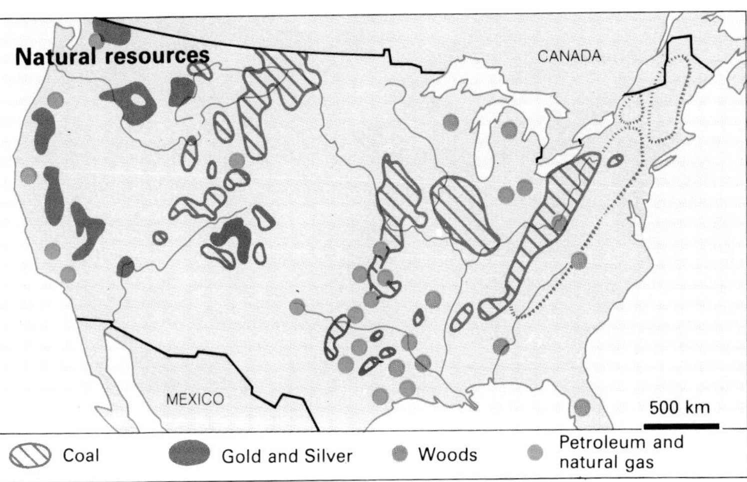

Natural resources
CANADA
MEXICO
500 km
Coal
Gold and Silver
Woods
Petroleum and natural gas

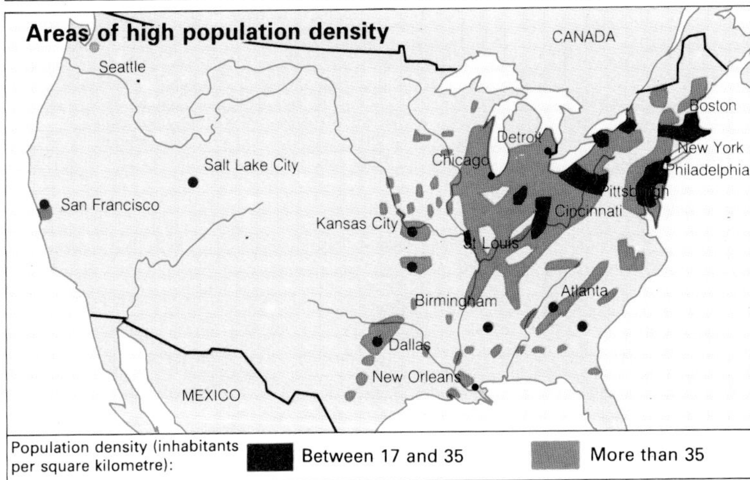

Areas of high population density
CANADA
Seattle
Salt Lake City
San Francisco
Kansas City
Chicago
Detroit
Boston
New York
Philadelphia
Pittsburgh
Cincinnati
St Louis
Birmingham
Atlanta
Dallas
New Orleans
MEXICO
Population density (inhabitants per square kilometre):
Between 17 and 35
More than 35

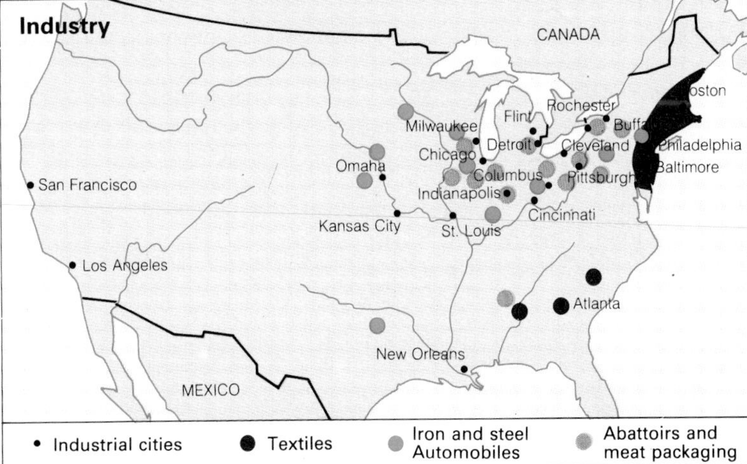

Industry
CANADA
Rochester
Boston
Milwaukee
Flint
Buffalo
Detroit
Chicago
Cleveland
Philadelphia
Omaha
Columbus
Pittsburgh
Baltimore
San Francisco
Indianapolis
Cincinnati
Kansas City
St. Louis
Los Angeles
Atlanta
New Orleans
MEXICO
Industrial cities
Textiles
Iron and steel
Automobiles
Abattoirs and meat packaging

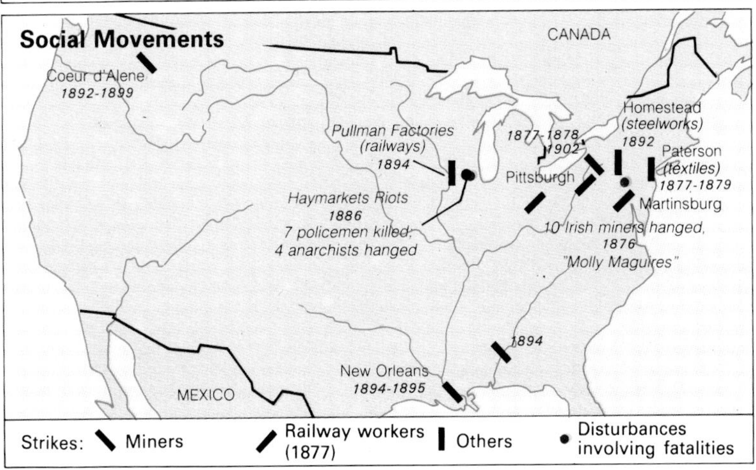

Social Movements
CANADA
Coeur d'Alene
1892-1899
Pullman Factories
(railways)
1894
Homestead
(steelworks)
1892
1877-1878
1902
Paterson
(textiles)
1877-1879
Pittsburgh
Martinsburg
Haymarkets Riots
1886
7 policemen killed,
4 anarchists hanged
10 Irish miners hanged,
1876
"Molly Maguires"
1894
New Orleans
1894-1895
MEXICO
Strikes:
Miners
Railway workers
(1877)
Others
Disturbances
involving fatalities

# The World Market before 1914

1. The New York Stock Exchange in 1899.

THE EXPANSION in international trade prior to 1914 was unprecedented, and developed at a much greater rate than in the succeeding decades of the twentieth century. The volume growth of world trade was 4.6% per annum from 1820 to 1913. Growth slackened somewhat in the years from 1873 to 1896, but picked up very strongly over the last twenty years preceding the War. This was only possible because of the rise in the number of steamships after 1870. The opening of the Suez Canal in 1869 resulted in major changes in commercial shipping routes. Sailing ships were banished from the routes to the Far East. Steam gave a considerable boost to the various Atlantic routes and increased the number of opportunities for new lines in the Pacific.

On the eve of the First World War, international trade was characterized by a dual hegemony: first, that of Europe itself, though it was in slight decline (from 67% in 1876–80 to 62% in 1913), and secondly that of the whole of the 'developed' world (the northwestern countries of Europe, North America and Australia: 63.5% in 1913). Two basic trading patterns, working in tandem, lay behind this twofold superiority. First, there was a 'classic' trading pattern based on the exchange of primary goods (raw materials and foodstuffs) in return for industrial products, which is what made the developed countries into the 'workshops of the world'. Second, there was a more recent trading pattern based on the trade in industrial products between the industrialized countries themselves. These two patterns complemented each other within the multilateral trading network that existed at the outbreak of the War. The industrial success of countries such as Germany, Sweden or the United States, with their efficient exploitation of technical innovations, fostered the development of exports from countries which were producers of primary products and gave them the means to purchase more traditional industrial goods (textiles in particular) which came from Great Britain, Belgium or France. In this way the system maintained its equilibrium in spite of its rapid growth: Great Britain had a trading deficit with continental Europe, the United States and Canada, and a surplus with India, Australia and the colonies in Africa. The equilibrium was restored by the deficit which, in turn, continental Europe and North America had with this third group of countries. Essentially, then, the equilibrium rested on the British trade surplus with the developing world, which reflects the somewhat 'archaic' nature of the structure of the country's exports, as it was also a major importer of German or American industrial goods. It must be said, too, that the British were the only country to maintain free trade in spite of the rising tide of protectionism which, after the great age of the free market in the 1850s and 1860s, spread across the world in the years following 1879, though the extent of European protectionism was much less wide-ranging than that in Russia or America.

International investment increased by a factor of approximately 7.5 times between 1870 and 1914. This was complementary to the growth in trade, as it enabled the development of the infrastructure necessary for the production and transportation of primary products. Great Britain owned 43% of these assets before the outbreak of war, while France had 20%, Germany 13% and the United States already 7%. These investments were traditionally directed towards infrastructure and public works, and towards the modernization of those emerging countries which had for the most part European populations (Russia in the case of France, and the dominions in the case of Britain). The colonies and countries with non-European populations were relatively neglected, but it was also the case, since the 1870s, that industrial investment was made directly by companies, which thus became 'multinational' companies, within the context of the transfer of technology amongst industrialized countries, at the head of which was the United States.

3. The loading of cotton bound for New Orleans on the Mississippi river, as seen by an American newspaper at the end of the nineteenth century.

4. The export of German products. An advertisement for Liebig's meat extract in Britain towards the end of the nineteenth century.

# 19th and 20th centuries

2. Opening of the Suez Canal, 17 November 1869.

*5. The* Frigorifique*, the first cargo-ship able to store food-stuffs by refrigeration. It crossed the Atlantic in 1876.*

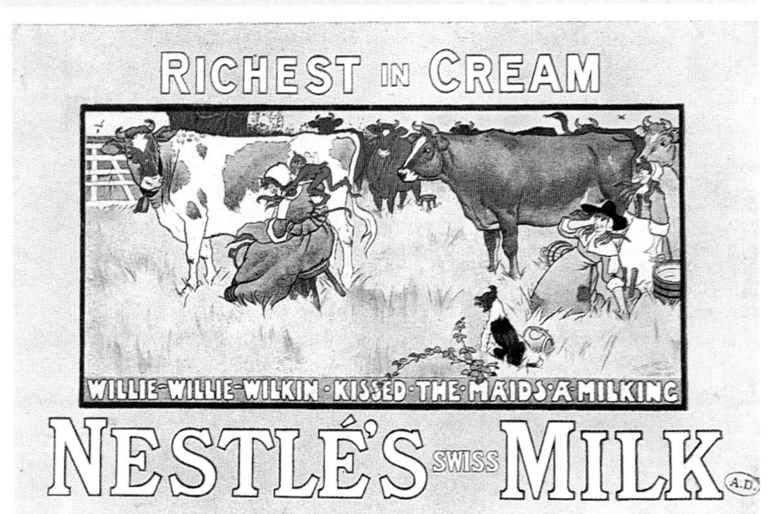

RICHEST IN CREAM
WILLIE-WILLIE-WILKIN-KISSED-THE-MAIDS-A-MILKING
NESTLÉ'S SWISS MILK


*6. The establishment of Swiss companies in Britain: an advertisement for Nestlé's condensed milk.*

# Towards the First World War

After its victory over France in 1871, Germany dominated European diplomacy to such a degree that, when a congress was arranged in 1878 to settle problems in the Balkans it was quite naturally held at Berlin.

Bismarck wished above all to maintain the European balance of power. France, isolated and weakened, was no longer a danger, even if she did experience periodic crises of revanchist nationalism. The major danger to stability lay in the fragility of the two great multinational empires, the Ottoman and the Austro-Hungarian. The Turks still controlled part of the Balkans, which the Austro-Hungarian Empire and Russia harboured designs upon, whilst in Austria-Hungary, the Slavic minorities – discreetly supported by Russia – were demanding independence. By arranging numerous meetings and agreements, Bismarck managed to prevent any direct confrontation between the Austrians and the Russians.

After 1890, William II broke with this prudent policy and openly opted for an alliance with Austria. Russia, which needed French capital to develop its industry, resigned itself to signing a military convention with Paris. Since the 1860s European expansion in Africa and Asia had greatly intensified, though Germany had played no part in it: it was William II's intention to acquire the military and economic means to enable Germany finally to pursue a genuinely global politics. In the Far East, and particularly in China, where they encountered competition from the USA and Japan, the Europeans managed to divide the country up quite comfortably into zones of influence. On the other hand, in the Near East and Africa they came into open confrontation. The reinforcement of the German war fleet and the territorial expansion sought by William II directly threatened Great Britain in Africa – where German possessions were sandwiched between territories under British control – and in the Persian Gulf. Although Germany was its principal trading partner in Europe, Britain accepted a *rapprochement* with France.

Europe found itself split into two coalitions, but the Triple Entente (Great Britain, France, Russia) was weakened by the internal difficulties experienced by Russia and was unable to co-ordinate its plans for military reorganization. William II, aware of the temporary superiority of the Triple Alliance (Germany, Austria-Hungary, Italy), applied increasing pressure. In Morocco, where he wanted to stem the tide of French penetration, he ran into concerted opposition from the other powers, who did not wish to see the African status quo threatened. By contrast, his unconditional support allowed Austria-Hungary to extend its territory and influence in the Balkans.

At the beginning of 1914, the Balkan peninsula constituted the only politically sensitive area in Europe. Russia had only one ally left there, Serbia, to whom she gave wholehearted support. The Austro-Hungarian Empire, encouraged by Bulgaria, was on the lookout for a pretext to remove this final obstacle. Ten years of tension had caused all the powers to reinforce their armed forces considerably, to tolerate fanatical support for war among the public, and to bind themselves by a complex system of accords which, if once triggered, might unleash a chain reaction that would prove irreversible. War was not in sight, but neither of the two coalitions was in a position to halt the mobilization process if it should once be set in motion.

*1. Colonial rivalry between France and Germany. A German cruiser blockades Agadir in the summer of 1911.*

**Wagner's *Ring* cycle performed at Bayreuth.** — **1876**

**Nietzsche's *Genealogy of Morals*.** — **1887**

**Kipling, *The Jungle Book*.** — **1894**

**10 May 1871:** Treaty of Frankfurt. France loses Alsace and part of Lorraine.
**1872:** Alliance between the three Emperors – German, Austrian and Russian – against revolutionary threats of any kind.
**1876–8:** Agitation in the part of the Balkans still under Ottoman rule. Russia goes to war against the Turks and, after her victory, seeks to consolidate her influence in the Balkans. Austria-Hungary and Great Britain displeased. In July 1878, the Congress of Berlin seeks to balance out influence within the Balkan peninsula. Bulgaria becomes independent. Austria-Hungary obtains control over Bosnia-Herzegovina.
**7 October 1879:** Dual alliance between Austria and Germany.
**1882:** Triple Alliance: Austria, Italy and Germany strike military pact.
**1885:** Germany forces recognition of her colonial rights in Africa.
**1887:** French nationalism revived under General Boulanger: tension between France and Germany.
**1889:** First French loan granted to Russia.
**1890:** William II dismisses Bismarck.
**December 1893:** The ratification of a Franco-Russian military agreement establishes a de facto alliance between the two powers.
**1894–5:** Sino-Japanese War. Japan acquires Formosa and protectorate over Korea.
**1898:** Germany, Great Britain, France and Russia come to an accord on the siting of naval bases in China. In the Sudan, French and British troops come face to face at Fashoda. The French troops, led by Marchand, withdraw. Hague Conference to restrain the arms race. The International Court will be founded two years later.
**1899–1902:** The Transvaal, the richest independent state in South Africa, refuses to submit to British influence. Great Britain subjugates it by force.
**1900:** Nationalist rising in China (Boxers), crushed by an international expeditionary force. The Ottoman Empire concedes to Germany the right to build a railway from Berlin to the Persian Gulf.
**1904–5:** Russo-Japanese War for control of Manchuria: the Japanese are victorious.
**8 April 1904:** Entente Cordiale: colonial agreement between Britain and France marks beginnings of a *rapprochement*.
**9 Jan 1905:** Revolution in Russia.
**1908:** Austria-Hungary annexes Bosnia-Herzegovina.

*4. Setbacks to Britain's imperial rule: the revolt of the Boers in the Transvaal and of the Boxers in China.*

**1912:** Balkan states fight victorious war against the Ottoman Empire.
**10 August 1913:** Treaty of Bucharest confirms Turkish withdrawal from the Balkans. Serbia fails to acquire access to the coast.
**1914. 28 June:** Assassination of an Austrian Archduke at Sarajevo in Bosnia. Austria-Hungary holds Serbia responsible. William II promises his support to the Austro-Hungarians in case of war.
**28 July:** Austria-Hungary declares war on Serbia.
**1st August:** Germany declares war on Russia.
**3rd August:** Germany declares war on France and enters Belgium.
**4th August:** Great Britain declares war on Germany.

# 1871–1914

2. Fashoda: the English wolf and the French Little Red Riding Hood, as seen by a German cartoonist.

3. Beginnings of the Entente Cordiale. Edward VII visits Paris, May 1903.

**Herzl, *The Jewish State.* Romain Roland's *Jean-Christophe*.**

**895** **1904–12**

5. Franco-Russian rapprochement. The French fleet putting in at Kronstadt, July 1891.

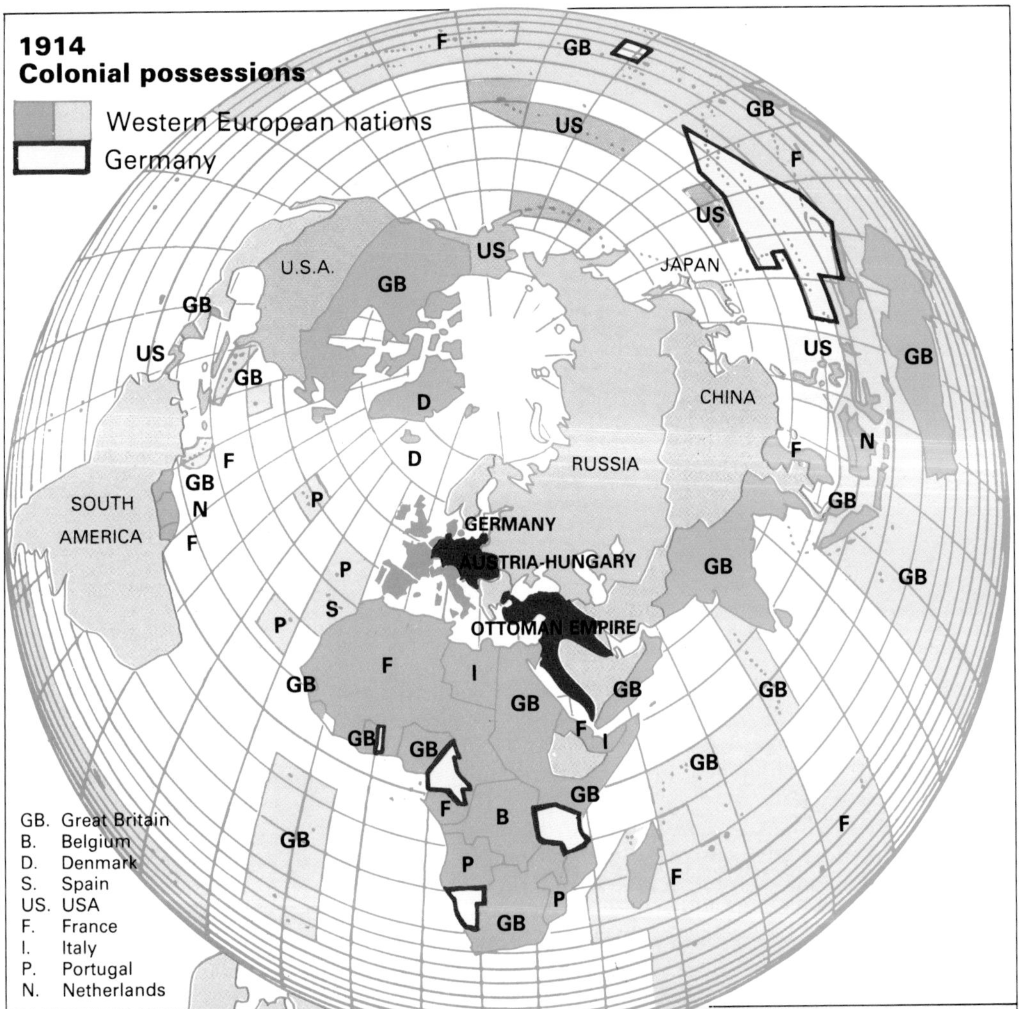

**1914**
**Colonial possessions**

Western European nations
Germany

GB. Great Britain
B. Belgium
D. Denmark
S. Spain
US. USA
F. France
I. Italy
P. Portugal
N. Netherlands

U.S.A.
SOUTH AMERICA
RUSSIA
JAPAN
CHINA
GERMANY
AUSTRIA-HUNGARY
OTTOMAN EMPIRE

**Conflicts in Europe**

Ottoman Empire in 1815
Balkan wars
Disputes and territorial claims

DENMARK
Schleswig-Holstein
Berlin
GERMANY
POLAND
BELGIUM
Eupen
Malmedy
Paris
FRANCE
Alsace Lorraine
AUSTRIA-HUNGARY
Vienna
Budapest
RUSSIA
Odessa
Trentino
RUMANIA
1908
Sarajevo
BOSNIA-HERZEGOVINA
SERBIA
BULGARIA
MONTENEGRO
Constantinople
ITALY
Rome
ALBANIA
Macedonia
OTTOMAN EMPIRE
GREECE
F. 1830
1912
Dodecanese
Cyprus
GB. 1878
ALGERIA
I. 1912
I. 1912
Crete
500 km
LIBYA
EGYPT

# The Great War in the West

1. The Chemin des Dames disaster, after the failure of the French offensive in April 1917, depicted by François Flameng.

2. 'Down with war!': anti-militarist poster before Italian intervention in 1915.

BETWEEN 1914 AND 1918 the high commands of both sides switched repeatedly between the strong point strategy – which consisted of attacking the enemy in an effort to break his resistance – and the weak point strategy, which aimed to disorganize him and reduce the number of his allies.

In 1914 the Germans attacked at the strong point in the west: this was the Schlieffen plan, which sought to encircle and destroy the British and French armies by an attack from the west. They failed in this, however, Joffre halting them on the Marne. Simultaneously, the Russians attacked at Gumbinnen, but the Germans repulsed them and Hindenburg was victorious at Tannenberg. Each side's powerful hammer blows, struck at the principal enemy's strongest point, proved costly and ineffective. No decisive victory was possible; in fact, they merely produced a general paralysis of fronts (the trenches). In 1915 both the Allied offensives in Champagne and Artois and the German and Austrian attacks in Poland came to nothing.

Given these conditions, it is not surprising that the protagonists thought up another strategy which aimed at the weak point in the enemy coalition. However, did the Allies really have to mount a massed attack on the Turks in the Dardanelles, while the enemy was camped at the gates of Noyon? And, in the opposing camp, was it really necessary for the Germans and Austrians to pursue the Serbs with such ferocity or seek to punish the Italians who had changed sides, at a point when the Cossacks were able at a stroke to reach the Hungarian frontier? In 1916 it was back once again to the strong point strategy, but neither at Verdun nor on the Somme nor in the east, nor for that matter on the Isonzo or at Asiago did anything decisive occur. It was the same in 1917 when even the Chemin des Dames or Passchendaele hardly changed the respective armies' positions and even the Russian Revolution left things unchanged in the east.

The war then took on a global dimension as the British mounted offensives in Egypt, Iraq and elsewhere in the Arab world, and as first Japan, then China entered the war and, even more importantly, as submarine warfare brought America into the conflict.

In Europe, the strong point strategy produced another failure for the Germans on the Marne. It was at its weakest points that the Central Powers' alliance was to fall apart, in spite of the Russian armistice. These were the Bulgarian and Turkish fronts. At the same time the Italians gained revenge for Caporetto at Vittoria Veneto and the massive arrival of the Americans showed the Germans that they could no longer hope to turn the situation in their favour. The first armistices were signed at the end of October and in November 1918.

**Sinking of the *Lusitania*.** — **7 May 1915**

**Year of Verdun** — **1916**

**V. Blasco Ibanez: *The Four Horsemen of the Apocalypse*** — **1916**

3. British militarist poster, 1914.

**1914. 4 August:** The Germans advance on Paris by way of Belgium.
***19 August:** Russian offensive aimed at relieving the French front.
**26–30 August:** German counter-offensive; Russian defeat at Tannenberg.
**6–12 September:** The Germans, halted on the Marne, withdraw to the Aisne.
**10 October–10 November:** The Germans and the Anglo-French seek to outflank each other on the west ('The race for the sea'). The front settles down on a line running through Ypres, Soissons, Reims and Verdun.
**5 November:** The Allies declare war on Turkey.
**1915. February:** German offensive; Russians defeated at Masurian Lakes.
**24 April:** Allies land in the Dardanelles.
**24 May:** Italy enters the war against Austria.
**August:** Austro-German offensive; Russians lose whole of Poland.
**October:** Austro-Bulgarian offensive against Serbia; fall of Belgrade (9 October).

**Dates relating to Russia given according to the Gregorian Calendar adopted in January 1918.*

**1916. 9 January:** Allies evacuate the Dardanelles.
**21 February:** Verdun offensive. German gains.
**June–August:** Russian offensive against Austria, repulsed with very heavy losses. Russian Army begins to break up.
**24 June:** Franco-British offensive on the Somme. Attempt to make a breakthrough thwarted.
**27 August:** Rumania declares war on Austria and Italy enters the war against Germany. Austrian offensive: fall of Bucharest.
**October–December:** French regain the positions captured by the Germans around Verdun. End of the Battle of Verdun.
**1917. 1 February:** Germany announces unrestricted naval warfare.
**12 March:** February Revolution in Russia. End of Tsarism. Provisional government promises to fight with Allied cause.
**6 April:** USA declares war on Germany.
**16 April–17 May:** French offensive between Soissons and Laon. German front holds fast.
**May–June:** Mutinies in the French Army.
**July:** Russian offensive. Total failure.
**7 November:** October Revolution in Russia.
**1918. 3 March:** Russia signs separate peace treaties with the Central Powers.
**May:** Germans break through Allied lines and reach the Marne.
**18 July–3 August:** Second Battle of the Marne; Germans are fought back.
**14 October:** Independence of Czechoslovakia: proclamation of union of Serbs, Croats and Slovenes; 24 October: secession of Hungary.
**27 October:** Italian victory at Vittorio Veneto.
**3 November:** Austro-Italian Armistice.
**11 November:** Armistice signed at Rethondes between the Allies and Germany.

# 1914–18

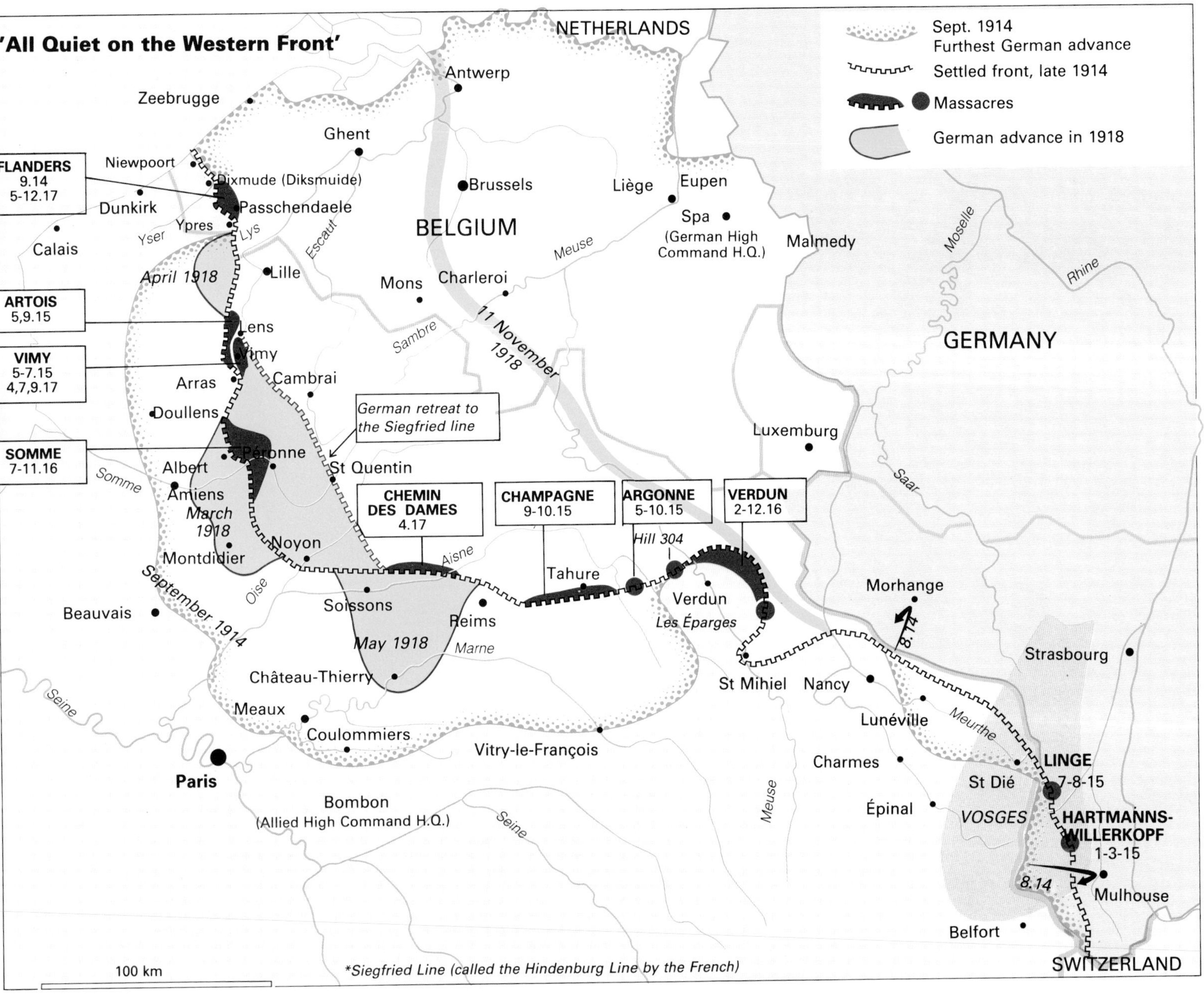

## 'All Quiet on the Western Front'

Sept. 1914
Furthest German advance
Settled front, late 1914
Massacres
German advance in 1918

FLANDERS 9.14 5-12.17
ARTOIS 5,9.15
VIMY 5-7.15 4,7,9.17
SOMME 7-11.16
CHEMIN DES DAMES 4.17
CHAMPAGNE 9-10.15
ARGONNE 5-10.15
VERDUN 2-12.16
LINGE 7-8-15
HARTMANNS-WILLERKOPF 1-3-15

German retreat to the Siegfried line

NETHERLANDS
BELGIUM
GERMANY
SWITZERLAND

Zeebrugge
Antwerp
Ghent
Niewpoort
Dixmude (Diksmuide)
Passchendaele
Dunkirk
Ypres
Calais
Brussels
Liège
Eupen
Spa (German High Command H.Q.)
Malmedy
Lille
Mons
Charleroi
Lens
Vimy
Arras
Cambrai
Doullens
Péronne
Albert
St Quentin
Amiens
Montdidier
Noyon
Soissons
Reims
Tahure
Hill 304
Verdun
Les Éparges
Luxemburg
Morhange
Strasbourg
St Mihiel
Nancy
Lunéville
Charmes
St Dié
Épinal
VOSGES
Mulhouse
Belfort
Beauvais
Château-Thierry
Meaux
Coulommiers
Vitry-le-François
Paris
Bombon (Allied High Command H.Q.)

April 1918
March 1918
May 1918
September 1914
11 November 1918
8.14

Yser
Lys
Escaut
Meuse
Sambre
Somme
Oise
Aisne
Marne
Seine
Moselle
Rhine
Saar
Meurthe

100 km

*Siegfried Line (called the Hindenburg Line by the French)

**L. Pirandello:** ***Ciascuno a suo modo.***

**1917**

**Death of Wilfred Owen.**

**4 November 1918**

**Death of Guillaume Apollinaire.**

**9 November 1918**

*4. French soldiers in the trenches, Verdun front, 1917.*

*5. Death of Baron Manfred von Richtofen, the German fighter ace, shot down near Corbie, 21 April 1918. Painted by an Allied soldier.*

# The Great War in the East and Across the World

*1. In the British rear: nationalist insurrection in Ireland. The Dublin General Post Office after the Easter Rising of 1916.*

During the Great War both sides employed strategies designed to disrupt or to stifle the other's efforts. Of these methods, the most widely employed was that of seeking to break up the opposing coalition. The main thrust of the Central Powers' policy consisted in an attempt to provoke non-Russian nationalities to revolt against the Tsarist empire. To this end, they published a Bulletin of the Nationalities of Russia, formed a Finnish legion and proclaimed the independence of Poland (in 1916). No one was deceived by these actions, but they nonetheless represented a blow against the Entente. Against Great Britain, the Germans lent support to the Irish nationalists, precipitating the 'Easter Rising' of 1916. In Belgium, Germany sought to weaken the Allied coalition by reawakening the ideal of Flemish nationhood: they even went so far as to form a National Council of Flanders. Lastly, the Austrians and the Germans attempted to provoke holy wars within their enemies' empires and, in Libya at least, they succeeded in fomenting a revolt against the Italians. They also lent aid to the Boer, St Moritz, who had hopes of regaining independence for his country. For their part, the Allies also acted in an indirect fashion against Hapsburg domination in Central Europe, promising independence, if they were victorious, to the oppressed nationalities (Croats, Slovenes, Czechs and Slovaks etc.). The only practical result of this policy was one massive desertion, that of the 29th Regiment of Prague, but it nevertheless weakened the morale and the cohesion of the Central Powers. The same policy produced more tangible effects in the Ottoman Empire, where the hopes raised in Armenia by the advance of the Russians led to the collective deportations and massacres of 1915, in which over a million people were killed. By contrast, the rising of the Arabs, aided by Colonel T. E. Lawrence, had positive effects for the insurgents, who entered Damascus alongside the British and reconstituted a nation that had been lost for several centuries.

To this general strategy of undermining the enemy's unity, we may add a second strategy, the attempt to suffocate him. From 1914 onwards the Allies sought to ruin the Central Powers' seaborne trade, thus destroying the foundations of their economy and provoking a crisis by creating shortages. The historical example set by Napoleon helped to revive the idea of blockade. When there seemed some danger that this strategy might have fatal consequences, the Austrians and the Germans responded with submarine warfare, which became rife after 1917. Instead of causing the Allies to throw in their hand and terrorizing the neutrals, this counter-attack merely stimulated the Allied naval effort and provoked US entry into the war.

These economic measures certainly had effects, but they are difficult to evaluate. No break-up of alliances occurred, and the war was won by military rather than economic means. Germany was able to offset the effects of the blockade for a long period, mainly because Great Britain, which believed its chances of victory would be improved by increasing its wealth, carried on 'business as usual' with the Germans through the neutral countries and also because Germany mobilized and rationalized its economy more quickly than the other belligerents. Through its attempts to imitate the German practice in this latter respect, the Russian economy deteriorated, and the resulting shortages were a major cause of the February 1917 revolution. The negative effects produced by submarine warfare had one essential consequence: the part played by US supplies and the arrival of a large contingent of American fighting men contributed to the Central Powers' demoralization and hastened their capitulation.

**Russians crushed at Tannenberg.**

**26 August 1914**

**The Germans take Warsaw.**

**5 August 1915**

**Freud, *Introductory Lectures on Psychoanalysis*; H. Barbusse, *Le Feu.***

**1916**

**1914. 25 August:** Allies establish blockade of Germany.
**December:** At Mecca, Arabs proclaim a holy war against the Sultan.
**8 December:** German naval defeat off the Falkland Islands.
**1915. January:** German zeppelins overfly London.
**18 March:** The Allies guarantee the Russians control of the Black Sea Straits.
**22 April:** First use of poison gas by the Germans.
**22 May:** Germany extends its submarine campaign to include merchant ships.
**July–August:** Massacres in Armenia.
**6 August:** Allies define their war aims at Chantilly: Alsace-Lorraine to be returned to France, German colonies to be divided up among the Allies with Britain as the principal beneficiary.
**1916. April:** Nationalist insurrection in Ireland – the 'Easter Rising' – repressed by the British.
**June:** The smaller nationalities meet at Lausanne.
**6 June:** Allies blockade the coasts of Greece.
**30 August:** Venizélos instals a government in Salonica.
**26 December:** The German government declares its willingness to participate in a peace conference.
**1917. 10 January:** Allies announce their war aims: restoration of Alsace-Lorraine to France, Belgian and Serbian sovereignty to be restored; principle of nationalities to be applied to all minorities.
**29 January:** Indirect response from Germany, which accepts modifications to its frontiers in favour of France and the establishment of an independent Poland under German influence.
**1 February:** Germany declares unrestricted submarine warfare.
**16 April:** Return to Russia of Lenin, whom the Germans have allowed through in the hope that he will hasten the onset of negotiations between Russia and the Central Powers.
**18 May:** Opening of a socialist conference at Stockholm which debates ways of bringing the war to an end.
**Spring–Summer:** British offensive in the Near East. Occupation of Baghdad.
**June:** Under Allied pressure, King Constantine of Greece, who is sympathetic to the Central Powers, is forced to abdicate. The new government declares war on Germany.
**22 December:** Beginning of peace negotiations between Russia and the Central Powers.
**1918:** American President Wilson defines the conditions for a durable peace, the Fourteen Points, which have to do mainly with the principle of nationalities.
**3 March:** Brest-Litovsk treaty between Russia and Central Powers: Russia accepts great territorial losses.
**11 November:** Armistice signed at Rethondes on the basis of Wilson's Fourteen Points.

*4. A scene from the British conquest of Palestine: Field-Marshal Edmund Allenby enters Jerusalem.*

# 1914–18

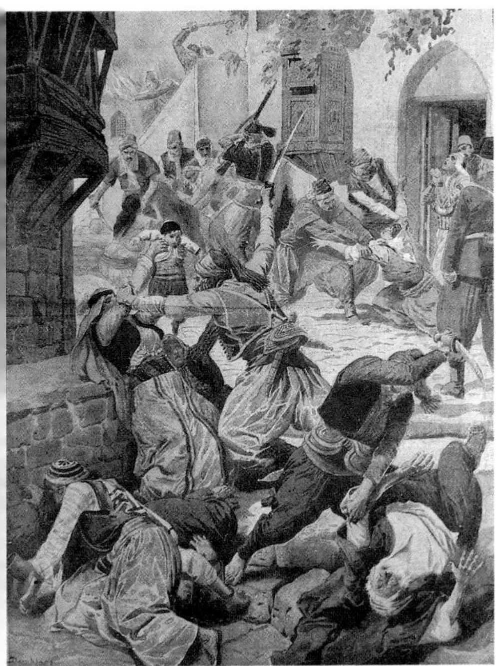

2. The Armenian massacres of 1915, as depicted in the French Petit Journal.

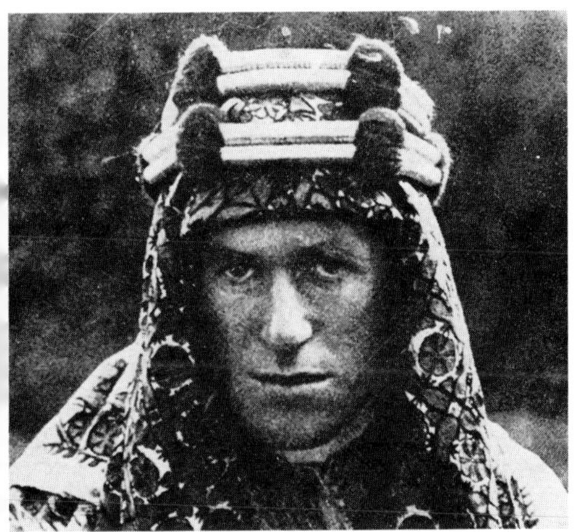

3. Colonel Thomas Edward Lawrence – 'Lawrence of Arabia' – at the head of troops allied to Great Britain in 1917.

**Ernst Jünger, *The Storm of Steel.***

20

Der „U“-Boot Krieg
Die durchschnittliche Monats-Leistung im 1. Halbjahr 1918
270000 Tonnen
630000 Tonnen
Gesamtneubau
160000 T
225000
275000
270000
630000

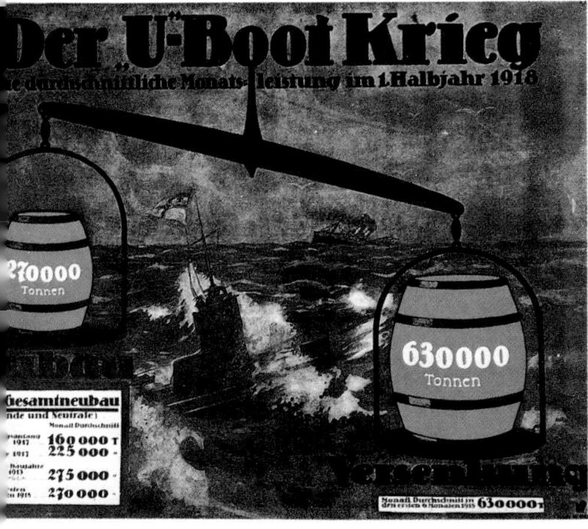

5. Submarine warfare, as seen by German propaganda in the early months of 1918.

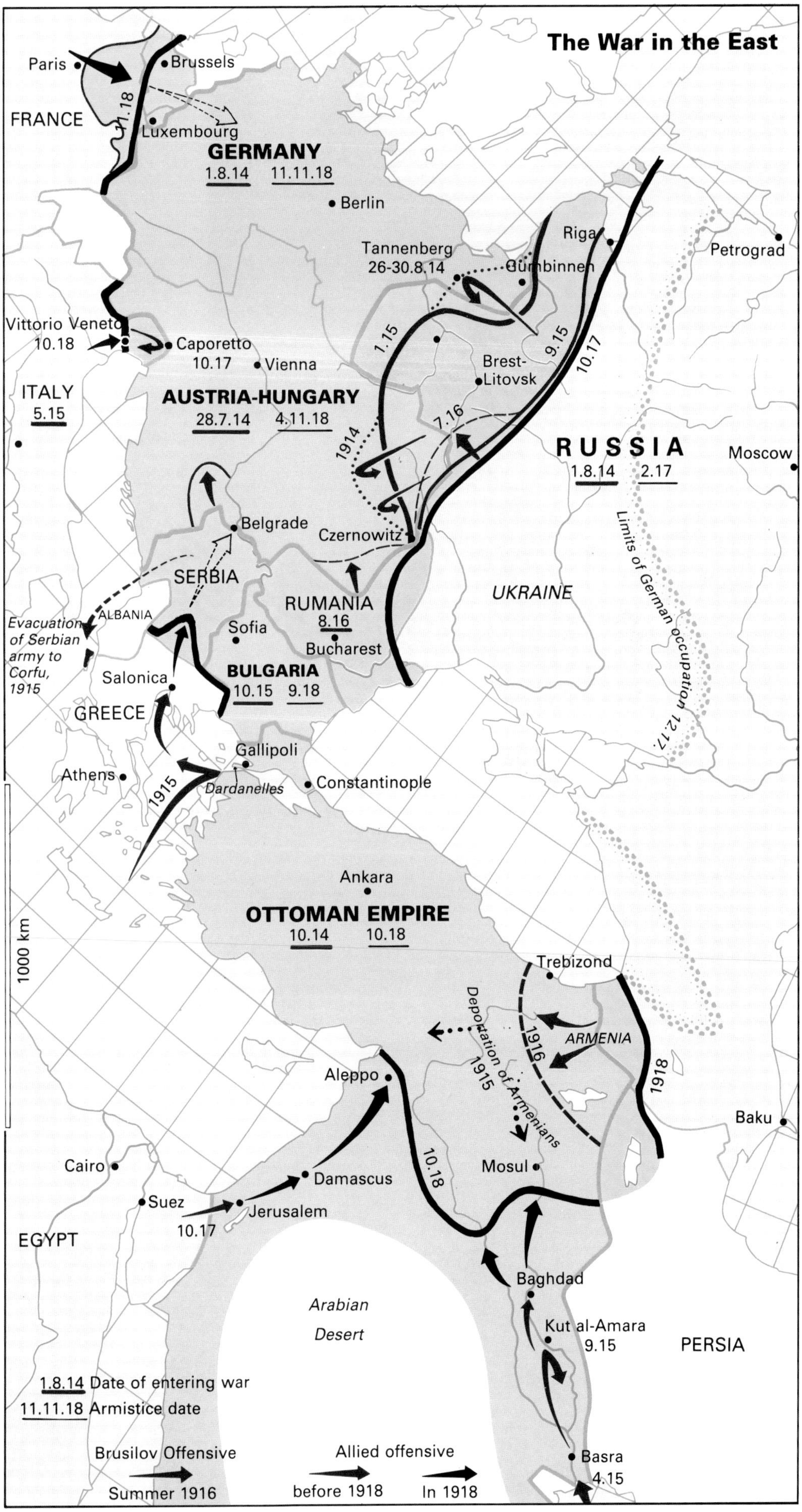

The War in the East
Paris
Brussels
FRANCE
11.18
Luxembourg
GERMANY
1.8.14 11.11.18
Berlin
Tannenberg
26-30.8.14
Gumbinnen
Riga
Petrograd
Vittorio Veneto
10.18
Caporetto
10.17
Vienna
1.15
Brest-Litovsk
9.15
10.17
ITALY
5.15
AUSTRIA-HUNGARY
28.7.14 4.11.18
7.16
1914
RUSSIA
1.8.14 2.17
Moscow
Belgrade
Czernowitz
SERBIA
Limits of German occupation 12.17
UKRAINE
RUMANIA
8.16
ALBANIA
Evacuation of Serbian army to Corfu, 1915
Sofia
Bucharest
Salonica
BULGARIA
10.15 9.18
GREECE
Gallipoli
Athens
1915
Dardanelles
Constantinople
1000 km
Ankara
OTTOMAN EMPIRE
10.14 10.18
Trebizond
Deportation of Armenians 1915
1916
ARMENIA
Aleppo
1918
Baku
10.18
Cairo
Damascus
Mosul
Suez
10.17
Jerusalem
EGYPT
Baghdad
Arabian Desert
Kut al-Amara
9.15
PERSIA
1.8.14 Date of entering war
11.11.18 Armistice date
Brusilov Offensive
Summer 1916
Allied offensive
before 1918
In 1918
Basra
4.15

# Revolution and Civil War in Russia

1. From left to right: Stalin, Lenin and Kalinin in February 1918.

2. Russian poster caricaturing the enemies of the revolution, 1917.

MILITARY DEFEATS, shortages and the hatred of autocracy constituted an explosive mixture, which, within five days in Petrograd, sealed the triumph of the revolution and the abdication of Nicholas II. A Soviet of Workers and Soldiers' Deputies was constituted which shared power with a provisional government made up of former Duma representatives. A. Kerensky was the living embodiment of the alliance between the 'bourgeois' and 'proletarian' revolutions. The new regime, which was incapable of winning the war and yet unable to put an end to it, and unable also to carry through the reforms which would have transformed the social order, found itself up against opposition from, on the one hand, the factory and soldiers' committees headed by Bolsheviks or anarchists and, on the other, that of the military high command and the big industrial bourgeoisie, who were intransigent in their resistance to the reforms desired by the socialists in the Provisional Government and the Soviets. The Mensheviks and Socialist-Revolutionaries were, as it turned out in any case, soon to lose their majority in these assemblies.

This situation explains why, after General Kornilov's failed *putsch*, the Soviets and workers' and soldiers' committees – led by the Bolsheviks under Lenin's guidance – were easily able to overthrow the Provisional Government in the October rising.

Subsequently, Lenin and Trotsky concluded the Treaty of Brest-Litovsk, which detached the Baltic states, Poland and part of the Ukraine from the old empire. At the same time the Bolsheviks, by dissolving the Constituent Assembly where they were in a minority, incited opposition from the other socialists and democrats, whilst the White generals raised the standard of rebellion in the south and, not long afterwards, in Siberia. The Allied powers gave assistance to the (White) volunteer army and landed British and Canadian troops at Archangel, Japanese and later American troops at Vladivostock and French troops at Odessa who, though they were still nominally at war, joined up with German forces in the Ukraine even before 11 November 1918. This foreign intervention discredited the White forces and contributed to the defeat of Denikin, Kolchak and Wrangel.

The revolution, which was for Russia a political and social phenomenon, seemed a good opportunity for the other nations of the old empire to recapture their freedom, an impression reinforced by the Bolsheviks' declaration of the peoples' right to self-determination. However, once the revolution was accomplished, it was pointed out that 'the right to divorce did not mean the necessity of divorce'. Lenin and Stalin accordingly broke up the nationalist movements in Georgia, the Ukraine, the Tartar regions and in Armenia (after they had saved the Armenians from being massacred by the Turks). At the end of the war and the civil war, only the Baltic states, Poland and Finland had succeeded in preserving their independence.

**V. Mayakovsky, *Man*.**

**In Finland, Lenin writes *The State and Revolution*.**

**Dissolution of the Constituent Assembly by the Bolsheviks.**

**1916** — **August 1917** — **6 January 1918**

***1917. 8 March:** Strikes begin in Petrograd: the situation gets out of the government's control.
**9 March:** Constitution of a Provisional Government with the support of the elected assembly (Duma). The soviet and government were to find themselves in competition.
**12 March:** Constitution of a Soviet (Council) of Worker and Soldier Representatives.
**16 April:** Return of Lenin, who takes over as leader of the most hard-line faction (Bolsheviks) of the Russian Workers' Social Democratic Party.
**17 April:** Lenin publishes his *April Theses*: calling for an immediate peace treaty, establishment of a republic of Soviets.
**16 June:** All Russia Congress of Soviets.
**July:** Provisional Government launches an offensive against the Germans; it is a total failure and a complete break-up of the army ensues.

*Dates are from the Gregorian Calendar.

**September:** Attempted counter-revolutionary *putsch*. The Provisional Government has to call on the Soviets to overcome it.
**6–7 November:** Bolshevik insurrection. Dissolution of the Provisional Government.

3. Kerensky, as a minister in the Provisional Government in March 1917.

4. Assault on the Winter Palace in Petrograd (today Leningrad) by the Bolsheviks, November 1917.

# 1917–21

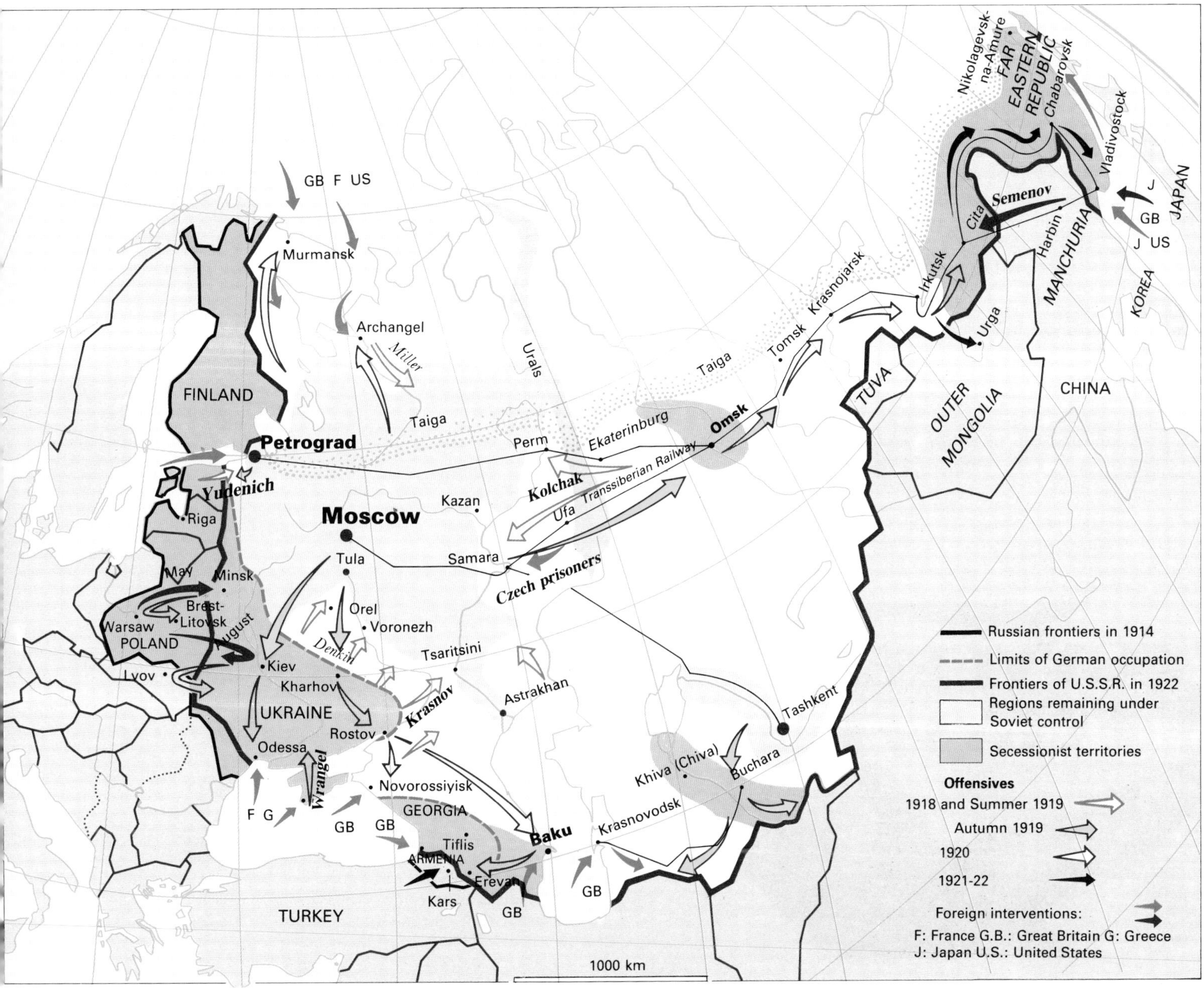

Russian frontiers in 1914
Limits of German occupation
Frontiers of U.S.S.R. in 1922
Regions remaining under Soviet control
Secessionist territories

**Offensives**
1918 and Summer 1919
Autumn 1919
1920
1921-22
Foreign interventions:
F: France G.B.: Great Britain G: Greece
J: Japan U.S.: United States

1000 km

**A. Kollontai, *Communism and the Family.***

**L. Trotsky, *Terrorism and Communism.***

1919 1920

**8 November:** Constitution of a Council of People's Commissars presided over by Lenin, who will exercise executive power. Confiscation of the large domains; end of war announced.
**1918. 6 January:** An elected Constituent Assembly meets. The Bolsheviks, who are in the minority, disperse it.
**15 January:** Creation of the Red Army based on the principle of voluntary service and the election of officers. These principles will not survive the pressures of the Civil War.
**3 March:** Treaty of Brest-Litovsk with the Central Powers: Russia cedes the Baltic provinces, its part of Poland and its protectorate over Finland.
**March–April:** The Allies land an anti-Bolshevik expeditionary corps at Murmansk.
**1919. 2 March:** Foundation of the Communist International (Comintern).
**May–September:** Counter-revolutionary offensive (supported by the Allies) against Petrograd and Moscow and on the Volga. In August, the victory of the Bolsheviks on the Volga marks the collapse of the counter-revolution.
**1920. July:** 2nd Comintern Congress. 21 points adopted which lay down strict conditions of membership for Communist parties.
**September:** Baku Congress for the liberation of the Eastern Peoples. Definition of a strategy to mobilize the East against the West.
**November:** The last Allied troops withdraw.
**1921. February:** Demonstrations by workers at Petrograd. Revolt of Bolshevik sailors at Kronstadt. The two movements are repressed.
**17 March:** The Congress of the Bolshevik party adopts a New Economic Policy (N.E.P.) tolerating private property and trade on a capitalist basis.
**18 March:** Treaty defining frontiers with Poland: commercial accord with Great Britain.

*5. The cruiser,* Aurora, *the sentinel of the revolution, on the Neva, October 1917.*

# The Aftermath of the First World War

Signed after months of laborious negotiation, the treaties that are given the name 'Treaty of Versailles' were almost immediately contested and were to end up being repudiated within two decades. Four of the principles which were invoked at Versailles explain this failure.

The first of these was the principle of nationalities. For centuries, within the Austrian, Russian and Ottoman Empires there had been oppressed minority groups labouring under the rule of a dominant community, which accorded them only minimal guarantees. In the nineteenth century these groups sought to emancipate themselves. During the war, the Western Allies took up their cause again, hoping thereby to weaken the Central Powers. However, within the Empires the minorities were intermingled; in fact it proved impossible to draw up political frontiers that were also linguistic ones. In only one case was the problem resolved by a massive population transfer: 400,000 Turks moved from Macedonia into Turkey and 1,300,000 Greeks were shipped from Asia Minor to Greece. This did not, however, diminish the hostility the two nations felt towards each other. Elsewhere, the minorities remained in their original homes. A large German population that had settled in the outer reaches of Bohemia became Czech; another group of Germans found themselves included in Poland, and in this case the problem was complicated by the granting of the port of Danzig, which had a mainly German population, to Poland. Paradoxically, the Treaty of Versailles would provide Hitler with one of his most effective propaganda themes.

To this thorny question of nationalities was added the problem of non-European territories. German colonies and the non-Turkish territories of the Ottoman Empire were divided up (in the form of colonies or mandates) between the victors. From this time onwards, the Middle East became a source of permanent difficulty for Britain and France.

The third problematic clause in the Versailles Treaty was the one dealing with Germany. Being judged responsible for the war, she was disarmed and condemned to pay reparations. A series of convoluted plans for paying reparations over half a century were devised and then abandoned. Germany, whose territory the Allies had not even reached at the signing of the Armistice in 1918 (the fighting took place on French soil), was still regarded, a decade after the Treaty, as the guilty party. The rejection of the Versailles *diktat* was to be the Nazi's first priority.

The final source of tension was the fact that no one was able to ensure that the new territorial divisions and the payment of reparations were respected. The United States immediately refused to ratify the Treaty. The League of Nations – a sort of world parliament – was not provided with any means of external action. As early as 1920, the Turks rebelled against their treaty (the Treaty of Sèvres), forcing its revision in the Treaty of Lausanne.

Between 1935 and the outbreak of war, Hitler's initiatives would be aimed at simply abolishing the Treaty (reintroduction of military service, remilitarization of the left bank of the Rhine, *Anschluss*, annexation of the German border region of Bohemia, claim upon the Polish corridor). It was the spirit of Versailles the Nazis sought to erase.

*2. The surviving orphans arriving in Greece in 1922, after the Turkish massacres of Greeks and Armenians.*

*1. 'To arms! To arms!': poster by R. Berény, for the Budapest Commune in 1919.*

**1920** Charlie Chaplin, ***The Kid.***

**1925** Eisenstein, ***Battleship Potemkin.*** Hitler, ***Mein Kampf.***

**1929** E. M. Remarque, ***All Quiet on the Western Front.*** E. Hemingway, ***A Farewell to Arms.***

*5. Rosa Luxemburg, the revolutionary whose life took her from a Jewish community in Poland to the Berlin uprising of 1919.*

**1919. 18 January:** Peace negotiations open in Paris.
**16 June:** Allied ultimatum demands Germany signs treaty.
**28 June:** Signature of the Treaty of Versailles. Germany loses Alsace-Lorraine to France and cedes Western Prussia to Poland: she accepts the existence of a 'corridor' across her territory that will give Poland access to the port of Danzig. She loses her colonies. Her army is limited to 100,000 men; the left bank of the Rhine is demilitarized. Germany acknowledges its responsibility for starting the war and undertakes to pay reparations.
**10 September:** Treaty of St. Germain-en-Laye. Austria, limited to its German-speaking territories, will not be allowed to unite with Germany.
**27 November:** Treaty of Neuilly. Bulgaria cedes Thrace to Greece and loses all access to the sea.
**1920. 4 June:** Trianon Treaty. Hungary is reduced to Magyar territory.
**10 August:** Treaty of Sèvres. Turkey loses its non-Turkish territories: the Straits and the Mediterranean coast of Asia Minor are occupied by the European powers. The Turkish national assembly refuses to ratify the treaty. A section of the army led by Mustafa Kemal decides to resist and the Greeks, given the task of implementing the treaty are defeated by the Turkish Army.
**25 August 1921:** After the rejection of the Versailles Treaty by the American Senate, the U.S. signs a separate pact with Germany. They neither recognize the League of Nations nor German reparations.
**1923. 11 January:** Because Germany fails to make its reparations payments, France and Belgium occupy the Rhineland. This action is fiercely criticized in Europe and the USA.
**24 July:** Treaty of Lausanne: Turkish sovereignty over whole of Asia Minor and the western region around Istanbul recognised.
**1924:** After American mediation, the Dawes Plan sets a total figure for German reparations payments and states how they are to be broken down.
**16 October 1925:** Locarno Pact: Germany guarantees French and Belgian frontiers, but refuses to give any commitment on its Eastern frontiers.
**1929:** Germany requests a re-scheduling of its debt, a revision of the Treaty which provides for payments until 1988.
**1932:** Lausanne Conference: reparations finally abandoned.
**14 October 1933:** Disarmament Conference. Germany, unable to obtain parity with other powers, leaves the conference and withdraws from the League of Nations.
**16 March 1935:** Re-introduction of compulsory military service in Germany – first open violation of the Treaty of Versailles.

# 1919–35

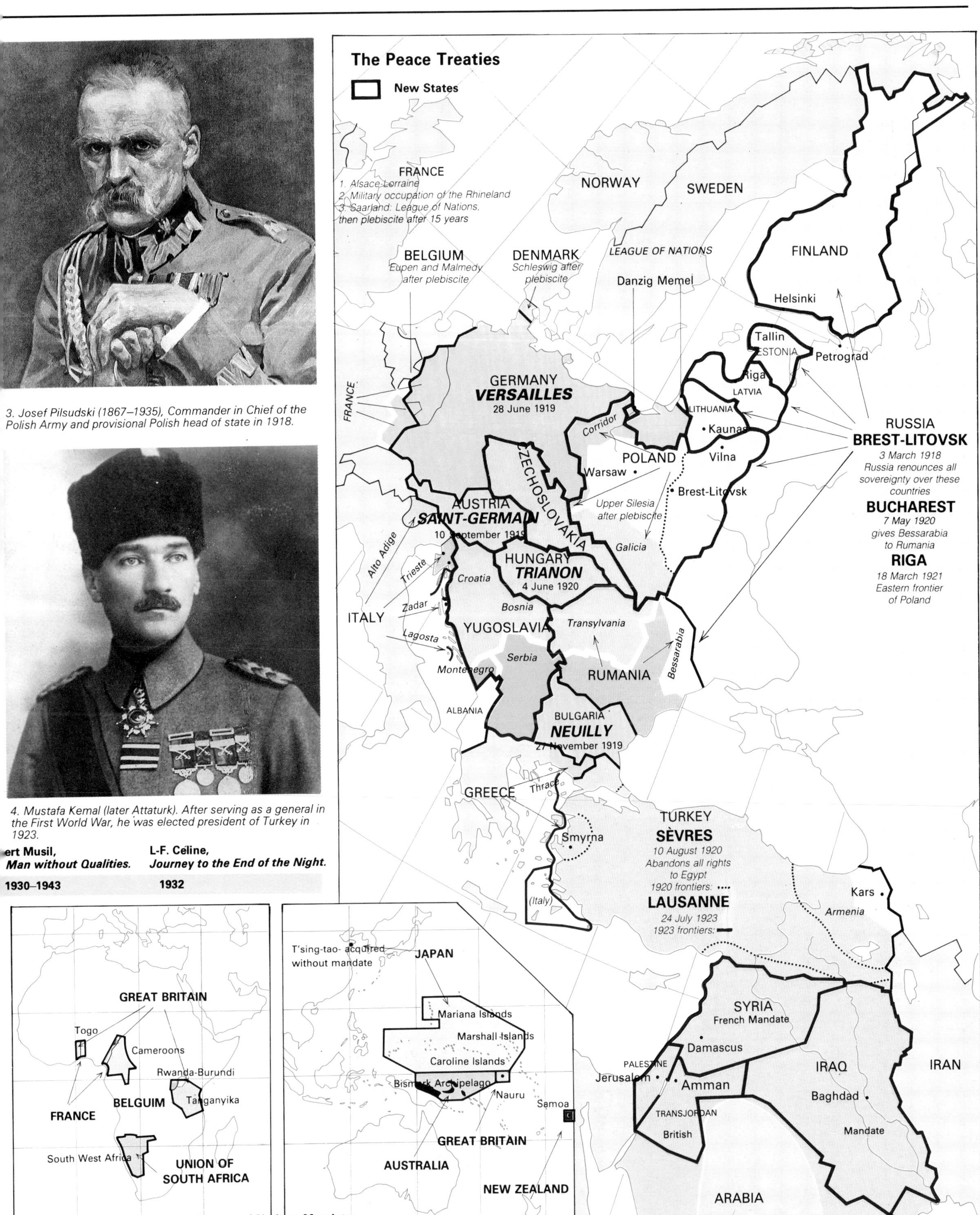


3. Josef Pilsudski (1867–1935), Commander in Chief of the Polish Army and provisional Polish head of state in 1918.

4. Mustafa Kemal (later Attaturk). After serving as a general in the First World War, he was elected president of Turkey in 1923.

**ert Musil,** **L-F. Celine,**
***Man without Qualities.*** ***Journey to the End of the Night.***

**1930–1943** **1932**

# Japan Opens its Frontiers and Embarks on a Policy of Conquest

1. Emperor Meiji arriving at the palace, print, late 19th century.

IN 1858, UNDER PRESSURE from the Western countries, the shogunate, despite its reservations, signed a number of unfavourable trade treaties with the foreign powers. Ports were opened up to trade, but traditional groups like the samurai, especially in the fiefs in the south-west, responded with a wave of xenophobia. Inflation made working conditions for ordinary people more difficult, and sparked off a number of revolts and violent protests. Those who argued for the end of the old regime of the Tokugawa prevailed and in 1867 the Shogun restored power to the Emperor.

Over a fairly short period of time the new Meiji state achieved major structural reforms, which aimed to put into operation the slogan 'Enrich the country, strengthen the army', and thus, it was thought, create the conditions necessary for the preservation of national independence. To guarantee the success of the slogan, it was argued, the country had to assimilate 'Western technology' without at the same time abandoning the 'Japanese spirit'. Within a generation, Japan was able to emerge successfully from its industrial revolution. The traditional social stratum of the samurai, who were already trained in the upkeep and management of feudal estates, occupied key positions in the civil service and in industry, with the aid of foreign experts. Japan's leaders, starting with Emperor Meiji himself, encouraged the adoption of Western methods and manners while some intellectuals translated and discussed books and ideas coming from the West.

By the very early years of the twentieth century Japan had become a major modern power. Over the period since 1890 the country had become a constitutional monarchy with a parliament. Legal reforms made it possible to model the legal system on that of the Europeans and to renegotiate the unfavourable treaties. Educational reforms were successful and all young Japanese enjoyed a school education. And, in the domain of scientific research, Japan enjoyed its first successes in this period. Japanese industrial growth, which up till then had been concentrated in textiles, from now on accelerated in the heavy industry sector. Like Western countries, Japan went through its moments of nationalist fervour and socialist trades union agitation. Symbolic of the country's success on the international stage were the Anglo-Japanese Alliance of 1902, the victory in the Russo-Japanese War of 1905, and the arrival of Japan as a colonial power with its annexation of Korea in 1910. From then on, Japan was able to have its voice heard internationally, as was for instance the case when

**MODERN TIMES** | **CONTEMPORARY PERIOD**

**1850** | **1860** | **1870** | **1880** | **1890**

**1853** **PERIOD OF 'THE END OF THE SHOGUNATE'** **1868** | **MEIJI ERA**

**1854:** Japanese–American Friendship Treaty signed. Japan ends its policy of isolation from the outside world.
**1858:** Trade treaties are signed with the major Western powers.
**1860:** Japanese Embassy opens in Washington.
**1866:** Military alliance formed between the fiefs of the south-west against the shogunate. There are more and more popular rebellions.
**1867:** Restoration of imperial power.
**1868:** First year of the new Meiji imperial régime. The last followers of the shogun capitulate.
**1869:** Tokyo, the former city of Edo, becomes the imperial capital.
**1871:** The fiefs are abolished and prefectures established. Emancipation of the *Eta Hinin*, or subordinate castes, is made official.
**1872:** Introduction of universal education. A conscript army is formed. The first railway line, from Tokyo to Yokohama, is inaugurated. Fukuzawa Yukichi publishes *Gakumon no susume*, supporting the idea of introducing Western science and ways of thinking.
**1873:** Land Tax reform.
**1876:** It is made illegal for former samurai to wear the sabre.
**1877:** A group of samurai, disappointed by the policies of the new régime, rebel in the south of the country. The new Imperial Army wins a victory over them.
**1881:** First paper money issued. The Liberal Party is formed, and the movement in favour of civil freedoms grows larger.
**1882:** Nakae Chomin translates Rousseau's *Social Contract* into Japanese.
**1884:** Popular rebellion in Chichibu to claim 'the freedom and rights of the people'.
**1885:** Tsubouchi Shoyo publishes *The Essence of the Novel*, which marks the beginnings of modern Japanese literature.
**1889:** Imperial constitution is promulgated. A rail link is established between Tokyo and Osaka.

3. A Chinese ship is destroyed by the Japanese.

**1890:** Parliament opens. The first major workers' strike takes place in Osaka.
**1895:** Japan defeats China.
**1897:** A team of Japanese scientists discover the dysentry bacillus.
**1901:** The Social-Democratic Party is formed.
**1902:** Anglo-Japanese Alliance is signed.
**1905:** Japanese victory over Russia. Treaty signed between Russia and Japan in Portsmouth, New Hampshire. Natsume Soseki publishes *I am a Cat*.
**1907:** Reform of primary schooling. All children now enjoy full-time education.
**1910:** Annexation of Korea. The first Japanese aeroplane is built.
**1914:** Japan declares war on Germany.
**1915:** Akutagawa publishes *Rashomon*.
**1919:** Japan takes part in the Conference of Versailles on the side of the victorious powers.
**1921–2:** Washington conference takes place. Japan is forced to reduce the power of its fleet.

# 1854–1941

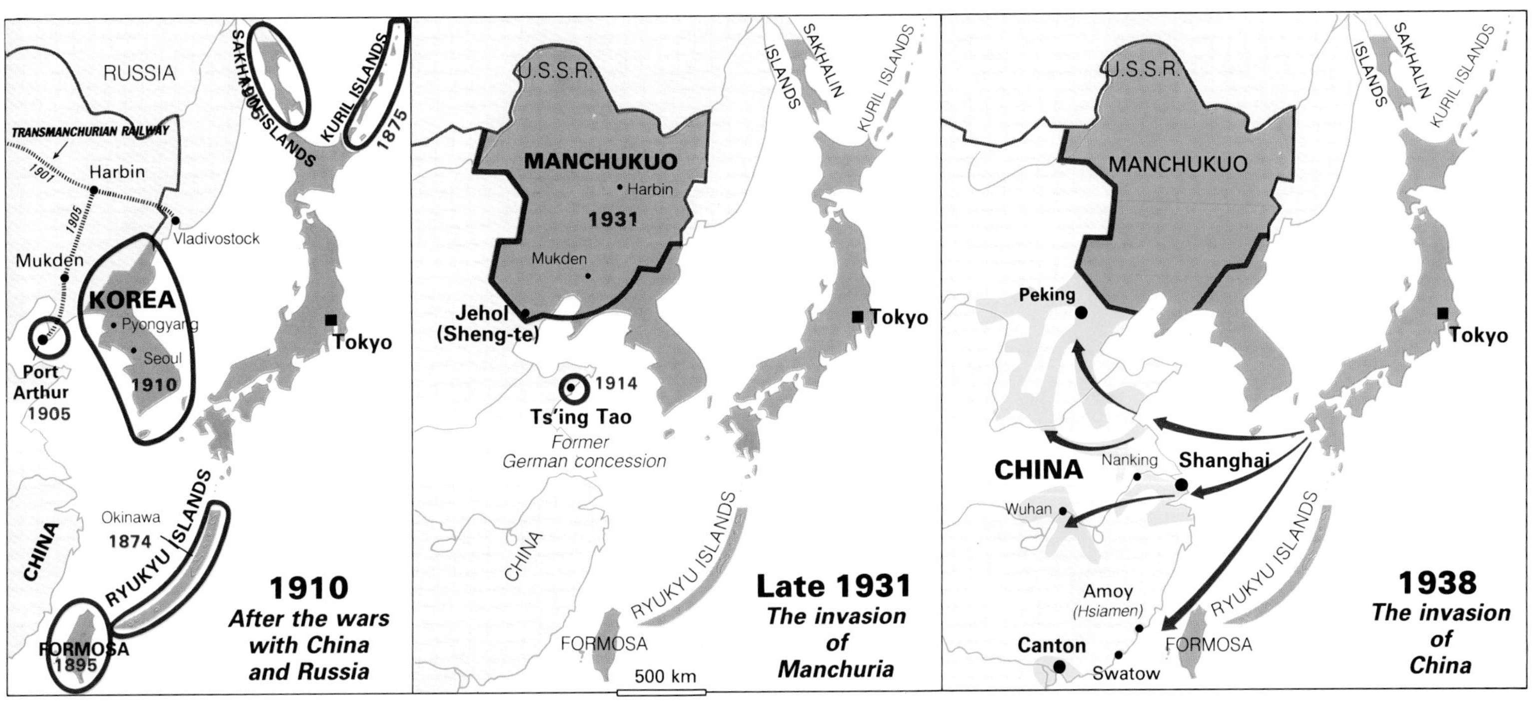

2. Old Japan: a group of young Japanese dressed as samurai warriors in 1910.

it sat with the victorious powers at the Conference of Versailles in 1919.

Between 1910 and 1920 public life was made more democratic. From 1913 onwards, parliamentary parties became the basis for government, while the trades union movement also grew stronger. Individualist values were the order of the day, and in the cities mass culture began to make an appearance. But this trend was blocked from the beginning of the 1930s by a resurgence of authoritarian and ultra-nationalistic views, which held sway amongst the military in particular. The economic slump, which affected the country after 1927, led some politicians to look to expansionism as a means of resolving the crisis. Losing control over their own rank-and-file activists, political parties were led into various military adventures on the continent of Asia, while, in the name of imperial values, repressive measures were taken against all those who disagreed with this change of direction, which was in fact supported by the majority of the population. Embroiled since 1937 in an unsuccessful war against China, in 1941 the military leaders launched the country into war against the United States by the attack on Pearl Harbor.

1900 | 1910 | 1920 | 1930 | 1940

TAISHO ERA | SHOWA ERA

1926

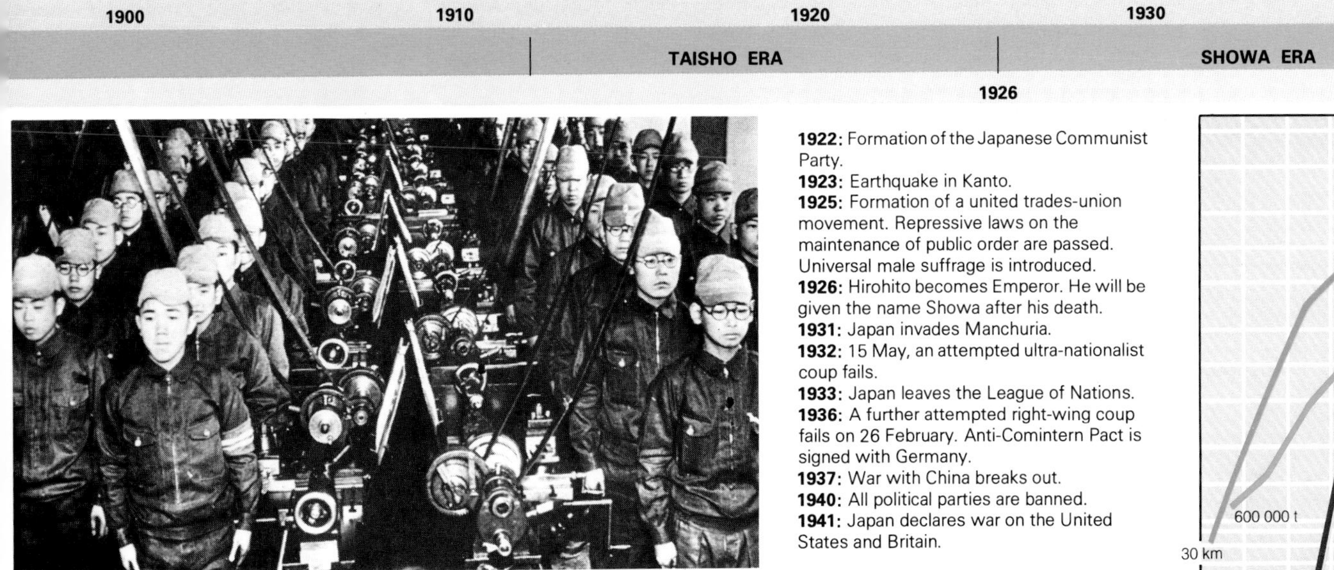

4. Modern Japan: students at work in an armaments factory during World War Two.

**1922:** Formation of the Japanese Communist Party.
**1923:** Earthquake in Kanto.
**1925:** Formation of a united trades-union movement. Repressive laws on the maintenance of public order are passed. Universal male suffrage is introduced.
**1926:** Hirohito becomes Emperor. He will be given the name Showa after his death.
**1931:** Japan invades Manchuria.
**1932:** 15 May, an attempted ultra-nationalist coup fails.
**1933:** Japan leaves the League of Nations.
**1936:** A further attempted right-wing coup fails on 26 February. Anti-Comintern Pact is signed with Germany.
**1937:** War with China breaks out.
**1940:** All political parties are banned.
**1941:** Japan declares war on the United States and Britain.

# China: From Nationalism to Communism

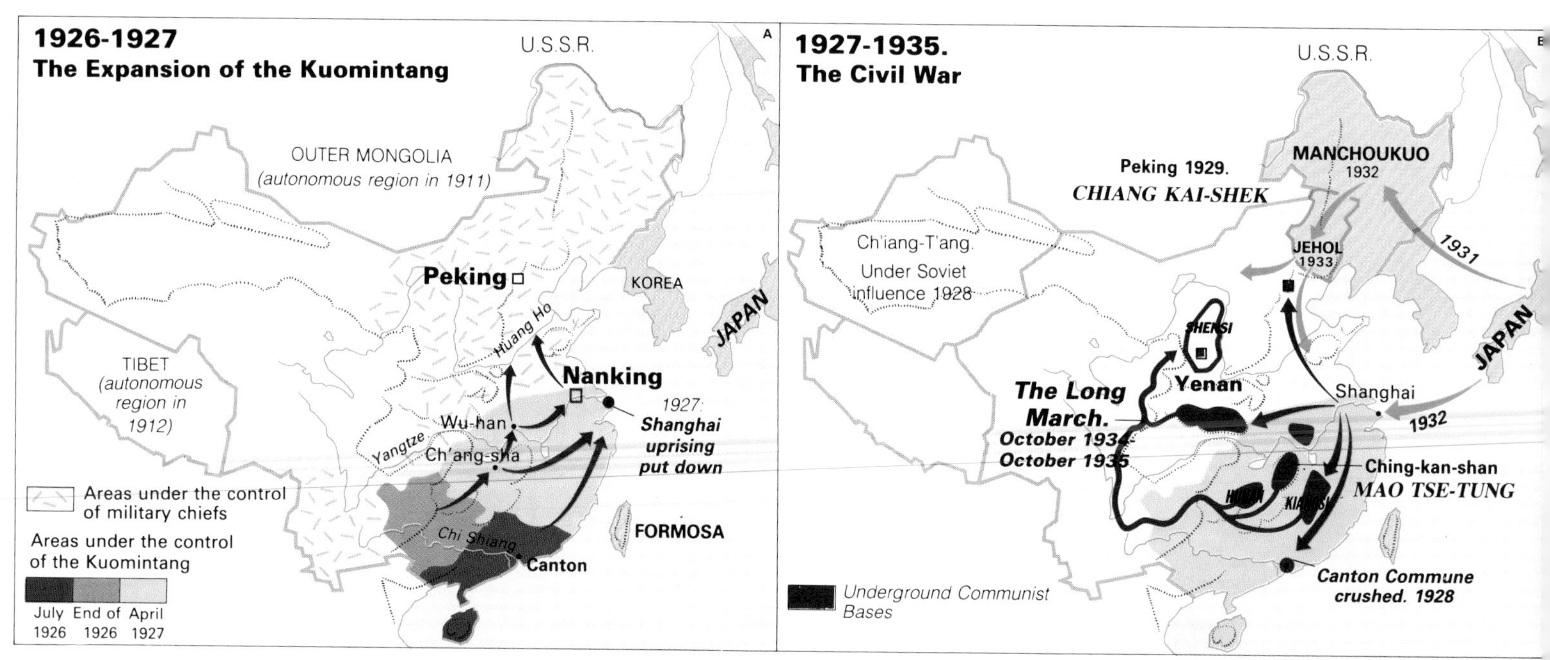


The Republic, which was transformed almost immediately into a dictatorship by overthrowing the dynastic order of the Manchus and the imperial system of government, deprived China of the last elements of cohesion. The sense of imperial unity having been torn away, society began to fall apart, revealing all the underlying contradictions which were at its centre. China's centrifugal tendencies re-emerged with the proliferation of warlords, held in check, however, by the dominant personal rule of Chiang Kai-shek. The penetration of foreign influences into Chinese society, in the dual shape of economic exploitation and political domination, produced their own antidote in the guise of the modernist and revolutionary ideas developing in the minds of the intellectuals and workers in the major ports. Urbane and sympathetic to Western ideas, the May Fourth Movement attacked all the outdated ideas of Confucianism and the Chinese tradition, while at the same time it reflected a genuine moment of national awareness. The same period as that which saw the gap widening between those enclaves of (relative) prosperity like Shanghai, Hong Kong, Canton, Tientsin etc., which were under foreign control, and the much poorer rural areas which were still very backward, also witnessed the confrontation between the China of the south, which was republican and progressive, and the China of the north, which was in the hands of a military clique. The confrontation between these

*1. March 1944. Modern warfare and the Great Wall of China.*

**May Fourth Movement of Modernist students and intellectuals.** **4 May 1919**

**Chinese Communist Party founded.** **1921**

**Death of the writer Lu Hsün** **1936**

**Nanking massacres perpetrated by the Japanese** **1937**

**1916:** Period of the warlords begins.
**4 May 1919:** Students demonstrate against the decision taken at the Versailles peace conference to leave the territories in China taken from the Germans in the hands of the Japanese.
**1921:** Chinese Communist Party founded. Sun Yat-sen proclaims the nationalist government in Canton.
**1924:** The Whampoa Military Academy established.
**1925:** Establishment of the General Labour Union for the whole of China. Death of Sun Yat-sen. Wave of strikes and boycotts of foreign goods.
**1926:** Chiang Kai-shek organises the Northern expedition. The Nationalist government moves its headquarters to Wu-han.
**1926–7:** Peasant revolts in Hunan. Mao Tse-tung argues they should be left to run their course.
**1927:** Shanghai uprising crushed. The Nationalist government established in Nanking. The Communists set up their base at Ching-kan-shan.
**1928:** Canton Commune is put down amidst much bloodshed, after the Huifeng uprising.
**1929:** Second Northern Expedition. Peking captured. Kiangsi Soviet declared.
**1930:** Failure of the policy advocated by Li Li-san, whom the Soviet Union repudiates.
**1930–4:** Nationalist campaigns to surround the bases of the Kiangsi Soviet.
**1931:** Japanese invasion of Manchuria.
**1932:** Shanghai attacked. Manchukuo set up by the Japanese with P'u-yi enthroned as emperor.
**1933–5:** Penetration of the Japanese in North China.
**1934:** Beginning of the Long March to break out of the Nationalist encirclement.
**1935:** Tsun-i conference adopts Mao Tse-tung as leader and acknowledges his leading role. Mao reaches Shensi with 8,000 survivors.
**1936:** Sian Incident. Chiang Kai-shek is captured and released only in return for a promise that he would join with the Communists in a common front against the Japanese.
**1937:** After a general offensive, the Japanese overrun all the major cities in North China. Shanghai, and then Nanking are occupied and 500,000 people are massacred by the Japanese.
**1938:** The Nationalists retreat to Chungking. The Japanese occupy Hankow and Canton. The Communists establish bases behind the Japanese lines (in Honan, Shantung and Chekiang).
**1940:** Wang Ching-wei establishes a collaborationist government with Japanese support in Nanking.
**1944:** Series of Japanese campaigns giving them control over Honan and South China.

*3. The Bridge over the Tatu River during the Long March.*

*4. The schoolteacher and the Mandarin: Chou En-lai and Mao Tse-tung in 1937.*

# 1916–49

two forces changed, with the northern expedition of Chiang Kai-shek, into a civil war between the two allies of the democratic front, the Kuomintang and the Chinese Communist Party, and finally culminated in the destruction of the workers' movement in a series of bloody massacres inspired by Chiang Kai-shek in Shanghai, Canton and Hunan. From Peking, from which he came in triumph after imposing his will on the generals, the Generalissimo returned to the south with nothing more to offer than bureaucratic corruption. It was the destiny of the Communist Party which would prove to be closest to that of China itself during the years to come, for it reflected most clearly the contrasts and paradoxes at work in the country. Forged in the urban environment, the revolutionary movement (helped a lot in this by the mistakes and dogmatism of their advisers in the Communist International) came to realize the impossibility of bringing about a workers' revolution, and forged itself into a peasant movement. P'eng Pai, in Canton, and Mao Tse-tung, in Hunan, were discovering the revolutionary potential of the rural areas at the very time when the movement of rebellion was being crushed in the cities. Later, Mao Tse-tung, in Kiangsi, by relying on traditional agrarian structures, found a rich fund of troops and activists as well as an operational base. The peasant revolution seemed threatened in its turn, though, when, driven back from their base, the communists were pushed back into the disinherited fringes of North Shensi (later to be known as the Yenan region). The Japanese invasion of China gave them a second chance by allowing them to apply the principles of guerilla warfare on a larger scale through opening a second united front against the Japanese. The day after the Japanese capitulation, the communists had at their disposal an infinitely greater number of soldiers and activists than they had ever had, even at the high point of the revolutionary period. Sapped by corruption, conservatism, and disorder, the nationalist regime, in spite of its initial military superiority, collapsed, leaving China in the hands of the communists.

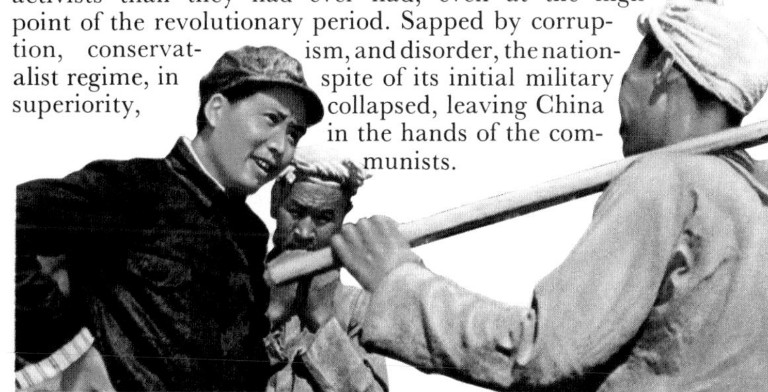

2. 'The Golden Age of Yenan': Mao Tse-tung talking with the peasants. Propaganda painting, 1939.

**Mao Tse-tung's lectures at the Yenan conference 'On Problems of Literature and Art'**

**1942**

**1945:** Japan capitulates. Manchuria is occupied by the Soviet Union. The Chinese Nationalists, with American support, take up the positions abandoned by the fleeing Japanese.
**1946:** The Soviets withdraw from Manchuria, after dismantling and shipping back to Russia much of the industrial machinery. The Marshall Mission delays the confrontation between Nationalists and Communists.
**1947:** The Nationalist forces go on the offensive after the failure of the conciliation mission, but the Communists win victories in Manchuria and North China.
**1948:** Lin Piao crushes the government forces in the whole of Manchuria.
**1949:** The victory at Huai opens the way to the Yangtze to the Communist armies. South China is conquered. The People's Republic of China is proclaimed in Peking. Chiang Kai-shek flees to Taiwan.

5. Scene of destruction after a Japanese bombing raid in Hankow, 1938.

6. The rout of the Nationalist armies, a scene from the 1949 War.

# The Great Depression

RECENT RESEARCH has made it clear how (if one excepts the USSR, which was undergoing its own specific crisis) the universal influence of the 1929 slump was at once the result of deep-seated strains and stresses in world capitalism, and the result of difficulties specific to certain countries. The crisis began in the United States, but it was also a continuation of the great European crises of the second half of the nineteenth century. Though fundamentally it was brought about by the low level of consumer spending, it was at the same time closely linked both to structural phenomena characteristic of the various countries and to the crisis in currency, credit and international trade which had been slowly developing since the Great War.

Indeed, even from before 1929, there had been many worrying symptoms. In France, for example, the warning signs had been flashing since 1928, in spite of the country's prosperity, as a result of the contradiction between a level of production which had entered into the 'capitalist' age and a level of consumption which was still held down by traditionally low wages. Inflation, which had been particularly spectacular in Germany, had ruined people living off savings or capital almost everywhere. The under-industrialized colonies suffered from the growing gap between agricultural and industrial prices. The financing of the war by inflation and the fall in the gold reserves kept the currencies, who had apparently been stabilized at the end of 1920, in a state of great fragility. The power of the banks, which specialized in the short-term investment of floating capital, had increased. It was eventually a fairly ordinary spate of speculation on Wall Street which, on 24 October 1929, sparked off the great crash. Stocks and shares continued to plummet until 1932.

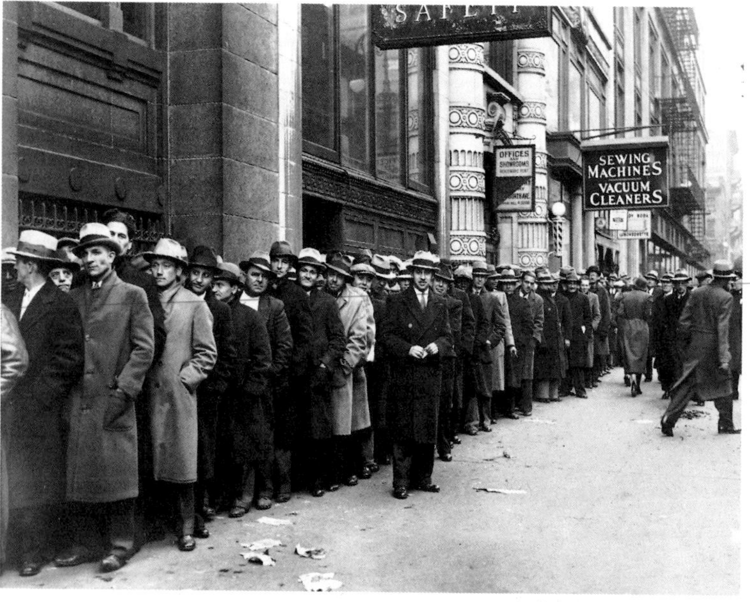


1. The New York unemployed in the dole queues, November 1933.

In its acute form, the crisis quickly spread throughout the world. Bankruptcies followed one after the other in all those countries that the credit system had tied to the United States, i.e. Austria (in May 1931), Germany (where the banks were forced to go 'on holiday' in the summer of 1931), Great Britain and then France. Trade collapsed, falling by 25% in three years.

The banking and business crisis precipitated the industrial crisis and made the plight of agriculture, already in a precarious position, even worse: the fall in agricultural prices was in excess of 50% in the United States, and that in world industrial output close to 40%. An enormous number of workers were thrown on to the dole: some 40 million in 1932. The Great Depression affected farmers not only in those countries where the capitalist economy was most highly developed (the United States and Canada), but also in those which were dependent on colonial powers. The lack of social security systems in many countries, and the weakness of independent trades union organizations for farm workers in the colonies or in the fascist countries (such as Italy) made the scale of human tragedy greater still.

As a result, social and political unrest was widespread. There were marches by the unemployed in the United States, in Great Britain and in France. There were uprisings in the colonies (like Vietnam), and a general radicalization of the suffering masses who could see with their own eyes the absurdity of a system in which, to 'maintain prices', corn was being burned and oranges destroyed while children were starving.

Confidence in the virtues of free enterprise was deeply shaken. In the world of business there was an urgent call to get the economy moving again at almost any price. In these conditions new political forces came to power almost everywhere. State intervention was advocated by businessmen and farmers, as well as workers, to an unprecedented degree. Almost everywhere the talk was of state planning of the economy.

Sometimes spurred on by violence spilling on to the streets (in Germany in 1931–2, in Vienna and Paris in 1934), different 'solutions' were devised according to how deep the crisis was and how the various forces in society lined up. What form these solutions took depended on the amount of support given to the various ideologies of the time, such as the New Deal in the United States, Nazism in Germany, or the Popular Front in France and Spain.

Total withdrawal into isolationism proved impossible. Nonetheless, the return to protectionism was general, notably in Great Bri-

**'Black Thursday' on Wall Street.** **24 October 1929**

**Great Britain abandons free trade.** **February 1932**

**Hitler comes to power.** **30 January 1933**

**Beginning of the New Deal.** **4 March 1933**

3. A Gaul defends the French franc against the pound and the dollar. Cartoon by A. R. Moritz, January 1924.

**1929. October:** Failure of the Hatry Bank in England.
**24 October:** 'Black Thursday' on Wall Street.
**1930. June:** Severe customs restrictions imposed in the United States.
**1931:** In Japan, the military forces the government to intervene in Manchuria.
**May:** The Kreditanstalt fails in Vienna.
**July–August:** The banks 'go on holiday' in Berlin.
**20 September:** Great Britain leaves the gold standard.
**December:** Germany embarks upon a policy of rapid deflation. On 13 December, Japan goes off the gold standard.
**1932. February:** Great Britain abandons free trade.
**August:** The Ottawa Imperial Conference sets preferential trade tariffs between Britain and the dominions.
**November:** F. D. Roosevelt elected President of the United States.
**1933. 30 January:** Hitler becomes chancellor of Germany.
**12 May:** The Agricultural Adjustment Act gives new powers to the American President.

4. The good ship Europe turns in distress to the dollar. German cartoon of 1926.

5. Zeus the capitalist: work or thunderbolts. Cartoon by Theodor Heine, December 1928.

# 1929–36

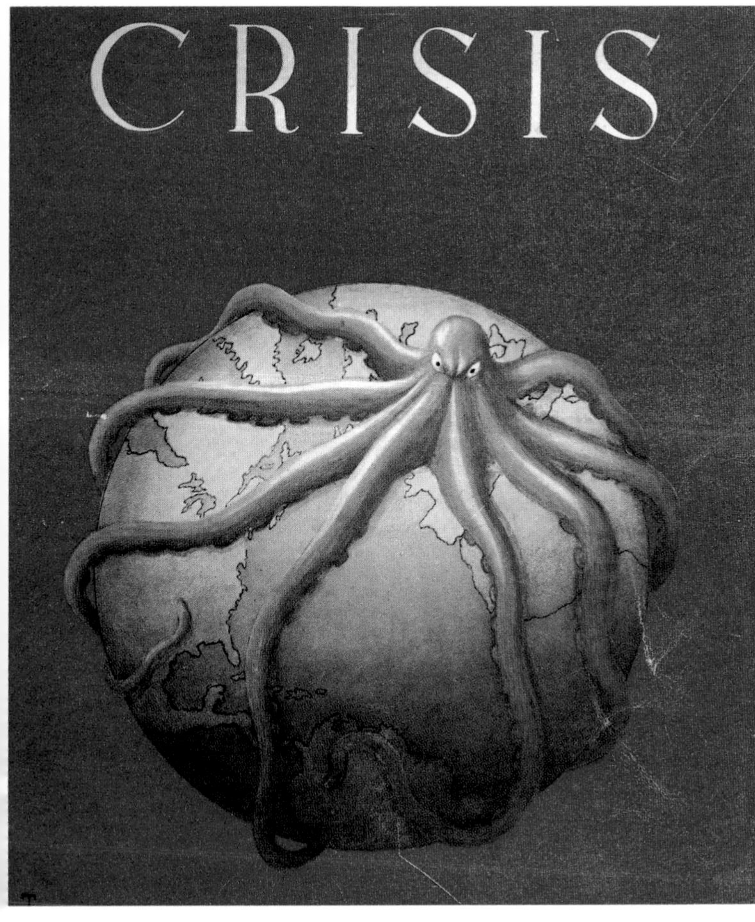


*2. The World Crisis as viewed by the German cartoonist Theodor Heine in 1941.*

tain, the home of free trade. The free convertibility of currencies was abandoned. All countries devalued their currency, France being the last to do so. Gradually, policies of deflation and austerity having shown their ineffectiveness, the wealthy nations turned towards public works (in the United States), towards increases in wages (in France) or closer links with the colonies (as in Great Britain), while in the 'proletarian countries' (Germany, Italy, Japan) governments chose the path of rearmament and preparation for war. Given such an economic climate, in some countries war had come to be considered as the 'natural' way out of the crisis.

**Matignon Accords.**

**7–8 June 1936**

**16 June:** The National Industrial Recovery Act sets the United States on a policy of public works.
**1934. January:** The dollar is devalued.
**6 February:** Right-wing extremists riot in Paris.
**1935:** France undertakes a policy of rapid deflation.
**1936 February:** J. M. Keynes, *The General Theory of Employment, Interest and Money.*
**4 June:** In France, the Popular Front Government comes to power with Léon Blum as prime minister.
**7–8 June:** A broad strike movement in France leads to the Matignon Accords between the Confédération générale de la production française (C.G.P.F.) and the Confédéderation générale du travail (C.G.T.).
**1st October:** The French franc is devalued.

*6. 'When will the crisis end?' Drawing by Autriac, October 1931.*

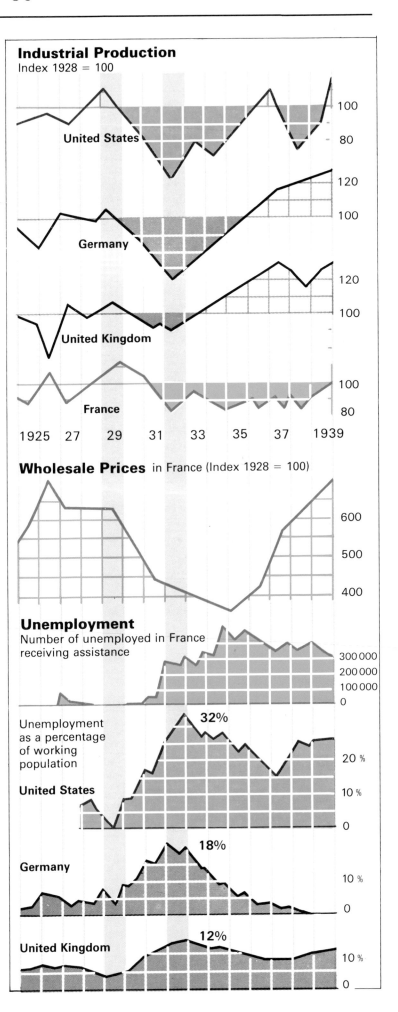

**Industrial Production**
Index 1928 = 100

United States — 100, 80
Germany — 120, 100
United Kingdom — 120, 100
France — 100, 80

1925 27 29 31 33 35 37 1939

**Wholesale Prices** in France (Index 1928 = 100)

600, 500, 400

**Unemployment**
Number of unemployed in France receiving assistance

300 000, 200 000, 100 000, 0

Unemployment as a percentage of working population

United States — 32% — 20 %, 10 %, 0
Germany — 18% — 10 %, 0
United Kingdom — 12% — 10 %, 0

# Fascism and the Popular Fronts in Europe

THE DAY AFTER the March on Rome in October 1922, Benito Mussolini was named head of government by King Victor Emmanuel III. After the Matteotti affair of 1924, which unsuccessfully attempted to strike a lethal blow against fascism, an initial period of uncertainty and 'legal dictatorship' was succeeded by the inauguration of a regime of personal power based on a single party, whose aim was the integration and regimentation of the Italian masses. Gradually, as the mechanism of dictatorship was set in place, Italy completed its transformation into a totalitarian state, the political centre extending its control over all sectors of economic, social and cultural life. This tendency increased after 1936 when the Ethiopian War – by means of which the regime sought to link up with the tradition of national grandeur inherited from the Roman past – forced the Duce to launch Italy on the road to autarchy and drove him to strengthen his ties with Nazi Germany.

*1. Striking workers dance at the Argenteuil car factories in Lorraine, 1936.*

*2. The Italian fascists celebrate the anniversary of the March on Rome in 1939.*

The wave of counter-revolution which submerged Europe after the First World War reached as far as Hungary, Lithuania, Poland, Spain and Portugal, all of which, in the twenties, were ruled by dictatorial regimes that had come to power in military coups. By contrast with Italian fascism, these deeply conservative regimes aimed only to consolidate or restore the power of the traditional social forces. In the course of the following decade there were indeed open conflicts between certain authoritarian regimes and the fascist movements representing the interests of the peasantry and the petty bourgeoisie. For example, King Carol II, faced in Rumania with the fascist upsurge embodied in Codreanu's Iron Guard (1931), dissolved all political parties by force (1938). In Bulgaria, Khimon Georgiev suppressed political parties and, in May 1934, set up a

**March on Rome.** — **27–28 October 1922**

**Primo de Rivera.** — **13 September 1923**

**Seventh Comintern Congress.** — **August 1935**

**Victory of *Frente Popular* in Spai[n]** — **16 February 1936**

**1922. 27–28 October:** March on Rome.
**29 October:** Mussolini becomes head of government.
**13 September 1923:** Miguel Primo de Rivera y Orbaneja comes to power in Spain following a military 'pronunciamento'.
**10 June 1924:** Socialist deputy Giacomo Matteotti murdered by fascists. In response, a section of the deputies refused to sit in the chamber ('withdrawal to the Aventine'), whilst many fascists left the party.
**3 January 1925:** Mussolini's speech to the Chamber claiming responsibility for events and proclaiming a dictatorship.
**1926. 3 April:** Rocco law on trade unions, which gave birth to the corporate state in Italy.
**May:** A coup d'état brought Gomes da Costa to power in Portugal. In 1928, Antonio de Oliveira Salazar emerged as the regime's 'strong man'. Became President in 1932 and introduced the nationalist, Christian *Estado Novo* constitution in March 1933.
**12–14 May:** Marshal Pilsudski's coup d'état in Poland; he marches on Warsaw at the head of soldiers faithful to his cause.
**November:** Laws for the defence of the state – so-called *fascistissime* laws. These set in place the apparatus of dictatorship.
**21 April 1927:** The Charter of Labour laid down the basic principles of the fascist regime's social organization.
**11 February 1929:** Lateran Treaty. Mussolini resolved the Roman question, which had remained in suspense since 1870. The Pope's sovereignty over the Vatican was recognized and a concordat established the position of the Catholic Church within the Italian state.
**28 January 1930:** Resignation of Miguel Primo de Rivera.
**March 1933:** Authoritarian, traditionalist regime comes to power in Austria. Chancellor Dollfuss outlaws all political parties in 1934.
**1934:** General Georgiev establishes a monarcho-military dictatorship in Bulgaria.
**16 May:** Karlis Ulmanis, head of the Peasant Union, carries out a coup d'état in Latvia.
**27 July:** Signature of a unity pact between the SFIO and PCF in France.
**October 1935–May 1936:** Italy conquers Ethiopia.

*3. A Republican dies during the Spanish Civil War.*

**1936. 16 February:** Victory of the Popular Front in Spain.
**3 May:** Victory of the French Popular Front.

*4. Armband of the Croix-de-Feu, a French Rightist political organization created in 1927 under the leadership of Colonel de la Rocque. It was to be outlawed in 1936.*

# 1922–39

dictatorship similar to that which Metaxas – with the assent of the sovereign – introduced in Greece (August 1936). In Austria, the authoritarian and traditionalist regime of Chancellor Dollfuss and of his successor, Schuschnigg, rid itself in 1936 of the Heimwehr, a fascist grouping that had been founded after the war.

Drawing the lessons from Hitler's rise to power, which had been aided by divisions within the Left in Germany, the Comintern adopted the strategy of Popular Fronts, in which it was no longer social democracy that was the main enemy but fascism. The communists had then to move closer not only to the socialists, but also to the bourgeois democratic parties. Several pacts on united action were signed in 1934, particularly in France, Spain and the Saarland and within the Italian émigré communities. In France, the Popular Front, which came to power in May 1936, immediately embarked upon important structural reforms and measures of social legislation. But economic difficulties and the unremitting hostility of the Right quickly put paid to Blum's government, which was forced out of power in June 1937. In Spain, after the Republicans' crushing electoral victory over the Monarchists, a republic was proclaimed. The elections of 16 February 1936 confirmed the victory of the *Frente Popular*, a combined movement of anarchists, communists and radicals, supporting the demands of the workers and peasants. But the assassination of the Monarchist leader, Calvo Sotelo, on 13 July gave the signal for a military rising under General Franco. A bloody civil war which lasted for three years until the capture of Madrid by Franco, was to set the Republicans against the Nationalists, who had their power base in the army, the clergy and the Phalange. This latter was a fascist-style movement founded in 1933 by José Antonio Primo de Rivera and backed with men and material by Germany, Italy and Portugal.

**Political regimes in Europe in 1938**

FINLAND
NORWAY
SWEDEN
ESTONIA
LATVIA
LITHUANIA
DENMARK
Polish Corridor
GERMANY
U.S.S.R.
IRELAND
UNITED KINGDOM
NETHERLANDS
Elbe
Vistula
GERMANY 1933
POLAND
BELGIUM
Rhine
Dnestr
CZECHOSLOVAKIA
AUSTRIA
HUNGARY
FRANCE 06/1936 04/1938
SWITZERLAND
RUMANIA
Danube
YUGOSLAVIA
BULGARIA
PORTUGAL 1926
ITALY 1922
SPAIN 02/1936 - 03/1939
ALBANIA
TURKEY
GREECE
MOROCCO
ALGERIA
TUNISIA
400 km

Liberal democracies
Countries governed at some point by Popular Fronts
Communist regimes
Fascist regimes
Authoritarian regimes

**First Blum government.**

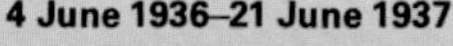

**4 June 1936–21 June 1937**

**Franco's forces capture Madrid.**

**28 March 1939**

*5. Adolf Hitler and Count Ciano sign the Pact of Steel on 22 May 1939, which transforms the political entente into a military alliance.*

The Left coalition won 369 seats against 236 won by the Right.
**17–18 July:** Beginning of the Spanish Civil War.
**4 August:** Metaxas's coup d'état in Greece.
**1 November:** Rome–Berlin Axis.
**1938. February:** King Carol II strikes to eliminate Codreanu's Iron Guard in Rumania.
**July:** Publication of the Manifesto for the Defence of the Race in Italy.
**October:** Education Charter.
**1939. 28 March:** General Francisco Franco takes Madrid and, on 18 October sets up his government there. The Civil War left more than one million dead.
**7 April:** Italy invades Albania.

*6. Léon Blum, miner's lamp in hand, acclaims the workers, 1937.*

# The USSR in the Age of Stalin

1. Iosif Vissarionovich Stalin. Propaganda poster.

THE 'RUDDERLESS YEAR', 1928, marks the irreversible passage from the Leninist to the Stalinist period. The forces of opposition to the one-party system were broken and the other institutions tamed. From this point on, the various oppositions within the Communist Party itself were destroyed (Bukharinite Right, Trotskyite Left), in confrontations which produced more surprise and indignation abroad than had previous efforts to bring factions into line. The same was true of the executions that accompanied these 'purges', which were more extensive than any previously carried out.

The Stalinist era was, moreover, characterized by great transformations which shaped the country for half a century.

The adoption of five-year plans to organize economic production was a spectacular innovation and one which seemed particularly rational when the crisis of 1929 broke in the West. The Soviet example was soon imitated, and several other countries adopted the idea of economic plans, whether of five years or some other period.

Industrialization gave priority to the production of heavy plant, which received three-quarters of investment. The symbols of this period of major public works, which were a subject of intense propaganda, were the great Zaporozhe and Dniepr dams, the huge Urals and Kuzbass industrial complexes, and the newly-built giant communications routes, such as the Turksib railway.

The collectivization of the countryside began with dekulakization, i.e. the persecution and extermination of the better-off (or merely refractory) peasants. This collectivization aimed at grouping peasants into the *sovkhozy*, which were organized as industrial enterprises, or into the *kolkhozy*, where the peasants retained a little individual plot of land but devoted the greater part of their time to the collective's land.

The reinforcement of the machinery of the state showed itself in the growing importance of the organs of control and repression, and in particular the NKVD (and the OGPU at its centre). This organization provided the inmates for the labour camps (known as Gulags), such as Kolyma, Karaganda, etc. The numbers of prisoners in these camps reached a figure of between five and eight million, depending on whose estimates one believes.

At the same time, the 1936 Constitution established the map of the Federation of the Republics of the Union, which rose from seven in number to eleven (fourteen after the war with the annexation of the three Baltic republics and Moldavia), whilst the number of autonomous republics rose to twenty, sixteen of which were in Russia.

This whole period can be summed up in three words: mobilization, reaction, repression. Society as a whole was mobilized in the most relentless manner and at a considerable cost in human sacrifice, symbolized in the emergence of such figures as the *Udarniki* (shock workers), the Stakhanovites and the *Mnogostanochniki* (elite workers), not to mention the *zeks* (Gulag deportees).

In the same period a traditionalist reaction occurred in favour of the family, academicism, the Soviet motherland and its new army. This phenomenon was connected with the slow 'plebeianization' of the army, following the accession to the state apparatus of popular elements who had entered the Soviets in 1917.

Lastly, the intensification of political terror on the eve of the war found expression in the 'show trials' which eliminated a number of Lenin's companions (Zinoviev, Kamenev, Radek, Bukharin) and generals like Tukhachevsky.

**1933** — **Birth of I. A. Yevtushenko.**
**1934** — **Maxim Gorky organizes the Writers' Union.**
**1935** — **Boris Souvarine publishes a biography of Stalin.**
**1936** — **André Gide publishes his *Return from the USSR.***
**1943** — **Birth of Lech Wale**

**April 1922:** Stalin becomes General Secretary of the Communist Party.
**21 January 1924:** Death of Lenin.
**24 April 1926:** Treaty with Germany.
**November 1927:** Trotsky expelled from the Communist Party: two years later, he will be exiled from the Soviet Union.
**October 1928:** Beginning of first Five-Year Plan. Suppression of private trade; collectivization of the countryside; iron and steel production doubled.
**February 1930:** Beginning of the campaign against the kulaks (so-called rich peasants); massive destruction of harvest, entire villages deported (10 million dead?).
**1933:** Second Five-Year Plan; call for emulation amongst workers.
**1934:** A. Zhdanov fixes the norms of Socialist Realism at the First Writers' Congress.
**18 September:** USSR enters League of Nations; in this way it marks its *rapprochement* with the democratic nations against Nazi Germany.
**1 December:** Kirov, a member of the Politburo, is assassinated; his death serves as a pretext for the incarceration of a large number of political prisoners.
**2 May 1935:** Franco-Soviet treaty of mutual assistance.
**1936:** 'Trial' of 'Left' opposition leaders (including G. Zinoviev and L. Kamenev).
**1937:** 'Trial' of Marshal Tukhachevsky and 31 other higher officers; the whole of the Soviet high command, which is suspected of opposition to Stalin, is disrupted.
**1938:** 'Trials' of 'Right' opposition, including Bukharin and Rykov.
**23 August 1939:** Non-aggression pact between Germany and the Soviet Union. Its secret clauses provide for a partition of Poland between the two countries.
**1941. 22 June:** Germans invade the USSR, encircle Leningrad and advance on Moscow.
**5 December:** Soviet counter-offensive. Moscow relieved.
**1942:** Germans attack towards the Black Sea and the Caucasian oil fields; in September, Stalingrad is encircled; in November, the Soviets relieve the town and launch a counter-offensive. From this point on, the Germans are constantly in retreat.
**1944. 1 August:** Warsaw rising.
**9 October:** Moscow conference. Britain and the Soviets divide up Europe into zones of influence.
**2 May 1945:** Berlin falls into Soviet hands.
**1946:** Stalin is Secretary of the Central Committee of the Communist Party, Prime Minister and Minister of War. Beginning of the fourth Five-Year Plan directed towards repairing the damage caused by the war.
**June 1948:** The Soviets blockade Berlin, forcing the Americans to organize an air bridge; the blockade lasts until May 1949. Split between Soviet Union and Yugoslavia in June.
**June 1950:** Outbreak of the Korean War.
**1951:** Launch of fifth Five-Year Plan directed towards the provision of electricity by huge hydro-electric dams.
**5 March 1953:** Death of Stalin. End of June, arrest of Beria.

3. Lavrenty Pavlovich Beria, the second most eminent Georgian, chief of the secret police.

# 1922–53

'The barque of love has shattered on the reefs of the daily ɪnd.' Vladimir Vladimirovich Mayakovsky, photographed at ː offices of Izvestia in 1927.

**L. Rajk is condemned to death.**

**24 September 1949**

Lev Davidovich Bronstein, known as Trotsky, arrives in exico, 1936.

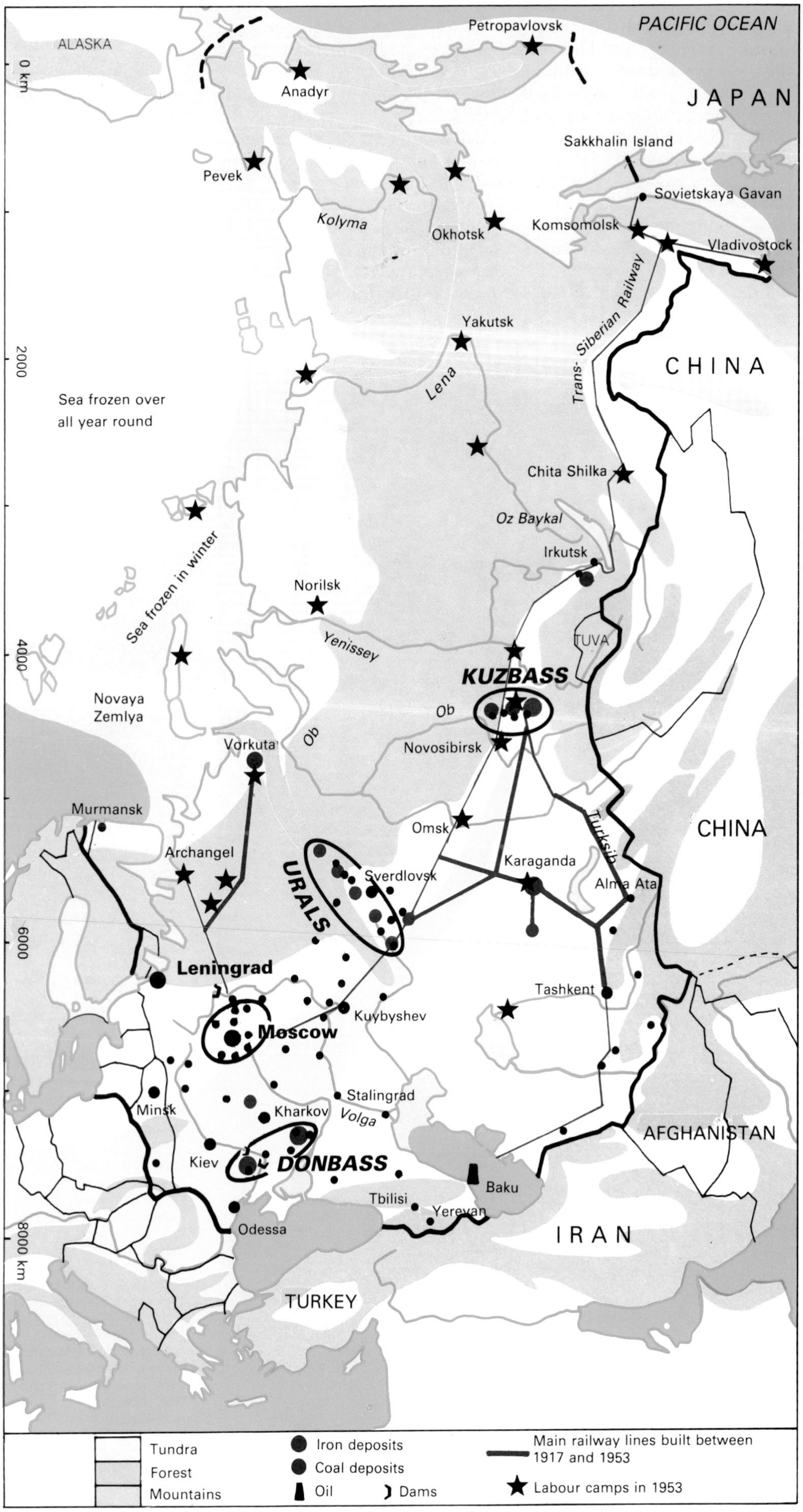

PACIFIC OCEAN
ALASKA
Petropavlovsk
Anadyr
JAPAN
Sakkhalin Island
Pevek
Sovietskaya Gavan
Kolyma
Okhotsk
Komsomolsk
Vladivostock
Trans-Siberian Railway
Yakutsk
CHINA
Lena
Sea frozen over all year round
Chita Shilka
Oz Baykal
Irkutsk
Sea frozen in winter
Norilsk
Yenissey
TUVA
KUZBASS
Novaya Zemlya
Ob
Novosibirsk
Vorkuta
Murmansk
Omsk
Turksib
CHINA
Archangel
URALS
Sverdlovsk
Karaganda
Alma Ata
Leningrad
Tashkent
Kuybyshev
Moscow
Stalingrad
Minsk
Kharkov
Volga
AFGHANISTAN
Kiev
DONBASS
Baku
Tbilisi
Yerevan
Odessa
IRAN
TURKEY
0 km
2000
4000
6000
8000 km

Tundra
Forest
Mountains
Iron deposits
Coal deposits
Oil
Dams
Main railway lines built between 1917 and 1953
Labour camps in 1953

# The United States: Prosperity, Crisis and Reform

IN THE DECADE after the First World War, the US enjoyed unprecedented prosperity, sustained by the Republican governments of Harding, Coolidge and Hoover. These were the boom years, during which the new industries (automobiles, aeronautics, electrical goods) began mass production, employing new, rationalized methods (Taylorism, production-line working).

This prosperity, however, concealed a number of weaknesses: incomes increased less (by 17%) than output (35%) and company profits (62%). Out of 27 million households, 6 million – most of them Black or immigrant households – lived in poverty. Agriculture experienced a permanent crisis of overproduction. The old sectors of industry stagnated. Profits were diverted towards frantic speculation on the Stock Exchange. In October 1929, the exaggerated rise in share prices relative to their real value caused the Wall Street Crash, which ushered in the Great Depression from which the USA would only recover thanks to the New Deal and war.

The Stock Exchange crisis quickly spread to the whole of the economy. Between 1929 and 1932, national revenue collapsed from 87 billion dollars to 39 billion. The unemployment figures rose from 1.5 million to 12 million. Ruined farmers lost their lands. This new poverty found its expression in the soup kitchens, shanty towns, the sight of homeless people wandering the streets, and general despair. In 1932, given the failure of Hoover's policies, the electorate put its faith in the Democrat, Franklin D. Roosevelt's promise of a New Deal.

The aim of the New Deal was to bring about a revival of free enterprise by means of pragmatic federal government intervention in all sectors of the economy: the control of the banking and monetary systems; aid to farmers and a reduction in agricultural production (AAA); the development of codes of fair competition in industry, together with collective agreements on reduced working hours and a minimum wage (NIRA); the commencement of huge public works schemes such as the Tennessee Valley Authority project. These initial measures were resisted by the business community and the Supreme Court ruled them illegal; but after 1936 Roosevelt called upon the support of broader sections of public opinion to push through bolder policies that were Keynesian in inspiration. He applied the principle of deficit funding to create new wealth and increase consumption levels. Thanks to a reshuffle of the Supreme Court, the principal measures of the first 'Hundred Days' were taken up again and reinforced.

1. In the days of Prohibition. *Anonymous painting, New York.*

*2. Work progressing on the world's biggest dam, Boulder City, Nevada, 1934.*

**The 'Red Scare'.** **1921**

**The Model T Ford.** **1924**

**The Wall Street Crash.** **October 1929**

*4. The anarchists Sacco and Vanzetti in court, 1921.*

**1920:** First commercial radio station.
**1921:** The 'Red Scare'. N. Sacco and B. Vanzetti are sentenced to death for murder, in spite of the lack of evidence. They will be executed in 1927.
**1924:** The Model T Ford priced at less than 300 dollars.
**1927:** First 'talking' cinema.
**1929:** 48 airlines in operation, serving 355 American airports. October: panic on the Stock Exchange. Hoover signs the Agricultural Marketing Act.
**1929–1932:** 85,000 companies bankrupted.
**1932:** 12 million unemployed. March of the 'Bonus Army' of ex-servicemen and civil servants on Washington. Reconstruction Finance Company founded.
Norris-La Guardia Act restricts the use of injunctions in labour disputes.
**1933–1945:** Franklin D. Roosevelt President.
**1933 March–June:** The 'Hundred Days'. Emergency Banking Act: the banks are closed and reorganized by the President. National Industry Recovery Act (NIRA): accords between industry, the federal government and the unions. Agricultural

*5. Franklin D. Roosevelt.*

These measures brought recovery in 1937, but it was short-lived. As soon as the federal government balanced its budget again, depression set in once more. From 1938 onwards the arms industry took up the slack from the industries that were in difficulty. The New Deal was a set of policies designed to attack the problem of depression; it was not a revolution. Though it succeeded in saving the American economy from bankruptcy, it was not able to find a market for the enormous productive potential of the USA. But for the Americans – and for the outside world – it represented a model for restoring harmony to a crisis-ridden economy and society. By imposing two countervailing forces to capitalism (trade unionism and the federal government), it reconciled a section of the intellectuals and workers to the American system. But confidence was still fragile, and it would take Pearl Harbor to persuade the American people to ally with the democracies in their war against Hitler.

*3. As the 'grapes of wrath' ripen . . . Refugees from Oklahoma reach California, August 1936.*

**F.D. Roosevelt: The landslide recedes**

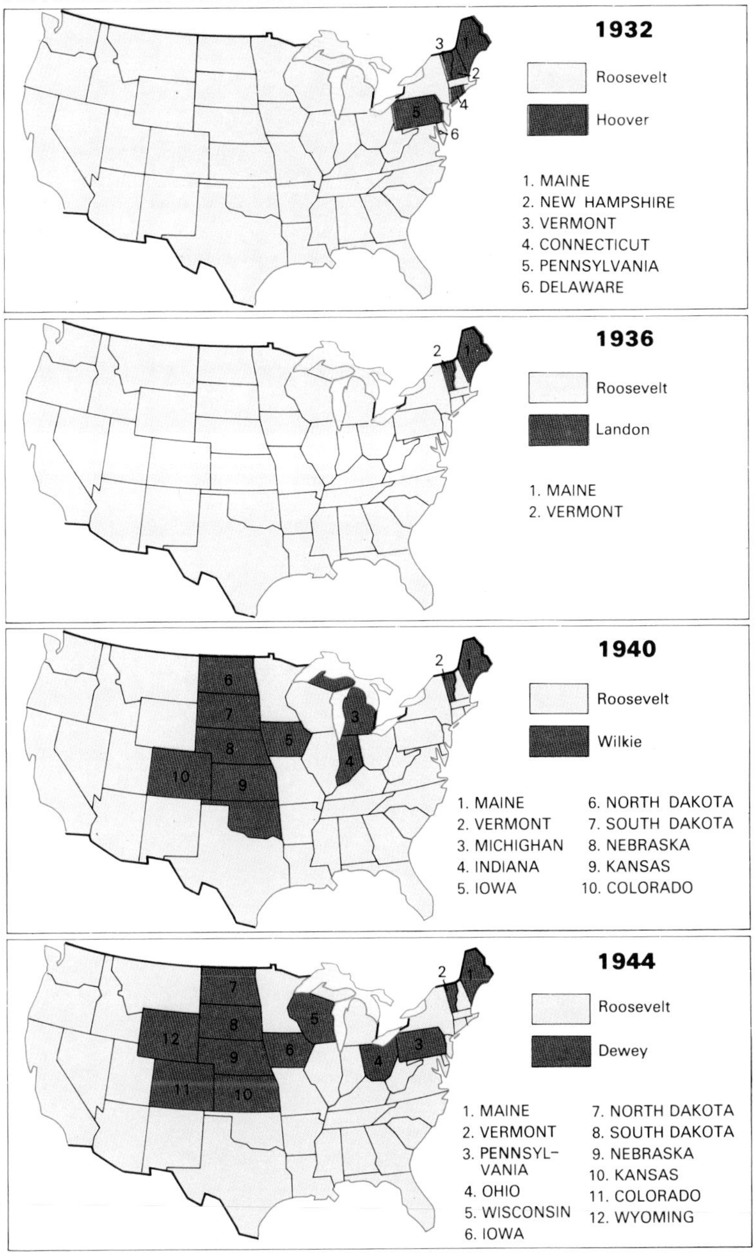

**1932**

Roosevelt
Hoover

1. MAINE
2. NEW HAMPSHIRE
3. VERMONT
4. CONNECTICUT
5. PENNSYLVANIA
6. DELAWARE

**1936**

Roosevelt
Landon

1. MAINE
2. VERMONT

**1940**

Roosevelt
Wilkie

1. MAINE
2. VERMONT
3. MICHIGAN
4. INDIANA
5. IOWA
6. NORTH DAKOTA
7. SOUTH DAKOTA
8. NEBRASKA
9. KANSAS
10. COLORADO

**1944**

Roosevelt
Dewey

1. MAINE
2. VERMONT
3. PENNSYL-VANIA
4. OHIO
5. WISCONSIN
6. IOWA
7. NORTH DAKOTA
8. SOUTH DAKOTA
9. NEBRASKA
10. KANSAS
11. COLORADO
12. WYOMING

**osevelt elected President.** **New Deal** **Pearl Harbor.**

**1932** **1933** **7 December 1941**

Adjustment Act (AAA): price control and assistance towards reducing agricultural production. Tennessee Valley Authority (TVA) giving development a regional dimension.
**1934:** Devaluation of the dollar. Abrogation of the Platt Amendment which had allowed the U.S. to intervene in Cuba.
**1935:** Creation of the Committee for Industrial Organization (CIO) and the Works Progress Administration, which, by 1939, will have employed 8.5 million people. The Supreme Court declare the AAA and the NIRA unconstitutional. The Wagner-Connery Act extends trade union rights and lays down the principle of collective conventions under the aegis of the federal government. First social security legislation.
**1935–7:** 'Neutrality' laws, prohibiting the sale of arms to a warring nation.
**1936:** Re-election of Roosevelt with a large majority. Second New Deal. Federal budget deficit of 3,500 million dollars.
**1937–41:** Roosevelt appoints 7 new judges to the Supreme Court.
**1937 spring:** Brief economic upswing. Sit-in strikes in the car industry. In a speech at Chicago, Roosevelt warns his fellow countrymen of the danger of a war in Europe.
**1938:** Unemployment reaches 19% of the employable population. Budget deficits accumulated over a five year period total 1 billion dollars.
**1939:** Modification of 'neutrality' laws.
**1941 spring:** The USA establishes a naval base in Greenland. 7 December: Japanese attack on the American base at Pearl Harbor. The USA goes to war against Japan.

*6. Eleanor Roosevelt (right) and a New Deal supporter in front of a poster for the National Industrial Recovery Act in August 1933.*

*7. The gangsters Bonnie and Clyde.*

# Hitler's Conquests: The Prelude to War

1. The 'Cathedral of Light', Nuremberg, 1st May 1939.

2. Hitler in Berlin, 1939.

IT TOOK THE FÜHRER less than a year to have his party declared the only legal one and bring into line all sectors of public life by intimidation and violence (the 'experimental' camp at Dachau was opened in March 1933 and was to be followed by five others before 1939). Once assured of compliance on the 'home front', Hitler then had the means to strike the final blows against the Versailles *diktat*, which he did with the reintroduction of compulsory military service and the remilitarization of the Rhineland. These shows of strength allowed him to assess Franco-British inertia and to achieve a *rapprochement* with the states of Southeastern and Central Europe, which the crisis had pushed into dictatorship. The (aerial) support that the Reich gave to Franco's forces in the Spanish Civil War laid the ground for a *rapprochement* with fascist Italy (the 'Axis'), which was formalized in the Pact of Steel.

Enjoying military superiority over the Western democracies, Hitler was able to move progressively towards the solution of the 'problem of Greater Germany'. The first stage in that solution consisted in annexing the lands inhabited by Germans. In the spring of 1938 the entry of the Wehrmacht into Austria provoked only verbal protestations in London and Paris. In Czechoslovakia, the last military and parliamentary bastion in Central Europe, Hitler supported the claims of the German-speaking Sudeten minority.

France and the USSR were prepared to honour their obligations on Czech independence (May 1938); however, out of a desire for 'appeasement', the British government refused to give any assurances. Once Prague had resolved to yield over the autonomy of the Sudetenland, Hitler doubled the stakes and called at the Nuremberg Congress for their annexation to the Reich. After the British prime minister, Neville Chamberlain, had made two trips to Germany, negotiation carried the day. Britain, France, Italy and Germany endorsed the Munich Agreement, which compromised the security of the democracies and dismantled Czechoslovakia (delivered up shortly afterwards to the appetites of the Poles and the Hungarians). On 15 March 1939, Bohemia-Moravia disappeared from the map. This new show of strength rounded off the second stage of Hitler's programme, the conquest of *Lebensraum* in the east. Now master of the Memel territory, occupied a week after Prague, Hitler's actions raised the question of what was to become of Danzig and the Polish Corridor. On this occasion, Paris and London could not retreat for fear of losing face among the smaller nations threatened by the Axis powers. The British government associated itself with the French guarantees to Poland, and negotiations commenced which even included the Soviets. These progressed slowly on account of reciprocal mistrust and as a result of the Polish refusal to allow the Red Army on to its soil. During this period, talks began in Moscow which were to lead to the Nazi-Soviet non-aggression pact, the secret clauses of which made provision for the division of Poland.

Hitler, therefore, had a free hand. After vainly attempting to sway the attitude of the British, with whom he offered to divide up the world, he ordered his forces to enter Poland on 1 September 1939. A final intervention by Italy could not prevent the outbreak of hostilities on 3 September.

| Hitler to power. | Reichstag fire. | Dachau camp opened. | Night of the Long Knives. |
|---|---|---|---|
| 30 January 1933 | 27 February 1933 | March 1933 | 30 June 1934 |

**1933. 30 January:** Hitler becomes chancellor.
**19 October:** Germany leaves the League of Nations Disarmament Conference.
**1934. 26 January:** German-Polish non-aggression treaty.
**1935. 13 January:** The Saarland returned to the Reich by plebiscite.
**16 March:** Reintroduction of compulsory military service.
**14 April:** Stresa Front (Britain, Italy, France) condemning the unilateral revision of treaties.
**2 May:** Franco-Soviet Pact.
**18 Nov:** League of Nations votes sanctions against Italy which had gone to war against Abyssinia on the 3rd October.
**1936. 7 March:** Military occupation of the Rhineland.
**18 July:** Beginning of the Spanish Civil War (–28 March 1939).
**1 November:** Proclamation of the Berlin-Rome Axis.
**25 November:** Anti-Comintern Pact between Germany and Japan.
**1937. 26 April and 31 May:** Guernica and Almeira.
**5 November:** The 'Hossbach Protocol' which lays down Hitler's future intentions.
**1938. 12–13 March:** Anschluss.
**24 April:** The Sudeten programme, 'the eight points of Karlovy Vary'.
**3 August:** Lord Runciman's mission to Prague.
**12–13 September:** Hitler's anti-Czech speech at Nuremberg and the Sudeto-Czech split.
**15 and 22–4 September:** Neville Chamberlain and Hitler meet at Berchtesgaden and Bad Godesberg.
**29–30 September:** Four-way international conference and Munich Agreement.
**2 October and 2 November:** Teschen ceded to Poland and Southern Slovakia ceded to Hungary with German backing.
**1939. 14–15 March:** Disappearance of Czechoslovakia. Slovakia proclaims its independence. Bohemia-Moravia becomes a Reich protectorate.
**23 March:** Lithuania cedes the Memel territory to the Reich.
**23 March:** British guarantees to Poland and

3. 'Strength through Joy', Nazi poster of 1936.

# 1933–39

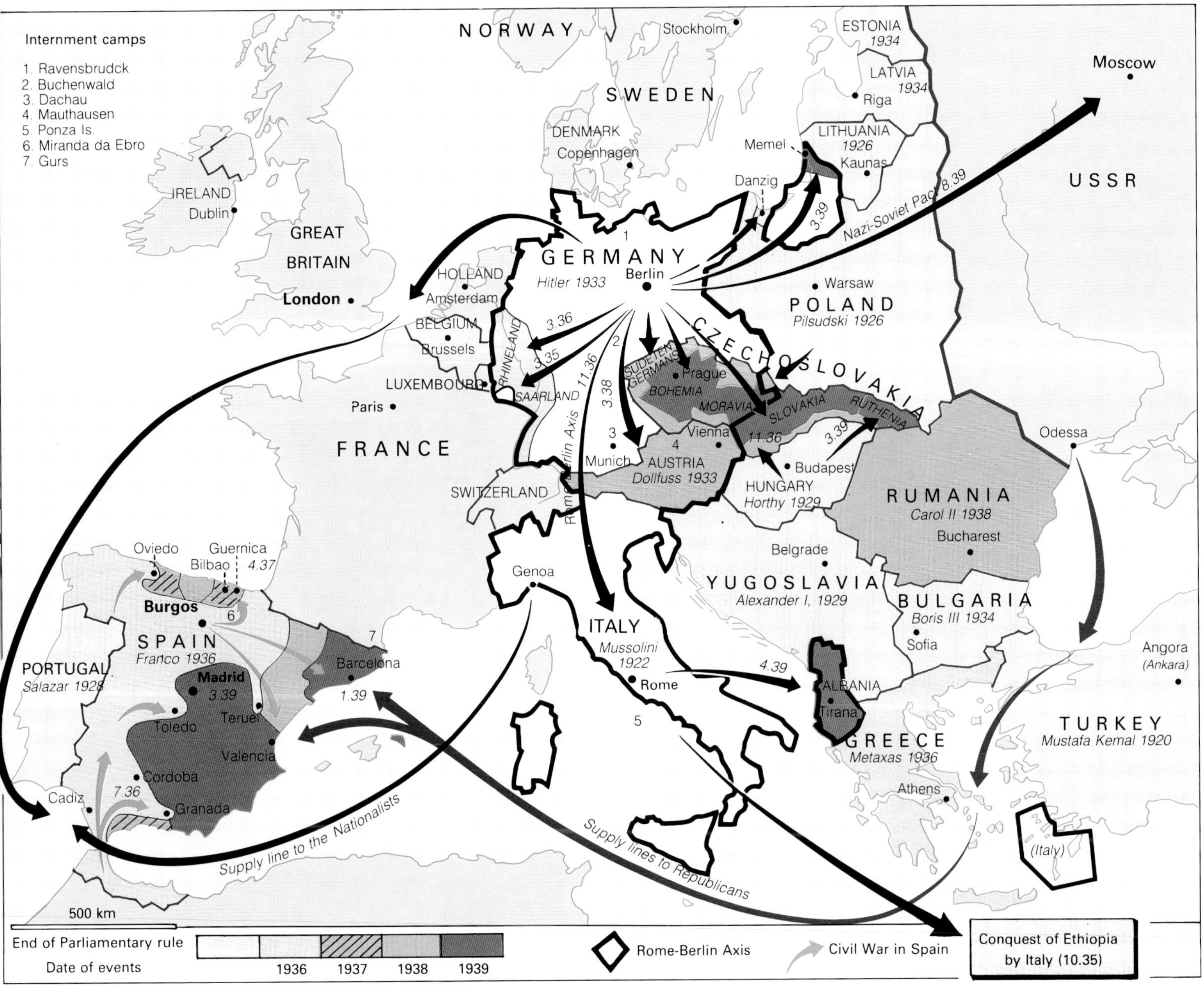

**Nuremberg Laws.**

**15 September 1935**

**Remilitarization of the Rhineland.**

**7 March 1936**

**Freud goes into exile in London.**

**4 March 1938**

Rumania.
**31 March:** Pledge of Permanent Mutual Guarantee between the United Kingdom and Poland.
**7 April:** The Italians occupy Albania.
**28 April:** Hitler repudiates his agreements with Britain and Poland.
**22 May:** Signing of the Pact of Steel, the military alliance between Germany and Italy.
**11 August:** Arrival of the Franco-British military mission in Moscow.
**23 August:** Nazi-Soviet Non-aggression Pact signed in Moscow.
**1 September:** Invasion of Poland. Danzig annexed by the Reich.
**3 September:** United Kingdom and France declare war on Germany.

*4. Hitler portrayed by Charlie Chaplin in* The Great Dictator, *1940.*

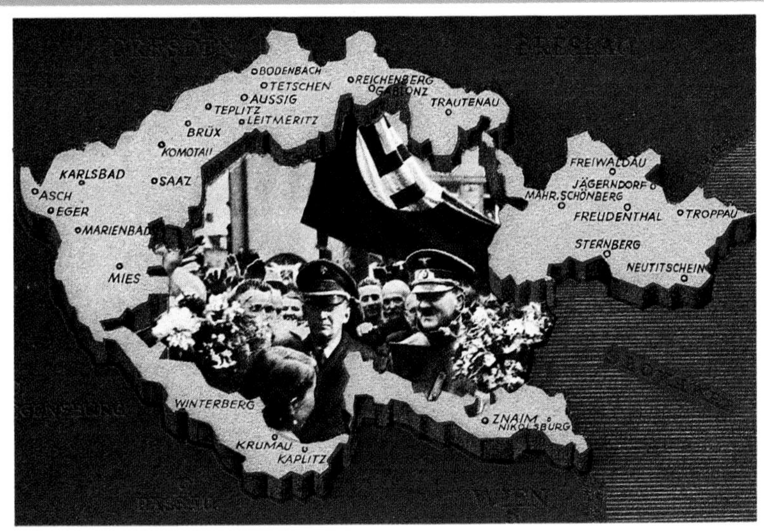


*5. The Nazis in Prague, 15 March 1939.*

*6. An orthodox Jew is arrested in Berlin, 1935.*

# The War in Europe and Africa

AFTER INITIAL SUCCESSES in Poland (September 1939), the lightning war (*Blitzkrieg*) began again the following spring, enabling the Germans to seize the Danish straits and the Norwegian coast, and subsequently the north-west of Europe (the Netherlands, Belgium and France were overrun in six weeks). After unprecedentedly heavy bombing raids on England, the focus of the war shifted for a year or two into the eastern Mediterranean and the Balkans, where Hitler wanted both to ensure that his Italian ally did not lose face and to prevent Great Britain re-establishing a foothold on the Continent. On 22 June 1941 the attack on the USSR (Operation Barbarossa) began, but after five months of the offensive the *blitz* began to show signs of petering out, the Germans having to confront, simultaneously, the problems of the Russian winter, the vastness of the territory and the weight of numbers ranged against them. Nevertheless, neither the Soviet counter-attack nor the Russian winter prevented the German's from advancing, between May and November 1942, as far as the Caucasus and the Volga.

1. Searching for the dead after a massacre in the Crimea, 1942.

Treated with varying degrees of harshness, either according to the imperatives of the conflict (as was the case with Vichy France and the puppet regimes of Norway and Croatia) or as a result of the exercise of the Nazi's racial doctrines (Poland, the USSR and Eastern Europe), the occupied countries were subjected to an implacably oppressive regime (eleven new concentration camps were built within the Greater Reich) and to intensive economic exploitation: this exploitation was most severe in the 'Ostlands' (the Ostland system organized agricultural production particularly in the east). The 'New Order' thus generated internal resistance movements which were to play an important role in the eventual liberation of Europe.

A turnabout in fortunes first became apparent at the end of 1942 and the beginning of 1943 with Montgomery's victory at El Alamein, the British and American landings in North Africa and Paulus's surrender at Stalingrad. Total war, to which the USA and the USSR (east of the Urals) had become converted, gave the Allies a superiority which they put to good effect, taking the initiative on all fronts. Whilst the Soviets forced their enemies into an 'elastic retreat' over the greater part of Russian territory, the Allied landings in Sicily (July 1943) brought about the fall of Mussolini, the capture of southern Italy and the surrender of the Badoglio government. In combination with the Red Army's operations, the landings in Normandy and Provence (6 June and 15 August 1944) made possible the liberation of a vast part of 'Fortress Europe' and forced Germany's satellites to sign armistices (autumn 1944).

The recourse to V1 and V2 rockets – first against England, then against Antwerp – and the counter-offensives in the Ardennes and around Budapest, did not halt the Allied advance. This began again, both in the east with a drive towards the Oder (January 1945), and in the west with the British, French and American forces crossing the Rhine (March). The desperate resistance of the leaders of the Reich could not prevent either the invasion of the country nor a general exodus of the population.

Powerless either to prevent the Allied armies from meeting up or to stop the Russians entering Berlin, Hitler took his own life in his bunker on 30 April. He left to his chosen successor, Admiral Doenitz, the task of negotiating with the Allies. The unconditional surrender of the German armies was ratified in Berlin on 8 May, having been signed at Reims on the 7th. It left a 'Year Zero' Germany in the hands of the Allied commanders-in-chief (USSR, USA, Britain, France).

**Fall of Warsaw.** 26 September 1939

**German offensive in the west.** 10 May 1940

**Operation Barbarossa.** 22 June 1941

**German capitulation at Stalingrad.** 2 February 1943

**1939. 26 September:** End of the Polish campaign. The country is partitioned between Germany and the USSR.
**1940. 30 November–12 March:** USSR attacks Finland.
**10 May:** General German offensive: the Netherlands and Luxenbourg are invaded.
**14 May:** French defences pierced near Sedan.
**28 May–4 June:** Battle of Dunkirk.
**7–8 June:** French lines breached.
**10 June:** Italy enters the war.
**22 and 24 June:** France signs armistice with Germany and Italy.
**10 July–31 October:** Battle of Britain.
**28 October:** Italians invade Greece.
**1941. 19 January–18 May:** British victories in East Africa.
**31 March–29 April:** Rommel's offensive in Libya.
**6 April–31 May:** German campaigns in Balkans and Crete.
**2–31 May:** Failure of anti-British coup in Iraq.
**22 June:** Germany and her allies invade the USSR.
**2 October–5 December:** Siege of Moscow.

4. Stukas over the Acropolis, May 1941.

**6 December–March 1942:** Soviet counter-offensive on the Moscow front.
**1942. 21 January–2 September:** Rommel's second offensive in Libya.
**8 May–2 July:** German offensive in the Crimea.
**12 May:** Fall of Sebastopol.
**5–10 July:** Rommel advances to El Alamein.
**23 October–4 November:** British victory at El Alamein. Afrika Korps routed.
**8 November:** Allied landings in North Africa.
**19 November–2 February 1943:** Battle of Stalingrad. German surrender.
**1943. 13 May:** Axis troops forced out of Tunisia.
**10 July–7 August:** Sicily campaign.
**25 July:** Fall of Mussolini (executed 28 April 1945).
**3 September:** Italian armistice. Allies in Calabria.
**Late 1943–Early 1944:** USSR's 1939 frontiers restored.
**1944. 11 May:** Allies assault the Gustav line in Italy.
**6 June:** Normandy landings.
**15 August:** Landings in Provence.

# 1939–45

*2. The Red Poster, 1944. The Nazi occupiers denounce terrorists among the immigrant labour force before shooting them.*

*3. The dead at Auschwitz.*

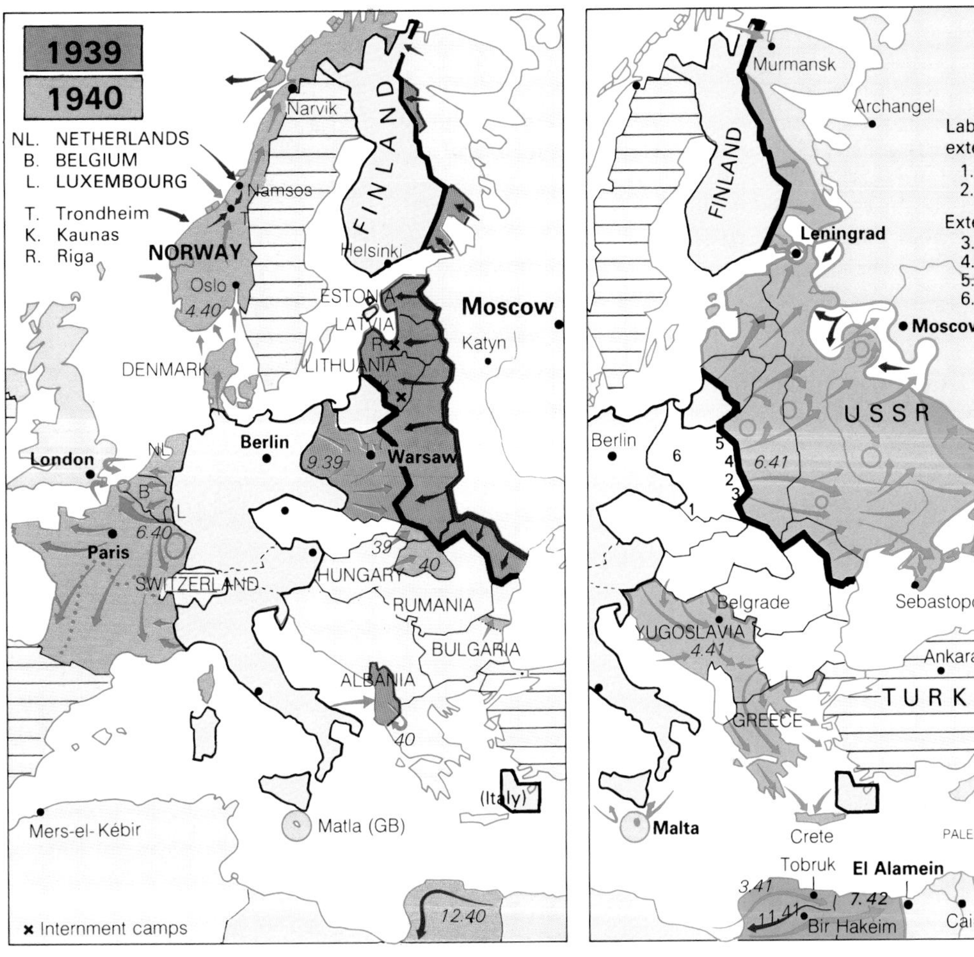


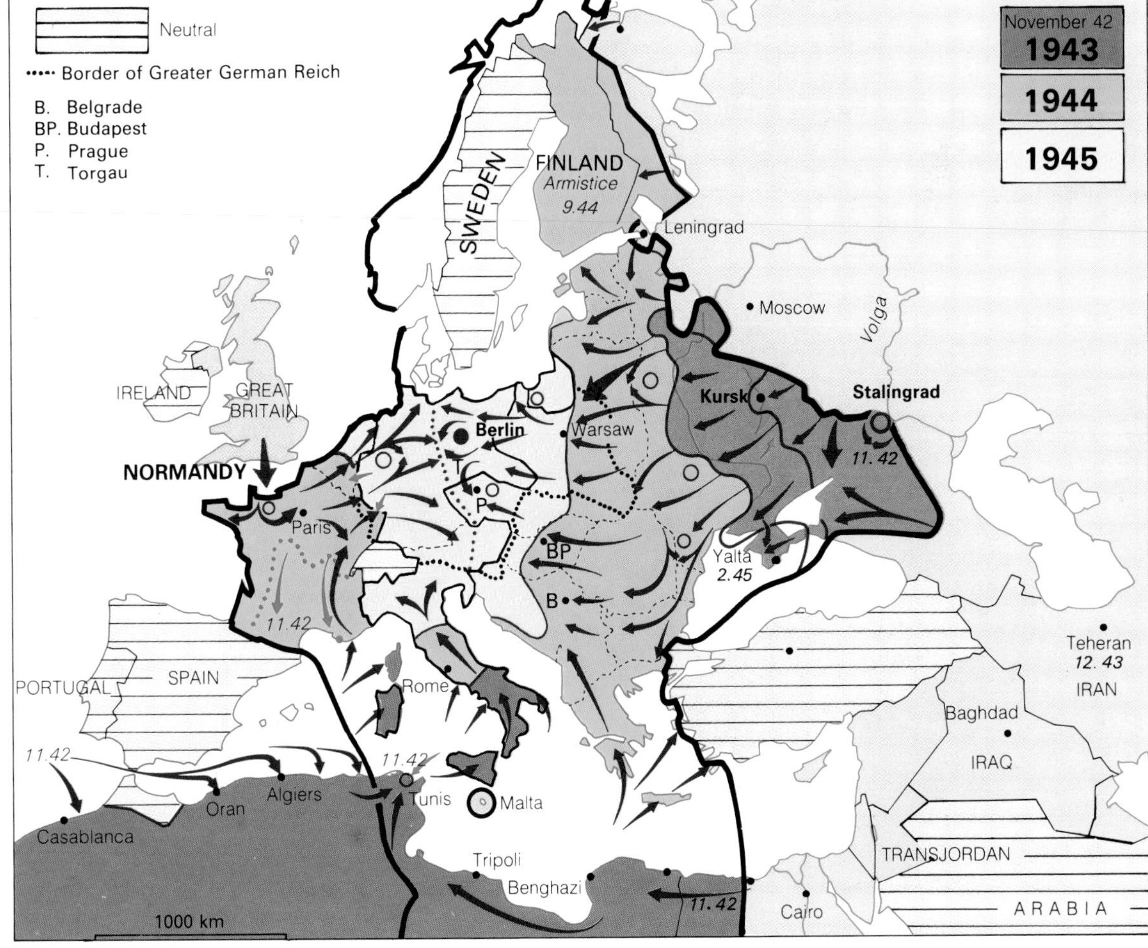


**…ration of Paris.** **Liberation of Auschwitz.**

**August 1944** **25 January 1945**

**July–October:** Soviets penetrate into German satellite states, which sign peace treaties (October–January 1945).
**16 December–27 January 1945:** German counter-offensive in the Ardennes.
**26 December–13 February 1945:** Soviets besiege Budapest.
**1945. 13 January:** Beginning of Soviet offensives in Germany.
**7 March:** Allies cross the Rhine.
**26 April:** Soviet and American forces meet.
**30 April:** Hitler commits suicide in his bunker.
**2 May:** Soviets enter Berlin. The Americans take Munich.
**7–8 May:** German surrender.

# The War: A Global Perspective

THE PLANISPHERE reveals the great disparity in size between the Axis partners and the Allied nations. The latter formed a bloc covering huge land masses, with the result that in some areas the Allies were able to develop their industrial potential safe from the enemy's strategic bombing campaigns (Canada, USA, the USSR east of the Urals). Their arms production (Great Britain included) was twice as great as the figure for the Greater Reich and Japan combined in 1941 and rose to three times that figure in 1943.

The Americans, who possessed the most powerful arms factories in the world, not only equipped themselves for a war on two fronts, they also became the 'arsenal of the democracies', and the Lease-Lend Bill (11 March 1941) was extended to include all their allies. The question of long-distance transport, therefore, became crucial. Two conditions had to be met for the United States to come to Britain's assistance. First, they needed ports backed up by air bases in the Middle East and Southern Africa in order to convey the material. Up until November 1942, when West Africa and Madagascar entered the war, the impossibility of using Dakar and Diego Suarez proved to be a stumbling-block. The British (and in September 1940 at Dakar the 'Gaullists') were ultimately forced to intervene, with varying levels of success. They succeeded only in occupying Diego Suarez, which fell on 6 May 1942.

The second condition was success in anti-submarine warfare, which was necessitated by the German *Rudeltaktik* (hunting in packs) in the Atlantic (and also in the Mediterranean and the Arctic Ocean). The situation was very difficult for the Allies until the beginning of 1943, when it began to improve as a result of technological developments and a naval building programme that outstripped losses. As a consequence, the Allies were able to carry out amphibious operations in Europe in 1944 and provide supplies for the forces on the Continent in the autumn.

By contrast, in the Pacific it was American submarines which held the initiative, attacking a Japanese merchant fleet that was ill-prepared for this type of warfare and whose losses soon exceeded the number of new ships launched. By the early months of 1945, Japan had lost all but 10% of the ships it possessed before the war (and these were its smallest vessels) and was threatened with economic asphyxiation.

The Second World War was fought out over long distances. Transport problems, therefore, assumed enormous importance and, as a further consequence, both submarine warfare and strategic bombing became particularly intense theatres of conflict.

*1. Identity checks in the Warsaw ghetto.*

*2. 'This war is a world war', De Gaulle, 18 June 1940.*

*3. Americans landing at Omaha Beach on D-Day.*

# 1939–45

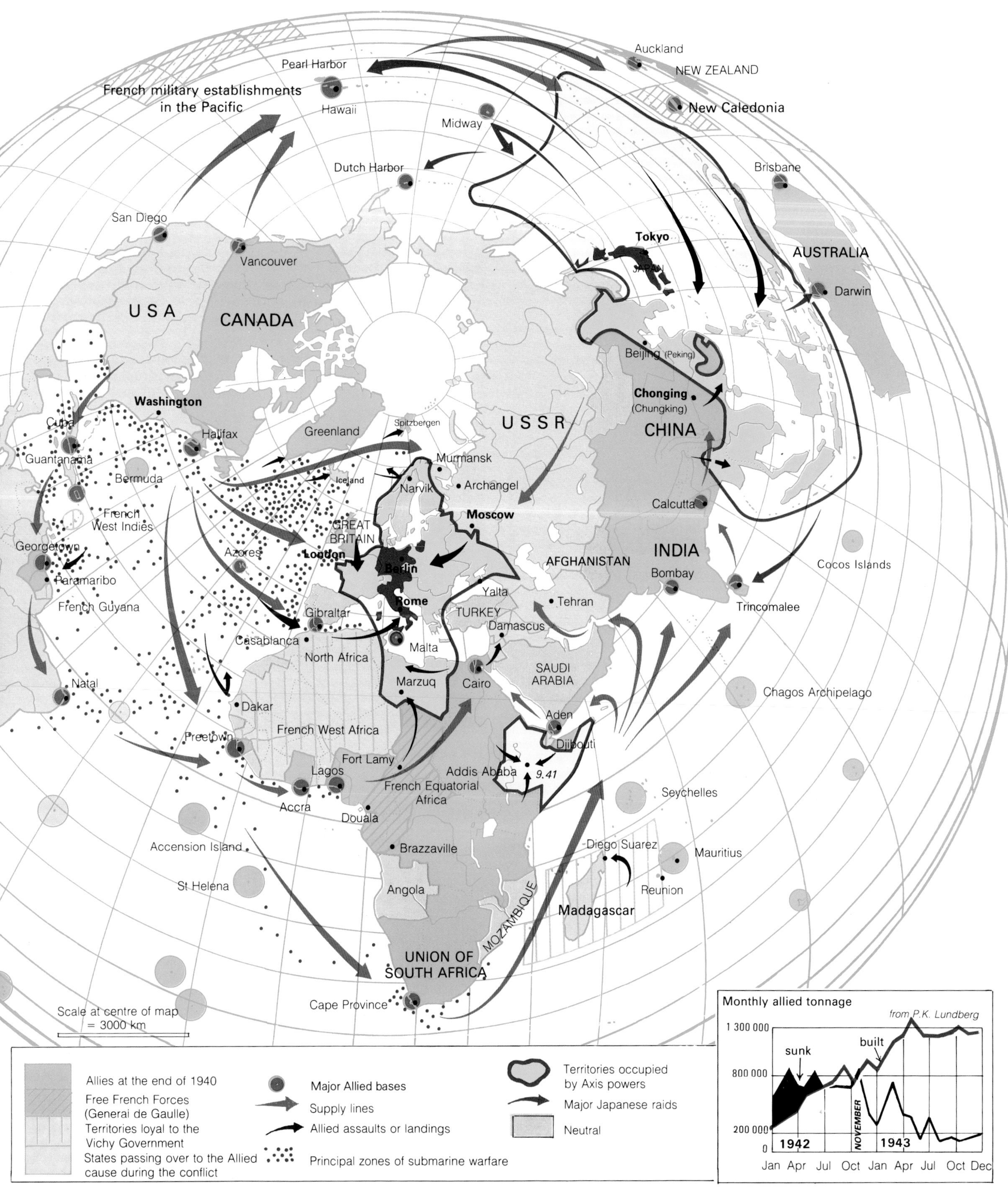

French military establishments in the Pacific
Pearl Harbor
Hawaii
Midway
Auckland
NEW ZEALAND
New Caledonia
Dutch Harbor
Brisbane
San Diego
Vancouver
Tokyo
JAPAN
AUSTRALIA
Darwin
USA
CANADA
Beijing (Peking)
Chonging (Chungking)
CHINA
Washington
Cuba
Guantanama
Halifax
Greenland
Spitzbergen
USSR
Murmansk
Bermuda
Iceland
Narvik
Archangel
Calcutta
French West Indies
GREAT BRITAIN
Moscow
London
Berlin
Georgetown
Paramaribo
French Guyana
Azores
Rome
Yalta
AFGHANISTAN
INDIA
Bombay
Cocos Islands
Tehran
Trincomalee
Gibraltar
TURKEY
Damascus
Casablanca
Malta
North Africa
SAUDI ARABIA
Natal
Marzuq
Cairo
Chagos Archipelago
Dakar
Aden
Djibouti
French West Africa
Freetown
Fort Lamy
Addis Ababa
9.41
Lagos
French Equatorial Africa
Seychelles
Accra
Douala
Accension Island
Brazzaville
Diego Suarez
Mauritius
St Helena
Angola
Reunion
MOZAMBIQUE
Madagascar
UNION OF SOUTH AFRICA
Cape Province
Scale at centre of map = 3000 km
Allies at the end of 1940
Free French Forces (Generai de Gaulle)
Territories loyal to the Vichy Government
States passing over to the Allied cause during the conflict
Major Allied bases
Supply lines
Allied assaults or landings
Principal zones of submarine warfare
Territories occupied by Axis powers
Major Japanese raids
Neutral
Monthly allied tonnage
from P.K. Lundberg
1 300 000
800 000
200 000
0
sunk
built
NOVEMBER
1942
1943
Jan Apr Jul Oct Jan Apr Jul Oct Dec

# The War in the Pacific

THE SURPRISE ATTACK on Pearl Harbor demonstrates the astonishing eagerness of the Japanese military establishment to take on the United States, who were hostile to Japanese penetration into China. It also reveals their determination to seize the resources of both Indochina and the Dutch East Indies, whose colonial rulers in Europe had fallen to the German Reich in 1940. The military occupation of Indochina, which posed a threat to Singapore and the South Seas (summer 1941), brought retaliatory measures from Roosevelt and the Commonwealth, spurring the bellicist party (Tojo) into action.

In a lightning war of only a few months' duration, the Japanese gained control of the American bases in the eastern Pacific and the main sources of raw materials in the south, and even threatened India and Australia. They may perhaps have expected to achieve a compromise peace with the Americans. The USA, however, riposted by bombarding Tokyo for the first time in the spring of 1942 and by fighting the air and sea battles of the Coral Sea and Midway. With its best units removed from the action, the Japanese navy was unable to prevent an Allied landing at Guadalcanal (Solomon Islands) in August of the same year.

*1. The Australians and Japanese do battle in the jungle of New Guinea (July 1943), painted by Ivor Hele.*

From then on the Japanese, with their communication lines over-extended and their forces too dispersed (in spite of temporary help received from the peoples they had 'liberated'), were unable to prevent the Allies carrying out a 'pincer' operation (1942–5). With General MacArthur at their head in the south, the Allies went from island to island, 'leapfrogging' those where the enemy contingents were too strong (these would later be forced to surrender when they had become encircled), and, eventually, reached the Philippines. With his 'task forces' (groups of aircraft-carriers, protection vessels and landing craft), Admiral Nimitz led the attack in the central Pacific, advancing from the Gilbert Islands as far as the Ryu Kyu. Like the British in Burma, the Americans came up against stubborn Japanese resistance (kamikaze suicide squads). At the beginning of 1945, as the Chinese were also launching an offensive, the US forces captured Iwo Jima and Okinawa, islands lying near to the Japanese archipelago. From these bases, their Flying Fortresses were able to bomb the nerve centres of Japan's war effort, as well as the supply ships arriving from Southeast Asia.

In spite of these threats, the Japanese leaders were not prepared to capitulate (they still held Indochina, the Dutch East Indies and the Chinese coasts): the American high command did not expect to be able to launch the final assault until 1946 and even then expected to suffer heavy losses (a million men).

The situation was resolved by President Truman's decision to drop the atomic bomb on Hiroshima and Nagasaki (6 and 9 August) and by the entry into the war of the USSR – it had been neutral since the treaty of 13 April 1941 – which marched into Manchuria and Korea. Emperor Hirohito decided to intervene personally and force his ministers and military leaders to agree to their country's surrender.

The act of capitulation, signed on 2 September aboard the battleship *Missouri* in the Bay of Tokyo, set the seal on bellicist Japan's defeat, but left a number of problems unresolved: Japanese occupation had dealt a fatal blow to European domination in Southeast Asia; in China, victory over the Japanese was to be followed by a confrontation between Chiang Kai-shek's nationalists and the communists led by Mao Tse-tung.

*2. Hiroshima six months after the bomb.*

| Pearl Harbor. | Fall of Singapore. | First American victory. |
|---|---|---|
| 7 December 1941 | 15 February 1942 | 7 June 1942 |

**1941. Spring–end of autumn:** US-Japanese negotiations.
**13 April:** Soviet-Japanese non-aggression pact.
**26 July:** Japanese assets in USA 'frozen'.
**29 July:** Japan obtains forces from Vichy France for the war in Southern Indochina.
**1 August:** Embargo on petrol exports.
**16–17 October:** The Tojo cabinet succeeds that of Prince Konoye in Tokyo.
**7 December:** Attack on Pearl Harbor; 8 December: Japan declares war on USA, Britain and the Commonwealth.
**10–11 December:** Japanese landings in the islands of Guam and Luzon.
**20 December:** Destruction of the *Prince of Wales* and the *Repulse*.
**1942. 18 January–17 March:** Occupation of Burma.
**15 February:** Capitulation of Singapore.
**8 March:** Occupation of Java; 7 April: Occupation of Sumatra.
**18 April:** First American bombing of Tokyo.
**4–8 May:** Battle of the Coral Sea (air and sea forces).
**8 May:** Surrender of Corregidor (Philippines).

*3. Destruction of the American fleet by the Japanese, 7 December 1941.*

**3–7 June:** American victory at Midway.
**12 June:** Japanese occupy Kiska (Aleutian Islands).
**7 August:** US landing at Guadalcanal (Solomon Islands).
**1943. 8 February:** Japanese evacuation of Guadalcanal.
**15 August:** Americans recapture Kiska.
**20 November:** American landings at Tarawa.
**1944. 31 January:** American landings in the Marshall Islands.
**20–23 May:** American landings in New Guinea.
**14 June:** Allied landings at Saipan.
**21 July:** Americans land at Guam.
**20 September:** Americans land at Leyte (Philippines).
**22–25 October:** Americans win air and sea battle at Leyte.
**1945. 23 January:** Reopening of the Burma Road to China.
**16 February–1 March:** Siege and capture of Corregidor.
**19 February–16 March:** Capture of Iwo Jima.
**1 April–21 June:** Battle of Okinawa.

# 1941–45

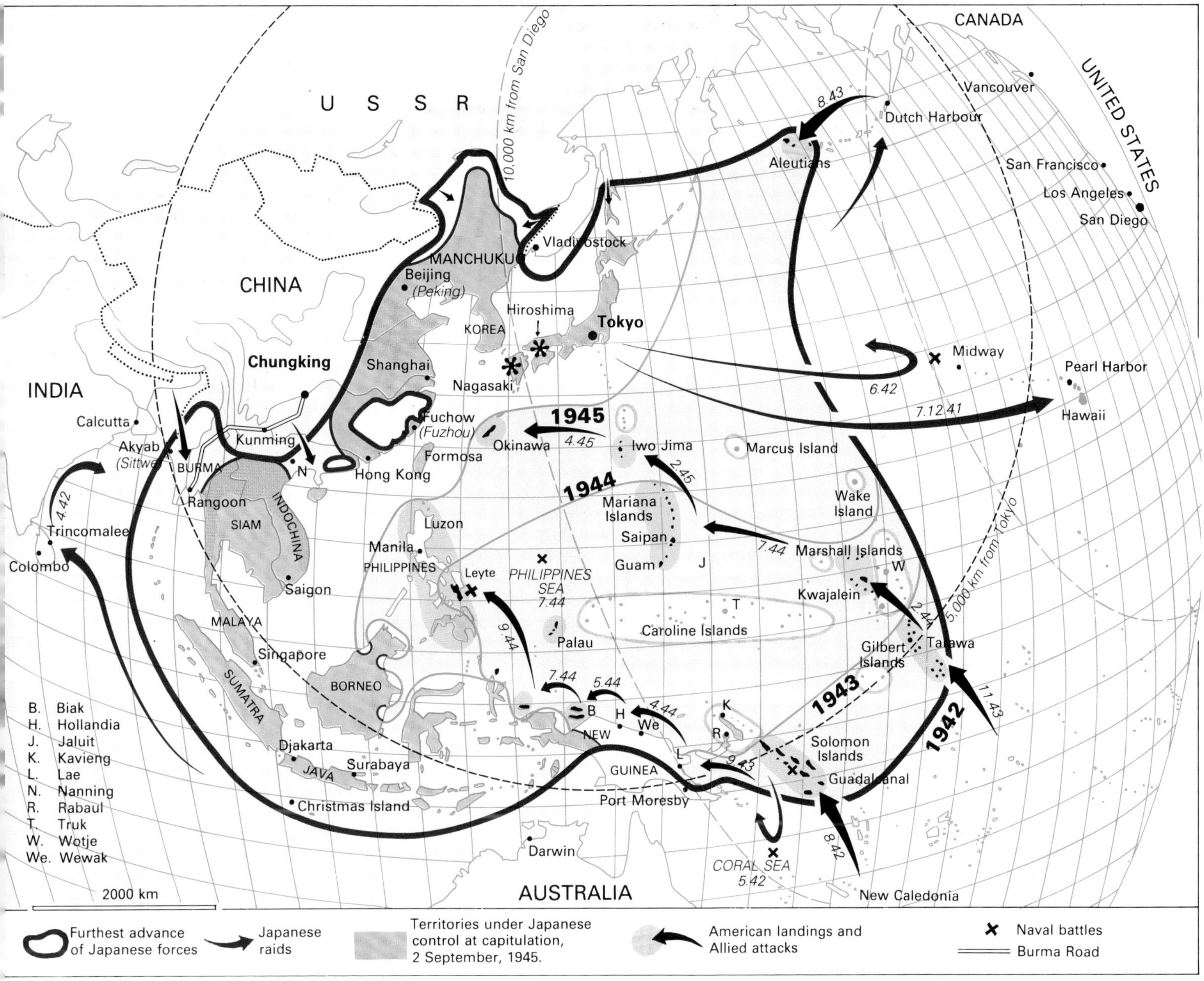

CANADA
UNITED STATES
U S S R
CHINA
INDIA
AUSTRALIA
10,000 km from San Diego
5,000 km from Tokyo
Vancouver
Dutch Harbour
San Francisco
Los Angeles
San Diego
8.43
Aleutians
Vladivostock
MANCHUKUO
Beijing (Peking)
KOREA
Hiroshima
Tokyo
Nagasaki
Midway
Pearl Harbor
Hawaii
6.42
7.12.41
Chungking
Shanghai
Calcutta
Akyab (Sittwe)
Kunming
BURMA
N
Fuchow (Fuzhou)
1945
Okinawa
4.45
Iwo Jima
2.45
Marcus Island
Formosa
Hong Kong
Rangoon
SIAM
INDOCHINA
1944
Mariana Islands
Saipan
Guam
J
Wake Island
7.44
Marshall Islands
W
Kwajalein
4.42
Trincomalee
Colombo
Luzon
Manila
PHILIPPINES
Leyte
PHILIPPINES SEA 7.44
Saigon
MALAYA
Singapore
Palau
9.44
T
Caroline Islands
2.44
Gilbert Islands
Tarawa
BORNEO
SUMATRA
7.44
5.44
B
H
4.44
We
NEW GUINEA
K
R
1943
11.43
1942
Solomon Islands
L
9.43
Guadalcanal
Djakarta
JAVA
Surabaya
Christmas Island
Port Moresby
Darwin
CORAL SEA 5.42
8.42
New Caledonia

B. Biak
H. Hollandia
J. Jaluit
K. Kavieng
L. Lae
N. Nanning
R. Rabaul
T. Truk
W. Wotje
We. Wewak

2000 km

Furthest advance of Japanese forces
Japanese raids
Territories under Japanese control at capitulation, 2 September, 1945.
American landings and Allied attacks
Naval battles
Burma Road

**Fall of General Tojo.** **16 July 1944**

**Atomic bomb.** **6 and 9 August 1945**

**14 April:** Americans take Bataan (Philippines).
**2 May:** Australians land in Borneo. British re-capture Rangoon.
**18 May:** Chinese re-take Fuchow.
**27 May:** Recapture of Nan-ning.
**14 July:** First naval bombardment of Japanese coasts.
**2 August:** Liberation of Burma completed.

**6 and 9 August:** Atomic bombs dropped on Hiroshima and Nagasaki.
**8 August:** USSR enters war against Japan.
**9 August:** Beginning of Soviet campaign in Manchuria.
**15 August:** Japanese delegation surrenders to the American general MacArthur at Manila.
**2 September:** Signature of Japanese capitulation aboard the *Missouri*.

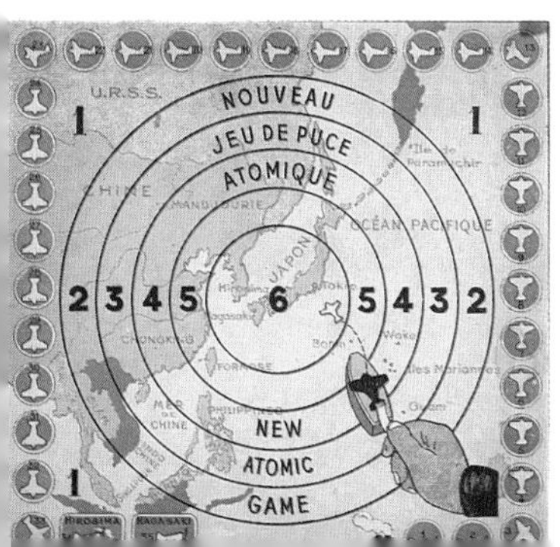

*5. The Japanese plenipotentiaries surrender on the battleship* Missouri*, 2 September 1945.*

# From Cezanne to Beckett

THE FIRST DECADES of the century saw a remarkable blossoming of artistic schools and movements. In Paris, after Seurat had given an intellectualist turn to Impressionism, the *fauves*, who were influenced by Van Gogh and Gauguin, rediscovered the expressive and emotive power of colour. The Cubists of the *Bateau-Lavoir* (Picasso, Braque, Juan Gris) took up Cézanne's legacy and transformed it, particularly through the use of collage. In Germany, the Expressionists (Kokoschka) enrolled poetry and painting in the cause of an anguish-laden rebellion, whilst Kandinsky and Klee (*Der blaue Reiter*) sought in pure colour the manifestation of an 'inner necessity'. Mondrian and Malevich were to extend this line of development into the most rarefied abstraction, whilst the Surrealists, more concerned with the imagination than with questions of technique, went in search of the 'convulsive beauty' of the dream-state which they hoped to find in 'transfigured' objects from everyday life (Ernst, Dali, Miró). After 1945 the United States was the most lively centre of avant-garde activity, particularly with movements like Pollock's 'Action Painting', even if certain tendencies there such as Pop Art maintained a somewhat ambiguous relationship with industrial society. It must be added that a list of schools and tendencies does not do complete justice to the contributions of the century's truly creative personalities, such as Matisse, Kandinsky, Klee and, above all, Picasso, who masterfully transmuted the various conflicting movements into 'periods' of his own life.

After the arabesques of Art Nouveau, architecture discovered the potential of reinforced concrete (Perret) and the beauty of stark forms. But the elegant and daring innovations of Van de Velde, Le Corbusier, Mies van der Rohe and Frank Lloyd Wright would subsequently give way to the monumental public architecture of Stalin's Russia, fascist Italy and Nazi Germany (Speer). After the Second World War, in spite of certain projects conceived on a grand scale (e.g. Niemeyer's Brasilia), the 'international style' came to dominate and, although design exerted a widespread influence, the Bauhaus ideal of a synthesis of all the plastic arts remained a utopian dream.

In the period in which Debussy, Ravel and Stravinsky were composing for the *Ballets russes*, Schoenberg and Webern launched music on the adventurous course of the atonal 'series'. In the same spirit, with his *Wozzeck*, A. Berg created twentieth-century opera. In France, the Group of Six (whose leading members were Poulenc, Honegger and Milhaud) were innovators who, nonetheless, respected traditional forms. After 1945, Messiaen seemed the master of contemporary music, though certain composers, while remaining faithful to the atonal (e.g. Boulez), were to experiment with radically new techniques, including concrete music (Schaeffer) and electro-acoustic or aleatory music (Berio, Stockhausen, Maderna, Xenakis). Finally, we should not forget the role played by jazz since its birth in New Orleans around 1910.

The hermetic but ambitious art of poetry sparkled with a rare brilliance in this period, both in France (Apollinaire, Valéry, Claudel, Breton, Éluard and Char) and in the rest of Europe (Rilke, Eliot, Yeats, Mayakovsky). Moreover, Expressionism and Surrealism sought to bring together poetry, painting and cinema in a common quest. In the work of Proust, Joyce and the Austrian, Musil, the traditional forms of narration were broken down. The novel remained, nonetheless, the privileged instrument of psychological analysis (Gide, Thomas Mann, Mauriac) and of social and political criticism (Aragon, Orwell, Céline), whilst also opening itself up to philosophical reflection in the work of Sartre and Camus and to phenomenological abstraction in the Nouveau Roman. It is through the novel, nowadays, that the Columbian writer (Garcia Marquez) or the Russian (Solzhenitsyn) makes his voice heard.

1. Les Demoiselles d'Avignon *by Picasso, 1907.*

| Death of Rimbaud | Debussy's *Pelléas et Mélisande.* | Proust, *Swann's Way.* | Death of Modigliani. | Kafka, *The Trial.* | Bunuel, *Un chien andal* |
|---|---|---|---|---|---|
| 1891 | 1902 | 1913 | 1920 | 1925 | 1928 |

2. La Montagne Sainte-Victoire *by Cezanne, c. 1905.*

**1890:** Death of Van Gogh.
**1891:** Gauguin in Polynesia.
**1895:** The Lumière brothers invent the cinetamograph.
**1896:** Puccini, *La Bohème* (vérismo).
**1897:** Klimt and the Vienna Secession.
**1900:** Exposition universelle (Paris).
**1902:** Debussy *Pelléas et Mélisande.* Rilke meets Rodin.
**1905:** *Die Brücke* (Dresden). Les fauves (Paris).
**1906:** Death of Cézanne.
**1907:** Picasso, *Les Demoiselles d'Avignon.*
**1908:** Richard Strauss, *Elektra.*
**1909:** *La Nouvelle Revue francaise.* The *Ballets russes* in Paris.
**1910:** *Der Blaue Reiter* (Munich), Marinetti, Futurism (Turin), Acmeism (Moscow).
**1912:** Schoenberg, *Pierrot Lunaire.*
**1913:** Stravinsky, *The Rite of Spring.* Proust, *Swann's Way.* Apollinaire, *Alcools.*
**1917:** Satie, Picasso, Diaghilev, *Parade.* Mondrian founds 'De Stijl'. Valéry, *La jeune Parque.*
**1918:** Cocteau and the Group of Six. Dada Manifesto.
**1919:** Gropius founds the Bauhaus.
**1922:** Joyce, *Ulysses.* Mural paintings in Mexico.
**1924:** Breton, *Surrealist Manifesto.*
**1925:** Berg, *Wozzek.* Kafka, *The Trial.*
**1926:** Éluard, *Capitale de la douleur.* Aragon, *The Paris Peasant.* Gide, *The Counterfeiters.*
**1928:** Brecht-Weill, *The Threepenny Opera.* Bunuel-Dali, *Un chien andalou.*
**1929:** Talking cinema. Faulkner, *The Sound and the Fury.* Claudel, *Le Soulier de satin.*
**1930:** Breton, *Second Surrealist Manifesto.* Musil, *The Man without Qualities.*
**1932:** Céline, *Journey to the End of the Night.*
**1933:** Malraux, *The Human Condition.*
**1934:** Socialist realism in the USSR. Aragon, *Les Cloches de Bâle.* Char, *Le marteau sans maître.*
**1937:** Picasso, *Guernica.* Exhibition of 'degenerate' art organized by the Nazis (Munich).
**1938:** Eisenstein-Prokofiev, *Alexander Nevsky.*
**1944:** Sartre, *In Camera.* Existentialism.
**1945:** Carné-Prévert, *Les Enfants du paradis.*
**1946:** Rossellini, *Païsa* (Italian neo-realism).

# 1890–1989

**ART NOUVEAU (MODERN STLYE, JUGENDSTIL)**
*Paris*, Guimard. *Nancy*, Gallé. *Barcelona*, Gaudi. *Brussels*, Horta, Van de Velde *Munich*, *Vienna*, Kilmt, *London*. Morris, Arts and Crafts. *Edinburgh*

**EXPRESSIONISM**
*Oslo*, Munch. *Brussels*, Ensor. *Arles*, Van Gogh. *Dresden*, Die Brücke. *Munich*, Der blaue Reiter. *Berlin*, Der Sturm, Neue Sachlichkeit around 1920. *Paris*, The Fauves Derain, Matisse, Vlaminck.

**DADA**
*Zurich*, Tzara 1916. *Berlin*, 1917. *Cologne*, Max Ernst, 1918. *Hanover*, Schwitters, Merz, 1919. *Paris*, 1920

**BAUHAUS**
*Darmstadt*, Behrens. *Weimar*, *Dressau*. *Berlin*, Le Corbusier.

**SURREALISM**
*Paris*, *Brussels*, *Prague*.

**FUTURISM**
*Turin*, *Moscow*.

**CUBISM and ORPHISM**
*Paris*.

**SUPREMATISM**
*St Petersburg*, Malevich.

**'DE STIJL'**
*Amsterdam*, Mondrian.

**CONSTRUCTIVISM**
*Moscow*, Pevsner.

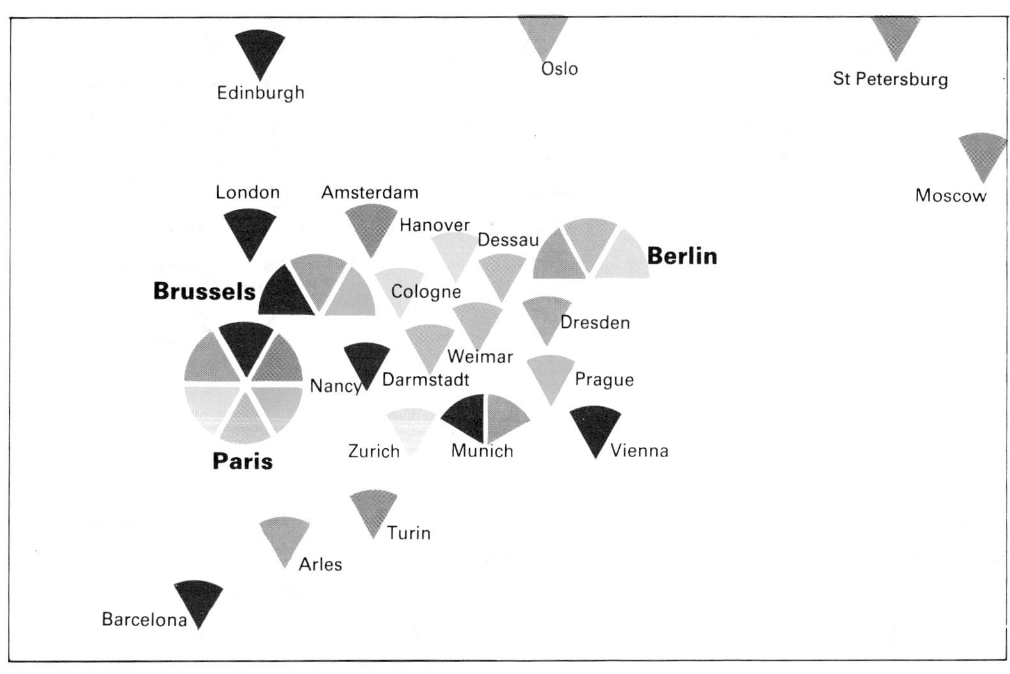


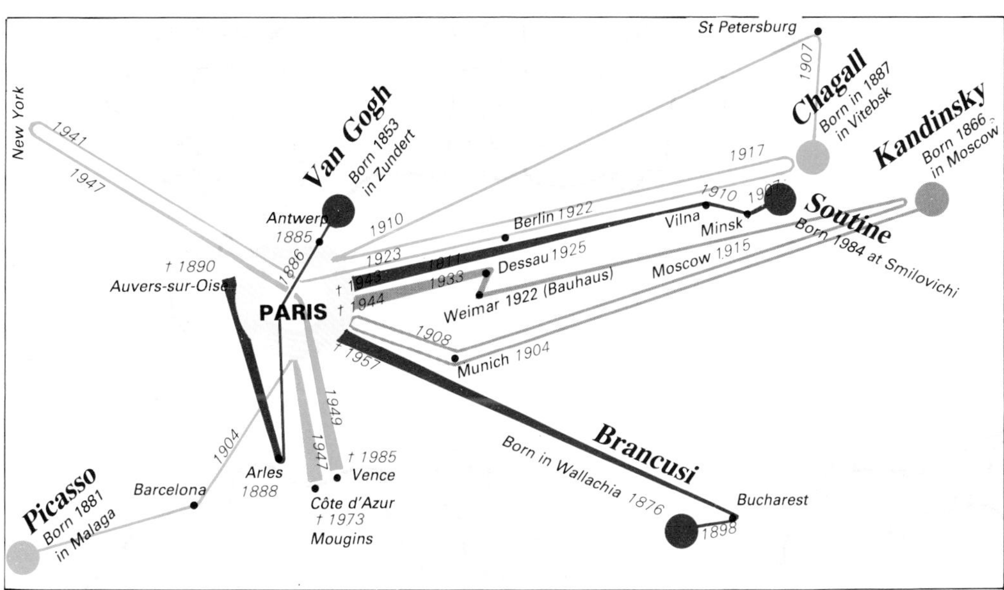


| 1942 | 1951 | 1955 | 1965 | 1985 | 1988 | 1989 |
|---|---|---|---|---|---|---|
| **Camus, *The Outsider*.** | **Beckett, *Molloy*.** | **Death of Nicolas de Staël.** | **Georges Perec, *Les Choses*.** | **Marguerite Duras, *L'Amant*.** | **Death of René Char.** | **Death of Salvador Dali.** |

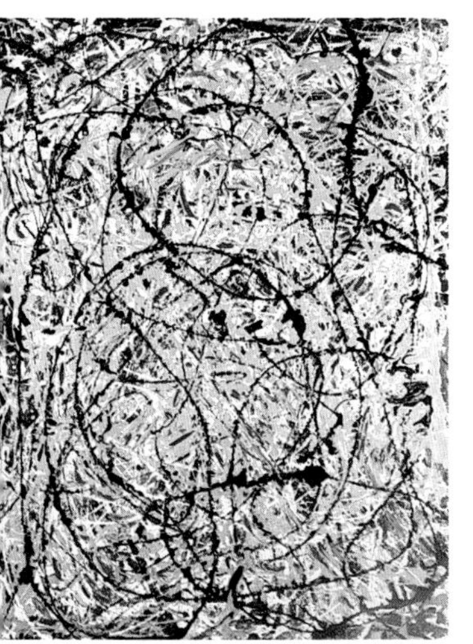

3. Watery Paths *by Jackson Pollock, 1947.*

**1947:** Camus, *The Plague*. Pollock, Action Painting.
**1950:** Discovery of Japanese cinema (Kurosawa).
**1953:** Beckett, *Waiting for Godot*.
**1954:** Fellini, *La Strada*.
**1955:** Boulez, *Le Marteau sans maître*.
**1956:** Bergman, *The Seventh Seal*.
**1957:** The Nouveau Roman.
**1959:** Godard, Truffaut, the *nouvelle vague*.
**1960:** Pop Art (Andy Warhol). *Tel Quel*.
**1967:** Garcia Marquez, *One Hundred Years of Solitude*. Hyperrealism.
**1968:** *Living Theatre* at Avignon. Solzhenitsyn, *Cancer Ward*.
**1969:** Beckett, Nobel Prize for Literature.
**1973:** Death of Picasso.
**1985:** Claude Simon, Nobel Prize for Literature.

*4. The National Gallery of Art, Washington, by the architect Pei, built in 1978.*

# From Riemann to Sartre

THE CLASSICAL PICTURE of a world regulated like clockwork has given way to a new vision of a constantly shifting universe. The phenomenology of the radiation, emission and absorption of light by matter has revealed a paradoxical entity, now wave, now particle, discontinuous and indeterminable: yet it is nonetheless subject to only four fundamental forces (gravitational, electromagnetic, weak and strong interactions), structured by a universal constant (Planck) and invariant for the observer in relative motion (Einstein).

This entity is Niels Bohr's atom. It contains a nucleus (protons and neutrons) which is positively charged, around which orbit negatively-charged electrons that balance its mass. These jump from one orbit to another, radiate, spin on their own axis and are magnetically charged, all according to Planck's constant. An atomic number can now be given to each of the elements in Mendeleyev's table of atomic weights: the periodic system indicates the orbits and the groups the electronic structure.

The experimental creation of energy-matter exchange by radiation gave rise to new industrial and medical techniques. Now the mainstay of the television set, the cathode tube was invented by Hittorf in 1869. At the phosphorescent end of a tube containing a vacuum, at the other end of which was an incandescent cathode, he observed the projected shadow of a cross placed in the middle; he thus discovered the cathode ray. In 1895 Röntgen studied the phenomenon of fluorescence on the outside of a cathode tube and discovered X-rays; thus was radiology born. In 1897 J. J. Thomson calculated the mass of these cathodic particles and discovered the electron; this was the beginning of electronics.

These results were only reached through new mathematical schemata: the notion of variety, the geometric object generalized to any number of dimensions, notions of metrics in Euclidian spaces with nil curvature and non-Euclidian spaces with positive or negative curvatures (Riemann); matrix theory (Cayley), theory of invariance

*1. The chemist and biologist Louis Pasteur towards the end of his life (c. 1890).*

*2. The physicist Albert Einstein in the USA in 1934.*

**1854** — **Riemann's hypotheses on the basic principles of geometry.**

**1896** — **H. Bergson's *Matière et Memoire.***

**1905** — **Einstein discovers special relativity.**

*4. The French mathematician Henri Poincaré (1854–1910), founder of algebraic topology.*

**1864:** Maxwell's equations governing the electromagnetic field, the transverse wave of which is light.
**1865:** Mendel's laws describe the discontinuous transmission of genetic inheritance.
**1869:** Periodic table of elements (Mendeleyev). The properties of chemical elements are periodic functions of their atomic weights. Elements are classified in order of increasing atomic weight, forming a table, with vertical columns representing the broad chemical groups (alkali metals, alkaline-earth metals etc) and the horizontal lines the periods. The gaps in the table have since been filled by the discovery of elements as predicted (scandium, gallium etc) and the artificial creation of elements beyond uranium, such as neptunium and plutonium.
**1888:** Institut Pasteur founded by international public subscription after the invention of rabies vaccination.
**1896:** Becquerel discovers radioactivity by neutralizing the phenomenon of phosphorescence and observing the spontaneous radiation of uranium salts.

**1900:** Planck's constant: energy is constituted of discrete units, quanta of energy, determined by a universal constant. $h = 6.55 \times 10^{-27}$ erg-second.

*5. The French philosopher Henri Bergson c. 1911.*

**1905:** Einstein's theory of special relativity. Measurements made with instruments in uniform relative motion are invariant under a given group of transformations of frames of reference (space–time co-ordinates) that vary in speed compared to the ultimate speed, that of light. Frames of reference will hardly be affected by motion on a human scale, where speed is low compared to that of light (300,000 km per second in a vacuum). But they are affected by motion at the atomic level, where speeds approximate to that of light; we can only conclude that rulers will shrink and clocks slow down.
**1916:** Einstein's theory of general relativity. Extends the principle of relativity to the accelerated motion of a frame of reference; this leads to the definition of gravitation by the curvature of space.
**1924–7:** Quantum mechanics: mathematical laws governing the movement of elementary particles in which wave and particle phenomena are linked through Planck's constant. The same equations, obtained with different mathematical schemata, led to different interpretations. For some people

# 1850–1945

*3. Scales of atomic weights of the Russian chemist Dmitry Ivanovich Mendeleyev: the blank spaces correspond to elements unknown at the time and discovered subsequently. From* Le Bulletin Scientifique, *Paris, 1879.*

| Séries | Groupe I | Groupe II | Groupe III | Groupe IV | Groupe V | Groupe VI | Groupe VII | Groupe VIII |
|---|---|---|---|---|---|---|---|---|
| — | — | — | — | — | — | — | — | — |
| | | | | $RH^4$ | $RH^3$ | $RH^2$ | RH | |
| | $R^2O$ | RO | $R^2O^3$ | $RO^2$ | $R^2O^5$ | $RO^3$ | $R^2O^7$ | RO |
| — | — | — | — | — | — | — | — | — |
| 1 | H = 1 | » | » | » | » | » | » | |
| 2 | Li = 7 | Be = 9.4 | B = 11 | C = 12 | N = 14 | O = 16 | Fe = 19 | |
| 3 | Na = 23 | Mg = 24 | Al = 27.3 | Si = 28 | P = 31 | S = 32 | Cl = 35.5 | |
| 4 | K = 39 | Ca = 40 | — = 44 | Ti = 48 | V = 51 | Cr = 52 | Mn = 55..... | Fe = 56; Co = 59; Ni = 59; Cu = 63. |
| 5 | (Cu = 63) | Zn = 65 | — = 68 | — = 72 | As = 75 | Se = 78 | Br = 80 | |
| 6 | Rb = 85 | Sr = 87 | ?Yt = 88 | Zr = 90 | Nb = 94 | Mo = 96 | — = 100..... | Ru = 104; Rh = 104; Pd = 106; Ag = 108. |
| 7 | (Ag = 108) | Cd = 112 | In = 113 | Sn = 118 | Sb = 122 | Fe = 125 | I = 127 | |
| 8 | Cs = 133 | Ba = 137 | ?Di = 138 | ?Ce = 140 | » | » | » | |
| 9 | » | » | » | » | » | » | » | |
| 10 | » | » | ?Er = 178 | ?La = 180 | Ta = 182 | W = 184 | » ..... | Os = 195; Ir = 197; Pt = 198; Au = 199. |
| 11 | (Au = 199) | Hg = 200 | Tl = 204 | Pb = 207 | Bi = 208 | » | » | |
| 12 | » | » | » | Th = 231 | » | Ur = 240 | » | » » » » |

under a given group of transformations (Klein), set theory (Cantor); the theory of dynamic systems (Poincaré).

Then there are the philosophical questions: firstly, determinism. A phenomenon is determined if, knowing its initial state and its rate of change, we can deduce its successive states, its trajectory. But the observation of elementary particles implies a margin of error of the same magnitude as the measurement to be effected (a photon is needed to spot an electron), so that the localization of the phenomenon and the determination of its velocity become incompatible, and the trajectory can only be arrived at statistically. The knowledge of a phenomenon cannot be both accurate and complete (Copenhagen School).

A second, more metaphysical question is that of meaning: the world is no longer the work of a rational God; yet subject to the laws of chance, with neither cause nor goal, it seems absurd. To the analytical philosopher (Russell, Wittgenstein, the Vienna Circle) such a question, like any metaphysical question, cannot be posed because it is meaningless. To the phenomenological philosopher (Bergson, Husserl, Heidegger, Sartre), man is the bearer of meaning because he chooses to be, because he is free.

**Bohr's atom.**

**1913**

*6. The British philosopher and logician Bertrand Russell, (1872–1970), author of the* Principia Mathematica, *towards the end of his life.*

*7. Ludwig Wittgenstein (1889–1951), Viennese philosopher who became a naturalized British citizen. A student of Russell, famous for his research on the foundations of mathematics.*

**Quantum mechanics.**

**1924–27**

(Broglie, Schrödinger), waves and particles are real, albeit mysterious, space–time entities. For others (Heisenberg, Dirac), they are only the probable outcome of particular measurements and have no physical reality.

**1934:** Frédéric and Irène Joliot-Curie discover artificial radioactivity.

**1939:** *Eléments de mathématique* (Bourbaki) A group of French mathematicians writing under the collective pseudonym of Bourbaki undertake the axiomatic reconstruction of the whole body of mathematics from a few key structures.

**Manhattan project produces atomic bomb.**

**January 1943**

*8. The French philosopher and writer, Jean-Paul Sartre (1905–1980).*

# From Alliance to Cold War

1. *The three men of Yalta from left to right: Churchill, Roosevelt, Stalin.*

IT IS GENERALLY BELIEVED that Roosevelt, Stalin and Churchill met at Yalta in February to divide up the world between them. Roosevelt, who was the initiator of the Conference, had, in reality, quite different objectives. In the first instance, he needed to ensure that the USSR would in fact enter the war against Japan once the Reich had capitulated. Stalin was happy to conclude a secret agreement with him to that effect, which involved in exchange the restitution to the USSR of the territory ceded by Tsar Nicholas II after the Russo-Japanese War of 1904–5.

Another objective was to build a 'United Nations Organization' whose goal was the indefinite preservation of the alliance between the victors over the Reich. Roosevelt had no doubt that America, which alone was capable of being an honest broker between 'British imperialism' and 'Soviet communism', would be its real leader. And in fact he had no difficulty in obtaining from Stalin and Churchill the formation – alongside a General Assembly open to all members on an equal footing – of a Security Council possessing broad powers for the maintenance of peace within which the five great powers (USA, Great Britain, USSR, France and China) would each have a permanent seat and a right of veto. The incessant interventions of this Council, particularly on the initiative of the USSR, paralysed the United Nations, which has proved powerless to prevent the outbreak of some 130 local conflicts since its inception.

The UN has been no more successful in preventing the formation, in the East and in the West, of two great antagonistic power blocs, which have no doubt only been restrained from coming into direct conflict on the battlefield by the fear of nuclear apocalypse. These blocs were, in fact, already in the course of being formed before Yalta, Stalin being clearly determined to conserve within his ambit all the territories occupied by the Red Army. Churchill himself had been to Moscow in the previous October and had reached an agreement on how the Balkans were to be divided up into zones of influence. This gave a free hand to the British in Greece, left Rumania and Bulgaria to the Soviets and divided Hungary and Yugoslavia equally between the two powers.

The agreement did not cover Poland, where two rival bodies – one in London, the other set up in liberated Poland by Soviet troops – disputed the government of the country. One of the major subjects of discussion at Yalta concerned the fusion of these two groups, which would not occur until the following June. The Americans then had to yield over the essential question for fear of endangering the prospects of Soviet participation in the war against Japan. There remained Czechoslovakia, which was not discussed at Yalta, Austria, on which the three great powers had reached an agreement (at Teheran in 1943) to restore its independence, and Germany.

At Teheran, there had been a plan for Germany to be dismembered into several regional states. This project was taken up again at Yalta. But, subsequently, Stalin had an unexpected change of mind. At Potsdam in July he met Truman, successor to Roosevelt (who had died in April), and Attlee, who had defeated Churchill at the polls; they decided to maintain a united but permanently demilitarized Germany, whose industrial power would be limited. Maintaining this unity would, however, have presupposed the continuing unity of the victor nations. From the moment the Cold War began to develop, the demarcation line from Czechoslovakia to the Far East between the occupying Soviet forces on the one hand and the British, French and American forces on the other ineluctably became a frontier between two Germanies, two Europes and, ultimately, two different worlds. To use Churchill's expression, it became an 'Iron Curtain'.

**Atlantic Charter.**

**14 August 1941**

**1941. 22 June:** Germany invades USSR.
**14 August:** Roosevelt and Churchill sign Atlantic Charter, recognizing the principles of self-determination for all peoples and excluding any territorial settlements that do not have the agreement of the parties concerned.
**7 December:** Attack on Pearl Harbor by the Japanese. United States at war.
**1 January 1942:** 26 countries at war against the Axis adopt a 'United Nations declaration', which echoes the terms of the Atlantic Charter and adds a clause on freedom of worship.
**1943. 22 May:** Dissolution of the Comintern (the Communist International founded at Moscow in March 1919).
**28 November–2 December:** Stalin-Roosevelt-Churchill Conference at Teheran. USSR adds its name to 'United Nations Declaration'. Agreement on the re-establishment of Austria's independence and on the principle of the division of Germany. Discussions on Poland come to no clear conclusion.
**1944. 1–22 July:** Bretton Woods

2. *De Gaulle in Moscow, December 1944. Molotov is to his left.*

**Teheran Conference.**

**28 November–2 December 1943**

Conference, which establishes the Gold Exchange Standard.
**23 July:** Constitution of a pro-Soviet Polish provisional government in opposition to the government in exile in London.
**9 October:** Agreement between Churchill and Stalin in Moscow on zones of influence in the Balkans.
**14 November:** Agreement between USSR, USA and Britain on zones of occupation in Germany.
**3 December–12 January:** First civil war in Greece. Bound by the agreement with Churchill, the USSR allows the British to crush the Communists.
**10 December:** De Gaulle signs a Mutual Aid pact with Stalin.
**1945. 4–11 February:** Stalin-Roosevelt-Churchill conference at Yalta. Agreement on the creation of the United Nations. Adoption of a 'declaration on post-war Europe' promising democratic institutions to all countries liberated from Nazi occupation. Confirmation of the return to the USSR of the eastern part of Poland that had been annexed since 1939 (as a result of the secret clauses in

# 1941–6

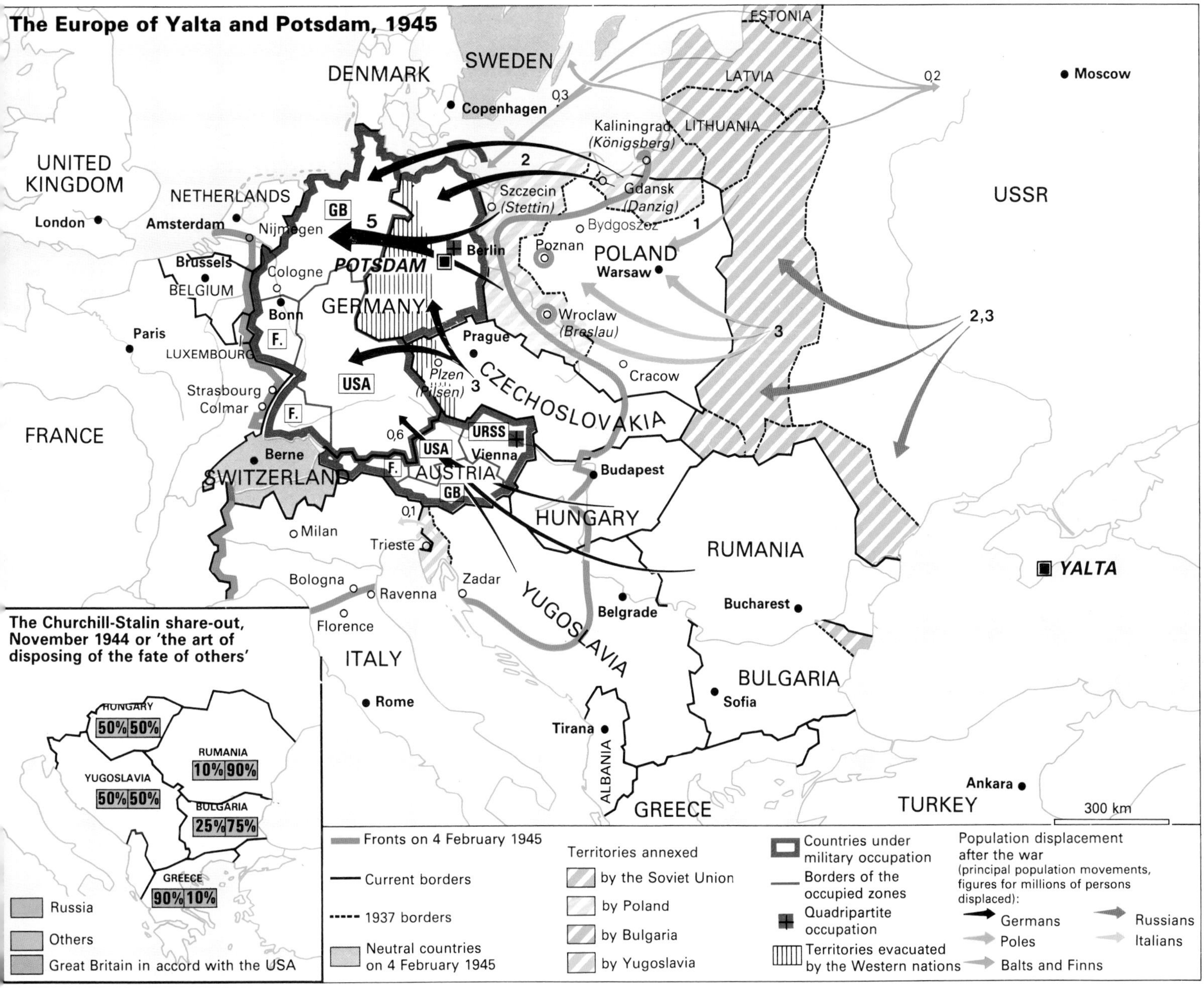

## The Europe of Yalta and Potsdam, 1945

DENMARK, SWEDEN, ESTONIA, LATVIA, LITHUANIA, UNITED KINGDOM, NETHERLANDS, BELGIUM, LUXEMBOURG, FRANCE, SWITZERLAND, GERMANY, POLAND, USSR, CZECHOSLOVAKIA, AUSTRIA, HUNGARY, RUMANIA, YUGOSLAVIA, ITALY, BULGARIA, ALBANIA, GREECE, TURKEY

Moscow, Copenhagen, Kaliningrad (Königsberg), Gdansk (Danzig), Szczecin (Stettin), Bydgoszcz, Poznan, Warsaw, Wroclaw (Breslau), Cracow, London, Amsterdam, Nijmegen, Brussels, Cologne, Bonn, POTSDAM, Berlin, Paris, Prague, Plzen (Pilsen), Strasbourg, Colmar, Berne, Vienna, Budapest, Milan, Trieste, Bologna, Ravenna, Florence, Zadar, Belgrade, Bucharest, YALTA, Sofia, Rome, Tirana, Ankara

GB, USA, F., URSS

300 km

### The Churchill-Stalin share-out, November 1944 or 'the art of disposing of the fate of others'

| | | |
|---|---|---|
| HUNGARY | 50% | 50% |
| RUMANIA | 10% | 90% |
| YUGOSLAVIA | 50% | 50% |
| BULGARIA | 25% | 75% |
| GREECE | 90% | 10% |

Russia
Others
Great Britain in accord with the USA

Fronts on 4 February 1945
Current borders
1937 borders
Neutral countries on 4 February 1945

Territories annexed
by the Soviet Union
by Poland
by Bulgaria
by Yugoslavia

Countries under military occupation
Borders of the occupied zones
Quadripartite occupation
Territories evacuated by the Western nations

Population displacement after the war
(principal population movements, figures for millions of persons displaced):
Germans
Poles
Balts and Finns
Russians
Italians

**Yalta Conference.** 4–11 February 1945 | **Potsdam Conference.** 17 July–2 August 1945 | **Churchill's Fulton speech.** 5 March 1946

the Nazi–Soviet Pact of the previous August), it being understood that Warsaw would receive substantial compensation at German expense. Long discussions on the merging of the two Polish governments and on the sum of reparations to be paid by Germany. Agreement on the conditions on which Russia was to join in the war against Japan.
**12 April:** Death of Roosevelt. Truman becomes President of USA.
**25 June:** Signature of the United Nations Charter.
**6 July:** The USA and Great Britain recognize the Polish government of national unity, of which S. Mikolajczyk, the president of the government in exile, becomes vice-president.
**17 July–2 August:** Conference at Potsdam between Stalin, Truman and Churchill (who is replaced during the conference, after his electoral defeat, by Attlee). Germany is to be permanently de-militarized and its industrial capacity reduced, but its unity will be maintained, power being provisionally exercised by the four Allied military commanders. Poland is to be allowed to continue to administer the part of Germany occupied by its troops. The definitive settlement of the frontier question is postponed till the negotiation of the peace treaty.
**6 August:** Hiroshima.
**8 August:** Soviet intervention against Japan.
**15 August:** Japan surrenders.
**17 August:** Soviet-Polish agreement on the Oder-Neisse frontier.
**1946. 5 March:** Churchill's anti-Soviet speech at Fulton. Beginning of the Cold War.

*3. Signature of the United Nations Charter at San Francisco.*
*– Andrei Gromyko and the Soviet delegation, 26 June 1945.*
*– Secretary of State Stettinius and President Truman, 28 June 1945.*

*4. General MacArthur and Emperor Hirohito, 15 October 1945.*

# Decolonization: Beginnings

To PARAPHRASE Lenin's famous words, it might be said that, 'a colonial power gives its colony the rope with which to hang it'. By imposing a new economic and social system, colonialism causes the break-up of traditional societies, but at the same time it produces agents of decolonization: networks of village leaders (the Indian maliks, the Algerian rural leaders), trade unionists in the towns (Tunisia), a civil and military petit bourgeoisie (Egypt and Black Africa). It introduces its colonies into the world economy, bends them to its needs, leaves them open to exploitation and arbitrary power. But it also exposes them to the wind of change, to new influences and models. Its schools, universities and factories create a group of men in its own image, cultural hybrids prone to feelings of frustration and malaise but also skilled in manipulating the ideas and weapons of the rulers. Eventually they will return to their own cultural heritage to forge a national identity: the Indian nation for which Gandhi fought was a Hindu *maharani*, Jinnah's Pakistan a Muslim 'Land of the Pure'; for Arab peoples seeking independence (with the exception of Syria and Iraq) Islam was the guiding principle (this was also the case for the followers of the Riff leader Abd el-Krim). But these élites are also – perhaps essentially – Western intellectuals; their model is the nation-state, their ideologies those of the West. This is the greatest paradox of colonialism. Western values inevitably lead to a condemnation of the colonial phenomenon.

1. Gandhi at the spinning wheel.

We need only think of the influence of Marxism, of the republican values inculcated by colonial French schoolteachers or the British liberalism absorbed at Oxford or Cambridge by Indian and African élites. The efficiency of the West, its sophisticated political and military organizations were imported by the colonies and eventually turned against the colonial powers themselves. Political parties sprang up everywhere to take on the political and ideological leadership of the masses, armies on the Western model assumed the lead in liberation struggles and lawyers employed all the sophistry of French or British law to argue their cause. Last, but not least, the language of the colonial powers and their cultural system proved an admirable way of unifying vast and disparate areas such as India, Africa and Southeast Asia.

As the West suffered repeated crises – the First World War, the Russian Revolution, the Depression, the Second World War – and became less and less sure of its moral position, colonized people found effective allies in anti-colonialist militants of all tendencies: progressive intellectuals, liberal politicians and churchmen. Even before the first wave of decolonization, colonialism had already lost the moral battle at home. It was considered economically out-of-date, politically unreformable and morally indefensible. The era of Kipling gave way to the idealism of Woodrow Wilson and the determined anti-colonialism of the Atlantic Charter. After the Bandung Conference there was no turning back: the Third World had made its appearance on the historical scene, and an era begun five centuries before with the dawn of European expansion had now come to an end.

**President Woodrow Wilson's Fourteen Points.** — **8 January 1918**

**Speech by Nguyen Ai Quoc (Ho Chi Minh) at Congress of Tours.** — **December 1920**

**Lyautey resident-general in Morocco.** — **1912–25**

**1855:** Indian Congress Party founded.
**8 January 1918:** Woodrow Wilson's 14 Points for Peace.
**1919:** Massacre at Amritsar (13 April) in India; Afghan independence war (Armistice 8 August). Emir Khalid's action in Algeria.
**1920:** Speech by Nguyen Ai Quoc (Ho Chi Minh) at Congress of Tours (25–30 December) in favour of liberation of colonial peoples. Founding of Liberal Constitutional Party in Tunisia (Destour). Congress of Eastern Peoples in Baku.
**21 February 1921:** Independence of Iran.
**1921–6:** Riff War in Morocco waged by Abd el-Krim against the Spanish and French.
**1922:** British create Emirate of Transjordan (July–September).
**1927:** Founding of Vietnamese National Committee (*Viet Nam Quoc Dan Dang*, VNQDD). Anticolonialist Congress of Brussels. Sukarno founds Indonesian National Party.
**1930. 10 February:** Yen Bai uprising in Vietnam at instigation of VNQDD.
**30 June:** (Relative) independence of Iraq.

2. Algerian sharp-shooters during the First World War.

**1931:** Association of Algerian Reformist Ulamas.
**1934:** Split between *Destour* and *Neo-Destour* in Tunisia. Founding of Moroccan Action Committee.
**1935:** Granting of limited autonomy in India: Government of India Act.
**1936:** Independence of Egypt (26 August). Founding of Algerian Muslim Congress. Treaties ending French mandate over Syria and Lebanon; French parliament refuse to ratify these. Arab anti-British and anti-Jewish revolt in Palestine.
**1937:** Founding of Algerian People's Party (Messali Hadj), offshoot of the *Mouvement de l'Etoile Africaine* (founded in 1926 by Ali Abd el-Kader).
**1939:** Indonesian People's Congress founded.
**1941:** Front for the Independence of Vietnam (Viet Minh) founded in May. Atlantic Charter plans emancipation of peoples under foreign domination (14 August). Abortive Nationalist and pro-German coup in Iraq by Rashid Ali.
**1943:** Ferhat Abbas: Manifesto of the Algerian People (10 February) demands end

3. Moroccan nationalist leader Abd el-Krim.

Independence dates before 1960 1960 onwards

Ex-colonial states

Possession: F GB US

Independence war

Major confrontation

Litigation

Trust Territory of the Pacific Islands (EU)

B Brunei 83
WF Wallis Island and Futuna Island
French trading stations in India:
C = Chandernagore K = Karikal M = Mahe
P = Pondicherry Y = Yanan

2000 km

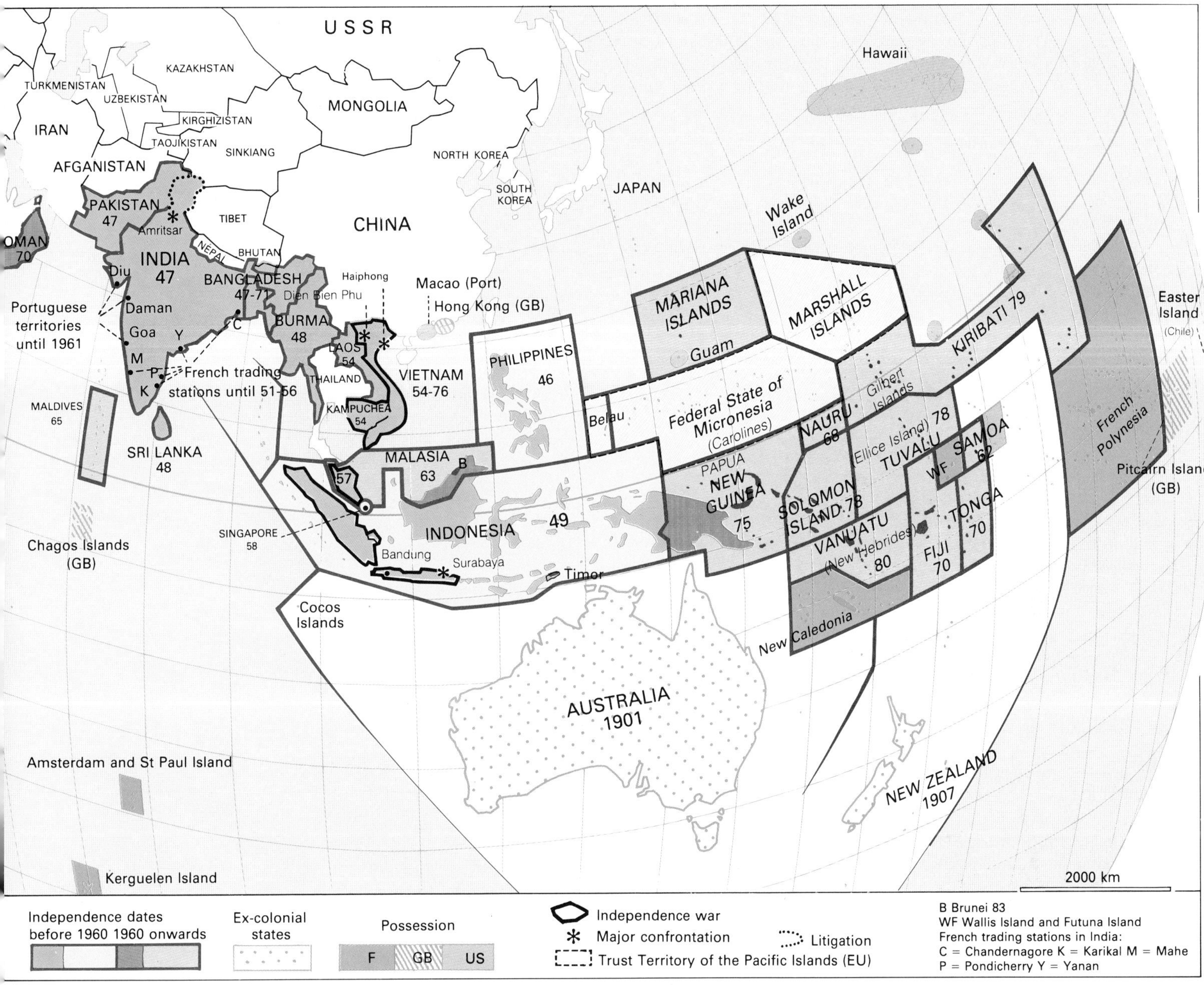

| **Algerian People's Manifesto.** | **General de Gaulle's Brazzaville speech.** | **Creation of Arab League.** |
|---|---|---|
| **10 February 1943** | **30 January 1944** | **22 March 1945** |

4. *24 March 1946: meeting between Ho Chi Minh and Sainteny.*

to French colonial rule. Dismissal of Muhammad al-Munsif, Bey of Tunis (May). **1944:** General de Gaulle's Brazzaville speech (30 January) praises colonial achievements, makes a brief allusion to necessity of 'emancipation'. Moroccan *Istiqlal* party issues independence manifesto. **1945:** Arab League founded (22 March) by Saudi Arabia, Egypt, Iraq, Lebanon, Syria, Transjordan and Yemen. Publication of Leopold Sedar Senghor's *'Defense de l'Afrique noire'* in French revue, *Esprit*, July 1945.

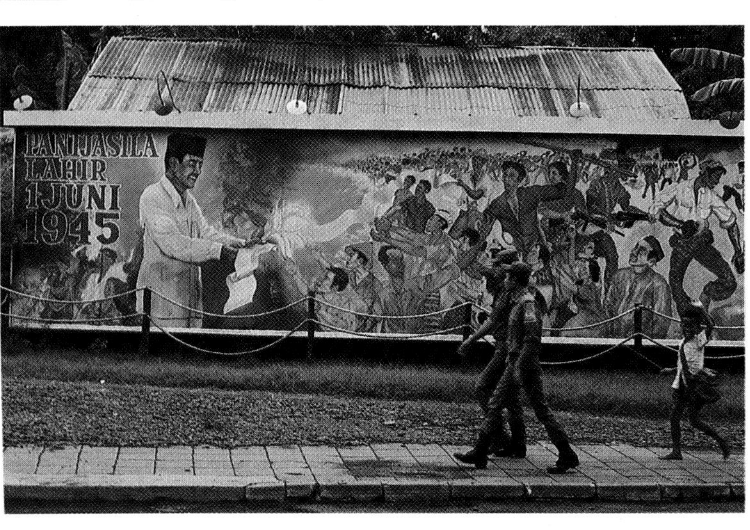


5. *Mural illustrating the Indonesian revolution of 1945.*

# Decolonization: The Main Stages

Decolonization is not a unitary phenomenon; it takes almost as many forms as there are countries seeking liberation. Forms of colonial domination varied from one power to another: the French, for example, practised active assimilation, while the British attitude was culturally élitist and tended to ignore the local cultures. 'Colonies' varied also, from old, sophisticated civilizations such as India and Southeast Asia to the tribal societies of Black Africa. Some were territories that sizeable European minorities regarded as their homeland such as Algeria, South Africa, and Palestine, not to mention South America where 'decolonization' began in the nineteenth century; some were colonies of pure exploitation; finally, there were lands directly under colonial administration, there were protectorates (Morocco, Tunisia) and there were territories under mandate (Syria, Lebanon, Palestine) enjoying a certain autonomy.

Four phases do stand out, however, taking into consideration the areas concerned, the degree of violence involved and the international context, these three variables being, of course, related.

Up to the end of the forties a few territories gained independence without actual liberation wars; these were countries under British or Dutch rule where élites had been ready to take over for some time (Egypt, India, Pakistan).

Next in line, in the fifties – with the Cold War contributing to a hardening of positions – were North Africa and Indochina. In Southeast Asia and Algeria the colonial power was only prepared to surrender after wars of extreme violence, which explains, at least partly, the militant character of the emergent states that took over.

The third phase, in the sixties, marks the emancipation of Black Africa: this usually took place without incident and with the consent of the outgoing colonial power.

Finally, the last of the Western empires were dismantled, comparatively painlessly, in the wake of the Portuguese 'carnation' revolution.

The effects of decolonization have been complex and ambiguous. It is easy to contrast the dignity of those still bound to the ex-colonial powers with ties of dependence (though Franz Fanon termed these neocolonials 'the wretched of the earth'), with the tinpot dictatorships that have sprung up in Africa and elsewhere, suffering tribal conflicts, famine and the suppression of human rights. Inadequately prepared and clumsily effected, decolonization forced societies into the ill-fitting mould of the nation-state. It tied them to a world market which drained their subsistence economies and exhausted them in the race to close the ever-widening technological, industrial and agricultural gap between themselves and the more developed countries. The various forms of fundamentalism appearing everywhere (Qaddafi, Khomeini, the Muslim Brotherhood, Ethiopian and Khmer Marxism) must be seen as the result of mismanaged transition to independence.

Decolonization may not have been a smooth process, but it is pointless to argue that it could have been easier. Freedom is not given, said Ferhat Abbas, it has to be fought for. Conditions of struggle are not conducive to the development of a well-regulated state. Even where independence was granted voluntarily, as in India or Africa, the colonial phenomenon left too deep a mark on the society and its way of thinking, the gap between ideal and reality was too great for the dream of 'successful' decolonization to come about. Rather than blame the past we ought now to turn our attention to the struggle for development, which undoubtedly will be a hard task.

(For a more detailed account of the decolonization of Southeast Asia see pp. 306/307.)

*1. Dream of an Algerian child, 1958.*

| **Brazzaville Conference.** | **Independence of State of Israel.** | **Coup d'état of "free officers" in Egypt.** |
|---|---|---|
| **30 January–8 February 1944** | **14 May 1948** | **23 July 1952** |

**1944:** Brazzaville Conference (30 January–8 February).
**1945:** Riots and massacres of Setif and Kabilie in Algeria (8 May). MacArthur receives Japanese surrender (15 August). Sukarno and Haata proclaim independence of Indonesia (17 August). Ho Chi Minh proclaims independence of Vietnam (2 September).
**1946:** Autonomy of Cambodia (Kampuchea) within the framework of the French Union (7 January). King Abdullah ('Abd Allah) proclaims independence of Transjordan (25 May). Independence of Philippines (4 July). Autonomy of Laos within French Union (27 August). Bamako conference and founding of RDA (Rassemblement Démocratique Africain, 18–21 October).
**1947:** Nationalist riots in Madagascar (30 March) and bloody repression. Independence of Indian Union and Pakistan (15 August). Populations are exchanged, communal conflicts. United Nations accepts plan for partition of Palestine (29 November).
**1948:** Independence of Burma (4 January). Gandhi assassinated by Hindu fanatic (30 January). Independence of Ceylon (Sri Lanka in 1971) (4 February). Creation of State of Israel (14 May), Arab invasion and start of first Arab-Israeli war (up to 20 July). Transjordan annexes West Bank of Jordan intended as nucleus of future Palestinian state; Israel and Egypt occupy the rest (16 December).
**1949:** Hashemite Kingdom of Jordan (January).
**1951:** Libyan independence (24 December).
**1952:** Coup d'état by 'Free Officers' in Egypt (23 July). King Farouk abdicates, beginning of Nasser government. Mau Mau terrorists in Kenya, British state of emergency (20 October).
**1953:** Muhammad Ben Yusuf, Sultan of Morocco, deposed (20 April).
**1954:** Fall of Dien Bien Phu (7 May). Geneva Accords put an end to French phase of Indochina war (20–21 July). Speech by Pierre Mendès France in Carthage recognizes Tunisian autonomy (31 July). Beginning of armed insurrection in Algeria. FLN (National Liberation Front) issues programme; declaration demanding independence (1 November).
**1955:** Afro-Asian conference of Bandung

*2. French-held prisoners after Dien Bien Phu.*

# 1945–87

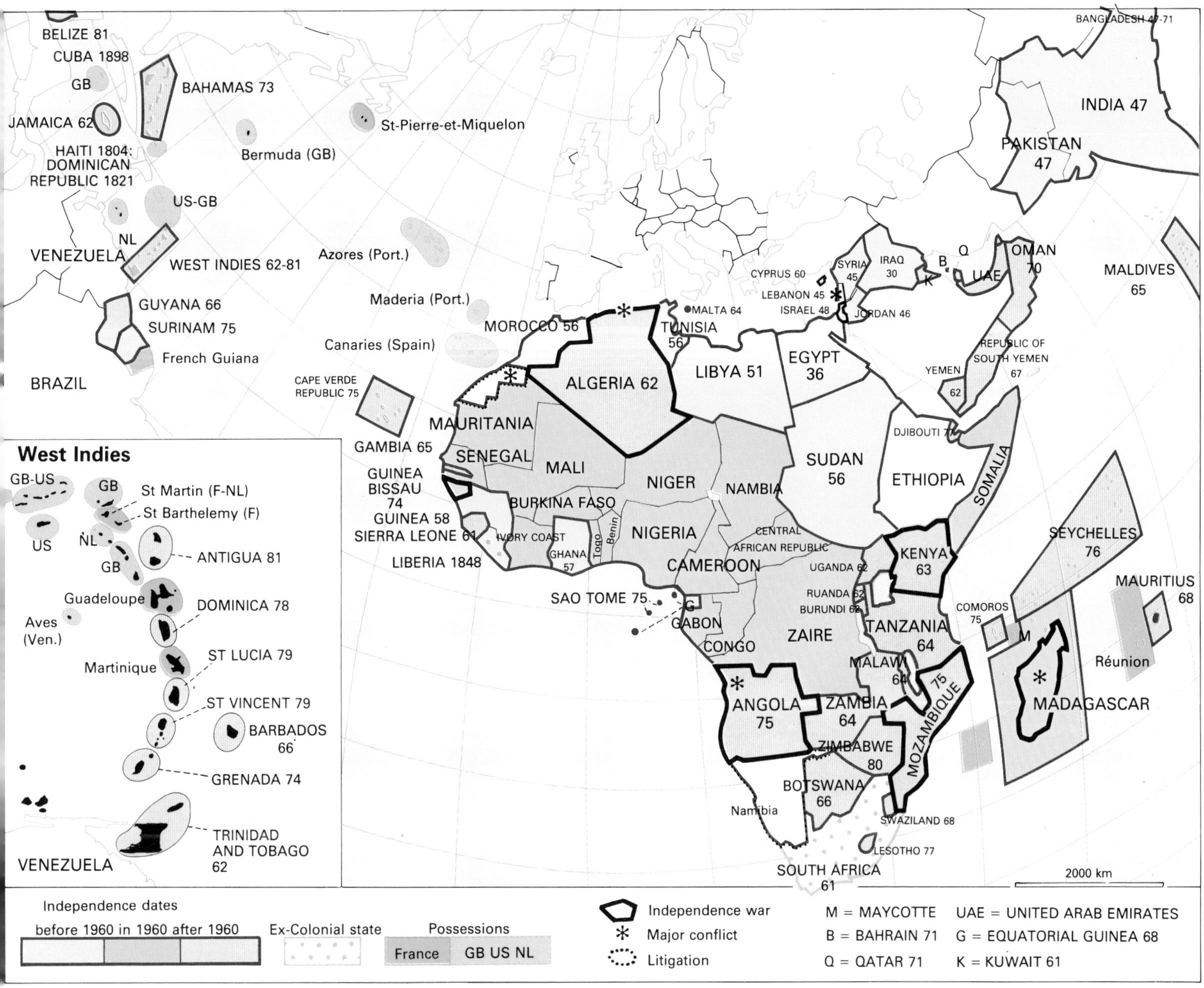

BELIZE 81
CUBA 1898
GB
BAHAMAS 73
JAMAICA 62
HAITI 1804: DOMINICAN REPUBLIC 1821
Bermuda (GB)
St-Pierre-et-Miquelon
US-GB
NL
VENEZUELA
WEST INDIES 62-81
Azores (Port.)
GUYANA 66
SURINAM 75
French Guiana
BRAZIL
Maderia (Port.)
Canaries (Spain)
CAPE VERDE REPUBLIC 75
MOROCCO 56
ALGERIA 62
TUNISIA 56
MALTA 64
LIBYA 51
EGYPT 36
CYPRUS 60
LEBANON 45
ISRAEL 48
SYRIA 45
IRAQ 30
JORDAN 46
B
Q
K
UAE
OMAN 70
BANGLADESH 47-71
INDIA 47
PAKISTAN 47
MALDIVES 65
REPUBLIC OF SOUTH YEMEN 67
YEMEN 62
MAURITANIA
GAMBIA 65
SENEGAL
MALI
NIGER
GUINEA BISSAU 74
GUINEA 58
SIERRA LEONE 61
LIBERIA 1848
BURKINA FASO
IVORY COAST
GHANA 57
Togo
Benin
NIGERIA
NAMBIA
SUDAN 56
ETHIOPIA
DJIBOUTI 77
SOMALIA
CENTRAL AFRICAN REPUBLIC
CAMEROON
UGANDA 62
KENYA 63
RUANDA 62
BURUNDI 62
SAO TOME 75
G
GABON
CONGO
ZAIRE
TANZANIA 64
SEYCHELLES 76
COMOROS 75
M
MAURITIUS 68
Réunion
MALAWI 64
ANGOLA 75
ZAMBIA 64
MOZAMBIQUE 75
MADAGASCAR
ZIMBABWE 80
BOTSWANA 66
Namibia
SWAZILAND 68
LESOTHO 77
SOUTH AFRICA 61
2000 km

**West Indies**

GB-US
GB
St Martin (F-NL)
St Barthelemy (F)
US
NL
GB
ANTIGUA 81
Guadeloupe
DOMINICA 78
Aves (Ven.)
Martinique
ST LUCIA 79
ST VINCENT 79
BARBADOS 66
GRENADA 74
TRINIDAD AND TOBAGO 62
VENEZUELA

Independence dates: before 1960 | in 1960 | after 1960
Ex-Colonial state
Possessions: France | GB US NL
Independence war
Major conflict
Litigation
M = MAYCOTTE
B = BAHRAIN 71
Q = QATAR 71
UAE = UNITED ARAB EMIRATES
G = EQUATORIAL GUINEA 68
K = KUWAIT 61

**Referendum on Algerian independence.** — **1 July 1962**

**Independence of Bangladesh.** — **16 December 1971**

**Independence of Angola and Mozambique.** — **June and November 1975**

**Independence of Zimbabwe.** — **18 April 1980**

(17–24 April) attended by 29 countries. Talks at La Celle–Saint-Cloud in France recognize Moroccan sovereign (6 November); Sultan returns to Rabat as Muhammad V, King of Morocco (16 November).
**1956:** Sudanese independence (1 January). *Pieds-noirs* riot in Algiers (6 February). French prime minister Guy Mollet resigns. Independence of Morocco (2 March) and Tunisia (20 March). Suez crisis. Nationalization of canal by Nasser (26 July) and Anglo-French-Israeli campaign from October to December.
**1957:** Battle of Algiers (January to October). Independence of Ghana (5 March).
**1958:** Conference of Independent African States at Accra, Ghana (15–22 April). De Gaulle visits Madagascar, French Equatorial Africa and French West Africa (20–28 August). Second Brazzaville speech proclaims right of colonized peoples to independence.
**1960:** Independence of Belgian and French Black African territories, Nigeria (Britain) and Mauritania (France).
**1961:** Independence of Sierra Leone (27 April), Tanganyika (9 December). Coup by Generals in Algiers (22–25 April). Anti-Algerian pogrom in Paris (17 October).
**1962:** Evian Accords (18 March). At the cost of thousands of victims, mainly Algerian, and the uprooting of one million *Pieds-noirs*, Algeria gains independence (1 July referendum). Independence of Ruanda and Burundi (1 July).
**1963:** Creation of Malaysia (Malaya and Singapore) on 16 December and independence of Kenya (12 December).
**1964:** Creation of Tanzania (Zanzibar and Tanganyika, 26 April). Independence of Malta (21 September), Malawi (ex-Nyasaland) on 6 July and Zambia (ex-Northern Rhodesia) on 24 October.
**1967:** Independence of People's Republic of South Yemen (29 November).
**1968:** Independence of Mauritius (12 March).
**1975:** 'Carnation' revolution in Portugal leads to independence of Angola (25 June) and Mozambique (11 November). Independence of Papua New Guinea (September).
**1976:** Spain leaves Western Sahara: beginning of Saharan question.
**1977:** Independence of Republic of Djibouti (27 June).
**1980:** Independence of Zimbabwe (ex-Southern Rhodesia) on 18 April.

*3. General Idi Amin, President of Uganda, 1972.*

# Fronts of the Cold War

THE PRINCIPAL VICTORS of the Second World War, the United States and the Soviet Union, now dominated the world. A rift between them quickly occurred, and the ex-allies began jealously to guard their zones of influence at the cost of a relentless arms race. Eventually, the balance of terror meant that the world's 'policemen' were forced into good behaviour; Cold War became 'peaceful coexistence', and the certainty that a nuclear holocaust would destroy them both resulted in a tactical neutralization of the ambitions of both sides. In the meantime, from 1946 to 1962, their rivalry shaped the history of international relations, in spite of efforts to rouse the conscience of the rest of the world against their hegemony (the United Nations was formed in 1945, followed by the Universal Declaration of Human Rights in 1948), and in spite also of the promising emergence of a 'non-aligned' movement in the Third World (the term dates from 1952), challenging the rationale of the power blocs, in particular since the Bandung Conference of 1955.

1. Nuclear obsession in the US: gas mask practice.

In reality the two super-powers were opposed in every way. From the Atlantic to the Pacific, the maritime empire of the 'free world' contrasted with the continental dominion of the 'socialist camp'. In the West, capitalism and freedom reigned. The East retorted with the 'classless society' and the endeavour to create a 'new man'. Moscow-style totalitarianism was loudly denounced in the West; the Atlantic camp took pride in its rapid recovery after the war and its economic vitality, often due to state intervention encouraging growth and a high standard of living. In answer to Western economic dynamism the Eastern bloc upheld the intrinsic superiority of 'peaceful' socialism over warlike imperialism. It invoked its concern to raise the consciousness of the masses and its tactical alliance with 'progressive' elements fighting 'Americanization' within Western societies. Conflict, both economic and territorial, between two world views assumed ideological and cultural dimensions, fuelling rival propaganda and mobilizing all forms of communication and mass culture, which were at that time developing to the furthest corners of the globe.

In the Cold War years (1946–62), confrontation several times came to a head. East-West relations became strained over Germany and the Marshall Plan for the reconstruction of Europe, and reached breaking point over the future of Berlin. In Korea and Indochina the confrontation became an armed one. 1956 was a pivotal year: crises within the People's Democracies and in the Near East revealed the capacity of the super-powers to 'contain' the antagonism. From 1957 to 1962, up to the short-lived but grim crisis brought about by the Soviet attempt to install missile bases in Cuba, directly threatening the United States, the loci of potential clashes became more decentralized. Decolonization, the emancipation of the People's Republic of China, and African and South American interests played a role in this process. The nuclear balance and the fact that the power blocs were no longer seen as monolithic paved the way for 'peaceful coexistence', which was a mark of the 1960s.

2. Arrival of American planes during the Berlin blockade, 1948.

**Marshall Plan.** **5 June 1947**

**Communist coup in Prague.** **25 February 1948**

**North Atlantic Treaty Organization.** **4 April 1949**

**1946. 20 January:** De Gaulle resigns from government.
**5 March:** At Fulton Churchill talks of an 'iron curtain' dividing Europe
**1947. 11 March:** Truman doctrine of containment of Communism.
**5 June:** Launching of Marshall plan.
**22–7 September:** Creation of Cominform (dissolved 17 April 1956).
**1948. 25 February:** Communist coup in Prague.
**20 June:** Berlin blockade (to 12 May 1949).
**28 June:** Exclusion of Yugoslavia from Cominform.
**1949. 25 January:** Economic union of Eastern countries in Comecon.
**4 April:** Signature of North Atlantic Treaty.
**5 May:** Creation of German Federal Republic (West Germany).
**14 July:** First Soviet Atomic bomb.
**1 October:** Proclamation of People's Republic of China.
**October:** End of civil war in Greece.
**25 June 1950–27 July 1953:** Korean War.
**1951. 1 September:** Defence treaty for Pacific between Australia, New Zealand and USA (ANZUS).
**8 September:** Peace declared between USA and Japan.
**1952. 1 November:** First American H bomb.
**1953. 12 August:** First Soviet H bomb.
**3 September:** Nikita Khrushchev becomes First Secretary of the Communist Party of the Soviet Union (until 15 October 1964).
**1954. 7 May:** Fall of Dien Bien Phu.
**20–1 July:** Geneva agreements on Indochina.
**8 September:** Creation of the Southeast Asia Treaty Organization.
**1955. 24 February:** Baghdad pact.
**17–24 April:** Bandung Conference.
**14 May:** Warsaw Pact.
**1956. 23 October–13 November:** Budapest rising and Soviet intervention in Hungary.
**29 October–6 November:** Second war between Egypt and Israel.
**5 November–22 December:** Suez expedition.
**1957. 25 March:** Treaty of Rome.
**1958. 4 November:** Khrushchev demands demilitarization of Berlin.

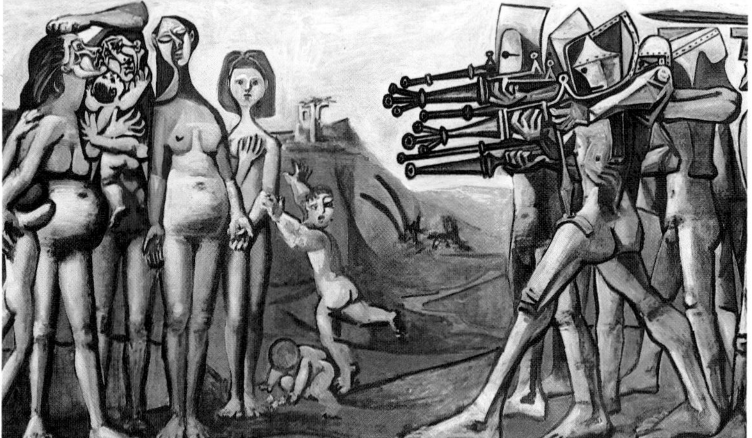

4. Massacres in Korea. *Painting by Picasso, 1951.*

# 1946–62

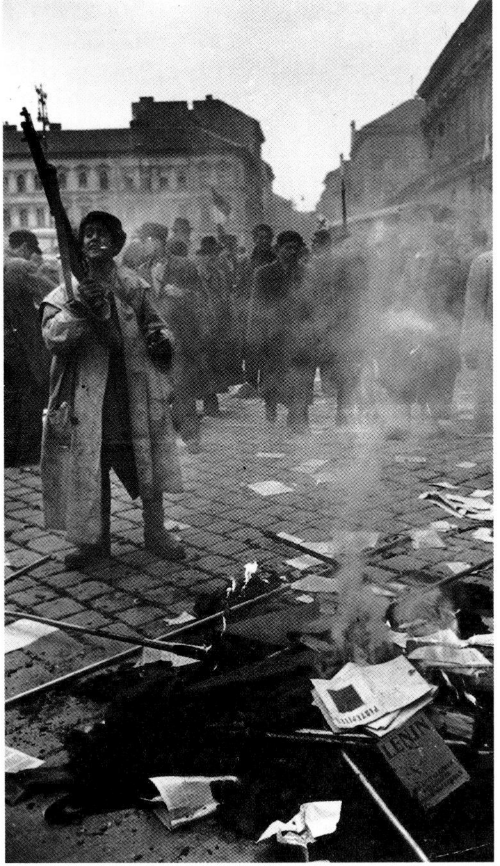
3. *Budapest in revolt: burning of Soviet books, 9 November 1956.*

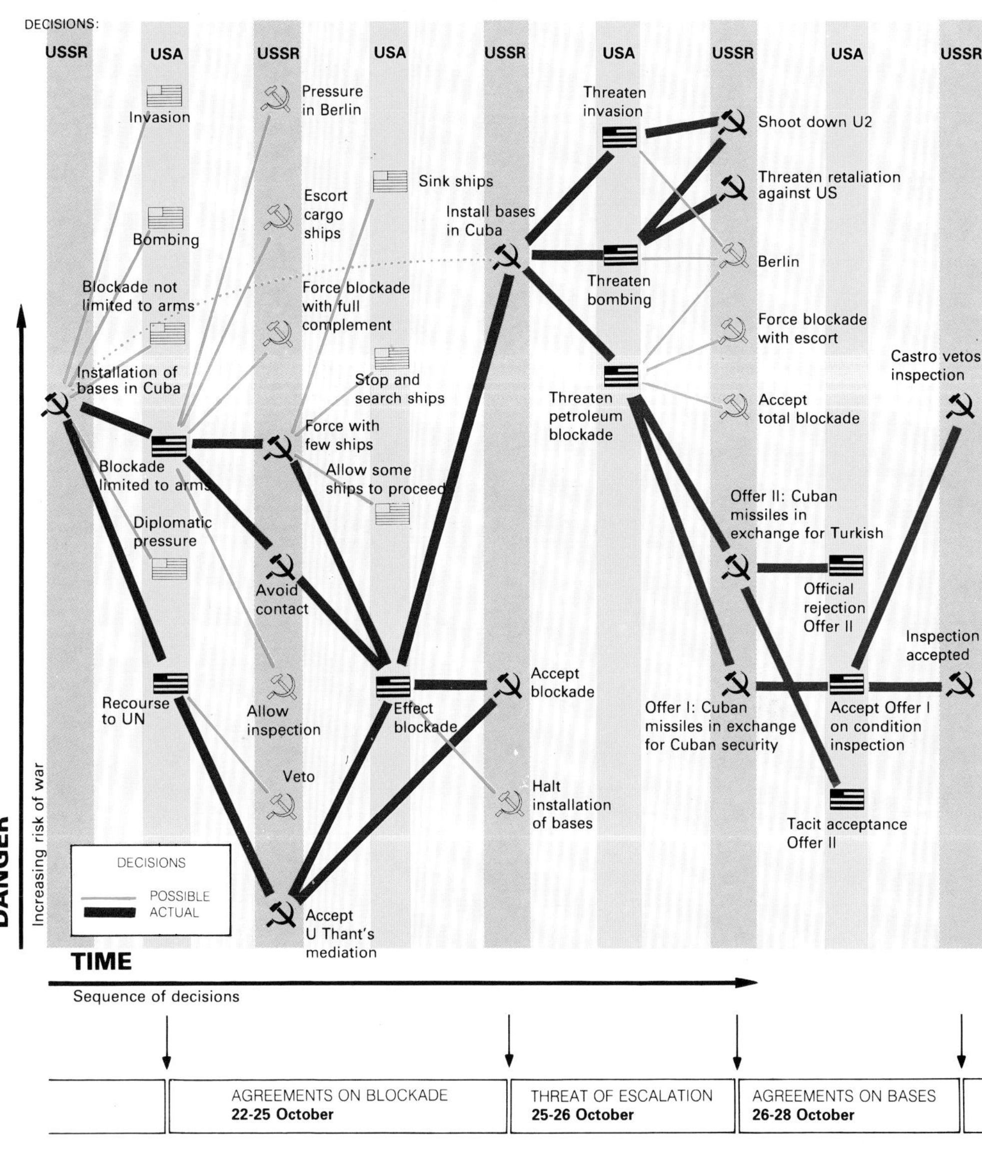


The Cuban Missile Crisis 1962
*An international crisis can be analysed step by step through tracing the decisions each protagonist makes in response to the other. The Cuban crisis is a good example.*

*Actual decisions are taken from many possible decisions, which are ranked according to their gravity, or the danger of war they represent. The succession of such bands of possibility provides a backdrop against which actual decisions mark the ups and downs of the conflict, its main stages and its most critical moments. On the chart, the role of various agencies is also shown, e.g. external agencies such as the UN.*
*From A. Joxe,* La crise cubaine de 1962: Eléments de décision au cours de la crise chaude.

**Budapest uprising.**
**23 October 1956**

**Berlin wall.**
**12 August 1961**

5. *Khrushchev and Eisenhower at the White House, September 1959.*

**1959. 15–18 September:** Khrushchev visits United States.
**1960. 13 February:** First French Atomic bomb.
**1 May:** American U2 spy plane shot down over USSR.
**June:** Founding of Lumumba University in Moscow.
**1961. 12 August–20 November:** Building of Berlin wall.
**1962. 18 October–2 November:** Cuban Missile Crisis.

6. *The French at Port Said during the Suez crisis, 5 November 1956.*

# Towards the Europe of the Twelve

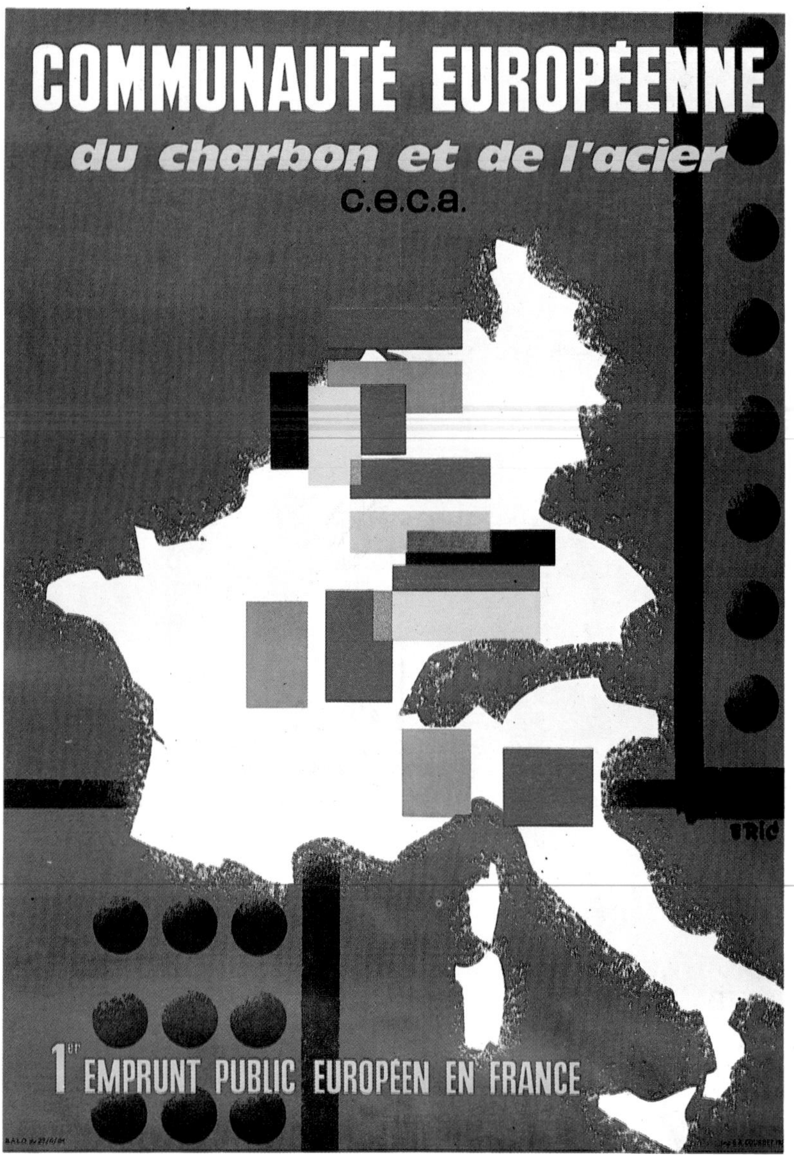


1. Poster for the European Coal and Steel Community (ECSC), 1964.

IN THE YEARS since 1945 Europe has had to come to terms with its inevitable decline. As a result of various factors, which include two world wars, the long process of decolonization, the Cold War, as well as two major economic crises, the first of which was the great slump of the 1930s and the second the economic recession which came in the wake of the monetary upheavals and oil crises of 1971–3, its centuries-old world supremacy has become a thing of the past. Today, Central and Eastern Europe are still cut off from the West by the Iron Curtain which fell in 1948, and in spite of the internal dissent which became evident with tragic consequences in Hungary, Czechoslovakia and Poland, the communist system, closely policed by the USSR, has exerted a baneful influence on precisely those areas where in the past Europe regularly found much of its energy and dynamism. In the West, which has sheltered under the nuclear umbrella of NATO since 1949, state nationalism has put an end to hopes for a federal Europe and made it impossible to imagine the setting up of a United States of Europe. From General de Gaulle to Mrs Thatcher, the logic of national sovereignty has run counter to any real devolution of power to supra-national bodies. What this has meant in reality has been a Europe dominated, as in the past, by France and Germany and riven by the assertion of divisive national interests.

Nevertheless, there have been many important positive achievements, including, for instance, the setting up of the ECSC and the ECU, as well as the founding of the EEC and the development of European space research. Admittedly, some of this was done initially through the use of American funds made available under the Marshall Plan, but nevertheless, with the formation of the (mainly agricultural) Common Market, and (since 1979), with the holding of direct elections throughout Europe to a single European Assembly (thus bringing together in one chamber representatives of most of the citizens of Western Europe), some of the fruits of Europe's tremendous post-War resurgence can clearly be seen. (Thirty glorious years of prosperity have, it should be added, also made possible the setting up of the welfare state which has begun the task of ironing out differences in society.) But, as is evidenced by the frequent stormy summit meetings and periodic tariff warfare, European unity remains precarious, all the more so as a result of the fatal blow to its political future inflicted by the French when they rejected the idea of a European Defence Union in 1954.

In sum, Europe has had both its successes and its failures: while it has been successful in the area of agricultural policy, it has shown itself impotent when it comes to protecting industry affected by the recession. It has performed badly in the realms of atomic research and new technology, and has suffered in this respect from the omnipotence of the dollar. In some ways it can be said that the Europe of the Community has suffered from having its priorities back to front. The

**Treaty of Paris leads to the founding of the ECSC.** **18 April 1951**

**Treaty of Rome leads to the founding of the EEC.** **22 March 1957**

**Franco-German Treaty.** **22 January 1963**

**General de Gaulle di** **9 November 19**

**16 April 1948:** OECE set up, later becoming, in December 1960, the OECD, Organization for Economic Cooperation and Development.
**9 May 1950:** Schuman plan for the European Coal and Steel Community (ECSC) put forward.
**18 April 1951:** ECSC established by the Treaty of Paris. First European steel produced in May 1953.
**31 August 1954:** French Parliament rejects the idea of the EDC (European Defence Community).
**1–3 June 1955:** Agreement signed in Messina, Sicily, for the formation of a Common Market. On 13 October Jean Monnet launches the Action Committee for the United States of Europe.
**25 March 1957:** Treaties of Rome and founding of the EEC and the European Atomic Energy Community (Euratom). Europe of the Six.
**1958. 13 May:** Uprising in Algiers.
**1 June:** General de Gaulle takes power in France. Appointed the first president of the French Fifth Republic, 8 January 1959.
**January 1960:** Great Britain launches EFTA (European Free Trade Association).
**1963. 14 January:** de Gaulle vetoes British entry into the Common Market.
**22 January:** Franco-German Treaty.
**19 December 1965:** de Gaulle is re-elected president.
**19 April 1967:** Konrad Adenauer dies.
**1968:** World-wide protest movement against Western society. 1 February sees the international student meeting in Berlin, and 22 March marks the beginning of the Paris 'événements'. By 22 May, 6 million workers were on strike in France. Industrial action was brought to an end with the Grenelle accords of 25–27 May. On 30 May the French parliament was dissolved, and on 23 and 30 June the Gaullists were re-elected with an overwhelming majority. In the Autumn, Italy underwent similar civil unrest.
**1969. 28 April:** General de Gaulle resigns.
**15 June:** Georges Pompidou elected President of France.
**21 October:** Willy Brandt elected chancellor of West Germany.
**30 January 1972:** 'Bloody Sunday' in Londonderry.

3. Three of the Junta of Colonels who took power in Greece on 21 April 1967.

**1 January 1973:** Europe of the Six becomes the Europe of the Nine (with the entry into the EEC of Denmark, Ireland and the United Kingdom).
**1974. 2 April:** Death of Georges Pompidou.
**25 April:** Military coup in Portugal restores democracy.
**16 May:** Helmut Schmidt becomes West German chancellor.
**19 May:** Valery Giscard d'Estaing elected to the French Presidency.
**24 July:** Democracy is restored in Greece after 7 years of military dictatorship.
**1975. 1 August:** Final Act of Helsinki Conference.
**20 November:** Juan Carlos I accedes to the throne of Spain.
**1976. 2 and 25 April:** New constitution drawn up, followed by general elections in Portugal.
**18 October 1977:** Death occurs in prison of Andreas Baader and Gudrun Ensslin, two of the leaders of the German Red Army Faction.
**1979. 3 March:** The ECU (European Currency Units) is created.

importance given to economic agreements has been no compensation for failures in social policy or for a political vacuum which has been filled only by a technocracy of Euro-experts. In a world where the price of trade and the course of history are settled outside Europe, there are those who argue that only a common political authority will reverse the relative decline of the old continent.

*2. Three of the founding fathers of Europe: A. De Gasperi, Konrad Adenauer and Robert Schuman, pictured here in Strasbourg, 11 January 1951.*

**Margaret Thatcher elected prime minister.**

**3 May 1979**

**16 March:** Death of Jean Monnet.
**3 May:** Margaret Thatcher returned as prime minister at the general election.
**7–10 June:** First direct elections to the European Assembly in Strasbourg.
**1981. 1 January:** Europe of the Nine becomes Europe of the Ten (with the entry of Greece into the EEC).
**10 May:** François Mitterand elected President of France.

**Beginning of the Europe of the Twelve.**

**1 January 1986**

**1982. 1 October:** Helmut Kohl elected chancellor of West Germany.
**1986. 1 January:** Europe of the Ten becomes the Europe of the Twelve (with the entry of Spain and Portugal).
**2 December:** Agreement among the Twelve on the unification of Europe.
**15–18 June 1989:** Strong abstention (41 %) from the European parliamentary elections.

*4. Anti-nuclear demonstration in Germany, 23 October 1983.*

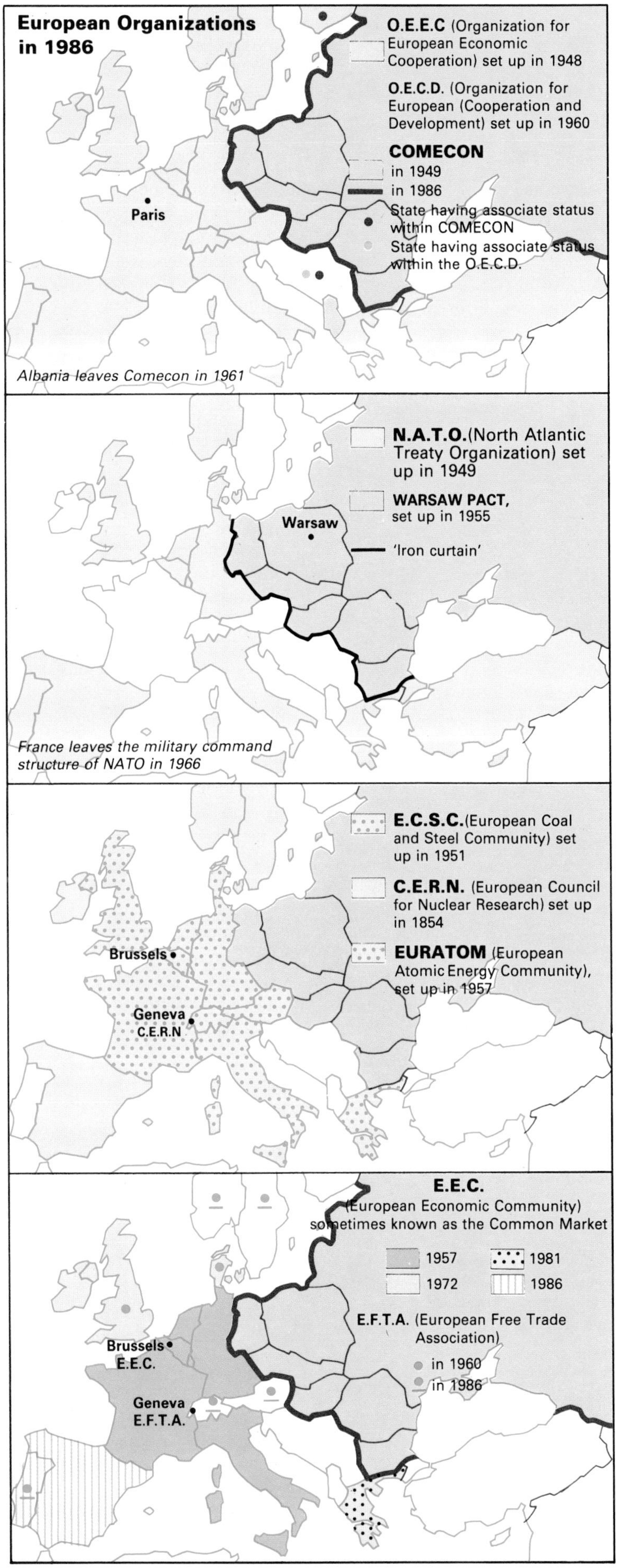

**European Organizations in 1986**

**O.E.E.C** (Organization for European Economic Cooperation) set up in 1948
**O.E.C.D.** (Organization for European (Cooperation and Development) set up in 1960
**COMECON**
in 1949
in 1986
State having associate status within COMECON
State having associate status within the O.E.C.D.
Paris
*Albania leaves Comecon in 1961*

**N.A.T.O.**(North Atlantic Treaty Organization) set up in 1949
**WARSAW PACT,** set up in 1955
'Iron curtain'
Warsaw
*France leaves the military command structure of NATO in 1966*

**E.C.S.C.**(European Coal and Steel Community) set up in 1951
**C.E.R.N.** (European Council for Nuclear Research) set up in 1854
**EURATOM** (European Atomic Energy Community), set up in 1957
Brussels
Geneva C.E.R.N

**E.E.C.**
(European Economic Community) sometimes known as the Common Market
1957
1972
1981
1986
E.F.T.A. (European Free Trade Association)
in 1960
in 1986
Brussels E.E.C.
Geneva E.F.T.A.

# Soldiers and Populists in South America

DURING THE Second World War, whether willingly or otherwise, all the countries of South America took part in the economic mobilization, spurred on by the USA (Brazil also provided troops).

At the end of the war there were revolutionary attempts to find solutions to social and economic problems. This was the case in President Arbenz's Guatemala in 1944, and in Bolivia in 1952 and Cuba in 1959. The first two enterprises failed, though only after thoroughgoing structural changes had been implemented (nationalization and land reform); the latter ended in the adoption of Soviet-style communism. The rural or urban guerilla movements which tried to extend the revolution to the entire continent were crushed at the end of the sixties and the beginning of the seventies. The 'legal Marxist' experiment of Allende's Chile also failed. A victim of economic crisis and 'social contradictions', weakened by the clandestine intervention of the CIA and undermined by its own errors and internal divisions, it was brutally brought to an end by a military coup. Authoritarian regimes under military control then became established in the cause of anti-communism (Brazil in 1964, Argentina in 1966, Chile in 1973 ...). Elsewhere other so-called 'progressive' military forces (in Peru in 1968, in Ecuador in 1972), often originating from the nationalist middle classes, but for all that still 'military', set about extending the role of the state.

Between 1965 and 1985 economic and social structures changed; some countries began living less off their mining and farming exports (apart from oil) and began to become industrialized (Brazil, Argentina). Towns grew phenomenally with the influx of rural migrants; unemployment and crime grew, and shanty towns sprang up.

Traditional governing groups such as the land-owning oligarchy gave way to newcomers who were in some cases connected with national industry, multinational companies and in others with overseas trade, for South America depends on the technology and capital of the more developed countries for its capital equipment. By the beginning of the 1980s this dependence had led to enormous debts, which in some instances brought countries to the brink of bankruptcy.

At the end of the seventies, military factions of the Left and of the Right had been discredited because they had so profoundly failed to solve the problems of countries in the grip of a crisis which was without precedent. Democracy is returning, and apart from Central America, which is torn apart by civil war, in which the major powers are active parties, only Paraguay and Chile have military governments. But the return of democracy does not necessarily mean that the difficulties of crumbling economies and societies torn apart by dissension have been resolved.

*1. Argentine democracy passes judgement on its military leaders, 12 September 1985.*

**E. Pettoruti paints *Quintet*.** — **1927**

**J. Amado: *The Violent Land*.** — **1942**

**Gabriela Mistral: Nobel Prize for Literature.** — **1945**

**1930:** Following the economic crisis a series of military uprisings (Argentina, Brazil, Peru ...)
**1932–35:** Chaco war between Bolivia and Paraguay.
**1937:** In Brazil, Getulio Vargas proclaims 'Estado Novo', a corporatist dictatorship, similar to European fascist regimes. He was overthrown in 1945 by a military coup d'état.
**1939:** Latin American neutrality in the Second World War.
**1942–5:** Progressive commitment of the South American continent to the United States. Strong reservations on the part of Argentina (coup d'état in 1943). Brazil sends an expeditionary force to Italy.
**1944:** *Fictions* by J. L. Borges.
**1945:** Peron's triumph in Argentina. Populist 'Justicialism' until 1955. Military government in Peru (until 1964).
**30 March-2 May 1948:** 'Bogotazo' in Columbia: riots in the capital: development of civil war in the country areas ('La violencia' 1949-57).
**1951–2:** Vargas elected president in Brazil on a programme of reforms (he commits suicide

*2. Juan Peron giving his speech of 1 May 1946.*

in 1954). Start of the Bolivian revolution: the National Revolutionary Movement in power until 1964.
**5 May 1954**: General Stroessner takes over power in Paraguay.
**1961–9:** Alliance for Progress created on President Kennedy's initiative.
**1964–7:** Military coup d'état in Brazil: anti-communist and technocratic dictatorship. Military coup d'état in Argentina.
**9 October 1967:** Ché Guevara, Castro's lieutenant, dies in Bolivia. Suppression of guerrilla forces organized by him.
**22 August 1968:** Paul VI at Medellin (Colombia): South American 'Vatican II'.
**1968:** 'Progressive' militarism (nationalizations, land reform, educational reforms ...) in Peru under General Velasco. Urban guerrillas in Argentina (the 'montoneros') and in Uruguay (the 'tupamaros'). Repression and military dictatorship in both countries.
**1970–3:** Experiment of Salvador Allende's Popular Unity government in Chile, overthrown by General Pinochet's coup d'état.
**September 1973:** Death of the Chilean poet N. R Reyes, known as Pablo Neruda.
**1973–8:** Succession of very repressive military governments. National security 'anti-subversive' doctrine.
**1978–85:** Return to pluralist democracy in most of the South American countries. Serious economic crisis.
**28 January–1 February 1981:** Border conflict between Peru and Ecuador.
**1982:** Falklands war between Argentina and United Kingdom. Occupation of the Islands by Argentina, 2 April. Surrender of Argentine forces 13 June.
**1983:** Assassination of Maurice Bishop, Prime Minister of Grenada, 19 October. Military intervention by America.
**18 October 1984:** Settlement of the Beagle canal conflict between Chile and Argentina: signing in the Vatican of a treaty ending the territorial differences which had existed between the two States since 1891.
**1985. 15 January:** Election of T. Neves in Brazil – return to democracy.
**3 November:** First free elections in

# 1930–89

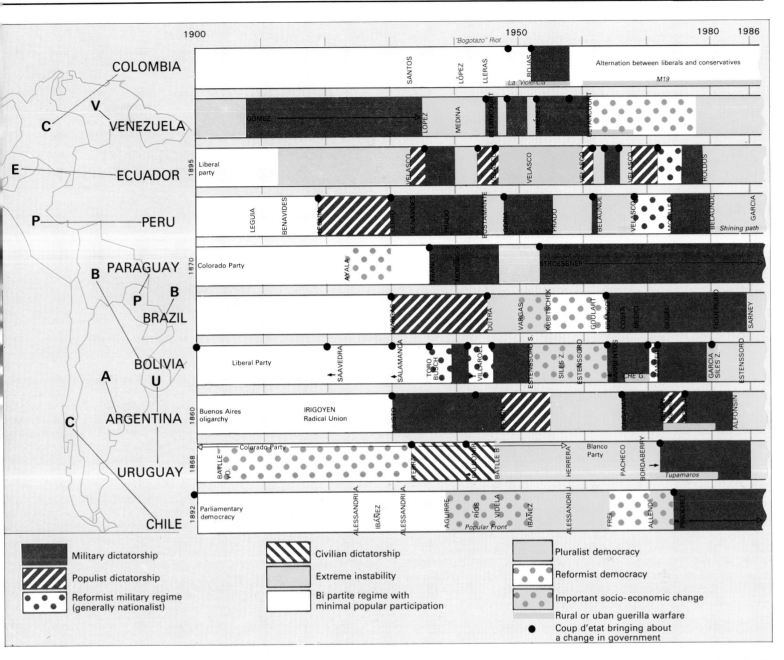

1900 1950 1980 1986

COLOMBIA — SANTOS, LÓPEZ, LLERAS, "Bogotazo" Riot, ROJAS, Alternation between liberals and conservatives, La Violencia, M19

VENEZUELA — GÓMEZ, LÓPEZ, MEDINA, BETANCOURT, JIMÉNEZ, BETANCOURT

ECUADOR — 1895 Liberal party, VELASCO, VELASCO, VELASCO, VELASCO, VELASCO, ROLDOS

PERU — LEGUIA, BENAVIDES, LEGUIA, CERRO, BENAVIDES, PRADO, BUSTAMANTE, ODRIA, PRADO, BELAUNDE, VELASCO, MORALES, BELAUNDE, GARCIA, Shining path

PARAGUAY — 1870 Colorado Party, AYALA, FRANCO, MORINIGO, STROESSNER

BRAZIL — VARGAS, DUTRA, VARGAS, KUBITSCHEK, GOULART, BRANCO, COSTA, MEDICI, GEISEL, FIGUEREIDO, SARNEY

BOLIVIA — Liberal Party, SAAVEDRA, SALAMANCA, TORO BUSCH, VILLAROEL, ESTENSSORO S., SILES Z., ESTENSSORO, BARRIENTOS, CHE G., BANZER, GARCIA SILES Z., ESTENSSORO

ARGENTINA — 1860 Buenos Aires oligarchy, IRIGOYEN Radical Union, JUSTO, PERON, ONGANIA, PERON, VIDELA, ALFONSIN

URUGUAY — 1868 Colorado Party, BATLLE Y O., TERRA, BALDOMIR, BATLLE B., Blanco Party, HERRERA, PACHECO, BORDABERRY, Tupamaros

CHILE — 1892 Parliamentary democracy, ALESSANDRI A., IBÁÑEZ, ALESSANDRI A., AGUIRRE, RÍOS, VIDELA, IBÁÑEZ, ALESSANDRI J., FREI, ALLENDE, PINOCHET, Popular Front

C V E P B P B A U C

Military dictatorship
Populist dictatorship
Reformist military regime (generally nationalist)
Civilian dictatorship
Extreme instability
Bi partite regime with minimal popular participation
Pluralist democracy
Reformist democracy
Important socio-economic change
Rural or uban guerilla warfare
Coup d'etat bringing about a change in government

**1967** Ernesto Sabato: ***Alejandra***

**1970** J. L. Borges: ***The Brodie Report.***

**1970** Beginning of Transamazonian Highway.

***1981*** M. Vargas Llosa: ***The War of the End of the World.***

3. *Strike in the tin mines, Bolivia.*

Argentina two years after the return to democracy.
**5 October 1988:** Despite the defeat of his referendum, General Pinochet of Chile announces his intention to finish his mandate in 1990.
**1989. 1 May:** First free elections in Paraguay following the overthrow of General Stroessner on February 2.
**14 May:** C. Menem succeeds R. Alfonsin in Argentina.

4. *The boots of the Chilean Army face a student demonstration, 12 July 1983.*

# The Restructuring of China

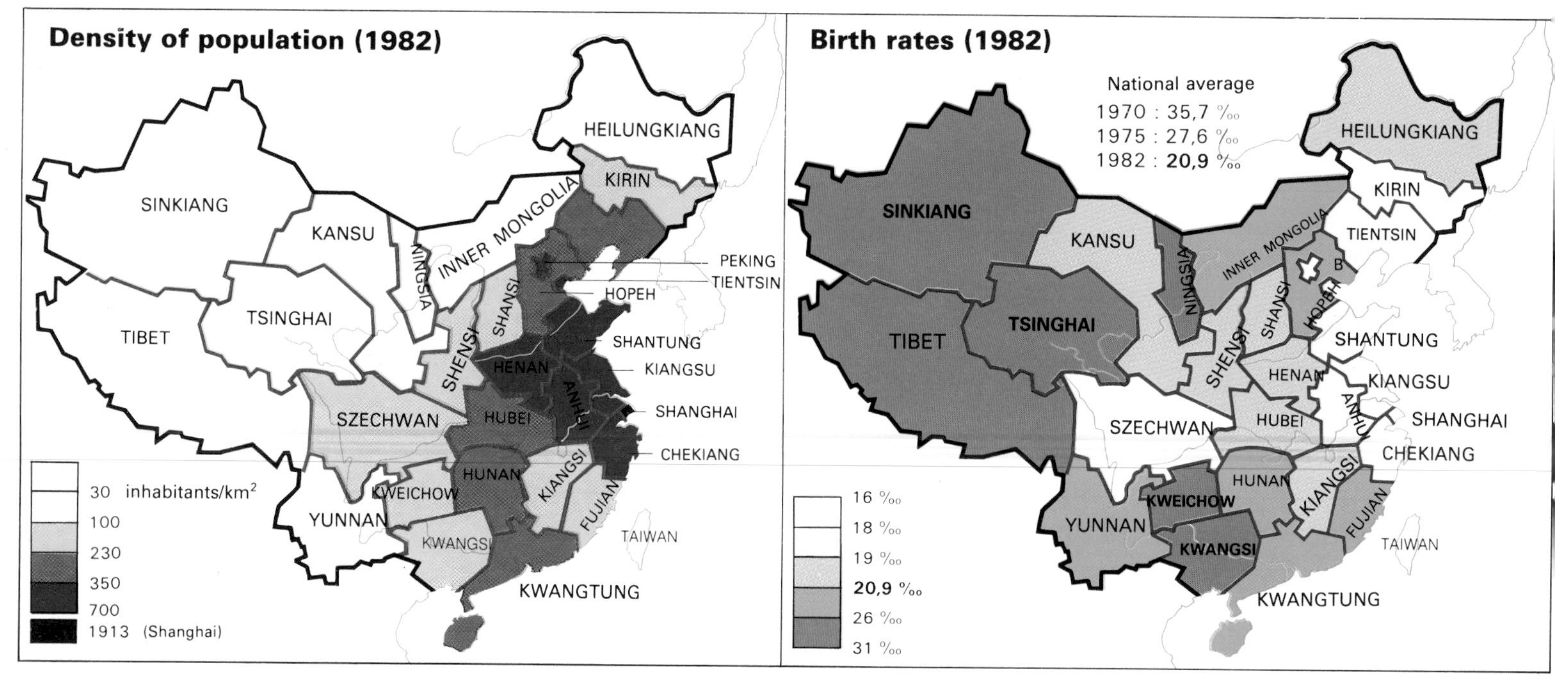


Chinese politics, after the arrival of the communists, were to fluctuate from one extreme to another and undergo a series of crises which in practice did no more than reflect the fundamental contradiction of the revolution, based as it was on a proletarian ideology but one reworked and subverted by the peasantry. The early years were spent getting the economy back into full production and securing the support of the population for the new regime (3 million executions took place to serve as an example). The currency was stabilized, moderate agrarian reform ensured satisfactory harvests, and a programme for industrial reconstruction was carried out, while at the same time campaigns for the mass mobilization of the population consolidated the power of the state and the party over the whole of society. The restoration of national unity allowed China to begin thinking once again of its ancient vocation of being the dominant power in the Far East. As a result, China intervened in Korea, and rebuffed the Americans later in Vietnam, invading the country itself after having aided first the Viet Minh and subsequently the Hanoi government against the French and the Americans; China similarly extended its influence into Tibet, crushing any wish for real autonomy, and risking an armed confrontation with India. This local imperialism came into conflict with Soviet expansionism, giving rise to the incidents over the disputed border territories on the Ussuri River and to Chinese support for Cambodia under Pol Pot.

The second phase in the Chinese revolution was marked by the extension of the socialist system of production, corresponding to the first five-year plan of Soviet inspiration. This led to the nationalization of industry and to the development of the farm co-operatives. With the achievement of the goals set out in the plan, which, in spite of some outstanding successes in some areas, Chinese leaders later had to admit were fundamentally unsuited to the reality of China, the time had come for what turned out to be the great agrarian disaster of the Great Leap Forward.

The plan was to bring about industrialization no longer at the expense of the rural areas but in the countryside itself, hand in hand with the peasants. The basic tool for this miracle was to be the people's commune, which was a huge economic and administrative entity (as well as being a way of controlling the population), and which meant that the workers could be mobilized for ambitious projects. The end result was catastrophic. After Mao Tse-tung had at first been manoeuvred into playing a less prominent role in party policy, the ruling group began to adopt a more realistic approach. But just as the country was recovering from the difficulties which the

**The Great Leap Forward.** **1958**

***The General History of Chinese Thought*, under the editorship of the historian Hou Wai-lu.** **1960**

**The Cultural Revolution begins.** **1966**

*4. During the 'rectification campaign' in 1958, the putting up of wall-posters.*

**June 1950:** Agrarian Reforms leading to the elimination of land-owners and the redistributior of land. Chinese troops intervene in Korea.
**1953:** First Five-Year Plan announced. The Korean War ends. The population of China is 583 million.
**1954:** New Constitution adopted.
**1955:** Co-operative farms developed.
**1956:** Total nationalization of industry and collectivization of 90% of the peasant population.
**1957:** The Campaign of a Hundred Flowers ends.
**1958:** The Great Leap Forward begins.
**1959:** The Lushan Plenum acknowledges the failure of the Great Leap Forward. Mao Tse-tung is replaced as head of state by Liu Shao-ch'i. The rising in Tibet is severely put down.
**1959–61:** Famine in the whole of China.
**1963:** Conflict between China and India.
**1964:** China explodes its first atom bomb.
**1966:** The Cultural Revolution begins. China is thrown into chaos. Liu Shao-ch'i is eliminated.

*5. Building of a dam near the Ming tombs, photographed by Henri Cartier-Bresson in 1958.*

# 1949–89

## Birth control and birth rate

*In 1953, the population of China was 583 inhabitants; in **1982** it had risen to **1,008 million inhabitants.** The aim for the year **2000 is not to exceed 1,200 million inhabitants.***

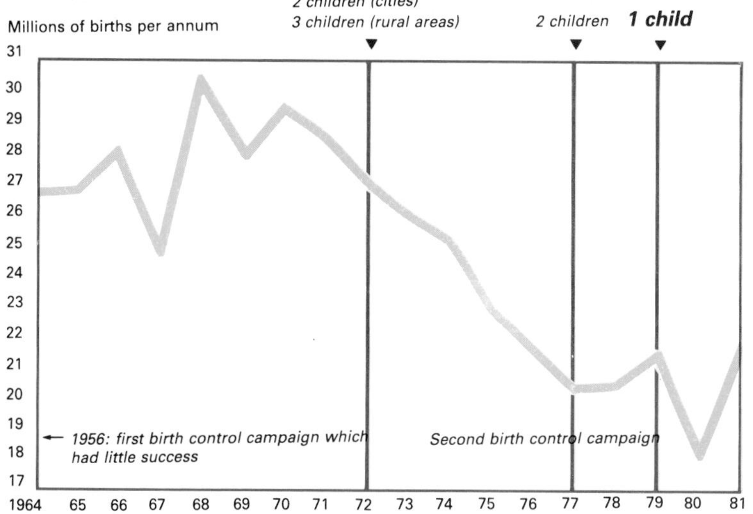

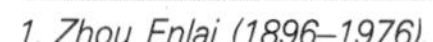
1. Zhou Enlai (1896–1976).

2. Deng Xiaoping (1904– ).

3. Tienanmen Square on the night of June 3-4, 1989.

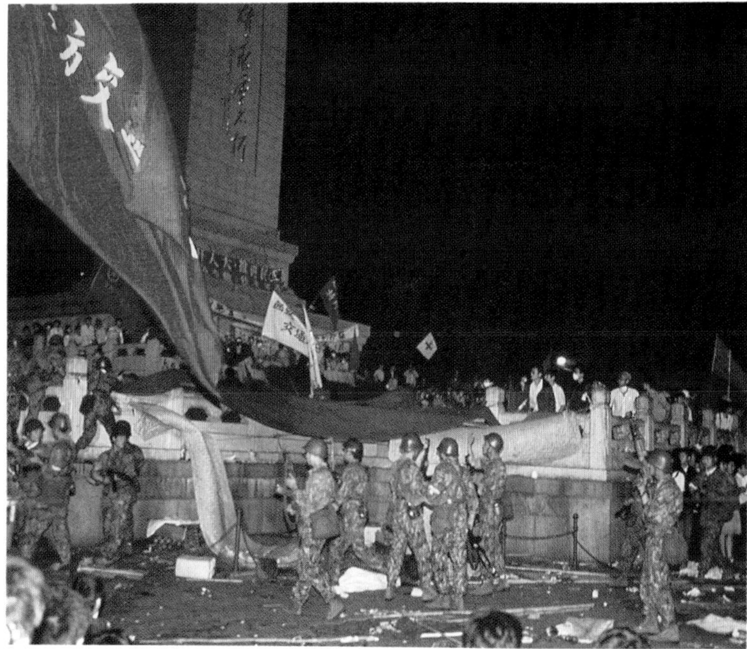

Great Leap Forward had caused (which ranged from famine to disorganized production and apathy on the part of the population), Mao was readying himself for the counter-attack. He embarked upon a series of mobilizing campaigns, each more popular than the one before, which eventually turned into the Cultural Revolution. While the Cultural Revolution did lead to the overthrow of Mao's main adversaries, it rapidly proved uncontrollable, and threw the country into total chaos. A semblance of order was restored only at the cost of fearsome repression on the part of the army. The factional struggles which had been rife in the party since the disasters of 1966 were to come to an end only with the total liquidation of the group who emerged from the Cultural Revolution, after the death of Mao Tse-tung. This victory of the realists and pragmatists, who represented the class of managers, technicians and workers, made it possible to adopt more flexible policies, better adapted to the true situation.

Between 1979 and 1989, under Deng Xiaoping, China underwent a very strong economic growth. However, these results were obtained during a climate of inflation and stirred the movement of democratic dispute. In 1979, 1982 and 1989, student movements denounced abuses by the regime and the corruption of high dignitaries of the party—but each time were silenced by violent repression.

**Campaign against Confucius and Lin Piao.**

**1974**

**Jiang Qu'ing is given a suspended death sentence.**

**1981**

**1967:** Production falls back. China explodes its first H-Bomb.
**1969:** IXth Congress of the Chinese Communist Party marks a wish to return to normal. Lin Piao designated as Mao's successor. Frontier incidents between China and the Soviet Union over the disputed border territories on the Ussuri river.
**1971:** Lin Piao dies in mysterious circumstances after attempting to overthrow Mao and take power.
**1973:** Teng Hsiao-p'ing rehabilitated. The campaign against Confucius and Lin Piao launched, masking the conflict between (on the one hand) the 'Gang of Four', the architects of the Cultural Revolution, and (on the other) the pragmatists (Chou En-lai, Teng Hsiao-p'ing).
**1975:** New Constitution promulgated. Chou En-lai, with the support of the moderates, consolidates his position.
**1976:** Death of Chou En-lai. Teng Hsiao-p'ing is disgraced. Hua Kuo-feng, the head of the secret police (the equivalent of the Soviet KGB), is appointed Prime Minister and Vice-President, showing that some compromise had been reached with the 'Gang of Four'. Violent riots break out in Peking in T'ien-an Men Square on 5 and 6 April on the occasion of the funeral of Chou En-lai, as a sign of the wish to put an end to the dictatorship of Mao's wife, Chiang Ch'ing. The death of Mao (9 September) brings about the fall of the 'Gang of Four' and the recall to power of Teng Hsiao-p'ing.
**1977:** XIth Congress of the CCP officially puts an end to the Cultural Revolution and sets out a programme of modernization.
**1978:** New Constitution. Teng Hsiao-p'ing consolidates his position. Peace treaty with Japan.
**1979:** New Democracy Movement (the Peking Spring) denounces the abuses of the régime and is severely repressed (Wei Ching-sheng is put on trial and sentenced to 15 years in prison); there are arbitrary arrests of dissidents such as Liu Ch'ing. China invades Northern Vietnam. Relations between China and America are normalized. Special economic zones are set up in the Canton region and firms established with joint Chinese and foreign capital.

6. Mao and his fourth wife, the actress Jiang Ouing.

**1981:** As a result of the economic reforms, agricultural production increases by 60% over 1978.
**1982:** The population of China reaches one billion.
**1985:** China signs a contract for the purchase of nuclear reactors from France.
**1986:** Despite the stated policy of "only one child," demographic growth is larger than predicted as the population exceeds one billion one hundred million.
**December 1986–January 1987:** Following student demonstrations in Shanghai and Peking, resignation of Hu Yao Bang, Secretary General of the CCP, replaced by Chao Tzu-yang.
**1989. 5–7 March:** Repression of the anti-Chinese uprising in Tibet.
**May–June:** Under the orders of prime minister Li Peng, "Spring" in Beijing is suppressed by tanks the night of June 3 and 4. Dismissal of Zhao Ziang.

# Crises in the Soviet Union

AT THE END of the Second World War the USSR had conquered Eastern Europe and the Balkans, with the exception of Yugoslavia, which had been liberated by communist partisans, and Greece. In the countries allied to Germany (Bulgaria, Hungary and Rumania) the occupying forces had no difficulty in setting up governments dominated by communists. Two liberated nations, Poland and Czechoslovakia, saw the formation of coalitions made up of all those who had resisted the Nazis. The communists, the only organized group, set up an effective propaganda system defending popular measures such as land reform. Making use of threats and promises and supported by Soviet troops, they eliminated the liberals. In 1948 the Iron Curtain was firmly in place and Europe was cut into two. The only changes of note were the creation of a Soviet republic in the Soviet zone of Germany and the secession of Yugoslavia, which refused to comply with directives from Moscow and broke away from the USSR in 1948.

The Soviet Union organized a military alliance (Warsaw Pact) with its satellite states and also imposed on them economic changes which were particularly advantageous to the USSR. Movements towards independence were repressed as soon as they appeared to be leading to liberalization and towards increased contacts with the West (Poland and Hungary in 1956, Czechoslovakia in 1968, Poland in 1981 – in this last case there was no obvious Soviet intervention). On the other hand, they were tolerated if they took place in the name of orthodox Marxism, even if they led to the extolling of local nationalism, as in the case of Albania and Rumania in 1961–2.

Although flexible in its alliances and prepared to support the Islamic revolution in Iran as well as the Cuban socialist regime, the Soviet Union is particularly uncompromising with countries sharing its borders; the invasion of Afghanistan (1979) is a case in point. It has constantly been building up armaments since 1945, and one-third of its budget is allocated to defence. Now it has achieved parity with the United States in terms of intercontinental missiles and has a clear lead in conventional weaponry, the USSR is advocating major reductions in the numbers of medium and short range nuclear missiles, in part so as to save cost and enable her to boost those other areas of the economy in which she currently lags well behind the West. In spite of vast resources and a wide variety of climates, agricultural production is regularly below target. Production levels in heavy industry are comparable to those in Europe or the USA, but everyday consumer goods are still rationed, the economic apparatus is paralysed by over-centralization, information is slow to circulate and computerization has made hardly any headway.

After the years of terror during the Stalin regime there has been a period of détente internally. At the Twentieth Party Congress of the Communist Party in 1956, Khrushchev's report denounced the excesses of the police state; subsequently, internment camps released their prisoners, the victims of purges were 'rehabilitated' and the majority of those convicted were set free. Conformity and acceptance of party directives are still the rule, however. Opponents, who are widely dispersed, are prevented from speaking out, persecuted (confinement for 'medical' reasons) or allowed to leave the country if they have achieved a certain notoriety.

After 20 years of "stagnation," Mikhail Gorbachev's arrival to power in 1985 is marked by the extent of his political and economic reforms and by a desire for detente with the United States. This liberalization clashed with the conservative regimes of certain sister countries and awakened strong tensions in bordering republics: the aspiration for self-determination in the Baltic states, inter-ethnic confrontations in Kazakhstan, Armenia and Uzbekistan, and ultimately the demolition of the Berlin Wall.

1. *Soviet tanks in the streets of Prague, August 1968.*

**Death of Boris Pasternak.** — **1964**

**M. Janscó: *Silence and a Shout.*** — **1967**

**Prague: suicide of J. Palach.** — **19 January 1969**

2. *Brankov (l) and Laszlo Rajk confessing their 'crimes', Budapest, 1949.*

**1944. August:** Entry of Soviet troops into Rumania.
**18 October:** Yugoslav partisans occupy Belgrade: prelude to the creation of a People's Federal Republic of Yugoslavia with Tito as president.
**28 October:** Capitulation of Bulgaria to the Soviets.
**1945. 20 January:** Hungary capitulates to the Soviets.
**July:** The conference of the Allied powers at Potsdam; Germany is divided into four zones.
**1947:** Founding of the Cominform, the centre of co-ordination of all communist parties.
**1948. February:** 'Prague Coup'. Under pressure from unions, a communist government was formed which eliminated all opposition.
**June:** Split between Soviet Union and Yugoslavia.
**1953:** Death of Stalin (5 March): Khruschev First Secretary of the Communist Party of the Soviet Union.
**1955. 14 May:** Warsaw Pact, military alliance of the European communist countries under Soviet leadership.
**26 May–2 June:** Khruschev and Bulganin in Belgrade.
**1956. February:** XXth Communist Party Congress; condemnation of the excesses of Stalinism; theory of peaceful coexistence between the rival blocs.
**June:** Workers' uprising in Poznan in Poland; unrest spreads. 'Polish October'; the Soviets intervene to control the movement.
**October–November:** Riot in Budapest against Soviet presence; the movement is repressed.
**1957. October:** First artificial satellite launched by the Soviets.
**November 1960:** International conference of Communist parties: open conflict between China and USSR.
**1961. 12 April:** The Russian, Gagarin, becomes the 'first man in space'.
**October:** Albania, which sees itself as keeping faith with the Stalin line, enters into conflict with the USSR. Rumania gives up collectivization thus showing its relative independence of Moscow.
**October 1964:** Dismissal of Khrushchev. Brezhnev and Kosygin take over the party and

# 1944–89

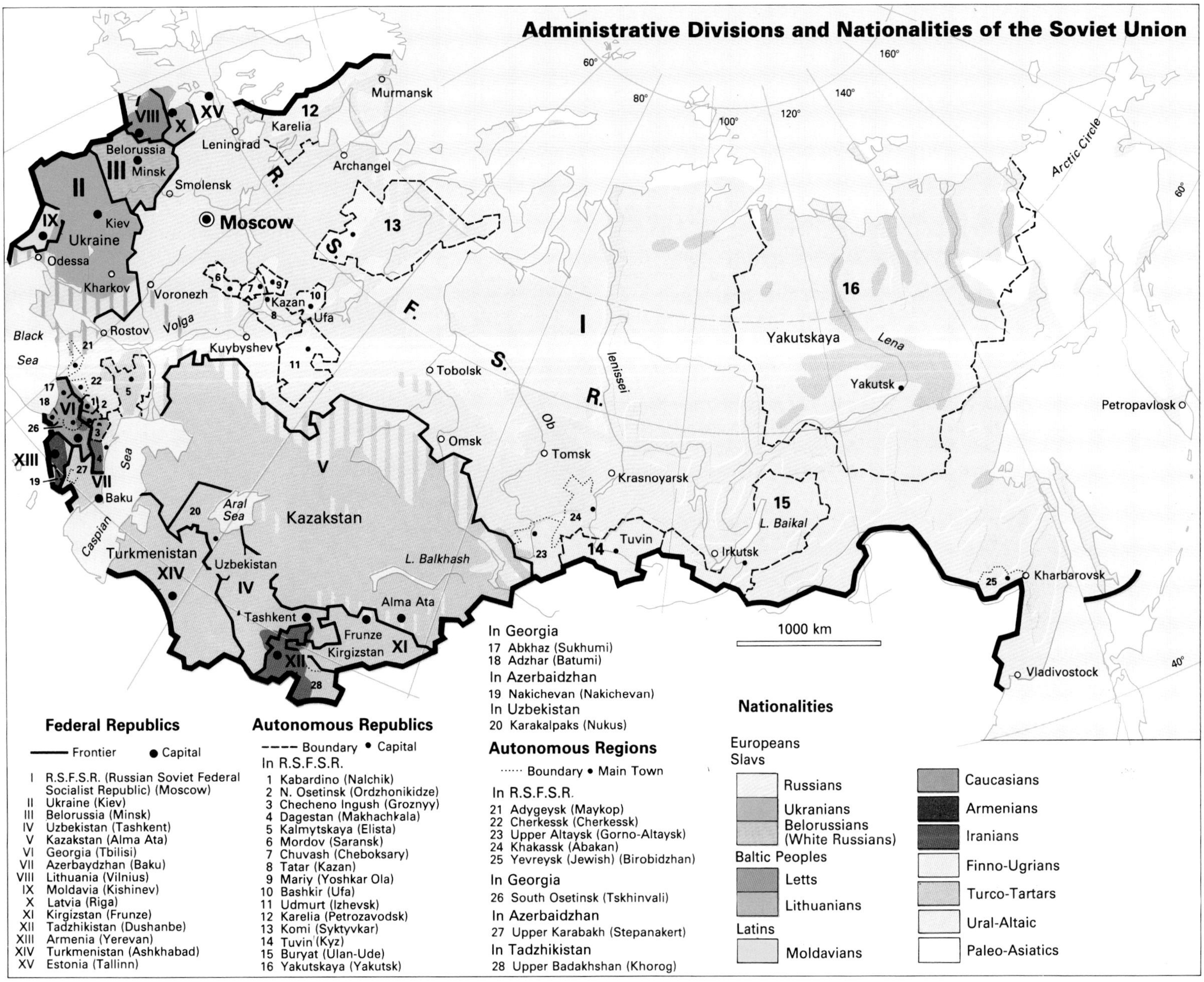

Administrative Divisions and Nationalities of the Soviet Union
Federal Republics
Frontier • Capital
I R.S.F.S.R. (Russian Soviet Federal Socialist Republic) (Moscow)
II Ukraine (Kiev)
III Belorussia (Minsk)
IV Uzbekistan (Tashkent)
V Kazakstan (Alma Ata)
VI Georgia (Tbilisi)
VII Azerbaydzhan (Baku)
VIII Lithuania (Vilnius)
IX Moldavia (Kishinev)
X Latvia (Riga)
XI Kirgizstan (Frunze)
XII Tadzhikistan (Dushanbe)
XIII Armenia (Yerevan)
XIV Turkmenistan (Ashkhabad)
XV Estonia (Tallinn)
Autonomous Republics
Boundary • Capital
In R.S.F.S.R.
1 Kabardino (Nalchik)
2 N. Osetinsk (Ordzhonikidze)
3 Checheno Ingush (Groznyy)
4 Dagestan (Makhachkala)
5 Kalmytskaya (Elista)
6 Mordov (Saransk)
7 Chuvash (Cheboksary)
8 Tatar (Kazan)
9 Mariy (Yoshkar Ola)
10 Bashkir (Ufa)
11 Udmurt (Izhevsk)
12 Karelia (Petrozavodsk)
13 Komi (Syktyvkar)
14 Tuvin (Kyz)
15 Buryat (Ulan-Ude)
16 Yakutskaya (Yakutsk)
In Georgia
17 Abkhaz (Sukhumi)
18 Adzhar (Batumi)
In Azerbaidzhan
19 Nakichevan (Nakichevan)
In Uzbekistan
20 Karakalpaks (Nukus)
Autonomous Regions
Boundary • Main Town
In R.S.F.S.R.
21 Adygeysk (Maykop)
22 Cherkessk (Cherkessk)
23 Upper Altaysk (Gorno-Altaysk)
24 Khakassk (Abakan)
25 Yevreysk (Jewish) (Birobidzhan)
In Georgia
26 South Osetinsk (Tskhinvali)
In Azerbaidzhan
27 Upper Karabakh (Stepanakert)
In Tadzhikistan
28 Upper Badakhshan (Khorog)
Nationalities
Europeans
Slavs
Russians
Ukranians
Belorussians (White Russians)
Baltic Peoples
Letts
Lithuanians
Latins
Moldavians
Caucasians
Armenians
Iranians
Finno-Ugrians
Turco-Tartars
Ural-Altaic
Paleo-Asiatics
1000 km
Moscow
Leningrad
Murmansk
Archangel
Smolensk
Kiev
Minsk
Odessa
Kharkov
Voronezh
Rostov
Volga
Kazan
Ufa
Kuybyshev
Tobolsk
Omsk
Tomsk
Krasnoyarsk
Irkutsk
L. Baikal
Yakutsk
Yakutskaya
Lena
Ob
Ienissei
Kharbarovsk
Vladivostock
Petropavlosk
Arctic Circle
Black Sea
Caspian Sea
Aral Sea
L. Balkhash
Kazakstan
Turkmenistan
Uzbekistan
Kirgizstan
Tashkent
Frunze
Alma Ata
Baku
Tuvin
Belorussia
Ukraine
Karelia
R.S.F.S.R.

Alexander Solzhenitsyn: *The Gulag Archipelago.* — 1974

Karol Wojtyla becomes Pope John Paul II. — 16 October 1978

M. Gorbachev becomes General Secretary. — 12 March 1985

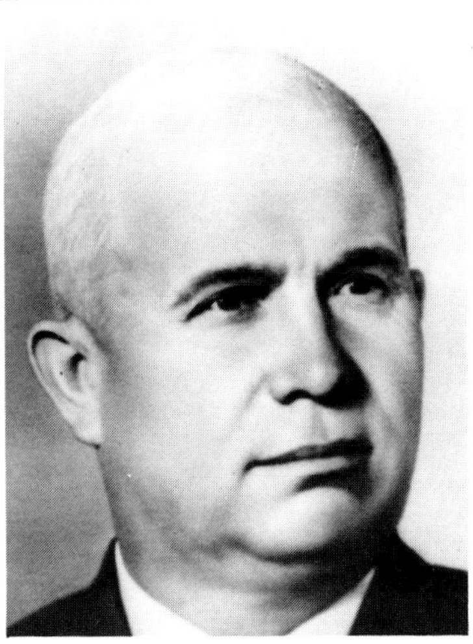

*3. Nikita Sergeivitch Khrushchev: First Secretary of the Communist Party of the Soviet Union. (Photo 1955).*

the government.
**January–August 20 1968:** "Prague Spring." Leaders sympathetic to the Soviets are swept aside, untill Warsaw Pact forces intervene.
**12 August 1970:** Moscow Agreement between Federal Republic of Germany and USSR recognizing the frontiers of the two Germanies.
**22 May 1972:** Visit of President Nixon to Moscow: Agreement on a freeze of strategic weapon arsenals.
**27 December 1979:** Soviet troops invade Afghanistan.
**31 August 1980:** Growth of the trade union "Solidarity" as strikes occur throughout Poland.
**12–13 December 1981:** General Jaruzelski imposes martial law on Poland.
**31 August–1 September 1983:** A South Korean Boeing is shot down in Soviet air space.
**1985. 12 March:** Mikhail Gorbachev General Secretary of the Communist Party of the Soviet Union.
**1986. 25 April:** Explosion at the Chernobyl nuclear plant (Ukraine).
**23 December:** A. Sakharov returns to Moscow after 6 years of exile in Gorky.
**1989. 15 February:** Final withdrawal of Soviet troops from Afghanistan.
**26 March–9 April:** First elections for multiple candidates in USSR.
**4–18 June:** Success of "Solidarity" in Polish legislative elections.
**November:** Ruling Communist parties in Hungary, East Germany and Czechoslovakia fall from power; the Berlin Wall comes down on November 9.
**14 December:** A. Sakharov dies in Moscow.
**26 December:** N. Ceausescu executed by the new government of Romania after a week of violent uprisings.

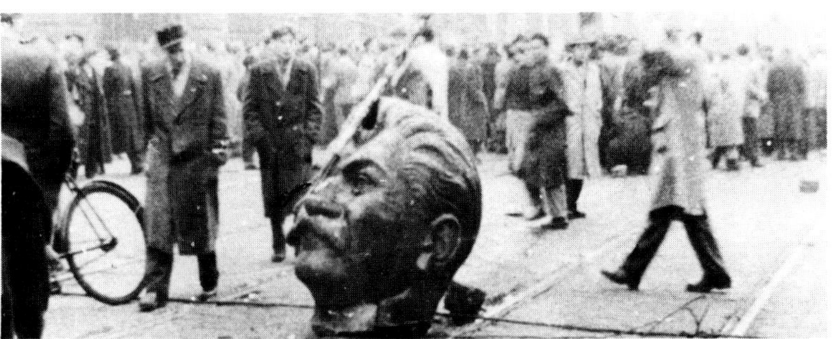

*4. Bronze statue of Stalin brought down, Budapest, late October 1956.*

# The United States from Truman to Bush

AFTER THE GOVERNMENTS of Harry Truman and Dwight Eisenhower, the United States was at the height of its power. However, some difficulties were beginning to appear: in the economy, which experienced several recessions; in the social fabric, with some 4 to 5 million unemployed and 20% of the population (which rose from 139 million to 180 million in the years 1945–60) below the poverty line; in deteriorating race relations, with Black revolts against segregation and exploitation; and in the political climate, which still bore the scars of McCarthyism.

When John F. Kennedy, the first Catholic President, was elected, he gave America a new dynamism with his 'new frontier' programme, renewing the struggle against poverty, abolishing segregation in public transport and restaurants, and providing aid to depressed areas and distressed towns. The 'new frontier' programme also had the moon as its goal through the Gemini and Apollo programmes, and aimed to assist the Third World to which Kennedy sent the volunteers of the Peace Corps. Aid to Latin America through the Alliance for Progress was not without political motivation. In Cuba, the CIA attempted without success to land at the Bay of Pigs, and the President was confronted with a missile crisis which he resolved by forcing Khrushchev to back down. The era of 'peaceful coexistence' did not prevent Kennedy from making a show of Western strength in Berlin and sending the first military contingents to South Vietnam to block the communist advance. Assassinated less than three years after his inauguration, Kennedy passed into legend. He gave Americans renewed hope and restored the image of the USA throughout the world. Lyndon Johnson finished off his work in the social field: social security, health, welfare and public housing programmes were all financed to a substantial degree by the federal government. Nonetheless, inflation continued to rise, university students continued their political protest, and the Black ghettoes caught fire. Richard Nixon, Gerald Ford and, later, Ronald Reagan were to reverse the Democrats' policies. Nixon, aided by his Secretary of State, Kissinger, launched successful foreign initiatives, promoting relations with

1. Student sit-in at Berkeley in 1964 for freedom of speech.

2. Racist demonstration by the Ku Klux Klan in the sixties.

**Death of Roosevelt.** — **12 April 1945**

**Outbreak of Korean War.** — **1950**

**Eisenhower President.** — **1953**

**Kennedy becomes first Catholic President.** — **1961**

**1945–53:** Harry S. Truman, President.
**1947:** Taft-Hartley Act restricting the right to strike.
**1950–53:** Korean War and McCarthyism.
**1953:** Execution of the Rosenbergs.
**1953–61:** Dwight D. Eisenhower, President.
**1953–4, 1957–8, 1960–61:** Economic recessions.
**1954:** Supreme Court rules social segregation in schools unconstitutional.
**1955:** Merger between AFL and CIO, the two major trade union federations.
**1958:** NASA created.
**1960:** CORE, Congress for Racial Equality.
**1961:** John F. Kennedy, President. Failure of the Bay of Pigs (Cuba) landing.
**1962:** Organization of the Peace Corps and of the Alliance for Progress in Latin America.
**22 November 1963:** John F. Kennedy assassinated at Dallas.
**1964:** Lyndon B. Johnson has 'Law against poverty' and law on Black civil rights passed.
**1964–7:** Riots in the Black ghettoes of Harlem, Newark, Detroit.
**1965:** Immigration law: quotas abolished; immigration of scientists and intellectuals promoted. Assassination of Malcolm X, ex-leader of the black Muslims. America intervenes against J. Bosch in Santo Domingo.
**1968:** Assassination of Martin Luther King.
**1969–74:** Richard Nixon, President.
**1969. 21 July:** Americans land on the moon.
**15–17 August:** Woodstock festival.
**9 May 1970:** 100,000 students demonstrate in Washington against the war in Vietnam.
**1970–2:** Laws passed on protection of the environment.
**15 August 1971:** Dollar inconvertible.
**1971–2:** Bombing campaign begins again in Vietnam.
**1971/73:** Devaluations of the dollar.
**21–28 February 1972:** Nixon visits China.
**1972/79:** SALT I and II agreements.
**27 January 1973:** Paris Accords on ceasefire in Vietnam.
**1973. 27 January:** Paris Accords on ceasefine in Vietnam.
**February–May:** Siege of Wounded Knee, occupied by the Sioux nation.
**1973–4:** Watergate Affair: Nixon resigns

4. John Fitzgerald Kennedy in the White House during the Cuban Missile Crisis.

5. Poster depicting Martin Luther King, winner of the Nobel Peace Prize in 1964.

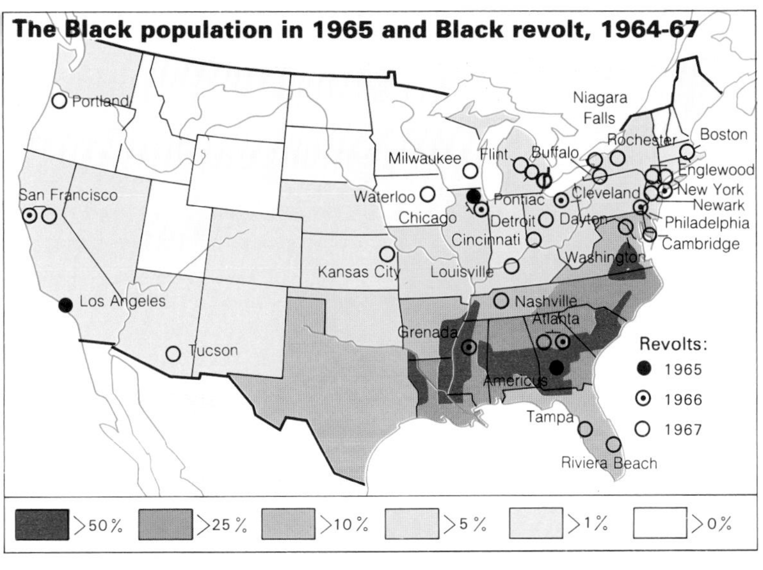


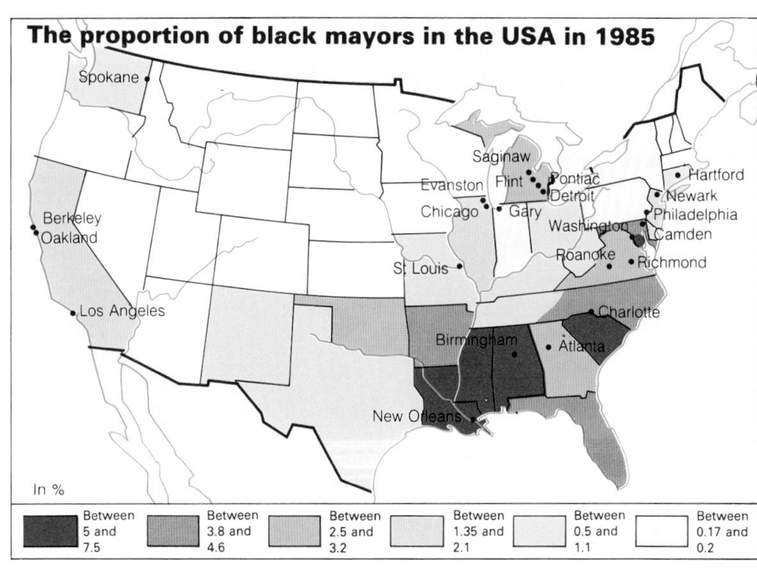


China, the SALT agreements with the USSR and, most importantly, withdrawal from Vietnam. At home, he gave priority to the struggle against inflation, but the oil crisis of 1973 was to lead America into 'stagflation'. When he resigned as a result of the Watergate scandal, Nixon caused a crisis of confidence, which his successor Gerald Ford proved incapable of surmounting. It was, therefore, to a little-known Democrat, Jimmy Carter, that the Americans gave the task, in their bicentenary year, of re-establishing the values proclaimed when they first won independence. However, in spite of his active role in the Middle East and his firm stand over the invasion of Afghanistan, Carter was judged too idealistic and he did not have the means to push through his policies. The election of Ronald Reagan in 1980 marked the victory of the conservative 'silent majority' tradition. During his first term Reagan succeeded in bringing down inflation. Business experienced an upturn and there was a fall in unemployment. But the reduction in taxes deprived the state of resources as military spending increased. Despite drastic reductions in social aid, the budget deficit and the foreign debt reached a new record. If, however, the creation of jobs followed a sustained rhythm, the social inequalities remained the same. In light of this problem, President Bush, during his inaugural address, stated his hope of making America "kinder and gentler."

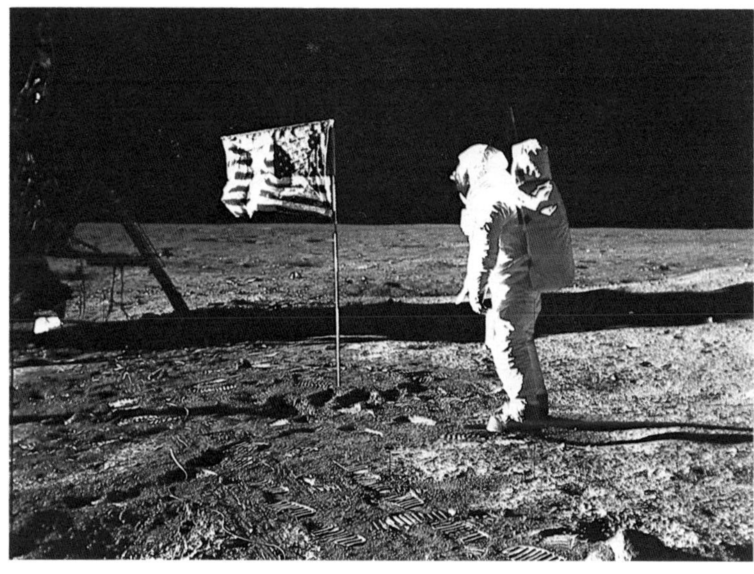
3. Edwin Aldrin, the second man to set foot on the moon, during the Apollo 11 mission in 1969.

**Nixon resigns.** **9 August 1974**

**Election of Reagan.** **November 1980**

after Senate investigation.
**1974–7:** Gerald Ford is President.
**1974:** Rise in price of imported oil.
**1975:** Onset of recession.
**4 July 1976:** Bicentenary celebrations.
**1977–81:** Jimmy Carter's Presidency.
**17 September 1978:** Camp David Accords between Egypt and Israel.
**1979:** Carter attempts to control American companies' oil prices.
**1979–81:** Iran hostages affair.
**1980:** Beginning of agricultural difficulties. Carter interrupts the shipping of wheat to the USSR to protest against invasion of Afghanistan.
**1981–5:** Ronald Reagan's first term.
**1981:** Wheat shipments to USSR recommence.
**1982:** Unemployment reaches 10% of the total employable population and 20% among Blacks.
**23 October 1983:** 230 American soldiers are killed by a "suicide truck" in Beirut.
**1985–1989:** Ronald Reagan's second term.
**1986. 28 January:** Explosion of the Challenger space shuttle.

6. First feminist demonstrations in New York.

**2 December:** The beginning of two investigative commissions on the "Iran-contra" affair.
**1987:** Inflation is at 4,4 % whereas in 1980 it had risen to 13.5 %.
**22 January:** Death of Andy Warhol.
**1988. May:** Unemployment returns to its level of 1974.
**8 November:** Election of George Bush.
**1989. 20 December:** American troops invade Panama to set up a new democratic government and to force General Noriega to stand trial in the US on drug charges.

7. Ronald and Nancy Reagan descending from the presidential plane.

# The Pacific: a Newly Dominant Region

*1. The sky-scrapers of Hong Kong, facing the sea and China.*

THE RUSSIAN THINKER Alexander Herzen once predicted that the Pacific would be the Mediterranean of the twentieth century. There may be some truth in his prediction, but the reality is more complex, especially in view of the fact that the population of the Pacific is particularly mixed. The economic growth of the last thirty years has in fact been confined to the north Pacific, from Singapore to Los Angeles, via Taiwan, South Korea and Japan.

The geopolitical importance of the Pacific region has become one of the major elements in the history of the twentieth century. 'Whoever controls the Pacific controls the world', said the American Senator Albert J. Beveridge in 1900. The Second World War was fully to confirm this view. In 1945 the Pacific, which was the only region to witness the explosion of an atom bomb, became an American ocean, defended by the largest fleet and by the most extensive military bases in history. As for the modernization process, it began with the Meiji era in Japan, the mining and oil booms in California, and the industrialization of Manchuria, and continued after 1945 with the ever-increasing growth in trade relations between the most densely populated and most powerful industrial countries in the world.

Since the 1950s, the dynamic of world history has become centred all the more firmly in the north Pacific. Dramatic changes have taken place in the political and social structure of the countries of the region: we have seen the setting up of new independent states, constitutional reform in Japan, agrarian reform in South Korea, Japan and Taiwan, and the intervention of various international agencies to promote the 'green revolution' in Southeast Asia. Today the north Pacific is the central focus of the world market, as may be seen from the recent change in the dominant pattern of United States foreign trade. In 1980, for the first time, trade between the United States and the Pacific zone (representing 117.6 billion dollars) was greater than trade with Western Europe (115.9 billion dollars). This historic reversal began no doubt much earlier, with the shift of the centre of gravity of US capitalism towards the west coast of America during the Second World War. The process continued with the enormous economic expansion of Japan in the 1960s, the extraordinary industrial take-off of the four newly industrialized countries of Asia – South Korea, Taiwan, Hong Kong and Singapore – and the slow and more haphazard industrialization of Thailand, Malaysia, Indonesia and the Philippines.

Between 1973 and 1981 the growth of these workshop countries together with Japan broke all historical records, with an average annual rate of 8% (during the same period North America managed 2.7% and the EEC countries 1.9%). The industrialization of the new industrial countries followed a common pattern: centralized planning by a military technocracy that was powerful at home but extremely vulnerable internationally, authoritarian control of the labour market and systematic exploitation of cheap labour, the massive injection of foreign capital, increasing specialization away from consumer goods towards basic industry and high technology (semiconductors, computers and telecommunications).

In this way a new economic, technological, cultural and political axis has developed around the United States and Japan. In less than half a century there has been a total displacement of the technical and industrial centres of world society towards the 'telectronic commonwealth' of the north Pacific. The third industrial revolution will have been the first not to have its origins on the Atlantic coast of Europe. The Greenwich meridian no longer marks the centre of the world. ...

| 1868 | 27 July 1953 | 16 September 1963 | 7 August 1965 |
|---|---|---|---|
| **Japan opens its frontiers and embarks on a policy of conquest of the world.** | **Armistice signed at P'anmunjom.** | **Malaysia formed.** | **Singapore declares its independence.** |

**1868:** Beginning of the Meiji era. Japan begins to industrialize.
**1894:** Japan annexes Korea.
**1904–5:** Russo-Japanese War.
**1931:** Japan occupies Manchuria and develops heavy industry.
**1941–5:** War in the Pacific: Japan attempts to establish a new order in the Pacific, and a co-prosperity sphere comprising Japan, Manchuria, Korea and North China. Industrial boom takes off in California.
**1946. 21 October:** Agrarian reform in Japan on the initiative of the American authorities.
**3 November:** New Japanese constitution.
**3 May 1947:** Measures are taken to break up the major economic concentrations in Japan. These are later abandoned in May 1949.
**1949. 21 June:** Agrarian Reform in South Korea.
**3 December:** Chinese Nationalist Government transfers to Taiwan.
**1950:** Hong Kong begins to industrialize.
**1950–3:** The Korean War leads to the consolidation of the partition of the country into two rival states.
**1951:** Peace treaties signed by the Allies (with the exception of the Soviet Union) and Japan: San Francisco Peace Treaty signed in San Francisco on 8 September.
**1953:** Agrarian reform in Taiwan.
**September 1954:** South East Asia Treaty Organization (SEATO) set up.
**1959:** Lee Kuan Yew comes to power in Singapore and adopts a policy of industrialization.
**1961:** Major-General Park Chung Hee comes to power in South Korea and embarks on a policy of accelerated industrialization.
**16 September 1963:** Malaysia formed.
**1963–75:** The Vietnam War acts as a stimulus to economic expansion in the neighbouring countries.
**1965. 11 February:** First Japanese satellite in orbit.
**9 August:** Singapore leaves Malaysia and becomes an independent state.
**November:** Ferdinand Marcos elected President of the Philippines.
**12 March 1966:** In Indonesia, General Suharto establishes military rule.
**August 1967:** Association of South East Asian Nations (ASEAN) set up.

*2. Futuristic architecture in Singapore.*

*3. A newly industrialized country: the nerve centre of a steel works in South Korea.*

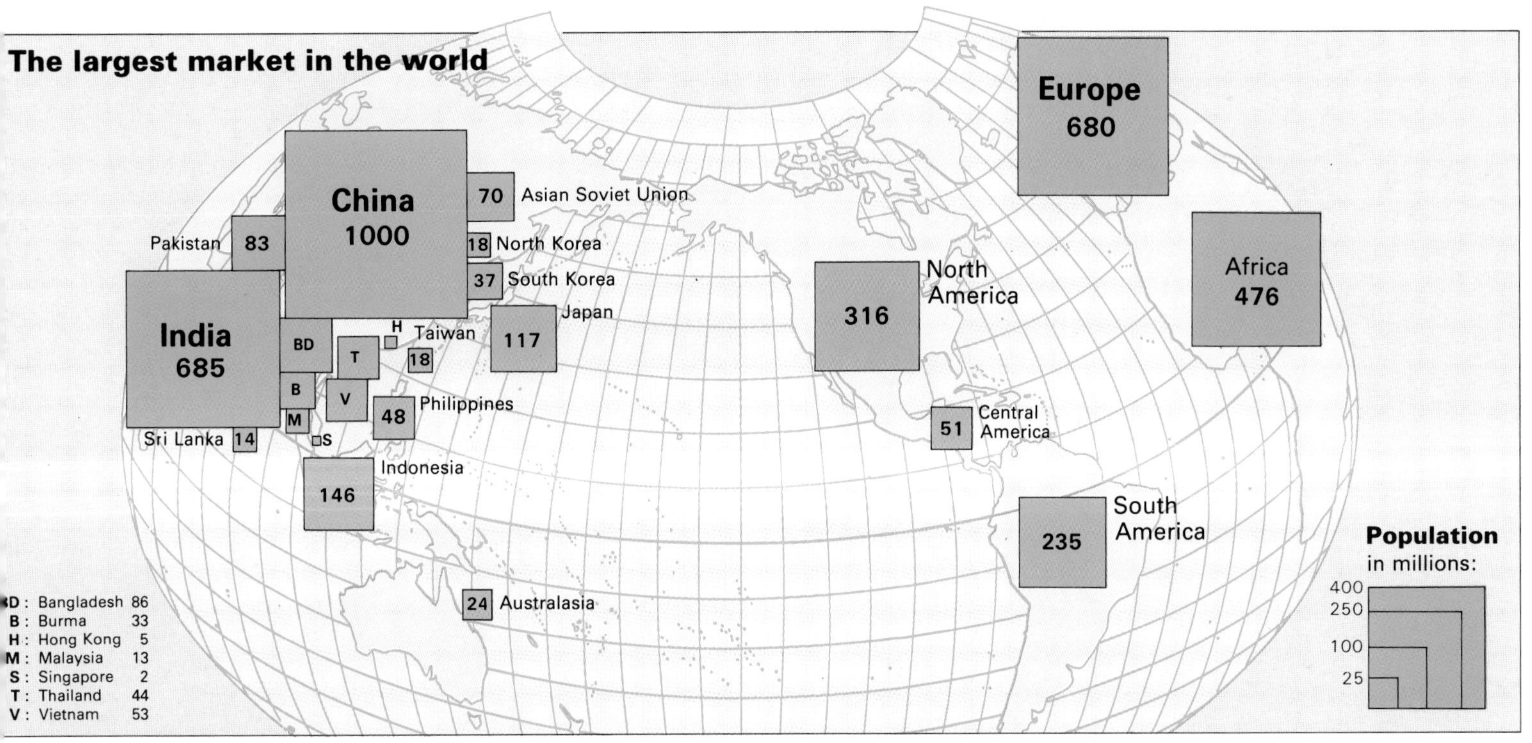


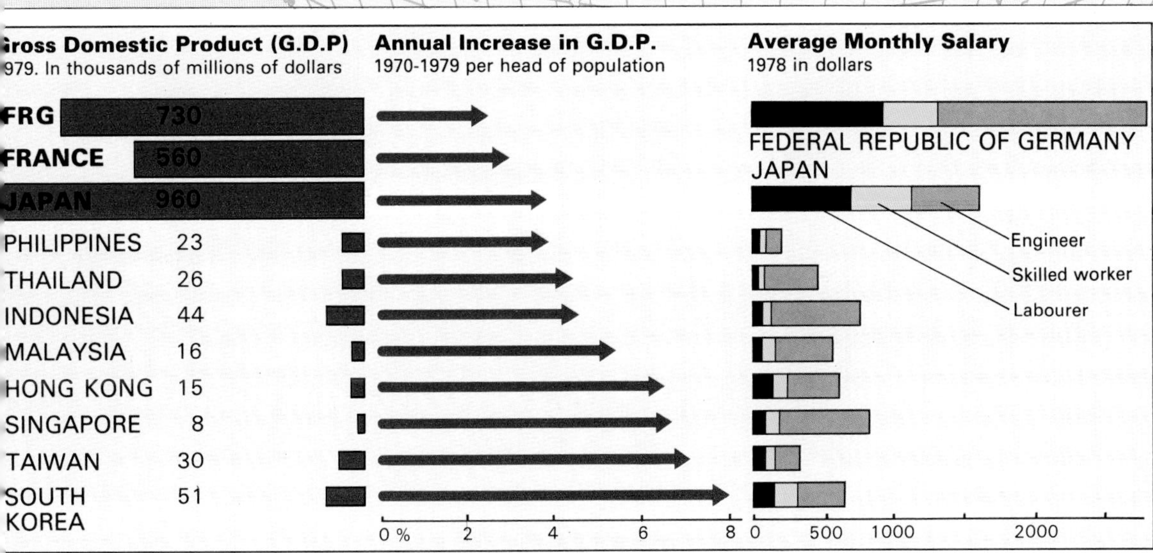


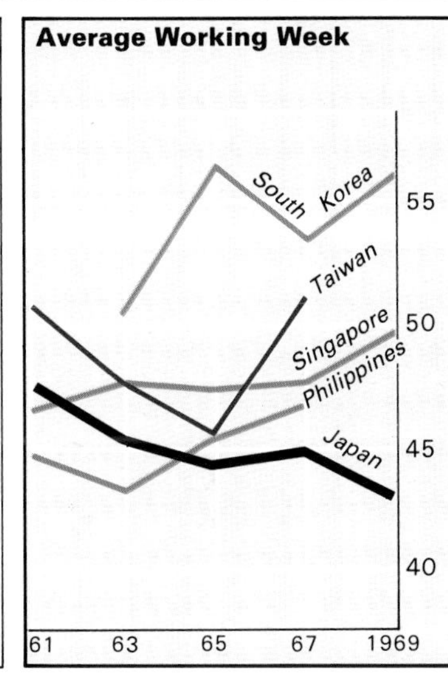


| eath of Hirohito | Sino-Japanese Peace and Friendship Treaty. | Anglo-Chinese Accord on Hong Kong. |
|---|---|---|
| 7 January 1989 | 12 August 1978 | 26 September 1984 |

968: Indonesian industry begins to expand
 textiles and plastics).
5 November 1970: Suicide of the
panese writer Yukio Mishima.
971. 31 October: Britain withdraws from its
ilitary commitments in the Far East.
3 December: Re-valuation of the Japanese
en.
72. 23 September: The Marcos
overnment declares martial law in the
hilippines.
) September: Normalization of relations
etween Japan and China.
972–80: Second phase of industrial
evelopment (heavy industry, chemicals,
otor-cars) in the 4 'new industrial countries'
f Asia.
1–12 January 1983: The first visit of a
panese head of state to South Korea
nce the war.
6 September 1984: Agreement signed
etween the British and the Chinese on the
eturn of Hong Kong to Chinese sovereignty
 1997.
986: End of the Marcos dictatorship in the
hilippines. On 26 February, Cory Aquino is elected president.

**1987:** Japan's balance of payments reaches a surplus of $87 billion (twice that of the Federal Republic of Germany).
**10–16 June:** Protests and "peace marches" in South Korea against President Chun and his designated successor, Roh Tae Woo.
**1988. 22 April–5 May:** Ouvea Affair in New Caledonia. Six servicemen and 17 separatists are killed.
**26 June:** Matignon accords between two rival factions on the future of New Caledonia.
**25 May 1989:** The Japanese prime minister, N. Takeshita, is implicated in a political-financial scandal and resigns. On July 23, the conservative Liberal Democratic Party, in power for 35 years, loses the senatorial elections.

*4. Japanese motocycles being unloaded in Dubai, in the United Arab Emirates.*

*5. Victory salute of Cory Aquino after her victory over ex-President Marcos in Manila, February 1986.*

# Africa: The Problems of Independence

After experiencing almost total subjection, most of the world's colonies acquired their independence in the same few years. For most of them, a new era began around 1960. It is, then, those cases where decolonization was not achieved that catch the eye: Portugal only yielded in 1974, White Rhodesia only gave way to Zimbabwe in 1980 and Namibia is still in the hands of South Africa, which remains a bastion of White power.

But the simple listing of when independence was achieved and on what legal terms can be misleading. Relations of dependence remain; they are built into the world market and political investment deci-

1. *UN soldiers in the Congo 1961.*

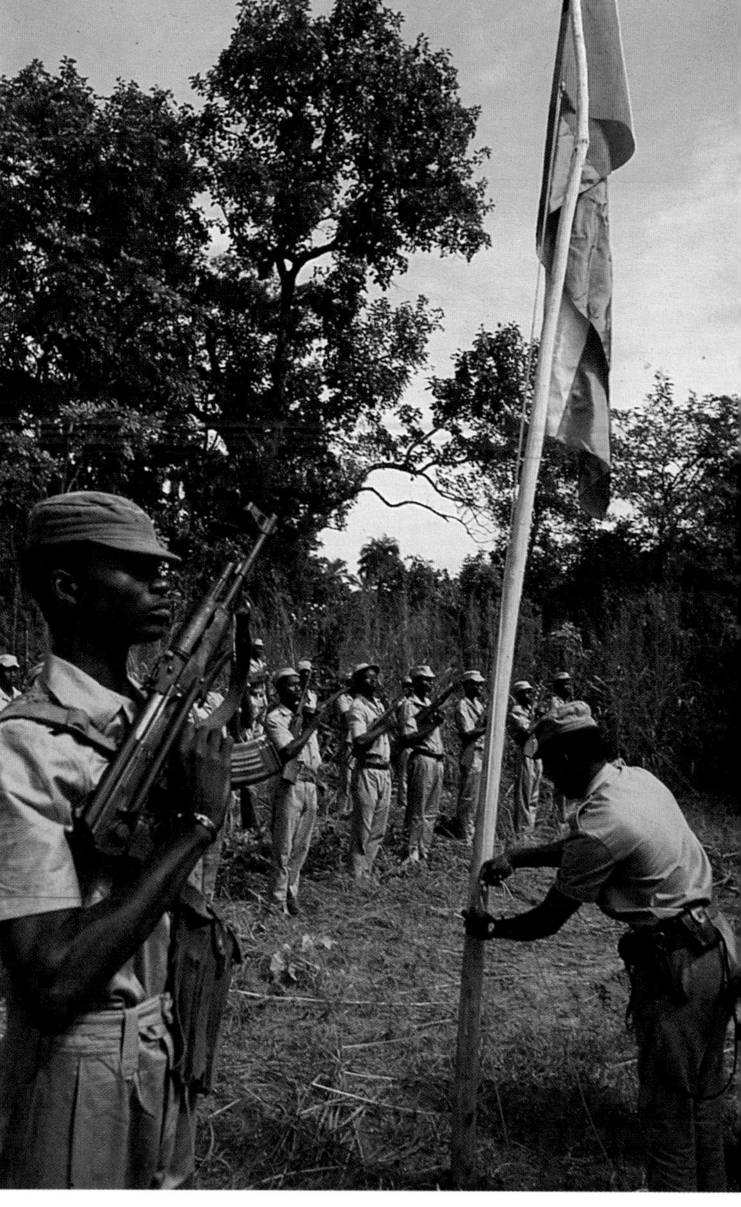

2. *Guerrillas from Bissau, Guinea 1974.*

**Independence of Ghana.**

**1957**

**Leopold Sedar Senghor.**

**1960–1981**

**1947:** Founding of the review *African Presence* under the aegis of Alioune Diop.
**1956:** First Congress of Representatives of Black Culture in Paris.
**15–22 April 1958:** Nkrumah calls the conference of Independent African States in Accra (Ghana), then the conference of African people.
**1958–72:** Rebellion in Southern Sudan. In 1972 the Nimeiri government recognizes its cultural and administrative autonomy.
**3 March 1960:** Rubgangwa the first black cardinal (Tanganyika).
**1960–5:** Clashes in Leopoldville, Congo; Katangan secession (11 July 1960–January 1963); assassination of Lumumba (17 January 1961); rebellion in the provinces; Western intervention; coup d'état by Mobutu (24 November 1965).
**1963–1964:** Chou En-lai tours Africa.
**22–23 May 1963:** Creation of the OAU in Addis Abada (annual meetings, permanent secretariat, commissions).
**1965:** White independence in Southern Rhodesia. Uprising in Northern Chad; beginning of a series of still-existing troubles.
**1963:** Chou En-lai tours Africa.
**22–5 May:** Creation of the OAU in Addis
**1967:** Nyerere expresses the socialist economic principles of Tanzania in a speech at Arusha.
**1967–70:** Secession of the Ibos (30 May 1967) in Nigeria after persecution and threats of deprivations; Biafra gives in (12 January 1970) after a terrible war in which support had come from differing sources..
**1969:** Siyad Barre comes to power in Somalia (21 October); socialist regime friendly to Russia (co-operation agreement, 1977); but geographic and political factors force him to seek American support (21 August 1980). Pan-African Festival, Algiers.
**1969–73:** Droughts and famines: political repercussions.
**1969–85:** Ganfar Mohammed el-Nimeiri in the Sudan. Political changes; he is ousted after demonstrations; provisional military Council.
**18 May 1972:** P. Tsiranana eliminated in Madagascar.
**1973:** UN and OAU recognize SWAPO (South

4. *The OAU conference at Lomé in 1981. From left to right: E. Eyadéma, D. Dacko, A. Ahidjo, F. Houphouet-Boigny.*

ons, superpower interests and geopolitics, the distribution of techni-al and ideological expertise and linguistic necessities. Neo-olonialism is not a policy like any other: it is the global situation of e age, though it takes different forms in different places, with arying implications and social costs. Moreover, two generations of olonization have dismantled and re-formed territories, societies and ultures. The new states have been unable to return to their pre-olonial traditions, and yet have found it equally hard to adopt the odern nation-state model of government, as this did not evolve from eir own historical processes.

The moderate/revolutionary distinction, which is entirely a matter f ideology is inadequate for understanding an emerging political eality in which the main factors are where the state functions effec-vely and where it is absent, and the relations between a dispersed ivil society and a concentrated political society. Ethnic particular-ms are not stubborn vestiges of the past: they enable present-day ocial groups to affirm their identity in relation to current issues.

Black Africa is a political arena for the great powers. France and reat Britain remain active and influential there, both by providing id and by initiating projects. They are present in the economic, ultural, military and political spheres, both in bilateral relations and rough large supra-national bodies. The two super-powers have also eveloped their modes of intervention, the United States becoming assively involved, the USSR having a more discreet – and, initially at least, less successful – presence. The East-West confrontation in its more pronounced form reached Africa around 1975, when the Portuguese withdrawal and radicalization of the Ethiopian revolution gave the USSR and Cuba the opportunity to acquire a firm foothold in Ethiopia and Angola. Interests originating in Mediterranean Africa and the Near East also still exert considerable influence.

The decolonization process has gone against the Pan-African ideal. Though efforts to unite states have come to nothing, the formation of loose regional groupings, or groupings on a technical basis, has been more successful. Since 1963 the Organization of African Unity (OAU) has offered all the African states a structure for concerted action which provides a solid response to a deeply felt aspiration, even though it also reveals the divisions between its members and fails to settle all their differences.

The most serious internal and international tensions have involved neighbouring countries and external powers, namely: sharp conflicts in Congo-Kinshasa (1960–5); defeat of the Ibo secession in Nigeria; recurrent troubles in Chad; two uprisings in southern Sudan; rebellion in Eritrea; the strains on the Somali frontiers, too narrow for its large people; the destiny of the former Spanish Sahara; resistance movements in Angola and Mozambique; uprisings among apartheid's subjects; and the various forms of pressure exercised by South Africa on all her neighbours, most notably Angola, Zambia and Malawi.

. First Black ghetto uprising in Soweto, 16 June 1976.

**di Amin ruler of Uganda.** **Independence of Mozambique.** **Race riots in Soweto.** **Ethiopia becomes Marxist under Mengistu.** **Independence of Zimbabwe.**

**971–80** **25 June 1975** **June 1976** **11 February 1977** **18 April 1980**

Vest Africa People's Organization) as the ole representative of the Namibian people.
**974:** Ethiopian revolution initiated by the rmy; deposition of Emperor Haile Selassie; and reform.
**975:** Malagasy socialist revolutionary harter. Inauguration of Tanzam Tanzania-Zambia) Railway built by the hinese, opening south west Zambia conomically and providing an outlet for ambian copper.
**975–6:** Spanish withdrawal from the ahara: shared between Morocco, the olisario Front and Mauritania: complex ilitary and political development: Republic f the Western Sahara recognized and isputed.
**976:** Uprising in Soweto, a Black African uburb of Johannesburg (South Africa). eturn to multi-party system in Senegal einforced in 1983) which had been rejected 1966.
**1 February 1977:** Mengistu takes over in thiopia: the USSR supports his regime.
**977–8:** Ogaden war between Somalia and thiopia.
**1980:** First intensive raids by South Africa into Angola.
**1984:** Death of Sékou Touré in Guinea and end of his rule. Signing of a cease fire between South Africa and Angola; Nkomoti agreement: Mozambique and South Africa agree not to support action against each other.
**1986. 14–15 February:** American air raid on Tripoli.
**19 October:** Accidental death of Samora Machel, Mozambique's chief of state.

*5. An artist's evocation of the massacres under the regime of A. S. Shagari, Nigeria 1981.*

**1987. 27 March:** Revival of Faya-Largeau, Libya's last stronghold in Northern Chad. Cease-fire between Colonel Qaddafi and Hissene Habre begins on 11 September.
**15 October:** Assassination of Captain Sankara in Burkina Faso.
**1988:** Zaire launches a five-year program of struggle against AIDS. The disease will touch more than 6 % of the urban population.
**25 June:** Protest of the community of Western African States against the stocking of toxic waste.
**4 August:** Catastrophic flooding of the Sudan.
**14–21 August:** Inter-ethnic massacres in Burundi.
**22 December:** Agreement on Namibia reached by South Africa, Cuba and Angola.
**1989. 22–28 March:** Confrontations between Mauritanians and the Senegalese in the cities of both countries.
**22 June:** Cease-fire between J.E. Dos Santos, the president of Angola, and J. Savimbi, head of the guerrilla group U.N.I.T.A.

# The Third World and Third World Independence Movements

In 1952, Alfred Sauvy, drawing an analogy with the Third Estate at the time of the 1789 French Revolution, began to call those emerging states and peoples who belonged neither to the Western nor the Eastern bloc the 'Third World'. Today the term is occasionally used in the plural to emphasize the heterogeneous nature of the different countries involved. The Third World movement, as set out at the moment of its inception at the Bandung Conference of 1955, was anti-colonialist and neutralist. Its aim was to bring together subjugated peoples and dominated states in the common defence of their political interests and territorial security; the idea was also to influence both the relations between states and the work of various

*1. Aswan Dam in Egypt.*

*2. The dry season near Makanah, in Senegal.*

international agencies in order that greater priority would be given to developmental issues. In the 1960s the Cuban revolution, the Vietnam war and the Palestinian problem gave rise to radical 'tricontinental' views of Third World revolution.

Various key ideas defined this theory of twentieth-century revolution. The peasant masses, it was argued, the 'wretched of the earth', constituted a huge potential force; 'power', Mao Tse-tung wrote, came 'out of the barrel of a gun', and therefore there had to be more and more Vietnams, and ever more centres of insurrection (what Che Guevara called the *focos* of revolution) had to be created. 'The global countryside' had to surround the 'global city' (as Mao Tse-tung put it), and the internationalism of the three continents became the main lever of the anti-imperialist struggle. The Third World, it was argued, was inventing a new historical path forward, new models of development, and was leading the way to the creation of a 'new man', as exemplified by the Chinese Cultural Revolution.

This body of doctrine did not survive the disappointments and

**Bandung Conference.** — **17–24 April 1955**

**Formation of the Organization of African Unity.** — **25 May 1963**

**War in Biafra.** — **July 1967–January 1970**

**Emperor Haile Selassie overthrown by a military coup in Ethiopia.** — **12 September 1974**

**Leopold Senghor, poet-president of Senegal, publishes, in French, his *Elégies majeures.*** — **1979**

**April 1951:** Mohammed Mosaddeq introduces a Bill for the nationalization of Iranian oil.
**17–24 April 1955:** Bandung Conference brings together for the first time 29 Third World countries and adopts a charter affirming equality between races and nations, and calling for peace and for a special United Nations Development Fund. The personalites of Nehru, Tito, Sukarno and Nasser are brought to the attention of world opinion.
**1960:** Sino-Soviet split. China rejects the notion of peaceful coexistence and claims leadership of the 'storm zone' between the two superpowers.
**1961. 17 January:** Patrice Lumumba, the figurehead of the independence and unity of the Congo, is assassinated. He becomes the first martyr of the Third World.
**1–6 September:** Conference of the non-aligned in Belgrade. The 25 initial countries increased, by 1979, to 95, meeting in Havana. At the United Nations U Thant becomes the first non-Western Secretary General.
**22–28 October 1962:** Cuban Missile Crisis. The Soviet Union backs down in the face of American protests and the image of 'Castroism' suffers its first blow.
**3–15 January 1966:** Conference of Solidarity between the peoples of Africa, Asia and Latin America held in Havana. It puts forward the idea of a revolutionary Third World movement spreading beyond the boundaries of individual countries.
**May 1968:** Protest movement is born from the campaign of solidarity with the Third World and from the struggle against American involvement in Vietnam.
**25 October 1971:** The People's Republic of China is admitted to the United Nations. As a result, Taiwan is expelled.
**1975:** Victory of the Khmer Rouge in Cambodia (17 April). The Vietcong arrive in Saigon on 30 April after 11 years of American involvement.
**1975–6:** Start of Vietnamese involvement in bordering countries: Laos, then Cambodia. Tension grows with China.
**1979:** Shah of Iran is overthrown (16 January). Ayatollah Khomeini returns to Tehran on 1 February. The Iranian Islamic revolution prefigures a series of upheavals in the Islamic world (like the revolution in the Sudan in 1985) and demonstrates the capacity of religious fundamentalism to mobilize the population.
**1980:** Start of the Iran-Iraq war. UNESCO adopts a report calling for a 'new world order' in information. This is opposed by the Western states.
**1982:** The Argentine army occupies the Falkland Islands (or Malvinas). In August the PLO is forced out of Lebanon.
**1983:** 146 national liberation organizations are counted in the Third World. Nigeria decides to deport one and a half million immigrants (17 January).
**1984. June:** The issue of immigration is used to an unprecedented degree by right-wing and extreme right-wing parties in the election campaign leading up to the European elections in France.
**31 October:** Indira Gandhi assassinated by a Sikh extremist. Violent clashes between communities in India.
**1985:** Unprecedented protests by the black population of South Africa against apartheid. Racism becomes an increasing problem in the West as a result of the economic crisis. The Vatican condemns the liberation theology developed by South American Church leaders since 1968. Democracy makes some inroads on military dictatorship, and there are elections for president in Brazil (January 1985), and Argentina (December 1983).
**8 August 1988:** End of the Iran-Iraq war.
**1988–1989:** Inter-ethnic confrontations and massacres in Africa (Burundi, Senegal, Mauritania).
**1989. 15 March:** The European Parliament approves the right of foreigners to vote in municipal elections.
**24 May:** François Mitterrand states that Paris unconditionally renounces the 16-billion-franc debt owed by 35 African states.
**May:** Beginning of negotiations in Paris on the future of Cambodia.

failures of the decade which followed. The countries of the Third World today do no not constitute a unified geopolitical bloc. This is because of the extreme diversity of social formations, culture and history to be found in the countries of the Third World, each of which has its own specific problems and strengths. In addition, the situations of various countries have become more and more diverse because of differing economic strategies, and as a result of their different experiences and results. While on the one side there are the petroleum exporting countries, there are others who remain vulnerable to all the fluctuations in the oil price; while on the one hand there are powerful new industrial countries emerging, on the other there are those still devastated by famine. The countries of the Third World are, moreover, divided up into regional organizations (like the Organization of African Unity) or religious and linguistic ones (like the Arab League, or the Islamic Conference), as well as political and military groupings. Finally, outbreaks of war between powers who share the same ideological system demonstrate the extent to which old ethnic conflicts or rivalries are hard to eradicate and how much the actions of states are dictated by *Realpolitik*. Without any unifying worldwide project and in the absence of any single undisputed leadership, neither tricontinentalism nor neutralism seems to represent a sufficiently powerful rallying force. Despite all the predictions to the contrary, Marxist revolutions in the Third World have most often failed or ended up producing repressive regimes.

The Third World is no longer what it was once thought to be. The reassertion by various communities of their particular national or ethnic identities – as is evidenced by the resurgence of Islamic fundamentalism (in the Iranian and Sudanese revolutions and elsewhere) – seems to be the chief characteristic of the 1980s.

**Restoration of democracy in Brazil.**

**1985**

*3. 17-24 April 1955: Bandung Conference, the leaders on the platform.*

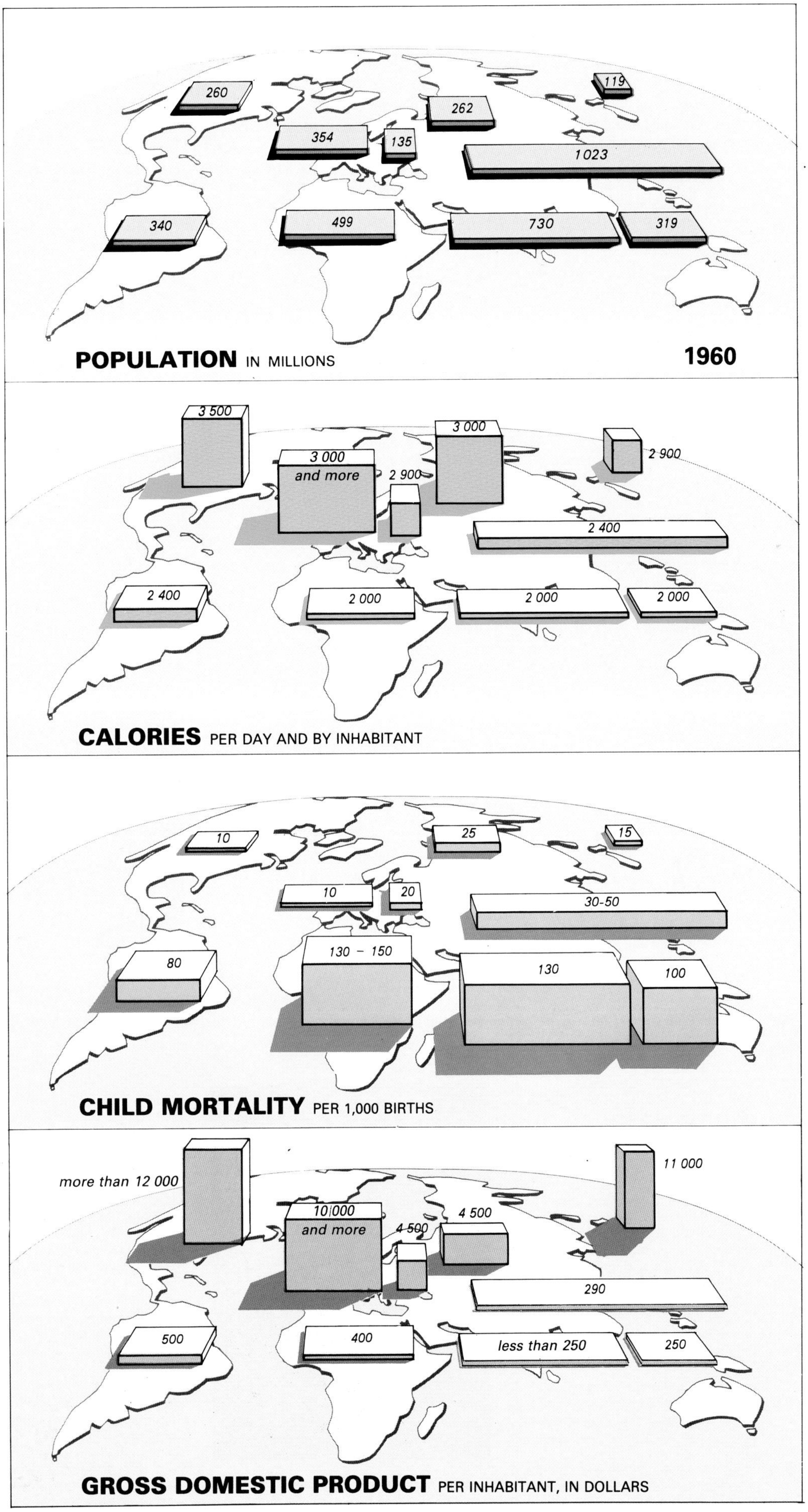

**POPULATION** IN MILLIONS **1960**

260
354
135
262
119
1023
340
499
730
319

**CALORIES** PER DAY AND BY INHABITANT

3 500
3 000 and more
2 900
3 000
2 900
2 400
2 400
2 000
2 000
2 000

**CHILD MORTALITY** PER 1,000 BIRTHS

10
10
20
25
15
30-50
80
130 – 150
130
100

**GROSS DOMESTIC PRODUCT** PER INHABITANT, IN DOLLARS

more than 12 000
10 000 and more
4 500
4 500
11 000
290
500
400
less than 250
250

# India since Independence

At the very moment of independence, the Indian subcontinent began to break up. The first step in this process was the partition of India and Pakistan. In spite of Gandhi and Nehru, who were both passionately committed to national unity, the Muslim League, under the leadership of Ali Jinnah, achieved its aim of setting up a separate Pakistan, 'the country of the pure', in those territories, in the Indus basin and in Bengal, where the majority of the population were Muslims. The partition sparked off several massacres of minority groups, and led to considerable waves of emigration: 7 million Muslims left the Indian Union to take refuge in Pakistan, and 5 million Hindus and Sikhs left Pakistan for the Indian Union. But while Pakistan became an almost exclusively Muslim country, the Indian Union retained a large Muslim minority (representing 10% of the population). In addition, the princely states (of which there were 562) occupied 45% of the territory of the Indian Union. The task of absorbing these different states into one and creating a solid and homogeneous federation was undertaken by Patel and brought to completion by 1956. The basic principle was that the different federal states should coincide with language areas. The federal language itself is English, though periodic attempts have been made to include Hindi as well, but this has always been rejected by the southern states. India is proud of its reputation as the largest democracy in the world. Each state has its own assembly, directly elected by universal suffrage, as well as its own government. The people also vote for the lower house of the central parliament (Lok Sabha), and the state assemblies choose a state chamber (Rajya Sabha). The central government is accountable to these twin chambers. In cases of emergency it can dissolve a state assembly and impose the President's rule, and the procedure has often been used. India remains a member of the Commonwealth. Its constitution, carrying on the work of Gandhi, makes it illegal to discriminate on grounds of religion, race or caste. The avowed goal of the government and the administration has been to abolish 'untouchability' and, by a system of quotas and facilities for university admission, to promote the integration of the disadvantaged castes. Marriage laws and laws concerning inheritance provide, at least in theory, for equality between the sexes. To these provisions must be added the huge network of agrarian reforms designed, in Nehru's mind, both to reduce social inequality and to develop production: for instance, the abolition of the *zamindar* system in which the landowner was also responsible for collecting taxes, the setting of a maximum limit for the ownership of lands, and the various attempts made to eliminate the problem of absentee landlords.

These were the ideals which inspired the founding fathers of modern India. It is true that some of these objectives have not been fully met, but the disasters predicted by the pessimists of the time have been averted. Admittedly, many characteristics of underdevelopment persist: as, for instance, the excessive growth of the population (which numbered 361 million in 1951 and 684 million in 1981), the predominantly rural nature of the country (where 70% of the population live in the villages), its vulnerability to natural disasters, like drought or flooding, the extreme poverty of a large section of the population, the often corrupt and inefficient administration, the undermining of the democratic system by systems of patronage and the disproportionate influence wielded by special interest groups. In some rural areas, the untouchables are over-exploited and are also the victims of physical violence. Slave labour has not yet entirely disappeared everywhere and the village money-lender remains a powerful figure.

And yet, India has become one of the great nations of the world. It has been able to maintain its territorial integrity and its unity, despite all the forces working against it, the democratic system (except for the interlude of the State of Emergency) has worked properly, and the numerous and often violent clashes between different ethnic groups and religious communities have not challenged the secular character of the institutions of the state. Thanks, above all, to the 'Green Revolution', the production of food has increased more quickly than the population (120% as compared to 90%), and India seems free of famine and enjoys self-sufficiency in food production. The road network has been extended five-fold, and electrical output has gone from 5 million to 122 million kW. The modernization of the rural areas and the development of industry have brought into existence a powerful middle class. India exports not only all types of industrial products but also qualified workers, technicians and engineers. A fresh Indian exodus has joined that, already centuries old, of its shopkeepers and tradesmen. Finally, India, up till now, has been able to follow a course of diplomacy which has allowed it to assert itself as the dominant force in the region and the voice of the Third World, without making it dependent in any permanent way on either of the two superpowers.

*1. A meeting in support of Bangladesh.*

**1951–6** First Five-Year Plan concentrates on irrigation works and starts agrarian reform.

**1955** The Bandung Conference: India emerges as leader of the Third World.

**1956–61** Second Five-Year Plan for heavy industry.

**15 August 1947:** India is granted independence and partitioned: the Indian Union and Pakistan are formed.
**30 January 1948:** A Hindu fanatic assassinates Gandhi.
**26 January 1950:** Constitution of the Indian Union promulgated.
**1952:** First general elections. The victory of the Congress Party is overwhelming. Nehru remains prime minister.
**1953:** State of Andhra Pradesh formed from the States of Madras and Hyderabad.
**1954:** Sino-Indian Agreement. Nehru and Chou En-lai proclaim the 'Five Principles of Peaceful Coexistence'. France's territories in India are transferred to the Indian Union. Pakistan joins the Southeast Asia Treaty Organization (SEATO).
**1957:** The Congress Party is once more victorious in the elections, except in Kerala, where the Communists are swept to power.
**1958:** General Ayub Khan takes power in Pakistan.
**1959:** The central government dissolves the State Assembly in Kerala and imposes the President's rule.

*2. Offerings after the death of Nehru in 1964.*

**1960:** The State of Bombay is divided up into Maharashtra and Gujarat.
**1961:** The Indian Army forces the Portuguese to leave Goa.
**1962:** War breaks out along the Himalayan frontier between China and India. China shows its superior strength.
**1964:** Death of Nehru, 27 May. He is succeeded by Lal Bahadur Shastri.
**1966:** Shastri dies in Tashkent during the conference called to settle the conflict between India and Pakistan over Kashmir. Indira Gandhi, Nehru's daughter, becomes prime minister. A series of poor harvests leads to a general recession. The rupee is devalued by 50%.
**1967:** In the elections the Congress Party wins in the central parliament, but in the majority of the state assemblies, various opposition parties are elected. The Communist Party splits into the pro-Moscow Communist Party of India (Marxist), which is at the head of the governments in Kerala and West Bengal, and the Maoist Party of the Naxalite extremists who engage in guerrilla warfare in West Bengal.
**1968:** The policy of five-year plans is abandoned. Greater support is given to private capital. The 'Green Revolution' enables the country to become self-sufficient in wheat.
**1969:** The banks are nationalized. Indira Gandhi has the right wing of the Congress Party expelled. In Pakistan, Yahya Khan takes power.
**1971:** Indira Gandhi wins the elections after campaigning with the slogan 'Eliminate Poverty'. Treaty of Peace, Friendship and Co-operation signed with the Soviet Union. East Pakistan rebels, India intervenes, defeats the Pakistani army and sees the setting up of an independent Bangladesh. In Sri Lanka, the rising of revolutionary youth violently quelled.
**1972:** Relations with Pakistan are restored. Zulfikar Ali Bhutto sets about reorganizing Pakistan after the war over Bangladesh. His aim will be to sever the country's links with the Americans.
**1974:** In May India explodes its first nuclear device.
**1975:** Indira Gandhi declares a State of

## One India or several?

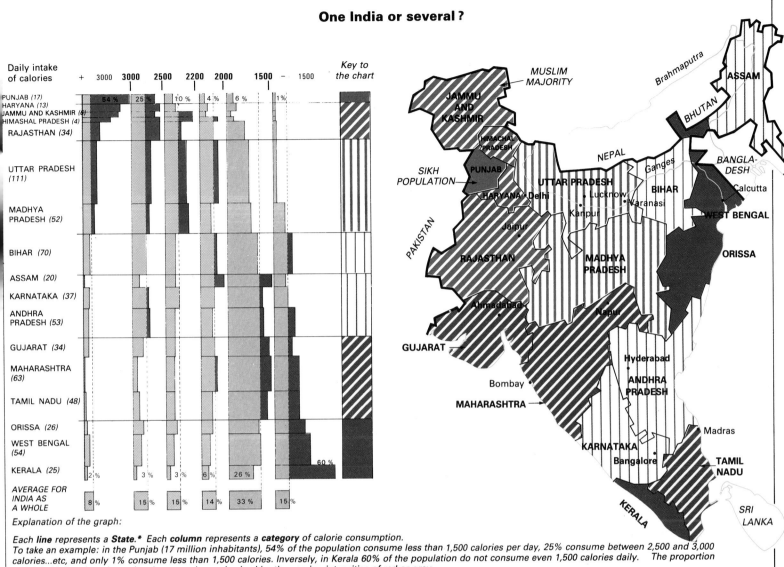

Daily intake of calories: + 3000 | 3000 | 2500 | 2200 | 2000 | 1500 | – 1500 | Key to the chart

PUNJAB (17) 54 % 25 % 10 % 4 % 6 % 1%
HARYANA (13)
JAMMU AND KASHMIR (6)
HIMASHAL PRADESH (4)
RAJASTHAN (34)
UTTAR PRADESH (111)
MADHYA PRADESH (52)
BIHAR (70)
ASSAM (20)
KARNATAKA (37)
ANDHRA PRADESH (53)
GUJARAT (34)
MAHARASHTRA (63)
TAMIL NADU (48)
ORISSA (26)
WEST BENGAL (54)
KERALA (25) 2 % 3 % 3 % 6 % 26 % 60 %
AVERAGE FOR INDIA AS A WHOLE 8 % 15 % 15 % 14 % 33 % 15 %

MUSLIM MAJORITY
JAMMU AND KASHMIR
HIMACHAL PRADESH
SIKH POPULATION
PUNJAB
HARYANA
Delhi
PAKISTAN
RAJASTHAN
Jaipur
UTTAR PRADESH
Lucknow
Kanpur
Varanasi
NEPAL
Brahmaputra
BHUTAN
ASSAM
Ganges
BIHAR
BANGLA-DESH
Calcutta
WEST BENGAL
ORISSA
MADHYA PRADESH
Ahmadabad
Napur
GUJARAT
Bombay
MAHARASHTRA
Hyderabad
ANDHRA PRADESH
Madras
KARNATAKA
Bangalore
TAMIL NADU
KERALA
SRI LANKA

*Explanation of the graph:*

*Each* ***line*** *represents a* ***State.**** *Each* ***column*** *represents a* ***category*** *of calorie consumption.*
*To take an example: in the Punjab (17 million inhabitants), 54% of the population consume less than 1,500 calories per day, 25% consume between 2,500 and 3,000 calories...etc, and only 1% consume less than 1,500 calories. Inversely, in Kerala 60% of the population do not consume even 1,500 calories daily. The proportion which is higher than the national average is emphasised by the varying intensities of red or grey.*
*Mentioned here are only the figures for these two examples and for the national average. Comparèd in this way the figures reveal the unequal distribution of India's wealth.*
**The height of each line is in relation to the population of the State concerened, and the number of inhabitants is shown within brackets*

**1961–6**
**Third Five-Year Plan for the development of ancillary industries for agriculture.**

**1968**
**The 'Green Revolution' begins. The policy of Five-Year Plans is abandoned.**

**1980**
**India begins exporting technical goods.**

**Since November 1984**
**Increased separatist agitation.**

Emergency. Elections are put off for a year, civil rights are suspended, and her opponents are put in prison. Under the influence of Sanjay Gandhi, Indira's son, a brutal campaign of birth control is pursued, leading to a programme of massive sterilization.
**1977:** At the elections the Congress Party is defeated by the non-communist opposition parties. The Janata Party, created by a follower of Gandhi, Jayaprakash Narayan, takes power. Morarji Desai, a strict Hindu, is prime minister (in March). In Pakistan, General Zia ul-Haq deposes Ali Bhutto, who is subsequently sentenced to death and hanged. The new régime in Pakistan intends creating an Islamic Republic.
**1979:** The Soviet occupation of Afghanistan sends refugees flooding into Pakistan (2.5 million in 1982).
**1980:** After a series of political crises, the central parliament is dissolved, and the elections see the triumphant, though unexpected, return to power of Indira Gandhi. Her son Sanjay is Secretary of the Congress Party, but dies in a plane crash in June. In Assam there are violent clashes between the

*3. Gandhi in 1947.*

indigenous population and the enormous mass of immigrants coming from West Bengal. Sikh separatism becomes active. India becomes an exporter of industrial equipment (machine-tools, railways, power-stations) to Southeast Asia, the Gulf States, Europe and Africa.
**1982:** Delhi hosts the Asian Games.
**1984:** Sikh extremists embark on a policy of terrorism and armed struggle. The Golden Temple in Amritsar, which had been occupied by Sikh activists, is stormed by the Indian Army. As a consequence of the desecration of the temple by Indian troops, Indira Gandhi is assassinated on 31 October by one of her Sikh body-guards. She is succeeded by her son Rajiv Gandhi. At the end of December, fresh elections give him a clear victory.
**3 December 1984:** In Bhopal, toxic gases escaping from a chemical plant cause the deaths of thousands of local inhabitants.
**October 1987:** Intervention of Indian troops in Sri Lanka to separate the Tamils and the Sinhalese.
**1 December 1988:** Benazhir Bhutto becomes prime minister of Pakistan.

*4. A Sikh demonstration, 1984.*

# The Third World and the West

1. Ernesto 'Che' Guevara: 'Two, three Vietnams!'

THE WORD 'UNDERDEVELOPMENT', much used since the 1950s, was coined in an attempt to account for a new phenomenon, one which in the eyes of sociologists, public opinion and politicians alike seemed to be the major characteristic of the non-industrialized world. The vocabulary of underdevelopment, however, like the notion of South as opposed to North, or of 'less developed areas', is problematic in its implications. It raises the question of whether it is accurate to speak of precapitalist societies as being 'backward' as well as the whole question of the effects on these countries of their confrontation with the West. Each developing country is clearly the end-product of a lengthy process which goes back at least to the end of the Middle Ages, and reflects a centuries-long history in the movement of capital, goods and people across the world. The argument still continues as to whether the empires of the West merely looted the Third World for their own benefit or whether those countries benefited from the shock of contact with the West. Whatever the truth of the matter, it is, in any case, apparent that one of the most important characteristics of the developing world is its large degree of dependence on the outside world, which manifests itself in a dependence on the international market (which does not function according to rules of equal and fair exchange), in technological dependence and in an increasingly pronounced dependence on other countries for food.

The various criteria which define underdevelopment reveal other underlying problems. In addition to the familiar imbalances between, say, the coastal regions and the interior, or between productive areas and areas important for their reserves (as Lyautey has argued), there remains the question of the massive urban transformation of these societies. There is no quantitative indicator which allows one to penetrate the mystery of the cities of the Third World: it is still unclear to the outside observer how people manage to live their lives and survive there. The destruction of the old social fabric and of rural communities does not always seem to produce new and acceptable alternatives. Those groups which belong to the modern sector are very much in a minority, and the ruling classes are merely elements in a system over which they have little control.

The broad mass of the people live in an in-between world, surviving in the underground economy, or as peasants who have been driven from the country to the edges of town-life. The possibilities that exist for integrating all these people into one society are limited, even perhaps entirely precluded, by development strategies. This is clear from the outcome of three decades of development policy for the developing world. There are the newly industrialized countries, but it may be wondered whether their growth has really taken off as yet. The Third World debt (which had risen to 800 billion dollars in 1984), the repayment of which now takes up one quarter of the gross domestic product of Third World countries (and therefore represents a huge loss of capital), in addition to the precarious nature of indus-

**Tricontinental Solidarity Conference in Havana.**

**January 1966**

**OPEC sets the oil crisis in motion by increasing prices dramatically.**

**17 October 1973**

4. Algiers in December 1960: a demonstration by Algerian nationalists.

**September 1960:** OPEC (Organization of Petroleum Exporting Countries) formed by five countries in Baghdad (Venezuela, Iran, Iraq, Saudi Arabia and Kuwait).
**1961:** UNO proclaims the first 'United Nations Decade for Development'.
**Easter 1967:** Pope Paul VI issues his encyclical letter *Populorum Progressio* ('Progress of the Peoples') which lays down the Catholic doctrine regarding problems of world development.
**1973:** Arab oil exporting countries set the first oil crisis in motion. Prices increase four-fold.
**May 1974:** United Nations declaration proclaiming its wish to set up a 'new international economic order' based on equal shares and cooperation between states. A fund is set up with a view to providing emergency aid and assisting world development.
**2 February 1975:** The EEC and 46 African, Caribbean and Pacific countries sign the Lomé Convention which is designed to organize trade relations between the countries. Since then, two further agreements have followed. The cycle of drought in the Sahel begins.
**1979:** Second oil crisis, prices double.
**1980:** Market interest rates reach 20% (compared to 10% in 1978).
**1981. September:** UNO Conference on 'less developed areas' held in Paris.
**22 October:** Cancun summit. 22 heads of state commit their countries to starting world-wide negotiations between rich and poor countries, and to the North–South dialogue.
**1982:** Mexico in crisis as a result of the country's foreign debt. This causes a series of suspensions of payments, followed by the intervention by the IMF which demands a reduction in public expenditure. International meetings on the issue of interest rates and the exchange rate of the dollar follow.
**1983:** Hunger riots in Brazil, then in Tunisia and Morocco (1984), the Sudan (1985), Algeria (1988) and Venezuela (1989). The budget cuts demanded by the IMF lead to an increase in the price of food-stuffs.
**7 June 1984:** London summit is devoted to Third World debt. In Ethiopia famine takes millions of victims.

tries which usually consist of sub-contracted work from abroad or of manufacturing goods for export, do set very real limitations on the economic future of the Third World. Despite all that the 'Green Revolution' and the use of appropriate technology have been able to achieve, the localized or regional progress which has taken place has neither put an end to malnutrition (2,311 calories per person are available for consumption in Africa, as opposed to 3,652 in the United States) nor avoided the present wave of famine. In thirty-two African countries out of thirty-eight, agricultural production per head of population has diminished over the last ten years. The under-fifteens represent between 37% and 45% of the population. Unless the developed world revises both its domestic and foreign relations priorities radically, the future for the Third World, it must be conceded, looks bleak, as what is ultimately at issue is the functioning of the entire world economic system.

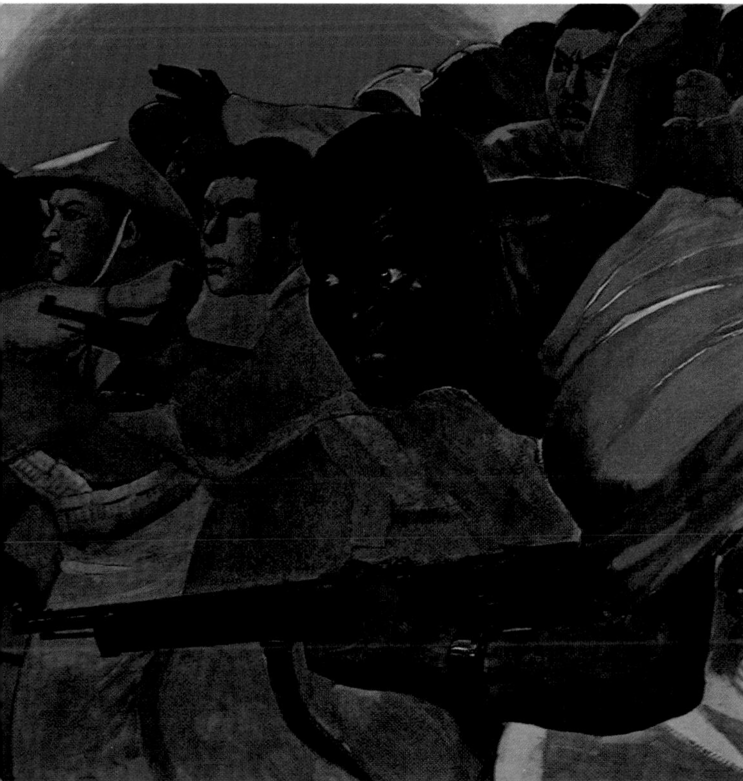

*2. The capitalist world surrounded, as seen by Chinese propaganda.*

*3. The funeral of Indira Gandhi in November 1984.*

**Lomé Convention.**

**2 February 1975**

**Hunger riots in Brazil, Tunisia, the Sudan.**

**1983–5**

**1986:** Foreign debt of Latin American countries rises to 350 % of their exports.
**19–21 June 1988:** Seven of the richest countries of the world hold a summit in Toronto and agree to a reduction of Third World debt. The problem is again addressed at the Paris summit in July 1989.

### Major International Bodies

**FAO** 1946 Food and Agriculture Organization.

**GATT** 1947 General Agreement on Tariffs and Trade.

**IBRD** 1946 International Bank for Research and Development (better known as the World Bank).

**IDA** 1960 International Development Association.

**IFC** 1956 International Finance Corporation.

**ILO** 1919 International Labour Organization.

**OECD** 1961 Organization for Economic Cooperation and Development.

**UNCTAD** 1964 United Nations Conference on Trade and Development.

**UNDP** 1966 United Nations Development Programme.

**UNESCO** 1946 United Nations Educational, Scientific and Cultural Organization.

**UNICEF** 1945 United Nations International Children's Emergency Fund.

**UNO** 1945 United Nations Organization.

**WHO** 1948 World Health Organization.

*5. A temporary anticolonial alliance: Chou En-lai and Nehru, 12 October 1954.*

# War in Southeast Asia

1. Vietnam in 1967: Vietcong prisoners during the battle for the Mekong Delta.

TOWARDS THE END OF THE 1950s, with the rivalry between the superpowers having crossed the nuclear threshold, and with the beginnings of détente in Europe, the axis of international conflict shifted to Southeast Asia. The geopolitical notion of 'Southeast Asia' only appeared around 1942, but this 'corner of Asia' had in reality been an unsettled part of the world for many years. In the nineteenth century the region was at once the most profitable area for the colonial expansion of classic imperialism by the British, the French and the Dutch and the theatre for their confrontation with China. From 1925–30 onwards strong communist parties were built up in the major urban centres, while the peasantry in Java, the Philippines and Vietnam lapsed into underdevelopment and poverty. The overthrow of the European colonial empires by the Japanese between 1940 and 1945, the First Indochina War and the painful process of decolonization in Indonesia and Burma created a power vacuum in the region, where as a result many important issues seemed to hang in the balance, from the future of the French Union (formed from France's former colonies) to the problem of what new social order would emerge in the newly formed states; uncertain, too, were the chances of neutralism in the area, as well as the credibility of the models of national construction and development that the United States wished to see followed in the Third World. Yet another destabilizing factor was the threat posed by the changing power relations between the USA, the USSR and China. The Indochina War became a 'world war fought on local territory'.

At the centre of the conflict was Vietnam. After the collapse of the plans for unification of the country provided for in the Geneva Accords of 1954, which the Americans refused to support, the war resumed in the south of the country. From 1955 the government led by Ngo Dinh Diem, with US backing, tackled the task of annihilating the communist opposition. In 1958 the National Liberation Front (NLF) was set up, and its guerilla army made rapid progress. Diem, who was unable to overcome the NLF and was swayed by the prospects of neutralism, was overthrown in 1963 as the result of pressure from the Americans, who sought, by intervening massively, though finally without success, to create in South Vietnam a military state like that in South Korea. The spectacular Tet Offensive launched by the North Vietnamese in February 1968 put paid to American policy, which had already been paralysed by the spread of the anti-war movement throughout the world. As a result, negotiations began in Paris.

It was feared that the whole region would become embroiled in the Indochinese conflict. This is indeed what happened to Laos after 1958, and to Cambodia in 1970. At the same time as large sections of the previously powerful Indonesian Communist Party were being massacred by the government, communist guerillas were gaining

| Ho Chi Minh proclaims the independence of Vietnam. | French garrison routed at Dien Bien Phu by the Viet Minh forces under General Giap. | Tet Offensive. | Paris Conference. | North-Vietnamese troops enter Saigon. |
|---|---|---|---|---|
| **2 September 1945** | **7 May 1954** | **January–March 1968** | **May 1968–March 1973** | **30 April 1975** |

**1926:** Workers' uprising organized by the Communist Party (PKI, Parti Kominis Indonesia) in Java.
**1930–1:** Indochinese Communist Party formed, village 'Soviets' set up in Nghe Tinh (North Annam). Peasant revolt in Burma.
**1940–5:** Overthrow of the colonial powers by the Japanese, and various countries declare their independence. In Indochina, the August 1945 Revolution leads to the proclamation of the Democratic Republic of Vietnam under the leadership of Ho Chi Minh (25 September). Anti-Japanese independence fronts are formed by the Communist Parties in Malaya, the Philippines and Burma.
**19 December 1946:** First Indochina War breaks out with French bombardment of Haiphong on 23 November, followed by Viet Minh attack on French troops in Hanoi on 19 December.
**1946–9:** Dutch fail to reconquer Indonesia, which becomes independent under President Sukarno.
**1948–60:** Emergency declared in Malaya, where the British put down the communist guerrillas. In the Philippines, the communist-led Hukbalahap Rebellion (1949) is brutally repressed. In Burma a communist insurrection breaks out which is joined by ethnic minority groups.
**10 December 1949:** Chinese People's Army reaches the borders of Indochina.
**1954. 7 May:** Defeat of the French at Dien Bien Phu.
**20–1 July:** Geneva Accords on Indochina.
**March 1958:** The NLF is formed in South Vietnam and the war resumes.
**July 1959:** War resumes in Laos.
**1 November 1963:** Ngo Dinh Diem is toppled and assassinated. He is to be followed by a succession of military governments in South Vietnam, notably by that of Nguyen Van Thieu in 1965.
**1965. 31 July:** Tonkin Gulf Incident leads to American escalation of the conflict in Vietnam.
**1 October:** Indonesian communists massacred in "Operation Gestapo".
**November 1967:** Beginnings of the Khmer Rouge guerrillas.
**1968. 30 January–Beginning of March:** In Vietnam, the North Vietnamese launch the

2. Indonesian communist survivors in Salembra prison in 1965.

Tet Offensive on 33 cities and towns, including Hue. The battle of Khe Sanh (from mid-February to 8 April) takes place in the Central Highlands.
**1968–70:** Phoenix plan in Vietnam: the destruction of the communist network in the South.
**1969:** Beginnings of the communist guerrilla war in the Philippines.
**18 March 1970:** In Cambodia, Prince Sihanouk is overthrown in a coup. Lon Nol takes power.
**21–8 February 1972:** President Nixon visits China.
**27 January and 2 March 1973:** Under the Paris Accords, it is agreed that a cease-fire be declared throughout Vietnam, North and South, that the Americans will withdraw all their troops from the country, and that Vietnam will gradually be reunified as one country.
**1975. 9 March:** North Vietnamese military offensive in Ban Me Thuot leads to the military collapse of the Saigon régime.
**17 April:** The Khmer Rouge enter Phnom Penh. The deportation of town populations to

ground in Thailand, and the Maoist 'New People's Army' was formed in the Philippines. The need to stop this widening of the conflict led the Nixon administration, under Secretary of State Henry Kissinger, to cut its losses by entering into direct negotiations with China (who thereby saw its own Indochinese ambitions recognized) and by deciding on the policy of the 'Vietnamization' of the conflict, which it attempted to achieve by exacerbating the tensions existing between the Chinese and the Vietnamese communists. The final end to the Vietnam War therefore merely brought about a change in the protagonists, and the first war in history between fellow-communist states, in 1978. This eventually culminated in the transformation of Kampuchea (Cambodia) into a 'sister republic' of Vietnam, a change which the Chinese unsuccessfully tried to prevent.

China henceforth had to content itself with 'bleeding Vietnam dry' by arming the Khmer Rouge guerillas. With the exception of the Philippines, the communist guerilla movement in Southeast Asia began to lose ground, and the 'corner of Asia' found itself firmly cordoned off. Vietnam itself, supported by the Soviet Union, which uses it as a strategic staging-post on the way to the Indian Ocean, finds itself today exhausted by the many years of struggle, but politically united. Though still in a state of preparedness for war, in 1985 Vietnam began the fifth decade of its independence. Tension in the region remains high.

**Vietnamese troops enter Phnom Penh.**

**7 January 1979**

the country begins.
**30 April:** The North Vietnamese Army takes Saigon.
**1976:** Formation of a single Socialist Republic of Vietnam; beginning of incidents between the Khmer Rouge and the Vietnamese that lead to a break in diplomatic relations (31 December 1977).
**1978. June:** Beginning of the exodus of the Vietnamese 'boat people'.
**1979. 1 January:** The Vietnamese army launches a generalized offensive against Cambodia.
**17 February–early March:** Chinese military offensive in the north of Vietnam.
**1988. 25 May:** Announcement of the withdrawal of half of the Vietnamese expeditionary corps in Cambodia.
**17 September:** The first day of the Olympic Games in Seoul. 160 countries are represented, with the exception of North Korea.
**1989. 2–3 May:** Meeting between Prince Sihanouk and Hun Sen, the prime minister of Cambodia, concerning the settlement of the Cambodian crisis. Further meetings take place in Paris in July.

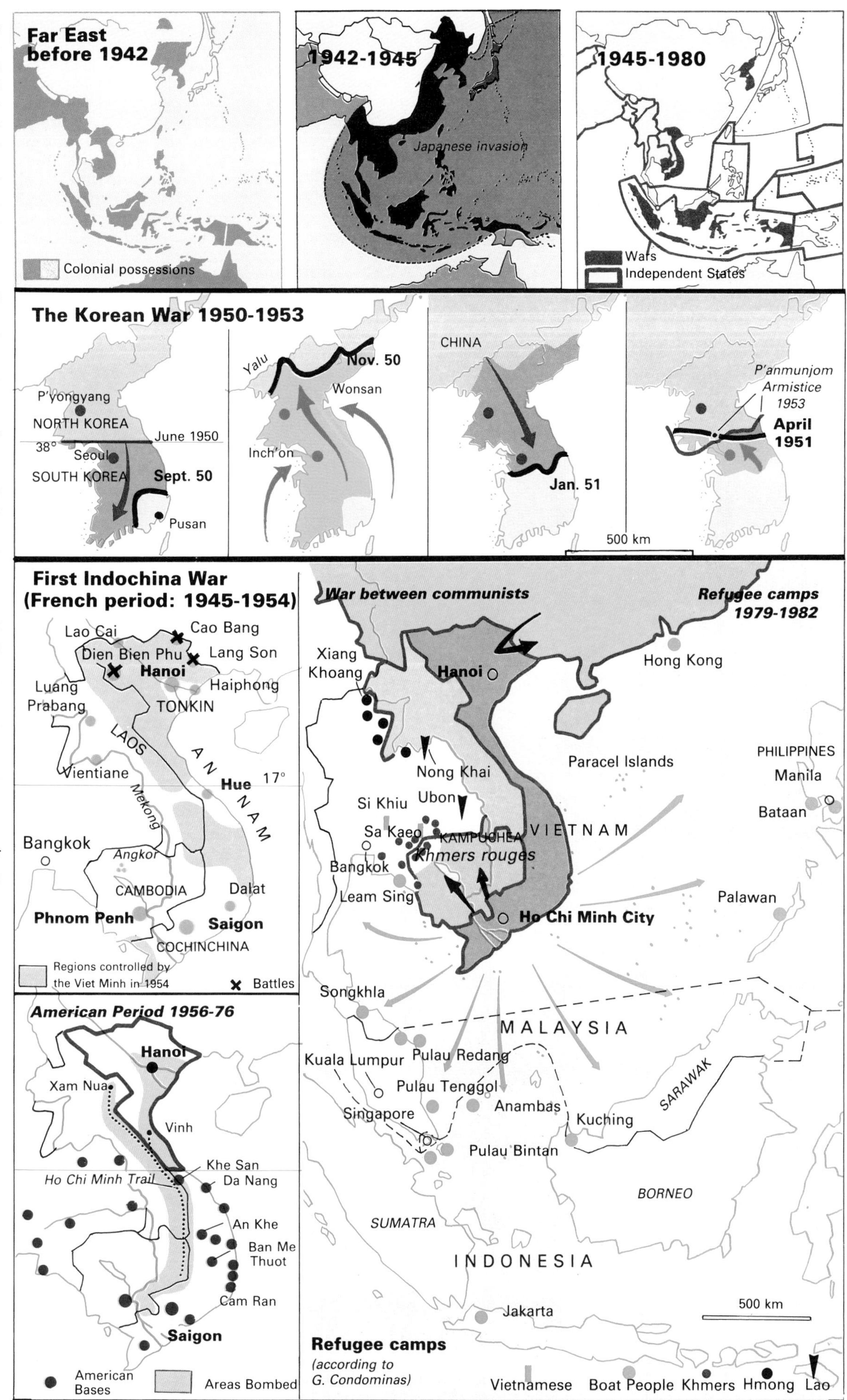

# The Muslim World from Ibn Sa'ud to Ayatollah Khomeini

A TENDENCY to try to remedy social ills by recourse to ethical and religious norms is a recurring feature of Muslim societies in time of crisis. The rise of Islamic fundamentalism, which is often referred to rather hastily as the 'political awakening of Islam', follows in this tradition. The steady forward march of secularization has not reduced the importance of religion, which continues, as before, to provide the terms by which the political authorities are judged.

The 'Islamic revolution' in Iran and the religious political movements which have put Islam at the centre of the world stage are, in the main, the consequence of a threefold failure: that of the reformist body of opinion within Islam, that of the nation-state, and that of the major economic models of our time, free-market capitalism and state socialism.

Since the eighteenth century the Muslim countries have seen a number of broad popular uprisings take place which were inspired and led by puritanical reformers such as Muhammad ibn 'Abd al-Wahhab (1703–97) in the Arabian Peninsula, Muhammad Ahmad ibn 'Ali al-Sanusi (1787–1857) in Libya, and Mahdi Muhammad Ahmad ibn Abd Allah in the Sudan. In each case the purpose of the uprising was to restore the true faith and to lay the foundations for a political order which would carry out divine law. The modern states of Saudi Arabia, Libya and the Sudan have their roots in these movements.

*1. Trial of the Muslim Brotherhood in Cairo 1954.*

At the end of the nineteenth century a major attempt was made by the Persian Jamal al-Din al-Afghani (1838–97) and the Egyptian Muhammad 'Abduh (1849–1905) to reform Islam and to awaken the Muslim peoples. Their aim was to respond to the challenge of Western colonial power and to restore to Islam the 'splendours of its early greatness'. Despite their rationalist tendencies, they were unable to relinquish religious dogma and apologetics totally. They had the effect of preparing the way for future nationalist movements throughout the Islamic world, from India to Morocco.

Confronted with the tasks of modernization and economic development, the newly independent Muslim states were unable either to emancipate themselves from religious ideology or to follow an original course, caught as they were between pro-Western secular movements on the one hand and Islamic fundamentalism which demanded a return to original Islam on the other. From 1928 onwards the association of the Muslim Brotherhood profited from the spontaneous beliefs of the masses and ushered in the age of fundamentalist protest against the secular modern state, rejecting the close links which existed between the ruling social groups and the imperialist powers. On the eve of the Nasserite revolution of 1952, the Brotherhood was the most powerful movement in Egypt and had close contacts in most of the other Muslim countries.

The rise of Arab nationalism, anti-imperialist and largely populist in emphasis, eclipsed for two decades all other politico-religious movements in the Middle East. But defeat in the 1967 Arab–Israeli war, together with the death of Nasser in 1970, left the way open for the return of religious leaders on to the political scene. Encouraged at first by governments because it kept the radical youth movement in check, fundamentalist protest grew strong on the disillusionment with progress, on the failure of various models of economic and social development and, in particular, on the absence of civil liberties. Consequently it itself became an important destabilizing factor.

In Iran, the religious hierarchy which was opposed to the 'modernization' experiment being pursued by the Shah was able to appropriate for itself the long tradition of struggle against tyranny in Iran and take the leadership of the movement which eventually overthrew the monarchy. The fundamentalists' victory provoked the protests made throughout the Arab world by the Shi'ite religious minority. As a result of the Israeli intervention in Lebanon in 1982, the Shi'ites became one of the major forces in that country.

Nevertheless, in spite of the constant reference to there being only one single community of believers (or *umma*), Islam is far from being monolithic. The plurality of Islamic states, the existence of various ethnic minorities within Islam, the various schismatic divisions which exist within these selfsame states (Sunni'ism, Shi'ism and so on), and the global pressures at work in the modern age, are all forces the 'awakening of Islam' must reckon with.

**Ottoman caliphate abolished.** 1924 — **Attempt on Nasser's life by the Muslim Brotherhood.** 1954 — **Coup d'état of Colonel Qadhafi in Libya.** September 1969 — **Formation of the 'Amal'.** 1975

**1924:** Mustafa Kemel, first President of the Turkish Republic, abolishes the Ottoman caliphate. Ibn Sa'ud drives Sharif Husayn from Mecca.
**1926:** Failure of the caliphate congress in Cairo and in Mecca.
**1928:** Association of the Muslim Brotherhood is formed in Egypt.
**1932:** Ibn Sa'ud becomes King of Saudi Arabia (he was to die in 1953).
**1941:** Jama'at al-Muslimun born in Pakistan.
**1948:** Egyptian Prime Minister an-Nuqrashi is assassinated.
**1949:** The Supreme Guide of the Muslim Brotherhood is murdered as an act of reprisal.
**1952:** In Jordan, the Islamic Liberation Party (ILP) is first formed.
**1954:** Attempt on Nasser's life. The Muslim Brotherhood is dissolved, and five of its leaders executed.
**December 1958:** Shi'ite religious leaders react strongly against the introduction of 'foreign ideas' into Iraq.
**1963:** Pro-Islamic activist groups formed in Syria. In Iran, there are demonstrations against the Shah.

*2. Nasser on the walls of the Aswan Dam which was opened in 1964.*

**1964. April:** In Algiers, Sheikh Bashir el-Ibrahimi attacks socialism.
**4 November:** The Shah forces Ayatollah Khomeini into exile.
**1965:** In Tehran, Ali Shariati is the new influential force within Islam.
**1966:** In Egypt, Sayyid Qutub, the leading theoretician of the Muslim Brotherhood is executed.
**1968:** The group al-Da'wa (the 'awakening') is formed in Iraq. There is a wave of arrests of Islamic activists in Turkey.
**1969:** The PLO attempts a coup in Jordan.
**1970:** In Aleppo, 83 'Alawite pupils at the military college are massacred. In Iraq the Shi'ite dignitary Muhsin al-Qazim is executed.
**22 October 1973:** Imam Musa as-Sadr founds the 'Movement of the Deprived' in the Lebanon. In Syria, Hafiz al-Assad abandons the secular state. In Tripoli, the Islamic conference is held under the auspices of Colonel Muamman al-Qadhafi.
**1975:** 'Amal' formed as the military wing of the Movement of the Deprived. There are Shi'ite riots in Iraq, and an attempted Islamic

*3. A suicide squad demonstrates in Iran. January 1984.*

# 1920–89

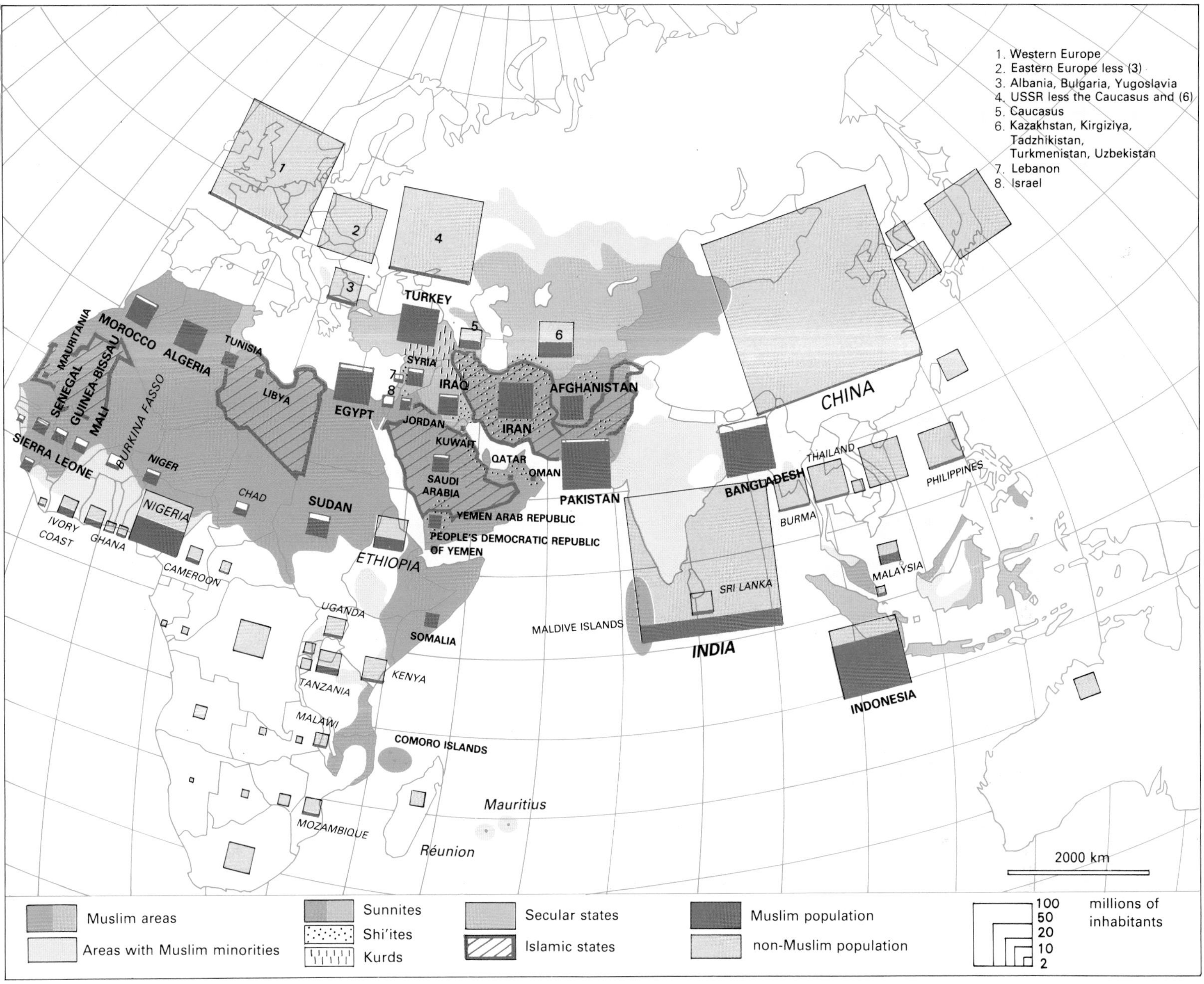

1. Western Europe
2. Eastern Europe less (3)
3. Albania, Bulgaria, Yugoslavia
4. USSR less the Caucasus and (6)
5. Caucasus
6. Kazakhstan, Kirgiziya, Tadzhikistan, Turkmenistan, Uzbekistan
7. Lebanon
8. Israel

TURKEY, MAURITANIA, MOROCCO, ALGERIA, TUNISIA, SENEGAL, GUINEA-BISSAU, MALI, BURKINA FASSO, LIBYA, SYRIA, IRAQ, AFGHANISTAN, EGYPT, JORDAN, IRAN, SIERRA LEONE, NIGER, KUWAIT, QATAR, OMAN, SAUDI ARABIA, PAKISTAN, CHINA, BANGLADESH, THAILAND, PHILIPPINES, CHAD, SUDAN, NIGERIA, IVORY COAST, GHANA, YEMEN ARAB REPUBLIC, PEOPLE'S DEMOCRATIC REPUBLIC OF YEMEN, BURMA, ETHIOPIA, CAMEROON, SRI LANKA, MALAYSIA, UGANDA, SOMALIA, MALDIVE ISLANDS, INDIA, KENYA, TANZANIA, INDONESIA, MALAWI, COMORO ISLANDS, Mauritius, MOZAMBIQUE, Réunion

2000 km

Muslim areas
Areas with Muslim minorities
Sunnites
Shi'ites
Kurds
Secular states
Islamic states
Muslim population
non-Muslim population
100 / 50 / 20 / 10 / 2 millions of inhabitants

**Islamic revolution in Iran.** **1979**

**President Sadat assassinated.** **6 October 1981**

**Death of Khomeini.** **3 June 1989**

uprising in Afghanistan.
**1977:** In Cairo, pro-Islamic terrorists kidnap and murder Dr el-Dahabi, the former Minister of Islamic Affairs.
**1978:** Demonstrations take place in Dakar against the celebration of Christmas and New Year.
**January–February 1979:** Ayatollah Khomeini returns to Iran in the midst of the Islamic revolution. The mosque at Mecca is occupied. In Senegal, N. Nyass founds the Party of God. There are several uprisings against the communist government in Afghanistan. Soviet troops invade towards the end of December.
**1980:** Violent clashes take place in Aleppo. About a thousand Islamic activists are massacred at Palmyra prison in Syria.
**6 October 1981:** The al-Jihad group assassinate the President of Egypt, Anwar al-Sadat. The Islamic Front attempts a coup in Bahrain. In Tunisia the Islamic Tendency Movement is formed.
**1982:** In Syria, there are violent clashes between the army and Islamic activists in Hamah. There are 12,000 civilian casualties.
**1983:** Pasdarans (guardians of the faith) begin to appear in Afghanistan. Islamic activists demonstrate in Algiers. The Islamic 'Jihad' terrorist group carries out a number of violent killings in the Lebanon. In Sudan, Islamic law is applied.
**1985:** In Khartoum Sheikh Muhammad Taha, the leader of the moderate Republican Brothers, who are opposed to the introduction of Islamic law, is executed.
**7 November 1987:** Bourgiba is dismissed by his prime minister, Zine el Abidine Ben Ali, who replaces him as head of state.
**October 1988:** Rioting and looting take place in Algiers and other cities. The army is responsible for the repression. President Chadli announces a referendum to reform the constitution.
**23–26 May 1989:** Egypt's official return to the Arab League.

*4. The attack on the American Embassy in Beirut, 18 April 1983.*

*5. Kurdish guerrillas in Iran, May 1985.*

# Wars in the Middle East

1. *The Egyptian president Anwar Sadat in Jerusalem in November 1977 with the Israeli prime minister Menachim Begin at the microphone.*

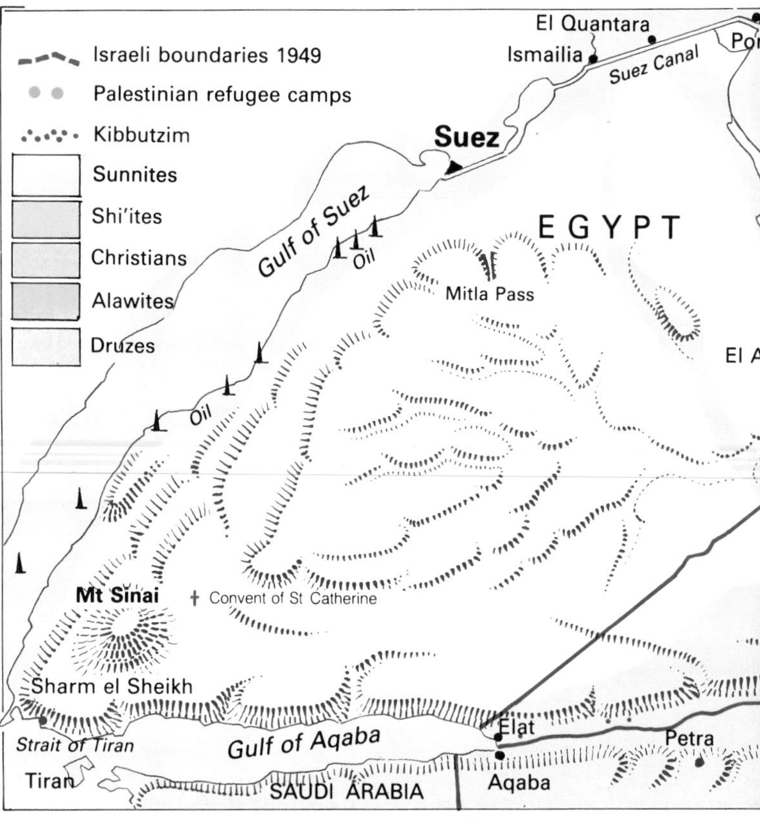


THE SPECTACULAR RISE of Nasserism which followed the nationalization of the Suez Canal in 1956 seemed to Israel and her Western allies a threat which had to be stopped. Three main factors determined the Israeli leaders' choice of a military course of action: Arab intransigence, Syria's ever more uncompromising stance and the birth of an autonomous Palestinian resistance movement. As a result, just a few weeks after the military putsch in Athens, the Six-Day War broke out. This event was to transform the political map of the Middle East profoundly. From this point on, Israel was to control the whole of what had been Palestine (Western Jordan, Gaza), as well as Sinai and the Golan Heights.

Aware of his military inferiority, Nasser was content to wage a war of attrition while he rebuilt his army. Sadat, his successor, continued this policy until October 1973, when his troops crossed the Suez Canal, causing the Israeli army to suffer its first setback. But this was only a tactical battle with limited objectives and Israel was not slow to reverse the situation. By the Camp David accords, Egypt recognized the state of Israel, while Israel in its turn withdrew from Sinai. Cut off from the Arab world, Egypt sought a place in the American camp, as it was the Americans who had gained most from the war, whereas the Russians, Syrians and Palestinians had been the main losers in the conflict. The armed Palestinian resistance organizations now took over the baton from defeated Nasserism, endangering the political balance in the countries where they were offered refuge. They clashed first with King Hussein of Jordan and were defeated. Forced to take refuge in Lebanon, they made that country their principal battlefield in the war with Israel. But at the same time they aroused old religious conflicts among the Lebanese, which were soon to develop into outright civil war.

There were as many objectives in this war as there were protagonists. For the Phalangists and their allies the Maronites, it was important to preserve the special identity of a Lebanon governed by

**Six Day War.**

**5–10 June 1967**

**Jordanian–Palestinian confrontation.**

**September 1970**

**28 May–2 June 1964:** Founding of the PLO (Palestine Liberation Organization).
**1967:** Syrian-Israeli frontier incidents and Palestinian attacks on Israel. The crisis puts Egypt in the front line.
**16–27 May:** Egypt obtains the evacuation of the UN peace-keeping force. Blockade of the Strait of Tiran and closing of the Gulf of Aqaba.
**5–10 June:** Surprise attack by Israel. Six Day War; annexation of Jerusalem.
**22 November:** Resolution 242 of the UN Security Council. Israeli forces retreat. Each state in the area is to have the right to defined and recognized frontiers.
**1968:** Jordanian-Israeli incidents. Battle of Karama (21 March). Iraq refuses to share the Shatt-al-Arab waters with Iran.
**1969:** Stepping-up of the war of attrition in the Suez zone. Lebanese-Palestinian confrontations and the Cairo agreements on Palestinian presence and the action of the fedayeen in Lebanon.
**1970. 17 September:** Jordanian-Palestinian confrontations. Cairo agreement between Hussein and Arafat (Yassar Arafat) 27 September.
**28 September:** Death of Gamal Abdul Nasser. Anwar el-Sadat succeeds him.
**13 November:** Coup d'état in Syria by Hafiz al-Assad.
**30 November 1971:** Iran annexes 3 islands in the Persian Gulf.
**1972. July:** Expulsion of Soviet military advisers from Egypt.
**5 September:** Palestinians kill 11 Israeli athletes at the Olympic Games.
**6–25 October 1973:** Fourth Israeli–Arab war (war of Yom-Kippur or war of Ramadhan).
**1974:** The belligerents agree to disengage.
**28 October:** Arab summit at Rabat: PLO is the only representative of the Palestinians.
**1975:** Several encounters between Palestinians and Israelis in Lebanon. Algiers agreement between Iraq and Iran.
**13 April:** Clashes between Palestinians and Phalangists near Beirut.
**5 June:** Re-opening of the Suez Canal.
**1976:** Civil war in Lebanon. At the request of the Lebanese Christians, Syria invades the country on 31 May.
**1977. 21 June:** Menachem Begin, Israeli prime minister. Active intervention by Israel in Lebanon. Iran–Iraq agreement and Khomeini is asked to leave Najaf (Iraq).
**19–21 November:** Visit of President Sadat to Jerusalem.
**1–5 December:** Formation of a Solidarity Front between Algeria, Libya, Syria, Southern Yemen and the PLO.
**1978. 14–21 March:** Israeli intervention in Southern Lebanon. United Nations peacekeeping force established in Lebanon.
**1979. February:** Islamic revolution in Iran.
**26 March:** Signing of the Israeli–Egyptian peace treaty in Washington.
**1980. July:** Jerusalem is proclaimed the capital of Israel.
**23 September:** Start of the Gulf War between Iraq and Iran.
**December 1981:** Annexation of Golan Heights by Israelis.
**1982. 6 June:** Israel invades Lebanon; Palestinian troops leave Lebanon (from 21 August). Fez Summit: King Fahd of Arabia's peace plan recognizes Israel unconditionally.
**14 September:** Beshir Gemayel, President-elect of Lebanon is assassinated.

2. *Egyptian soldiers during the Yom Kippur war, October 1973.*

Famagusta
CYPRUS
Taurus
Adana
TURKEY
Gaza
Tel-Aviv
Haifa
Akko (Acre)
Sour (Tyre)
Saida (Sidon)
Jubail (Byblos)
Tripoli
Iskendarum (Alexandrette)
Antakya (Antioch)
Nazareth
El Quneitra
ieba
Hebron
Jericho
Nablus
Ba'albek
Lataki
Beirut
PALESTINE
ISRAEL
LEBANON
Lake Tiberias
Mt Lebanon
Orontes
Aleppo (Haleb)
Jerusalem
Jordan
Golan
Mt Hermon
Litani
Beqaa
Hama
Homs
Dead Sea
Yarmuk
Damascus
Amman
JORDAN
Jebel el Druz
SYRIA
100 km
Euphrates

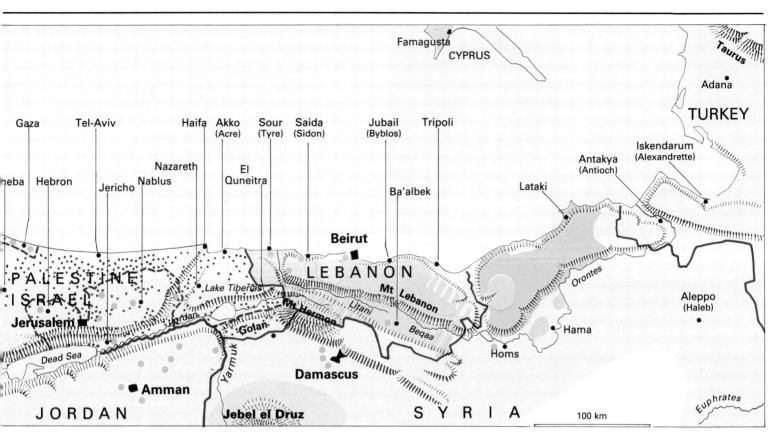

Christians and turned towards the West, and hence to expel the Palestinians. The latter had initially enjoyed the support of the Moslem factions, the Sunnis, Shi'ites and Druzes. But for the intervention of Syria in 1976, they would have gained the upper hand. Syria – seeking to pursue its own interests and re-form the old state of Greater Syria (including Lebanon, Palestine and Jordan) – prevented the emergence of a victor. Israeli intervention in 1982 eliminated Palestinian resistance in Lebanon, but in objective terms it gave the advantage to the Druzes and the Shi'ites, who advocated 'Arabization' and an end to the division of power on religious lines. A compromise agreement to this effect was signed at Damascus in December 1985. Whether the Syrians will be able to enforce it or not is another matter; American and Israeli intentions will also play a part.

It is often said that the Middle East is an area of perpetual conflict. Nothing better illustrates this than the Iran–Iraq War. Ever since the Erzerum Treaty of 1847 between Persia and the Ottoman Empire, frontier disputes (over questions of navigation on the Shatt-al-Arab) have been at the centre of relations between Iraq and Iran. The war is not new, but the historical circumstances in which it arose are. After signing the (unfavourable) Algiers agreement, the Ba'athite government in Baghdad took advantage of the internal strife which had accompanied the Islamic revolution in Iran to launch its army against that country. Saddam Hussein thought he might regain the Arab-speaking province of Khuzistan and the islands in the Straits of Ormuz at no great cost, prevent a Shi'ite revolt against his regime and thus give Iraq the leading role in the Arab world. He miscalculated. The war reinforced Khomeini's power and the Iraqi troops were driven out of the territory they had occupied. The two sides became bogged down in a bloody war in which nearly a million have died. The war has solved nothing, has been financially ruinous and has damaged the international standing of the two protagonists. It is still far from clear what its precise consequences will be.

**art of civil war in Lebanon.** — **976–**

**Camp David Agreements.** — **17 September 1978**

**Gulf War: Iran–Iraq.** — **1980–**

**War between the Shi-ites and the Palestinians in Lebanon.** — **1986**

*3. The ravages of the Iran–Iraq war seen from the Iranian side, October 1980.*

Israel reacts by occupying West Beirut. Massacre of Palestinians (who were surrounded by Israeli forces) by the Phalangists at Sabra and Shatila (16–17 September). Demonstration in Israel against the war in Lebanon. A multinational peacekeeping force (U.S., France, Italy) enters Beirut.

**1983. May:** Israeli-Lebanese agreement on a withdrawal of all foreign forces.

**23 October:** The peacekeeping forces come under attack (288 killed). They leave Lebanon soon after.

**1984. March:** Lebanon revokes earlier Israeli–Lebanese agreement.

**13 September:** In Israel, an agreement of national unity is made between the Likud and Labor parties. Each party will govern for a period of two years.

**1984–5:** PLO re-establishes relations with Egypt and Jordan.

**Since 1985:** Western hostages held in Lebanon.

**9 December 1987:** Beginning of the uprisings in Israeli occupied territories.

**8 August 1988:** Cease-fire between Iran and Iraq puts an end to nine years of war.

*4. The Chatila refugee camp in Beirut after the massacres perpetrated by the Phalangists, September 1982.*

**1989. 21 March:** The Christian force's hideout in West Beirut is blockaded and bombed after General Aoun is assigned to the war against the Syrian occupation.

**2–4 May:** Yasser Arafat visits Paris. The PLO charter is declared "invalid."

# Western Europe

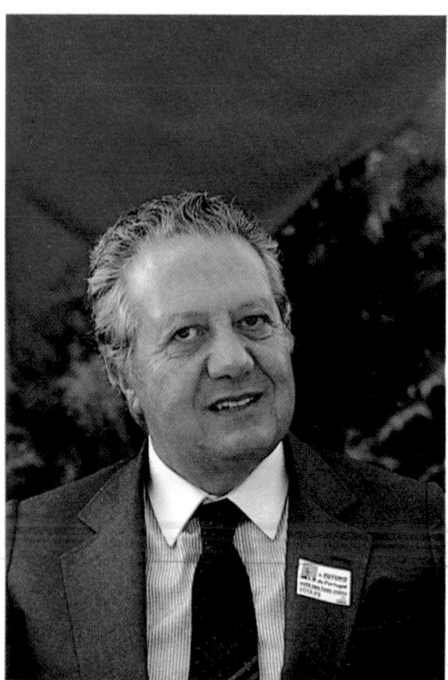

1. Mario Soares, Portuguese president.

2. Margaret Thatcher, British prime minister.

3. Helmut Kohl, West German chancellor.

4. François Mitterand, French president.

Politics is today suffused with history as never before. The ceremonies held to commemorate the victory over Nazism (8 May 1945), so numerous in West Germany and France, serve a useful function in recalling to people that the Europe they live in has had to win its liberty. Pluralism and the alternation of different political parties in government remain the basic political values of these countries. Over the last forty years, every moment of international tension, in particular every threat from the East (e.g. the Soviet SS-20s affair), has invariably seen these countries ranged within the Western camp. In the 1984 municipal elections in the GDR, 99.88 per cent of votes were cast for the communist state's single list: around the same time, the reasonable rate of participation (average sixty per cent) and the liveliness of the debate in the second European parliamentary elections revealed how democratic practices have become a pleasantly routine feature of the political landscape in the Europe of the Ten (now Twelve with Spain and Portugal having entered the Community).

Nevertheless, enormous difficulties remain. The economic crisis is still omnipresent, even though West Germany succeeded in 'hitching itself', at an early stage, to the American economic upturn. Everywhere unemployment has generated a 'new poverty'; the destruction of the old industrial fabric has produced an enforced redeployment of human and industrial resources that has been far from easy; companies are straining under the pressures of fierce international competition; currencies are forced to conform to the law of the dollar; energy has become only marginally less expensive; and investors in high-technology have been seduced by the prospect of greater returns in the USA and Japan. Strikes (e.g. the British miners' strike), anxieties among EEC farmers, racism (the presence of immigrants has been used to stir up trouble in whole regions of France, Great Britain, Switzerland and West Germany) and disquieting declines in the birth-rate (except in Ireland) have all served to compound the negative social effects of the economic depression. Institutions such as the unions, the church, the community and even the family have been challenged. Mass-consumption cultural products have flooded in from the USA, threatening to disfigure the identity of the old continent. Even sport, that modern bridge between nations, has degenerated into a series of violent clashes between young supporters.

In this sombre landscape, the ruling politicians have had limited scope for manoeuvre. In France, West Germany and Great Britain, socialists, Christian democrats and conservatives all face the same problems with more or less equal chances of success. Political Europe, which the EEC has played down too much, is progressing slowly, from failed 'summits' to the discreet exercise of 'overriding authority'. Finland, Switzerland, Sweden and Austria have renewed their pact of neutrality in case of 'misadventure'. And everywhere, terrorism, with its aim of destabilizing society, has also become a threat to the

5. Philipe Gonzalez Marquez, Spanish prime minister.

6. The leaders of the group of 7 at the Louvre, 14 July 1989.

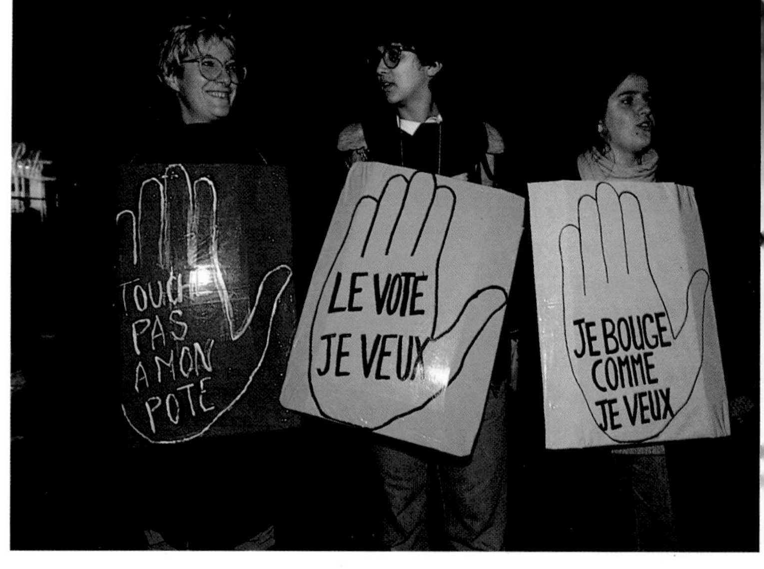


7. Anti-racist demonstration in Paris, December 1985.

democracies. Its rough and ready International, which has its roots in the violence ravaging the Near East, arms both foreign and native commando squads, in which the extremes of Left and Right come together (a phenomenon also seen in the false debates over the concentration camps). In the face of this threat, political Europe has essentially meant the European police forces. In their turn, the regionalist movements (Irish, Corsican and Basque) have not shrunk from engaging in criminal attacks.

The European elections of June 1984 do suggest, however, that the threat of totalitarianism is diminishing in Europe, as is confirmed by the socialist takeovers in the old dictatorships of Greece and Spain. Everywhere, the dominant choice has been for a conservative, liberal or Christian democratic centre-right or for a centre-left in which social democrats could be more effective arbitrators. Everywhere – except in Greece and Italy, and to a lesser degree in Portugal – the communists are in decline (in Finland they have split). New political influences are making themselves felt, with the Greens in West Germany, Belgium and the Netherlands, and with the revival in popularity of the peace movements ('Better Red than dead'), particularly in Northern Europe. However, it must unfortunately be acknowledged that regionalists of the extreme Left are making ground in Italy and Denmark and the extreme Right have received an unprecedented hearing in France as a result both of immigration and the climate of urban insecurity.

Should we conclude, therefore, that democracy has become more fragile in Western Europe? Perhaps this is the case if we look at the political relations of force and examine the logic of the violence that is ravaging the continent. This would, however, be to neglect other positive factors: the growth of individualism, which is producing a profound renewal of each citizen's relationship to the political sphere; the forward march of culture and education; and the sense of a common future which is growing among the young.

8. A press conference given by the military wing of ETA.

9. Paris, May 1968.

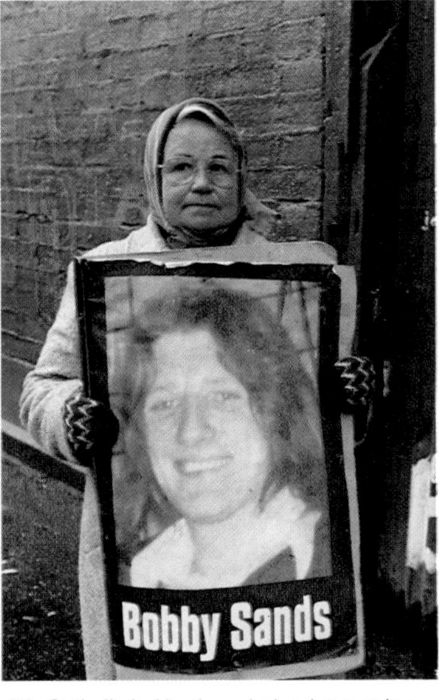


10. Catholic in Northern Ireland mourning Bobby Sands, May 1981.

11. Poster denouncing the National Front, a British party of the extreme right.

12. Italy, May 1978: the funeral of Aldo Moro.

# Science and the State

*1. Dwarf mouse, the result of genetic manipulation at the Jackson Laboratory in Maine, United States, 1982.*

SCIENCE HAS BECOME a concern of the state because it lies at the heart of contemporary military and civil technology. There follow, by way of illustration, three examples of this, extreme cases where state-sponsored programmes are linking together both research laboratories and industrial plants in common ventures.

Our first example is to be found in the development of the atom bomb. Fearing the worst from the uranium project of their German colleagues during the Second World War, a group of European émigré scientists in the United States, supported by their British colleagues who wanted to devote their time to developing radar, persuaded Roosevelt to adopt a project for the development of nuclear weapons. Set up in 1943 under the leadership of General Groves and the physicist J. Robert Oppenheimer, the Manhattan Project had as its object the development and construction in Los Alamos of two nuclear bombs, one to be made from uranium 235 at Oak Ridge, and the other from plutonium at Hanford. 150,000 people were employed at the Experimental Research Centre and in the factories producing fissile material. The project itself cost two billion dollars (the equivalent of the entire output of the motor-car industry at the time) and resulted in 1945 in the explosion of a plutonium bomb in the New Mexico desert. The scientists had suggested to President Truman that the experiment be carried out in public so that it might have a deterrent effect, but this was not done, and so on 6 August 1945 'Little Boy' was dropped on Hiroshima, killing half of the population over an area of 12.5 square kilometres. On 9 August 'Fat Man' was exploded over Nagasaki, with the same devastating effect, but spread over only 3.5 square kilometres, since a mountain spur divided the city into two and protected it in part from the force of the blast.

Our second example is to be found in the field of rocket technology. After the Second World War the United States and the Soviet Union each took over a part of the German research team responsible for developing the V2 rocket, but whereas the Americans were to rely on their B-52s to deliver the atomic bomb, the Soviet Union used rockets which in 1955 Korolev was able to adapt for use in space and for the putting into orbit of man-made satellites. The A1 rocket, developed from the R7 missile, put Sputnik I into orbit, then, on 12 April 1961, Vostok I, with Yury Gagarin on board. A month later, recognizing the Soviet lead in manned flight and pressing for the introduction of piloted missions, President Kennedy launched the Apollo moon programme, announcing that its goal was the landing of a man on the moon before the end of the decade. In carrying out the project, NASA spent 20 billion dollars (half of its entire budget), undertaking ten trials, four of which were manned, and co-ordinated the work of 400,000 people in several hundred different universities. On 21 July 1969 Neil Armstrong became the first man on the moon, with, he said, what was 'one small step for a man, one giant leap for mankind'.

Our final example focuses on the so-called 'Star Wars' programme. While today the dissident scientist Andrei Sakharov, the father of the Soviet H-bomb, continues to experience severe restrictions on his activity despite his recent release from internal exile, Edward Teller, his American counterpart, is the guiding force behind the Strategic Defence Initiative (SDI) announced by President Reagan on 23 March 1983. The aim of SDI is to deploy both on the ground and in space, before the end of the century, laser beam weapons capable of destroying Soviet missiles at each of the three stages of their trajectory. In 1985 1.4 billion dollars had been spent on it, and 5,000 people were at work on it in 260 companies and laboratories.

**First atomic reactor built in the USA.**

**1942**

**First laser invented.**

**1960**

**1942:** First atomic reactor built in the United States. Such reactors work by setting off a controlled nuclear chain reaction by bombarding fissile material with neutrons. The heat given off is used to drive turbines to generate electricity (1951) or for the propulsion of submarines (1953). Canada (1945), USSR (1946), Great Britain (1947) and France (1948) will follow ...
**1945:** First atomic bomb exploded in the United States. A non-nuclear explosive charge is used to bombard fragments of fissile material which thus reach a critical mass and spark off a chain reaction in a fraction of a second. The USSR (1949), Great Britain (1952), France (1960), China (1964) and India (1974) will later join the nuclear club ...
**1946:** First generation of electronic tube computers based on the model of the Electronic Numerical Integrator and Calculator (ENIAC) and having a computing speed of 1/40 second.
**1952:** First thermonuclear H-bomb exploded in the USA. The A-bomb uses the fission of heavy nuclei, while the H-bomb uses light

*3. Portrait of Yury Alekseyevitch Gagarin, first Soviet citizen into space, as pictured on the cover of his official biography published in Moscow in 1981.*

nuclei. The USSR (1953), Great Britain (1957), China (1967) and France (1968) will all explode H-bomb devices in turn. Research is under way to achieve sufficient temperature for fusion by other methods than the explosion of an A-bomb. The aim is to harness for peaceful civil uses the very same thermonuclear energy as that which powers the sun.
**1957:** First man-made satellite put into orbit by rocket power by the Soviet Union. The United States (1958), France (1965), Japan and China (1970), Great Britain (1971) and India (1980) will follow.
**1959:** Second generation of transistorized computers based on the IBM 1401 with a computing speed of 10 microseconds.
**1960:** Invention of the laser. The laser is an apparatus for the amplification of a light wave passing through a layer of excited atoms and stimulating the emission of a light beam of the same frequency, in the same direction, and in phase, in accordance with the equations of quantum mechanics. Contained within two reflective surfaces, the stimulated

*4. France opts for atomic power: here one sees the production of plutonium at Marcoule (Gard), where the factory has been in production since 1958.*

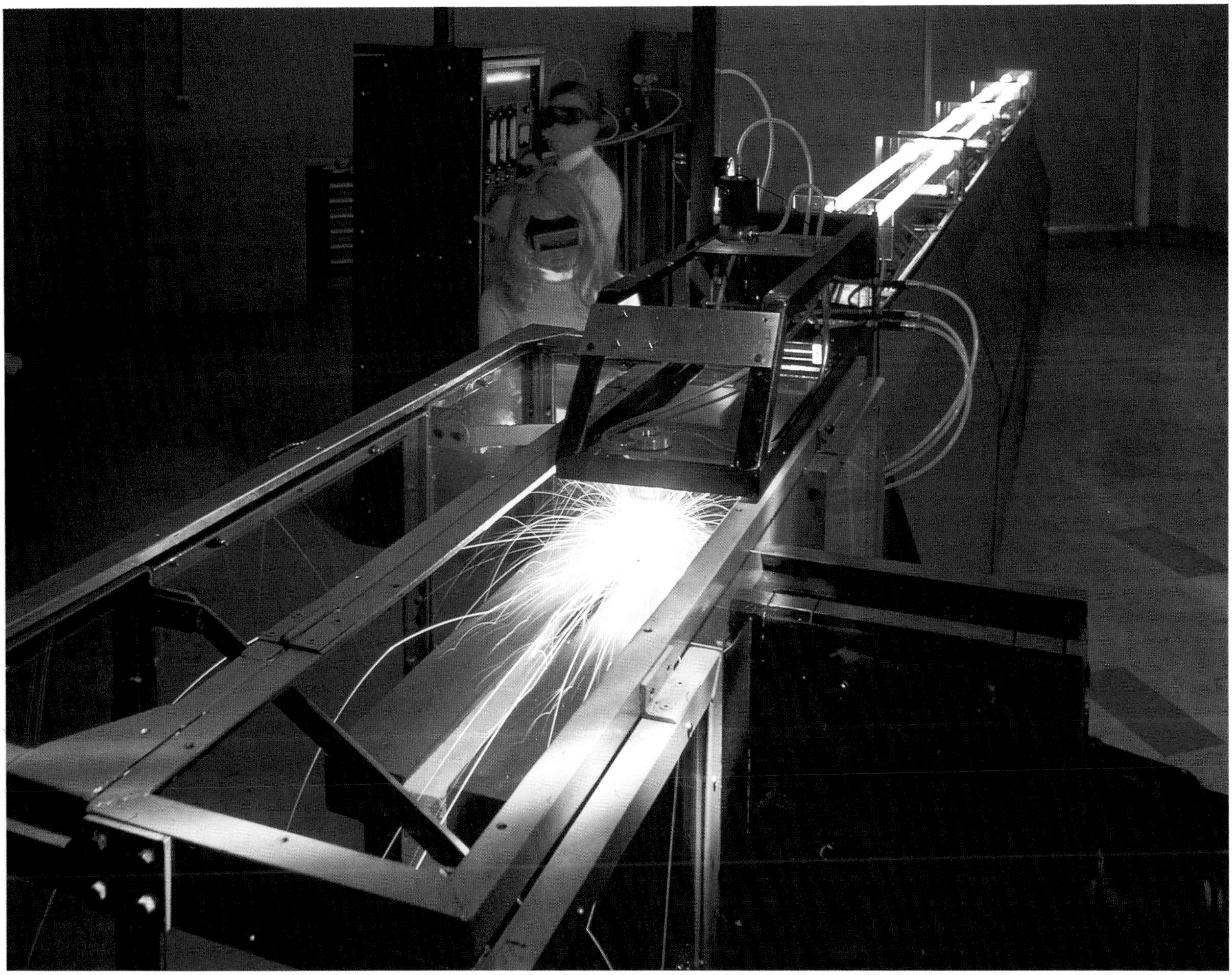

*2. Industrial application of the laser: here the laser is being used to cut steel.*

**Neil Armstrong becomes the first man on the moon.**

**21 July 1969**

**Launch of the European space rocket *Ariane.***

**1979**

**Launch of the American Space Shuttle.**

**1981**

**AIDS: identification of the disease.**

**Summer 1981.**

*5. Cape Canaveral: the departure of the American Space Shuttle, 18 June 1983.*

light passes through the layer of excited atoms several times, which has the cumulative effect of transforming the amplifier into a generator of coherent light of such a small degree of divergence and such intensity that the laser may be used as a surgical instrument, industrial tool, or even a ray gun ...

**1965:** Third generation of computers with integrated circuits, an off-shoot of the Apollo project, based on the IBM 360, having a computing speed of 5 nanoseconds. The fourth generation will appear in 1981.

**1967:** Soviet Soyuz-Saliut-Progress space programme for a manned spacecraft, manned orbiting space station and automatic cargo ship.

**1979:** Launching of the European space rocket *Ariane.* First satellite put into orbit in 1981. Studies begin on the project for a manned orbiting space station.

**1980:** World-wide eradication of smallpox. The smallpox virus, which has no animal carriers, is eliminated after an international vaccination campaign organized by the World Health Organization (WHO).

**1981:** Launching of the American Space Shuttle, which is propelled by rockets into space, orbits like a manned cargo vessel and lands like a glider and thus can be reused.

**199?:** Fifth generation of computers with artificial intelligence becomes indispensable for the planned American SDI.

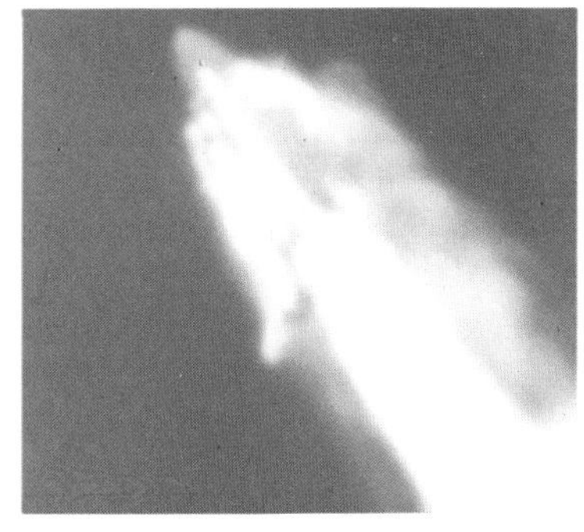

*6. Explosion of the Space Shuttle,* Challenger, *a few seconds after firing, January 27 1986.*

# Oil and Raw Materials

UNTIL AFTER the Second World War, mankind drew upon nature's resources with an easy conscience. But at the beginning of the seventies it became clear that supplies of certain strategic raw materials were finite, and concern about this has become a major source of disquiet.

In terms of mineral ore, more than 90% of world production is supplied by only two or three countries. The main areas specializing in particular ores are the USSR, South Africa and Canada (platinum); Australia and Brazil (titanium ore); South Africa, Zimbabwe and USSR (chromium ore); Zaire, Zambia and Cuba (cobalt); North Africa, USSR and Gabon (manganese ore); the USA, Canada and Chile (molybdenite).

Raw materials providing energy – coal, oil and natural gas – pose different problems.

Coal was the key source of energy for nineteenth-century industrialization, and it will doubtless be of vital importance in the twenty-first century. It is found in many parts of the world and reserves are nearly one hundred times greater than those of oil. In 1984 they represented 11,606,382 million tonnes, to which can be added a further 2,528,944 million tonnes of lignite. 60% of all coal is to be found in the USSR alone, and 90% of world reserves occur in the USSR, the USA and China.

But in the space of a century it is oil that has come to occupy the predominant place. Its 'flexibility' and above all its price, which is constantly falling in absolute terms (and sometimes even in money terms), make it the most highly taxed raw material (at twice the rate of luxury goods) and the one that attracts most controversy. The largest reserves were, in fact, discovered by foreign companies. Production was in the hands of the 'seven sisters' (Exxon, Mobil, Socal, Gulf, Texaco, Shell, BP) before the producing countries awoke to realities – a situation which led to frequent confrontations, and to the creation in 1960 of OPEC (Organization of Petrol Exporting Countries).

1. The Soviet Urengoi-Novopskov gas pipe-line under construction.

The tempting prices for crude, which the creation of OPEC brought about, have encouraged countries to invest even at the risk of running themselves heavily into debt (as in the case of Mexico). But the amount of extra oil produced and the decrease in consumption forced OPEC initially to reduce production and then subsequently to flood the market, which brought about the fall in the price of crude oil. As a result, developing countries are not gaining from their resources in real terms because they are not sufficiently diversified to allow any freedom in managing them.

What is most significant, is where the concentration of oil wealth is to be found: 85% of the oil discovered to date has been found in twenty-two oil-rich areas which contained initially more than 1.5 billion tonnes of oil. The largest is the Arab-Iranian basin in the Middle East, which forms what amounts to a 'ring' with the other large oil-producing areas. During the last few years the average cost of discoveries by the most active international oil companies has been between five dollars and fifteen dollars per barrel.

Natural gas, which is more widely distributed than oil, was thought to be a cheap replacement fuel until recently. In the long term the largest known deposits which have not yet been developed are in the Middle East and the USSR. By the year 2000 OPEC, holding 72% of world supplies, will have control of the world oil market and joint control with the USSR of the world's gas supplies. A progressive increase in world consumption is likely and alternative energy (coal and nuclear energy) cannot completely replace oil (as we approach the year 2000 some forty to fifty reactors a year are to be closed).

In the final analysis, energy is less a problem of wealth than of power: in spite of sensationalist declarations, quite obviously there is no lack of resources; there are only conflicts between nations for domination. One can only hope that the ever-increasing interdependence of the world economic markets will ensure that a genuine desire for peaceful coexistence, rather than the search for advantage, becomes the primary motivation of our political leaders in the future.

| **Creation of the Anglo-Persian Oil Company.** | **'Red Line' agreement between Americans and British.** | **Nationalization of Iranian Oil.** | **First Oil Crisis.** |
|---|---|---|---|
| **14 April 1909** | **31 July 1928** | **February 1951** | **16 October 1973** |

**29 May 1901:** Concession contract granted by the Shah of Persia to W. K. D'Arcy which grants him the 'special and exclusive right', amongst others, 'to prospect for, obtain, work, develop, render suitable for trade, remove and sell oil, natural gas, asphalt, ozocerite throughout the entire Persian Empire for a period of 60 years'. In fact, the Shah excluded five provinces – Azerbaijan, Gilân, Mâzandaran, Astarabad and Khorosan – in order not to upset Russia.
**31 August 1907:** Great Britain and Russia conclude an agreement relating to Persia, Tibet and Afghanistan.
**14 April 1909:** Founding of the Anglo-Persian Oil Company which buys the companies founded by D'Arcy. Its capital is fixed at 2 million pounds.
**23 October 1912:** Agreement between the Turkish Petroleum Company and the Deutsche Bank. The capital of the Turkish Petroleum Company increases from £50,000 to £80,000, divided as follows; Deutsche Bank 25%, National Bank of Turkey 20%, Gulbenkian 15%, Sir Ernest Cassel 15%, Royal Dutch Shell 25%.

3. The Kofflefontein diamond mines, South Africa.

**9 May 1915–15 May 1916:** Sykes-Picot agreements.
**19–26 April 1920:** San Remo conference which draws up the Treaty of Sèvres between the Allies and Turkey (10 August 1920).
**24 July 1923:** Lausanne Treaty. The protocol refers to certain concessions.
**5 June 1926:** Treaty between Great Britain, Iraq and Turkey.
**31 July 1928:** British and Americans sign the so-called Red Line Agreement by which the American monopolies obtain 23.75% of the shares of the TPC (Turkish Petroleum Company).
**8 June 1929:** TPC becomes IPC (Iraq Petroleum Company). The IPC and its subsidiaries are made up of 5 companies: Anglo-Iranian Oil Company (23.75%), Compagnie française des pétroles (CFP) (23.75%), Royal Dutch Shell (23.75%), Near East Development Corporation (American) comprising Standard Oil (11.875%), Socony-Vacuum and Gulf Oil (11.875%), Calouste Sarkis Gulbenkian (5%).
**1938:** Nationalization of oil in Mexico.

*2. Rotterdam, Holland, the main oil importing port in the world.*

**Second Oil Crisis.**

**1979**

**Sheik Yamani, Saudi Oil Minister dismissed.**

**29 October 1986**

**February 1951:** Mossadeq nationalizes Iranian Oil.
**3 February 1954:** IPC and the Iranian government sign a fifty-fifty agreement.
**September 1960:** Creation of OPEC which brings together Venezuela, Iran, Iraq, Saudi Arabia and Kuwait.
**16 October 1973:** Unilateral decision to fix the price of oil taken by OPEC at Teheran.
**Between January 1979 and November 1980:** The price per barrel rises from 13.3 to 32 dollars.
**1984. 10–11 July:** OPEC fixes the official price at 29 dollars per barrel and production at 17 million barrels per day.
**31 October:** OPEC decides to reduce production to 16 million barrels per day.

*4. A power station in Pennsylvania.*

1968 1974 1981 1984

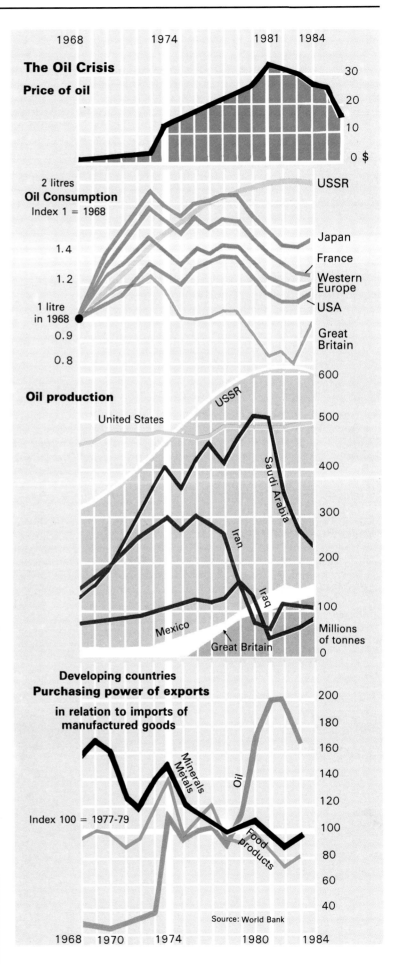

**The Oil Crisis**

**Price of oil**

30
20
10
0 $

2 litres
**Oil Consumption**
Index 1 = 1968
1.4
1.2
1 litre
in 1968
0.9
0.8
USSR
Japan
France
Western Europe
USA
Great Britain

**Oil production**

600
500
400
300
200
100
Millions of tonnes
0
USSR
United States
Saudi Arabia
Iran
Iraq
Mexico
Great Britain

**Developing countries**
**Purchasing power of exports**
**in relation to imports of manufactured goods**

200
180
160
140
120
100
80
60
40
Index 100 = 1977-79
Minerals Metals
Oil
Food products
Source: World Bank

1968 1970 1974 1980 1984

# Détente and Nuclear Strategy

THE POST-WAR ERA witnessed the birth of two new empires: the American empire, based on the free market economy, and extending throughout the world by virtue of its sea-power; and the Soviet empire, dependent on the idea of the centrally planned economy, and existing as a continental entity, primarily a Eurasian one. Within a short space of time the two military alliances, NATO and the Warsaw Pact, both maintaining an integrated command structure in peacetime, began to treat Europe as an arena of confrontation, but also of possible equilibrium. The two leading countries in the alliances, the USA and the USSR, adopted the policy of using nuclear weapons in case of attack, which produced reciprocal nuclear stalemate. Each country remains free, nonetheless, within its own sphere of influence, to carry out repression by military force or impose military dictatorship in any area where political or social movements threaten the Eastern or Western empire. As a result military strength has become one of the foundations of co-existence, and the arms race has become a permanent feature. The arms race itself has followed three phases, each based on a different type of military technology and each more expensive than the one before. Each of these phases has in turn been accompanied by wars and –fruitless– negotiations on disarmament. After the destruction of Hiroshima, the nuclear bomb was considered as a weapon of war, more powerful than any other. During the Cold War, the bombers of the Strategic Air Command (SAC) threatened 300 Soviet cities with destruction, thus claiming to deter any attack from the other side (the strategy depended on the threat of massive retaliation). The nuclear monopoly initially enjoyed by the United States, and later, after the Soviet Union had its own bomb, its nuclear superiority over the Soviet Union, did not lead to the use of nuclear arms in Korea; rather, it was thought that the role of the atomic bomb was to compensate for the regional superiority of the USSR within Europe. Prospects for disarmament seemed remote.

After 1955 the American mainland became vulnerable to attack from Soviet bombers and especially from Soviet missiles. The era of peaceful coexistence had begun. With Sputnik, the Soviets at first had a technical lead in the field of intercontinental ballistic missiles (ICBMs), but the Americans were able to produce more modern medium range missiles, such as their submarine-launched ballistic missiles (SLBMs) which were invulnerable to attack and which were targeted on the Soviet Union from the seas surrounding Europe and Asia. The Americans effectively prevented the Soviet Union from threatening the USA from Cuba and at the time gave up the idea of targeting the USSR from within Europe. Both countries abandoned the development of anti-missile missiles. The balance of power rested on the enormous destructive power of thousands of missiles, accumulated in great numbers to maintain sufficient forces for reprisal even if the enemy were to attack by surprise (the strategy known as deterrence by MAD or 'mutually assured destruction'). Britain, France and China took the course of maintaining a national nuclear capability, independent of the two superpowers. The American doctrine of 'flexible response' did nothing to stop the United States from losing the Vietnam war. The two superpowers first presented grand 'plans for general and total disarmament'. Then after 1962 they moved towards more limited agreements which were to be called Arms Control Agreements. The SALT I and SALT II (Strategic Arms Limitation Talks) agreements were signed simply as a way of moderating the arms race.

From 1974 weapons, whether nuclear or not, became 'intelligent', meaning that they began to incorporate computerized automatic guidance systems. The technology of multiple warheads became more important, as the number of missiles had been fixed in the SALT II agreement. In addition, cruise missiles are now being deployed on land and at sea, and American B-52s and B-1s equipped with them. Weapons have become more accurate, more reliable and

**1946-57: Bombers and Military Divisions**

Soviet Advances
Western Repression
Neutral

Number of Warheads in 1955
USA 1,050
USSR 340

KOREA
GUATAMALA
Indo-China
Algeria
Suez
Kenya

Bombers
Divisions

**War in Indo-China.** 1946–54

**Korean War.** 1950–3

**Suez Crisis. Crushing of the Hungarian uprising by Soviet tanks.** 1956

**Cuban Missile Crisis.** 1962

**1 December 1959:** Antarctic Treaty prohibiting nuclear explosions or disposal of radioactive waste in Antarctica.
**20 September 1961:** Soviet Union–United States Statement of Agreed Principles concerning disarmament negotiated by Zorin and McCloy.
**1963. 16–25 July:** Agreement on the establishment of the 'hot line' between the United States and the Soviet Union.
**5 August:** Partial Nuclear Test — Ban Treaty signed (by Great Britain, the Soviet Union and the United States) banning nuclear tests in the atmosphere, in outer space and under water.
**1967. 27 January:** Outer Space Treaty demilitarizes space.
**14 February:** Tlatelolco Treaty prohibits nuclear weapons in Latin America.
**1 July 1968:** Treaty on the Non-Proliferation of Nuclear Weapons signed.
**1971. 11 February:** Sea-bed Denuclearization Treaty.
**30 September:** Agreement on measures to reduce the risk of outbreak of nuclear war between USA and USSR (Nuclear Accidents Agreement).
**1972. 10 April:** Biological Warfare Convention prohibits the development or possession of biological weapons.
**16 May:** SALT I Treaty signed, on the use of anti-ballistic missiles (ABMs).
**November:** Opening of the SALT II negotiations.
**22 June 1973:** US–USSR Agreement on the Prevention of Nuclear War.
**1974. 3 July:** US-USSR Treaty on the limitation of underground nuclear weapons tests.
**24 November:** Joint declaration by the United States and the Soviet Union on strategic arms (Vladivostock Agreement).
**1 August 1975:** Final Act of the Helsinki Conference on Security and Co-operation in Europe.
**16 July 1976:** Agreement between France and the Soviet Union on the prevention of the accidental or unauthorized use of nuclear weapons.

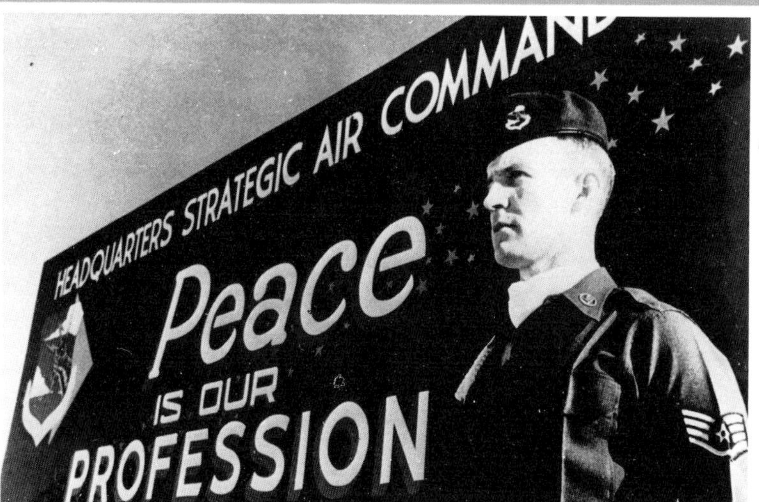


*2. Headquarters of the Strategic Air Command.*

# 1959–89

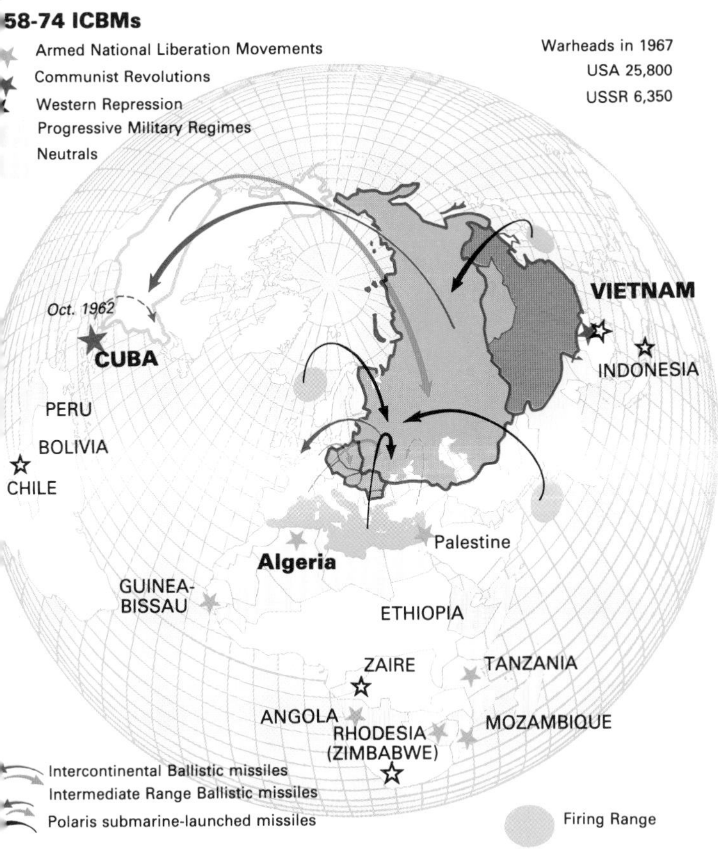


**1975-85 Multiple Warheads**

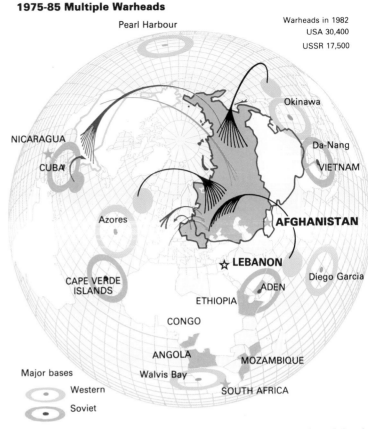

Warheads in 1982
USA 30,400
USSR 17,500

Pearl Harbour
Okinawa
Da-Nang
VIETNAM
NICARAGUA
CUBA
Azores
AFGHANISTAN
LEBANON
CAPE VERDE ISLANDS
Diego Garcia
ADEN
ETHIOPIA
CONGO
ANGOLA
MOZAMBIQUE
Walvis Bay
SOUTH AFRICA
Major bases
Western
Soviet

more numerous (there are now about 10,000 on each side). Deterrence is no longer guaranteed by MAD, and, according to present-day NATO strategists, can be maintained only by the alliance's belief in its own 'capacity to win a limited nuclear war'. 40,000 targets have been assigned in the USSR.

These developments continue to be the source of great alarm to public opinion (especially after 1980), in particular in the United States (with the Nuclear Freeze Movement), in Great Britain (with the Campaign for Nuclear Disarmament and other peace groups) and in the German Federal Republic (with the Peace Movement and the Green Party). Major demonstrations have been held to call a halt to the arms race. Despite this, early 1987 saw the Reagan administration breaching the SALT II agreement (signed under President Carter but never ratified by Congress) and thus far the Strategic Arms Reduction Talks (START) have made little progress. With the deployment of Cruise and Pershing in Europe, and the research undertaken for the Strategic Defence Initiative (SDI), or 'Star Wars', the arms race has been set off on a new spiral. The dealings between Reagan and Gorbachev in 1985, reinforced by subsequent Soviet initiatives, perhaps represent new hope of détente in East-West relations. But the growth in the sales of arms to the Third World and the wars in the Southern Hemisphere, increase the dangers of non-nuclear conflict.

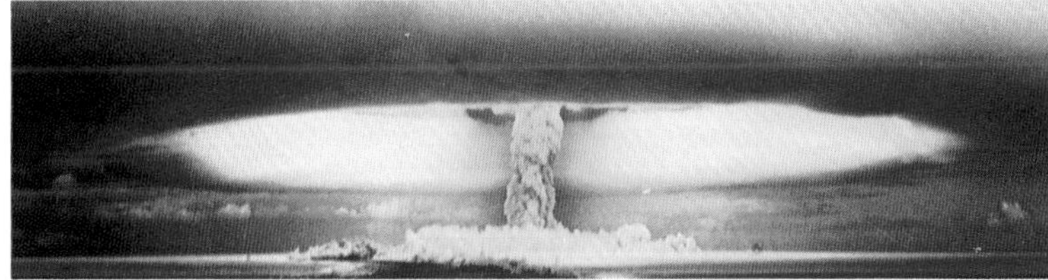

*1. French nuclear explosion on Muroroa Atoll, 1983.*

**Vietnam War.**

**963–75**

**Invasion of Czechoslovakia by the Warsaw Pact nations.**

**1968**

*3. Missiles on parade in Red Square, 7 November 1984.*

**War in Afghanistan.**

**1979–**

**18 June 1979:** SALT II Treaty between the Soviet Union and the United States on the limitation of strategic arms.
**11 November 1980–9 September 1983:** Madrid Conference.
**13 May 1982:** President Reagan makes proposals for START (discussions on the reduction of strategic arms).
**1983. 23 November:** Deployment of Pershing II missiles begins in the Federal Republic of Germany.
**8 December:** Suspension *sine die* of START talks.
**17 January 1984:** Stockholm Conference.
**19–20 November 1985:** Talks held in Geneva between Gorbachev and Reagan.
**11–12 October 1986:** U.S.-Soviet summit at Reykjavik.
**7 December 1988:** M. Gorbachev announces a unilateral reduction of 500,000 Soviet armed forces and the withdrawal of 10,000 tanks from Eastern Europe by 1991.

*4. Meeting between Reagan–Gorbachev, 19–20 November 1985.*

# World Population Development

*1. Indian women.*

SINCE THE BEGINNING of this century population growth has speeded up. In 1900 there were 1,634 million people in the world; there were 2,530 million in 1950, and today there are 4,845 million. A figure of six billion is forecast for the end of the century, and it is unlikely that it will level off at less than eight or nine billion in the middle of the next century.

In the nineteenth century, Europe and its colonial populations had the highest growth rate in the world. An initial drop in fertility (1880–1940) was followed by a short-lived recovery in 1945–65. Now these areas are in crisis: the birth rate is nearly everywhere too low to ensure replacement, which inevitably means an aging population. Although these countries, along with the USSR and Japan, make up 24% of world totals, they only account for 13.9% of births.

Third World countries, on the other hand, are still at stages two and three of demographic evolution: mortality fell rapidly up to 1970 and only then did fertility begin to drop in some countries. Their population went from around 1,700 million in 1950 to around 3,600 million in 1985, their proportion of world totals from two-thirds to three-quarters.

At present China and the whole of Southeast Asia are heading for a state of equilibrium: their natural population growth only remains a positive figure because of the inertia of demographic phenomena. In Latin America, too, fertility is on the decline. The term 'population explosion' can only really be applied to the Arab world and to Africa, which beats all world records for birth (and death) rates.

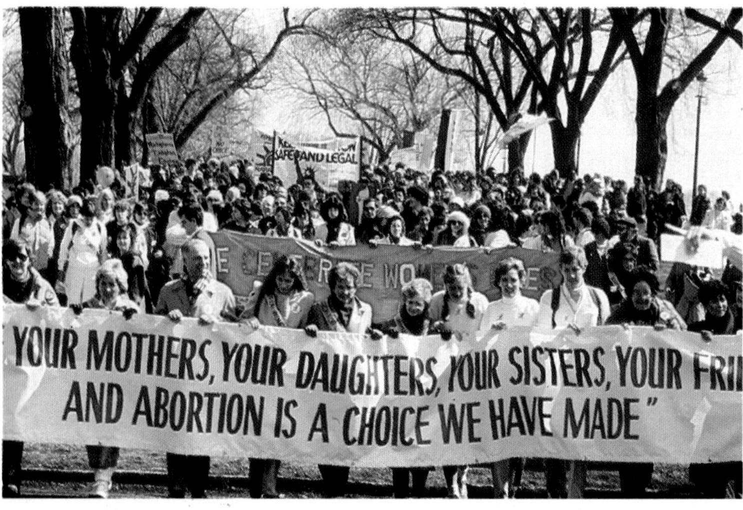


*2. Pro-abortion demonstration, Washington, 3 September 1985.*

**A: Fertility rates in 1985**

The figures represent the average number of children a woman would have in her lifetime according to fertility rates recorded in a given year. The replacement of generations is only ensured if this figure is at or above 2.1.

| | |
|---|---|
| **WORLD** | **3.7** |
| **Africa** | **6.3** |
| North Africa | 6.0 |
| West Africa | 6.4 |
| East Africa | 6.8 |
| Central Africa | 6.1 |
| Southern Africa | 5.2 |
| **Asia (minus USSR)** | **3.7** |
| Southwest Asia | 5.9 |
| South Asia | 5.0 |
| Southeast Asia | 4.5 |
| East Asia | 2.1 |
| **Oceania** | **2.7** |
| **South and Central America** | **4.2** |
| Central America | 4.9 |
| Caribbean | 3.3 |
| Tropical South America | 4.2 |
| Temperate South America | 3.1 |
| **Northern America** | **1.8** |
| **Europe (minus USSR)** | **1.8** |
| Northern Europe | 1.8 |
| Western Europe | 1.6 |
| Eastern Europe | 2.1 |
| Southern Europe | 1.9 |
| **USSR** | **2.4** |

*Population et societés* bulletin July–August 1985.

**B: Yearly natural population increase 1950–85 by main region**

The natural rate of increase is the difference between the birth rate and the death rate. It is expressed here in percentages.

| | 1950–55 | 1965–70 | 1984–85 |
|---|---|---|---|
| **WORLD** | **1.8** | **2.1** | **1.7** |
| More developed regions | 1.3 | 0.9 | 0.6 |
| Less developed regions | 2.1 | 2.6 | 2.0 |
| **Africa** | **2.2** | **2.6** | **2.9** |
| Algeria | 2.0 | 3.0 | 3.3 |
| Kenya | 2.8 | 3.3 | 4.1 |
| **Asia** | **2.0** | **2.5** | **1.8** |
| Japan | 1.4 | 1.1 | 0.7 |
| China | 2.2 | 2.8 | 1.1 |
| India | 1.8 | 2.2 | 2.1 |
| **Oceania** | **2.4** | **2.0** | **1.3** |
| **Latin America** | **2.6** | **2.7** | **2.3** |
| Mexico | 2.8 | 3.2 | 2.6 |
| Brazil | 2.9 | 2.8 | 2.3 |
| **Northern America** | **1.8** | **1.1** | **0.7** |
| **Europe** | **1.5** | **0.9** | **0.3** |
| France | 0.8 | 0.8 | 0.4 |
| West Germany | 0.9 | 0.7 | −0.1 |
| USSR | 1.7 | 1.0 | 1.0 |

**C: World population at the end of the century**

Demographic projections are estimates of the future size of populations based on the hypothetical evolution of their fertility and mortality. The United States Bureau of Census published three sets of projections in 1978 based on data recorded in 1975.

**Population in year 2000**

| | upper estimate | medium estimate | lower estimate |
|---|---|---|---|
| **World** | **6796** | **6350** | **5921** |
| More developed regions | 1377 | 1323 | 1274 |
| Less developed regions | 5419 | 5027 | 4647 |
| **Africa** | **847** | **814** | **759** |
| **Asia and Oceania** | **3951** | **3630** | **3359** |
| **Latin America** | **677** | **636** | **580** |
| **USSR and Eastern Europe** | **480** | **460** | **442** |
| **Western countries and assimilated immigrant populations** | **842** | **809** | **781** |

# 1950–2000

## World population in 1985

• = 500,000 people

**Fertility***

6
4
2,1

## Natural increase

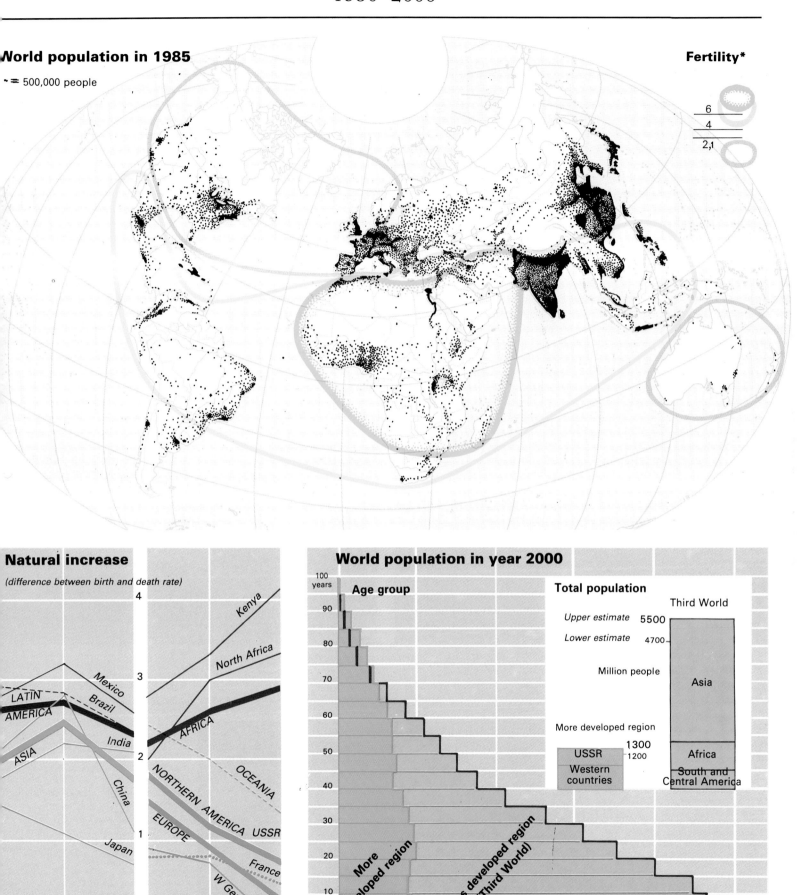

*(difference between birth and death rate)*

4
3
2
1
0

Mexico
LATIN AMERICA
Brazil
India
ASIA
China
Japan
Kenya
North Africa
AFRICA
OCEANIA
NORTHERN AMERICA
USSR
EUROPE
France
W Germany

1950 1965 1984 1950 1965 1984

## World population in year 2000

100 years
Age group
90
80
70
60
50
40
30
20
10
0

**Total population**

Third World
*Upper estimate* 5500
*Lower estimate* 4700
Million people
Asia
Africa
South and Central America

More developed region
1300
1200
USSR
Western countries

More developed region
Less developed region (Third World)

0 100 200 300 400 500 M

Source: US Bureau of Census

*Average live births per woman based on the fertility rate for a given year (in this case 1985). Below 2.1 replacement is not ensured.

# The World Economy in Continuing Crisis

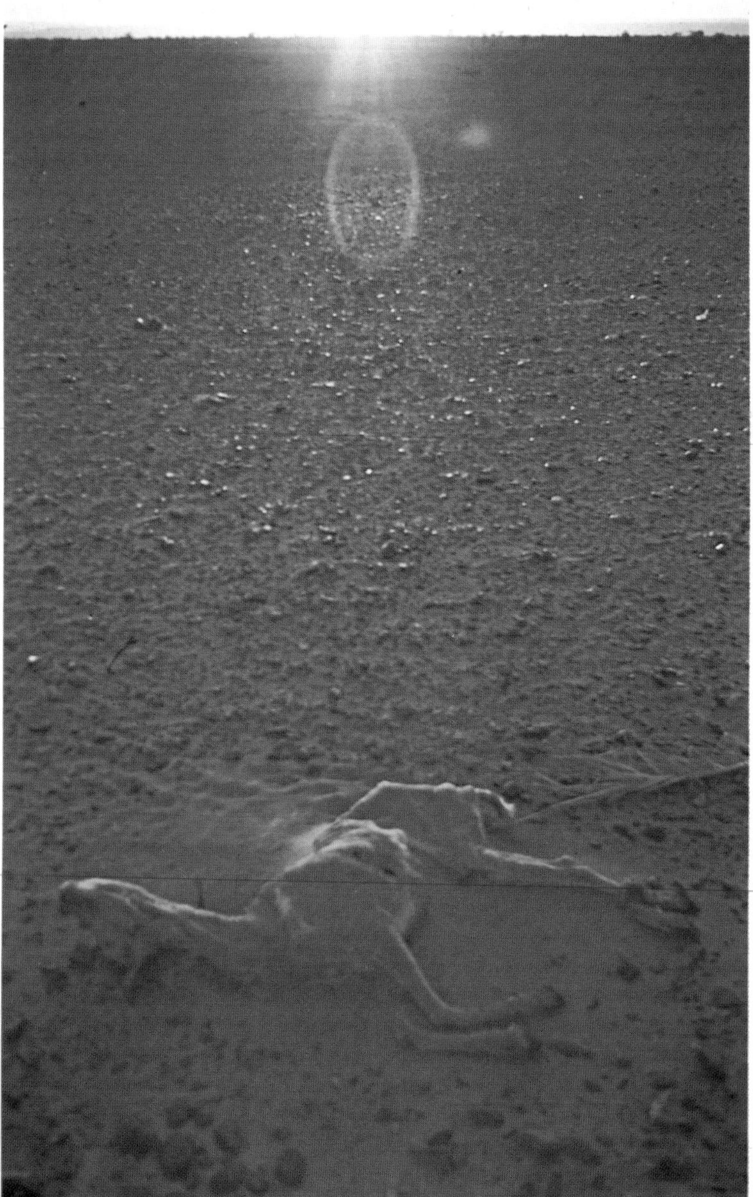

1. *Drought in the Sahel: livestock is decimated.*

THE LONG PERIOD of post-war prosperity produced an atmosphere of heightened optimism. In the West, economists were interested in growth, not in crises. In the East, vague generalizations on the 'overall crisis of capitalism' made it possible to avoid any precise view of the future. Gierek had even laid plans, from 1970 on, to build, with money borrowed from the West and paid back with goods sold to the West, an industrial 'second Poland'. Against this background it was inevitable that the economic crisis of 1974 also became a crisis of ideas. A total misjudgement had been made about the possibility of a major recession. Subsequently more mistakes were made about how long the crisis would last.

Today, one thing seems certain: long-term economic depressions do exist, and short-term crises, in the context of such breakdowns in the economic system, take on a seriousness that they do not have during periods of prolonged expansion.

But pointing up former illusions should not lead one to paint a rosy picture of the 'thirty glorious years' (1945–1974) and a bleak one of the decade after. The years from 1957 to 1961 and the years from 1964 to 1967 produced noticeable recessions, while 1976–9 and 1983–4 were clearly better than other moments in the crisis. In the same way it would be wrong to underestimate the differences between the present crisis and earlier crises. In the first place, social security systems, at least in the industrialized countries, are clearly much better. Secondly, the important part played more or less everywhere by the underground or 'black' economy suggests that statistical

2. *A meeting of OPEC.*

**1945–74:** The 'thirty glorious years' of economic prosperity.
**1945–9:** Years of reconstruction.
**1950:** Korean War breaks out. Huge surge of economic activity takes place in the West. Investments in communist countries increase.
**1950–7:** Years of rapid growth in communist China.
**1967:** Devaluation of the pound.
**15 August 1971:** Devaluation of the dollar, collapse of the international monetary system set up at Bretton Woods in 1944.
**1973:** The price of oil increases sharply ('First Oil Crisis') as a consequence of the devaluation of the strong currencies and the break-up of the international monetary system. The oil price is also a weapon used by the Arab world after the 1973 war with Israel. American oil companies make huge profits and Western banks begin recycling petro-dollars, particularly in the form of loans to the Third World.
**1974:** The beginning of the recession is signalled by the slowing of growth throughout the world. Between 1971–1975 and 1976–1980 the annual rate of growth of the GDP of the Soviet Union falls from 6% to 4%. For the period 1981 to 1985 an average of 3.5% is predicted. From 1972 to 1982, the rate of growth in the capitalist world (including Japan) is 2.5% on average. This rises in 1983–1984 to 3.3%. Stock prices plummet temporarily. Famine rages in Ethiopia and in the Sahel.
**1974–5:** Industrial production in the West falls considerably. First marked rise in unemployment figures.
**1976–9:** Uncertain years with contradictory indications as to the outcome of the crisis.
**1978–9:** Fall of the Shah of Iran at the hands of the Islamic revolution.
**1978–83:** Serious famine in northeast Brazil.
**1979–80:** Second Oil Crisis brings a fresh increase in oil prices.
**Since 1980:** The dollar, weakened in the 1970s at the same time as American influence itself, reinforces its position. American interest rates rise and capital pours into the country. The consequences of these events are often likened to those of a third 'oil crisis'. The recession worsens in the West.

4. *A family in Harlem.*

# 1974 . . .

results should not be taken too literally. Finally, it must also be said that until the 1980s, at any rate, trade, and particularly international trade, had suffered comparatively little from the recession. Moreover, the form and intensity of the crisis have varied greatly from country to country.

In the communist countries (with the exception of Poland, which has been very seriously affected, and China, which is in the midst of changing to more pragmatic policies), the burden of debt has been much less than in the Third World, and real unemployment seems less pronounced than in countries with market economies, but traditional shortages have become more serious, and rates of growth have fallen back (even though they have been higher, it appears, than in the West). In the developing world, in addition to the famines which have ravaged the population in some areas, the size of the international debt is so enormous that the world, at times, has been close to an economic catastrophe of monumental proportions, and the rise of poverty, with all the despair and threats of explosion it implies, has been quite alarming.

There has been, of course, no shortage of attempts to explain or to find the meaning of the crisis. Some observers are content simply to compare the present recession with various long-term cycles which can be seen to have existed in the past: from 1849 to 1873 there was a positive phase, from 1873 to 1893 a negative one; 1893 to 1913 was positive once more, while 1913 to 1945 was negative. And the present crisis comes in the wake of the positive phase from 1945 to 1974.

Other commentators point to demographic factors: according to this view, the baby boom of the 1940s and 1950s was the reason for post-war prosperity, and the fall in the birth-rate is said to have brought about a breakdown in growth. It is worth noting, however, that affluence in the West was quite unaffected by demographic decline in the 1960s and the first half of the 1970s. Many other analysts place the emphasis on changes in technology, since these, it is argued, are what sparked off and sustained expansion after the Second World War, and the upturn in the economy will be correspondingly dependent on the arrival of a fresh wave of technological innovation. But it can be shown that this new technological age was upon us, even before the onset of the economic crisis, at the end of the 1960s, in the shape of nuclear and computer technology, and today we seem to have travelled further down the same path with developments in biotechnology and robotics.

Finally, it can be argued that it is worth considering the socio-political and cultural changes of the end of the 1960s and 1970s, i.e. the questioning of the value of work and of industrial discipline, the decline or collapse of economic planning and of the planned economy itself, and the breakdown in the international monetary system under pressure from the enthusiastic defence of national and ethnic identities.

*3. Ayatollah Khomeini, the head of the Iranian Islamic revolution.*

*5. Steelworkers demonstrating for their jobs at Longwy (France) in August 1979.*

The economic situation in Poland gets worse.
**1982:** Mexico defaults on its international debt. Bankruptcy is only barely avoided.
**1983:** Third World debts have increased three-fold since 1975. World agricultural production falls as a result of drought and the world recession. There are riots and looting in São Paulo, in Brazil. Polish industrial production falls to its 1973 level.
**1983–4:** Partial economic recovery, particularly in the USA.
**1984:** Drought and famine in Black Africa and Ethiopia (where the movement of refugees increases the number of victims).
**1985:** America voices its concern about the strength of the recovery. In 1985, the number of unemployed as a percentage of the working population reaches 7 or 8% in the United States and the Federal Republic of Germany, 11 or 12% in France, Great Britain and Italy.
**1992?:** According to some analysts, the real recovery will not take place before about 1992; only then will the sequence of poor or bad years come to an end. But, between now and then, it is unlikely that the world will see years as bad as 1974 and 1975, or even as bad as 1980, 1981 or 1982.

# Picture Credits

VI-IX
1. Paris, Bibl. nat./Ph. H. JOSSE
2. London, British Museum/Archives LIDIS-BREPOLS.
3 and 4. Paris, Bibl. nat./Ph. EXPLORER ARCHIVES.

2-3
1, 2 and 3. Ph. CH. LÉNARS-EXPLORER.
4. Liège, Musée Curtius/Ph. CH. MAHAUX-EXPLORER.
5. Ph. CH. LÉNARS-EXPLORER.

4-5
1. Vienna, Naturhistorisches Museum/ Ph. E. LESSING-MAGNUM.
2. Ph. G. MARTIN-GUILLOU-EXPLORER.
3. Ph. CH. LÉNARS-EXPLORER.

6-7
1. Ph. A. BORDES-EXPLORER.
2. Ph. H. JOSSE.
3. Ph. M. CAMBAZARD-EXPLORER.
4. Saint-Germain-en-Laye, Musée des Antiquités nationales/Ph. E. LESSING-MAGNUM.
5. Périgueux, Musée du Périgord/Ph. J.-M. LABAT-EXPLORER ARCHIVES.
6. Saint-Germain-en-Laye, Musée des Antiquités nationales/Ph. GIRAUDON.

8-9
1. Paris, Musée de l'Homme/Ph. E. LESSING/MAGNUM.
2. Ankara, Archaeological Museum/Ph. G. DAGLI ORTI.
3. People's Republic of China, Ph. BULLOZ.
4. Stockholm, Historiska Museet/Ph. G. DAGLI ORTI.

10-11
1 and 2. Ph. G. DAGLI ORTI.
3. Ph. FERRERO-J.-M. LABAT-EXPLORER.
4. Paris, Musée de l'Homme/Ph. E. LESSING-MAGNUM.
5. Ph. G. DAGLI ORTI.
6. Athens, National Archaeological Museum/Ph. G. DAGLI ORTI.
7. Ph. J.-M. LABAT-EXPLORER.

12-13
1 and 2. London, British Museum/ Archives LIDIS-BREPOLS.
3. Baghdad, Iraq Museum/Ph. E. LESSING-MAGNUM.
4. London, British Museum/Archives LIDIS-BREPOLS.
5. Ph. I. MORATH-MAGNUM.

14-15
1. Ph. G. DAGLI ORTI.
2. Ph. P. TÉTREL-EXPLORER.
3, 4 and 5. Cairo, Egyptian Museum/Ph. G. DAGLI ORTI.

16-17
1. Ph. S. FIORE-EXPLORER ARCHIVES.
2. London, British Museum/Ph. BRIDGEMAN-GIRAUDON.
3 and 4. London, British Museum/ Archives LIDIS-BREPOLS.
5. London, British Museum/Ph. E. LESSING-MAGNUM.

18-19
1 and 2. Ph. G. DAGLI ORTI.
3. Ankara, Archaeological Museum/Ph. G. DAGLI ORTI.
4. Damascus, National Museum/Ph. G. DAGLI ORTI.
5. Ph. G. DAGLI ORTI.
6. Ankara, Archaeological Museum/Ph. G. DAGLI ORTI.

20-21
1. Ph. G. DAGLI ORTI.
2. Iraklion, Archaeological Museum/Ph. G. DAGLI ORTI.
3. Athens, National Archaeological Museum/Ph. G. DAGLI ORTI.
4 and 5. Athens, National Archaeological Museum/Ph. BRIDGEMAN-GIRAUDON.
6. Athens, National Archaeological Museum/Ph. G. DAGLI ORTI.

22-23
1. Ph. S. FIORE-EXPLORER.
2 and 3. Ph. CH. LÉNARS-EXPLORER.
4. Ph. S. FIORE-EXPLORER.
5. Ph. J.-L. NOU-EXPLORER.
6. Ph. S. FIORE-EXPLORER.
7 and 8. Ph. J.-L. NOU-EXPLORER.

24-25
1. Ph. CH. LÉNARS-EXPLORER.
2. London, British Museum/Archives LIDIS-BREPOLS.
3. Ph. RODGER-MAGNUM.
4. Paris, Musée du Louvre/Archives LIDIS-BREPOLS.
5. Vienna, Kunsthistorisches Museum/ Ph. E. LESSING-MAGNUM.
6. Paris, Bibl. nat./Archives LIDIS-BREPOLS.

26-27
1. Ph. E. LESSING-MAGNUM.
2. London, British Museum/Archives LIDIS-BREPOLS.
3. Ph. E. LESSING-MAGNUM.
4 and 5. London, British Museum/ Archives LIDIS-BREPOLS.

28-29
1. Ph. PH. BEUZEN-EXPLORER.
2. Ph. E. LESSING-MAGNUM.
3. Ph. S. FIORE-EXPLORER.
4. Luxor, Museum/Ph. G. DAGLI ORTI.
5. Cairo, Egyptian Museum/Ph. G. DAGLI ORTI.
6. Paris, Musée du Louvre/Archives LIDIS-BREPOLS.

30-31
1. People's Republic of China/Ph. H. JOSSE.
2. People's Republic of China/Ph. BULLOZ.
3. People's Republic of China/Ph. CH. LÉNARS-EXPLORER.
4. People's Republic of China/Ph. E. LESSING-MAGNUM.
5. People's Republic of China/Ph. LAUROS-GIRAUDON.

32-33
1. Copenhagen, Nationalmuseet/Ph. E. LESSING-MAGNUM.
2. Ph. E. LESSING-MAGNUM.
3. Graz, Steiermärkisches Landesmuseum/Ph. E. LESSING-MAGNUM.
4. Aix-en-Provence, Musée Granet/Ph. G. DAGLI ORTI.
5. London, British Museum/Ph. E. LESSING-MAGNUM.

34-35
1. Paris, Musée du Louvre/Ph. R.M.N.
2. Ph. CH. LÉNARS-EXPLORER.
3. Tunis, Musée du Bardo/Ph. EDIMEDIA.
4. Carthage, Musée nationale/Ph. CH. LÉNARS-EXPLORER.
5. Paris, Bibl. nat./Ph. EXPLORER ARCHIVES.
6. London, British Museum/Archives LIDIS-BREPOLS.

36-37
1. Paris, Bibl. des Arts décoratifs/Ph. G. DAGLI ORTI.
2 and 3. Ph. G. DAGLI ORTI.
4. Baghdad, Iraq Museum/Ph. G. DAGLI ORTI.
5. Paris, Bibl. nat./Photothèque HACHETTE.
6. Athens, Acropolis Museum/Ph. G. DAGLI ORTI.

38-39
1. Rome, Museo Nazionale Romano/Ph. G. DAGLI ORTI.
2. Vienna, Naturhistorisches Museum/ Ph. E. LESSING-MAGNUM.

40-41
1. Ph. CL. BÉRARD.
2. Iraklion, Archaeological Museum/Ph. G. NIMATALLAH-ARTEPHOT.
3. Photothèque HACHETTE.
4. Athens, National Archaeological Museum/Ph. G. NIMATALLAH-ARTEPHOT.
5. Thebes, Archaeological Museum/Ph. E. LESSING-MAGNUM.
6. Athens, National Archaeological Museum/Ph. G. NIMATALLAH-ARTEPHOT.

42-43
1. Ph. G. DAGLI ORTI.
2. Athens, Acropolis Museum/Ph. G. DAGLI ORTI.
3. Istanbul, Archaeological Museums/ Ph. E. LESSING-MAGNUM.
4. Châtillon-sur-Seine, Archaeological Museum/Ph. G. DAGLI ORTI.
5. Paris, Bibl. nat./Ph. E. LESSING-MAGNUM.

44-45
1. Ph. G. DAGLI ORTI.
2. Teheran, Archaeological Museum/Ph. H. JOSSE.
3. Teheran, Archaeological Museum/Ph. G. DAGLI ORTI.
4. Ph. G. DAGLI ORTI.
5. Teheran, Archaeological Museum/Ph. G. DAGLI ORTI.

46-47
1. Ph. G. DAGLI ORTI.
2. Paris, Bibl. nat./Ph. EXPLORER ARCHIVES.
3. Boston, Museum of Fine Arts/Ph. EXPLORER ARCHIVES.
4. Athens, National Archaeological Museum/Ph. G. DAGLI ORTI.
5. Ph. R. PERCHERON-ARTEPHOT.
6. Athens, Acropolis Museum/Ph. L.-Y. LOIRAT-EXPLORER ARCHIVES.

48-49
1. Paris, Bibl. nat./Photothèque HACHETTE.
2. Naples, National Archaeological Museum/Ph. G. NIMATALLAH-ARTEPHOT.
3. Paris, Bibl. nat./Ph. EXPLORER ARCHIVES.
4. Mexico, National Anthropological Museum/Ph. G. DAGLI ORTI.
5. Rome, Capitoline Museum/Ph. G. DAGLI ORTI.
6. Dijon, Chartreuse de Champmol/Ph. G. DAGLI ORTI.
7. Naples, National Archaeological Museum/Ph. G. DAGLI ORTI.
8. Paris, Musée du Louvre/Ph. H. JOSSE.

50-51
1. Paris, Bibl. nat./Ph. EXPLORER ARCHIVES.
2 and 3. Thessalonika, University Museum/Ph. T.A.P.-EXPLORER ARCHIVES.
4. Ph. P. VIDAL-NAQUET.
5. Delphi, Archaeological Museum/Ph. BRIDGEMAN-GIRAUDON.

52-53
1. Rome, Museo Nazionale di Villa Giulia/Ph. G. DAGLI ORTI.
2. Ph. CH. LENARS-EXPLORER.
3. Capua, Museo Provinciale Campano/ Ph. G. DAGLI ORTI.
4. Rome, Museo Nazionale di Villa Giulia/Ph. G. DAGLI ORTI.

54-55
1. People's Republic of China/Ph. E. LESSING-MAGNUM.
2. People's Republic of China/Ph. LAUROS-GIRAUDON.
3. Ph. R. BAUMGARTNER-EXPLORER.
4. People's Republic of China/Ph. E. LESSING-MAGNUM.
5. Paris, Musée Cernuschi/Ph. EXPLORER ARCHIVES.
6. PEOPLE'S Republic of China/Ph. CH. LENARS-EXPLORER.

56-57
1. Ph. C.B.O.-GIRAUDON.
2. Ph. J.-L. NOU-EXPLORER.
3. Ph. G. DAGLI ORTI.

58-59
1. Ph. F. SCIANNA-MAGNUM.
2. Benevento, Museo del Sannio/Ph. G. DAGLI ORTI.
3. Paris, Musée du Louvre/Ph. H. JOSSE.

60-61
1. Ph. CH. LÉNARS-EXPLORER.
2. Mainz, Römisch-Germanisches Zentralmuseum/Ph. E. LESSING-MAGNUM.
3. Paris, Musée du Louvre/Ph. H. JOSSE.
4. Paris, Musée du Louvre/Ph. EXPLORER ARCHIVES.

62-63
1. Lyon, Musée de la civilisation gallo-romaine/Ph. H. JOSSE.
2. Ph. J. DUPONT-EXPLORER.
3. Trier, Rheinisches Landesmuseum/ Ph. LAUROS-GIRAUDON.
4. Nîmes, Maison Carrée/Ph. P. TÉTREL-EXPLORER.

64-65
1. Archives LIDIS-BREPOLS.
2. Paris, Bibl. nat./Archives LIDIS-BREPOLS.
3. Rome, Museo Cristiano Lateranense/Ph. ALINARI-GIRAUDON.
4. Urbino, Museo Arcivescovile/Ph. ALINARI-GIRAUDON.
5. London, by courtesy of the Bible Society/Ph. BRIDGEMAN-GIRAUDON.

66-67
1. Rome, Vatican Museum/Ph. E. LESSING-MAGNUM.
2. Ph. H. CARTIER-BRESSON-MAGNUM.
3. Ph. R. BAUMGARTNER-EXPLORER.
4. Sarnath, Museum/Ph. LAUROS-GIRAUDON.
5. Mexico, National Anthropological Museum/Ph. G. DAGLI ORTI.

68-69
1 and 2. Brescia, Museo dell'Età Cristiana/Ph. GIRAUDON.
3. Ph. R. PERCHERON-ARTEPHOT.
4. Troyes, Musée des Beaux-Arts et d'Archéologie/Ph. G. DAGLI ORTI.

70-71
1. Teheran, Archaeological Museum/Ph. G. DAGLI ORTI.
2. Ph. S. FIORE-EXPLORER ARCHIVES.
3. Paris, Musée du Louvre/Ph. H. JOSSE.
4. Paris, Musée Guimet/Ph. GIRAUDON.
5. Paris, Musée Guimet/Ph. LESSING-MAGNUM.
6. Paris, Musée Guimet/Ph. LAUROS-GIRAUDON.

72-73
1. Paris, Bibl. nat./Archives CLAM!
2. Ph. LAUROS-GIRAUDON.
3. Berne, Bernisches Historisches Museum/Ph. F. FAILLET-ARTEPHOT.
4. Paris, Musée de Cluny/Ph. H. JOSSE.
5. Berne, Bernisches Historisches Museum/Ph. F. FAILLET-ARTEPHOT.

74-75
1. Venice, Biblioteca Nazionale Marciana/Ph. G. DAGLI ORTI.
2. Ph. G. DAGLI ORTI.
3. Ph. G. DAGLI ORTI.
4. Paris, Musée de Cluny/Ph. H. JOSSE.
5. Paris, Bibl. nat./Ph. EXPLORER-ARCHIVES.
6. Ph. E. LESSING-MAGNUM.

76-77
1. Ph. CH. LÉNARS-EXPLORER.
2. Ph. PH. BOUSQUET-EXPLORER.
3. Paris, Musée du Louvre/Ph. LAUROS-GIRAUDON.
4. Ph. G. DAGLI ORTI.
5. Tunis, Bibl. nat./Ph. LAUROS-GIRAUDON.

78-79
1. London, Victoria and Albert Museum/Ph. BRIDGEMAN-GIRAUDON.
2. Paris, Bibl. nat./Ph. EXPLORER ARCHIVES.
3. Ph. G. DAGLI ORTI.
4. London, British Museum/Ph. BRIDGEMAN-GIRAUDON.
5. Paris, Bibl. nat./Ph. EXPLORER ARCHIVES.
6. Parisn Bibl. nat./Archives TALLANDIER.

80-81
1. Oslo, Norsk Sjøfartsmuseum/Ph. KNUDSENS-GIRAUDON.
2. Ph. P. TÉTREL-EXPLORER.
3. London, British Museum/E.T. ARCHIVE.
4. Oslo, Norsk Sjøfartsmuseum/Ph. KNUDSENS-GIRAUDON.

82-83
1. Ph. JAFFRE-DUROU-EXPLORER.
2. Paris, Musée Guimet/Ph. GIRAUDON.
3. People's Republic of China/Ph. BULLOZ.
4. Ph. JAFFRE-DUROU-EXPLORER.
5. People's Republic of China/Ph. LAUROS-GIRAUDON.
6. Paris, Musée Guimet/Ph. E. LESSING-MAGNUM.
7. Commission for the Protection of Japan's Cultural Heritage/Ph. EXPLORER ARCHIVES.

84-85
1. Nara, Todai-ji/Ph. OGAWA-ARTEPHOT.
2. Rome, Museo Nazionale d'Arte Orientale/Ph. G. DAGLI ORTI.
3. Ph. CH. LÉNARS-EXPLORER.
4. Kyoto, Horyu-ji/Ph. OGAWA-ARTEPHOT.
5. Paris, private collection/Ph. G. DAGLI ORTI.

86-87
Illustration BERTIN.
1. Paris, Musée Guimet/Ph. G. DAGLI ORTI.
2. Ph. INVERNIZZI-GIRAUDON.
3. Ph. G. DAGLI ORTI.
4. Ph. CH. LÉNARS-EXPLORER.
5. Ph. G. BOUTIN-EXPLORER.

88-89
1. Aix-la-Chapelle, Trésor de la cathédrale/Ph. E. LESSING-MAGNUM.
2. Paris, Musée de Cluny/Ph. E. LESSING-MAGNUM.
3. Ph. B. BARBEY-MAGNUM.
4. Paris, Bibl. nat./Ph. EXPLORER ARCHIVES.

90-91
1. Paris, Bibl. nat./Photothèque HACHETTE.
2. Ph. CH. LÉNARS-EXPLORER.
3. Istanbul, Topkapi Library/Ph. G. DAGLI ORTI.
4. Paris, Musée Guimet/Ph. G. DAGLI ORTI.
5. Ph. CH. LÉNARS-EXPLORER.
6. London, British Museum/E.T. ARCHIVE.
7. Paris, Bibl. nat./Ph. EXPLORER ARCHIVES.

92-93
1. Paris, Bibl. nat./Ph. H. JOSSE.
2. Conques, Trésor de l'église Sainte-Foy/Ph. GIRAUDON.
3. Paris, Archives nationales/Ph. BULLOZ.
4. Paris, Musée du Louvre/Ph. LAUROS-GIRAUDON.
5. Ph. J.-L. CHARMET.
6. Ph. G. MARTIN-GUILLOU-EXPLORER.

94-95
1. Paris, Bibl. nat./Photothèque HACHETTE.
2. Ph. D. DORVAL-EXPLORER.
3. Paris, Musée de Cluny/Ph. H. JOSSE.

96-97
1. Moscow, State Tretyakov Gallery/Ph. J. MASSON-ÉD. CERCLE D'ART.
2. Ph. C. CAPA-MAGNUM.
3. Moscow, State Tretyakov Gallery/Ph. A.P.M.
4. Ph. A.P.N.

98-99
1. Paris, Musée de Cluny/Ph. H. JOSSE.
2. Paris, Bibl. nat./Photothèque HACHETTE.
3. Vienna, Kunsthistorisches Museum/ Ph. E. LESSING-MAGNUM.
4. Ph. M.-J. LEROY-EXPLORER.

100-101
1. Paris, Bibl. nat./Photothèque HACHETTE.
2. Paris, Musée du Louvre/Ph. GIRAUDON.
3. Ph. LAUROS-GIRAUDON.
4. Paris, Bibl. de l'Arsenal/Ph. GIRAUDON.
5. Paris, Musée de Cluny/Ph. H. JOSSE.
6. Paris, Bibl. nat./Photothèque HACHETTE.

102-103
1. Ph. PUJEBET-EXPLORER.
2. London, British Museum/E.T. ARCHIVE.
3. Bayeux, Musée de la Tapisserie de la Reine Mathilde/Ph. G. DAGLI ORTI.
4. Ph. F. MAYER-MAGNUM.
5. Ph. B. GÉRARD-EXPLORER.
6. Paris, Musée de Cluny/Ph. H. JOSSE.

104-105
1. Paris, Musée du Louvre/Ph. H. JOSSE.
2. Dublin, Trinity College Library/Ph. BRIDGEMAN-GIRAUDON.
3. Paris, Bibl. nat./Archives TALLANDIER.
4. Paris, Archives nationales/Ph. J.-L. CHARMET.
5. Montecassino, Abbey Library/Ph. GIRAUDON.
6. Admont, Abbey Library/Ph. E. LESSING-MAGNUM.

106-107
1. Urbino, Galleria Nazionale delle Marche/Ph. LAUROS-GIRAUDON.
2. Ph. CH. MAHAUX-EXPLORER ARCHIVES.
3. Paris, Archives nationales/Ph. BULLOZ.
4. Ph. L.-Y. LOIRAT-EXPLORER.
5. Madrid, Museo del Prado/Ph. G. DAGLI ORTI.
6. Berne, Burgerbibliothek/ Burgerbibliothek photo.

108-109
1. Ph. G. DAGLI ORTI.
2. Paris, Bibl. nat./Ph. GIRAUDON.
3. Ph. G. DAGLI ORTI.
4. Ph. E. LESSING-MAGNUM.
5. Ph. G. DAGLI ORTI.
6. Ph. E. LESSING-MAGNUM.

110-111
1. Ph. CH. LÉNARS-EXPLORER.
2. Istanbul, Topkapi Library/Ph. G. DAGLI ORTI.
3. Oxford, Bodleian Library/Ph. EXPLORER ARCHIVES.
4. Toulouse, Musée Paul Dupuy/Ph. LAUROS-GIRAUDON.
5. Paris, Bibl. nat./Ph. J.-L. CHARMET.

112-113
1. Paris, Archives nationales/Ph. BULLOZ.
2. Paris, Musée Guimet/Ph. H. JOSSE.
3. Istanbul, Topkapi Library/Ph. G. DAGLI ORTI.
4. Ph. M. KOENE-EXPLORER.

114-115
1. Tokyo, National Museum/Ph. ZAUHO PRESS-ARTEPHOT.
2. Paris, private collection/Ph. G. DAGLI ORTI.
3. Ph. G. ZAWADZKI-EXPLORER.
4. Lyon, Musée historique des tissus/Ph. GIRAUDON.

116-117
1. Ph. G. DAGLI ORTI.
2. Ph. S. FIORE-EXPLORER.
3. Bombay, Prince of Wales Museum of Western India/Ph. J.-L. NOU-EXPLORER.
4. Ph. J.-L. NOU-EXPLORER.

118-119
1. Ph. G. PERESS-MAGNUM.
2. Castres, Musée Goya/Ph. G. DAGLI ORTI.
3. Oxford, Bodleian Library/E.T. ARCHIVE.
4. Agen, Bibl. municipale/Ph. H. JOSSE.
5. Paris, Archives nationales/Ph. J.-L. CHARMET.

120-121
1. Ph. F. JALAIN-EXPLORER.
2. Ph. H. VEILLER-EXPLORER.
3. Paris, Musée du Louvre/Ph. G. DAGLI ORTI.
4. Gerona, Cathedral Museum/Ph. ORONEZ-ARTEPHOT.
5. Ph. B. BORAUD-EXPLORER.

# Picture Credits

122-123
1. Ph. J.-P. LAMOUR-EXPLORER.
2. Ph. M. CAMBAZARD-EXPLORER.
3. Ph. LAUROS-GIRAUDON.
4. Chantilly, Musée Condé/Ph. GIRAUDON.
5. Paris, Musée du Louvre/Ph. G. DAGLI ORTI.
6. Lyon, Musée historique des tissus/Ph. GIRAUDON.
7. Paris, Archives nationales/Ph. GIRAUDON.

124-125
1. Paris, Bibl. nat./Ph. EXPLORER ARCHIVES.
2. Siena, Palazzo Pubblico/Ph. G. DAGLI ORTI.
3. Paris, Musée du Louvre/Ph. G. DAGLI ORTI.
4. Paris, Bibl. nat./Ph. EXPLORER ARCHIVES.
5. Ph. G. DAGLI ORTI.
6. Paris, Bibl. nat./Ph. EXPLORER ARCHIVES.

126-127
1. Paris, Bibl. nat./Archives TALLANDIER.
2. Avignon, Palais des Papes/Ph. G. DAGLI ORTI.
3. Paris, Bibl. polonaise/Ph. J.-L. CHARMET.
4. Naples, Museo e Gallerie Nazionali di Capodimonte/Ph. GIRAUDON.

128-129
1. Palermo, Galleria Regionale di Sicilia/ Ph. LAUROS-GIRAUDON.
2. Paris, Bibl. nat./Archives TALLANDIER.
3. Madrid, Museo del Prado/Ph. G. DAGLI ORTI.
4. Paris, Bibl. de l'Arsenal/Ph. J.-L. CHARMET.
5. Modena, Biblioteca Estense/Ph. GIRAUDON.

130-131
1. Ph. J. VALENTIN-EXPLORER.
2. Paris, Bibl. nat./Ph. EXPLORER ARCHIVES.
3. Ph. BOUTIN-EXPLORER.
4. Ph. CH. LÉNARS-EXPLORER.
5. Ph. CL. WEINMANN-A.A.A. PHOTO.
6. Ph. CH. LÉNARS-EXPLORER.

132-133
1 and 2. Ph. G. DAGLI ORTI.
3. Oaxaca, Regional Museum/Ph. G. DAGLI ORTI.
4. Madrid, Museo de América/Ph. G. DAGLI ORTI.
5. Jalapa, Anthropological Museum/Ph. G. DAGLI ORTI.

134-135
1. Ph. G. DAGLI ORTI.
2. Lima, Museo del Oro del Peru/Ph. G. DAGLI ORTI.
3. Lima, Museo Nacional de Antropologia y Arqueologia/Ph. G. DAGLI ORTI.
4. Ph. G. DAGLI ORTI.

136-137
1. Lisbon/Ph. H. JOSSE.
2. Philadelphia, Museum of Art/Museum photo.
3. Vienna, Kunsthistorisches Museum/ Ph. H. JOSSE.

138-139
1. Madrid, Museo de América/Ph. OROÑOZ-ARTEPHOT.
2 and 3. Lisbon, Monastero de Jeroninos/Ph. H. JOSSE.
4. Paris, Bibl. nat./E.T. ARCHIVE.
5. Madrid, Bibl. Nacional/Ph. G. DAGLI ORTI.

140-141
1. Amsterdam, Rijksmuseum/Ph. A. HELD-ARTEPHOT.
2. Paris, Bibl. nat./Ph. EXPLORER ARCHIVES.
3. Paris, Bibl. des Arts décoratifs/Ph. EXPLORER ARCHIVES.
4. Paris, Bibl. nat./Ph. GIRAUDON.
5. Versailles, Musée national du château/Ph. GIRAUDON.

142-143
1. Vienna, Österreischische National Bibliothek/Ph. Bibliothek.
2. Paris, Ecole nationale supérieure des Beaux-Arts/Ph. BULLOZ.
3. London, Victoria and Albert Museum/Ph. BRIDGEMAN-GIRAUDON.
4. Florence, Uffizi/Ph. GIRAUDON.
5. Paris, Bibl. nat./Ph. LAUROS-GIRAUDON.
6. Clermont-Ferrand, Musée du Ranquet/Ph. LAUROS-GIRAUDON.

144-145
1 and 2. Paris, Bibl. nat./Ph. EXPLORER ARCHIVES.
3. Private collection/Ph. J.-L. CHARMET.
4. Paris, Bibl. nat./Photothèque HACHETTE.
5. Paris, Bibl. des Arts décoratifs/Ph. J.-L. CHARMET.

146-147
1. Palermo, Galleria Regionale di Sicilia/ Ph. LAUROS-GIRAUDON.
2. Paris, Bibl. des Arts décoratifs/Ph. EXPLORER ARCHIVES.
3. Ph. EXPLORER ARCHIVES.
4. Florence, Santa Maria Novella/Ph. SCALA-FIRENZE.
5. Paris, Bibl. nat./Ph. EXPLORER ARCHIVES.
6. Orléans, Musée des Beaux-Arts/Ph. LAUROS-GIRAUDON.

148-149
1. Florence, private collection/Ph. ZUCCONI-ARTEPHOT.
2. Lima, Museo de Arte/Ph. G. DAGLI ORTI.
3. Siena, Pinacoteca Nazionale/Ph. EXPLORER ARCHIVES.

150-151
1. Paris, Bibl. du Protestantisme/Ph. J.-L. CHARMET.
2. Heidelberg, Kurpfalzisches Museum/Ph. LAUROS-GIRAUDON.
3. Paris, Bibl. du Protestantisme/Ph. LAUROS-GIRAUDON.
4. Winterthur, Kunstmuseum/Ph. BURKHARD-ARTEPHOT.
5. Ph. J.-L. CHARMET.
6. Florence, Uffizi/Ph. BRIDGEMAN-GIRAUDON.
7. Munich, Alte Pinakothek/Ph. ARTOTHEK-GIRAUDON.
8. Lugano, Thyssen-Bornemisza collection/Ph. BRIDGEMAN-GIRAUDON.

152-153
1. Paris, Musée Carnavalet/Ph. LAUROS-GIRAUDON.
2. Ph. J.-L. CHARMET.
3. Paris, Bibl. nat./Ph. J.-L. CHARMET.
4. Paris, Bibl. nat./Ph. I.R.L.
5. Rome, Palazzo Barberini/Ph. A. HELD-ARTEPHOT.

154-155
1. Moulins, Musée d'art et d'archéologie/Ph. LAUROS-GIRAUDON.
2. Madrid, Museo del Prado/Ph. BRIDGEMAN-GIRAUDON.
3. Madrid, Museo de América/Ph. GIRAUDON.
4. Ph. GIRAUDON.

156-157
1. Greenwich, Royal Naval College/ EXPLORER ARCHIVES.
2. Amiens, Musée de Picardie/Ph. LAUROS-GIRAUDON.
3. Versailles, Musée national du château/Ph. GIRAUDON.
4. London, Guildhall Library/Ph. BRIDGEMAN-GIRAUDON.

158-159
1. Naples, Museo Nazionale di San Martino/Ph. G. DAGLI ORTI.
2. Clermont-Ferrand, Musée Bargoin/Ph. LAUROS-GIRAUDON.
3. Paris, Bibl. des Arts décoratifs/Ph. J.-L. CHARMET.
4. Paris, Bibl. nat./Ph. J.-L. CHARMET.

160-161
1. Paris, Musée du Louvre/Ph. H. JOSSE.
2. Paris, I.N.R.P./Ph. J.-L. CHARMET.
3. Paris, Bibl. nat./Ph. J.-L. CHARMET.
4. Munich, Bayerische Staatsgemäldesammlungen/Ph. BLAUEL-Photothèque HACHETTE.
5. Paris, Archives du Quai d'Orsay/Ph. J.-L. CHARMET.

162-163
1. Istanbul, Topkapi Library/Ph. G. DAGLI ORTI.
2. Venice, Museo Correr/Ph. GIRAUDON.
3. Ph. GIRAUDON.
4. London, Victoria and Albert Museum/Ph. BRIDGEMAN-GIRAUDON.
5. Ph. G. DAGLI ORTI.
6. Istanbul, Topkapi Palace/Ph. G. DAGLI ORTI.

164-165
1. Private collection/E.T. ARCHIVE.
2. Ph. M. PELL-MAGNUM.
3. Lisbon/Ph. H. JOSSE.
4. Paris, Bibl. nat./Archives TALLANDIER.
5. Paris, Bibl. nat./Ph. J. DESMARTEAU-EXPLORER.

166-167
1 and 2. Ph. CH. LÉNARS-EXPLORER.
3. Paris, Musée Guimet/Ph. GIRAUDON.
4. Paris, private collection/Ph. G. DAGLI ORTI.
5. Oporto, Museu Nacional de Soares dos Reis/Ph. GIRAUDON.

168-169
1 and 2. London, Victoria and Albert Museum/Ph. BRIDGEMAN-GIRAUDON.
3 and 4. Ph. J.-L. NOU-EXPLORER.
5. Ph. CH. LÉNARS-EXPLORER.

170-171
1. Ph. J.-L. CHARMET.
2. Paris, Bibl. nat./Ph. J.-L. CHARMET.
3. Ph. G. DAGLI ORTI.
4. London, Museum of Mankind/Ph. BRIDGEMAN-GIRAUDON.

172-173
1. Ph. E. LESSING-MAGNUM.
2. Toledo, San Tomé/Ph. LAUROS-GIRAUDON.
3. Granada, Cathedral/Ph. OROÑOZ-ARTEPHOT.
4. Ph. SCALA-FIRENZE.
5. Rome, Santa Maria delle Vittorie/Ph. G. NIMATALLAH-ARTEPHOT.
6. Chantilly, Musée Condé/Ph. LAUROS-GIRAUDON.
7. Madrid, Escorial/Ph. OROÑOZ-ARTEPHOT.

174-175
1. Versailles, Musée national du château/Ph. H. JOSSE.
2. Versailles, Musée national du château/Ph. LAUROS-GIRAUDON.
3. Paris, Bibl. nat./Ph. LAUROS-GIRAUDON.
4. San Francisco, The Fine Arts Museums, California Palace of the Legion of Honor/Ph. H. JOSSE.
5. Paris, Hôtel des Monnaies/Ph. LAUROS-GIRAUDON.
6. Versailles, Musée national du château/Ph. H. JOSSE.

176-177
1. Rennes, Musée des Beaux-Arts/Ph. H. JOSSE.
2. Paris, Bibl. nat./Ph. LAUROS-GIRAUDON.
3. Paris, Musée du Louvre/Ph. H. JOSSE.
4. Paris, Bibl. des Arts décoratifs/Ph. J.-L. CHARMET.

178-179
1. Moscow, State Historical Museum/ Ph. A.P.N.
2. Moscow, State Historical Museum/ Ph. EDIMEDIA.
3. Paris, Bibl. nat./Ph. LAUROS-GIRAUDON.
4. Moscow, State Historical Museum/ Ph. A.P.N.
5. Moscow, Rublyov Museum/Ph. A.P.N.

180-181
1. Photothèque HACHETTE.
2. Paris, Bibl. nat./Ph. J.-L. CHARMET.
3. Paris, Institut Tessin/Ph. J.-L. CHARMET-EXPLORER ARCHIVES.
4. Uppsala Universitet/Ph. Universitet.
5. Paris, Institut Tessin/Ph. J.-L. CHARMET-EXPLORER ARCHIVES.
6. Ph. A.P.N.

182-183
1. Paris, Musée de la Marine/Ph. G. DAGLI ORTI.
2. Paris, Bibl. nat./Ph. EXPLORER ARCHIVES.
3. Paris, Bibl. nat./Ph. GIRAUDON.
4. Paris, Archives nationales, section outremer/Ph. J.-L. CHARMET.
5. Ph. GIRAUDON

184-185
1. Oporto, Museu Nacional de Soares dos Reis/Ph. G. DAGLI ORTI.
2. Postdam, Sans-Souci/Ph. LAUROS-GIRAUDON.
3. Paris, Bibl. nat./Archives TALLANDIER.
4. Vienna, Kunsthistorischesmuseum/ Ph. MEYER-ARTOTHEK-GIRAUDON.
5. Versailles, Musée national du château/Ph. LAUROS-GIRAUDON.

186-187
1. Geneva, Institut et musée Voltaire/Ph. EXPLORER ARCHIVES.
2. Paris, Bibl. des Art décoratifs/Ph. J.-L. CHARMET.
3 and 4. Private collection/Ph. EXPLORER ARCHIVES.

188-189
1. Ph. G. KREMER-EXPLORER ARCHIVES.
2. Paris, Bibl. des Arts décoratifs/Ph. J.-L. CHARMET.
3. Montpellier, Musée Atger/Ph. G. DAGLI ORTI.

190-191
1. Liverpool, Walker Art Gallery/Ph. Photothèque HACHETTE.
2. Paris, C.N.A.M./Ph. H. JOSSE.
3. London, British Library/Ph. FLEMING-Photothèque HACHETTE.
4. Paris, Bibl. nat./Photothèque HACHETTE.
5. Stafford, Staffordshire County Council/Ph. P. ROGERS-Photothèque HACHETTE.

192-193
1. Moscow, State Historical Museum/ Ph. A.P.N.
2. Private collection.
3. Éd. HOA-QUI.
4. Paris, Institut Tessin/Ph. J.-L. CHARMET-EXPLORER ARCHIVES.
5. Cholet, Musée des Guerres de Vendée/Ph. LAUROS-GIRAUDON.

194-195
1. Paris, Bibl. nat./Ph. H. JOSSE.
2. London, Trade Union Congress/Ph. BRIDGEMAN-GIRAUDON.
3. Ph. MARY EVANS.

196-197
1. Paris, Bibl. nat./Ph. J.-L. CHARMET.
2. Paris, Bibl. nat./Ph. EXPLORER ARCHIVES.
3. THE BETTMANN ARCHIVE.
4. Blérancourt, Musée national de la co-opération franco-américaine/Ph. G. MULLER-PHOTOTHÈQUE HACHETTE.
5. Washington, The National Gallery of Art/Ph. LAUROS-GIRAUDON.

198-199
1. Paris, Musée Carnavalet/Ph. H. JOSSE.
2. Private collection/Archives TALLANDIER.
3. Paris, Musée Carnavalet/Ph. H. JOSSE.
4 and 5. Paris, Musée Carnavalet/Ph. LAUROS-GIRAUDON.

200-201
1. Versailles, Musée national du château/Ph. LAUROS-GIRAUDON.
2. Paris, Musée de l'Armée/Ph. H. JOSSE.
3 and 4. Ph. EXPLORER ARCHIVES.
5. Paris, Bibl. nat./Ph. LAUROS-GIRAUDON.

202-203
1. Paris, Musée Carnavalet/Ph. H. JOSSE.
2. Paris, Bibl. nat./Ph. EXPLORER ARCHIVES.
3. Paris, Bibl. des Arts décoratifs/Ph. J.-L. CHARMET.
4. Paris, Bibl. nat./Ph. EXPLORER ARCHIVES.
5. Paris, Musée Carnavalet/Ph. LAUROS-GIRAUDON.
6. Paris, Bibl. nat./Ph. EXPLORER ARCHIVES.

204-205
1. Paris, Musée Carnavalet/Ph. J.-L. CHARMET.
2. Versailles, Musée national du château/Ph. G. DAGLI ORTI.
3. Paris, Bibl. des Arts décoratifs/Ph. G. DAGLI ORTI.
4. Vienna, Federal Chancellery/Ph. ALPENLAND-Photothèque HACHETTE.
5. Paris, Bibl. nat./Archives CLAM!
6. Paris, Bibl. nat./Ph. EXPLORER ARCHIVES.

206-207
1. Callao, Military Museum/Ph. G. DAGLI ORTI.
2. Rio de Janeiro, Museu Historico Nacional/Ph. G. DAGLI ORTI.
3. Bogotá, Museum of 20 July/Ph. G. DAGLI ORTI.

208-209
1. Ph. HENRIQUES-MAGNUM.
2. Mexico/Ph. G. DAGLI ORTI.
3. J. Meyer Collection.
4. Mexico, Museo de Historia Natural/ Ph. G. DAGLI ORTI.
5. Ph. S. MEISELAS-MAGNUM.

210-211
1. Naples, Museo Nazionale di San Martino/Ph. G. DAGLI ORTI.
2. Frankfurt, Historisches Museum/Ph. H. JOSSE-Photothèque HACHETTE.
3. Paris, Musée Carnavalet/Archives TALLANDIER.
4. Paris, Bibl. nat./Ph. LAUROS-GIRAUDON.
5. Rome, Museo del Risorgimento/Ph. G. DAGLI ORTI.

212-213
1. Paris, Musée Carnavalet/Ph. J.-L. CHARMET.
2. Rouen, Musée des Beaux-Arts/Ph. LAUROS-GIRAUDON.
3. Berlin, Nationalgalerie/Ph. BILDARCHIV PREUSSISCHER KULTURBESITZ.
4. Barcelona, Museo Picasso/© SPADEM, 1986.

214-215
1. Ph. MARY EVANS.
2. Ph. G. DAGLI ORTI.

216-217
1. Paris, Bibl. Hist. de la Ville de Paris/Ph. GIRAUDON.
2. Paris, Musée Carnavalet/Ph. J.-L CHARMET.
3 and 4. Ph. J.-L. CHARMET.
5. Société Michelin/Archives CLAM!
6 and 7. Ph. J.-L. CHARMET.

218-219
1. Artist's collection: Grand-Mére-Paris © SPADEM, 1986/Ph. J.-L. CHARMET.
2 and 3. Ph. J.-L. CHARMET.
4. Paris, Bibl. nat./Ph. H. JOSSE.
5. Essen, Deutsches Plakatmuseum/Ph J.-L. CHARMET.
6. Ph. J.-L. CHARMET.

220-221
1, 2 and 3. THE BETTMANN ARCHIVE.
4. Private collection/Ph. GIRAUDON.
5. Chicago, Historical Society/Archives TALLANDIER.

222-223
1. Ph. G. N. Barnard, 1865/THE BETTMANN ARCHIVE.
2. Ph. EDIMEDIA.
3. Ph. EXPLORER ARCHIVES.
4. Washington, National Collection of Fine Arts/Ph. EDIMEDIA.

224-225
1. Brescia, Museo del Risorgimento/Ph G. DAGLI ORTI.
2. Ph. H. JOSSE.
3. Milan, Pinacoteca di Brera/Ph. GIRAUDON.
4. Paris, Musée Carnavalet/Ph. J.-L. CHARMET.
5. Paris, Musée Carnavalet/Ph. G. DAGLI ORTI.
6. Budapest, Museum of Military History/Ph. J.-L. CHARMET.

226-227
1. London, Victoria and Albert Museum/Ph. E.T. ARCHIVE.
2. Ph. E.T. ARCHIVE.
3. Ph. J.-L. CHARMET.
4. Private collection/Ph. J.-L. CHARMET.

228-229
1. Paris, Musée Carnavalet/Ph. J.-L. CHARMET.
2. Private collection/Ph. J.-L. CHARMET.
3. Ed. IRIS-Archives TALLANDIER.
4. Paris, Bibl. des Arts décoratifs/Ph. J.-L. CHARMET.
5. A. Fildier Collection/Archives TALLANDIER.

230-231
1. Essen, coll. Friedrich Krupp Gemeinschaftsbetriebe/Ph. coll.-Photothèque HACHETTE.
2. A. Fildier Collection/Archives TALLANDIER.
3. Paris, Bibl. nat./Ph. H. JOSSE.
4. Ph. J.-L. CHARMET-EXPLORER ARCHIVES.

232-233
1. Paris, Musée des Deux Guerres mondiales/Ph. G. DAGLI ORTI.
2. Private collection/Ph. J.-L. CHARMET.
3. Paris, Bibl. nat./Ph. J.-L. CHARMET.
4. Sigmund Freud Archive/Archives TALLANDIER.
5. Moscow, State Historiical Museum/ Ph. A.P.N.
6. Venice, Galleria Internazionale d'Arte Moderna di Ca' Pesaro/Ph. G. DAGLI ORTI.

234-235
1. *The Illustrated London News*/Ph. G. DAGLI ORTI.
2. Paris, Musée national des Arts africains et oceaniens/Ph. H. JOSSE.
3. Ph. A.D.P.C.-EXPLORER ARCHIVES.

236-237
1. Private collection/Ph. EDIMEDIA.
2. Paris, Bibl. nat./Archives TALLANDIER.
3. Vincennes, Bibl. du Service historique de la Marine/Ph. G. DAGLI ORTI.
4. Paris, Bibl. nat./Archives TALLANDIER.
5. C. Dars Collection/Ph. EDIMEDIA.

238-239
1. *The Illustrated London News*/Ph. J.-L. CHARMET.
2. *Le Petit Journal*/Ph. J.-L. CHARMET.
3. Liverpool, City Museum and Art Gallery/Ph. J.-L. CHARMET.
4. Paris, Bibl. des Arts décoratifs/Ph. J.-L. CHARMET
5. Collection SIROT-ANGEL.

240-241
1. THE BETTMANN ARCHIVE.
2. Private collection/Ph. F. G. MAYER-Photothèque HACHETTE.
3. THE BETTMANN ARCHIVE.

242-243
1. The Bettmann Archive/Photothèque HACHETTE.
2. Compiègne, Musée du Second Empire/Ph. H. JOSSE.
3. Paris, Bibl. nat./Ph. H. JOSSE.
4. Paris, Bibl. des Arts décoratifs/Ph.

# Picture Credits

J.-L. CHARMET.
5. Photothèque HACHETTE.
6. Paris, Bibl. des Arts décoratifs/Ph. J.-L. CHARMET.

244-245
1. Photothèque HACHETTE.
2. *Le Petit Journal*/Ph. J.-L. CHARMET.
3. *Le Petit Parisien*/Archives TALLANDIER.
4. *L'Illustré National*/Ph. J.-L. CHARMET-Archives TALLANDIER.
5. Paris, Bibl. nat./Ph J.-L. CHARMET.

246-247
1. Paris, Musée de l'Armée/Ph. H. JOSSE.
2. Nanterre, B.D.I.C./Photothèque HACHETTE.
3. Ph. E.T. ARCHIVE.
4. Photothèque HACHETTE.
5. Canberra, Australian War Memorial/ Ph. E.T. ARCHIVE.

248-249
1. Ph. J.-L. CHARMET.
2. *Le Petit Journal*/Ph. J.-L. CHARMET.
3. Archives TALLANDIER.
4. Ph. KEYSTONE.
5. Essen, Deutsches Plakatmuseum/Ph. J.-L. CHARMET.

250-251
1. Nanterre, B.D.I.C./Ph. G. DAGLI ORTI.
2. Paris, Musée des Deux Guerres mondiale/Ph. G. DAGLI ORTI.
3. Nanterre, B.D.I.C./Ph. G. DAGLI ORTI.
4. Ph. KEYSTONE.
5. Paris, Musée des Deux Guerres mondiales/Ph. G. DAGLI ORTI.

252-253
1. Private collection/Ph. J.-L. CHARMET.
2. Ph. KEYSTONE.
3. Paris, Bibl. polonaise/Ph. J.-L. CHARMET.
4. Archives TALLANDIER.
5. Coll. VIOLLET.

254-255
1. Paris, Bibl. nat./Ph. J.-L. CHARMET.
2. Ph. HARLINGUE-VIOLLET.
3. Private collection/Ph. J.-L. CHARMET-EXPLORER ARCHIVES.
4. Ph. LAPI-VIOLLET.

256-257
1. Archives TALLANDIER.
2. Ph. J.-L. CHARMET.
3. Ph. MAGNUM.
4. Ph. J.-L. CHARMET.
5. Ph. R. CAPA-MAGNUM.
6. Washington, National Archives and Records Service/Ph. EDIMEDIA.

258-259
1. Ph. ASSOCIATED PRESS-Photothèque HACHETTE.
2. Ph. J.-L. CHARMET.
3. *Le Petit Journal*/Ph. J.-L. CHARMET.
4. *Kladdezadatsch*/Ph. J.-L. CHARMET.
5. *Simplicissimus*/Ph. J.-L. CHARMET.
6. *Lecture pour Tour*/Ph. J.-L. CHARMET.

260-261
1. Paris, Bibl. nat./Photothèque HACHETTE.
2. A. Brissaud Collection/Archives TALLANDIER.
3. Ph. R. CAPA-MAGNUM.
4. Private collection/Ph. J.-L. CHARMET.
5. Paris, Bibl. nat./Ph. S.A.F.A.R.A.-Archives TALLANDIER.
5. Ph. R. CAPA-MAGNUM.

262-263
1. Paris, Bibl. nat./Ph. J.-L. CHARMET.
2, 3 and 4. Ph. KEYSTONE.

264-265
1. New York, Museum of the City of New York/Photothèque HACHETTE.
2. Ph. KEYSTONE.
3. Ph. D. Lange, Washington, Library of Congress/GAMMA.
4. Ph. UPI/BETTMANN NEWSPHOTOS.
5. Archives TALLANDIER.
6. Ph. KEYSTONE.
7. Ph. THE BETTMANN ARCHIVE.

266-267
1. Ph. USIS-Archives TALLANDIER.
2. Ph. LIFE-Archives TALLANDIER.
3. Stuttgart, Würtembergische Landesbibliothek/Ph. J.-L. CHARMET-EXPLORER ARCHIVES.
4. Archives INTERPRESS.
5. Silvain Collection/Archives TALLANDIER.

268-269
1. Ph. D. BALTERMANTS-ICP-MAGNUM.
2. Ph. J.-L. CHARMET.
3. Ph. KEYSTONE.
4. Private collection/Ph. J.-L. CHARMET.

270-271
1 and 2. Ph. KEYSTONE.
3. Ph. CAPA-MAGNUM.

272-273
1. Canberra, Australian War Memorial/ Ph. E.T. ARCHIVE.
2. Ph. U.S. AIR FORCE/E.T. ARCHIVE.
3. Ph. USIS-Archives TALLANDIER.
4. Private collection/Ph. J.-L. CHARMET.
5. American Cultural Centre/Archives TALLANDIER.

274-275
1. New York, MOMA/Photothèque HACHETTE © SPADEM, 1986.
2. Tokyo, Bridgestone Bijutsukan/Ph. LAUSAT-EXPLORER ARCHIVES.
3. Rome, Galleria Nazionale d'Arte Moderna/Ph. G. DAGLI ORTI, D.R.
4. Ph. M. RIBOUD-MAGNUM, D.R.

276-277
1. Archives LAROUSSE-GIRAUDON.
2. Ph. KEYSTONE.
3. Ph. J.-L. CHARMET.
4. Paris, Bibl. nat./Ph. EXPLORER ARCHIVES.
5. Paris, Bibl. nat./Archives TALLANDIER.
6. Ph. M. RIBOUD-MAGNUM.
7. Coll. C. SJÖRGEN D.R.
8. Ph. H. CARTIER-BRESSON-MAGNUM.

278-279
1. Ph. UPI-BETTMANN NEWSPHOTOS.
2. Archives TALLANDIER.
3. Ph. UPI-BETTMANN NEWSPHOTOS.
4. Ph. KEYSTONE.

280-281
1. Ph. A.F.P.
2. Autochrome Lumière/Archives TALLANDIER.
3 and 4. Archives TALLANDIER.
5. Ph. F. MAYER-MAGNUM.

282-283
1. Coll. J. Charby/Ph. EDIMEDIA.
2. Ph. E.C.P./ARMÉES-Archives TALLANDIER.
3. Ph. MAGNUM.

284-285
1. Ph. KEYSTONE.
2. Ph. UPI-BETTMANN NEWSPHOTOS.
3. Ph. E. LESSING-MAGNUM.
4. Paris, Musée Picasso/Ph. R.M.N. © SPADEM, 1986.
5. Ph. UPI-BETTMANN NEWSPHOTOS.
6. Ph. D. SEYMOUR-MAGNUM.

286-287
1. Paris, Bibl. nat./Ph. LAUROS-GIRAUDON.
2. Ph. KEYSTONE.
3. Ph. B. BARBEY-MAGNUM.
4. Ph. J. GAUMY-MAGNUM.

288–289
2. Ph. KEYSTONE.
3. Ph. S. SALGADO-GAMMA.
4. Ph. TH CAMPION-GAMMA.

290–291
1. Ph. E. HAAS-MAGNUM.
2. Ph. XINHUA-GAMMA.
3. Ph. K. IMAEDA-MAGNUM.
4. Ph. CHRIS MARKER-EDIMEDIA.
5. Ph. CARTIER-BRESSON MAGNUM.
6. Coll. C.J. Bucher/TALLANDIER.

292-293
1. Ph. MAGNUM.
2, 3 and 4. Ph. KEYSTONE.

294-295
1. Ph. UPI-BETTMANN NEWSPHOTOS.
2. Ph. S. LISS-LIAISON GAMMA.
3. Ph. UPI-BETTMANN NEWSPHOTOS.
4. Ph. E. ERWITT-MAGNUM.
5. Ph. EDIMEDIA.
6. Ph. UPI-BETTMANN NEWSPHOTOS.
7. Ph. E. ERWITT-MAGNUM.

296-297
1 and 2. Ph. J.-P. NACIVET-EXPLORER.
3. Ph. F. MAYER-MAGNUM.
4. Ph. J.-L. NACIVET-EXPLORER.
5. Ph. R. BURRI-MAGNUM.
6. Ph. S. MEISELAS-MAGNUM.

298-299
1. Ph. M. RIBOUD-MAGNUM.
2. Ph. G. CARON-GAMMA.
3. Ph. KOSI-GAMMA.
4. Ph. D. LAINE-GAMMA.
5. Ph. ABBAS-GAMMA.

300-301
1. Ph. G. DAGLI ORTI.
2. Ph. H. VEILLER-EXPLORER.
3. Ph. E. HAAS-MAGNUM.

302-303
1 and 2. Ph. M. RIBOUD-MAGNUM.
3. Ph. H. CARTIER-BRESSON-MAGNUM.
4. Ph. R. RAI-MAGNUM.

304-305
1. Ph. E. ERWITT-MAGNUM.
2. Washington, Library of Congress/Ph. EDIMEDIA.
3. Ph. T. SENNETT-MAGNUM.
4. Ph. N. TIKHOMIROFF-MAGNUM.
5. Ph. M. SILVERSTONE-MAGNUM.

306-307
1. Ph. J. GRIFFITHS-MAGNUM.
2. Ph. F. MAYER-MAGNUM.

308-309
1. Ph. KEYSTONE.
2. Ph. B. BARBEY-MAGNUM.
3. Ph. JEUNE AFRIQUE-GAMMA.
4. Ph. AN NAHAR-GAMMA.
5. Ph. B. BARBEY-MAGNUM.

310-311
1. Ph. A. DE BORCHGRAVE-GAMMA.
2. Ph. J.-P. BONNOTTE-GAMMA.
3. Ph. A. MINGAM-GAMMA.
4. Ph. CH. HIRES-GAMMA.

312-313
1. Ph. F. LOCHON-GAMMA.
2. Ph. F. APESTÉGUY-GAMMA.
3. Ph. B. BREESE-LIAISON-GAMMA.
4. Ph. F. APESTÉGUY-GAMMA.
5. Ph. CH. VIOUJARD-GAMMA.
6. Ph. POOL BICENTENAIRE-GAMMA.
7. Ph. ABBAS-MAGNUM.
8. Ph. VELEZ-GAMMA.
9. Ph. J.-P. REY-GAMMA.
10 and 11. Ph. J. SUTTON-GAMMA.
12. Ph. M.-L. DE DECKER-GAMMA.

314-315
1. Ph. E. HARTMANN-MAGNUM.
2. Ph. A. HOWARTH-DAILY TELEGRAPH-EXPLORER.
3. Ph. J.-L. CHARMET.
4. Ph. H. CARTIER-BRESSON-MAGNUM.
5. Ph. GREENWOOD-LIAISON-GAMMA.
6. Ph. EDWARD-LIAISON GAMMA.

316-317
1. Ph. TASS.
2. Ph. A. SAUCEZ-EXPLORER.
3. Ph. K. KRAFFT-EXPLORER.
4. Ph. F. GOHIER-EXPLORER.

318-319
1. Ph. E.C.P./ARMÉES-GAMMA.
2. Ph. KEYSTONE.
3. Ph. JASMIN-GAMMA.
4. Ph. GAMMA.

320-321
1. Ph. B. GLINN-MAGNUM.
2. Ph. T. SENNETT-MAGNUM.

322-323
1. Ph. J.-P. PAIREAULT-MAGNUM.
2. Ph. J. GRIFFITHS-MAGNUM.
3. Ph. ABBAS-MAGNUM.
4. Ph. R. BURRI-MAGNUM.
5. Ph. R. KALVAR-MAGNUM.
6. Ph. RIO BRANCO-MAGNUM DIST.

# Index